second edition

CORRECTIONS

PHILOSOPHIES, PRACTICES, AND PROCEDURES

PHILIP L. REICHEL
University of Northern Colorado

ALLYN AND BACON Boston | London | Toronto | Sydney | Tokyo | Singapore

Editor-in-Chief, Social Sciences: Karen Hanson
Developmental Editor: Lisa Ziccardi
Series Editorial Assistant: Sarah McGaughey
Marketing Manager: Judeth Hall
Production Editor: Christopher H. Rawlings
Editorial-Production Service: Omegatype Typography, Inc.
Composition and Prepress Buyer: Linda Cox
Manufacturing Buyer: Megan Cochran
Cover Administrator: Linda Knowles
Text Design: Carol Somberg/Omegatype Typography, Inc.
Electronic Composition: Omegatype Typography, Inc.

A Pearson Education Company
160 Gould Street
Needham Heights, MA 02494

Internet: www.abacon.com

Between the time Web site information is gathered and published, some sites may have closed. Also, the transcription of URLs can result in typographical errors. The publisher would appreciate notification where these occur so that they may be corrected in subsequent editions.

Library of Congress Cataloging-in-Publication Data

Reichel, Philip L.
Corrections : philosophies, practices, and procedures / Philip L. Reichel.— 2nd ed.
p. cm.
Includes bibliographical references and index.
ISBN 0-205-31512-7
1. Corrections—United States. I. Title.
HV9471 .R435 2001
365'.973—dc21

00-029322

Printed in the United States of America

10 9 8 7 6 5 4 3 2 1   05 04 03 02 01 00

Photo credits appear on page 634, which constitutes an extension of the copyright page.

Dedication

To my parents
Joe Reichel and Virginia Reichel

Brief Contents

CONTENTS

CHAPTER 13

CHAPTER 14

Preface

The area of corrections, in addition to law enforcement and the court system, is often identified as a primary component of the criminal justice process. This term applies to educational and vocational programs for criminal offenders as well as the application of the death penalty. Issues in corrections are studied and discussed by journalists, reporters, legislators, criminal justice practitioners, scholars in a variety of disciplines, and citizens in general. One goal of this book is to describe and explain those issues so that we can understand their importance and their implications. An increasing number of citizens are impacted directly by crime and the government's response to it, and many people are affected at least indirectly through the use of taxes to support corrections programs. Everyone can benefit from an increased understanding of corrections.

Major Concepts and Themes

Of the many different ways to inform readers about this topic, I have chosen to rely especially on three concepts: **philosophies, practices,** and **procedures.** In this manner, the reader will come to understand the reasons (the philosophies) behind our application of different penal sanctions (the practices) and the particular paths (the procedures) that have been chosen to achieve social control in the United States. In addition to the traditional coverage of these concepts (via description, examples, and statistics), this text also integrates historical and international material. This approach reflects my belief that an understanding of our own procedures is increased when those procedures are placed in a historical context and when they are compared and contrasted with strategies used in other settings, including other countries. In addition to the historical and comparative themes, this book provides a more integrated look at female offenders than other corrections textbooks. The need for an integrated focus on female offenders is not merely a reaction to past disregard—although it certainly is that in part. Instead, it is the result of the increased presence and impact that women are having on the corrections system. Finally, attention to issues of race, ethnicity, and social class are included throughout the text in order to inform the reader of the impact these topics continue to have on the philosophies, practices, and procedures of corrections in the United States.

Organization of the Book

This book includes fifteen chapters that are distributed among three parts.

- **Part 1, Punishment Philosophies and Penal Eras.** These four chapters introduce the general topic of corrections (Chapter 1), the five punishment philosophies that provide a recurring theme for the book's material (Chapter 2), and the development of the penal system prior to the twentieth century (Chapter 3) and during the twentieth and twenty-first centuries (Chapter 4).
- **Part 2, Punishment Practices and Procedures.** This part begins a detailed look at corrections with a discussion of sentencing (Chapter 5). To set the stage

for a discussion of individual sanctions, Chapter 6 presents the penalties of corporal and capital punishment. Following this chapter, the focus changes to intermediate sanctions such as probation, community service, and day reporting centers (Chapter 7). The discussion then moves to confinement sanctions (short-term confinement in jails and boot camps [Chapter 8] and long-term confinement in state and federal prisons [Chapter 9]). Part 2 concludes with institutional management (Chapter 10), which includes a review of issues such as inmate labor and the management of special-needs inmates.

- **Part 3, Contemporary Issues.** This part not only elaborates on some topics introduced in Part 2 but also introduces new topics of current interest. Although most offenders sentenced to confinement are adult males, there are important issues and problems related to the imprisonment of women (Chapter 11) and juvenile offenders (Chapter 12). Also, regardless of the offenders' sex or age, there are difficult and significant issues related to the offenders' release from confinement (Chapter 13). Chapter 14 considers what, if any, rights prisoners and crime victims have today. Using a review of various corrections programs, Chapter 15 discusses the importance of recognizing that the success of a corrections program depends on what goal we were hoping to accomplish—which reflects back on the text's opening emphasis on correctional philosophies.

Pedagogical Features

Several specific features are included in this text to help enhance the learning experience.

- **Historical Perspective Boxes.** These discussions use historical material to highlight or expand on particular topics being covered in the chapter.
- **Cross-Cultural Corrections Boxes.** To provide students with an international perspective, these discussions highlight chapter topics as they appear in other countries.
- **Spotlight on Contemporary Issues Boxes.** The material in these boxes expands on chapter topics, highlighting what is currently newsworthy and what may impact future practices and procedures in corrections.
- **Issues of Fairness Boxes.** These boxes address gender, race, ethnicity, or social class issues. Each feature presents information on how correctional philosophies, practices, or procedures might be impacted by extralegal factors.
- **Correctional Links.** Each boxed feature contains Internet-related information relevant to the material in that box. This feature may be used by students to gather more information on the topic, or it can be used by instructors as Internet activities or assignments. Because Web addresses are likely to change, a Web site for this text (www.abacon.com/reichel) will provide continuously updated URL information.
- **Help Wanted Ads.** To inform students about career opportunities in the corrections area, employment ads are distributed throughout the text. These features resemble actual ads so that students can become aware of the variety of corrections positions available. Incorporated into each ad are one or two links to additional information.
- **Key Terms and Concepts.** At the end of each chapter is a list of key terms and concepts from that chapter. These items, which are in bold type in the text, are further identified as concepts that the student should recognize and understand after reading the chapter.
- **Discussion Questions.** Located at the end of each chapter, these questions are designed to stimulate conversation in the classroom. Instructors can use

the questions to encourage further study by students, to link the chapter material to local circumstances, or to gauge the students' level of understanding of the chapter material.

- **Tables and Figures.** Sprinkled throughout each chapter are tables and figures that provide current statistics and information on the topics being covered. The material in the tables and figures has a direct relevance to the subject matter and is often linked to a particular reference in the text.
- **Writing Style.** The narrative writing style smoothly transitions into story-like examples that help make sometimes complex ideas a bit more accessible. Also, I attempt to achieve gender neutrality by alternating between the use of the male and female pronoun.

SUPPLEMENTS

- Instructor's Manual and Test Bank
- Computerized Test Bank
- Companion Web site with online practice tests (www.abacon.com/reichel)
- Power Point presentation
- Allyn and Bacon Video Library

ACKNOWLEDGMENTS

This edition of my book is the result of an opportunity provided by Karen Hanson, my editor at Allyn and Bacon. I greatly appreciate her support and enthusiasm. I would also like to thank Lisa Ziccardi, my developmental editor. Lisa kept me motivated and on task, but was especially helpful in providing insightful and practical suggestions for improving the book.

Once the research and writing endeavor starts, the author's family and friends enter the process, whether they wish to or not. My wife, Eva Marie Jewell, was true to her name and remained a gem throughout this process, despite fixing more than her share of meals, tackling extra household chores, and spending more nights and weekends in solitary endeavors than she might otherwise have liked. I must also thank our sons, Scott Reichel and Matt Reichel, who continue to be constant joys in our lives and who make their parents very proud. Finally, I wish to express appreciation for the encouragement and support provided in recent years by Janet Alcorn, Mark Alcorn, Colleen Fitzpatrick, John Fox, and Brian Stutts. Each has been helpful in unique ways that range from encouraging high standards of professional activity to making sure there were periods of amusement to balance those periods of toil. It is a pleasure to count them among my friends.

I would also like to thank the following reviewers: Leanne Fiftal Alarid, University of Missouri–Kansas City; Meena Allen, New Mexico State University; Henry DeLuca, Westfield State College; Pam Hart, Iowa Western Community College; Homer C. Hawkins, Michigan State University; Ronald G. Iacovetta, Wichita State University; James W. Marquart, Sam Houston State University; Donna Massey, Florida State University; Michael R. Olson, Frostburg State University; Barbara Owen, California State University–Fresno; Lynda J. Pintrich, Middlesex Community College; Jerome Rosonke, Northern State University; Donald Walker, Kent State University; and Anthony Zumpetta, West Chester University. These reviewers made many important suggestions that I have tried to incorporate as the various drafts took form. I thank them all for their hard work and am pleased to have them listed in this acknowledgment.

part one

Punishment Philosophies and Penal Eras

KEY THEMES

The Historical Perspective

The International Perspective

Issues of Fairness

CRIME AND CORRECTIONS

Crime Rates and Imprisonment Rates

Correctional Philosophy, Policy, and Imprisonment Rates

CORRECTIONS AND THE CRIMINAL JUSTICE SYSTEM

Law

Police and Courts

Corrections

SUMMARY

KEY TERMS AND CONCEPTS

DISCUSSION QUESTIONS

chapter 1

Corrections and the Criminal Justice Process

Katharina Dallinger lived during the Middle Ages in what is now known as Western and Central Europe. Unfortunately, she had a well-deserved reputation for minding everyone's business but her own. One spring, just before the annual festival, Katharina outdid herself by gossiping without any pretense of subtlety. Her neighbors finally had enough, and Katharina was sentenced to wear a dragon mask with big ears (she heard everything), spectacles (she saw everything), a big nose (she stuck her nose into other people's business), and a big mouth and long tongue (everything she heard was maliciously told to others).

Several centuries after Katharina had to wear the dragon mask, an English court found John Mosley guilty of poaching fish and sentenced him to be hanged. But, like many of his condemned fellows, John avoided the gallows by "volunteering" to be transported to the American colonies where he was sold, in the same manner as a slave, to the highest bidder. Had John been born 150 years later in the new American state of Pennsylvania, he may have benefitted from the work of Quakers who fought against capital and corporal punishment and helped establish long-term confinement as a punishment; in other words, John might have been confined in a solitary cell where he would spend hours thinking about the wrongs he committed.

Similar family stories continue through the ages with accounts of people such as Ida O'Hare who, as the nineteenth century ended, was sentenced to the men's prison in Wyoming. Women inmates lacked a separate facility as well as work or educational opportunities. Ida's sister, Elizabeth, had stayed in their birth state of Massachusetts even though she was no less criminal than her sibling. Elizabeth's sentence placed her in the recently established Massachusetts Reformatory Prison for Women, where she learned housewifely skills in a pleasant, cottage-like setting. Elizabeth's thirteen-year-old son, Mark, had the misfortune of being born into a family of criminals but was at least lucky enough to have committed his crime in Massachusetts. In the same year that his mother was sent to the reformatory, Mark was placed on probation under the supervision of one of the country's first paid probation officers. Had the probation statute not been passed a year earlier, the thirteen-year-old would have been sent to the state prison.

These historical and international examples of punishments show a variety of penal sanctions used in society. Each specific practice (shaming, hanging, transporting, incarceration, probation) supports a particular philosophy (deter, avenge, incapacitate, rehabilitate) and follows a certain procedure (informal folk approach or formal court process). *Corrections: Philosophies, Practices, and Procedures* elaborates on these themes in an attempt to understand the reasons (the philosophies) behind the application of different penal sanctions (the practices) and the particular ways (the procedures) chosen to achieve societal goals.

Key Themes

Throughout this book, you will notice three recurring themes: attention to history, discussion of penal sanctioning in countries throughout the world, and consideration of fairness issues relating to women, racial and ethnic minorities, and

During the Middle Ages, especially in the area that is now Germany, masks of shame were used to degrade offenders by making them look ridiculous.

social class. Many of us do not understand or appreciate the historical and international perspectives of corrections. Nor do we fully realize the impact female offenders and issues related to race, ethnicity, and social class have on contemporary corrections. Following is a brief explanation of why these topics are emphasized in this book.

The Historical Perspective

Whoso desireth to know what will be hereafter, let him think of what is past.

—Sir Walter Raleigh

Picture a prison in which inmates follow a regimen of strict discipline that requires them to march in lockstep, maintain downcast eyes, and be involved in constant activity under the watchful eyes of their guards. Is this one of the new military-style boot camp prisons you may have heard about? No; this was the situation at the Auburn, New York, prison during the 1820s. Now imagine a state government that releases its convicted felons to a private business, which feeds and houses the prisoners, gives them jobs, and makes a profit on the care and custody of them. Are you thinking that this must be a new trend toward privatization, in which private contractors take control over state prisoners? No again; this example refers to Kentucky's decision in 1825 to lease the state's prison and its prisoners to an enterprising businessman, who got free labor in return for paying the state $1,000 plus half the net profit from inmate labor (Feeley, 1991).

Most of us have at least one school subject for which we cannot see any relevance. Over time, though, we often find those subjects are more relevant than we imagined. We have greater appreciation for the required math class when we agonize over bounced checks and a checkbook we cannot balance. Similarly, we have more appreciation for history when we wonder how elected officials could possibly think their "new" plan for reducing crime will work today when it didn't work 100 years ago. Of course, it is possible to make too strong an argument for a respect for history. For example, today's social, cultural, and economic situations may be so different from those of a century ago that ideas that failed earlier will succeed today. The point is not that we should avoid resisting old ideas, but that we should consider new ideas in their historical context. An appreciation for history gives us more than a knowledge of the mistakes and successes that have already occurred in relation to the topic being considered; it helps us to appreciate how those experiences can help in anticipating future problems and solutions.

A police inspector visiting from England once explained to my class his frustration with police administrators who constantly try to be innovative but just as regularly ignore the experiences of others who have already tried similar things. To make his point, the inspector referred to the *cave syndrome,* which he explained as follows. Chief Constable A comes up with a new idea (or takes credit for a new idea) and enters a tunnel (the mouth of the cave) believed to lead to that new idea. Chief Constable B hears about what A is doing, but instead of waiting for A to come out of the cave and report his findings (success or failure), B heads into the cave on his own. In time, word spreads to Chief Constable C who, not wanting to appear backward, starts heading into the cave as well. But when C gets halfway in, he meets A coming back out. A says to C, "Don't bother continuing, the idea didn't work." But C says to himself, "I've already invested a lot of money and I don't want people to think it was wasted," so he continues into the cave anyway—soon to meet B, whose experience C is also likely to ignore.

Similar cave-and-tunnel stories could be told about people in most occupations throughout the world. This does not suggest that it is human nature to ignore the lessons of history; rather, it suggests that frustration commonly results

Chain gangs, which were reintroduced in several states in the mid-1990s, are groups of inmates that work outside a prison while being shackled together by chains around their ankles.

HISTORICAL PERSPECTIVES

The Reemergence of Chain Gangs

Having a historical perspective allows us to understand how mistakes and successes of the past can help us anticipate future problems and solutions. These "Historical Perspective" boxes will highlight previous philosophies, practices, and procedures that are relevant to contemporary issues.

The first chain gangs appeared in Georgia in 1866. Colvin (1997) explains that they were a result of the punishment of criminals being transferred from the state penitentiaries—which were destroyed in the Civil War—to the counties. The counties forced the men to work in chain gangs in which inmates were shackled to each other by leg-irons connected to a common chain. "Workdays were long and hot, meals were meager, convicts slept chained together often without shelter, and time could be arbitrarily added to the sentence of forced gang labor by county sheriffs" (Colvin, 1997, p. 220). Because the chain gangs proved profitable for the counties—partly because they provided a way to control the black labor force—other southern states soon followed Georgia's lead. The importance of controlling the black labor force is supported by Rafter's (1990) report that black female prisoners, as well as black male prisoners, were assigned to southern prison chain gangs. Comparatively few white men and virtually no white women were given chain gang assignments (Johnson, 1997). It wasn't until the 1950s and 1960s, when states began regaining control over prisoner punishment and when the civil rights movement brought civilized sensibilities to the treatment of southern blacks in all settings, that chain gangs disappeared.

But, like Freddy Krueger and Jason Voorhees, chain gangs reappeared from apparent death. In 1995, Alabama became the first state to reinstate chain gangs—then dropped them for financial reasons in 1999. Following Alabama's lead, several other states (e.g., Arizona, Florida, Iowa, Maine, and Massachusetts) added chain gangs (Bureau of Justice Assistance, 1998; Zipp, 1999) to their corrections practices. Although in their first appearance chain gangs were used for profit, contemporary chain gang proponents are more likely to support the practice as a shaming sentence.

Chain gangs have been a popular theme in movies. Read about or watch *I Am a Fugitive from a Chain Gang* (***www.filmsite.org/iama.html***) and *Cool Hand Luke* (***www.filmsite.org/cool.html***) and then discuss which features of the chain gang are so appealing that state legislators want to return to those practices. Can chain gangs be used in a way that avoids the problems suggested in these old movies?

when contemporary policy is based on earlier experiences without any attempt to learn from those experiences. You might wonder, for example, if Alabama, Arizona, and Florida fully considered the reasons that chain gangs were discontinued in the 1930s before deciding in the 1990s that they would be an economical deterrent to crime (see "The Reemergence of Chain Gangs").

Conscious efforts are made in this book to provide a historical context for discussing contemporary issues. If through those efforts you come to believe that "the more things change, the more they remain the same," then one goal of this text will be achieved. This statement is not a cynical suggestion that it is futile to try to resolve corrections-related problems. Rather, history can reassure us that we have made it through similar problems in the past and are likely to do so again. The 1990s were not, for example, the first decade in U.S. history in which prison crowding was of great concern. The goal of a historical perspective is neither to make you simply throw up your hands at the uselessness of it all nor to make you cover your eyes and assume that the problems will go away just as they did before. Instead, an appreciation for history offers an opportunity to learn from earlier experiences with similar problems, to reuse things that worked in the past, and to modify responses that did not work earlier but may be adapted to work today. For these reasons a sense of history is an important part of this book.

The International Perspective

> *If criminal justice is studied only within the boundaries of our country, without taking into consideration foreign ideas and experiences, it will reduce significantly the knowledge and possible approaches to solving our problems.*
>
> —Richard J. Terrill

The benefits of an international perspective are both provincial and universal. Provincial benefits arise from having a point of contrast to judge your way of doing something. As long as everyone believes that internal combustion engines are the only reasonable way to move vehicles, there will be no self-propelled alternatives to automobiles. If legislators believe that long-term imprisonment is the only reasonable way to reduce crime, there will be no community alternatives to imprisonment. Innovative ideas can certainly come from a country's citizens, but innovations are also generated in other countries. If people look only to the local community for answers to puzzling questions, they may miss opportunities for adapting ideas.

As you will see in Chapter 3, during the 1860s Americans were debating the advantages and disadvantages of the Auburn, New York, and the Pennsylvania prison systems. These models of prison operation were the only options at that time; there was little movement toward a new system that was different from either of these standards. Then people began hearing about a penal system being used in Ireland (and, as it turned out, in Australia as well) that approached imprisonment from a different perspective. This Irish system innovation was to play an important role in the development of long-term imprisonment in the United States. Even if Americans eventually would have devised a version of the Irish system on their own, they did not need to.

In addition to its provincial benefits, an international perspective is becoming increasingly necessary as countries become interdependent. Cross-national crime is expanding as criminals ignore or easily avoid country boundaries when committing or fleeing from their crimes. Politicians, criminal justice officials, and average citizens are becoming more aware of a need to cooperate with officials in other countries as everyone tries to combat crime. To work together, the people of different countries will have to understand other justice systems. The result of cooperative efforts may not, and possibly should not, be the equivalent to world prisons holding criminals from many countries. But on a smaller scale it might be desirable for bordering countries to share administrative and financial costs of a prison or some other corrections program. For example, should the United States and Mexico build and jointly operate a prison somewhere along the border that would hold one country's citizens who commit a crime in the other country? Should Canada and the United States (or a border province and a border state) share the administration and cost of a probation-like program for their respective citizens who cross the border to commit crimes? In either scenario, all of the involved countries, states, or provinces would have to understand and appreciate the justice and corrections process in the other jurisdictions.

In addition, an international perspective can allow citizens of one country to come to the rescue of fellow citizens—criminals though they might be—who may be subjected to inappropriate sanctions in another country. Consider the following scenes.

> A prisoner is locked in a cave and forced to rely on insects for sustenance. A detainee is suspended by a rack tied to his wrists and ankles inches from the ground. Another prisoner's penis is nailed to a wooden table. (Preston, 1992, p. 134)

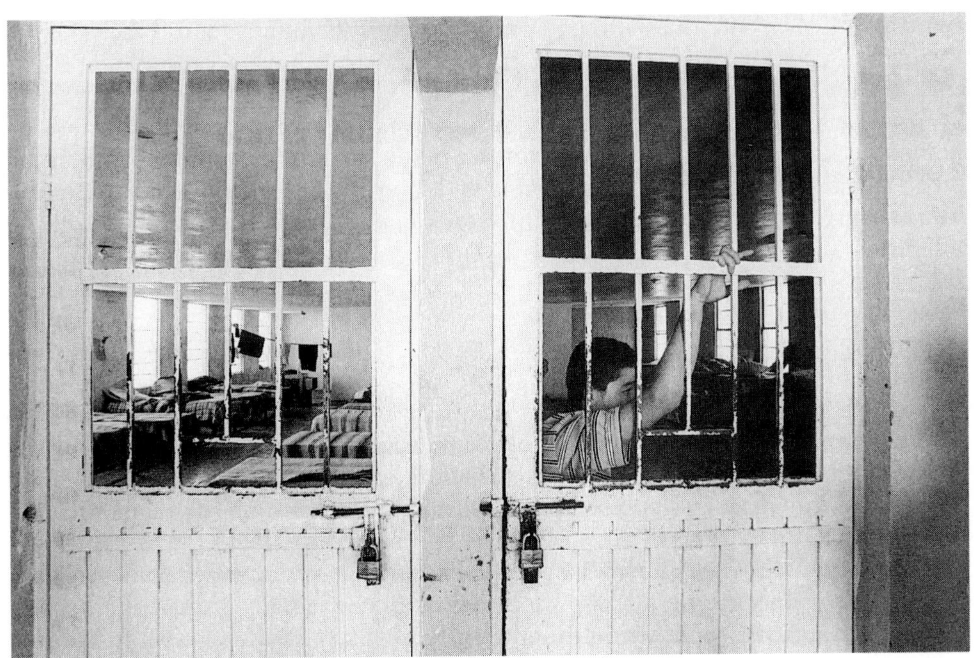

As crime increasingly occurs across national boundaries, inmates like this one in Mexico may serve their sentences in prisons jointly operated by bordering countries such as Mexico and the United States.

Are these scenes from a medieval dungeon? No, Preston explains, they are examples of abuse and torture that U.S. citizens have claimed to suffer at the hands of arresting and prison authorities in other countries.

The United States currently has prisoner transfer treaties with nearly fifty countries (State Department, 1999). Under these treaties, nationals convicted of crimes in one country can return to their own country to complete their sentences under more familiar living and cultural conditions. The receiving country has no authority to reopen the issue of guilt or innocence; nor can it change the imposed sentence length. It can, however, administer the sentence according to its own statutes and regulations—including the decision about what type of supervision the offender receives.

The U.S. Parole Commission considers a release date and the terms and conditions of supervision for exchanged offenders who may be released to the community. Prisoners' claims of abuse and torture become important because Congress has told the Parole Commission to consider such circumstances, as well as harsh prison conditions, when deciding release date and supervision requirements. Commission officials try to confirm claims made by the exchanged prisoner by determining if the prisoner had earlier filed a complaint with the American Embassy or with a court official in that country, or if there was some medical documentation supporting the charges. Knowledge of the justice systems in other countries can help U.S. officials make informed decisions about the claims of exchanged prisoners. Possibly more important, widespread knowledge of punishments in other countries would also help visitors to those countries know what to expect if they commit a crime during their stay.

Of course, citizens of other countries may find some sanctions and prisoner treatment in the U.S. justice system to be inappropriate. Most notable is the continued use of the death penalty in many states and its authorization, though without recent implementation, at the federal level. Several countries refuse to extradite to the United States any person who might be subject to the death penalty. Execution, from the perspective of those countries, is an inappropriate punishment. They are not willing to participate in such unacceptable sanctioning by releasing persons in their custody to U.S. officials if those people could be sentenced to death.

Similarly, there are examples of prisoner treatment that other countries can point to as illustrations of abuse and torture in the American system. As elaborated on in Chapter 11, human rights groups and lawyers filing class action suits are identifying many examples of sexual misconduct and abuse—especially of women offenders—in U.S. prisons.

Issues of Fairness

Injustice anywhere is a threat to justice everywhere. We are caught in an inescapable network of mutuality, tied in a single garment of destiny. Whatever affects one directly, affects all indirectly.

—Martin Luther King, Jr.

Concern about the differential application of justice depending on one's gender, race, ethnicity, or social class should be a concern to all. But despite the eloquence and accuracy of Martin Luther King, Jr.'s words, an undeniably fair justice system has not existed in either past or contemporary times. Of course, that does not mean that society should cease striving toward the elimination of injustice. But it does mean that society must sometimes be reminded when and where injustice exists. The topic of injustice in the contemporary criminal justice process is discussed in this book under the general topic of fairness. Specifically this book concentrates on fairness as it relates to gender, race, ethnicity, and social class.

Fairness and Gender. Crime, criminality, and corrections have historically been regarded as almost exclusively male phenomena. Silence on the issues of female criminality and societal response to female offenders has been rationalized as resulting from the small percentage of female offenders, the presumption that crimes

The increasing number of women in prison requires a more specific focus on female offenders than has been provided in the past.

by women present less of a threat to society than do crimes by men, and a belief that women who are sentenced to punishment do not present problems much different from those of men. That historical perception is no longer acceptable, and the explanations for silence on these issues are no longer accurate.

Boritch (1997) notes that researchers could once point to a scarcity of theory and research on female criminality, but not any longer. Similarly, any claim about an absence of studies about women in the corrections system can no longer be made. The theory, research, and information are being developed and published by women and men in criminology and penology. In addition to academic figures, politicians and practitioners are increasingly interested in—and aware of—crime and corrections material with a focus on women.

Textbooks, of course, must reflect this trend by incorporating material about women offenders in books that were typically only about men in the corrections system. Often that increased attention results in only one chapter devoted to women offenders. This book includes such a chapter because, as you will see in Chapter 11, some issues are most clearly handled separately. However, the increase in available information now allows more integrated coverage of women and men in the corrections system. To that end, attention to female offenders is a focus throughout this text.

The need for an integrated focus on female offenders is not merely a reaction to past disregard. Instead, it is the result of the increased presence of women and the impact that they are having on the corrections system. In the mid-1990s there were more women arrested, convicted, and sent to prison than ever before. Female offenders, who made up 3.8 percent of the state and federal prison populations in 1975, made up 6.3 percent in 1995. The nature of crimes for which women are convicted has also changed (see Table 1.1). An increasing percentage of women are sentenced to prison for drug offenses rather than for the property and morals offenses that were more common twenty years earlier (Coordination Group on Women, 1998).

TABLE 1.1: Adult Female Offender Profiles in 1975 and 1995

1975	1995
Women represented 13 percent of all arrests in the nation.	Women represented 19 percent of all arrests in the nation.
Women were incarcerated primarily for larceny, forgery, embezzlement, and prostitution.	Women were incarcerated primarily for drug-related offenses and larceny.
Women constituted 10 percent of all arrests for violent crime.	Women constituted 14 percent of all arrests for violent crime.
Women represented 5 percent of offenders serving federal prison sentences and 4 percent of offenders serving state prison sentences.	Women represented 7 percent of offenders serving federal prison sentences and 6 percent of offenders serving state prison sentences.
Seventy-three percent of incarcerated women had one or more dependent children.	Sixty-one percent of incarcerated women in the federal system and 67 percent in the state systems had one or more children under age eighteen.

Source: Coordination Group on Women. (1998). *Women in criminal justice.* Washington, DC: Office of Justice Programs.

In 1994 the Coordination Group on Women was established in the Office of Justice Programs to update a 1975 report completed by the Law Enforcement Assistance Administration Task Force on Women. The 1975 report discussed the lack of attention given to gender-specific services for women in federal and state criminal justice systems; it attributed that deficiency to inadequate awareness of women's special needs, to the priority given to male-specific programs, and to a general absence of information about women in the criminal justice system. In its 1998 report, the Coordination Group on Women noted that the gender-specific needs of female offenders have not changed since 1975, nor, for the most part, has the criminal justice system's relative inattention to the needs of this population. The report also provides suggestions for action (see "Recommendations for Responding to Female Offenders"), which will be expanded on in later chapters, but for now the report simply offers support for the need to pay specific, and sometimes separate, attention to issues that women offenders present in the corrections system.

Fairness and Race, Ethnicity, and Social Class. In addition to the increasing numbers of women in the corrections system, there are also increasing numbers of racial and ethnic minorities. Because of the occasional conflation of these terms, the feature "Why Hispanic Is Not a Race" on page 12 briefly distinguishes between **race** and **ethnicity** for statistical purposes. Social class (specifically, fairness related to persons in the lower socioeconomic strata) is also identified as a fairness issue. As with gender issues, the topics of race, ethnicity, and social class demand attention in any analysis of contemporary corrections. A quick look at some numbers helps explain why this is true.

The U.S. Census Bureau (see the Web site at www.census.gov) shows that as the twentieth century ended, the U.S. population comprised 82 percent whites, 13 percent blacks, 1 percent American Indian/Alaska Native, and 4 percent Asian/Pacific Islander. In addition, 11 percent of the population was identified as being of Hispanic origin. Given this distribution, a similar distribution would be expected among persons arrested, in jail, on probation, and so on, for criminal behavior. When the percentages do not match, it may be that one of the groups is either over- or underrepresented in the arrest, jail, or probation statistics. Or that group is said to be disproportionately represented.

Table 1.2 on page 13 shows overrepresentation of blacks and Hispanics at several stages in the criminal justice process. The current disproportionality is disturbing in itself, but even more so because the overrepresentation has been getting worse. Brown, Langan, and Levin (1999) report that persons whose racial background is not white have increased among convicted felons. In 1988 blacks, American Indians/Alaska Natives, and Asian/Pacific Islanders together were 14 percent of the population age eighteen or older and 43 percent of persons convicted of a felony. In 1996 those same groups accounted for 16 percent of U.S. adults and 47 percent of those convicted. Similarly, between 1990 and 1998 the percentage that blacks made up of all persons on probation increased from 31 to 35 percent. During the same period, the percentage that Hispanics comprised of all people on probation decreased from 18 percent to 15 percent. Of all the people on parole in 1990, 18 percent were Hispanic, and 47 percent were black. In 1998 the percentage of Hispanics on parole rose to 21 percent while the percentage of blacks on parole fell to 44 percent. Despite the decreasing percentages of Hispanics on probation and blacks on parole, most analysts express concern about the continued overrepresentation of blacks and Hispanics in all stages of the criminal justice process and the continued increase in some of the stages.

Although there is virtually no disagreement about these numbers, there is considerable disagreement about what they mean. Is the overrepresentation of blacks

ISSUES OF FAIRNESS

RECOMMENDATIONS FOR RESPONDING TO FEMALE OFFENDERS

Adult female offenders have needs that differ from those of men; these needs stem in part from female offenders' disproportionate victimization from sexual or physical abuse and their responsibility for children. Female offenders are also more likely to be addicted to drugs and to have mental illnesses. Many states and jail jurisdictions, particularly those with small female offender populations, have few special provisions, either in management or programming, for meeting the needs of women. Although some improvements have been made since 1975, largely because of litigation and increased attention to women's issues overall, a great deal needs to be done to ensure that women are treated fairly as they move through every phase of the criminal justice system (Coordination Group on Women, 1998, p. 2).

Recommendations from the OJP Coordination Group on Women

- Continue gender-specific programming for adult and juvenile female offenders.
- Collect more gender-specific data at every point in the criminal justice process to establish an accurate profile of the female offender.
- Ensure that specialized training is provided to law enforcement personnel, including the development of emergency services, alternatives to arrest, and mental health crisis intervention. Train staff on women's issues, listening skills, and services that are available to women in the community.
- Encourage the expansion of intermediate sanctions and community programs that address the criminogenic behaviors of female offenders.
- Develop state department of corrections policy standards for community release specific to female offenders, and develop staff training curriculums to prepare probation and parole officers to manage women's many needs in the community.
- Emphasize the study and management of older female offenders, since their numbers are expected to increase.
- Allocate more resources to provide the necessary program opportunities to return female offenders to the community.
- Offer mental health and substance abuse treatment programs to women in jails and prisons.
- Assess and provide additional services for women who have histories of physical and sexual abuse.
- Encourage visitation rights, parenting programs, and other opportunities for mothers and children to be together. (Coordination Group on Women, 1998, p. 14)

Read the complete report by the Coordination Group on Women at ***www.ojp.usdoj.gov/reports/98Guides/wcjs98/welcome.html.*** Chapter 1 in the report provides information on crimes for which women are arrested. What were the top five crimes for which women were arrested in 1975? How does that list compare with the top five in 1995?

and Hispanics at the arrest and conviction stages a result of greater criminality on their part, or does it reflect a bias by police and prosecutors? Are blacks and Hispanics disproportionately represented in jail, in prison, and on parole (but not quite so disproportionately represented for probation) because they have been sentenced for more serious offenses or because they have been discriminated against in the courtroom? In other words, are people being treated fairly regardless of such nonlegal and inappropriately used factors as race, ethnicity, gender, and social class? A goal of this book is to bring some of these issues and topics to your attention (even though they are often raised without being answered) because they will continue to influence corrections policy in the twenty-first century.

With promises of a historical perspective that can explain the present and forecast the future, an international perspective that offers provincial and universal advantages, and issues of fairness that focus attention on gender, race, ethnicity,

ISSUES OF FAIRNESS

WHY HISPANIC IS NOT A RACE

Because most scholars define race in terms of biological characteristics and ethnicity in terms of cultural characteristics, statistics are usually gathered with this division in mind. In most of the studies and reports used in this book, distinction by race is made in terms of four categories: (1) white, (2) black, (3) American Indian/Alaska Native, and (4) Asian/Pacific Islander. Sometimes, usually because of insufficient numbers to support distinction, the last two categories are combined as "Other." These are racial categories in the sense that persons in each group are identified (usually through self-categorization) as sharing biological or anatomical characteristics with others in that group.

Unlike the biological distinctions for race, ethnicity typically describes cultural differences. In this manner, people of a particular ethnic group may share a common cultural tradition, history, religion, dress, language, or they may have other common traits. Obviously, *ethnicity* is a broader term than *race,* because people with different biological characteristics can share a common culture, religion, language, and so on. This becomes important for statistical purposes in corrections because one particular ethnic group in the United States, Hispanics, has received increased attention as members of that group comprise an increasing proportion of the U.S. population. That group, like any other ethnic group, can include people of different races. It is possible, for example, to have white Hispanics, black Hispanics, Native American Hispanics, Asian Hispanics, and so on.

When presenting statistical information that distinguishes probationers, prisoners, parolees, and so forth on the basis of racial or ethnic categories, it is not possible to include Hispanics in the same table or chart as whites, blacks, American Indians/Alaska Natives, and Asian/Pacific Islanders because there would be double counting. That is, if you tally five Hispanic persons among the whites, then count three black Hispanics among the blacks, you cannot count those same eight people again under Hispanic. To lessen the potential for double counting, government statistics typically provide two types of statistics. One distinguishes among the four racial categories, and the other distinguishes Hispanic and non-Hispanic. Occasionally, as in Table 1.2 along the "jail" row, the groups are combined and renamed "white non-Hispanic," "black non-Hispanic," "Hispanic," and "Other."

There are several interesting government documents that provide information about specific ethnic and racial groups. Read *We the American . . . Hispanics* at ***www.census.gov/apsd/wepeople/we-2r.pdf.*** Go to Figure 4 of that report and identify what percentage of your state population was Hispanic in the 1990 census. Read the report *American Indians and Crime* at ***www.ojp.usdoj.gov/bjs/pub/pdf/aic.pdf.*** How does the rate of violent victimization of American Indians compare with that for other U.S. racial or ethnic groups?

and social class, we are ready to discuss the philosophies, practices, and procedures directing corrections in the United States. The journey starts with a consideration of the link between crime and corrections.

CRIME AND CORRECTIONS

In June 1994 the United States passed the 1 million mark in its prison population—no one celebrated. Four years later there were 1.8 million people incarcerated, and the nation was well on its way to starting the twenty-first century with a prison and jail population of 2 million. As one pundit put it, "For the land of the free, the United States puts an extraordinary number of its citizens behind bars" ("A Land of Bondage," 1999, p. 3).

When probation and parole—the primary forms of community supervision—are included, about 6 million people were under some form of correctional su-

TABLE 1.2: Indicators of Overrepresentation of Blacks and Hispanics at Different Stages in the Criminal Justice System (percentage of stage total)

	RACIAL CATEGORIES*			ETHNIC CATEGORY
	White	Black	Other	Hispanic (any race)
General Population	82	13	5	11
Violent crime arrests (1997)[1]	57	41	2	not available
Property crime arrests (1997)[1]	65	32	3	not available
Felony violent crime convictions (1996)[2]	52	46	2	not available
Felony property crime convictions (1996)[2]	59	39	2	not available
Felony drug crime convictions (1996)[2]	45	53	2	not available
Jail inmates (1998)[3]	41 (non-Hispanic)	41 (non-Hispanic)	2	16 (1998)
Probationers (1998)[4]	64	35	2	15
Prison inmates (1997)[5]	48	49	3	18
Parolees (1998)[4]	55	44	1	21

* The designations *white, black, American Indian,* and *Hispanic* are the preferred terms by members of these groups as indicated in a 1995 survey by the Bureau of Labor Statistics and the Bureau of the Census (see www.bls.census.gov/cps/racethn/1995/stat40rp.htm).

[1]Uniform Crime Reports 1997 and Table 43.

[2]Brown, J. M., Langan, P. A., & Levin, D. J. (1999). *Felony sentences in state courts, 1996* [NCJ 173939]. Washington, DC: Bureau of Justice Statistics.

[3]Gilliard, D. K. (1999). *Prison and jail inmates at midyear 1998* [NCJ 173414]. Washington, DC: Office of Justice Programs.

[4]Bonczar, T., & Glaze, L. E. (1999). *Probation and parole in the United States, 1998* [NCJ 178234]. Washington, DC: Bureau of Justice Statistics.

[5]Beck, A. J., & Mumola, C. J. (1999). *Prisoners in 1998* [NCJ 175687]. Washington, DC: Bureau of Justice Statistics.

pervision at the end of the century (Bonczar & Glaze, 1999). That total showed an increase of over 35 percent from the 1990 numbers. The total U.S. population also was growing during that period, but by the decade's end about 3 percent of the adult population was incarcerated or on probation or parole. In 1990 the rate was 2.3 percent. Bonczar and Glaze (1999) also point out that most of the increase was a result of more people being put in jails and prisons rather than under community supervision. Specifically, the percentage of the correctional population on probation and parole declined from 74 percent to 69 percent, while the percentage in jails or prisons increased from 26 percent to 31 percent. Not only is America putting more people under correctional supervision, but it is also incarcerating them more often. In fact, the United States is putting so many people in prison that it has one of the world's highest incarceration rates. This situation presents several interesting questions: Why are there more people under correctional supervision? Why are there continually greater numbers, among those under correctional supervision, specifically in jails and prisons? Finally, why does the United States imprison a greater proportion of its population than do other countries? Explanations for America's world standing can help answer the first two questions as well as the final question.

Figure 1.1 shows that the United States has one of the highest incarceration rates in the world. Figure 1.2 shows that the United States has also had a consistent and,

FIGURE 1.1

Imprisonment Rates for Selected Countries, 1995

Source: Biles, D. (1995). Prisoners in Asia and the Pacific. *Overcrowded Times, 6*(6), 5–6; Bureau of Justice Statistics. (1997). *Correctional populations in the United States, 1995* [NCJ 163916]. Washington, DC: Bureau of Justice Statistics; Mauer, M. (1997). *Americans behind bars: U.S. and international use of imprisonment, 1995.* Washington, DC: The Sentencing Project; Walmsey, R. (1997). *Prison populations in Europe and North America* (HEUNI paper no. 10). Helsinki, Finland: The European Institute for Crime Prevention and Control.

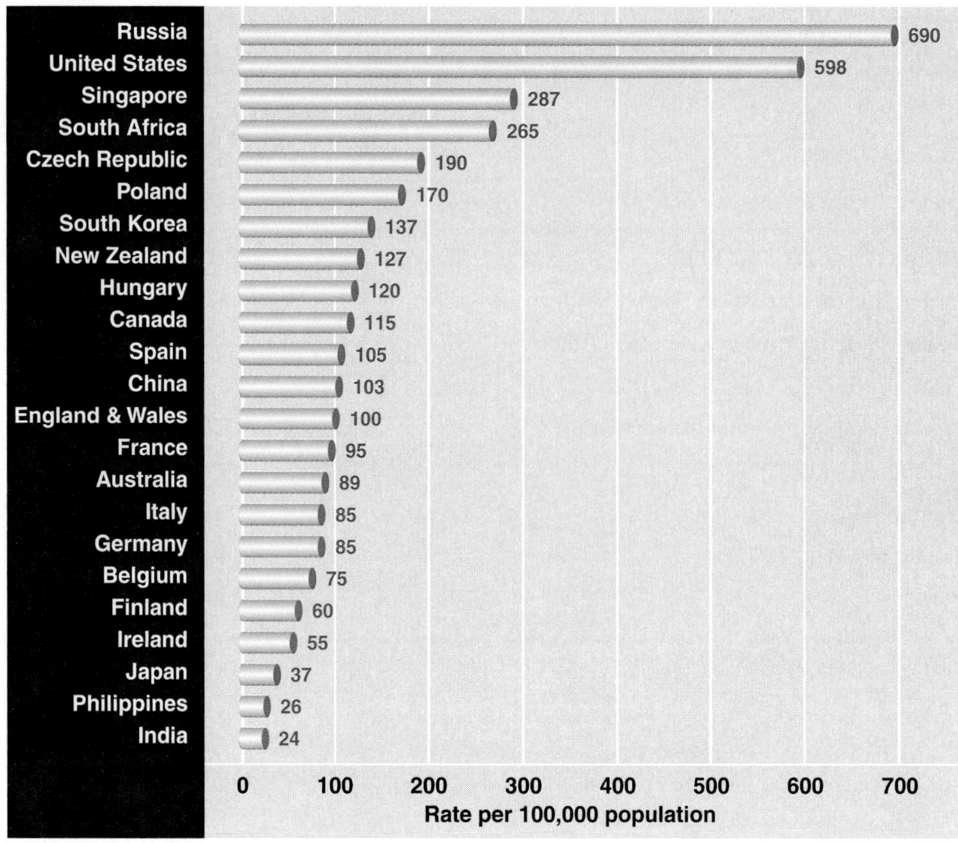

since about 1980, a dramatic increase in its prison population. These two conditions, America's standing worldwide and its own long-term trends, present questions about the use of imprisonment in the United States. This book will try to answer a few of them.

Russia's high incarceration rate (see Figure 1.1) might be explained by its political instability, the transition to an uncertain economic future, and the rise of organized crime (Mauer, 1994), but such reasons are unlikely explanations for a high incarceration rate in the United States. Suggestions for conditions affecting the number of people imprisoned, in any country, have included such variables as the crime rate, prison capacity, unemployment rates, age composition of the general population, and changes in correctional philosophy or policies—including changes in sentencing practices (Duffee, 1989). We will look at the possible role of the crime rate and changes in correctional philosophy and policies as explanations for the United States' position in Figure 1.1 and the trends shown in Figure 1.2.

Crime Rates and Imprisonment Rates

An increase in crime would seem to be the most obvious explanation for an increase in people being placed under correctional supervision. However, during the 1990s the U.S. crime rate actually declined. The 1998 crime statistics from the Federal Bureau of Investigation's annual Uniform Crime Report showed that crime was down for the seventh straight year. The rate of violent crimes reported to law enforcement agencies was the lowest it had been since 1987, and murder was at its lowest rate since 1967. Property crime rates were 13 percent lower than the 1989 rates.

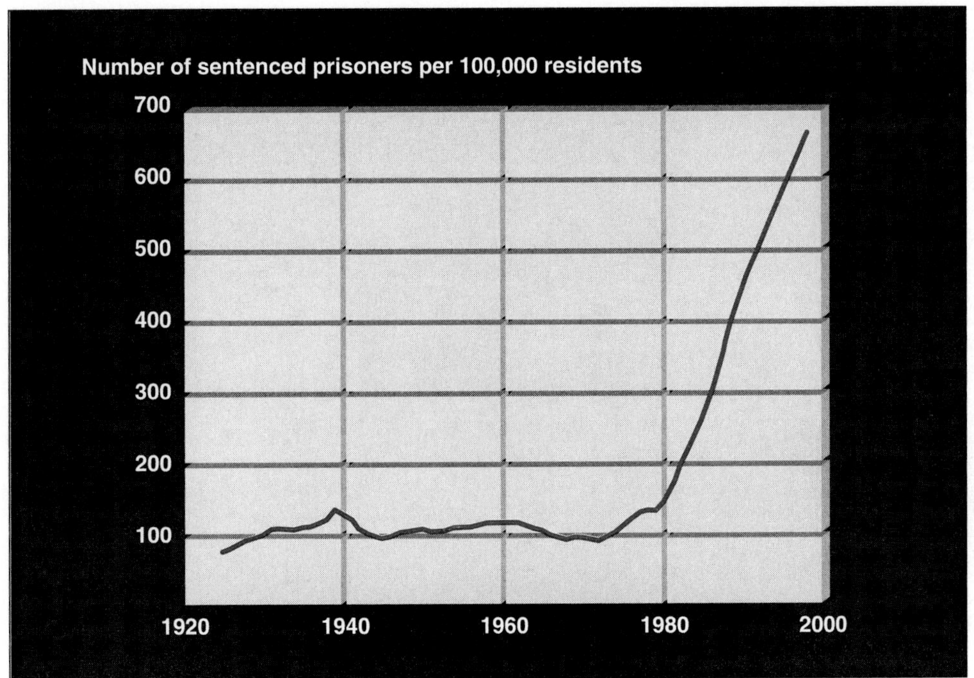

FIGURE 1.2

Sentenced Prisoners in State and Federal Institutions in the United States on December 31, 1925–1998

Note: The rates for the period before 1980 are based on the civilian (nonmilitary) population. Since 1980, the rates are based on the total resident population.

Source: Adapted from Maguire, K., & Pastore, A. L. (Eds.). (1995). *Sourcebook of criminal justice statistics—1994* [NCJ 154591]. Washington, DC: Bureau of Justice Statistics. Figure 6.4. Beck, A. J., & Mumola, C. J. (1999). *Prisoners in 1998* [NCJ 175687]. Washington, DC: Bureau of Justice Statistics.

Why, some ask, are we locking more people up when the crime rate is down? Well, others respond, maybe crime is down because we are locking the criminals up! As you might imagine, both the question and the answer are more complicated than they appear. Although it may seem obvious that the amount of crime in a state or country will drive its imprisonment rate, the relationship is not that clear-cut. Some studies have found no consistent relationship between crime and incarceration rates, while others report that high crime rates tend to precede high incarceration rates, which are then followed by lower crime rates (Duffee, 1989, pp. 40–42).

One problem in drawing conclusions about a relationship between crime rate and incarceration rate is an assumption that all crimes have the same probability of receiving a prison sentence. For example, the overall crime rate may increase without an accompanying increase in prison sentences because most of the crime increase was in the area of property crime, which may not be as likely to result in imprisonment. On the other hand, the overall crime rate could fall as the incarceration rate increased if the number of violent crimes increased and the number of property crimes (and, therefore, the overall crime rate) decreased. Mauer (1994) has addressed these points and presents some interesting findings.

International crime and victimization surveys have shown that crime rates in the United States are not substantially higher than crime rates in other industrialized nations (Mauer, 1994; Reichel, 1999). The overall crime rate as well as rates for property crimes and some assaultive crimes in the United States were found to be similar or even lower than those rates in Australia, Canada, France, and New Zealand. As Figure 1.1 shows, however, the incarceration rates in those countries were considerably lower than the incarceration rate in the United States. There was, however, an important difference in the area of violent crime, especially murder. Murder rates in the United States are generally five to ten times the rates in European countries. Because violent offenders are more likely than nonviolent offenders to receive a prison sentence, the United States' higher violent crime rate should result in a higher imprisonment rate. But even if violent crime in general,

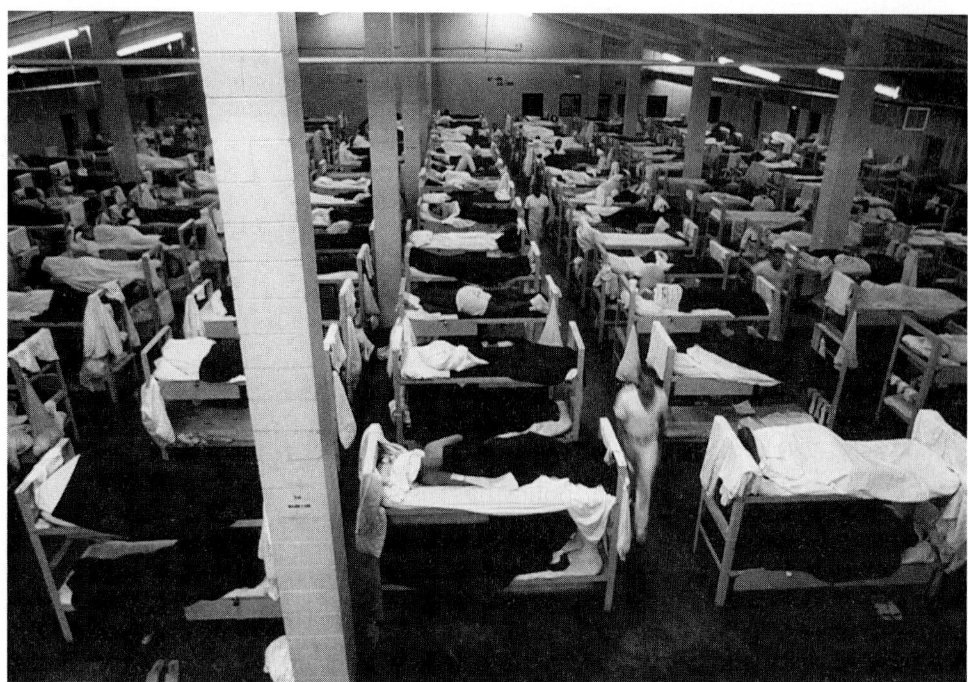

As more and more offenders receive sentences to incarceration, jails and prisons across the country experience overcrowding.

and murder more specifically, explains some of the difference in incarceration rates between the United States and other industrialized countries, it does not explain the increasing use of imprisonment in the United States itself. Those recent increases are linked instead to changing policies toward drug offenders, and that takes us to the next variable.

Correctional Philosophy, Policy, and Imprisonment Rates

As noted in several parts of this book, since the 1970s jurisdictions throughout the United States have taken an increasingly tough position toward crime. The Retributive era and a just deserts philosophy increased prison sentence lengths and applied mandatory prison sentences to several crimes. These "get tough" policies and their accompanying philosophies of retribution and incapacitation were not always applied across the board, however. Violent crimes and drug offenses were particularly targeted by the police (thereby increasing arrests), the legislators, and the courts (increasing penalties and prison sentences). As a result, one explanation for the growth in the prison population since 1980 is an increase in the number of persons arrested for violent crimes and for drug law violations. Among the four major crime categories (violent, property, drug, and public order), drug offenses were responsible for most of the increase between 1980 and the early 1990s (Gilliard & Beck, 1994). During the 1990s, violent crime offenses accounted for the largest growth in the state inmate population (Beck & Mumola, 1999).

The increasing number of violent criminals and drug offenders being sent to prison is not the only reason for the growth of America's prison population. Another explanation, also linked to changing correctional philosophies and policies, is the number of persons returned to prison after being released conditionally. In addition to new court commitments, prison admissions also include those persons who have had their parole, or other conditional release, revoked and are being returned to prison. Since 1990 the relative size of the two main sources of prison admissions has changed. Court commitments accounted for 82 percent of state prison admissions in 1980 but only 62 percent in 1997 (the remainder were admissions who were escapees, transfers, and so on). Over the same period of time, admissions who were parole violators increased from 17 percent to 35 percent (again, the remainder being other types of admissions). This increase in conditional release violators accounted for more than one-third of the growth in the total admissions to state prisons (Beck & Mumola, 1999; Gilliard & Beck, 1994).

So how do we explain the United States' position in Figure 1.1 and its prison population trends in Figure 1.2? Based on the prison admission data provided by the Bureau of Justice Statistics (Beck & Mumola, 1994), we might propose the following:

- Although the United States does not seem to have a higher crime rate than do several other industrialized countries, its higher violent crime rate, especially murder, may result in more persons receiving prison sentences.
- Application of a "get tough" policy has resulted in more offenders of all types being sentenced to prison, especially violent criminals and drug offenders.
- An increasing number of persons released from prison on parole, or some other type of conditional release, are being returned to prison as conditional release violators.

These factors may not explain all aspects of U.S. imprisonment policies, but they certainly offer some explanation for the country's position worldwide and its growing prison population since 1980. The feature "Where Are They All Coming From?" offers some other explanations, and Chapters 7 and 8 will also consider this question.

CORRECTIONS AND THE CRIMINAL JUSTICE SYSTEM

The criminal justice process has three components: police, courts, and corrections. Ideally, the three parts work in partnership as they respond to law violators and achieve their individual and collective goals. When the agencies operate in this fashion, they approach what has been called the *criminal justice system model.* In an ideal system, whether it is biological, social, political, economic, or some other type, the various parts work independently and collectively so that the whole can function in a healthy manner. Some people suggest that it is more appropriate to describe a criminal justice nonsystem model, because the police, courts, and corrections agencies seem at times to operate at cross-purposes, with more redundancy than efficiency, and with considerable conflict among and within agencies. Here the **criminal justice system** is defined as a loose confederation of agencies whose general goal is the control of crime. We first discuss law because it is common to all three systems.

Law

In order to know what [the law] is, we must know what it has been, and what it tends to become.

—Oliver Wendell Holmes, Jr.

Each society has a legal system that can generally be grouped into one of four legal families or traditions: civil law, common law, socialist law, and Islamic law (Fairchild, 1993; Reichel, 1999). Each of these legal traditions has an interesting, intriguing history (as illustrated in the feature on page 19). However, at this time

Spotlight ON CONTEMPORARY ISSUES

Where Are They All Coming From?

The last two decades of the twentieth century saw dramatic increases in America's prison population. During that period the United States consistently had one of the world's highest incarceration rates—typically coming in second behind Russia among countries for which data were available (Reichel, 1999, p. 260).

A number of explanations have been offered for the increase in prisoners. They can be divided most simply into the following logical explanations: (1) more people are entering prison and (2) fewer people are leaving. The "more people coming in" factors include:

- There has been an increase in the number of parole violators being returned to prison and in the number of new commitments to prison. The impact of this increase on the number of people coming into prison is elaborated on in Chapter 9.
- Explanations for why more people are entering prison are linked primarily to changes in punishments attached to certain crimes and in sentencing practices and lengths. For example, more jurisdictions are using sentencing practices that require imprisonment for some types of crimes (violent and drug offenses, especially). Also popular are sentences that require a specified minimum time to be spent in prison. Chapter 5 provides coverage of these issues.

The "fewer people leaving" factors include:

- In addition to having more people enter prison, there are fewer people being released to make room for the new arrivals. Annual release rates of inmates dropped from 37 percent in 1990 to 31 percent in 1997.
- Not only are more coming in and fewer being released, but while in prison, the men and women are staying longer. In 1990 the average time served was twenty-two months, and in 1997 it had increased to twenty-seven months (Beck & Mumola, 1999).
- A small but growing number of inmates will serve twenty or more years in prison before their release—and some won't leave prison until they die. The impact of this decrease in the number of people leaving prison is also addressed in Chapter 9.

This increased use of imprisonment has not had a similar impact on everyone. As we will see in later chapters, the increase has been especially high for women and black males. Data such as these reemphasize the importance of covering the topic of fairness as it relates to corrections issues.

Read "The Prison Population Bomb" at ***www.demographics.com/publications/ad/96_ad/9602_ad/ad880.htm.*** To what does that article attribute the greater prison boom in states in the South and West as opposed to those in the Northeast and Midwest? Read Amnesty USA's report at ***www.amnestyusa.org/rightsforall/women/factsheets/drugs.html.*** In what way is the increase in the number of women being sent to prison a result of the war on drugs?

we will focus mainly on the U.S. legal system. The United States is most closely associated with the common law tradition, yet there are certain distinctions in the way laws are developed and enforced that require explanation.

Because laws are complex, it is difficult to summarize the key portions that are relevant to corrections. In the following material are terms and concepts that help us understand corrections and the law. Rather than being a separate component of the criminal justice system, law is that system's core. Without law there would be nothing for police to enforce nor any punishment for the courts to apply. But particular aspects of law that are more relevant to criminal justice in general, and to corrections more specifically, must be clarified.

Criminal Law versus Civil Law. The law can be divided into **civil law** and **criminal law.** In its original meaning, civil law referred to the code of laws collected by the Roman emperor Justinian in his *Corpus Juris Civilis* around A.D. 350. This initial concept of laws as a collection of written codes provided by a political authority had considerable influence over the next 2,000 years.

While Europe was developing a system of laws based on pronouncements from rulers and legislators, English kings were claiming that laws are simply customs

Cross-Cultural Corrections

The Islamic Legal Tradition

Of the four contemporary legal traditions, the least well known to many in the United States is the Islamic tradition. Compared with the other legal traditions, Islamic law is uncommon in its singularity of purpose. Islam recognizes no distinction between a legal system and other controls on a person's behavior. In fact, Islam is said to provide all the answers to questions about appropriate behavior in any sphere of life.

Three categories of crime are distinguished in the *Shari'a:* hudud, quesas, and ta'azir. *Hudud,* which are offenses against God, require mandatory prosecution and must be punished in the manner prescribed in the *Qur'an* (the holy book of Islam) or the *Sunna* (the statements and deeds of the Prophet Muhammad). The seven hudud crimes are adultery or fornication, defamation, drinking alcohol, theft, highway robbery, apostasy (the rejection of Islam by one professing Islamic faith), and rebellion or corruption of Islam. The punishments for hudud crimes include death by stoning for a married person committing adultery, hand amputation for theft, and whipping for persons using alcohol (Sanad, 1991).

Quesas crimes are less serious than hudud crimes and more serious than ta'azir crimes. They are similar to what other criminal codes call crimes against persons and include acts such as voluntary and involuntary homicide, assault, and battery. Punishment for these crimes can be either acts of retaliation by the victim or the victim's family (e.g., eye for an eye) or financial compensation by the offender to the victim or the victim's family.

The least serious of Shari'a crimes are the *ta'azir.* Included in this category are all offenses not identified as either hudud or quesas crimes. Examples of ta'azir crimes are petty theft, homosexuality, eating pork, neglect of prayers, and acts damaging to the public interest. A ta'azir penalty can be execution but is more likely to be whipping, imprisonment, or a fine.

Like all religions, Islam has sects, the *Shi'ite* and *Sunni* branches being the primary ones. Even within the sects, different schools of thought developed regarding legal questions. As a result, Islamic law is not uniformly applied throughout Islamic countries any more than civil, common, or socialist law is consistent across nations following those traditions. Countries such as Jordan and Kuwait have both civil and Islamic aspects in their legal systems while other nations combine Islamic and common traditions (e.g., Kenya and Nigeria) or even have a socialist aspect (Algeria). Muslim countries providing the most clear examples of widespread use of Islamic law include Afghanistan, Iran, Iraq, and Saudi Arabia.

Despite variation in the way Islamic law is interpreted and applied, media reports often portray it as a harsh and inflexible system that is inappropriate in today's world. Certainly there are criminals who have been amputated, beheaded, and stoned under Islamic law. But there have also been criminals whose punishment has been set aside because of their victim's forgiveness. In fact, the Qur'an encourages forgiveness with the same vigor that it advocates retaliation. That point, which becomes more clear in Chapter 2's discussion of compensation, is good to keep in mind as a counterbalance to media-inspired notions of Islamic law (Reichel, 1999, p. 103).

Go to Professor Godlas's Islamic studies page at ***www.arches.uga.edu/~godlas/practices.html,*** and scroll down to the section on Islamic law. What are the four schools of law identified within Islamic law? Go to the page maintained by the USC Muslim Students Association at ***www.usc.edu/dept/MSA/law/shariahintroduction.html.*** How are the terms *Shari'ah* and *Fiqh* distinguished?

that have become so repetitive as to be compulsory—that is, customs have the force of law. The laws in England came not from the dictates of a ruler or even a legislature; instead they came from the people as a result of certain principles and rules said to be common throughout the land. Because of these different sources of law, one of the world's major legal families is called the common legal tradition (based on ancient and continuous custom), and another is the civil legal tradition (based on written pronouncements of rulers and legislators).

U.S. citizens typically do not refer to civil law as the civil legal tradition that is based on historical and contemporary European legal systems. Instead the term is thought of as a contrast to criminal law. And for our purposes that is exactly how it is conceived.

Under the common law tradition, the concept of criminal law developed with the belief that the state has a legal personality. Historically the courts were justified in settling disputes among private individuals only because the lord of the manor (and eventually the monarch) had an interest in the case. From the lord's perspective, "when you steal from my servant, you steal from me, and when you physically harm my servant, you harm me." In this way the state (in the form of the lord or monarch) takes a legal personality, and the harm done to the individual is seen as a harm to the public (the state).

The tradition of individual harm having a public component is illustrated in the way criminal cases are identified. It is the state (or commonwealth, or people) versus the defendant. That is, the defendant's accused harm is considered to have been a wrong against the public in general rather than the individual victim alone. But consider another type of harm. If your landlord has promised to paint your apartment during semester break but does not, you have clearly been harmed as an individual. But have your fellow citizens been harmed as well? Although your apartment may be an eyesore, it probably falls short of being a public nuisance. In this case the state does not see itself as having an interest in the harm done. It is considered to be a matter between you and the landlord.

Although different in terms of the wrong done—public or private—the two types of harm deserve a hearing before an impartial judge or jury. The harm considered to have a public component falls under the criminal law, while the harm done to you as an individual is handled by the civil law. In the United States, both state and federal courts are responsible for hearing each type of case. In fact, in the same courtroom on the same day, a judge may hear a criminal case in the morning and a civil case that afternoon. Although there are clearly different procedures and outcomes under each type of law (see Table 1.3), each is handled at the same courthouse.

TABLE 1.3: Distinguishing Features of Criminal Law and Civil Law

CRIMINAL LAW	CIVIL LAW
The wrong that was committed was a public wrong.	The wrong that was committed was a private wrong.
Action is initiated and controlled by a government official (the prosecutor) at the government's expense.	Action is initiated by the injured party (through a hired attorney) and at the individual's expense.
The personalities involved are the state as prosecutor and the accused as defendant (e.g., *Colorado v. Bertine*).	The personalities involved are the person bringing the action as the plaintiff and the person accused of wrongdoing as the defendant (e.g., *Schneider v. Jewell*).
The prosecutor has to prove a defendant's guilt *beyond a reasonable doubt* (almost certainty).	The plaintiff has to show by a *preponderance of evidence* (more than half the evidence) that the defendant is liable for damages.
A decision against the defendant can result in a range of punishments including a fine at one extreme and imprisonment, or even execution, at the other.	A decision against the defendant can result in payment of money damages or loss of property, but because we no longer have debtors prisons, the defendant is not at risk of imprisonment.
The public is the recipient of any decision against the defendant (e.g., the citizens get the satisfaction of knowing the convicted offender will be on probation for two years).	The private individual who brought suit against the defendant is the recipient of any decision against that defendant (e.g., the defendant must pay the private individual $1,000).

We are interested only in what happens when a crime or public wrong has occurred. That does not mean that there are no important links among the types of law concerning victims and offenders. In fact, an offender is subject to legal action in both civil and criminal court. Even though the harm done to an assault victim, for example, is considered a harm to the public as well, there is no doubt that the victim also suffered a private wrong. So, in addition to being charged with a crime (public wrong), an offender might also be charged with a civil action (private wrong). A good example of such a case is that of O. J. Simpson who was prosecuted for murder but acquitted by a jury in a criminal trial. However, a jury in a civil trial determined that he was responsible for the harm done to Nicole Brown Simpson and Ronald Goldman. As a result of the civil trial, O. J. Simpson was ordered to pay millions of dollars in damages to the victims' relatives. But, as Table 1.3 explains, the public is neither involved in the initiation of such cases nor responsible for the punishment handed down. The public is, however, clearly responsible for initiating criminal cases and for exacting the prescribed punishment. Therefore, this book concentrates on criminal rather than civil law violations.

Substantive and Procedural Law. Laws must serve two purposes. First, the rules must be defined—this is called **substantive law.** Second, the manner in which enforcement is accomplished must be prescribed—this is called **procedural law.** Both substantive criminal law and procedural criminal law are important to corrections. Defining the rules is accomplished by state legislatures and by the U.S. Congress. The results are presented in tomes such as a state's criminal (or penal) code and the United States Code (Title 18).

For example, the federal government defines, in part, the crime of counterfeiting and forgery of postage stamps, postage meter stamps, and postal cards in the following way:

> Whoever forges or counterfeits any postage stamp, postage meter stamp, or any stamp printed upon any stamped envelope, or postal card, or any die, plate, or engraving

The two trials of O. J. Simpson show how cases going through criminal court (where Simpson was found not guilty of murder) and civil court (where he was found liable for the death of Ronald Goldman and for committing battery against Nicole Brown Simpson) differ in procedures and may result in different outcomes.

> thereof; or Whoever makes or prints, or knowingly uses or sells, or possesses with intent to use or sell, any such forged or counterfeited postage stamp, postage meter stamp, stamped envelope, postal card, die, plate, or engraving; or . . . Shall be fined under this title or imprisoned not more than five years, or both. (18 U.S. Code Chap. 25 §501)

Notice that this example of substantive criminal law contains both an explanation of the actions constituting the crime and a stipulation regarding the punishment for persons committing this crime. These are ingredients of all substantive law, whether state or federal. The assumption is that everyone should be able to determine, in advance of his or her actions, whether those actions constitute a crime and what the punishment could be for that crime.

While substantive law defines what is criminal and stipulates a punishment, procedural law identifies the process that must be followed when the government interacts with citizens at various stages in the criminal justice process. This concern about government intrusion into citizens' lives has been a key issue since the country began. After creating the new Constitution of the United States, some framers expressed concern that the document contained the seeds of a tyranny by government. Discussion focused on adding a bill of rights to restrict the powers of the new federal government. The proponents' voices were so strong that the first Congress to meet following the adoption of the new Constitution submitted twelve amendments for consideration by the states. Ten of those were ratified by 1791, and they have become known as the Bill of Rights.

For purposes of criminal law, the Fourth (protection against unreasonable searches and seizures), Fifth (protection against double jeopardy and self-incrimination, and the requirement for due process), Sixth (providing for such things as the right to a speedy and public trial before an impartial jury, and for the assistance of counsel), and Eighth (prohibiting excessive bail, excessive fines, and cruel and unusual punishment) Amendments have particular relevance. The others are not unconnected to criminal law but typically have a more tangential

After creating the Constitution of the United States, the framers of this new document ratified ten amendments that became known as the Bill of Rights because they established the rights of U.S. citizens in relation to the powers of the new federal government.

link. For example, the First Amendment references to restrictions on religion, speech, press, assembly, and petition have been controversial in trial proceedings (conflicts between a free press and a fair trial) and confinement of prisoners (may Satanists practice their religion while in prison?).

What these amendments share in common is an attempt to stipulate the circumstances under which the government may intrude into citizens' private lives for purposes of assuring social order. In other words, they lay down the procedures—as in procedural criminal law—that police, courts, and corrections officials must abide by when initiating and taking action against a citizen.

The Bill of Rights is not the only source of procedural criminal law. Other examples include state constitutions, state criminal or penal codes, case law, and administrative regulations. In Chapter 14, on prisoners' rights, we will have occasion to return to several of these sources. Also in Chapter 14 is an elaboration of the Fourteenth Amendment. Because of that amendment's overall importance in criminal procedure, it receives brief mention here in the feature "How Did That Case Get There?"

Crime Control versus Due Process. Rules of criminal procedure must somehow juggle at least two aspects of freedom that are important to any criminal justice system: (1) Individual citizens must be free from wrongdoing by their fellow citizens, and (2) individual citizens must be free from wrongdoing by their government. Ideally, both objectives can be achieved in a way that balances a citizen's right to move freely throughout the country (the first goal) while allowing the government to monitor those movements to assure the citizen has no evil intent (the second goal). Packer (1968) distinguishes between these goals by referring to a crime control model and a due process model.

The **crime control model** assumes that freedom is so important that every effort must be made to repress crime, while the **due process model** assumes that freedom is so important that every effort must be made to ensure that criminal justice decisions are based on reliable information. Each model seeks to guarantee social freedom. One does so by emphasizing efficient processing of wrongdoers, while the other emphasizes effective restrictions on government invasion in the citizen's life. Who is the greater threat to our freedom? "The criminal trying to harm us or our property," says the crime control model. "The government agents such as police officers and prosecutors," says the due process model. Both criminals and government agents can invade our interests, take our property, and restrict our freedom of movement. Social freedom requires that the law-abiding citizen be free from unjustifiable intrusion by either criminals or by government agents. Unfortunately, it does not appear possible to achieve both goals simultaneously. One is emphasized at the expense of the other, but neither can be identified as qualitatively better (Cole, 1986; Reichel, 1999).

Both models are important at every stage of the criminal justice process. For corrections, the crime control model influences everything from reasons (philosophies) for punishment to the type and length of sentences given (practices and procedures). The due process model affects the quantity and quality of protection (also philosophies) afforded persons under correctional sanction (probation, jail, prison, etc.) and influences the way (more practices and procedures) corrections officials interact with offenders (e.g., revoking probation, disciplining prisoners). Obviously aspects of both crime control and due process will be discussed throughout this book.

Felonies and Misdemeanors. A final distinction must be made before leaving the topic of law. The crimes for which a person might be convicted are generally identified according to their level of seriousness. The least serious are termed **petty**

HISTORICAL PERSPECTIVES

How Did That Case Get There?

Have you ever wondered how the federal government gets involved in decisions made by state courts? Presumably our decentralized system of criminal justice means that each state develops and enforces its own laws. So, if one state says it's okay for the police to look in the glove compartment of a car to see if it contains a stash of shotguns, how can the U.S. Supreme Court determine that procedure to be inappropriate? Similarly, if a state chooses to execute by electrocution persons convicted under state law of a capital offense, what business would the U.S. Supreme Court have in telling that state it must use a different method? The only obligation a state has, you might argue, is to be true to its own state constitution, penal code, case law, and administrative guidelines. And if procedural law from those sources allows police to search containers that can't possibly hold the items for which they are supposedly searching, and allows the appropriate authorities to execute a murderer with an electric chair, then why should the federal government (in the form of the U.S. Supreme Court) care?

When drafted, the U.S. Constitution was not intended to protect individual citizens from the unfair enforcement of state laws. In the spirit of states' rights, and with greater fear of the federal government than of the state government, citizens expressed interest in controlling only the federal government. U.S. Supreme Court Chief Justice Marshall explained the prevailing opinion in the 1833 *Barron v. Baltimore* decision by noting that the framers of the U.S. Constitution would have specifically said the Bill of Rights applied to the states if the framers had so intended. Instead, Marshall argued, the amendments are clearly designed to limit only behavior by the federal government in its interactions with citizens.

That view held until after the Civil War when protection of citizen rights gained new concern and attention. The Thirteenth Amendment abolished slavery, but in response to continued violation of rights, Congress adopted the Fourteenth Amendment in 1868. The portion of the amendment affecting criminal justice reads: "No State shall . . . deprive any person of life, liberty, or property, without due process of law. . . ." Since the amendment's adoption, the meaning of the phrase *due process* has been a point of controversy. One resolution rests on the theory that the provisions of the Bill of Rights are incorporated into the due process clause of the Fourteenth Amendment and, therefore, are applicable to the states as well as the federal government. This legal theory has served as the basis for many U.S. Supreme Court decisions. The Court selectively has made certain Bill of Rights stipulations binding on state governments. In this manner, the U.S. Supreme Court can tell any state how to proceed (due process) when trying to deprive a citizen of life, liberty, or property. Because of the Fourteenth Amendment, the procedural conditions of amendments such as the Fourth (e.g., police can't search for items in locations where those items could not possibly be) and Eighth (e.g., the Court might some day consider execution by electrocution to be cruel and unusual) must be followed by state governments in criminal proceedings.

Go to "A Roadmap to the U.S. Constitution" at ***hyperion.advanced.org/11572/issues/past/incorporation.html,*** and read the explanation about incorporation and the Bill of Rights. Which amendments in the Bill of Rights have not yet been incorporated? Choose one of the cases hyperlinked on this page, and explain which amendment that case incorporated.

offenses (infractions, in some jurisdictions). For these crimes the maximum penalty is typically a fine or short term in jail. More serious crimes are **misdemeanors** (including petty offenses in jurisdictions that do not use the petty offense category), which are typically punishable by a fine and/or up to one year in jail (in a few jurisdictions, such as Colorado, it could be up to two years in jail). The most serious crimes throughout U.S. jurisdictions are **felonies.** The penalty for these offenses could be a fine, one year or more in prison, life imprisonment, or, where it is authorized, death.

Because they are more likely to involve incarceration, we will be dealing primarily with misdemeanors and felonies. It is important also to remember that punishments other than jail (for misdemeanors) and prison (for felonies) are possible for both types of crimes. For example, misdemeanants and felons might both receive community service sentences or be placed on probation.

Having identified the importance of law to the criminal justice system, it is also necessary to briefly mention how the first two components (police and courts) of that system interact with the third component (corrections).

Police and Courts

The strategies used to control crime and the philosophies on which those strategies are based are the nucleus of this book. Chapter 2 introduces five philosophies of punishment: deterrence, incapacitation, rehabilitation, retribution, and restoration. You will discover that each philosophy relies on particular strategies to achieve its goal. Because the penal philosophy being touted as the most desirable changes from decade to decade and region to region, it is not surprising that the philosophy currently in favor also changes among and within the three system components. So U.S. society can go through periods when the police act as if deterrence is the paramount response to criminals, while the courts emphasize retribution, and corrections officials operate programs set up to rehabilitate. As if that were not complicated enough, inconsistency can occur even within components so that, for example, wardens might try to operate prisons that attempt to rehabilitate offenders while at the same time relying on correctional officers who firmly believe in retribution.

The lack of agreement on a philosophy of punishment means the police, courts, and corrections agencies may each have a different approach to social control. Because activities in each component affect what happens in the other components, lack of agreement can cause problems. When the police crack down on crime by increasing arrests, the courts may respond by putting more people in prison. Increasing prison populations may mean that those institutions have to cut back on rehabilitation and training programs and serve primarily as warehouses for ever-increasing numbers of prisoners. Crowded prison conditions may require the early release of inmates who return to their communities only to commit new crimes and be arrested—once again—by the police, who start the process all over.

Because the activities in one component affect those in the other two, it is difficult to discuss corrections without addressing the role of law enforcement and the courts. For example, the police not only influence who is eventually handled by corrections agencies but also actually "work with" persons who are on probation, parole, or completing another aspect of a sentence. Anecdotes of police officers helping juvenile delinquents straighten out their lives, or encouraging a drug-addicted prostitute to get cleaned up and to find a legitimate job, occur often enough to remind us that police work has a corrections role. Some communities are implementing specific police–corrections partnerships that formalize the link between these two system components (see Parent & Snyder, 1999).

The corrections role of the courts is even more easily seen than that of the police. Most obvious is the judge's sentence, which formally initiates the corrections process. Less obvious are the efforts that avoid a formal court process as much as possible. For example, Chapter 5 explains the use of *mediation*—the offender and victim meet with a third party (typically not a judge) to try to rectify the harm caused by the offender in a manner that is satisfactory to all parties.

It is the court's formal role that has the most direct influence on the corrections component. In addition to handing down the sentence for an offender, the judge can also be involved in discussions related to any plea bargains that might have been offered, and in modifications of a sentence such as taking someone off probation and placing him or her in prison. Also, as noted in the earlier discussion of procedural criminal law, the courts are actively involved in determining the

Help Wanted

In addition to boxed material relevant to the major themes of this book, you will also find occasional "Help Wanted" boxes that draw your attention to career opportunities in corrections. The job titles and descriptions are similar to ones you will encounter in seeking a corrections career, but specifics will vary by agency. Included in each "Help Wanted" ad is Internet or other contact information about an agency or agencies that might have a position like the one described. The ad is not, of course, an offer of employment from any agency.

For both general and criminal justice–specific career information, check out the career page at *www.cjed.com/career.htm.*

obligations that corrections officials such as probation officers, correctional officers, and wardens may have as they interact with offenders under their control. Later chapters expand on all these issues.

Corrections

Corrections, the third component of the criminal justice system, refers to the network of local, state, and federal government agencies having responsibility for preconviction and postconviction custody, supervision, and treatment of persons accused or convicted of crimes. The term also applies to the correctional facilities where those people are held (e.g., jails and detention centers for the accused; and jails, halfway houses, or prisons for the convicted) and to the correctional programs in which they participate (e.g., pretrial services, community service, probation, work release, and parole). Finally, the term refers to the corrections personnel (e.g., correctional officers, probation officers, prison counselors, and wardens) who are responsible for the custody, supervision, and treatment duties.

The corrections system, including its facilities, programs, and personnel, is an increasingly large and expensive part of American society. There are some 5,000 correctional facilities in the United States, of which there are about 3,300 local jails (administered by counties and sometimes cities), 1,400 state prisons, 125 federal prisons, and 175 private facilities (Beck & Mumola, 1999; Harlow, 1998; Thomas, 1999). Included in the state and federal prison numbers are facilities such as boot camps, prison farms and camps, and community-based facilities such as halfway houses, work release centers, and treatment centers.

The cost associated with correctional activities varies by year and government level, but consider the following for the nation's fifty-two adult correctional agencies (fifty states, District of Columbia, and federal government) during 1997 (Camp & Camp, 1997):

- The fiscal year 1997 budget for all fifty-two agencies totaled nearly $30 billion (up from $18 billion in 1991) for an average of about $556 million per agency.
- The average agency's budget represented nearly 5 percent of the jurisdiction's total budget—ranging from a high in Alabama of 17.4 percent to a low of 0.002 percent in the Federal Bureau of Prisons.
- The average daily cost per confined inmate in 1996 was $54.25 (up from $48.07 in 1990) in all adult agencies—ranging from Alaska's high ($105.27) to Alabama's low ($25.52).

Similar data for probation and parole agencies result in the following (Camp & Camp, 1997):

- The fiscal year 1997 budget for probation and parole agencies throughout the nation totaled more than $4 billion for an average of $60 million (up from $34 million in 1992).
- The average daily cost per probationer/parolee in 1996 was $3.51.

For points of comparison, Table 1.4 shows that the national per capita expenditures for corrections are less than that for police protection but greater than the expenditures for judicial and legal activities. Also, although it is not a direct comparison, you might be interested in knowing that the $19,800 estimated annual cost per confined inmate (the average per day cost of $54.25 × 365 days) compares with a $6,600 annual per pupil cost in U.S. public elementary and secondary schools (Geddes, 1998) and a $7,100 annual per passenger cost for public transportation (e.g., bus, tram, light rail, heavy rail, commuter rail) in the United States ("U.S. Urban Public Transport Summary of National Trends, 1983–1995," 1995). Some pundits have also pointed out that with the average annual tuition and room

TABLE 1.4: Direct Expenditures for Correctional Activities of State Governments and Percent Distribution by Type of Activity, United States, Fiscal Years 1980–1994[a] (dollar amounts in thousands)

		INSTITUTIONS				OTHER CORRECTIONS		
				Capital Outlay				
Fiscal Year	Total Direct	Total	Direct Current	Construction	Other	Total	Direct Current	Capital Outlay
1980	$4,257,509	$3,410,933	$2,869,492	$482,652	$58,789	$846,576	$824,439	$22,137
1981	4,843,857	3,886,234	3,276,441	533,419	76,374	957,623	927,529	30,094
1982	5,559,792	4,480,490	3,848,893	544,300	87,297	1,079,302	1,038,299	41,003
1983	6,323,240	5,135,550	4,488,027	557,237	90,286	1,187,690	1,122,558	65,132
1984	7,178,011	5,913,323	5,114,702	695,198	103,423	1,264,688	1,213,602	51,086
1985	8,336,040	6,927,619	5,932,686	858,856	136,077	1,408,421	1,335,947	72,474
1986	9,877,577	8,246,279	6,708,440	1,342,807	195,032	1,631,298	1,558,933	72,365
1987	10,732,880	8,843,089	7,587,706	1,077,207	178,176	1,889,791	1,722,418	167,373
1988	12,403,648	10,364,051	8,648,292	1,486,461	229,298	2,039,597	1,926,136	113,461
1989	13,854,499	11,617,138	9,661,969	1,724,021	231,148	2,237,361	2,099,149	138,212
1990	15,842,063	13,321,228	11,145,405	1,921,846	253,977	2,520,835	2,301,633	218,202
1991	17,789,540	14,995,912	12,497,915	2,235,632	262,365	2,793,628	2,591,245	202,383
1992	18,750,826	15,657,098	13,599,703	1,813,405	243,990	3,093,728	2,874,716	219,012
1993	19,091,342	15,965,881	14,239,710	1,479,871	246,300	3,125,461	2,999,462	125,999
1994	21,266,053	17,741,937	15,776,174	1,695,718	270,045	3,524,116	3,319,462	204,654
Percent Distribution								
1980	100%	80.1%	67.4%	11.3%	1.4%	19.9%	19.4%	0.5%
1981	100	80.2	67.6	11.0	1.6	19.8	19.1	0.6
1982	100	80.6	69.2	9.8	1.6	19.4	18.7	0.7
1983	100	81.2	71.0	8.8	1.4	18.8	17.8	1.0
1984	100	82.4	71.3	9.7	1.4	17.6	16.9	0.7
1985	100	83.1	71.2	10.3	1.6	16.9	16.0	0.9
1986	100	83.5	67.9	13.6	2.0	16.5	15.8	0.7
1987	100	82.4	70.7	10.0	1.7	17.6	16.0	1.6
1988	100	83.6	69.7	12.0	1.8	16.4	15.5	0.9
1989	100	83.9	69.7	12.4	1.7	16.1	15.2	1.0
1990	100	84.1	70.4	12.1	1.6	15.9	14.5	1.4
1991	100	84.3	70.3	12.6	1.5	15.7	14.6	1.1
1992	100	83.5	72.5	9.7	1.3	16.5	15.3	1.2
1993	100	83.6	74.6	7.8	1.3	16.4	15.7	0.7
1994	100	83.4	74.2	8.0	1.3	16.6	15.6	1.0

[a]Detail may not add to total because of rounding.

Source: U.S. Department of Justice, Bureau of Justice Statistics. *Justice expenditure and employment extracts: Trends since 1980* [NCJ 175704]. Washington, DC: forthcoming. Table 10. Table adapted by SOURCEBOOK staff. Available: www.ojp.usdoj.gov/bjs/eande.htm#data.

and board costs at a public four-year college running about $7,300, it is cheaper to provide a bachelor's degree for a person than to keep that person in prison. In fact, it is even cheaper to finance tuition and room and board (about $18,500 per year) at a private four-year college ("Education Costs by Institution," 1998).

It is time to begin looking at America's corrections system in greater depth. The following chapters will consider the facilities, programs, and personnel that make up the corrections component of the criminal justice system. But before considering the specifics of these practices and procedures, the philosophies on which the corrections system is based need to be explained. That background is the subject of Chapter 2.

SUMMARY

KEY THEMES

This chapter introduces key terms and concepts that will be recurring throughout the text. First, it notes the importance of three perspectives that influence this book's content and approach.

- Taking a historical perspective, we know the mistakes and successes that have already occurred in relation to a particular topic. Thus, we can appreciate how these experiences help us anticipate future problems and solutions.
- Taking an international perspective is important in today's world, not only because cross-national crime makes it necessary for countries to understand other justice processes, but also because we can learn from each other's successes and failures. The historical and international perspectives are used throughout the text as a way to highlight how looking back and looking abroad can help us to look forward.
- Being aware of the importance of issues of fairness related to gender, race, ethnicity, and social class is necessary because of the increasing presence of women and other minorities in the criminal justice system.

CRIME AND CORRECTIONS

The link between crime and corrections is addressed, and a few suggestions are made about ways to explain the increasing imprisonment rate at a time when crime is declining.

CORRECTIONS AND THE CRIMINAL JUSTICE SYSTEM

This chapter concludes by placing corrections in the context of the criminal justice system as a whole.

- Law is distinguished as either criminal or civil law. It is further divided according to whether it defines crime and sets a punishment (substantive law) or stipulates the process to be used in taking action against a citizen (procedural law).
- Two models used to help understand the complexities of procedural law are the crime control and the due process models. Each is important and necessary in the way society applies the law.
- *Corrections*—a term that refers to facilities, programs, and personnel—is an increasingly large and expensive part of U.S. society.

Key Terms and Concepts

civil law (p. 18)
corrections (p. 26)
crime control model (p. 23)
criminal justice system (p. 17)
criminal law (p. 18)
due process model (p. 23)
ethnicity (p. 10)
felonies (p. 24)
misdemeanors (p. 24)
petty offenses (p. 23)
procedural law (p. 21)
race (p. 10)
substantive law (p. 21)

Discussion Questions

1. In studying corrections and the criminal justice process, what are the advantages of taking a historical perspective?
2. In studying corrections and the criminal justice process, what are the advantages of taking an international perspective?
3. Provide some examples of the truth in Martin Luther King, Jr.'s quote: "Injustice anywhere is a threat to justice everywhere."
4. Do you think American society currently places a greater emphasis on the crime control or the due process model? Explain why and offer some examples.
5. In addition to comparing the annual cost of keeping a person in prison to the cost of public education and public transportation, what are some other types of expenditures that you think would make interesting comparisons? Try to find the data allowing you to make those comparisons.

SOCIAL CONTROL

SANCTIONS

Sanction Direction

Sanction Styles

Sanction Types

PHILOSOPHIES OF PUNISHMENT

Deterrence

Incapacitation

Rehabilitation

Retribution

Restoration

SUMMARY

KEY TERMS AND CONCEPTS

DISCUSSION QUESTIONS

chapter 2

PHILOSOPHIES OF PUNISHMENT

Jerrod has been found guilty of burglary. He broke into a home while the residents were at a movie, and he stole a VCR worth $225. This is Jerrod's second conviction on burglary charges. As an eighteen-year-old adult, he received six months probation for the first offense. He completed that probation successfully two months ago. As the judge in the present case, you must punish Jerrod. Which of the following best expresses what you believe your personal motivation will be as you determine the appropriate punishment? Choose only one!

1. The punishment must be unpleasant enough that Jerrod is discouraged from committing another crime.

2. The punishment must be one that makes it physically unlikely, if not impossible, that Jerrod will commit another crime for at least a specific number of months or years.
3. The punishment must be one that provides opportunities for Jerrod to make better choices in the future so that he is unlikely to need or want to commit another crime.
4. The punishment must be one that is comparable to the punishment others would get for a similar crime and is of reasonable severity considering the nature of the offense. Whether that punishment results in subsequent behavior change in Jerrod is less important than making sure Jerrod is punished.
5. The punishment must be one that not only sanctions the crime but also takes into consideration Jerrod's victim and the members of the community where the burglary occurred. In fact, if the victim and community members are willing, you will seek their advice regarding Jerrod's punishment and his reintegration in the community.

Well, what is your philosophy of punishment? Do you lean more strongly toward punishment for deterrence (choice "1"), incapacitation ("2"), rehabilitation ("3"), retribution ("4"), or restoration ("5")? In all likelihood you felt restricted by the request to choose only one response. And, realistically, your philosophy may change depending on the circumstances of the offense and/or the characteristics of the offender. But our immediate goal is to understand better just what options exist for any individual or collective punishment philosophy. This chapter explains the five philosophies and tells how they are important to each of us personally and as members of society.

SOCIAL CONTROL

One is absolutely sickened, not by the crimes that the wicked have committed, but by the punishments that the good have inflicted; and a community is infinitely more brutalized by the habitual employment of punishment than it is by the occasional occurrence of crime.

—Oscar Wilde

Oscar Wilde seemed not to accept any rationale for punishment—he would have liked a "none of the above" response for the punishment philosophy question! His position is rather extreme by most people's standards in most parts of the world.

Debates about punishment have not dealt with whether it should be applied but rather center on reasons for applying it—and in turn influence the punishment used. This chapter begins with a general discussion of social control and then explores the topic of sanctions.

The topic of social control can be approached from at least two directions. Some theorists are interested in why people conform to the status quo. The question asked by these philosophers and scientists is: "Why do people behave themselves?" Emile Durkheim (1964), for example, studied the nature of social bonds holding people together in groups. He hypothesized that the division of labor (the number of different jobs done by different persons) in a society gave society its order, harmony, and solidarity. In primarily rural and agrarian societies, he argued, everyone had a similar job (e.g., farming), and as a result they shared similar beliefs and values. After all, if an economic, political, or educational condition favored one farmer, it was likely to favor the others. In these communities people behaved themselves because they all agreed on the same norms and values.

But people continued to behave themselves even as the division of labor grew. Instead of everyone farming, some people are now bankers, merchants, and factory workers. No longer is a particular economic or political condition that benefits one person necessarily going to benefit all the others. The differences among these citizens do not, however, mean that their society lacks cohesion or order. The specialization brought by the division of labor means that people are no longer self-sufficient. Now they must depend on each other for items they no longer own or produce. So, social control exists in these societies not because people are so alike but instead because they depend on each other.

Of course, we know that there are people in all types of communities who violate the norms. Those are the people whom other social control theorists find intriguing. They ask the question: "Why do people misbehave?" Both sides of this social control coin are important and interesting, but this chapter will be concentrating on the "why people misbehave" side. Before doing so, however, some concepts helpful in understanding all aspects of social control will be reviewed.

Sociologists refer to society's guidelines for people's behavior as being **norms.** These norms are of three specific types: **folkways, mores,** and **laws** (Sumner, 1907). The types of norms are best understood by looking at how society responds when one type of norm is violated. For example, when a folkway is violated, the members of society are displeased but do not demand harsh punishment of the offender. Good examples of folkways are the rules of etiquette set down in different cultures. If your culture expects you to eat with utensils rather than your hands, the person shoving fistfuls of food into his or her mouth is violating a folkway. Other dinner guests may shake their heads at such crudeness, but the worst that is likely to happen is that the "offender" will not be invited to a similar dinner by that hostess. Violations of rules of etiquette typically result in little more than chiding or scolding.

Mores are norms that members of society take a little more seriously. If folkways are considered desirable behavior, mores are expected behavior. In the 1970s, streaking around U.S. college campuses in the nude was an occasional practice—it even continued into the late 1990s as the Princeton University Nude Olympics. Because the wearing of clothes in public is considered more than simple etiquette by most Americans, the streaking fad can be considered to have violated social mores. In some communities the response to streakers went beyond simple chiding or scolding; instead, the streakers were rebuked and reprimanded. Some communities were so upset with streakers that they tried to charge them with violating the law, the third type of norm. Often, however, the laws against public nudity required the offender to be acting in a lewd and lascivious manner—attributes difficult to apply to the streakers. At Princeton, for example, university officials have tried to ban the annual event as being dangerous to the students (there have been incidents of alcohol poisoning) and the community (in a few years students left campus and committed minor offenses in the city) but not because students are running around naked.

There are some norms that society sees as such necessary guidelines for behavior that they are made into laws. Society considers violation of its laws as the most serious norm infraction and responds with its most serious penalties. Although offenders of the law may be chided and scolded, and rebuked and reprimanded, they will also receive formal punishment administered by government authorities. That formal punishment is technically a **sanction,** which refers to techniques a society uses to enforce its norms.

SANCTIONS

Sanctions are categorized in several ways. They might be divided by their direction (positive or negative), their style (formal or informal), or their type (physical, economic, or social/psychological). The topic of corrections, as part of a criminal justice system, is primarily concerned with formal, negative sanctions of all three types. But before concentrating on formal negative sanctions, this section briefly considers each characteristic of sanctions in general.

Sanction Direction

Because sanctions simply refer to the ways a society tries to enforce its norms, they can technically be either positive or negative. **Positive sanctions,** such as rewards, will presumably encourage the continuation of norm-abiding behavior. When people are asked back to parties, are congratulated on doing a good job, or receive extra pay for exceptional work, they are receiving positive sanctions. On the other hand, **negative sanctions** are used to discourage norm-violating behavior. Being ignored by friends, being demoted for poor work, or getting fined for misbehavior are examples of negative sanctions.

It could be argued that positive sanctions are more effective at encouraging norm-abiding behavior than negative sanctions are at discouraging norm-violating behavior, but such debates are better left to learning theorists in psychology. That is not to say that such issues are unimportant to the area of corrections. For example, we will see in later chapters that Alexander Maconochie, as director of an Australian prison colony, allowed prisoners the opportunity for early release from prison by taking days off their sentence at the end of each month they showed good behavior. This positive sanction rewarded prisoners who showed norm-abiding behavior. U.S. prisons that adapted Maconochie's idea accepted the concept but preferred a negative sanctioning approach. Prisoners entering American prisons were, and essentially still are, given time off their sentences upon their arrival at the prison doorstep. If the prisoners do not misbehave while in prison, they are released (often on parole) earlier than provided for by their actual sentences. But, if the prisoners misbehave, some of those "days off" can be added back on to the time they must spend in prison. In this manner, prison officials are using negative sanctions to discourage norm-violating behavior.

Deciding whether to give prisoners days off their sentence after they have shown good behavior, or adding days back on to their sentence when they exhibit bad behavior, may seem as futile as determining whether the chicken or egg came first. But each approach may have different consequences that link to topics such as rehabilitation, reintegration, and even social control within the prison. Despite the intriguing and important questions presented by the positive versus negative sanctions debate, the criminal justice system in the United States is basically built around the use of negative sanctions. As a result, this book is primarily about the negative sanctions that society uses in an attempt to enforce those norms called laws.

Sanction Styles

Because everyone in society has the ability to sanction everyone else, it is not surprising that some sanctions will be very informal in nature. When one friend frowns at another who has just said something inappropriate, or when teammates join in "high-fives" after a great play, **informal sanctions** are being handed out. These informal sanctions are the ones individuals encounter earliest in their lives and continue to be the most frequent throughout life. Family members, friends, neighbors, and even enemies are able to sanction us informally by exhibiting everything from friendly or hostile greetings to throwing their arms around our waist or their fist into our face. What all these sanctions have in common is that they occur without the official backing of any group—they simply represent the feeling and reaction of an individual, or maybe a casual group of individuals. They are, in this manner, informal sanctions.

When a person representing some explicit group of people (such as the school we attend, the company we work for, or the government where we reside) sanctions us, it becomes a **formal sanction.** The distinction between informal and formal is not clear-cut, and realistically does not need to be, but we should appreciate the difference in style that is represented. For purposes of criminal justice in general, and corrections more specifically, we must understand that formal sanctions are of central concern. Informal sanctions may actually be more effective at controlling behavior (we abide by norms so we are not on the receiving end of our parents' or friends' wrath) than are formal sanctions (we are not impressed by penalties imposed by the principal or the judge), but this book focuses on the formal sanctioning process used in the criminal justice system.

Sanction Types

Having identified formal negative sanctions as the primary concern in this book, this section can now look more closely at different versions of these sanctions. Physical sanctions are the simplest and most direct of the three sanction types. They involve some kind of reinforcing stimulus applied to the person's body. When a misbehaving child is spanked, or a well-behaved child is hugged, physical sanctions are being used. For purposes of criminal justice, formal negative physical sanctions are handed down by justice officials and include incarceration in jail or prison, restrictions on a person's movement in the community, and the most extreme example, execution. We will review examples of each type, and a few others throughout this book.

Financial rewards and punishments are another popular way that members of society try to influence each other's behavior. Regular patrons at a restaurant provide positive economic sanctions to the owners, whereas boycotts of certain products are efforts to express negative financial sanctions. Fines, payment of financial restitution, and even forced community service are examples of the kinds of formal negative financial sanctions that the criminal justice system can dispense. As with physical sanctions, specific examples of formal negative financial sanctions will be considered in later chapters.

When a person is made to feel bad, good, accepted, or rejected, social/psychological sanctions are being used. These are most clearly seen in their informal style because they are used daily as we interact with each other. Smiles, frowns, hand gestures, invitations, scolding, and cursing give verbal and nonverbal cues about how one person evaluates another's behavior. People being sanctioned in these ways are made to feel either proud, favored, and appreciated or guilty, ashamed, and snubbed. They have, in other words, had their social setting or their psychological well-being affected. People experience formal negative social/psychological sanctions from having their name printed in the local paper after a shoplifting or drunk driving conviction, being required to wear an electronic monitoring bracelet that occasionally shows beneath their pant leg, or being stared at by college students on a tour of the state prison where they currently reside.

It will occur to you that the three sanction types are not always so easy to distinguish. Isn't a person who has to pay a fine (a financial sanction) likely to be embarrassed (a social/psychological sanction)? Doesn't a person confined in jail (a physical sanction) miss opportunities to make money (a financial sanction), and possibly lose friends (a social/psychological sanction) as a result of the conviction? The answer, of course, is that one particular sanction may actually incorporate aspects of all three types. But the reason for distinguishing them is not so we can assign a judge's sentence to one of three categories of sanctions. Instead, it gives us a way to easily show the various types of impact the sentence might have. So, as the rest of the book considers the ways society has chosen to provide formal negative sanctions, we can appreciate how those sanctions might affect the offender physically, economically, or socially/psychologically.

Because the sanctions most relevant to the justice system tend to be negative ones, use of the word *sanction* in this text will be synonymous with the terms *penalty* and *punishment*. But it is good to remember that just as sanction has a positive side, the concepts of penalty and punishment might also have positive consequences that their names belie. For example, later this chapter will discuss the rehabilitative and restorative aspects of punishment. If you think of punishment as having only negative consequences, it might be hard to associate punishment with supportive programs. But if you remember that punishment, like sanction, simply refers to society's attempt at encouraging norm-abiding behavior, the link to concepts such as rehabilitation and restoration seems less strange. The rest of this chapter will look first at some philosophies or rationales that have been offered over the years for punishing law violators. Then the chapter will review the various ways that societies have sanctioned, or punished, those persons who have broken the norms called laws.

Philosophies of Punishment

Philosophies, justifications, reasons, or rationales for punishment have been pondered, proposed, and debated for centuries. We will consider several of these philosophies because they will help us understand some of the techniques and processes used in response to society's criminals. Specifically, we will concentrate on the philosophies of deterrence, incapacitation, rehabilitation, retribution, and restoration (see Table 2.1).

Keep at least two things in mind as you begin this review: (1) Philosophies of punishment are more like recurrent themes than new ideas, and (2) there is never a time when everyone agrees that a single punishment philosophy is appropriate. First, because all the justifications have been around for a long time, new arguments are most likely just reappearances of their older versions. For example, in 1776 Myuart de Vougians referred to the punishment rationales of rehabilitation, restoration, and deterrence when he said that the aim of punishment should be

TABLE 2.1: Characteristics of the Punishment Philosophies

	DETERRENCE	INCAPACITATION	REHABILITATION	RETRIBUTION	RESTORATION
Does punishment focus on the act or actor?	Act	Act	Actor	Act	Actor and victim
Is punishment applied as reactive or proactive?	Primarily reactive	Reactive and proactive	Primarily proactive	Primarily reactive	Primarily reactive
Is punishment applied as an end in itself or to achieve some other goal?	Has the goal of discouraging repeat offense and preventing crime in the first place	Has the goal of preventing continued criminal acts by restricting the offender's freedom of movement	Has the goal of changing the offender into a law-abiding citizen	An end in itself	An end in itself but also has the goal of restoring the balance that the offender has upset

to "(a) correct the offender; (b) repair the wrong caused by the crime if possible; and (c) deter the evil-minded by the example and fear of similar punishments" (Sellin, 1967, p. 20).

Second, although one or two punishment philosophies may hold center stage in a particular time period, there are always people who disagree about the appropriateness of those in vogue and promote the desirability of the ones waiting in the wings. That's why it is difficult to identify any particular justification as being dominant during a specific time period. For purposes of explanation, the five basic punishment philosophies need to be described as if they might exist independently and can at times hold a dominant position. But remember that the various punishment rationales constantly intermingle in the minds of citizens and in the way penal sanctions are applied.

With these warnings in mind, we now begin a review of the five basic philosophies of punishment. Their importance in understanding the theory and practice of corrections is emphasized by how they relate to the main ideas in several of the following chapters. In Chapters 3 and 4, for example, the philosophies are used to help explain the penal system eras through which corrections has passed. In Chapter 15, the philosophies are the points for discussion of what, if anything, works in corrections. In other words, the concepts of deterrence, incapacitation, rehabilitation, retribution, and restoration are the structure for society's system of penal sanctions and for this book.

Deterrence

Following the older demonological and theological explanations for crime, the classical school of criminology provided one of the early theories of criminality. It may be more accurate to say that the classical school provided an early theory of correction. When Cesare Beccaria, an eighteenth-century Italian criminologist, published *Essay on Crimes and Punishments* in 1764, he was proposing as much a system of justice as an explanation of crime. Following the lead of Jeremy Bentham, an eighteenth-century British philosopher who argued that actions are moral if they are useful or utilitarian, Beccaria believed punishment should be used only to achieve good. A clear example of good would be a reduction in crime. If punishment helps bring about such a reduction, then punishment is serving a utilitarian purpose. The idea that punishment, or the threat of it, keeps people in line is so ingrained in many people that it is easy to forget that it is simply one of many theories about human nature (see the feature "Forget All Those Theories You Learned in School!").

Deterrence is the term applied to the utilitarian principle that says punishment's aim is to prevent future offenses by example to both the offender and to others. In other words, punishment preserves the social order (1) by showing the criminal that his action was undesirable because it brought him more pain than pleasure, and (2) by showing others who are considering a criminal act that they also will suffer painful consequences if they commit a wrong. That first function of punishment is called **specific deterrence,** whereas the second is **general deterrence.**

Specific Deterrence. When punishment is applied to someone who has already misbehaved, its aim is to discourage that specific person from offending again. Because the offender is still a rational, hedonistic person with free will, the punishment should convince her that the pain associated with the crime outweighed any pleasure she may have received from committing the crime.

The lack of a specific deterrent effect might be due to problems society has in achieving some of the key requirements of an effective deterrence system. It can be argued, as in Chapter 15, that punishment can act as a deterrent only when it is accomplished with certainty, severity, and swiftness. For purposes of specific deterrence, this means that having caught offender Jones—and wanting to deter her from future acts—society's punishment must be unavoidable, it must be severe enough that Jones considers it more painful than any pleasure she got from the act, and it must be applied to Jones soon after the crime occurred. Each of these conditions is problematic, and as a result specific deterrence is hard to accomplish. Certainty can reasonably be achieved only if citizens are willing to be constantly monitored so that all criminal acts are known to the authorities and can thereby be punished. Severity may be possible today, but there is the problem that "severe" for one person may be "mild" to another. Swiftness of punishment could likely be achieved only by restricting the due process currently provided defendants and the rights to appeal now granted to convicted offenders.

If conditions such as certainty, severity—in just proportion—and swiftness are necessary for punishment to effectively operate as a specific deterrent, and Beccaria claimed that they were (Maestro, 1973, p. 29), we can understand better why there are few studies showing a specific deterrent effect of punishment. But what about a general deterrent effect? Unfortunately, if you are hoping to find such an effect, Beccaria said the same conditions are necessary for punishment to serve as a general deterrent.

General Deterrence. When the aim of punishment is to discourage other people from committing a crime in the first place, it is said to have a general deterrence function. As the Christmas season approaches, local department stores may seek to deter shoplifting by increasing their willingness to press charges against shoplifters. The store manager believes that the publicity resulting from media reports about shoplifters being prosecuted and punished will discourage other people from shoplifting. If people who hear about "Christie the Booster" getting sentenced to three months in jail for shoplifting decide not to shoplift, the punishment of Christie has a general deterrence role—even if it fails to specifically discourage Christie from further crime.

HISTORICAL PERSPECTIVES

Forget All Those Theories You Learned in School!

One of the more interesting, if not irritating, things I have come to expect in twenty-plus years of teaching occurs when a former student checks in with me a few months after his or her graduation. If that student has found employment in law enforcement, at some point in our conversation I expect to hear something such as the following: "During the first few weeks on the job I had several officers tell me to forget all those theories I learned in school. The only thing I need to know, they explained, is that people commit crime because they want to and they don't think they'll be punished."

Sometimes the student says this with disappointment that she has coworkers who don't appreciate social or behavioral science. Other students make the comment with glee and seem to hope that I will encourage my department to change the curriculum to remove all reference to theory. But regardless of the motivation to tell me the story, the more important point is that "Officer Naysayer" is in fact supporting a theory. The idea that criminals respond to punishment, or its threat, is simply one of many theories about human nature. What the officer is really saying is: "Forget all those theories you learned in school, except the one I believe!" Let's take a brief look at Officer Naysayer's favorite theory, classical theory.

The classical school's argument is based on three notions: free will, rational calculus, and hedonism. In contradiction to such prevailing explanations of human behavior as demonology ("the devil made him do it"), classical theorists believe people's behavior results from conscious decisions by those people. In other words, humans have free will that allows them to behave in ways of their own choosing. Both law abiders and law violators use their respective free will to decide how they will behave. The decision itself results from weighing pros and cons associated with the behavior being considered. Because humans are rational beings, the classicists argue, they calculate the consequences of an act before it is committed. This rational calculus involves an estimate of the rewards to be gained from the act as they match up against any possible penalties associated with the act. Finally, because humans are hedonistic, they constantly seek to gain pleasure and avoid pain. Therefore, when people choose to act in a particular way, they first consider the pros and cons of that behavior (rational calculation) and then choose (free will) the act that gives them more pleasure than pain (hedonism).

If these assumptions about human behavior are correct, the classical theorists argue, an effective system of social control is one that sets penalties for undesirable acts at a level at which they present more pain than pleasure to people considering them. So, if I am thinking about stealing a radio, I will weigh the pleasure the radio will give me against the pain I will receive when caught and decide that the eventual pain is not worth it.

You have probably already discovered some of the problems with this view of human behavior, even if Officer Naysayer hasn't. For example, what if I am not convinced the penalty will actually be applied? If the punishment lacks certainty, I may not see it as outweighing the pleasure the radio will give me. Or what if I don't see the proposed penalty as being as severe as did those who made it the punishment for theft? Something you see as being very punitive may not be considered so bad from my perspective. Like all theories, the one held by Officer Naysayer must be critically evaluated and respected for both its drawbacks and its benefits.

Read more about the classical school of criminology at ***www.crimetheory.com/Theories/Classical.htm.*** According to the social contract, what are the four steps to a well-ordered society? Do the exercises at "Fit the punishment to the crime" link. Did you agree with the punishments suggested by Beccaria?

For society's punishment of "Christie the Booster" to have a deterrent effect on the behavior of Smith, Martinez, Chen, Brown, and others, they will all have to believe that (1) it is certain they will be punished, (2) the punishment will be severe enough that they consider it to be more painful than any pleasure the act will give them, and (3) the punishment will be administered soon after their wrongful act. In addition to those three conditions, Newman (1985) adds the requirement of publicity because that condition is necessary for Smith and the others to know about Christie's punishment.

If people refrain from committing a crime because they fear the punishment they might receive, that punishment is serving a deterrent function.

Just as certainty, severity, and swiftness are difficult to achieve for purposes of specific deterrence, they are also problematic for general deterrence. Publicity, however, is more attainable today with our advanced media technology. But if the public is informed less about criminals being punished and more about the problems of making arrests and getting convictions (a lack of certainty), the increased use of what are seen as lenient penalties (a lack of severity), and the excessive time it takes for punishment to actually be applied (a lack of swiftness), the existence of publicity may be more harm than help in having punishment be a general deterrent.

Before leaving the concept of general deterrence, it is important to consider an interesting and controversial aspect of this philosophy. Pollock-Byrne says the idea of general deterrence is interesting "because there does not necessarily need to be an original crime" (1989, p. 132). In other words, for general deterrence to work, it is not necessary that only guilty people be punished.

Intriguing as the argument of punishing an innocent person to achieve general deterrence might be, Newman (1985) says that Bentham would not have accepted it as a legitimate aspect. Although punishing innocent people might help achieve general deterrence, any system of ethics would reject the practice. But that does not necessarily mean that people cannot be punished for something they have not yet done. As seen later, both incapacitation and rehabilitation are philosophies of punishment that might apply punishment on the assumption that a person will misbehave in the future.

We have used the concepts of certainty, severity, swiftness, and publicity to show some of the problems of using punishment, either specific or general, to deter behavior. Of course, it is also possible that the deterrence philosophy of punishment suffers from a more fatal problem—its very core assumptions may be wrong. Maybe people are not rational, calculating individuals using free will to achieve pleasure and avoid pain. If this is the case, all the certainty, severity, and swiftness that society can muster will be to no avail. Irrational people, or those whose behavior is determined by biological, psychological, or social factors rather than through free will, are not going to be deterred by punishment (Katz, 1988).

Incapacitation

When **incapacitation** is used as a punishment, a person's ability to move about freely is impaired or restricted. Historically the incapacitation of criminals has been through imprisonment. The idea is that by removing a criminal from free society, that person is prevented from continuing to cause harm to people or property. Because the prisoner's freedom of movement is taken away, society is protected from his or her misbehavior. Although imprisonment is the classic way to incapacitate offenders, recent technological advances offer other ways to restrict an offender's freedom of movement. For example, chemicals or surgery might be used to keep an offender in check. Or technology might allow authorities to electronically monitor an offender's whereabouts. These old and new means of incapacitation are discussed in later chapters, but they are considered briefly here to expand the understanding of the philosophy of incapacitation.

Incapacitation through Imprisonment. Zimring and Hawkins (1995) believe that incapacitation was the dominant official justification for punishment during the 1980s and 1990s. The increase in state and federal prison populations during those decades seems to support their argument. The penal philosophy of incapacitation by imprisonment has aspects that appeal to both liberals and conservatives, who tend to disagree more about the appropriate scale of imprisonment than its actual use. A liberal crime control policy, for example, might reserve imprisonment for those very few offenders who must truly be locked away for society's protection. In 1973 the National Council on Crime and Delinquency suggested that number could be as low as 100 persons in each state (Zimring & Hawkins, 1995, p. 10). Imprisonment, in other words, is acceptable on a limited scale. Crime control from a conservative perspective sees imprisonment as not only acceptable but desirable on an extensive scale for a wide range of offenders. From this perspective, imprisonment is thought to have benefits of protecting society from criminals whether or not any rehabilitation or specific deterrence occurs.

Zimring and Hawkins (1995) refer to the minimalist rationale of liberals as highlighting **selective incapacitation,** wherein imprisonment is reserved for a select group of especially dangerous repeat offenders who must be incapacitated to protect society. The conservative's expansionist rationale is called **general incapacitation,** because it favors a broad use of imprisonment as a way to achieve large gains in crime prevention by locking away even run-of-the-mill felons.

Both selective incapacitation and general incapacitation are based on the premise that a small proportion of the criminal population commits a large percentage of the crime. If that small number can be removed from society—that is, incapacitated—the crime rate will decline while they are imprisoned. Even if the assumption is correct, the problem of distinguishing those criminals who fall into the small and overly active population from the run-of-the-mill offenders is not an easy task. Selective incapacitation has often relied on an ability to distinguish the two groups on the basis of individual characteristics, whereas general incapacitation more often relies on characteristics of the crime itself.

Cohen (1983) explains that selective incapacitation requires individualized sentences based on predictions that particular offenders will commit serious offenses at a high rate if they are not locked away. As a result, because of their assumed future criminality, some offenders will be imprisoned for longer periods than will others convicted of the same offenses. Of course, some people find such a sentencing policy to be quite unfair. For example, retributivists believe people should be punished only for things they have already done. Punishment should be deserved, they argue. Also, selective incapacitation may result in too many false positives, wherein an offender is incorrectly included among the likely to repeat group. But although these "punishment should be deserved" and "too many false positives" arguments might tarnish the luster of selective incapacitation, the problem of discrimination is more often used to discredit the strategy.

Bias and discrimination play a role in selective incapacitation when trying to define the criteria for identifying individual dangerousness. For argument's sake, assume that persons most likely to continue their criminal behavior will be those who come from a low-socioeconomic area of the inner city, are high school dropouts, and are unemployed. If these characteristics are included among those used to identify persons likely to continue their involvement in crime, there is a potential for discrimination by race and ethnicity. Unfortunately, in contemporary U.S. society there is a disproportionate number of African Americans and Latinos who are unemployed high school dropouts living in low-income areas of the inner city. Not all of them, however, commit crimes. Even those who are criminal may not be any more likely to continue their criminal involvement than is a European American offender with a high school diploma who is living in suburbia. The point is, currently there is insufficient data regarding the causes of crime to accurately identify any individual characteristics of the people most likely to continue their criminal ways. Available data show only characteristics that identify persons sharing common circumstances, such as unemployment and dissatisfaction with school. Some of them may commit serious crimes over a prolonged time period, but many may not. This is, of course, an aspect of the "false positive" criticism, but it is also a bias and discrimination problem because many of the false positives will be people from certain racial and ethnic categories.

It has been argued that a policy of general incapacitation avoids the problem of racially and ethnically biased sentencing that selective incapacitation presents (but see the feature "Discrimination and Incapacitation"). General incapacitation does not require the identification of the individual characteristics of persons most likely to continue to commit serious offenses. Under a strategy of general incapacitation, people are sentenced to prison based on what they did rather than who they are. For example, if members of a community decide that drug offenders present a serious and continued threat to the public safety, they can develop a policy of longer prison terms for anyone convicted of a drug offense. In this manner, Anglo drug dealer Petterson and Hispanic drug dealer Jaramillo both receive long prison sentences. Presumably, the educational level, employment status, and neighborhood of residence of Petterson and Jaramillo will not influence the length of imprisonment. In this manner, Petterson and Jaramillo are punished because the community believes drug offenders are dangerous—not because it thinks either Petterson or Jaramillo are necessarily dangerous individuals.

Zimring and Hawkins (1995) agree that imprisoning whole categories of offenders for purposes of incapacitation may resist stereotypes of dangerousness, but they are not so sure that general incapacitation can avoid the problem of overprediction, or false positives. That is, giving longer prison sentences to all drug offenders (or robbers, or thieves, etc.) will mean some people will be imprisoned for an unnecessarily long time. Even ignoring the ethical aspects of that situation, the mere cost involved in constructing prisons to house these offenders presents a problem to proponents of general incapacitation.

The value of selective and general incapacitation as punishment rationales continues to be debated. As with all the rationales, a key to deciding if incapacitation is a desirable basis for making punishment decisions will ride on how effectively it achieves its goal. The answer may depend on what is meant by effective (see "Has Imprisonment Lowered the Crime Rate?" on page 45). Consider, for example, the problem of replacement. If Petterson completes 100 drug deals a year in his community, the effect of his imprisonment would be 100 fewer drug deals

ISSUES OF FAIRNESS

DISCRIMINATION AND INCAPACITATION

Whether the policy is that of selective or general incapacitation, there seems to be the possibility of discrimination based on race and ethnicity. Consider the example of American Indian offenders.

American Indians are among the nation's poorest and least educated groups. Any sentencing policy that assumes poor, uneducated offenders are likely to be repeat criminals will mean that American Indian offenders are more likely to end up in jail and prison for longer periods than might a non-Indian offender who commits the same crime. But even a general incapacitation policy—one focusing on characteristics of the crime rather than of the offender—could result in discrimination against American Indians. Greenfeld and Smith (1999) explain that in 1997, American Indians were held in local jails at a rate higher than any other racial group. They also note that American Indians have a rate of arrest for alcohol violations (DUI, liquor law violations, and public drunkenness) more than double the national rate. There does not appear to be any research to support the following speculation, but what if local sentencing laws or practices encourage (require?) judges to incarcerate persons convicted of alcohol violations whereas persons convicted of other similar-level crimes are placed on probation? That seemingly unbiased policy that reacts to the offense rather than the offender may still result in discrimination against a particular group.

Similar concerns have been expressed about a sentencing policy that sets longer prison term sentences for crack cocaine convictions than for powder cocaine offenses. If crack cocaine users are more likely to be African American and powder cocaine users more likely to be European American (see DiMascio, 1997; Isokoff, 1995), African American offenders will receive longer sentences than will white offenders—although they have the same drug in common.

Read the report "American Indians and Crime" at **www.ojp.usdoj.gov/bjs/pub/pdf/aic.pdf.** Are American Indians more or less likely than people of other races to experience violence at the hands of someone of a different race? How do American Indians compare with African Americans, Asian Americans, and European Americans in terms of their per capita rate of being in the care or custody of correctional authorities?

in that community. But what if drug dealer Tanaka begins to service Petterson's former clients and essentially makes 100 more drug sales than he does when Petterson is around? The community has lessened Petterson's criminal behavior but has not lowered the amount of crime occurring because Tanaka has replaced Petterson. Has imprisonment achieved the goal of incapacitation? The answer seems to be "yes" regarding Petterson, but "no" in terms of the community's crime rate.

However, even Petterson's punishment may cause other problems because incapacitation may provide him with opportunities to learn techniques for committing other offenses. To the extent that prisons might be "schools for crime," offenders may complete their prison sentences with greater knowledge about ways to commit an even wider variety of crimes. Although incapacitation may have disabled Petterson's drug dealing, it could have enabled his foray into areas such as auto theft or burglary. These questions provide a basis for discussion in Chapter 15 of whether incapacitation and the other rationales work. But before leaving this topic, it is important to consider the possibility that incapacitation can be achieved without resorting to imprisonment.

Incapacitation through Technology. The idea that an offender's freedom of movement might be effectively restricted by technology rather than imprisonment has been discussed at least since the 1960s. In his 1962 novel, *A Clockwork Orange,* Anthony Burgess describes a version of chemotherapy that allows the violent hoodlum,

Following the incapacitation argument that imprisoning drug offenders will lower the number of drug crimes, many U.S. jurisdictions have passed laws making imprisonment a more likely punishment for drug offenses.

Alex, to be free in the community while rendering him unable to follow through on his evil impulses. As seen in Chapter 8, scientists were proposing as early as 1964 that offenders be regulated in the community via electronic monitoring devices. In 1978 sociologist Marlene Lehtinen was wondering if medical research might allow authorities to implant tranquilizers under the skin of violent offenders as a way to reduce their aggression. Although recognizing them as barbaric and probably unrealistic, Lehtinen (1978) also suggested that technologies that would temporarily blind or cripple offenders might serve as effective incapacitation. Some of these ideas from the 1960s and 1970s are included among the biomedical measures Dinitz (1987) calls critical organ surgery and drug treatment.

Restricting a person's freedom of movement through surgery on his body is, of course, extremely intrusive. But operating on critical organs of persons suffering from afflictions such as uncontrollable aggression has had its advocates. In 1921 the U.S. Supreme Court held involuntary surgical castration to be unconstitutional (Dinitz, 1987), but in some states offenders today can volunteer to be castrated as part of a plea agreement or as an alternative to mandatory chemical castration. But in the decade or so preceding the Court's decision, castration was used in several states as a way to control sexually aggressive males. Dinitz explains that no one knows how many men were castrated, and no one bothered to study the postcastration lives of the offenders. In Europe, where castrations were performed on sex offenders for several decades in the twentieth century, reports showed an average 2 percent postcastration reoffense rate compared with a 50 percent relapse rate among those offenders prior to their castration (Meyer & Cole, 1997).

Surgery on specific regions of the brain has also enjoyed a level of popularity since the Nobel Prize was won in 1949 for successes with prefrontal lobotomies. Dinitz notes that neurosurgeons have claimed a marked calming effect on acting-out patients who underwent hypothalotomies, and that surgical interventions performed in the mid to late 1960s were conducted to reduce such emotional disturbances as aggression. Advocates of psychosurgery continue to suggest that a

Spotlight ON CONTEMPORARY ISSUES

Has Imprisonment Lowered the Crime Rate?

The concept of incapacitation is simple—when offenders are locked up, they cannot commit crimes outside of prison. A result of increased incapacitation should be a lowering of the crime rate. During the 1990s the crime rate did in fact decrease while the incarceration rate grew dramatically. Clearly, some argued, incapacitation must work!

But, as you probably guessed, the analysis is not so simple. People believing a low crime rate is a result of a high imprisonment rate point especially to the impact incapacitation has on certain crimes. Allen Beck, chief statistician for corrections at the Bureau of Justice Statistics, agrees that incarceration prevents a certain amount of crime—for example, domestic assault, armed robbery, serial murder, rape, burglary, and auto theft—because those crimes are more often committed by high-frequency offenders who would be repeating their acts if they were in the community rather than in prison (Krane, 1999). Other crimes, however, such as drug trafficking, are less affected by locking up the offender because there is usually someone else ready to take that person's place moving and selling the drugs.

Others argue that the high imprisonment rate is simply one of several reasons for the decreasing crime rate. More aggressive policing in urban areas such as New York City is offered as a reason for declining crime, as are stricter probation and parole monitoring, increased efforts to keep guns away from criminals, and a prolonged strong economy. The argument here is that there is no single cause for crime, and there is no single cause for its decline.

Because even those who do not view a lower crime rate as a direct result of a higher imprisonment rate do agree that incarceration plays some role in crime's decline, it seems that incapacitation does work.

Go to the National Center for Policy Analysis Web site at ***www.ncpa.org/pi/crime/crime33b.html*** and click on several of the links under the topic of incarceration rates. Especially look at the item "Incapacitating career criminals lowers crime rate." What statistics are provided regarding the effect imprisonment has had on burglary and robbery rates?

propensity toward violence can be stopped with surgical techniques, but so far not many have hopped on that bandwagon. Dinitz acknowledges that psychosurgery may someday become "a legitimate procedure in the treatment of certain behaviorally deviant humans who cannot be contained or managed by other less intrusive means; . . . [but he hopes] that more is known before psychosurgery achieves such legitimacy" (1987, p. 8). Neither castration nor psychosurgery is likely to be among the new technologies used to incapacitate offenders in the near future because the effects of each can often be achieved today through drug intervention.

The other biomedical intervention identified by Dinitz (1987) is drug therapy. One well-known drug treatment for criminal offenders is the use of antabuse to treat alcoholics and excessive drinkers. By causing a severe and unpleasant physical reaction to even very small amounts of alcohol, antabuse forces abstinence. Similarly, methadone, a synthetic narcotic, is given to addicts to block the euphoric action of heroin and cause less severe and hazardous withdrawal symptoms. Less familiar drug treatments have tried to duplicate the effects of therapeutic castration and even psychosurgery.

Cyproterone acetate, a compound developed in the late 1960s, was used in the treatment of sexually aggressive male offenders by reducing or eliminating sexual behavior but not necessarily affecting aggression. Because cyproterone's actions are reversible and because such side effects as general feminization and obesity are minimal, Dinitz suggests this type of drug therapy would be accepted as a legitimate form of medical intervention. More recently, the drug depo-provera, which is an FDA-approved contraceptive for women, has been used to eliminate the ability of men to sustain an erection. During the 1990s, several states enacted chemical castration legislation that requires offenders to receive depo-provera injections

Spotlight ON CONTEMPORARY ISSUES

Chemical Castration of Sex Offenders

In 1996 California passed the nation's first law to require chemical castration of repeat child offenders. The amendment to Section 645 of the Penal Code provides that any person convicted twice of specified sex offenses, in which the victim is under age thirteen, must receive medroxy progesterone acetate (identified as depo-provera) treatment upon parole. The medication, which is administered by injection, has the effect of lowering the testosterone level and blunting the sex drive. Several states (e.g., Georgia, Florida, Texas, and Wisconsin) have followed California's lead and either allow or require chemical castration for sex offenders.

Criticism of the procedure takes several forms. Some civil liberties groups consider chemical castration to be barbaric and unconstitutional. Meisenkothen (1999) reviews some of the legal arguments and concludes that such a sanction can be constitutionally sound, although much of the current legislation, especially California's, falls short of that goal. Other critics argue that the treatment is ineffective and fails to provide for public safety.

Proponents argue that chemical castration is a humane and effective treatment for some sex offenders when used in conjunction with counseling therapy. Because the medication decreases—but does not prevent—erections and ejaculation, proponents are quick to note that chemical castration is not appropriate for all sex offenders. The medications used for chemical castration decrease the offender's sexual drive and provide an opportunity for him to engage in cognitive-behavioral tasks that recognize and control unacceptable sexual urges. But some sex offenders are motivated by anger, hatred, or power rather than by sex. Those people will not be affected by chemical castration because their crimes do not rely on sexual urges or fantasies.

Even when it is applied in appropriate cases, chemical castration must be accompanied by counseling. Effective therapy includes group or individual sessions in which the offenders learn to recognize the internal (such as loneliness or boredom) and external (such as drugs or alcohol) triggers that cause their behavior (Seligman, 1996). The medication in combination with the therapy allows the person time to engage strategies that avoid or counteract the triggers.

Meyer and Cole (1997) report that the two most common medications used for chemical castration (depo-provera and androcur) seem to reduce recidivism. Reoffense rates averaging 27 percent (depo-provera studies) and 6 percent (androcur studies) were found among offenders undergoing chemical castration treatment. Comparison groups, using either a control group or the pretreatment behavior of the offenders themselves, typically reported reoffense rates above 50 percent.

Contemporary legal and medical arguments suggest that chemical castration can be a useful and appropriate response to some sexual offenders. In combination with psychological therapy it is a safe and effective way to drastically curb the recidivism rate of some sex offenders. It would seem prudent, however, that legislators create chemical castration sanctions only after determining the particular type of offender for which that treatment can be effective and when providing for therapy to accompany the medication.

Read the *San Francisco Examiner* story on California's law at ***www.sfgate.com/cgi-bin/article.cgi?file=/examiner/archive/1996/09/15/METRO7595.dtl***. What are some of the weaknesses identified in the California law?

(see "Chemical Castration of Sex Offenders"). Drugs for controlling violent or aggressive behavior resulting from psychiatric problems include thorazine and prozac. As with chemical castration, the reversibility of psychotropic drugs makes them preferable to the permanence of psychosurgery.

Another nontraditional incapacitation technique receiving considerable attention is electronic monitoring. This book will consider this version of technological incapacitation in detail in Chapter 8, but a brief description is warranted here as well. As early as 1964, suggestions were being made for using technology to assist in the supervising of offenders released to the community. By 1983, devices had been developed that could monitor the presence or absence of a person at a particular location. One version of the device consists of a miniaturized transmitter strapped to the offender's ankle or wrist. The transmitter sends a signal at regular intervals over a range of some 200 feet. The signal is picked up by a monitor located in the offender's home. The monitor relays the signal via phone lines to a central computer. This computer then compares the signal (or, if the offender is not home, the lack of signal) with the offender's work/curfew schedule and alerts correctional officials to any unauthorized absences. In other words, electronic technology has restricted the offender's freedom of movement and provided incapacitation without traditional imprisonment.

Whether incapacitation is sought through imprisonment or technology, society is assuming that it can protect itself by identifying, in advance, persons most likely to commit crimes. Selective incapacitation, especially, uses punishment proactively by seeking to restrict the movement of persons who are probably dangerous. In this manner, attention is directed toward the offender rather than the offense. Even collective incapacitation, which supposedly ignores individual characteristics in favor of crime characteristics, still proposes a proactive application of punishment. As Zimring and Hawkins (1995) explain it, punishing categories of offenders because society believes their crime is one that is likely to be repeated is just as much a wholesale prediction of dangerousness as is punishment based on the belief that a specific person is likely to repeat criminal behavior. Using punishment proactively, because of assumed future violations, is an even more clearly entrenched principle of the next justification of punishment—**rehabilitation.**

Help Wanted

Job Title: Electronic Monitoring Specialist (EMS)

Position Description: EMS employees conduct intakes, review and explain terms and conditions of electronic monitoring, document client activities pursuant to the court order and case plan, and meet with offenders on a regular basis in accordance with the level and type of electronic monitoring.

Qualifications: This position requires strong customer service and data entry skills. The successful applicant will be dependable, detail oriented, and able to excel in a fast-paced environment. Bilingual skills are highly desirable.

For examples of career opportunities in this field, check the employment opportunities section on the Web sites for BI Incorporated ***www.bi.com/*** and for Advanced Business Sciences, Inc. at ***www.abscomtrak.com/***.

Rehabilitation

Rehabilitate, according to the *American Heritage Dictionary,* means "to restore to good health or useful life, as through therapy and education." *Webster's Unabridged Dictionary* says *rehabilitate* means "to put back in good condition; to reestablish on a firm, sound basis." Being this precise in defining terms is unusual in this text but probably necessary for this particular term. Some cynics in the general public, as well as some employed in corrections, often scoff at the term *rehabilitate* as being silly and inappropriate. Rehabilitate, they argue, means to "return something to its prior state." Therefore, people who want to rehabilitate criminals simply wish to put the offender back in society the way he or she was when arrested—that is, they want to return the offenders to their prior state. Of course, persons who dismiss the concept by simply suggesting the term does not mean what proponents think it does are trying to attack an idea by rejecting a word.

In addition to problems associated with the meaning of rehabilitation, there are some people who would not accept rehabilitation as either a form of, or justification for, punishment. It just does not seem right to think of efforts to "restore someone to good health" as being a type of punishment. But consider the point raised by Weihofen (1971) who argues that any measure that deprives people of their liberty against their will is essentially punitive in nature—no matter how well-intentioned are the authorities administering the measure.

English author C. S. Lewis is even more specific. In criticizing the rehabilitation rationale, Lewis noted that people might criticize him for using the word *punishment* when discussing rehabilitation because proponents of rehabilitation are wanting only to heal, not punish, offenders. Lewis disagreed, suggesting that

> to be taken without consent from my home and friends; to lose my liberty; to undergo all those assaults on my personality; . . . [and] to know that this process will never end until either my captors have succeeded or I grow wise enough to cheat them with apparent success—who cares whether this is called Punishment or not [since] it includes most of the elements for which any punishment is feared—shame, exile, bondage. (Lewis, 1971, p. 304)

The idea being expressed by both Weihofen and Lewis is that anytime a person is deprived of his or her liberty, as when being placed in prison or even on probation, that person is being punished. Even if the prison experience includes educational and vocational training, substance abuse classes, and Wednesday night movies, the convicted have lost their liberty and are being punished.

Having argued that *rehabilitate* is an appropriate term in the context of corrections, and a proper term to link with the concept of punishment, this chapter can move on to a more specific discussion of how rehabilitation operates as a punishment rationale. That is accomplished by identifying the three key ingredients of rehabilitation (see Figure 2.1) and, in doing so, distinguishing among terms that are sometimes confused: *reclamation, reformation,* and *rehabilitation.*

Rehabilitation as Reclamation. The idea of punishment for purposes of rehabilitation is possibly the newest of the five punishment rationales, but even this newcomer has a lengthy history. In its earliest form, rehabilitation was more accurately called **reclamation** because the goal was to rescue wrongdoers from the evil that had overcome them. Offenders were to be reclaimed or brought back to the correct ways of living. Because those correct ways were based in morality, it is not surprising that religion often played a role in the reclamation process. For example, Chapter 3 describes late-nineteenth-century versions of this reclamation as influencing the Pennsylvania Quakers in their attempt to use imprisonment as the preferred method of punishment. A goal of imprisonment, for the Quakers, was to reclaim the offender's soul.

In addition to religious motives, reclamation also has a secular base in the sense of humanitarianism—or a belief in promoting human welfare through the elimination of pain and suffering. In addition to reclaiming souls, the Quakers believed that imprisonment would be a humane alternative to corporal and capital punishment. This humanitarian perspective provided a necessary but not sufficient step in a movement toward the rehabilitation philosophy.

FIGURE 2.1

The Building Blocks of Rehabilitation

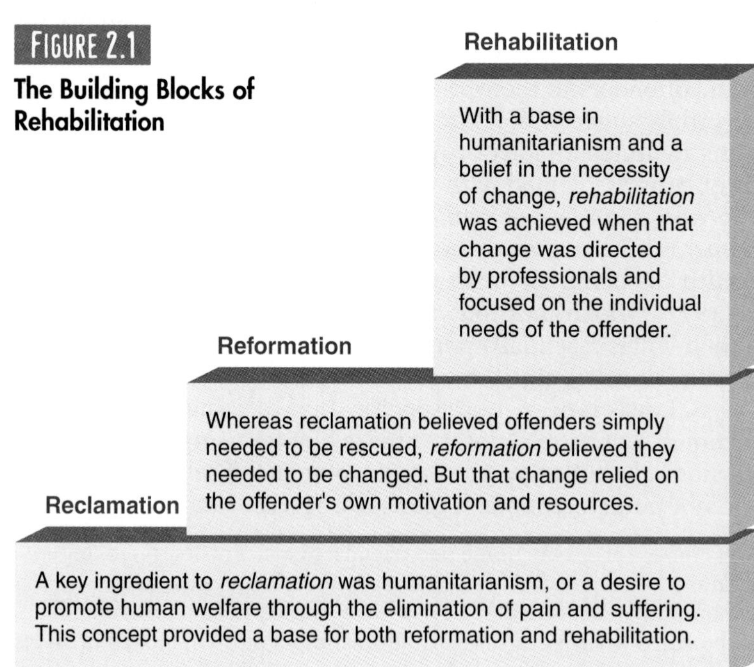

In the late nineteenth century, Pennsylvania Quakers played a major role in establishing imprisonment as the preferred sanction to capital and corporal punishment.

Rehabilitation as Reformation. The link between humanitarianism and rehabilitation is more clearly seen in the late nineteenth century when **reformation** was becoming a popular term. Whereas reclamation had both sacred (saving souls) and secular (humanitarianism) aspects, reformation was essentially a secular concept. In addition, reclamation was assumed to occur without the need for specific changes in or by the offenders. Instead, offenders were rescued from their evil ways by being given the opportunity to realize their errors and simply letting their natural goodness return. Reformation, on the other hand, suggests that specific changes must occur in the offenders in order for them to take a new and improved form. The distinction is between being rescued (reclaimed) and being changed (reformed).

It is this idea of changing the offenders that provides another step in the building of a rehabilitation philosophy. However, in contrast to rehabilitation, the process of reformation assumed the offenders were responsible for changing themselves. That is, given the opportunity to change from bad to good, the offenders will make that change through their own devices. Society's obligation was to provide—in a humanitarian setting—educational, vocational, and religious opportunities for the offenders. But the offenders were primarily responsible for identifying which opportunities would be of most assistance in their particular cases. Only when others got involved in developing individual treatment plans for specific offenders did *rehabilitation* become the appropriate term to describe the punishment philosophy being used.

Rehabilitation as Individualized Treatment. Although the building blocks of rehabilitation are clearly found in the humanitarianism of reclamation and reformation's interest in changing the offenders, it was not until the twentieth century that individualized treatment allowed rehabilitation to occur. The focus of debate during this period was twofold. Skeptics had to be convinced that offenders really could be changed, and proponents had to be convinced that the change could occur in a variety of settings—including prison.

In his 1968 book, *The Crime of Punishment,* psychiatrist Karl Menninger deplored the prison system of the day for not stimulating or even expecting a change to take place in the criminal. The prisoner, he argued, should emerge from the prison experience "a different person, differently equipped, differently functioning, and headed in a different direction from when he [entered prison]" (Menninger, 1971, pp. 246–247). To the citizen who doubted that this change could be achieved with criminals, Menninger recalled that the public used to doubt that change could be accomplished in the mentally ill. Although no one believed a hundred years ago that mental illness could be cured, today everyone knows (or should know, Menninger argued) that mental illness is curable in most cases. This comparison of criminality with mental illness is important for more than simply analogy because it goes to the heart of the rehabilitation argument as it appeared during the 1960s and 1970s. That is, criminal behavior is comparable to an illness and can be treated in a similar manner. This medical model of corrections, discussed in further detail in Chapter 4, gave its proponents a flag to rally around, but it was also ammunition for the critics of rehabilitation.

Criticism of Rehabilitation. Even before its heyday in the 1950s and 1960s, rehabilitation was being criticized for its narrow-minded and illiberal position. What, you say? Rehabilitation illiberal? Haven't we always linked proponents of rehabilitation with the tolerant and broad-minded social worker types who wish only to set the wrongdoer along a law-abiding path to the greater benefit of both offender and society? Such a view of rehabilitation is possible, some critics argue, only when the viewer keeps one eye closed. The point of controversy centers on rehabilitation's proactive rather than reactive use of punishment. More specifically, when rehabilitators try to change offenders into something different than they were upon entering the justice system, the offender's freedom as an individual is being taken away. Denying someone his or her individual freedom is a very illiberal, intolerant thing to do.

In the late 1940s, C. S. Lewis warned readers about the dangerous illusion created by what he called humanitarian theory although he is clearly writing about the rehabilitation rationale of punishment. Lewis claimed the "humanity" being proposed was actually a cruel and unjust penal system because "things done to the criminal, even if they are called cures, will be just as compulsory as they were in the old days when we called them punishments. . . . [T]his doctrine, merciful though it appears, really means that each one of us, from the moment he breaks the law, is deprived of the rights of a human being" (Lewis, 1971, p. 302).

The persistence of Lewis's criticism is seen in the writings of attorney and law professor Nicholas Kittrie. Whereas Lewis, writing in the 1940s, was warning of problems that rehabilitation might bring, Kittrie was describing what he saw as problems that rehabilitation had already brought. Using terms such as *enforced therapy* and referring to the "therapeutic state," Kittrie (1971) expresses great concern about a policy of designating undesirable conduct as an illness rather than a crime. He argues that the therapeutic state should arouse fear because it seeks to impose controls over people who should actually be free from societal intervention. Furthermore, that fear is well placed because the therapeutic state has access to tools of human control that threaten individual liberty (Kittrie, 1971, p. xvii).

The tide was turning against rehabilitation—or at least its medical model and therapeutic approach. And, as described in Chapter 4, by the 1970s rehabilitation as a punishment philosophy seemed to have fewer and fewer adherents. But what did critics want instead? Some preferred an approach that focused on the offense rather than the offender. Lewis, for example, argued for a system based on just deserts. What the criminal deserves is considered instead of focusing on what will cure him or her or deter others (Lewis, 1971). Fortunately, at least for Lewis, such a rationale for punishment already existed in the form of retribution.

Retribution

If he who breaks the law is not punished, he who obeys it is cheated. This, and this alone, is why lawbreakers ought to be punished: to authenticate as good, and to encourage as useful, law-abiding behavior. The aim of criminal law cannot be correction or deterrence; it can only be the maintenance of the legal order.

—Thomas Szasz

A person who claims that a wrongful act must be repaid by a penalty that is as severe as the wrongful act is arguing for **retribution.** In its more crude form, retribution was the vengeance, or revenge, exhibited in feuds between individuals and families. In its contemporary form, retribution differs from its primitive ancestor in three important ways. Retribution is (1) a formal penal sanction seeking (2) equity and (3) just deserts. As a formal penal sanction, retribution should be applied only when a law or formal code of conduct has been violated. Revenge might occur in response to a much wider variety of transgressions. And, although individuals might take revenge on someone as a form of individual retaliation, retribution is more accurately the province of an office representing the public as a whole. For example, Lynn, as a private citizen, might revenge a wrong done to her automobile by flattening the tires on the car of Laura, the culprit. But if a judge, representing the community, sentences Laura to probation for the damage she caused to Lynn's car, the judge is imposing a formal sanction backed by the authority of the people's government. Lynn's act was revenge, but the judge's act was retribution.

Even more important aspects of retribution, but not of revenge, are the concepts of **equity** and **just deserts.** For purposes of retribution, similar crimes and similar criminals should be treated alike—that is, there should be equity of punishment. Two people who, each for the first time, commit burglary should receive similar sentences. In the reverse, persons who commit their first burglary should not receive a punishment similar to that received by persons who commit their third burglary.

Just deserts requires punishment to be proportional to the seriousness of the offense and the culpability of the offender. A person who assaults another person should be punished more severely than a person who causes damage to property. A person who purposefully and knowingly struck another in the face with a beer bottle should receive a harsher punishment than a person who recklessly ran toward a door and, while doing so, hit another in the face with a book.

In addition to distinguishing retribution and revenge, we can also immediately set retribution apart from the other punishment philosophies by noting retribution's lack of interest in preventing crime. Deterrence, incapacitation, and rehabilitation all have a utilitarian aspect. That is, each hopes that punishment will achieve some goal—have some utility. For deterrence, punishment is imposed to either keep criminals from reoffending or to prevent others from committing a crime in the first place. Proponents of incapacitation believe punishment can be used to protect society, for at least the period of incapacitation, from the continued misbehavior of the criminal. And the followers of rehabilitation propose that punishment can change people from criminals to law-abiding citizens. Retributivists, however, do not care if criminals or others are deterred, if society is safer while a criminal is locked up, or whether offenders are rehabilitated. Their concern is simply that society carries out its moral obligation to punish people who commit a crime.

To be fair it should be noted that retributivists certainly do not mind if punishment results in crime prevention. However, any prevention that occurs as a result of imposing punishment on an offender is simply a secondary result that is welcome but was neither sought nor intended. Does this sound cruel and inhumane? An increasing number of authors, politicians, and citizens do not seem to think so—or at least do not care if it is.

Graeme Newman (1985) has been a particularly noted proponent of retribution. He claims, for example, that saying "a wrongful act must be punished" is a simple statement of fact. Because never in history have wrongful acts, when defined as such, been rewarded, their punishment can be considered a part of the natural order. In fact, retributive punishment might even be a social law following the **norm of reciprocity.** Without reciprocal arrangements between individuals and groups or organizations, much of economic and social life would not be possible. In that sense, punishment is a natural response, or reciprocation, to a wrongful act. This link to reciprocity highlights an important aspect of retribution: It should only be applied after, never before, a wrongful act has occurred and a person has been appropriately convicted.

It is not uncommon for retribution to be viewed as a primitive justification for punishment that cares little about the individual and supports the view that social interests have primacy over individual rights. Interestingly, however, it can be argued that of all the justifications for punishment, the retributive position is most supportive of individual rights. The retributivist recognizes each individual as a rational person choosing to behave as he or she wishes. Under the norm of reciprocity, the individual chooses to misbehave, and society must reciprocate by punishing that misbehavior—not by changing the individual. The retributive philosophy leaves the individual intact. The offender is not treated as a means to an end (e.g., to achieve general deterrence) or as someone needing to be changed (e.g., specific deterrence or rehabilitation). As Newman (1985) explains it, by punishing individuals, their right to deviate is upheld; and by refusing to change them, that right is even further bolstered. Looked at this way, retribution becomes a liberal principle against the conservative, conformity-prodding principles such as deterrence and rehabilitation.

In its pure form then, a retributive rationale sees punishment as part of the natural order wherein individuals are allowed to misbehave; but when they do, society is required to punish them. There is no interest in using punishment to change the offender or to influence the behavior of others. Very simply, if you do wrong, society will punish you. If, after your punishment, you do wrong again, society will punish you again. This reciprocal arrangement continues without end, or, more likely, until one side or the other gets tired and chooses not to continue.

Probably the most difficult problem presented by a retributive philosophy of punishment is determining exactly what the just punishment is for a particular offense. Ellis and Ellis (1989) highlight this obstacle by noting that both the crime and the penalty must somehow be measured—crime for its seriousness and penalty for its desert. Of course, deterrence theorists had a similar problem because that philosophy also required a correspondence between crime and penalty. That is, for deterrence to occur, the penalty had to be fixed at a level just harsh enough to convince the offender, or potential offender, that the pain would outweigh the pleasure. There is a difference, however, between the deterrence and retribution view of correspondence between crime and penalty. Where deterrence requires correspondence in order to accomplish a goal of crime prevention or reduction, retribution requires correspondence in the sense that an offender justly deserves a certain severity of punishment (Ellis & Ellis, 1989). So, we are back to the problem of deciding which penalty a crime deserves or merits.

Measuring the seriousness of a crime may seem rather straightforward. After all, state legislators provide such measures when they identify offenses as misdemeanors or felonies, and when they provide levels within those two categories such as class 1 felony and class 4 misdemeanor. If you prefer a measurement that relies on a broader consensus of a community, Sellin and Wolfgang (1964) provide a crime seriousness index that shows a fairly high degree of consistency in the way people rank various crimes according to their seriousness. But even if one of these strategies were acceptable to retributivists, they would be left with the more difficult problem of measuring the penalty.

Determining when a penalty has provided criminals with their just deserts is no small task. We could ask members of the public to rate the unpleasantness of a given penalty, or to rank penalties according to their level of severity. Neither of these techniques accounts for the individual differences that certainly arise when one person's penalty is another person's mere inconvenience. But more importantly, these approaches seem better suited to deterrence purposes when trying to find a penalty to prevent or reduce crime. What is really needed is a way to determine what kind (type, level, etc.) of penalty a particular criminal act deserves. So far the closest retributivists have come to matching the penalty to the crime is the principle of ***lex talionis,*** or the law of retaliation. The classic example of this principle is stated in the Bible: "And if any mischief follow, then thou shalt give life for life, eye for eye, tooth for tooth, hand for hand, foot for foot, burning for burning, wound for wound, stripe for stripe" (Exodus 21:23–25). A similar principle is stated in the Qur'an: "And [as for] the man who steals and the woman who steals, cut off their hands as a punishment for what they have earned" (5:38).

Punishment as talion (equivalence of crime and its punishment) exists today primarily in the form of the death penalty for homicide. Similar equivalence for other crimes and penalties seems unlikely in contemporary society, so today's retributivists are more likely to argue for **proportionality.** Nigel Walker (1991) has succinctly described how retributivists conceive of proportionality.[1]

Walker suggests that proportionality of crime and penalty for the retributivist can be thought of as two ladderlike scales whose rungs correspond (see Figure 2.2). On the penalty ladder, each rung indicates different levels of severity increasing in order from the lowest rungs to the higher ones. Unfortunately, we cannot assume that the distance between each rung indicates any standard progression. In this manner, the third rung might indicate a fine, the fourth could mean a probation sentence, and the fifth could require nine months in jail. But is the progression of severity between the third and fourth rungs, or even between the fourth and fifth, of similar degree? Possibly more important, is a jail sentence always more severe than a fine or probation? Maybe an offender would actually choose confinement in order to avoid financial hardship. In other words, the ladder's rungs are not only loose, but they may also be interchangeable.

Ideally, the other ladder would be a harm ladder, in which the rungs are well-defined harms. But this ladder remains poorly defined by retributivists. Instead, the second structure more often is a crime seriousness ladder. Its rungs consist of offenses distinguished by their legal definitions: murder, robbery, theft, and so on. Again, the rungs may imply a rank order of seriousness (though, as on the penalty ladder, individuals may differ in their assessment of seriousness), but the distance between rungs cannot be taken to show similar degrees.

To achieve proportionality, the retributivist says, the two ladders are fitted together so that a rod of proportionality could be balanced on corresponding rungs

[1]From Walker, N. *Why punish?* (Oxford: Oxford University Press, 1991). Used by permission of Oxford University Press.

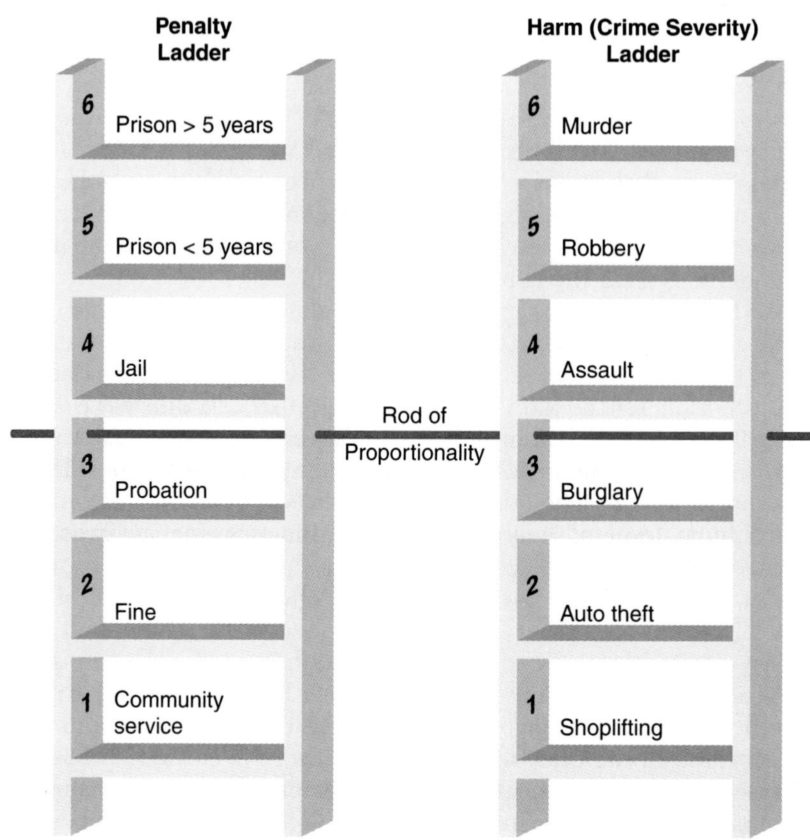

FIGURE 2.2
Retribution and Proportionality
Ideally, retributivists would like to have proportionality between the punishment and the crime. This might be possible if one could truly determine equivalence between a particular penalty (typified by a rung on the penalty ladder) and a particular crime (a rung on the harm ladder). But, unlike the nicely balanced rod of proportionality shown here, the rungs on each ladder are not so easily aligned.

of the two ladders. In this way, the punishment (penalty rung) will match the offense (harm rung). But because of problems such as inconsistent intervals among rungs within and between the ladders, the best a retributivist can claim is that the ladders provide consistency among judges using the ladders. That is, when several judges use the coupled ladders to determine sentences, the penalties will be similar as the harm rung and penalty rung match up. But consistency is not the same as proportionality, and Walker suggests the retributivists have been unable thus far to provide a way to measure both crimes and penalties in order to ensure offenders get their just deserts.

Another aspect of retributive philosophy deserves mention. It is possible to view the norm of reciprocity as trying to restore equilibrium. Just as the balance is unequal when your friend has invited you to dinner but you have not yet returned the favor, so is it unequal when a criminal has caused the victim harm to his or her person or property. Punishment, in its reciprocal role, can help restore the balance that the criminal has upset. When punishment is considered in this light, a new aspect of the sanction and a new rationale under which it can be discussed emerge as the fifth, and last, punishment philosophy—restoration.

Restoration

The focus of punishment philosophies thus far has been on either the offender (rehabilitation) or the crime (deterrence, incapacitation, and retribution). Increasingly in U.S. jurisdictions calls are made for a penal philosophy that features the harm done to the victim when deciding an appropriate punishment for the offender. **Restoration** is a punishment rationale that attempts to make the victim and the community "whole again" by restoring things, as much as possible, to how they were before the crime occurred. This return to equilibrium provides a link between retribution and restoration because each philosophy is based on the norm of reciprocity as described earlier while discussing Newman's (1985) work. A difference between the two lies with the focus on what the offender deserves (retribution) versus what the victim deserves (restoration).

Traditionally the American justice system and others have taken the view that the victims of crime are compensated for the harm done to them simply by knowing that the offender is being punished by the courts. In recent decades that level of compensation and the argument itself have been criticized by victims, legislators, various advocate groups, and the public in general. But, like many other issues, the question of what is due the victim has been addressed in earlier times and in wide-ranging places. This review of the restoration philosophy begins with a comment about its central role in other justice systems around the world. Because the victim is often made whole again by receiving compensation from the offender, restoration in its general sense and compensation as a specific aspect will both receive our attention.

Restoration and Compensation in Saudi Arabia. Although it may seem to be a new punishment rationale from a North American perspective, the idea that justice requires that the victim be made whole again and that equilibrium be regained actually has a rich and widespread history. This is one of those areas in which the Western industrialized countries can benefit from the knowledge and experiences of their less industrialized neighbors. The feature "Restoration in Nigeria and Gambia" offers examples of African traditions that provide a basis for restorative justice, but here we consider a restorative aspect of Islamic law.

Saudi Arabia presents an aspect of reparation that is interesting to consider, but in order to do so, it must first be placed in the religious context of Islamic law. The boxed feature titled "The Islamic Legal Tradition" in Chapter 1 explained basic aspects of law in Islamic countries. You will recall that Islamic law operates as an intrinsic part of Islamic faith. Other legal traditions can point to important religious aspects in that tradition's evolution, but the Islamic legal tradition is unique in its view that law and faith cannot be separated.

Islamic law, called the Shari'a (the path to follow), consists of the writings in the Qur'an (Islam's holy book) and the Sunna (Muhammad's statements and deeds). Because of its divine origin, the Shari'a can be viewed as a moralizing instrument that directs Muslims as to the proper behavior in their daily lives. It is also important to know that the Shari'a does not identify some crimes as public wrongs whereas others are private wrongs. In other words, the emphasis is on the individual, both as victim and as offender. The state does not have a separate legal personality, so wrongs are actions against the individual rather than against the government. Obviously, this view of crime sets the stage for a very victim-oriented legal system.

Because the state has not replaced the individual as the victim of criminal acts in Islamic society, the Shari'a allows and even encourages nonlegalistic response to misbehavior. Criminal complaints are often resolved through arbitration even before a police record is made. Even such serious crimes as homicide may never be brought to formal trial because the Qur'an condones at least two types of responses that do not involve the court system: retaliation and compensation.

Retaliation by a victim's family is an accepted response to murder under Islamic law. The Qur'an explains that "retaliation is prescribed for you in the matter of the slain; the free for the free, and the slave for the slave, and the female for the female" (2:178). Similarly, any intentional, serious, but nonlethal harm inflicted on a human body can also be responded to with retaliation. The Qur'an repeats the Torah's

Cross-Cultural Corrections

Restoration in Nigeria and Gambia

Adeyemi (1994) presents Nigeria as an example of how the tradition of restoration continues in today's Africa. Some countries formally abolished the application of unwritten custom as their criminal justice system was influenced by colonial powers. But some aspects of the traditional justice system were so entrenched that they had to be included in the new penal codes and the criminal procedure. Nigeria is an example of a country that has incorporated aspects of the traditional restoration process into its contemporary system. But even when custom has been incorporated into statute, traditional ways of handling problems are not easily set aside.

Adeyemi found that it was hard to determine just how often cases were handled under a philosophy of restoration because Nigeria, and several other African countries, provide for compounding procedures. Compound, in its legal sense, refers to a compromise. When a crime is compounded, the victim agrees not to seek prosecution of the offender on condition that the offender compensates (usually financially) the victim. Cases that Adeyemi could document indicate that in a large number of instances crimes are never brought to the attention of authorities because victims (or their families) and offenders work things out on their own. Interestingly, these are not simply for minor cases. Thefts, assaults, and even homicides and rapes were all diverted from the formal criminal justice process.

Another grouping of countries described by Adeyemi are those that continue to let customary law operate alongside their statutory law. Gambia is an example because its native, or customary, courts operate within the recognized criminal justice system, although they are organizationally separate from the statutory courts. Compensation in Gambia is ordered by the courts as a penalty in addition to any fine that might be imposed. Importantly, the native courts are three times more likely to use compensation than are the Western courts (Adeyemi, 1994).

Canada is another country that has found that restorative justice principles fit nicely with indigenous justice methods. Read the *Christian Science Monitor* story at ***www.csmonitor.com/durable/1998/11/12/fp53s1-csm.shtml*** and identify why restorative justice is especially popular in Canada's western provinces as a response to juvenile offenses.

version of retaliation in noting that "life for life, eye for eye, nose for nose, ear for ear, tooth for tooth, and wounds equal for equal" (5:45). But an important distinction between Islam's version of retaliation and a pure lex talionis is that the Qur'an clearly tempers retaliation by encouraging forgiveness. For example, the "life for life" verse continues by noting that "if any one remits the retaliation by way of charity, it is an act of atonement for himself" (5:45). Expression of that charity or forgiveness is found in the concept of compensation in the form of ***diyya.***

When retaliation is not used in response to murder or for felonies against the person, it is typically replaced by diyya. Al-Sagheer believes that diyya is best defined as "money paid to a harmed person or his heir in compensation for a felony committed against him" (1994, p. 85). Although diyya may have a deterrent function, it is considered a way to rid society, including the victims and their families, of any grudges toward the offender. It attempts, in other words, to make the victim and the community whole again.

Rules govern the cases in which diyya can be applied, the amount to be paid, and by whom it is paid (Al-Sagheer, 1994). For example, in cases in which a human life has been taken, the diyya amount varies from the equivalent of one hundred camels for a Moslem male to the equivalent of fifty camels for a Moslem woman. Payment is typically made by the offender or the offender's blood relatives, but the burden of payment may occasionally fall to the Saudi Arabia State Treasury (e.g., when the offender has not been identified).

So far our examination of the philosophy of restoration has concentrated on its compensation aspect and has implied that it occurs primarily at the instigation of the victim or victim's family. Turning to the application of restoration in the contemporary United States, it is evident that compensation remains an important ingredient, but it takes on a more formal process involving other people than just the victim and offender or their families.

Contemporary Aspects of the Restoration Philosophy. Western societies also have a tradition of compensation and restoration. The *wergild* was essentially an Anglo-Saxon version of diyya, as was the ancient Germans' use of compensation for homicide as a way to avoid the harm that feuds brought to the community. In fact, the desire to avoid the devastating effects of the blood feud is the primary reason Weitekamp (1993) offers for the early appearance of a restoration philosophy in any prestate or early state society. Weitekamp's reference to government is not simply a casual remark. In actuality, the link between restoration and government is central to understanding why victims came to have a decreasing role in the criminal justice process of Western nations.

Prior to the organization of the state, the many small, interdependent, and economically cooperative communities existing where nations now locate could not afford to lose any member of the group. As Michalowski (1985) points out, killing, expelling, or in any way making unproductive a member of the community would threaten the group's very survival. All community members, wrongdoers included, were needed to keep the group viable. Understandably, restoration through compensation to victims was a reasonable penal philosophy because it truly did make the victim and community whole again. But as governments developed, the leaders and rulers began taking an active role in resolving conflicts among the people. Progressively, the interests of the state began replacing those of the victim. Crime came to be a social wrong rather than a private harm, and society rather than the victim became the focus of the justice process.

With the shift in focus came shifts in justifications, rationales, or philosophies of punishment. Concern was now on ways to protect society, and ideas about deterrence, incapacitation, and rehabilitation sprang forth. By the end of the twelfth century, the erosion of reparative justice was complete (Schafer, 1970, p. 8). Wright (1991) sees victims as once again beginning to have an important role in the administration of justice by the eighteenth century (primarily through initiating prosecution and deciding charges), but it was not until the 1970s that a real focus on victims returned to prominence in countries such as England, Canada, and the United States.

Restorative Justice and the Balanced Approach. The increased attention to victims of crime that occurred in the 1970s tended to emphasize the compensation and restitution aspects of restoration. And, as this review has suggested, these topics are important and recurrent themes in any discussion of a restorative philosophy of justice. What has been missing in this text's examination of restoration has been discussion of the process by which today's victim and community are made whole again. Attention to this aspect is actually the key to using the term *restoration* rather than just borrowing more traditional terms such as *compensation, reparation,* or *restitution.* Each of the other words refers primarily to a reimbursement being made by the offender to the victim. But restoration, as a punishment philosophy, is more than that.

As the twenty-first century begins, there are indications that a penal philosophy of restoration will take a prominent role. The label attached to this philosophy is restorative or community justice and its initial proponents include people such as Howard Zehr (1985), Mark Umbreit (1989), and Martin Wright (1991). While the terms *restorative justice* and *community justice* are used interchangeably in many U.S. communities, the preference in this book is for the term *restorative justice.*

To achieve the goal of repairing, to the degree possible, the damage caused by the offender to both the victim and the community, the restorative justice model

Help Wanted

Job Title: Restorative Justice Project Team Leader

Position Description: The team leader will develop and lead a restorative justice effort by establishing and providing services such as victim–offender mediation (VOM), victim awareness classes, and outreach. The position also requires a variety of professional, communication, and logistical work to provide restorative justice services in conjunction with the juvenile court, law enforcement, businesses and directly to the community.

Qualifications: Applicants should have experience in the restorative justice field, including service as a victim–offender mediator, and experience providing training and curriculum. A bachelor's degree from an accredited college or university with course work in conflict resolution, restorative justice, communications, and related fields is required.

For career opportunities in restorative justice, visit the Restorative Justice Project's job page at *www.fresno.edu/pacs/rjjobs.html.*

relies on a balanced approach (Bazemore & Umbreit, 1997). This approach begins with the understanding that the community needs and expects (1) crime to be sanctioned, (2) offenders to be rehabilitated and reintegrated, and (3) the community to be protected. The balanced approach meets those needs and expectations by seeking a balance of resources (time, money, staff, attention) allocated to (1) creating opportunities for holding offenders accountable to crime victims and communities, (2) identifying the social, financial, emotional, occupational, and cognitive capabilities of offenders, and (3) improving community protection and public safety.

One popular technique in using the balanced approach to achieve restorative justice is a **mediation** process by which victim, offender, and community representatives work out their version of what would be a fair or just way to restore the balance that the crime upset (more details in Chapter 5). For example, a juvenile caught shoplifting at the local grocery store might be brought before a community group composed of the merchant, a community member, and the juvenile. Under the direction of a mediator, who may be from the juvenile court or some local nonprofit agency, the merchant explains how she has been harmed by the juvenile's act. The community member might complain about the price increases resulting from theft in the store. When it seems that the juvenile understands the harm that he caused, takes responsibility for his actions, and expresses remorse, the three participants can discuss what punishment should be imposed. The agreed upon sanctions might include apologies, loss of shopping privileges, payment for, or return of, the items stolen, and so on. The goal, however, is less the sanction than the attempt to repair the damage.

The restoration philosophy, like the other philosophies, has its critics. Retributivists often see it as too lenient, proponents of deterrence do not think it can deter (either specifically or generally), and incapacitationists fail to see how society is protected from continued harm. Some people are concerned that restorative justice will increase the number of people brought under the net of social control. In this view, called **net-widening,** there is concern that programs designed as alternatives to the traditional process actually end up bringing more people into the system. Even victim advocates are not always sure about the benefits of restorative justice. Mediation, for example, may prove to be an additional burden to the already stressed victim. Also, restorative justice programs are criticized as lacking clarity regarding their aims. But as Wright (1991) points out, the current system and its various programs are certainly open to the same charge. What becomes evident is the realization that a restoration philosophy of punishment, like all the other punishment rationales, may please some people but certainly will not please everyone.

Restorative Justice and Discrimination. One particular criticism of restorative justice deserves special attention—the suggestion that it can promote discrimination. Some critics of the restorative process warn that it may perpetuate existing social inequities when one party has greater economic, intellectual, political, or physical power than the other. Proponents respond that the restorative process relies on all participants negotiating in good faith and not using mediation to legitimize an unfair solution. Relying on good faith and achieving fairness are not always compatible, the critics retort.

People in a weaker or subordinate position (such as students to school officials or employees to employers) may be under pressure to accept too little in the hope of obtaining an agreement and being left alone. Or weaker parties (such as persons with fewer financial resources) may argue for what they think they can get rather than what they think is fair. For example, when an economically middle-class bully takes lunch money from an economically lower-class classmate, the victim may agree to simply a return of the money taken rather than asking for an apology, a return of the money taken, plus an extra week of lunch money. In other words, weaker parties, whether victim or offender, may accept agreements that give them much less than they could have obtained if the power imbalance did not exist. Even mediators could influence the outcome if they are of a higher social standing than one or both participants. As Merry puts it, "Mediation can end up a new forum in which the predominantly middle-class helping professionals are invited to supervise and control the private lives of the working class" (1989, p. 239).

These are valid concerns, and restorative justice proponents note that the programs and procedures must be continually evaluated to make sure they are operating in as nondiscriminatory a fashion as possible. Some authors have also noted that restorative justice is certainly no more likely to discriminate than is the traditional formal justice process. In fact, it may even have the potential to be more responsive to cultural diversity. Maxwell and Morris (1996), for example, suggest that restorative justice processes may challenge misconceptions in cases involving racial strife and could even increase understanding among different subcultures—goals the traditional justice system does not even attempt. As Bright (1997) reminds us, social injustices in society are bound to influence any system of justice, including restorative justice. However, because restorative justice involves the community members in an attempt to resolve the problem, the possibility for engagement and interaction may provide opportunities to address even broader issues such as inequalities, discrimination, and prejudice.

SUMMARY

SOCIAL CONTROL

The field of corrections is at its most basic level interested in questions of social control and the techniques or sanctions society uses to enforce violation of the laws.

SANCTIONS

- Although sanctions can be either positive or negative, the U.S. criminal justice system tends to rely on negative sanctions.
- Although sanctions can also be either informal or formal, the emphasis in this text is on formal sanctions.
- Three types of sanctions are physical, financial, and social/psychological sanctions. Examples of many formal negative versions of all three sanction types will be discussed throughout this book.

PHILOSOPHIES OF PUNISHMENT

The question "why punish?" may seem to deserve no more elaboration than the answer "because," but there really are practical considerations linked to whatever answer is given. This chapter focuses on five primary answers, which are identified as punishment philosophies.

- Deterrence, which can be either specific (the aim is to discourage that person from reoffending) or general (the aim is to discourage others from offending in the first place), focuses on the act and applies punishment reactively.
- Incapacitation, which restricts a person's ability to move about freely, focuses on the act and applies punishment both proactively and reactively.
- Rehabilitation, which attempts to use a treatment plan and therapy to provide offenders with opportunities to become law-abiding members of society, focuses on the offender and applies punishment proactively.

- Retribution focuses on the act and applies punishment reactively with equity and in a way that makes it proportional to the seriousness of the offense and the culpability of the offender.
- Restoration, which applies punishment with a balanced approach involving the offender, victim, and community members, focuses on both the offender and the victim and applies the punishment reactively.

Key Terms and Concepts

deterrence (p. 38)
diyya (p. 56)
equity (p. 51)
folkways (p. 33)
formal sanction (p. 35)
general deterrence (p. 38)
general incapacitation (p. 41)
incapacitation (p. 41)
informal sanction (p. 35)
just deserts (p. 51)
laws (p. 33)
lex talionis (p. 53)
mediation (p. 58)
mores (p. 33)
negative sanction (p. 34)
net-widening (p. 58)
norm of reciprocity (p. 52)
norms (p. 33)
positive sanction (p. 34)
proportionality (p. 53)
reclamation (p. 48)
reformation (p. 49)
rehabilitation (p. 47)
restoration (p. 55)
retribution (p. 51)
sanction (p. 34)
selective incapacitation (p. 41)
specific deterrence (p. 38)

Discussion Questions

1. Quotes from Weihofen and from Lewis seem to assume that rehabilitation necessarily involves loss of liberty. Does it? Explain your answer.
2. What is the legitimacy of Newman's position that retribution is actually a liberal or enlightened penal philosophy?
3. Prepare an argument that shows not only guilty people need to be punished in order for general deterrence to work.
4. Describe changes that would be necessary in society to allow the conditions of certainty, severity, and swiftness to be implemented at a level where deterrence would work at its best.
5. In what way can the Islamic diyya restore the balance that was upset by an offender's act? What cultural differences most likely exist between Saudi Arabia and the United States that would make it difficult for U.S. jurisdictions to implement a diyya-like procedure?

PUTTING PHILOSOPHIES INTO PRACTICE

WELLSPRING ERA (MIDDLE AGES TO 1800s)

Transportation

Hospice Facilities

Houses of Correction

John Howard and Reforms in England

Early U.S. Institutions

From Pillory to Penitentiary

PENITENTIARY ERA (1800s TO 1860s)

The Pennsylvania System

The Auburn System

REFORMATORY ERA (1860s TO 1900s)

The Irish System

Disillusionment

PRISON DEVELOPMENT IN THE SOUTH AND WEST

Developments in the American South

Developments in the American West

SUMMARY

KEY TERMS AND CONCEPTS

DISCUSSION QUESTIONS

chapter 3

EARLY PENAL SYSTEM ERAS

The authors of a report on the poor condition of their country's prison system complain about the heavy cost to the treasury of maintaining prisons. Adding to the problem, prison discipline is minimal, and the convicts leave prison more corrupt than when they entered. The authors go on to tell of another country's prison system that not only shows a financial profit but does so under humane conditions. We might assume that the first country is the United States. But where is the second country, and how do we hire its director of corrections?

Actually, the United States is the envied country. The authors, Alexis de Tocqueville and Gustave de Beaumont, are complaining about the prison system of their own nineteenth-century France. Throughout the 1800s, prisons in the United States were often cited with admiration by foreign visitors. The U.S. facilities built for long-term incarceration were a novelty to many Europeans, who were more used to less secure buildings designed for short-term detention.

Beaumont and Tocqueville were among the more famous of the visitors, especially because of a book, *Democracy in America,* that stemmed from Tocqueville's journey. But it was the pair's report on prisons (Beaumont & Tocqueville, 1964) that reflects an appreciation for a system that the public might otherwise assume has always been discredited. In his journal account of their visit to Sing Sing Prison in New York on May 29, 1831, Tocqueville wrote about the effects of prison discipline, which he said included (1) the health of the prisoners, (2) their extreme concentration on work, (3) the revenue the state gets from their work, and (4) perhaps the moral reform of some prisoners (Tocqueville, 1981, p. 209). With hopes of taking the French prisons to a similar status, Beaumont and Tocqueville explained to French officials why they considered the American system superior to the French system, and they suggested ways the American ideas could be implemented in France.

America's nineteenth-century experience, even experiment, with penitentiaries was the result of a variety of penal sanctions that had been used since the country's colonial days. Those early penitentiaries have, in turn, influenced the penal sanctions that we now find in the twenty-first century. This chapter reviews those sanctions as they developed in Europe and the United States. After looking at the preeighteenth-century period, the Wellspring era, we will look more closely at the prisons visited by Beaumont and Tocqueville and then conclude the chapter with the first modification of those penitentiaries—the reformatory.

Putting Philosophies into Practice

Having philosophies or justifications for punishment is not sufficient to establish a penal system. Those philosophies must be put into practice through agencies, institutions, and procedures in order for them to have an effect. Although it would be convenient and straightforward to show how each philosophy has had its turn at the penal system helm, reality is more complicated. Philosophies of punishment overlap and exist concurrently—although they may contradict each other.

New York's Sing Sing Prison was one of the eighteenth-century prisons visited by Frenchmen Beaumont and Tocqueville as they sought information about the new American idea of long-term imprisonment as a punishment for crimes.

Similarly, the agencies, institutions, and procedures set up to implement the philosophies change over time, but the variation has not been random over the years. In fact, as suggested in the discussion of the five philosophies, although all seem to exist together, one or two seem to have prominence during particular times. Using the development of the U.S. penal system as a model, the chapter now looks at the history of punishment philosophies and the methods used to implement them. As you read, remember that all five of the philosophies have existed together over the decades. When one or two of the philosophies are identified with a particular era, it is to analyze and describe that era rather than argue that other philosophies were ineffective or discarded.

In this discussion six penal system eras are covered: Wellspring, Penitentiary, Reformatory, Industrial, Rehabilitation, and Retributive. Because clear-cut events seldom mark the end of one era and the beginning of another, decades are used to identify each period's birth and decline. The punishment philosophies covered in Chapter 2 help describe events and policies in each era. As Table 3.1 shows, all the philosophies influence every era, but only one or two become particularly important during an era. In the following discussions, you will learn how these prevailing philosophies help in setting one era apart from the others.

TABLE 3.1: Prison System Eras and Their Philosophies*

WELLSPRING ERA (Middle Ages to 1800s)	PENITENTIARY ERA (1800s to 1860s)	REFORMATORY ERA (1860s to 1900s)	INDUSTRIAL ERA (1900s to 1930s)	REHABILITATION ERA (1930s to 1970s)	RETRIBUTIVE ERA (1970s to present)
Deterrence	Deterrence*	Deterrence*	Deterrence*	Deterrence	Deterrence*
Incapacitation	Incapacitation*	Incapacitation	Incapacitation*	Incapacitation	Incapacitation*
Rehabilitation	Rehabilitation	Rehabilitation*	Rehabilitation	Rehabilitation*	Rehabilitation
Restoration	Restoration	Restoration	Restoration	Restoration	Restoration
Retribution	Retribution	Retribution	Retribution	Retribution	Retribution*

Although all five philosophies are present during each era, one or two are often emphasized (shown by "").

Wellspring Era (Middle Ages to 1800s)

By the time of the American Revolution, the colonists had already experienced aspects of each of the five punishment philosophies. There was, however, no consistent or structured penal system by which the philosophies could operate. Instead, the period preceding 1800 is best understood as one that served as the wellspring from which specific philosophies and methods emerged. In the American colonies and other places, a variety of methods were tried that helped set the stage for the more bureaucratic endeavors to follow.

Key features of the **Wellspring era** include the use of corporal punishment, capital punishment, and exile. Corporal punishment and capital punishment have remained popular in several countries of the world, and each receives detailed attention in Chapter 6. Exile came to play a very important role for countries such as England and is presented here as an important aspect of the Wellspring era. Noticeably absent from this listing of early penalties is punishing offenders by locking them up in secure buildings. But the Wellspring era provided necessary precursors to this idea of jails and prisons, and those early places of confinement are also discussed in this section. We begin by looking at a method of social control that simply rids the community of its scoundrels by sending them somewhere else.

Transportation

Attempts to rid a community of crime by tossing out the criminals have a certain appeal. This "out of sight, out of mind" philosophy had its initial form in the **banishment** of wrongdoers from the village, expulsion to sea as a galley slave, and eventually through **transportation** to faraway lands. Banishing misbehaving villagers meant there was no need to worry about that person's future behavior (see the feature "No Welcome Mat Here!"). Similarly, transportation of criminals had as one goal the removal of criminals to a place they could do no harm. But, although banishment had little economic impact on the sending village other than being a very cheap method of social control, transportation was touted as having specific economic benefits.

Transportation was used by European countries such as France (especially to French Guiana), Russia (to Siberia), Portugal (to places such as Mozambique and Brazil), and Italy (to islands off the Tuscan coast). South American countries such as Chile and Ecuador (to islands in the Pacific) also transported criminals (Barnes & Teeters, 1943). But the country attracting the most attention has been England, which used transportation for economic purposes.

The first indication of transportation's use in England was in 1598 when, plagued by unemployment at a time when labor was lacking in the new American colonies, officials decided to ship some offenders to the colonies. Although such activity continued on a primarily informal basis, transportation did not become an official aspect of England's punishment system until specific laws were passed by Parliament in the seventeenth century. The acts provided that persons found guilty of just about any felony could be sent to the West Indies or to American plantations as laborers (see "A Land of Bondage" on page 66). But despite the existence of such laws, transportation as a major component of the British penal system did not occur until the eighteenth century. With the passage of the Transportation Act of 1718, transportation became a possible substitute for execution or was used as a punishment in its own right.

The actual transporting of the criminal was a duty given to individuals, usually ships' captains, who contracted for rights to the prisoner's labor. Ships' cap-

Spotlight ON CONTEMPORARY ISSUES

No Welcome Mat Here!

Banishing offenders from the community did not end in the Wellspring era. Quite the contrary, there are vestiges of the practice in many contemporary U.S. sanctions. For example:

- In 1992 five members of the Tonawanda Band of Seneca Indians were summarily convicted of treason by tribal officials. Each was sentenced to permanent banishment from the Tonawanda Reservation and were told their names were removed from the tribal rolls, their Indian name was taken away, and their lands would become the responsibility of the Council of Chiefs. They were told to leave immediately and that they would be walked to the outer borders of the Tonawanda territory (*Poodry v. Tonawanda Band of Seneca Indians;* 85 F.3d 874, 2d Cir. 1996).
- In 1999 the Oregon Court of Appeals upheld Portland's drug-free zone ordinance (passed in 1992) that identifies areas of the city with serious drug problems. Anyone arrested on drug charges within one of the zones can also be issued an exclusion notice that prohibits that person from entering the drug-free zones for ninety days. If they are convicted of the charges, they face an additional one-year exclusion. Prostitution-free zones, instituted in 1995, work similarly (Green, 1999). The court, by the way, did not consider the ordinance to be banishment.
- Under the Interstate Compact agreement, state prisoners can be transferred from their home state to a host state. Because this practice results in prisoners being removed from their families and communities, it has been referred to as a form of banishment or exile (Wilber, 1999). Although the trading among states is typically for control purposes (e.g., break up the inmate leadership), it can have a humanitarian bent when inmates are actually transferred to a state where their friends and family reside.
- Many states are passing sex offender notification laws that require citizens to be informed when a convicted sex offender moves into their neighborhood. In his comments on one such law, Judge Becker of the U.S. Court of Appeals (3rd Circuit) noted that offenders may have no refuge from the sometimes severe effects of notification. Moving to another state is increasingly not an option because most states now have some form of community notification. Must the offender seek voluntary exile to another country? Judge Becker says, "Notification has become, at least for that offender, akin to banishment" (www.app.com/doc2/megan/no.htm).

Read about the Tonawanda banishment case at ***www.tourolaw.edu/2ndcircuit/may96/95-7490.html*** and, for more on banishment in Native American justice, see ***www.ableza.org/ward/ban.html.*** The Portland drug- and prostitution-free zones are explained at ***www.oregonlive.com/news/99/04/st041509.html.*** Read about the Interstate Compact agreement at ***www.drc.ohio.gov/web/compact.htm.*** Do you think the American justice system should be flexible enough to allow for inclusion of Native American justice ideals in some cases? Which type of cases? Do you agree or disagree with the establishment of drug- and prostitution-free zones? Why?

tains could transfer that right to another person, so when transport ships arrived in the colonies the captains auctioned prisoners off to the highest bidders. Historians estimate that some 50,000 prisoners were transported, primarily from England and Ireland, to the American colonies before 1775 (Christianson, 1998; Hughes, 1987; Shaw, 1966). When the American Revolution stopped transportation to England's former colony in North America, the British turned to their new colony of Australia. In the United States the prisoners had become indentured servants, and the British government gave up all responsibility for them. In Australia, the government took responsibility for shipping the prisoners and continued to have control over them after their arrival in Australia.

From 1788 to 1868, over 160,000 convicts were transported from England and Ireland to the British colonies in Australia. Both men and women were among the transportees—at least until 1851, when the transportation of women ended. During the entire transportation period, about 24,000 of the transportees were women,

HISTORICAL PERSPECTIVES

A Land of Bondage

In his fascinating book *With Liberty for Some,* Scott Christianson (1998) makes the interesting argument that prisoners did as much as free men and women to establish the United States as a nation.

Whereas Australians for the most part accept their history as a prison colony, U.S. citizens—with the notable exception of blacks—still cherish the idea that the country was founded by hardy individualists who rejected the oppressions of a rigid European order to build a better society in the New World ("A Land of Bondage," 1999). Christianson, however, points out that a large proportion of white immigrants to early America arrived in chains as prisoners, indentured servants, or bonded laborers.

By the end of the seventeenth century, three main classes (besides the Native Americans) had emerged in the North American colonies. Black slaves occupied the lowest rung, convicts and other white servants were somewhat better off (primarily in their chances for eventual freedom), and free white persons comprised the most privileged group. The growth of America was the result of hard work by all three classes—especially the slaves, convicts, and servants, some would argue—rather than simply the efforts of some idealized group of hardy individualists voluntarily coming to the colonies in search of opportunities.

Read the fact sheet on indentured servants at ***falcon.tamucc.edu/~kmahar/indentsv.htm.*** What was the age range of the indentured servants? What were their typical occupations? Read about the life of indentured servants in Virginia at ***curry.edschool.virginia.edu/curry/dept/cise/soc/resources/jvc/unit/econ/servantlife_bkgd.html.*** With what benefits were the English enticed to "sign on" with the Virginia Company? Read about transported convicts at ***www.stratfordhall.org/ed-servants.htm.*** How did politics and religion play a role in the transportation of convicts?

typically in their teens and early twenties. The percentage of women was especially high during the first decade of the 1800s, when over 80 percent of all convicts transported were women, but fell to less than 20 percent of all transportees in the 1820s (Convicts in Australia, 1987).

The initial increase in women transportees was linked in part to a hope that the women would act as a moralizing influence over Australia's coarse masculine society of settlers and ex-convicts. But the expected positive influence did not materialize, and one colonial official admitted, "The influence of female convicts is wholly valueless upon male convicts; women of depraved character do them no good whatsoever" (quoted in Zedner, 1995, pp. 330–331). Apparently such officials did not see the assignment of the transported women to brothel work, or simply marrying them off to male convicts and settlers, as playing a role in the women's self-concept and in how they were perceived by others. As Zedner explains, life in the Australian colonies for transported women made it all but impossible for even well-intentioned women to retain their character (1995, p. 331). Disillusioned with the inability of the women to have a positive influence, fewer and fewer provinces would accept female transportees, and by midcentury they were not accepted anywhere in Australia.

Although the felons transported to Australia remained prisoners rather than becoming indentured servants, the penal colony governor could assign a convict to a free settler who would put the prisoner to work. Most convicts were lent out as laborers to the settlers, who then gave the prisoner food and shelter in return for his or her work. Those prisoners who were left unassigned—maybe one in ten—were kept by the British government in penal colonies and put to work on public projects (Hughes, 1987).

Norfolk Island, about a thousand miles east of Sydney, became the most notable penal colony. Captain Arthur Phillip was the first governor of this penal settlement, and his charges turned out to be difficult to handle. The convicts tried to

Although many countries transported their criminals to other places, England was especially likely to ship offenders to other places such as the new American colonies and later to Australia.

escape, were unimpressed with threats of capital punishment, fought among themselves, and generally presented major problems for Captain Phillip. Dressler (1969) reports that the discipline imposed at Norfolk Island was unbearable. He tells of a Catholic priest who arrived there in 1834 to find convicts who had been sentenced to death (for participating in an uprising), falling on their knees to thank God for their release from this life. Other convicts, who had been reprieved, were weeping because they were forced to continue living. The convicts' situation began improving when Alexander Maconochie was transferred from the penal colony of Van Diemen's Land (i.e., Tasmania) in 1840 to be the governor at Norfolk Island. Because his important contributions to the development of penal philosophy and procedures are most directly related to release from imprisonment, detailed discussion of Maconochie is delayed until Chapter 14. Instead, we turn to another key feature of the Wellspring era—the forerunners to penitentiaries.

As the Middle Ages were ending in the fifteenth century, and public officials were taking responsibility for punishing offenders, there was little need for jails or prisons to house offenders for the long term. Offenders were typically subjected to corporal punishment, capital punishment, or exile. Johnston (1973) found examples of imprisonment being used as punishment for some minor offenses as early as the fourteenth century, but more typically when offenders were put in secure buildings such as dungeons, it was to prepare them for the torture that would soon extract a confession, to await their execution or banishment, or even to coerce payments of debts. The idea that long-term imprisonment in a secure facility could be used as a punishment for convicted felons did not fully occur until the nineteenth century. But the prenineteenth-century institutions serving as forerunners to the modern penitentiary provided important philosophies and practices that continue to have an impact today.

As we will see in the discussion of the Penitentiary era, there were two important themes in the development of imprisonment as punishment. One was the idea that convicts should be isolated. This practice could encourage penitence and prevent cross-contamination of evil ideas. A second theme was that prisoners should be required to work. Such labor would deter them from future crime and could provide a profit for the institution. These themes had parallel development during the sixteenth and seventeenth centuries, which can be traced through the hospice facilities, representing the isolation theme, and the houses of correction, representing the work theme.

Hospice Facilities

The idea of an institution in which wrongdoers could be punished with long-term incarceration was first used in Europe during the sixteenth century. There were examples of confinement places in ancient and medieval times (see Peters, 1995), but it was the sixteenth-century Europeans who provided specific models for the modern prison by creating single-purpose institutions in which inmates performed forced labor (Spierenburg, 1995). The influence of the church was especially important as an emphasis on penitence, and reflection in monastic cells was prescribed for the wayward. By 1653 (at Italy's Hospice de San Filippo dé Neri) vagrant and wayward boys were placed in solitary cells to encourage correction and penitence. The French Benedictine monk, Dom Jean Mabillon (1632–1707), was one of the first to propose that misbehavior should be responded to by having the disobedient follow the principles of monastic life, which he identified as isolation, work, silence, and prayer (Eriksson, 1976). Between 1690 and 1695 Mabillon drafted a plan (not published until 1724) for an institution that would reform and correct criminals by using these principles. He made his argument by suggesting that

> penitents might be secluded in cells like those of the Carthusian monks, and there employed in various sorts of labor. To each cell might be joined a little garden, where, at appointed hours, they might take an airing and cultivate the ground. . . . (T)he solitude of prisoners' lives should be unbroken, except by the visits of the Superior or some person deputed by him to exhort and console them. (quoted in Barnes & Teeters, 1943, p. 476)

Despite the precedent of the Hospice de San Filippo dé Neri, the first institution said to have set the stage for penitentiaries was built for misbehaving boys in 1704 at Rome. The **Hospice of St. Michael** was established by Pope Clement XI as a place where the boys could be kept busy at hard work during the day and locked in their cells at night. We do not know what role, if any, Mabillon played in the hospice's philosophy (although he was in close touch with the Vatican and had the opportunity to make suggestions), but the Hospice of St. Michael became the first reform and correctional institution to follow Mabillon's principles of isolation, work, silence, and prayer (Eriksson, 1976).

The boys slept alone but worked together at spinning and weaving in the halls of the hospice. While at work, they were chained by one foot to their work benches and listened (supposedly) as monks read aloud from religious texts. The actual number of incorrigible boys was only fifty, while other parts of the facility housed some two hundred orphan boys and over five hundred aged and infirm men and women. In 1735 a prison for women was added, according to the single-cell method (Barnes & Teeters, 1943; Eriksson, 1976). Because of this diverse population, the Hospice of St. Michael was not truly a penitentiary. That term is reserved for institutions housing only convicted criminals. But it did provide an architectural design that was a forerunner to the modern penitentiaries. The rectangular structure had outside rooms or cells arranged on three tiers. Each cell contained a mattress, a latrine, an outside window, and a solid door with a small opening. These cells faced a large center hall, which was used as a workroom, dining room, and chapel (Johnston, 1973, p. 12).

Besides setting an architectural precedent, the Hospice of St. Michael followed procedures, such as complete silence while the boys were at work and separation into individual cells when not at work, that influenced the direction that full-fledged penitentiaries would eventually take.

Houses of Correction

As hospice facilities were providing the idea of seclusion, **houses of correction,** which began appearing in the late sixteenth century, were emphasizing the importance of work. The first of these houses of correction, or **workhouses,** was in England. In 1553 Edward VI turned a royal palace in the town of Bridewell over to London city officials. In 1557 the former palace opened as a workhouse in which the ever-increasing number of London's vagrants, beggars, and corrupt men and women could be kept. Not all the persons placed in Bridewell got there by the authority of magistrates, however. Husbands, parents, and masters could also have disobedient and wayward wives, children, and servants taken to the workhouse (Dobash, Dobash, & Gutteridge, 1986). The workhouse proved a success, and Parliament soon ordered that every county should construct a similar house of correction. Parliament's goal was to deter those sent to the house of correction from leading an unruly life by forcing them to do hard work at disagreeable tasks. The prisoners, who were paid for their labor, worked as bakers, spinners, and menders; made such items as pins, lace, and gloves; and, in the case of female offenders, had to cook, clean, and launder for both male and female inmates (Barnes & Teeters, 1943; Dobash et al., 1986).

The term **Bridewell House,** after the prototype at Bridewell, came to be used for all English versions of the workhouse. The idea also quickly spread to the European continent and houses of correction were built in cities such as Amsterdam (1596), Copenhagen (1605), Bremen (1608), Bern (1614), and Hamburg (1622). Spierenburg (1995) notes that the geographic concentration of these early prisons in the European north reflected the rarity there of galley servitude. In France, Spain, and most Italian states, sentences to the galley became common from about 1500 onward, and galley servitude came to represent a mostly criminal punishment befalling convicts, and especially, beggars and vagrants (Spierenburg, 1995). The northern European areas were using confinement to forced labor in the houses of correction in the same way that Mediterranean countries used the galley.

A particularly significant version of the workhouse was erected in 1773 at Ghent, in what would become Belgium. The **Maison de Force** had reformation as its goal and hard work as its means. This idea that labor could be a positive technique to change behavior was different from the view at most workhouses, where labor was made as undesirable as possible to deter offenders from future crimes. But Jean Jacques Philippe Vilain, the Maison de Force's first director, saw labor and vocational training as an important way to put prisoners in a position to earn an honest living upon their release (Barnes & Teeters, 1943). With this perspective, Vilain was anticipating a key feature of prison labor as it would be viewed during the Industrial era of the U.S. penal system. Beyond presenting new views about the role of labor, Vilain also developed a rudimentary classification system that separated felons from misdemeanants and vagrants. Also, women and children had separate quarters away from each other and from the men.

With the procedures developed at institutions such as the Hospice of St. Michael and the Maison de Force providing the ideas of separating prisoners and putting them to work, the concept of punishment through imprisonment was ready to move to the next stage. In England this was accomplished through the efforts of John Howard, who is credited with formalizing the penitentiary system.

John Howard and Reforms in England

John Howard (1726–1790) is often considered the greatest prison reformer of modern times. His life was dedicated to the cause of humanity, and his success in that effort is best expressed in the Latin inscription on his gravestone that reads, "Whoever thou art, thou standeth at the tomb of thy friend" (quoted in Eriksson, 1976, p. 32). His legacy of improving prison conditions and of helping prisoners and ex-convicts continues today through the efforts of the John Howard Association founded in 1901.

In 1773 John Howard was elected high sheriff of Bedfordshire, England. Through this position, he was made aware of the deplorable conditions existing in the English gaols (jails) and prisons of his day. Because of Howard's attacks on the prevailing system, in 1774 Parliament corrected some abuses and tried to improve the sanitary conditions of the gaols. Howard, however, believed there still had to be better ways to house offenders. In 1775 he left for the European continent to see what could be learned from the institutions operating there. Over the next year or so, Howard visited institutions in cities such as Paris, Amsterdam, Mannheim, Ghent, and Rome. In some parts of Europe he found conditions to be as bad as they were in England, but other places impressed him with their treatment of the convicts. He was especially influenced by what he saw at Rome's Hospice of St. Michael, and at Ghent's Maison de Force.

At Ghent, Howard noted that prisoners' cells had a sleeping bench and appropriate bedding, and that the prisoners themselves were given adequate food, allowed to perform work, and could attend daily religious services. Such procedures stood in stark contrast to conditions in England, where Howard had found prisoners being forced to sleep on a damp dungeon floor or required to go hun-

John Howard is considered a great prison reformer because of his efforts to improve conditions in English jails and prisons.

gry because they could not afford to buy food from their jailer. He was also impressed with the classification and separation procedure that Vilain had set up. At the Hospice of St. Michael, Howard was quite taken with the monastic philosophy of doing penance in seclusion. He returned to England with a wealth of new information and immediately set about advocating changes to the operation of English gaols and prisons.

In 1777 Howard published a book entitled *The State of Prisons in England and Wales*. The book was well received and went through five editions in as many years. Noted contemporaries of Howard, including Montesquieu, Voltaire, and Beccaria, were impressed with his arguments, and they helped his ideas reach a wide audience. Eventually that audience included the English Parliament, which used Howard's book to provide the basic principles underlying the **1779 Penitentiary Act** (Barnes & Teeters, 1943; Dobash et al., 1986):

- Prisoners should be housed in secure and sanitary facilities.
- Those facilities should undergo systematic inspection.
- Fees for basic needs and services, such as food, should be abolished.
- Discipline at the facilities should follow a reformatory regime.
- The facilities should be built for solitary confinement and operated on the basis of silent contemplation and continuous labor.

The first facility in England specifically set up to carry out Howard's reforms and the Penitentiary Act was the **Gaol at Wymondham.** Built in 1785, the gaol used cells to separate different types of offenders, placed women and men in different parts of the building, and provided separate areas for the prisoners to work and sleep.

The developments of the late eighteenth century in the use of imprisonment as punishment occurring in England and on the European continent were being matched by changes taking place in the former American colonies. With this background in topics such as transportation and the benefits of solitude and hard work, this chapter is ready to follow the Wellspring era to the seventeenth- and eighteenth-century America.

Early U.S. Institutions

Many facilities have laid claim to being the first prison in the American colonies (Powers, 1985). But like their English and European cousins, early American facilities cannot truly be called prisons or penitentiaries in the same sense that we use these terms today in referring to state or federal facilities for confining persons convicted of crimes. Specifically, those early institutions were usually under local jurisdiction, housed both convicted and unconvicted persons, and even held persons violating civil as well as criminal codes. The local jurisdiction status and a population of both convicted and unconvicted persons made the facilities more like today's jails than prisons or penitentiaries. The first U.S. facility to specifically house only offenders convicted of crimes from throughout the state's jurisdiction was not established until 1785. In that year the Massachusetts legislature made **Castle Island** in Boston harbor a repository for convicted—and only convicted—criminals from all over the state (Hirsch, 1992; Powers, 1985). However, the various facilities called jails, gaols, prisons, and penitentiaries that were forerunners or contemporaries to Castle Island are important to the movement toward the Penitentiary era and deserve attention.

The Massachusetts Bay Colony was established by English settlers in 1630. Within two years, the colony's General Court (the legislature) had decided Boston needed a house of correction. The Boston Prison, as the new wooden structure was

FIGURE 3.1

A Time Line of Early American Jails and Prisons

For an interesting state-specific history, see New York Correction Time Line at www.correctionhistory.org/html/timeline/html/timeline.html.

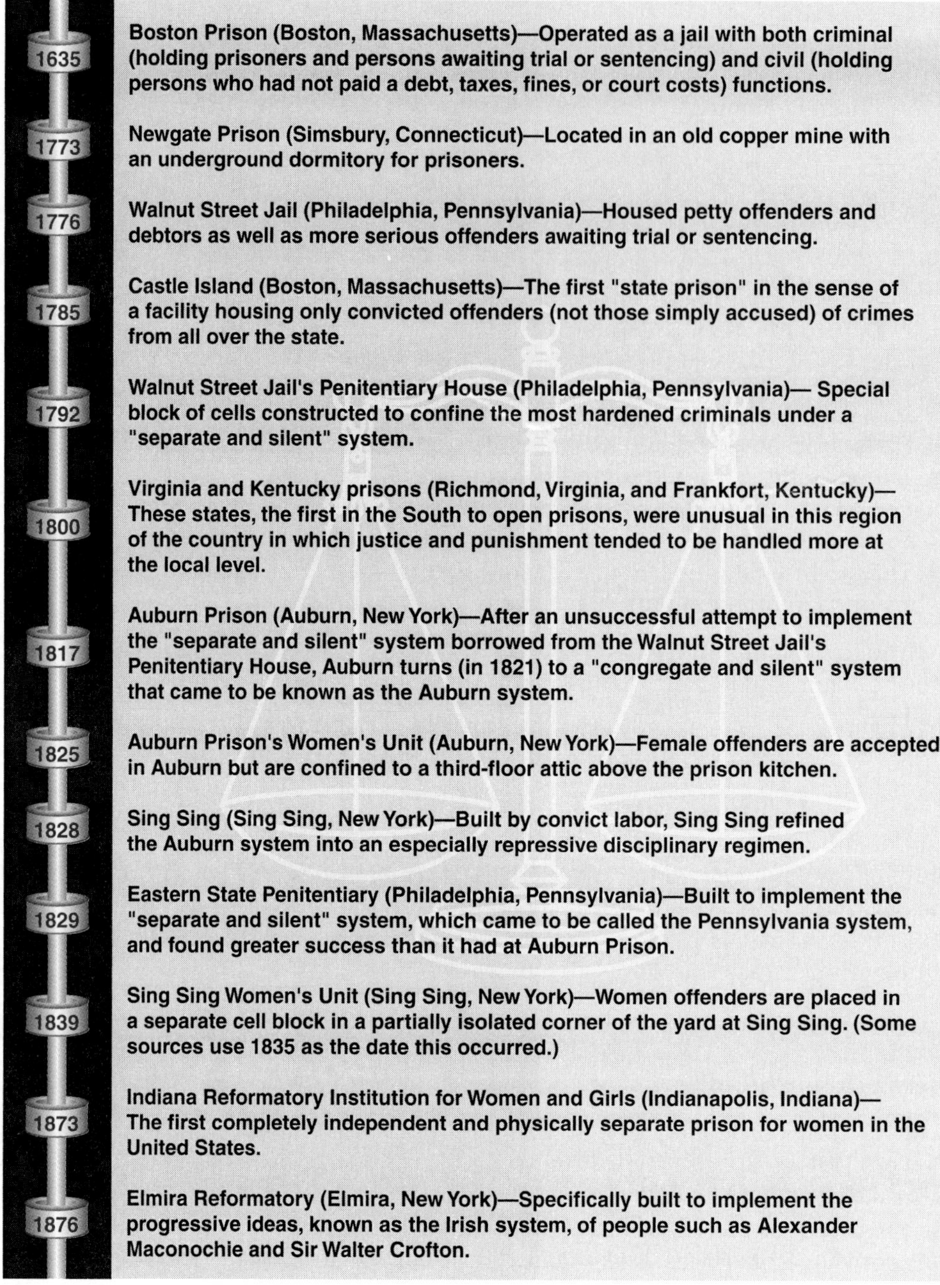

1635 Boston Prison (Boston, Massachusetts)—Operated as a jail with both criminal (holding prisoners and persons awaiting trial or sentencing) and civil (holding persons who had not paid a debt, taxes, fines, or court costs) functions.

1773 Newgate Prison (Simsbury, Connecticut)—Located in an old copper mine with an underground dormitory for prisoners.

1776 Walnut Street Jail (Philadelphia, Pennsylvania)—Housed petty offenders and debtors as well as more serious offenders awaiting trial or sentencing.

1785 Castle Island (Boston, Massachusetts)—The first "state prison" in the sense of a facility housing only convicted offenders (not those simply accused) of crimes from all over the state.

1792 Walnut Street Jail's Penitentiary House (Philadelphia, Pennsylvania)— Special block of cells constructed to confine the most hardened criminals under a "separate and silent" system.

1800 Virginia and Kentucky prisons (Richmond, Virginia, and Frankfort, Kentucky)— These states, the first in the South to open prisons, were unusual in this region of the country in which justice and punishment tended to be handled more at the local level.

1817 Auburn Prison (Auburn, New York)—After an unsuccessful attempt to implement the "separate and silent" system borrowed from the Walnut Street Jail's Penitentiary House, Auburn turns (in 1821) to a "congregate and silent" system that came to be known as the Auburn system.

1825 Auburn Prison's Women's Unit (Auburn, New York)—Female offenders are accepted in Auburn but are confined to a third-floor attic above the prison kitchen.

1828 Sing Sing (Sing Sing, New York)—Built by convict labor, Sing Sing refined the Auburn system into an especially repressive disciplinary regimen.

1829 Eastern State Penitentiary (Philadelphia, Pennsylvania)—Built to implement the "separate and silent" system, which came to be called the Pennsylvania system, and found greater success than it had at Auburn Prison.

1839 Sing Sing Women's Unit (Sing Sing, New York)—Women offenders are placed in a separate cell block in a partially isolated corner of the yard at Sing Sing. (Some sources use 1835 as the date this occurred.)

1873 Indiana Reformatory Institution for Women and Girls (Indianapolis, Indiana)— The first completely independent and physically separate prison for women in the United States.

1876 Elmira Reformatory (Elmira, New York)—Specifically built to implement the progressive ideas, known as the Irish system, of people such as Alexander Maconochie and Sir Walter Crofton.

called, opened in 1635 and served the entire Massachusetts Bay Colony for eighteen years. Between 1652 and 1776, eleven other similar facilities opened in the Bay Colony, so that each of the twelve counties was maintaining its own jail. These early jails served various functions, such as housing prisoners of war (e.g., Indians, French, and eventually British soldiers) and political prisoners (Quakers, Jesuits, and Loyalists). The most notable of the jails' noncriminal roles was confining people who had not paid a debt, taxes, fines, or court costs. Hirsch notes that imprisonment for debt in those days served a different purpose than today. Specifically, debtors were confined "to pry open the purse rather than to chastise debtors" (Hirsch, 1992, p. 7). This point was made clear in the policy that released delinquent debtors from jail whenever their debts were paid in full, or upon convincing the judge that they were bankrupt. Despite these civil duties, the main function of the early jails was for pretrial and presentence detention—but because of these civil duties, the early jails were different from the prisons and penitentiaries they preceded.

Besides performing functions different from modern prisons, early American jails were also distinct in their structure and administration. Hirsch (1992) describes the colonial jails as unimpressive buildings with thin wooden planks, often rotted through, attempting to hold up to thirty prisoners. Jail administrators paid little attention to the inmates' physical health and essentially no attention to their comfort (see the feature "An Underground Prison").

The first U.S. state prison was established in 1785 when Massachusetts converted an old fortress on Castle Island for use as a place of confinement to hard labor for convicted criminals from around the state (Hirsch, 1992; Powers, 1985). From 1785 to 1798, Castle Island served as the Massachusetts State Prison. Around 280 prisoners, either committed by the courts or transferred from other institutions, served time at Castle Island. But, as if confirming the newness of this idea of long-term imprisonment, over the thirteen years some forty-five prisoners escaped from their confinement. Obviously, authorities still had things to learn about making facilities secure enough to house persons for purposes other than pretrial detention, but the establishment of places for long-term imprisonment at hard labor had begun in the United States.

From Pillory to Penitentiary

What would be your reaction to an announcement by legislators that because the cost of prison construction has grown too great, imprisonment is no longer a viable response to crime? Instead, the announcement continues, starting next Monday the

HISTORICAL PERSPECTIVES

An Underground Prison

Although Castle Island lays claim to being America's first state prison, the award for early America's most structurally unique prison most likely goes to the State of Connecticut. Newgate Prison (named after London's famous Newgate Prison) at Simsbury, Connecticut, opened in 1773 and was made the state prison in 1790. New York State's first prison, which opened in 1797, was also known as Newgate but technically was the Greenwich State Prison. The Connecticut prison was both earlier and more unusual because it was located in an old copper mine with an underground dormitory. Using a long ladder, inmates got to their sleeping quarters by descending from the earth's surface, down the solid rock passageways, to a cavern described as twenty-one feet long, ten feet wide, and less than seven feet high.

Sleeping platforms—boards covered with straw—were positioned on the cavern's sides and niches. At dawn the men were taken to the surface where they spent the day at hard labor. Authorities tried to continue mining operations after the first prisoners arrived, but the idea was soon abandoned and inmates were instead put to work making nails, barrels, shoes, wagons, and doing other odd jobs. While at work, the prisoners were chained at the ankles and sometimes at the neck by a collar attached to an iron chain suspended from the ceiling (American Correctional Association, 1983; Barnes & Teeters, 1943).

Read about the original Newgate Prison in London at ***www.spartacus.schoolnet.co.uk/LONnewgate.htm.*** What was the link between Tyburn Tree and Newgate Prison? How were the prisoners divided up in the redesigned Newgate Prison? Also review the history of New York prisons at ***www.correctionhistory.org/html/timeline/html/timeline.html.*** What facilities did New York use to house prisoners prior to using Greenwich State Prison?

state will use electronic technology and drug therapy to control convicted offenders who will now be allowed to remain in their communities. Quite likely you would be appalled by the audacity of the elected officials who thought such a dramatic change in policy can occur so rapidly.

Obviously, such changes in punishment philosophies, practices, and procedures require time. Citizens and legislators would have to modify their general ideas about punishment and would have to be willing to replace the familiar and comfortable, if inadequate, system of imprisonment with an untested alternative. How would proponents of such a change go about achieving it, and what are some problems they would face? Actually, similar questions have confronted Americans before. The transition from corporal and capital punishment to the use of imprisonment presented Americans of 200 years ago with similar problems. Understanding the response of our predecessors helps prepare us for the inevitable struggles that accompany change on such a grand scale.

The first institutions used for long-term imprisonment reflected the hesitancy legislators felt in making the jump from corporal and capital punishment to prisons and penitentiaries. Existing facilities, such as the old copper mine in Simsbury, Connecticut, or the former barracks on Castle Island, were used to avoid large monetary expenses on the untested idea. Rather than completely changing the criminal codes to make imprisonment the only punishment option, incarceration was more often an alternative to, rather than a replacement for, the old corporal punishments. For example, when Massachusetts established Castle Island as the state prison, the sanction of imprisonment and hard labor was often just one of several options available to the judge. Arson against a building other than a dwelling, for example, had always been punished by whipping. The revised statute of 1785 allowed sentences to hard labor, either for life or a specified number of years, the pillory, whipping, imprisonment, a fine, or some combination of these (Hirsch, 1992, p. 57). Obviously the legislators were not anxious to rely only on the newfangled notion of imprisonment to respond to criminals. Furthermore, Massachusetts judges reflected similar hesitancy by only infrequently imposing imprisonment at hard labor as the punishment for a crime.

The new idea of imprisonment and hard labor as an alternative to corporal and capital punishment is especially evident in the activities of Pennsylvania Quakers. In 1787 the Quakers helped establish the Philadelphia Society for Alleviating the Miseries of Public Prisons. This group was essentially a response to the Pennsylvania penal code of 1786, which abolished capital punishment (except for treason and murder) and substituted punishment at hard labor. Importantly, the hard labor punishment did not have to take place in a prison. In fact, an immediate result of the new code was the placement of convicts in road gangs to work on city streets. Dressed in brightly colored clothing and chained to each other or to heavy cannonballs, the prisoners presented a public spectacle of suffering that some found inconsistent with the new humanitarianism of the time (Sullivan, 1990). Complaints from the public pressured the legislature to look for other ways to impose the hard labor sanction. The Society for Alleviating the Miseries of Public Prisons seized the opportunity to argue that the idea of solitude should accompany that of hard labor. They saw an opportunity to carry out their ideas in Philadelphia where an institution suitable for imprisonment to solitude and hard labor already existed.

When it first opened in 1776, Philadelphia's **Walnut Street Jail** housed in large rooms rather than cells petty offenders and debtors on one side and more serious offenders waiting to be tried or sentenced on the other side (McKelvey, 1977). Men and women prisoners intermingled freely; one critic of the sexually mixed jail noted its "promiscuous and unrestricted intercourse, and universal riot and debachery" (quoted in Freedman, 1974, p. 78). Not helping the situation was the

Philadelphia's Walnut Street Jail opened in 1776, and in 1792 a penitentiary house addition was opened. The Penitentiary House provided solitary confinement for the more hardened criminals who now received prison terms rather than death sentences.

common practice of allowing jail keepers to sell alcohol to the inmates. Terror reigned among the prisoners as exemplified by the pastime known as "strip or pay." For that activity, newly admitted inmates could choose between treating all the other inmates to a drink or stripping themselves of their clothes, which were then sold to pay for a round or two (Eriksson, 1976).

During the American Revolution, the jail became a military prison and then reverted to its city jail status. With the new penal code of 1786, and the public's displeasure with having convicts on the city streets, Quakers and others suggested the Walnut Street Jail be expanded to have a new role. The pleas were successful, and in 1790 the legislature ordered that a special block of cells be built at the Walnut Street Jail. Construction was completed in 1792, and the new penitentiary house addition to the jail confined the most hardened criminals in single cells. In theory, if not practice (see Eriksson, 1976, p. 46), the prisoners were kept strictly isolated from each other and from other prisoners, and made to work at hard labor. As the eighteenth century came to a close, the dual themes of solitude and labor were firmly established, and each theme continued to be important in the next era when full-fledged penitentiaries were finally established.

PENITENTIARY ERA (1800S TO 1860S)

The initial establishment of a penal system in the United States (for a note on Canada, see "Development of a Women's Prison in Canada") relied on institutions to implement the punishment philosophies. Rather than choosing just one philosophy from the Wellspring era, the new country sought incapacitation and

Cross-Cultural Corrections

Development of a Women's Prison in Canada

Canadian correctional facilities are found at the federal, provincial, and municipal levels. However, under the two-year rule offenders receiving a sentence over two years fall under the jurisdiction of the federal corrections system. Sentences under two years are the responsibility of the provinces.

As in so many countries, the comparatively small number of female offenders in Canada meant that women were initially placed in prisons that had been built for men. The Kingston (Ontario) men's penitentiary, built in 1835, received its first two women prisoners within one year of its opening. They were confined in a small attic space and essentially considered a nuisance and inconvenience by prison officials. The women, who were denied access to the workshop and recreational facilities provided for male inmates, spent their time making and mending prison clothing (Boritch, 1997).

In 1849, following reports of cruel discipline, starving women, and even driving one woman insane through excessive punishment, recommendations were made for constructing a suitable building for federal female inmates. But it took another sixty-five years before a separate facility for women was built within the existing penitentiary walls. Some twenty years later, in 1934, a separate women's federal penitentiary—the Prison for Women (P4W)—was built across the road from the men's penitentiary.

For several decades recommendations have been made that P4W inmates be transferred to provincial facilities. Finally, in 1990, the Task Force for Federally Sentenced Women made recommendations that are being acted upon. The Correctional Service of Canada is building five small, regional, federally operated facilities across the country (Edmonton, Alberta; Kitchener, Ontario; Truro, Nova Scotia; Jolliete, Quebec; and the Okimaw Ohci [Thunder Hills] Healing Lodge, Saskatchewan). These prisons will not only reduce travel time for prisoners' family members but will also give the women inmates better access to community services and provide programs specifically designed for women.

The new regional facilities are made architecturally different from most of the men's prisons by using apartment-like units and incorporating a nursery. Their location near a city allows for closer ties with local resources, such as chapters of the Elizabeth Fry Society (named for the nineteenth-century English prison reformer). The Thunder Hills Lodge in Saskatchewan is specifically designed for aboriginal women. There is a relatively high native female population in federal women's prisons, so this facility provides those women with healing opportunities such as counseling with elders and the use of sweat lodges (Boritch, 1997; Griffiths & Verdun-Jones, 1994).

Go to the Correctional Service of Canada's site for Federally Sentenced Women at *www.csc-scc.gc.ca/text/prgrm/fsw/fsw_e.shtml,* and read some of the reports on programs available for female offenders. Then read about the Okimaw Ohci (Thunder Hills) Healing Lodge at *www.csc-scc.gc.ca/text/prgrm/fsw/healing/toce.shtml.* How are aboriginal principles being implemented in both the planning and operation of the Healing Lodge?

deterrence in the confines of an institution. An emphasis on institutions is not really surprising because punishment to this time had primarily occurred in the community—especially in the form of public displays of capital and corporal punishment. In that context, turning toward institutions as the place to start formalizing a penal system seemed very appropriate.

The stress on incapacitation and deterrence is reflected in the words of New York and Louisiana statesman Edward Livingston (1764–1836), who wanted to have the following words inscribed over every murderer's cell door:

> In this cell is confined, to pass his life in solitude and sorrow, A. B., convicted of the murder of C. D.; his food is bread of the coarsest kind, his drink is water, mingled with his tears; he is dead to the world; his cell is his grave; his existence is prolonged, that he may deter others from the indulgence of hatred, avarice, sensuality, and the passions which led to the crime he has committed. (quoted in Barnes & Teeters, 1943, p. 514)

In this view of the purpose of imprisonment is found the basic philosophy of that period in the United States' developing penal system called the **Penitentiary era.**

The Penitentiary era is identified by two parallel views of operating a prison (American Correctional Association, 1983). Both were based on the idea that regimens of silence and penitence would prevent cross-infection and encourage positive changes in behavior. The systems' names come from the first locations of their use: Pennsylvania and Auburn (New York).

The Pennsylvania System

Eastern State Penitentiary opened in 1829 in Philadelphia, Pennsylvania. Built on the site of a cherry orchard, and called Cherry Hill by the locals and the prisoners, it was designed with seven cell blocks radiating from a hublike center. A corridor ran down the center of each cell block, with the cells positioned on each side of the corridor. Each cell had a back door to a small, uncovered yard where prisoners were allowed to exercise for two brief periods each day. The prison's design was important to the idea that correction was best achieved when prisoners were kept separate from each other and required to remain silent. This **separate and silent** strategy, key words distinguishing the **Pennsylvania system,** assumed offenders would more quickly repent and reform if they could reflect on their crimes all day.

During its earliest days, the rule of silence was strictly followed as inmates were not allowed to see or talk with each other. Prison officials, the occasional prison inspector, and members of the Philadelphia Prison Society's Visiting Committee were the only visitors allowed. Actually, it was the members of the visiting committee that some criminologists believe provided Eastern State Penitentiary with its most notable accomplishment (Barnes & Teeters, 1943). The visitors made monthly treks to the prison in all kinds of weather and without convenient means of transportation. In addition, they met as a group at least once per month to make their reports and discuss their ministrations—an appropriate term because the visits were primarily religious in nature. Visits were held in the inmate's cell and lasted about fifteen minutes. The Philadelphia Prison Society's visitors were charged with gathering information in several areas during each of their visits. Besides checking on the inmates' general health, the number in the infirmary, and how many were on the list of the insane, the visitors also kept track of information such as the number of inmates discharged and the manner of the discharges, the

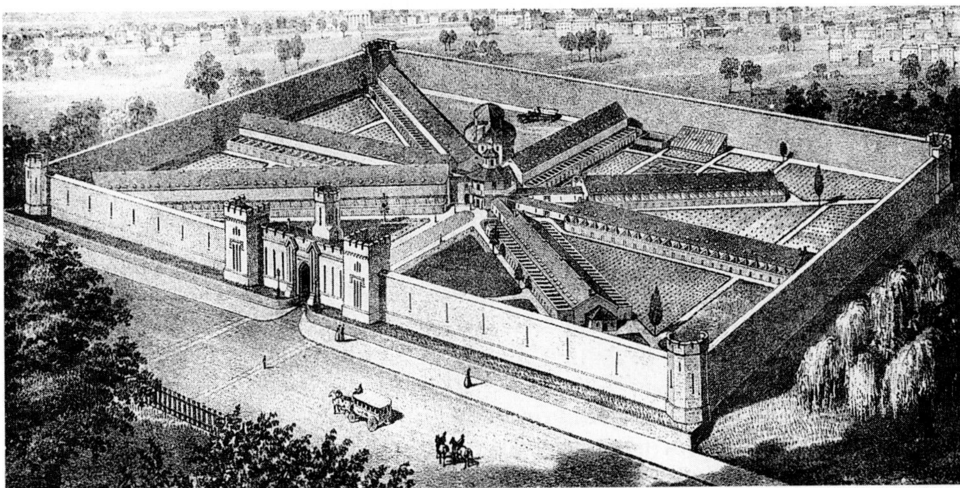

Eastern State Penitentiary in Philadelphia was designed by architect John Haviland with cell block spokes jutting from a central hub. The design made it easy to watch the inmates and promoted the philosophy of solitary confinement and silence.

number of books on loan from the library, and how many inmates were receiving instruction from the teachers.

Critics of the Pennsylvania system argued that the practice of separation (termed *solitude* by the system's proponents) produced insanity in the prisoners. This argument was difficult to refute because reality kept providing examples of prisoners who developed mental problems during their incarceration. The founders of the system were admittedly ignorant of the basic tenets of disciplines such as psychology, sociology, and social work. But those disciplines were not well established in the early and mid-1800s, so it is probably more appropriate to view the Pennsylvania system backers as well-intentioned rather than as inhumane. Mental retardation and mental disease were considered the same by most laypeople, and attempts to explain how either version of this "insanity" came about were difficult.

Borrowing the concept of solitude from the Wellspring era, proponents of the Pennsylvania system had hoped to stop what they saw as the training in crime that prisoners received at those institutions in which inmates had close and constant contact with each other. To eliminate the contamination, especially of first offenders, separation seemed the only reasonable solution. In the early twenty-first century, many behavioral scientists would agree with this centuries-old position, but the problems Eastern State Penitentiary officials had in maintaining the integrity of their system would probably be just as difficult today.

Barnes and Teeters (1943) note that it was physically impossible to keep prisoners entirely apart. Inmates developed ingenious methods to communicate with each other (such as tapping out codes on the water pipes within the cells), but even such shrewdness was soon unnecessary because the officials themselves provided contact among the prisoners. From the beginning, Warden Samuel Wood used the convicts as servants in his home, and very soon two men were put in each cell so that one might learn a trade from the other. Possibly most important in affecting how the prison was made to operate, then as now, the legislature's building appropriations never kept pace with the ever-increasing prison population, so that doubling of prisoners in single cells became necessary. The separate and silent system soon proved a failure, although some could argue it never received a fair chance.

Criticism that it caused mental problems in the inmates and the inability to maintain separation of prisoners were important factors in the Pennsylvania system's demise. But another criticism seemed to take priority in the debates between its champions and its critics: The separate and silent system was very costly. As the system developed at Eastern State Penitentiary, prisoners were allowed to work in their cells at various handicrafts. They made shoes, caned chairs, and knitted hose, but the cell size (18 feet long, 8 feet wide, and 16 feet high) made it difficult to get much production from its single occupant. Even when two prisoners were working in the cell, the profits that could be gained by the prison for their labor were small. Fortunately, for those wanting an economically self-supporting prison, another option was developing at Auburn, New York.

The Auburn System

The Auburn prison opened in 1817 in Auburn, New York. In 1821 Auburn officials borrowed the separate and silent strategy from the Walnut Street Jail for use at the new prison. This meant the Auburn prison actually used the Pennsylvania system before the Eastern State Penitentiary even opened, but it did not prove very successful in New York. The Auburn design, with cells built back to back on five tiers within a hollow building and doors opening out on galleries, did not allow for individual exercise yards. Continual confinement in their cells without access to an outside area and without the distractions of work created mental and physical problems for the inmates. Officials soon decided the separate and silent strategy from Pennsylvania was not working, and the experiment was abandoned as a failure in 1823.

The alternative that Auburn officials turned to was a modification of the Pennsylvania system in which inmates were locked in separate cells at night but allowed to work and eat together, in silence, during the day. This **congregate and silent** policy, which was often enforced with flogging, provided the key words distinguishing the **Auburn system.** The spread of evil ideas among prisoners could be prevented, Auburn proponents argued, by separating prisoners at night and enforcing strict silence in the shops and dining hall during the daytime. That silence was enforced through regulations such as lockstep marching, downcast eyes, constant activity when out of the cells, and prohibitions against prisoners ever being face to face (Barnes & Teeters, 1943).

Shortly after the Auburn system was implemented at the Auburn prison, the New York legislature authorized construction of another prison near New York City in Sing Sing, New York. (In 1906 the city's name was changed to Ossining in an attempt to avoid the stigma brought by the penitentiary.) With great confidence in his system of discipline, Warden Elam Lynds volunteered to have his Auburn prisoners transferred to the new site so they could build the prison. Construction began in 1825, and within three years their hard labor under strict and silent discipline provided New York State with an inexpensively built institution with cells for over five hundred convicts, a cookhouse, blacksmith and carpenter shops, and a chapel room.

Between the 1820s and 1860s policymakers, penologists, and politicians debated the merits of the Pennsylvania and Auburn systems. Proponents of the Pennsylvania strategy claimed it was superior because it was easier to control prisoners, it gave more consideration to individual needs, it provided more opportunity for meditation and repentance, and it avoided cross-contamination of prisoners by maintaining strict separation. The single cells for sleeping, eating, and working; the solitary exercise yards; the restricted and carefully selected visitors; and even the hood placed over the head of a new prisoner being marched to his cell were all precautions against contamination (Rothman, 1971). The end result, in theory, was an opportunity to reform because the prisoner's solitude not only halts the progress of corruption but also encourages the prisoner to recognize the wrongs of his ways.

Supporters of the Auburn system claimed it was superior because it was cheaper to construct and carry out, it provided better vocational training, it was less damaging to the prisoner's mental health, and it produced more money for the state. On this last point, Conley (1980) contrasts the craft-oriented labor at Eastern State Penitentiary with the factory-oriented labor at Auburn and concludes that Pennsylvania had adopted an outdated labor system. The Auburn model, on the other hand, proposed a labor system that could provide the state with a way to exploit convict labor in order to defray institutional expenses, and possibly earn a profit for the state. With full appreciation of New York's direction, the American states yielded to economics and the Auburn system was eventually adopted for most of the country's prisons.

In the early 1830s visitors from around the world came to visit the U.S. penitentiaries to gather information they hoped would be helpful as their own countries decided how to use long-term incarceration. Not surprisingly, like their U.S. counterparts, foreign visitors disagreed about which prison system seemed the best (Eriksson, 1976). The Marquis de Lafayette from France preferred Auburn's congregate system (possibly a result of his own three years of solitary confinement in an Austrian prison). Swedish social reformer Frederika Bremer liked the Pennsylvania system. Often, however, the visitors saw advantages of both the Pennsylvania and Auburn systems. Frenchmen Gustave de Beaumont and Alexis de Tocqueville considered the Pennsylvania system the better of the two because of moral grounds and management simplicity, but they concluded that the Auburn system had the important advantage of economic benefits. English Commissioner of Prisons William Crawford favored the Pennsylvania system in principle but feared its high costs. By the mid-1830s most of the visitors were highlighting the benefits of the separate and silent system to their home countries, but no one encouraged wholesale adoption of the Pennsylvania system. Instead, modified versions were set up throughout Europe.

An interesting aspect of comparative studies is to observe the way that countries are constantly trading ideas and adapting each other's procedures. Although developments in the United States had dramatic influence over the spread of penitentiaries, especially in European countries, the next era for America's penal system was heavily influenced by activities in those countries that had just been learning from the United States a few decades earlier. There were, of course, home-grown efforts as well, but the **Reformatory era** in America owes a great deal to activities that first occurred in other countries.

Reformatory Era (1860s to 1900s)

When reviewing the history of penal institutions, the term **reformatory** is used in referring to a particular system of prison discipline that incorporates a more humanitarian approach to confinement and has an interest in preparing inmates for their eventual return to the community. Reformatory procedures and institutions called reformatories presented different views about prison discipline and administration than were found in the penitentiaries that developed in the first half of the nineteenth century. As we will see, the first American reformatory was at Elmira, New York. The procedures used there developed from activities in Europe, Ireland, and Australia, as well as efforts in the United States. After reviewing some changes that occurred in how prisoners should be treated, we will look more closely at some procedures developed to prepare prisoners for release in the community.

The United States had been at the forefront in putting into operation the first penal philosophies for long-term imprisonment of criminals. But after about fifty years of little more than debate about the merits of the Auburn and the Pennsylvania systems, things were stagnating in the United States, and some prison reformers began looking for new approaches. It soon became apparent that since the 1830s some people had focused their attention less on handling the prisoner in confinement and more on ways to prepare the prisoners for their eventual return to the community. This new focus, which was appealing to many in post–Civil War America, featured an approach that came to be called the **Irish system.**

The Irish System

Beyond a more humanitarian approach to imprisonment, key features of the Reformatory era included an emphasis on education and trade training, indeterminate sentences, and early release from prison. In addition to their occasional presence on the European continent, these traits had already been introduced in Australia and Ireland when they came to the attention of U.S. citizens. The Irish system provided an intriguing option to the Auburn and Pennsylvania systems at a time when many people were looking for alternatives.

The Irish system resulted from the work of Scotsman Alexander Maconochie and Irishman Walter Crofton. Maconochie moved from London to the British penal colony of Van Diemen's Land (Tasmania) in 1836 and immediately took an active interest in the operation of that colony. In 1840 he was placed in command of the penal colony on Norfolk Island. It was there that he developed an administrative philosophy that would have significant impact on penal administration around the world.

Alexander Maconochie. Maconochie's philosophy of punishment varied considerably from the conventional views of his time. He condemned a penal system based on terror; instead, he saw punishment as a necessary evil used only for the prevention of greater evil. His proposals for improvement rested on two fundamental beliefs: (1) "brutality and cruelty debase not only the person subjected to them, but also the society which deliberately uses or tolerates them for purposes of social control," and (2) "the treatment of a wrongdoer during his sentence of imprisonment should be designed to make him fit to be released into society again, purged of the tendencies that led to his offense, and strengthened in his ability to withstand temptation to offend again" (Barry, 1958, p. 72). A system of punishment should train offenders to return to society as honest, useful, and trustworthy members. Punishment, then, could be used as a means to prevent crime, but its most direct and immediate purpose should be to reform the criminal.

From this philosophy, Maconochie created the **mark system** to achieve the goal of reform. Punishment could be severe but only as a means to strengthen character. Because a variety of circumstances determine how long it takes each criminal to become a useful and law-abiding citizen, the term of imprisonment should be indefinite. Maconochie's first proposal, therefore, was that criminal punishments should consist of task and not time sentences; instead of being sentenced to imprisonment for a specific time, the offender should be imprisoned until he completed a specified amount of labor (Barry, 1958; Eriksson, 1976). To achieve this, the prisoner had to attain a fixed number of "marks of commendation" before his period of detention could be ended. Others had expressed similar ideas, but Maconochie introduced them into practice.

Upon first arriving at the prison, offenders would undergo a short period of restraint and deprivation, accompanied by moral and religious instruction, with the purpose of inducing humility and penitence. Upon completion of that stage, they would enter a stage designed to develop powers of industry and self-control. Rather than being given such things as shelter, food, and clothing, prisoners would be required to "purchase" such items with the marks they compiled through labor and good behavior. If prisoners misbehaved, punishment would be fines in marks and withdrawal of privileges rather than the traditional corporal punishment or enforced labor.

After showing exemplary behavior through the accumulation of marks, prisoners could join with five or six other prisoners to participate in joint work projects. With progression through the various stages, offenders would have fewer and fewer restraints placed on their movements. By the final stage, the detention resembled as much as possible the conditions prisoners encounter upon release. "The fundamental principle was: nothing for nothing; everything must be earned" (Barry, 1958, p. 75).

Maconochie's system was not really original, because he borrowed ideas from, and gave credit to, John Howard, Jeremy Bentham, Benjamin Rush, and others. But making use of the ideas of others does not diminish his stature as a penal reformer because it was Maconochie who—despite disbelief and mockery—combined the ideas into a rational system and successfully set up that system.

Sir Walter Crofton. Crofton, who is discussed in greater detail in Chapter 14, became director of the Irish prison system in 1854. Crofton had studied the innovations Maconochie used a decade earlier and was favorably impressed with their basic features. Following his belief that prisons should work toward reforming their prisoners, Crofton borrowed Maconochie's ideas about a mark system and progressive stages. To those he added his own idea of placement in a completely open institution that would help prepare prisoners for their eventual return to the free community under a **ticket-of-leave** (early release from prison) that was subject to revocation if the prisoner misbehaved.

Under Crofton's direction, the **intermediate system**—as Crofton called it—gained considerable attention and received extensive praise during the 1850s and 1860s. The Civil War (1861–1865) understandably distracted U.S. citizens from matters of prison systems, but it was not long after the war's end that this topic became well discussed. The most influential of these exchanges was in 1870. In that year, Americans got a chance to hear firsthand about the operation of Crofton's system when the American Prison Association (now the American Correctional Association) met in Cincinnati for its first National Prison Congress. One hundred thirty delegates from twenty-four states heard some forty papers presented by penal reformers and administrators.

Zebulon Brockway and the Elmira Reformatory. Sir Walter Crofton described his Irish system in a paper presented at the National Prison Congress. His arguments were well received; they influenced both the direction of the meeting and the development of a reformatory philosophy in the United States. Another presenter, Zebulon Brockway, also made quite an impact on the delegates at the congress. Since 1861, Brockway had been director of the Detroit House of Correction, which had been commented upon by several people as a praiseworthy institution. Brockway advocated classification of prisoners by age, sex (see "Women Offenders in the Reformatory Era"), and offense and saw great benefit in the use of indeterminate sentences (see Chapter 5). By the end of the meeting, the views of people such as Crofton and Brockway had been adopted in a declaration of principles that still stands as a progressive document of correctional goals. The view that society should take responsibility for its criminals and their rehabilitation began to take hold. The reformation of offenders would be achieved "through religion, education, industrious work habits, and the aid and supervision of convicts after discharge" (Sullivan, 1990).

The enthusiasm generated at the meeting finally resulted in the 1876 opening of a facility at Elmira, New York, specifically built to carry out these progressive ideas from Australia and Ireland. The **Elmira Reformatory** received offenders ranging from sixteen to thirty years old who were serving their first prison term. Under the direction of Zebulon Brockway, the Elmira Reformatory differed from existing prisons by placing greater emphasis on reforming the inmates, providing more extensive trade training, and increasing opportunities for academic education. Sentences were indeterminate, with fixed minimum terms, and the inmates had the possibility for parole. Maconochie's mark system was also borrowed; inmates were placed into one of three classes depending on their achievement and conduct. They entered at the second grade and after six months were demoted to third grade for bad conduct or promoted to first grade as they earned marks. Only those at first grade were eligible for parole. Paroled inmates remained under the jurisdiction of reformatory authorities for another six months. During that time, parolees had to report on the first day of every month to an appointed guardian (volunteer citizens who were the forerunners of parole officers) and provide an account of their situation.

ISSUES OF FAIRNESS

WOMEN OFFENDERS IN THE REFORMATORY ERA

During the first part of the Penitentiary era, there was seldom any separation of men and women offenders. Offenders of both sexes and all ages were often housed together in large rooms where the strong preyed on the weak. Beginning in the 1830s, segregation of the sexes was accepted in principle but not always in practice. In response to an increasing number of female offenders in the early 1830s, New York finally (in 1835) moved its women offenders from Auburn to a separate cell block in a partially isolated corner of the yard at Sing Sing prison. The women's unit at Sing Sing set the stage for what would be the continued mistreatment of female prisoners by putting them in hot, crowded, and unsanitary conditions, and then subjecting them to corporal punishment and forcing them into prostitution (Barnes & Teeters, 1943; Pollock-Byrne, 1990).

Women and men prisoners were separated increasingly often after the 1830s, but it was not until the Reformatory era that states made concerted efforts to house women in physically separate units from the men. Some states actually built prisons just for female offenders (e.g., Indiana and Massachusetts in the 1870s), but more often the women's units were within the walls of men's prisons.

Although the lack of clear records makes it hard to substantiate, there is good reason to suspect that black women prisoners did not benefit as much from the differential response. The belief that women were worthy of reform may have referred mainly to white women. Nineteenth-century women's reformatories may have accepted only white women, leaving black female offenders to serve their sentence in the women's—and sometimes men's—custodial prisons. In the twentieth century black women were more likely to be admitted to reformatories but were usually segregated in cottages of their own (Rafter, 1990).

Another Reformatory era change in the way states handled their women prisoners is considered as important as placing them in separate facilities—women were being placed in charge of the women's prisons. In 1822 Maryland had become the first state to hire a female jail keeper, and in 1827 Connecticut hired a woman to supervise the female department of the state prison. The norm, however, was for men to be administrators and guards in the women's facilities. Women began arguing that females were better equipped than males to reform and supervise female inmates. Finally, in the 1870s women reformers were seeing the fruits of their arguments as more and more states provided matrons for women's prisons (Freedman, 1974; Pollock-Byrne, 1990).

Read M. Kay Harris's article at ***www.taft.cc.ca.us/cja/cja34_Harris.htm***. In her discussion of the women's reformatory, Harris describes the aim of the reformatories as preparing the residents to be dutiful wives, mothers, and educators of children. How were the reformatory programs and activities designed to achieve this goal?

Disillusionment

The new approach began spreading across the country, with states borrowing the Elmira model. But the enlightened ideas of the 1870s had to meet the realities of the same time. The progressive-stage system, which encouraged good behavior, personal reformation, and early release, had to exist in a system of punitive discipline and strict regimentation. Because of that situation, the grading and promoting of inmates became a mechanical and ineffective way of encouraging reformation. Similar problems occurred with another key aspect of the reformatory—vocational education. Despite lofty claims, the reformatories did not have impressive systems of vocational instruction, did not make use of any testing to find out which inmates might benefit from vocational or trade training, and typically received inadequate funding to maintain a satisfactory vocational education program (Barnes & Teeters, 1959).

By the end of the nineteenth century enthusiasm for the reformatory concept had been dampened. One reason the reformatory ideals had trouble was the setting in which they were being tried. The first three reformatories (Elmira, New York; Concord, Massachusetts; and Huntingdon, Pennsylvania) were all opened in buildings that were originally built as maximum-security prisons for adult felons. The economic benefits of using existing structures meant that many states tried the reformatory ideas in settings that were more conducive to tight security and hard labor than to progressive stages and vocational training. Barnes and Teeters (1959) attribute the decay of the reformatory program to the forbidding atmosphere of steel cages and high, gloomy walls that made it impossible to develop true reformatory ideals.

The problems of inappropriate facilities, haphazard program application, and inadequate funding resulted in the reformatories becoming more like junior prisons than the enlightened alternative proposed by reformers at the Cincinnati congress. As the century ended, vocational training was about the only aspect of the reformatory philosophy that officials stressed—but even that survived less for purposes of education and training than as a way for the prison to make a profit. And that profit motive was strong enough to take hold of prison philosophies around the country and bring the U.S. penal system into a new century and a new era.

PRISON DEVELOPMENT IN THE SOUTH AND WEST

Thus far this chapter gives the impression that the history of America's prison development was restricted to the northeastern part of the country. Beginning with the colonial forerunners to prisons, and moving through the first state prisons in Massachusetts (Castle Island) and Connecticut (Newgate Prison), all the action in imprisonment seems to have been in the Northeast. The clash between the Auburn and Pennsylvania systems kept attention on prison development in the Northeast during the first two-thirds of the nineteenth century, and even the response to that debate (Elmira Reformatory) failed to move attention away from New York and the surrounding states.

Obviously, the rest of the country did not just wait around for the northeastern states to decide what form U.S. imprisonment would take. The other states and territories were certainly influenced by what was happening in places such as Massachusetts, New York, and Pennsylvania, but they also realized there were unique circumstances at home that often required modification, replacement, and even rejection of the prison systems developing in the Northeast. For a different perspective, we will consider the history of state prisons in two other parts of the country: the South and the West.

Developments in the American South

By 1835, most of the states had revised their criminal codes to substitute imprisonment for the traditional corporal punishments. But in many of those jurisdictions, the administration of justice was left to local authorities instead of being centralized at the state level. The reliance on local authority was especially entrenched in the South, where the role of county government and the position of sheriff were of greater consequence than either were in the North. The Carolinas, especially, relied on the counties to administer justice—usually in the form of corporal and capital punishments. A few states tried the penitentiary idea, with Virginia, Kentucky, and Maryland opening state prisons during the first decade of the nineteenth century. Georgia established a prison in 1817, Tennessee in 1831, and Louisiana in 1835, but by the mid-1800s state prisons in the South were still more talked about than a reality (Colvin, 1997). The southern preference remained one of having justice and punishment dispensed at the county rather than the state level.

But the principle of decentralization was not the sole or even primary cause of differences between southern and northern penal developments. Another was the role played by religion. Colvin (1997) explains that in the North, several religious groups promoted penitentiaries as a means of salvation through the implanting of self-discipline. But southern evangelicals had little use for the penitentiary—which, after all, was not even mentioned in the Bible—preferring instead the application of corporal and capital punishment.

In addition to a preference for decentralization and the absence of religious support, the development of penitentiaries in the South was also influenced by the Civil War. First, the war interrupted whatever movement southerners had been making toward developing a penitentiary system. The postwar years in the northern states found those citizens turning toward humanitarian concerns and saw the developments of prison societies and boards of charity that had prison conditions as primary areas of concern. In the southern states, efforts were directed toward rebuilding their homes and communities rather than toward philanthropic endeavors aimed at their law violators.

Finally, economic differences between the North and the South influenced developments in punishment (Colvin, 1997; McKelvey, 1977).[1] While the industrial North put its prisoners to work under labor systems designed to produce a product, the agricultural South was making greater use of a lease system (described in detail in Chapter 4) that provided labor to plantation owners and others. Expanding prison populations in the North were handled by enlarging the buildings housing the prisoners and providing a place for their labor. Increasing prison populations in the South were handled by leasing more prisoners out to employers, who could then build more work camps and push farther into the mountains, swamps, or mining regions. Also important from an economic point was the absence of a strong labor union movement in the South. While the unions of the North fought to limit convict labor's competition with job opportunities for free laborers, there was little organized effort directed against the use of convicts working in the southern fields, forests, and construction sites.

Even with the distractions of reconstruction and the economic and political pushes toward decentralization, it is possible that southerners could have moved toward state penitentiaries like those in the North. But many of the southern states found themselves, after the War between the States, without the prisons they had built before the war started. Georgia's state prison was burned down by the northern army, and the fledgling prisons in other states were either similarly destroyed or torn down. Unfortunately, the law violators were not willing to wait for prisons to be rebuilt. Something had to be done with the regular criminals and the increasing number of vagrant and sometimes desperate freedmen. Southerners turned to the old lease system that had served them well before the war and, realistically, could substitute for the economic benefits of slavery. Arguments have been made that imprisonment in the postwar South quickly came to take the place held by slavery in the antebellum South (Colvin, 1997; Hindus, 1980). Statistics showing that blacks soon made up over 90 percent of the total criminal population

[1]From McKelvey, B. *American prisons: A history of good intentions* (taken from pp. 25–31; 197–233). Copyright © 1977 by Patterson-Smith. Permission from Patterson-Smith for extended use.

in the Deep South help to support that thesis. The lease system put convicts in the role of exploited laborer and prison wardens in the role of slaveholder.

Labor in areas such as farm work, road construction, and turpentine extraction requires workers to be dispersed over a wide area. Rather than being conveniently housed in a big building, prisoners need to be where the crops are grown, the road built, and the pine trees sapped. In other words, prison labor in the South did not lend itself to having prisoners located at a single state penitentiary, where they could make boots, buttons, barrels, and brooms. Instead, smaller work camps with housing for about 100 prisoners who could be transported to the work site each day was more reasonable and economical.

McKelvey (1977) uses Georgia's experience as typical of the Deep South. General T. H. Ruger took over the state government in 1868 and found 100 convicts on his hands. Because the old prison was now in ruins, Ruger promptly leased the convicts to a railroad builder. The succeeding governor continued the practice and by 1876—when its prisoners numbered 1,110—Georgia had developed a leasing program by which its convicts were leased among three companies on contracts lasting twenty-five years. Each company paid the state $25,000 per year for the labor.

Mississippi legislators voted down a proposal for a new penitentiary in 1876; instead, they leased the entire population to a company that quickly discovered it could sublease the convicts at even higher rates. No check was made on the resulting fate of the penal slaves. Similarly, Arkansas and Tennessee turned their prisons over to leaseholders who first employed the convicts within the prison walls but eventually were allowed to develop work camps away from the prison grounds. By 1880 all the former Confederate states and Kentucky had leased out a major portion of their criminal populations. When reformers sought to end leasing, the taxpayers prevented any change. The tragic system continued as former slaves "awoke from rosy dreams of freedom and forty acres and a mule to find themselves shackled to the task of rebuilding the wealth of the South in hopeless penal slavery" (McKelvey, 1977, p. 207).

A common theme at the southern prison camps was a demand for economy. One-story wooden huts usually housed a hundred or more prisoners who were forced to sleep, often shackled, on crude bunks around the walls. Water was scarce, bathing nearly impossible, sanitary arrangements crude, and disease rampant. Death or escape was the only quick means of relief for the prisoners. An 1882 report showed a total of 1,100 men had made successful escapes in the two previous years in southern states. That number presents an interesting contrast to the sixty-three escapes in one year committed by northern convicts. Similarly, compare the average death rate of 14.9 per thousand in northern prisons to the 41.3 per thousand in the South (McKelvey, 1977, pp. 209–210).

Leasing's end was brought about not so much by new humanitarian concerns as by reduced profits. By the end of the nineteenth century, states were finding that other labor systems were proving beneficial. Experiments with penal plantations were especially encouraging. Louisiana, Mississippi, and Texas were among the first states to experiment with the use of prisoners on large farms and plantations. These states began purchasing farmland and buying plantations where prisoners would work for the state rather than for private contractors or lessees. The penal plantation became entrenched in southern penology and influenced the direction imprisonment would take in the twentieth-century South.

The Louisiana State Penitentiary at Angola is an example of the southern penal plantation. As described by Rideau (1992a), Louisiana purchased an 8,000-acre plantation in 1901 to add to its existing levee camps and the penitentiary at Baton Rouge. The plantation purchase was originally made to give the state a source of income. That goal was not easily achieved; boll weevils ravaged the cotton crop, and several floodings from the Mississippi River caused other damage and

Unlike their northern counterparts who were busy manufacturing items, inmates in the South worked on farms, built roads, and extracted turpentine from pine trees. As a result prison labor in the South did not lend itself to having prisoners located at a single state penitentiary. Instead, smaller work camps were built, and prisoners were transported each day to the work site.

crop loss. But the system was maintained, and by 1922 the Angola plantation had increased to 18,000 acres. Sugar cane had replaced cotton as the principal crop, and sugar refining became the primary work activity—supplemented by other agricultural work as well as lumbering and manufacturing. Today the Louisiana State Penitentiary at Angola retains its plantation format with four camps, the main prison, and a reception center housing over 4,500 male prisoners who continue to work the traditional areas. But in addition to the facilities at Angola, Louisiana now also has four correctional centers, two correctional institutes, two work training facilities, and one correctional institute for women.

Developments in the American West

The earliest prisons in the West were not strongly influenced by the developments in New York and Pennsylvania. When California achieved statehood in 1850, it already had a population of 90,000 and was finding the old Spanish jails to be inadequate for its needs. The legislature voted to build a penitentiary and turned that task and the eventual care of the convicts over to a leaseholder. A site was selected at San Quentin, and with convict labor California's first prison was built. In 1855 over 300 men crowded the two buildings that made up the prison, and by 1873 two more cellhouses were added as the population exceeded 900. By 1880 over 1,300 prisoners were packed into San Quentin.

The problems of crowding at San Quentin, and at Folsom when that prison opened in 1880, highlight what McKelvey (1977) sees as California's worst failure in the area of imprisonment—poor prison accommodations. The total prison population was about twice the capacity of facilities, but a more important problem concerned the type of offender being put in prison. California tended to place a larger portion of its lesser offenders into prisons than was the practice in the East. Classification processes were inadequate for separating the criminally naive from the more hardened offenders, and no system of correctional discipline was used to control, reward, or encourage the inmates.

But bad as the crowding in California prisons was, the conditions to the north were of even greater concern. To handle its law violators, the Washington Territory used leasing (starting in 1877) to a mill owner, who worked the prisoners during the day and then herded them "through a trapdoor into a log pit to spend the nights in mutual corruption and suffocation" (McKelvey, 1977, p. 229). Conditions in the pit were so terrible that McKelvey suggests the "structure was possibly the worst prison in America since the closing of Connecticut's old copper mine nearly a century before" (p. 229).

Some of the territories chose to transfer their criminals to other states rather than build their own prisons. In Wyoming Territory, federal authorities built a wooden prison at Laramie, but expenses forced the territorial legislature to contract first with the Nebraska state prison, and then with the Illinois prison at Joliet, to house its criminals. Upon attaining statehood in 1890, Wyoming officials leased the entire institution at Laramie to a private party, but by 1898 an Auburn-style structure had been built at Rawlins. Oklahoma's criminals—who multiplied even more rapidly than its citizens (McKelvey, 1977)—were sent off to the penitentiary in Kansas, where they were jammed into crowded cells when they were not digging coal in the mine pits.

In the southwestern territories, Arizona opened its territorial prison at Yuma in 1876, and the inmates were soon presented with interesting contrasts. On the amenities side, the prison had a generator that supplied electricity to the prison and to the town of Yuma, and allowed for large blowers to help circulate hot air in the main cell block—a convenience most of the town residents did not have. In addition, the prison had a library that was open to the public as well as to the inmates and the guards (Trafzer & George, 1980). Contrasted with these niceties were the bare necessities the inmates were allowed to have: two each of underwear, handkerchiefs, and towels; two pairs of socks; one pair of shoes; an extra pair of pants; a toothbrush, comb, toothpick, and bedding; and the assorted books and tobacco. In addition, the desert climate meant these items might be shared with cockroaches, black widows, and the occasional scorpion.

Like most western prisons in the late 1800s, the Territorial Prison at Yuma, Arizona, held both men and women. Among the more notorious women at the Yuma prison was Pearl Hart, shown here expressing the attitude that may have encouraged the court to give her a prison sentence.

Typical of most western prisons, the Yuma facility held both men and women. Records indicate they came from over twenty different countries, as well as including American-born blacks, Mexicans, whites, and Indians. Their offenses ranged from stage robbery and cattle rustling to rape and murder. Sentences of varying lengths were imposed, including death and life imprisonment, but pardons were common and few prisoners served out their complete sentences (Trafzer & George, 1980). By 1909 (almost three years before statehood), the Territorial Prison at Yuma had become too small to handle the increasing number of Arizona criminals. The property was returned to the city, and the prisoners were transferred to a new prison at Florence.

Possibly the most successful states to develop stable prison systems in the West were Colorado, Utah, and the Dakotas. McKelvey suggests the success of these states was due to their ability to keep open the channels of eastern influence and their participation in the congresses of the National Prison Association. From each source, these western states were kept informed about eastern debates, experiments, and theories regarding penal administration. For example, when the National Prison Association held its 1895 congress in the Rocky Mountain west, Colorado officials were able to brag about having the first adult reformatory, the first board of charities, the only separate prison building for women, the only effective parole law, and the only genuine grading system west of the Mississippi River (McKelvey, 1977).

During the twentieth century other western states, most notably California, came to play a prominent role in directing penal policies and procedures across the nation. The East no longer had a hold on innovation, and both independent and collaborative efforts by each of the fifty states created facets of the U.S. penal system. But while this brief history is informative in itself, its importance for this chapter is to remind us about the cycle of history. Problems of crowding, complaints about prison conditions, and concerns over prison labor systems are not new in American history. Although it would be nice to explain that society has learned from history and can now handle these problems with efficiency and expertise, it is more accurate to say that society has not. Contemporary problems are typically seen by the media, the public, legislators, and even corrections professionals as being unique to this time.

SUMMARY

PUTTING PHILOSOPHIES INTO PRACTICE

This chapter and the next present the development of the U.S. penal system as occurring over six penal eras: Wellspring, Penitentiary, Reformatory, Industrial, Rehabilitation, and Retributive. The first three eras, taking us to the end of the nineteenth century, were covered in this chapter.

WELLSPRING ERA (MIDDLE AGES TO 1800s)

- A variety of philosophies and strategies were tried in the American colonies and in other parts of the world.
- Sanctions such as corporal and capital punishment, banishment, and transportation were popular in most countries.
- During this time we also see the early stages of imprisonment as a penal sanction. Hospice facilities and houses of correction set a precedent for later jails and prisons through their belief in the value of isolating those who had misbehaved (the hospice facilities) and the benefits of work (the houses of correction).

PENITENTIARY ERA (1800s TO 1860s)

- This era was identified to a great extent by the debates over the merits of two competing penal systems.
- The Pennsylvania system, as it operated at Eastern State Penitentiary in Philadelphia, emphasized separation (isolation) and silence of the prisoners.
- The Auburn system, at the prison in Auburn, New York, agreed with silence among the prisoners but believed they could be allowed to work together during the day.
- The Auburn system, especially for financial reasons, ended up serving as a model for the prison system in most of the other American states.

REFORMATORY ERA (1860s TO 1900s)

- The Reformatory era began as reformers implemented ideas from Europe—especially those associated with the Irish system.
- Key features of the Irish system included such practices as indeterminate sentencing, the mark system, and early release from prison.
- These procedures provided the basis for contemporary probation and parole.

PRISON DEVELOPMENT IN THE SOUTH AND WEST

- Conditions influencing the different development of prisons in the South included the southern preference for decentralization of justice to the county level, the absence of religious support for penitentiaries as a replacement for corporal and capital punishment, the destruction caused by the Civil War, and an economy based in agriculture rather than industry.
- Western territories and states experienced serious overcrowding and other problems as they began using imprisonment as a response to law violators. States that were most successful in developing a penitentiary system were those that kept themselves informed about—and learned from—eastern debates, experiments, and theories regarding penal administration.

KEY TERMS AND CONCEPTS

1779 Penitentiary Act (p. 71)
Auburn system (p. 79)
banishment (p. 64)
Bridewell House (p. 69)
Castle Island (Massachusetts) (p. 71)
congregate and silent (p. 79)
Elmira Reformatory (p. 82)
Gaol at Wymondham (p. 71)
Hospice of St. Michael (p. 68)
houses of correction (p. 69)
intermediate system (p. 82)
Irish system (p. 80)
Maison de Force (p. 69)
mark system (p. 81)
Penitentiary era (p. 77)
Pennsylvania system (p. 77)
reformatory (p. 80)
Reformatory era (p. 80)
separate and silent (p. 77)
ticket-of-leave (p. 82)
transportation (p. 64)
Walnut Street Jail (p. 74)
Wellspring era (p. 64)
workhouses (p. 69)

Discussion Questions

1. Are the two important themes in the development of imprisonment as punishment (i.e., prisoners should be isolated, and prisoners should work) still important today? In what way, or why not?
2. If we can agree that conditions at Newgate Prison in Connecticut were horrible, why did people continue to commit crimes at the risk of being sent to Newgate?
3. Highlight what you consider to have been the major advantages and disadvantages of both the Pennsylvania and the Auburn systems.
4. The chapter points out that some authors believe the Philadelphia Prison Society's Visiting Committee was the most notable accomplishment of the Eastern State Penitentiary. Should the services the visitors provided still be offered in today's prisons? Should those services be the responsibility of volunteers, such as the visitors, or the responsibility of only jail and prison officials?
5. Are economically self-sufficient prisons desirable in today's society? Are they possible today? Why or why not?

chapter 4

Modern Penal System Eras

Shortly after I arrived at Graterford, I discovered that my fellow inmates made a point of "playing the opposites." This game involves reverse psychology, where prisoners state the opposite of their actual feelings when asked by someone in authority to voice a preference or an opinion. A common occasion for playing the opposites is when an inmate is being interviewed by a counselor or employment officer for a job assignment. . . . As a general rule, inmates don't receive the jobs that they request. Consequently, a more savvy convict won't hint at his preference; instead, he misleads the staff member into believing that he would hate being assigned to a work detail that he secretly desires.

The conversation [might] sound like this:

Officer: Okay, where do you want to work?

Inmate: I worked as a clerk in the library the last time I was here and I got burned. The job was too demanding and I couldn't get enough free time.

Officer: So are you saying you don't want a clerk's job?

Inmate: Yeah, I guess so. I don't think I could take working as a clerk anymore. I need something easier—you know, a no-brain job—so I can work on my legal papers and stuff like that.

Officer: So where do you want to be assigned?

Inmate: How about the kitchen? That's a pretty simple job and I get to eat real good. I think I'd like to work in the kitchen this time 'round. I got a couple of friends who work in the kitchen who can show me the ropes.[1]

Whether the story of playing the opposites is a prison myth or an effective way to manipulate the system, it serves to highlight some important issues that have affected the modern penal eras. The problem of inmate labor has been responded to in several ways since the establishment of the nation's first prisons. This chapter reviews some of the labor systems that have been used and notes some of the problems and successes of each. Also in this chapter is a review of a period of years in which rehabilitation was the prevailing punishment philosophy. The idea that inmates' opinions about their work assignments might even be asked or considered is a reflection of that era. Finally, people who were irritated by the story about playing the opposites—seeing it as simply another example of criminals cunningly manipulating an indulgent system—will understand the country's eventual movement to a retributive philosophy of punishment.

[1]From Hassine, V. (1999). *Life without parole.* Los Angeles: Roxbury.

TWENTIETH AND TWENTY-FIRST CENTURY ERAS

Chapter 3 described the Wellspring, Penitentiary, and Reformatory penal system eras. Those eras extended from the Middle Ages through the end of the nineteenth century. Over those centuries exist examples of the five penal philosophies of deterrence, incapacitation, rehabilitation, retribution, and restoration. This chapter continues the discussion by presenting the penal system eras occurring in the twentieth and twenty-first centuries. As we look at the Industrial, Rehabilitation, and Retributive eras, all five of the punishment philosophies will still be apparent. But, as was true in the early penal system eras, one or two philosophies seem to take a more prominent role during certain decades.

The importance of remembering that all five penal philosophies existed during each penal era will be increasingly apparent as the discussion focuses on contemporary times. Several of the defining characteristics of the three twentieth-century penal eras will likely retain importance in the twenty-first century. For example, prisoner labor (central to the Industrial era) continues to be an important concern for prison administrators, private companies, labor unions, and the prisoners themselves. Similarly, rehabilitation components such as **classification, treatment,** and **intervention** strategies are key aspects of contemporary corrections—although not as central as they were during the Rehabilitation era. Finally, the Retributive era of the present day is a complex time that emphasizes the age-old philosophy of retribution tempered with concerns for proportionality of punishment. It is also a time of searching for alternatives to imprisonment as the primary method for handling serious felony offenders. It is that search for alternatives that not only provides links to the other punishment philosophies but may also be setting the stage for the next penal system era.

INDUSTRIAL ERA (1900S TO 1930S)

Identifying a particular span of years as the **Industrial era** of America's prison system can be misleading. After all, labor has had a significant role since the Wellspring era—why should it suddenly be so important that it defines a separate era in our prison system? The answer lies in events occurring at the end of the nineteenth and beginning of the twentieth centuries. Over a forty-year period, prison labor moved from an activity whose primary purpose was to benefit the state to an activity that might benefit the prisoner. Especially during the first thirty years of the twentieth century, prison labor experienced dramatic changes in the type of labor most often used, the profitability of the labor, and labor's primary purpose. Those topics are used here to describe the Industrial era of the U.S. prison system.

Types of Labor Systems

In 1887 the second annual report of the Bureau of Labor was presented to the U.S. Congress (House of Representatives, 1887). Labor Commissioner Carroll Wright devoted the entire report to the subject of convict labor. In the report's introduction Wright gave one reason for such a focus. He explained that convict labor was presenting the United States with a dilemma: "(H)ow shall convicts be employed in useful labor without unduly competing with labor outside penal institutions, either in the wages of labor or in the price of products?" (House of Representatives, 1887, p. 3). Much of the twentieth century's first quarter was spent trying to answer that question by manipulating everything from the employment of prisoners to the marketing of their products. The difficulty in solving this dilemma continues today at the beginning of the twenty-first century in the search for a way to balance the desire to put prisoners to useful labor without having the products of that labor provide undue competition to private enterprise.

Six types of labor systems are typically identified: public account, contract, piece-price, lease, public works and ways, and state use. The types are first distinguished on the basis of the market for the goods each produces. The first four are **open market** systems because their products are sold, either by private companies or by the state, to any prospective buyers. The last two types—public works and ways and state use—are **sheltered market** systems because their products are only for the state's benefit. As Table 4.1 shows, the types also differ according to whether public or private entities maintain and discipline the prisoners, supervise their employment, and control the sale of the product. Because several of these labor systems continue today, as seen in Chapter 10, it is important to look at each more closely.

The Lease System. Leasing is one of the oldest labor systems in the United States because it is related to indentured service as found in the colonies. Its use specifically for prisoners (ignoring criminals transported to the colonies from England and required to work for private individuals) is documented as early as 1798 in Massachusetts. The **lease system** was especially popular in the South after the Civil War when prisoners worked in turpentine camps or sugar cane plantations. States outside the South, such as Wyoming, Montana, New Mexico, and Arizona, also made significant use of leasing, but the system's extreme example probably occurred in 1894 when Tennessee leased its entire prison population to the Tennessee Iron and Coal Railroad for a yearly payment of $100,000 (Sullivan, 1990). By the 1920s leasing was used in only an insignificant number of prisons, and by 1936 the practice had been abolished in every state—although some county jails retained leasing for many more years.

The lease system was one of the most controversial of the six labor systems. For a specified sum and for a fixed time, the institution would lease a prisoner to a private individual. That lessee was then usually responsible for feeding, clothing, and disciplining the prisoner while that prisoner labored at whatever activity

TABLE 4.1: Prison Labor Systems

SYSTEM	MARKET AREA	MAINTENANCE AND DISCIPLINE OF PRISONERS	CONTROL OF EMPLOYMENT	CONTROL OF SALE OF PRODUCTS
Lease	Open	Private	Private	Private
Contract	Open	Public	Private	Private
Piece-price	Open	Public	Public	Private
Public account	Open	Public	Public	Public
State use	State	Public	Public	Public
Public works and ways	State	Public	Public	Public

Source: From Sutherland, E. H., Cressey, D. R., & Luckenbill, D. F. (1992). *Principles of criminology* (11th ed.). Dix Hills, NY: General Hall. Copyright © 1992 by General Hall. Adapted with permission of the publisher.

Construction of the Erie Canal, shown here around 1825, became an early example of the convict lease system when the New York legislature authorized the canal builders to use prisoner labor.

was specified by the terms of the lease. In 1886 prisoners were leased to work in such industries as mining, tobacco, furniture, and carriage construction. In 1905 mining, clothing, and lumber were popular industries for leasing inmates.

Because the lessee controlled the conditions under which inmates worked, the potential for abuse was considerable. Chaneles (1985) reports on the conditions of Alabama leased convicts in the 1880s and 1890s when most were working in coal mines. The pens in which they were confined at night were declared by an investigating committee to be unfit for human habitation. The committee's report noted, among other things, that the prisoners "breathed and drank their bodily exhalations and excrements" (quoted in Chaneles, 1985, p. 113). In 1893 and 1894, tuberculosis and pneumonia were identified as the cause of more than one-half of the deaths among the felony convicts working in the coal mines.

Leasing was typically terrible when operated by state prisons and often horrible when used by county jails. In 1901 in Alabama the *Montgomery Advertiser* told of seventeen white men and three black men securely handcuffed and tied together with a rope as they were taken to work in coal mines. The men had been arrested at gun point and, without even a pretense of a trial, were taken to jail where they were kept for four or five weeks before being sent to a one- to three-month stretch working in the mines (Chaneles, 1985, pp. 118–119). The newspaper, remarking that such treatment recalled stories of suffering that used to come from Siberia, suggested that the arrests (for unlawfully riding on trains) may have been the result of paying the man making the arrests two dollars for each arrest rather than by any misbehavior of the twenty men.

Also in 1901 the *Mobile Register* reported that a deputy sheriff had recently arrested eighteen men, receiving a fee for each arrest. All eighteen were sent to the mines, but fourteen of them had not received a trial. But not all "offenders" were appropriate for leasing to the mine owners. "A little negro boy, dirty and ragged was arrested and as he was not worth sending to the mines, the Deputy sold him to a farmer for one dollar" (Chaneles, 1985, p. 118).

Women were also leased out for labor in camps and mines, but even more often they were provided to the locals as domestic servants. In the midnineteenth century, training at Massachusetts's Lancaster Industrial School for Girls focused on domestic skills, and at age sixteen the girls were assigned to suitable families as indentured domestic servants. They were expected to remain in that capacity until reaching age eighteen (Colvin, 1997). Because many of the women leased as domestics were black, Butler suggests it helped "freeze African American women in their role as domestic workers" (1997, p. 191). The lease system, Butler argues, pressured black women to feign passivity when they worked for white families or face returning to prison. In this way leasing reinforced the fundamental use of women, especially black women, as domestics.

If you think the leasing system sounds a bit like slavery, you would be sharing the opinion of many. In fact, the leasing system's growth and popularity in the South after the Civil War is easily attributed to the need for a labor system that could provide workers to replace slave labor. But it would be unfair and misleading to attribute such motives to only one region of the country and to a particular time period. The possible link between slavery and prison labor is much older than the post–Civil War period and much broader than the southern region of the country.

A connection between the institutions of slavery and the penitentiary is proposed by Christianson (1998), Hindus (1980), and Hirsch (1992). None of those authors restrict their argument to the lease system as they explain the association between convict labor and slavery. Similarly, it is important to remember that throughout history slaves and masters have been of any—and often the same—race and ethnicity. As a result, the examples in the following discussion are not always of the lease system nor only of black prisoners. But the topic of prison labor as slavery is important enough to digress for a moment from the specifics of leasing. And, because the lease system is most obviously like slavery, discussion at this point seems appropriate.

We saw in reviewing the Wellspring era that the penitentiary existed in conceptual and incomplete form in several parts of the world prior to the nineteenth century. When it made its modern appearance in the 1820s, it did so as one of several social institutions existing or developing at the time. Politics, religion, and philanthropy were certainly important in the penitentiary's eventual form, but so was America's institution of slavery.

When New York legislators decided to authorize construction of a state prison in Auburn, the history of slave labor seems to have been fresh in their minds. In early 1817 in New York State, two controversial public issues had converged: the decision to build the Erie Canal and the abolition of African slavery. Opponents of the canal aligned with abolitionists in an effort to remove African slaves from potential economic exploitation in the canal venture. Canal supporters found an alternative labor source—unpaid prisoner labor.

On April 15, 1817, the New York legislature passed a law authorizing the builders of the canal to use as much inmate labor as they wished exclusively for work on the canal. The state government would provide for the care and custody of prisoners, but the builders had to abide by two conditions: (1) Inmates would work on the canal without pay for a period of not less than six months; and (2) escaped convicts would be apprehended, brought before a court, and upon conviction banished from New York State on pain of death. The same law provided for the construction of a state prison in the rural village of Auburn—conveniently located along the proposed route of the canal (Chaneles, 1985).

Some of the prisoners forced into labor on the canal were African slaves, but they were the minority. As Chaneles describes the canal workers:

> Most were white, Irish youngsters, nearly all without families in New York, freshly deposited by sailing ships in the slums, orphanages, debtor's prison, and almshouses of New York City. All were subject to the intense anti-Catholic hatred at the time. They were arrested literally within days of their arrival, mainly on charges of drunkenness,

Because the lease system required prisoners to work away from the prison, mobile cages were often used for convict transportation and sleeping.

> hastily convicted in sizable groups, hastily marched to the prison brigs for the voyage to Albany [to be carted by ox-drawn wagon to Auburn]. . . . Within two years the basic system was working efficiently: daily arrests and convictions on the New York City docks and shipment north, daily release from Auburn for labor on the canal with fresh replacements assured.[2] (1985, pp. 56–57)

Similarities between slavery and convict labor extended beyond the comparable treatment of each population. From language (both convicts and slaves were supervised by an "overseer") and dress (both had to wear distinctive garb), to assumptions about character (if they were not restrained, it was assumed that both convicts and slaves would resort to criminal ways) and effort (slaves and convicts sabotaged materials and tools and sought ways to avoid their required work), there were many points on which the two populations could be compared (Hirsch, 1992). Even when contrasts seem obvious, there remains some similarity. For example, slaves had to resign themselves to perpetual captivity whereas convicts served a definite term of imprisonment. But high rates of recidivism suggest that many convicts were perpetually in the prison. On another point, slaves can be distinguished as being the private property of an individual master whereas prison inmates labored under the supervision of the state. Yet under the lease system, prisoners were also "sold" to individuals (although via newspaper advertisements rather than the indignity of an auction block) who then controlled that convict's labor.

A strong argument can be made (see Christianson, 1998; Colvin, 1997; Hirsch, 1992) that the penitentiary and slavery were alike in many ways. Given the similarities, it seems surprising that disgust with the institution of slavery was not accompanied by aversion to penitentiaries and forced labor. But quite the contrary; as slavery receded, the penitentiary and convict labor grew. Often the very people (e.g., Benjamin Rush and Thomas Eddy) who argued that slavery must be abolished on moral grounds were at the same time strong proponents of penitentiaries with hard labor. How did these activists reconcile their antislavery position with their desire for penitentiaries?

[2]Chaneles, S. (Ed.). (1985). *Prisons and prisoners: Historical documents.* New York: Haworth Press. Reprinted by permission of the publisher.

Hirsch (1992) suggests that people such as Benjamin Rush could plead for the destruction of slavery while pushing for the construction of penitentiaries by distinguishing the circumstances that brought each population to their respective institution. The primary argument was that penal slavery was different from chattel slavery because those subjected to penal slavery had brought the situation onto themselves through their own actions. John Locke, for example, argued that slavery could be imposed only when a person violated the natural law that the civil government was created to uphold. Criminals, therefore, can be justly subjected to slavery because they took themselves outside the social contract and lost such natural rights as protection against enslavement. Following Lockean theory, penitentiary advocates were always careful to propose these institutions only for convicted offenders. Debtors and pretrial detainees, for example, who had in the past been kept along with criminal convicts would not be appropriate for the penitentiaries because hard labor was an integral feature of those facilities.

This digression from the specifics of the leasing system serves as a reminder that as loathsome as leasing might seem today, its similarity to slavery was in part consistent with America's history of imprisonment and was neither limited in time (e.g., post–Civil War) nor place (e.g., the South). With that caution, it is time to look more closely at leasing as a particular prison labor type.

Table 4.2 shows that leasing was already accounting for only a small percentage of the number of prisoners employed as the Industrial era began. Although 20 percent of prisoners employed in 1885 were under the lease system, by 1903 to 1904 the number had declined to only 7 percent. Changing attitudes toward leasing can be inferred from the reports issued by the Department of Labor in 1886, 1896, and 1906. In the first two reports the lease system was simply described along with the other five systems. No comment was made about the humanitarian aspects or abuses associated with leasing or any other labor system. But the

TABLE 4.2: Number of Prisoners Employed by Type of Labor System

	1885[a]		1895[b]		1903–1905[a]		1923[b]	
Labor System	Number of Prisoners Employed	Percent of Total	Number of Prisoners Employed	Percent of Total	Number of Prisoners Employed	Percent of Total	Number of Prisoners Employed	Percent of Total
Lease	9,104	20	6,869	18	3,652	7	0	0
Contract	15,670	35	10,599	28	16,916	33	6,083	12
Piece-price	5,676	13	7,537	20	3,886	8	3,577	7
Public account	14,827	33	13,410	35	8,530	17	13,526	26
State use	c	c	c	c	12,044	24	18,850	36
Public works and ways	c	c	c	c	6,144	12	9,763	19
Total	45,277	101	38,415	101	51,172	101	51,799	100

Note: Figures are compiled from House of Representatives (1887, 1896, 1906) and Bureau of Labor Statistics (1925).

[a]Data for 1885 and 1905 include state prisons, reformatories, and county institutions.

[b]Data for 1895 and 1923 include state and federal prisons and reformatories.

[c]Work under state use and public works and ways was counted under the public account system in 1885 and 1895.

Labor Department's twentieth annual report, presented to Congress in 1906, said the only possible argument for the convict lease system was the state's poverty and its inability to provide housing, food, guards, and suitable work for the prisoners. The report continued by noting that other than being convenient and cheap, the lease system had nothing in its favor and served only to demoralize both the convict and the public (House of Representatives, 1906, pp. 16–17).

The commissioner of labor was not so much leading the charge against leasing as he was reporting the prevailing opinion of citizens, politicians, and prison officials of the time. The abuses and inhumanity of leasing were becoming increasingly apparent and unacceptable. By 1923 the Department of Labor was reporting that no state or federal prisoners were being employed under the lease system (Bureau of Labor Statistics, 1925), but it was 1936 before every state had formally abolished the practice of leasing (Sullivan, 1990). However, the feature "Leasing Today" suggests leasing may still be present in a modified format.

States moving away from the lease system often turned to public account, state use, or public works and ways. But the contract system, as seen in Table 4.2, was the prison labor type that employed the greatest number of prisoners as the Industrial era began.

The Contract System. The **contract system** was used as early as 1807 in Massachusetts but did not become widely popular until about 1820 (Sutherland, Cressey, & Luckenbill, 1992). New York state prisons—such as Auburn and Sing Sing—

Spotlight ON CONTEMPORARY ISSUES

Leasing Today

The term *inmate leasing* correctly conjures up undesirable images. So, it is understandable that it is seldom used when referring to contemporary labor programs. However, at least one contemporary program seems to have much in common with the old leasing system.

Under the lease system, a prison "rents" a prisoner to a private individual for a specified sum and for a fixed time. That private individual, who could assign the prisoner to work details as the lessee saw fit, took responsibility for feeding, clothing, and disciplining the prisoner. Compare that situation with the Oregon Inmate Work Program called Private Partnerships.

The Private Partnership program teams Oregon's Inmate Work Program with private-sector businesses to employ inmate labor both inside and outside the prisons. It is the outside prison work venue that most closely reflects the old leasing system, and Oregon actually refers to the program as "inmate labor leasing." But, in an example of how a historically abusive program can be adapted to more modern and humane situations, Oregon's leasing system seems a far cry from those found 75 to 100 years ago.

According to the Oregon Department of Corrections Web site (see the URL that follows), the projects that inmates might do are flexible, and private businesses are encouraged to make suggestions for consideration by the Prison Industries Board. An important key to distinguishing this contemporary version of leasing from its historical cousin is the joint involvement of both public and private sectors in the maintenance, discipline, training, and hiring of the inmates. As Table 4.1 shows, the old leasing system relied on the lessees to hire whom they wished, to determine work assignments, and to be responsible for the prisoners' discipline and maintenance. Oregon's version of leasing requires the involvement of both public and private sectors in the arrangement—therefore, prisoners are never at the sole mercy of the private enterprise.

Visit Oregon's Inmate Work Program's Web site at ***www.doc.state.or.us/wrkprgms***. What are some of the types of work in which the inmates engage? Also take a look at California's Joint Venture Program at ***www.cdc.state.ca.us/program/jvppg.htm***. What are the program's major components?

adopted this labor system by which private employers contracted with prison officials who provided inmates as laborers for the employers. The private employers could then sell the goods on the open market. Contracting was very profitable for the institution and maintained its popularity as a primary labor system throughout most of the nineteenth century.

Under the contract system of labor, the state feeds, clothes, houses, and guards the prisoners. A private individual or firm contracts with the state to have prisoners provide their labor, at or near the prison, to produce goods for the contractor. The contractor pays the state for the prisoners' labor, supplies the necessary raw materials, and provides supervisors to monitor and direct the prisoners' work. In 1906 the Department of Labor suggested the contract system was far superior to the lease system so far as the prisoners' welfare is concerned (House of Representatives, 1906). This claim was based on the state maintaining responsibility for the general care of the prisoners and thereby lessening the potential for abuse.

Contracting's popularity at the start of the twentieth century was essentially a carryover from its widespread use between 1825 and 1840. Its expansion occurred when merchant-capitalists started making their presence known. Using the cheap labor found in cottage industries, sweatshops, and prisons, the merchant-capitalist was able to provide a link between manufacturers and customers. New York state prisons such as Auburn and Sing Sing adopted the contract system, and the successes at those places encouraged other states to seek profits through convict labor. The system came under increased criticism in the 1880s as labor unions expressed their displeasure with jobs being taken by inmates when law-abiding citizens were looking for work.

In addition to the complaints of labor unions, contract prison labor was also criticized for its brutality. Because prisoners under contract labor were under the complete power of their keeper, many convicts suffered under conditions that were designed to extract their last ounce of labor. Christianson (1998) tells about prison authorities in New Jersey pouring alcohol on epileptics and setting them afire to detect possible faking as prisoners sought to avoid the harsh labor conditions. In Ohio, in 1878, unproductive convicts had to sit naked in puddles of water and re-

Using inmate labor to make shoes was an especially popular industry in the late 1800s. But the prisoners did not have the advantage of the twentieth-century machines shown here.

ceive electric shocks from an induction coil. Convicts who did not put forth the appropriate effort, or tried to avoid work completely, were subjected to tortures including the lash, the paddle, the dark cell, and the cooler. In the 1880s, New York officials admitted that some Sing Sing convicts had actually jumped off the upper tiers of the cellhouse and broken their legs in an effort to escape being paddled (Christianson, 1998, p. 184).

By 1885, 35 percent of the employed state and county prisoners were under the contract system (see Table 4.2). They were making boots and shoes (an especially popular industry in many of the state prisons), brooms, barrels, cigars, and wagons. When the Industrial era began, prisoners were under contract for those same items and were also busily building railroads, making buttons, and working stone quarries. But as the Industrial era was drawing to a close in 1923, only 12 percent of the employed prisoners were under the contract system as they made baskets, brooms, work pants and shirts, furniture, and shoes, and worked in coal mines. The complaints of labor unions and public outrage at some of the conditions under which contract labor occurred were finally taking their toll.

The Piece-Price System. The **piece-price system** was a modification of the contract system by which labor was paid for on the basis of output rather than for the number of hours worked. Although this labor type had been used in New Jersey and Pennsylvania prisons in the late eighteenth and early nineteenth centuries, its greatest development came in the 1880s and 1890s as the contract system went into decline. The primary difference between the two systems lies in the responsibility for supervising the prisoners at work—the state under the piece-price system and the private agent under contracting (see Table 4.1).

Near the end of the nineteenth century, the piece-price system was used for 20 percent of the employed prisoners, but during the Industrial era it accounted for only 7 or 8 percent (see Table 4.2). Like the contract system, the piece-price system's decline is attributed to increased complaints from free labor and outside industry. Because both systems produced goods that were sold on the open market, they shared the criticism of presenting unfair competition. The goods being made under the piece-price system (e.g., brooms, chair caning, clothes, shoes, hosiery, and furniture) were similar to items produced under the contract system and, therefore, brought complaints from similar labor groups and businesspeople.

The Public Account System. So far as the prisoner is concerned, there is very little difference between the piece-price system and **public account system.** Because the two systems differ only in whether the sale of the product is controlled privately or publicly (see Table 4.1), the prisoners' actual conditions of employment, supervision, and maintenance remain the same. The public account system also shares much in common with the state use and public works and ways labor types. In fact the sole difference is public account's open market as opposed to the sheltered market for state use and public works and ways. The three systems are so alike in the way they maintain, discipline, and control prison laborers that the Department of Labor did not distinguish state use and public works and ways as separate labor systems until its 1906 report (see Table 4.2).

As also shown in Table 4.2, the number of prisoners employed under the public account system remained remarkably consistent prior to and during the Industrial era. Although declining from essentially one-third of the prisoners employed in 1885 and 1895 to about one-fourth in 1923, the 1885 and 1895 figures were boosted by prisoners technically engaged in state use and public works and ways labor. With that in mind, it is probably safe to say that the public account system showed greater consistency in use than did any other labor system during the late nineteenth and early twentieth centuries.

Prisoners under public account systems worked on items similar to those in other prison labor types (e.g., making bricks, brooms, and chairs, and working in mines). But because states using the public account system were engaged in regular manufacturing to compete on the open market with private industry, the prisoners often found themselves engaged in such hard-core industries as textiles, iron works, farm machinery, and binder twine. The last product, binder twine, is often cited as the best example of success through a public account prison labor system.

After his 1925 tour of twenty-eight state prisons, Austin MacCormick described Minnesota's prison at Stillwater as "the best prison plant of its kind in America with the best organized industrial system" (1926, p. 599). The product being manufactured at Stillwater was binder twine, and the method being used was the public account system. In 1891 Minnesota farmers, who were angry with what they considered the extortionate price of twine, convinced officials to begin producing a more reasonably priced twine with prison labor. By 1906 the enterprise earned over a $200,000 profit for the prison, and Minnesota ranked first among the states on the value of goods produced under the public account system (House of Representatives, 1906). Minnesota remained successful throughout the Industrial era (and after) with the binder twine industry, employing an average of 487 prisoners who produced twine valued at over $2 million in 1923 (Bureau of Labor Statistics, 1925).

The State Use System. Under the **state use system** the state is engaged in the manufacture or production of goods, as in the public account system, but the use of the goods produced is limited to state institutions. Under this sheltered system, prison-produced goods would not compete directly with private business or with employment of free labor. In 1923 the principal goods produced, as measured by value, were farm, garden, dairy, and livestock products; clothing; auto tags; and textiles.

States were encouraged to adopt the state use system as a response to complaints from free labor and private businesses. Those complaints, which are reviewed a bit later, spurred growth in both the state use and the public works and ways systems during the Industrial era. As Table 4.2 shows, those two labor types increased from being simply a portion of the public account system in 1885 and 1895 to accounting for over one-third of the employed prisoners at the start of the Industrial era and over one-half as the era was drawing to a close. This movement to sheltered market systems for prison labor was a direct result of protests from citizen laborers and businesspeople.

The free laborers complained about the competition provided by prison labor, whereas private business disapproved of the competition from prison-made products being sold on the open market. In the labor commissioner's twentieth annual report (House of Representatives, 1906), the state use system was lauded for meeting three types of interests:

- The financial interest of the state is met by having the state produce items for its own consumption rather than having to buy them from outside sources. In this way the cost of maintaining state institutions is partially met by employment of prisoners, and the reliance on taxation is reduced.
- The general interest of the convict is satisfied because prisoners are able to produce articles they will consume themselves. Presumably their labor will be more motivated when they perform work they will benefit from directly.
- The interests of free labor and private industry are recognized when the state uses prisoners to make products that will not compete directly with those on the open market.

Along with these benefits of the state use system, the labor commissioner's report recognized that there would also be some problems. Especially notable is the increased idleness of prisoners when states rely on the state use labor system. Because the demand for the prisoner-made products is limited, the prisoners cannot as a rule be worked to their full capacity. For example, in 1885, 6 percent of the prisoners were identified as sick or idle (the two were combined as one category) whereas in 1903 to 1904, 12 percent of the prisoners were idle (3 percent were identified as sick). The number who were idle dropped to 6 percent in 1923 (the number sick remained at 3 percent), but it was apparent to prison officials that increased idleness would be one result of movement away from the open market type of labor systems (Bureau of Labor Statistics, 1925; House of Representatives, 1887; House of Representatives, 1906). Today state use remains the most popular form of prison labor used to produce goods. The disadvantage of this system remains the inability to provide productive labor for all the inmates. Because of its important contemporary use, discussion of the state use system continues in Chapter 10.

The Public Works and Ways System. In 1658 convicts were used for public works projects in Virginia; and in 1718 prisoners cleared the swamps for what is now New Orleans (Funke, Wayson, & Miller, 1982). Walnut Street Jail inmates were put to work on the city streets in the early nineteenth century. That makes the **public works and ways system** one of the country's oldest prison labor types. It is similar in concept to the state use system because it involves a sheltered market, but it differs in the kind of labor engaged in by the prisoners. Whereas inmates laboring under state use are manufacturing common items such as furniture and clothing, those engaged in public works and ways are constructing or repairing public buildings, public roads, parks, and other permanent public structures.

In the 1906 Department of Labor report, public works and ways was recognized as allowing the construction of items that would most likely be delayed or never undertaken for lack of necessary funding. There were problems, however, because labor at construction sites provided more opportunities for escape—hence, greater costs for guarding—and exposed the prisoners to the gaze of the public, which "penologists admit to be against the best interests not only of the public but of the convict as well" (House of Representatives, 1906).

In 1923 building construction with prison labor was valued at over $3.5 million, while road construction was valued at nearly $12 million (Bureau of Labor Statistics, 1925). Road construction, or "road gangs," were primarily used in Florida, Georgia, North Carolina, and Virginia. Each of those states employed over 60 percent of their convicts in the construction or maintenance of roads. As shown in Table 4.2, public works and ways had a prominent role during the Industrial era, accounting for 12 percent of the employed prisoners in 1903 to 1904 and 19 percent in 1923. And, like the state use system, public works and ways continued to have an important role in prison labor during the subsequent penal system eras. In Chapter 10 the public works and ways labor system's contemporary use is examined.

Purposes of Prison Labor

For what purpose are prisoners put to work? It appears that at least three purposes are easily identified: punishment, profit, and rehabilitation. It is also apparent that the axiom claiming idle hands are the devil's workshop has been a consistent reason to keep prisoners busy. From the warden's point of view then, prison labor can reduce convicts' opportunities to disrupt the prison order or to spend hours planning ways around prison rules. Such administrative purposes for putting prisoners to work are appropriate and should be noted. However, the other three—**labor for punishment, labor for profit,** and **labor for rehabilitation**—have more specific goals and will be the focus of the next discussion.

Labor for Punishment. In cases in which hard labor is part of the sentence, it seems primarily to have a punitive purpose. In those instances it is probably irrelevant whether the labor is productive. In England, for example, authorities at jails and houses of correction developed unproductive machines just to keep the prisoners working. Especially notable were the treadwheel and the crank. The treadwheel, which was invented about 1818, consisted of twenty-four steps that were arranged around a cylinder like the floats of a paddlewheel. After completing thirty revolutions, taking about fifteen minutes, a bell rang and the twelve men stepped off the wheel and were replaced by twelve more. While off the wheel, the men could sleep or read but were not allowed to talk to each other (Barnes & Teeters, 1959, p. 525).

The treadwheel might occasionally operate for a purpose, such as grinding corn or pumping water, but more often its turning accomplished nothing. The crank, on the other hand, was invented about 1846 at a London prison and had no productive function at any time. It was described as consisting of a metal box with a handle jutting from one side. As the handle was turned, a counter on the box recorded the number of revolutions. Varying amounts of resistance when turning the handle could be accomplished by adjusting the metal band that circled an axle in the box. The typical resistance required 4 to 11 pounds of pressure for the cranker to turn the handle. According to one account, with resistance set at about 5 pounds for boys and 10 pounds for men, a person could make about 10,000 revolutions a day with ordinary effort. The prisoner's meals typically depended on a certain number of revolutions being turned, with 1,800 revolutions for breakfast and 4,500 for dinner. It was not unusual for men to turn the crank for long hours in their cells at night to make up for time lost during the day (Barnes & Teeters, 1959, p. 527).

There are some examples of nonproductive labor being used in early American prisons, like the treadwheel at Newgate Prison in Connecticut, but most uses

Convicts sentenced to hard labor at the treadwheel usually accomplished nothing more than making sure the wheel kept turning.

of convict labor have served a productive function. In some cases that productive function has been aimed at the economic well-being of the prison, but at other times the emphasis has been on the welfare of the prisoner.

Labor for Profit. Having economically self-sustaining prisons was a goal of state legislators and prison officials since the profits resulting from the Auburn system were cited as a distinct advantage of that approach over the Pennsylvania system. In fact, between 1830 and 1870, the idea of imprisonment as punishment was able to spread throughout the United States primarily because of the profits being realized from the contract and lease systems (see the feature "Women Offenders during the Industrial Era"). As the nineteenth century was drawing to a close, the lease system was responsible for a smaller percentage of the value of goods produced by inmate labor, but the contract system was still bringing in some 43 percent of the total value.

During the Industrial era, the profitability of contract and lease systems declined (as a percentage of the whole) whereas that of the public account, piece-price, state use, and public works and ways systems increased. Especially notable was how the state use and the public works and ways systems increased both their total value of goods produced and their percentages of the total. During the mid-1800s many prisons made a profit through inmate labor, but in the Industrial era prisons found it increasingly difficult to pay their own way. In its 1906 report, the Department of Labor noted that although convicts as a whole were a burden on the public, prisoners in Alabama, Florida, Mississippi, and Virginia were actually a source of profit (House of Representatives, 1906). If one allowed credit for labor performed by prisoners on public works and ways, Georgia, Louisiana, Missouri, North Carolina, and South Carolina also saw a profit from prisoner labor. But despite those examples of what appeared to be a profit, the Department of Labor concluded that the cost of apprehension and conviction probably exceeded the immediate profit shown even in these states.

The profitability of prisons continued to decline after the Industrial era. For example, the total value of goods produced decreased (without adjusting to constant dollars) from $74 million in 1923 to $57 million in 1940. It was not a coincidence that during that same time period, the percentage of prisoners employed in open market systems decreased from 45 percent to 12 percent (Funke et al., 1982). The sheltered market systems were just not able to provide as much profit for the prisons as were the open market labor types. As the profit motive failed, the purpose of inmate labor was increasingly directed toward the welfare of the prisoner.

Labor for Rehabilitation. Labor to benefit the prisoner rather than the prison has a recurring rather than constant history in the United States. During the Reformatory era, prison labor played a key role in attempts to prepare prisoners for their eventual release. Policies such as the ticket-of-leave, good time, and conditional pardons initially depended on the quality and quantity of a prisoner's labor. Sentences came to be linked less to the concept of an appropriate amount of time having to be served and more to the necessary completion of labor. But by the end of the nineteenth century, prison labor was used less as a reward (such as early release from prison) and increasingly used as a way to control prisoners and give economic support to the institution. Inmate labor for the purpose of benefitting the prisoner took a back seat to the idea of labor for profit during the Industrial era. But as the profitability of prison labor declined in the 1920s, prison officials began returning to the idea of prison labor as rehabilitative.

By 1925 the idea of prison labor having a rehabilitative purpose had been set so far aside that the Department of Labor took time to comment that "if imprisonment is intended to transform the man, to redeem him, to rehabilitate him, then the kind

ISSUES OF FAIRNESS

WOMEN OFFENDERS DURING THE INDUSTRIAL ERA

The convict leasing system was abhorrent for both men and women, but women often suffered greater abuse. Colvin (1997) explains that women—virtually all black and about 7 percent of the prisoners in southern convict lease camps—were seldom separated from men when leased out. Occasionally men and women were actually chained together and occupied the same bunks. Given such conditions, it is not surprising that women prisoners were frequently raped by male convicts and guards.

The situation for women convicts in the North was better only in the sense that conditions were cruel rather than sadistic. As the Industrial era came into full swing, when prisoners were expected to aid in the financial support of their institution, women were often considered a liability. Rafter (1990) quotes administrators and reformers of the time as complaining that women prisoners did not provide labor that met the expenses of their unit, nor did many believe that women's labor could ever be profitable. Experiences at New York's Bedford Hills Reformatory and at the Massachusetts Reformatory for Women confirmed those beliefs (or at least confirmed society's lack of acceptance of these women and lack of appreciation for the type of labor they performed). Women released from those institutions could not obtain jobs—despite their reformatory training in such skills as hat making, machine knitting, stenography, chair caning, bookbinding, and so on. Employers refused to hire the former inmates because they feared they would contaminate other employees. This argument Katherine Bement Davis, director at Bedford Hills, found ironic because those employers didn't hesitate to take these same prisoners into their homes where they would have frequent contact with the employers' children as domestic servants (Colvin, 1997; Freedman, 1981). In the absence of a market for either their products or themselves, women prisoners were relegated to labor and training that continued to be domestic in nature.

Of course, the complainers ignored the fact that differential treatment in the kind of work women prisoners were allowed to do was less lucrative by its very nature. Had women been contracted for some of the high-profit tasks given to the men, the women may well have been able to earn their keep. The attitudes and ignorance faced by women during this time are probably no better illustrated than by a recommendation that a dairy industry be developed at a women's prison. "Milking cows, the formulator of this policy argued, is an excellent activity for female inmates because women have a natural affinity for udders!" (quoted in Rafter, 1993, p. 9).

Go to the Web reproduction of *150 Years in the Forefront: The Women's Prison Association and Home*, and read the selection on "Changing Needs, Modern Era" at ***www.correctionhistory.org/html/chronicl/wpa/html/wpathree2.htm.*** Comment on how this selection responds to the claim made by some that "the Depression did not affect women as much as it did men."

of work he does is of material importance" (Bureau of Labor Statistics, 1925, p. 16). Prisons for adults, more so than juvenile reformatories, were criticized for failing to provide work experiences that would benefit the prisoners after their release from confinement. The point was made by noting that "a man trained only to stitch one particular seam on an apron or shirt will have difficulty in getting a place in an apron or shirt factory filled mainly or exclusively by women" (Bureau of Labor Statistics, 1925, p. 17). The Department of Labor concluded that legislators and prison officials should give careful consideration to providing industrial training that could accomplish rehabilitation goals.

But the movement to labor as rehabilitative was going to take some time. In 1926 MacCormick complained that Minnesota's Stillwater prison, noted for the profitability of its binder twine industry, "seems directed to the production of goods, not men" (1926, p. 600). In 1931 Howard Gill criticized prison administrators for being "more concerned with developing a profitable system than in directing it toward the reformation of the individual" (1931, p. 83). But while MacCormick and Gill were expressing frustration with the lack of attention to the needs of the prisoner, they were also foretelling a new stage in America's prison history. The time seemed right for the prison system to leave behind its emphasis on industry and profits and to move into a new era.

REHABILITATION ERA (1930S TO 1970S)

Although he wrote it about 100 years earlier, Alexander Maconochie anticipated the central principle of the Rehabilitation era in this argument:

> When a man breaks a leg, we have him into a hospital, and cure him as speedily as possible, without even thinking of modifying his treatment so as to make his case a warning to others. *We think of the individual, not of society.* But when a poor fellow-creature becomes morally dislocated, however imperious the circumstances to which he may have fallen a victim, we abandon all thought of his welfare, and seek only to make "an example" of him. *We think of society, not of the individual.* I am persuaded that the more closely and critically we examine this principle, and whether abstractly, and logically, or above all Christianly and politically, the more doubtful it will appear;—Yet it lies at the root of nearly all our Penal Institutions, and the reasoning on which they are founded. (quoted in Eriksson, 1976, p. 88)

The argument that people should "think of the individual, not of society" identifies the focus of prison activities during the **Rehabilitation era.** Although people such as Maconochie were making pleas for such a focus many decades earlier, it took until the 1930s before we can say U.S. prisons pushed this penal philosophy to the forefront.

Launching the Rehabilitation Era

America's prisons were urged into the Rehabilitation era through the efforts of several agencies, organizations, and individuals. The four particular "nudgers" considered here are those people called **progressive reformers,** the annual congresses of the **American Prison Association** (now the American Correctional Association), the **Wickersham Commission** (named for its chairman, George Wickersham), and the **Federal Bureau of Prisons.** These sources provided U.S. prisons with the essential ingredient of the Rehabilitation era—a medical model that views criminals as persons who are "ill" and need treatment.

Progressive Reformers. Although this section starts a discussion of the Rehabilitation era in the 1930s, important developments were occurring in the late nineteenth century that must also be mentioned. In the 1890s, a general reform movement known to history as progressivism began sweeping the country. That movement combined several trends that had emerged earlier in the century: the Christian fervor of the Social Gospel Movement; the rise of a new professional class; the use of scientific methodology in social sciences; industrialism; and the tendency to depend on government intervention to solve social problems (Sullivan, 1990). These trends had resulted from early nineteenth-century growth in the cities and from the associated problems of urbanism and large-scale industrialization prevalent in the late nineteenth century. Progressives devised new ideas and solutions to social problems by seeing those problems as products of the environment rather than the individual. To solve the problems, efforts must be directed toward changing society rather than changing the individual. Because such a massive project required substantial resources, reformers turned to the government and public agencies to intervene in the country's social and economic affairs.

With an evangelistic spirit and scientific means, the progressive reformers saw themselves as impartial experts gathering and analyzing social data that would allow them to uncover laws of human behavior. Newfound knowledge in medicine, such as the germ theory of disease, bolstered the idea that individuals are not totally responsible for what happens to them. Illness began to replace free will to explain why antisocial behavior occurs. The resulting biological view of a "sick" society permitted the reformers to adopt a medical metaphor for treatment of offenders. The resulting medical or treatment model of prison reform dominated penology from the 1930s to the 1970s during the Rehabilitation era.

American Prison Association. The annual congresses held by the American Prison Association in the 1930s played an important role in moving U.S. prisons into the Rehabilitation era. Papers and discussions at the 1930 congress in Louisville included reference to scientific studies showing high levels of recidivism among persons released from some of the country's prisons. Also at that congress, and for the next several annual meetings, delegates heard about the problems of implementing prison labor programs under the restraints of the Hawes-Cooper Act (see Chapter 10) and the generally harsh economic consequences brought by the Depression. As if recidivism and labor issues were not enough, presenters at the meetings also reported that few, if any, existing educational programs could be considered effective (McKelvey, 1977).

Fortunately, at the same time scientists and prison officials were reporting on the frustrating aspects of U.S. prisons, there were also reports about new developments that seemed promising. Papers at the 1930 congress reported on experiments with classification in New Jersey prisons. F. Lovell Bixby's paper, for example, described how classification in New Jersey had moved from "a passive plan to separate dissimilar inmates into a positive effort to promote individualized treatment" (McKelvey, 1977, p. 300). By the 1933 congress in Atlantic City, several states were reporting on new developments in classification and educational programs. But innovations by the states were overshadowed by the pioneering efforts of the Federal Bureau of Prisons, which was taking the lead among the country's prison systems in moving to an emphasis on rehabilitation.

The Wickersham Commission. The late 1920s and early 1930s presented many challenges for Americans in general and prison officials more specifically. The stock market crash in 1929 and the economic depression that followed presented a bleak environment for the general public. Prison riots in Illinois, Colorado, Kansas, and New York forced prison officials to realize that convicts also saw their situation as hopeless. In its 1931 report, the Wickersham Commission (the National Commission on Law Observance and Enforcement) confirmed prisoner complaints by documenting the widespread idleness in almost all state prisons, the failure of nearly every attempt to develop a prison factory system that did not rely on contract labor, the use of arbitrary rules and punishments dealt out to prisoners, and the absence of any meaningful programs for inmates (Sullivan, 1990).

The commission did not, however, provide only complaints. The crime problem could and should be responded to, the commission argued, by rehabilitating the criminal. This rehabilitation would be accomplished through scientific classification, segregation, meaningful work, and effective vocational and educational training. Those techniques may sound familiar because they were also the presumed basis for the Reformatory era. But remember a primary lesson learned from the study of history is that the more things change, the more they stay the same.

There were, of course, some important differences in how the Rehabilitation era tried to implement the principles first championed in the Reformatory era. Especially new in the twentieth century was the setting in which reform, now rehabilitation, was to occur. At the forefront for changes in prison design was the new (established in 1930) Federal Bureau of Prisons.

Federal Bureau of Prisons. The history and current role played by the Federal Bureau of Prisons is discussed in detail in Chapter 9. Here the discussion is about how the bureau helped bring about the Rehabilitation era. Most simply stated, the federal government was clearly in the lead position when it came to implementing new prison methods during the 1930s (Barnes & Teeters, 1959; McKelvey, 1977; Sullivan, 1990).

Under the direction of Sanford Bates, the Federal Bureau of Prisons (BOP) set up a training school for prison officers; upgraded educational, disciplinary, and industrial programs; and implemented a comprehensive classification program. Those undertakings had significant impact on developments in the state prison systems, but it is another federal innovation that is emphasized in this section—changes in prison architecture.

Recall that one explanation for the failure of the reformatory concept and the ending of the Reformatory era was the attempt to achieve reform ideals in facilities that were built for quite different purposes. As the Rehabilitation era was getting under way, officials realized that the goals of rehabilitation were more likely to be achieved if they were undertaken in a setting other than the maximum-security penitentiaries built in the nineteenth century. While his assistants Austin MacCormick and James V. Bennett worked on education, discipline, and labor programs, Sanford Bates turned his attention to the building of new federal prison facilities.

The number of federal crimes increased in the 1920s, and one result was an increase in the number of federal prisoners. Bates responded to the need for places to put the extra prisoners by converting some old World War I army posts into prison camps. At these camps, bootleggers and moonshiners got a chance to perform useful services, such as road work, while confined at minimum-security institutions (McKelvey, 1977). But it was Bates's interest in medium-security institutions that had even greater impact on the direction of prison architecture in the United States.

Bates, MacCormick, and Bennett had committed themselves to developing a federal prison system that tried to treat convicts as individuals. Believing that maximum-security penitentiaries were inappropriate for many aspects of individual treatment, Bates became intrigued with alternatives to the traditional design of prisons—which really had not changed since John Haviland designed the Eastern Penitentiary at Philadelphia. Building on what he saw during a tour of European prisons, and with the help of New York architect Alfred Hopkins, Bates began plans for a new prison to be built at Lewisburg, Pennsylvania. This new facility would be designed in a manner that allowed administrators to implement the concept of classification more completely than had traditional prison designs.

The U.S. Penitentiary at Lewisburg, which opened in 1932, was built in a telephone pattern as used in France in 1898 (see Figure 4.1). Johnston (1973) argues that the design was first used at London's Wormwood Scrubs Prison (1874–1891), but the Lewisburg design was definitely based on the French prison near Paris. The telephone-pole design featured a long connecting corridor extending from the administrative building past dining rooms, shops, and dividing the cell blocks in a manner that had them extending from a central stick like the arms of a telephone pole. With this layout some of the cell blocks could be designed as medium-security outside cells, whereas others were maximum-security inside cells, and still another cell block could house inmates achieving honor status in dormitory-style

FIGURE 4.1

The U.S. Penitentiary, Lewisburg, Pennsylvania (1932)

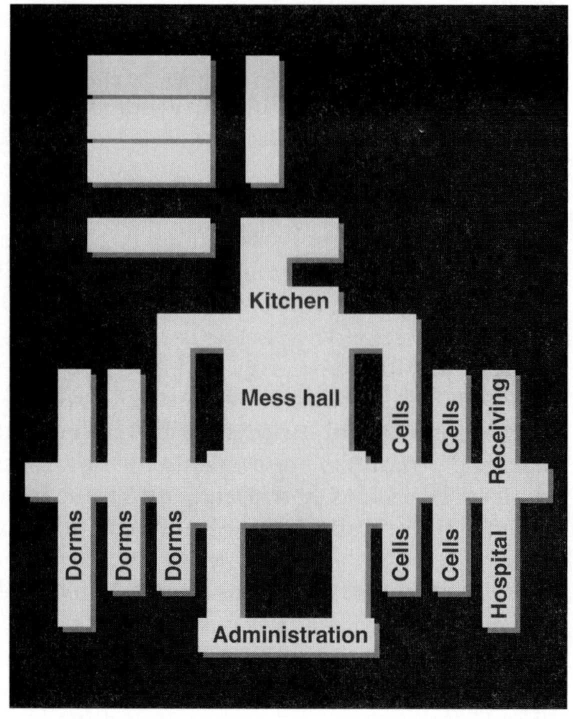

rooms (McKelvey, 1977). In this way prison officials gained the flexibility needed to treat prisoners according to individual needs under different security levels resulting from new developments in classification—a key ingredient of the **medical model.**

The Medical Model

The progressive reformers, the American Prison Association, the Wickersham Commission, and the Federal Bureau of Prisons had in common a belief that criminal behavior was pathological. Criminals were not so much "bad" as they were "ill." Because of that, offenders should be responded to as people who are sick. As MacNamara explained, the medical model as applied to corrections assumes the offenders are sick (physically, mentally, and/or socially). Their crimes are symptoms of their sickness (1977, pp. 439–440).

Following the medical metaphor, society's response to the criminal should include three stages (see Abadinsky, 1994):

- *Examination.* A case history is developed (e.g., a presentence investigation report) to identify the causes or sources of the "illness."
- *Diagnosis.* Professionals use information from the examination stage to identify an individual offender's particular version of the illness. After officials agree on the diagnosis, the offender can be assigned to one or several categories holding other offenders with similar problems (e.g., substance abuse, poor education, minimal vocational skills, etc.).
- *Treatment.* After determining the nature of the "sickness" and identifying the category into which the illness places the offender, officials must develop a treatment plan that will allow the offender to "get well" and be able to return to the community as a law-abiding and productive citizen.

Using these stages, imagine an offender whom professionals conclude has committed a crime because she came from a dysfunctional family (the source of the illness) and then dropped out of school and began using drugs (placing her in a category holding other offenders with similar "symptoms"). Such an offender may be assigned to a treatment program that includes academic instruction and therapy for substance abuse.

The medical model was the orienting philosophy of the Rehabilitation era. And, just as the U.S. penal system today includes features of each prior era, aspects of the medical model continue to influence the way society responds to convicted offenders. This is especially true with the importance the medical model placed on personal histories of the offenders. The written records of those histories reflected information considered relevant to the offender's illness and its "cure." The use of presentence investigation reports (see Chapter 7) and other versions of case histories continues to reflect an interest in identifying which particular problems an offender has.

In addition to the continued use of case histories, the basic idea of treating offenders remains part of the American penal system. Just because we passed through the Rehabilitation era, America's penal system has not stopped using personal histories or trying to treat offenders. The major difference today is that the medical model is no longer the orienting philosophy. Treatment has become something that is made available to those wishing to take advantage of it rather than something that all offenders must undergo. But in its heyday treatment was the goal of corrections systems around the country.

Treatment programs to make offenders better were developed in a number of areas. Academic programs were the treatment for persons lacking basic educational abilities, whereas vocational training was the remedy for those presumably choosing a career in crime because they did not have marketable job skills. Others, it was argued, engaged in criminal acts because they were morally deficient (treatment = religious training), abused a variety of substances (treatment = therapy groups), or had mental health problems (treatment = group and individual counseling). Most of the treatment efforts developing or expanding during the Rehabilitation era remain an important part of contemporary federal and state prison systems, but there is no longer a central theme around which the prisons are organized. Chapters 7's coverage of community corrections highlights the contemporary versions of the examination and treatment stages as they operate without a direct link to the medical model. Those topics do not need additional coverage here. But the other stage in the medical model, diagnosis, is a topic that needs elaboration. That is because diagnosis, in different forms and by different names, was prominent before the Rehabilitation era and continues to have an integral role today. Using its contemporary name, *classification,* we will use the diagnosis stage to highlight the medical model's importance to the Rehabilitation era.

Classification

Separating prisoners into groups based on certain common characteristics has been practiced since at least the eighteenth century. Although housing men and women offenders in different parts of the same facility was common in the early houses of correction and hospices, it did not take long for authorities to realize that separation beyond the simple one based on sex was going to be necessary.

As early as 1773, the Maison de Force at Ghent reserved each of its housing units for a specific type of offender. In eight self-contained, trapezoid-shaped units, which together formed a giant octagon, prisoners were separated by sex and, within each sex, by age, degree of criminality, and length of sentence (Johnston,

Help Wanted

Job Title: Classification Officer

Position Description: Classification officers perform correctional casework in an institutional setting; develop, evaluate, and analyze program needs and other data about inmates; evaluate progress of individual offenders; coordinate and integrate inmate training programs; develop social histories; and evaluate positive and negative aspects in each case situation.

Qualifications: Classification officers must be able to communicate orally and in writing and should have knowledge of casework theory, methods, and guidelines, as well as knowledge of case management services in a correctional setting. Applicants must be able to use clinical assessments; to write clinical reports; and should have knowledge of psychological problems associated with drug addiction.

Classification officers, or similar titles, are typically found in all state departments of correction. Their duties are similar to those described here. At the federal level this position is called a correctional treatment specialist. For more information visit the Bureau of Prisons employment site at ***www.bop.gov/recruit.html***, and go to the "major professions and qualifications" section.

1973). However, it was not until the twentieth century that classification was viewed as a crucial element in operating a penal system. For purposes of this discussion, classification's modern history begins with the efforts of F. Lovell Bixby, a psychologist in charge of the classification division for New Jersey's prisons.

In the late 1920s, Bixby developed a classification procedure that standardized the testing of newly sentenced offenders throughout New Jersey's diverse prison facilities. He prepared various reporting forms in order to standardize information that had been gathered on each new arrival and tried to identify some of their personality traits, work skills, and educational needs. Using the collected data for each prisoner, Bixby divided them into groups requiring minimum, medium, or maximum security (McKelvey, 1977). Bixby's experiments in New Jersey became known to Sanford Bates just as he was taking the new Federal Bureau of Prisons to a leadership role among America's prison systems. In 1934 Bates hired Bixby as an assistant director for the BOP and placed him in charge of developing a federal classification program.

The classification system developed by Bixby used **classification committees** in each of the federal prisons. Because of the great distances separating the federal institutions from each other, each institution had to handle prisoners with a variety of needs and of different security levels. The classification committees were composed of professionals representing a variety of areas (such as psychiatry, psychology, social work, religion, education, and security). Shortly after his arrival at the prison, the offender was interviewed by each of the committee members (or their representatives) individually. When all examinations and interviews were completed, the committee members met and decided what assignments (e.g., work area, educational level, vocational training, therapy groups, or security level) should be made for each inmate. In this way, individualized treatment programs were developed for each offender—as the medical model proposed.

Although classification began receiving general acceptance in the 1940s, by the 1950s it was being implemented throughout the country's prisons as a way of achieving two goals: segregation and diagnosis. The segregation goal was a continuation of classification's earliest use in which offenders are separated from each other on the basis of some characteristic such as sex, age, or even race. By segregating prisoners according to, for example, minimum-, medium-, and maximum-security levels, officials hoped to lessen the negative influence of the prison social structure. Also, by placing less serious offenders in minimum- and medium-security institutions, treatment officials could make use of the free community to provide positive influence through tactics ranging from work release programs to sports competition between inmates and local teams.

Whereas the segregation goal was a reminder of classification's earliest uses, the diagnosis goal was more directly linked to the new uses of classification in the medical model. The procedure for classification to make a diagnosis and determine a treatment program basically followed Bixby's original procedure using classification committees at each individual prison. But in the 1950s and 1960s, some states were expanding the number and type of prisons they used to house prisoners and needed to determine which particular institution was most appropriate for each new prisoner. Those states began using centralized **reception and diagnostic centers** to perform classification tasks that included medical, educational, vocational, and psychological testing. After gathering information about the offender, staff at the reception and diagnostic center would determine which state institution would be most appropriate given that prisoner's individual needs.

Classification today continues to play an important role in the institution and for various types of community corrections. But the medical model, individualized treatment, and even the concept of rehabilitation were increasingly criticized in the 1970s. The challenger to rehabilitation's primary role emphasized a different punishment philosophy—retribution. Although the idea of retribution was not new, it began to have such prominence in the criminal justice system as a whole, and the punishment strategy more specifically, that it can be identified as the newest and current era in the U.S. penal system.

RETRIBUTIVE ERA (1970S TO PRESENT)

The strength of the medical model and the duration of the Rehabilitation era were noted in the 1960s when the President's Commission on Law Enforcement and the Administration of Justice proclaimed that "as with disease, so with crime" and that prison's "main focus was on the individual—on correcting him" (President's Commission on Law Enforcement and the Administration of Justice, 1967, pp. 3 and 164). But even as the President's Commission was issuing its report, the end of such a view was nearing. By 1976 Andrew von Hirsch was explaining that when a person commits a crime, he "gains an unfair advantage over all others in the society—since he has failed to constrain his own behavior while benefiting from other persons' forbearance from interfering with his rights" (1976, p. 47). Society's response, Ernest van den Haag (1975) argued, should be retributive in an effort to "enforce the law and to vindicate the legal order" (p. 11). Obviously, things were changing.

Opinions such as those of von Hirsch and van den Haag signaled the end of the Rehabilitation era and the start of a new era with different perspectives about criminals and how society should respond to them. Because the new era seemed to emphasize the idea that those who commit crimes deserve to be punished, the term *retribution* has been applied to the post-Rehabilitation era. The **Retributive era** began taking hold in the 1970s and remains strong as the twenty-first century begins. This text will look at this current era by reviewing circumstances that brought it about, the impact it has had on policy and procedures, and in which direction it is likely to go.

Sources of the Retributive Era

By the mid-1950s the ideology of rehabilitation was firmly rooted in U.S. prisons. The term *penology* was replaced with *corrections*, prisons became correctional institutions, and guards were correctional officers. Even the American Prison Association changed its name in 1954 to the American Correctional Association. But by the end of the 1960s, events in the social, political, and academic arenas had called into question the whole idea of rehabilitation. A complete review is neither possible nor necessary, but in the following discussion we consider some activities that influenced the decline of the Rehabilitation era and the growth of the Retributive era.

Social Events. A distinctive feature of the Rehabilitation era was a strong belief in the institution as the most effective means for treating offenders (Empey, 1982). Such optimism was part of a general hopefulness found among U.S. citizens, especially in the post–World War II years and continuing into the early 1960s. But assassinations of John F. Kennedy (1963), Robert Kennedy (1968), and Martin Luther King, Jr. (1968), combined with protests over the war in Vietnam, demonstrations on college campuses, riots in urban areas, and other expressions against the status quo made it clear that the hopefulness starting the decade had changed to hopelessness by its end. Many among the American public became disillusioned with, and cynical about, their government, schools, religion, and even the traditional family. The authority and abilities of institutions linked to these important aspects of society were questioned and opened to challenge on a national basis. Mental hospitals were emptied, school curricula and organization were modified, programs to combat poverty and racism were initiated, Eastern religions became popular, and communes were started. Not surprisingly, the way society handled its criminals was also challenged, and correctional institutions were a clear target of the controversy.

Unfortunately, at least in terms of having a clear and consistent philosophy of punishment, prisons in the 1960s were finally accepting the values of free society just when the white middle class, upon whose values prison reforms had been modeled, were rejecting them. Institutions were no longer seen as effective in treating offenders. Interestingly, this position had advocates from both ends of the political spectrum. Liberals, consistent with their challenges to social institutions, saw little need for treating criminals in prison because that kind of environment was not conducive to human improvement. Conservatives, even while supporting U.S. social institutions, complained that the promises of rehabilitation had not been forthcoming, either inside the prisons or out in the community. When persons of different political persuasions find themselves agreeing on an issue, even though for different reasons, the potential for action on that issue is increased. In a sense, the Rehabilitation era's confidence in the prison and in changing the offender had little chance against a political coalition of this type.

Political Events. Accompanying a growing disillusionment with their social institutions, Americans in the 1960s were forced to confront a variety of social problems that had been festering for decades, if not centuries. Especially relevant to the breakdown of the Rehabilitation era and the growth of the Retributive era were the politicalization of prisoners in general, black prisoners specifically, and of crime as a principal social problem.

In the 1960s prisoners began realizing they could exert power through legal suits and riots. Traditionally the state and federal courts had kept a hands-off policy when it came to the way prison officials carried out their duties. That changed in the 1960s, when the U.S. Supreme Court began hearing cases brought by prisoners who were complaining that their civil and constitutional rights were being violated while in prison. The court not only heard these cases, but the prisoners were winning them.

In addition to an ability to influence the conditions of their imprisonment through the courts, prisoners also began using the less subtle technique of rioting. Thirty-nine prison riots in 1969 and fifty-nine the next year (e.g., see Sullivan, 1990) forced prison officials, politicians, and the general public to see that something was wrong with the U.S. penal system. Prisoners had entered the political arena and were getting attention.

Whereas prisoners in general were engaging in riots and taking prison officials to court, minority prisoners especially were becoming increasingly vocal in their demands. To the extent that prison society is a microcosm of free society, it is not surprising that the civil rights movement was affecting race relations inside the walls just as it was on the outside. Throughout the late 1950s, the Black Muslim organization, also known as the Nation of Islam, began working its way into prisons around the country, and by the early 1960s Muslim leader Elijah Muhammad had recognized (at San Quentin prison) the first Black Muslim prison group (see the feature "Black Muslims" on page 118). The organization instilled a sense of worth and pride in blacks, whether in prison or not, and used a high degree of organizational discipline and cohesiveness to help the movement gain strength among blacks around the country. Another important group becoming active in the 1960s was the Black Panther party (founded in 1966), which initially operated

Among the political events shaping prisons in the 1960s was the increased influence that the Nation of Islam, or Black Muslims, had on African American prisoners. Black Muslim leaders such as Malcolm X encouraged feelings of self-worth and pride among black people, whether in prison or not.

as a militant political organization advocating violent revolution to achieve African American liberation. The Black Panthers, who were more prone to violence than were the Black Muslims, were especially active in highlighting the negative treatment blacks received at the hands of the criminal justice system—especially by the police but also by prison officials.

One result of the spread of Black Muslim and Black Panther philosophy was that blacks in prison came to identify themselves as political prisoners. Using the techniques of civil suits and riots, black prisoners began influencing policy and procedure in U.S. prisons. Lending credibility to the argument that black prisoners were political prisoners, the 1960s saw an increase in the black prison population. Between 1960 and 1970, the percentage of blacks in state and federal prisons increased from 37 percent to 41 percent (Cahalan, 1986). It did not seem to be simply a coincidence that more blacks were being sent to prison just when the civil rights and black power movements were taking hold.

If you see yourself as a political prisoner of an oppressive government, you are not likely to be inclined to participate in programs developed by that government to "treat" you. Even if you do not consider yourself a political prisoner, you may not look favorably on treatment programs offered by institutions and agencies whose authority and abilities are being challenged by many in society's middle-class majority. Think about how difficult it would be to treat a person with diabetes if that person did not want treatment and would not cooperate with any aspects of a treatment plan. In a similar manner, when the prison version of a medical model has to work with inmates who do not want treatment, whether they see it as further oppression or futile efforts of an ineffective institution, the treatment program is not going to get very far.

In this time of assassinations, riots, and protests, politicians were forced to take a new view of America's people, programs, and problems. One of those problems

HISTORICAL PERSPECTIVES

Black Muslims

In 1946 teenager Malcolm Little began serving a ten-year prison sentence for a string of burglaries in Boston. Following suggestions from his brothers, Philbert and Reginald, Malcolm began reading about a new religion, the Nation of Islam, that was attracting attention in the black quarters of some American cities.

The Nation of Islam, also known as the Black Muslim movement, had been founded in Detroit in 1930 and added notions of black supremacy to the traditional beliefs of Sunni Islam. The movement's growth began in earnest between 1946 and 1947 under the direction of Elijah Muhammad, who had taken over the organization and moved its base to Chicago. Elijah Muhammad was released in 1946 from federal prison where he had served three and one-half years for draft evasion. (Black Muslims were forbidden to kill unless ordered to by Allah, so during World War II some followers were imprisoned for refusing to serve in the military.)

Malcolm Little studied the Qur'an in his cell and eventually wrote to Elijah Muhammad expressing his interest and faith in the Nation of Islam. Shortly after Little's parole from prison in 1952, he dropped his "slave name" and became Brother Malcolm X. Continuing to identify with black convicts, Malcolm X often used prison metaphors in his speeches. By the early 1960s, the Nation of Islam had attracted as many as 100,000 members, many of them urban males who had been in prison and who now shunned drugs and other vices (Christianson, 1998, pp. 245–247).

Go to the study guide for Malcolm X at ***www.brothermalcolm.net/studyguide.html.*** In what way is radical ideology a black tradition? From the Nation of Islam's on-line site, read about the Muslim program at ***noi.org/program.html.*** From the section "What the Muslims Want," identify three topics related to criminal justice.

needing a fresh perspective was crime. As the nation's crime rate began increasing in the 1960s, the public demanded that something be done. President Johnson responded by convening the Commission on Law Enforcement and the Administration of Justice, which issued a general report (*The Challenge of Crime in a Free Society*) in 1967. The difficulty in responding to the crime problem was highlighted when it became apparent that many of the President's Commission's recommendations were similar to those made forty years earlier by the Wickersham Commission—the lack of progress was obvious. An important difference did exist, however. Whereas the Wickersham Commission had recommended rehabilitation of the offender as a solution to the crime problem, the President's Commission was emphasizing treatment of society. Crime, the commission argued, grew out of such social conditions as poverty, unemployment, inadequate housing, and poor academic education. The President's Commission did not reject, or suggest abolishing, treatment programs in prison, but it served to turn attention away from rehabilitation and the medical model as the only way to respond to crime. That notion was advanced further by research and theories from the social sciences.

Academic Events. By the mid-1970s, the complaints and suspicions that politicians, the public, and even prisoners had expressed regarding the idea of rehabilitation were receiving support from the social sciences. Theorists and researchers from psychology, sociology, political science, and other disciplines had turned their attention to crime and the criminal. The result was often a very critical commentary on rehabilitation as a goal for corrections. The harshest criticism was saved for the medical model itself. For example, MacNamara argued that the medical model's basic premise was also its basic flaw—the belief that offenders are "sick" when in fact they are as "normal" as most nonoffenders. The difference, according to MacNamara, is that offenders are inadequately socialized and forced to live in a world where they are subject to abuse, brutalization, discrimination, and exploitation. For these reasons, no program of education, vocational training, or health therapy will bring about a "cure" because they cannot reverse twenty or thirty years of antisocial conditioning (MacNamara, 1977, p. 441).

Probably the most famous report on the inadequacy of treatment programs resulted from an analysis of research conducted on treatment programs between 1945 and 1967 (Lipton, Martinson, & Wilks, 1975). In his summary of their findings, Martinson said that "with few and isolated exceptions, the rehabilitative efforts that have been reported so far have had no appreciable effect on recidivism" (1974, p. 25, italics omitted). Although his summary asked the question, "Does nothing work?" (p. 48), the phrase became a statement: "Nothing works!" Martinson and his colleagues are often cited as placing the last shovelful of dirt on the Rehabilitation era's grave. "Nothing works" became the flag around which politicians and others could rally in their efforts to get the criminal justice system out of the treatment business.

Martinson's alternative to rehabilitation and treatment was to emphasize deterrence. He favored increased use of community corrections for offenders at low risk for repeating their crimes, whereas imprisonment would be used only for the hard-core offender. In addition, because indeterminate sentencing and parole boards were useful only under a philosophy of rehabilitation, Martinson favored the abolition of both. Support for these and similar positions began coming in from other social scientists (see MacNamara, 1977). For example, Norval Morris (1974) proposed that all rehabilitation and treatment programs be entirely voluntary, that the range of judicial discretion in sentencing be reduced, and that terms of imprisonment be determined by the seriousness of the offense rather than on guesses about the offender's likelihood for recidivism. Like Morris, David Fogel (1975) maintained that sentencing discretion of judges should be limited and replaced with a model that linked the sentence to characteristics of the offense rather than to those of the offender. Ernst van den Haag (1975) suggested that we respond to crime in a manner that balances temptation against swift and certain punishments. Minor crimes may result in fines, whereas more serious offenders could be imprisoned for one or two years. Indeterminate imprisonment or even exile would be reserved for incorrigibles. Andrew von Hirsch (1976) advocated eliminating both indeterminate sentences and parole while emphasizing that offenders "deserve" to be punished in proportion to the seriousness of their offense. James Q. Wilson (1975) argued that imprisonment, including swift and certain short terms, can be effective and should be used.

It must be noted that these authors cannot simply be placed in the "lock 'em up and throw away the key" camp. Although their views downplay any important role for rehabilitation, they temper their proposals by reserving prison for clearly dangerous offenders and recidivists, encouraging the use of community corrections when appropriate, and suggesting gradual reentry to the community (although not via a parole board) after a prison term is served. Such arguments may sound very conservative, but as noted in Chapter 2 when discussing retribution as a philosophy of punishment, basing punishment on the offense rather than the offender can be a liberal rather than conservative notion. Such a policy accepts the criminal's "freedom" to commit a crime and society's responsibility to punish that act. The fact that seemingly conservative ideas, such as abolishing indeterminate sentences and parole while rejecting a role for rehabilitation, have liberal aspects and proponents helps explain some of the confusion regarding the United States' current penal system. People who prefer clearly black-and-white issues are forced to consider the possibility that something they have always assumed was white (e.g., rehabilitation) is at best gray because it has aspects that may be harmful for both the offender and for society.

A Convergence. As social, political, and academic events converged, people from different perspectives found themselves advocating similar changes to America's justice process and the penal system. The changes were most clearly seen in attitudes toward indeterminate sentencing—the nucleus that allowed the medical model, classification, treatment, and other ingredients of the Rehabilitation era to operate. Liberals argued that the indeterminate sentence (see Chapter 5) was unfair because people convicted of the same crime would get different sentences. Therefore, it should be replaced with the more equitable determinate sentence. Conservatives argued that the indeterminate sentence was undesirable because lenient parole boards were releasing inmates too early. Therefore, it should be replaced by the determinate sentence, so the public can be assured a criminal will serve the time appropriate for the crime. When both liberals and conservatives are seeking the same changes, despite having different reasons for the adjustment, the changes are likely to occur. The first state where these strange bedfellows were able to achieve success was in California.

In 1976 the California legislature passed a bill, effective in 1977, declaring that the "purpose of imprisonment for crime is punishment" (quoted in Sullivan, 1990, p. 124). Because California's Indeterminate Sentencing Act, which had been in effect for about sixty years, was considered inconsistent with imprisonment's newly stated purpose, determinate sentencing returned to California. California's declaration that imprisonment is for punishment arguably marked the end of the Rehabilitation era and the formal beginning of the Retributive era. Other states followed California's lead. Throughout the 1980s, the call for changes in sentencing laws swept the country.

Aspects and Impacts of the Retributive Era

Because the Retributive era continues today, many of its aspects are covered in the remaining chapters when contemporary conditions and situations are described. As you will see in coming chapters, the basic philosophy behind the current penal system has two aspects: (1) The punishment should be inflicted as something the offender deserves in order to repay society for damage caused, and (2) the sentence should protect the public by including punishment so unpleasant that potential offenders will refrain from crime and actual offenders will abstain from additional criminal behavior. Rehabilitation of the offender is of secondary importance—it is wonderful if it happens, but the penal system will not be structured around attempts to achieve it. Of the two aspects, the first, a just deserts position, is most clearly retributive. The second aspect, punishment should provide protection by being unpleasant, is more closely linked to deterrence. But, as we have seen in each of the eras, several punishment philosophies often exist simultaneously.

Just Deserts in the Retributive Era. Even though punishment today includes a "protect society" or deterrence objective, it is still part of the Retributive era because the justice system's first concern is that of just deserts—criminals must get what they deserve for the crime they committed. The importance of this position is evident in many of the changes occurring over the last several decades. It was first apparent in the movement away from indeterminate sentences, begun in California in the 1970s. The just deserts rationale was seen even more clearly in the 1980s, when states and the federal government began increasing sentence lengths, imposing mandatory sentencing laws by which convictions for some crimes required a prison sentence, and creating sentencing guidelines as a way to ensure equitable punishment for similar crimes and criminals. These issues are discussed at greater length in Chapter 5's coverage of sentencing, but they have also affected such areas as parole (see Chapter 13) and prison conditions (see Chapter 9).

In addition to changes in sentencing strategies, such as moving from indeterminate to determinate length, an interest in just deserts for criminals is also found in the types of sentences that are given. Consider, for example, the sentence given to Raymond Thomas. In 1993 Raymond Thomas was convicted of shooting Reggie Haines in the forehead at point-blank range. At the time of sentencing, Reggie had progressed from months in a wheelchair to walking with a cane. Judge Lynn Tepper, in Dade City, Florida, decided twelve-year-old Raymond should get a taste of the life he had created for sixteen-year-old Reggie. At Raymond's sentencing in early 1994, Judge Tepper told Raymond he would have to move around in the same world as Reggie. *The Denver Post* quoted Judge Tepper's decision: "You will go to the bathroom in a wheelchair. . . . You will get in and out of bed, eat, try to drink from the water fountain in a wheelchair" ("Wheelchair to Be Boy's Punishment," 1994). After two days in the wheelchair, Raymond would move to a walker for a week and then had to walk using a cane. Judge Tepper's hope was that Raymond would come to appreciate what his victim had to go through to get where he was at the time of sentencing. In addition to the wheelchair/walker/cane requirements, Raymond's sentence also required that he write an essay about his experience and send it with a letter of apology to his victim, stay in the custody of the state's department of health and rehabilitative services until his nineteenth birthday, live in foster care, receive home schooling, attend regular counseling sessions, visit a prison, pay restitution to Reggie's family, and perform 200 hours of community service.

Deterrence in the Retributive Era. Because the desire to use punishment as a way to protect society is also present today, there are several areas in which this aspect has had important impact. Of course, protecting society can be achieved in several ways. The rehabilitation philosophy tries to protect society by treating offenders and changing them into law-abiding members of society. Alternatively, incapacitation advocates claim that society is protected by isolating offenders in secure buildings, away from free society, as was done in the Penitentiary era. Proponents of deterrence say that when the pains of punishment outweigh the pleasures of the crime, society is protected by deterring both potential offenders (general deterrence) and the actual offender (specific deterrence). Rehabilitation and treatment are downplayed in the Retributive era, so today's version of protecting society is closer to the incapacitation and deterrence models.

A new variable has appeared in the present that was not as widespread in the early eighteenth century—the number of spaces available in prisons today is not sufficient for the number of criminals that legislators, prosecutors, judges, and some members of the public want to send to prison. As a result, new alternatives to imprisonment are being tried around the country. These alternatives are often community-based programs, but unlike their forerunners from the Rehabilitation era, the newer programs emphasize protecting the public over an interest in treating the offender. This position fits well in the Retributive era because the idea is one that says to offenders, "We would like to put you in prison because that is what you deserve, but we don't have room for all of you. So some of you will be allowed to stay in the community—but you will stay there under our watchful eye." This view has given rise to programs such as intensive supervision probation, electronic monitoring, and home confinement (see Chapter 8), which provide increased surveillance of the offender. Other contemporary programs reflect the Retributive era by telling the criminal, "You deserve to be put in prison, but crowding prevents putting all of you in there for as long as you deserve. So some of you will get more intense punishment over a shorter time and others can stay in the community but will be kept someplace other than your homes." (See Chapter 8's coverage of boot camps and halfway houses.)

Although the Retributive era does not actively promote rehabilitation, neither does it try to prevent it from occurring. As a result, today's corrections system still includes probation, parole (in most states), and even treatment programs (e.g., academic and vocational education, and individual and group counseling) in prisons. Furthermore, the "were it not for overcrowding" types of programs (e.g., home confinement and halfway houses) also have a treatment component even if officials do not emphasize it when speaking to the public. The point is, the Retributive era has returned the U.S. penal system (including the community component) to a philosophy found in the early stages of the Wellspring era. Not surprisingly, we have also learned things from each of the intervening eras. Our contemporary response to criminal offenders still includes aspects of deterrence, rehabilitation, incapacitation, and restoration—with an emphasis on retribution philosophy during this time period. But if history teaches us anything, we are more likely to continue our journey by moving to a new era than by staying forever in this one.

Next Up, the Restorative Era?

The United States enters the twenty-first century with the Retributive era still having controlling influence over sentencing and penal policy. But the Retributive era will eventually be replaced. When that will happen, and what the replacement will be, is only conjecture at this point. But several things occurring at the end of the twentieth century lead some to believe that "next up" will be an emphasis on restorative or community justice. As described in Chapter 2, restoration is a philosophy that believes punishment's goal must be to make the community and victim whole again. It is linked to the retributive philosophy through the norm of reciprocity, and it is this link that makes a **Restorative era** the likely candidate to follow the Retributive era.

Borrowing especially from traditional community-based ideas, restorative justice works on the premise that crime is more than a violation of the law. Crime causes harm to victims, the community, and even to the offender. That harm, restorative justice proponents explain, is too often ignored by contemporary justice procedures and programs. Rather than concentrating on whether an act violated the law and whether the accused was culpable, justice requires that attention be paid to questions such as: What is the harm? What needs to be done to repair the harm? Who is responsible for the repair? When questions such as these become the focus of the justice system, society is forced to identify the interests common to the victim, community, and offender (see Figure 4.2). The response—that is, the sentence or punishment—should be something that addresses the common interests and serves to restore things, to the extent possible, to the way they were before the harm occurred.

Answers to the harm, repair, and responsibility questions are best obtained outside the traditional court setting and without use of the traditional court procedures. Instead, restorative justice requires a setting that encourages the active participation of those directly involved: the victim, the community, and the offender. The process is designed to treat offenders as persons accountable for their actions yet assuring them that they remain desired members of the community. Victims must be allowed an opportunity to affirm the harm done to them, and members of the community should be able to express and explain the collateral harm the offender's act caused. Because the typical criminal court setting and procedures are not designed to achieve these goals, where might the Restorative Justice era get its start?

Examples of restorative justice are most often found in the juvenile justice system. This is simultaneously surprising and expected. It is surprising because the Retributive era has encouraged reforms to juvenile justice that allow increased

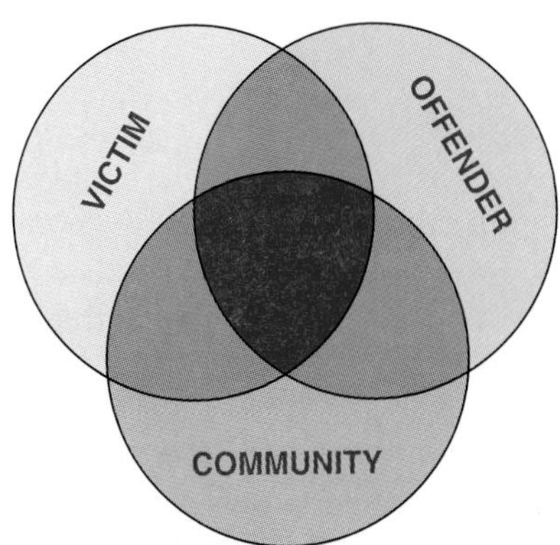

FIGURE 4.2

Common Ground

Restorative justice tries to find the area of interest common to the victim, community, and offender. The process then provides a response to the crime that addresses the needs of all three.

numbers of juvenile offenders to be handled through the adult system and that holds those juveniles remaining in the juvenile system more accountable for their actions. Yet at the same time, the traditional informality in juvenile courts and the general public support for alternative responses to youth crime make the juvenile justice system an ideal setting for restorative justice experimentation (Bazemore, 1998). By the end of the 1990s, at least twelve states had adopted legislation incorporating the language of restorative justice and/or the balanced approach. Even more states had legislation or policy referring to these positions as a guiding philosophy for implementing juvenile justice. If the changes in penal philosophy and practice that are occurring in juvenile justice foretell the next penal era, what might the justice system look like in the next ten or twenty years?

Possible Aspects of a Restorative Justice Era

To achieve its goal of making things whole again, restorative justice borrows heavily from some of the world's oldest justice systems. In its attempt to return the victim and the community to positions of influence, restorative justice supports ideals present in the earliest attempts at achieving justice. In fact, some of the preferred procedures for implementing restorative justice include indigenous ones from tribal and aboriginal systems in parts of the world where Westerners do not normally look for innovation (see "Tribal Justice").

As restorative justice ideas spread, it is not surprising that a variety of practices are put forward as exemplifying the philosophy. Of course, just as there is disagreement regarding the best ways to achieve deterrence, incapacitation, rehabilitation, and retribution, we should expect different interpretations of the best procedures for attaining restoration. Some people argue that shaming sentences (discussed in Chapter 5) are prime examples of restoration, whereas others see such sentences as purely retributive. Others say victim–offender mediation (discussed in Chapter 5) is the embodiment of restorative justice, but others argue that mediation's usefulness is restricted to nonviolent property offenses and, therefore, does not have a broad enough application to support a penal system based on restorative justice. Similarly, restitution (discussed in Chapter 7) is offered as a key sanction in achieving restoration, but critics say restitution also has limited application and too often exists without a clear purpose.

Even with the lack of consensus about specific programs, it is certain that any movement toward restorative justice must include procedures and programs that give victims an increased role in the justice process and that encourage offenders to take responsibility for their acts. That means that some version of victim–offender mediation will be included and that sanctions will emphasize both

Cross-Cultural Corrections

Tribal Justice

Carey Vicenti, when chief judge in the Jicarilla Apache tribal court, described how the Jicarilla Apache people approach justice as a community affair (Vicenti, 1995). He notes that the tribal court will address the *mens rea* of individuals brought before it but explains that such a determination actually has limited usefulness. Rather than concentrating on the guilt of the individuals, the tribal court is more interested in the fate of the individuals and the restoration of their spirits and their reintegration into the community. It is this approach that makes many tribal and indigenous systems models of restorative justice.

Vicenti contrasts the contemporary American view of justice with the Jicarilla Apache view by noting that American society relegates the question of justice to just one institution. The Indian views all aspects of the individual and society as inseparable. Every action by a person is considered to have meaning and implication to the individual and to that person's interactions in society. To believe that the law and its courts stand apart from the rest of society seems absurd.

Persons interested in incorporating restorative ideals to contemporary American justice may be well served to look at traditional American Indian justice systems. Vicenti is encouraged that after decades of forcing American Indian society to rely on non-Indian justice, there are indications that American Indians are increasingly allowed to integrate traditional values and procedures into their tribal courts. Even more encouraging, for proponents of restorative justice, traditional American justice may finally be seeing virtue in its own indigenous system.

Read about the Navajo Nation Courts at ***www.law.harvard.edu/News/navajocourts.html.*** How does the stated vision for the Navajo Nation Courts compare with the way the Jicarilla Apache people approach justice? Describe the organization and jurisdiction of the Navajo Nation Courts.

offender accountability and restitution. Whether such restorative justice policies and procedures will define the next penal era remains to be seen. But, as a new century begins, it seems that restorative justice is best positioned to take over as the Retributive era faces its inevitable decline.

SUMMARY

TWENTIETH AND TWENTY-FIRST ERAS

Three penal system eras have been identified during the twentieth century. Just as the penal system eras prior to the twentieth century laid foundations for contemporary and future responses to lawbreakers, so too did those in the twentieth century.

INDUSTRIAL ERA (1900s TO 1930s)

Different versions of inmate labor systems were tried during the Industrial era, and those systems continue to influence contemporary prison labor. The chapter discussed the following systems:

- Leasing
- Contract
- Piece-price
- Public account
- State use
- Public works and ways

REHABILITATION ERA (1930s TO 1970s)

- The Rehabilitation era directed attention more toward the offender than the offense. Groups important in implementing this era were:
  - Progressive reformers
  - American Prison Association (now American Correctional Association)
  - Wickersham Commission
  - Federal Bureau of Prisons
- The medical model was the orienting approach of the rehabilitation philosophy, and classification was the specific technique for carrying out the medical model.

RETRIBUTIVE ERA (1970s TO PRESENT)

Beginning around the 1970s, several events converged to give the U.S. penal system a retributive focus.

- These events were identified as including:
  - Social events leading to a disillusionment in social institutions.
  - Political events leading to more politically aware and legally astute inmates—especially black inmates.
  - Academic events that suggested, or were interpreted as suggesting, rehabilitation was not working.
- The result of these events is a contemporary penal system with two particular aspects:
  - Punishment should be inflicted as something the offender deserves (i.e., just deserts).
  - The sentence should protect the public by including punishments that will deter both the offender and potential offenders.

NEXT UP, THE RESTORATIVE ERA?

- The chapter concludes with a forecast of the next penal system era as one reflecting restorative justice. That philosophy differs from others by paying less attention to issues such as whether an act violated the law and whether the accused was culpable and instead concentrates on the following questions:
  - What harm has been done?
  - What needs to be done to repair that harm?
  - Who is responsible for the repair?
- The response (sentence) should result in a punishment that recognizes the interests of the victim, community, and offender as it attempts to restore things, to the extent possible, to the way they were before the harm occurred.

KEY TERMS AND CONCEPTS

American Prison Association (p. 109)
classification (p. 95)
classification committees (p. 114)
contract system (p. 101)
Federal Bureau of Prisons (p. 109)
Industrial era (p. 95)
intervention (p. 95)
labor for profit (p. 105)
labor for punishment (p. 105)
labor for rehabilitation (p. 105)
lease system (p. 96)
medical model (p. 112)

open market (p. 96)
piece-price system (p. 103)
progressive reformers (p. 109)
public account system (p. 103)
public works and ways system (p. 105)
reception and diagnostic centers (p. 114)
Rehabilitation era (p. 109)
Restorative era (p. 122)
Retributive era (p. 115)
sheltered market (p. 96)
state use system (p. 104)
treatment (p. 95)
Wickersham Commission (p. 109)

Discussion Questions

1. What are some pros and cons regarding the notion of having prisoners engaged in nonproductive labor, such as breaking up rock that will never be used?
2. How can prisoners be provided the opportunity for productive labor without giving rise to complaints from private companies and labor organizations?
3. What are some arguments for why private companies and labor organizations should support prison labor even if it means limited loss of sales or loss of jobs in the free world?
4. Using information from other classes in sociology, psychology, criminal justice, and social work, what are some arguments supporting the basic concepts of the medical model?
5. What aspects of the Retributive era are most appealing to people today, and what aspects are the least appealing?
6. What are some local or national examples that might support the chapter's suggestion that the next penal system era might emphasize the restorative philosophy?

part two **PUNISHMENT PRACTICES AND PROCEDURES**

chapter 5

SENTENCING

In Osaka, Japan, Rei Yahiro complains to police officer Kasai-san that Takehiro Kawamura has been verbally assaultive toward her while they were in the bar across the street. Kasai-san listens to both Yahiro and Kawamura, then decides that the issue is best resolved by having Kawamura make a formal apology to Yahiro. Sanctioning Kawamura in this way is not only embarrassing to Kawamura but also provides an expression of remorse to compensate Yahiro.

Ingrid Strindberg is before a Swedish judge to be sentenced on charges of theft. The judge has received information about Ingrid's personal finances and has decided to punish her with a fine instead of three months in prison.

After appropriate calculations to determine an amount that will leave Ingrid economically deprived, yet not destitute, and that will reflect the seriousness of the crime, Judge Gustafson imposes a fine of 1,600 krona.

In a moment of youthful exuberance, Lung Hing and his friend Lee Chan engage in acts of vandalism by damaging cars parked on a Singapore street. Following Singapore's tough laws, Judge Yew sentences the boys to four months in prison and to a caning. The caning will consist of six strokes of a cane to each boy's bare buttocks. The caning, which will leave permanent scars, will be administered by a martial arts expert.

In Casablanca, Morocco, Ahmed Hassan has been convicted of stealing two watches from a safe in Muhammad Al-Dokheal's home. Because the watches had been in a place of safekeeping and were worth over 10 dirhams, the judge in the local Islamic court imposes the required punishment for serious crimes—amputation of Hassan's hand at the wrist.

The preceding scenarios show some of the ways a society can respond to law violators. In some cases the police may find an acceptable way to handle the case; in others the prosecutor may determine an appropriate response. Usually, however, citizens think of judges as the people deciding the correct response to a law violator. But even then the variation remains broad—including things such as fines, corporal punishment, imprisonment, or amputation. This chapter concerns the topic of **sentencing,** which refers to the process of a court imposing a penalty on a person convicted of a crime. By that definition, the situation described earlier from Japan is not considered a sentence. Those from Sweden, Singapore, and Morocco are imposed by judges in those countries and, therefore, qualify as sentences.

We approach this topic by looking at the basic sentencing systems used in the United States. After exploring some special features of those systems, we then consider specific types of sentences available to U.S. judges. The chapter concludes with a review of sentencing systems and types in other countries.

The Two Basic Sentencing Structures

Decentralization of criminal justice procedures to the state level makes it difficult to describe a basically American police, court, or corrections system. Nowhere is that problem more evident than when discussing approaches to sentencing convicted offenders. U.S. Department of Justice publications consider sentencing as possibly "the most diversified part of the Nation's criminal justice process" (Zawitz, 1988, p. 90). Attempts to classify sentencing into several types of practices are doomed to failure because inevitably there are states with hybrid systems straddling the boundary between categories. But because the alternative is to describe fifty-one different systems, academics and practitioners have tried to place the different approaches under a limited number of categories.

In 1996 the Bureau of Justice Assistance (BJA) conducted a national survey in order to, among other things, classify each state according to the type of sentencing practice used. The lack of consensus regarding the meaning of terms such as **indeterminate sentencing** and **determinate sentencing** required the BJA to develop operational definitions that would bring consistency to the data collected from each state. Although the BJA chose to identify five separate practices, three of those (mandatory minimum sentencing, presumptive sentencing guidelines, and voluntary sentencing guidelines) can actually be used within either indeterminate sentencing or determinate sentencing. For our purposes, only two sentencing structures are identified (indeterminate and determinate), and other practices are discussed as examples of special sentencing practices (see Figure 5.1).

Help Wanted

Job Title: Federal Judicial Center Employee

Position Description: To meet its mission as the research and education agency of the federal judicial system, the Federal Judicial Center seeks employees to assist in the continuing education and training of federal judges, court employees, and others.

For specific information on jobs with the Federal Judicial Center, click on "employment opportunities" at *www.fjc.gov/*.

Indeterminate Sentencing

Although it followed fixed or determinate sentencing in U.S. history (see "History of Indeterminate Sentencing"), indeterminate sentencing provides the background for an understanding of today's resurgence of determinate sentencing.

In its most extreme form, indeterminate sentencing would simply have a judge hand the offender over to corrections officials and let those officials determine the length of sentence. Conceivably, some offenders could be released the same day they arrive; others would spend their natural life in prison. Instead of a judge trying to guess in advance how long it will take for an offender to reform, the decision to release offenders is made by officials who are watching their

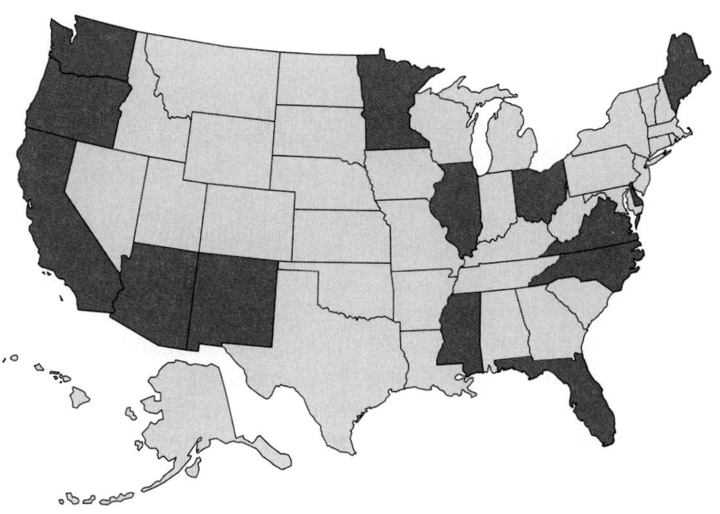

FIGURE 5.1

Types of Sentencing Practices by State, February 1996

HISTORICAL PERSPECTIVES

History of Indeterminate Sentencing

During the first hundred years of sentencing in the United States, the various states largely held to the position that offenders should be sentenced to a specific penalty (corporal or capital punishment). With the growing use of prisons for punishment, the idea of specific penalties remained and offenders were sentenced to prison for a definite time period. A prisoner was released from confinement only when he or she had completed the years, months, and days stipulated in the judge's sentence. By 1876 some prison officials had become convinced that a fixed penalty, called determinate sentencing, prevented the reformation of offenders by keeping prisoners confined regardless of their efforts toward improvement. A new sentencing strategy developed, known as indeterminate sentencing, that allowed officials other than the sentencing judge to determine when a prisoner should be released from confinement.

As you may recall from reading Chapter 3, Alexander Maconochie believed criminals could be reformed, but he also realized that one could not determine in advance just how long that reformation would take. He implemented a process of applying open-ended sentences (basically, indeterminate sentences) that allowed the offender to obtain an early release from confinement by showing good behavior and earning marks. Prisoners who acquired the necessary number of marks could have their sentences terminated. Maconochie's early version of an indeterminate sentence became known to Sir Walter Crofton while he was director of the Irish prison system. Crofton adopted the mark system but modified Maconochie's early release by making it a conditional release (essentially called parole today) that allowed officials to return released offenders to prison if they misbehaved in the community.

Both Maconochie and Crofton advocated the idea that offenders' prison behavior rather than just their crime should affect the timing of their release. The idea continued to spread to countries beyond Australia and Ireland, and in 1876 New York State opened the Elmira Reformatory using the Irish system philosophy. Under the direction of superintendent Zebulon Brockway, Elmira accepted young first offenders on an indeterminate sentence with a maximum term that was no greater than the penalty fixed for offenders sent to the state's regular prisons. A reformatory offender would be released from confinement by a board of managers based on the inmate's institutional behavior.

Visit the Web site for Families Against Mandatory Minimums, and read about the history of sentencing at ***www.famm.org/about3.htm#3***. What were the Boggs Acts that were passed in the 1950s, and what criticisms did they receive in the 1960s? Read the history of Elmira Reformatory at ***www.geocities.com/MotorCity/Downs/3548/facility/elmira.html***, and identify specific examples of education and work programs provided at Elmira.

progress and determining the optimum point for release in the community. Although this absolute indeterminate sentencing process might seem most consistent with having a sentence fit the individual offender's needs, it was a more restricted version that caught on around the country.

Limits to indeterminate sentencing in the United States are provided both by state legislatures and by judges. State legislatures are responsible for enacting the criminal laws in their respective jurisdictions. As part of that duty, legislators assign the punishment for those committing a particular crime. Each jurisdiction will have its own method of assigning punishments, but the states are consistent in that each determines the statutory penalties identifying the punishment to be given offenders convicted of crimes in that jurisdiction. Sometimes those penalties are linked to specific crimes; for example, in one state a person convicted of auto theft may be sentenced to at least one year but no more than three years. In other states the punishments may be linked to a class of offenses that includes many specific crimes. For example, auto theft may be categorized as one of several class 2 felonies—and all class 2 felonies are punishable by a sentence of one to three years.

Whether the statutory penalties are linked to specific crimes or to classes of felonies (or misdemeanors), the state legislatures typically identify a minimum and maximum time period within which sentences must fall. Occasionally, especially for misdemeanors and less serious felonies, only maximum penalties are set.

When judges impose indeterminate sentences, they are also setting limits on the penalty. But the judge's sentence must fall within the **statutory penalty** set by the legislature. If the statutory penalty requires that auto theft receive a punishment between one and three years, the judge must impose a minimum and maximum between those numbers. So, sentences such as one to two years, two to three years, or even the full one to three years would be possible. But a sentence such as six months to four years could not be imposed in that jurisdiction. Once the sentence is given, its termination is determined by corrections officials on the basis of the offender's rehabilitation. It is the difficulty of identifying a point when prisoners are rehabilitated that caused many states to abandon indeterminate sentencing. To many of the states, the old fixed or determinate sentence was more reliable.

In 1996 indeterminate sentencing was the dominant sentencing structure in the United States with thirty-six states and the District of Columbia classified as having that sentencing practice (see Figure 5.1). The BJA included New York with the indeterminate sentencing states because the majority of inmates receive an indeterminate sentence although determinate sentencing is used for New York's repeat violent felony offenders.

Determinate Sentencing

As described by Abadinsky (1994), twentieth-century dissatisfaction with indeterminate sentencing first surfaced in 1971, when the Quaker-sponsored American Friend's Service Committee (AFSC) published an attack on indeterminate sentencing and parole. The criticism struck at the very heart of indeterminate sentencing—the idea of individualized sentences. Although the proponents of indeterminate sentencing praised the notion that sentences should vary according to individual needs, the AFSC complained that emphasis on the individual ignores factors such as poverty and discrimination. Furthermore, despite their best efforts, behavioral sciences have not advanced to the point that anyone is able to tell when a person has been rehabilitated and, therefore, ready for release to the community. In the mid-1970s, reviews of research on rehabilitation supported the AFSC position by suggesting that treatment efforts were not working. Criticism also began building against the ability of parole boards to release offenders early (a key aspect of the indeterminate sentencing process) and toward the necessary inequalities in sentencing that individualization brings.

The attack on excessive discretion by parole boards and on apparent sentencing inequalities seemed to doom indeterminate sentencing. People on the political right asserted that the parole boards were releasing prisoners too early. Those on the political left said persons convicted of the same crime received very different sentences. Both sides complained about indeterminate sentencing until the system eventually had few supporters. The result was a return in many states to the old system, in which the judge sentences offenders to a fixed period of time within the statutory limits determined by the legislature. For example, the legislature may decide a person convicted of assault must be punished for a period of between two and five years. Under determinate sentencing, the judge must impose a flat sentence for a specific amount of time. Sentences such as two and one-half years probation or four years imprisonment would be acceptable. Sentences of one year or of five and one-half years would not be possible because the time falls outside the statutory penalty.

Several states have found determinate sentencing to be a satisfactory way to restore justice by reducing discretion. In 1996 fourteen states were classified as having determinate sentencing (see Figure 5.1). However, several states included among those fourteen allow for indeterminate sentencing for certain types of crimes (e.g., some California offenders might receive a sentence of twenty-five years to life with the possibility of parole). Those states were included in the determinate sentencing group because that is the type of sentence a vast majority of the offenders receive in those states.

FOUR SPECIAL SENTENCING PRACTICES

Although there are just two sentencing structures used in the United States, the variation in American sentencing procedures results from the way jurisdictions modify their indeterminate or determinate sentencing structure with one or more special sentencing practices. Sentencing guidelines and mandatory minimum sentencing are two strategies that relate to the amount of discretion the judge has when setting sentence length or type. Taking into consideration aggravating and mitigating circumstances, a third strategy provides a way for judges to increase or decrease a sentence because of special conditions associated with the offense or the offender. Grouped under a fourth strategy called *methods for reducing sentence time* are procedures that allow the early release of prisoners so that room is available for newly arriving inmates.

Sentencing Guidelines

Some jurisdictions modify their basic sentencing structure with the use of **sentencing guidelines.** When guidelines are used in an indeterminate sentencing state, they direct the judge to a range of years that have been deemed appropriate for the case at hand. When guidelines are used in determinate sentencing jurisdictions, the judge sets a fixed sentence that falls within a range found in the guideline.

Two types of sentencing guidelines are identified. Under **presumptive sentencing** guidelines, it is "presumed" that judges will issue a sentence that falls within a range established for an offender in a particular case. In 1996 there were ten states identified as presumptive (see Table 5.1 on pages 134–135). In some jurisdictions (seven in 1996) the guidelines are voluntary in that they simply suggest possible sentences to judges.

Two jurisdictions using presumptive guidelines have received considerable attention and will be used here to describe more fully the use of guidelines. Minnesota and the federal government use sentencing guidelines that arrange presumptive penalties in the cells of a matrix. In both jurisdictions, the guidelines are created by sentencing commissions that determine suitable sentences for particular crimes and offenders.

As Table 5.2 shows (see page 136), the Minnesota **sentencing grid,** or matrix, is composed of ten rows (I through X) identifying crime severity levels. The grid's other dimension is made up of seven columns that identify the offender's criminal history score, which is based on items such as number of prior convictions and whether the offender was under correctional supervision when the current offense occurred. In the cells resulting from this two-dimensional array are numbers (months) that tell judges what the sentencing commission considers the ideal sentence for a particular crime committed by an offender with a particular criminal history score. Dividing the grid is a solid line that distinguishes cells requiring incarceration (cells above and to the right of the line) from cells that allow the judge to sentence the offender to probation or up to one year in jail (cells below and to the left of the line). For example, if an offender with a criminal history score of two is convicted of nonresidential burglary, she could receive a sentence up to eighteen months probation. On the other side of the incarceration line, if an offender with a criminal history score of two is convicted of aggravated robbery, he could receive a sentence of sixty-eight months in prison. Note, however, that for the aggravated robber the judge could impose a prison sentence as low as sixty-four months or as high as seventy-two months and still be within the guidelines.

Federal sentencing guidelines went into effect in late 1987. The guidelines were a reaction to such things as the view that sentencing for purposes of rehabilitation had failed, and that offenders convicted of similar crimes were receiving very different sentences. The guidelines are also a response to complaints from prisoners that the uncertain release dates caused by indeterminate sentences constitute cruel punishment (Tjoflat, 1991). Congress responded to these and other complaints by passing the 1984 Comprehensive Crime Control Act, which established a seven-member U.S. Sentencing Commission. The commission was told to establish uniform federal sentencing guidelines, and in November 1987, those guidelines took effect.

Like the Minnesota guidelines, the federal sentencing guidelines (see Table 5.3 on page 137) are on a grid composed of rows (the offense level) and columns (the criminal history category). The offense level is determined by considering things such as the seriousness of the crime, public concern generated by the crime, and how frequently the particular offense is occurring in the community and the nation. The base offense level can be adjusted either upward or downward by factors linked to the victim, the number of coparticipants, or any special skills the offender used to commit the crime (Campbell, 1991; Tjoflat, 1991). Dividing the grid are lines marking four zones (A through D) that identify the type of sanction available for the sentencing range that results from the intersection of offense level and the criminal history score.

The criminal history category is composed of offender factors that are the result of points assigned for characteristics such as the role in the offense, criminal record, and commitment to criminal activity. For example, a criminal record is translated into a criminal history score by assigning points for prior convictions. The score can be adjusted upward or downward based on items such as how recent the offense is, or whether the crime occurred while the offender was under any form of criminal sentence.

Upon determining the appropriate offense level and criminal history category, the judge can move to the applicable point at which row and column meet and find the guideline range. The guideline range not only provides minimum and maximum months for the sentence but also indicates what type of sanctions are available because the range falls in one of four zones. Sanctions available in zone A are a fine, probation, or imprisonment. Possible zone B sanctions are probation with a confinement condition such as home confinement or residential community corrections, a split sentence, or imprisonment. Sanctions linked to zone C are a split sentence or imprisonment. In zone D the sanction is imprisonment (U.S. Sentencing Commission, 1998). By referring to Table 5.2, you can see that an offender falling into criminal history category III who is convicted of a level 15 offense should receive a sentence to prison, or possibly to a boot camp, lasting from twenty-four to thirty months.

Help Wanted

Job Title: Sentencing Commission Researcher/Analyst

Position Description: The researcher/analyst will develop and refine a simulation model to estimate the impact on court and correctional resources of any changes in sentencing proposed by the commission. The position also requires working with research contractors to understand sentencing and corrections data and ensure their work is responsive to the needs of the commission.

Qualifications: Candidates must have the necessary educational background to fulfill the research requirements of the position and demonstrate an ability to organize and express thoughts clearly.

This type of position is typically available in states with sentencing commissions. Visit the State Sentencing Commission's contact list at *www.ussc.gov/states/nascaddr.htm* for places to write regarding job opportunities with sentencing commissions.

TABLE 5.1: U.S. Sentencing Practices, February 1996

STATE	DETERMINATE SENTENCING	INDETERMINATE SENTENCING	TYPES OF SENTENCING GUIDELINES	MANDATORY MINIMUM PRISON SENTENCING
Alabama		◆		◆
Alaska		◆		◆
Arizona	◆			◆
Arkansas		◆	Voluntary/advisory	◆
California	◆			◆
Colorado		◆		◆
Connecticut		◆		◆
Delaware	◆		Presumptive	◆
District of Columbia		◆		◆
Florida	◆		Presumptive	◆
Georgia		◆		◆
Hawaii		◆		◆
Idaho		◆		◆
Illinois	◆			◆
Indiana		◆		◆
Iowa		◆		◆
Kansas		◆	Presumptive	◆
Kentucky		◆		◆
Louisiana		◆	Voluntary/advisory	◆
Maine	◆			◆
Maryland		◆	Voluntary/advisory	◆
Massachusetts		◆	Under study	◆
Michigan		◆	Under study	◆
Minnesota	◆		Presumptive	◆
Mississippi	◆			◆
Missouri		◆	Voluntary	◆
Montana		◆	Under study	◆
Nebraska		◆		◆

TABLE 5.1: Continued

STATE	DETERMINATE SENTENCING	INDETERMINATE SENTENCING	TYPES OF SENTENCING GUIDELINES	MANDATORY MINIMUM PRISON SENTENCING
Nevada		◆		◆
New Hampshire		◆		◆
New Jersey		◆		◆
New Mexico	◆			◆
New York		◆		◆
North Carolina	◆		Presumptive	◆
North Dakota		◆		◆
Ohio[1]	◆		Presumptive	◆
Oklahoma		◆	Voluntary/advisory	◆
Oregon	◆		Presumptive	◆
Pennsylvania		◆	Presumptive	◆
Rhode Island		◆		◆
South Carolina		◆		◆
South Dakota		◆		◆
Tennessee[2]		◆	Presumptive	◆
Texas		◆		◆
Utah		◆	Voluntary/advisory	◆
Vermont		◆		◆
Virginia	◆		Voluntary/advisory	◆
Washington	◆		Presumptive	◆
West Virginia		◆		◆
Wisconsin[2]		◆		◆
Wyoming		◆		◆
Total	14	37	17	51

[1]Ohio abolished indeterminate sentences in July 1996.

[2]Tennessee and Wisconsin continue to have sentencing guidelines; the sentencing commissions were abolished in 1996.

Source: From Bureau of Justice Assistance. (1998). *1996 National survey of state sentencing structures* [NCJ 169270]. (Exhibit1-1, prepared by National Council on Crime and Delinquency). Washington, DC: Department of Justice.

TABLE 5.2: Sentencing Guidelines Grid
Presumptive Sentence Lengths in Months

Italicized numbers within the grid denote the range within which a judge may sentence without the sentence being deemed a departure. Offenders with nonimprisonment felony sentences are subject to jail time according to law.

SEVERITY LEVEL OF CONVICTION OFFENSE		CRIMINAL HISTORY SCORE 0	1	2	3	4	5	6 or More
Murder, second degree (intentional murder; drive-by shootings)	X	306 *299–313*	326 *319–333*	346 *339–353*	366 *359–373*	386 *379–393*	406 *399–413*	426 *419–433*
Murder, third degree Murder, second degree (unintentional murder)	IX	150 *144–156*	165 *159–171*	180 *174–186*	195 *189–201*	210 *204–216*	225 *219–231*	240 *234–246*
Criminal sexual conduct, first degree Assault, first degree	VIII	86 *81–91*	98 *93–103*	110 *105–115*	122 *117–127*	134 *129–139*	146 *141–151*	158 *153–163*
Aggravated robbery, first degree	VII	48 *44–52*	58 *54–62*	68 *64–72*	78 *74–82*	88 *84–92*	98 *94–102*	108 *104–112*
Criminal sexual conduct, second degree (a) and (b)	VI	21	27	33	39 *37–41*	45 *43–47*	51 *49–53*	57 *55–59*
Residential burglary Simple robbery	V	18	23	28	33 *31–35*	38 *36–40*	43 *41–45*	48 *46–50*
Nonresidential burglary	IV	12[1]	15	18	21	24 *23–25*	27 *26–28*	30 *29–31*
Theft crimes (over $2,500)	III	12[1]	13	15	17	19 *18–20*	21 *20–22*	23 *22–24*
Theft crimes ($2,500 or less) Check forgery ($200–$2,500)	II	12[1]	12[1]	13	15	17	19	21 *20–22*
Sale of simulated controlled substance	I	12[1]	12[1]	12[1]	13	15	17	19 *18–20*

☐ Presumptive commitment to state imprisonment. First-degree murder is excluded from the guidelines by law and continues to have a mandatory life sentence. See section II.E. Mandatory Sentences for policy regarding those sentences controlled by law, including minimum periods of supervision for sex offenders released from prison.

■ Presumptive stayed sentence; at the discretion of the judge, up to a year in jail and/or other nonjail sanctions can be imposed as conditions of probation. However, certain offenses in this section of the grid always carry a presumptive commitment to a state prison. These offenses include third-degree controlled substance crimes when the offender has a prior felony drug conviction, burglary of an occupied dwelling when the offender has a prior felony burglary conviction, second and subsequent criminal sexual conduct offenses and offenses carrying a mandatory minimum prison term due to the use of a dangerous weapon (e.g., second-degree assault). See sections II.C. Presumptive Sentence and II.E. Mandatory Sentences.

[1]One year and one day.

Source: From Minnesota Sentencing Guidelines Commission. (August 1999).

The federal guidelines have been controversial since the commission began work on them. One controversy, reducing sentencing disparity, is addressed in the feature "Sentencing Guidelines and Racial Disparity" on page 138. Another controversy, the guidelines' constitutionality, continued until 1989 when the U.S.

TABLE 5.3: Sentencing Table (in months of imprisonment)

	Offense Level	CRIMINAL HISTORY CATEGORY (CRIMINAL HISTORY POINTS) I (0 or 1)	II (2 or 3)	III (4, 5, 6)	IV (7, 8, 9)	V (10, 11, 12)	VI (13 or more)
Zone A	1	0–6	0–6	0–6	0–6	0–6	0–6
	2	0–6	0–6	0–6	0–6	0–6	1–7
	3	0–6	0–6	0–6	0–6	2–8	3–9
	4	0–6	0–6	0–6	2–8	4–10	6–12
	5	0–6	0–6	1–7	4–10	6–12	9–15
	6	0–6	1–7	2–8	6–12	9–15	12–18
	7	0–6	2–8	4–10	8–14	12–18	15–21
	8	0–6	4–10	6–12	10–16	15–21	18–24
Zone B	9	4–10	6–12	8–14	12–18	18–24	21–27
	10	6–12	8–14	10–16	15–21	21–27	24–30
Zone C	11	8–14	10–16	12–18	18–24	24–30	27–33
	12	10–16	12–18	15–21	21–27	27–33	30–37
Zone D	13	12–18	15–21	18–24	24–30	30–37	33–41
	14	15–21	18–24	21–27	27–33	33–41	37–46
	15	18–24	21–27	24–30	30–37	37–46	41–51
	16	21–27	24–30	27–33	33–41	41–51	46–57
	17	24–30	27–33	30–37	37–46	46–57	51–63
	18	27–33	30–37	33–41	41–51	51–63	57–71
	19	30–37	33–41	37–46	46–57	57–71	63–78
	20	33–41	37–46	41–51	51–63	63–78	70–87
	21	37–46	41–51	46–57	57–71	70–87	77–96
	22	41–51	46–57	51–63	63–78	77–96	84–105
	23	46–57	51–63	57–71	70–87	84–105	92–115
	24	51–63	57–71	63–78	77–96	92–115	100–125
	25	57–71	63–78	70–87	84–105	100–125	110–137
	26	63–78	70–87	78–97	92–115	110–137	120–150
	27	70–87	78–97	87–108	100–125	120–150	130–162
	28	78–97	87–108	97–121	110–137	130–162	140–175
	29	87–108	97–121	108–135	121–151	140–175	151–188
	30	97–121	108–135	121–151	135–168	151–188	168–210
	31	108–135	121–151	135–168	151–188	168–210	188–235
	32	121–151	135–168	151–188	168–210	188–235	210–262
	33	135–168	151–188	168–210	188–235	210–262	235–293
	34	151–188	168–210	188–235	210–262	235–293	262–327
	35	168–210	188–235	210–262	235–293	262–327	292–365
	36	188–235	210–262	235–293	262–327	292–365	324–405
	37	210–262	235–293	262–327	292–365	324–405	360–life
	38	235–293	262–327	292–365	324–405	360–life	360–life
	39	262–327	292–365	324–405	360–life	360–life	360–life
	40	292–365	324–405	360–life	360–life	360–life	360–life
	41	324–405	360–life	360–life	360–life	360–life	360–life
	42	360–life	360–life	360–life	360–life	360–life	360–life
	43	life	life	life	life	life	life

Source: From U.S. Sentencing Commission. (1998).

ISSUES OF FAIRNESS

SENTENCING GUIDELINES AND RACIAL DISPARITY

According to proponents, sentencing guidelines would help reduce sentencing disparity by decreasing the possibility that irrelevant characteristics—such as the offender's race, ethnicity, or gender—could influence sentencing. Instead, the sentence would be determined only by such relevant factors as the offense and the offender's criminal history.

Senna and Siegel (1999) and Parent, Dunworth, McDonald, and Rhodes (1996) reviewed research on how guideline sentencing has been doing and found mixed results. In both Minnesota and Washington, racial, ethnic, and gender differences in sentencing declined after guidelines were implemented. However, that movement toward sentencing neutrality was tempered by findings of continued racial disparity in sentencing that seems to be the result of factors such as race-specific crimes. For example, possession of crack cocaine is punished more severely under federal guidelines than is possession of powder cocaine. Because blacks are more likely to possess crack and whites and Hispanics powder, black cocaine offenders receive harsher sentences than do white and Hispanic cocaine offenders. Also, black offenders were more likely to be charged with weapons violations and, hence, more likely to receive prison terms than were European American offenders. Furthermore, black offenders are more likely than whites to have prior records as juveniles. Because some guidelines give enhanced sentences for prior juvenile conviction, longer sentences for black offenders may result. Clearly racial disparity in sentencing continues even under guidelines. If there is good news in the continued presence of racial disparity under guidelines, it may be that the disparity results more from correlated factors such as race-specific crimes rather than from apparent prejudice on the part of judges.

Results such as these have led some people to conclude that sentencing guidelines have not yet shown themselves to have many of the positive aspects anticipated by proponents. It seems likely, though, that guidelines will continue to be used because the federal government is following that path and the U.S. Supreme Court has upheld their use.

Go to the Sentencing Project's search page at ***www.sentencingproject.org/search/search.html***, and enter the keywords *crack* and *cocaine*. Read several of the "Commentaries" and "News and Updates" that are produced by the search. What type of arguments are made regarding the impact of different punishments for crack and powder cocaine? Do you think there is subtle racism in harsher crack sentences?

Supreme Court (*Mistretta v. U.S.*) held that Congress had acted appropriately and that the commission's guidelines could be applied nationwide. But even after the Supreme Court's decision, disagreement continues, often with the passion demonstrated by U.S. District Court Judge G. Thomas Eisele, who views the current guidelines as a "dark, sinister, and cynical crime management program [that has] . . . a certain Kafkaesque aura about it" (Eisele, 1991, p. 20).

A particularly controversial item is the argument that guidelines have taken sentencing discretion away from judges and given it to prosecutors. In Minnesota (Miethe & Moore, 1988), both prosecutors (95 percent) and judges (85 percent) believed judicial discretion decreased under guidelines, but fewer prosecutors (14 percent) than judges (46 percent) believed guidelines resulted in increased discretion for the prosecution. At the federal level, Judge Eisele (1991) suggests the guidelines place the real sentencing power with the prosecutors because of the role they play in determining the offense charged—which in turn highly influences the sentence range. Federal prosecutor Thomas Zeno (1991) disagrees with such a position by suggesting that guidelines actually had little impact on the prosecutor's role in sentencing. Before guidelines, prosecutors influenced a sentence by selecting particular charges, by making plea offers, and through their speeches to the court. Zeno (1991) points out that federal judges still have the power to accept or reject plea bargains, to decide the precise sentence within the guideline range, and to determine if there should be a departure from the guidelines. The controversy continues as indicated in a 1996 survey (Johnson & Gilbert, 1997) in which nearly three-quarters of the federal district judges surveyed believed the prosecutor has the greatest influence on the final guideline sentence. It appears that the various actors in the federal court system will continue to debate the impact and desirability of guidelines, but it is also apparent that guidelines will remain for the foreseeable future.

Mandatory Minimum Sentencing

Another feature that helps provide the variety in U.S. sentencing practices is the **mandatory minimum sentence.** Sentencing practices are often discussed in terms of sentences to prison. Actually, judges usually can choose from several sentencing types (such as fines, probation, or residential community corrections), and some of those types (especially those linked to probation) are governed by the jurisdiction's overall sentencing structure. For example, in an indeterminate sentencing state the judge may sentence the offender to probation for a period of one to three years—keeping the statutory limits in mind. In a determinate sentencing state the sentence could be (again, depending on the statutory limits) a flat two years on probation.

The possibility of a judge imposing a term of probation rather than time in prison did not always sit well with some citizens. During the 1970s and 1980s, the get-tough-on-crime philosophy often criticized judges' decisions to impose a nonprison sentence on offenders whom the public viewed as deserving or needing prison. Complaints were especially forceful in indeterminate sentencing states because those judges had the most discretion.

Lawmakers responded to public concern by deciding that judges should not have the discretion to impose anything other than imprisonment for some crimes and offenders. Legislation was passed to make a prison sentence mandatory for such cases. Today, these **mandatory sentences** are especially popular for violent crimes and drug trafficking, as well as for repeat felony offenders and for offenders who used a firearm when committing the crime. All states and the District of Columbia presently employ some version of mandatory minimum sentencing laws (see Table 5.1). Mandatory sentencing is most commonly used for repeat or habitual offenders (forty states), crimes committed using a deadly weapon (thirty-eight states and the District of Columbia), drug possession/trafficking (thirty-six states and the District of Columbia), and, in thirty-one states, for drunk driving (Bureau of Justice Assistance, 1998, pp. 6–7).

In addition to laws requiring a prison sentence, the term *mandatory sentencing* is linked to legislation that excludes certain offenders from being considered for parole (sentences "without possibility of parole"), to laws requiring that a certain percentage of the sentence be served ("truth in sentencing"), and to the so-called "three strikes and you're out" legislation. The last two of these warrant additional discussion.

Truth in Sentencing. Ditton and Wilson (1999) point out that "the amount of time offenders serve in prison is almost always shorter than the time they are sentenced to serve by the court" (p. 1). State prisoners released in 1990 had served an average of 38 percent of their sentence length. By 1996 the average had increased to 44 percent of the sentence length—but that was still lower than many citizens believed appropriate. One reason for discharging prisoners sooner than their sentence would indicate was the need for a release valve that made room for new arrivals. The "get-tough" policies of the 1970s and 1980s, such as sentencing guidelines and mandatory minimum sentences, resulted in an average prison population growth of 7 percent annually between 1990 and 1997 (Gilliard, 1999).

Many states did not have enough prison beds to handle all the new admissions but procedures such as good time and earned-time reductions (both discussed later in this chapter) and parole release (see Chapter 13) allowed existing prisoners to be released early so there was room for the newcomers—the result being a difference between the offenders' sentence and the time in prison that they actually served. Citizens of Washington State were the country's first to demand that there be more accuracy or "truth" in the sentence given and the time served in prison. In 1984 Washington passed the first **truth-in-sentencing law,** and by the end of the 1990s many other states had followed.

The biggest obstacle to keeping prisoners incarcerated for a greater percentage of their sentence was the insufficient number of prison beds available. The U.S. Congress came to the states' assistance by authorizing funding to construct or renovate state prisons and jails so that more prisoners could be confined for a greater percentage of their sentence. To receive these Violent Offender Incarceration and Truth-in-Sentencing Incentive (VOI/TIS) grants, states must require persons convicted of *Uniform Crime Report Part I* violent crimes (i.e., homicide, aggravated assault, forcible rape, or armed robbery) to serve not less than 85 percent of the prison sentence. Table 5.4 shows the status of truth-in-sentencing requirements. By mid-1999 twenty-eight states and the District of Columbia met the federal 85 percent requirement, and the remaining states all had some type of minimum requirement.

The impact of truth-in-sentencing laws is difficult to determine at this time. One reason is the absence of agreement on the laws' objectives. If the goal is mainly retributive—keep the prisoner in prison longer—then the laws are probably succeeding. As noted earlier, prisoners released in 1996 had served more of their sentence than had the average prisoner released in 1990. And, with the new 85 percent requirement, Ditton and Wilson (1999) predict that the minimum term for violent offenders will increase by fifteen months. If the goals are incapacitative, then truth in sentencing might also be considered a success because the nation's crime rate has been declining. However, as noted in Chapter 2, many reasons are offered for the declining crime rate and keeping in prison longer those people most likely to commit further crime is just one possibility. But proponents of punishment for deterrence will have to wait to determine if truth-in-sentencing laws are achieving either general or specific deterrence. Because the laws are relatively new in many states, there has not been enough time to determine whether a longer prison sentence will deter that individual from future criminal behavior or will deter others who hear about the longer sentences from committing a crime in the first place.

"Three Strikes and You're Out" Laws. The "hot topic" in sentencing during the mid-1990s was actually a revisiting of early versions of mandatory minimum sentencing. Turner, Sundt, Applegate, and Cullen (1995) note a 1926 New York State law requiring life imprisonment for third-time felony offenders. By 1968 twenty-three states had enacted legislation that allowed habitual offenders to be sentenced to life imprisonment after being convicted of a specified number of offenses. The word *allowed* is important because it identifies a difference between many of the three-strikes laws and the earlier habitual offender legislation. Although the intent of both is to ensure that more severe punishment will follow subsequent convictions, the three-strikes version typically (though not always) requires rather than allows repeat offenders to receive life imprisonment. So, although laws that target repeat and habitual offenders are not new, their current incarnation requires some specific comment.

TABLE 5.4: Truth-in-Sentencing Requirements, by State

MEET FEDERAL 85% REQUIREMENT		50% REQUIREMENT	100% OF MINIMUM REQUIREMENT	OTHER REQUIREMENTS
Arizona	Missouri	Indiana	Idaho	Alaska[c]
California	New Jersey	Maryland	Nevada	Arkansas[d]
Connecticut	New York	Nebraska	New Hampshire	Colorado[e]
Delaware	North Carolina	Texas		Kentucky[f]
District of Columbia	North Dakota			Massachusetts[g]
Florida	Ohio			Wisconsin[h]
Georgia	Oklahoma[b]			
Illinois[a]	Oregon			
Iowa	Pennsylvania			
Kansas	South Carolina			
Louisiana	Tennessee			
Maine	Utah			
Michigan	Virginia			
Minnesota	Washington			
Mississippi				

[a]Qualified for federal funding in 1996 only.

[b]Effective July 1, 1999, offenders are required to serve 85 percent of the sentence.

[c]Two-part sentence structure (two-thirds in prison; one-third on parole); 100 percent of prison term required.

[d]Mandatory 70 percent of sentence for certain violent offenses and manufacture of methamphetamine.

[e]Violent offenders with two prior violent convictions serve 75 percent; one prior violent conviction, 56.25 percent.

[f]Effective July 15, 1998, offenders are required to serve 85 percent of the sentence.

[g]Requires 75 percent of a minimum prison sentence.

[h]Effective December 31, 1999, two-part sentence; offenders serve 100 percent of the prison term and a sentence of extended supervision at 25 percent of the prison sentence.

Source: From Ditton, P., & Wilson, D. J. (1999). *Truth in sentencing in state prisons* [NCJ 170032]. Washington, DC: Office of Justice Programs.

Under the title of **"three strikes and you're out,"** laws were passed first in Washington State (1993) then a few months later in California (1994). By early 1996 twenty-five states had enacted laws specifically addressing repeat and habitual offenders. The "three strikes and you're out" moniker is more a catchy phrase than a helpful descriptor because the states vary widely on what is meant by "three," "strikes," and "out." Despite variation in the way states have implemented three-strikes legislation, Clark, Austin, and Henry (1997) identified some similarities as follows:

- All three-strikes laws authorize—or in some cases, mandate—longer periods of incarceration for those convicted of violent crimes. Violent felonies such as murder, rape, robbery, arson, aggravated assault, and carjacking are typically

Showing more disrespect than remorse, Richard Allen Davis was sentenced to death for murdering twelve-year-old Polly Klaas in Petaluma, California. Because Davis had already served several prison sentences, California citizens used Polly's murder to have legislators pass one of the nation's first "three strikes and you're out" laws as a way to keep dangerous criminals behind bars.

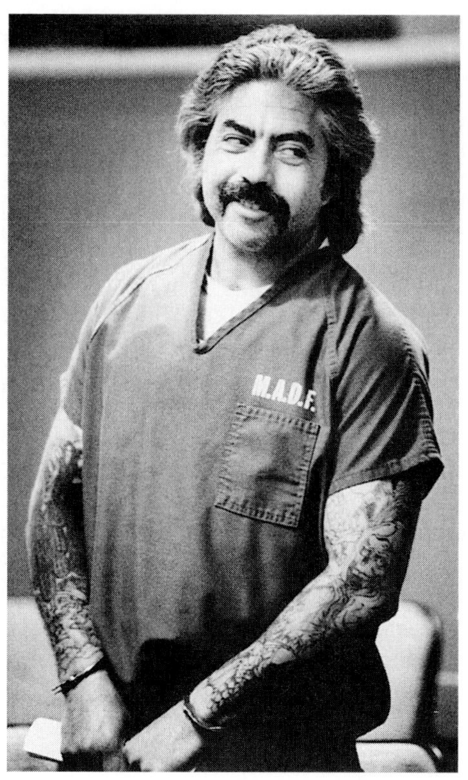

included. Less common are drug sales (e.g., California, Indiana, and Louisiana), escape (Florida), treason (Washington), and embezzlement and bribery (South Carolina).

- All but one of the states (Kansas) had preexisting laws that targeted repeat violent offenders, so the breadth of those preexisting statutes will to a large extent determine the impact of the new laws in each state. Early evidence suggests that, with the exceptions of California and possibly Georgia, most of the laws will have minimal impact on the state's prison system.
- All of the statutes either increase the period of incarceration for violent crime, expand the number of crimes that are included in the violent crime category, or both. In some instances laws simply changed the period of incarceration for a particular crime from a range to a mandatory fixed number of years (Clark, Austin, & Henry, 1997).

Table 5.5 highlights the differences in what counts as a strike (ranging from any felony to specific felonies), how many strikes are needed (ranging from two to four), and what it means to be out (ranging from doubling the regular penalty to life in prison without parole).

The newness of three-strikes laws means there has not been much evaluation of their impact. Initial reports suggest that except for California the laws are having little effect. Washington State, which expected about forty to seventy-five three-strikes cases per year, had totaled only 121 convictions between December 1993 and September 1998. Other states had as few as zero persons incarcerated under their three-strikes laws, and only six states had more than thirty convictions by 1998 (Dickey & Hollenhorst, 1998).

The California exception is a dramatic one—by July 1998 over 40,500 offenders were admitted to the California Department of Corrections (CDC) for either a two- or three-strikes sentence (see the California strike zones defined in Table 5.5). Of that number, 89 percent were sentenced under the two-strikes provision (Dickey

TABLE 5.5: Examples of Variations in State Strikes Laws

STATE	STRIKE ZONE DEFINED	STRIKES NEEDED TO BE "OUT"	MEANING OF "OUT"
California	Any felony if one prior felony conviction is from a list of strikeable offenses	Two	Mandatory sentence of twice the term for the offense involved
	Any felony if two prior felony convictions are from a list of strikeable offenses	Three	Mandatory indeterminate life sentence, with no parole eligibility for twenty-five years
Kansas	Any felony against a person	Two	Court may double term specified in sentencing guidelines
	Any felony against a person	Three	Court may triple term specified in sentencing guidelines
Pennsylvania	Murder, voluntary manslaughter, rape, involuntary deviate sexual intercourse, arson, kidnapping, robbery, aggravated assault	Two	Enhanced sentence of up to ten years
	Same offenses	Three	Enhanced sentence of up to twenty-five years
South Carolina	Murder, voluntary manslaughter, homicide by child abuse, rape, kidnapping, armed robbery, drug trafficking, embezzlement, bribery, certain accessory and attempt	Two	Mandatory life in prison with no parole eligibility
Utah	Any first- or second-degree felony	Three	Court may sentence from five years up to life
Virginia	Murder, kidnapping, robbery, carjacking, sexual assault, conspiracy to commit any of the above	Three	Mandatory life in prison with no parole eligibility

Source: Adapted from Clark, J., Austin, J., & Henry, D. A. (1997). *"Three strikes and you're out": A review of state legislation* [NCJ 165369]. National Institute of Justice Research in Brief. Washington, DC: Office of Justice Programs.

& Hollenhorst, 1998). But even these numbers are not as great as had been originally projected. Clark et al. (1997) report that after an initial period of adjustment that saw additional case processing time, greater jail populations, and an increase in jury trials, some California counties have learned to absorb the increases brought by the law, and the number of two- and three-strikes cases entering the CDC was even leveling off by 1997.

In addition to a better ability to handle strikes cases at the county and state levels, some have attributed the "less than expected" impact of California's laws to actions by prosecutors and judges that allow offenders to avoid being "out" even if they technically have enough strikes. At the prosecutor's level, this is accomplished when they subtract an infraction (i.e., striking a strike) to avoid invoking the long mandatory sentence and to secure a guilty plea in exchange (Dickey & Hollenhorst, 1998; Levinson, 1995). Discretion at the judges' level comes from a California Supreme Court ruling (*People v. Romero,* 13 Cal. 4th 497; 1996), that gives judges the authority to ignore in three-strikes cases a prior conviction when a minimum sentence of twenty-five years would be too severe.

To the extent that three-strikes laws were passed to ensure that offenders convicted repeatedly of serious offenses would be removed from society for long periods of time, even life, the analysis to date suggests those laws are having little impact. With only a few states reporting any significant use of the laws (Dickey & Hollenhorst, 1998), it is not surprising that analysts are concluding that, with the exception of California, most of the laws will have minimal impact on the state prison systems (Clark et al., 1997).

Aggravating and Mitigating Circumstances

A goal of determinate sentencing, sentencing guidelines, mandatory minimum sentences, and three-strikes provisions is to reduce the discretion of judges. That is partly an attempt to achieve fairness in sentences given to different offenders convicted of similar crimes and in sentences given by different judges throughout a jurisdiction. In addition, reducing discretion is a way the legislature can have greater impact on sentencing and presumably assure their constituents that stiff penalties will be imposed when necessary. But in most of those jurisdictions the judges still have some discretion available because they are often allowed to take aggravating and mitigating circumstances into consideration.

Legislatures have realized that they cannot anticipate all the different aspects of a particular case. Deciding that all convictions of robbery with a weapon will require a prison term of eight years may sound reasonable as a general principle. But what happens when the convicted robber not only carried a weapon but also repeatedly kicked the victim while the victim was lying face down on the sidewalk? Is the determinate or presumptive eight-year sentence harsh enough for this case? On the other hand, what if the convicted robber had no prior criminal record and engaged in this crime only at the urging of his older brother, who has two prior robbery convictions? Should the younger brother receive the same eight-year sentence as his older brother?

Because some cases are more serious or less serious than the standard incident, legislatures often allow judges to vary from the determinate or presumptive sentence when either aggravating or mitigating circumstances are present. **Aggravating circumstances** refer to situations that require a tougher sentence, whereas **mitigating circumstances** are situations requiring a lighter sentence. Similarly, under sentencing guidelines the judge is often allowed to impose a sentence outside the guidelines if circumstances of the case warrant such departure.

When aggravating or mitigating circumstances lead a judge's sentence to depart from the determinate or guideline sentence, many jurisdictions require the judge to provide written justification for the deviation. Actually, departures occur fairly often. Looking at the Federal Sentencing Guidelines, for example, we find that in 1996 about one-third of all sentences departed from the guidelines. About 33 percent were downward and 1 percent were upward departures (Maguire & Pastore, 1998, Table 5.35). Most of the downward departures were the result of a motion by the government for a reduced sentence because of the defendant's substantial assistance to authorities.

In addition to using different sentencing features with the three sentencing systems, sentencing in the United States also gets its diversity from the ways used to reduce the actual time offenders spend under their sentence.

Methods for Reducing Sentence Time

Determinate sentencing, mandatory minimum sentencing, and truth-in-sentencing laws have reflected a just deserts trend. A result of those sentencing practices and of things such as increased statutory penalties has been crowded prisons in many jurisdictions. To make sure there is space available to imprison new arrivals, the states and federal prison systems must release offenders currently in confinement. Several little "tricks of the trade" have been used over the years to help make sure there is room for newly sentenced prisoners.

Jail Time. Defendants often are kept in jail while awaiting their trial—and sometimes that can be quite a wait. For defendants pleading not guilty to the charges brought against them, the Speedy Trial Act of 1974 requires the federal government to hold a trial within 100 days of arrest. State jurisdictions have restrictions ranging from Minnesota's 60 days (between indictment and trial) to Indiana and Massachusetts's 365 days (between arrest and trial). The most frequent time limit is 180 days, either from arrest to trial or indictment to trial, as set in nine states (Zawitz, 1988).

Six months may seem a long time to wait for a trial, but the actual time is often even longer. Speedy trial limits can be ignored in certain situations, such as when the delay is caused by requests from the defense. In 1994 the average time between arrest and sentencing was 190 days for defendants pleading guilty and 269 days for defendants going to trial (Maguire & Pastore, 1998, Table 5.63).

Not all defendants will be in jail between arrest and trial or even arrest and sentencing. But for those who have been in jail, it is quite possible that they have been locked up for six months before they even begin to serve an actual sentence. This situation of **jail time** presents both fairness and practical issues. Regarding fairness, should the defendant's eventual sentence take into consideration the time already spent in jail? For practical purposes, couldn't crowded jail and prison conditions be lessened if sentences were shortened by taking jail time into consideration?

States have responded differently to the issue of jail time, but most have chosen to give inmates some credit for time served before sentencing. In some jurisdictions the offender must make a formal request to the judge, asking that jail time be deducted from the sentence imposed. In other jurisdictions the presentence jail time is automatically deducted from the eventual sentence.

Good Time. The concept of **good time,** which is also discussed in Chapter 14, refers to a reduction of days from a sentence as a result of statutory provisions, the offender's good behavior, or extra work by the offender. Good time, like jail time, essentially addresses issues of fairness and practicality. To reward good behavior (a fairness matter) and to encourage compliance with institutional rules (a practical matter), prison inmates usually have the opportunity to cut down their sentence length through good-time deductions.

Good time typically falls into three categories: statutory good time, earned good time, and meritorious good time. **Statutory good time** is usually given automatically when inmates serve their time without problems. When inmates receive good-time credit as the result of good behavior, or through participation in work or education programs, it is often called **earned good time.** A few states reward **meritorious good time** to inmates who perform exceptional acts or services such as fire fighting or working in emergency conditions (Davis, 1990). For example, whereas qualified California inmates in any of the state's facilities and programs might potentially perform a heroic act suitable for a meritorious time reduction, those assigned to the Conservation Camp program have increased opportunities to be heroic. The men and women in that program live and work in some of the state's most secluded wilderness areas and provide a large force of trained crews for wildland fire fighting and other natural disasters, and for search and rescue missions.

Although good-time deductions were originally given only after a period of good behavior, many states automatically deduct the good time the day the offender arrives at prison (Davis, 1990). As long as the inmate behaves, his or her release date

Because they more often find themselves in dangerous situations, such as fighting fires, inmates assigned to the California Conservation Camp programs have increased opportunities to earn meritorious good time for heroic efforts.

will be the actual sentence less the good-time deduction. For example, in a jurisdiction in which good time amounts to one-third of the sentence, offenders sentenced to six years will be told upon entering prison that they will be released in four years as long as they maintain good behavior. When inmates misbehave, they lose part of their good-time deduction. Their release date is then figured from the actual sentence less the good time that was not taken away by prison officials. So an inmate who loses six months of good time for misbehavior will be released after serving four years and six months of a six-year sentence.

Other states using good time (Hawaii, Montana, and Utah reported no good-time deductions in 1996 and Wisconsin has "bad time," which allows the adding of time to the mandatory release date) deduct it from the sentence only after it has been earned by the inmate (Bureau of Justice Assistance, 1998). Not only can this earned good time be withheld in the first place, it can also be taken away (except in a few jurisdictions) as a disciplinary measure. Consider an example in which inmates can earn up to forty-five days credit per month. In this way, a five-year sentence could be served in three years and four months. Misbehaving inmates may not receive their forty-five days at the end of the month, or they could even lose days already earned if the prison disciplinary board sees fit.

Good time is easily seen as correction's carrot for good behavior because the deductions will affect either parole eligibility (primarily indeterminate sentences) or the discharge date (determinate and some guideline sentences). The inmates' fear of losing good time, therefore, gives prison officials an impressive disciplinary tool for controlling prisoner behavior. But good time also has a management aspect; it is useful in coping with prison crowding. Longer prison sentences obviously increase the prison population. Legislators can use good time to reduce the impact of increasing sentence length by boosting the number of good-time deductions an inmate can earn. In this way legislators can appease the public's demand for longer sentences (increase burglary from three years to five years) yet keep the prison population at a reasonable level (increase good-time credit from ten days to fifteen days per month).

With jail-time and good-time deductions, it is difficult to know exactly how long a person's sentence to prison will actually be. The public might be pleased to hear that an offender convicted in a highly publicized rape case was sentenced to ten years in prison. You can appreciate the citizens' surprise when they read in the paper just four years later that the guy is being released from prison. If the offender had been in jail for nine months between his arrest and sentencing, received one day of good-time credit for each day served once he got to prison, and had additional earned good-time credit for participating in training programs, it is quite possible that he could serve a ten-year sentence in less than five years.

Concurrent Sentencing. Both jail time and good time are techniques that effectively reduce the time offenders must serve on their sentences. Another way to reduce sentence time is through **concurrent sentencing,** which is a strategy that can be used by the judge. When offenders plead or are found guilty of several offenses (or several counts of the same offense), they are subject to sentencing on each crime or count. If Anna is charged with trespass, burglary, and theft, she could risk eight years in prison if her jurisdiction has, for example, sentencing guidelines suggesting one year for trespass, three years for burglary, and four years for theft.

For a number of reasons, including public relations, prosecutors may believe it is desirable to gain a conviction on each charge. But the prosecutor also knows that multiple sentences will mean that Anna takes up space in prison for eight years (ignoring jail time and good time). During periods of crowding, the prosecutor may want to avoid having property offenders occupying prison space that could be used for violent offenders. This is Anna's third felony conviction, however, and it seems that harsh action is necessary. An option the prosecutor has is to request that the judge sentence Anna on each charge but then have the sentences run concurrently. Normally an offender will serve multiple sentences one after the other (i.e., consecutively). If sentenced consecutively, Anna would serve eight years in prison. If the judge has the sentences run concurrently, Anna will serve all three sentences at the same time and will essentially have four years (the longest of the three sentences) rather than eight years to serve.

Jail time, good time, and concurrent sentencing give legislators, judges, and prison officials ways to help control the number of inmates in prison. Furthermore, especially in the case of good time, control can also be exerted over the inmates' behavior while in prison. All of these techniques have been around for decades, but they have become especially helpful under determinate and presumptive sentencing. Those sentencing systems have increased state and federal prison populations to the point that prisoners must be released to make room for the next group coming in. With the aid of jail time, good time, and concurrent sentencing, justice officials can reflect a just deserts response to criminals (lock 'em up) while still allowing the system to operate (let 'em out) in a reasonably efficient manner.

This discussion of basic sentencing systems and some features of those systems provides a general framework for understanding how sentences are imposed. Although much of the foregoing uses imprisonment to explain the sentencing system or feature, we must realize that imprisonment is simply one of several forms the sentence can take. This becomes apparent as we consider the variety of sentence types available under each sentencing system.

SENTENCE TYPES

As shown in Table 5.6 on page 149, a wide variety of sentence types are available to judges. Although sentencing guidelines and mandatory minimum sentencing place some restrictions on the sentence types that can be imposed, judges still have significant discretion in the sentencing process (see "Shame on You!" on page 150 and "A School for Johns" on page 151). Importantly, judges are not restricted

Judges are not restricted to giving standard sentences such as probation or imprisonment. Shown here are Tonya Kline (left) and her mother Deborah Harter. In 1995 a South Carolina judge ordered Tonya to be tethered to one of her parents instead of going to a juvenile detention facility.

to using just one of the sentence types. Some types obviously cannot occur together (e.g., a person could not be executed and placed on probation), but for the most part several different sentence types can be included as part of the actual sentence. Consider, for example, Keith's case. After Keith's conviction for burglary, Judge Jewell requests a presentence investigation from the probation department. The results of that investigation tell Judge Jewell that this is Keith's second conviction for burglary in the past three years. For the first conviction Keith was placed on probation for nine months, and he successfully completed that sentence without incident. Believing that this second conviction requires a harsher punishment, Judge Jewell sentences Keith to probation again but with the special condition that he reside at the local halfway house. The sentence also requires Keith to pay restitution of $500 to the victim of his crime and to perform fifty hours of unpaid labor that will benefit his community. This sentence, which uses probation, residential community corrections, restitution, and community service, is a reasonable example of combining sentence types.

The sentence types listed in Table 5.6 are considered formal sanctions because they are typically imposed by the court following rules set by the legislature. In addition to such formal sanctions, there are examples of **informal sanctions** increasingly being used. They are called informal because they rely on persons not directly affiliated with the court—or at least not acting in the role of traditional court officials. This chapter on sentencing concludes with a brief look at informal sanctions and with an introduction to formal sanctions, which are the focus of the book's remaining chapters.

Informal Sanctions: Compensation and Mediation Examples

Society's formal response to criminal behavior is the focus of this book, but a formal response is not the only means of social control. Informal social control techniques are considered by some people to be more effective than formal action

TABLE 5.6: Sentence Types

Death penalty	For the most serious crimes, such as murder, the courts in most states may sentence an offender to death by lethal injection, electrocution, exposure to lethal gas, hanging, or other method specified by state law [*see Chapter 6*].
Incarceration	The confinement of a convicted criminal in a federal or state prison or a local jail to serve a court-imposed sentence. Confinement is usually in a jail, administered locally, or a prison, operated by the state or federal government. In many states, offenders sentenced to one year or less are held in a jail; those sentenced to longer terms are committed to a state prison [*see Chapters 8, 9, and 10*].
Probation	The sentencing of an offender to community supervision by a probation agency, often as a result of suspending a sentence to confinement. Such supervision normally entails specific rules of conduct while in the community. If the rules are violated, a sentence to confinement may be imposed. Probation is the most widely used correctional disposition in the United States [*see Chapter 7*].
Split sentences, shock probation, and intermittent confinement	A penalty that explicitly requires the convicted person to serve a brief period of confinement in a local, state, or federal facility (the "shock") followed by a period of probation. This penalty attempts to combine the use of community supervision with a short incarceration experience. Some sentences are periodic rather than continuous; for example, an offender may be required to spend a certain number of weekends in jail [*see Chapters 7 and 8*].
Restitution and victim compensation	The offender is required to provide financial repayment or, in some jurisdictions, services in lieu of monetary restitution, for the losses incurred by the victim [*see Chapter 7*].
Community service	The offender is required to perform a specified amount of public service work, such as collecting trash in parks or other public facilities [*see Chapter 7*].
Fines	An economic penalty that requires the offender to pay a specified sum of money within limits set by law. Fines often are imposed in addition to probation or as an alternative to incarceration [*see Chapter 5*].

Source: Adapted from Zawitz, M. W. (Ed.). (1988). *Report to the nation on crime and justice.* (2nd ed.) [NCJ 105506]. Washington, DC: Department of Justice, Bureau of Justice Statistics.

when trying to encourage law-abiding behavior. If you avoid criminal behavior out of respect for the values and norms of family or friends, informal controls are most likely having a greater impact on you than are the laws designed to punish your misbehavior. When Donna "chooses" not to steal because it would be the wrong thing to do, it might be argued that she is being "controlled" by informal forces such as parental values rather than formal forces such as section 18-3456 of her state's penal code.

Theories of criminal behavior show us that understanding where and when crime occurs, and who and why people commit it, is infinitely more complicated than simply distinguishing informal and formal social control efforts. But citizens in many countries around the world, including the United States, are more often looking toward informal punishments as a way of responding to criminal behavior. Sometimes these efforts lie totally outside the formal control process, but increasingly they are offered as options within that formal process. Moderate sanctions seem especially well suited to informal justice, so this discussion begins with a few examples of that type before moving to the formal moderate sanctions.

Chapter 2 discussed the importance of concepts such as retribution and restoration in establishing community responses to law violators. With their firm

Spotlight ON CONTEMPORARY ISSUES

Shame on You!

The 1990s saw a resurgence in the use of sentences that had a goal of shaming or degrading the offender. The concept fits well with the just deserts philosophy and retribution because shaming sentences are often meant to reflect the crime. However, shaming has a much longer history than its recent application might indicate. Ancient societies used punishments that included public denunciation, and from the twelfth to sixteenth centuries English criminal law made liberal use of shaming display punishments such as the pillory, branding, public stocks, and ducking stools. On the European continent, degrading punishments included tarring and feathering, wearing degrading garments, and stone-carrying. This last punishment, which was inflicted mostly on women, required the offender to carry a stone hung round her neck and then walk a prescribed distance and route lined with onlookers who provided verbal and even physical abuse (e.g., egg throwing). Should the stone (weighing, depending on the crime, as little as 25 pounds or as heavy as 200 pounds) be set down along the way, a fine would be assessed against the offender or, more accurately, the offender's husband (Hinckeldey, 1993).

Contemporary versions of colonial scarlet letters are found in bumper stickers that drunk drivers must place on their cars to identify themselves to other drivers, or to the signs that some child molesters have been required to wear or place in their front yard, announcing to all their offense. Instead of being placed on public display in the stocks, today's offenders may be required to wear prison stripes as they work on chain gangs or a sandwich board, proclaiming their crime, as they walk up and down a sidewalk.

Shaming punishments are sometimes linked to corporal punishment, which is covered in Chapter 6. However, in the context of shame and punishment you can read from the first edition of Graeme Newman's *Just and Painful: A Case for the Corporal Punishment of Criminals* at ***www.albany.edu/~grn92/jp00.html.*** Read Newman's chapter "A Punishment Manifesto." Are there situations in which Newman favors humiliation of the offender? Also read his chapter "Pain Is Not Evil." Why does Newman believe the application of punishment should be essentially public?

basis in tradition, retribution and restoration have influenced the idea of justice in countries throughout the world. In precolonial Africa, for example, justice systems rarely used imprisonment to react toward law violators. Instead, emphasis was on community participation and victim-centered sanctions of compensation. Custody of the offender was avoided, and offenders were required to remain in the community and try to return affairs to their standing before the offender's misbehavior. Other countries, such as Japan and Germany, give their formal justice officials the discretion to handle some cases informally. There are even examples of countries, such as China, in which a courtlike procedure follows what appears to be a formal court process but is actually a component that acts in place of the courts (see "China's Mediation Committees" on page 152). Following are some examples of these informal responses to misbehavior.

African Countries. Colonial powers pushed nearly all sub-Saharan African countries to set up Western criminal justice systems. This westernization of African justice required, among other things, that Africans begin viewing crime as a dispute between the government and the criminal rather than holding the traditional view of crime as a clash between the victim and the offender. Precolonial African societies used both corporal and capital punishment (see Milner, 1969), but the preferred response to criminal behavior was through **compensation.** Under the precolonial process, community members required offenders to compensate victims for the wrong done. Through this compensation the victim was made whole again, and balance was returned to the community.

ISSUES OF FAIRNESS

A SCHOOL FOR JOHNS

Despite the obviousness of it "taking two to tango," the woman is traditionally the only person arrested and punished in the typical prostitution case. That tradition is changing in several communities around the country. Places such as Aurora, Colorado, are publishing in the local newspaper photographs of men arrested for soliciting prostitution. But one of the more unique ways to include men when punishing the crime of prostitution is to involve the prostitutes themselves.

Nieves (1999) and Leslie (1999) tell about "john schools" in San Francisco and St. Paul, Minnesota. San Francisco's version (more formally, the First Offender Prostitution Program) was started in 1995 by a former prostitute with the assistance of a police lieutenant and an assistant prosecutor. Modeled after the daylong traffic schools for bad drivers, the john school is trying to drum some sense into those who perpetuate it. The technique is similar to the "scared straight" programs in which older offenders try to convince youngsters to change their ways. Nieves provides an example of what the johns hear while attending the school:

> Angel Cassidy, a dark-haired woman in her early 30s who started working the streets when she was 14, told the men that she lied when clients would ask if she was a heroin addict. "I'd have needle tracks all up and down my arms and say no," she said. She would have unprotected sex, she said, even though she had had several venereal diseases. She fantasized about maiming the men. (Nieves, 1999)

The day's course of study also included a lecture on the laws against soliciting, color slides showing the affects of venereal disease, rebukes from people living in prostitution-plagued neighborhoods, and a few more lectures by angry ex-prostitutes who hurled insults at the men and told them how they had wanted to "stick a knife in you."

The St. Paul program, modeled after San Francisco's, hopes the program will force men who buy sex to consider the impact of their illegal behavior and to understand that prostitution is not a victimless crime. As one of the judges who will be sentencing men to the john school says, "The communities where this takes place suffer immensely, people get AIDS, marriages break up, wives, mothers and children are solicited. They're all victims" (Leslie, 1999).

Although no one expects the programs will stop prostitution, the john school coupled with other procedures—such as outreach programs to help prostitutes find an alternative to street life—may reduce the level of street prostitution.

Visit the St. Paul Police Department's "prostitution reduction" page at ***www.stpaul.gov/police/prostitution.html.*** What are the reasons given there for creating this Web page? Do you agree or disagree with the reasons provided?

Compensation was deemphasized by the Western criminal justice systems, which instead championed the benefits of deterrence, rehabilitation, and incapacitation. In Nigeria, for example, the British brought administrative pressure on the native courts to understand that the restitution of stolen property, or even the return of an abducted person, were not sufficient penalties. The British opinion that restitution and compensation were insufficient penalties for crime was made clear in the early 1900s, when colonial officials were encouraged to always add a "punishment" to restitution (Milner, 1969).

The British view of compensation being nonpunitive took hold in the formal court system created by the colonists. The native courts, which were allowed to remain active for certain crimes, imposed compensation more often than did the formal courts (Milner, 1969). But the official justice process began emphasizing such penal objectives as deterrence and reformation. The lingering effects of colonialism means even today's postcolonial African countries find themselves in the paradoxical situation of having the courts infrequently order compensation in a

Cross-Cultural Corrections

China's Mediation Committees

Informal justice in places such as Africa, Japan, and Germany highlight ways that officials can divert people from the formal social control process. But the eventual informal sanctions used in these situations are still the result of action by the formal agents of social control. China offers an interesting example of informal justice that avoids any link to the formal or official agencies of social control.

Clark (1989) provides a detailed description of local negotiation of conflict in China. He realizes that Westerners may feel ill at ease with neighbors, fellow workers, and other acquaintances taking a significant interest in the behavior of people around them. The Chinese, however, see responsibility both to others and for others as an obligation shared by everyone. As a result, conflict among a few citizens becomes a concern and responsibility for many citizens.

The organizational structure of Chinese society moves from the broad national level to the smallest level of the neighborhood committee, which typically consists of four subcommittees. One of those subcommittees is the mediation committee, whose size (usually twelve or more local citizens) provides one mediator for a group of families (Clark, 1989).

Persons serving as mediators are elected by fellow citizens. The mediators receive training on legal aspects of their new position and on the techniques of conflict resolution. Technically, the mediators do not handle criminal cases, but Clark (1989) found some mediator's cases (such as minor theft) to be ones that could clearly have been handled under the criminal code.

It is not clear at what point mediators will intervene in a dispute because most mediations are unrecorded—lending, of course, to the informality of the process. But when mediators do get involved, their role is to encourage talk and to be persuasive. With their knowledge of local conditions, mediators gather extensive information about the situation even before direct intervention. Because of this early and purposeful start, it is unlikely that mediators could ever receive a case about which they did not already have significant information (Clark, 1989). But an early start does not mean there will be an early solution. As Clark notes, mediators are aware that the entire community, not just the disputants, must live with the mediator's decision. Because of that, mediation may involve several weeks and many meetings before resolution.

Participants at the mediation sessions include the conflicting parties and the mediator, but may also involve others on the mediation committee, legal advisors, Communist Party officials, or interested neighbors. Disputants are each encouraged to tell their own story without fear of interruption or challenge, and the mediator then attempts to find common ground that will allow for a settlement.

China's social control process is being made more formal as the official legal system evolves. But efforts are being made to ensure the informality of out-of-court mediation even when social control becomes more closely linked to professional justice actors.

Read Article 111 in the Constitution of the People's Republic of China at ***www.qis.net/chinalaw/prccon5.htm#chap35,*** and identify the structure and duties of the "residents' committees and villagers' committees." You might also find interesting the formal court system in China. Go to ***www.chinatoday.com/law/supreme.htm,*** and identify the three responsibilities of China's Supreme People's Court.

cultural environment that regards compensation as an integral part of dispute settlement (Adeyemi, 1994).

But, even as they did under colonial rule, African citizens typically have other social control options available than just the formal ones provided in the modern court system. The native, or customary, courts still have only limited jurisdiction in criminal matters, but these more informal sanctioning systems can make greater use of the African tradition of compensation.

In those African countries where they operate, **customary courts** are part of the criminal justice system but function within a structure based on custom rather than statute. That attention to custom means the native courts are more likely to rely on the tradition of compensation than are the courts that make up the more formal justice process. In Nigeria and Gambia, for example, Adeyemi (1994) reports that native courts use compensation three times as much as do the Western-type courts in those countries. Furthermore, some 20 percent of unintentional homicide, 60 percent of theft, 40 percent of rape and defilement, and 67 percent of assault cases were settled through compensation without resorting to the formal criminal process (Adeyemi, 1994).

It seems unfortunate that the tradition of compensation has been essentially transferred out of the modern justice system in African countries. With restorative justice and compensation becoming popular ideas around the world, it would have been quite helpful to be able to analyze procedures that had been operating for centuries in countries such as Nigeria and Kenya. But because colonial powers imposed a Western-type justice system throughout Africa, today's African countries merely have an older tradition rather than extended formal application of compensation's role in modern justice systems.

Japan. As with any society, Japan is influenced by cultural traits that are important in providing a context within which the Japanese people behave (see Reichel, 1999). Two such cultural traits, contextualism and harmony, are especially important in understanding the Japanese preference for informal justice.

Standards of morality and ethics in Japan are decided by reference to the group rather than to rigid legal codes. Because of this, what is moral can vary depending on the situation or context in which people find themselves. There are not, in other words, absolute standards of morality that dictate proper behavior for all situations. This acceptance of contextualism means that there may be times when another important cultural trait, harmony, is upset.

The Japanese socialization process emphasizes the importance of maintaining harmony in social situations. Of course, complete and continual harmony can only be an ideal, so many Japanese become adept at portraying harmony even when it does not exist. As a result, observers may see social relations only as the actors want them to appear rather than how they actually are.

Putting the concepts of contextualism and harmony together, there are situations (contexts) in which deviant behavior (disharmony or conflict) may occur, but the actors want to handle the situation so that harmony is achieved—or at least appears to be achieved. In this manner, the offender and victim and the primary groups each represents can avoid the embarrassment of appearing unable to maintain harmony by putting a harmonious face on the situation.

Informal social control techniques more easily lend themselves to portraying and achieving harmony than do formal control techniques. When conflict is dealt with by formal arrest, court appearance, and required reporting to probation officers, it is difficult to convince anyone involved that this is a harmonious situation. But if the conflict is handled informally between the victim, offender, and control agent, it is possible to portray and even achieve harmony. Because informal sanctions are more likely than formal ones to be private, indirect, and ambiguous, they can be virtually invisible to society. Consider, for example, some typical responses by police and prosecutors in Japan.

In Japan, self-worth and identity stem primarily from the groups to which a person belongs. This significance of group membership is accepted by most Japanese, as are the obligations that accompany group membership. One of those obligations is to avoid embarrassing the group. If a person does act in an embarrassing way, as when committing a crime, the offender should do his or her best to avoid public display of the misconduct (i.e., avoid the appearance of disharmony).

The police, of course, are fully aware of this pressure to avoid embarrassing one's family, friends, colleagues, and so on. They use this knowledge to successfully handle many criminal events informally. The use of an apology is a particular

Police officers in Japan exemplify informal justice when, instead of making an arrest, they allow the accused to apoligize to the victim of a minor crime.

favorite of police officers on the beat. Bayley (1991) gives several examples of police accepting apologies as a reason to halt further processing of a case. Drunks, traffic offenders, and minors smoking in public are examples of persons who could be asked to apologize to the law-abiding citizens who may have been harmed or offended by the misconduct. The conflict could also be on a more personal level, as the following example suggests:

> Late one night [police] officers were summoned by a young woman to save her from a man who, she said, had tried to force her to come to a hotel. It turned out that they had had an affair some time before and he, meeting her by accident, wanted to resume it on the spur of the moment. The woman was both furious and scared. The man, flashily dressed in a pink shirt and white slacks, was very embarrassed and steadfastly maintained that he had only asked her to come for a cup of tea. Discounting his denials, [the police] lectured him sternly about using threats. Then the officers arranged that if he apologized to the woman and wrote a letter saying he would not do this again, the woman would sign an undertaking that she would not press charges. Taken into the room where the woman was, he shuffled his feet reluctantly and with bad grace mumbled "Sumimasen ne"—"I'm really sorry." (Bayley, 1991, p. 127)

Although people in the United States may consider giving an apology to be an easy way out for the offender, an apology from the Japanese is an admission of having failed in their obligation to the group. It is not easy to admit that one has disrupted the harmony or jeopardized his or her group standing. For the Japanese, an apology can be a punishment for the now-embarrassed offender and an expression of remorse to compensate the victim.

The Japanese preference for informal handling of misbehavior seems linked to aspects of their cultural heritage. But do not assume that a society's willingness to use informal sanctions requires a preexisting tradition. A popular option in Germany actually goes against the German tradition of formally prosecuting all convictable cases.

Germany. Since 1975, prosecutors in Germany can use an interesting alternative to the formal criminal processing of misdemeanor offenders. This option is particularly intriguing in Germany because it emphasizes the trend toward informal sanctioning, although German tradition has always required prosecutors to bring formal charges in every case in which evidence was sufficient for conviction.

As described by Weigend (1993), section 153a of the German Code of Criminal Procedure is based on the idea that the public interest in prosecution can be satisfied by having the offender make a payment or perform another action that will benefit the public. Under section 153a, misdemeanor offenders can avoid a criminal trial and a conviction, thereby avoiding a criminal record, by paying a sum of money to the victim, a charitable organization, or the state. "By compensating the victim, or by giving to charity, the defendant implicitly acknowledges his responsibility for the offense [while showing] his willingness to act in a socially commendable way" (Weigend, 1993, p. 15).

Although this procedure may look like a fine, the German statute very carefully avoids any such reference because linking the compensatory payment to a fine would present serious legal problems (see "That'll Be Eight Packs of Diapers, Please" for an American version of a donation program). The payment under section 153a precedes conviction, so imposing a fine (i.e., a sentence) before conviction would clearly violate the presumption of innocence and have prosecutors rather than judges setting sentences. To avoid such complications, payments under section 153a require the prior consent of the defendant and are, therefore, considered voluntary—unlike a fine sentence, which does not require or seek the offender's consent.

Spotlight ON CONTEMPORARY ISSUES

That'll Be Eight Packs of Diapers, Please

Josh, a student in a college town, was sentenced on misdemeanor charges of drinking under age—not a particularly unusual offense in many college towns. The sentence, however, was unusual. Dunn (1999) reports that the judge's order that Josh perform twenty-four hours of community service was actually completed by Josh in less than one hour. Instead of serving his time picking up trash or assisting at a local homeless shelter, Josh bought eight packs of diapers that he then donated to a local nonprofit agency.

Donation programs are popping up in local jurisdictions across the country as court officials seek alternative sentences. The Weld County, Colorado, program in which Josh was sentenced is operated by Intervention Community Corrections Program, which is responsible for supervising some of the people sentenced to probation and community service. Under the donation program, offenders have the option to work off their public service by purchasing items from a list of food, clothing, and other goods. The purchased items are donated to any nonprofit agency needing them. In its first four months of operation, the program collected more than $27,000 worth of food, clothing, diapers, shoes, and other items (Dunn, 1999). Equally important, the program reported 100 percent compliance in its initial four months compared with the typical 67 percent compliance of those completing community service by working.

The amount to be spent by the offender is computed by multiplying the number of hours the person is sentenced to perform by the minimum wage of $5.15 per hour. Josh had a sentence of twenty-four hours so he had to spend $123.60 and then bring his purchases and receipt to the program office. With confirmation that the requirements were completed, Josh was considered to have met his community service obligation.

Donation programs exemplify the type of punishment that might result from conferencing programs. Go to the RealJustice site at ***www.realjustice.org/Pages/whatisconferencing.html***, and identify how conferences could be used by the police, courts, or corrections agencies. Can conferencing also be used to respond to inappropriate behavior in schools and the workplace?

Weigend (1993) explains that either the prosecution or the defense can initiate the conditional dismissal under section 153a. Most often it is the prosecutor who proposes dismissal (with a judge's approval in more serious cases) and suggests an appropriate amount to be paid, although the defendant can make a counteroffer. The victim need not be consulted before dismissal is offered to the defendant. The defendant is not required to confess guilt but only to agree to the proposed disposition. When the defendant submits proof that the required payment was made, or work assignment fulfilled, the prosecutor dismisses the case and no criminal record is made of the incident.

Over 240,000 conditional dismissals were given in 1989 in (West) Germany. Traffic offenses, shoplifting, and other petty property offenses were typically handled through voluntary money payments. Because U.S. citizens often view misdemeanors as involving trivial matters, it is important to note that German law categorizes actions such as aggravated assault, fraud, extortion, and most economic and environmental offenses as misdemeanors (Weigend, 1993).

German critics of conditional dismissal are bothered by the increased discretion section 153a gives to prosecutors and by the haggling over how much the dismissal will cost. This would be less of a concern in the United States, where there is a long tradition of unlimited prosecutorial discretion and of bartering on both charges and sentences. Another argument of the critics is not so easily dismissed in either Germany or the United States. Because the conditional dismissal allows defendants to avoid possible conviction and any criminal record of the event, there is a question regarding how voluntary the consent to make payments can be. The prosecutor's offer to dismiss in exchange for payments may be an offer the accused cannot refuse—even if they are innocent or otherwise unconvictable. Although these criticisms are important considerations, Weigend concludes that when "properly limited to minor offenses . . . conditional dismissal is a sensible solution with obvious advantages for all concerned" (1993, p. 16).

Help Wanted

Job Title: Mediation Project Assistant

Position Description: Perform a variety of support, logistical, case, and volunteer management duties related to a restorative justice project. Perform initial intake steps for mediations and other cases. Train volunteers and interns in office procedures.

Qualifications: Experience providing support services in an office environment. Mediation/restorative justice experience (including volunteer and intern) is preferred. College-level coursework in a related field is highly desirable.

For examples of career opportunities in this field, visit the Conflict Resolution Resource Center at ***www.conflict-resolution.net*** and see its job listing.

Mediation in the United States. Before the twelfth century, victims were very clearly the people who suffered harm from the actions of others. Crime was a conflict between the person claiming harm and the person accused of causing the harm. With the growth of the state, initially as the monarch, crime became viewed as a harm primarily against the government. The person actually being harmed received less and less attention as crime was increasingly considered a conflict between the offender and the state (the new victim). Punishment became seen as something that required the offender to pay a debt to society rather than to the person actually harmed.

The philosophy of restorative justice argues that the person who was violated by a crime must be considered the primary victim, while the state is reduced to the status of secondary victim. When this is accomplished, crime again becomes a conflict between people (victim and offender), and punishment now requires the offender to pay a debt to the person harmed instead of to an abstract entity called the state. This can be done through a variety of procedures, but those most common in Western societies over the past several decades have involved victim–offender mediation. A review of some American versions will provide one example of how informal justice is approached in the United States.

Victim–offender mediation programs take several forms, but they are most often used in cases of property offenses committed by first-time offenders who are juveniles (see "Can One Mediate Abuse?"). This may seem too restrictive to be considered much of a trend, but it is important to remember that the United States' crime problem is primarily one of property offenses committed by persons under age twenty-one. Therefore, efforts directed at those specific crimes and offenders seem very well placed.

ISSUES OF FAIRNESS

CAN ONE MEDIATE ABUSE?

As the principles of restorative justice and the practice of victim–offender mediation grow in popularity, questions are increasingly asked about the kind of offenses that are appropriate for mediation. Victim–offender mediation programs (VOMP), which are also called victim–offender reconciliation programs (VORP), typically begin with property crimes as their concern. Mediation can be and certainly is being carried out with major violent crimes as well (e.g., see "Facing Up to Murder," 1999), but minor assaults are more often the extent to which mediation is currently used as a response to nonproperty offenses.

Of the violent crimes for which mediation could be a response, spouse abuse is one of the most controversial. Klein (1998) explains that a primary difficulty in using VOMP for abuse cases is the type of relationship often found between victim and abuser. Persons opposed to mediation in abuse cases believe the imbalance in the relationship means that any negotiation or mediation that takes place between the parties will only reinforce and perpetuate the ongoing abuse. This imbalance is a feature distinguishing abuse crimes from most other offenses. In domestic cases the victim remains at far greater risk than, for example, does the victim in stranger crimes. Furthermore, because acts of domestic violence are part of a repeatedly occurring behavior pattern, it is unlikely that any "right relationship" or harmony existed before the specific act of violence now being addressed. There is, in other words, no balance for restorative justice to restore!

Although recognizing that abuse cases present special circumstances, Klein (1998) does not believe they are always inappropriate for mediation and restorative justice. Instead, he argues, the emphasis in domestic cases must "... begin with victim restoration—restoring the victim as an independent, capable, strong, empowered individual—all the elements the abuser tried to take from the victim.... First and foremost, to be restored, the victim must be able to live without fear and threat from the abuser" (Klein, 1998).

These are goals in which domestic violence intervention advocates (who often reject the possibility of mediation in abuse cases) would agree with VOMP proponents. But it may be more difficult to find agreement regarding treatment of the offender. Ideally, abusers should sit down, apologize to their partners, leave the victims' and their children alone—or continue to live together in peace and harmony. But because batterers, more than other criminals, are likely to believe they did nothing wrong, it may be very difficult to get them to accept responsibility for their actions. Because that acceptance of responsibility is a necessary ingredient for mediation and restorative justice, it may be that VOMP will not be effective in abuse cases. Klein wonders if it is possible to be partially restorative (toward the victim and community) and partially retributive (toward the offender). Is that the closest society might be able to come in using mediation for abuse cases?

Read some of the comments on the appropriateness of restorative justice for family violence cases at ***www.justice.govt.nz/pubs/reports/1998/restorative_justice/chapter_5.html.*** What else can you think of that would present problems with using restorative justice in abuse cases? Having read and thought about the problem, do you think restorative justice can be used in family violence cases? Other information about mediation is available from the victim–offender reconciliation program at ***www.vorp.com.***

Mark Umbreit, who conducted an empirical review of victim–offender mediation, gives us information helpful in understanding this application of restorative justice. As described by Umbreit (1994), the mediation process begins with an offender being referred by justice officials (probation staff, judges, or prosecutors) to a victim–offender mediation program. Many programs admit only offenders who have entered a formal admission of guilt, but some programs accept cases before such a declaration, when the offender is under deferred prosecution or another diversion effort.

Cases accepted in the program are assigned to a mediator who meets, separately at first, with both the victim and the offender. This allows the mediator to become familiar with each party's story, to explain the program, and to encourage participation. Typically the offender's consent to participate is gotten first, and then the mediator asks if the victim is willing to take part. After securing the agreement of both victim and offender, the mediator schedules a face-to-face meeting. At this meeting, the mediator explains his or her role, announces any ground rules that may be in effect, and explains the topics of the meeting.

As described in "In the Yard Again," the first part of a mediation session focuses on the facts and feelings related to the crime, with the victim usually going first. Distressing questions that might have haunted the victim for months (such as "Why me?", "How did you get into the house?", and "Were you stalking us and planning to come back?") can be asked and answered. This unique opportunity for crime victims to express their feelings directly to the person who violated them is considered by victims to be the most important aspect of the mediation process—even more important than receiving restitution for the losses (Umbreit, 1994).

Offenders also have an unusual opportunity in the mediation process. Although they are admittedly in an uncomfortable position, they can display human dimensions to their character (such as remorse) that cause the victims to see the offender in a broader and more complex manner. The process, in other words, al-

Spotlight ON CONTEMPORARY ISSUES

In the Yard Again

The following mediation meeting took place in a pleasant room in a neighborhood church. None of the participants are members of this particular church. The offender, Brian, is a fifteen-year-old white male charged with battery. The victim, Sarah, is a fourteen-year-old white female. She was struck in the leg by a pellet fired by the offender from his air rifle. The offender is accompanied by his mother; the victim, by her mother and stepfather. Also present is the mediator.

The offender is hesitant and avoids making eye contact with anyone. He finally finds a spot on the floor at which to stare. The victim anxiously fiddles with her hands. After the introduction, the mediator explains the ground rules for the meeting, as well as her role as mediator. She invites both sides to be respectful and open to telling their stories. The mediator invites Sarah to begin.

"I was in my own yard working in the garden. I was bent over weeding when I felt a sharp sting in my right leg. Some blood was oozing from my leg." The victim seems to lose concentration and is close to tears.

The mediator elicits more of Sarah's story. "What did you do then?"

"I turned around and saw him and his friend running toward his house. He had a gun in his hand. I thought, 'My God, he shot me!' And I started screaming."

"What happened then?"

The victim's mother responds. "I heard the screams and dashed out of the house to see what was wrong. A little blood was coming from her wound, but she was screaming almost beyond control. I got her into the house where we washed the wound. I felt a tiny hard lump and found the pellet but could not get it out."

"I called the police," chimed in the victim's stepfather, "and we took her to the trauma center at the hospital. Medical staff calmed her down and very simply removed the pellet. We then went home with a still very frightened girl on our hands. It was a helluva thing to happen: we had just moved in the weekend before."

"Brian, why don't you tell us what happened that morning?" asked the mediator.

Without glancing up, Brian responds, "Well, me and my friend were in the backyard shooting around. I didn't really aim at her. I didn't really think the gun could shoot that far."

"You didn't really want to hurt me?"

"No. I didn't think we could hit you even if I tried."

"Didn't you hear me yell?"

"Yeah."

"Well, then, why did you run away?"

"We were scared. Real scared. Thought maybe we had really hurt you."

Silence ensues. Victim and offender seem to feel that they have little to add.

lows both victim and offender to "deal with each other as people . . . rather than as stereotypes and objects" (Umbreit, 1994, p. 9).

During the second part of the mediation session, the losses incurred by the victim are reviewed, and discussion centers on ways to make things right. Umbreit (1994) reports that in 95 percent of all mediation sessions a written restitution agreement is successfully negotiated and signed by the victim, offender, and mediator. In those few cases in which an agreement is not reached, the case is returned to the referral source, and the offender will most likely be placed in a different program.

The first North American efforts at victim–offender reconciliation occurred in 1974 in the province of Ontario, Canada. In 1978 Elkhart, Indiana, began the first U.S. program. By the late 1990s there were some 300 victim–offender mediation programs in the United States and at least 26 in Canada (Umbreit, 1998). The idea is catching on around the world with over 100 programs in both Germany and Finland and at least 1 program in Australia, France, and South Africa. Two countries, Austria and New Zealand, have victim–offender mediation programs available in all their jurisdictions (Umbreit, 1998).

But not everyone sees the spread of mediation as based on firm ground. Weitekamp (1993) argues that victim–offender reconciliation programs promise more

---

The stepfather points out to the offender that things could have been worse. "You could have put out an eye: you could have blinded her."

"I know. I know. That's why we were so scared," the offender moans. "I'm sorry it happened. It was stupid." Both mothers are visibly moved by Brian's comments.

The mediator moves the discussion toward possible restitution. "I am sure that your apology is appreciated, Brian, but how else might you begin to repay Sarah and her family for the pain and suffering that they went through because of you?"

"I don't know."

Turning to Sarah's parents the mediator asks, "How much were the hospital bills?"

"Ah, $750 with a $300 deductible," Sarah's mother replies. "If he could repay the deductible," the victim's stepfather suggests, "we could call it even."

"Can you do that?" asks the mediator. The offender nods. The mediator continues. "With your paper-route job, you could pay $50 a month for six months. Is that OK with you?"

"Yeah, I can do that."

"Is that OK with everyone else?" The mediator looks around as all nod agreement.

As the mediator begins to fill out a contract form, the offender's mother says, "I think that $50 a month is fair, but I don't think it is enough given what we are trying to do here and given the amount of personal trauma that Brian caused Sarah and her family. I think he should have to do something more personal."

The mediator looks at Brian. "Do you have any ideas?"

"He could do my homework for a month," says Sarah with a relaxed smile.

"No, that won't be needed," chuckles Sarah's mother, "but some help with the yard would certainly be appreciated. And we do want to be good neighbors."

As the mediator writes up the contract there is some side discussion. The offender's mother talks about how embarrassing all of this has been and how she has punished Brian. "There is no more air rifle, ever."

All parties sign the contract. The mediator thanks everyone for coming and for being so cooperative. The families go out together, and the last comment heard was that of the offender's mother. "Now maybe I can go out in the yard again and look across the fence."

View a directory of mediation programs in the United States at ***ssw.che.umn.edu/ctr4rjm/Resources/VOMSurv/VOMSurv.htm.*** Does your state have a victim–offender mediation program? Click on your state, or another one of your choice, and determine which specific program is closest to your location. Visit or write that program for information on how it operates.

Source: From Umbreit, M. S. (1994). *Victim meets offender: The impact of restorative justice and mediation.* Monsey, NY: Criminal Justice Press. Reprinted with permission.

than they have delivered, and Umbreit (1994) notes that existing programs still have several problems. Some difficulties can be summarized as follows:

- Victim–offender mediation programs are applied in an unsystematic manner at the discretion and initiative of criminal justice administrators who support the programs at very different levels (Weitekamp, 1993). In the United States and Canada, for example, over 2,000 new laws and procedures for victim restitution and mediation were passed between 1975 and 1990. Unfortunately, there was no strategy uniting the laws and procedures, so that programs varied considerably from one jurisdiction to another. Not only was there little consistency in program application, implementation of the programs was often at the discretion of police, prosecutors, or judges rather than being mandatory.
- Some proponents of mediation programs put them forward as alternatives to imprisonment, but they do not seem to have that type of impact at all (Weitekamp, 1993). That is probably because the typical program client (first-time property offenders) would not be likely to receive a prison sentence anyway. But, the critics argue, if mediation programs do not provide an alternative to incarceration, their impact will be small.
- Program descriptions imply that offender participation in the mediation process is totally voluntary. Umbreit (1994) believes actual practice presents a different story because offenders are told that participation in mediation will mean they can avoid further formal prosecution. The "choice" of diversion from prosecution over traditional court appearances and traditional punishment may not be much of a choice ("Restorative Justice," 1998).
- The restorative justice theory does not claim to be applicable only to certain victims and offenders. But the reconciliation and mediation programs built on that theory are too often available in only certain cases. Specifically, juvenile, nonminority, and middle-class offenders are more often admitted to programs than are adults, minorities, and lower-class offenders (Weitekamp, 1993).
- As victim–offender mediation programs expand, they are likely to follow the path of other innovations and become more concerned with securing funding and establishing routine procedures than in achieving restorative justice (Umbreit, 1994). Growing out of this loss of vision could be the additional problems of taking only the "easy" cases and the tendency to widen the net so that persons whom the justice system would not otherwise have handled are now brought into the process.
- Mediation programs are often difficult to evaluate because they are set up without concrete goals and are often combined with other criminal justice and welfare programs (Weitekamp, 1993). Obviously, conducting a program evaluation when it is not clear what the program was to accomplish, and when subjects are simultaneously involved in other programs, is a methodological nightmare.

Those criticisms are each relevant and demand attention, but their complaints are focused mainly on problems of implementation. None of them attacks the core concept of informal justice. But there are those who see real problems stemming from an attempt by society to rely on informal over formal justice in general, or on mediation over litigation more specifically. Although he is more concerned with civil law than criminal law, Auerbach (1983) raises some interesting points in a book he titled *Justice Without Law?*—with the question mark being key. He argues that in societies with a formal justice system, informal justice is inevitably used to suppress the disadvantaged. Alternatives to formal justice, such as victim–offender mediation, can create a two-track justice system that dispenses informal justice to society's disadvantaged, while those with power get to use the formal justice system. "Justice according to law will be reserved for the affluent" (Auerbach, 1983, p. 144).

An argument similar to Auerbach's is made by Joseph and Carton (1992) in their analysis of law in the future as portrayed in the television series "Star Trek: The Next Generation." Law professors Joseph and Carton are intrigued by the apparent displacement in the future of legal formalism with informal procedures. "Star Trek" writers suggest to the viewers that in the twenty-fourth century people can rely "on the evolved goodness of the people involved [in a dispute] and on informal mechanisms of dispute resolution" (Joseph & Carton, 1992, p. 84). But several episodes of the series make it clear that informal justice is not always successful in arriving at accurate factual findings, nor in protecting individual rights. Because of that, formal justice must occasionally come to the rescue and save the television hour, if not the real-life day.

What Auerbach and Joseph and Carton seem to share is an appreciation for the formal system of justice. It has served society well in the past and will most likely serve society well in the future, so it is no surprise that it becomes a central feature in examining corrections.

Of the formal punishments used to sanction wrongdoers, fines have the potential to be a very severe sanction; but at least in the United States, the use of fines is at best only moderate in severity. Also, it will soon become apparent that U.S. jurisdictions tend to use punishments in combination. That is, although it is possible that a person's only punishment could be a fine or restitution, judges are more likely to impose sentences that make use of several types of punishment. This becomes increasingly noticeable when discussing intermediate sanctions such as probation and community service. However, the discussion begins with individual sanctions such as those covered in this section: suspended sentence, restitution, and fines.

Formal Sanctions: Fine and Day-Fine Examples

The idea of punishing offenders financially, called a **fine,** predates the Code of Hammurabi and remains popular today in many countries. The fine's advantages as a criminal sanction help explain its popularity (see Hillsman, 1990; Morris & Tonry, 1990):

- Fines have unmistakably punitive and deterrent purposes.
- Fines are sufficiently flexible (varying from small change to economic capital punishment) to reflect both the seriousness of the offense and the offender's resources.
- Fines can be combined with other sanctions when multiple sentencing goals are sought.
- Fines do not necessarily undermine the offender's ties to family and community.
- Fines are relatively inexpensive to administer and can even be financially self-sustaining or income producing.
- Fines can be tailored to the offender's assets and income to make up roughly comparable financial burdens.
- Fines can be collected with the same vigor and ruthlessness that characterize neighborhood finance companies.

Despite the fine's impressive list of advantages, it has never really caught on in the United States as a punishment for serious kinds of offenses. U.S. jurisdictions use fines primarily for traffic offenses and less serious high-volume crimes such as misdemeanors and ordinance violations. Because these kinds of offenses are so numerous throughout the United States, fines are actually the most frequently used sanction in the nation. But the key is that fines are viewed as appropriate for the high-volume, inconsequential offenses and not for felony-level crimes. Morris and Tonry (1990) find it ironic that "a society that relies so heavily on the financial incentive in its social philosophy and economic practice should be so reluctant to use the financial disincentive as a punishment of crime" (p. 111).

In a survey of different types of courts around the country, researchers found that judges in courts of limited jurisdiction (such as traffic court) imposed a fine, usually in combination with another penalty, in an average of 86 percent of their cases whereas general jurisdiction judges (e.g., judges in trial courts) imposed fines 42 percent of the time (Hillsman, Mahoney, Cole, & Auchter, 1987). These numbers, which may seem high at first glance, pale when compared to percentages in Western Europe. Hillsman (1990) reports that in the former West Germany, 81 percent of all adult criminal cases and 75 percent of all nontraffic criminal offenses were disposed of by a fine as the sole penalty. A fine was the sole penalty in only 36 percent of the limited jurisdiction and 10 percent of the general jurisdiction U.S. courts. In Sweden, fines are used in 83 percent of all criminal prosecutions and 65 percent of all nontraffic criminal offenses.

Why are American judges hesitant to use fines as the only penalty, or for cases other than traffic and misdemeanor offenses? The answer seems to center on beliefs by prosecutors and judges that fines are unsuited for the poor, ineffective against the rich, and generally too difficult to collect (see "DebtCollect"). Of course these "answers" simply require another question: Are fines possible in Europe but not in the United States because Europe's poor have more money, their rich are more affected by loss of funds, or their collection techniques are more effective? Because fines are finally receiving increased positive attention in the United States, we will look more closely at these issues by reviewing the use of fines in the United States and then looking at European procedures that may serve as a positive example for U.S. jurisdictions.

Fines in the United States. Most state penal codes currently set maximum and sometimes minimum amounts of fines for particular crimes or classes of offenses. The maximums have tended to be low, but "get tough" positions have led some legislatures to increase the top amounts. Even with the rather low maximums, the fine amounts actually imposed by judges tend to be well below the statutory limit (Hillsman et al., 1987). Several researchers attribute that situation to both philosophical and operational problems.

Philosophical problems with the use of fines in the United States include the idea that fines cannot be set high enough to be a credible punishment in the public's eyes, and that the fine discriminates against the poor. Regarding the view that fines are not punitive enough, Morris and Tonry (1990) ask us to consider an automobile factory worker earning $35,000 a year who has his own home, a motor boat, a recreational vehicle, and is generally considered financially secure. Unfortunately, the guy becomes quarrelsome and disrespectful when he drinks and has been convicted on several occasions of minor assault and damaging property. Having gone through previous suspended sentences and community service, he now finds himself charged again with assault and facing twelve months in jail.

What if, instead of the jail sentence, he is fined the equivalent of one year's after-tax pay? That amount might come to $25,000 and, if he has not been good at saving money for a rainy day, it may require that he sell items such as the motor boat and RV and remortgage his house. Cruelly punitive, you say? Morris and Tonry (1990) suggest it is no more cruel than would be a year in jail. More important, the financial penalty may even better serve sentencing goals such as retribution and deterrence. The substantial penalty sends deterrent signals and is unarguably punitive. At the same time, however, the man may be able to keep his job, could be surrounded by a supportive family, and will be reminded of his crime each month when bills need to be paid.

Spotlight ON CONTEMPORARY ISSUES

DebtCollect

Morris and Tonry (1990) agree that collection is a key, but they believe American ingenuity and entrepreneurship could make it all work. They believe an effective system could be operated under the control of court administrators, but they also suggest we consider involving the private sector. The simplest way to do that would be to refer unpaid fines to collection agencies on a commission basis. A more complex arrangement might have unpaid fines sold to a finance company that could buy them at a discount from face value. The company then assumes all risk of nonpayment in a manner similar to the way financing an automobile or appliance is sometimes handled.

Morris and Tonry (1990) provide an example using a fictitious company called DebtCollect. DebtCollect agrees to collect all fines between $100 and $10,000 that are not paid within one week of sentence imposition. The company will give the court three-quarters of the amount it collects. The 25 percent discount is justified by the saving of administrative costs and the likely increased rates of successful collection.

DebtCollect must use the same methods of debt collection it uses to collect civil debts, which in most states can include legal action such as seizing property and the garnishment of wages. Because it is important that the court keeps its promise and enforces its sentences, DebtCollect should refer to the court all fines not actually collected. The court regains responsibility for the collection of the fines and might decide to impose other penalties allowed for nonpayment.

It appears that successful collection of fines is not as serious a problem as some U.S. policymakers may think. But the more difficult problem may be one of setting fines that willing offenders can reasonably pay.

Go to section 11 of the *Victims' Rights Sourcebook* at ***www.ncvc.org/law/SBOOK/ch11.htm***. Read the "Improving the rates of collection" section, and identify any techniques suggested here that could also be used to improve collection rates of fines that have been given as criminal sentences.

The example of fining an offender who has an annual income of $35,000 seems to confirm the idea that fines can be effective only for those with money. In fact, studies have found that judges often believe poor offenders cannot pay fines (Hillsman et al., 1987). As a result poor offenders, seen by judges as unlikely to be able to pay a fine, get sentenced to jail instead (Hillsman, 1990). This tendency to jail poor offenders and fine more affluent ones makes the fine an unfair sentence. But proponents of the fine argue that the unfairness is a result of the way fines are handled in the United States rather than any innate unfairness of the fine itself. One example is the tariff system for determining fines.

Most American judges use a limited range of fine amounts because of constraints caused by the **tariff (or fixed-fine) system** prominent in various states. The tariff system is based on informal understandings that the same or similar fine amounts should be imposed on all defendants convicted of a particular offense (Hillsman, 1990; McDonald, 1992a). Thus, the "going rate" in one jurisdiction for disorderly conduct may be a fine of $200—regardless of the offender's financial situation. The statutory range on fines for disorderly conduct may actually be from $100 to $600, but to make them within reach of poorer defendants the judges set the tariff toward the low end. As a result, fines are seen as weak penalties because they cluster near the bottom of the permissible range.

Proponents of the increased use of fines as sole sentences in U.S. jurisdictions believe problems such as discrimination against the poor and views of fines as only a weak punishment can be rejected on seeing how other countries use the fine. Several countries in Europe provide especially good examples.

Day Fines in Europe. Because the tariff or fixed-fine system is based on the severity of the offense without concern for the offender's financial situation, it is understandable that judges and the public look skeptically on the fine as a penalty for crime. Setting a fixed amount that is high enough to deter financially secure offenders will result in an amount so high that poor offenders cannot reasonably receive the penalty. On the other hand, setting a fixed amount that is within the financial ability of poorer offenders will be little more than a slap on the wrist for criminals with greater financial resources.

If fines are linked to a person's ability to pay, it seems reasonable to assume that fines could better meet their punitive and deterrent goals. Variable fining systems are not a new concept; they date at least to thirteenth-century England, but their most recent version was proposed by a Scandinavian criminologist. Called **day fines,** this variable fining idea was implemented in Finland in 1921, Sweden in 1931, Cuba in 1936, Denmark in 1939, and West Germany and Austria in 1975 (Hillsman, 1990). Because the day-fine procedures in Sweden and Germany have received the most attention in recent years, we concentrate on them here.

The basic idea behind day fines is to separate the calculation of the fine penalty into two components. In the first, the fine amount is linked to the severity of the crime. In the second, the fine is adjusted to the offender's financial circumstances. In this manner, more serious offenses warrant higher fines, but what is high will depend on the offender's finances. Judges decide how much punishment an offender deserves for a particular crime by identifying the offense as requiring a certain number of punishment units. Those punishment units are translated into monetary terms by, for example, making one punishment unit equal to one day's pay. So, a sentence of ten punishment units, or ten day's pay, will result in a large day fine for high-income offenders and a smaller amount for lower-income people (McDonald, 1992a). But despite the differing amounts, the penalty should weigh equally on both offenders.

Sweden and Germany take this basic approach and modify it to suit each country's particular objectives. In Sweden, the day fine is meant to economically deprive offenders in the sense that they are in an economic jail. The Germans, on the other hand, see day fines as a replacement for imprisonment and, therefore, use the fines even for serious offenses.

Because Swedish day fines are primarily intended for less serious offenses, the possible punishment units range only from 1 to 180. The punishment units are converted to a monetary unit by taking a person's gross annual income and then subtracting business expenses, maintenance, or living expenses. That amount is divided by 1,000, and the resulting figure is a quantity equal to about one-third of the offender's daily income. After a few more adjustments, the Swedish judges have a day-fine system with fine amounts ranging from about $5 to nearly $2 million.

Under the German system, day-fine units range as high as 360. The value of each unit is set by statute as the offender's net daily income with no deductions for financial responsibilities. This straightforward calculation emphasizes the idea that offenders are avoiding jail for a day by paying a day's wages.

Both Sweden and Germany make significant use of their day fines. About half of all property and violent crime convictions in Sweden result in day fines. In Germany, three-quarters of all property offenses and two-thirds of all violent crimes receive fines (Hillsman, 1990). Obviously, both countries are pleased with the day fine as a criminal penalty, but there are some difficulties in establishing day fines as a workable sentence. We will consider some of these problems by looking at the prospect for day fines in the United States.

Day Fines in the United States. The idea of day fines seems like a natural for the United States and its free enterprise economy. And the day fine's success in several Western European countries suggests that it may deserve the attention of U.S.

policymakers. Day fines have been experimented with in several U.S. jurisdictions (see Tonry, 1997), but most attention has been given to the attempts in the New York City borough of Staten Island and in the municipal court of Milwaukee, Wisconsin. Both jurisdictions found that a workable day-fine system could be developed for regular use in courts. McDonald (1992a), in summarizing the findings of research on the two projects, determined that day fines were used without slowing the normal pace of court operations, without lessening (and sometimes actually increasing) collection rates, and without increasing recidivism. Following is a look at one of the experiments more closely.

On August 12, 1988, Judge Rose McBrien of the Staten Island Criminal Court imposed the first U.S. day fine (Greene, 1992). To get to that point, the Vera Institute of Justice spent more than a year preparing a framework for testing the feasibility of using day fines in a U.S. court. The Vera Institute planners were confronted with three difficult problems:

- How should punishment units be assigned to each crime?
- How would the resulting day-fine units be matched to the offender's ability to pay?
- How will the day-fine sentences be enforced and the money collected?

Following Germany's lead, the Staten Island day-fine units were set in a range from 1 to 360 days for all offenses. There was a cap of 120 day-fine units for misdemeanors, but felonies could be punished up to the 360-day maximum. Working first with the misdemeanors, each offense was assigned a presumptive number of day-fine units ranging from a low of 5 units (e.g., disorderly conduct) to the maximum of 120 (e.g., sexual misconduct). Judges were given a reference table to assist them in using day fines (see Figure 5.2), but the Staten Island experiment neither required the judges to impose day fines nor forced them to follow the table's suggestions.

After deciding how many day-fine units they would assign to each crime, the Vera Institute planners moved to the even more difficult task of matching day-fine units to the offender's ability to pay. A key to making this match is having accurate information about the offender's financial resources. In Sweden, courts have legal access to offenders' tax records (although the courts rarely use that approach) whereas the German courts do not have tax information directly available. American courts are in a situation similar to those of Germany because the Internal Revenue Service cannot reveal tax information for the purposes of sentencing. But as we have seen, day fines work in Germany despite possible difficulties in obtaining accurate financial means information. The Vera Institute planners decided that some German techniques may also work in the United States.

As it turned out, the Staten Island court was already gathering financial information on the accused. To aid in making pretrial release decisions, reports were prepared about each arrestee's employment; length of employment; name, address, and phone number of the employer; hours worked per week; and take-home pay. The report on unemployed defendants told the duration of unemployment, whether he or she had ever worked, and if the defendant was in school. Added to this information were details about additional sources of income, financial responsibilities, and people who are financially dependent on the defendant.

Having concluded that information was already available for finding out a defendant's financial means, the planning group decided that the value of each day-fine unit should be based for all offenders on daily net income after adjustments for basic personal needs and family responsibilities (Greene, 1992). Because this formula would apply even to defendants who were destitute, the planners provided additional discounts for persons living in poverty. A resulting chart provided

FIGURE 5.2

Staten Island Day-Fine Unit Scale (Partial)

PENAL LAW CHARGE*	TYPE OF OFFENSE**	NUMBER OF DAY-FINE UNITS DISCOUNT - PRESUMPTIVE - PREMIUM
	E. Stolen Motor Vehicle: Range of 20–60 DF (Car value scaled as for petit larceny)	
	$1,000 or more	51 - **60** - 69
	$700–$999	42 - **50** - 58
	$500–$699	34 - **40** - 46
	$300–$499	25 - **30** - 35
	$150–$299	17 - **20** - 23
	$1–$149	13 - **15** - 17
220.03 AM	Criminal Possession of a Controlled Substance 7: Range of 35–50 DF	
	A. Possession of cocaine, heroin, PCP, LSD, or other "street jobs"	42 - **50** - 58
	B. Criminal possession of valium, methadone, or other pharmaceutical drugs	30 - **35** - 40
221.05 vio	Unlawful Possession of Marijuana	13 - **15** - 17
221.10	Possession of Marijuana 5	13 - **15** - 17
230.00	Prostitution	13 - **15** - 17
240.20 vio	Disorderly Conduct	13 - **15** - 17
240.25 vio	Harassment	13 - **15** - 17
240.30 AM	Aggravated Harassment 2	42 - **50** - 58
240.37 B BM	Loitering for Prostitution	13 - **15** - 17
265.01 AM	Criminal Possession of a Weapon 4: Range of 35–60 DF	
	A. Criminal Possession of a Firearm	51 - **60** - 69
	B. Criminal Possession of Any Other Dangerous or Deadly Weapon	30- **35** - 40
110/265.01 BM	Attempted Criminal Possession of a Weapon 4: Range of 15–25 DF	
	A. Criminal Possession of a Firearm	21 - **25** - 29
	B. Criminal Possession of Any Other Dangerous or Deadly Weapon	13- **15** - 17

*AM = Class A Misdemeanor; BM = Class B Misdemeanor; vio = Violation

**DF = Day Fines

Source: From Vera Institute of Justice. (1996). *How to use structured fines (day fines) as an intermediate sanction* [NCJ 156242]. Washington, DC: Bureau of Justice Assistance.

judges with an IRS-like "tax table" to aid in assigning a monetary value to each day-fine unit (see Figure 5.3).

A remaining problem was how to identify and handle any income the offender might have from illegal activity (see Bureau of Justice Assistance, 1996).

FIGURE 5.3

Staten Island Valuation Table (Complete Table Has Net Daily Income from $3 to $100)

	DOLLAR VALUE OF ONE DAY-FINE UNIT, BY NET DAILY INCOME AND NUMBER OF DEPENDENTS NUMBER OF DEPENDENTS (INCLUDING SELF)							
Net Daily Income ($)	1	2	3	4	5	6	7	8
36	20.20	16.63	13.07	10.69	8.32	5.40	4.50	3.60
37	20.76	17.09	13.43	10.99	8.55	5.55	4.62	3.70
38	21.32	17.56	13.79	11.29	8.78	7.52	4.75	3.80
39	21.88	18.02	14.16	11.58	9.01	7.72	4.87	3.90
40	22.44	18.48	14.52	11.88	9.24	7.92	5.00	4.00
41	23.00	18.94	14.88	12.18	9.47	8.12	5.12	4.10
42	23.56	19.40	15.25	12.47	9.70	8.32	5.25	4.20
43	24.12	19.87	15.61	12.77	9.93	8.51	7.09	4.30
44	24.68	20.33	15.97	13.07	10.16	8.71	7.26	4.40
45	25.25	20.79	16.34	13.37	10.40	8.91	7.42	4.50
46	25.81	21.25	16.70	13.66	10.63	9.11	7.59	4.60
47	26.37	21.71	17.06	13.96	10.86	9.31	7.75	4.70
48	26.93	22.18	17.42	14.26	11.09	9.50	7.92	6.34
49	27.49	22.64	17.79	14.55	11.32	9.70	8.08	6.47
50	28.05	23.10	18.15	14.85	11.55	9.90	8.25	6.60
51	28.61	23.56	18.51	15.15	11.78	10.10	8.41	6.73
52	29.17	24.02	18.88	15.44	12.01	10.30	8.58	6.86
53	29.73	24.49	19.24	15.74	12.24	10.49	8.74	7.00
54	30.29	24.95	19.60	16.04	12.47	10.69	8.91	7.13
55	30.86	25.41	19.97	16.34	12.71	10.89	9.07	7.26
56	31.42	25.87	20.33	16.63	12.94	11.09	9.24	7.39
57	31.98	26.33	20.69	16.93	13.17	11.29	9.40	7.52
58	32.54	26.80	21.05	17.23	13.40	11.48	9.57	7.66
59	33.10	27.26	21.42	17.52	13.63	11.68	9.73	7.79
60	33.66	27.72	21.78	17.82	13.86	11.88	9.90	7.92
61	34.22	28.18	22.14	18.12	14.09	12.08	10.06	8.05
62	34.78	28.64	22.51	18.41	14.32	12.28	10.23	8.18
63	35.34	29.11	22.87	18.71	14.55	12.47	10.39	8.32
64	35.90	29.57	23.23	19.01	14.78	12.67	10.56	8.45
65	36.47	30.03	23.60	19.31	15.02	12.87	10.72	8.58
66	37.03	30.49	23.96	19.60	15.25	13.07	10.89	8.71
67	37.59	30.95	24.32	19.90	15.48	13.27	11.05	8.84

Source: From Vera Institute of Justice. (1996). *How to use structured fines (day fines) as an intermediate sanction* [NCJ 156242]. Washington, DC: Bureau of Justice Assistance.

For example, the income of a prostitute may be difficult to determine, but Greene (1992) explains that judges could use their discretion in determining the offender's economic resources, just as they already do in setting bail. Even if a good estimate of finances is made, what is to prevent the offender from engaging in illegal acts to pay the fine? Fining prostitutes, for example, may result in the court taking the role of a "state pimp" by encouraging the illegal activity so the fine can be paid. One Staten Island judge confronted this problem by basing a day fine for prostitutes on an estimate of the wages commanded by persons employed in Staten Island's domestic labor market—a career the judge encouraged each fined prostitute to consider (Greene, 1992).

The last major problem to deal with was how day-fine sentences would be enforced and the money collected. Understanding that fines left unpaid lack punitive value, the Vera Institute planners were determined that the new program would be at least as successful in collecting fines as was the old procedure. Because collection rates in New York City courts of limited jurisdiction stood at an impressive 75 percent within one year of sentencing, the planners had a high standard to meet.

Beginning with the assumption that most offenders would not be able to pay their fine at sentencing, plans were made to have installments designed to get full payment in the shortest possible time. It was felt that this goal could best be achieved by establishing a day-fines officer, who would have sufficient authority to enforce payment by offenders and who could closely monitor the payment efforts. Preliminary data suggest that the planners were successful in their efforts because collection rates did not appear to decline with the coming of day fines. In fact, estimates were that general-fund revenues derived from fines would significantly increase under the new system (Greene, 1992).

As more communities experiment with day fines (see Bureau of Justice Assistance, 1996), successful collection becomes more well established. Current procedures for collecting day fines include (1) setting reasonable and appropriate terms of payment (preferably within a three-month period) and communicating those terms clearly to offenders; (2) making it as convenient and easy as possible to pay fines (e.g., accept cash, personal checks, money orders, cashiers' checks, or credit cards); (3) using incentives to encourage prompt payment (such as discounts for early payment); and (4) when payments are not made on time, taking swift action (e.g., see Figure 5.4) to persuade offenders to comply with the terms of their sentences (Bureau of Justice Assistance, 1996, pp. 29–32).

The day fine in U.S. courts is still in its infancy, but reports from courts such as those in Staten Island and Milwaukee suggest that this European tradition can be effectively adapted in the United States. If that occurs, examples such as the following one from Staten Island court records may be the norm rather than sounding unusual.

> Joseph Burke [name is changed] was prosecuted for stealing a car. He was arraigned for grand larceny (a class E felony); possession of stolen property (a class E felony); and unauthorized use of an auto (a class A misdemeanor). He pleaded guilty to attempted unauthorized use of an auto (a class B misdemeanor).
>
> Mr. Burke is 21 years old. He is single and lives with his mother, to whom he contributes support. He works at a restaurant and reports take-home pay of $180 per week. He was sentenced to pay a ten-unit day fine, and his unit value was set at $11.78. His fine totals $115. He was given an installment schedule for payment and has paid his fine in five payments over 3 months. (Greene, 1992, p. 36)

The day fine seems to have good potential in U.S. court jurisdictions. Possibly there are other sentencing systems and sentence types around the world that could also be adapted in the United States. But even if other ideas are not transferable, it is good to see the variety of ways that sentencing can be carried out.

FIGURE 5.4

Sample Notice Concerning Fine Payments Owed

Polk County Attorney

John P. Sarcone
County Attorney

Address Reply to
Room 408, Courthouse
Des Moines, IA 50309-4242
515-286-3737

Date

John R. Smith
1234 Yourstreet
Yourcity, IA 50300

RE: Polk County Criminal Docket Number ___________

Dear John:

The Polk County Clerk of Court has advised us that your scheduled fine payment of $___________, which was due on ___________ has still not been received, thus making your account seriously delinquent.

Your continued failure to comply with the Court ordered payment of this fine WILL result in action(s) being taken against you. These actions could include, but are not limited to, garnishment of your wages, garnishment of any income tax refund due you, seizure of certain items of personal property, the placement of a lien on any real property that you own, the filing of a criminal charge of Contempt of Court against you and a warrant being issued for your immediate arrest.

To avoid these consequences, you must <u>immediately</u> bring or mail the past due fine payment to the Polk County Clerk of Court, Room 201, Polk County Courthouse, 5th & Mulberry Streets, Des Moines, IA 50309.

If you have a legitimate reason for not making this payment, please contact me at (515) 286-2259.

Yours Truly,

A. McDaniel/C. Ver Heul
Structured Fines Officer

Source: From Vera Institute of Justice. (1996). How to use structured fines (day fines) as an intermediate sanction [NCJ 156242]. Washington, DC: Bureau of Justice Assistance. Reprinted with the kind permission of the Polk County (Iowa) County Attorney's Office.

SUMMARY

TWO BASIC SENTENCING STRUCTURES

There are two basic sentencing strategies used in the United States:

- Indeterminate sentencing, wherein a judge sentences the offender to a minimum and maximum penalty (such as two to four years imprisonment) for which the boundaries do not fall outside limits set by the state legislature.
- Determinate sentencing, which requires the judge to impose a flat sentence (staying within any statutory limits the legislature has set) rather than a range of years.

FOUR SPECIAL SENTENCING PRACTICES

Either basic sentencing strategy can be modified with special sentencing practices that include:

- Sentencing guidelines, which can be either
  - Presumptive—It is presumed the judge will issue a sentence falling within a range established for an offender in a particular case, or
  - Voluntary—The guidelines simply suggest sentences to the judge.
- Mandatory minimum sentencing specifies certain crimes (e.g., drug offenses or committing crimes with a deadly weapon) and certain offenders (e.g., repeat or habitual offenders) for which a prison sentence must be given. Aspects of mandatory minimum sentencing include:
  - Truth in sentencing, which ensures that a certain percentage of the prison sentence will actually be served, and
  - "Three strikes and you're out" laws, which typically require a sentence to life imprisonment given after an offender has been convicted of a specified number and/or type of felonies.
- Circumstances that allow a judge to vary from legislative required sentences can be either:
  - Aggravating—That is, the events of the crime or the circumstances of the criminal are such that a more severe penalty than is required can be applied.
  - Mitigating—That is, the events of the crime or the circumstances of the criminal are such that a less severe penalty than is required can be applied.
- Methods for reducing sentence time include:
  - Jail time, in which convicted offenders are given credit toward their sentence for time they served in jail while awaiting trial and sentencing.
  - Good time, which allows prisoners to reduce days from their sentence because of their good behavior or extra work, or as a result of legislative laws.
  - Concurrent sentencing, which allows an offender to serve multiple sentences all at one time (i.e., concurrently).

SENTENCE TYPES

- Some sanctions can be applied in an informal manner, as is done in some African countries where compensation is paid to crime victims or in Germany where offenders make a donation to a charity. Victim–offender mediation programs in the United States can also be examples of applying informal moderate sanctions.

- Formal sanctions rely on judges for their application. Fines are examples of this type. Day fines may grow in popularity in the United States as a sanction that has punitive aspects and provides some equability among persons of varying incomes.

Key Terms and Concepts

aggravating circumstances (p. 144)
compensation (p. 150)
concurrent sentencing (p. 147)
customary courts (p. 152)
day fine (p. 164)
determinate sentencing (p. 129)
earned good time (p. 145)
fine (p. 161)
good time (p. 145)
indeterminate sentencing (p. 129)
informal sanctions (p. 148)
jail time (p. 145)
mandatory minimum sentence (p. 139)
mandatory sentences (p. 139)
meritorious good time (p. 145)
mitigating circumstances (p. 144)
presumptive sentencing (p. 132)
sentencing (p. 128)
sentencing grid (p. 132)
sentencing guidelines (p. 132)
statutory good time (p. 145)
statutory penalty (p. 131)
tariff (or fixed-fine) system (p. 163)
"three strikes and you're out" (p. 141)
truth-in-sentencing law (p. 140)
victim–offender mediation (p. 156)

Discussion Questions

1. In the debate over indeterminate and determinate sentencing, some of the strongest opponents of indeterminate sentencing were the prisoners. Why would prisoners so greatly dislike indeterminate sentences?
2. A recent criticism of sentencing statutes that require prison terms for some drug offenses is that the laws have a more negative impact on black offenders than on white offenders. Specifically, in jurisdictions in which crack cocaine results in a harsher penalty than does powder cocaine, African American offenders are often punished more severely than white offenders. What would be some solutions to this problem?
3. What could be some key issues raised by persons wanting to show that three-strikes legislation violates either the Eighth or the Tenth Amendments to the U.S. Constitution?
4. What are some arguments for why judges should be allowed to take aggravating and mitigating circumstances into consideration when imposing a sentence? What are some arguments for why they should not?
5. For whom besides the inmates might jail-time and good-time credit be a desirable thing?
6. If the practice of preventive imprisonment does not result in a person being locked up for any longer than he or she would have been after a finding of guilt, has any harm really been done?
7. Discuss the implications of Joseph and Carton's argument that, at least as viewed by writers of "Star Trek" episodes, informal justice may not be successful in accurate fact-finding or in protecting individual rights.
8. Can fines be made so punitive that the public would accept them as an alternative to probation or jail? What are some problems when using fines in that way?
9. Is the increased use of day fines in the United States a practical option? What must be done to make the day fine acceptable to the public as a formal sanction?

chapter 6

CORPORAL AND CAPITAL PUNISHMENT

Instead of sending a drug offender to prison, a South Carolina judge took off his belt in court and handed it to the teen's grandmother. The judge said, "Grandmama, take this belt and take him into my office and whip him good." The judge, defendant, grandmother, and a deputy went into the judge's chambers for the punishment. Witnesses said ten to twelve loud smacks were heard. When they returned, the young man appeared sheepish and his grandmother looked pleased. The judge then accepted the teen's guilty plea and sentenced him to two years in prison but suspended it upon the service of five years' probation. The teen also had to finish high school, be on house arrest for six months, and perform 250 hours of public service ("Judge Gets Grandmother to Whip Offender," 1995).

Reactions to that story will range from, "That's not legal!" to "Why don't more judges do that?" Is there a place for corporal punishment in contemporary American society? This chapter does not answer that question, but it does present information that may help you come up with your own answer. Similarly, this chapter covers the topic of capital punishment by reviewing arguments typically addressed in the debate between abolitionists and retentionists. At the chapter's end you will have information on both corporal and capital punishment that allows you to clarify your personal opinion. We begin with a look at the broad topic of physical sanctions, which encompasses both corporal and capital punishment.

Physical Sanctions

Physical sanctions provide the greatest extremes of all sanction types. Most people seek out the positive ones, such as hugs and pats on the back. The negative ones, however, are to be avoided. As explained in Chapter 2, the criminal justice process relies more on negative sanctions than on positive sanctions. Most of those negative sanctions have a social/psychological aspect such as embarrassment, loss of friends, or disrupted family relations, and some have an economic feature such as fines and community service, but many of them rely primarily on a physical element. Because physical sanctions involve action toward a person's body, they include sentences that restrict that body's freedom to move about—probation or imprisonment, for example—as well as sentences that affect the body itself, such as amputation or execution. This chapter focuses on the second grouping of negative physical sanctions—those directed toward the body itself. They are referred to as corporal and capital punishments, and they provoke some of the most divisive and emotionally charged positions people take regarding penal sanctions.

This chapter looks at corporal and capital punishments before considering sentences such as fines, probation, and imprisonment because they preceded these other types of physical sanctions. Chapter 3 explained that contemporary punishments such as imprisonment were offered by some reform groups as humanitarian alternatives to corporal and capital punishment. But the newer types of physical sanctions never completely replaced the older ones. Most jurisdictions in the United States still authorize the death penalty as a criminal sanction and, although examples are harder to find, corporal punishment still has its proponents.

TORTURE

Because the concept of **torture** is sometimes linked with the topics of corporal and capital punishment, this discussion must begin by clarifying its meaning. In its historic use, torture referred to a procedure used to extract confessions of guilt or to disclose incriminating information about others (Barnes, 1972; Langbein, 1978). More recently, torture still refers to a technique of interrogation, but it also can refer to the inflicting of "intense pain to body or mind for purposes of punishment" (*Black's Law Dictionary*). This chapter is primarily interested in torture and punishment, but to place the term in its correct context, its use for interrogation is briefly considered.

Torture for Interrogation

Pain forces even the innocent to lie.

—Publilius Syrus

Despite warnings such as this one delivered by Publilius Syrus twelve centuries earlier, pain was an important aspect of European criminal procedure from the middle of the thirteenth century to the middle of the eighteenth century. Interestingly and importantly, torture during that time was a routine technique that the criminal courts permitted against suspected criminals as a way to get them to confess. As Langbein (1978) explains it, torture became an ingredient of the medieval law of proof during the thirteenth century as a replacement for trial by ordeal. Prior to 1215, when the Roman Catholic Church effectively destroyed the practice, ordeals were the common method for determining guilt or innocence in criminal matters.

Persons accused of crime were required to undergo an ordeal that subjected them to some physical feat. The deed, it was assumed, could be successfully performed only with the help of God. Because God would help the innocent but not the guilty, successful completion of the ordeal provided absolute certainty of the accused's guilt or innocence. Under ordeal by fire, the accused had to carry a hot iron for a distance of nine feet or walk blindfolded and barefoot over the red-hot blades of plows. Ordeals by water required the accused to place his or her hand into boiling water, pick a stone out of boiling water, or to be bound thumb to toes and tossed into water (Moore, 1973). Innocent people were those whose hand or feet were healing properly three days after ordeal by fire or boiling water, or whose bound body sank (and was then retrieved) when tossed into water. God identified the guilty people by not healing their wounds or by having the water reject their bodies (i.e., their bound bodies floated).

In 1215 Pope Innocent III forbade the clergy to assist in ordeals of water and fire. In doing so, he forced the courts to come up with a new way to determine guilt or innocence. People were understandably distressed about having human judges replace God in the judgment seat, so great effort was made to eliminate human discretion as much as possible (Langbein, 1978). The procedure established in Italy and soon accepted in much of the rest of Europe required that conviction be based on two unimpeachable eyewitnesses. Without two such witnesses, a criminal court could not convict the accused who denied the claims against them. But if the accused voluntarily confessed to the crime, the court could convict them without eyewitness testimony. The problems with this law of proof soon became apparent as Europeans learned they had set the safeguard too high. The level of proof was only effective in cases involving crime committed in the presence of others or by repentant criminals (Langbein, 1978).

Because it was difficult to get around the "two eyewitnesses" rule, officials began concentrating on conviction by confession. To regulate the process by which a confession was extracted, the law of torture was developed—permitting torture as a way to generate a confession. Only those persons who were very likely guilty—for example, there was only one eyewitness or there was circumstantial evidence—could be examined under torture. In addition, the accused had to repeat the confession at a time when they were free from torture during a hearing one or two days later. Because persons recanting their confession could be reexamined under repeated torture, the accused learned quickly enough that further agony in the torture chamber could be avoided only by confirming the confession at the time of the ratification hearing.

The use of torture to elicit a confession lasted into the eighteenth century (Langbein, 1978) primarily because the two-witness rule left European courts without a more tolerable alternate way to establish guilt. As the civil and common legal traditions continued to evolve, procedures such as examining magistrates, lay judges, and jurors came to provide the means of determining guilt or innocence. This does not mean that all police officials, any place in the world, have stopped using torture as a way to extract a confession or other kinds of information, but today such practices are typically pursued outside the law.

Torture for Punishment

Many forms of punishment inflicted on those found guilty of a crime have been painful in the extreme and are literal examples of torture (Barnes, 1972; Swain, 1931, 1995). But as Newman points out, "pain is not (necessarily) torture" (Newman, 1995, p. 149). Torture refers not only to applying physical pain to a person's body but also implies extralegal motives on the part of the person inflicting the pain; for example, some political objective is sought. And, although it has not been defined, the courts have said torturing suspects, defendants, or offenders would be unconstitutional. But although prohibiting torture, the courts have consistently allowed the infliction of physical pain as punishment for crimes—and even as a disciplinary measure for misbehaving prisoners. The key is not whether punishment is painful; rather, the courts' concern is whether it is cruel and unusual.

The Eighth Amendment to the U.S. Constitution prohibits cruel and unusual punishment. Unfortunately, the framers of the Constitution did not go on to define or describe cruel or unusual. The courts have also avoided any specific definition of cruel and unusual—but they have tried to provide some examples of what it is or is not. Collins (1993, p. 81) summarizes the resulting guidelines that courts take into consideration when deciding if a punishment is cruel and unusual. Judges are to determine, for example, whether the contested punishment:

- Shocks the conscience of the court.
- Violates the evolving standards of decency of a civilized society.
- Imposes punishment that is disproportionate to the offense.
- Involves the wanton and unnecessary infliction of pain.
- Shows deliberate indifference to the needs (usually medical and safety) of the prisoner.

You will note that the infliction of pain is not prohibited. Wanton and unnecessary pain is prohibited, but administering pain itself is not cruel and unusual under either historical or contemporary court rulings. But consider for a moment the "evolving standards of decency" guideline.

The federal courts have ruled that execution, presumably the ultimate infliction of pain, is not cruel and unusual (*Gregg v. Georgia*) but that whipping, as either a penalty for crime or to enforce prison discipline, is (*Jackson v. Bishop*, 1968). How do the courts go about determining standards of decency? The primary sources are the various state legislatures because they represent the will of the people. Because so many states have passed capital punishment statutes, the court assumes that society endorses that form of punishment. But in the 1968 *Bishop* decision, the court of appeals found—among several other reasons—that public opinion was against whipping because only two states still permitted the use of the strap (Palmer, 1991).

This idea of corporal and capital punishment as being cruel or unusual at different times and under different standards presents some interesting points for consideration. If all versions of inflicting pain that are correctly identified as torture are dismissed and only those methods of inflicting pain that are solely for purposes of punishment are kept, at least some authors suggest both corporal and capital punishment can be appropriate contemporary sanctions. That point will be examined more closely later.

CORPORAL PUNISHMENT

Corporal punishment refers to any kind of punishment of, or inflicted on, the body (*Black's Law Dictionary*). Although that means imprisonment is technically an example of corporal punishment, the term more often brings to mind things such as whipping, amputation, and branding. Similarly, execution is certainly a punishment inflicted on the body, but as the ultimate sanction it has its own identity as capital punishment. After reviewing some of the forms that corporal punishment has taken over the years, we will consider the controversial topic of using corporal punishment as a contemporary alternative to imprisonment.

Forms of Corporal Punishment

In Chapters 3 and 4, we examined how the primary philosophies of punishment are reflected over five penal eras progressing from the Middle Ages to the present. The emphasis in those periods was on imprisonment and how that sanction was influenced by rationales such as retribution and rehabilitation. But interestingly, the different rationales are reflected in various types of corporal punishment as well. As you read about punishments such as the pillory, the stocks, and branding, consider some of the goals each sanction was to achieve. The public nature of these punishments certainly suggests a goal of general deterrence, and a few, such as mutilation or amputation, had very clear purposes of specific deterrence. But there are also aspects of retribution—throwing things at people locked in the pillory must have satisfied the desire for vengeance in more than a few villagers—and even incapacitation: Cutting off a thief's hands may result in more than specific deterrence; it may actually prevent him or her from committing that particular crime again. Even restoration, in the spirit of restoring a sense of balance to the community, might have been a reason for some of these physical sanctions. Because this discussion of corporal punishment concludes with a consideration of its contemporary role as a legitimate sanction, think about what penal goals could be served by these punishments as you read their classic descriptions.

The Pillory and the Stocks. The **pillory** consisted of a wooden frame set on a post with holes for the offender's head and hands. In this structure the more serious offenders, such as those committing fraud and cheating, were locked and exposed to public ridicule at best—and rotten vegetables and stones at worst. Petty offenders, on the other hand, were put in the **stocks.** These devices were also wooden frames, but they had holes to secure the offenders' feet and sometimes their hands. Use of the pillory began declining in England during the eighteenth century, but use of the stocks continued at least until the middle of the nineteenth century for crimes such as gambling on Sunday and—especially—for drunkenness.

In colonial America, the stocks had a rather ominous start when the Boston magistrates commissioned a carpenter to build a set. Upon completion, the stocks were immediately filled by that very carpenter, who had charged too much to build them. Seventeenth-century colonists used the stocks for such petty offenses as slandering, signing a rebellious petition, bigamy, stealing yarn, vagrancy, resisting a constable, and stealing an Indian child—perceived as a petty offense at the time. In England, however, drunkenness was by far the most common offense for which a person was put in the stocks during the seventeenth and eighteenth centuries.

Authorities disagree about whether the stocks and pillory were originally intended as punishment themselves or as a way of displaying the prisoner to the public. But whatever the original reason, this public punishment came to create quite a draw and often had theatrical qualities (Swain, 1931, 1995). In fact, the riotous celebrations at these public punishments eventually brought calls for reform and quests for other forms of punishment. That set the stage for reformers to suggest a look at imprisonment as a less barbaric punishment.

Branding. Another popular punishment was **branding** of the forehead, cheek, shoulder, or hand. This practice was well established in history as far back as Roman times when criminals were branded with some appropriate mark on their forehead. Barnes (1972) explains that in medieval France the criminal was branded on the shoulder with the fleur-de-lis emblem, and in England a letter-brand, usually on the face, was used to indicate the crime a person had committed.

Colonial Americans followed the English lead and applied a brand that would tell others what the offender had done. For example, James Nayler, the "Mad Quaker," had his tongue bored through, and the letter *B* (for blasphemer) stamped on his forehead with a hot iron (Newman, 1985). In Maryland, where branding was widely used well into the eighteenth century, *M* stood for manslaughter, *T* for thief, and *R* for rogue. Such action was very stigmatizing and left the recipient with a criminal record visible to the entire community. By the eighteenth century the hand was the most common place to brand an offender, and it became customary to have defendants in court raise their hands to show whether they had any previous convictions. Newman suggests it is quite likely that this practice "was the forerunner of the modern swearing of witnesses requiring one hand on the Bible but the other raised with an open palm" (1985, p. 118).

Similar to branding was the use of "scarlet letters." For this punishment a letter or inscription stating the crime was sewn onto garments of the criminal. During the seventeenth century, this practice was especially common for blasphemers and drunkards.

The pillory, the stocks, and branding have all played significant roles in the history of corporal punishment. But one other form persisted—at least in the Western world—longer than the others, and it still occasions great controversy. This punishment is the topic of the next section.

Whipping.

> *He who spares the rod hates his son, but he who loves him is diligent to discipline him.*
>
> —King Solomon, Proverbs 13:24

> *Hold you there, neither a strange hand nor my own, neither heavy nor light shall touch my bum.*
>
> —Sancho Panza, in Cervantes's *Don Quixote*

Whether you lean more toward King Solomon's or Sancho Panza's view of **whipping,** there are uncounted numbers of people supporting your position. And the courts have not provided much help in clarifying the matter. The U.S. Supreme Court has ruled that whipping as punishment for criminals violates the Eighth Amendment's prohibition against cruel and unusual punishment (*Jackson v. Bishop*). But the reasonable use of corporal punishment is permissible in schools (*Ingraham v. Wright,* 1977). It seems that society's evolving standards of decency have a schizophrenic quality. Maybe a look at the history of whipping will offer a better understanding of whipping's role in contemporary society.

Whipping is one of the oldest and most often used forms of corporal punishment. It was widely used in the sense that it was part of the experience of the bulk of ordinary people throughout the history of Western civilization. This was especially true during the three centuries beginning at 1600. Newman (1985) suggests that most spectators of public whippings had personally experienced a whipping either as a child or as a servant. It was, therefore, a universal punishment rather than a community-centered one such as the pillory and the stocks.

In 1530 Parliament passed the Whipping Act, and it became the preferred punishment for vagrants. The act required that vagrants " 'be tied to the end of a

The whipping post at the New Castle (Delaware) County Jail, shown here in 1897, was combined with a pillory.

cart naked, and beaten with whips throughout such market town or other place, till the body shall be bloody by reason of whipping'" (Newman, 1985, p. 120). In the 1597 revision of the Whipping Act, the offender was stripped only to the waist rather than naked, and was then tied to a whipping post rather than a cart. This form of punishment increased in popularity over the next two centuries and reached its peak in the early American colonies, where it continued to be used well into the twentieth century.

The instruments of whipping have been quite varied over time and place (Swain, 1931/1995). Sticks, canes, rods, straps, and rubber hoses are some of the more popular flogging devices. Variations on the theme included the cat-o'-nine-tails (it left marks like the scratches of a cat), which was a lash consisting of nine knotted cords or thongs of rawhide fastened to a handle. But the standard whip was the method preferred in those American colonies and states that used this form of corporal punishment. Delaware provides the classic example of the crimes punished by whipping, the number of lashes imposed, and the constant debate over whipping's merits. Although it certainly was not the only American colony or state to punish its criminals this way, Delaware's persistence in using whipping has made that state a popular example (see "Red Hannah").

Corporal Punishment in Contemporary Society

Corporal punishment and imprisonment (and, as we see later, capital punishment) are all sanctions imposed for some reason. Appreciating that reason permits a better understanding of the policies, procedures, and consequences of corrections both past and present—it may also help in anticipating the future direction of punishment. Also, it seems that the methods of sanctioning change more over time than do the reasons for sanctioning. If imprisonment and capital punishment are still used because they are believed to exact retribution or achieve deterrence, rehabilitation, incapacitation, or restoration, is it possible that corporal punishment might return as a favored sanction because it also can meet punishment goals? Judging from the support some U.S. citizens expressed when Singapore officials had Michael Fay caned, the answer might be yes. Even more clearly, when Alabama officials returned to the use of chain gangs and put prisoners to work on the rock pile, some suggested corporal punishment had come to the mid-1990s.

But, you might argue, the direction that sanctions seem to be taking is toward more community-based penalties as a way to relieve prison crowding. And, as we will see in Chapters 8 and 9, there is excellent support for that argument. But some authors have suggested that corporal punishment might also be a reasonable alternative to imprisonment. The ideas of Hannah Long (1998) and Graeme Newman (1995) are offered as examples.

Long comes to support corporal punishment after concluding that incarceration is a source of individual injustice because judges can give offenders penalties of equal time but not of equal severity. The inequable severity of incarceration, Long argues, results from the different ways individuals respond to the prison experiences of sexual violence and humiliating prison conditions, and to the inmate's mental health, life expectancy, and HIV status (1998, p. 349). Greater equability can be achieved with punishment that relies on application of acute pain rather than on sentencing to long-term imprisonment—as long as it is clear that the painful punishment:

- does not result in permanent physical damage,
- is of brief duration, and
- the offender is fully informed of these facts and the approximate intensity of the pain he will feel. (Long, 1998, p. 351)

HISTORICAL PERSPECTIVES

Red Hannah

Robert Caldwell (1947) gave his book about whipping in Delaware the title *Red Hannah*, after the name black prisoners in southern Delaware gave the red-painted post at which they were whipped. But even before the posts were named, whipping was well established as a punishment for criminals. The first recorded instance of public whipping in Delaware took place in 1654. More than 300 years later, in 1964, whipping was imposed as a punishment by a Delaware court, although the governor refused to let it be carried out. In the intervening years, the whipping post had been both applauded and condemned by citizens of all characteristics and occupations.

From 1776 to 1829, the debate focused on corporal punishment versus the establishment of a penitentiary system. Caldwell describes the frustration of reformers during these years who were consistently blocked in their attempts to have a penitentiary built and to revise the criminal code so that imprisonment replaced corporal punishment as the primary sanction. In the remainder of the nineteenth century, some modifications were made. The whipping of white women convicted of larceny was abolished in 1855, and in 1883 judges could omit whipping when sentencing children convicted of larceny. In 1889 the whipping and pillorying of women convicted of any crime was abolished by the Delaware legislature. Also, newspapers increasingly expressed opposition to the whipping post, and Delaware governors granted more and more pardons as the only way to reduce the number of whippings meted out.

Delaware entered the twentieth century without a state penal institution. A workhouse in New Castle County had been established in 1899, but rather than making imprisonment a substitute for corporal punishment, whipping was now applied to prisoners as a means of discipline and additional punishment. The continued strength of whipping as punishment was also seen in the new criminal code in 1915, which added even more crimes (e.g., burglary at night and wife beating) to the list of offenses punishable by whipping (Caldwell, 1947). By the mid-1930s, action toward whipping was directed more at its public nature than its consequences. People were prohibited from having a camera at or near the whipping post. In 1941 one of the most important changes occurred when petty larceny was removed from the list of crimes punishable by whipping. Because a large percentage of the whippings in Delaware were inflicted for that crime, its removal from the list marked the start of a noticeable decline in punishment by whipping.

Visit the World Corporal Punishment Research Web site at ***www.corpun.com,*** and read the "News Highlights." Find out what countries have recently applied corporal punishment as a punishment for crime. For what crime was the punishment applied? Which method was used? Visit the LAW's Hall of Horror at ***wwlia.org/horror.htm,*** and identify two corporal punishment methods other than whipping that have been used in the past.

Long notes that considerable research would be required to identify the most equable technique of imposing pain, but she suggests that might include radiant heat, cold pressure (e.g., immersing the offender's hand or limb in ice water), pressure, external or internal chemical introduction, or electricity. After administration of the acutely painful punishment, Long explains, offenders should be permitted or required to enroll in rehabilitation, treatment, and education programs that are suited to their needs.

The subtitle for Newman's book, *Just and Painful,* is *A Case for the Corporal Punishment of Criminals.* His argument is essentially that corporal punishment (such as whipping, but especially electric shock) should be considered as a reasonable alternative to imprisonment. Newman understands that his proposal runs counter to court rulings on acceptable punishment and, for the most part, lacks widespread public support. But, he suggests, both the courts and the public are berating corporal punishment without having a clear understanding and appreciation of its potential benefits.

Part of Newman's defense of corporal punishment consists of general responses to equally broad criticisms. For example, some people claim that whipping creates penological problems and makes adjustment to society more difficult. Newman responds that when compared to the difficulties of societal adjustment

In 1994 Michael Fay, shown here with his stepfather Marco Chan, was convicted in Singapore of vandalism, criminal mischief, and possession of stolen property. Fay was punished with four strikes of a rattan cane and twelve weeks in jail.

and penological problems created by imprisonment, those created by corporal punishment pale in significance. In addition, corporal punishment is said to be easily subject to abuse in the hands of the sadistic and the unscrupulous. So, Newman argues, is any other punishment. As long as the sentence is carried out as it was imposed, there should be no abuse. But what about the cruelty of too much or too frequent whippings? Knowing the point when whipping passes from a permissible punishment to one that is cruel and unusual is a problem Newman acknowledges, but he suggests the same criticism applies to prison. When does confinement cease to serve its legitimate purpose and begin to be spiteful instead?

The claim that corporal punishment is cruel and unusual is one to which both Long and Newman respond. Newman believes the courts have consistently confused corporal punishment with torture under the mistaken belief that any punishment that causes immediate bodily pain is torture. Although some of the bloody corporal punishments of the past might correctly be called cruel, it is not appropriate to dismiss all infliction of pain as examples of cruelty. Newman offers corporal punishment as something that does not cause any lasting damage to the body (except that it hurts) and as such is not really cruel.

Newman finds claims about cruelty in corporal punishment to be especially ironic when presented by persons favoring the status quo of imprisonment, which he says includes the abuse of individuals through the brutality of prison violence, neglect, harsh diet, and mental torture. Supporting Newman's claim were accusations in the late 1990s of brutality at Corcoran State Prison (California) where guards were accused of setting up gladiator-style battles among inmates for the guards' entertainment and in arranging a prison-cell rape to punish an inmate. Although such action by correctional officers is certainly uncommon across the country, even its infrequent occurrence might call into question how much crueler corporal punishment could be. Newman would not close down the prisons because he believes they provide a necessary last resort. But when imprisonment is used, he suggests that the few prisons allowed to exist be "extremely harsh places, reserved only for the terrible few" (1995, p. 181).

In place of heavy reliance on imprisonment, Newman would substitute corporal punishment. The particular methods of corporal punishment that he champions are electric shock and whipping. Under Newman's punishment manifesto (1995, p. 179), most property crimes would result in electric shock to the offender. Electric shock is less violent in its application (at least in comparison to other corporal punishments), and it can be scientifically controlled and calibrated to ensure an appropriate level is administered. Violent criminals would receive a violent punishment such as whipping, which is flexible enough to provide that violence in measured levels as a response to different types of crimes. Whenever possible, however, Newman prefers that the punishment reflect the crime.[1] Persons who beat up another should receive a beating themselves. Those who risk the lives of others should have their own lives put at risk. And those who killed should be killed—but before considering that particular sanction, the following section takes a brief look at how corporal punishment is used in other parts of the world.

Corporal Punishment in Other Countries

The most civilized are as near to Barbarism as the most polished steel to rust. Nations, like metals, have only a superficial brilliancy.

—Antoine Rivarol

Mutilation, including amputation, is a form of corporal punishment still used in several countries. Libya's "purification laws" allow sentences of flogging and amputation; army deserters in Iraq have had their ears severed—allegedly without the use of anesthetic—and thieves have had their hands amputated; and in Saudi Arabia in 1998 at least two people convicted of theft had a hand amputated (Amnesty International, 1999b). In 1996 Iran amputated the fingers on six recidivist thieves while other convicted thieves were reportedly forced to watch (Amnesty International, 1996).

The prevalence of Middle Eastern countries as examples of sentences to mutilation is linked to provisions of Islamic justice. Using the Islamic Republic of Iran as his example, Darius Rejali explains that "the Islamic Penal Code provides for amputation in cases of recidivism, particularly with respect to crimes such as theft or robbery" (1994, p. 124). Apparently the amputation procedure is sometimes accomplished by an electric guillotine that severs a hand in a tenth of a second. Rejali believes the amputation device is an example of attempts to have better coordination of punishment between medical and political authorities. He offers an example of a 1990 amputation of four fingers from a convicted thief's right hand, which had been postponed earlier because the convict was suffering from high blood pressure.

In addition to the notoriety many Islamic countries receive regarding their use of amputation, citizens of other countries are also appalled, delighted, or at least intrigued by their methods of execution. Beheading is a common technique, but Islamic law also prescribes stoning as the means of carrying out a death penalty. The extent to which stoning is used to execute a condemned prisoner is difficult to verify, but Rejali (1994) suggests that at least in Iran, the percentage of executions

[1]Newman, G. (1995). *Just and painful.* (2nd ed.). Albany, NY: Harrow and Heston. Reprinted by permission of the author.

by stoning is a small proportion of all executions. But this discussion is shifting focus from corporal punishment to capital punishment, which requires a more specific introduction.

CAPITAL PUNISHMENT

The topic of **capital punishment** gives rise to some of the most emotional, yet academically interesting, debates of any criminal justice issue. The breadth and depth of potential issues to address in this area are too many to mention, let alone tackle in one section of one chapter of one book. The solution chosen here is to begin by covering the ways capital punishment has been applied over the centuries and in different places. That narrative is not provided to produce either disgust or titillation. Instead, a look at the way capital punishment has been imposed can provide an understanding of some contemporary issues in debates over the death penalty. For example, in *Weems v. United States* (1910), the U.S. Supreme Court held that cruel and unusual punishment, in terms of the Constitution's Eighth Amendment, must be interpreted in relation to contemporary concepts. Beheading was considered neither cruel nor unusual as recently as 1812 in Louisiana. Will twenty-first-century Americans look back in horror at the practice of lethal injection as used by their twentieth-century ancestors?

Forms of Capital Punishment

In addition to the variation in the type of crimes for which it is applied and the number of occasions on which it is used, the death penalty has come in many forms. Some of them were intended to be as cruel as possible; others were thought to be relatively painless. This chapter arbitrarily categorizes the means of capital punishment into three types: **death by natural elements, death by animal and insect,** and **death by instrument** (also see "Burning and Hanging Witches").

Death by Natural Elements. Death from exposure to the natural elements (earth, air, water, and fire) is one of the oldest ways to impose the ultimate penalty. Death by earth (e.g., burying alive) has been less frequent than the other three, but each has seen its time of popularity. Probably the most well-known version of death by exposure to air is the method of crucifixion. As used in the Middle East, classical Greece, parts of the Roman Empire, portions of Europe during the Middle Ages, and as recently as nineteenth-century Japan, crucified offenders were hung on a tree or a constructed cross. There they were left to die of exposure or starvation, although impaling or piercing with a spear might be used to bring a quicker death.

Also well known was death by fire as offenders were burned, often at a stake. Burning was especially popular in Europe from the fourteenth to the eighteenth centuries as the Christian church sought out examples of witchcraft. In England and the American colonies, witches were more likely to be hanged than burned. Burning was especially horrible for medieval Christians because it destroyed the body, and without a proper Christian burial of the body, a person could not spend eternity in heaven (Kronenwetter, 1993).[2]

Death by water was occasionally accomplished by not providing any water (death from thirst) but was more often the result of too much water (death by drowning), or of water that was too hot (death by boiling). Under Roman law, a

[2]Kronenwetter, M. (1993). *Capital punishment: A reference handbook.* Santa Barbara, CA: ABC-CLIO. Used with permission of the author.

ISSUES OF FAIRNESS

BURNING AND HANGING WITCHES

Both men and women have been accused of being witches. However, throughout history and across cultures the term *witch* has applied primarily to women who, with the help of Satan, harm people, animals, and things. Witch mania was extensive during the thirteenth to seventeenth centuries in Germany, France, Italy, and Spain. In those times, Merzbacher (1993) explains, typical characteristics of witches included red hair, certain moles, and nonobservance of holy days—all of which might identify a man or a woman. However, another characteristic, given sex roles of the period, pointed more often to women, that is, an "aversion to cooking and washing" (p. 184). And, because witches also were likely to have an "aversion to men," it is not surprising that women were more often accused. Punishment for witches included flogging and banishment, but many of those convicted on the European continent were burned. Because fire was seen as having the power to purge and devour all evil, it was the preferred method for handling witches. Witches were typically burnt on hills so the smoke that arose, and with it the witch's evil, could be carried away by the wind (Merzbacher, 1993, p. 141).

England also had its witches, or at least those so accused, and they too were mostly women. Ives (1914, 1970) suggests ordinary witch cases were best explained as the result of such things as hysterical subjects or private enemies. However, two other explanations may help explain the greater number of women among the accused. Using the term *wise women,* Ives says midwives traditionally resorted to charms, salves, and various medications that, especially when they worked, made the practitioner subject to accusations of trafficking with the devil. Also, many of the women were old and had outlived family and friends. They were left helpless and solitary and were often "... unclean from infirmities, eccentric in wisdom, crazy with delusions, palsied in limbs, or wandering in mind" (Ives, 1914, 1970, pp. 77–78). They were, in other words, easy marks for those hunting witches.

Unlike the continental punishment of burning, witches in England were hanged. Because the American colonies followed English law, the most famous witches in American history were also punished by hanging. The Salem witch trials were held in 1692 after some girls who had become friendly with a slave woman named Tituba began acting strangely—screaming, falling into convulsions, and barking like dogs. Other Salem girls began acting similarly, and the townspeople quickly seized on witchcraft as the cause and identified Tituba and two other women as the culprits. As fear spread so did the accusations, and between June and October of 1692 fourteen women and four men went to the gallows (D'Amario 1999). Obviously, many factors must be considered when seeking an explanation, but because we are concentrating on the link between women and accusations of witchcraft, Freidman (1993) makes a relevant point when he comments on most of the witches being older women: "In some subtle and not so subtle ways, the war against witches was also a war against women: or at least against disorderly, troublesome, deviant women" (p. 47).

Experience the witch trials at the National Geographic's interactive site at ***www.nationalgeographic.com/features/97/salem/***. Did you survive? You will also find interesting information at the Salem Witch Museum's site at ***www.salemwitchmuseum.com/learn2.html*** and at the Famous American Trials site at ***www.law.umkc.edu/faculty/projects/ftrials/salem/salem.htm***.

sentence to drowning was enhanced for persons who murdered their parents by having the parricide thrown into the water after being tied into a sack that also contained a dog, a cock, a viper, and an ape (Laurence, 1960). Adding special twists to the standard punishment is seen rather often around the world when the offender murdered his or her own parents.

Death by Animal and Insect. Death by animal and insect has been accomplished "naturally" by placing offenders outside in the hot sun, where their bodies are eventually assaulted by insects and ravenous birds. Sometimes the person was first skinned alive (flaying), then placed upon a sharp stick (impaling) like a grotesque scarecrow enticing rather than repelling the birds. Rather than waiting for a decaying body to attract insects, some versions of execution have the offender placed in a box with his or her limbs and head protruding through holes in the wood. Those extremities were then smeared with milk and honey to attract small animals and insects that would set about devouring the offender.

Death by larger animals has been accomplished through the classic punishment of being thrown to the lions to be eaten and the less well-known method of tossing the offender before the elephants to be trampled. Elephants have also been trained to crush a person's head with the weight from a foot. Horrendous as these techniques may have been, some believe they pale in comparison to being drawn and quartered, which involves tying horses to each arm and leg. The horses are then led in four different directions, each horse taking a limb with it as they pull.

Death by Instrument. Many different instruments or devices have been used for execution over the centuries. Some, such as the cross, have already been mentioned. But in this category of execution methods are those techniques that rely specifically on some apparatus or gadget to bring about death. The most simple of these instruments have included stoning the condemned (used in England into the tenth century and prescribed by law today in a few Islamic countries), flogging (whipped to death), running the gauntlet (forced to run along a path while being hit with rods of various types), sawing (the person was hung up by the feet and then divided vertically with the saw), pressing (heavy weights are applied to a board resting on the prone offender's chest, slowly crushing him), and by mallet (blows to the head from a well-slung mallet like the Italian *mazzatello*).

One of the most notable instruments of execution has been the sharp blade as used to separate the offender's head from its body (Abbott, 1994). This technique is notable not only because of its wide use but also because it provides the basis for the term *capital punishment.* Kronenwetter (1993) explains that the Latin word *capitalis,* which means "the head," provides the root for the English words *capital* and *decapitation.*

Beheading was practiced in ancient Greece and Rome, in several parts of Asia, and throughout much of Europe. Today it remains an official method of punishment in Belgium, the Congo, Mauritania, Saudi Arabia, Qatar, the United Arab Emirates, and the Arab Republic of Yemen (Kronenwetter, 1993). Axes and swords have been the traditional instruments for beheading, but some countries have used a decapitation machine such as the guillotine. Because a missed stroke by the executioner can result in enormous pain, those most likely to value the machine's increased precision are probably the machine's victims.

More recent execution instruments have included bullets from rifle fire, the electric chair, and deadly chemicals (lethal injection). An interesting aspect of these contemporary techniques is their assumed movement away from cruelty. As noted earlier in this chapter, the U.S. Supreme Court operates on the understanding that ideas of what is cruel and unusual will vary over time. Because of that, the Court does not consider the death penalty to be cruel and unusual in itself although some methods of carrying it out might be cruel. This idea of changing concepts of cruelty requires some elaboration because it has influenced the contemporary use of capital punishment and enters into some of the debates that we cover later.

Concerns about Cruelty

Beheading by the guillotine was presented in 1789 as a preferred execution method in a civilized society because it was swift, sure, and relatively painless. According to Paris physician Joseph Guillotine (who, despite persistent rumors, neither invented nor died by the machine bearing his name), "My victim will feel nothing but a slight sense of refreshing coolness on the neck. We cannot make too much haste, gentlemen, to allow the nation to enjoy this advantage" (quoted in Trager, 1979, p. 342). But a quote from another physician who observed a French execution seems to suggest something different:

> Immediately after the head was severed and dropped into the basket, I took charge of it. The facial expression was that of great agony, for several minutes after decapitation. He would open his eyes, also his mouth, in the process of gaping, as if he wanted to speak to me, and I am positive he could see me for several seconds after the head was severed from the body. There is no doubt that the brain was still active. . . . His decapitated body which was previously fastened by a strap upon a bench, was in continuous spasmodic and clonic convulsions, lasting from five to six minutes, also an indication of great suffering. (quoted in Barnes, 1972, pp. 235–236)

Electrocution was first used as a method of capital punishment in the United States on August 6, 1890, when New York State executed William Kemmler. It also was proposed as a relatively painless way to die because death would be virtually immediate. After strapping the condemned into a wooden chair, copper electrodes are attached to his or her head and legs. At the assigned time, a massive electrical charge is passed through the electrodes, causing the body's internal organs to burn and producing respiratory paralysis and cardiac arrest (Kronenwetter, 1993). But from that first electrocution, there were doubts that this would be a painless death. The first jolt of electricity given to Kemmler lasted only 15 seconds—enough to give rise to a purplish foam around his lips but not enough to cause death. With a second flow of electricity, lasting four minutes, the odor of burning flesh, singed hair, and a momentary blue flame at Kemmler's spine announced the successful execution.

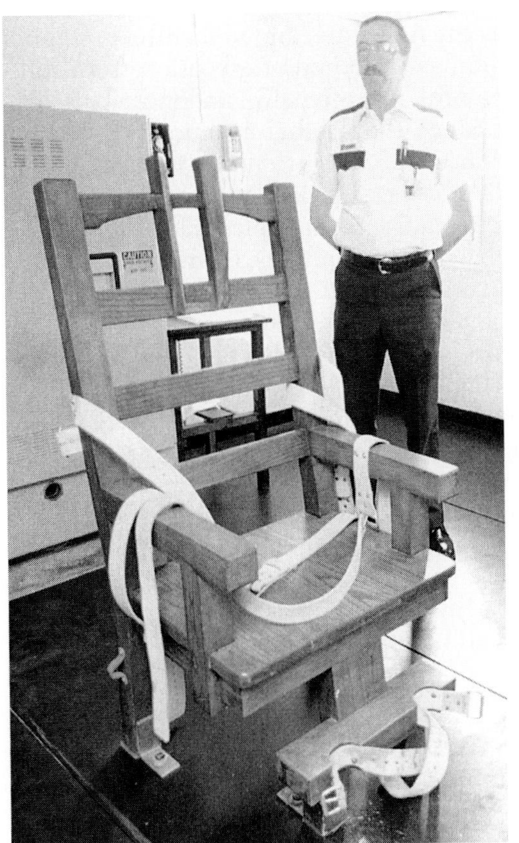

On at least three occasions in the 1990s, Florida electrocutions resulted in shooting flames or spurting blood from the condemned men. In January 2000, responding to criticism from a variety of sources, the Florida legislature provided lethal injection as an alternative to electrocution—with the condemned prisoner choosing between the two methods. Also in early 2000 Georgia legislators voted to replace electrocution with lethal injection for capital crimes committed after May 1, 2000. That left Alabama and Nebraska as the only states in which electrocution is the sole means of execution.

Proponents of the electric chair argued that the person being electrocuted loses consciousness and the sensation of pain as soon as the electricity begins to flow. Harold Hillman, an English physiologist and an expert in electrical burns, suggests that electrocution is quite likely very painful because the burns at the points of contact are quite severe. He suggests the body fluids must heat up to a temperature close to the boiling point of water in order to generate the steam, or wisps of smoke, which witnesses often note after an electrocution (quoted in Wikberg, 1992, p. 294). It seems those searching for a more humane method of execution would have to look beyond both beheading and electrocution.

In his 1972 book on punishment, first published in 1930, Barnes relates tortuous descriptions of executions by beheading and electrocution. Following those descriptions, Barnes supports a switch to lethal gas, which he says is a painless form of meeting death. His preference was to do away with capital punishment entirely, but until that time he argued that humanitarian sentiment must support lethal gas as the preferred method of execution (1972, pp. 245–246).

Some have suggested that the gas chamber presents more torture to the spectators than to the condemned because it is not a pleasant thing to watch. Persons who had observed many hangings considered the lethal gas execution they watched to be "the most terrible thing I've seen" and suggested there was "nothing humane about it." A prison physician declared hanging to be "much simpler and much quicker." A prison guard admitted "it was pretty awful watching those men stare at you" (quotes from Barnes & Teeters, 1943, p. 420).

The most recent version of a humane execution is actually a return to one of the oldest. More than 2,300 years ago Socrates drank a cup of poisonous hemlock, and in 1982 Charlie Brooks, Jr. received lethal injections of sodium thiopental (an anesthetic), pancuronium bromide (a muscle relaxant designed to paralyze), and potassium chloride (to stop the heart). He died, as planned, from the overdose of sodium thiopental, and in this way dying was presumed to be "no more traumatic than falling asleep" ("A New Executioner," 1981, p. 80).

The execution of Brooks made Texas the first state, and in fact the first jurisdiction in the world, to use lethal injection as a method of execution. Texas officials lauded the new technique as less painful, less offensive, and more palatable ("A 'More Palatable' Way," 1982, p. 28). Since 1982, lethal injection has become the technique of choice in most of the states with death penalty statutes. Adding to the Texas arguments, officials in other states claim that lethal injection is also quicker, more certain, and, as a Louisiana state senator explained, it "minimizes the cruelty in taking a life" (quoted in Wikberg, 1992, p. 284). By mid-2000, thirty-six states and the federal government had authorized lethal injection for execution. Fifteen states allow either lethal injection or an alternative method with most of those states leaving the choice up to the condemned prisoner.

But execution by lethal injection has had its share of problems. In 1985 a Texas executioner spent forty minutes and made twenty-three separate "needle pokes" in the prisoner's arm while trying to find a vein suitable for inserting the needle. By the Supreme Court's view of contemporary standards, lethal injection is no more cruel than is death by electrocution, lethal gas, hanging, or firing squad. But because contemporary standards change, U.S. citizens in future generations may use the following descriptions to depict death by lethal injection in the same manner—and elicit similar reactions—that the methods such as flaying and impaling, the garrote, and beheading were presented here.

> *Rickey Ray Rector (Arkansas, 1992)*—It took medical staff more than 50 minutes to find a suitable vein in Rector's arm. Witnesses were not permitted to view this scene, but reported hearing Rector's loud moans throughout the process. During the ordeal, Rector (who suffered serious brain damage from a lobotomy) tried to help the medical personnel find a vein. The administrator of the State's Department of Corrections medical

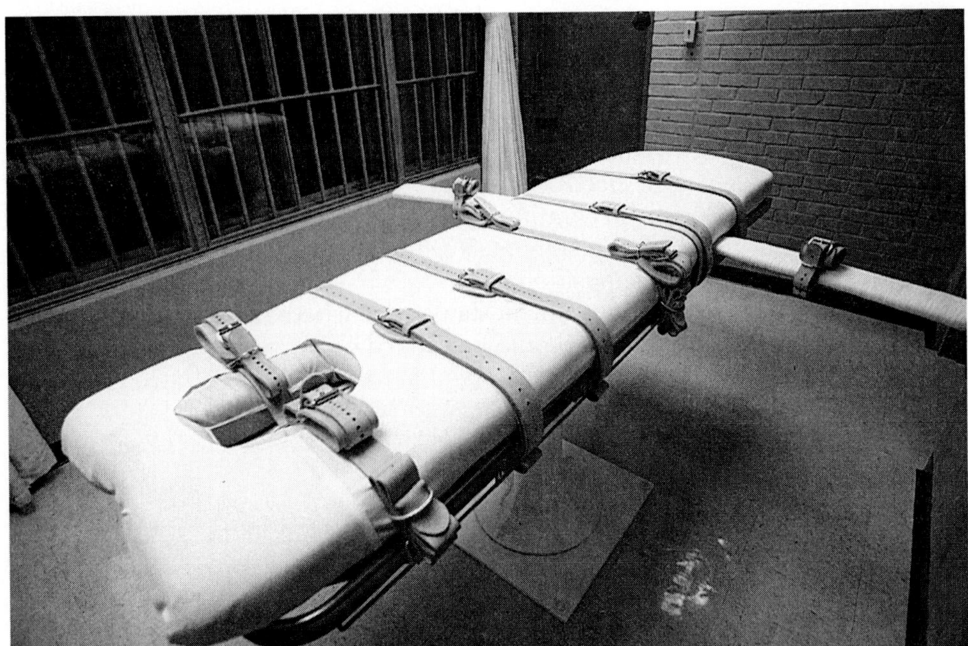

Since its first use in Texas in 1982, lethal injection has become the most popular method of execution in the United States. In early 2000 there were thirty-six states using lethal injection as the sole method of execution or as one of several authorized methods.

programs said (paraphrased by a newspaper reporter) "the moans did come as a team of two medical people that had grown to five worked on both sides of his body to find a vein." The administrator said "that may have contributed to his occasional outburst."

Emmitt Foster (Missouri, 1995)—Foster was not pronounced dead until 30 minutes after the executioners began the flow of the death chemicals into his arms. Seven minutes after the chemicals began to flow, the blinds were closed to prohibit the witnesses from viewing the scene; they were not reopened until three minutes after death was pronounced. According to the coroner, who pronounced death, the problem was caused by the tightness of the leather straps that bound Foster to the gurney; it was so tight that the flow of chemicals into his veins was restricted. It was several minutes after a prison worker finally loosened the strap that death was pronounced. The coroner entered the death chamber twenty minutes after the execution began, noticed the problem, and told the officials to loosen the strap so that the execution could proceed.

Scott Carpenter (Oklahoma, 1997)—Two minutes after the lethal chemicals began flowing into the body of Scott Carpenter at 12:11 a.m., he began to make noises, his stomach and chest began pulsing, and his jaw clenched. In total, his body made 18 violent convulsions, followed by 8 milder ones. His face, which first turned a yellowish gray, had turned a deep purple and gray by 12:20 a.m. He was officially pronounced dead at 12:22 a.m. (Radelet, 1999)

It may be that cruelty, like beauty, is in the eye of the beholder. There are people today, in the United States and other parts of the world, who believe the death penalty could be conducted with many of the techniques used in the past, and the end result would be more justice than savagery. They are not, in other words, distracted by the possibility that execution results in pain. Kronenwetter (1993) quotes one commentator from the Washington Legal Foundation as saying "pain and discomfort are an inherent and necessary aspect of legal punishment," whereas another suggests that condemned criminals "are not entitled to die with no pain whatsoever" (p. 52). During a Louisiana debate over the switch from the electric chair to lethal injection, a state representative asked, "Why should we be concerned about doing it in a humane manner? . . . Shouldn't we be doing it to set an example instead of saying you just fall asleep and go away for killing people?" (quoted in Wikberg, 1992, p. 285).

The U.S. Supreme Court, although abiding by the view that standards of cruelty change over time, has forbidden punishments that involve torture (such as being disemboweled, drawn and quartered, or burned alive) but has allowed the death penalty by hanging or electrocution (21 Am Jur 2d, Criminal Law, §627). It seems likely that the Court will continue to be asked if various forms of execution constitute cruel or unusual punishment. Regardless of their decision, there will be citizens who voice their opposition.

Debate over how capital punishment should be carried out is surpassed in passion only by the debate over if it should be carried out. We turn our attention to that controversy in an attempt to understand better the issues related to this divisive sanction.

Debating Capital Punishment

> *If we are to abolish the death penalty, I should like to see the first step taken by my friends the murderers.*
>
> —Alphonse Karr

> *The death penalty is an excessive and unnecessary punishment that violates the Eighth Amendment.*
>
> —Justice Thurgood Marshall

These quotes—from Karr for the retentionists and Marshall for the abolitionists—reflect the great distance between persons wishing to retain the death penalty and those wishing to abolish it. The points of debate have been identified in a variety of ways and cover a wide range of issues (see "Debating Capital Punishment"). This discussion looks at the issues of specific and general deterrence, fairness, and retribution.

The Deterrence Debate. The death penalty seems to obviously serve as a specific deterrent. The executed person will not commit another crime. But specific deterrence is still an appropriate topic for discussion if it is approached from another angle. For example, what if execution is not the only way to achieve specific deterrence? If some punishment short of the death penalty can deter the offender from continued criminality, does that weaken the argument that execution is necessary for specific deterrence? As a reminder, people who support the death penalty as just deserts will not care if it deters the offender or others. But those people who argue that the death penalty is necessary to prevent the offender from committing other crimes, especially murder, should be interested in other sanctions that can achieve a similar goal. For that reason, the possibility that specific deterrence can be achieved without resorting to the death penalty must be considered.

The 1972 *Furman v. Georgia* decision had the effect of nullifying death penalty sentences around the country. This presented researchers with the rare occurrence of what is called a natural experiment. Social scientists often find it difficult to use an experimental design to study relationships among variables. Because the experimental design requires precisely controlled conditions, the subjects (humans) in social science research make it difficult and sometimes unethical to set up many experiments. It would, for example, be unethical (and possibly dangerous to the community) to randomly assign some offenders to probation, suspended sentence, or prison just to see the impact of each sanction on things such as deterrence or rehabilitation. Similarly, public opinion would not—and should not—allow the ex-

Spotlight ON CONTEMPORARY ISSUES

Debating Capital Punishment

The chapter reviews several topics on which retentionists and abolitionists base their respective arguments. In addition to those, the following areas are also the basis for disagreement:

- The expense of capital punishment versus life imprisonment—as long as unlimited appeals are allowed, the court proceedings associated with death penalty cases will continue to make the execution process more expensive. But the Anti-Terrorism and Effective Death Penalty Act of 1996 (Title 28, U.S.C. §2244(d)) restricts the access state prisoners have to federal courts when seeking habeas corpus review. A result may be fewer appeals at the federal level for state prisoners receiving a death sentence. Also there are reports that an increasing number of death row inmates are dropping their appeals and opting to be executed. Willing (1999) explains that sixty-eight prisoners executed in 1998 said they wanted to die compared with six in 1997.
- The possibility that capital punishment actually increases the murder rate—the "brutalizing effect"—by attracting criminals so filled with self-hatred that they commit capital crimes so they will be executed by the state. Execution, for them, is a form of suicide (see Van Wormer, 1995).
- The problems presented by executing people who are mentally retarded or mentally ill. The U.S. Supreme Court ruled that executing a mentally retarded person is not unconstitutional (*Penry v. Lynaugh,* 1989), although jurors can take that condition into account as a mitigating factor. And, although the U.S. Supreme Court prohibits the execution of a person found to be insane at the time set for the execution (*Ford v. Wainwright,* 1986), a mentally ill person can be executed if he or she understands the punishment and why it has been ordered.
- The possibility of executing an innocent person is enough reason for some people to ban the use of death sentences. Others suggest that the horror of a rare mistake is outweighed by the benefits of execution when it is appropriate. Since 1973, over eighty people in the United States have been sentenced to death and then freed from death row when it became clear they were innocent or that they were wrongfully convicted. Florida, with twenty death row survivors, leads the nation in wrongful death sentences, but Illinois (where twelve condemned inmates had been freed from death row in twelve years) was second (Freedberg, 1999; Mills & Armstrong, 1999). Many of the convictions were thrown out as a result of exoneration by DNA testing.

Many places on the Internet provide interesting, accurate, and current information that will help you develop arguments for your pro or con position on capital punishment. The California Department of Corrections provides information about the state's death row inmates and about California executions since 1978 at ***www.cdc.state.ca.us/issues/capital/capital.htm.*** You can read about Harris County, Texas (the "capital of capital punishment"), at ***www.csmonitor.com/durable/1999/07/29/p1s4.htm.*** Read about the extent of wrongful murder convictions at ***sun.soci.niu.edu/~critcrim/wrong/wrong.html.*** For the most complete and current statistics on capital punishment visit the Death Penalty Information Center at ***www.essential.org/dpic/firstpage.html.***

ecution of some offenders and the return to the community of others, just so we can study aspects of the death penalty. Occasionally a situation occurs that gives researchers an opportunity to study relationships among variables without having to manipulate the situation. Such a natural experimental situation resulted from the *Furman v. Georgia* decision when some persons who were to have been executed were eventually returned to the community. This meant it would be possible to observe the behavior of persons who were supposed to have been executed but instead were punished with a term of incarceration. If those offenders went on to commit other crimes, one might argue that specific deterrence could have been better achieved by their execution. On the other hand, if those offenders did not continue their criminal ways, it might be argued that specific deterrence had been achieved with incarceration.

After the *Furman* decision, more than 600 offenders nationwide had their death sentences commuted. Those Furman-commuted offenders typically received a life imprisonment sentence in place of the death sentence, and as a result most of them eventually became eligible for parole. Marquart and Sorensen (1988) were interested in the postrelease performance of Furman-commuted offenders. Their study of 28 such offenders in Texas compared those offenders with a control group of 109 violent offenders who had received a life sentence for crimes of murder or rape. The research question was whether the Furman releasees, as compared with the control group, inflicted injury on others after their release from prison. The researchers found that when technical violations were excluded, six (6 percent) of the life sentence group and four (14 percent) of the Furman releasees did commit a new (known) felony while free in the community. The four new felonies committed by the Furman group included two burglaries, one rape, and one murder. The murder occurred when one of the Furman releasees murdered his girlfriend and then committed suicide. The new felonies by the life sentence group included four burglaries, one robbery, one rape, but no murders.

Upon comparing the recidivism of twenty-one people in the Furman group who had committed murder only to other studies of recidivism among first-degree murderers, Marquart and Sorensen determined that the Furman offenders were returned to prison at a similar rate. That is, the offenders who were to have been executed behaved similarly after release from prison as did other released murderers. The authors conclude that because nearly all the released Furman inmates proved to be good "risks" in the free community, "executing the offender to protect society is not a valid response to violent crime or a legitimate sentencing policy" (Marquart & Sorensen, 1988, p. 690). But what about the four new felonies committed by that group—especially the murder and the rape? We return to that point after looking at a broader study of Furman releasees.

The study of Furman-commuted inmates was extended to a national level by Vito, Koester, and Wilson (1991). At the time of their 1987 survey, thirty-five releasees (19.7 percent of 177) had been returned to prison. The recidivism rate was primarily the result of nonviolent offenses such as parole violations and burglary, but eight parolees were returned after committing a violent crime of murder (3), robbery (3), rape (1), or kidnapping (1). Overall, the 19.7 percent reincarceration rate of the Furman releasees falls in the middle of the range (9.7 percent to 29.0 percent) of reported reincarceration rates of paroled murderers followed in other studies. But even though the Furman releasees performed better than many would have expected, Vito et al. (1991) leave us with the same question Marquart and Sorensen ask in their study: Does the murder of three citizens—one being the Texas murder noted by Marquart and Sorensen—constitute an acceptable level of risk? Stated a bit differently, would executing 478 persons (the total of Furman-commuted inmates in the nationwide study) in order to prevent three additional homicides be a reasonable or an extraordinary measure?

The idea that people will be deterred from committing murder if they can expect to be executed themselves seems inherently logical. In fact, a belief that the death penalty provides a general deterrent is one of the oldest reasons for its use. Executions were held in public with a deliberate intention of persuading those who might be thinking about committing murder, or some other capital crime of the time, to decide against such behavior. But murder and other crimes continued, and the public executions themselves were often a stimulus to criminal behavior.

Espy (1980) relates descriptions of public executions that invariably seemed to invite thefts and encourage fights among the spectators. Such misbehavior among the supposed "students" at the gallows classroom led more and more people to wonder if the lesson was being learned. Finally, in 1936 at Owensboro, Kentucky, the last public execution in the United States was held. A crowd estimated between 10,000 and 20,000 gathered to watch a nineteen-year-old black man be hanged for the rape and murder of a seventy-year-old white woman (Espy, 1980; "10,000 Witness," 1936). The combination of a disorderly crowd and scathing criticism from the national media resulted in this event being the last of its kind in the United States.

Even when the death penalty is imposed in a private setting, reason seems to suggest that it should deter persons from doing something that could result in their execution. That belief goes back to the logic of the classical school, in which people such as Beccaria and Bentham (see Chapter 2) argued that under conditions of certainty, severity, and swiftness, punishment can effectively keep the rational person from committing a crime. Issues of certainty, severity, and swiftness are admittedly important, but an overriding matter is the assumption of rationality. Abolitionists argue, for example, that murder is seldom a rational act. Quite the contrary; it typically occurs in the heat of the moment and frequently involves alcohol or drugs in the victim, offender, or both. This lethal mix does not create a setting for rational decision making. If a punishment only deters when the potential offender can rationally weigh the pros and cons of a proposed act, the death penalty will not deter the majority of murders—because they are emotional, not rational acts.

Retentionists respond to the rationality argument by suggesting that the death penalty's deterrent effect is achieved through the socialization process. Throughout his or her life, the individual comes to internalize the association of act and penalty. Good behavior becomes something that occurs naturally rather than something that results from constant weighing of pros and cons throughout the day. Goldberg (1991) uses an analogy of angry husbands to make the point. Most husbands, he argues, slam doors, shout, or sulk when they are angry. Some husbands, when angry, murder their wives. "The question is not what deterred the person who did murder (nothing did), but what deterred the person who didn't" (Goldberg, 1991, p. 114). The slamming, shouting, sulking husband has presumably instilled a psychological resistance to murder—not because he makes a rational decision in the heat of the moment but because he has internalized the link between killing and the death penalty.

Interesting though the philosophical debate on deterrence might be, much of the discussion about deterrence and the death penalty has relied on statistics. Use of statistical analysis is especially popular among abolitionists because the evidence has consistently supported the position that the death penalty does not serve as a general deterrent to murder. Actually, it is more accurate to say that it is no more a deterrent than is a prison sentence. Kronenwetter (1993) notes that as long ago as 1919, statistical studies were showing that there was no measurable relation between the homicide rate and the existence or absence of the death penalty. Since then, researchers have repeatedly failed to find a general-deterrent effect in executions. Even in Texas, where executions have been most frequent among the death penalty states, Sorenson, Wrinkle, Brewer, Marquart, and James (1999) found that data from 1984 through 1997 showed "the number of executions did not appear to influence either the rate of murder in general or the rate of felony murder in particular" (pp. 489–490). The authors conclude, as has the vast majority of other studies on deterrence and capital punishment (see Peterson & Bailey, 1998), that factors other than execution are responsible for the variation and trends in murder rates.

A few studies claim to have found a deterrent effect. From his nationwide study of capital punishment in the midtwentieth-century United States, Ehrlich (1975) suggested that eight murders were prevented by each execution. His findings have been roundly criticized, and attempts at replication have failed to confirm a deterrent effect (Paternoster, 1991). The greatest damage to Ehrlich's study came from a board of experts commissioned by the National Academy of Sciences to review his findings. They determined that it offered no useful evidence for a deterrent effect of capital punishment (Kronenwetter, 1993).

The statistical evidence so far is on the side of the abolitionists. Paternoster (1991) summarizes the research in this way: "After years of research with different methodologies and statistical approaches, the empirical evidence seems to clearly suggest that capital punishment is not a superior general deterrent" (p. 241). But even with statistics on their side, abolitionists have trouble responding to the retentionists' point that only the times when the death penalty has not deterred can be counted because only then is there something to count. There is no way of knowing when it did deter because there is nothing to count when the murder does not happen.

The Fairness Debate. A number of issues are raised when discussing the fairness of the death penalty. Many of those issues are based on statistics that show the death penalty is applied most often to men, disproportionately to blacks and Hispanics, and invariably to poor defendants (see the feature "Is the Death Penalty Class Biased?"). Women, whites, and rich people also commit capital crimes, but they have not been executed quite as regularly. Other fairness issues are raised during discussions about executing juveniles.

Dobash, Dobash, and Gutteridge (1986) point out that at times in history, women have been subjected to more severe punishments for the same offense as men. During the Middle Ages women could be burned to death for adultery or murdering their spouse, but adultery was sometimes not even considered an offense for men. Even when there was equity in the death sentence, the means of execution was often hanging for men but burning (presumably a more agonizing death) for women.

The execution of women in the United States has not followed a Middle Ages tradition of bias either in application or in method. The first woman known to have been executed in the United States was Jane Campion, who was hanged for an unstated crime in 1632 in Virginia. Since then there have been more than 560 documented instances of actual execution of female offenders in U.S. jurisdictions. That number constitutes less than 3 percent of the approximately 19,200 confirmed executions since 1608. Since 1880 the percentage of women sentenced to death has consistently been between 1 percent and 3 percent of the total (Cahalan, 1986; Snell, 1998). It appears that over the years the percentage of women executed has been less than the percentage at risk of execution (see "You're a Pretty Good Man, Eva" on page 197). If a sex bias does exist in the application of the death penalty, it may be one that favors women. Although women account for about 3 percent of all executions since 1608, only five females have been executed since 1977 (less than 1 percent).

Racial and ethnic discrimination in applying the death penalty has been an easily documented situation for many years. Traditionally, the bias has been recognized as relating to the race and ethnicity of the offender; more recently, attention has turned to the race and ethnicity of the victim. We look first at characteristics of the offender.

Statistics on Hispanics sentenced to death have been asked for in official statistics since only 1977. As a result, historical data about minority populations are restricted primarily to information about African Americans. Official statistics on capital punishment and death row populations are provided by the Department of Justice (e.g., see the annual bulletin titled *Capital Punishment*) under a program that started in 1926. Much of the historical data, however, begins with 1930 information. Cahalan (1986) uses census data and a variety of other sources to provide information on executions and illegal lynchings from as early as 1882. From these sources, we find some clear patterns regarding blacks and the death penalty.

Between 1882 and 1962 (the last report of a lynching), 4,736 illegal lynchings were reported in the United States. Of those lynchings 73 percent were of black persons, with the regional breakdown showing 67 percent black in the Northeast,

ISSUES OF FAIRNESS

IS THE DEATH PENALTY CLASS BIASED?

One searches our chronicles in vain for the execution of any member of the affluent strata of this society.
—Justice William O. Douglas

There may be many reasons why the death penalty is imposed mostly on society's poor and lower class, but one reason is glaringly obvious: "They can't afford good lawyers." Because a good, experienced lawyer will improve the defendant's chances at each stage in the legal process, "the better the lawyer, the better the defendant's chances of escaping execution" (Kronenwetter, 1993, p. 36). Or, as author Stephen Bright (1994) subtitled one of his articles: "The Death Sentence Not for the Worst Crime but for the Worst Lawyer."

Blaming the defense lawyer in cases in which the death penalty is imposed is essentially a condemnation of public defenders and court-appointed attorneys as not being good or experienced lawyers. Certainly there are good, well-trained, and imminently qualified public defenders and court-appointed attorneys handling death penalty cases around the country. But there are also public defenders and court-appointed attorneys who have exceedingly high case loads or may not have worked many death penalty cases. In a study of death penalty cases in Texas, researchers found that capital defendants with court-appointed lawyers were more than twice as likely to receive a death sentence as were those able to hire their own attorneys (Kronenwetter, 1993).

The characteristics of persons on death row seem to reflect those of the poor and lower class in society as a whole. Although most of the criminal justice system's clients are poor, death row inmates are among the poorest. They also have completed less formal education, are less employable, often show abnormal emotional characteristics, and display a variety of substance abuse problems (Endres, 1991). Unfortunate and unfair as it is, persons with those characteristics elicit little sympathy from justice system officials, jurors, or the general public. We know that punishments for other crimes, such as marijuana possession, have eased as the behavior includes more and more of the middle class. Those offenders do draw sympathy from officials, jurors, and the community with a result being a lessening of penalties associated with the behavior. Endres (1991) wonders, as have many others, how long the death penalty would have lasted if most of those executed had reflected typical middle-class characteristics.

Proponents of the death penalty argue that inequities in the application of the death penalty should draw criticism of its application, not of its use. As van den Haag (1991) argues, "If guilty whites or wealthy people escape the gallows and guilty poor people do not, the poor or black do not become less guilty. . . . nor do they deserve less punishment because others did not get the punishment they deserve" (p. 158).

Download and read Stephen Bright's article "Counsel for the Poor: The Death Sentence Not for the Worst Crime but for the Worst Lawyer" at ***schr.org/reports/docs/counsel3.pdf.*** Do you think Bright makes a convincing argument? What changes could be made in death penalty cases to ensure an adequate defense? There is other information at the Southern Center for Human Rights Web site that you will find interesting. Check it out at ***schr.org/center/index.html.***

83 percent in the South (with South Carolina's 98 percent the highest of any state), 36 percent in the North Central, and 5 percent in the West (Cahalan, 1986).

America's black population has not fared much better when legal executions are considered. Blacks constituted between 10 and 12 percent of the total U.S. population during the twentieth century. The percentage varies by region of the country with the highest proportion consistently being in southern states. In fact, when statistics comparing executions under state authority are presented as a rate per 100,000 nonwhites in each region of the country, the South had the lowest rate for the decades of the 1890s, 1900s, 1910s, and 1920s. In the 1930s, 1940s, 1950s, and 1960s, the South's rate of executions per nonwhite population was consistently second to the West's rate (Cahalan, 1986). These data are misleading because

Karla Faye Tucker, shown here reading her Bible in the visiting room of a Texas prison, was executed in 1998 for her role in a double murder. By mid-2000 five women (two in Texas) had been executed in the United States since the death penalty was reinstated in 1976.

blacks were being lynched in the South at a much higher rate than any other region, so it can be assumed that fewer black citizens were even brought before the legal authorities.

It is important to understand that evidence of racial discrimination in the United States is not restricted to southern states. Because most of the executions—since their resumption in 1977—have occurred in southern states, it is not appropriate to compare rates of blacks executed in the South to their rates in other regions. But if we look at persons under a sentence of death, we find large enough numbers to draw some conclusions. At the end of 1997 there were 1,406 persons under sentence of death in the United States (Snell, 1998). Table 6.1 (see page 198) shows that in the Northeast, 60 percent of those persons were black, whereas the Midwest had 51 percent black, the South was 43 percent black, and the West was 30 percent black. In every region, the proportion of blacks under sentence of death exceeded their percentage of the region's population. But look at how the percentages compare to the proportion of black citizens in each region.

When we compare the percentage of blacks in a region's total population to that region's percentage of blacks sentenced to death, we find that the South, though still disproportionate, has a lower ratio than the other regions. Clearly, the percentage of blacks sentenced to death exceeds their proportion of each region's black population. But it is important to understand that any racial discrimination causing such disproportion is not restricted to just one region of the country. Racial disproportionality on the country's death rows is found everywhere in the United States and as a result has been the basis for criticism of the death sentence.

In a report on race and the death penalty, Amnesty International—USA (1999) concluded that there is no evidence "that current legal safeguards eliminate racial bias in the application of the death penalty." The report notes the potential for

ISSUES OF FAIRNESS

"YOU'RE A PRETTY GOOD MAN, EVA"

In 1930 Eva Dugan was executed for the murder of the Arizona rancher with whom she was living. As she was being escorted through the prison doors on her way to the gallows, she told a guard, "Don't hang onto my arm that way. They'll think I can't walk." A few steps later she asked one of her guards, "Why are you so attentive tonight?" He did not answer, but the guard on her other side said, "You're a pretty good man, Eva." "You're not a better one," she flashed in reply (quoted in Gillespie, 1997, p. 4). Eva was decapitated at her hanging because a debilitating muscle disease had weakened her neck. The beheading outraged the public, and hanging as a form of execution was banned in Arizona (O'Shea, 1999).

Whether because of gender roles and expectations or other complex reasons, women have not been executed in the United States as often as their number on death row suggests they could be. Since 1973 women have averaged about 2 percent of the total number of inmates on death row in the United States. But rather than comprising 2 percent of the persons executed, women make up 0.005 percent of the total. Since 1900 only 0.5 percent of all twentieth-century executions were of women (Streib, 1999a).

In 1984 North Carolina executed Velma Barfield, and she became the first woman executed in the United States since the resumption of executions in 1977. By mid-2000 other women had been executed—two in Texas, one in Florida, and one in Arkansas.

As of June 1999 (see Streib, 1999a):

- Three states (Florida, North Carolina, and Texas) account for one-third of all death sentences for female offenders.
- Most of the women (38 percent) on death row are in the thirty to thirty-nine age category although 10 percent are over age sixty.
- In 1999 a federal judge overturned the death sentence of a seventy-eight-year-old woman believed to have been the nation's oldest woman on death row ("Oldest Woman," 1999).
- Most of the women under sentence of death were white (53 percent), with 36 percent being black and 11 percent Latina.
- Most of the victims were men (56 percent).

Go to the most current issue of the Bureau of Justice Statistics publication, *Capital Punishment*, at ***www.ojp.usdoj.gov/bjs/cp.htm.*** How many people were executed in the year covered by the publication? What were the three states in which the most executions occurred? If any women were among those executed, what information can you find about the circumstances of their crime(s)? Even more current information is usually available from Professor Victor Streib (Ohio Northern University) who makes his report "Death Penalty for Female Offenders" available electronically at ***www.law.onu.edu/faculty/streib/femdeath.htm.*** Find your state in Streib's report or a neighboring state if yours does not have the death penalty, and read about the crimes of any women sentenced to death in your state.

racial bias linked to prosecutorial discretion because it is unreasonable to think individual prosecutors are not influenced by the racial divisions affecting American society. To support the existence of prosecutorial bias, the report notes that only 2 percent of the nation's district attorneys are nonwhite and also cites studies showing prosecutors in some jurisdictions seem to selectively apply the death penalty on the basis of race (Amnesty International—USA, 1999). However, as an editorial in the *New York Post* notes, because the death penalty can only be sought when aggravating circumstances are present, it is possible that such circumstances appear disproportionally by race ("Amnesty International Is Dead Wrong," 1999). If that is true—and at least one study suggests it may be (see Rothman and Powers, 1994)—prosecutors may bring death penalty charges against black defendants more often because of the circumstances of their alleged crime rather than because of their race. The issue, like so many linked to the death penalty, is

TABLE 6.1: Proportion of Blacks under Sentence of Death to Their Share of the Population, 1997

	BLACKS IN THE POPULATION (%)	BLACKS AMONG THOSE SENTENCED TO DEATH (%)	BLACKS SENTENCED TO DEATH COMPARED TO BLACK POPULATION OF REGION
United States	13	42	3 to 1
Northeast	12	60	5 to 1
Midwest	10	51	5 to 1
South	19	43	2 to 1
West	5	30	6 to 1

Source: Table compiled from data in *Statistical Abstracts of the United States, 1994* (Bureau of the Census) and *Capital Punishment 1997* (Bureau of Justice Statistics, NCJ 172881).

complex! And, not surprisingly, the issue of race has been an important factor in some U.S. Supreme Court decisions. We return to this topic later when considering court decisions on the death penalty.

In Chapter 12, the text reviews the long-held belief that juveniles and adults do not share equal responsibility for their actions. Suffice it to note here that American jurisdictions, following England's lead, accepted very early on that a person must be of a certain age before he or she is able to have criminal intent. The age was not completely arbitrary (being first based on the Church of England's position that a person under age seven could not commit a sin), but there have never been solid arguments to support one age over another. Because common law prefers to punish as criminal only those persons who have knowingly and intentionally committed a crime, there has been a tradition of excluding from criminal responsibility those persons acting without knowledge or intention. Of course, the problem comes in trying to identify the offenders who fall into the category for exclusion. In the absence of tests or other evaluation techniques that can measure a person's level of responsibility or maturity, legal systems around the world have relied on age as the distinguishing criterion. Inexact and inaccurate as it is, persons under a certain age are considered immature and irresponsible whereas persons over that age are deemed mature and responsible.

The age distinction for criminal responsibility in most American jurisdictions is between seven and twelve, with age ten the most frequently used point at which a person is said to have become criminally responsible. Individuals committing their crime, including murder, when they were under that jurisdiction's age of criminal responsibility cannot be punished with the prescribed sanction for criminals. By definition they cannot be criminals. But in addition to an age of criminal responsibility, all American jurisdictions have also set an age when a person becomes an adult for purposes of criminal prosecution. As a result, there is a period between a state's age of criminal responsibility (e.g., age ten) and an age of adult status (e.g., age eighteen) when offenders are prosecuted by the juvenile justice system instead of the adult justice system. But for some kinds of offenses, jurisdictions have decided the act is so serious that they allow juveniles above the age of criminal responsibility to be transferred to the state's adult court system. This transfer process is covered in Chapter 12, so here it is simply noted that murder is among those crimes for which a juvenile can be prosecuted as an adult. When that happens, the juvenile is then subject to any punishment that an adult might receive for the same offense. The youngest person executed in the United States was Hannah Ocuish, a twelve-year-old Indian girl, who was hanged in 1786 in Connecticut for murdering a six-year-old white girl. In contemporary times

American jurisdictions have set at least age sixteen as the minimum age a person should have reached, when the crime was committed, before that person is subject to the death penalty (see Table 6.2).

The constitutionality of executing persons who were juveniles when they committed their crime is fairly clear (Streib, 1999b). In *Thompson v. Oklahoma* (1988), the Court ruled that it would be unconstitutional to execute offenders who were age fifteen or younger at the time of their crime. In *Stanford v. Kentucky* (1989), the U.S. Supreme Court held that there is no constitutional prohibition against the death penalty for crimes committed at age sixteen or seventeen. With the legal authority to conduct such executions firmly established, the execution of persons who were juveniles when they committed their crime began increasing during the 1990s. Between 1973 and mid-1999, a total of 180 juvenile death sentences were imposed in American jurisdictions. Two-thirds of those were for seventeen-year-old offenders and one-third of the sentences were for offenders ages sixteen and fifteen (Streib,

TABLE 6.2: Minimum Age Authorized for Capital Punishment, 1999[1]

AGE 18	AGE 17	AGE 16
California	Georgia	Alabama
Colorado	New Hampshire	Arizona
Connecticut	North Carolina	Arkansas
Illinois	Texas	Delaware
Kansas		Florida
Maryland		Idaho
Nebraska		Indiana
New Jersey		Kentucky
New Mexico		Louisiana
New York		Mississippi
Ohio		Missouri
Oregon		Montana
Tennessee		Nevada
Washington		Oklahoma
Federal		Pennsylvania
		South Carolina
		South Dakota
		Utah
		Virginia
		Wyoming

[1]The U.S. Supreme Court decision *Thompson v. Oklahoma*, 487 U.S. 815 (1988) effectively set age sixteen (at the time of the crime) as the youngest age at which a state can authorize execution of an offender. States that do not specify an age in their state statutes are included here under age sixteen by default in accordance with the *Thompson* decision.

Source: From Snell, T. L. (1999). *Capital punishment 1998* [NCJ 179012]. Washington, DC: Bureau of Justice Statistics.

1999b). By mid-1999, 13 of the 140 sentences had resulted in executions. Twelve of those executed were age seventeen at the time of their crime, and the youngest at the time of his execution was age twenty-four (Jay Pinkerton in Texas). Sean Sellers, the sole person executed for a crime committed at age sixteen, was age twenty-nine at the time of his 1999 execution in Oklahoma.

There has been a dramatic increase in the number of murder arrests of persons under age eighteen in recent years. Arrests of persons under age eighteen on charges of murder and nonnegligent manslaughter increased 51 percent from 1987 to 1996. During the same period, the number of arrests for persons over age eighteen had *decreased* 10 percent (Maguire & Pastore, 1998). Violent crime, especially murder, is increasingly committed by younger offenders. During this Retributive era, it seems likely that more juvenile death sentences will be imposed and more persons executed who were juveniles when committing their crime. Questions about the fairness of executing juveniles, who presumably have less culpability than do adults, are likely to be countered with statements about the fairness of having an equal response to all offenders, regardless of age, who commit heinous crimes where aggravating factors outweigh any mitigating ones.

The Retribution Debate. The last capital punishment topic discussed here is that of *lex talionis*—the "eye for an eye, tooth for a tooth" position. In many ways this is the most difficult of the points to debate because technically it provides no basis for debate. Newman (1985) says retributivists—the prime supporters of this view—are often asked the trap question, "Why must a wrongful act be punished?" It is a trap for the retributivist because any reply will provide a utilitarian response and, of all the punishment philosophies, retribution is the only one that is nonutilitarian. If the retributivist tries to answer a question such as "Why should the death penalty be used?" the response will inevitably lean toward things such as deterrence, public safety, or reinforcing the moral order. But each of these answers has a utilitarian aspect and the retributivist does not require, or even want, such a link.[3]

Newman (1985) suggests the only nonutilitarian response available to retributivists is "Because the act was wrong." But that response merely restates the assertion. That is, retribution claims that a wrongful act must be repaid by punishment, so saying that the reason for punishment is to repay the wrongful act is merely redundant. Unless, of course, the statement "A wrongful act must be punished" is a statement of fact rather than simply an assertion. And, Newman suggests, that is exactly what the statement is. In fact, he argues that saying "A wrongful act must be punished" verges on being a social law. The resulting problem, as you can appreciate, is finding another position to take in order to have a debate. If retributivists say that punishment, the death penalty, for example, is inherently right—even required, the only "other side" one could take is to claim the statement is not a fact, let alone a social law. This becomes more of a philosophical discussion than a utilitarian debate. That is not a bad thing; it just means that the "discussers" must remember not to get hung up on topics such as what punishment achieves. In other words, even if there was clear and convincing evidence that the death penalty is not needed to achieve specific deterrence, does not provide general deterrence, and is applied in a biased manner, the retributivist would still favor capital punishment because it is the "right" thing to do. An example of this position emerged during the discussion about the wealthy escaping the gallows while the poor are executed. Van den Haag (1975) and others say that im-

[3]Newman, G. (1985). *The punishment response* (2nd ed.). Albany, NY: Harrow and Heston. Reprinted by permission of the author.

proper application of a punishment does not make the punishment wrong—it makes the application wrong.

But there are self-described retributivists who are against the death penalty. They arrive at that position by emphasizing the difficulty of exactly matching crime and penalty. As noted in the Chapter 2 discussion of retribution and proportional punishment, there are many limitations to achieving a strict principle of lex talionis. Paternoster (1991) highlights three that lead some retributivists to be abolitionists.[4] First, rigid adherence to the lex talionis principle of equality would mean that the death penalty is appropriate only for murder. Crimes of rape, kidnapping, and armed robbery, all of which have been capital offenses at one time, would not be punished by execution. On the other hand, all murderers should receive the death penalty. In a later discussion of court decisions on the death penalty, it is shown that the death penalty today typically is reserved for murders committed in combination with an aggravating circumstance such as killing a hostage, murder for money, or killing in a heinous manner. But even if the murder included an aggravating circumstance, the death penalty may not follow; the judge or jury must also make sure there are no mitigating factors that outweigh the aggravating factors. This means that under contemporary legal requirements, the principle of equality is tempered with a dose of mercy (Paternoster, 1991).

A second limitation to achieving true lex talionis is that ridiculous and uncivilized punishments would be required because society cannot always treat criminals exactly as they treated their victims. We do not rape the rapists, set fire to the arsonists, or steal from the thief. Nor can we administer several executions to the multiple murderer. Related to this point is Paternoster's third limitation—the principle of equality cannot be met in instances of brutal murder. A strict "eye for an eye" would require that brutal murderers be treated brutally by tormenting those who tortured, dismembering those who cut up their victims, and so on. Such behavior by the state would require imitation of the very acts the public so intensely despises.

These limitations on applying a strict version of lex talionis do not convince some retributivists that their rationale for punishment is unworkable. Rather than tossing aside a belief about punishment being just deserts, the abolitionist retributivists argue for **proportional retributivism.** Rather than requiring an exactly similar punishment for a criminal, "proportional retributivism requires only that the worst crime in any society be punished with the worst penalty" (Paternoster, 1991, p. 258). In abandoning the requirement of lex talionis, this version of retribution would require that a murderer receive the most severe penalty that society currently would morally tolerate. That punishment must be severe enough so as not to trivialize the victim's injury. Consider, for example, a prison sentence for rapists. Ten years in prison is not equivalent injury for one who has raped another; but it is a severe enough penalty that it does not do an injustice to the victim. Similarly, life imprisonment without the possibility for parole does not duplicate the harm to the murder victim, but it is not a penalty that is out of proportion to murder.

Some of the points around which retentionists and abolitionists frame their arguments have now been considered. There are others, of course, and as we set about developing or solidifying personal opinions about this ultimate sanction, it is important to consider both sides of as many arguments as possible. We turn now to some data on which that opinion must act.

[4]From Paternoster, R. (1991). *Capital punishment in America.* San Francisco: Jossey-Bass.

Help Wanted

Job Title: Social Science Analyst

Position Description: The social science analyst is responsible for assessing and implementing research projects to increase the understanding of significant criminal justice problems. Specific duties include integrating a wide variety of contemporary research studies and findings to identify critical program issues; designing research projects; preparing research program materials such as solicitations and requests for proposals; preparing and managing the review and selection of research grants, contracts, and/or cooperative agreements; responding to requests for information and assistance concerning related research activities; and acting as principal author and technical resource on special assignments, task forces, and committees.

Qualifications: General requirements for the position include a degree in behavioral or social science or a related discipline. Specific requirements include an ability to develop, design, and conduct social and behavioral research, particularly in criminal justice. Ability to present ideas, findings, and recommendations effectively both orally and in writing is essential to the position.

Positions similar to the social science analyst are common at local, state, and federal levels where criminal justice statistics are gathered and analyzed. One source for information about such positions at the federal level is at ***www.usajobs.opm.gov/*** where you can select "current job openings" and then do an "agency job search" in the Office of Justice Programs.

Capital Punishment in the United States Today

This section considers the contemporary status of capital punishment in the United States by looking at issues such as where it is imposed, who tends to receive it, and the methods by which it is applied. Then some of the legal questions concerning death penalty statutes are discussed by reviewing relevant court decisions.

Statistics. Statistics about capital punishment are provided by many organizations and the media as well as the federal Bureau of Justice Statistics (BJS). The BJS statistics (e.g., *Capital Punishment 1997*) have the advantage of consistency and accuracy but a disadvantage in the area of timeliness—their data are about one year old by the time of publication. More timely information can be found on the Internet using search terms to find organizations such as the Death Penalty Information Center.

In 1995 New York became the thirty-eighth state to authorize capital punishment. The thirteen jurisdictions, including the District of Columbia, without the death penalty are shown in Figure 6.1. Statistics from the Death Penalty Information Center (2000) show that by mid-2000 over 630 executions occurring since 1977 took place in thirty-one states with Texas and Virginia accounting for 46 percent of those. Of the inmates executed during that period, 56 percent were white, 35 percent were black, 7 percent were Hispanic, and 2 percent were Native American and Asian American.

Table 6.3 (see page 204) shows the method of execution, the number of persons executed, and the number of persons under sentence of death. In studying the table, note that lethal injection has been adopted as the method of choice in most jurisdictions. Where more than one method is authorized (lethal injection is always one choice), the choice is generally left to the condemned prisoner. It was just such a decision that was made in January 1977 when Utah executed Gary Gilmore by firing squad and ended a nearly ten-year moratorium on executions.

Gilmore's 1977 execution was the first one in the United States since 1967. Because executions carried out after the U.S. Supreme Court's 1976 decision in *Gregg v. Georgia* (discussed later) were to have been imposed in a more equitable manner, capital punishment statistics are often presented in a pre- and post-Gregg manner. Executions between 1930 and 1977 were usually of blacks (54 percent), men (99 percent), and took place in the South (60 percent). Most of the 3,859 executions were for murder (86 percent, with blacks accounting for 49 percent of these executions), and 12 percent were for rape in which blacks accounted for 90 percent of the executions (Department of Justice, 1978). From 1977 through 1999, most of the executions were of whites (56 percent), men (all but 5), and took place in the South (80 percent) (Death Penalty Information Center, 2000). All executions since 1977 have involved a murder charge.

A switch from executions to persons under sentence of death also reveals some interesting patterns. At the end of 1998, states in the South (a region with about 35 percent of the nation's adults) held 55 percent of all inmates under sentence of death. About 55 percent of the national total under sentence of death were white prisoners, nearly 99 percent were men, and 10 percent were of Hispanic origin (Snell, 1999). Because the percentage of people executed since 1977 who are non-Hispanic blacks (36 percent) is less than it was before 1977 (54 percent—including black Hispanics), and because it is now close to the percentage of non-Hispanic blacks who have been sentenced to death during that time (41 percent), there seems to have been some improvement in the death penalty's application. Importantly, however, black people still make up a much higher percentage of the death row population than they do of the population as a whole. That point has been one of several grounds for claims in the courts about the constitutionality of the death penalty.

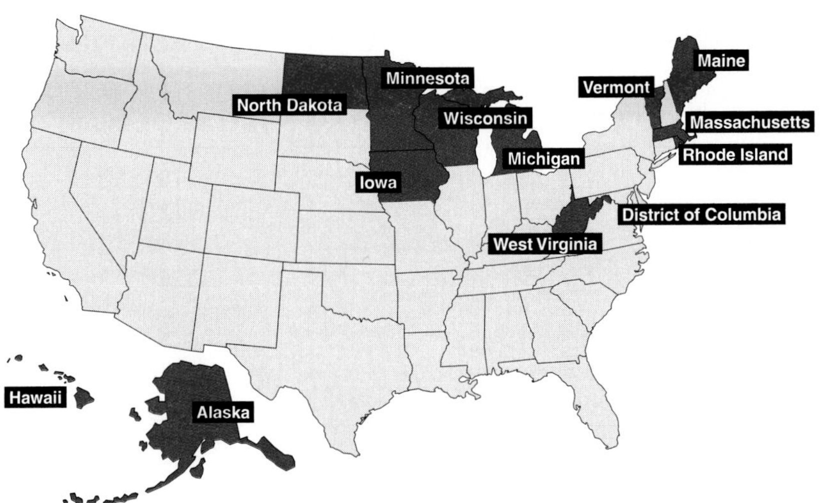

FIGURE 6.1

U.S. Jurisdictions without Death Penalty Statutes

Court Rulings. Between 1930 and 1949, the number of executions in the United States ranged from 199 in 1935 to 117 in 1945. Between 1950 and 1967, the number consistently declined from a high of 105 in 1951, to 47 in 1962, 15 in 1964, and 2 in 1967. The declining number of executions, reaching zero from 1968 through 1976, resulted from increasing legal challenges to the death penalty. During this moratorium the states with death penalty statutes were unsure about the Supreme Court's view of the constitutionality of the laws, so they refrained from any executions. Their concern was well founded because the 1972 *Furman v. Georgia* decision by the Court held that the death penalty as it was then being used amounted to cruel and unusual punishment.

What is referred to as the *Furman* decision actually involved three cases that the U.S. Supreme Court heard together: *Furman v. Georgia, Jackson v. Georgia,* and *Branch v. Texas.* The other two cases deserve brief mention before looking at *Furman.* Jackson, a twenty-one-year-old black man, was convicted of raping a white woman. He had entered the house after the husband left for work and, while holding scissors against the woman's neck, demanded money. She could not find any money and, after she failed in an attempt to get control of the scissors, Jackson raped her while keeping the scissors against her neck. Jackson, who had escaped from a work gang in the area, was at large for three days and during that time had committed several other property and violent crimes. A court-appointed psychiatrist said Jackson was of average education, average intelligence, and was not mentally deficient, schizophrenic, nor psychotic. Branch, also a black man, entered the home of a sleeping sixty-five-year-old white widow and raped her while holding his arm against her throat. Afterwards he demanded money and, although searching for thirty minutes, the victim found little. Branch told the victim he would return and kill her if she told anyone what had happened. Branch, who had the equivalent of five and a half years of grade school education, had been found to be borderline mentally deficient (*Branch v. Texas,* 408 U.S. 238; 1972).

Furman—a twenty-six-year-old black man with a sixth grade education—tried to enter a private home at night. Furman was surprised by the homeowner while in the act of burglary. While trying to escape, Furman shot and killed the homeowner with one pistol shot fired through a closed kitchen door from the outside. At his trial, Furman said he accidentally tripped over a wire while backing away causing the gun to fire.

Prior to his trial, Furman was committed to the Georgia Central State Hospital for a psychiatric exam on his plea of insanity. Initially, the superintendent

TABLE 6.3: Executions and Death Sentences by States with Death Penalty Statutes, December 1999

	METHOD OF EXECUTION	EXECUTIONS SINCE 1977	NUMBER OF PERSONS UNDER SENTENCE OF DEATH[3]
Alabama	Electrocution	22	185
Arizona[1]	Lethal injection; lethal gas	21	121
Arkansas[1]	Lethal injection; electrocution	22	40
California[1]	Lethal injection; lethal gas	8	561
Colorado	Lethal injection	1	5
Connecticut	Lethal injection	0	7
Delaware[1]	Lethal injection; hanging	10	18
Florida[1]	Lethal injection; electrocution	46	389
Georgia[1]	Lethal injection; electrocution	23	134
Idaho[2]	Lethal injection	1	21
Illinois	Lethal injection	12	160
Indiana	Lethal injection	7	43
Kansas	Lethal injection	0	3
Kentucky[1]	Lethal injection; electrocution	2	39
Louisiana	Lethal injection	25	87
Maryland[1]	Lethal injection; lethal gas	3	17
Mississippi	Lethal injection	4	63
Missouri[1]	Lethal injection; lethal gas	42	83
Montana	Lethal injection	2	6
Nebraska	Electrocution	3	9
Nevada	Lethal injection	8	89
New Hampshire[2]	Lethal injection	0	0
New Jersey	Lethal injection	0	16
New Mexico	Lethal injection	0	5
New York	Lethal injection	0	5
North Carolina	Lethal injection	15	224
Ohio[1]	Lethal injection; electrocution	1	199
Oklahoma[2]	Lethal injection	24	149
Oregon	Lethal injection	2	27
Pennsylvania	Lethal injection	3	232
South Carolina[1]	Lethal injection; electrocution	24	67
South Dakota	Lethal injection	0	3
Tennessee[1]	Lethal injection; electrocution	0	101
Texas	Lethal injection	214	462
Utah[1]	Lethal injection; firing squad	6	11
Virginia[1]	Lethal injection; electrocution	76	31
Washington[1]	Lethal injection; hanging	3	17
Wyoming[2]	Lethal injection	1	2
Total		632	3,652

[1]These states authorize more than one method of execution with lethal injection always being one type. The actual method used is stipulated depending on the date of sentencing with those condemned before the stipulated date being allowed to select the method.

[2]These states authorize other methods of execution if the primary method (the one shown in this table) is ever found to be unconstitutional, cannot be given (New Hampshire), or is "impractical" (Idaho).

[3]As of January 1, 2000. Detail may not sum to total because some inmates have a death sentence in more than one state.

Source: From Snell, T. L. (1996). *Capital punishment 1998* [NCJ 179012]. Washington, DC: Bureau of Justice Statistics. Updated with information from the Death Penalty Information Center, May 2000, available at www.essential.org/dpic.

reported that the diagnostic staff had concluded that Furman's diagnosis was of mental deficiency, mild to moderate, with psychotic episodes associated with convulsive disorder. The physicians agreed that Furman was not presently psychotic but said he was incapable of cooperating with his counsel in preparing his defense. Furthermore, the staff believed that he needed further psychiatric hospitalization and treatment. However, at a later time the superintendent reported that, although the staff diagnosis was the same, he concluded that while Furman was not currently psychotic, he knew right from wrong and was able to cooperate with his counsel in preparing his defense. All the jury knew about Furman was that he was black, twenty-six years old, and worked at an upholstery shop. After deliberating about ninety minutes, the jury returned a verdict of guilt and a sentence of death (*Furman v. Georgia,* 408 U.S. 238; 1972).

In *Furman v. Georgia,* the U.S. Supreme Court determined that the death penalty was cruel and unusual. Two of the justices said it is cruel and unusual in all cases, but the majority said it was cruel and unusual because it was imposed in an arbitrary and capricious manner. Justice Douglas, taking the arbitrary and capricious position, said it was not possible to determine from the facts of these three cases that these defendants were sentenced to death because they were black. However, he expressed concern that the laws left the decision of death or imprisonment to "the uncontrolled discretion of judges or juries" and in doing so, "people live or die, dependent on the whim of one man or of 12" (*Furman v. Georgia,* 408 U.S. 238; 1972).

In the *Furman* case, three of the five justices in the majority took the position that the death penalty was cruel and unusual because it was applied arbitrarily. The other two justices in the majority believed the death penalty was cruel and unusual in itself. Had the second position been held by the majority, the death penalty would essentially have been abandoned throughout the United States. But, the "arbitrary" position left the door open for laws that would allow for nonarbitrary use of the death penalty. Said differently, in the *Furman* decision, the Court's ruling was not against capital punishment itself, only against the way it was being imposed. Under that reasoning, states assumed, death penalty statutes that removed the arbitrary nature of executions would be constitutional.

Because each Court justice wrote a separate opinion in *Furman,* it was not immediately clear just what kind of death penalty law would be acceptable to the Court. Two major types of laws were tried by different states: mandatory and guided discretion. The mandatory laws tried to completely eliminate discretion in capital sentencing by requiring the death penalty upon conviction of specific crimes. Those types were held unconstitutional in a series of 1976 rulings (see *Roberts v. Louisiana* and *Woodson v. North Carolina*).

The guided discretion statutes require juries to administer capital punishment after considering both aggravating and mitigating circumstances. These statutes were upheld by the Court in several other 1976 rulings (*Gregg v. Georgia; Jurek v. Texas;* and *Proffitt v. Florida*), but the Georgia decision is typically cited as initiating the guided discretion era. The Georgia, Texas, and Florida statutes each require a bifurcated trial, with the first stage being the traditional trial to determine guilt. When guilt is established, the second stage takes place to decide the sentence—death or life imprisonment. It is during the second stage that guided discretion occurs; this is when the sentencing authority hears about aggravating and mitigating factors that will affect the sentencing decision. In Georgia the sentence is determined by the jury. In Florida juries make advisory sentencing recommendations by majority vote, but the actual capital-sentencing discretion lies with the trial judges. The judges, who are given specific and detailed guidance to assist them in making the life imprisonment or death decision, must justify a death penalty decision with written findings. Texas also leaves the actual sentence up to the jury because the way the jury responds to specific questions required by the statute determines what sentence the trial judge must impose (Palmer, 1991).

Further refinements to the death penalty laws have included decisions such as *Coker v. Georgia* (1977) wherein the death penalty was deemed disproportionate, and therefore unacceptable, to the crime of rape of an adult woman. Under *Lockett v. Ohio* (1978), the Court ruled that the sentencing authority must be allowed to consider every possible mitigating factor rather than being limited to a specific list of factors. In its *Godfrey v. Georgia* (1980) decision, the Court found that some aggravating circumstances, such as a reference to the crime being "outrageously or wantonly vile, horrible, or inhumane," were too broad and vague.

It would appear that the issue of capital punishment's constitutionality has been settled with *Gregg v. Georgia,* and faces only refinement and clarification from subsequent decisions. In addition to the clarifications in the *Coker, Lockett,* and *Godfrey* decisions, the Court has decided questions such as these:

- Who can be excluded from the jury in death penalty cases? *Lockhart v. McCree* (1986) held that prospective jurors opposed to the death penalty may be removed for cause.
- Who cannot be executed? *Ford v. Wainright* (1986) prohibits the execution of a mentally ill person.
- Who can be executed? *Tison v. Arizona* (1987) allows the death penalty to be imposed on offenders who did not specifically intend to kill the victims.
- What role can the victim have in the sentencing process? *Payne v. Tennessee* (1991) allows a "victim impact" statement to be admitted in the sentencing phase of a death penalty case.

Despite some views that post-Gregg death penalty questions will simply involve refinement and clarification, abolitionists have certainly not given up their goal of removing, or finding unconstitutional, death penalty statutes in the United States. A major—though ultimately unsuccessful—challenge was based on claims that the death penalty was imposed in a discriminatory manner depending on the race of the victim. Although the race of the offender has been a prime target to show bias in imposing the death penalty, attention to the race of the victim is a more recent concern. In *McClesky v. Kemp* (1987), the U.S. Supreme Court dealt directly with this issue. McClesky, a black man who had been convicted of murdering a white police officer, used a study by Baldus, Pulaski, and Woodworth (1983) in his claim that he was being discriminated against on the basis of his race and that of his victim. The Baldus study (as it has come to be called) found a large racial disparity in the way Georgia juries had imposed the death penalty between 1973 and 1978. For example, Baldus and his colleagues found that offenders charged with killing a white were 4.3 times more likely to be sentenced to death in Georgia than those charged with killing a black.

McClesky argued that if killers of whites were being disproportionally sentenced to death, then they had been denied equal protection under the Fourteenth Amendment. In addition, if it was possible that an irrelevant factor (race) entered into the sentencing decision, then the death penalty was being imposed in an arbitrary and capricious manner in violation of the Eighth Amendment as applied in *Furman v. Georgia* (Paternoster, 1991). The Court rejected McClesky's claims, deciding that a statistical study suggesting that racial considerations entered into capital sentencing in Georgia does not establish purposeful discrimination—which the Court said a successful Fourteenth Amendment claim must show. In addition, the justices noted that although the Baldus study found a correlation between race factors and sentencing, it did not prove that race entered into the sentencing decision. But even to the extent that there is some risk of racial discrimination, any sentencing procedure that provides for discretion—which the Court-approved systems certainly do—will inevitably have some inconsistency. Therefore, the Court said there was no Eighth Amendment violation either.

As they attempt to halt executions in the United States, abolitionists are likely to turn toward at least three other areas. One would be to get state legislators to remove the death penalty statutes. In recent years action by legislators has been in the opposite direction; Kansas passed a death penalty statute in 1994, and New York did the same in 1995. But the possibility of abolishing capital punishment at the state level remains an option for abolitionists. Another area still open to abolitionists is to challenge death penalty statutes as violating the state rather than the federal constitution. There have been occasions when state supreme courts have held death penalty statutes unconstitutional under the state constitutions, but revision of the statute by legislators typically resolves the problem. It is possible, however, that state courts might find that certain wordings in a state constitution are such that capital punishment would not be permitted under that constitution.

A third area for future action by abolitionists has the potential to be the most fruitful. The U.S. Supreme Court has recognized the importance of considering society's evolving standard of decency when deciding what constitutes cruel and unusual punishment. Because of that policy, it is possible that citizens of the future will be as appalled at any form of execution as some of today's citizens are about earlier forms such as beheading or drawing and quartering. At that time, the U.S. Supreme Court might be asked to find the death penalty unconstitutional because our future citizens would consider it cruel and unusual.

Public Opinion and the Death Penalty. The idea that capital punishment could be abolished because it doesn't have the public's support may seem far-fetched, but it is actually quite plausible. Because of the Court's interest in considering society's evolving standard of decency when deciding what constitutes cruel and unusual punishment, public opinion will make a difference.

According to the Harris poll, in the years preceding the *Furman* decision public support for the death penalty generally stayed under 50 percent. By the time of the *Gregg* decision (1976), public support had increased to 67 percent. Since then, it has not been below 50 percent and was at 71 percent in 1999 (Maguire & Pastore, 1998). Generally, more men than women favor the death penalty, and more whites than blacks. But there is indication that people may also be willing to have an alternative to capital punishment. When the Gallup poll asks if people believe the punishment for murder should be the death penalty or life imprisonment with absolutely no possibility of parole, the number choosing the death penalty has been less than 60 percent since the mid-1980s. A similar question was presented by surveyors at Sam Houston State University that asked respondents, who had already said they favored capital punishment, if they would still favor the death penalty if they knew that murderers would be given a true life sentence without the possibility of parole. Seventy-six percent said they would still favor the death penalty (Maguire & Pastore, 1998). So, although support for the death penalty may drop when another option is given, it seems that most U.S. citizens today are proponents of capital punishment.

The abolitionists respond to these seemingly discouraging statistics by referring to what has been called the Marshall hypothesis. Supreme Court Justice Marshall, in his opinion for the *Furman* decision, said that the public lacks knowledge about the death penalty and its effects. He then suggested that an informed public generally would oppose the death penalty. Believing Justice Marshall to have been on to something, abolitionists often direct their attention toward public education. And their efforts may not be misplaced because some research suggests that educating the public can reduce support for capital punishment—but it is seldom reduced to less than a majority (Bohm, Clark, and Aveni, 1991; Bohm, Vogel, & Maisto, 1993).

Despite the strength of a retentionist position in the polls, there are some indications that people are becoming dissatisfied with one particular problem associated with the death penalty—the possibility of mistake. Although people can debate whether the death penalty is cruel and unusual punishment for a murderer, it is hard to imagine anyone who would not agree that it is cruel and unusual punishment for an innocent person. And as more states execute more people the likelihood increases that innocent people will be among those executed. Research by Radelet, Bedau, and Putnam (1992) found twenty-three cases since 1900 in which innocent people were executed.

In addition to the execution of innocent people, there have been numerous close calls. Since 1973, over eighty people have been released from death row with evidence of their innocence (Death Penalty Information Center, 2000). In fact, between 1977 and 1999 the state of Illinois found itself in the disconcerting position of having voided the death sentences of the same number of men (twelve) as they had executed.

Some defenders of the death penalty simply point to these close calls as examples of the system working—they were caught in time, the argument goes. Some of the condemned were cleared with new trials, some had their convictions overturned on appeal, and in about eight cases DNA proved their innocence. Reliance on the justice system to catch its own errors before tragedy occurs may be misplaced, however. In the Illinois exonerations, it was not a diligent justice system that identified the condemned men's innocence but rather a journalism professor and his students.

Journalism students under the direction of Northwestern University professor David Protess have been the essential ingredient in the release of three of the twelve exonerated men in Illinois. In 1996 students from Protess's investigative reporting class helped free four men who had collectively served sixty-five years for rape and murder. Two of those men were on death row. In 1999, working with a private investigator, Protess and his students tracked down witnesses who changed their testimony implicating Anthony Porter in a 1982 double-murder case. The Northwestern investigative team found the man who witnesses said had actually committed the murders and got him to do a videotaped confession in which he claimed he had killed in self-defense. Porter, who had come within two days of being executed in 1998, had his conviction officially reversed in 1999 (Death Penalty Information Center, 2000; Harrington, 1999; Lehmann, 1999).

Is the stage being set for a twenty-first-century U.S. Supreme Court ruling that finds capital punishment to be cruel and unusual? As more examples of innocent people being sentenced to death and even executed come to light, it may well push public opinion against the death penalty. In the absence of clear public support, the Court may decide that society in the twenty-first century has come to view the possibility of executing innocent people as cruel and unusual punishment. Were that to happen, the death penalty would undoubtedly be ruled unconstitutional. An alternative, of course, would be to improve the judicial process so those mistakes are never made. Or there is always the position that the execution of the occasional innocent person is simply an unfortunate cost that is outweighed by the great benefit derived from capital punishment. Once again we are left with our own personal punishment philosophy to direct the choice we would make. But eventually, all those personal philosophies influence society's position, legislators' action, and the courts' decisions.

Capital Punishment around the World

Capital punishment has a history of use across the ages and around the world. Anthropologist Keith Otterbein (1986) actually considers capital punishment to be a "universal cultural trait" in a manner similar to the universal presence of religion and the family. He attributes its universality to a notion common among cultures that a "dangerous individual must be disposed of through the use of the death penalty" (1986, p. 48). Otterbein's research led him to make four generalizations about capital punishment (1986, pp. 45 and 107):

- Capital punishment is a cross-cultural universal; although exceptions may exist, the evidence shows that most if not all societies, at one time or another, will use the death penalty.
- Capital crimes are most likely to be offenses that directly threaten people—homicide, stealing, violations of community religious norms, and sexual offenses.
- Disposal of the wrongdoer is the reason most frequently found for executing a community member.
- In the vast majority of cultures, most members of the community accept capital punishment as an appropriate sanction.

Where capital punishment is not used, Otterbein argues, the community members must find an alternative method to dispose of individuals who threaten the community. The communities most likely to accept alternatives to capital punishment are those where citizens have stable, mature governments in which crime and fear of crime are not the major concerns. But presumably, where crime and the fear of crime become major concerns, even mature, stable communities may turn to capital punishment as the ultimate protection against threatening individuals.

An International Overview. According to Amnesty International (AI) data, as of April 1999 over half the countries in the world (figured at 195 by AI) have abolished the death penalty in law or practice (Amnesty International, 1999a). The 105 countries counted as abolitionist include 68 that have abolished the death penalty for all crimes, 14 that have abolished it for all but exceptional crimes (such as those contrary to military law), and 23 countries that are abolitionist de facto because they have not carried out any executions for at least ten years. AI estimates that more than two countries a year on average have abolished the death penalty in law since 1976 or, having abolished it for ordinary crimes, have gone on to abolish it for all crimes.

Retention and abolition show considerable variation by and within regions of the world. The North American countries include one country (Canada) that has abolished the death penalty for all crimes and two countries (United States and Mexico) with differences by state jurisdiction. All the former British colonies in the Caribbean have death penalty statutes. Over half the estimated 200 death row prisoners in that region are in Jamaica and Trinidad. In 1999 Trinidad hanged nine men—the first executions there in five years—and Jamaica was said to be ready to resume hangings after a more than ten-year break in executions in that country (Bohning, 1999). Latin American countries show considerable variation, with about one-half of the countries having abolished capital punishment and the other half choosing retention.

Western European countries seem primarily to have abolished the death penalty for all crimes. As Central and Eastern European countries moved toward democratization in the 1990s, many—including Bulgaria, the Czech Republic, Estonia, Hungary, and Slovakia—abolished the death penalty for all offenses. In 1999 Boris Yeltsin, despite overwhelming public support for the death penalty, commuted over 700 death sentences on Russia's death row. His action was interpreted as more of a foreign policy move than a domestic one because it could serve to bring Russia into the European mainstream and improve ties with Western European countries (Paddock, 1999).

Countries of the Middle East generally retain the death penalty, with some (Iran, Pakistan, and Iraq) using it rather frequently. Saudi Arabia imposes death sentences by beheading for murder, rape, drug trafficking, and armed robbery. On the African continent, the death penalty is still widespread, although since 1989 countries such as Namibia, Mozambique, and South Africa have abolished it for all crimes. On the other hand, Uganda executed 28 men on one evening in May 1999 and had more than 1,000 prisoners still on death row ("Uganda Defies," 1999).

The countries of Asia and Australasia also are more likely to be retentionist than abolitionist. In Australia, where use of the death penalty is a matter left to the states, all jurisdictions have abolished capital punishment. It has also been abolished in New Zealand. It is retained but infrequently used in places such as India, Japan, Singapore, and Thailand and is retained and more frequently used in Pakistan and Taiwan. The feature "Japan's Execution Protocol" highlights Japan as an interesting example, not so much for its infrequent use of capital punishment as for the protocol followed.

By AI figures, 80 percent of all known executions during 1998 took place in four countries: China (over 1,000 known executions), the Democratic Republic of Congo (over 100), the United States (68), and Iran (66 known). AI also notes that hundreds of executions were reported in Iraq, but confirmation could not be made (Amnesty International, 1999c). All countries are likely to have interesting stories regarding their historical use and contemporary attitudes toward capital punishment, but one country in particular seems to demand closer attention—China.

The Death Penalty in China. In China many offenses are punishable by death; it is not unusual for more than 1,000 executions to take place during one year. AI recorded nearly 2,500 death sentences and almost 1,800 executions in China during 1994 (Amnesty International, 1995a). In one day in September 1994, forty-three people were reported executed in the city of Wuhan, Hubei province. This was presumably the largest mass execution in the city since the anticrime crackdown of 1983. In addition to having the death penalty applied for crimes of violence, the Chinese also execute persons for property and public order offenses such as thefts of farm animals and agricultural machinery, corruption, and taking bribes. China's willingness, even eagerness, to use the death penalty provides an opportunity to look more closely at some of the topics covered in this chapter. Specifically, China's experience with capital punishment in the context of Otterbein's conclusions gives more insight into the issues of deterrence and retribution.

Earlier we saw that Otterbein (1986) concluded that countries most likely to retain or return to capital punishment for protection against threatening individuals are those nations in which crime and the fear of crime are major concerns. To the extent that is true, it may help explain increased use of capital punishment in some U.S. jurisdictions, the reintroduction of death penalty statutes in jurisdictions that had previously abolished it (e.g., some American states, Papua New Guinea, and the Philippines), and the occasional calls for its reinstatement in jurisdictions currently without it (e.g., England, Canada, and New Zealand). Until an interested researcher tests correlations among variables such as a country's crime rate, citizen perception of crime as a problem, dates of abolishment and reintroduction, and legislative attempts at reinstatement, one can only wonder about Otterbein's conclusion. But to the extent that it appears crime rates are increasing—or the perception of crime as a major problem is increasing—in places where the death penalty has been reintroduced or has received more discussion, it seems at least reasonable to suggest the link is an appropriate area for research. This is not the place to undertake such a study, but as anecdotal support for Otterbein's position we can look at the Chinese example.

Cross-Cultural Corrections

Japan's Execution Protocol

One criticism of capital punishment, at least as carried out in U.S. jurisdictions, is its planned and purposeful nature. The condemned is given a specific time and date that he will die and, although he can hope for a last-minute reprieve, he essentially spends his last weeks knowing that death awaits. But is it more cruel to know exactly when you will die—and be forced to sit idly by until the moment arrives—or to know you are scheduled to die but not if it will be this afternoon or ten years from now?

A 1995 Amnesty International report noted that almost sixty Japanese prisoners under sentence of death have spent years—some more than two decades—wondering if they will be arbitrarily chosen for a secret hanging. Executions are carried out in Japan at a secret time and location without any warning to the prisoners or notification to their families or lawyers. In fact, there is minimal confirmation of who was hanged. In 1998 the justice minister announced plans to disclose when executions have occurred and the number of people involved—but not the names of those executed nor the place of execution.

The decision about when a prisoner is to be executed is made by Japan's minister of justice. Amnesty International found the selection for execution to be apparently random, with no clear reason why a particular prisoner is chosen to die. Some have been under sentence of death for nearly thirty years, and several of them are over age seventy.

In addition to expressing concern about an execution process that is conducted in secret and applied at random, Amnesty International was also disturbed about the conditions of Japan's death row. Lights are never switched off, video cameras monitor the prisoners twenty-four hours a day, and strict rules require those sentenced to death to do things such as sit in the middle of the cell in one of three authorized positions.

In 1993 seven persons were executed, and in 1994 two more were chosen to have their death sentences imposed.

Because the Japanese government does not provide information about executions, there is no official source to which the public has access to the application of the death penalty in Japan. In the absence of official data, information is retrieved from unofficial sources such as Amnesty International. Go to *www.amnesty.org/ailib/countries/indx322.htm,* and read some of the recent reports and news releases about executions in Japan. AI is, of course, against any application of the death penalty, but what specific concerns does the organization express about its use in Japan?

Source: From Amnesty International. (1995). "Japan prisoners on death row wait for secret random execution" [AI Index ASA 22/06/95]. (London: Author.). Adapted with permission.

Lepp (1990) explains that during the late 1970s, China experienced a significant jump in its crime rate, and Chinese leaders began using the death penalty more frequently. Crime continued to rise, and with the launching of an anticrime campaign in the early 1980s, China resorted to the death penalty even more frequently. Foreign press estimates suggest that between 1983 and 1986, anywhere from 7,000 to 14,000 executions were carried out (Lepp, 1990). In early 1987, Chinese officials announced there had been a substantial drop in the number of crimes in the first half of 1986. The anticrime campaign had struck a "ruthless blow," Communist Party officials said, and in response the campaign's intensity was reduced throughout 1987. But serious crime increased again in 1988, and the government returned to the frequent use of the death penalty. The correspondence of ups and downs in the crime rate with increased and decreased use of capital punishment seems to support Otterbein's contention that the death penalty is linked to actual or perceived levels of crime. Because crime statistics in the People's Republic of China are suspect—primarily because they are not made available to researchers for analysis—and because government policy, Communist or otherwise, does not necessarily reflect public opinion, it is inappropriate to draw conclusions from the Chinese example. But the Chinese experience certainly presents food for thought among those interested in possible relationships between a country's use of capital punishment and the actual or perceived rate of serious crime in that country.

Linked to Otterbein's conclusion that the death penalty is retained or reinstated when citizens fear serious crime is the broader issue of deterrence. There is a Chinese saying that one should "kill the chicken to frighten the monkey." Lepp (1990) explains that expression reflects a traditional faith in the power of punishment as a deterrent. The practical application of this belief is found in the Chinese custom of using degrees of punishment to achieve degrees of deterrence. The centuries-old "five punishments," which basically remain today, started with five degrees of beating with a light stick (ranging from ten to fifty blows) and increased in severity to two degrees of death (strangulation or decapitation). Two degrees of a death punishment were seen as possible because strangulation, although it was the more prolonged and painful death, was considered less severe than decapitation. That perception was based on social and religious views of the body, which saw decapitation as being disrespectful to one's parents. By the early eighteenth century, a sentence of strangulation was usually commuted to exile but the term *strangulation* was still used—presumably for deterrent effect.

The tradition of harsh punishment to achieve general deterrence remained after the Communist Party took control in 1949 and declared the People's Republic of China. Following the preferred tradition in other socialist countries, Chinese officials turned to a single pistol shot to the back of the head as the method of execution. But to emphasize the deterrent goal of the executions, China has made sure that executions are well publicized and accompanied with appropriate propaganda. As expressed by one Chinese court official, "by killing one we educate one hundred" (quoted in Lepp, 1990, p. 1015). News of executions is spread throughout the country with the aid of television, radio, and the press, and occasionally an execution is carried out in public or a corpse might remain exposed after the punishment.

Although deterrence seems to be the primary justification for capital punishment in China (Lepp, 1990), retribution also has an important role. The highly publicized process of punishment—sometimes including the public parading of condemned prisoners with head bowed and placards hung from their necks to announce their crime—is as much an outlet for vengeance and outrage as it is a means of deterrence. Evidence of such feelings is often found in the pronouncement of death sentences that include a declaration by the court that "the people are extremely indignant." In other sentences in which the punishment is life or long imprisonment the court may simply announce that the people are only "very indignant" (Lepp, 1990, p. 1022).

There is a final point to make regarding China's use of the death penalty. In an interesting twist to what appears to be a harsh and vengeful system, Chinese law permits suspension of the death sentence in certain situations (Felkenes, 1989; Lepp, 1990). The Chinese criminal law says that "In the case of a criminal element who should be sentenced to death, if immediate execution is not essential, a two-year suspension of execution may be announced at the same time the sentence of death is imposed. . . ." (The criminal law, 1984, Article 43). Even more interesting, during this period of suspension the offender is to undergo "reform through labor" and, if he or she is found to have truly repented, the sentence should be reduced to life imprisonment. If the court determines that the offender has demonstrated meritorious service in addition to having truly repented, the sentence should be reduced to not less than fifteen and no more than twenty years. At the end of the two-year suspension, if there is verified evidence that the condemned person has "resisted reform in an odious manner," the death penalty is to be carried out (The criminal law, 1984, Articles 43 and 46).

The policy of *sihuan zhidu,* "death sentence with a reprieve," has been used primarily for political prisoners (most notably for Mao Zedong's widow), for young offenders, and for pregnant women (Lepp, 1990). The sentence is presented by Chinese officials as evidence of a desire to combine punishment with leniency. Despite the possibility for and the actual use of a death sentence with a reprieve, Lepp suggests there are no vocal groups in China advocating the abolition of capital punishment.[5]

SUMMARY

PHYSICAL SANCTIONS

This chapter reviews some of the most controversial punishments used in the United States and other countries: corporal and capital punishments. Both are examples of physical sanctions.

CORPORAL PUNISHMENT

- Types include the pillory and the stocks, branding, mutilation, and whipping.
- Long and Newman argue for the contemporary use of penalties such as electric shock and whipping. Their suggestions may have some support among members of the American public, but most contemporary examples of corporal punishment are found in countries other than the United States.

CAPITAL PUNISHMENT

Although contemporary U.S. jurisdictions do not authorize corporal punishment, most states do provide for the possibility of capital punishment.

- Debates about the merits of capital punishment have focused on issues of deterrence, fairness, and retribution.
- Regarding the fairness issue, some people are especially concerned about the preponderance of men who are executed (fairness and sex), whereas others point to the disproportionate number of executions of minorities (fairness and race) and poor people (fairness and finances). Concerns are also expressed about the execution of juveniles (fairness and age).
- Over half the world's countries are considered abolitionist by Amnesty International. Of those countries still using capital punishment, some 80 percent of the executions are conducted in China, the Democratic Republic of Congo, the United States, and Iran.

KEY TERMS AND CONCEPTS

branding (p. 178)
capital punishment (p. 184)
corporal punishment (p. 177)
death by animal and insect (p. 184)
death by instrument (p. 184)
death by natural elements (p. 184)
mutilation (p. 183)
pillory (p. 178)
proportional retributivism (p. 201)
stocks (p. 178)
torture (p. 175)
whipping (p. 179)

[5]Lepp, A. W. (1990). Note, the death penalty in late imperial, modern, and post-Tiananmen China. *Michigan Journal of International Law, 11,* 987–1038. Reprinted by permission of the author.

Discussion Questions

1. With which parts of Newman's defense of corporal punishment do you agree? With which parts do you disagree?
2. Of the many discussion issues that Singapore's use of caning encourages, explain your position regarding (a) whether corporal punishment deters certain kinds of criminal behavior; (b) whether support for caning in U.S. jurisdictions is actually as widespread as media reports suggested it was during Michael Fay's ordeal; and (c) why some U.S. jurisdictions allow the spanking of misbehaving school children but do not allow the whipping of criminals.
3. Explain your opinion regarding the U.S. Supreme Court's conclusion that what is cruel and unusual will vary over time. If you disagree with the Court, which of the methods of execution would you find acceptable today? Why would you choose those? If you agree with the Court, what methods currently in use should be banned? Why should they be banned?
4. Explain which of the three general debate issues (deterrence, fairness, and retribution) is of most importance in forming your personal opinion regarding the death penalty. What issues that were not covered in the chapter are important to you?
5. Discuss the merits of Japan's execution protocol (not informing the condemned of the exact date and time of the execution) versus the procedure in U.S. jurisdictions (having a prolonged countdown—which even then could result in a last-minute reprieve—to a predetermined date and time).

chapter 7

Intermediate Sanctions

Last summer, Sara Smith and Janet Jones were walking home from the movie theater when they passed the Lyle house. Sara knew the Lyles were away for the weekend, so on a whim she and Janet decided to see if they could get in the house just to look around. With minimal effort the young women were able to find an unlocked window, which they opened and used to enter the house. A compact disc player in the family room was just too tempting for these eighteen-year-olds. They took the CD player and left through the open window. Unfortunately for them, their running while holding the CD player attracted the attention of Police Officer Lubow, who was on routine patrol in the neighborhood. Upon questioning, Sara and Janet immediately confessed to taking the CD player.

The young women were charged with criminal trespass, burglary, and felony theft. They subsequently pled guilty to burglary and felony theft (trespass charges were dropped by the prosecutor). Because of the guilty plea, no trial was held, and no evidence or defense was presented. To aid in determining the most appropriate sentence for Sara and Janet, Judge Hays asked the probation department to prepare a report that gave him information about the two offenders. With the aid of this report and its accompanying recommendation from the probation officer, Judge Hays sentenced Sara and Janet in a manner that ensured safety for the community and also served to lessen the likelihood that Sara and Janet will repeat the criminal behavior.

Probation Officer Dave Gutierrez conducted interviews with Sara and Janet, with their respective families, and with other people (e.g., teachers, neighbors, and employers) having knowledge of each young woman's character. Gutierrez determined that Sara, who had two prior convictions for burglary, had not responded to previous efforts to change her behavior through community sanctions. His report on Sara recommended that Judge Hays sentence her to the Department of Corrections for incarceration. Janet, however, had no prior convictions and received very positive evaluations from the various people Gutierrez interviewed. Gutierrez believed that incarcerating Janet would be overly harsh and serve no real purpose. He did not feel Janet presented any threat to citizens or their property, but because she had shown a tendency to follow friends into illegal ventures, he felt Janet should be supervised while under restricted liberty in the community. Finally, to make sure Janet realized that her behavior had been a serious violation worthy of some level of punishment, Gutierrez believed Janet should be threatened with incarceration should she not abide by the requirements of her release in the community. Gutierrez, therefore, wanted to recommend a sentence that had four objectives: (1) It should be more humane than incarceration, but (2) the possibility of incarceration should be present if Janet failed to abide by (3) the conditions that would be set for her release in the community. But most important, Gutierrez wanted to be sure (4) that an official of the court would be supervising Janet to help her complete the requirements of the sentence. To achieve these objectives, Gutierrez determined the best sentence would be probation.

After reading Gutierrez's report, Judge Hays agreed that Sara should be turned over to the Department of Corrections and that Janet should be sentenced to probation. Sara's sentence is more appropriate for later chapters, but Janet's sentence is a clear example of what this chapter calls prison alternatives.

A Need for Alternative Sentences

This chapter deals with sentences that try to address an offender's misbehavior without resorting to imprisonment. Chapter 5 discussed sentences such as fines and restitution, which are often viewed as moderate penalties. Chapters 8 and 9 look at sentences that involve confinement and are often viewed as severe penalties. Not surprisingly, these extremes fail to provide enough choice to handle all types of crimes and criminals coming before the sentencing judges.

Over the years, sentences that are more strict than fines yet less severe than imprisonment have developed. Today these **intermediate punishments** are of two types. One category has come about primarily as a substitute for imprisonment. As prison populations have grown, some jurisdictions have determined that it is no longer possible to imprison all those persons that the government wishes it could lock up. Some of these resulting **prison substitutes,** such as intensive probation supervision and day reporting centers, are discussed later in this chapter. Other intermediate sanctions are designed for those offenders whom the government may not want to imprison but who deserve or need a penalty harsher than fines or restitution. Rather than being substitutes for prison, these penalties are **prison alternatives.** Several of these penalties are the topic of this chapter. Both types of intermediate punishments involve supervision of the offender in the community rather than in a traditional jail or prison. Because of that, it is first necessary to look at the general concept of community corrections.

Community Corrections

Community corrections is more accurately called community-based correctional services. But in the interest of simplicity and without significant loss of meaning, the shorter term is used. The variety of programs that fit under the broad meaning of community corrections seems limited only by the imagination. There are other programs (such as work release, weekend detention, or shock incarceration) that involve community supervision, but they also rely on some level of incarceration in jail or prison. The term *community corrections* is used for those programs that depend on correctional resources available in the community and require the offender to abide by certain conditions while at liberty in the community.

Community corrections has received increased attention in recent years because of concerns about prison crowding. That portrayal is, however, misleading.

The philosophy behind community corrections predates contemporary concerns about prison crowding and does not rely on any kind of link to incarceration. As Smylka (1981) explains, community corrections provides meaningful ties between offenders and their local environment in a way that gets offenders involved with a network of relationships that can provide most of the goods and services they need to live in the community.

The very essence of community corrections is a program's ability to encourage those meaningful ties to the community. From this perspective, community corrections may be appropriate as an alternative to incarceration, as an effort toward reintegration after incarceration, or even for offenders who would never even be considered appropriate for jail or prison. It is, in other words, a self-standing aspect of a correctional system that may have a link to the incarceration part of the system, but it certainly does not depend on that link for its existence.

Having claimed that community corrections has a separate standing within a corrections system, it is necessary now to back away from that position a little. This is because, as noted earlier, the contemporary view of community corrections is inevitably linked to conditions of prison crowding. Proponents of community corrections argue that it should not be so, but they realize that conditions today place community corrections in the same sandbox as incarceration. When legislators, policymakers, and corrections officials discuss community corrections programs, it is most often in terms of such punishment rationales as retribution or possibly restoration. The rehabilitation aspect, implied in the "meaningful ties" concept, is not rejected—it just is not highlighted; often it is not even a program goal. Instead, the programs are offered to the public as retributive in the sense that they provide "just" punishment for certain acts. In this way, community corrections programs that existed in the past as primarily rehabilitative are joined today by other programs that emphasize the just deserts aspect of retribution while, importantly, decreasing reliance on incarceration. Examples of this perspective are found in the growth of community corrections acts around the country.

Community corrections acts (CCAs) are state laws that use financial incentives to encourage local agencies to develop and operate alternatives to imprisonment. A few of the acts stress rehabilitation (e.g., in Oregon), but more typically they target misdemeanants who would be put in jail and felons who would otherwise go to prison. In the early 1970s, Minnesota became the first state to adopt a CCA. By 1995, twenty-five states had passed similar legislation.

Michigan's CCA (effective in 1989) is a good example of the view that community corrections should relieve prison crowding. The Michigan law directs local advisory boards to develop and implement community corrections plans that substantially reduce the use of prison sentences for felons. Michigan's success in achieving that goal is reflected in numbers showing a decrease in prison dispositions from 37.2 percent of all sentences in 1989 to 29.3 percent in 1993 (Clark, 1995). The types of programs to which offenders are being diverted in Michigan and in most of the other CCA states include community service work, electronic monitoring, day reporting, probation, and specific treatment programs that address problems such as substance abuse and employability. Most of these programs are discussed in this chapter, but it is appropriate to begin with the best known of the list, probation.

PROBATION

Probation is a familiar term to most people. Although some may confuse probation with parole, most people understand that someone who receives a probation sentence must abide by certain conditions or risk being sent to prison.

Forerunners to Probation

Rather than being the result of deliberate legislation or judicial action, probation came about from gradual growth through which existing legal practices were modified and elaborated upon. The legal practices being modified were based in English common law and resulted in the arrival of probation at similar times in both England and the United States. In both countries, probation developed out of methods used for the conditional suspension of punishment; so this review of probation's origins must examine those methods of postponement. The most notable are benefit of clergy, judicial reprieve (suspended sentence), and recognizance.

The Benefit of Clergy. Between the eleventh and fourteenth centuries, two separate court systems operated in England. The state courts (secular courts) enforced the common law, and the ecclesiastical courts enforced the church law. Occasionally, members of the clergy were accused of violating the common law. Because many violations at that time were punished by death, there were efforts by the accused and their representatives to have the punishment rather than the offender suspended. Initially, members of the clergy (ordained clerks, monks, and nuns) could have their cases transferred to church courts on the basis of **benefit of clergy,** which claimed that only the church courts had jurisdiction over its clergy. The result of such transfer was to reduce the punishment to which the accused could be subjected.

By the late twelfth century, Henry II (1133–1189) was succeeding in his efforts to strengthen the Crown's power. He began insisting that ordained persons accused of violating the secular law should be tried in King's Court. In a compromise, the church agreed to let the state court hear cases against members of the clergy, but only if the state presented no evidence against the clerics. Furthermore, clerics could give their own versions of the alleged offense and could present witnesses to corroborate their testimonies. Not surprisingly, it was difficult to convict a person when only positive information and nonincriminating evidence were given to the court (Dressler, 1969).

The persons to which benefit of clergy applied changed over time, as did the court setting in which it occurred. After beginning as a mechanism available only to ordained representatives of the church, benefit of clergy was extended during the fourteenth century to any defendant who could read. Reading was a skill usually only possessed by the clergy and some of the upper class, so it was assumed that a person who could read must be linked to the church and should be granted benefits of that position. Proof of ability to read was shown by having the accused read a passage from the Psalms. Typically, a passage from Psalm 51 ("Have mercy upon me, O God, according to thy loving kindness: according unto the multitude of thy tender mercies blot out my transgressions") was required. Dressler (1969) notes that abuse of the system began occurring with regularity, and the reading test eventually became a fiction. Defendants either memorized the verse, or clerks of the court simply told the judge that defendants could read even when they could not (Chute & Bell, 1956).

Expansion of benefit of clergy to almost every accused person, and the resulting abuses of the procedure, indicated the beginning of its end. Parliament began to stipulate that certain crimes should be felonies without benefit of clergy and finally succeeded in abolishing the practice altogether with the Criminal Law Act of 1827.

Judicial Reprieve or Suspended Sentence. It is probably pushing the point to cite benefit of clergy as a forerunner to probation. Although the benefit may exemplify a technique that is more humane (the first objective noted earlier for probation), the practice of bona fide probation involves a suspension—instead of dismissal—

of a harsher punishment. That aspect of probation more clearly comes from the techniques known as judicial reprieve.

Judicial reprieve refers to a temporary suspension of either the imposition or execution of a sentence. At the judge's discretion, sentencing can be delayed (**suspension of imposition**) for a person who has pled or been found guilty, or a sentence that has been imposed will not be carried out (**suspension of execution**). Under English common law, the reprieve was typically given for a specific purpose. Most often it was to allow the convicted person a chance to apply to the Crown for a pardon. Because the suspension was only temporary, convicted people who did not receive a pardon had a sentence imposed or executed. In addition, judges could grant judicial reprieve in cases in which they were not satisfied with the verdict, or when they felt the evidence was suspicious. In these situations, what was supposed to be only a temporary stay could actually mean the case never continued beyond that stage.

Because judicial reprieve affects the imposition or execution of a sentence, it is an obvious forerunner to probation and provides other components of the probation process. In addition, while awaiting word about a possible pardon, the person under judicial reprieve was usually allowed to remain at liberty in the community.

Recognizance. The term **recognizance** refers to a commitment a defendant makes to a judge, by which the defendant promises to appear in court at a specified time while the court allows the defendant to remain at liberty in the community. When this obligation is backed only by the defendant's word, it is called **personal recognizance,** and the defendant is said to have been released on his own recognizance (ROR). If the obligation is backed by a third party, the defendant is said to have surety or bail, and that person serving as surety has the duty to return the offender to court if a new offense is committed or the defendant fails to comply with conditions of the release.

The earliest use of recognizance in the United States occurred in the Municipal Court of Boston in 1830. Judge Oxenbridge Thacher occasionally allowed a defendant to remain at liberty on a promise (recognizance) to appear before the court at any time the judge might request. Judge Thacher's hope was that the defendant would avoid any further violation of the law. The effect was that no sentence was pronounced against the defendant—unless the promise to behave was not achieved. This process, called **laying on file,** was Massachusetts's procedure for suspending sentence under recognizance and after a guilty plea or verdict (Chute & Bell, 1956).

Recognizance had a humane aspect (like benefit of clergy originally) and included the idea of suspension of sentence with freedom in the community (as did judicial reprieve), but it also added features that brought the justice system even closer to the idea of probation. Specifically, recognizance set conditions for the defendant's liberty and made possible the revocation of that liberty if the conditions were not met. But a final ingredient was still missing; although a person serving as surety may have an interest in the defendant's behavior, the defendant was under no supervision or guidance from the court. When a court supervision aspect was added, the procedure now called probation was achieved. But even that supervision was not an overnight happening. Its first stages occurred in the United States in Massachusetts, so we must turn our attention to activities in that state to appreciate probation's development.

Massachusetts and the Origin of Probation

Massachusetts provided the site for the first practical demonstration of probation, the first use of the term *probation* as a legal procedure, and the enactment of the first probation law.[1] Specifically, the efforts of Boston shoemaker John Augustus are cited as essential for the movement toward formalization of probation as a sentence.

It seems likely that the persons serving as sureties in recognizance cases provided aid and supervision to the released offender. But documentation of such activity was not provided until John Augustus published the story of his labors as a surety for 1,102 men, women, and children between 1841 and 1851. As a result of his documentation, and his use of the term *probation* in reference to the time defendants spent under his supervision (Augustus, 1972, p. 5), Augustus is generally considered the founder of modern probation.

In his book, John Augustus describes being in Boston's police court one morning in August 1841.

> . . . when the door communicating with the lock-room was opened and an officer entered, followed by a ragged and wretched looking man, who took his seat upon the bench allotted to prisoners. I imagined from the man's appearance that his offense was that of yielding to his appetite for intoxicating drinks, and in a few moments I found that my suspicions were correct, for the clerk read the complaint, in which the man was charged with being a common drunkard. The case was clearly made out, but before sentence had been passed, I conversed with him for a few moments, and found that he was not yet past all hope of reformation. . . . I bailed him by permission of the Court. He was ordered to appear for sentence in three weeks from that time. He signed a pledge and became a sober man. . . . The Judge expressed himself much pleased with the account we gave of the man, and instead of the usual penalty—imprisonment in the House of Correction,—he fined him one cent and costs, amounting in all to $3.76, which was immediately paid. The man continued industrious and sober, and without doubt has been by this treatment, saved from a drunkard's grave.[2] (Augustus, 1972, pp. 4–5)

In this account of the first probation client and the first probation officer are the important elements of official probation:

1. Information is gathered from and about the client.
2. The probation officer draws conclusions regarding the client's suitability for probation and then makes a recommendation to the court regarding disposition of the client.
3. While under probation, the client undergoes treatment directed by a probation officer.
4. On successful completion of probation, the client is rewarded by not having to suffer more severe punishment in the form of incarceration.

This chapter returns to these elements later, but first discusses more about the activities of Augustus.

John Augustus was born in 1785 in Woburn, Massachusetts. Eventually he moved to Boston where he opened a shoe shop near the courthouse. Chute and Bell (1956) suspect Augustus began visiting the Boston courts because of his membership in an abstinence society that was promoting temperance and reclaiming drunkards. During his first year of serving as surety in police court, Augustus bailed only men charged with drunkenness. In mid-1842 he began to take women who had been similarly charged. By 1843 his efforts had expanded to men and women charged with a variety of offenses, and he also began accepting children. Because the country's first juvenile court was still fifty-six years from realization, his efforts to assist children meant they could avoid jail and other

[1]The following discussion draws heavily from the work of Chute and Bell (1956). Reprinted with the permission of Simon & Schuster from *Crime, Courts, and Probation* by Charles Lionel Chute and Marjorie Bell. Copyright © 1956 by Marjorie Bell, renewed.

[2]Reprinted with the permission of Patterson Smith Publishing from *John Augustus, First Probation Officer,* Montclair, N.J. Copyright © 1972 by the publisher.

John Augustus, a Boston shoemaker, is credited with establishing the basis for probation as a sentence for criminal offenders. Through his voluntary efforts, offenders were provided with bail, counseling, and supervision upon being released to the community.

punishments then being offered without concern for age. In 1843 Augustus expanded his efforts to Boston's Municipal Court, and between that and the police court he documented ten years of assistance wherein 1,102 persons were bailed with 674 of those being men and boys, and 428 being women and girls (Augustus, 1972, p. 41).

Like the probation officers to follow him, Augustus had certain criteria by which he made decisions regarding those persons for whom he would stand as surety. Augustus confined his efforts "mainly to those who were indicted for their first offense, and whose hearts were not wholly depraved, but gave promise of better things" (Augustus, 1972, p. 19). He took into consideration the person's character, age, and surrounding influences (Augustus, 1972, p. 34) when deciding if the prisoner was likely to benefit from probation.

The type of assistance extended by Augustus also anticipated that offered by later probation officers. By providing bail for a temporary suspension or postponement of sentence, Augustus was able to help his charges find homes, secure employment or ensure school attendance, and soothe family problems. The results of his labors are not as well documented as the procedures, but Augustus claimed only 1 of his first 1,100 cases had a forfeited bond. Chute and Bell (1956) refer to a friend of Augustus who notes that only 10 out of nearly 2,000 persons proved ungrateful of Augustus's efforts. Regardless of the actual numbers of people he assisted, John Augustus provided the base for an aspect of modern justice that has grown beyond what even he could have anticipated.

Probation Expands and Spreads

Probation is considered to be an American invention, especially by people in the United States. However, activities occurring in England in the early 1840s paralleled those in Massachusetts at that time. The main difference between the two approaches was in the supervision provided offenders while they were in the community. Probation in the United States relied on a formal and organized supervision process. Probation in England became an additional responsibility for persons such as magistrates and police officers rather than the duty of a person specifically responsible for probation. The two approaches to probation (i.e., with or without formal supervision) provided a choice for other countries interested in this new alternative to jail and prison. After considering probation in the United States, we will look at its growth in England and other parts of the world.

Probation in the United States. The first law actually providing for paid probation officers supervising both children and adults was enacted by the Massachusetts legislature on April 26, 1878. This law was limited to Suffolk County (Boston and a few adjacent towns), but in 1880 a new statute permitted the appointment of a probation officer in every Massachusetts city and town. These initial probation officers were considered advisors to the court and were responsible for investigating cases and recommending probation, as appropriate, to the judge. By the end of the century, Massachusetts law provided for mandatory statewide salaried probation service and made the disposition of probation available, at the court's discretion, to all persons charged with any level of offense (Chute & Bell, 1956).

Probation's success in Massachusetts became known in other states as alternatives to prison were being considered for first offenders. Most states were already using release on recognizance and suspension of either execution or imposition of sentence for persons not seen as needing or deserving imprisonment. The biggest problem with simple recognizance or suspension of sentence was the absence of any effective control over the offenders, who were released to the community. Finally, Vermont (in 1898) and Rhode Island (in 1899) passed probation laws that incorporated features of the Massachusetts law while providing some important innovations (Chute & Bell, 1956). Vermont, for example, adopted a county plan wherein each county court appointed a probation officer who would investigate cases at the court's request. After conviction and imposition of sentence, and regardless of age or offense, Vermont courts could impose probation for the time period that the court desired.

Rhode Island's innovations included placement of probation services as a state-administered system (rather than city or county), and a requirement that at least one of the appointed state probation officers be a woman (Chute & Bell, 1956). Rhode Island also differed from either Massachusetts or Vermont by excluding the possibility of probation for persons charged with the serious offenses of murder, robbery, rape, arson, or burglary.

With the turn of the century, probation began spreading beyond the New England area (e.g., Michigan and California in 1903), and by 1910 probation laws were in place for both adults and children in nineteen states. In 1925 a statute authorizing probation in federal courts was passed, and by 1954 all but one of the forty-eight states had an adult probation law (Mississippi was the exception), and all forty-eight had enacted probation laws for juveniles (Chute & Bell, 1956).

As the twenty-first century begins, probation in the United States continues to serve as the primary sanction for criminal offenders. Figure 7.1 shows that since 1985 probation, prison, parole, and jail populations have each shown steady increases, but probation's growth certainly stands apart. Nearly 60 percent of the almost 6 million adults under correctional supervision are on probation.

Most of the persons on probation are men (79 percent), but the 21 percent female population gives probation a larger proportion of women than any other correctional population (Bonczar, 1997). For example, women are about 11 percent of the local jail population, 6.5 percent of the prisoners; and 12 percent of the people on parole. As discussed in Chapter 11, the increased use of community sanctions (probation in this case) is consistent with some suggestions for differential handling of female offenders because they are less likely to present a risk to the community. Table 7.1 also shows that most probationers are white, non-Hispanic, and have been placed on probation as the result of a felony offense. Also interesting, probation today is more likely to be a directly imposed sentence rather than a condition of a suspended sentence. Probation clearly plays an important role in contemporary corrections. After briefly reviewing its use in other countries, this chapter will return to the specific discussion of probation in the United States.

Probation in England. Probation in England developed in a manner similar to its progression in the United States. In early 1841 Matthew Hill, a court recorder in Birmingham, added supervision by relatives or volunteers to the existing practice of releasing offenders to their parents or trade master after one day's imprisonment. In his book about his experiences, Hill explains that beginning in 1841, he would identify juvenile offenders who were not wholly corrupt and hand them over to persons willing to act as guardians (Timasheff, 1941). So, while John Augustus was identifying persons in Boston appropriate for his guardianship, Matthew Hill was identifying persons in Birmingham appropriate for assigning to a guardian. In both instances the beginnings of probation are seen.

FIGURE 7.1

Adults on Probation, in Jail or Prison, or on Parole, 1985–1998

Source: Adapted from Bureau of Justice Statistics. (1999). *Correctional populations in the United States, 1996* [NCJ 170013]. Washington, DC: Author. Update to 1998 with Bonczar, T. (1999). *Probation and parole in the United States, 1998* [NCJ 178234]. Washington, DC: Bureau of Justice Statistics.

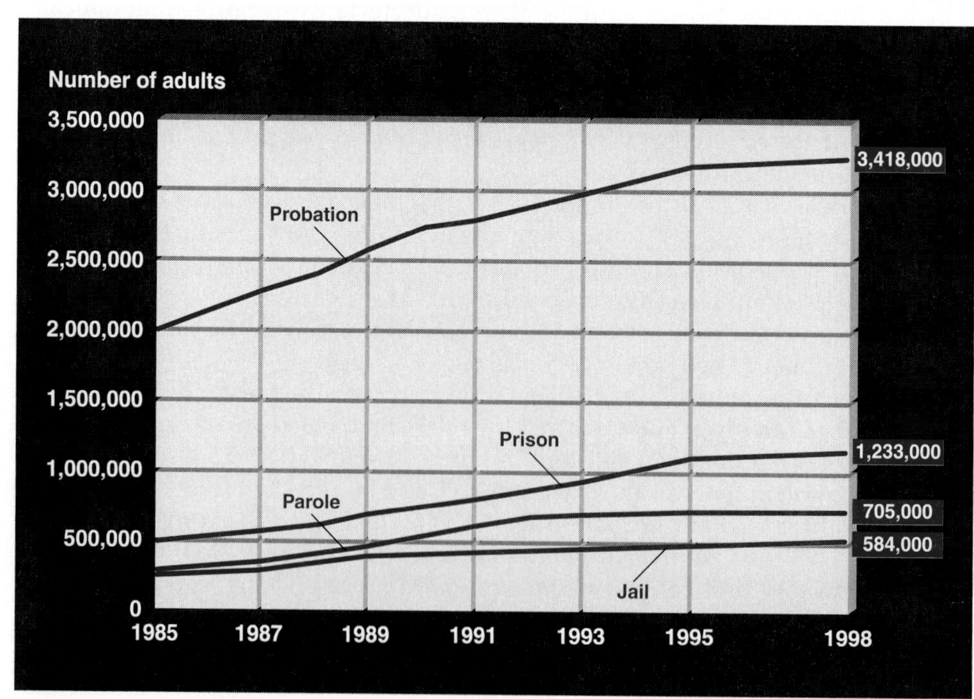

TABLE 7.1: Characteristics of Adults on Probation, 1990 and 1998

CHARACTERISTIC	1990 (%)	1998 (%)
Sex		
Male	82	79
Female	18	21
Race		
White	68	64
Black	31	35
American Indian/Alaska Native; Asian/Pacific Islander	1	2
Hispanic Origin		
Hispanic	18	15
Non-Hispanic	82	85
Status of Probation		
Sentence suspended	41	27
Imposition suspended	14	10
Direct imposition of probation	38	51
Split sentence	6	10
Other	1	2
Status of Supervision		
Active supervision	83	77
Inactive supervision	9	9
Absconded from supervision	6	10
Supervised out of state	2	2
Other	not available	2
Types of Offense		
Felony	not available	57
Misdemeanor	not available	40
Other infractions	not available	3

Source: Adapted from Bonczar, T. (1999). *Probation and parole in the United States, 1998* [NCJ 178234]. Washington, DC: Bureau of Justice Statistics.

Probation continued to develop in England at a pace similar to its growth in Massachusetts. Whereas Massachusetts made probation formal with legislation in 1878, an English statute followed in 1879. There was, however, an important difference between the two jurisdictions' use of probation. Whereas the Massachusetts law provided for paid probation officers, the English model avoided the use of organized supervision and the assignment of officials specifically responsible for probation. Instead, English magistrates, police officers, and volunteers were expected to watch over the cases (Timasheff, 1941). Not until 1907 did the English

Parliament pass a bill providing for appointment of paid probation officers to supervise those offenders placed on probation.

The use of organized supervision in Massachusetts and the preference for unorganized supervision in England provided two models that other countries could consider as the concept of probation grew. A brief review of probation's development in countries not linked to English common law shows some of the different directions the American and English innovation took.

Probation around the World. Nicholas Timasheff (1943) provides an interesting and complete review of probation's development in continental Europe, Latin America, Asia, and Africa. Because community sanctions and penalties in other parts of the world are considered later, it is important to have an understanding of the origin of this basic form of community release in other countries. Probation in continental Europe lagged behind its development in Massachusetts by some forty years. Timasheff (1943) suggests the reasons for this delay were the severing of ties to historical institutions and procedures (e.g., benefit of clergy and recognizance) that had given common-law countries an important base from which to work. Furthermore, the civil legal tradition's predominance in continental Europe meant judges had less freedom to experiment with punishment and sentences than did their counterparts in the common legal tradition. Thus, the introduction of probation could come about only through legislation in countries with a civil legal tradition.

France was among the first European countries to enact a law containing aspects of probation (in 1891), but it was not until 1958 that French law allowed for a formal sentence to supervised probation. France's 1891 legislation was influenced by the English law of 1879 and had been under discussion by the French parliament since 1884 when Berenger introduced it in continental Europe (Timasheff, 1943). In its final form, French probation was used for persons who had not previously been sentenced to prison for either a misdemeanor or felony but in the current case had received a prison sentence or a fine. This probation, therefore, was of the "suspended execution of sentence" type. The suspension term was five years (the longest sentence midlevel courts could impose) and could result in offenders being placed in prison if they committed another offense. This is not, however, a true example of probation because the law did not provide for supervision of the probationer's behavior. When supervised probation was implemented in 1958, France finally had a formal probation procedure.

Other countries adopted procedures reminiscent of probation's origin in the United States, but still were without the supervision aspect. Belgium's 1888 law called for probation through suspension of sentencing rather than France's suspension of execution; parts of Switzerland passed laws in 1891 that directed benevolent societies to help the offenders find jobs—a nod toward supervision; and in Germany, probation took a form more accurately seen as conditional pardon (Timasheff, 1943). Eventually the American model—as Timasheff calls probation with organized supervision—grew in popularity. Countries such as Denmark (in 1905) were placing offenders under the supervision of the Prisoner's Aid Society, whereas Hungary (in 1908) used either salaried officers or volunteers to supervise behavior. The aspect of supervision took strong hold in Europe; by 1940 only Finland, Estonia, and Romania had failed to include provisions in their criminal law for care and guidance of probationers (Timasheff, 1943).

Because of their historical and legal ties to continental Europe, Latin American countries followed a similar path that built first on the use of suspended execution of sentence and only later incorporating supervision. The penal codes of Costa Rica (1924), Mexico (1921), and Colombia (1936) provided for supervision by authority, but that authority was essentially a kind of police surveillance rather than guidance by a probation officer (Timasheff, 1943). Countries of Asia and Africa often had probation enforced during colonizations (e.g., French and Dutch colonies emphasized the suspended sentence aspect) or by nations keeping the country in semi-independent status (e.g., in the 1930s probation in the Philippine Islands incorporated the American use of supervision). Asian and African countries having independent status in the first several decades of the twentieth century showed variation in probation as diverse as that found on the European continent. Probation was possible in Egypt only to those who had never been imprisoned for over one week and had never before received probation. In both Japan and China, you could receive probation multiple times as long as you had never been sent to prison. The Chinese law of 1912 allowed for supervision by the police, charitable organizations, government officials, members of the public, or even the offender's relatives (Timasheff, 1943).

By the midtwentieth century, it was obvious that the idea of probation was one whose time had come. It was equally obvious, however, that there would be variations on the basic theme as different countries, and different sections of a single country, modified the Massachusetts and English models. Before turning to some of those alternatives (e.g., community service orders and day reporting centers), it is important to understand better some specifics regarding the way probation currently operates.

Components of Probation

As noted earlier, when John Augustus reported on his first years of providing probation services, he described activities that even today define the main components of probation:

1. On gathering information from and about the offender, a probation officer draws conclusions regarding the offender's suitability for probation and recommends a disposition to the court.
2. While on probation and under the supervision of a probation officer, the client receives services that encourage or enable law-abiding behavior.
3. While on probation, the client is rewarded by not being imprisoned but is also penalized through restrictions placed on his or her behavior and movements as monitored by the probation officer.

These three components are often called **investigation, service,** and **surveillance.** Each deserves a closer look in order to understand probation.

Investigation. Probation is not an appropriate sentence for everyone. For some offenders, the conditions of probation are more punitive and restrictive than the offense or offender requires. For others, probation may not provide the supervision deemed necessary to protect the public or to exact retribution. The problem is determining which persons, of all those eligible for probation, should actually receive this sentence.

The interest in giving probation to those persons most likely to benefit from it has been an important aspect of this sentencing strategy since its inception. John Augustus gave his services to those he believed were not "past all hope of reformation" (Augustus, 1972, p. 4), whereas Matthew Hill sought guidance for those individuals "not wholly corrupt" (quoted in Timasheff, 1941, p. 13). But how do the courts identify such persons?

Some jurisdictions have statutory restrictions on who can receive probation; for example, murderers might not be considered. Others may have formal or informal guidelines that essentially require probation for some crimes or criminals, for example, certain misdemeanor or felony first offenders. Generally, however, determining appropriateness for probation is accomplished by the probation officer in preparing a presentence investigation report.

Presentence investigation (PSI) refers to a method of developing information about a convicted offender that examines that offender's prior record as well as relevant personal and family data. The investigation, which is typically done by a probation officer, results in a **PSI report** that summarizes the information and is used by a judge to help determine an appropriate sentence.

Building on the early twentieth-century interest in individualized study of offenders, people such as William Healy (director in 1910 of the Juvenile Psychopathic Institute at Chicago) encouraged investigation and classification as necessary steps to understanding and helping offenders (see Healy, 1915). This technique of social casework and accompanying treatment became popular among probation services. In 1924 probation officers such as Hans Weiss (Boston Juvenile Court) were praising the usefulness of social casework in forming a diagnosis "based on careful investigation and of working out a plan of treatment in close cooperation with court-clinics" (quoted in Cohn & Ferriter, 1990, p. 16). In 1949 the PSI received legal sanction when the U.S. Supreme Court declared the PSI report to be a valid instrument (*Williams v. New York*). Armed with professional and legal support, the PSI and its accompanying report spread throughout the country and today is a standard tool—especially for felonies, but also for some misdemeanors (Bonczar, 1997).

Ideally, the PSI requires the probation officer to gather information from a variety of sources. In addition to interviewing the person who has pled or been found guilty (in a few cases the PSI may occur prior to adjudication of guilt), the officer preparing the PSI should include information about the person's home environment, family life, work history, education, substance abuse, physical and mental health, criminal history, and other relevant factors (see "Topics Covered in a PSI Report"). That information may come from case files but is considered more helpful if received through direct contact with family, friends, employers, teachers, ministers, and others with direct knowledge of the offender.

After using his interviewing and investigative skills, the probation officer writes the PSI report, concluding it with an evaluative summary that briefly explains the person and her situation to the sentencing judge. The probation officer also recommends a sentence to the judge, and research suggests judges are likely to impose the recommended sentence as often as 95 percent of the time (Cromwell & Killinger, 1994, p. 56). Such a high level of concurrence may be influenced by factors such as the probation officer recommending what he has come to know the judge is likely to do anyway, and by the probation officer conforming to a plea agreement that was struck with the prosecutor. But in fairness to the hard work and dedication of probation officers charged with producing PSI reports, it must also be acknowledged that judges recognize those efforts and express their confidenced in the probation officers by agreeing with recommended sentences.

Although the PSI report's primary use is to assist judges in determining the most appropriate sentence for a particular offender, it is also helpful to probation officers charged with supervising the offender when probation is the resulting sentence. In addition, institutional corrections personnel make use of the PSI report when the offender receives a sentence requiring incarceration. In those instances, the PSI report can assist in the classification process to determine appropriate custody and institutional assignment as well as to help design a treatment plan. Finally, the PSI report might help paroling authorities decide if the offender is ready for release, as indicated by attitude change (e.g., is remorse now being shown when it seemed absent at the time the PSI was conducted?) and release plans (e.g., what did the PSI report say about the offender's older brother, with whom the offender

Help Wanted

Job Title: PSI Report Writer

Position Description: The PSI report writer will compile information about a convicted offender for whom the court requires a presentence investigation report to assist in determining an appropriate sentence. The PSI report writer will gather client information from sources that include interviews with the client and the client's family, friends, employers, and others having relevant knowledge of the client. This information will then be summarized in a standard format for presentation to the judge prior to sentencing. The report will include a recommended sentence from the PSI report writer.

Qualifications: Applicants should have a bachelor's degree with major coursework preferably in criminal justice, sociology, psychology, social work, or a related field. Written and verbal communication skills are a clear requirement for this position. Experience with interviewing and/or interviewing techniques is preferred.

In some probation departments PSI report writing is a duty given to entry-level employees. From that position the employee may move to other probation officer duties. In other jurisdictions the PSI Report writer may be contracted out to a specific agency. For an example of the duties and requirements for probation officers and presentence investigation officers, see the Web site for Nevada's Division of Parole and Probation at *www.aci.net/noyes/pnp/ppfrmops.html.*

Spotlight ON CONTEMPORARY ISSUES

Topics Covered in a PSI Report

Although report styles vary among jurisdictions, the following categories are typical of the ones found in many PSI reports. In an actual PSI report, a one- or two-paragraph narrative under each category heading describes the client's circumstances for that category. A fictional example of a concluding narrative is given for the recommendation category.

- official version of the present offense
- client's version of the offense
- the crime's impact on the victim
- similar offenses by the client
- disposition of codefendants
- pending actions against the client
- criminal history
- social history (e.g., family, educational, military, and marital data)
- home investigation
- employment and financial condition
- additional information and treatment issues (e.g., physical and mental health, prior treatment, and bad habits)
- character references received in the client's behalf
- recommendation

Mr. Doe pled guilty to aggravated assault and is being held at the county jail while awaiting sentencing. His social history and criminal history suggest that he prefers to live off the proceeds of others instead of accepting responsibility for himself. He is thirty-two years old and lives rent free with no source of support other than his wife's Social Security income and food stamps. Although this is Mr. Doe's first charge on a violent offense, his lengthy history of property crimes and his serious substance abuse problem suggest he has some critical problems. He successfully completed one previous probation sentence, but problems have not been addressed adequately.

It is the recommendation of the probation department that Mr. Doe be placed on probation for three years after completing a jail sentence. Specifically, the department recommends that Mr. Doe:

1. Serves ninety days flat time in the county jail.
2. Enters, upon his release from jail, an outpatient treatment program for substance abuse and be required to submit to random urine screens.
3. Finds and maintains full-time employment and not terminate employment without the consent of his probation officer. In addition, he should provide for his own support and room and board.

Read the requirements for items to be included in Utah's presentence investigation reports at ***www.le.state.ut.us/~code/TITLE76/htm/76_03030.htm.*** How do those items compare with the topics expected to be covered in PSIs for your state? Look at Table 6 in the BJS report *Characteristics of Adults on Probation, 1995* at ***www.ojp.usdoj.gov/bjs/abstract/cap95.htm,*** and determine whether it is likely or not likely that a person charged with a misdemeanor property offense would have had a PSI completed prior to his or her sentencing.

plans to live?). These purposes of the PSI report—that is, advising judges on sentencing, probation officers on supervision, institutional personnel on classification and treatment, and paroling authorities on release decisions—make the report an important tool in the justice process.

Service. Beginning with the efforts of John Augustus to help his charges find homes, secure employment, and generally better themselves, probation has been offered as a way to rehabilitate or reintegrate offenders. These goals have been in conflict over the years with other punishment objectives such as incapacitation and retribution, but the rehabilitation philosophy remains predominant (Champion, 1990).

Probation is seen by some as being too lenient and without deterrent value. Interestingly, similar sentiments were expressed when probation was first introduced. The response of John Augustus to such criticism is as appropriate today as it was in 1852. Critics complained that bailing on probation was undesirable and served as an incentive to crime because "the law is robbed of its terrors, and its punishments, and there is nothing therefore, to deter" offenders from repeating their

When clients meet with their probation officer, their progress on probation is reviewed, and suggestions are made to provide them with treatment opportunities.

crimes (Augustus, 1972, p. 99). Augustus rejected such claims as relying too much on stereotypes:

> Individuals and communities generally are but too prone to infer evil of a class, if they but occasionally observe it in individuals; if a person who has been bailed, or received the leniency of the court, proves false to his promises of amendment, people are ever ready to predict that all others will conduct in a similar manner. (Augustus, 1972, pp. 99–100)

So, although there will always be individuals who do not benefit from probation, Augustus warns that it should not be assumed that everyone granted probation will fail. To encourage the likelihood of success, probation has a treatment component that is essential to the whole idea behind the sentence.

Probation departments can be organized in a variety of ways, but quite often they use one of two approaches to provide services to their clients: the **casework approach** or the **brokerage approach.**

Think for a moment about what you believe a probation officer does. If things such as counseling the client about his drug or alcohol problems, meeting with a client and her parents to help them build a positive relationship, or advising clients about managing their finances more effectively come to mind, you are suggesting a casework approach to probation services. This approach assumes the probation officer will play a treatment role and have direct contact with the client.

In many ways, the casework approach is the classic way to offer probation services. Augustus and the other early volunteers took a personal interest in their clients and helped them find jobs, stay in school, refrain from drinking alcohol, and overcome family problems. Today's probation departments that follow the casework approach still use the probation officer as a counselor who takes direct responsibility for treating clients. In other departments, the probation officer does not actually treat the client but instead serves as a link to community services. Under that approach the probation officer is said to be serving as a broker.

The brokerage approach has at least two advantages over the casework approach. First, few people on probation have only one or two problems that must be addressed. Consider, for example, John's case. The PSI identifies John as a substance abuser without job skills who dropped out of school and has low self-esteem, accompanied by an inability to maintain positive social relations. Assigning John to one probation officer who will counsel him in each of those areas may be unreasonable. Under a brokerage approach, rather than independently tackling all John's problems, the probation officer operates as an intermediary between John and various community services. In this way the probation officer refers John to a substance abuse program, arranges for vocational training and preparation for high school equivalency testing, and directs him to community counseling services for assistance with self-image and social relations. Obviously, the broker probation officer must be very knowledgeable about community services and how to access them.

It could be argued that all John's problems are linked to his substance abuse. On that basis a casework probation officer would not really have to address the other problem areas because addressing the substance abuse problem would allow the others to be overcome. And in fact some probation departments use the casework approach for exactly that reason. But this brings us to the second advantage of the brokerage approach—it is more efficient for midsize and small probation departments. Probation services in metropolitan areas may have enough substance abusers, sex offenders, or mentally ill clients to warrant a casework approach in which probation officers have a caseload composed only of persons with one of these problems. But midsize and small departments have trouble justifying the use of probation officers who are qualified to counsel only the occasional, for example, sex offender. It is more efficient for those departments to use probation officers as brokers who know when and where to refer sex offenders as well as substance abusers, the mentally ill, and any other client.

Whether a probation department relies on casework, brokerage, or some combination of these approaches, the issue of **caseload** must be addressed. Ideal or optimum caseloads have been suggested to be as low as thirty-five and as high as fifty (Champion, 1990). The assumption has been that an individual probation officer can be expected to handle only a certain number of clients at a time. A problem with this strategy is that clients may require different amounts of the probation officer's time and energy. For example, the conditions of Maria's probation may require her to see her probation officer only once a month, whereas David has serious problems and is under maximum supervision requiring weekly meetings with his probation officer. Randomly assigning cases to probation officers simply on the basis of balancing caseloads at thirty-five, forty, or fifty may result in Probation Officer Jones having thirty Marias while Probation Officer White has thirty Davids. Attempts to avoid such problems have led to interest in workloads rather than caseloads.

The idea behind **workload** is to balance probation officers' labor on the basis of the effort required to handle their cases rather than on the actual number of cases themselves. In this way, Probation Officer White may have a workload of 25 cases, all of which require a lot of assistance and maximum supervision. In the same department, Officer Jones has a workload with 150 cases with few behavioral problems and requiring only minimum supervision. The effort required of both White and Jones is now ideally equitable, and each officer's clients can receive appropriate treatment.

As suggested earlier, the number of cases handled by each probation officer is influenced by both the amount of treatment or services the client needs and by the level of supervision or monitoring required. The monitoring of probationers brings us to the final component of probation—surveillance.

Surveillance. Probation officers have two roles that in some ways conflict with each other. On one hand, they are expected to be a supportive caseworker for the client to confide in and turn to for advice and assistance. On the other hand, the

Help Wanted

Job Title: Probation Officer

Position Description: Entry-level probation officers will perform a variety of duties in either the juvenile or adult division. Work includes supervision of probationers, report writing, coordination with law enforcement and social service agencies, as well as other assigned duties.

Qualifications: Minimum qualifications include a bachelor's degree in behavioral science, social science, criminal justice, or related field. Must have no felony convictions and be able to possess a driver's license at time of appointment. Background check and drug testing will be conducted as part of the pre-employment screening process.

For examples of career opportunities in this field, visit the American Probation and Parole Web site at ***www.appa-net.org/jobs.htm,*** and review the types of probation positions being advertised. There is also a variety of federal-level probation positions that can be reviewed at the Federal Judiciary Web site at ***www.uscourts.gov/employment/opportunity.html.***

probation officer is the court's representative, charged with enforcing the conditions of the offender's sentence and with bringing violations of those conditions to the court's attention—thereby placing the offender at risk of being sent to prison. It is not easy to serve simultaneously as advisor and enforcer (see "Female Probation Officers"). But as parents and teachers will attest, it can be accomplished with hard work and dedication.

Sentences to probation typically include certain conditions that the probationer agrees to abide by in return for remaining at liberty in the community. These probation terms and conditions may simply consist of general rules applying to all persons released on probation or may be special conditions tailored to an offender's particular needs. As indicated in Figure 7.2, the general rules or standard conditions require probationers to do such things as regularly work or attend school, obtain permission before leaving the jurisdiction, avoid association with persons having a criminal record, meet with the probation officer on a regular basis, and pay fees toward their supervision.

In addition to the standard ones, special conditions may be required of some probationers. Table 7.2 shows that payment of fees, fines, and court costs are the most frequent special condition, followed by substance abuse treatment and employment and training. Other special conditions include topics covered in later chapters. For example, the probationer may be assigned to an intensive probation supervision program (discussed next) or to a residential community corrections facility (see Chapter 8).

ISSUES OF FAIRNESS

FEMALE PROBATION OFFICERS

Probation officers are required to take the roles of both nurturer and enforcer. These are roles that society typically expects of parents and teachers as well. Possibly because of sex-role stereotyping, the jobs of parenting, teaching, and probation work are ones to which women are often attracted or directed. In 1997 women were 55 percent of the staff in the nation's probation agencies and 50 percent in those jurisdictions with combined probation and parole agencies. Women made up 48 percent of the country's parole agencies' staff and an average of 30 percent of the staff in adult correctional agencies (Camp & Camp, 1997, pp. 109, 172–173).

Paternalistic and/or statutory restrictions prior to the 1970s often meant that women interested in the corrections field had few, if any, options. Klosak offers Michigan as an example in which women were specifically prohibited, until the early 1970s, from "working inside the security perimeter in men's prisons, from supervising male parolees or probationers, or even from applying for a corrections officer job in a men's facility" (NIC Information Center, 1993, p. 20). Contemporary percentages suggest that earlier restrictions on women in probation are being overcome, but it is difficult to determine if women are making gains only at the entry-level and midlevel staff positions, or are also becoming supervisors. Morton reviewed national data from 1989 to 1990 and found that only a few women in community corrections were in top-level administrative positions around the country (NIC Information Center, 1993, p. 5). Anecdotal data might suggest there is an increased number of women in such positions today, but the absence of a national study means we do not know for certain.

Visit the Blacks in Illinois History page at ***www.ieanea.org/features/bhm/blkhisti.html***, and identify the person who, in 1913, became the first black woman probation officer in the nation. Then go to the Women in Criminal Justice Hall of Honor site at ***www.cj.msu.edu/~outreach/azm/hof.html***, and determine how Denise Quarles and Tekla Miller were important to probation. For an interesting review of significant events for women in the United States regarding their experiences with the law (including practicing it as a profession), see the time line provided at ***members.aol.com/aacdrcnnea/lawtime.htm.***

FIGURE 7.2

Typical Probation Terms and Conditions Agreement

________________ COURT, ________________ COUNTY ________________, COLORADO

Case No. ________________ Div/Ct. Room ________________ ML NO. ________________

CONDITIONS OF ________________ **FOR THE OFFENSE(S) OF** ________________

GRANTED ON ___/___/___ to ___/___/___

THE PEOPLE OF THE STATE OF COLORADO v. ________________, Defendant

You shall be supervised by the probation department for a period of _______ months/years and shall comply with the following conditions and those listed on the reverse side of this form. You may be supervised in specialized programs, as determined by the probation department, with additional conditions imposed.

As a condition of supervision, you shall pay the following amounts:

Victim compensation cost (VCMP)	$_______	Drug offender surcharge (DRUG)	$_______
Victims assistance surcharge (VAST)	$_______	Special advocate surcharge (SPAD)	$_______
Restitution (REST)	$_______	Sex offender surcharge (SXOF)	$_______
Sheriff cost (ASSF)	$_______	Youthful offender surcharge (YTHO)	$_______
Attorney fees (ATYF)	$_______	Substance abuse assessment fee (DSAS)	$_______
Supervision fee (SUPV)	$_______	PSI drug testing fee (DTST)	$_______
ADDS fee (ALCV)	$_______	Other	$_______
Fine (FLNF/MISD)	$_______	Other	$_______
Court costs—docket fee (CRTC)	$_______	Other	$_______
LEAF fee (LEAF)	$_______	TOTAL	$_______

A cost of care reimbursement may be assessed in addition to the amounts above and may be a continuing obligation after probation is terminated.

The total amount is to be paid by ________________ or at the rate of __________ per __________ beginning ________________ to the Clerk of ________________ Court at ________________

________________.

ADDITIONAL CONDITIONS: You shall participate in, cooperate with, pay any fees required, and successfully complete the following, as indicated:

- ❒ 1. Substance abuse evaluation/treatment
- ❒ 2. Mental health evaluation/counseling or treatment
- ❒ 3. Community corrections for __________ beginning ________________
- ❒ 4. Community service of __________ hours completed by ________________
- ❒ 5. Electronic monitoring for __________ days
- ❒ 6. Jail for ________________ beginning ________________
- ❒ 7. Work release for ________________ beginning ________________

____
Judge Date

I have received a copy of these conditions and have read them carefully with full understanding. I understand that, if I violate these conditions, I may be brought before the court for revocation and imposition of sentence.

________________ ________________
Defendant Date Probation Officer/Witness Date

Continued

Source: From Colorado Judicial Department.

FIGURE 7.2

Typical Probation Terms and Conditions Agreement (continued)

STANDARD CONDITIONS

1. You shall not violate any local, state, or federal law.
2. You shall not harass, molest, intimidate, retaliate against, or tamper with any victims of or any prosecution witness to the crime.
3. You are required to register as a sex offender if you are convicted of an offense involving unlawful sexual behavior, pursuant to Section 18-3-412.5 of the Colorado Revised Statutes.
4. You shall maintain a permanent residence and shall report any change of address, as directed by the probation officer.
5. You shall not leave the State of Colorado without written permission from the probation officer or the court.
6. You shall report to the probation officer at reasonable times, as directed by the court or the probation officer, and permit the probation officer to visit you at reasonable times at home or elsewhere.
7. You shall answer all reasonable inquiries by the probation officer.
8. You shall report any law enforcement contacts to the probation officer immediately.
9. You may be required to notify third parties of your criminal record, as directed by the probation officer.
10. You shall maintain or seek suitable employment or faithfully pursue a course of study or vocational training and shall report any change in employment or educational status, as directed by the probation officer.
11. You shall support your dependents and meet your other family responsibilities, including any obligations for child support or spousal maintenance.
12. You shall not possess any firearm, explosive or other destructive device, nor any other dangerous weapon, unless you obtain written permission from the court.
13. You shall not use alcohol (to excess)* or use unlawfully any controlled substance or other dangerous or abusable drug or substance.
14. You shall submit to substance testing at the direction of the probation officer, and it may be at your expense.
15. You shall obtain counseling or treatment for drug abuse, alcohol abuse, or a mental condition and shall remain in a specified residential facility if necessary for that purpose, as required by the court or the probation officer. You may be responsible for the costs of the program.
16. You shall comply with any other requirements of the probation officer in order to meet the conditions imposed by the court.

*Strike as appropriate.

As you review the standard and special conditions in Figure 7.2, you find some that seem to emphasize deterrence (e.g., paying a fine or submitting to searches on demand) whereas others seem to have a rehabilitative aspect (e.g., obtain vocational training or participate in drug or alcohol treatment). Because the probation officer is charged with making sure these conditions are carried out, the dual nature of the officer's role (advisor and enforcer) is apparent.

TABLE 7.2: Conditions of Sentences of Adult Probationers, by Severity of Offense, 1995

		SEVERITY OF OFFENSE	
Condition of Sentence	Total	Felony	Misdemeanor
Any Condition	98.6%	98.4%	98.9%
Fees, Fines, Court Costs	84.3%	84.2%	85.1%
Supervision fees	61.0	63.9	59.8
Fines	55.8	47.4	67.9
Court costs	54.5	56.4	54.5
Restitution to Victim	30.3%	39.7%	17.6%
Confinement/Monitoring	10.1%	12.9%	6.3%
Boot camp	0.5	0.8	0.1
Electronic monitoring	2.9	3.2	2.0
House arrest without electronic monitoring	0.8	1.1	0.5
Curfew	0.9	1.6	0.0
Restriction on movement	4.2	5.3	2.9
Restrictions	21.1%	24.0%	16.0%
No contact with victim	10.4	11.8	8.2
Driving restrictions	5.3	4.3	5.8
Community Service	25.7%	27.3%	24.0%
Alcohol/Drug Restrictions	38.2%	48.1%	23.7%
Mandatory drug testing	32.5	43.0	17.1
Remain alcohol/drug free	8.1	10.4	5.2
Substance Abuse Treatment	41.0%	37.5%	45.7%
Alcohol	29.2	21.3	41.0
Drug	23.0	28.3	14.8
Other Treatment	17.9%	16.1%	20.9%
Sex offenders program	2.5	3.9	0.2
Psychiatric/psychological counseling	7.1	8.9	4.7
Other counseling	9.2	4.4	16.4
Employment and Training	40.3%	45.4%	34.4%
Employment	34.7	40.9	27.3
Education/training	15.0	15.5	15.1
Other Special Conditions	16.5%	19.0%	12.6%
Number of probationers*	2,558,981	1,470,696	982,536

Detail may not sum to total because probationers may have more than one condition on their sentences, and totals may include items not shown in the table. Excludes 61,579 probationers (2% of all adults on probation) for whom information on conditions of probation were not reported.

Source: From Bonczar, T. (1997). *Characteristics of adults on probation, 1995* [NCJ 164267]. Washington, DC: Bureau of Justice Statistics.

Intensive Probation Supervision

An especially popular condition to attach to probation today is the intermediate sanction know as **intensive probation supervision (IPS).** This sanction's identity is complicated by parole programs having similar designs that are called, for example, intensive parole supervision (still IPS). For simplicity, the text uses the IPS designation and, given the focus of this chapter, restricts discussion to probation, not parole programs.

As its name suggests, IPS is designed to provide greater supervision than regular probation. Offenders on IPS will typically have very frequent contact (daily or at least many times during the week) with their probation officer. In addition to these increased encounters, IPS might place greater restrictions on the offender than would regular probation. For example, IPS clients may be more frequently subjected to unscheduled checks for drug use, required to stay at their residences during certain hours of the day, or be placed on electronic monitoring.

The combination of increased contact between probation officers and probationers and increased restrictions on the probationers' activities highlight two aspects of IPS. On one hand, it can be considered a probation-enhancement strategy wherein high-risk probationers on regular probation are placed under increased supervision. On the other hand, IPS can be considered a prison-diversion technique in the sense that it becomes an alternative sanction for offenders who would otherwise go to prison.

Probation-Enhancement IPS. **Probation-enhancement IPS** was first tried in the 1960s in attempts to increase probation officers' abilities to treat their clients under the medical model by providing smaller caseloads. With fewer clients, the argument went, probation officers could diagnose the trouble and see that clients received appropriate treatment. Actually, the term *IPS* was not being used for these programs, but they were certainly examples of the *intensive* and *probation* parts of today's buzzword.

The term **case management probation** is probably more accurate for the intensive probation programs operating during the Rehabilitation era. Under a caseload strategy, each probation officer is assigned a small enough number of cases (usually between 35 and 50) so that each client can receive individualized attention. Fifteen probation officers in the department might, therefore, each have around 42 cases, so that all 630 persons currently on probation will have a probation officer who can give them the necessary attention and treatment.

In the mid-1960s, some researchers began wondering if they could develop empirical support for the theoretical assumption that smaller caseloads made for more effective probation (Carter, Robison, & Wilkins, 1967; Robison, Wilkins, Carter, & Wahl, 1969). In what was called the San Francisco Project, researchers had federal probation authorities assign offenders to one of four caseload types. The intensive caseload had 20 to 25 offenders per probation officer, the ideal caseload had 40 to 50 offenders per officer, the normal caseload ranged from 70 to 130, and the minimum caseload consisted of several hundred probationers. At the end of two years, the violation rates from each caseload group were compared. There was no significant difference among the violations in the minimum, normal, and ideal caseloads (each had violation rates around 23 percent). Interestingly, the intensive caseload violations were different—but in an unexpected direction. Instead of having more success on probation as a result of receiving more attention from the probation officer, persons assigned to the intensive caseload group had a violation rate of 38 percent.

The higher violation rate for probationers in the intensive caseload group resulted primarily from a high proportion of technical violations. In fact, when technical violations were excluded from the analysis, there were no significant differences among the violation rates from the four caseload types. Apparently, having fewer clients gave probation officers increased opportunities to observe and respond to violations such as having improper associates or unauthorized absences. The officers seemed to use the increased time for each client as a way to check on compliance with the terms and conditions of probation rather than as an opportunity to assist in the client's rehabilitation.

But the results of the San Francisco Project were not all bad news for the proponents of treatment. One benefit was a new focus on the topic of client-to-officer ratios. As people discussed the implications of the San Francisco Project, as well as other studies finding that smaller caseload sizes did not increase the likelihood of success on probation, attention turned to a new concept of workload. As discussed earlier, the concepts of caseload and workload are similar, but the workload strategy takes into consideration the differing time requirements needed by various offenders.

The concept of workload has continued today as probation-enhanced IPS replaces the earlier case management probation. Somewhat ironically, the tendency for small caseloads to result in increased technical violations, considered undesirable under a treatment orientation, fits nicely with the incapacitation goals of the Retributive era. Probation-enhanced IPS assigns a smaller number of clients to a single probation officer, although each officer still has a standard workload. The officer can then more closely monitor the offender's actions and, secondarily, provide a better opportunity for rehabilitation.

Prison-Diversion IPS. The increasing penalties and prison crowding that accompanied America's movement into the Retributive era generated a new look at probation programs with small caseloads. If the probation-enhancement programs emphasize the *I* and *P* of IPS, then the **prison-diversion IPS** most certainly highlights the *I* and the *S*. The stress on *intensive* and *supervision* fits well with a sentencing strategy that emphasizes specific deterrence and incapacitation (Lurigio & Petersilia, 1992). Increased surveillance of the offender should, the argument goes, deter the offender from further criminal acts because the likelihood of detection and punishment is increased. Also, close scrutiny of the offender can achieve incapacitation objectives that presumably ensure public safety.

Intensive supervision programs are increasingly the focus of evaluation studies (see "Evaluating IPS"), and Georgia's program has been particularly well studied. The Georgia program, which also was one of the country's first, is a good example of the prison-diversion type of IPS because it was created to shift prison-bound offenders into a community setting without jeopardizing public safety.

In 1981 Georgia received the dubious distinction of having the world's highest per capita incarceration rate (Erwin, 1990). Inevitably, the strains on state prison facilities and budgets made it clear that alternatives had to be found for some of the offenders the judges believed should be sentenced to prison. Georgia officials were confronted with a need to satisfy two seemingly contradictory goals:

> (1) restraining the growth of prison populations and associated costs by controlling selected offenders in the community and (2) at the same time, satisfying to some extent the demand that criminals be punished for their crimes. (Erwin & Bennett, 1987, p. 1)

A number of alternatives to incarceration were developed (winning Georgia several awards in 1987 for innovations in government), but the most notable was the IPS program started in 1982.

Under Georgia's version of IPS, two officers (a probation officer and a surveillance officer) supervise a caseload of twenty-five, although in some jurisdictions an extra surveillance officer is added and the caseload is increased to forty

Spotlight ON CONTEMPORARY ISSUES

Evaluating IPS

Between 1986 and 1989, fourteen intensive probation supervision (IPS) programs in nine states were evaluated by the Rand Corporation under commission of the National Institute of Justice. A study of those programs provides what may be the largest random experiment in corrections ever undertaken in the United States because each site provided both an experimental and control group of offenders. The study's goal was to determine how participation in an IPS affected offenders' subsequent criminal behavior. Some results from the study are provided by Petersilia and Turner (1993).

Areas in which IPS seems more effective. At all fourteen sites, the IPS program provided more stringent supervision than was given to offenders in the control group. Persons under IPS had more face-to-face and telephone contacts with their supervisors, received more law enforcement checks and drug and alcohol tests, and had more monitoring of their employment. The increased scrutiny of IPS clients meant they were more often caught in technical violations of their probation or parole contract than were persons under regular supervision. This suggests that IPS can be an effective intermediate sanction that allows offenders to serve their sentence in the community without placing the public at undue risk.

Areas in which IPS seems less effective. IPS programs did not seem to have much impact on offender recidivism. Persons on IPS "were not subsequently arrested less often, did not have a longer time to failure, and were not arrested for less serious offenses than control group members" (Petersilia & Turner, 1993, p. 5). However, these findings must be interpreted in the knowledge that closer supervision means greater likelihood of detection. In other words, IPS offenders may have been committing the same number or even fewer crimes than persons on routine supervision, but their misbehavior was more likely to be found out.

Read the evaluation of Colorado's intensive probation supervision program at *www.ncjrs.org/pdffiles/166822.pdf* (page 11). What answers do the evaluators give to these questions about the program: Does IPS divert offenders from prison? Does IPS protect the public? What are the successful treatment and surveillance components of IPS?

probationers. Because the program goal is to "incarcerate" offenders in the community without increasing risk to the citizens, the supervision standards are designed to emphasize control first and treatment only secondarily. For example, probationers are subjected to five contacts per week with a team officer, mandatory curfews that are enforced by frequent home visits, mandatory and verified employment, and unscheduled drug screening and alcohol breath tests. The question, of course, is how successful these procedures have been in helping Georgia achieve the goals of restraining growth in prison populations and budgets, satisfying the public's demand that criminals be punished, and avoiding any increased public safety risk to the community.

Researchers at Georgia's Office of Research and Evaluation have been diligent in their efforts to answer these and many other questions about the IPS program. A brief review of some of their early findings gives a useful summary of this particular version of prison-diversion IPS.

The first comprehensive study of the Georgia program looked at the 2,322 people put on IPS between 1982 and 1985. The researchers concluded that IPS was an option that satisfied public demand for a tough response to crime while avoiding the costs of prison construction (see Erwin, 1990; Erwin & Bennett, 1987). Specifically, the evaluators determined:

- The program did divert offenders from prison. Because Georgia's IPS program is designed to handle offenders who would otherwise go to prison, it was important to confirm that program participants were actually those kinds of offenders. The evidence showed a 10 percent reduction of felons sentenced to prison from 1982 through 1985 and confirmed that the IPS offenders were more like those in prison than those on regular probation.

- Public safety risk was not increased. More IPS probationers violated the conditions of their probation than did regular probationers. But as the San Francisco Project showed, if probation officers are watching their clients more often and more closely, more violations will be observed and acted upon. Possibly more important, the IPS probationers' rate of subsequent serious crime was lower than that for either a sample of released prisoners or a sample of high-risk regular probationers.

Despite what appears to be a glowing report, Georgia's program has received some criticism. Even though IPS offenders had characteristics similar to those in Georgia's prisons, they were still primarily nonviolent property offenders and drug- and alcohol-related offenders. In the period from 1982 through 1985, only 9 percent of the IPS probationers had been convicted of violent personal crimes. Although critics accept Georgia's IPS program as being one of prison diversion, they wonder why Georgia is subjecting those kinds of offenders to prison in the first place. In other words, the critics say that prison is certainly a more controlled environment than these offenders may need (at least in terms of public safety), but even an IPS program may be too restrictive.

Release from Probation

Table 7.3 identifies six categories by which a person can exit probation status. Two of those are important for this text's purposes: (1) successful completion of the sentence or (2) revocation of the sentence. But because release from probation is necessarily linked to the length of probation, it is necessary to begin by understanding how the probation sentence is figured.

Length of Probation. Because probation is a sentence, its duration or length often has both legislative and judicial aspects. As discussed in Chapter 5, legislators can set minimum and maximum limits on sentences, including those for probation. However, judges actually impose the sentence and, therefore, have the power to fix the actual length of a probation sentence.

TABLE 7.3: Ways That Adults Leave Probation, 1990 and 1998

ADULTS LEAVING PROBATION	1990	1998
Successful Completions	69	59
Returned to Incarceration (Revocation)	14	17
With new sentence	3	9
With the same sentence	11	9
Absconders	7	3
Other Unsuccessful	2	9
Death	(less than 0.5)	(less than 0.5)
Other	7	11

Source: Adapted from Bonczar, T. (1999). *Probation and parole in the United States, 1998* [NCJ 178234]. Washington, DC: Bureau of Justice Statistics.

The legislative limits for probation are often the same as the statutory minimum and maximum for the offense if the offender had been imprisoned rather than placed on probation. But the recent trend has been to set statutory limits for probation that are actually less than those used when the offender is sent to prison. For example, recommendations from a variety of professional associations and commissions (see Cromwell & Killinger, 1994) suggest that probation terms should be fixed and relatively short (e.g., five years for a felony conviction and two years for a misdemeanor), even if the maximum term for imprisonment for the same offense is longer.

Rather than fixing the maximum length of probation at a term of something like five or two years, jurisdictions have been more likely to give judges the authority to modify the term of probation after initial sentencing. When circumstances warrant—for example, the probationer is showing improvement but the probation officer wants to keep her on probation until a new treatment program is completed—some jurisdictions allow judges to extend the term of probation. Generally this must be done during the time limits of the original probation term. Under other circumstances, the probationer may deserve to have the term of probation reduced. This type of situation brings up for discussion the previously mentioned ways that a person can be released from probation.

Successful Completion of Probation. Table 7.3 shows that 59 percent of the adults on probation in 1998 were released from probation as successful completers. The typical way in which a sentence to probation is successfully completed is for the probationer to spend the required amount of time (e.g., two years) under the conditions of probation. When that time is up, probation is over.

In some situations a probationer may be released early from the probation sentence. Courts in some jurisdictions have authority to reduce the term of probation at the request of the probationer or the probation officer. This authority is recognized as an appropriate feature of the rehabilitative aspect of probation. If probationers do not need probation services for the originally set time period, discharging them early not only rewards their good behavior and efforts but also allows the probation department to direct resources toward more difficult cases.

Revocation of Probation. As you may recall from the examples of probation conditions noted in Figure 7.2, probationers are required to avoid any further criminal conduct as well as to abide by the general and special conditions that are part of the probation contract. If a probationer does commit a new criminal act, the original probation can be revoked on the basis of a **new crime violation.** If the probationer fails to abide by any of the general or special conditions of probation, that probation can be revoked on the basis of a **technical violation.** Importantly, neither type of violation results in automatic revocation. Instead, probation officers typically are required to tell the court of any new crime violations and may report any technical violations. In both situations, the court makes the final decision regarding the revocation. Table 7.4 shows some reasons for which probationers are taken to a disciplinary hearing.

In the case of new crime violations, the local prosecutor has the authority to charge and prosecute the offender on that new crime but cannot order the offender's probation revoked and have him sent to prison. To save the citizens the time and expense of a new trial, however, prosecutors may be willing to avoid prosecuting on the new crime in exchange for the offender having his probation revoked and being sent to prison for the crime for which he was originally placed on probation. Although the offender is not technically punished for the new crime, the less strict rules of evidence in revocation hearings (a preponderance of evi-

TABLE 7.4: Reasons for Disciplinary Hearings of Adult Probationers, by Severity of Most Serious Offense, 1995

		SEVERITY OF OFFENSE	
Reason for Disciplinary Hearing[a]	Total	Felony	Misdemeanor
Absconded/Failed to Maintain Contact	41.1%	43.3%	37.6%
New Offense	38.4%	43.2%	31.0%
Arrested	30.4	34.9	23.5
Convicted	13.9	15.8	10.5
Failure to Pay Fines or Restitution	37.9%	34.1%	43.0%
Drug/Alcohol Violation			
Failure to attend/complete treatment program	22.5%	17.5%	33.0%
Positive drug test	11.2	14.3	5.6
Alcohol abuse	2.7	2.9	2.7
Violation of Confinement Restrictions			
Failure to do jail time/return from furlough	2.5%	2.5%	2.8%
Violation of home confinement	1.3	1.6	0.6
Other Violations			
Failure to complete community service	8.5%	9.5%	6.7%
Other	6.8	6.9	6.7
Number of probationers[b]	457,279	297,481	144,550

[a]Detail adds to more than total because some probationers had more than one disciplinary hearing, while others had a single hearing with more than one reason.

[b]Excludes probationers who never had a disciplinary hearing or for whom information on disciplinary hearings was not reported.

Source: From Bonczar, T. (1997). *Characteristics of adults on probation, 1995* [NCJ 164267]. Washington, DC: Bureau of Justice Statistics.

dence rather than proof beyond a reasonable doubt) will mean that the offender can be put in prison more quickly and more certainly by revoking the probation than by prosecuting and possibly convicting him on the new charge.

Prior to 1972, the procedures for revoking probation varied from one jurisdiction to another. In some places, probationers were granted a revocation hearing—if nothing else, an opportunity to give their own version of events. Other jurisdictions simply sent probationers to prison by means of a revocation order. The absence of procedural protection was so flagrant that one observer wrote, "there is no other area of law, except perhaps the civil commitment of the mentally ill, where the lives of so many people are so drastically affected by officials who exercise a virtually absolute, unreviewed discretion" (Cohen, 1968, p. 5).

The absence of procedural protection was not considered a constitutional violation because such protection was deemed necessary only during criminal prosecution. Once the defendant was convicted, the general view was that criminal prosecution had ended and procedural protections no longer applied (Miller, 1994). The point was clearly made in one of the first U.S. Supreme Court decisions relevant to **probation revocation.** In the 1967 *Mempa v. Rhay* decision, the Court

Probation can be revoked if persons sentenced to probation do not comply with the terms and conditions of their sentence. In 1999 a California judge sentenced actor Robert Downey, Jr. to three years in prison for violating probation from a 1996 drug conviction.

ruled that a probationer whose probation officials wanted to revoke and who they wanted to send to prison was entitled to counsel at a revocation hearing. But the only reason such a procedural safeguard was necessary was that the probation was of the "suspended imposition of sentence" type. That is, the judge had not actually imposed a sentence, so the criminal prosecution stage was not complete (Miller, 1994). Had the probationer been under a "suspension of execution of sentence" situation, counsel would not be necessary at a revocation hearing because that hearing would not be part of the criminal prosecution.

The view that procedural protections were not warranted during probation revocation was not successfully challenged until 1972, when the U.S. Supreme Court issued a decision in *Morrissey v. Brewer.* The *Morrissey* decision actually dealt with parole revocation (see Chapter 13), but a year later the Court's ruling in *Gagnon v. Scarpelli* (1973) applied the basic procedures outlined in the *Morrissey* decision to the probation revocation process. As a result, procedures for both probation and parole revocation are typically discussed using both the *Morrissey* and *Gagnon* decisions.

The parolee in *Morrissey* did not try to argue that the revocation process was still part of criminal prosecution and, therefore, deserving of all the protections one would have at trial. Instead, he argued that he was entitled to at least some kind of procedure that would help ensure the fairness of the revocation process (Miller, 1994). The Court agreed and set forth procedures it considered minimally necessary to conduct a fair revocation process. Specifically, probation revocation must include a two-stage process consisting of a preliminary hearing and a revocation hearing. The preliminary hearing in the probation revocation process serves to determine whether there is probable cause or reasonable grounds to believe that the probationer committed acts that constitute a violation of probation. If the hearing officer believes there is probable cause or reasonable grounds to believe probation conditions were violated, officials can continue to detain the probationer and will move toward the second stage of the process: the revocation hearing.

The revocation hearing is a formal undertaking that the U.S. Supreme Court has been careful to emphasize is not equal to a criminal trial. For example, if the probationer is being accused of violating probation by committing a new crime, she does not first have to be found guilty of that new offense. Because the revocation hearing is not a crime new crime only requires evidence that as a whole shows it is more probable than not that the probationer committed the new crime. That standard of proof, which is called **preponderance of evidence,** is less strict than proof **beyond a reasonable doubt,** which is the standard required in a criminal trial. This latter standard is harder to achieve because it requires that the judge be fully satisfied or entirely convinced of the probationer's guilt in the new crime.

As noted earlier, even though the revocation process is not equal to a criminal trial, the U.S. Supreme Court has ruled that fairness requires certain procedural safeguards. The minimum due process rights identified for parolees in *Morrissey v. Brewer* and applied to probationers in *Gagnon v. Scarpelli* must be followed. The Court identified these rights as including:

- written notice of the claimed violations
- disclosure of the evidence against the probationer or parolee
- an opportunity to be heard in person and to present witnesses and documentary evidence
- the right to confront and cross-examine adverse witnesses (unless the hearing officer finds good cause for not allowing confrontation, such as a risk of harm to the witness)
- a neutral and detached hearing body
- a written statement by the fact finders as to the evidence relied on and the reasons for revoking probation or parole

Noticeable by its absence in this list is any reference to a right to counsel in the revocation process. The Court reached no decision on that issue in *Morrissey v. Brewer* but did address it in *Gagnon v. Scarpelli.*

Because the Court viewed probation revocation as essentially informal, flexible, and economic when contrasted with a criminal trial, it was hesitant to impose a requirement for representation by counsel at the hearings. But the justices were also concerned about the occasionally complicated revocation case in which the facts may be in dispute. So, although the Court believed "participation of counsel will probably be both undesirable and constitutionally unnecessary in most revocation hearings" (*Gagnon v. Scarpelli,* 411 U.S. at 790), the justices agreed that fundamental fairness requiring decisions about representation of counsel be handled case by case. The Court gave no specific guidelines as to how the decision should be made, but generally the state should provide counsel when the probationer or parolee requests counsel, is disputing the charges, and is incapable of speaking effectively for himself.

The U.S. Supreme Court and the various state courts continue to deal with issues related to the revocation process. One decision is of particular interest here because it brings us to the next chapter topic. In 1983 the U.S. Supreme Court in *Bearden v. Georgia* ruled that probation could not be revoked merely for failure to pay a fine as required by probation conditions—assuming the probationer exhausted all reasonable attempts to pay the fine. In such situations, the Court said alternatives other than imprisonment must be considered. This particular case is interesting because it highlights the need for other community sanctions. If probation is the only community sanction, what should be done with those people who are not successful on probation yet still may not deserve or benefit from prison? One choice is a sentence to community service.

COMMUNITY SERVICE ORDERS

In its most general meaning, a **community service order** (CSO) sentences offenders to carry out unpaid work for the general good of the community. This sanction may serve as a default for failure to comply with another sentence (e.g., not paying a fine), or it may be a specific sanction either standing alone or combined with other punishments. In the United States, community service tends to be combined with other punishment, often in conjunction with probation. In England and many other European countries, the CSO is more often a formal sentence used as an independent punishment (see "Community Service in England and Wales").

The contemporary use of community service orders is usually linked to their appearance in one of two places—Alameda County, California, in 1966, or their introduction in England in 1972. But the CSO undoubtedly has a much richer heritage than either of those dates imply. For example, there is documentation from the Middle Ages that some German towns allowed offenders to work for the community (e.g., clean the town canal) in order to avoid fines. As early as the seventeenth century, community work was used in Germany as a separate sentence as well as the default when a fine was not paid (van Kalmthout & Tak, 1988). Despite that history, it was not until the late 1960s that community service really appeared (or reappeared) as a sanction receiving serious attention.

The use of CSOs in the United States began in Alameda County, California, in 1966 as a punishment for traffic offenders. The idea had immediate appeal as an intermediate sanction, especially for white-collar offenders, and it began spreading to other U.S. jurisdictions. News stories today tell of convicted doctors being ordered to provide services in locations lacking medical care, of traffic offenders being assigned to hospital emergency rooms to observe the injuries they risk imposing on others, and of substance-abusing celebrities being ordered to lecture students on the danger of drugs and alcohol (Morris & Tonry, 1990, p. 152). In each instance, the punishment is designed to benefit the community through the expenditure of time and effort by the offender. It is these elements of punishment for the offender and reparation to the community that give community service its appeal.

When community service is ordered in U.S. jurisdictions, it is often a condition of probation and included among several other sanctions the probationer must follow. In this manner, a probationer may be required to complete a number of community service hours while also attending GED classes, paying a fine, and participating in treatment programs for substance abuse. When American jurisdictions use CSOs as the sole sanction, it tends to be for misdemeanant offenders and only seldom for adult felons and juveniles (Hudson & Galaway, 1990).

A sentence to community service or having community service as a condition of probation is promoted as having several benefits for the courts, the community, and the offenders. The courts benefit from having another option between fines and imprisonment because neither of those extremes offers appropriate responses to all offenders. The community benefits by having services performed that may have been needed but for lack of money or personnel may not have gotten done. In addition, the community is compensated in a small way for harm it received from the offender. Finally, the offender benefits by being able to maintain normal social contacts, by being able to stay employed or in school, and by getting a feeling of self-confidence in his or her working and earning capacity. Despite those benefits, Tonry (1997) laments that community service is the most underused intermediate sanction in the United States.

Identifying benefits of community service is easier than determining who should receive the sanction and deciding issues such as work assignments and re-

Cross-Cultural Corrections

Community Service in England and Wales[3]

As part of a participant observation study, Anthony Vass completed 220 hours of community service in England by working at activities as various as constructing a children's playground, gardening, and looking after elderly couples. To emphasize the punitive nature of community service orders (CSOs), Vass (1990) explains that after the euphoria of having escaped a harsh punishment, such as imprisonment, wears off, the offenders begin to realize they may not have been let off so easily. They are obliged to work for the community doing things they may not like; to be under surveillance; to be punished further if they fail to comply; and to have lost some control over their leisure time. A frequent response to this new reality is absenteeism, which may run as high as 25 percent of all attendees per month (Vass, 1990). As many as half of those absences are for reasons that are considered unsatisfactory or unreasonable.

The problem of absenteeism in England is one that seems endemic to community service programs and requires officials to respond sternly so that offenders will take the sentence seriously. In England the initial response to absenteeism is through the mail, with home visits as follow-ups. Vass describes the frustration community service officers have in trying to work with an offender who just does not seem to take the CSO seriously. He relates the story of ZA, whom the officer finally had to visit at home because ZA had not been impressed by several letters requesting that he complete his community service.

> ZA failed to attend again. A home visit was made. He came to the door looking very sorry for himself stating that he had attended a party and had eaten some strange food, which made him feel unwell. He was going to the doctor who is apparently open on Sundays. At that evening he drove past me in a car. He stopped. I asked him where he was going. He said that he had just been to the doctor's but he was closed and he was on his way home. However, the road he was on meant that there was no way he was on his way home; he was therefore told to get a medical certificate because he was getting himself in deeper and deeper trouble with his excuses. (Vass, 1990, p. 123)

The officer's response to ZA may seem too tolerant to some. But rather than seeing such tolerance and informal exchanges as simply avoiding the inevitability of harsher sanctions, Vass suggests the officer's patience is promoting the basic reason for even having community sanctions. As he explains it: "Hard as it may seem, tolerance of some rule-breaking, and, overall, some discretion and elasticity in the way offenders are treated are necessary and integral parts of the administration, organization and enforcement of laws" (Vass, 1990, p. 131).

Read how the Dorset Probation Service operates its community service component at *www.dorset-cc.gov.uk/probatn.htm.* What are some examples of the work assignments for offenders in this program?

[3]This summary of Vass's study takes, by necessity, some of his words out of context. Material is taken from Vass, A. (1990). *Alternatives to prison: Punishment, custody, and the community.* London: Sage Publications. Copyright © 1990, by permission of Sage Publications, Ltd.

sponses to noncompliance. Generally, such questions are addressed during five stages of community service program implementation: (1) site development, (2) intake, (3) placement, (4) supervision, and (5) termination (see Hudson & Galaway, 1990; Probation Division, 1989).

Site Development

The success of a community service program depends on the availability of a sufficient number of project places at which the work will be performed. Governmental and nonprofit organizations typically serve as work sites in jurisdictions throughout the United States. United Way organizations, Boy Scouts and Girl Scouts, Boys and Girls Clubs, city offices of parks and recreation, and local volunteer offices provide information about community needs. Hospitals, convalescent homes, mental health facilities, public parks, public streets, and public schools are examples of popular work sites.

Work sites usually make use of community service workers in one of two ways (Hudson & Galaway, 1990). The most common practice has offenders being referred directly to a community agency that then handles the work placement and supervises completion of the community service hours. A less popular procedure has a group of offenders assigned to a specific agency to complete a particular project. For example, four offenders may repair playground equipment at a city park. When the group project approach is used, each offender is likely to work at several different sites before the work obligation is completed. Offenders assigned as individuals to a particular agency are more likely to complete all their hours at that agency. Under both situations, officials must make sure the work being done is something that is not otherwise likely to be completed. This is an important point because community service programs do not want to displace paid workers and thereby cause a negative reaction from the public.

Intake

As noted earlier, community service in American jurisdictions tends to be used as a condition of probation rather than as a separate sentence. In those situations it becomes one of several sanctions being applied to the offender. In Hudson and Galaway's (1990) study of U.S. community service programs, these "combined sanction" versions were typically used for felony-level offenders. The two researchers also found some programs for which community service was the sole sanction. But they noted that, unlike the English model that often uses CSOs as the only sanction for serious offenders, U.S. jurisdictions tended to use community service as the sole sanction primarily in misdemeanor cases.

Because community service does not really enjoy widespread or serious use in the United States when compared to its use in other countries, not much attention has been paid to intake criteria. Hudson and Galaway (1990) found that

Offenders sentenced to community service perform work that benefits the community and improves the offenders' self-confidence in their working and earning abilities.

most programs do not have written criteria defining the population of eligible offenders or defendants. When community service is combined with other sanctions, eligibility tends to be determined by the primary sentence (e.g., probation) rather than having specific standards for the community service condition. When community service is its own sentence, existing programs usually rely on the judge's discretion rather than unique program assignment criteria.

Placement

As noted earlier, offenders sometimes are placed at a work site in groups. In those cases, placement decisions are less critical. When the work assignments are made for individuals, matching the offender to appropriate work sites must be approached more carefully. Successful placement should take into consideration: (1) the sentencing objectives of the court, (2) the characteristics of the offender, and (3) the needs of the agency (Probation Division, 1989).

Two approaches are possible when considering the court's sentencing objectives. In one approach, offenders are placed at work sites at which they are likely to have pleasant experiences. The hope is that such placements will lead to an increase in self-esteem, create positive ties to the community, and have other similar benefits. Under the other approach, offenders are assigned to unpleasant tasks on the assumption that such chores will deter future criminal behavior (Hudson & Galaway, 1990).

Attention to the offender's characteristics and circumstances requires consideration of issues such as availability of transportation, offender interests and skills, and the offender's employment or school schedule. Similarly, the placement decision must take into account the needs of the work site. Some agencies may have work that requires special skills or a commitment of a certain number of hours. The number of community service hours the offender must complete is usually determined by the sentencing judge based on factors such as the type of offense. Placement decisions must be made so that the agency's needs (e.g., a twenty-hour work project) correspond to the sentence.

Supervision

Because supervision of group tasks is linked to the specific project the offenders are working on, supervision changes as the work site changes. In the more common situation in which an individual offender is placed with a specific agency, supervision of the offender usually falls to the agency itself. The staff is responsible for monitoring the offender's hours, confirming that all the time claimed was actually finished, making sure the work performance is satisfactory, and generally overseeing the offender's actions while at the work site.

If problems arise, the agency staff notifies the community service staff, which handles enforcement as they do in England—with warning letters, personal visits, and referral to court. To ensure that the program operates smoothly, the agency and the community service staff must communicate frequently throughout the placement time period. This interaction highlights the community aspect of the sanction and may give citizens a sense of shared responsibility for responding to offenders.

Termination

When community service is a condition of probation, noncompliance with the work requirement may constitute a technical violation of that probation. Generally, this kind of noncompliance results in action other than revocation (Probation

Help Wanted

Job Title: Community Service Caseworker

Position Description: The caseworker is responsible for any and all activities surrounding the placement of offenders in community service work and the accurate reporting of this work to the courts. The caseworker will meet with clients to determine their work history and work skills and will then identify a work site reasonably close to the client's home, school, or place of employment. The caseworker will plan and schedule work projects, inspect and prepare reports, and may be required to participate in projects that require lifting heavy objects and operating motorized equipment.

Qualifications: Education, training, or work experience in natural resources, construction, or remodeling is helpful. Crew leaders should have supervisory experience working with adults and/or juveniles.

For examples of career opportunities in this field, read about community service in New York City at ***www.ci.nyc.ny.us/html/prob/html/commserv.html.***

Division, 1989), such as adding other conditions to the probation contract or making existing conditions (e.g., curfews) more strict. When the CSO is its own sentence, noncompliance might result in alternate sentences such as fines or imprisonment.

Upon successful completion of the CSO, the offender's sentence is considered to be over. If the community service obligation was simply a requirement of probation, as is primarily true in the United States, completion merely marks the end of one condition. But an increasing number of people are encouraging U.S. jurisdictions to follow the British lead and make community service more of a stand-alone sentence. As Tonry (1997) explains:

> For offenders who do not present unacceptable risks of future violent (including sexual) crimes, a punitive sanction that costs much less than prison to implement, that promises comparable reoffending rates, and that presents negligible risks of violence by those who would otherwise be confined has much to commend it. (p. 12)

RESTITUTION

Under a community service order the offender is paying back the community for harm and injury caused by the crime. Some intermediate sanctions involve a payback that hits the offender's billfold rather than involving a time commitment. These sanctions are called **restitution.**

The idea that offenders should compensate their victims for the harm suffered by the victim is one of the oldest principles of justice. Proponents effectively argue that restitution compensates the victim's loss, is efficient, focuses the offender's attention on the wrongfulness of the crime and on its human consequences, and may provide a sense of vindication to the victim. But in practice restitution programs have been plagued by several problems (Weitekamp, 1992). First, most restitution programs are used only for property offenders or first-time offenders, or are further restricted to first-time property offenders. Second, although restitution is often proposed as an alternative to incarceration, it is rarely used in that context. More typically, restitution is an add-on sanction to probation. The fact that most restitution programs are designed for juveniles rather than adults is yet another indication that officials do not consider this sentence to be a prison alternative. Finally, restitution programs too often favor white and middle-class offenders, whereas minority offenders are admitted to the programs in disproportionately small numbers.

Not everyone, of course, considers it a problem to restrict restitution to property offenders, first-time offenders, or juveniles, or to use restitution as additional punishment rather than an alternative to prison. Most people would agree that getting offenders to actually pay the restitution is an issue that will help decide the effectiveness of restitution programs. In 1988 the American Bar Association began a study (Davis, Smith, & Hillenbrand, 1991) of restitution enforcement to determine if courts were having problems in collecting restitution. The researchers were especially interested in finding out how successful enforcement efforts were, which factors were affecting compliance, and which offenders were most likely to pay restitution.

In their evaluation of seventy-five restitution programs throughout the United States, Davis et al. (1991) found that program directors reported an average of 67 percent of offenders paid their restitution sum in full. But from the researchers' own inspection of case records at four program sites, they learned that a more accurate estimate would be that about 42 percent of offenders had full compliance.

Davis and his colleagues do not suggest that the program directors lied about success rates. Instead, the discrepancy was most likely a result of different procedures to determine compliance rates. Faith in their own calculations led Davis et al. (1991) to suggest that compliance with restitution orders is a problem around the country.

Turning their attention to factors that seem to increase compliance, the researchers found the most successful programs were those in which the court allowed for the offender's financial means when deciding the restitution amount and made serious efforts to enforce the order and collect the payment. Finally, the analysis of programs found that the offenders most likely to make full payments were the ones having strong community ties. Offenders who were employed or in school, had lived in their neighborhoods a longer time, and had a telephone were more likely to pay restitution than were offenders without such ties (Davis et al., 1991). If those characteristics are more often linked to white and middle-class offenders, Weitekamp's (1992) criticism that restitution programs discriminate against minority and poorer offenders is supported.

Some type of victim restitution program exists today in every state, but many programs seem to operate without concern for their purpose, target group, efficiency, or effectiveness. Possibly the growth of restorative justice and victim–offender mediation will give restitution programs a clearer philosophical base and a stronger desire to evaluate programs.

Help Wanted

Job Title: Restitution Collector

Position Description: This entry-level position provides new employees in the corrections field with an opportunity to gain experience working with adult offenders who have been ordered to pay restitution as part of their sentence. The restitution collector coordinates with other professionals involved with the offender's case (e.g., probation officers and community corrections personnel) to work out a payment schedule for the client and to collect and properly document all client payments.

Whereas restitution collection may be the sole duty in some positions, it is also likely to be one of several duties associated with careers in probation or community service. At *www.nvc.org/infolink/info66.htm* you can read about restitution and gain an understanding of how it is structured.

DAY REPORTING CENTERS

The **day reporting center,** called **probation centers** in England and Wales, and **attendance centers** in Australia, is an intermediate sanction blending high levels of control with the delivery of specific services needed by offenders. In this way offenders are subjected to pressure and control without sending them to prison, while simultaneously offering them help and assistance. In 1990, thirteen day reporting centers (DRCs) were identified in the United States. By mid-1994 that number had increased to 114 (Parent, Byrne, Tsarfaty, Valade, & Esselman, 1995), and there is every indication to expect continued growth in the coming years. Because the emergence of DRCs in U.S. jurisdictions relied on the experience of similar programs in Great Britain, this chapter begins with those forerunners, but you will also find the feature on "Attendance Centers in New South Wales" to be interesting.

Probation Centers in England and Wales

The seeds of DRCs were sown in the 1960s and 1970s in England and Wales, and in New Zealand. The motivators in England and Wales were concerned about the growing prison population and conditions inside the prisons, and a disenchantment with traditional individualized casework (Mair, 1993a). In an attempt to respond to those issues, Parliament provided for day training centers in a 1972 Criminal Justice Act. These centers were to divert offenders whose problems seemed linked to social inadequacies and subject them to intensive, structured training.

After a few false starts and a new authorization in 1982, English probation centers increased in popularity. By 1985 there were eighty such facilities in England and Wales. Currently the centers serve persons who are required to attend as part of their probation order, but the centers also accept persons on regular probation who attend voluntarily.

Cross-Cultural Corrections

Attendance Centers in New South Wales

As described by Caruana and Allanson (1991), the Australian state of New South Wales (NSW) first established attendance centers in the Sydney area in the mid-1980s. Those initial centers were essentially experimental, but their benefits quickly became apparent. In 1987 the legislature amended the community services act to include an attendance center possibility. Because of its legislative link to community service, the majority of clients at the attendance centers are under either a dual CSO and attendance center order or a CSO only. The remainder are on recognizance from the court and are required to attend for purposes of education and development, or are simply on referral from the caseloads of probation officers.

The attendance centers of NSW are seen as providing judges a sentencing alternative to prison with a program emphasizing rehabilitation and reintegration. Attendance centers are designed to address individual needs of the offender and to assist offenders in bringing about positive changes in their attitudes and behavior. This general goal is accomplished through programs with four separate components.

During induction the program's first component, the process of thrusting responsibility onto the offender, begins. Offenders are made aware of their legal obligations, the center's rules, and the roles and responsibilities of the center's staff. The second component—the core program—consists of topic areas such as employment, money management, and personal development, and takes about twenty hours to complete. Offenders attend sessions on each specific topic and receive information and counseling that emphasize their need to take responsibility for developing more productive attitudes and behavior.

The third program component is called the satellite program. These programs address individual needs in group settings and are primarily directed toward self-development and employment. Basic education, the final component, is focused on offenders who are not functionally literate.

Unlike the probation centers in England and Wales, the attendance centers in NSW are only indirectly linked to probation. A distinguishing feature of community service work orders is whether they are a stand-alone sentence or simply a condition of probation. American jurisdictions tend to use community service as a probation condition, whereas England and Wales use it more often as a sentence on its own. Similar options present themselves when considering ways to operate reporting centers. As the name implies, probation centers in England and Wales are technically an aspect of probation rather than a stand-alone sentence. In NSW, required attendance at a community center can be a condition of community service (a stand-alone sentence in NSW) rather than being an aspect of probation.

In addition to administering attendance center orders, the New South Wales Probation and Parole Service is responsible for several other programs. Go to its Web site at *www.dcs.nsw.gov.au/probation/*, and read about at least three other programs the service operates. How similar or different are they from probation-related programs in your state?

In a review of clients ordered to attend the probation centers, Mair (1993) found that nearly 95 percent were male, and 73 percent of clients were under age 25. Their offenses were primarily burglary or theft (66 percent), and the vast majority (98 percent) had prior convictions.

Depending primarily on the size of the facility, probation centers will handle from ten to fifty offenders with a staff composed of full- and part-time probation officers as well as other staff and volunteers. Each center sets its own program and its times of operation. Mair (1993) explains that some centers emphasize control whereas others are more therapy oriented, but they all tend to focus activities around four main elements:

- social and life skills (e.g., appropriate releases of anger and filling out job applications)
- arts and crafts classes (e.g., painting and music)

- health and welfare activities (such as dealing with substance abuse and applying for welfare benefits)
- participation in sports

It may seem that receiving a probation center order would be an "easy out" for a person convicted of a crime and potentially on the way to prison. For strictly punitive purposes (such as retribution), the probation center does seem more lenient than a prison sentence. But for therapeutic purposes, the center's impact on the offender may be more powerful than that of either prison or regular probation because contact and interaction with officials in the center are so much more intense. For example, a person receiving a sixty-day order may go to a center that is open three days each week and, therefore, take twenty weeks to complete the order. When you compare the time spent with probation officers and staff in the center to the approximately 1 hour per week the client sees the probation officer when on regular probation (Vass, 1990), you can clearly see that the center's 480 contact hours (24 hours/week × 20 weeks) are more intense than regular probation's 20 hours.

When compared to contact with officials in prison, the 480 hours at a probation center cannot stand up to the 2,240 prison hours (112 waking hours/week × 20 weeks) if it is argued that the prisoner who is awake is in constant contact with some kind of prison official. But when contact with security officials is omitted from the equation, those in prison would actually be fortunate to see treatment officials even 1 hour per day for 5 days per week. Therefore, a more accurate comparison between probation center therapeutic contact and prison therapeutic contact hours might place the center's 480 against the prison's 100.

The experience with probation centers in England and Wales has been reasonably positive. Mair (1993) reports reconviction rates over a two-year period as ranging from 45 to 75 percent, depending on the center. Although recognizing that such rates look high, he argues that the clients are often high-risk offenders with numerous prior convictions. Furthermore, the probation centers are effective in diverting—and that in itself warrants, in some people's view, a positive evaluation.

Day Reporting Centers in the United States

Programs similar to probation centers and attendance centers are relatively new in U.S. jurisdictions. Parent et al. (1995) explain that officials in Connecticut and Massachusetts concurrently but independently learned about British day centers in 1985 and began considering their adoption in the United States. Nine years later, twenty day reporting centers (DRCs) were operating in Connecticut (the highest number in any state), and another ninety-four DRCs were found spread across twenty-one other states.

Where DRCs do exist, some important similarities and differences are apparent between the U.S. versions and their cousins in England and Wales. First, American DRCs typically follow the English form and are linked to probation, although some accept parolees, parole violators, persons on pretrial release, and persons on early release from a jail sentence or on furlough from prison.

Another difference between DRCs and probation centers is more philosophical in nature. Massachusetts and New York City, for example, use DRCs as an enforcement tool for persons who are not abiding by conditions of their probation. In this way, DRCs are used as a control option for probation agencies wishing to enforce their conditions but confronted with prisons that are too crowded to accept probation violators (McDevitt & Miliano, 1992). This purpose for DRCs is, of course, more obviously punitive than probation centers, which have a control

Help Wanted

Job Title: Day Reporting Center Officer

Position Description: The DRC officer will perform a variety of case management and general supervision duties with a caseload of adult offenders whose sentences require daily reporting to the DRC office. Because DRC clients come from a variety of jurisdictions and agencies (e.g., federal, state, probation, parole), the DRC officer must ensure that the required procedures for each entity are followed for the appropriate case. Because some clients will be on electronic monitoring, the DRC officer may assist in the supervision of the electronic monitoring program.

Qualifications: Applicants should have knowledge of investigative and interviewing techniques, and of sociopsychological factors influencing human behavior. The ability to communicate effectively orally and in writing and to prepare accurate reports and maintain records is essential to the position.

For examples of career opportunities in this field, visit Web pages for day reporting centers in North Carolina at *www.henderson.lib.nc.us/county/drrc/* and in North Dakota at *www.sharehouse.org/dayrep.htm.* DRC jobs are sometimes posted on the careers section of Corrections.com at *database.corrections.com/career/index.asp.*

aspect but emphasize a therapeutic goal. In contrast to the Massachusetts and New York City examples, other DRCs seem to share the treatment philosophy of their British forerunners. In their 1994 survey of fifty-four DRCs in the United States, Parent and his colleagues found support for a more therapeutic goal. The primary objective of the DRCs that responded to the questionnaire was "to provide offenders with access to treatment or services" (Parent et al., 1995, p. 9).

Obviously there are differences among the nation's DRCs regarding the clients accepted, the programs offered, and the importance given to either control or treatment. Despite the variation, certain features of newer American DRCs are identified by Parent et al. (1995) as including the following characteristics:

- Accepts primarily male offenders who are on probation or have violated conditions, who abuse alcohol and other drugs, and who pose a low risk to the community.
- Aims primarily to provide treatment and other needed services to offenders and to reduce jail or prison crowding in its community.
- Is open five days (about 54 hours) each week and has a program duration of about five months.
- Serves fewer than 100 offenders at any one time.
- Maintains a strict level of surveillance and requires more contacts with offenders than is required by the most intensive form of community supervision otherwise available in the jurisdiction.
- Directs successful offenders through three phases with increasingly less stringent requirements . . . [and] monitors offenders for a total of nearly 70 hours per week.
- Tests offenders for drug use at least five times each month during the most intensive phase.
- Provides numerous services on-site to address clients' employment, education, and counseling needs . . . , [and] refers offenders off-site for drug abuse treatment.
- Requires offenders to perform community service.
- Costs about $20 per day per offender. (p. 40)

The DRCs are in their second decade of operation in U.S. jurisdictions, but very little is known about how successful they have been or are likely to be. An evaluation of the Cook County (Chicago) DRC, which serves as an alternative to pretrial detention for offenders charged with nonviolent crimes, showed positive results with almost two-thirds of participants successfully completing the program (Lurigio, Olson, & Swartz, 1998). But regardless of their eventual evaluation, DRCs are an interesting example of how ideas from other countries can influence program development in the United States.

SUMMARY

A NEED FOR ALTERNATIVE SENTENCES

- Intermediate punishments are those sanctions falling between simple fines and imprisonment.
- Some of those sanctions seem to emphasize a control or punishment aspect.
- Others called community sanctions are geared more toward providing assistance and seeing the offender successfully reintegrated into the community.

COMMUNITY CORRECTIONS

Community sanctions are the topic of this chapter and are grouped in four categories.

- probation
- community service orders

- restitution
- day reporting centers

PROBATION

- Probation is one of the oldest types of community sanction.
- Probation has roots in common-law activities such as benefit of clergy, judicial review, and recognizance.
- Probation operates through its components of investigation, service, and surveillance.
- Intensive probation supervision is a specific type of probation in which the offender is subjected to closer scrutiny and greater restriction than are persons on regular probation.

COMMUNITY SERVICE ORDERS

- Although community service has historical roots, its modern version is usually dated to the early 1970s in England and Wales.
- Judges sentence offenders to perform unpaid labor that benefits the community.
- Community service operates in some jurisdictions as a stand-alone sentence (often referred to as a community service order or CSO).
- In other jurisdictions it is simply a condition of probation.
- The program is most effective when serious consideration is given to issues such as matching offender and work site, supervising the clients, and following up with other sanctions when the offender's community service efforts are unsatisfactory.

RESTITUTION

- Restitution requires the offender to make financial payments to the victim or the community (either directly or indirectly through the court) as compensation for the harm caused by the offender.
- Restitution programs work best when the offender's financial situation is taken into consideration when determining the amount of restitution.
- Offenders with close ties to the community are most likely to fulfill their restitution obligation.

DAY REPORTING CENTERS

- Day reporting centers (DRCs), like community service, can be linked to other community sanctions but are most often an aspect of probation.
- The basic idea is to create a more structured environment for offenders who are at liberty in the community.
- A goal is to provide assistance to the offender while still protecting the public's safety.

Key Terms and Concepts

attendance centers (p. 249)
benefit of clergy (p. 219)
beyond a reasonable doubt (p. 243)
brokerage approach (p. 230)
caseload (p. 231)
case management probation (p. 236)
casework approach (p. 230)
community corrections (p. 217)
community service order (p. 244)
day reporting center (p. 249)
intensive probation supervision (IPS) (p. 236)
intermediate punishments (p. 217)
investigation (p. 227)
judicial reprieve (p. 220)
laying on file (p. 220)
new crime violation (p. 240)
personal recognizance (p. 220)
preponderance of evidence (p. 243)
presentence investigation (PSI) (p. 228)
prison alternatives (p. 217)
prison-diversion IPS (p. 237)
prison substitutes (p. 217)
probation center (p. 249)
probation-enhancement IPS (p. 236)
probation revocation (p. 241)
PSI report (p. 228)
recognizance (p. 220)
restitution (p. 248)
service (p. 227)
surveillance (p. 227)
suspension of execution (p. 220)
suspension of imposition (p. 220)
technical violation (p. 240)
workload (p. 231)

Discussion Questions

1. Determine whether your state has a community corrections act and identify the goal of that act (e.g., rehabilitation, relieve overcrowded jails and prisons, etc.). If your state does not have a CCA, discuss whether it should.
2. Some people suggest that presentence investigation reports too often include only negative information about the offender. Discuss whether you believe such an argument is correct; if it is, what are the implications of sentencing individuals using mostly negative information about them?
3. What are some possible explanations for why probation, of all types of correctional sanctions, has the largest percentage of female offenders?
4. Discuss the advantages and disadvantages of both the brokerage and the service approaches to probation.
5. In your community today, should probation officers place more emphasis on their service role or their enforcement role? Justify your position.
6. Distinguish between prison-diversion and probation-enhancement versions of IPS, and explain which version you believe would be more acceptable in your community.
7. What are some desirable and undesirable aspects of having U.S. jurisdictions make greater use of community service orders, day reporting centers, or both?

chapter 8

Short-Term Confinement

Like most workers in the year 2022, Offender Monitoring Officer Ginger Spry doesn't have to go far to reach her office. After a quick trip upstairs in her condominium, she sits before her computer terminal and begins her job of monitoring and correcting the behavior of the 250 criminal offenders in her caseload. As she begins scrolling through her cases to decide whom she'll check on, she remembers stories in her justicology courses about the old days when probation officers (as the OMOs were called back then) had to check on their cases in person. Ginger can't imagine how such an inefficient system was able to operate. There was no way probation officers could keep weekly, let alone daily, track of their clients. And what if one of your clients was violating conditions of his or her probation? If punishment wasn't administered immediately, how could the clients learn not to engage in acts that violated the community incapacitation agreement—or whatever it was called back then—that they signed? Luckily, Ginger thinks, she never has to worry about those things.

Putting aside such historical musings, Ginger focuses her attention on Marlin Mean's name as her client list continues across the screen. Marlin is new to community incapacitation, so Ginger has been checking on him every two or three hours. Upon giving her computer a voice command to find him, Ginger is presented with current information about Marlin. The transmitter/evaluator/receiver that has been surgically implanted in Marlin, as for everyone under community incapacitation, begins supplying Ginger's computer with information about Marlin's position (he is upright and walking), location (he is heading north on Orwell Avenue), and physiology (blood analysis indicates alcohol consumption; urine analysis indicates cocaine ingestion). It has been a bad night for Marlin—but it's about to get worse. Because alcohol and drug use are prohibited under the agreement Marlin signed, Ginger tells her computer to enter an alcohol and drug (A&D) violation into his file. She decides immediate action is necessary because Marlin is new to the program and apparently needs to be convinced that his OMO means business.

Within minutes, the computer indicates that the physiological conditions are correct, confirms that Marlin has violated the community incapacitation agreement, and gives Ginger a menu of choices for her response to his misbehavior. She quickly skips over the ancillary responses such as "violation report placed in client's file," and "notification of violation relayed to client," and jumps to the more serious ones. Ginger makes her choice, telling the computer to "issue an electric jolt" to Marlin—that will get his attention and let him know that his OMO is on the job. While waiting for Marlin to get to a communication center where he and Ginger can be in visual and audio contact, Ginger returns to her list of clients to decide whom she'll check on next.

A far-fetched scenario? Not really, when we consider that technological changes are occurring at a pace that gives us ways to handle offenders today that were seldom imagined even two decades ago. Even today, video phones enable probation and parole officers to "see" their clients without leaving their office. Companies are marketing laboratory equipment that probation and parole officers can use to get instant information about their clients. Clients are told to breathe into a breathalyzer tube while the officer watches over the video phone. In minutes, the officer knows the exact amount of alcohol in the client's breath. You may be thinking of Ginger and Marlin's story as science fiction, but given the rapid rate that technology is advancing, by the year 2100 it could sound as historical as the twentieth century's straight probation procedures!

This chapter's general focus is on short-term confinement. Traditionally that topic has been restricted to coverage of jails. But today communities have more options than just the jail to achieve incapacitation as an aspect of short-term confinement. Technology is an important aid to providing incapacitation without walls, and discussion begins with a key feature in that technology.

Electronic Monitoring

A goal of both short-term and long-term confinement is to restrict the offender's freedom of movement. That incapacitation has traditionally been accomplished by placing offenders in jails for a relatively short period (typically less than one year) or in prisons for a longer period, conceivably for life. Technological advancements in the last several decades have encouraged people to look at incapacitation (restricting an offender's freedom of movement) as something that can be accomplished without the use of high walls or razor wire fences. As described in this chapter's opening, a tool that is increasingly used for this purpose is **electronic monitoring.** Its importance in corrections requires a discussion of this relatively new device.

Today's version of yesterday's science fiction, at least in the area of short-term confinement in the community, is electronic monitoring (EM). Although it was first proposed as early as 1964 (Schwitzgebel, Schwitzgebel, Pahnke, & Hurd, 1964), EM was not actually used in the United States until 1983 by a New Mexico judge inspired by a "Spiderman" episode in the newspaper comics. Since its arrival on the corrections scene, controversy about EM has grown as rapidly as its use. Although EM is spreading to other countries, it is not always as quickly accepted as it has been in the United States (see "Electronic Monitoring in Canada"). After briefly explaining the technology of EM, we will consider some of the philosophical, legal, and administrative issues related to its use.

The Technology

Electronic monitoring technology is constantly being improved. There are two basic types of EM equipment: active devices and passive devices (a third type is a hybrid combining aspects of the basic two). The active devices use a transmitter that is attached to the offender's ankle or, rarely, to the wrist. The transmitter emits a continuous signal up to a 200-foot radius, although the range is adjustable to accommodate various conditions and restrictions. The signal is picked up by a receiver, usually attached to the offender's home telephone. The receiver is programmed to expect the transmitter's signal during those hours of the day that the offender is supposed to be at home (e.g., between 6:00 P.M. and 7:00 A.M.). If the

Cross-Cultural Corrections

Electronic Monitoring in Canada

The speed at which electronic monitoring (EM) and home confinement spread throughout U.S. jurisdictions in the 1980s might be expected to have been repeated in other countries. After all, aren't new ways of doing things always better than the old? Actually, Corbett and Marx (1991) refer to such thinking as the "fallacy of novelty." The delusion is said to occur when decisions are based on newness rather than on data that suggest either the new will work or the old has failed. Related to the fallacy of novelty is the "vanguard fallacy." Here it is assumed that if the big guys are doing it, it must be good.

Corbett and Marx use these fallacies and several others to encourage "a spirit of responsible conservatism, which asks us to pause in the face of any proposed change" (1991, p. 412) to make sure it is needed, is appropriate, and does not bring more problems than it solves. It seems that other countries have agreed with Corbett and Marx's position more so than have U.S. jurisdictions. Electronic monitoring schemes were being hurriedly introduced and quickly adopted throughout the United States in the 1980s. Because there really was no evaluation evidence showing that EM met any of its claimed goals (e.g., reduce prison crowding, lower justice system costs), the best explanation for its rapid spread might be the idea that if it's new, it's better. Conversely, EM's slow start in some other countries might suggest the kind of "responsible conservatism" championed by Corbett and Marx. Consider, for example, electronic monitoring—or the lack of it—in Canada.

Canada's oldest electronically monitored home confinement (EMHC) program is in Vancouver, British Columbia. It has received positive evaluations in such areas as reducing jail population, long-term cost-effectiveness, minimal equipment problems, few violations by program participants, and a positive evaluation from the offenders being monitored (Schulz, 1991). But despite positive evaluations in Vancouver, few other Canadian jurisdictions had adopted EMHC by 1991. Alberta, the first Canadian jurisdiction to investigate the possible uses of EMHC, had not started a program by mid-1991. Saskatchewan began using EMHC in conjunction with an IPS program in 1990, but the EMHC component is considered only a small part of the program. In Ontario, the city of Toronto began a pilot project in 1989, but the EMHC program was phased out until the provincial government could better evaluate the program's potential.

Some reasons for the apparent hesitancy, at least by U.S. standards, of Canadian jurisdictions in adopting EMHC are similar to those expressed in the United States. Some people simply are unconvinced of the need for EMHC; maybe they have not been duped by the fallacy of novelty. Others express concerns related to issues of privacy, appropriateness, consent, and the target population. But there are also some practical considerations that Canada's more rural areas must face. In the northern part of British Columbia, for example, the demographics prevented officials from simply copying Vancouver's program. The northern region's small, isolated communities included people either without telephones or sharing party lines. The EMHC program was modified rather than simply dismissed as unworkable by using equipment that avoided the usual reliance on telephone lines. Instead, a computer in the offender's home receives messages from an anklet transmitter and then sends those messages to a tape recorder. The tapes are sent to the regional office, where staff members determine if the offender violated any of the program conditions.

Whether it be for reasons of finances, civil liberties, or simple rejection of the belief that new things are invariably better, EM did not spread as quickly in some of the countries most like the United States. That does not mean that other industrialized countries will not come to use monitoring technology to the same extent that it is used in the United States, but it is interesting to think about why "advances" in this area are received very quickly by some countries and more cautiously by others.

Go to *www.criminallawyers.ca/newslett/aug97/rondinelli.htm* where you will find an interesting article written by Vincenzo Rondinelli. What new issues and concerns are expressed in Rondinelli's article that don't appear in this chapter?

signal is not received when it should be, a computer sends a report of the violation to a central computer accessed by corrections officials. When the signal appears or reappears, the officials are contacted once again.

Passive EM devices differ from the active ones primarily in the absence of a continuous signal from a transmitter to a receiver. Instead, a computer makes ran-

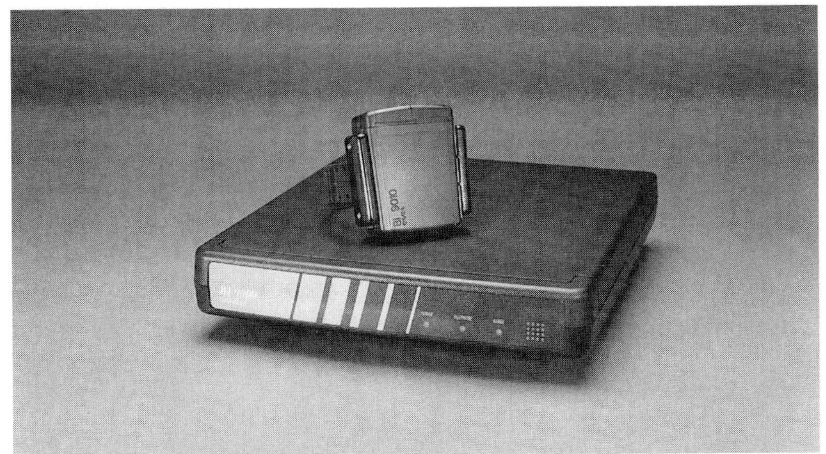

(a)

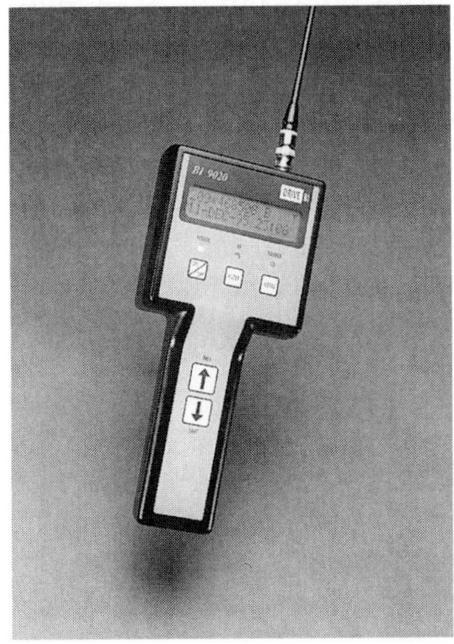

(b)

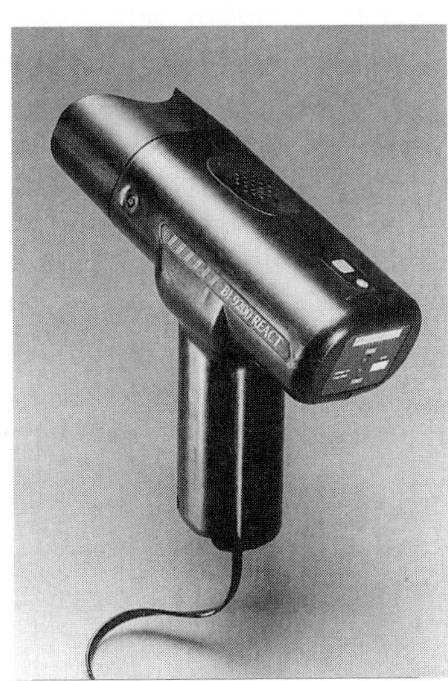

(c)

An electronic monitoring package might consist of a bracelet transmitter and field monitoring device (a), a portable monitoring unit (b) to "find" the bracelet-wearer at work or school, and an alcohol compliance device (c) to conduct remote breath alcohol checks.

dom (or programmed) calls to the offender's home. Under some programs, the offender has an ankle or wrist transmitter similar to the active device. But instead of emitting a continuous signal, this transmitter's signal is received only in response to the computer's phone call. Upon answering the phone and determining the computer has called, the offender verifies his or her presence at home by placing the transmitter on the verifier box. Alternative methods of confirmation allow the offender to provide voice verification or visual verification by still-picture video phone (Hofer & Meierhoefer, 1987; Schmidt, 1991).

An often overlooked point when discussing EM technology is the level of security it provides. It is surprising to people who are only casually familiar with EM that today's equipment really cannot prevent violations—of course, neither can any other community supervision program. EM's purpose is to provide absence/presence monitoring at a single location, usually home or work. This service is more than can be provided with traditional labor-intensive supervision. It does not ensure (nor is it designed to) complete security through constant knowledge of the offender's location when away from the monitoring site. But when the offender is not where he or she is supposed to be, corrections officials will know of the violation. Under traditional manual community monitoring, those officials were not as likely to be aware of absences.

Philosophical, Administrative, and Legal Issues

When used as a tool to restrict, deter, and discover behavior, EM seems more effective and efficient than traditional manual, labor-intensive means. But its use is not without controversy. Even though the level of intrusion and surveillance seems minimal, EM programs and technology receive considerable discussion centered on philosophical, administrative, and legal topics.

Who Should Be Placed on EM? In its first several years of use, monitorees were mostly probationers for whom EM was made a condition of probation. By 1989 its use had expanded to parolees and for pretrial, presentence, and deferred prosecution programs (Renzema & Skelton, 1990). It is that second grouping that causes some concern because there may be greater potential for threats to public safety when persons other than probationers and parolees are placed under EM.

Use of EM prior to sentencing, trial, or even prosecution causes some people to express concerns for public safety because authorities may not be as familiar with the offender's (or the accused's) background and personality. For example, by the time a probationer is placed on EM, the probation department has already conducted an investigation into topics such as the offender's drug and alcohol use. Furthermore, while awaiting sentencing, many offenders have stopped or significantly reduced any substance abuse or criminal behavior because they are in a controlled environment, (e.g., in jail) or are on their best behavior to increase the chances for probation. If such offenders are eventually placed on EM, they have already had a period of adjustment to an abuse- and crime-free lifestyle. Also authorities are aware of the potential problems each particular offender might have or might present to the community. When persons are placed on EM before sentencing, trial, or prosecution, the amount of information court officials have is reduced, even if the person has been through the system before, and the person's substance abuse or criminal activity may not have been interrupted much. In other words, the pretrial and preconviction uses of EM place into a community-based program persons about whom court officials have little information and who may not have had much interruption in their deviant lifestyle.

The Potential for Net-Widening. The phenomenon known as **net-widening** describes a situation in which a program has the effect of bringing more people under control of the criminal justice system than would otherwise be included. If EM can be demonstrated as an inexpensive way to control troublemakers, persons whom prosecutors and judges would have not bothered with in the past could now be placed in the criminal justice system without raising concerns about adding to crowded prisons or increasing costs to the public. Renzema and Skelton (1990) report that research has not found net-widening to be a problem with sentenced offenders; most would have been put in jail or prison were it not for EM. But they admit the possibility that some unconvicted offenders may find themselves under greater restrictions than they would if EM were not available. Lilly (1993) also reported that initial concerns about net-widening so far seem to have been unwarranted because it seems to be used instead of jail rather than as an alternative to conventional probation.

The Potential for Discrimination. An early concern about EM was the fear that it would be something made available to middle- and upper-class offenders but not to poorer ones. Because EM's primary advantage from the offender's perspective is the chance to avoid imprisonment, the potential for discrimination on the basis of income received considerable attention. Renzema and Skelton (1990) identified the four ways EM might discriminate against the poor:

- a requirement that monitorees have jobs
- a requirement that monitorees have telephones
- a requirement that monitorees have fixed residences to which they can be restricted
- a requirement that offenders pay a fee to be in the EM program

Obviously, each of these requirements is more easily met by persons with some level of financial security and stability.

Jurisdictions using EM have made specific attempts to reduce the discriminatory aspects of the requirements placed on persons being considered as monitorees. The employment requirement, for example, is typically flexible enough to excuse persons with medical conditions that prevent them from holding a job, persons who have been laid off, and mothers of small children. The phone requirement is often resolved through time-payment agreements with the telephone companies to provide lines with restricted service. With the increased use of cellular telephones, which can be supplied by the agency during the EM time period, this issue is even less important.

The other two requirements are less easily dismissed. The homeless poor, by definition, are not going to have a fixed residence. When EM is used as a condition of home confinement (as discussed later), these people are clearly discriminated against. If technology eventually allows the monitoring of persons throughout, for example, an area of several miles, maybe the fixed residence requirement can be more flexible. At present persons without homes, or without relatives or friends who would provide use of their homes, may very well end up in jail or prison when they would otherwise be placed on EM.

In the early 1990s, most EM programs charged the monitorees a fee. That requirement presented serious problems for poor offenders. Renzema and Skelton (1990) reported that monthly fees ranging from $100 to $300 were required in half the programs operating in 1989. Today EM costs are often included in a jurisdiction's regular budget as an ongoing expense. When charges are assessed to the offender, it may be as part of the sentence itself in the form of a supervision fee. Probably the clearest rejection of the claim that EM will be used for middle- and upper-class offenders is the feedback from corrections officials, who note that most of their EM clients are similar in economic status to the clients in the traditional community corrections programs (personal communication, February 1996).

Legal Issues Related to EM. Renzema and Skelton (1990) were surprised to find that by 1989 the use of EM had generated very little litigation and had not received any serious legal challenge. Potential legal issues that were raised in the mid-1980s have not presented the kind of problems many people had anticipated, and now these problems seem unlikely to appear (Renzema, 1992). For example, does EM provide an inappropriate level of surveillance? The answer must depend on the situations in which EM is used. Both probation and parole, for example, have surveillance as a clear condition of the program. Because surveillance is already an aspect of the program, the use of technology to enhance its effectiveness cannot be easily dismissed. On the other hand, if surveillance is not a purpose of the program, EM may not be appropriate. For example, is surveillance an accepted aspect of deferred prosecution or of pretrial release?

Other legal questions concern issues of privacy (is there any violation of Fourth Amendment protection involving security in one's home?), self-incrimination (do monitored offenders incriminate themselves?), and personal humiliation or degradation (is an EM bracelet so humiliating or degrading that it constitutes cruel or unusual punishment?). How the courts would respond to claimed violations in such areas remains to be seen because EM has seldom been challenged by offenders being monitored. Reasons for the lack of court challenges to EM might be attributed to several mitigating factors (Friel, Vaughn, & del Carmen, 1987; Renzema & Skelton, 1990):

- Many probationers in EM programs have volunteered (although it might be considered a forced choice because the alternative is incarceration), so they are on shaky legal ground if they complain about a program in which they chose to participate.
- Because monitorees have often consented to be monitored, any claim of an unconstitutional invasion of privacy is indefensible.
- Existing use of EM technology is not as invasive as it can be, and it will not be seriously challenged unless it comes to involve surveillance that, for example, intercepts conversations, visually monitors offenders, or requires surgically implanting various devices.

Factors such as these have allowed EM usage to expand during the 1990s without significant legal challenge. Whether that will continue to be the case in the twenty-first century is likely to depend on the third factor—How intrusive will EM technology become? The most significant technological advance since the mid-1980s has been the creation of "drive by" systems that allow authorities to determine from an automobile if the monitorees are where they should be (Lilly, 1993). This development has not, however, attracted much complaint about an inappropriate level of surveillance.

EM Today and Tomorrow

EM grew so rapidly in the 1980s that, by 1989, monitoring programs were operating in thirty-seven states, the District of Columbia, the Commonwealth of Puerto Rico, and for pretrial release in the federal government. Since 1990, all states have had at least one EM program. The EM programs in these jurisdictions were monitoring nearly 6,500 offenders who were under the control of either public or private corrections programs (Renzema & Skelton, 1990). By 1993 there were estimates that anywhere between 50,000 and 70,000 people were being monitored each day in the United States (Lilly, 1993). Current estimates of the number of persons under EM are increasingly difficult to get. One reason for this is that EM is less novel today; courts and corrections officials see it as simply another tool rather than as a specific program. Estimating the number of EM units in operation on a given day in a state or in the country might be as difficult as getting a count of the radar units in use by police seeking speeders. When counts are available, they tend to be program or facility specific. For example, Gilliard (1999) reports that in mid-1998 nearly 11,000 people were in an EM program under community supervision by the nation's jails.

The most recent comprehensive survey of the use of EM is based on a 1989 study (Renzema & Skelton, 1990). In the sample group of offenders, most monitorees were male (90 percent), under age thirty (58 percent), and had been convicted of a property offense (32 percent). In a 1987 survey of monitorees, most had been convicted of driving under the influence of alcohol (33 percent) whereas property offenders made up only 18 percent of the monitorees. Just as there seemed to be a greater willingness to place property offenders under EM, there was also an increase between 1987 and 1989 in the percentage of violent offenders among those monitored (from 6 percent to 12 percent). Renzema and Skelton express mixed feelings about the increased use of EM for more serious offenders.

On one hand, the trend makes genuine diversion from jail and prison more likely and shows that judges have increased confidence in the EM programs and the technology. On the other hand, Renzema and Skelton were concerned in 1990 about the ability of some jurisdictions to manage more serious offenders given their existing equipment and operating procedures.

EM's initial popularity was linked to crowded jail and prison conditions. Because crowding continues into the twenty-first century, it is not possible to determine if EM usage will decline when jail and prison space becomes available. But, as Figure 8.1 shows, EM programs have now expanded to include persons not yet prosecuted or offenders not yet sentenced, so the tool may already have progressed so far that it will remain an option even if crowding is no longer a problem. As its use continues to expand, there will be more and more questions to answer. For example, we will probably want to know if EM represents the beginnings of a change in social control techniques as dramatic as the replacement of corporal and capital punishment by imprisonment. Also, do you suppose EM can be useful in changing rather than just temporarily suppressing criminal behavior? Will EM be used to simply widen the net of social control so that persons not currently handled by the justice system can be restricted with only minimal cost to the government? Answers to such questions await sufficient data and interested researchers. Until then it can only be reported that EM is increasingly used as an important part of such community penalties as home confinement and intensive supervised probation.

HOME CONFINEMENT

The idea of punishing misbehaving people by restricting them to their own living area dates at least to the first time parents sent a misbehaving child to his or her room. The use of similar confinement for law violators is certainly a more re-

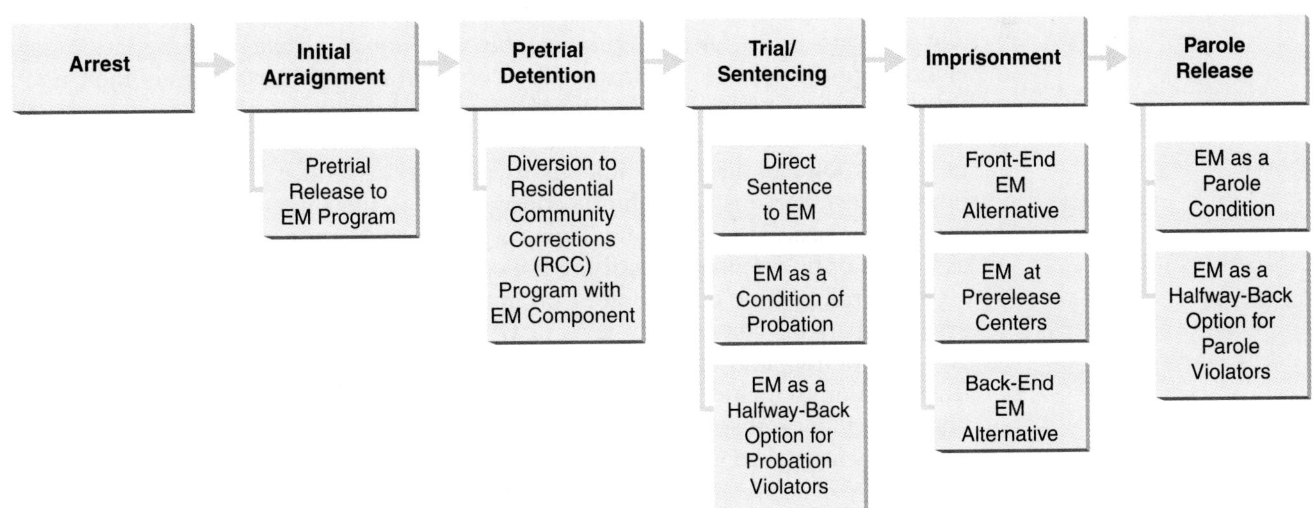

FIGURE 8.1

Key Decision Points Where Electronic Monitoring Is Being Used

Source: From Bureau of Justice Assistance. (1989). *Electronic monitoring in intensive probation and parole programs* [NCJ 116319]. Washington, DC: Department of Justice.

cent event. Since the 1970s, home confinement has become a popular way for authorities to handle some criminals. Its beginning resulted from a search for alternatives to crowded jails and prisons, but its growth was aided by the appearance of electronic surveillance, which gave members of the public a sense of security. Today home confinement continues to be used as a punishment for convicted offenders and as a way to handle some people not yet sentenced or even convicted. It is often used in conjunction with EM because the monitoring provides a mechanism to enforce the home confinement penalty.

The term **home confinement** is used to refer to any condition imposed by a judge that requires an offender to remain in his or her residence for any portion of the day. Because "any portion of the day" is the standard, the curfew conditions can range from nighttime hours through any nonworking hours, to continuous twenty-four-hour-a-day incarceration. That variation can result in quite varied levels of control, so Hofer and Meierhoefer (1987) distinguish three types of home confinement:

- **Curfew.** Under curfew types of home confinement, offenders must be at their residences during limited, specified hours, generally at night. In addition, many of these strategies require offenders to participate in treatment, training, or drug testing programs; community service; or paying fines or restitution.
- **Home detention.** Home detention requires offenders to remain at home at all times, except for such purposes as employment, school, treatment, medical emergencies, or approved shopping trips. When strictly enforced, home detention is stricter than curfew and affords greater control over offenders' activities.
- **Home incarceration.** The most severe form of home confinement is home incarceration. As if they were in prison, offenders must remain at their residences at all times with very limited exceptions (e.g., religious services or medical treatment). Visitors to the home are restricted, offenders cannot work outside the home, and they may not even make shopping trips. The goal very clearly is to punish offenders and to maintain control over their movements.

Noticeably absent from this review of terms is *house arrest.* Although we occasionally see *house arrest* used interchangeably with *home confinement,* the latter term is more appropriate because most offenders confined to their homes in the United States have been convicted of crimes (exceptions being cases of pretrial detention). House arrest also has some negative connotations from its use in some countries to silence political dissent. Unlike many political dissenters who are placed under house arrest, persons under home confinement in the United States have received certain due process protections. Therefore, house arrest may not be as appropriate as home confinement in describing the community penalty discussed here.

Generally, home confinement programs have been used for low-risk offenders (e.g., persons convicted of DWI or DUI), but Sherman, Gottfredson, MacKenzie, Eck, Reuter, and Bushway (1997) note that some jurisdictions are expanding this sanction to include parolees and other serious offenders. As an overview, this chapter will look at some of the advantages and disadvantages attributed to home confinement in the United States.

Advantages of Home Confinement

Sentences to home confinement have several advantages that make this a popular sanction. The sentence seems cost-effective, is flexible, and has several social and humanitarian benefits. When offenders are truly prison bound, the state not only saves the yearly cost of housing the offender but can also reduce the pressure to build new prisons. A compounding factor to consider, however, is whether the offender is also under electronic monitoring. If the lease cost for the monitoring equipment is paid by the state rather than by fees charged to the offender, the cost of home confinement will increase, but it still seems cost-effective. Nationwide figures (Petersilia, 1988) show that home confinement programs without EM cost anywhere from $1,500 to $7,000 per offender per year. Home confinement with EM costs $2,500 to $8,000. When compared to the annual operating cost of $15,500 (Maguire & Pastore, 1994) per inmate that states averaged in 1990, home confinement is cost-effective whether or not EM is included.

If the public is just as safe as they would be were the offender imprisoned, then home confinement may achieve that desired result in a more cost-effective manner. The same is true for other purposes that punishment might have. If the offender under home confinement is deterred from future criminal acts, is able to develop skills and attitudes that support a law-abiding lifestyle, or is required to compensate the community without having to spend time in jail or prison, then home confinement might be considered cost-effective. As with all types of alternative sanctions, cost-effectiveness depends on the sanctions being compared and the goals to be achieved. In general, however, cost-effectiveness is typically offered as an advantage of home confinement over placement in jail or prison.

An aspect of home confinement's flexibility lies in its potential for use at many points in the criminal justice process. Although it might be thought of as a way primarily to punish convicted offenders, home confinement is also used as an aspect of pretrial release and as a condition to receiving a suspended sentence. But its flexibility is even more apparent as either a sole sanction or when linked to other penalties. For some offenders, home confinement may be a sufficient punishment in itself. For others, confinement to their home may be only one part of a sentencing package that tries to serve several purposes. To protect the community and to ease community outrage, offenders can be confined to their residences but allowed to go to work so they can pay restitution or complete community service. Such a sentencing package might meet purposes of deterrence, retribution, rehabilitation, and restoration.

Some social or humanitarian benefits of home confinement include giving the offender an opportunity to stay employed and help provide financial support to the family. In addition, home confinement does not disrupt the family and family networks in the same manner that imprisonment might. A less obvious benefit of confinement in one's home is the ability to avoid the corrupting influences, stigmatizing effects, and physical and psychological damage that might accompany a stay in jail or prison. Finally, there are categories of persons that might be more humanely handled by home confinement than by placement in a prison. For example, the terminally ill, physically handicapped, or highly contagious offenders may be candidates for a sentence to their residences. Other offenders may be appropriately placed under home confinement for a specified time (e.g., offenders needing medical attention including pregnant women) but kept in jail or prison at other times in their sentences.

Disadvantages of Home Confinement

Few things, if any, can claim only advantages. Home confinement is no exception. Like other community penalties, home confinement has the potential for net-widening, selecting participants in a biased manner, compromising public safety, and violating citizens' rights. As noted in the discussion of EM, net-widening refers to a situation of placing persons under greater control than they would have been if the program did not exist. If people who would otherwise be placed on regular probation are placed instead under home confinement, the home confinement program can be said to have unnecessarily widened the social control net. The other side of that coin is the net-narrowing that occurs in the social control option of imprisonment. To the extent that home confinement is an alternative to prison, some offenders will receive a less severe penalty by being confined to their residences than they would get if home confinement did not exist. In these cases the net of imprisonment has been narrowed so that people do not receive as harsh a penalty as they would or, some argue, should. So, depending on your perspective, home confinement has the disadvantage of net-widening if people are being controlled by the government more so than they would without the program, or the disadvantage of net-narrowing if people are receiving less severe punishment than they otherwise would.

The argument that home confinement programs are biased toward particular categories of offenders comes primarily from the selection criteria used to identify program participants. Criteria for program placement often exclude offenders with a history of violence (including domestic violence), chronic drug or alcohol problems, or an unstable employment record. Of course, other criteria as well as offender and offense characteristics are also considered (see Hofer & Meierhoefer, 1987), but the result is often a program filled with nonviolent property offenders having regular employment and good family relations. Many offenders with those characteristics are from the middle and upper classes economically and are more often from the white-Anglo majority than from America's racial and ethnic minorities. If this is true (the answer awaits further research), it can be argued that home confinement programs are available to offenders based more on aspects of class, race, and ethnicity than on type of offense.

Another disadvantage of home confinement programs is that public safety may be compromised. Criminals who are confined to their homes are more easily able to continue criminal behavior than if they were confined to a prison. This seems especially true, for example, of drug abusers and dealers, although it might be less true for burglars. Even when home confinement is combined with EM, authorities cannot assure the public that offenders will refrain from criminal activity. In addition, because many home confinement programs allow offenders to leave their residences for activities such as work and shopping, it is possible that crimes can be committed even when offenders are legitimately away from home.

Finally, it is important to realize that home confinement may have disadvantages in terms of possible violations to civil liberties. Like the privacy issues that ask if EM compromises security in one's home, some people wonder if home confinement might violate aspects of the U.S. Constitution. Ball, Huff, and Lilly (1988) consider, for example, what is implied when homes are converted into jails and when a significant portion of society lives under the constant realization that their movement is being monitored. Those kinds of questions must be asked in order to sensitize us to potentially larger implications associated with "homes as prisons" and "living under an ever watchful government eye." Less philosophical questions may need more immediate answers. For example, is unauthorized absence from home confinement an "escape" punishable as a separate crime? Should time spent in home confinement be deducted from any incarceration sentence that might later be imposed?

As with EM, home confinement has not received much legal challenge. But waiting to answer questions only when forced to is seldom a sound practice. As home confinement and electronic surveillance continue to expand as social control techniques, the issues being raised today by program critics may be asked tomorrow by persons subjected to the programs. Renzema (1992) warns us that the civil libertarian's nightmares could come true if future prison space is saved for the more serious offenders while home confinement is increasingly used for the less serious ones. To prevent an Orwellian-like situation of constant surveillance and an unveiled home, groundwork must be laid by passing laws regulating the use of home confinement and EM and by taking prompt corrective action when any abuses occur in the programs.

Home confinement and electronic monitoring are comparatively new techniques for short-term confinement of offenders. The more traditional method is to hold people in secure facilities designed to both detain suspects awaiting trial and to confine convicted offenders as a form of punishment. In the United States a single-facility type performs both these functions—the jail.

Jails: The Detention Function

The primary focus of this chapter is on the use of short-term confinement as a penal sanction. However, the structure of criminal justice in the United States is such that the premier facility for short-term confinement of offenders—the jail—is also the facility where persons are held while awaiting trial. Discussion of the jail begins with its pretrial detention function.

When authorities arrest a person suspected of having committed a crime, two conflicting goals are put in motion: those of the community and those of the suspect. The community, which believes it has been harmed by the suspect, is interested in ensuring that the suspect will appear for trial and, meanwhile, will refrain from harming members of the public and their property. The suspect is, among other things, interested in preparing a defense against the charges brought by the community and in avoiding damage to such areas as employment, school, and family life. The community's goals seem best achieved if the suspect is confined in a jail or is at least closely monitored in the community. The suspect's goals are most easily realized if he or she has complete freedom of movement and choice of associates. The resulting dilemma has forced jurisdictions to develop systems of pretrial release and pretrial detention that try to balance the interests of both the community and the suspect. This section looks at approaches that have been tried, discarded, modified, or proposed in the United States especially but also in some other countries.

Pretrial Release

When efforts to balance community and suspect interests result in the suspect's release in the community, reference is being made to **pretrial release.** Under pretrial release, the suspect is released from custody for all or part of the time before or during prosecution. That release is conditioned upon the defendant's agreement to return to court at the appointed day and time. Sometimes that agreement is simply the defendant's promise to appear; at other times the agreement is backed by a financial obligation. But whether the guarantee put up is a verbal promise, money, or property, that security is called **bail.** Generally these bail types fall into one of two categories: financial or nonfinancial.

Financial Types of Pretrial Release. Release from jail under a financial obligation often involves a **bail bond.** The bail bond is a written agreement presented by the defendant, who agrees to pay a cash bail bond (money) or a property bail bond (property) to the court if the defendant fails to attend required court appearances. Because not all defendants have the money or property necessary to secure the

Under a commercial bail system, a professional bondsman agrees to serve as surety for a defendant in return for a fee paid by the defendant to the bondsman.

bail, another person, acting as surety, is allowed to pay the money or put up the property for the defendant. Of course, just as the defendant may not have the necessary money or property, neither may the defendant's family or friends. In those cases it may be possible for another person, the bail bondsman, to secure the defendant's release by telling the court that the bondsman will pay the required sum if the defendant fails to appear. Bondsmen agree to serve in this capacity as a way to make money because the defendant has to pay the bondsman a certain sum to gain the bondsman's financial support.

When bail bonding allows a person to make money by serving as surety for a defendant, the process becomes commercial bail. Although the commercial bail system still requires money from the defendant, the fee charged by the bondsman is considerably less than the bail amount set by the court (e.g., the bondsman may charge only 10 to 15 percent of the total bail amount). As a result, the defendant has a better chance at securing money for the bondsman than in getting the total amount required by the court. When defendants who placed their own cash or property bond appear for court, they will have the cash returned or property bond released. Defendants who used a bail bondsman, however, will not get back any of the fee paid to the bondsman when they appear for their court date.

Financial bail has been criticized as being discriminatory toward low-income people. Poor defendants may be required to stay in jail simply because they lack financial means for release on bail rather than because of any danger they present to the community. But criticism of financial bail becomes especially intense when commercial bail and the bondsmen are discussed. In 1922 Harvard law professors Roscoe Pound and Felix Frankfurter said commercial bail prostitutes the administration of justice and has spawned the disreputable professional bondsman, who makes money by exploiting the poor (Devine, 1991). Despite such an indictment, commercial bail bonding has remained popular in the United States. Only recently have U.S. jurisdictions (e.g., Kentucky and Wisconsin) moved toward eliminating bail bondsmen. Other countries, however, have been forceful in prohibiting the growth of commercial bail. Canada, for example, has laws with the deliberate purpose of prohibiting commercial bail bonding. Similarly, England and many Australian jurisdictions have passed laws that specifically attempt to prohibit the development of commercial bail bonding.

Where financial bail in general or commercial bail more specifically is not used, the courts must rely on nonmonetary incentives to ensure the defendant's appearance in court. Many countries have had great success with these nonfinancial kinds of pretrial release. They seem particularly desirable when jurisdictions are concerned that the "bail or jail" decision is determined solely, or even primarily, by the defendant's finances.

Nonfinancial Types of Pretrial Release. According to a national sample of felony cases in state courts in the nation's seventy-five largest counties, 62 percent of the defendants were released before case disposition and 38 percent were detained (Reaves, 1998). Figure 8.2 shows that most of the defendants in the sample were released under either financial or nonfinancial conditions. Of the 38 percent detained until their case disposition, most (82 percent) had a bail amount set but did not post the money required to secure release. The most frequent nonfinancial release procedure was release on recognizance (ROR), which is based simply on the defendant's promise to appear for trial. It is a kind of bail by which defendants personally acknowledge, without the backing of money or property, their obligation to appear in court. The only other types of nonfinancial pretrial release used in these jurisdictions were conditional release (defendant is released on a promise to fulfill some requirement such as staying employed, maintaining a curfew, or participating in a treatment program) or release on an unsecured bond (defendants are released without having to make any payment but are liable for the full bail amount if they fail to appear).

If U.S. jurisdictions follow the trend in other countries, conditional release may become increasingly popular. In France, for example, some pretrial defendants are released under *contrôle judiciaire,* which serves as a middle ground between jail and simple release on bail (Gerety, 1980). Designed as a way to encourage more liberal use of pretrial release by magistrates and to provide social services to the defendant, *contrôle judiciaire* allows the subject to be released in the community as long as certain conditions are followed. The conditions are similar to those imposed on offenders placed on probation and include items such as remaining in a specified area, reporting to justice officials, or relinquishing one's passport and driver's license. Reporting to officials is also a typical bail condition in New Zealand and Tasmania, whereas restrictions on movement and surrendering passports are often part of bail in South Australia (Devine, 1991).

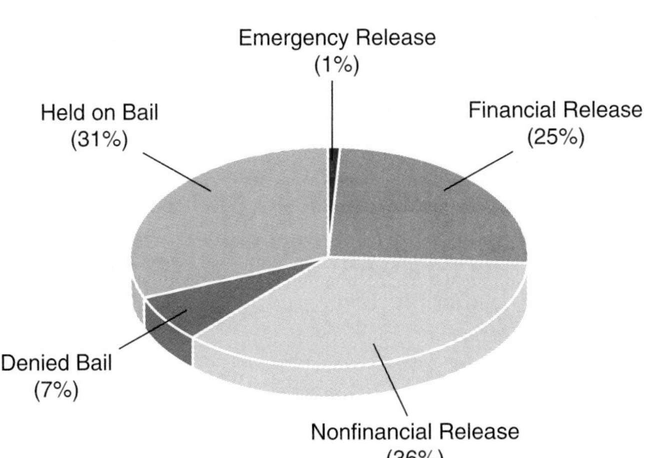

FIGURE 8.2

Types of Pretrial Release

Source: Adapted from Reaves, B. A. (1998). *Felony defendants in large urban counties, 1994* [NCJ 164616]. Washington, DC: Bureau of Justice Statistics.

Also growing in popularity, at least in common-law countries, is the use of criminal penalties to gain compliance with the terms of bail. England, Canada, and most Australian jurisdictions, for example, have attached criminal penalties to those who avoid their court appearance (Devine, 1991). In England, Canada, and New South Wales, defendants who break their promise to appear in court are guilty of absconding and can be punished with imprisonment, a fine, or both. This threat of punishment for absconding is the primary means in these jurisdictions for getting defendants to keep their promise to appear in court at the appointed time.

Pretrial Service Programs. There is obviously a variety of financial and nonfinancial versions of pretrial release. Also available to the judge or magistrate who is deciding what to do with the defendant is placement in a detention facility. But before looking at the detention option, this section will take a closer look at the decision-making process itself.

In the early 1960s, the Vera Institute of Justice, a private foundation concerned about pretrial detention issues, began the Manhattan Bail Project to increase pretrial release opportunities. Using law students from New York University, the Manhattan Bail Project, in cooperation with the courts, began conducting interviews with defendants awaiting their bail hearing. Working on the assumption that persons with close ties to the community would be likely to appear for their trial date, the project staff identified those persons who "scored" high on community ties criteria and recommended them for ROR. The project was considered successful and served as one of the first programs that are now grouped under the title of pretrial services.

Help Wanted

Job Title: Pretrial Services Officer

Position Description: Gather and verify background information concerning defendants and make recommendations on the amount of bail and the conditions to be met by defendants allowed to remain at liberty in the community while awaiting a court hearing. Pretrial services officers also supervise defendants released on bail in order to monitor and intervene with the defendant's compliance to the conditions of release.

Qualifications: Applicants should have a bachelor's degree in the social sciences, knowledge of community services, and be well skilled in both oral and written communication.

For examples of career opportunities in this field visit the U.S. Courts (Northern District of Indiana) Web site at ***www.innd.uscourts.gov/html/pretrial.html*** and the Maryland Pretrial Release Services Program at ***www.dpscs.state.md.us/pds/prsp.htm.***

Pretrial services incorporate the practices and programs that help judges and magistrates make the release/detention decision by providing them with summaries of data about the personal background of the defendant (Henry, 1991). These services are important because the decisions about who remains in jail are not always made in an informed fashion. Pretrial services grew quickly after the Manhattan Bail Project was begun and are now available in one form or another in most U.S. jurisdictions (Lee, Cole, & Buchele, 1998; McElroy, 1998).

Pretrial service programs divide their work efforts into two areas: identification and supervision. Under their identification service, pretrial programs screen defendants for those eligible for pretrial release, interview the eligibles to determine the extent of their community ties, and recommend to the judge which eligible defendants are likely to keep their court date and to stay out of trouble. Because jail crowding might require judges to release defendants who are not really good candidates, the recommendations may also include suggestions for conditions the judge should impose to increase the odds that a questionable defendant will appear and refrain from crime.

The supervision segment of pretrial services includes monitoring the pretrial releasees' behavior, notifying (reminding) defendants about upcoming court dates, determining the appropriate response to any violations linked to the pretrial release that the defendants may have, and providing defendants with social service program information. It is important to note that pretrial services staff are technically neither law enforcement nor corrections employees. They do not have arrest authority and have no right to "rehabilitate" someone who has yet to be convicted of anything (Marsh, 1994). But their work, which has always been important, is increasingly necessary as jurisdictions try to deal with the greater numbers of people entering the justice system.

Behavior of Pretrial Release Defendants. Whether the pretrial release procedures are effective in achieving the community's goals of safety and court appearance depends on how much compliance is expected. Data from a 1994 sample of felony cases in state courts showed that about 15 percent of all released defendants were rearrested while on pretrial release (Reaves, 1998). The community goal of keeping its members free from harm while the defendant awaits trial was achieved in about 85 percent of the cases.

The failure-to-reappear rate in the 1994 national sample was 24 percent of the released felony defendants. (See Table 8.1.) This suggests that the community's interest in ensuring the defendant's appearance at trial may not have been very successful, but two-thirds of the "no-shows" had been found and returned to court by the end of the one-year study. The other one-third (7 percent of all those who had been released) remained fugitive (Reaves, 1998).

There is no agreed-upon percentage for determining successful pretrial release policies. The 15 percent rearrest rate (9 percent of the rearrests were for a new

TABLE 8.1: Released Felony Defendants Who Failed to Make a Scheduled Court Appearance, by Most Serious Arrest Charge, 1994

		PERCENTAGE OF RELEASED FELONY DEFENDANTS IN THE SEVENTY-FIVE LARGEST COUNTIES WHO—			
			Failed to Appear in Court		
Most Serious Arrest Charge	Number of Defendants	Made All Court Appearances	Total	Returned to Court	Remained a Fugitive
All Offenses	31,154	76	24	17	7
Violent Offenses	7,059	85	15	11	4
Murder	106	92	8	8	0
Rape	277	90	10	9	2
Robbery	1,661	81	19	14	5
Assault	3,799	84	16	11	5
Other violent	1,216	90	10	7	3
Property Offenses	9,911	75	25	18	8
Burglary	2,042	76	24	17	7
Theft	3,873	73	27	19	8
Other property	3,996	76	24	17	8
Drug Offenses	11,490	71	29	20	9
Trafficking	4,568	73	27	18	9
Other drug	6,922	69	31	22	9
Public-Order Offenses	2,693	82	18	13	6
Weapons	1,242	84	16	11	5
Driving related	848	77	23	16	7
Other public order	603	85	15	10	4

Note. Data on the court appearance record for the current case were available for 99 percent of cases involving a defendant released prior to case disposition. All defendants who failed to appear in court and were not returned to the court during the one-year study period are counted as fugitives. Some of these defendants may have been returned to the court at a later date. Detail may not add to total because of rounding.

Source: From Reaves, B. A. (1998). *Felony defendants in large urban counties, 1994* [NCJ 164616]. Washington, DC: Bureau of Justice Statistics.

felony) in the 1994 sample is quite likely a greater number than many in the public sector are willing to accept. Similarly, having one-third of the defendants on pretrial release not show up for the trial is surely an unacceptably high percentage for some citizens. Others, however, will look at the 85 percent of the pretrial releasees who were not rearrested, and at the 76 percent who made all court appearances, and see those numbers as representing a reasonable risk. These people argue that in exchange for living in a society in which persons merely accused of a crime have the ability to maintain their family, work, and community ties while assisting in the preparation of their defense, citizens must be willing to accept a procedure that is less than 100 percent effective.

Pretrial Detention

Important issues of pretrial detention are easily grouped with the classic who, what, where, and why queries. We begin with an explanation of where people are detained, then look at why they are being detained, and conclude with a description of who they are and what impact the detention has on their involvement with the criminal justice system.

Pretrial Detention Facilities. The typical pretrial detention facility in the United States is the local jail. Some jurisdictions, such the federal government, are using the term *detention center,* but for the most part, the country's jails have maintained their name and purpose. **Jails,** which are distinguished from prisons in several important ways (see Table 8.2), are confinement facilities usually operated by city or county governments and typically managed by that government's law enforcement agency. For example, the city police department administers the city jail, and the county sheriff manages the county jail. Not all cities and counties operate their own jails, but those that do not have made some arrangement with another entity for jail services.

In the United States, five states have state jail systems (also called integrated jail–prison systems) rather than the more typical local jail systems. In those states—Connecticut, Delaware, Hawaii, Rhode Island, and Vermont—the state government is responsible for the administration and operation of jails located throughout the state. Except for five locally operated jails, Alaska also has a state jail system.

TABLE 8.2: Some Differences between Jails and Prisons

JAILS	PRISONS
Operated by local governments (except in Connecticut, Delaware, Hawaii, Rhode Island, Vermont, and parts of Alaska)	Operated by state or federal government
Hold convicted misdemeanants (usually on sentences up to one year)	Hold convicted felons (usually on sentences of one year and more)
Typically hold males and females in separate units of the same facility	Typically hold males and females in separate facilities
Serve as a detention facility for persons not yet convicted of a crime	Serve as a custody facility for persons already convicted and sentenced

Jails have a controversial place in the U.S. justice system in part because of the jail's confusing role but also because of the physical condition of many jails (see also "Jails in History"). Beginning with one of the country's first jails (Philadelphia's Walnut Street Jail, which opened in 1773), there have been complaints about management issues and poor living conditions. In 1871 the Board of State Commissioners said of the Adams County Jail in Illinois that it was "difficult to imagine any place more unfit to confine human beings than this jail, dark, damp, and extremely filthy" (quoted in Charles, Kethineni, & Thompson, 1992, p. 56). In 1959 Barnes and Teeters wrote that of all the places criminals are kept, jails were "the vilest from the standpoint of sanitation; the most absurd from a functional point of view; and the most inefficient in administration" (Barnes & Teeters, 1959, p. 387). By 1992 a review of jails noted that although there had been "many attempts in recent years to improve the condition of jails, many jails are still old and plagued with inadequate security, space, and environmental problems" (Charles et al., 1992, p. 56). There seems to have been little progress from the 1770s to the 1990s.

The lack of attention paid to the jail is especially curious because jails have been called the most important part of the American correctional system (Charles et al.,

HISTORICAL PERSPECTIVES

Jails in History

Barnes and Teeters (1959) suggest that "modern" jails originated in 1166, when Henry II ordered the construction of a gaol (jail) at the Assize of Clarendon. Its original function was holding suspected or arrested offenders until they could be tried by the courts. Developing around the same time as early English jails were the houses of correction or Bridewells. While the jails were built as detention places, the houses of correction were established specifically as places of punishment. In the eighteenth century these two types of institutions gradually merged, and they were often found under the same roof, being administered by the same keeper (Barnes & Teeters, 1959). In this way, the jail came to have a second function of short-term confinement for petty and misdemeanor offenders.

Responsibility for the jails fell to the English shire-reeves (sheriffs). Typically that duty was delegated to a "keeper," who then had the responsibility of caring for both the jail and its occupants. Rather than receiving a salary, the keeper's (or even the sheriff's where the duty had not been transferred) income came from fees attached to the jail's operation. Inmates, or their family or friends, paid the keeper for maintenance, light, heat, sleeping mats, and even food. The more people in the jail, and the longer they stayed, the greater was the keeper's income.

The fee system continued without much published criticism until the 1770s, when John Howard was named sheriff at Bedfordshire. This notable prison reformer found the jail system in England to be disgraceful. He worked hard to improve the physical conditions of English jails and to end the practice of paying fees for basic services. Howard was successful in bringing about changes in England, but by the time Parliament passed the Penitentiary Act (1779), the American colonists had already implemented the earlier version of a jail system.

Jails were established in the American colonies as soon as people began gathering together in one location. One of the earliest jails was erected in 1653 at York Village, Maine; one at Williamsburg, Virginia, dated from 1701 (Barnes & Teeters, 1959). Because the jails existed primarily for pretrial detention or to hold offenders until a sentence was carried out (presentence detention), they were not particularly secure facilities. Rather than using individual cells, those being detained were housed in small rooms, typically without heat, where they awaited their fate. Conveniently, because that fate was often corporal punishment, close to the jail were the stocks, pillory, and occasionally the whipping post.

For an idea of what some of the early Bridewell houses looked like, visit ***ireland.iol.ie/~thu/bridewel.htm***, and see the photos and read the description of the Bridewell at Tipperary. How many prisoners did this old jail hold?

Jails, which are typically operated by city or county governments, are among the oldest features of the criminal justice system.

1992) or are claimed to be at least as important as the state prison (Barnes & Teeters, 1959). The 567,000 persons held in the nation's local jails in 1997 was double the number held just ten years earlier (Maguire & Pastore, 1998, Table 6.23). During the 1990s the annual average increase in the number of persons held in local jails (4.5 percent) was similar to that for state and federal prisons (5.7 percent), yet public attention and media scrutiny seem focused only on the prisons (Gilliard, 1999). If jails are in fact as important to the operation of the U.S. justice system as are prisons, such disregard is undesirable.

Help Wanted

Job Title: Detention Officer

Position Description: Detention officers work throughout the facility to supervise, secure, control, and care for inmates at the detention center. The officer will observe the conduct and behavior of inmates to prevent disturbances and escapes, will maintain direct contact with inmates to provide prompt resolution to their problems, and will write detailed reports in regard to incidents and/or events within the facility.

Qualifications: Applicants must be high school graduates, cannot have a felony conviction or be on probation, and must pass a security investigation.

For examples of career opportunities in this field, check the job bank for the American Correctional Association at ***www.corrections.com/aca/jobbank.html***, and read about jobs with the New York City Department of Corrections at ***www.ci.nyc.ny.us/html/doc/html/jobframe.html***.

Jails Today. Of the over 3,300 local jails around the country today, the majority (about 57 percent) are considered "small" because they hold fewer than 50 inmates. About 31 percent are "medium" facilities, holding 50 to 249 people; 10 percent are "large," with populations of 250 to 999; and about 2 percent are "mega" jails, holding over 1,000 people (Perkins, Stephan, & Beck, 1995). The nation's two largest local jail jurisdictions, Los Angeles County and New York City, together held nearly 39,000 inmates in 1998—about 7 percent of the national total (Gilliard, 1999).

Because of differences in the way jurisdictions keep records, it is difficult to make accurate status distinctions among persons held in jail. Although you might think each jail would know who among its residents are unconvicted and who are convicted, the situation is not so simple. You might think of jails only as places where persons are held awaiting trial or are serving short-term confinement sentences, but contemporary jails serve many purposes, including (Gilliard, 1999):

- receive individuals pending arraignment and hold them awaiting trial, conviction, or sentencing
- readmit probation, parole, and bail-bond violators and absconders
- temporarily detain juveniles pending transfer to juvenile authorities
- hold mentally ill persons pending their movement to appropriate health facilities
- hold individuals for the military, for protective custody, for contempt, and for the courts as witnesses
- release convicted inmates to the community upon completion of sentence
- transfer inmates to federal, state, or other authorities
- house inmates for federal, state, or other authorities because of crowding of their facilities
- relinquish custody of temporary detainees to juveniles and medical authorities
- sometimes operate community-based programs as alternatives to incarceration
- hold inmates sentenced to short terms (generally under one year). (p. 5)

As that list suggests, a person in jail could be unconvicted and awaiting trial, waiting for a transfer to another agency or jurisdiction, or being held for possible revocation of her probation or parole. Similarly, a jail resident could be convicted but not yet sentenced or convicted and waiting for transfer to a prison. Best estimates in recent years suggest that about 57 percent of the nation's adult jail inmates were unconvicted (awaiting court action on their current conviction), and the other 43 percent were serving a jail sentence, awaiting sentencing, or serving time for probation or parole violation (Gilliard, 1999).

Reason for Pretrial Detention. Traditionally, release on bail (either financial or nonfinancial) has been denied to suspects when there is good reason to believe they will not appear in court at the assigned date and time, or when it seems likely they will continue to do harm in the community. That means we would expect to find among the pretrial detainees three categories of persons: (1) those suspects whom judges believed were likely to flee, (2) people whom judges thought might commit crimes if they remained free in the community, and (3) persons who were granted but could not afford release on financial bail. Together these three categories comprise an estimated 57 percent of the adult jail inmates, but national statistics are not available on the percentage that each category comprises in the jail population (Gilliard, 1999; Harlow, 1998). Persons in category 3 were discussed as we considered nonfinancial bail alternatives. Individuals in category 1 are the primary focus of this section. But suspects in category 2 present a somewhat different situation. Technically they are simply under pretrial detention, but the implication is that they must be detained primarily because it is assumed they will commit crimes if they are not kept in jail. In other words, these people are put in custody for acts they have not yet committed and may not ever commit. The specific term applied to this situation is **preventive detention.** Before discussing the broader issue of pretrial detention, this chapter will consider aspects of its preventive branch.

Preventive detention involves the pretrial incarceration of an accused person who is considered likely to commit crimes if returned to the community. So, to prevent the crime from ever occurring, the punishment comes first. Of course, we are playing with words here because the due process clause of the Fourteenth Amendment prevents the punishment of pretrial detainees (Cohen, 1988, p. 321). But just what constitutes punishment? Are persons not yet found guilty of anything being punished when their freedom of movement is restricted? The U.S. Supreme Court provided an answer to those questions in *United States v. Salerno* (1987) when it upheld the constitutionality of preventive detention as provided for in the federal Bail Reform Act of 1984. The justices based their decision in part on their belief that rather than being used as a punishment, preventive detention was intended as a legitimate way to protect the community.

The crucial question, you might argue, is whether preventive detention keeps crimes from ever occurring. Unfortunately it is a difficult question to answer because we can never know how those who were put under preventive detention would have behaved in the community. What is clear, however, is that laws allowing preventive detention have expanded in recent years so that over half the states permit preventive detention and the denial of bail for persons charged with certain serious crimes. Data from a 1994 national sample (Reaves, 1998) show murder defendants (43 percent) were the most likely to have been denied release on bail, followed by defendants charged with rape (10 percent) or robbery (10 percent). The reasons for not being released certainly include preventive detention aspects, but some jurisdictions may also have statutory restrictions on bail for these crimes.

Regardless of whether persons are being detained because they cannot afford bail, because they are considered unlikely to appear at the appointed time, or because their release would endanger the community, the impact of that detention will be important.

Some Impacts of Pretrial Detention. One reason for concern about the conditions of jails is that over half the people confined to them have not yet been found guilty of anything (Gilliard, 1999). This is not meant to suggest that convicted criminals are more deserving of confinement under unsanitary or otherwise unsuitable conditions. But confinement in some of the world's jails may seem especially inappropriate for people simply accused of a crime and presumably not yet subject to punishment. Should persons merely suspected of having committed a crime be subjected to the same kinds of conditions (such as confinement in small cells) and circumstances (such as strip searches) as persons already convicted? In other words, do pretrial detainees have constitutional protections that might require them to be treated differently while in jail?

Although the broad question of offenders' rights is discussed in detail in Chapter 14, two cases are appropriate for this chapter. In *Bell v. Wolfish* (1979) and in *Block v. Rutherford* (1984), the U.S. Supreme Court decided that courts should treat jails and prisons the same for purposes of inmates' rights. The Court's reasoning was that institutional order and security are similar whether the institution houses pretrial detainees or convicted prisoners. As a result, it is acceptable to double-bunk, restrict the mail, search the cells, and conduct body cavity searches on pretrial detainees (*Bell v. Wolfish*). In addition, pretrial detainees do not have a right to contact visits (visits during which the inmate and visitor are allowed to touch), nor must cell searches by jail staff be conducted in the presence of the detainee (*Block v. Rutherford*). The Court has found no reason to differentiate between pretrial detainees and convicted prisoners in the area of constitutional rights, despite the presumption of innocence that is afforded the pretrial detainee.

In addition to undesirable physical and psychological impacts that the circumstances and conditions of pretrial detention may have on some people, there are other impacts that link more directly to the adjudication process. Although the persons detained are not likely to be comforted in this knowledge, the median time (in the country's seventy-five largest counties) from the original felony arrest to adjudication of that charge was less (except for murder charges) for detained than for released defendants (Reaves, 1998). But the news was not all good for the detained defendants. Although their cases were usually handled more quickly, the conviction rate for detained defendants was 79 percent compared to a 67 percent conviction rate for released defendants. Furthermore, of the detained defendants who were convicted, about 88 percent received a jail or prison sentence but only 51 percent of the convicted released defendants were sentenced to incarceration (Reaves & Perez, 1994). So, it appears that in return for having their cases adjudicated more quickly, detained defendants are more likely than released defendants to be convicted and, when convicted, to be incarcerated.

Is it the jail-versus-bail distinction that explains a higher conviction rate and an increased chance of a sentence to incarceration for detained defendants? This would be especially bothersome if detention were the result of a lack of money instead of a belief that the defendant would flee or cause harm (see "Do the Rich Get Bail and the Poor Get Jail?"). But Reaves (1998) reports that defendants who were detained had a more serious criminal history than did defendants who were released and were being charged with a more serious offense. Those detained were more likely to have had a prior arrest, a prior conviction, and were charged with a violent crime. It seems reasonable that the increased likelihood of conviction and incarceration reflects the differences in prior arrests, convictions, and types of crime. Because one of the conviction options is a jail sentence, it is time to consider the second function of jails.

ISSUES OF FAIRNESS

DO THE RICH GET BAIL AND THE POOR GET JAIL?

As the chapter points out, persons who have been detained while awaiting adjudication are more likely than those who were free in the community to be convicted and, when convicted, to receive a jail or prison sentence. Because pretrial release status is linked to case disposition and sentence, it is a subject of concern to practitioners, policymakers, and researchers. If the correlation between jail or bail and the eventual outcome of the case is a result of extralegal factors such as social class, race, and ethnicity, the situation is especially troublesome.

The link between social class and a defendant's ability to secure pretrial release seems obvious when a jurisdiction relies on financial rather than nonfinancial release models. In *Stack v. Boyle* (1951) the U.S. Supreme Court found bail to be a pretrial right that helps to prevent the defendant from being punished prior to conviction and allows the defendant to participate in preparing his or her defense. Because of that, the Court said bail should be set in an amount that is generally set for similar offenses. The bail amount should not be frivolous, unusual, or beyond a person's ability to pay under similar circumstances.

Even with the *Stack* decision, bail practices were criticized across the nation as penalizing indigent defendants. The growth of pretrial service programs, which lessen the reliance on financial release methods, certainly benefits indigent defendants who might otherwise remain in jail for lack of bail money. But even with the *Stack* decision and the newer pretrial release programs, a national sample found that many of the defendants in pretrial detention (82 percent) did in fact have a bail amount set—they just could not secure the required funds (Reaves, 1998).

Because the bail amount presumably depends on the crime for which the defendant is charged (the more serious the offense the higher the bail), it is possible that the people held on bail are simply charged with more serious crimes. If that is the case, one can argue that any discrimination regarding who is released is a result of an appropriate factor (crime seriousness) rather than an inappropriate one (poverty). And, in fact, the data seem to support that argument because defendants who were detained had an average bail amount that was three times that of defendants who secured release (Reaves, 1998).

The fairness of bail is not a topic that will soon be resolved. Even with the data showing the average bail amount was higher (suggesting more serious charges) for persons held on bail, that same data also remind us that about 33 percent of the defendants with bail set at under $5,000 were unable to post the amount needed for release. Is it fair that even a small percentage of unconvicted poor defendants are kept in jail to await their day in court while unconvicted rich (or at least "not as poor") defendants are released on bail?

Read *Felony Defendants in Large Urban Counties, 1994* at ***www.ojp.usdoj.gov/bjs/pub/pdf/fdluc94.pdf.*** Look at Tables 15 and 16 (p. 18). For which crime did the greatest percentage of felony defendants have a bail amount under $5,000? Do you believe the bond amounts set for persons charged with drug offenses are appropriate when compared with the amounts set for persons charged with violent offenses or property offenses?

JAILS: THE CONFINEMENT FUNCTION

As already noted, jails have been the subject of much criticism over the last several centuries. Typically that criticism was to no avail because modern jails, like their predecessors, tend to be overcrowded, underfunded, and understaffed. The staff that are present are too often underpaid and untrained. The physical facilities themselves are outdated, and the environment for both inmates and staff is generally charged with stress, violence, and hostility (Zupan, 1991). But there are indications of some changes for the better as the twenty-first century begins. After looking at some characteristics and concerns of contemporary jails, this section will consider the modifications being brought by facilities called the *new generation jails.*

Contemporary Issues for Jails

By the end of the 1990s the number of persons under jail supervision was nearly 700,000 people. At the start of the decade there were about 400,000 in jail. Even allowing for the increase in the nation's general population, these numbers are depressing because they show that the jail population has increased from 163 jail inmates per 100,000 population in 1990 to a rate of 219 in 1998 (Gilliard, 1999). The steadily increasing jail population (averaging almost 5 percent annually during the decade) results in several important questions. First, how is the increase explained? Second, who are the people making up the jail population? Third, what impact do the increased number and the population characteristics have on jail management?

Factors Affecting the Growing Jail Population. In 1998 about 665,000 persons were under jail supervision in the nation's local jails. Most of those (90 percent) were actually confined in jail, but 10 percent were under jail supervision in alternative programs outside the jail facility such as home confinement, day reporting, community service, or various work and treatment programs (Gilliard, 1999). Explanations for how these people came to be under jail supervision include an increase in the number of arrests, increasing felony convictions, a trend toward sentencing more felons to jail, and the use of jails as a holding area for state and federal prisoners.

One reason given for the increasing jail population is an increase in the number of arrests. The *Uniform Crime Reports, 1997* indicates arrests for all offenses were up 16 percent from 1988 to 1997. Arrests for index property crimes had actually declined by 8 percent during that period, but index violent crime arrests increased 23 percent. Notable increases in the nonindex crimes were found for drug abuse violations (up 48 percent) and for offenses against family and children (up 109 percent). The increase in arrest numbers resulted in more admission to local jails and, therefore, increased jail populations.

Also important to the population increase has been an increase in convictions. Brown et al. (1999) report that between 1988 and 1996 there was an increasing likelihood of arrest leading to conviction in state courts. Also there has been an increase in the number of felons being sentenced to jail. Between 1988 and 1996 the number of felons receiving a state prison sentence actually declined, but that drop was accompanied by an increase in the percentage receiving jail sentences with 25 percent of the convicted felons sentenced to jail in 1988 and 31 percent in 1996. It is important to note, however, that felons sentenced to jail received about the same average sentence length (six to seven months) throughout the 1988 to 1996 period. This suggests that while an increase in the number of felons sentenced to jail might explain the jails' growing population, that growth is not a result of longer sentences (Brown et al., 1999; Perkins, Stephan, & Beck, 1995).

As with the increase in arrests, some types of offenses have been especially prominent in this trend toward increased likelihood of receiving a jail sentence. In 1983, 9 percent of the jail inmates were there for a drug offense. By 1989 that percentage had increased to 23 percent. However, the rapid increase seen in the 1980s did not continue in the 1990s, and by 1996 the number of jail inmates being held for a drug offense was 22 percent (Harlow, 1998). Even without a continued increase, the continued impact of the 1980s' harsher reaction to drug offenders explains some of the increase in the jail population during the last two decades.

An increasing number of arrests and increasing likelihood of those arrests leading to conviction, and the trend of sentencing more felons to jail explain some of the growth in jail population. But also important has been the need for jails to hold inmates for state and federal authorities. In a classic ripple effect, the crowding in state and federal prisons has an effect on most other parts of the criminal justice system. When the process works correctly, convicted persons who are sentenced to imprisonment are kept in the local jail, for the jurisdiction in which they were sentenced, until they are released to the receiving authorities. When the conviction is in state court, officials from the state department of corrections (or the equivalent agency) should be ready to receive their new ward within a few weeks of sentencing. Similarly, the Federal Bureau of Prisons should be receiving persons convicted in federal court fairly soon after the sentence is imposed. In recent years both state and federal authorities have had to delay accepting newly sentenced prisoners because there has often been no room in the prisons.

About 12 percent of all jail inmates are prisoners being held for state or federal authorities. That percentage is up from about 8 percent in 1983 but remained constant in the 1990s. Many of those inmates being held for transfer remained in jail because of crowding in state or federal prisons. The others were still in jail for things such as having special security needs, participating in special programs, or waiting for transfer or early release paperwork to be completed (Perkins et al., 1995). Although the state and federal governments pay the local jails for housing their prisoners, the jails seldom see this as a beneficial situation. In some cases local officials have brought legal action against their state government for failure to take the state prisoners from the jail.

Although the foregoing factors are typically mentioned when explaining the growing jail population, one other explanation deserves attention—primarily because it is often ignored. Since the late 1960s, and especially in the 1970s, there has been a movement of mental health decarceration. Thousands of former and potential mental patients were removed from or kept out of the nation's state mental hospitals (Winfree & Wooldredge, 1991, p. 64). Many of those people seem to have ended up in the nation's jails instead. Some authors have proposed an alternative institutionalization thesis that explains some of the growth in jail populations as coming from the use of jails to house persons formerly kept in mental hospitals. Numbers to support that position are reflected in the dramatic increase in the percentage of the total jail population that suffers from mental illness (see "Mentally Ill and Jail"). But this leads us to a discussion of the characteristics of people in jail, so let us move more formally to that topic.

Characteristics of the Jail Population. Most of the local jail inmates are male and are black or Hispanic. Table 8.3 (see page 281) shows that these characteristics remained constant during the 1990s with white, non-Hispanics always accounting for less than half the percentage of jail inmates.

A survey of jail inmates completed in 1996 provides some interesting facts (Harlow, 1998):

- *An increasing percentage of the jail population is female.* Although jail inmates are predominantly male, the number of women is increasing at a faster rate than that of men.
- *Offenses vary between men and women.* Male inmates are nearly twice as likely as female inmates to be in jail for a violent offense. Women are more likely than men to be in jail for a drug offense and for fraud or theft.
- *Nearly 60 percent of jail inmates are members of racial or ethnic minorities.* After rising during the 1980s, the percentage of blacks and Hispanics has not changed substantially in the 1990s.
- *Offenses vary among blacks, whites, and Hispanics.* Proportionately, more black and Hispanic inmates than whites are in jail for drug offenses, and black inmates are somewhat more likely than white or Hispanic inmates to be in jail for a violent offense. A greater percentage of white inmates than either blacks or Hispanics is in jail for property offenses and public order offenses (especially DWI or DUI).

Spotlight ON CONTEMPORARY ISSUES

Mentally Ill and Jail

Based upon self-reports of either a mental or emotional condition, or an overnight stay in a mental hospital or program, 16 percent of the nation's jail population is estimated to be mentally ill (Ditton, 1999). The percentage identified as mentally ill in jail was especially high for white non-Hispanics (22 percent); females (23 percent); and persons age forty-five to fifty-four (23 percent).

The national sample also found that the mentally ill were more likely than other offenders to have committed violent offenses. However, Ditton is quick to point out that this does not necessarily mean that mentally ill offenders are more violent than other offenders—in fact, some studies suggest that released mental patients are no more likely than other residents in the same neighborhoods to engage in violence. Instead, Ditton suggests, police could find it easier to catch violent criminals who are mentally ill; juries might be more willing to convict mentally ill defendants, and judges may be more inclined to sentence them to confinement than to release them on probation ("A Quarter-Million Mentally Ill," 1999).

The possibility that mentally ill defendants are more likely to be caught, convicted, and confined is one of the reasons that declining use of mental hospitals is offered to explain part of the growing jail population. The fact that nearly one-third of the mentally ill in jail reported a period of homelessness in the year prior to their arrest (Ditton, 1999) emphasizes the lack of appropriate facilities in the United States for many of our mentally ill citizens.

John Belcher (1988) studied homeless mentally ill people in an effort to understand the interactions those people have with the criminal justice system. The difficulties of street life, the tendency not to comply with aftercare arrangements, and the difficulties associated with impaired mental functioning often result in displays of odd behavior by many of these people. That odd behavior places homeless mentally ill people in direct conflict with many societal norms, and as a result they are frequently involved with the criminal justice system. In many states, unless individuals are overtly suicidal or homicidal, the state hospitals will not admit them. Police officers are left to decide whether to let the people wander back to the void of street life or detain them in jail.

The jail may be a refuge for the homeless mentally ill, but it is a refuge without treatment or even prolonged shelter because these people are quickly released. As Belcher puts it: "Wandering aimlessly in the community, psychotic much of the time, and unable to manage their internal control systems, these [chronically homeless mentally ill people] found the criminal justice system was an asylum of last resort" (p. 193). Belcher encourages more structured and rigorous action by community mental health professionals as a way to reduce the frequent encounters the homeless mentally ill people have with the criminal justice system.

A prisoner provides an interesting commentary about mentally ill convicts in San Quentin. Read his story at ***www.wco.com/~aerick/catj.htm.*** Do you think the mentally ill should be housed in the same area as non-mentally ill prisoners? Should they be in jails and prisons at all? Get the document on "Providing services for jail inmates with mental disorders" at ***www.ncjrs.org/pdffiles/162207.pdf.*** What are some of the specific needs of inmates with mental health problems? What are some of the new programs and policies being used in jails to respond to these needs?

- *Drugs and alcohol play a prominent role in the lives of convicted jail inmates.* During the month before their offense over half of convicted jail inmates report having used illegal drugs, and about one-third said they were using drugs at the time of the offense. About 16 percent report having committed their crime to get money for drugs. Over 60 percent of convicted jail inmates said they consumed alcohol regularly, and 41 percent were using alcohol at the time of the offense.
- *Women more so than men report past physical or sexual abuse.* Nearly half of all female jail inmates report that they had been physically or sexually abused prior to their current admission to jail (see Table 8.4). Abuse of the men was more likely to have occurred prior to age eighteen whereas women continued to be abused as adults.

TABLE 8.3: Sex, Race, and Hispanic Origin of Local Jail Inmates, Midyear 1990–1998

	PERCENTAGE OF JAIL INMATES								
Characteristic	1990	1991	1992	1993	1994	1995	1996[a]	1997	1998
Total	100.0	100.0	100.0	100.0	100.0	100.0	100.0	100.0	100.0
Sex									
Male	90.8	90.7	90.8	90.4	90.0	89.8	89.2	89.4	89.2
Female	9.2	9.3	9.2	9.6	10.0	10.2	10.8	10.6	10.8
Race/Hispanic Origin[b]									
White, non-Hispanic	41.8	41.1	40.1	39.3	39.1	40.1	41.6	40.6	41.3
Black, non-Hispanic	42.5	43.4	44.1	44.2	43.9	43.5	41.1	42.0	41.2
Hispanic	14.3	14.2	14.5	15.1	15.4	14.7	15.6	15.7	15.5
Other[c]	1.3	1.2	1.3	1.3	1.6	1.7	1.7	1.8	2.0

Note. Detail may not add to total because of rounding.

[a]Data for 1996 were based on all persons under jail supervision.

[b]Data on race/Hispanic origin were reported for 89.7 percent of all inmates in 1990, 91.1 percent in 1991, 97.6 percent in 1992, 85.1 percent in 1993, 95.8 percent in 1994, 97.1 percent in 1995, 99.3 percent in 1996–1997, and 99.6 percent in 1998.

[c]Includes American Indians, Alaska Natives, Asians, and Pacific Islanders.

Source: From Gilliard, D. K. (1999). *Prison and jail inmates at midyear 1998* [NCJ 173414]. Washington, DC: Bureau of Justice Statistics.

TABLE 8.4: Physical or Sexual Abuse before Current Admission, by Sex of Jail Inmates, 1996

	PERCENTAGE OF JAIL INMATES		
Abused before Admission	Total	Male	Female
Ever	16.4	12.9	47.5
Before age 18	14.3	11.9	36.6
After age 18	4.7	2.3	26.7
Physically Abused	13.3	10.7	37.2
Sexually Abused	8.7	5.6	37.1
Raped	6.6	3.7	32.2
Completed	5.4	3.0	26.6
Attempted	1.2	0.7	5.6

Note. Detail adds to more than total because some inmates were abused both before and since age eighteen or were both physically and sexually abused.

Source: From Harlow, C. W. (1998). *Profile of jail inmates 1996* [NCJ 164620]. Washington, DC: Bureau of Justice Statistics.

So, these are some of the characteristics of people making up the jail population. Obviously there are important points raised by each of these highlighted characteristics, but only a few can be addressed here. This section tackles them in the context of jail management and focuses on women in jail and on issues of safety and security.

Jail Management and the Female Offender. It is becoming increasingly difficult for jails to ignore the problems associated with female inmates. Their numbers are increasing too rapidly for administrators to maintain the "head-in-the-sand" response that identifies many jails. Although there are several gender-specific concerns associated with female inmates (e.g., high rates of substance abuse and mental illness, physical health problems, and parenting and child care issues), problems associated with histories of physical and sexual abuse are often highlighted in the literature.

Vesey, De Cou, and Prescott (1998) suggest that the coercive environment and procedures in jails present particular problems for women inmates who have histories of abuse. This is because those women may perceive the environment and procedures as dangerous and threatening. In response to that misperception, the women may withdraw, fight back, experience a worsening of psychiatric symptoms or physical health problems, engage in self-injury, or find access to illegal substances. It behooves jail administrators, Vesey et al. argue, to understand the genesis of these behaviors in order to respond appropriately or, better yet, reduce the likelihood they will appear to begin with.

Because they were created with male inmates in mind, the security and treatment practices in jails may unintentionally create crisis situations for female inmates. Examples of standard procedures that are harmless, even if irritating, for male inmates but that may remind women of prior experiences of abuse might include intimate touching (e.g., strip searches); threatened use of force (e.g., crisis response teams); observing threats, assaults, or use of physical force (e.g., inmate–inmate or inmate–staff violence); isolation (e.g., administrative or medical isola-

Increasing numbers of both male and female inmates have forced some jails to construct "tent cities" as temporary housing.

tion); and locked rooms or spaces and the use of restraint devices (e.g., handcuffs or shackles). Add to those features of the jail the appearance of uniforms and male officers and the presence of fear based on lack of information and it is not surprising that women with histories of physical and sexual abuse experience increased stress and vulnerability. When the response to these triggers is turned outward, there may be an escalation of violence in the women's unit of the jail.

Vesey et al. (1998) understand that jails have a mandate to provide secure and humane conditions of confinement. And they do not suggest that women should not be in jail. Instead, they suggest modification to the jail environment and procedures that can accommodate the special needs of women detainees and convicts. A few such recommendations follow (Vesey et al., 1998):

- *Information disclosure.* Both women and men should have a detailed understanding of what will happen during their time of incarceration, but jail administrators should be aware that each group may need different kinds of information. For example, female inmates especially will want information regarding their children and what child care arrangements have been made.
- *Regimentation, lack of privacy, and unquestioned response to authority.* Jails must provide a secure environment for the safety of both inmates and staff. However, security measures developed to control male inmates may not be necessary or appropriate for female inmates. Because most female offenders are arrested for nonviolent crimes, they may not need the same high-security supervision that men require. Keeping cell doors unlocked or open, allowing greater interaction among the women inmates, and training staff in nonthreatening management techniques may actually result in a more tranquil women's unit.
- *Treatment services.* Incarcerated women, more so than incarcerated men, report that they want someone to talk to—not necessarily someone to solve their problems, just someone who will listen. Women inmates, especially those who are victims of abuse, also tend to find single-gender group treatment activities preferable to mixed-gender groups. Recognizing and responding to these preferences may allow jail staff to provide a more effective treatment response to their female inmates. (pp. 52–53)

Because persons in jail should not leave in worse condition than when they arrived, Vesey et al. encourage jail administrators to give active consideration to the unique characteristics and needs of female inmates. Doing so may minimize further injury and aggravation of health problems. It may also provide a safer environment for staff and other inmates while lessening the harm to the individual inmate that will accompany a jail term.

Jail Management and Issues of Safety and Security. Compared with prisons, jails present greater safety and security risks to both staff and inmates because jail officials do not know as much about the people they are guarding. Persons in prison have typically been incarcerated in jail before arriving at prison, have undergone several weeks of evaluation and observation before being placed in the general population, and have in several ways become accustomed, if not adjusted, to confinement. Jails, on the other hand, receive people who may never have been in such a situation, persons who are under the influence of alcohol or drugs at the time of their arrival, and people who range from the most violent in society to those who would never resort to violence. The jail population presents jail officials with some unique situations requiring close attention to issues of safety and security.

Persons brought to jail by police officers or sheriff's deputies typically find their first stop to be an intake area in which jail staff complete the appropriate forms and conduct initial searches for contraband. The booking process is likely to include photos, fingerprinting, impounding of valuables, checks for outstanding warrants and criminal record, and an interview session to gather personal information. After jail officials have a better idea of who the new arrival is, and of his

Help Wanted

Job Title: Classification Clerk

Position Description: The classification clerk performs a variety of duties that include checks of incoming and outgoing inmate files, preparing the domestic relations court list, calculating inmate good time credits, scheduling state prison transports, and maintaining weekend work release files. An especially important duty is completing the inmate assessments, which will assist in determining appropriate living placement of the inmate and serve as an initial check on the inmate's psychological stability.

Qualifications: Applicants must be high school graduates, but some college coursework is preferred. Successful applicants should be able to work easily with others and should be comfortable in an ethnically and racially diverse environment.

For examples of career opportunities in this field, check the careers section of Corrections.com at ***database.corrections.com/career/index.asp***, and visit specialized pages such as that for the Polk County (Florida) Sheriff's Department at ***www.polksheriff.org/jobs/descriptions/0805.html.***

or her criminal history, the inmate is often subjected to a strip search and a delousing shower. During the admission process, the inmate is given opportunities to contact friends, relatives, attorneys, or bondsmen. As admission continues, jail staff gather information to help determine things such as the inmate's security risk, suicide potential, and medical needs. Because jails must provide all security levels, the clothing issued to inmates during admission is color coded (e.g., maximum-security inmates may wear orange uniforms whereas minimum-security inmates may wear blue), so staff can quickly identify inmates who are in the wrong locations or who may present safety risks.

The process of classifying jail inmates is not as elaborate as that for new arrivals at prison (see Chapter 10), but some of the goals are the same. In both settings the staff members try to identify certain needs (e.g., medical, psychological, social, and educational) the inmates have and any risks (e.g., the potential for harming themselves, other inmates, or staff) the inmates might present. Because the jail is for short-term confinement, concern is more often with the risks than with the needs. That does not mean that jails fail to provide medical, psychological, social, or educational services because in fact they do. But because sentences to jail are usually for less than one year, with an average of six to seven months, it is difficult to develop short-term programs addressing what are often severe social-psychological and educational deficiencies.

One area that is not ignored by jail officials is suicide prevention. This falls under the risk identification area of classification because the jail officials are responsible for protecting inmates from both each other and from themselves. In 1983 suicide was the most frequent cause of death among jail inmates. By the early 1990s, deaths by suicide had fallen to second place behind illness and natural causes (excluding AIDS-related deaths). Table 8.5 shows that death rates among jail inmates fell by more than one-third from 1983 to 1993, with suicide rates reflecting an especially sharp decline. Explanations for that decline await an interested researcher, but other studies may lead to some hypotheses. For example, Winfree and Wooldredge (1991) found that suicides will most likely continue to occur among jail populations regardless of changes in jail clientele (male only, adult only), levels of crowding, or turnover rates. But because suicides are often a matter of opportunity, having fewer full-time staff relative to the size of the inmate population could result in an increase of suicides over time. When staff are present in sufficient numbers, for prolonged periods, and have been trained to recognize and respond to troubled inmates, suicide can be reduced. Jail suicide rates may have declined between 1983 and 1993 because staff presence and training lessened the opportunities for successful suicides.

In addition to labor-intensive ways to reduce jail suicides, there is reason to believe that physical changes can also have a positive impact. Although inmates have been very ingenious in finding ways to commit suicide (a Texas inmate rewired an electric hospital bed to make it the reclining equivalent of the state's electric chair), hanging is by far the most frequently used method (Stone, 1990). Using items such as shirts, strips of cloth, belts, shoelaces, and electrical cords, inmates have found a variety of places to attach their hanging instrument. Stone (1990) analyzed suicides in Texas jails and found typical "points of attachment" to be cell crossbars, vent and window grates, shower rods, and privacy partitions. Although it is hard to remove many of the hanging instruments such as shirts and cloth that can be torn into strips, it is less difficult to eliminate many of the points of attachment. Possibly, new jail construction played a role in reducing suicides from 1983 to 1993 by designing jails with solid walls and doors (taking away the crossbars) and by using fine mesh screens to replace grates.

The suggestions for why jail suicides may have declined since 1983 have highlighted two interesting points regarding jail management. The first deals with the

TABLE 8.5: Deaths per 100,000 Inmates in Local Jails, by Cause, 1983 and 1993

	NUMBER OF DEATHS PER 100,000 JAIL INMATES	
Cause	1983	1993
Total	232	149
Illness/natural cause (excluding AIDS)	88	67
Acquired immune deficiency syndrome	(data not available)	15
Suicide	129	54
Homicide	5	4
Other	9	9

Source: From Perkins, C. A., Stephan, J. J., & Beck, A. J. (1995). *Jails and jail inmates 1993–94* [NCJ 151651]. Washington, DC: Bureau of Justice Statistics.

importance of having staff available to watch inmates, and the second suggests that the way a jail is constructed can influence safety and security. These points are interesting because they have been the primary topics of attention for discussion of what is called the new generation jail.

New Generation Jails

American jails seem no longer willing or able to elude reform efforts. The high cost of maintaining the status quo is no longer acceptable to judges, jail administrators, or inmates. The most important result of the newest reform efforts is what are called **new generation jails.** The term has both theoretical and applied aspects because it assumes certain relationships exist between the inmates' behavior and their environment (the theoretical side), and explains how changes in jail architecture and in inmate supervision can have positive results in jail management. The growing importance of the new generation approach requires a closer look at its underlying philosophy and its practical consequences.

Prior to the mid-1970s, jails throughout the United States had much in common with their historical ancestors—in fact, some of them were old enough to have been those very ancestors. Charles et al. (1992) reported that of the 308 jail facilities they surveyed, 12 were over 100 years old and 86 were between 25 and 100 years old. Some of the sanitary and physical conditions had improved since the country's first jails, but their basic features had stayed very much the same. A jail reform movement was said to have occurred between 1973 and 1983, when 1,000 new jail facilities were built (Zupan, 1991). But the design of those facilities was basically the same as the jails built in the eighteenth century, and the end result was more of the same rather than the beginning of a new era. But that period did include the first examples of those jails to be identified as new generation. Beginning with the opening of the Contra Costa County (California) Jail in the 1970s—and continuing with new jails in Tucson, Arizona; Portland, Oregon; and Las Vegas, Nevada—the new generation design and philosophy began influencing jail construction and renovation across the country.

Zupan (1991) explains the popularity of new generation jails as resulting from their offer of having new ways to deal with old and persistent problems. Drawing primarily from Zupan's work, and that of a few other authors, this section will

Help Wanted

Job Title: Programs Counselor

Position Description: Programs counselors perform professional, supervisory, and administrative correctional counseling work in the jail facility. Specific responsibilities may include serving as correctional counselor for jail inmates, transporting inmates within the secure jail facility, informing inmates about programs available in the jail facility, and conducting or arranging for others to conduct therapeutic programs appropriate for inmate needs in areas such as substance abuse, education, and life skills.

Qualifications: Knowledge of and ability to carry out individual and group counseling with special emphasis on agency counseling. Knowledge of the referral process to take advantage of community services available to jail inmates. Master's degree in counseling or related field is preferred. Bachelor's degree in an appropriate field may be acceptable.

For examples of career opportunities in this field, check the job bank for the American Correctional Association at *www.corrections.com/aca/jobbank.html,* and visit state pages such as that at *www.wsja.addr.com/* for the Washington State Jail Association.

consider the underlying theory of new generation jails, the importance of architectural design to solving practical problems, and some recent evaluations of this new approach.

The Philosophy Underlying New Generation Jails. The new generation jails are designed and operated with a primary goal of reducing violent and destructive behavior by the inmates. Because such behavior has undesirable effects on staff and inmate safety and because it increases costs associated with facility maintenance, attempts to lessen the occurrence and severity of violence and destruction are most welcome. The new generation approach is based on the assumption that violent and destructive behavior is engaged in by inmates who are attempting to control and manipulate an environment that fails to provide for their critical human needs. Proponents of the new generation philosophy argue that the inmates' inclination and need to engage in illegitimate behavior can be greatly reduced through the use of appropriate architecture and the implementation of inmate management practices that provide for critical needs such as safety, privacy, personal space, and dignity (Zupan, 1991).

The two key ingredients to the new generation approach are architectural design and inmate supervision. The importance of architectural design may seem to be a strange thing to concentrate on, but it has been accepted as an integral part of jail and prison construction since the nineteenth century (see "The Importance of Architectural Design"). The aspect of inmate supervision may also elicit an "of course" response in persons who see it as being little more than a situation of a couple of guards watching a group of prisoners. But, like architectural design, inmate supervision is more complicated than it might first appear.

Zupan (1991) has described the design of U.S. jails and prisons over the last several hundred years as **linear facilities.** Linear refers to an architectural design using the rectangular shape, in which single- or multiple-occupancy cells are aligned along corridors. This design type has required an **intermittent surveillance** model of inmate supervision. Because the linear facility makes difficult—maybe even impossible—the continuous supervision of inmate activities by custodial staff, inmates are left unsupervised for long periods. Presumably, heavy metal doors, bars, and other security devices will prevent inmate escapes and assaults on staff. Similarly, indestructible furnishings and fixtures should prevent acts of vandalism by the inmates. But it has become increasingly clear that reliance on such devices and equipment can provide only limited control over inmate behavior.

> It cannot prevent assaults, rapes, or even homicides between unsupervised inmates assigned to multiple-occupancy cells or who are in isolated areas of the common dayroom or tank. It cannot prevent formation of inmate groups or gangs, inmate suicides, vandalism or property damage. In sum, the linear/intermittent surveillance architectural design cannot prevent the types of behavior and activity that make jail incarceration a brutal and violent experience for inmates, and, in fact, the structure of the facility actually contributes to institutional disorder by providing opportunities for inmates to engage in aberrant behavior without fear of detection. (Zupan, 1991, p. 5)

The new generation jails are an alternative to the linear design and intermittent surveillance model. For that reason, they present the most significant modification in prison architectural design, certainly since the telephone-pole pattern and possibly since the Auburn and Eastern State layouts. This is accomplished through the use of a podular architectural design and through direct supervision of inmates by custodial staff. These features lead some to use the term **podular direct** jails interchangeably with new generation jails. The result is a facility that looks very different from the traditional linear design and offers a unique form of interaction between inmates and correctional officers.

HISTORICAL PERSPECTIVES

The Importance of Architectural Design

The physical structure of jails and prisons has been recognized as an important feature since the Wellspring-era facilities laid the groundwork for imprisonment as punishment. As we saw in Chapter 3, the belief that solitary confinement was a desirable aspect for responding to wrongdoers resulted in the earliest facilities having individual cells, often lined along a corridor that guards could stroll as they checked on their wards. The biggest decision that planners of new prisons had to make during much of the nineteenth century was whether the cells would be built back to back—following the inside design of Auburn—or on the outside of the cell block, as was done at Eastern State Penitentiary. The decision could not be made lightly because the chosen design effectively determined which penal philosophy the prison would follow. Pennsylvania's separate-and-silent system had been shown to be most effective when prisoners could leave their cell for individual exercise in a personal yard behind their cell. Because an inside cell design did not provide for private exercise, the structure at Auburn included separation and silence at night but allowed the prisoners to congregate and work during the day. In other words, from the penitentiary's very beginning its architectural design influenced the type of prison management, inmate supervision, and penal philosophy that the officials would follow.

As noted in Chapter 4, the next significant change in prison design did not occur in the United States until the twentieth century, when the U.S. Penitentiary at Lewisburg opened in 1932. As McKelvey (1977) described the new telephone-pole design, a long corridor extended from the administrative building past dining rooms, shops, and other essential facilities. The corridor also bisected the cell blocks or housing units so that on one side of the main "pole" were two medium-security cell blocks holding outside cells, and one cell block with maximum-security inside cells. On the other side of the pole were three dormitory blocks providing housing for minimum-security and honor inmates. With this design, prison officials were able to handle a variety of security types while maintaining centralized control.

Learn more about Eastern State Penitentiary at ***www.easternstate.com/*** where you can even take a virtual tour of the old prison. Find the history page at the site, and identify the architect who designed Eastern State Penitentiary and then go to the Philadelphia Architects Page at ***www.ushistory.org/architects.html*** and read more about him.

Prior to the late 1970s, most jails and prisons were built in a linear design. In this design, single or multioccupancy cells are aligned along corridors.

Most jails and prisons built since the 1980s have used a podular design. This design places inmates in a small housing unit (a pod or module) containing about sixteen to thirty rooms or cells.

Under the podular design, inmates are placed in a small housing unit containing about sixteen to thirty rooms or cells. These rooms are often on two levels, so that upon entering the housing unit (called a pod or module) one can look across an open area and see two rows of eight to fifteen cells each. One or two inmates are assigned to each cell, so the maximum number of inmates in a particular pod might range from thirty-two to sixty. There may be four or five such pods grouped together in a manner that allows two adjacent pods to share a common wall, but does not allow the inmates of different pods to see or interact with each other. Separating inmates in this manner places them into smaller and more manageable groups than does the traditional cell block design. In addition, because the inmates will eat, play games, watch television, and make phone calls all in their pod, there is never a time that staff should have more than about sixty inmates together at one time. For recreation that cannot be conducted in the housing pod (such as basketball or volleyball games), residents of one pod at a time can be taken to a nearby recreation pod where their number remains at a manageable level. Because the number of inmates always remains at a manageable level, the safety of both staff and inmates is greater than in facilities where hundreds and even thousands of inmates can gather together on the "big yard" for recreation or in the mess hall for meals.

The Importance of Inmate Supervision. In addition to a unique architectural design, new generation jails make use of a different type of inmate supervision. Because the inmates are gathered in relatively small pods, custodial staff can be assigned to a particular pod for an entire shift. Positioned, for example, in the open area of the pod, correctional officers have direct supervision over and interaction with the sixteen to sixty inmates in that pod. This **direct supervision** style of inmate surveillance provides for continuous rather than intermittent supervision. That supervision in turn lessens the opportunities for prohibited inmate behavior and activities.

With the elimination of the old physical barriers, such as bars and guards in isolated observation areas, the inmates and officers can now intermingle in relative freedom. In this way, control lies in the hands of institutional staff rather than with the inmates—as it often does when officials rely too much on things (bars, indestructible furniture, etc.) rather than people (correctional staff) to control inmate behavior.

It is apparent that the success of the new generation philosophy depends on the skills of correctional officers assigned to the pods. Ideally, these officers will receive extensive training in interpersonal communication and social interaction. They must also be familiar with principles of crisis and conflict management, problem solving, and other aspects of human relations (Zupan, 1991).[1] Unfortunately, staff hiring, assignment, and training have not also kept pace with developments in facility management philosophy. Schmalleger (1995) notes that some of the podular direct jails are staffed by old-style managers, and that staff assigned to direct supervision are not always prepared for the new skills needed to make direct supervision successful. In addition to problems associated with staffing, the new generation jails have also been criticized for their ability to meet the needs of female inmates as well as they do the male inmates. In the next section both those issues are addressed as well as noting that the overall evaluation of podular direct jails has been positive.

Evaluations of the New Generation Approach. Research has generally shown that new generation jails provide facilities that are cost-efficient, job enriching for the staff, safer for both staff and inmates, and more humane than are traditional facilities (Pellicane, 1991; Stohr, Self, & Lovrich, 1992; Zupan, 1991). In addition, studies have found fewer assaults (both inmate to inmate and inmate to staff) in podular direct jails and a reduction in inmate destruction and vandalism to jail property. Both staff and inmates—or at least male inmates—give positive evaluations to the results of the new generation philosophy. But despite these positive evaluations, in a few areas researchers have expressed concern about the use and future of podular direct jails. This can be seen in studies on the impact of jail crowding and on the application of the new generation philosophy to women inmates.

A central premise of the new generation philosophy is the importance of having inmates grouped in numbers that allow for direct supervision. Although many podular direct jails were built with pods designed for one person per room, increased admissions, more sentences to jail, and the need to hold convicted inmates until there is room for them in state prisons have all conspired to increase the number of inmates housed in the pods. Double bunking is rather standard in many facilities, and in some inmates sleep on cots in the dayrooms. As the number of inmates in each pod exceed the original capacity, the benefits of direct supervision are reduced. In addition, staff satisfaction, which studies such as those by Zupan (1991) found to be high, can suffer as correctional officers become frustrated in their efforts to use direct supervision skills in a setting where a high inmate population make them less effective.

The importance of having correctional officers with appropriate skills was highlighted in research by Stohr et al. (1992), who report that in-service training in interpersonal communication and in problem solving were the two most highly valued types of training received by employees of new generation jails. But, as important as training is to the officers, Stohr et al. found that crowded jail conditions can override employee satisfaction and lead to high rates of turnover. High levels of employee turnover present a problem for any agency, but it is especially problematic when the agency has invested significant time and expense to train the employees and to provide them opportunities to acquire and develop specialized skills. If the new generation philosophy is to maintain its popularity and effectiveness, officials will have

[1]Zupan, L. L. (1991). *Jails: Reform and the new generation philosophy.* Cincinnati, OH: Anderson. Reprinted with permission of the Anderson Publishing Company.

to find ways to counter the negative effect that pod crowding has on staff satisfaction and the use of direct supervision.

Another area that requires caution as officials make increased use of podular direct jails is the possibility that the new generation philosophy has different effects on male and female inmates. Jackson and Stearns (1995) conducted the first research specifically looking at gender differences and podular direct jails. They noted that although it makes sense that the more humane, peaceful, and safer environment provided in new generation jails has similar benefits to both men and women, there were no studies to confirm that belief. To their surprise, female inmates at a podular direct facility in California preferred the old, traditional jail over the new generation version in several important areas.

Using a version of simple pretest–posttest research design, Jackson and Stearns (1995) surveyed male and female inmates who were transferred from a traditional jail to a new podular direct facility. Both men and women inmates had positive evaluations for the way the new jail offered increased privacy and safety, but there were significant gender differences in other areas. For example, the women held more positive attitudes toward the old jail than the new in the areas of social stimulation, emotional feedback, and activity. They also gave lower evaluations to the correctional officers at the podular direct facility than they had at the old jail. Males, on the other hand, generally had more positive evaluations on all areas after their transfer to the new jail.

Jackson and Stearns suggest that the less positive evaluation that women gave the podular direct jail may be a result of the new generation philosophy itself. That philosophy tries to lessen the development and intensity of interpersonal networks or peer groups that can develop in an institution. Because such groups can encourage inmate control of a facility, the new generation philosophy uses direct supervision to interfere with the development of these relationships among inmates. The result is a leveling of inmate hierarchies of power and the lessening of domination by particular individuals or groups. Males in general benefit from, and do

Podular design jails separate inmates into smaller and more manageable groups than is possible in the traditional cell block design. Because the inmates watch television, make phone calls, and participate in treatment activities all in their pod, the number of inmates always remains at a manageable level, and the safety of both staff and inmates is more easily achieved.

not resent, this control by jail officials. The result may not be the same for women, however. As seen in Chapter 11, studies of females in confinement find that women tend to develop close, cooperative, family-like relationships with a small number of other inmates. The resulting social organization, compared to that of men's institutions, is less violent, less likely to involve gang relations, and less likely to result in racial divisions. The problem is that podular direct supervision assumes all versions of inmate social organization are bad. But that may be true only of the social organization developed in men's facilities. If inmate associations in women's jails and prisons are nonviolent and mutually supportive, they may not need to be discouraged in attempts to increase staff and inmate safety.

The women surveyed by Jackson and Stearns evaluated the correctional officers at the podular direct jail at a significantly lower level than the officers at the old jail. Because the podular direct officers were successful at penetrating or thwarting the anticipated or desired relationships among inmates, the women were denied their preferred type of social organization. Because that type of organization is not seen as presenting the same type of safety and security concerns as does the social organization in men's facilities, Jackson and Stearns wonder if the new generation jail is trying to fix something that isn't broken. Their research encourages us to ask if a new approach will have the same impact on both male and female inmates.

Although jails have been the classic example of short-term confinement, some comparatively new sanctions have also come to serve that purpose. Boot camp programs and halfway houses have received widespread attention as ways to incapacitate offenders without relying on the traditional jails or prisons. We will look at each of the sanctions as we continue our consideration of short-term confinement.

SHOCK INCARCERATION AND BOOT CAMPS

> "Rise and shine, skinheads!"
>
> Hours before the hot sun claws across the Southern sky, the sorry young men hit the barracks floor. It is 4:30 A.M. Breakfast is hours away. Their day will not end until lights go out at 10 P.M.—if they are lucky. If not, spot inspections will shatter the sleep of the utterly drained.
>
> Waking hours are broken mainly into half-hour intervals. They are miserable half-hours—calisthenics and marching drills and more calisthenics and more marching drills, cleanups and inspections and more cleanups and inspections for this collection of head-shaven misfits in combat fatigues.
>
> Their days are a series of rewards and punishments. Their reward is the absence of punishment, the absence of mental and physical harassment. The punishment comes in the form of withering, in-your-face verbal abuse and dirt-in-your-face pushups—pushups, always and forever. Both can leave the hardest hard guys in collapse on the ground and, according to one witness, "cryin' like babies for their mommas."[2] (Reinhard, 1988, p. 1)

Sound like a day in the life of a new Marine recruit? Same principle—different setting. The description is a reporter's view of life at Louisiana's "boot camp" for young felony offenders. Officially, Louisiana calls it the Intensive Motivational Program of Alternative Correctional Treatment (IMPACT). In other places similar programs are officially the Disciplinary Rehabilitation Unit (DRU), Regimented Inmate Discipline (RID), or other titles lending themselves to convenient acronyms. But the terminology popularized by the media in the 1980s seems to

[2]Reprinted with the permission of *The Oregonian*.

A boot camp program uses military-style discipline, hard work, and tough physical conditioning to encourage offenders to maintain a crime-free lifestyle after their release.

have been accepted by default—*boot camp corrections.* Some purists may use *shock incarceration* as the general term incorporating all these programs, but increasingly the public, politicians, academics, and corrections personnel are following the media's lead and referring to them as boot camps. For our purposes the following distinction is made:

- **Shock incarceration** refers to a philosophy that a military regimen including hard work and physical conditioning helps build desirable character traits in offenders.
- **Boot camp corrections** refers to a program that uses military-style discipline and activities, in combination with more traditional corrections programs, to achieve specific goals.

Both the philosophy and program are important topics for discussion, and each will receive attention as issues related to this version of short-term incarceration are considered. Specifically, this section will look at the history and spread of boot camps throughout the country, how offenders are chosen for participation in boot camps, how the programs are generally structured, and some problems or criticisms associated with shock incarceration.

An important topic that is not covered here concerns how successful boot camps are in reaching their goals. The attention given to shock incarceration since the early 1980s has produced a considerable amount of research that evaluates how well boot camp programs have achieved their goals. The last chapter of this book takes a close look at several corrections programs in an attempt to answer the question, "What works?" Because of the interest they have generated, the results of several boot camp program reviews are included in Chapter 15. Accordingly, boot camp goals are mentioned in this chapter only in general terms and without evaluation.

The History and Current Status of Boot Camps

Throughout the evolution of boot camp programs, the philosophy of shock incarceration has remained the same. It is sometimes confused with the term **shock probation,** which was in use before shock incarceration came on the scene, but there are important differences. Under shock probation an offender is placed in jail or prison for a relatively short time, then released to the community under probation status. Presumably, the experience of confinement will "shock" the offender into a crime-free lifestyle. Because humans show a remarkable ability to adjust to a variety of settings and physical conditions, it is important to release the offender before she or he adapts to prison life.

Shock incarceration is similar to shock probation because it is based on the idea of using a relatively short period of incarceration. But the "shock" in "incarceration" is more than simply a brief stay in jail or prison followed by release to the community. Instead, boot camp participants are kept separate from the regular inmate population and must participate in highly structured activities that are not available to other inmates. After experiencing the shock of intense drills, ceremony, physical conditioning, and hard work, the offender is placed in the community with—presumably—a new attitude toward self and others. Because young, first offenders are likely to be the most impressionable among prison arrivals, shock incarceration is often geared toward that population.

The first boot camp programs were developed in Georgia and Oklahoma in 1983, although the idea of military-style imprisonment dates at least to the late nineteenth century and the Elmira Reformatory. The idea of felons being placed in a highly structured military-style environment quickly caught the media's attention, and word of the programs traveled around the country. Legislators looking for alternatives to imprisonment that still had the appearance of punishment were intrigued with this new concept for corrections. They were not even disheartened when they heard that in exchange for placement in the military regimen, the offenders were given the opportunity to have their length of imprisonment reduced. The "carrot" of reduced punishment seemed worth the "sticks" of strict discipline, physical training, and hard work.

Florida, Louisiana, Mississippi, New York, and South Carolina soon followed the lead of Georgia and Oklahoma. Boot camp programs have been established in over thirty states and in the Federal Bureau of Prisons. The programs continue to attract media attention and have been the subject of considerable research and close scrutiny by legislators. Legislators in some states (e.g., Arizona, California, and New Hampshire) have discontinued boot camp programs—generally for financial reasons but also with concern that the programs are not reducing recidivism (Allen, 1997).

Boot Camp Selection and Discharge

Inmates are assigned to boot camp programs either by direct sentence from a judge or through selection by corrections officials. In their review of programs, MacKenzie and Souryal (1994) found the entry decision was by direct sentence in about half the programs. In the remaining programs, the judge recommends placement and the Department of Corrections (DOC) must approve, or the DOC selects offenders and the judge approves—and some jurisdictions use a combination of these methods. Also, most programs require the offender to agree—that is, volunteer—to be placed in a boot camp. This is especially true in jurisdictions in which entry is by DOC selection; but even where assignment is by direct sentence, the judge might first have to get the offender's consent.

The voluntary aspect of shock incarceration usually extends to departure from the boot camp program as well. Of course, the goal is to graduate all those who start the program. More realistically, there will be those who decide on their own that they cannot make it—and those for whom others make that same decision. The former case, voluntary dropouts, are allowed in over half the programs. Those dropouts are typically transferred to a regular prison to complete their sentence. When others decide that offenders are not appropriate for the boot camp program, they can be removed or dismissed from the program and sent to another facility. Completion rates vary quite a bit across the country. In their concentrated study of eight programs, MacKenzie and Souryal (1994) reported graduation rates ranging from about 49 percent in Florida to around 90 percent in Georgia, Oklahoma, and Texas.

So what happens to those who complete a boot camp program? If most programs rely on volunteers to keep the programs populated, there must be some potential reward for the participant. Why would people willingly subject themselves to weeks of verbal harassment, strict discipline, hard work, and hours of calisthenics? Volunteers to the military are hoping for things such as valuable education and training, or are starting a career. Volunteers for shock incarceration are hoping for early release from a prison sentence. Less cynically but not necessarily more accurately, boot camp corrections volunteers may hope the ordeal will give them experiences and attitudes to help them straighten out their lives.

Although the carrot enticing volunteers is early release from prison, that prize is not necessarily automatic. In some jurisdictions, boot camp graduates are automatically released on probation, in others release is to parole, and in still others release is to a residential community facility that serves as a transition to the community. But in some jurisdictions, the decision about what happens to boot camp graduates is made by a judge after the offender has undergone shock incarceration. In Colorado, for example, boot camp graduates are automatically given an opportunity for sentence reconsideration. This means the offenders go back before a judge who, taking the boot camp experience into consideration, can choose any one of these remedies:

- Place the offender on probation.
- Recommend the offender to community corrections.
- Modify the length of the sentence but keep the offender in a prison setting.
- Refuse any reconsideration of the original sentence.

If the judge refuses to reconsider the sentence, the offender completes the remainder of the original sentence under the authority of the DOC.

The Structure of Boot Camps

The philosophy behind shock incarceration assumes, in part, that the unpleasantness of the boot camp experience will make inmates want to avoid serving further time in prison. Presumably, a brief period of incarceration under harsh physical conditions and strenuous manual labor will shock the younger and less serious criminally oriented offender out of a future life of crime. In addition, the boot camp experience may enhance the offender's ability to live a law-abiding life as a result of the self-control, self-esteem, or educational experience gained from successful program completion. But most would agree that boot camps are not for everyone. Before considering the operation of boot camps, it is important to comment on the criteria for program participation.

Program Eligibility. Boot camps have been designed primarily for young, male offenders convicted of nonviolent offenses. In their review of state boot camps, MacKenzie and Souryal (1994) found that 62 percent of the programs would take only persons convicted of nonviolent crimes, whereas the remainder accepted those with either nonviolent or violent convictions. Other eligibility criteria often include age minimums (typically sixteen to eighteen), age maximums (most often twenty-three to twenty-five), and restrictions linked to prior criminal history. For example, the convicting offense must be the first felony offense or the first sentence to state prison.

Both males and females are allowed to participate in boot camp programs in about half of the states surveyed by MacKenzie and Souryal (1994). But even where females could participate, the number of beds available to them was limited. MacKenzie (1993) also reported some coed programs, in which males and females sleep in separate quarters but are integrated for most other activities. In other jurisdictions, female offenders attend completely separate programs.

Program Characteristics. The length of boot camp programs is usually within the range of 90 to 180 days (e.g., see "A New York Boot Camp"). During that period, the activities occupying the offenders' time will always include physical conditioning and hard work, but increasingly they also include education and rehabilitation efforts. The traditional boot camp program provides a highly regimented agenda involving strict discipline, drill and ceremony, and physical training. While marching, shining shoes, and doing push-ups, the inmates are learning discipline, self-esteem, determination, punctuality, cooperation, and attention to detail. They are, in other words, learning they can control their bodies, their tongues, and their actions.

The work assignments at boot camp usually involve hard physical labor (such as clearing land, digging ditches, or draining swamps) in addition to facility maintenance and housekeeping. At some boot camps the inmates are also involved in projects benefiting the community that might include cutting firewood for elderly citizens or separating recyclables.

Although discipline and physical activity are important features of all the programs, many are now adding significant numbers of hours spent in more treatment-oriented activities. Essentially all programs now incorporate some drug education or a combination of drug education and treatment. But the amount of time devoted varies from as few as fifteen days to programs with everyday attention to drug education or treatment (MacKenzie & Souryal, 1994).

Help Wanted

Job Title: Boot Camp Drill Instructor

Position Description: The drill instructor is responsible for maintaining a paramilitary environment designed to enhance the physical and psychological well-being of criminal offenders while providing continual guidance regarding personal habits, hygiene, discipline, daily living skills, and acceptable behavior. Instructors will conduct scheduled and random military inspections of offenders and their living quarters and participate and lead in physical fitness programs.

Qualifications: Applicants must undergo a background check, pass a drug screening test, maintain military grooming standards, and be physically fit. Military experience is desirable but not necessary.

For examples of career opportunities in this field, check the careers section of Corrections.com at ***database.corrections.com/career/index.asp***, and read the job description at the Collier County (Florida) Sheriff's Office at ***www.naplesnet.com/sheriff/job6.htm.***

Boot Camp Problems

The problems associated with boot camp corrections are often related to topics of discrimination, abuse, net-widening, and aftercare. Because participation in boot camp programs requires a physically fit person, strict medical requirements typically restrict program eligibility to those capable of a high level of physical conditioning and work. The possibility of race discrimination has been suggested in the *African American Male Research* journal because of the disproportionate number of black males in juvenile boot camps ("Spread of Boot Camps," 1996). Sex discrimination is also receiving increased attention as seen in the feature "Women Offenders in Boot Camp" on page 297. But let us look at the issues of net-widening and aftercare.

Net-widening refers to the potential for a program designed as an alternative to incarceration to attract persons who would actually have received less supervision rather than those for whom the program was designed. As Burns and Vito (1995) put it, "A major purpose of the program would be defeated if judges were sentencing offenders to the boot camp program who were good candidates for either probation or a split sentence" (p. 64).

Reports of a net-widening effect are often linked to the procedure used to assign people to boot camp programs. When boot campers are chosen by a state's DOC, the selection is being made from among those already sentenced to prison.

Spotlight ON CONTEMPORARY ISSUES

A New York Boot Camp

To qualify for boot camp in New York, offenders must be under age thirty-five and have a sentence making them eligible for parole within three years of admission to the Department of Correctional Services (DOCS). In addition, they must not have committed a violent or sexual offense or been previously sentenced to an indeterminate sentence. As described by Clark, Aziz, and MacKenzie (1994), all offenders meeting these requirements are sent to an orientation and screening center, where DOCS staff interview the offenders and tell them about New York's boot camp program. Interested prisoners must volunteer for the program, then undergo mental and physical examinations to identify any health problems that would prohibit them from participating. During the evaluation period, offenders are introduced to some of the boot camp activities to better inform them about what they can expect.

New York's programs are all located in remote wooded areas that afford opportunities of hard outdoor labor. A new platoon, with about fifty to sixty offenders, enters one of the programs each month. They proceed through the 180-day program as a unit.

During the first two weeks, inmates learn the basics of physical training, drill and ceremony, and discipline. The focus in this orientation and evaluation stage is on strict discipline and attention to detail. Most volunteer dropouts occur during this period. Inmates have no free time, no visits to the commissary, and no time for watching television. In addition, inmates are allowed no packages from home, no magazines, no newspapers, and no radios.

Consistent with shock incarceration goals of physical training and hard work, the boot camp participants spend 26 percent of their time at physical training, drill, and ceremony; and 33 percent at hard labor on facility or community projects. Work projects include cutting firebreaks in the forest, maintaining public-use areas, and helping in community clean-up projects.

Offenders can be removed from the boot camp program for legal, medical, disciplinary, or adjustment problems. They may also drop out voluntarily. About 37 percent of the offenders entering New York's programs fail to complete the boot camp program and are sent to regular prisons, where they complete their original sentence.

The Office of Legislative Research for the Connecticut General Assembly prepared an informative report on prison boot camps. Read the report at ***www.cga.state.ct.us/olr/decemberreports/98-r-1470.htm,*** and summarize the report's review of boot camp recidivism rates.

In that situation there can be little criticism of net-widening because the prison sentence is imposed before a boot camp decision is made. In jurisdictions in which judges can sentence directly to boot camp, the possibility of net-widening is a more reasonable concern. Research on those states provides inconsistent findings. MacKenzie (1994), for example, reports that the Georgia program admitted a substantial number of offenders who would otherwise have been on probation. On the other hand, Burns and Vito (1995) found that during the first year of the Alabama boot camp program, there was no indication of net-widening. Upon comparing Alabama samples of persons on probation or in prison (under a split sentence) to those in the boot camp program, Burns and Vito determined that had the boot camp program not been available, those in boot camp would have been sent to prison. The Alabama boot camp, in other words, was serving as an alternative to prison and not as simply increased control for persons who would otherwise be on probation or have a split sentence.

The problem of transition to the community for boot camp graduates is one of growing concern and attention. During the boot camp experience and upon release to the community, program participants often show positive attitude change, increased self-respect and self-confidence, and are in very good physical condition. But it seems difficult for graduates to hold on to their improved attitudes, opinions about themselves, and good health after they leave the highly structured and supportive environment of the boot camp. Staff members at halfway houses that

ISSUES OF FAIRNESS

WOMEN OFFENDERS IN BOOT CAMP

Although outright discrimination, when states have programs only for males, occurs less often now than in the 1980s, there are still unresolved issues regarding shock incarceration and women. The major problem centers on issues of program modification for women. Whether the program is coed or is developed for women only, critics complain that boot camps need to be modified to meet the women's needs. Marcus-Mendoza, Klein-Saffran, and Lutze (1998) note that the very premise of boot camps (i.e., teaching discipline and responsibility so crime will not be recommitted) may not even be applicable to women because no research supports the position that female offenders are lacking in discipline and responsibility.

Whether the program is military or treatment oriented, men and women are too different to assume that one program will fit both sexes. Sharp (1995) and Gowdy (1996) review problems identified with both coed programs and the unmodified programs originally established for men. Much of the criticism focuses on the additional stress women might feel when put in an environment in which most of the participants and staff are men. Some research found that in coed boot camp programs the drill instructors are harsher, the stress is greater, activities are restricted, and sexual misconduct may occur (MacKenzie, Elis, Simpson, & Skroban, 1996). In addition, some practices that may be acceptable for men are questionable when applied to women. For example, in American society and most likely many others, forcing a woman to shave her head is a more humiliating experience than it is for a man. Some programs take this into consideration by having women boot campers simply crop their hair short.

But another military regimen issue has broader implications. Carol Shapiro, a former official with the New York City corrections department, argues that strict military programs are no place for women who have a history of abuse by men. "The last thing such an inmate needs is a male drill instructor screaming in her face" (quoted in Sharp, 1995). MacKenzie et al. (1996) reiterate this concern when they quote a woman who had recently decided to leave a boot camp as saying: "I was physically and mentally abused and just being here reminds me of it" (p. 240). Another inmate said: "For the two months I was here, I cried because it triggered all that stuff from my childhood that I just started remembering when I came here" (p. 240).

Despite these concerns, there are many men and women who believe the advantages of women in boot camps outweigh the disadvantages. Cheryl Clark, New York's director of shock incarceration, understands the potential for—and reality of—problems associated with boot camps for female offenders. However, Clark (1996) relates positive testimonials by women graduates of New York's shock incarceration program and suggests that "carefully designed boot camps for women have much to offer, physically, mentally, and spiritually" (p. 317). Even recognizing the potential problems presented by having male drill instructors yelling at women with histories of abuse, Clark says it is possible to be highly confrontive (an appropriate behavior in boot camp, she argues) without being abusive (an inappropriate behavior in boot camp or anywhere else).

Get MacKenzie et al.'s article on boot camps for women at ***www.uncg.edu/edu/ericcass/bootcamp/DOCS/bcamps14.htm***, and find the section on potential advantages of the camps for women. Do you agree with the authors regarding these advantages? Do you think the advantages outweigh the disadvantages?

receive boot camp graduates offer stories about the boot campers' solid posture deteriorating in proportion to their decreased use of "sir," "ma'am," and other indicators of ceremony and respect for authority. Pride in self and in their accomplishments and abilities also seemed to wither away as they experienced increased interaction (and teasing) from other halfway house residents who had not been through the boot camp. Castellano and Plant (1996) explain the importance of aftercare in shock incarceration programs and identify Maricopa (Arizona) County and New York as having two of the best examples.

New York's AfterShock program, which is operated by the Division of Parole, has the goal of continuing in the community the supervision intensity found in the boot camp setting. Along with close supervision, parolees receive opportunities and programs designed to improve their chances for successful reintegration (Castellano & Plant, 1996; Clark, Aziz, & MacKenzie, 1994). Parole officers (POs) supervising boot camp graduates have reduced caseloads (twenty-five graduates to one PO) and are able to have increased contacts with their clients. These parolees have priority access to community services (such as educational and vocational training), relapse prevention counseling, and are guaranteed a job on release.

Evaluation of graduates from New York's program suggests the boot camp experience itself, the AfterShock component, or some combination of both are achieving some positive results. In a study that compared the return-to-prison rates of program graduates with offenders who had not gone through or had started but not completed the boot camp experience, the graduates had the smallest return rate. Measured at intervals of twelve, twenty-four, and thirty-six months after release from prison, boot camp graduates consistently had the lowest return rate of the groups being compared (Clark et al., 1994).

As more jurisdictions realize the importance of supervising boot camp graduates in their return to the community setting, the AfterShock program is likely to be closely watched and evaluated. But other interesting modifications of traditional boot camps will also interest legislators, corrections officials, and the public. Some of these changes are dramatic enough that they suggest a new generation of boot camps is on the horizon.

New Generation Boot Camps

Some examples of modifications in the traditional boot camp program are actually expansions of the shock incarceration concept to other settings. For example, at the Valdosta Correctional Institution (Georgia), which is a close-custody prison, modified boot camps are used for inmates presenting special management problems. The intensive therapeutic program (ITP) operates for disruptive inmates, and the mental health program (MHP) is geared toward disruptive inmates who have been diagnosed as mentally ill (MacKenzie, 1993). Prisoners in ITP follow a regimen of strict discipline and drills, and must adhere to a code of ethics, maintain their personal living quarters, and follow high standards of personal hygiene. The program goal is to teach these disruptive inmates some more acceptable ways to deal with frustration, anger, and fear. Prisoners in Valdosta's MHP follow a similar regimen and adhere to comparable standards. The MHP was developed in consultation with mental health professionals to provide a treatment response for disruptive inmates who are seriously mentally ill.

An important aspect of the Valdosta ITP and even more so the MHP programs is their attention to treatment. Although most of the boot camps operating today have added treatment aspects to the traditional military regimen, the next generation of boot camps will most likely have an even greater treatment component. The review in Chapter 15 of research evaluating boot camps suggests that the military component by itself does not really do much in changing prisoners. Rather than relying only on shaved heads and push-ups to change criminal behavior, the research is showing that strong treatment elements inside prison and coordinated follow-up efforts in the community are critical. The programs now operating and those being developed that realize the importance of treatment and aftercare can be called **new generation boot camps** (Sharp, 1995).

Like their predecessors, new generation boot camps are high-impact programs relying on a regimented structure and strict discipline. Unlike the traditional boot camps, the newer ones incorporate programs to help inmates make the transition back to the community: education, counseling, substance abuse programs, life skills classes, and job training. Campbell (1996) and Sharp (1995) give an example of a newer generation boot camp in their summaries of the Work Ethic Camp (WEC) at McNeil Island, Washington.

McNeil Island's WEC follows a nonmilitary model that allows a relationship to develop between inmates and their supervisors that is more like one between employee and employer than between military recruit and drill instructor. With the emphasis on hard work, WEC inmates—ages eighteen to twenty-eight, and both men and women—spend eight-hour days pulling weeds, repairing fences, and cleaning and painting the ferries that travel from island to mainland. Inmates who successfully complete their first month at WEC can choose from other prison jobs, including work at the recycling yard or cleaning up in the meat-packing center. When they are not working, the prisoners are engaged in such activities as adult education classes, anger management, planning for life after prison, substance abuse counseling, and victim awareness.

When inmates at traditional boot camps break a rule, they will probably do push-ups or some other physical conditioning. Rule violation at the WEC may require extra physical work but more likely will involve psychological attempts at attitude change. Sharp (1995) gives the example of an inmate who utters a racial slur. Instead of push-ups, that inmate may have to write an essay on the cultural contributions of the ethnic group he or she demeaned. It is a different version of boot camps than was first presented to the public in the 1980s, but modifications may be necessary and welcome.

Residential Community Corrections Facilities

The use of a specific facility that allowed offenders to maintain community contact yet be closely supervised by authorities has a history in the common-law tradition dating from the eighteenth century. As early as 1788, the Philanthropic Society of London had organized several small cottages for children who were arrested for begging or stealing (Goldfarb & Singer, 1973). In 1914 British judges were authorized to require some young persons placed on probation to reside in a hostel as a condition of probation. Both the cottages and the hostels were considered halfway houses in the sense that they were a midpoint between liberty in the community and deprivation of liberty in a prison. Continued misbehavior by those at the cottages or hostels could result in the offender being moved from that halfway point all the way to the path's end, where full imprisonment awaited. These facilities were, therefore, known as halfway-in houses. In the United States, officials were at first less concerned about providing a facility that was an alternative for those heading to prison and more interested in facilities that would help offenders leaving prison in adjusting to their new freedom in the community. These halfway-out houses—less concisely but more politely called halfway-out-of-prison houses—were established as early as 1845, when Quakers opened New York's Isaac T. Hopper Home, and in 1864, when Bostonians opened an asylum to house women discharged from jails and houses of correction (Goldfarb & Singer, 1973). Facilities serving this halfway-out function saw considerable growth in the twentieth century and remain popular today. But their purpose and activity are more appropriately discussed in Chapter 14, which covers postinstitutional penalties.

The term *halfway house* (encompassing both the halfway-in and halfway-out functions) has fallen out of favor in recent years. As the variety and mission of community facilities expanded, the term *halfway* was seen as too restrictive. Not only did it imply that imprisonment was a situation the offenders awaited or already experienced, it also failed to identify the correctional function that newer versions were incorporating. The contemporary term, **residential community corrections** (RCC), avoids any implications that imprisonment is linked to the facility, its program, or the participants, and also highlights the corrections role emphasized at most of these facilities.

The concept of RCC includes those facilities that were, and occasionally still are, called halfway houses. These traditional halfway houses use a regular staff to provide residents with direct services such as counseling and drug abuse treatment, and to encourage a link with other services such as academic education and vocational training. The emphasis tends to be on rehabilitation. The newer residential facilities often place less emphasis on treatment and concentrate instead on enforcing rules and assuring compliance with court orders, such as paying restitution. As Table 8.6 shows, the differences between today's residential facilities and the traditional halfway house extend beyond the treatment versus security emphasis. But despite such differences, the overriding feature of "required living at a designated facility" is the common attribute that allows both types of facilities to be discussed as one type of intermediate sanction. The features described in Table 8.6 suggest that it is not possible to describe an average residential facility—there is simply too much variation in population, program offerings, and clientele.

Help Wanted

Job Title: Residential Case Manager

Position Description: The residential case manager works in a residential community corrections facility while performing a variety of case management and general client supervision duties. The case manager is responsible for assisting clients to accomplish goals (e.g., paying restitution, participating in treatment, and maintaining proper client behavior) during their placement. Specific duties can include gathering and verifying client intake information, assessing client needs and potentials and then identifying staff and community resources available to meet those needs, and providing clients with job seeking information and techniques.

Qualifications: In addition to having their bachelor's degree in social work, criminal justice, corrections, psychology, or counseling, applicants should have knowledge of investigative and interviewing techniques and of sociopsychological factors influencing human behavior. An ability to read and process large volumes of written material is a necessity, as are oral and written communication skills.

For information about career opportunities in this field, check the home page for the International Halfway House Association at ***www.iccaweb.org/ICCA_Info/icca_ info.html*** and at the employment opportunities page for the Minnesota Association of Community Corrections Act Counties at ***www.maccac.org/employme.htm.***

Evaluation of Residential Community Corrections

Latessa and Travis (1992) note the paucity of research on RCC programs and suggest this may be a result of (1) the few corrections-specific residential facilities in operation, (2) the fact that many of the facilities are privately operated and may not be willing or able to facilitate research, (3) the often great differences in the programs offered and clients served among the facilities, and (4) the problems of developing an adequate comparison group for follow-up studies. From the studies that have been completed, Latessa and Travis indicate there is at least support for the following observations:

- Residential community correctional groups display greater service needs than do regular probation or parole groups.
- Many of these needs, such as psychiatric and drug/alcohol abuse history, are related both to positive adjustment and to new criminal convictions.
- Offenders in residential facilities are more likely to receive a variety of treatment and counseling services than are offenders on traditional probation or parole.
- Offenders from residential facilities do no better and no worse than offenders on probation in the areas of subsequent convictions and in positive social adjustment.

These observations are more supportive of residential community corrections than they might appear. As Latessa and Travis point out, the offenders in community residential facilities had characteristics that would suggest they presented a higher risk of recidivism and lower levels of social adjustment than did offenders on probation. Because the eventual outcome was one of no difference between the groups, and because the residential group received more treatment interventions, it seems reasonable to claim that the halfway house group benefitted from the residential community corrections program. More conclusive support and any findings showing failure must wait for additional research on this expanding version of short-term confinement.

TABLE 8.6: Comparing Traditional Halfway Houses and Residential Community Corrections

Residents at both types must live at the facility but are generally allowed to leave without escort during specific hours for approved purposes.

TRADITIONAL HALFWAY HOUSES	RESIDENTIAL COMMUNITY CORRECTIONS
Provide a treatment-oriented atmosphere.	Provide a security-oriented atmosphere.
Enforcement of rules and regulations shows tolerance.	Enforcement of rules and regulations is rigid.
Clients are either being diverted from prison or are recently released from prison.	Clients range from persons as yet unconvicted to prison inmates under prerelease status or on parole.
Full treatment services are provided at the facility or through community programs.	Treatment services range from full-service programs to situations where no direct services are available to residents.
Facility size tends to be small with only ten to twenty residents.	Facilities may house less than ten residents but will also include those with resident populations in the hundreds.

Source: Adapted from information in Latessa, E. J., and Travis, L. F. "Residential Community Correctional Programs," in *Smart sentencing: The emergence of intermediate sanctions* (pp. 166–181) by J. M. Byrne, A. J. Lurigio, and J. Petersilia (Eds.), 1992, Newbury Park, CA: Sage.

SUMMARY

The traditional means use to incapacitate offenders (i.e., restrict their freedom of movement) has been to place them in secure facilities. However, technology now allows a level of incapacitation to occur outside the walls. Electronic monitoring is the prime example of this new technology, and its use in conjunction with the sanction of home confinement is especially popular. But jails continue to be the main method for short-term confinement of persons suspected of committing a crime and for persons sentenced to confinement for short periods of time. Also growing in popularity are the use of boot camps and residential community corrections facilities as alternate places for short-term confinement.

ELECTRONIC MONITORING

Important issues related to the use of electronic monitoring include:

- Who should be placed on EM?
- What is the potential for net-widening or placing certain offenders under tighter control than they would otherwise be placed?
- Does EM discriminate against certain offenders?
- What legal issues are raised by the use of EM?

HOME CONFINEMENT

Home confinement, which includes the use of curfew, home detention, and home incarceration, has both advantages (e.g., is cost-effective, flexible, humanitarian) and disadvantages (e.g., causes net-widening, has a bias toward middle- and upper-income offenders, and compromises public safety).

JAILS: THE DETENTION AND CONFINEMENT FUNCTIONS

- Jails have two primary purposes. The first—pretrial detention—is to detain people awaiting trial, transfer, or a hearing on probation or parole revocation. The other purpose—confinement—is to be a secure holding facility for persons convicted of a crime.
- A growing jail population since the 1980s has required jail managers to pay closer attention to problems presented by female offenders and to issues of safety and security.
- An important reform effort that helps address these and other issues is the movement toward new generation jails. These jails have a different physical structure and a different management philosophy than the traditional jails.

SHOCK INCARCERATION AND BOOT CAMPS

- Boot camps are programs using military-style discipline and activities to implement a philosophy of shock incarceration.
- The shock incarceration philosophy, in turn, suggests that a military regimen of hard work and physical conditioning will build desirable character traits in offenders.

RESIDENTIAL COMMUNITY CORRECTIONS FACILITIES

Residential community corrections facilities, the contemporary incarnation of halfway houses, share an interest in rehabilitation and reintegration with the old halfway houses, but they also emphasize an incapacitative and sentence-enforcing function.

KEY TERMS AND CONCEPTS

bail (p. 267)
bail bond (p. 267)
boot camp corrections (p. 292)
curfew (p. 264)
direct supervision (p. 288)
electronic monitoring (p. 257)
home confinement (p. 264)
home detention (p. 264)
home incarceration (p. 264)
intermittent surveillance (p. 286)
jails (p. 272)
linear facilities (p. 286)
net-widening (p. 260)
new generation boot camps (p. 298)
new generation jails (p. 285)
podular direct (p. 286)
pretrial release (p. 267)
preventive detention (p. 275)
residential community corrections (p. 300)
shock incarceration (p. 292)
shock probation (p. 293)

DISCUSSION QUESTIONS

1. For which offenders and under what type of sanctions would you favor the use of electronic monitoring?
2. Discuss the accuracy of Corbett and Marx's ideas about the "fallacy of novelty" and the "vanguard fallacy." Other than electronic monitoring and home confinement, what might be some examples of these fallacies in operation?
3. The U.S. Supreme Court has ruled in *Bell v. Wolfish* and in *Block v. Rutherford* that jails and prisons are to be treated the same for purposes of inmates' rights. What are some arguments for treating differently at least those persons

in jail as pretrial detainees? Do people who have not been found guilty of anything have more rights than those who have been found guilty?

4. Discuss the extent to which you believe homeless mentally ill people in your community are involved with the criminal justice process. What options should the police have when dealing with such people?
5. Should boot camp programs be modified for female offenders? Discuss some of the modifications that could be made, and explain why they would be appropriate changes.
6. Anecdotal information from some practitioners suggests that boot camp graduates perform very well in community corrections settings for the first several weeks or months after completing boot camp. After a while, however, their attitudes and behavior are less distinguishable from non–boot campers. What could be done to make the positive influence of boot camp last longer?

THE DUAL PRISONS SYSTEM

Problems in Counting Prisoners

Characteristics of State and Federal Prisoners

Characteristics of State and Federal Prisons

SOCIAL STRUCTURE AND INTERACTION IN PRISON

Social Structure and Interaction in Men's Prisons

Social Structure and Interaction in Women's Prisons

Explanations for Prison Subculture

SEX AND VIOLENCE IN PRISON

Sex in Prison

Personal Violence in Prisons

Riots: Collective Violence in Prisons

Managing Violence

IMPRISONMENT IN OTHER COUNTRIES

Imprisonment around the World

Race, Ethnicity, Nationality, and Imprisonment

SUMMARY

KEY TERMS AND CONCEPTS

DISCUSSION QUESTIONS

chapter 9

Long-Term Confinement

Prison can be compared with the microwave oven in my kitchen at home—it destroys you on the inside long before its effects are evident on the outside. . . . Prison is coldness. It is a den of indifference and spiritual emptiness. It is a place where you learn to hate. I find myself thrust into a city of strangers with whom I have nothing in common except my incarceration. Once in a while you find a friend in prison; sometimes, if you're inordinately lucky and spend a long time looking, you may find more than one. But no one in prison really cares about you. . . . Loneliness breeds and thrives in the belly of the monster known as prison. (Metzger, 2000, pp. 138–139)

That was the view of prison provided by inmate Diane Hamill Metzger, as she wrote from Baylor Women's

Correctional Institution in New Castle, Delaware. In that short passage are several important themes for understanding prisons in the United States. One is the point that prison does actually change a person. Few would deny that individuals leave prison as different people. And change is exactly what judges, legislators, and the public—at least those operating from a rehabilitation or specific deterrence philosophy—were hoping would occur. But that change is seldom for the better. Instead of releasing a rehabilitated or reformed prisoner who now wishes to join the ranks of the law-abiding, the adjustments an individual makes in order to survive a prison sentence too often result in a released ex-con who is psychologically damaged, socially challenged, and bitter. Even those who may have been described in that manner before entering prison are not likely to be released with less severe versions of those characteristics.

One explanation for the negative impact prison has on many inmates is the social structure of the prison itself. That structure is a key theme in this chapter, and understanding the structure will help us appreciate better the comments Diane Metzger makes about loneliness, strangers, and the occasional friend. But before considering social interaction in prison, it is necessary to clearly understand who the prisoners are and in what type of facilities they are kept.

The Dual Prisons System

The United States has a dual prisons system with structures at the federal and state levels. Just as the state and federal courts are structured somewhat alike in our dual court system, there is similarity in the organization, operation, and problems found in prisons at the federal and state level. We begin with a description of the prisoners confined in state and federal facilities and then look at the facilities themselves.

Problems in Counting Prisoners

It is not as easy as you might imagine to get information about the characteristics of state prison inmates. Some information is straightforward. For example, we can be fairly certain about data categorizing inmates as either male or female and information reporting the prisoners' age. But other information that might seem at first glance to be easily obtained and reported may actually be more complicated. The Bureau of Justice Statistics (BJS), a component of the Office of Justice Programs that in turn is linked to the Department of Justice, gathers and distributes most of the statistical information related to state and federal corrections. But our dual system means there are no requirements for the federal government and the various state governments to agree on definitions of terms.

Consider race and ethnicity, for example. When states report demographic information to the BJS, they might be asked to categorize their population as being (1) white, not of Hispanic origin; (2) black, not of Hispanic origin; (3) Hispanic origin (separated as either white or black and including persons of any Spanish culture or origin); (4) American Indian/Alaska Native; or (5) Asian/Pacific Islander. What the BJS gets back may be quite different. A few states report race as being "white" or "nonwhite." Other states have coded Asians/Pacific Islanders or American Indians/Alaska Natives as "unknown." *Hispanic origin,* a term that can apply to persons of any race, is coded in some states as a racial category rather than an ethnic one. Some states give Hispanic origin a more restricted application than the BJS intends by, for example, including among Hispanics only those of Mexican origin or only persons of Puerto Rican birth or parentage (Bureau of Justice Statistics, 1999; Perkins, 1994).

As if differences in terminology for prisoner characteristics do not present enough problems for the BJS, it must also try to account for variation in answers to one of the most basic questions—who is a prisoner? You might think that question could be answered by saying it is anyone who is involuntarily in a prison. That answer would distinguish those prisoners from, for example, jail inmates who either are awaiting trial or sentencing, or are serving a sentence on a misdemeanor charge. But six states (Alaska, Connecticut, Delaware, Hawaii, Rhode Island, and Vermont) have a combined prison and jail system—although Alaska has five jails operating local lockups. When asked to report their populations, these jurisdictions typically provide data that include both prison and jail populations. To lessen the possibility of including in its counts of prisoners those individuals who are not serving a sentence (e.g., they are in jail awaiting trial), BJS reports often refer to "sentenced prisoners," who are defined as prisoners with sentences of more than one year.

Despite problems of varying definitions for terms and characteristics, to say nothing of different reporting practices, the BJS does its best to provide accurate and informative statistics on all aspects of corrections in the United States. BJS publications typically include a methodology section that explains terms and definitions, reporting differences, and other technical information to help the reader interpret the statistical information. For present purposes, we need only understand that data presented here are the result of the best efforts by the BJS (the source for most of the tables and figures in this chapter) to provide accurate information from diverse sources.

Characteristics of State and Federal Prisoners

The combined state and federal prison population in the United States is primarily male (about 94 percent), non-Hispanic (about 82 percent), middle-aged (over one-third are in their thirties and nearly half are between ages thirty and forty-four), and of minority race (about 49 percent black and another 3 percent categorized as "other") (Beck & Mumola, 1999).

The racial composition of U.S. prisons has been particularly troublesome over the years and shows no signs of becoming less so. As explained in Chapter 1, when categories of persons are proportionately represented in a sample, their percentage is similar in both the general population and the sample. Disproportionality occurs when the sample has a greater or lesser percentage of that group than does the general population. In 1980 the percentage of black state and federal prisoners was 47 percent (Snell, 1995b). As Table 9.1 shows, that percentage increased to 49 percent by 1997. During the same time, the percentage of blacks in the general population increased from 12 percent to 13 percent. In other words, the percentage of blacks in the prison population has become increasingly disproportionate.

Although U.S. prisons remain primarily non-Hispanic, there has been a dramatic increase in the Hispanic prison population. The BJS reports that between 1980 and 1992, the Hispanic prison population nearly doubled from 8 percent to 14 percent at a time when Hispanics in the general population only increased from 7 percent to 10 percent (Bureau of Justice Statistics, 1995). Table 9.1 shows that the Hispanic prison population has now increased to 18 percent although Hispanics in the general population increased only to 11 percent.

Like race and ethnicity, the number of men and women in the prison population is disproportionate to percentages in the general population. To accurately reflect their general population percentage, we would expect females to make up about 50 percent of the prison population. In 1998 women accounted for 7 percent of all prisoners nationwide (see Table 9.1). That percentage is comparatively small, but it is important to note that the number of females has been increasing rather dramatically. Between 1990 and 1998, the number of female inmates rose more rapidly (up 108 percent) than did the number of males (up 74 percent). We look more closely at this trend in Chapter 10.

TABLE 9.1: Estimated Number of Adults in Prison by Sex, Race, and Ethnicity

	TOTAL	PERCENTAGE	PERCENTAGE INCREASE SINCE 1990	PRISONERS SENTENCED TO MORE THAN ONE YEAR
Sex (1998)				**Per 100,000 Residents**
Male	1,217,592	93.5	74	885
Female	84,427	6.5	108	57
Race (1997)				**Per 100,000 Residents of Each Group**
White	578,000	47.9	56	491 (males) / 32 (females)
Black	584,400	48.9	61	3,253 (males) / 192 (females)
Other	33,098	2.7	265	–
Ethnicity (1997)				**Per 100,000 Hispanic Residents**
Hispanic	213,100	17.8	64	698
Non-Hispanic	982,398	82.2	61	–
State and Federal Prison Population				**Per 100,000 Residents**
(1990)	739,980	100.0	–	297
(1997)	1,195,498	100.0	62	445
(1998)	1,302,019	100.0	76	461

Source: Adapted from Beck, A. J., & Mumola, C. J. (1999). *Prisoners in 1998* [NCJ 175687]. Washington, DC: Bureau of Justice Statistics.

To help see the degree of disproportionality in the prison population, Table 9.1 also provides the imprisonment rates by sex, race, and ethnicity. Especially noticeable is the rate for black males, which exceeds 3,000 per 100,000 black males in the general population. When the BJS breaks the imprisonment rate down by age category, the result is even more troublesome. In 1997 over 8,600 black males ages twenty-five to twenty-nine were incarcerated for every 100,000 black males in that age group in the general population (Beck & Mumola, 1999). A very high but still distant second were Hispanic males ages twenty-five to twenty-nine with a rate of over 2,700 per 100,000 Hispanic males of that age in the general population. The highest rate for white males was in the category of ages thirty to thirty-four with an imprisonment rate of 950 per similar category in the general population. You will recall that possible explanations for these disproportional rates were suggested in earlier chapters as including increased numbers of drug offenders receiving prison sentences (Chapters 1 and 8) and sentencing disparity (Chapter 5) that gives harsher sentences for offenses such as crack, cocaine, and weapons violations—with which minority offenders are more likely to be charged.

Federal Prisoners. Because of the way statistics are gathered and presented, it is difficult to make general statements about the characteristics of state prisoners without including federal prisoners. For that reason, the preceding section describes prisoners in both state and federal facilities. However, because federal prisoners comprise less than 10 percent of all U.S. prisoners, the characteristics described earlier most accurately reflect state prisoners.

Although we don't have national statistics describing only state prisoners, we do have specific information on federal inmates. Despite being confined in facilities spread across the country, federal prisoners are under a central authority and are, therefore, more easily characterized than are state prisoners. Information from the **Federal Bureau of Prisons** (described later) shows that the nationwide increase in imprisonment that began in the mid-1980s had just as significant an impact on the number of prisoners in federal facilities as it did on those in state prisons. The increase in federal prisoners resulted from reductions in good-time allowances, elimination of parole, required mandatory minimum sentences, and changes in the federal sentencing law. You can appreciate the impact of such developments by looking at Table 9.2, which shows changes in the federal prison census that amounted to a 125 percent increase during the 1990s.

The Bureau of Prisons' (BOP) inmate population is changing in composition as well as number. In 1999 30 percent of the bureau's population were not U.S. citizens—representing an increase of more than 600 percent since 1980 (Bureau of Prisons, 1990). Less dramatic but still notable is the increasing proportion of female offenders. In 1990 7.1 percent of the federal inmates were female. By 1999 females made up 7.5 percent of the BOP's population. But despite these changes, federal inmates remain primarily male (92.5 percent), white (58 percent), non-Hispanic (69 percent), and U.S. citizens (70 percent). Table 9.2 shows that drug offenses are the largest single category of crimes among the sentenced BOP offenders. Figure 9.1 expands that point by showing how the percentage of sentenced prisoners who are drug offenders has changed over time. The dramatic increase starting in the 1980s is a direct result of the war on drugs.

Female Federal Offenders. Although the number of female offenders housed in federal prisons has increased at a faster rate in the last decade than has the rate for male inmates, women still compose only 7.5 percent of the total federal prison population. That small percentage is the main reason given for why BOP facilities, policies, programs, and services have not been designed with the unique needs of female inmates in mind.

TABLE 9.2: Bureau of Prisons Statistics

	SEPTEMBER 1999	DECEMBER 1990
Total Population[1]	132,538	58,659
Number of Institutions	94	67
Inmates by Security Level		
Minimum	25.0%	23.3%
Low	34.0%	22.5%
Medium	21.6%	28.7%
High	12.1%	13.0%
Unclassified	7.3%	12.5%
Gender		
Male	92.5%	92.9%
Female	7.5%	7.1%
Race		
White	58.0%	64.9%
Black	38.8%	32.7%
Asian	1.6%	0.9%
Native American	1.6%	1.5%
Ethnicity		
Hispanic	31.3%	26.1%
Citizenship		
United States	70.0%	75.4%
Mexico	14.4%	5.9%
Colombia	3.3%	5.1%
Cuba	2.2%	5.2%
Other/unknown	10.1%	8.4%
Average Inmate Age	37	37
Type of Offense (Top 5 in 1999)		
Drug offenses	58.5%	54.2%
Firearms, explosives, arson	9.0%	5.8%
Robbery	8.0%	13.3%
Immigration	6.5%	0.8%
Property offenses	5.7%	7.4%

[1]The total population (i.e., sentenced and detained) includes all inmates in BOP custody—those in BOP facilities and those in contract facilities. All other numbers pertain to inmates in BOP facilities only.

Source: Adapted from Bureau of Prisons "Quick Facts" Web site at www.bop.gov/fact0598.html; Bureau of Prisons. (1990). *State of the bureau 1990.* Washington, DC: Federal Bureau of Prisons.

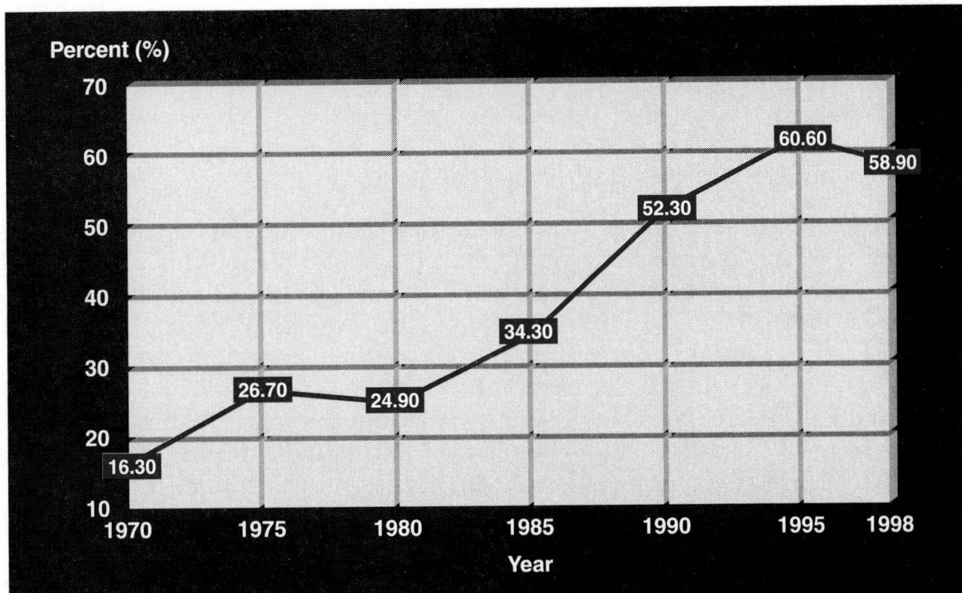

FIGURE 9.1

Percentage of Sentenced Prisoners Who Are Drug Offenders (1970–1998)

Source: Adapted from Bureau of Prisons. (1999, September 30). Federal Bureau of Prisons Quick Facts. www.bop.gov/fact0598.html, accessed November 5, 1999.

In addition to differences in numbers, men and women under BOP control differ on several other characteristics (Bureau of Prisons, 1998). The women offenders are more likely to be serving time for drug offenses (65 percent of the females compared with 59 percent of the males), tend to have committed less serious crimes, have less serious criminal histories, and have a lower security level than male offenders (1 percent of the females are high security compared with 14 percent of the males). Because they are more likely to be at a lower security level, more women (14 percent) than men (9 percent) are housed in community corrections facilities under contract with the BOP.

Among the special needs of women offenders is the issue of placement. The BOP recognizes that the placement of women offenders is especially problematic because research shows that inmates with strong family relationships are more likely to reintegrate successfully into society after release from prison (Bureau of Prisons, 1998, p. 3). To take advantage of the positive effects of strong family ties, inmates should be situated where those ties can be maintained and even strengthened—despite being in prison. At the state level, relatives often have to travel many miles and several hours to visit prisoners. At the federal level, because facilities are spread throughout the country, relatives may have to travel hundreds of miles, taking several days in a car or bus for a visit. Both male and female federal prisoners are confronted with these obstacles to family visits, but because female inmates are more likely to return to caring for their children, they (and their children) may face even greater difficulties when visits are hindered.

The small number of female inmates and the great expanse of territory the BOP must cover make it prohibitively expensive to establish facilities for women in every state. As a result the bureau has a small number of facilities for women offenders (about fourteen facilities at ten different locations) but provides comprehensive programs and services at those facilities. That, of course, does not respond to the placement issue, but there are some changes at the BOP that may allow more women offenders to be in closer proximity to relatives. Specifically, low-security and minimum-security facilities (therefore, more economical to construct and operate) have been established in Texas, Florida, and California. Because one criterion, in addition to their security level, considered when assigning women to these facilities is their release destination, the BOP is attempting to provide less travel distance for relatives of those women.

Characteristics of State and Federal Prisons

There are over 800 state correctional institutions across the country. Of that number, nearly 90 percent are designated for men, about 9 percent for women, and around 1 percent are coed. Wyoming, with the country's lowest population, operates just 2 institutions—one for men and one for women. More populous states require a greater number of institutions, but the link is not direct because institution size is more relevant than is number. For example, California, Texas, New York, and Florida are our most populous states, but they vary in number of institutions from 33 in California to 49 in Florida, and 51 in New York to 60 in Texas (American Correctional Association, 1999). But despite the differences in number of institutions, these four states have the largest prison populations (see Table 9.3) because their institutions tend to have greater capacity.

Another way to look at prison use in each state is to compare incarceration rates. As Table 9.3 shows, New York and Florida, despite having the third and fourth (among states) largest prison populations, are not among the top ten jurisdictions in incarceration rates. California and Texas, on the other hand, have large general populations, large prison populations, and high rates of incarcerating residents.

State Facilities. States with more than one prison for men and one for women are likely to designate the various institutions according to security levels. Table 9.4 provides a few examples of security classifications in California's prisons. Generally, prisons for men are classified as being minimum-, medium-, or maximum-security facilities. As the California examples show, some facilities incorporate

TABLE 9.3: Prison Populations and Incarceration Rates, 1998

TEN JURISDICTIONS WITH THE LARGEST PRISON POPULATIONS		TEN JURISDICTIONS WITH THE HIGHEST INCARCERATION RATES	
State	Number of Inmates	State	Prisoners per 100,000 Residents
California	161,904	Louisiana	736
Texas	144,510	Texas	724
Federal	123,041	Oklahoma	622
New York	72,638	Mississippi	574
Florida	67,224	South Carolina	550
Ohio	48,450	Nevada	542
Michigan	45,879	Alabama	519
Illinois	43,051	Arizona	507
Georgia	39,252	Georgia	502
Pennsylvania	36,377	California	483

Source: Adapted from Beck, A. J., & Mumola, C. J. (1999). *Prisoners in 1998* [NCJ 175687]. Washington, DC: Bureau of Justice Statistics.

TABLE 9.4: A Sample of California Prisons for Male and Female Adult Felons

FACILITY	OPENED	CAPACITY	1998 AVERAGE DAILY POPULATION	SECURITY LEVEL
California Institution for Men (Chino)	1941	3,078	6,311 males	Min
California Institution for Women (Corona)	1936 (in Tehachapi)	1,026	1,783 females	Max, Med, Min
California Rehabilitation Center (Norco)	1963	2,314	4,066 males 858 females	Med
California State Prison (San Quentin)	1852	3,281	5,883 males (including those in a reception center and at boot camp)	Max, Med, Min
Central California Women's Facility (Chowchilla)	1990	2,004	3,605 females (includes reception center and security housing unit)	Max, Med, Min
Folsom State Prison (Repressa)	1880	2,072	3,820 males	Med, Min

Source: Adapted from American Correctional Association. (1999). *Directory of juvenile and adult correctional departments, institutions, agencies and paroling authorities.* Laurel, MD: American Correctional Association. Adapted with the permission of the American Correctional Association, Laurel, Maryland.

several security levels. Because fewer women are in prison, most states have just one institution with all three security levels for confining women, although California has three institutions specifically for women.

Minimum-security prisons range from large drug rehabilitation centers to small farm, road, and forestry camps across the rural United States. Because inmates assigned to these facilities typically have the best security classification, the absence of walls, fences, guard towers, and obvious security measures is not unusual. Such facilities seem desirable for offenders showing little threat to themselves or others because the inmates have considerable personal freedom and are often given opportunities for work furloughs and educational release.

Since the 1930s, much of the construction in corrections has been alternatives to the maximum-security style. The first **medium-security prisons** were hard to distinguish from maximum-security ones, but more recent medium-security facilities reflect a campus design with attractive residence areas made up of single rooms or dormitories rather than cells. Newer medium-security prisons are typically smaller, require a less regimented routine by the inmate, and often have fences with razor wire and electronic sensors rather than walls.

Traditionally, **maximum-security prisons** are fortress-like structures with high stone walls surrounding a grouping of buildings that serve as cell blocks, mess halls, laundry rooms, gymnasiums, and so on. Guard towers are usually attached to the walls at the corners and other strategic places. The "Big House," as the maximum-security prison built in the nineteenth century is often called, was the prototype maximum-security prison. Designed for the fullest possible supervision, control, and surveillance of inmates, the Big Houses rank any consideration of individual or social needs as secondary to security requirements.

Today's version of maximum-security prisons often rely on a fence perimeter rather than high walls. The fence achieves security with the use of razor wire that is coiled at the top, and occasionally from ground to top, on an otherwise typical-looking chain-link fence about thirteen feet high. Security is increased by running a double fence, with several yards of ground in between the fences, along the facility perimeter. Whereas maximum-security prisons with high walls rely primarily on

Today's medium-security prisons are often built in a campus style with administration, education, housing, and other buildings spread across an attractive open space. A secured perimeter, typically razor wire, around the group of buildings allows inmates to walk unescorted from building to building.

human observation to monitor the perimeter, the newer prisons use electronic sensing devices and video surveillance to alert officials about breaches in the fence perimeter. The newest addition to perimeter security is a move in some states toward electric fences that can deliver a lethal jolt to prisoners attempting an escape (see "Fences That Kill" on page 316).

Although it seems a contradiction in terms, some states and the federal government have classified a few prisons as "supermaximum" security. These **super-**

Contemporary prison perimeters are secured with coils of razor wire on a typical chain-link fence. Security is increased by running a double fence, with several yards of ground in between the fences, along the facility perimeter. Electronic sensing devices and video surveillance may also be used to alert officials about breaches in the fence perimeter.

Traditionally, maximum-security prisons are fortress-like structures with high stone walls along which guard towers are strategically placed. Shown here is the inside of a maximum-security prison.

max prisons (or what some states call control units, secured housing units, and even maxi-maxis) are modeled after the U.S. Penitentiary at Marion, Illinois. That facility, which opened in 1963, went to permanent lockdown status in 1983 and became the highest-security prison in the United States. Since then many states have followed the federal lead and have modified existing prisons or built new ones to allow implementation of the control unit philosophy. Because Marion was not built as a lockdown facility, the federal government eventually constructed a prison specifically designed as a supermaximum security facility. That Administrative/Maximum Penitentiary, which is one of four facilities at the Federal Correctional Complex in Florence, Colorado, now holds many of the federal government's most dangerous or troublesome inmates (see "A Federal Correctional Complex" on page 317).

A supermax facility, which can be either a high-custody housing unit within a secure facility or an entire secure facility, isolates inmates from the general population and from each other. Inmates assigned to these units have typically committed grievous crimes, repetitive assaultive behavior in another prison, threatened or actual escape from a high-custody facility, or have incited or threatened to incite a disturbance in a correctional facility (Riveland, 1999, p. 6). Distinguishing features of the supermax or control unit philosophy are:

- Prisoners are kept in lockdown status (confined to a single cell) for twenty-two to twenty-three hours per day rather than the thirteen-hour average in typical maximum-security prisons.
- Isolation and control are achieved through securely designed cells in which the prisoner eats, sleeps, and participates in severely restricted activities that might include listening to the radio or completing correspondence courses.
- When allowed to leave the cell, the prisoner is fully shackled and flanked by guards.
- Visitors and visits are restricted in number and time.

Spotlight ON CONTEMPORARY ISSUES

Fences That Kill

In 1999 Colorado opened a new 2,445-bed prison in the northeastern part of the state. Although it happened to be the state's largest and newest prison, it was the facility's fence that earned the most attention—especially from human rights organizations. The 13-foot-high razor wire fence surrounding the prison at Sterling, Colorado, is designed to administer a 600-volt jolt if touched. On second contact, a fatal 6,000-volt jolt is delivered (Chen, 1999; Finley, 1999).

Lethal fences are still rare at U.S. prisons. California, which in 1993 installed electrified fences capable of killing fleeing inmates, had reported no escapes or fatalities through the fences by 1999. Missouri was also using lethal fences at a few prisons in 1999.

The justification for lethal fences is primarily as a cost-saving measure. California officials claim the fences saved nearly $34 million in their first five years of use. Colorado officials estimate the Sterling prison fences, which cost $1.7 million to construct, will save the state $1.2 million in other construction costs and $750,000 a year in reduced staffing expenses (Chen, 1999). The cost savings is a result of not needing to construct or staff traditional guard towers from which correctional officers have traditionally monitored and protected the perimeter.

Human rights organizations express concern about the use of electrified fences and other electroshock devices (e.g., stun guns and stun belts) because, they argue, such devices have the potential to be frequently and capriciously used. Prison officials respond that, at least in terms of lethal fences, they have always had the authority to use lethal force in keeping people from escaping custody. The old technology was a correctional officer with a shotgun in a tower, and the new technology is a lethal jolt of 6,000 volts.

Read about other monitoring and surveillance systems being used in prisons at ***www.nlectc.org/SpecialAnnouncements/jackson.html.*** The achievement of which four goals is considered to be the basic role of a perimeter security system? Also visit ***www.apbnews.com/cjsystem/behind_bars/1999/01/11/fence0111_01.html.*** How were high-tech and low-tech devices used at South Carolina's Lee Correction Facility to ensure safety?

Human rights organizations and other critics argue that the supermax prisons are primarily political responses to a perceived public desire for meaner and harsher treatment of prisoners. They argue that the use of sensory deprivation and restricted human contact simply dehumanizes people who will eventually be returned to society. Proponents respond in much the same way as did an official in charge of a new supermax facility in Texas who told reporters that "It's sad to say, but there are some people who deserve to be treated like animals" (quoted in American Civil Liberties Union, 1997).

In addition to the "tough on crime" explanation for the growth in supermax prisons, Riveland (1999) explains that supermax facilities show a prison management trend for troublesome inmates away from a dispersion approach and toward a concentration approach. The dispersion approach, which was popular in the past, had prison administrators spread their troublemakers around the system or in various units of the prison. Sometimes they might even be sent to other states or to the Federal Bureau of Prisons. The goal was to prevent troublemakers from working together and also enabled officials to break up cliques and gangs. Under a concentration approach, troublemakers are grouped together in special units (supermax or control units) in which their activities and movements are severely restricted and highly monitored. As a result, the argument goes, the general prison population is more easily and safely managed because the troublemakers have been removed.

Supermax prisons and the concentration approach present a variety of cost (they are very expensive to build and maintain), ethical (do they dehumanize?), and legal (some critics complain they are unconstitutional in whole or part) issues.

Spotlight ON CONTEMPORARY ISSUES

A Federal Correctional Complex

In 1991 the BOP began constructing the first **Federal Correctional Complex (FCC).** The complex, located in Florence, Colorado, uses a new design concept with several correctional facilities of different security levels at a single site. Benefits of the complex include the obvious financial savings such as lower construction and operating costs, but also have personnel advantages because staff members can have career mobility without making geographic moves.

The Federal Correctional Complex at Florence consists of a Federal Prison Camp (FPC), a Federal Correctional Institution (FCI), a U.S. Penitentiary/High Security (USP/HS), and a U.S. Penitentiary/Administrative Maximum (USP/ADX). The prison camp is a minimum-security facility with no perimeter fencing. The 512 inmates (listed capacity) are double-bunked in open dormitories. The FCI is a medium-security prison designed in a campus plan with razor wire protecting its perimeter. The 744 inmates (listed capacity) are housed in four separate units and move about the FCI campus as they go to the dining unit, gymnasium, visiting area, classrooms, chapel, work area, and so on.

Of the two U.S. penitentiaries at the complex, the high-security unit (USP/HS) has a listed capacity of 744. Seven guard towers surround the housing units, recreational areas, prison industry shops, and other necessary units. But it is the other penitentiary at FCC Florence that has raised the most controversy. The USP/ADX replaces the USP at Marion, Illinois, which in turn had replaced the island penitentiary of Alcatraz as the confinement facility for America's most dangerous prisoners. The USP/ADX differs from both those facilities, however, because it is the first specifically designed administrative maximum-security facility ever to be built by the BOP. Because the 484 inmates (listed capacity) represent different custody classifications, the facility must provide six levels of security. Availability to support services, such as visitation, recreation, and education, varies according to each inmate's security placement.

The inmates housed at USP/ADX are those people considered the greatest security risks in the federal prison system. Actually, we could even say they are the "greatest security risks in the country" because some state prison systems contract with the BOP to house prisoners that a state is unable to handle. Drug lords, international spies, cop killers, and prison gang leaders are among the kinds of prisoners found at USP/ADX.

Go to the Bureau of Prisons' facility information page at ***www.bop.gov/facilnot.html.*** Click on the region that includes your state, and identify the federal prison facilities closest to you. Do you have penitentiaries, prison camps, or correctional institutions? What are the security levels of the facilities nearest your hometown?

But despite such questions the twenty-first century begins with increasing numbers of these ultrasecure prisons.

In addition to institutions, states also place prisoners in community facilities (about 300 nationwide), work release centers (about 175), farms and work camps (about 170), and prerelease centers (about 60). Of these placement types, the community facilities are most likely to be coed (about one-third of the facilities) and the farms/work camps are least likely (less than 1 percent). The farms and work camps are still popular in the South, but western states also take advantage of such facilities and even add the use of ranches. Inmates at farms produce dairy products, grain, and vegetable crops, whereas those on ranches are involved in cattle raising and horse breeding. The most popular work camps are forestry camps, where inmates maintain state parks and fight forest fires, and road gangs that involve road construction and repair.

The variety of prisoners and prisons found within and among the state prison systems is repeated in part at the federal level. Although it is under a single administration, the federal prison system still has considerable diversity in its inmates and in the facilities in which they are confined.

In 1933 the Federal Bureau of Prisons took control of the Army disciplinary barracks on Alcatraz Island in San Francisco Bay. Until its closing in 1963, the U.S. Penitentiary at Alcatraz served as a maximum-security, minimum-privilege prison holding federal prisoners considered especially troublesome and dangerous.

Federal Prisons. The Federal Bureau of Prisons was established in 1930 as part of the Department of Justice. The new bureau had three goals: (1) ensure consistent, centralized administration of the federal prison system; (2) professionalize the prison service; and (3) provide more progressive and humane care for federal inmates (Bureau of Prisons, 1991). For seventy years the BOP has sought to achieve these goals and in doing so has often served as a model for state correctional systems. We will look at the history of the BOP and characterize its inmates and prisons.

During the United States' first 100 years, there were virtually no federal prison facilities. Most offenders convicted of violating federal laws were placed in state prisons and county jails. After the Civil War, the number of federal offenders began expanding, and the states and counties increasingly complained about the burden of housing federal criminals. In 1891 Congress responded to those complaints by authorizing the construction of three federal penitentiaries. Two were east of the Rocky Mountains—Atlanta, Georgia, and Leavenworth, Kansas, were finally decided upon—and one was west, eventually at McNeil Island, Washington. These penitentiaries, as well as a detention center, a youth facility, and a women's reformatory, operated as part of the federal prison system under the authority of the Justice Department.

Cahalan (1986) reports that the number of federal prisoners housed in federal institutions took a significant jump in the late 1920s. In 1910 there were 1,904 federal prisoners, in 1923 there were 4,664, and in 1930 there were 12,964. The nearly threefold increase in numbers from 1923 to 1930 is partly attributed to new laws that made more acts federal crimes. Especially important was the Volsted (or Prohibition) Act, passed in 1919; its enforcement alone caused crowding in the handful of federal prisons existing at the time.

In addition to crowding problems, federal prisons in the 1920s were plagued by inconsistent, haphazard administration (Bureau of Prisons, 1991). Much of the blame for that condition was due to the wardens, who were political appointees operating with no central direction as they applied their individual policies and procedures. Finally, in 1930, Congress decided to provide the needed centralization by establishing the BOP to manage and regulate all federal prisons. The new bureau quickly began to build or acquire new institutions in an attempt to relieve the crowding (see "Alcatraz: Then and Now"). That expansion continues today as the BOP builds new facilities, reconditions older ones, and expands into the area of community corrections.

By the mid-1990s, the BOP had grown to an organization of over 25,000 employees responsible for operating more than seventy-five institutions. From the bureau's central office in Washington, DC, the director and assistant directors oversee

HISTORICAL PERSPECTIVES

Alcatraz: Then and Now

The name Alcatraz, which comes from the Spanish word *Alcatraces,* is usually defined as meaning "pelican" or "strange bird." The island sits in San Francisco Bay and was used in the early 1850s as a U.S. Army fortress to protect the bay. Within only a few years some military prisoners were housed on the island, and in 1909 the original fortress was torn down and the basement level served as the foundation for a new military prison. From 1909 through 1911, the military prisoners on Alcatraz built the new prison that would become known as "The Rock."

Shortly after the newly created Federal Bureau of Prisons provided centralized administration of federal prisons and developed a classification scheme to identify inmate needs and risks. Young lawbreakers went to reformatories to learn a trade, other less serious offenders went to minimum-security conservation camps, the sick and mentally ill went to a new federal medical center, and the hardened criminals went to penitentiaries. Even in the penitentiaries, however, the Rehabilitation era meant those convicts had work assignments, learned skills, received academic education, and could earn early release under parole.

Not everyone was pleased that penitentiary inmates were being viewed with compassion and were considered treatable. To appease those concerns, and to help ensure the success of the bureau's new classification program, the BOP opened a maximum-security, minimum-privilege prison to deal with prisoners identified as troublesome, incorrigible, and generally public enemies. Alcatraz Island seemed to be an ideal site for this new prison, and in 1933 the BOP took control of the island and its military disciplinary barracks from the U.S. Army (Bureau of Prisons, n.d.; Gazis-Sax, 1997).

From 1933 until its closing in 1963, the U.S. Penitentiary at Alcatraz had an average population of 260 to 275—it never reached its capacity of 336. Prisoners were housed in single cells that were about five feet wide, ten feet long, and some seven feet high. Each cell had a folding bunk, a chair, a toilet, a shelf, and a washbasin. As described by Gazis-Sax (1997), each man was allowed items such as a drinking cup, nail clippers, soap, toilet paper, whisk broom, a sack of tobacco, and a corncob pipe. Allowable and common personal items included musical instruments, law books, art supplies, and playing cards.

By 1963 it was becoming apparent that Alcatraz was too expensive to continue operating. It was nearly three times more expensive to operate than any other federal prison—primarily for the same reason it made a great penitentiary, its physical isolation. Food, supplies, water, fuel, and nearly everything else had to be taken to Alcatraz by boat. The island prison was closed on March 21, 1963, and its occupants were distributed among the other federal penitentiaries.

In 1969 the island was claimed by a group of Native Americans who had hopes of creating a Native American cultural center and education complex on the island. The small group of leaders was unable to protect the island and its property from damage caused by thousands of people coming to the island, so in 1971 the U.S. Marshalls removed the remaining Native Americans from the island. In 1972 Congress created the Golden Gate National Recreation Area, and Alcatraz Island was included as part of that new National Park Service unit. It is open to the public and has become one of the most popular Park Service sites (Bureau of Prisons, n.d.).

Visit the site dedicated to Alcatraz during the Warden Johnston years (1933–1948) at ***www.alsirat.com/alcatraz/ns2/index.html.*** From the chronology link go to the year 1946. How did the number of psychopaths at Alcatraz compare with the number in other federal prisons? At the Bureau of Prisons' Alcatraz page ***(www.bop.gov/alcatraz.html)*** determine how many escape attempts were made from Alcatraz. Have all men who attempted escape been accounted for? Finally, read about Alcatraz today at ***www.nps.gov/alcatraz/index.html.***

Help Wanted

Job Title: Federal Bureau of Prisons Employee

Position Description: The Bureau of Prisons (BOP) employs people in a variety of positions ranging from academic/vocational instructors and correctional officers to chaplains and counselors. The nationwide location of BOP facilities means opportunities are available throughout the country.

Qualifications: Applicants should have the appropriate professional certification or college degree relevant to the job being sought.

For examples of career opportunities in this field, visit the BOP Web page for employment at *www.bop.gov/recruit.html.*

BOP activities around the nation. For management purposes, the country is divided into six geographic regions, each with a regional director. This regionalization, which began in 1973, provides greater coordination of the bureau's widely dispersed staff and of the diverse program areas.

The federal prison system currently consists of more than ninety institutions. The most well known of the federal facilities are the U.S. Penitentiaries (USP), but over half the facilities are Federal Correctional Institutions (FCI), and the next greatest number are Federal Prison Camps (FPC). In addition to these institutions, the BOP has contracts for operating Community Corrections Centers (CCC) around the country. These centers provide bed space for inmates who are nearing the end of their sentence, or who are serving short terms of confinement in the community. There are also Comprehensive Sanctions Centers (CSC) that provide programs designed to meet the needs of offenders on supervision who have reverted to substance abuse and for inmates who are returning to the community after long-term incarceration for serious crimes.

Since 1990, BOP officials have sought alternatives to the traditional facilities as a means to lessen prison crowding and to provide appropriate punishments for less serious offenses. Such alternatives as home confinement, electronic monitoring, day reporting systems, and community work programs have been especially popular. One innovative community procedure sends inmates to an urban work camp program during the last eighteen months of their sentence. Qualifying inmates are assigned jobs with a nearby federal agency (e.g., the Department of Defense). When they are within six months of their release date, these inmates are assigned to the prerelease component of the CCC.

In 1991 the BOP opened its first version of a boot camp facility. Located at the USP Lewisburg (Pennsylvania), this Intensive Confinement Center (ICC) houses minimum-security male offenders in a highly structured program of work, education, physical conditioning, and life skills development. An ICC for female offenders, which opened in 1992 in Bryan, Texas, provides a similarly structured program. The ICC programs teach inmates self-discipline and self-respect while preparing them for a successful postrelease adjustment in the community. Assignment to the ICC is voluntary and requires the sentencing judge's permission; but in exchange for successfully completing the six-month program, the inmates are allowed to finish their sentence in community-based facilities rather than the more secure institutions.

Now that you have an understanding of the characteristics of state and federal prisons and prisoners, it is time to return to the comments that began this chapter. You will recall that inmate Diane Metzger lamented the destructive and lonely aspects of prison. In the next sections we will examine this concept of a social structure that results from the interaction of prisoners—with each other and with their prisons.

Social Structure and Interaction in Prison

Prison might be seen as an unnatural environment because its physical structure restricts a person's freedom of movement and choice, and because its social/psychological aspects require unusual social interactions and uncommon individual adjustments. Remarkably and irritatingly, the deterrence and retribution proponents say—people somehow adjust to the strange environment that is prison. The remainder of this chapter looks at several aspects of the prison and its prisoners. We first consider the social structure to which the inmates must adapt. We then discuss some ways in which prisoners choose to respond to that structure, looking especially at sex in prison, instances of personal violence, and examples of prison riots. The chapter concludes with a discussion of imprisonment in other countries.

In 1980 John Irwin wrote that "most of our ideas about men's prisons are mistaken because they fix on a type of prison—the Big House—that has virtually disappeared during the last twenty-five years. . . . We must clear the air of false visions, distinguish the Big House as a type, and then move toward an analysis of succeeding types of prisons" (1980, p. 1). Despite Irwin's plea to break from the belief that "Big House equals prison," contemporary reports in the media, television, movies, and novels suggest that many Americans still think of the following description when they think of prison:

> The floor was concrete. So was the ceiling, some thirty feet above our heads. Two tiers of cells ran along the walls with solid steel doors painted battleship gray. In the middle of each door was a small barred window with a slot at the bottom to shove in food tins. I could see faces looking out at us from many of the windows. . . . The cell was about nine feet long and seven feet wide. Directly opposite the door was a heavily barred window which overlooked a yard. A toilet was mounted on the wall near the door, and just above it was a wash basin and single faucet. Two metal slabs jutted out from the wall, each fitted with what could pass for a mattress. A thin gray blanket and a sheet were folded at the foot of the top bunk. (Griswold, Misenheimer, Powers, & Tromanhauser, 1970, pp. 13, 15)

That description from an ex-con's first impressions of the Illinois State Penitentiary at Joliet could easily have been from the maximum-security prison, or Big House, in most any other state at the time. It was San Quentin in California, Sing Sing in New York, Jefferson City in Missouri, Cañon City in Colorado, and so on across the country. Designed for the fullest possible supervision, control, and surveillance of inmates, at these prisons any considerations of individual or social needs were secondary to security requirements.

In the 1970s there were prisons, especially those of the minimum- and medium-security type, that did not fit the Big House stereotype. By the 1980s even some maximum-security prisons had a very different look and feel about them. The following description is more accurate for prisons built within the last several decades, including those for maximum security:

> A sunlit room with carpeted floors, attractive, soft furniture covered with fabrics of muted grays combined with bright blues and reds. Men joke around ordinary card tables while playing checkers. In a corner, several watch TV while sitting on an upholstered couch. The uniformed officer strolls by and stops to chat. An inmate asks her to open the door to his room so he can use the toilet. The room has a bed, sink, desk with desk lamp, and window with a view of the city street below. (Werner, Frazier, & Farbstein, 1993, p. 1)

Making a distinction between the Big House prison and the contemporary prison is important because each prison type reflects a different social structure. Of course, different social structures will mean differences in behavior and interactions between and among prisoners and prison officials. As we look at aspects of the prison's social structure, it will be necessary to distinguish between social structures produced in the Big House and those produced in the contemporary prison (no one has come up with a colorful name for contemporary maximum-security prisons).

Before continuing, it is important to note that the following material applies most directly to maximum-security institutions—especially those for men. A primary reason for that is the basic sociological premise that social structures arise most clearly and develop most fully in social settings in which there are long-term relations among people. It is important, however, not to overstate that point. Prisons of all types and security levels present a social structure to which inmates and staff must adapt. And many of the comments made here about topics such as inmate unity versus fragmentation, sex in prison, and prison violence will apply to many or even most prisons. It is appropriate to keep in mind, however, that examples of prison social structure and inmate adjustment that most clearly follow the descriptions offered here will most often be found in maximum-security facilities because those places provide more opportunity for a particular structure to develop.

Social Structure and Interaction in Men's Prisons

In the 1930s Donald Clemmer (1958) studied changes that inmates undergo during their confinement. Borrowing from the term **socialization,** which refers to the process by which people in a society learn what is expected of them and what they can expect of others, Clemmer referred to the process by which the prisoners learn the norms of life in prison as being **prisonization.** The prison, Clemmer argued, contains an **inmate subculture** with norms, values, and beliefs that can be distinguished from those in general society. The prison society is a subculture in the sense that it exists within the dominant culture and, therefore, shares some aspects of that culture (e.g., prisoners often value democratic ideals and capitalism), yet it also has its own distinct norms, value system, and even language.

The inmate subculture affects the life of each prisoner because the prison operates as a total institution. Goffman (1961) developed that concept to refer to a place that completely encapsulates the lives of the people who work and live there. The prison was offered as an example of a **total institution** because every detail of the prisoners' lives was handled within the institution and according to institutional rules. The prisoners had little communication with the outside world, and even that limited contact was filtered through the prison staff.

The concepts of total institution, inmate subculture, and prisonization dominated the corrections literature until the 1970s and 1980s. Few researchers had reason to disagree with the accuracy of the concepts, at least not until it was becoming clear that they did not apply as well to the contemporary prison as they did to the Big House. As early as 1961, John Irwin was telling Donald Cressey that "Goffman's thesis was baloney" (Cressey, in Irwin, 1980, p. x), but it was not until the mid-1970s that more widespread challenges to both Clemmer and Goffman's explanations were questioned. James Jacobs (1976), for example, encouraged persons studying prison violence to begin looking outside the prison walls as they searched for explanations about what was happening inside the walls. Irwin (1980) was describing how much of what occurs in prison is a result of what had happened, and was happening, outside of prison. By the early 1990s, prisons were being reconceptualized as "not-so-total" institutions (Farrington, 1992).

Critics of Clemmer and Goffman's concepts do not necessarily believe the prisons were never total institutions or that prisoners do not undergo a prisonization process into an inmate subculture. Instead, the view increasingly is that those concepts described a prison type that is less frequently found today in the United States, although it may still be accurate for our older prisons and for prisons in other countries (see "Social Structure and Interaction in Poland"). Contemporary prisons, on the other hand, have quite a bit of contact with the outside world (making the concept of total institution less applicable) and seem to be made up of several independent groups (making the concept of an agreed-upon inmate subculture less applicable). One way to distinguish the two versions of prison social structure is to look at organization of the inmates themselves. In the

Cross-Cultural Corrections

Social Structure and Interaction in Poland

The inmate social structure in Polish prisons varies somewhat depending on factors such as the prison's security level, the region of Poland where the prison is located, and the period (prereform or postreform) being discussed. The description provided here will be incomplete, and even incorrect, for some Polish prisons, but the goal is to provide an overview rather than to conduct an in-depth analysis. With that caution in mind, we begin by describing an inmate subculture in men's prisons with three groups or classes. At the top of the hierarchy are the "grypsmen" (also called "git-men," "men," or "people"). Below them are the "clean mugs" ("festmen" or "suckers"). At the bottom are the "dirty mugs" ("cwels" or "damaged"). Attached to these inmate roles are specific expectations for one's own behavior and for the way prisoners behave toward each other. The result is an inmate social system called the "hidden life" or the "second life."

Assignment to an inmate role is accomplished shortly after a person's arrival at a prison. There is initially a democratic nature to the assignment process; almost any new prisoner wishing to do so can become a member of the grypsing group. The grypsmen establish and impose the rules of the hidden life. The code includes rules such as never taking advantage of another grypsman, observing strict personal hygiene, avoiding all contact with the guards, never snitching, and never helping the prison staff. To become a member of this group, a prisoner must know all the rules and the consequences of their violation. At the end of an informal educational process, the inmate must pass tests of intellectual ability, strength of character, resistance to pain, and shrewdness. Kamiński and Gibbons (1994) provide an example of a test called "prison car."

> A [new prisoner] is thrown under the bed while two prisoners press him to the wall with stools. A third prisoner commands "Get him in first gear—second—third," causing increasing pressure. The appropriate reaction [expected] from the screaming and helpless [neophyte] is, "Put it in neutral." (p. 111)

Inmates who fail to make the grypsing ranks become clean mugs. The clean mugs have a lower ranking in the inmate hierarchy, are not as cohesive as are the grypsmen, and are less antagonistic toward prison staff. What they have in common with the grypsmen is a belief that those below them in the hierarchy, the dirty mugs, are contaminated. The dirty mugs, typically representing only 1 or 2 percent of a prison's population, exist primarily for sexual exploitation. They are often grypsmen and clean mugs who have been evicted from their group. But the category also includes prisoners who have been raped, are mentally retarded, submissive, or dependent.

The hidden life, especially before political reform began in Poland during the late 1980s, determined both general and specific ways that a prisoner would serve his time in a Polish prison. Even after the political reforms and the subsequent prison reforms, the hidden life continues to direct social interactions among the prisoners (Płatek, 1990).

Professor Andrzej Adamski provides an interesting Web site on Poland's criminal justice system. Read about Poland's prisons at ***www.law.uni.torun.pl/publikacje/aadamski/raport/#VIII***. How many prisons and prisoners does Poland have? How does Adamski describe the condition of the buildings and cells?

Big House, structure was built around inmate leaders. In contemporary prisons, structure is often built around prison gangs or factious inmate groups.

Structure of Inmate Leaders. The inmate subculture has several aspects. We will consider only two: the rules and inmate roles. **Inmate roles** are especially important because they help identify who the leaders are and help define how the inmate's world is organized. But first we must understand the rules guiding inmate behavior.

For Clemmer, the key ingredient of the prison subculture was the **inmate code.** The code is informal and unwritten, but by word of mouth it is widely known. It identifies a system of norms that directs the inmate's behavior even more than the formal prison rules do. Sykes and Messinger (1960) examined descriptions of the inmate code that had been provided by several authors and suggested that the main principles can be classified roughly into five major groups:

- Don't interfere with the interests of other inmates. This norm warns inmates to "Never rat on a con," "Don't be nosy," "Don't have a loose lip," and "Don't put another inmate on the spot."
- Keep out of quarrels or arguments with fellow inmates. The classic line, "Do your own time," falls under this part of the code in which inmates are told simply to "Play it cool," and "Don't lose your head."
- Don't exploit other inmates. Prisoners are warned not to take advantage of one another by dictums such as "Don't steal from cons," "Don't break your word," "Don't welsh on debts," and "Be right."
- Maintain yourself and keep your dignity. This directive tells inmates to "Be tough," "Be a man," "Don't weaken," and "Don't whine."
- Don't give respect or prestige to the prison staff or to the world for which they stand. This aspect of the code is especially harmful to rehabilitation efforts because it tells the inmates that officials are wrong and prisoners are right. Inmates are cautioned to "Be sharp," and "Don't be a sucker."

In addition to identifying the norms by which inmates are to abide, the inmate subculture also identifies certain achieved roles (earned by their own efforts) that are ascribed roles (assigned based on some characteristic) that one might have in prison. As you might imagine, there is some variation around the country, but the differences tend to be more in the names used for the roles than in the roles themselves (see Table 9.5).

The role an inmate takes will also determine his standing in a hierarchy of prestige. At the top of the stack are the "Right Guys," who obey the inmate code, oppose staff and institutional rules, cooperate with each other, and present an aura of coolness and toughness. Clemmer described them as the more intelligent, urbanized, sophisticated offenders. They provide the leadership in the inmate subculture. Close to the top are the "Merchants" and "Politicians," who owe their high status to their ability to control scarce resources (the merchants) or to their skill at manipulating other inmates and staff (the politicians). At the bottom of the hierarchy are the "Rats," "Squealers," "Rapos," "Queens," and "Punks." The "Dings," or "Dingbats," are so far out of the loop that they are essentially ignored by all and fall outside this informal social structure. Placement of the remaining roles is not so clear-cut. "Outlaws" and "Toughs" are respected because they are a constant threat. The "Square Johns" are mostly ignored by the leaders, but they are certainly more accepted than those at the bottom of the hierarchy (Clemmer, 1958, p. 107; Irwin, 1980, pp. 12–14).

When the inmate code with its resulting hierarchy of roles was well established, the prison society had a cohesion and structure that provided a type of order that was as much the doing of the inmates themselves as the prison officials. Sykes (1958) described the situation as one in which the prison officials give up a certain level of control to the inmate leaders in exchange for the leaders' assistance in maintaining a peaceful and orderly prison. But the resulting order was not one that necessarily benefited all prisoners. This was, after all, an inmate society that reflected the color and ethnicity of the society as a whole—it was white and non-Hispanic.

Structure of Factions and Prison Gangs. In his forward to Irwin's 1980 book, criminologist Donald Cressey made clear his dislike of the contemporary prison by writing that if he had to do prison time and could choose the type of prison in which to do it, he certainly would not select the contemporary prison (p. vii). Without romanticizing the Big House, Cressey explains that he was swayed by Irwin's analysis of Big House prisons as places where inmates had a level of personal security and unity that meant he would not have had "to look around every corner

TABLE 9.5: Some Inmate Roles in Men's and Women's Prisons*

MEN'S PRISON ROLE	DESCRIPTION	WOMEN'S PRISON ROLE	DESCRIPTION
Right Guy	Abides by the norms of prisoner society by following the inmate code and opposing staff and institutional rules.	Real Woman	Responsible and loyal inmate who is in control of herself and her actions as she upholds the inmate code.
Square John	Identifies with the administration and behaves in accordance with the prison's official social system.	Inmate Cop or Square	Follows the prison rules because she is in a position of authority over other inmates through a work assignment, or is an "accidental" criminal with no connection to prison society.
Con Politician	Moves easily between staff and inmate norms by playing both sides to his advantage.	Stars and Daddies	Provides entertainment and tension release yet receives critical comments from other prisoners for needing to be in everything and to be seen.
Merchant	Places his own well-being over that of fellow inmates by selling goods in short supply.	King Pins and Big Spenders	The "big shots" in the prison economy because of their access to money and supplies.
Tough	Quick to quarrel with other prisoners and because of that he gives rise to both fear and respect among fellow inmates.	Jive Bitch	A troublemaker who creates unrest among inmates, especially through distortion of facts.
Rat or Squealer	Betrays fellow inmates and the inmate society.	Snitcher	Violates the code of confidence.
Queen	Takes a passive and submissive role in a homosexual encounter because he wants to (male prostitute) or prefers to (gay inmate).	Lesbian	Involved in homosexual relations because she prefers them to heterosexual ones.
Punk	Takes a passive and submissive role in a homosexual encounter because he is coerced.	Punk	Acts like a "female" in the manner stereotypically expected by men. The role elicits a combination of anger and ridicule from the inmates.
Wolf	Takes an active, aggressive, "masculine," role in a homosexual encounter.	Stud Broad	Takes a "masculine" role in a homosexual encounter.
Rapo	Serving a sentence for sexual acts such as incest and child molestation. Occupies the very bottom of the inmate status hierarchy.	Femme	Takes a "feminine" role in a homosexual encounter.
Ding or Dingbat	Behaves with so much inconsistency and lack of reliability that he cannot be assigned to another role. May be considered crazy but harmless.	Mother	Assures the internalization of prison values and norms by other inmates by providing motherly advice.

*The roles in men's and women's prisons are presented here in parallel fashion for ease of reading rather than to suggest that they are parallel. Certainly, there are some equivalents (like Right Guys and Real Women) but these should be read as examples under each prison rather than as comparing the men's term with the parallel women's term.

Source: Roles in men's prison are from Irwin, J. (1980). *Prisons in turmoil.* Boston: Little, Brown and Company; Schrag, C. Some foundations for a theory of corrections. In D. Cressey (Ed.). (1961). *The prison: Studies in institutional organization and change.* (pp. 309–357). New York: Holt, Rinehart and Winston; and from Sykes, G. (1958). *The society of captives: A study of a maximum-security prison.* Princeton, NJ: Princeton University Press. Roles in women's prisons are from Giallombardo, R. (1966). *Society of women: A study of a women's prison.* New York: John Wiley and Sons; and from Heffernan, E. (1972). *Making it in prison: The square, the cool, and the life.* New York: Wiley-Interscience.

to see if someone was waiting to stick a knife in my throat" (Cressey, in Irwin, 1980, p. viii). A similar feeling of safety may be missing in contemporary prisons because their social structure operates in the context of fragmented inmate groups rather than around a stable and recognized inmate subculture. A particularly good way to view this new structure is to look at the role played by factions and prison gangs.

As early as 1980, sociologists recognized that the inmate subculture of the Big House was being replaced by a prison environment in which inmates are organized in activist, racial, and ethnic groups for purposes of both defense and attack (Irwin, 1980, p. vii). An important impact of this factionalization has been a less widespread acceptance of the inmate code. Prisoners in the Big House tended to agree with the basic tenets of the inmate code and with the inmate roles the code generated. Certainly there were violations of the code by some inmates, but those violations were noted and the deviant prisoner had to face sanctions from fellow inmates ranging from ostracism to death. One reason the code was widely known, accepted, and enforced was that certain inmate leaders—the "Right Guys"—made it so. Their elite status (see Clemmer, 1958) brought them respect, and their allegiance to the code brought respect to it as well.

After World War II, changes that were occurring throughout society were also affecting prison life. Chief among these was increased division among inmates. Initially the division was along racial lines, with the most notable example being the separatist movement defined by the Black Muslims in the mid-1950s (see discussion in Chapter 6). Irwin (1980) describes the separation of Black Muslim prisoners from other prisoners as resulting in the Muslims forming "groups of highly committed, disciplined black prisoners who shaved their heads, kept themselves impeccably neat, maintained a cold but polite attitude to other prisoners, refused to eat pork, congregated together wherever possible, and listened to other Muslims deliver the teaching of Elijah Muhammad" (pp. 68–69). They often had hostile words, Irwin explains, but seldom provoked violence.

By the 1960s, black prisoners were reflecting the same rage against whites and white society that was exhibited by blacks in general society. As black prisoners developed new identities, experienced new levels of rage, and increasingly asserted themselves in the daily operation of prisons, racial hostilities and racial violence increased (Irwin, 1980). The inmate subculture was no longer widely accepted, nor were its primary adherents afforded leadership status by all the prisoners. New leaders were emerging among prison groups that were increasingly divided along racial lines. Divisions along lines of ethnicity, at least in California, were not as quick to arise. Irwin explains that Chicanos, especially those from Los Angeles, had grown up associating with Anglos, and although some Anglos disliked Chicanos, they also feared and respected them because it was assumed that Chicanos would quickly use violence when insulted or threatened. Relations between Chicanos and blacks were even less harmonious because "Chicanos were more deeply prejudiced and hostile than whites were toward blacks" (Irwin, 1980, p. 51).

As the separation by race and ethnicity continues, inmates are divided into more and more factions. As a result, any inmate code that exists seems relevant only to inmates of certain factions rather than to all inmates. Sutherland et al. (1992, p. 526) explain that whites do not think they should interfere with the interests of other whites, whereas blacks believe that playing it cool applies only to relationships among blacks, and Latinos think that the code means only that they should not exploit other Latinos.

As if these divisions were not enough, there are also factions within each of the factions, so that the tenets of the code often are seen as applicable only to the inmates who belong to a specific gang or clique. Jacobs (1977) makes the point with an example from Stateville, a maximum-security prison in Illinois: "Gang members simply see nothing wrong with 'ripping off' independents. The fact that they occupy adjoining cells does not seem to offer a basis for solidarity" (p. 157). Borrowing from a tenet of the inmate code, Jacobs (1977) goes on to note that "while at one time inmates may have endorsed the principle of 'doing your own time,' the gangs endorse the morality of 'doing gang time' " (p. 157). Because it appears that "doing gang time" continues to define the social structure of contemporary prisons, let us consider prison gangs more closely.

Doing Gang Time in Today's Prisons. Implied in the statement that today's inmates are doing gang time instead of just doing time are two important ideas. First is that gangs are power-wielding groups in many of today's prisons, and the behavior of both inmates and prison staff will be affected by that fact. Second, even if a prisoner does not belong to a gang, he will still be doing gang time because his adjustment to the prison world is going to be influenced by the actions of the gangs.

The Washington State Penitentiary at Walla Walla provided the first documented prison gang when the Gypsy Jokers organized there in 1950 (Fong, 1990), but growth of prison gangs is more closely tied to the racial conflicts of the late 1950s and the 1960s. Irwin (1980) and Orlando-Morningstar (1997) describe a link between racial hostility in society, increased factions among prisoners, and an eventual rise in prison gangs. The history begins in the 1960s in California when lowriders came into prominence. The term *lowrider* originally applied to hoods who rode around in their cars, slouched down in their seats. When used in prison, it was a derogatory label given to "young hoodlums, many of them state-raised, who formed cliques, hung around the prison yard, and 'talked-shit,' or bragged about their exploits and capabilities" (Irwin, 1980, p. 75).

The prison lowriders were more violent than the average prisoner, stole from other prisoners, and were more racially prejudiced than the general population. Many of them grew up in youth prisons that were racially segregated and hostile. When racial hostilities broke into the open in the 1960s, the lowriders became open racists. Some white lowriders wore swastika tattoos and called themselves Nazis. Some black lowriders also displayed open racism. Chicano lowrider groups were ambivalent about their racial position, showing more hostility toward blacks than whites, and instead seemed to focus more on drugs than racial hatred. When the young Chicanos fought, it was more likely over obtaining drugs or controlling drug trafficking (Irwin, 1980, pp. 75–76).

In 1957, at a juvenile training school in southern California, a tightly knit clique of Chicano youths organized the Mexican Mafia. That prison gang began taking over other California prisons and developed a violent reputation. Other Chicano prisoners, mostly from northern California, sought protection from the Mexican Mafia and organized La Nuestra Familia in 1965. The gangs have had a violent rivalry for thirty years as each tries to control drug trafficking inside prison, but Orlando-Morningstar (1997) explains that the rivalry between the two was easing in the late 1990s.

As the violence of the Chicano gangs escalated, black and white prisoners moved to consolidate and expand their own groups. Two gangs, the Aryan Brotherhood and the Black Guerrilla Family, rose to prominence for their violent activities. Eventually the Aryan Brotherhood formed an alliance with the Mexican Mafia while the Black Guerrilla Family affiliated with La Nuestra Familia. Although maintaining clear rivalry, gang alliances became increasingly popular in the 1980s as a feature of doing business in prison. According to Orlando-Morningstar (1997), prison gangs conduct business across racial, ethnic, and political boundaries in order to divide prison activities, maximize drug-trafficking profits, and avoid violent confrontations.

Data from 1992 indicate that over 47,000 inmates throughout the country are members of some 755 gangs or cliques operating within prisons throughout the

United States. Street gangs that are infiltrating correctional institutions today include the Bloods, Crips, Jamaican Posse, Vice Lords, Hells Angels, Skinheads, and Latin Kings—and there continues to be more and more overlap between groups defined as prison gangs and those identified as street gangs. The prison gangs offer the street gang members protection in and out of prison, and some street gang members become prison gang members when incarcerated. After release from prison, they may return to their former street gangs but will retain some allegiance to the gangs they joined in prison (Orlando-Morningstar, 1997).

In the Big House prisons, an inmate subculture with recognized leaders and a widely accepted code helped provide a degree of order in the prison—at least as long as prison officials were willing to recognize and occasionally reward the inmate leaders for their assistance in keeping order. But with the emergence of gangs, the prison subculture no longer has the simple division of inmates against staff. Allegiance is less to an all-encompassing inmate subculture than it is to specific gangs and cliques. And, as with street gangs, divisiveness intensifies power struggles and a result is a seemingly relentless cycle of attack and defend.

But what is it the prison gangs are struggling over? Gangs in prison are organized primarily for purposes of controlling the institution's drug transactions, gambling, loan-sharking, prostitution, extortion, and debt-collection rackets. In addition, they provide protection for their members from other gangs and instill a sense of macho camaraderie as they intimidate other inmates (Clear & Cole, 1994; Fox & Stinchcomb, 1994). What they do not provide are inmate leaders with widespread legitimacy. As Irwin (1980) describes the "new convict identity," the "Right Guy" and other higher-status roles have been pushed aside and replaced with toughness and raw power. That toughness has in turn "pushed out most other attributes, particularly the norms of tolerance, mutual aid, and loyalty to a large number of other regulars. . . . Toughness . . . means, first, being able to take care of oneself in the prison world, where people will attack others with little or no provocation" (pp. 192–193). And because "taking care of oneself" is ironically more fully accomplished with the assistance of others, the significant role played by gangs and cliques in today's prisons is likely to continue in the foreseeable future.

Social Structure and Interaction in Women's Prisons

The social structure and social interaction occurring in women's prisons can also be discussed in terms of topics such as an inmate code and the resulting inmate organization. Alarid (1996, 1999) and Pollock-Byrne (1990) note that women prisoners may very well have different values and a different inmate code, but researchers have invariably relied on the male inmate code—and one from forty to fifty years ago at that—to measure prisonization in both male and female prisons. Not surprisingly, the result is confusion and contradiction regarding the features of an inmate code among female prisoners. For example, Pollock-Byrne's review of the literature found that the "Do your own time" dictum is more often followed by males in prison than by females. The subcultural norms in women's prisons do not seem to prohibit or discourage getting involved in another woman's problems. Negatively, this means that women "spread rumors and gossip about one another's activities as a form of social control or merely as a social pastime" (Pollock-Byrne, 1990, p. 131).

The research on women's prisons also suggests that interaction with correctional officers is not prohibited for female inmates as it is for the men. For women, the interaction with correctional officers and staff is more casual and social. There is even some indication that female prisoners look to staff, as well as to each other, for support and nurturance.

To exemplify the difficulty of identifying and describing an inmate code for women's prisons, we can note research by Mahan (1984) that contrasts with the review presented by Pollock-Byrne. In her study of two New Mexico minimum-security institutions for women, Mahan identified two important components of an inmate code: (1) "Don't rat," and (2) "Mind your own business." To exemplify the first provision, Mahan offers examples of women telling her that prisoners seen talking with correctional officers are "snitches" and are violating the code. The second dictum suggests that the "Do your own time" mandate in the men's code is also applicable in women's prisons.

Research by Owen (1998) in the Central California Women's Facility (the world's largest female facility) also indicates that women prisoners support a male version of the convict code with statements such as "Do your own time" and "Don't snitch," and discourage each other from interacting with staff. But Owen also found that some bending of the rules might be tolerated among the prisoners—especially the younger ones. The ambivalence at least some women feel over a strict interpretation of the code was described by one of Owen's (1998) subjects who explained that a main part of the code is "Don't snitch," but she quickly added: "It is good to tell for certain things, like if someone gets jumped or somebody got stabbed" (p. 178).

Another aspect of differences in inmate subculture that has brought more agreement among researchers than the topic of inmate codes is the topic of inmate organization. As we have seen, the social organization of contemporary men's prisons is shaped primarily by the structures of prison gangs and prison cliques, with race and ethnicity being important defining variables. A result of this situation is fragmented leadership by which ties are mostly based on racial or political allegiances. The situation is different in women's prisons, in which the social organization is based on make-believe families, friendships, and homosexual liaisons with race and ethnicity taking an insignificant role. Instead of grouping together in gangs and pseudopolitical organizations, women group themselves in familial units, cliques, or dyads. "Their advocacy is emotional and personal; their allegiance is to a few rather than to many" (Pollock-Byrne, 1990, p. 138). The same conclusion was drawn by Owen from her research at the Central California Women's Facility. Owen says that even with increasing numbers of young women claiming gang membership on the streets, she found very little support for typical gang membership inside. Instead, social relationships in today's women's prison continue to be based primarily on "prison families and emotional dyads that can and do cross racial and ethnic lines" (Owen, 1998, p. 137).

One of the most widely documented aspects of the social structure of women's prisons is a fabricated kinship network that has been variously called artificial families, fantasy families, pseudofamilies, make-believe families, prison families, and so on. Owen (1998), Propper (1982), and many others use the term **play families** to refer to the short-term and long-term relationships among women in prison that borrow the structure, terminology, and function of families in the general society. In this manner, inmates might take the role of mother, daughter, sister, and so on, and build relationships with each other based on stereotypical concepts of that role in society.

An important point to make about play families is that a discussion of them is not the same thing as discussing homosexuality in women's prisons (a topic covered later in this chapter). Despite being written about since the early twentieth century, homosexual behavior among female inmates is mistakenly associated with their practice of calling each other by family names such as sister, mother, daughter, and even father, brother, or uncle. Having made that point, however, it is also necessary to note that two women prisoners operating as part of a play family may very well be involved in a homosexual relationship—but so too may women prisoners who have no link to a play family at all. A play family exists and operates in a woman's prison with or without accompanying homosexual behavior. In other words, homosexual relationships are neither a sufficient nor necessary condition for a play family's existence.

The most frequent role networks are mother–daughter and sister–sister. Mothers, especially, may have several daughters for whom they listen to problems and offer advice. Interestingly, Pollock-Byrne points out that the relationships created in the play family probably do not represent the women's real-life experiences. Instead, the play mother may be a better mother to her inmate daughters than she was to her own children before imprisonment. And, in sister–sister or other dyad linkages, the inmate couple may seek a romantic bond that neither woman ever before experienced. That is because many women in prison have had only poor and exploitive relationships with men, so this experience may be their first in which the bond is one of affection and romance rather than sex (Pollock-Byrne, 1990, p. 149).

Because the play families are seldom segregated by race or ethnicity, and because they exist for purposes of affection and affiliation rather than power, the level of violence is lower in female prisons than in contemporary men's prisons. But with changes brought by the drug culture, increased numbers of women in prison, changes in the composition of those offenders, and general modification of societal values and expectations for women, it seems likely that this version of social structure will be modified in the years to come (see Alarid, 1999).

Explanations for Prison Subculture

Ever since it was proposed that a distinct subculture exists in the prison setting, there have been attempts to explain its origin. The first explanations relied on what is called a **deprivation model.** In this approach, the inmate subculture is said to be the result of people being confined. Upon entering prison, the inmate is isolated from family and friends, no longer has personal possessions, has to get permission for such taken-for-granted tasks as shaving and bathing, and has no freedom of movement. Sykes (1958) describes these kinds of conditions as the **pains of imprisonment.** The norms, values, beliefs, and roles that make up the prison subculture are the results of adaptations to these five deprivations:

- *Deprivation of liberty.* Not only are the inmate's movements restricted to the prison, but the inmate is also separated from family, relatives, and friends.
- *Deprivation of goods and services.* The average inmate lives in a harsh, spartan environment that is painfully depriving.
- *Deprivation of heterosexual relationships.* Regardless of one's sex or sexual preference, people generally desire and benefit from interactions with people of the opposite sex. In a same-sex environment, prisoners are deprived of the opportunity to see themselves in that half of the mirror that is held by the other gender.
- *Deprivation of autonomy.* The inability to make choices and the unlikelihood of getting explanations for the rules they must follow reduce prisoners to the weak, helpless, dependent status of childhood.
- *Deprivation of security.* Being thrown into prolonged intimacy with persons who often have histories of violent, aggressive behavior is very anxiety producing.

Because all prisoners share the pains, the argument goes, they naturally come together to reduce the deprivations and the pains by establishing a subculture that allows them to have status, be loyal to something, and have a sense of cohesion.

The deprivation model relies heavily on the prison itself to explain the development of the subculture. Under the deprivation model all persons entering the prison, regardless of their individual personalities and social backgrounds, should experience the pains of imprisonment and seek the comfort of the inmate social structure. An experiment by Philip Zimbardo is sometimes used to portray the deprivation model (see "The Pathology of Imprisonment"), and the experience he describes certainly suggests that specific conditions of imprisonment might give rise to certain social/psychological adjustments. However, not everyone accepts the premise of the deprivation model.

In the preceding discussion of John Irwin's work, we learned that Irwin believed the prison structure in the Big House was modified over the years by changes occurring outside the prison. Consistent with this approach to under-

Spotlight ON CONTEMPORARY ISSUES

The Pathology of Imprisonment

Social psychologist Philip Zimbardo (1972) conducted an experiment to gain an understanding about what it means psychologically to be a prisoner or a prison guard. He selected about two dozen young men to be part of this study. By a flip of a coin, half were designated as prisoners, the others as guards. The guards were told they could make up and continually revise as necessary their own formal rules for maintaining law, order, and respect. The prisoners were unexpectedly picked up at their homes, searched, handcuffed, fingerprinted, booked, and taken blindfolded to the jail. At the jail, they were stripped, deloused, put into a uniform, given a number, and put into a cell with two other prisoners.

The prisoners expected to live in the cell for the next two weeks, but at the end of only six days the mock prison had to be closed down. Zimbardo explains that after that relatively short time span, it was no longer apparent to most of the subjects—or even the researchers—where reality ended and role-playing began. Most of the subjects had indeed become prisoners and guards and were no longer able to clearly differentiate between role-playing and self. Zimbardo (1972) describes the changes as follows:

> There were dramatic changes in virtually every aspect of their behavior, thinking and feeling. In less than a week the experience of imprisonment undid (temporarily) a lifetime of learning; human values were suspended, self-concepts were challenged and the ugliest, most base, pathological side of human nature surfaced. We were horrified because we saw some boys (guards) treat others as if they were despicable animals, taking pleasure in cruelty, while other boys (prisoners) became servile, dehumanized robots who thought only of escape, of their own individual survival and of their mounting hatred for the guards. . . .
>
> By the end of the week the experiment had become a reality. . . . The consultant for our prison . . . , an ex-convict with 16 years of imprisonment in California's jails, would get so depressed and furious each time he visited our prison, because of its psychological similarity to his experiences, that he would have to leave. A Catholic priest who was a former prison chaplain in Washington, D.C., talked to our prisoners after four days and said they were just like the other first-timers he had seen. (p. 5)

Attempting to make sense of the events, Zimbardo reminds us that individual behavior is more the result of social forces and situational circumstances than of specific personality traits. When the power and pervasiveness of situational controls over behavior are underestimated, dire consequences may result. Contemporary prisons provide forces and circumstances that give rise to pathological behavior in both prisoners and guards. A result, Zimbardo (1972) concludes, is an environment "guaranteed to generate severe enough pathological reactions in both guards and prisoners as to debase their humanity, lower their feelings of self-worth and make it difficult for them to be part of a society outside of their prison" (p. xx).

The "Stanford Prison Experiment" continues to receive considerable discussion today. Read a recent *Stanford News* article about the experiment at ***www.stanford.edu/dept/news/relaged/970108prisonexp.html.*** What role did Christina Maslach have in stopping the experiment, and how does she view her actions today?

standing prison society, Irwin also suggests that the inmate subculture itself is the result of norms, beliefs, and values brought in from the outside. Under this **importation model,** elements of the prison subculture come into the prison as new prisoners arrive. Rather than being stripped of their outside status upon entering prison, Irwin argued, inmates bring a great deal of behavioral baggage with them to prison and retain it during their stay (Irwin, 1980; Irwin & Cressey, 1962).

Having described the social structure and inmate interactions that are found in prison and having considered some explanations for the prison subculture's origin, we are ready to look at that subculture in greater detail. Two areas of behavior are especially relevant because they are of great concern to the prisoners themselves and of fundamental interest to the general public: sex and violence.

SEX AND VIOLENCE IN PRISON

The deprivation model and the importation model have dominated discussion of the prison subculture for decades. Both have their proponents, but increasingly people are recognizing that each model most likely complements rather than contradicts the other. You will see examples of each in operation as we consider some other aspects of prison subculture. Watch for how the deprivation model might help explain occurrences of homosexuality in men's prisons and of prison riots. The importation model, on the other hand, seems to provide an explanation for occurrences of prison rape in men's prisons and for play families in women's prisons. But instead of relying on only one or the other approach, we might find that things such as homosexuality, riots, prison rape, and play families are the result of an interaction of both the pains of imprisonment and of the baggage brought in with the prisoner.

Sex in Prison

It is important to begin this section with a distinction between terms. Traditionally, more attention has been given to the study or description of sexual violence in prisons than to consensual sexual behavior. Specifically, rape of one male prisoner by one or more other male prisoners has been the extent of some discussion on sex in prison. As will be pointed out later, rape in prison, just like rape outside of prison, is not a sexual act—it is an act of violence. For that reason, prison rape and sexual assault in general are topics covered later under a heading of "personal violence in prisons." Here the concern is with consensual sex in the prison setting. Of course, there is an immediate problem in trying to distinguish, especially in prison, between consensual and forced sex. When a prisoner agrees to sexual behavior with a same-sex fellow prisoner, how do we know that he or she is not just agreeing out of fear of what a refusal would bring? We don't know, and that presents a problem for any discussion of consensual sex in prisons. But it seems more important not to confuse the violence of prison rapes with the occurrence of voluntary sexual activity—even at the risk of counting among the "voluntary" or "consensual" acts some that more accurately are coerced.

One other term needs clarification before continuing. *Homosexuality* refers to both a sexual orientation and to a sexual activity. Very interesting discussions can develop regarding whether any person who has engaged, now engages, or has even fantasized about engaging in same-sex sexual relations is homosexual. Also, is a person who was entirely heterosexual in behavior before entering prison and who returns solely to that orientation after exiting prison correctly considered a homosexual if he engaged in same-sex sexual acts while in prison? Interesting as such questions are, they are not relevant to the following material. For our purposes, homosexuality is being used in reference to sexual activity regardless of the preferred sexual orientation of the participants. When the discussion requires clarification of one's sexual orientation, the terms *straight* (for heterosexuals of either sex), *gay* (for male homosexuals), and *lesbian* (for female homosexuals) are used. With these cautions in mind, we will consider consensual sex in men's prisons and then in women's prisons.

Sexual Behavior and Male Prisoners. Consensual sex in prison presents an interesting topic for considering whether the deprivation model or the importation model offers the better explanation for this aspect of the inmate subculture. Under the deprivation approach, as described earlier when listing the pains of imprisonment, being deprived of heterosexual relationships is a pain of imprisonment that helps form an inmate subculture. What was unacceptable on the outside (homosexuality) becomes acceptable under the conditions of deprivation found in prison. The inmate subculture develops norms and attitudes that are more tolerant of homosexual behavior under conditions of confinement. But just how frequent an occurrence is homosexuality in a prison for men? Because all the inmates experience the same conditions of deprivation, we might assume that the instances of homosexual behavior are quite high, but research does not generally support this assumption.

Much of the information on the frequency of sex in prison has been anecdotal. In a description of his time in Sing Sing prison in the early 1960s, Manual Torres recognizes the prevailing belief that homosexuality is widespread and running rampant in prison. Torres points out that the reality is much more complex:

> Many cons never play any sexual games in prison. Sometimes the inmate identity is almost nonsexual by nature of the experience. Some lead a monastic life, and for them the prison becomes a monastery where they read, contemplate, and pray. But, overall, there is no standard sexual orientation to prison life. In fact, guys like us used to deliberately steer clear of sexual traps in the joint. I never had any sex life at all, extending beyond myself, that is. I was too busy with drugs and with the accompanying hustle to bother about getting into homosexuality. (Rettig, Torres, & Garrett, 1977, p. 98)

By Torres's admittedly unscientific estimates, 30 percent of the prison population was into some type of homosexual adjustment on a regular basis, another 20 percent might have a homosexual encounter once or twice during their stay, but easily 50 percent stay clear of sexual activity.

A more scientific study over thirty years later suggests that Torres's estimates may not have been too far off. In 1994 Saum and his colleagues interviewed male inmates at a Delaware prison regarding their experiences with and knowledge of homosexuality in prison. Just over half (51.5 percent) of the subjects reported ever having heard from other inmates or correctional officers of consensual sex taking place during their previous year of imprisonment (Saum, Surratt, Inciardi, & Bennett, 1995). Possibly more interesting, over one-third (35.6 percent) said they had never heard of consensual sex occurring during that previous year. When the men were asked who had actually witnessed consensual sex in prison over the previous year, only about one-fourth (24.8 percent) said they had seen such behavior. As they reviewed their data, Saum et al. concluded that there is a myth of pervasive sex in prison, a myth the inmates themselves seem to hold, but that although homosexual contact in prison certainly occurs, it is probably not as widespread as people believe.

The idea that many, and more likely most, male prisoners do not engage in homosexual behavior while in prison presents a dilemma for the deprivation model. If all male prisoners are equally deprived in the prison setting, why isn't homosexuality a more common occurrence? Enter the importation model with an explanation—homosexual behavior is not common in prison because some previously held values, norms, and beliefs that the prisoners bring with them to prison do not support that behavior. The importation model could explain the less than pervasive presence of homosexuality in prison as a result of previously held values against homosexual behavior. When those values are part of the baggage brought in with the inmate, that inmate does not easily start engaging in homosexual behavior just because he is now deprived of heterosexual encounters. But an even more interesting explanation of why homosexuality is not as widespread in prisons as the public, and even many prisoners, might believe it is comes from a combination of the deprivation and importation approaches.

Sexual behavior, whether homosexual, heterosexual, or autoerotic, is often accompanied by environmental stimuli. In a typical situation, people rely to some extent on triggers such as clothing, music, food, flowers, darkness, privacy, and so on to set the stage for a sexual encounter. These sexual triggers are brought with prisoners into the prison setting (the importation model), but that setting does not have sexy clothing, romantic music, fine dining, candlelit rooms, or private areas (the deprivation model). When considered in this manner, it is more the presence of any sexual activity that needs explaining rather than the need to explain the presence of homosexual behavior. But it is exactly this kind of complexity that suggests the need to consider aspects of the inmate subculture from both a deprivation and an importation approach.

A final point before leaving the topic of sex in men's prisons: There is an understandable assumption that sexual encounters in a men's prison will have to be either homosexual or autoerotic in nature. Saum et al. report, with admitted surprise, that over 11 percent of the men in their sample claimed to have had sex with females during the previous year of imprisonment—all instances reportedly without any coercion on either side. Because the women involved were correctional officers, visitors, or female inmates attending classes at the male prison, there are many new questions raised by this finding. Some of those questions are linked to the topic of **conjugal visits,** but the claims of consensual sexual activity between female correctional officers and male inmates is a topic that awaits additional verification and explanation.

Sexual Behavior and Female Prisoners. The earlier discussion of social organization in women's prisons highlighted the role of play families. You will recall that participation in a play family may involve but does not require homosexual activity. However, the presence of play families makes it difficult to discuss sexual behavior in female prisons without making reference to the play families. As Pollock-Byrne (1990) put it: "Much of what has been described as [homosexuality in women's prisons] does not even include a sexual relationship. Rather, the women involved receive the affection and attention they need in a dyad with a sexual connotation" (p. 144).

When homosexual behavior, whether tied to a play family or not, occurs in girls' institutions and women's prisons, it is invariably consensual, although Owen (1998) found several examples of exploitative relationships in the California prison. In addition, the types of relationships that develop seem not to have changed much over the years. Most of the women prefer a female role (called *femmes*) as they compete for the favors of the few who assume the male role (*little boys, butches,* or *stud-broads*). But most of the interactions involve relatively innocent love relationships that are confined to holding hands or kissing. "Fewer women engage in actual lesbian affairs, and these take place more often in institutions for adults rather than in juvenile institutions" (Pollock-Byrne, 1990, p. 145).

During a conjugal visit, inmate and spouse are allowed to spend private time together on the prison grounds—usually in trailers, houses, or private rooms specifically provided for the visit. Although conjugal visits are common in European and Latin American prisons, fewer than ten U.S. states have correctional agencies that permit conjugal visits.

Homosexual behavior and play families in female institutions present another opportunity to consider the deprivation and importation approaches for understanding the inmate subculture. Because the structure and organization of the inmate subculture differ somewhat in men's and women's prisons, the models must be able to account for those variations. The deprivation approach might suggest that although men and women experience some of the same pains of imprisonment, there are also areas where the "pains" differ. Pollock-Byrne (1990) suggests that the most severe pain for women in prison is the severing of family ties and friendship. Because this is a significantly different deprivation for women than it is for men, the inmate subculture in women's prisons has developed in response to that deprivation by providing opportunities to replace the lost ties with homosexual behavior that emphasizes affection over sex, and with play families. But why, we might ask, don't the women simply meet these attachment needs by forming prison gangs and cliques? The importation model may provide an answer.

According to the importation approach, homosexual behavior and play families in girls' institutions and women's prisons may be the result of societal sex roles being brought into the facilities by the inmates. Gender seems to be a perfect example of an importation factor because our conceptions of what it means to be feminine and masculine are certainly shaped by societal forces outside prison. Because of this, even if women and men prisoners were being deprived of exactly the same things and in exactly the same manner, we might still expect them to react differently and to develop different inmate subcultures (Pollock-Byrne, 1990). If women in American society are still viewed—by women as well as men—as gaining their status and acceptance in the context of a family and its accompanying roles, the existence in prison of affection-based homosexuality and affiliation-based play families should be expected. That is, in a setting in which the traditional mechanism for women to have status and acceptance has been stripped away (the deprivation model), a seemingly natural response would be for those women to bring into that setting (the importation model) a structure that creates an opportunity to regain their status and acceptance.

Presumably, as women's conceptions of gender roles change and as opportunities to gain status and acceptance are broadened from the traditional reliance on family, the inmate subculture should look different than is currently described. In fact, such changes in the social world of imprisoned women may already be taking place. But until researchers become more interested in women's prisons, we are not able to identify what, if any, those changes might be.

Personal Violence in Prisons

> *I either committed a crime or had a crime done to me every day I was in jail. Once you go to prison you belong there.*
>
> —Socrates Fortlow (from the pen of Walter Mosley)

Violence in prison takes several forms. There are instances of inmates harming other inmates, of inmates harming correctional officers and other staff, and of prison personnel harming inmates. In 1996 almost 30,000 assaults by inmates against inmates and nearly 14,000 assaults by inmates against staff were reported (Camp & Camp, 1997). In a few states the reported assaults against staff exceeded the number reported against inmates, but the standard was for assaults against inmates to be more frequent (an average of 642 assaults against inmates compared with 327 assaults against staff), to be more likely to require medical attention (an average of 84 staff assaults and 264 inmate assaults), and to be more often referred for prosecution (41 inmate assaults on average compared with 35 staff assaults).

Prison officials have a duty under the Eighth Amendment to protect prisoners from assault by other prisoners, but the officials are not automatically liable for any such assaults that occur. Liability is increased when the damage is sufficiently serious (see *Rhodes v. Chapman,* 1981; *Wilson v. Seiter,* 1991), and when the officials are shown to have exhibited a deliberate indifference to the inmate's health or safety (identified in *Estelle v. Gamble,* 1976, and further defined in *Farmer v. Brennan,* 1994). Officials are said to have been deliberately indifferent when they knew about the possibility of a specific assault and did nothing to prevent it. The key and, therefore, the problem are determining specific examples of deliberate indifference.

Consider, for example, the case of *Farmer v. Brennan* (1994). In 1989 federal prison authorities placed Dee Farmer in the general population at a prison in Terre Haute, Indiana. That would not normally give rise to a legal suit by an inmate, but Farmer, who was born male, had undergone estrogen therapy, had breast implants, and had unsuccessful "black-market" surgery to remove his testicles. As a result, Farmer was a male inmate who projected feminine characteristics. Putting him among the general prison population, Farmer argued, showed deliberate indifference to his high vulnerability to sexual attack. The Supreme Court said that Farmer, whose suit had been dismissed by two lower courts, should be given an opportunity at the trial court level to show that the beating and rape he suffered at the penitentiary were the result of deliberate indifference to his need for special protection. The Supreme Court returned the case to the district court with instructions for the district court to consider deliberate indifference as the equivalent of acting recklessly—with recklessness being "defined" as involving something more than mere negligence but less than an actual intent to bring about the harm that occurred.

The obligation to provide a safe environment for prisoners and staff is something corrections officials are concerned about for moral as well as legal reasons. The mere fact that prison rapes occur suggests that, despite the efforts of officials, the prison is a violent place that puts its occupants in dangerous situations.

Violence in Men's Prisons. Accounts of personal violence in prisons typically use men's prisons as the study site. The violent acts are most often explained as linked to racial conflict, drugs, and sexual orientation. Irwin (1980) and Jacobs (1977), for example, cite the growth of racially and ethnically identified gangs as important causes of prison violence. Drugs have been seen as contributing to prison violence, primarily because of their link to economic transactions (e.g., not paying for drugs or stealing drugs) but also as a result of the drug's effects, which may increase violence in those who are predisposed to violence (Bowker, 1977). But it is probably violence associated with sexual orientation that has gained the most attention by the media, if not by the researchers.

Violence toward gay men in prison, specifically because they are gay, has linked homosexuality to some violent acts and is clearly a point of concern for some prisoners, their family, and for prison officials (Bowker, 1980; Wooden & Parker, 1982). But sexual assault by straight men (as self-defined) of other straight men (especially a young first offender) is a particularly violent and fear-invoking event—although it may not be as frequent an event as the public, and even other prisoners, believe it to be (Saum et al., 1995; Smith & Batiuk, 1989).

Early explanations for prison rape relied on the deprivation model and suggested the rapes were a result of sexual deprivation in the prison setting. Louisiana prisoner Wilbert Rideau explains that the prison population consists of men whose sexuality, sense of masculinity, and sexual frame of reference are primarily structured around women. In the absence of women, weaker inmates are made to assume the role of "women" and thereby reinforce the stronger inmates' sense of manhood and personal importance. The weaker inmates gratify the needs that, in the outside world, would presumably be satisfied by women (Rideau, 1992b, pp. 74–75).

Reliance on the deprivation model began changing in the 1970s as feminists were succeeding in redefining the rape of women as an act of power rather than an act of sex. Similarly, people began looking at prison rapes differently and started finding very clear indications of those rapes as also being expressions of power and anger rather than of sex (see "Prison Rape: Are White Males a Minority?"). In one of the most recent studies of prison sexual assaults, Struckman-Johnson, Rucker, Bumby, and Donaldson (1996) report that the incident rate for coerced sex was 22 percent for male inmates in their survey of two maximum-security state prisons. Results of their study led the researchers to conclude that half of the assaulted prisoners had been forced to have intercourse, with about one-fourth of all incidents qualifying as "gang rape." Struckman-Johnson et al. did not attempt to determine the motivation behind the reported assaults. But because anal sex was involved in half of the most serious assaults, and because stranger inmates were usually among the perpetrators, it seems that power and anger—more so than sexual gratification—could have been a motivation.

There is no reason to believe that the search for an explanation of prison rapes will result in an answer more quickly or easily than has the search to understand the complexities of rapes outside prison. Probably the soundest advice thus far was offered by Bowker (1980) who suggests that it would be a mistake to search for the causes of prison rape by looking only at the rapist. Sexual deprivation within prison may contribute to rape's frequency, but it is likely the least important causal factor. Instead, he argues, prison rapes result from the lack of social outlets for playing masculine roles. Participation in a consensual homosexual relationship is not an example of the traditional masculine role. But—in a perverted and unfortunate way—rape is considered by too many men as a display of machismo.

Violence in Women's Prisons. Kruttschnitt and Krmpotich (1990) note that little is known about violence in women's prisons, but they provide some interesting information based on their review of the limited literature. The most frequently cited

ISSUES OF FAIRNESS

PRISON RAPE: ARE WHITE MALES A MINORITY?

Violent crime tends to be intraracial. That is, people are primarily violent toward others of their own race. Much of that phenomenon is the result of life in a rather segregated society in which people of the same racial group live near and socialize with others of that race. As a result, when violence between people occurs, it will more likely be white on white, black on black, and so on.

An interesting aspect of sexual assault in men's prisons is that it is likely to be interracial—specifically, a black aggressor and a white victim. This phenomenon is used by some people to support the thesis that prison rape, like rape on the outside, is often an expression of power and anger rather than an attempt at sexual gratification. Consider the following argument:

> Outside prison the female victim's minority status (women have less power in society than do men) make them targets for the male rapist's misguided display of power and misplaced anger. Inside prison, where expressions of power through gender are meaningless since everyone is male, power may take on a race component. White males in prison (where power shifts in the prison social structure result in white males having minority status) become victims of black prisoners who use sexual assault to show their power and express their anger.

There are several problems with that argument—not the least of which is the idea that blacks have more power in prison than do whites. But accept the premise for a moment and consider the implications it has for explaining prison rapes.

Carroll (1974) suggested that explanations for interracial sexual assaults in prison are imbedded in the sociohistorical context of black–white relations in the United States. In the outside world, rape is an expression of power by men against women. In the prison world, inverted as it is, rape is an expression of power by blacks against whites. Support for this type of analysis was first offered by Carroll when he explained that at least 75 percent of the rapes in an Eastern prison he studied were black assailants and white victims—a situation he explained as resulting from black rage directed at white institutions. Scacco (1975) also seemed to adopt a **black rage theory** based on reports to him that black aggressors attacked their victims to get back at whites. Wooden and Parker (1982) report that most voluntary homosexual liaisons in prison are intraracial, but most prison rapes are interracial with black aggressors and white victims. They also suggest a link between black hostility toward whites and the inversion of power that these rapes can express.

Another explanation for prison rapes, especially black on white, might be called a **vulnerability theory.** In this approach, certain persons are chosen as rape victims because they appear vulnerable. Alarid (2000) found that white non-Hispanic men felt the most pressure to join a protection group, but Lockwood (1980) notes that even when white prison gangs or cliques do form, they are less powerful, less cohesive, have less potential for violence, are less likely to retaliate when a member is wronged, and generally inspire less fear in exploiters. As a result, whites may be seen as vulnerable when they are loners and when they are members of a group—they are, in that sense, a minority.

Go to the Web site for the organization Stop Prisoner Rape at ***www.spr.org.*** Here you will find news, stories, and advice from survivors and links to articles, lectures, and legal information. One of the items at that site is entitled *Rape of Males* (***www.spr.org/docs/malerape.html***). Read the material under the heading "Jail Rape," and explain how the rape of males in confinement differs from the rape of males in the community.

variable linked to female prison violence is homosexuality. Studies conducted at women's prisons in the 1960s and 1970s were rather consistent in finding that violence often stemmed from such situations as broken homosexual relationships, moves by staff to separate homosexual couples by relocating one to a different part of the prison, and the tensions of a lovers' triangle. The play family structure also provided and even encouraged some types of situations that resulted in violent encounters.

Whereas race and race relations are considered important variables to explain violence in men's prisons, less is known about how the racial composition of women's prisons affects the institutional environment (Kruttschnitt & Krmpotich, 1990). Some studies have found black women to be inmate leaders and, at least in a juvenile facility, to have gained dominance through aggressive roles. In their study of aggression at a Minnesota women's facility, Kruttschnitt and Krmpotich (1990) found that whites were less aggressive than minorities, but the relationship was not statistically significant and the authors do not believe much should be made of the correlation. At this time it is most accurate to say that women's prisons have not yet received sufficient attention to allow even general comments to be made regarding a link between violence and race.

Riots: Collective Violence in Prisons

Collective action can take the same forms in prison that it does outside prison. Prisoners have engaged in hunger strikes, work slowdowns, and voluntary lockdowns (refusing to leave their cells). But the type of collective action that occasions the most publicity and causes the most damage to property and harm to people is the riot.

A **prison riot** is a situation that represents the prison officials' loss of control over a large number of prisoners in a sizable area of the prison for a substantial amount of time (see Useem & Kimball, 1989). Because of the physical harm they can cause, the property damage they can produce, and the public reaction they can generate, these disturbances deserve a closer look.

The first thing to know about prison riots is that they are as old as prisons themselves. Some of the earliest riots took place within years of the opening of the first prisons. In the spring of 1776—within eighteen months of receiving its first prisoner—a log house built over the main entrance to the underground prison at Newgate, Connecticut, was set on fire in an escape attempt by the convicts. Other destructive riots occurred until late 1780, when the prison was placed under the supervision of a military guard (Dean, 1979; Phelps, 1845). In the 200-plus years since then, riots have continued to be occasional and sometimes frequent events in the prison environment despite the fact that prisoners do not have a history, or even a single example, of having won—either in a short-term sense of maintaining their freedom, or in the long-term sense of drawing lasting attention to their plight (Fox & Stinchcomb, 1999). The obvious question is why do they keep occurring? It will not surprise you to hear that the answer is not a simple one.

Montgomery and Crews (1998) categorize the dominant theories explaining prison riots into eleven typologies. Some of the theories assume riots are beyond the control of prison officials whereas others suggest actions by the prison administration may actually encourage a riot. Some theories propose specific conditions or variables that can cause a riot whereas others pay little attention to the role of specific variables. Other theories highlight the role that people outside the prison can play, and others emphasize how the conditions of the prison itself lead prisoners to view violence as their best response to adverse conditions or to the achievement of change.

Two of the theories suggest that riots pass through specific stages. The "theory of riot causation" identifies five stages—a preriot state through a termination stage in which prison officials recapture the prison. This theory places considerable responsibility for riots on the breakdown of administrative control and operation of the prison and on the erosion of the prison's security system (Montgomery & Crews, 1998). The second theory that proposes specific stages in a prison riot is the "time bomb theory." This theory assumes that while riots will only occur where predisposing conditions exist, the riot itself is produced by a spontaneous event. Montgomery and Crews (1998) explain that this theory cannot explain riots that are premeditated and/or deliberate, but it provides insight into the collective actions of the inmates and administration involved in a prison riot. Because we are interested in the collective aspect of prison riots, the time bomb theory deserves closer attention.

The time bomb theory was presented by noted penologist Vernon Fox (1971), who suggested five stages through which riots progress: outbreak, organization, confrontation, termination, and reaction. His proposal, with some modification, serves as the basis for our analysis of riots in men's prisons.

The Outbreak Stage. Prison riots are the result of both predisposing and precipitating causes. The predisposing factors are the underlying conditions that provide the foundation for an eventual riot. The precipitating causes, or triggering events, refer to one or several specific events that actually start the riot. We do not need to spend much time on the precipitating factors since they are unlimited in type and their identification is not especially helpful in understanding the patterns of a riot. For example, a riot might be triggered by such things as the action of a correctional officer, a change in administrative policy, the kind of food provided to the inmates, or racial tensions in the prison. Initial reports on the February 2000 riot at California's Pelican Bay prison suggested that the bloody riot in the exercise yard was a result of mounting racial tensions between Latino and African American inmates (Tamaki & Gladstone, 2000).

But to say that a specific event, or even a combination of events, was the cause of a riot is too simplistic. More likely, the event that triggered the actual riot did so because of certain conditions that already existed in the prison. To understand why the riot occurred, it is necessary first to understand those conditions.

Table 9.6 identifies confrontation with other inmates, confrontation with staff, and gang-related incidents as frequent causes of contemporary prison riots. But for a more specific analysis consider the work of Boin and van Duin (1995) who categorize the predisposing causes of a prison riot in two ways. The first, the deprivation approach, says that prisoners riot because of conditions in the prison. Fox originally described this first phase with the analogy of a bomb: "The way to make a bomb is to build a strong perimeter and generate pressure inside. Similarly, riots occur in prisons where oppressive pressures and demands are generated in the presence of strong custodial containment" (Fox, 1971, p. 10). The Pelican Bay prison riot in February 2000 occurred at a high-tech maximum-security prison that had just five years earlier been found by a federal judge to have a pattern of brutality and neglect. At the time of the riot the prison, which was built to house 2,280 inmates, was overcrowded by more than 1,000 prisoners (Wallace, Podger, & Van Derbeken, 2000). Although a complete understanding of the Pelican Bay prison riot awaited more intense study, early reports suggested that such conditions were examples of oppressive pressures that could eventually "explode" into a riot.

Elaborations of Fox's "powder keg" or "bomb" theory include the idea of relative deprivation. Under this version of the deprivation approach, conditions in the prison may not be so terrible, but the prisoners believe the conditions are significantly worse than at other comparable prison environments. They are, in other words, relatively deprived. Another variant of the deprivation approach suggests that a riot is used to attract the attention of outsiders, especially the media, to the bad conditions of the prison.

Another way to categorize the predisposing causes is with a breakdown approach. The classic version of this approach emphasizes the social structure of the prison by highlighting the relationship between prisoners and prison officials. The assumption here is that order in prison occurs only when the prisoners themselves agree to have order. Prison officials, in other words, must rely on the consent and cooperation of the prisoners to maintain an orderly environment. In one version of this approach (see Sykes, 1958), prison order is said to be "bought" from pow-

TABLE 9.6: Reported Underlying Causes of Prison Riots, 1980–1995

	NUMBER	PERCENTAGE
Confrontation with other inmates*	389	42.3
Unknown causes	140	15.2
Rules or regulations violations	97	10.6
Racial tension	81	8.8
Gang related*	52	5.7
Confrontation with staff*	38	4.1
Multiple factors	35	3.8
Security issues	30	3.3
Institutional food	28	3.1
Mass escape attempts	10	1.1
Alcohol and drug related	10	1.1
Rumors	9	1.0
Total	919	100.0

*These three incident types were the only ones showing an increase during the time period considered the final trigger for the occurrence of the violent event. The other events showed no clear trends.

Source: Montgomery, R. H., Jr., & Crews, G. A. (1998). *A history of correctional violence: An examination of reported causes of riots and disturbances.* Lanham, MD: American Correctional Association. Used with the permission of the American Correctional Association, Lanham, Maryland.

erful inmates who operate an unofficial inmate government. In exchange for the recognition and respect of prison officials, these inmate leaders keep order for authorities. When there is a disruption in the relationship between prisoner leaders and prison officials, riots may result.

Boin and van Duin (1995) suggest there is yet another way to categorize predisposing causes—a management approach. The deprivation approach emphasizes the role played by prison conditions and the breakdown approach emphasizes the importance of prison leaders, but neither of these views the role of prison administrators as especially significant. Taking a position that "management matters," Boin and van Duin suggest that prison management influences at least two key factors that could result in a prison riot: (1) prison living conditions and (2) the state of security.

At prisons in which the inmates believe that the living conditions are good and that a high level of security exists, the chances that inmates will start a riot are relatively low. At the other extreme, when inmates believe that the conditions are bad and that institutional security is low, the prison is susceptible to triggers that can inflame the institution at any given moment. Falling between those extremes are situations where the prison is vulnerable to a riot because living conditions are bad or because sloppy security leaves room for inmates to start a riot.

Whether the predisposing factors that trigger a precipitating event are best understood using a deprivation, breakdown, or management approach, there will be certain activities in which the inmates participate during this outbreak stage. Some of the inmates will seek safety and remove themselves from the rioters. Others, Cressey suggests, will rejoice in their newfound freedom and partake in binges of drinking, drug taking, and property damage (Sutherland et al., 1992). In this initial stage, hostages may be threatened, harmed, or even killed. There may also be violence among inmates as old grudges are settled. Eventually, a sense of reality penetrates the surroundings, and the riot proceeds to its next stage.

The Organization Stage. After the binges subside, any continuing violent acts are likely to be instances of power grabbing by individual prisoners or by inmate groups. During the 1950s and 1960s, this stage of prison rioting typically involved the "cooler" heads among the inmate leaders, or the "Right Guys" as described earlier. They would come forward and explain to the other inmates that any revolutionary schemes or escape plots that might have existed earlier must now be set aside in favor of peaceful negotiations (Sutherland et al., 1992). During the 1970s this stage had examples that ranged from well-organized inmate groups (rather than individual inmate leaders) that took control of the prison in Attica to the apparent absence of any person or group taking control of the New Mexico penitentiary riot.

During the last thirty years, several prison riots have been especially notable for their violence or duration. Along with a 1987 riot at the federal penitentiary in Atlanta and a 1993 riot at the prison in Lucasville, Ohio, the 1971 uprising at New York's Attica Correctional Facility and the 1980 riot at the New Mexico penitentiary in Santa Fe are considered the most notorious in recent years. On September 9, 1971, inmates at Attica took over cell blocks and killed four fellow prisoners. The state police moved in on September 13, and in the fifteen minutes it took to reclaim the prison, thirty-nine inmates were killed and more than eighty were wounded. Something that made this riot different from riots in the 1950s and 1960s was its political component. Prisoners in the earlier riots often challenged what they saw as an abuse of power in the prison system; but the prisoners at Attica were challenging the very ideology and structure of both the penal system and the larger society (Hawkins & Alpert, 1989).

Attica presents an example of a riot where the organization stage involved a unified group of militant inmates who seemed to have control over the riot—possibly even during the outbreak stage. This was very different from the pre-1970 riots that more typically involved confrontations between prison officials and the inmate leaders of a unified prisoner subculture over issues like inmate privileges. But the inmate solidarity and politicalization shown at Attica did not turn out to be a blueprint for future prison riots. By the decade's end, riots were showing still another variation from their pre-1970s' version. The prison riot at New Mexico's state penitentiary provides the most publicized example.

On February 2, 1980, inmates at the New Mexico State Penitentiary in Santa Fe began what would be a thirty-six-hour riot. Before it was over, 33 inmates were dead, and over 100 others were beaten and sexually assaulted by fellow prisoners. There were some similarities in the predisposing conditions leading up to both the Attica and the New Mexico riots (see Colvin, 1992), but the most startling item for purposes of the organization stage was the absence of organization. Whereas inmates at Attica showed considerable unity of purpose and action against authorities, the prisoners at New Mexico showed fragmentation and violence against each other. Several of the prison riots since 1980 suggest that the case of splinter groups in the Santa Fe example has been followed more often than has the case of the unified inmates at Attica. This situation makes it difficult to proceed to the next stage of prison riots because it is not always clear exactly who is confronting whom.

The Confrontation Stage. Once the inmate rioters have organized around the leaders of the inmate subculture, or around a unified inmate group that has taken control, a confrontation takes place between the inmate leaders and prison authorities. At this point, assuming the riot has not already been extinguished by prison officials, bargaining strategies develop, and the negotiation process begins. Typically the inmates have a list of demands for prison or state officials. Those demands may include anything from better food and safer working conditions to revisions of prison policies or even modification of good-time and parole procedures. In any event, the two sides exchange their ideas about how the insurrection can be resolved.

As in the organization stage, the New Mexico rampage presents a contradiction to the orderly flow of these stages of a riot. No generally recognized list of demands was ever issued to administrators at New Mexico, and the group of inmates that eventually ended up acting as negotiators had little influence over other inmates or the course of the riot (Useem & Kimball, 1989). But confusion about which, if any, inmates were in charge was in keeping with the disorganized and fragmented nature of the New Mexico riot itself. And the absence of agreed-upon leaders highlighted the disunity of these prisoners and may have revealed the direction prison riots would take during the 1980s and 1990s. As Sutherland et al. (1992) explain, the infighting and political apathy of the New Mexico riot reveal "the extent to which relations among inmates have become increasingly fragmented in recent years" (p. 546). An aspect of that fragmentation is the increased numbers and growing influence of prison gangs. As long as the gangs are competing for a superior position in the prison subculture, it will be difficult for any inmate group to have the widespread support necessary to successfully negotiate during a prison riot. In the absence of inmate leaders who represent a solid inmate subculture (pre-1970s riots) or a well-organized inmate group with a specific agenda (the Attica riots), riots at prisons in which gangs compete for power are likely to be uprisings of pointless property destruction and unorganized attempts to gain public sympathy for inmate-perceived brutality.

The Termination Stage. Riots are terminated when custodial control is regained by the authorities. In a study of 255 riots that occurred in the United States between 1900 and 1995, Montgomery and Crews (1998) report that most were ended with the use of force or just with a show of force—negotiation with inmates was a close third. The process can be deadly and can take only minutes, as at Attica, or it can be peaceful and last several hours, as in Useem and Kimball's (1989) description of the termination of a 1986 riot at the West Virginia Penitentiary.

The Reaction Stage. A stage following termination may seem superfluous, but it is actually an important final phase. After authorities regain control, the public and government officials typically clamor for explanations and want assurance that precautions are taken, or changes made, that will prevent another riot in the future. Suggestions flow easily from editorial writers, talk show hosts, academics, and people with a variety of other credentials. Official investigation committees may be formed and serious efforts made to identify the problems that led to the riot. Too often, however, prison officials, politicians, journalists, and the public are satisfied when a precipitating event has been clearly identified. It is easy and convenient to print a headline that says the riot occurred because, for example, inmates did not like the way correctional officers searched their cells. If such an explanation satisfies all government and prison officials, there may never be an attempt to address the predisposing conditions. When predisposing conditions remain unresolved, even if the precipitating event has been identified, we should not be surprised if riots continue.

Managing Violence

So far we have concentrated on how prisoners respond or adjust to life in prison. The prison, in the sense of prison officials or management, also responds and adjusts to the prisoners. We are especially interested in the prison response to violence and other maladaptive behavior by the prisoners. After all, as was noted earlier, prison officials have a legal mandate, and probably a moral one as well, to do their best to ensure the safety of those persons placed in their keeping. In addition, the safety of prison employees must be considered as officials find ways to handle problems presented by prison gangs, acts of personal violence, and by riots. Some responses by prison officials have used classification techniques to weaken the influence of gang leaders. With this strategy, persons identified as disruptive influences are classified to particular prisons, to special sections within prisons, or to certain security levels. Under a divide-and-conquer philosophy (or at least one of separate and ameliorate), prison officials try to reduce the impact of gangs and gang leaders by impairing the group's leadership structure. Because primary group affiliation is most easily maintained with frequent face-to-face contact, a policy that limits the interaction between leaders and their gangs might weaken both the gangs' and the leaders' power.

Another response by prison officials to problems presented by the contemporary prison social system is to modify the physical structure of the prison. The old cell block–style prisons contributed to the development of a unified social system with widely acknowledged leaders by allowing all the prisoners to interact with each other. In the big yard, at the work sites, in the mess hall, and in the cell houses, inmates could easily find out who was doing what to whom—and what the reaction would be. The inmate code, because it was informal and unwritten, depended on dissemination by word of mouth. Of course, that is more easily accomplished when people are in close and frequent contact.

For all the advantages the old cell block–style prisons had in promoting a common inmate code, it also facilitated violence among combating factions as the prison structure became increasingly gang dominated. Whereas before the open areas and large grouping of inmates made it easy to spread the word, those same characteristics now made it easy to spread the violence. The new generation jails described in Chapter 8 may be changing that. The new design relies on pods containing, usually at the most, about 60 prisoners. For example, if you have one prison designed around five modules with each module containing five separate pods and each pod holding 50 prisoners, you quickly have a prison with a capacity for 1,250 inmates. That is not large by the standards of the cell block prisons, and in all likelihood states will need to maintain several of the old facilities. But the podular-direct facilities can make it more difficult for hostile gangs to interact. In addition, riots might be more easily contained to a small number of prisoners in a smaller area under the new design type.

IMPRISONMENT IN OTHER COUNTRIES

The degree of civilization in a society can be judged by entering its prisons.

—Dostoyevsky

Dostoyevsky's view on society and its prisons was undoubtedly influenced by his exile to Siberia in 1849, where he served four years at hard labor. But even people who have not spent time in a prison are likely to agree that a country's use of imprisonment and conditions within those prisons will reveal something about the citizens of that country. We conclude this chapter with some general comments on and a few specific examples of imprisonment.

Imprisonment around the World

It is obviously difficult to make general comments about prison use and conditions around the world—but it has been attempted. Often the result is a negative evaluation. For example, the Human Rights Watch (1993) concluded that prisoners worldwide "are confined in conditions of filth and corruption, without adequate food or medical care, with little or nothing to do, and in circumstances in which violence—from other inmates, their keeper or both—is a constant threat" (p. xv).

Other authors lament the undesirable aspects of imprisonment in all countries by reminding us that "much remains to be done to humanize prison conditions," although "there is no doubt that significant progress has been made in comparison with the cruelty and extreme misery found by John Howard two centuries ago" (Neudek, 1991, p. 712).

As a brief overview of some aspects of the various imprisonment systems operating today, we will concentrate on one topic already covered in this chapter: the problems of minority groups in prisons.

Race, Ethnicity, Nationality, and Imprisonment

In this chapter and several others, you will note that the racial and ethnic composition of U.S. prisons has a disproportionate number of black and Hispanic Americans. In addition, an increasing number of prisoners, especially in the federal system, are noncitizens. This problem of disproportional minority representation is not unique to the United States. That does not mean the disproportionality is unimportant; rather, it suggests that it is a very widespread problem that cannot simply be dismissed as country specific.

Although making up only 12 percent and 10 percent, respectively, of the nation's total population, American blacks and Hispanics account for about 49 percent and 18 percent of its prison population. Table 9.2 shows that by 1999, noncitizens in the federal system had increased to 30 percent. Similar disproportional representation of minorities is found in other countries. Dünkel and van Zyl Smit (1991) note that foreign prisoners have become a greater problem for many European countries since the opening of country borders in the early 1990s. In some Council of Europe countries (e.g., France, the Netherlands, and Sweden) the proportion of foreigners had already exceeded 20 percent by the late 1980s. Other countries, including Belgium and Switzerland, had over 30 percent foreigners in their prison systems. Statistics in the mid-1990s suggest that racial and ethnic minorities continue to be a high proportion of the prison population in many countries.

The number of ethnic minorities in Italian prisons almost doubled between 1988 and 1992, so that they made up more than 10 percent of the total prison population. But by late 1992, the proportion was approaching 20 percent (Ruggiero, 1995). When you know that ethnic minorities make up only 2 percent of Italy's general population, the disproportion of that percentage becomes apparent. France has seen a similar increase in foreign prisoners as the percentage of non-French-born inmates increased from 18 percent in 1975 to 31 percent in 1993 (Gallo, 1995). In Sweden, the proportion of foreign inmates has remained around 20 percent since the mid-1970s, but their composition has changed from mostly other Scandinavians (especially Finnish) to now being mostly other Europeans and non-Europeans (Leander, 1995). A small majority (52 percent) of prisoners in the Netherlands are white Dutch (van Swaaningen & de Jonge, 1995). About 11 percent of the foreign inmates were from Suriname, and another 11 percent were from other non-European countries (especially Africa, Latin America, and the Middle East).

Some authors suggest that a disproportionate representation of ethnic minorities in these countries may be the result of selective criminalization practices or selective prosecution of certain ethnic group minorities (Dünkel & van Zyl Smit, 1991, p. 741). Others believe it is not so much a discriminatory justice system that gets a person to prison as it is the typically poor social and economic status that foreigners and ethnic minorities have in many countries (Ruggiero, 1995). Both explanations are similar to ones debated in the United States, and it is increasingly obvious that each country's minority groups present similar problems and concerns to each country.

SUMMARY

THE DUAL PRISONS SYSTEM

- Prisons operate in the United States at both the state and federal levels. The combined state and federal prison population is primarily male, non-Hispanic, middle-aged, and of minority race.
  - The percentage of blacks and Hispanics is increasingly disproportional to their numbers in the general population.
  - The number of men and women in the prison population is also disproportionate to percentages in the general population, with males making up the majority of prisoners. However, the percentage of women prisoners is growing at a faster pace than the percentage of men.
- Prisons are typically categorized by security level. From least to most secure, they are minimum, medium, maximum, and supermax.
- In addition to institutions, states also place prisoners in community facilities, work release centers, farms and work camps, and prerelease centers.
- The federal prisons are operated by the Federal Bureau of Prisons (BOP), which is part of the Department of Justice.
  - Federal inmates are primarily male, white, non-Hispanic, and U.S. citizens. Drug offenses are the largest single crime category for federal offenders.
  - The number of female offenders housed in federal prisons has increased at a faster rate in the last decade than has the rate for male inmates, but women still compose only 7.5 percent of the total federal prison population.

SOCIAL STRUCTURE AND INTERACTION IN PRISON

- In both state and federal prisons, the inmates come to participate in an inmate subculture that results from a prisonization process wherein new prisoners come to learn the norms and values associated with prison life.
- The norms and values of the inmate subculture are the result of deprivation brought by the prison itself and through an importation of street norms and values into the prison.
- The social structure of men's prisons has changed from one oriented around inmate leaders to one built on factions and gangs—many of which have race and ethnicity as an essential ingredient.
- The social structure of women's prisons is less influenced by race and ethnicity but continues to reflect a structure built on traditional female roles linked to the family.

SEX AND VIOLENCE IN PRISON

Of the many features of prison life that arise from the prison's social structure, sex and violence have attracted considerable attention.

- Consensual sexual behavior occurs in both men's and women's prisons, but it is the personal violence associated with nonconsensual sex and other forms of assault that are particularly troublesome to prison inmates and staff.
- When collective violence, a riot, occurs in prisons, it typically follows a five-stage progression from outbreak through organization, confrontation, termination, and reaction.

IMPRISONMENT IN OTHER COUNTRIES

There are many differences in how countries of the world structure and use imprisonment, but a common theme seems to be the disproportionate incarceration of each country's minority group members.

KEY TERMS AND CONCEPTS

black rage theory (p. 338)
conjugal visits (p. 334)
deprivation model (p. 330)
Federal Bureau of Prisons (BOP) (p. 309)
Federal Correctional Complex (FCC) (p. 317)
importation model (p. 332)
inmate code (p. 323)
inmate roles (p. 323)
inmate subculture (p. 322)
maximum-security prisons (p. 313)
medium-security prisons (p. 313)
minimum-security prisons (p. 313)
pains of imprisonment (p. 330)
play families (p. 329)
prisonization (p. 322)
prison riot (p. 339)
socialization (p. 322)
supermax prisons (p. 314)
total institution (p. 322)
vulnerability theory (p. 338)

DISCUSSION QUESTIONS

1. Although many citizens are aware of increasing prison populations, they may not understand that the increase is especially due to the greater likelihood of certain offenders (e.g., drug offenders and burglars) more often receiving a prison sentence. Do you believe the offenders identified in this chapter as targets of the get-tough policy are the kinds of offenders toward whom the public really wants to get tough?
2. Discuss some reasons for the disproportionate numbers of minority group members in U.S. prisons—and seemingly in the prisons of other countries as well.
3. What are some problems and possible solutions to simultaneously using classification for management and classification for treatment?
4. What are some advantages and disadvantages of having prison industries that make a profit for the state?
5. Explain why you agree or disagree with Dostoyevsky's quote about a country's prisons being used to judge the society.

chapter 10

INSTITUTIONAL MANAGEMENT AND PROGRAMS

"Good morning, Warden," your assistant announces as you step into your office. "It looks like you have a busy day!"

"I'm afraid so," you respond while taking a seat at your desk. You remember glancing at your appointment book last night before leaving the office, and you are hoping now that the day isn't really going to be as packed as you thought. You are wrong, as the list of activities clearly reminds you. "This is why I get the big bucks!" you find yourself thinking.

8:30 A.M. Meet with assistant warden for security about complaints from women correctional officers regarding their acceptance by the male officers.

9:00 A.M. Do weekly presentation to the newly arriving inmates.

9:30 A.M. Meet with assistant warden for correctional programs about changes in the classification system for identifying the risks and needs of new inmates.

10:30 A.M. Meet with chaplain about requests from prisoners for changes in food offerings to better accommodate religious dietary restrictions.

12:00 P.M. Lunch meeting with committee of state legislators who want to get rid of weight lifting in the prisoners' recreation program.

1:30 P.M. Meet with directors of academic and vocational programs and encourage coordination of schedules to allow inmates to take academic classes while enrolled in vocational classes.

2:00 P.M. Go to the Prison Industries building to review progress in increasing production of school desks that will be sold to school districts in the state.

2:30 P.M. While at the Prison Industries building, meet with representatives from local private companies who are interested in hiring inmate labor to package their products for shipment to buyers.

3:30 P.M. Meet with students on tour from the local college who have questions about management problems presented by the presence of prison gangs.

4:00 P.M. Meet with the health services supervisor about trying to contain costs associated with health care for the increasing numbers of elderly inmates.

4:30 P.M. Meet with reporter from the local newspaper who wants an opinion about the recent legislation that allows the state to contract with private companies for correctional facilities.

As you look over the day's activities, the last one catches your eye, and you wonder if by 4:30 you might be ready to get out of this mess and join a private company as a consultant—or better yet, become a reporter and spend your day asking people why problems haven't been solved rather than being the one who has to solve them!

Our fictional warden does indeed have a busy fictional day! And, like all managers, she is going to have to find a way to answer all the questions, provide leadership and direction, and make sure the prison's mission statement is adhered to by all her staff. To appreciate the variety of activities in which prison administrators are involved, we will take a closer look at each of the topics the warden will have to address as her day progresses. But first, however, it is important to understand the organizational context in which prison management occurs.

Organizational Structure

Figure 10.1 shows a likely organizational chart for our fictional prison—Elm Tree Medium-Security Prison. At the highest level is the director of the state's Department of Corrections (DOC). Because the state has a separate Department of Youth Services, there are no juvenile facilities under the control of the DOC director. Those persons who do report directly to the DOC director are the assistant directors of correctional institutions, prison industries, and community corrections. Because Elm Tree Medium-Security Prison is an adult correctional facility, our warden reports directly to the assistant director for correctional institutions. Our warden as well as the wardens of the state's three other facilities—each of which has an organizational structure similar to the one we are following—are all on the same organizational level.

Prisons are obviously large organizations that are part of an even more complex bureaucracy that makes up a state's Department of Corrections. Although there is much to learn about that larger bureaucracy, our attention is focused on what happens in one particular facility. Of course, even focusing on one institution does not allow a complete review of that facility and all the management issues an administrator must face. Because choices must be made, this chapter looks specifically at some issues facing prison administrators as they manage their staff, programs, and inmates. The particular style an administrator uses to address management issues will have a significant impact on employees and inmates. But rather than spending time on management styles, we will focus on what are arguably the two most important areas for prison management: the staff and inmate programs. The key to each of these areas is staffing, so our attention is specifically directed toward management issues related to the staff responsible for security and to those responsible for treatment. After reviewing the roles played by these important prison employees, we will consider the specific management issues of prison industries, prison gangs, special-needs inmates, and private corrections.

FIGURE 10.1

Organizational Chart for a Hypothetical Medium-Security Prison

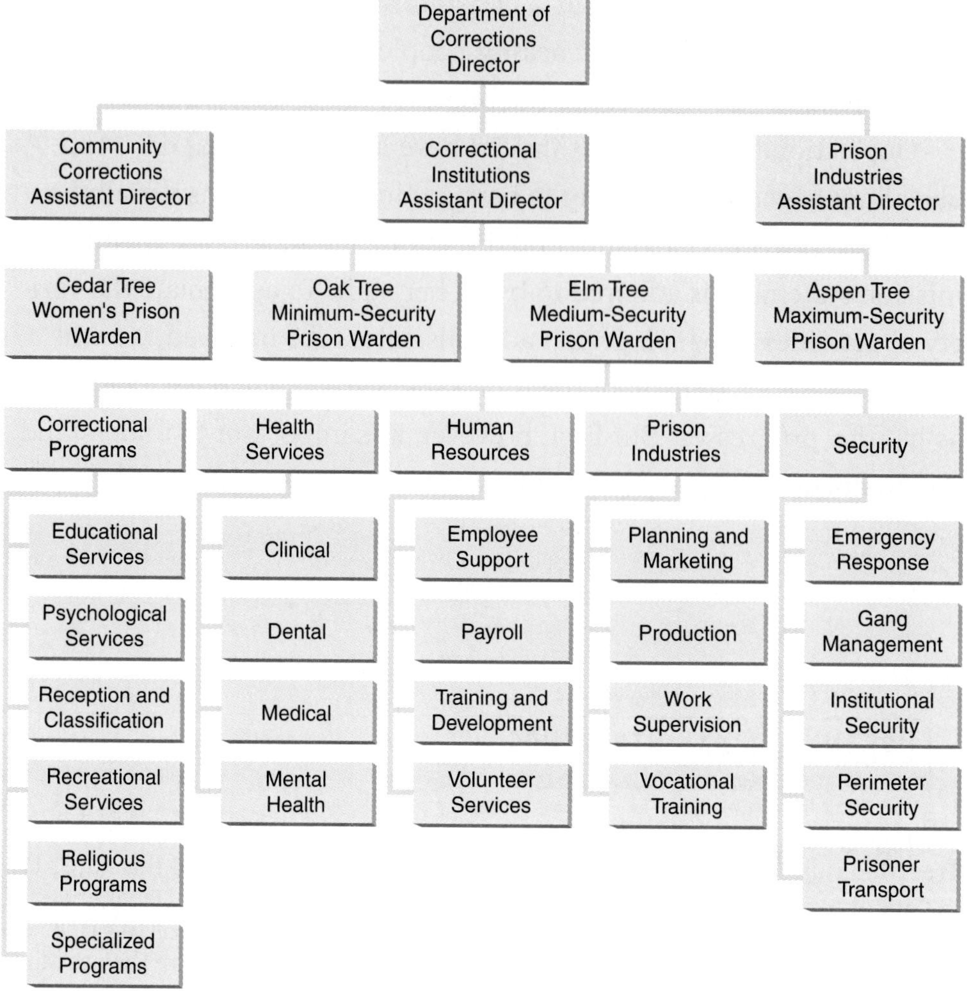

CORRECTIONAL OFFICERS

The successful operation of a prison requires a number of people filling a variety of positions. The positions include upper-level administrators such as directors of the Department of Corrections; wardens and assistant wardens; midlevel administrators such as security captains and program directors; and line staff such as correctional officers and treatment personnel. Because of their direct involvement with the prisoners, we will focus our attention on the correctional officers and treatment staff.

From Watchman to Correctional Officer

Those persons responsible for supervising the activities of jail and prison inmates have had a number of different names over the years. Lombardo (1981) explains that in early prison history, "watchmen" were charged with being on the lookout for breaches of the peace in institutions holding criminals of the day. Also early on were the "keepers," literally the "keepers of the keys," who were in charge of the keys for the whole institution. But eventually the watchman and keeper roles were expanded from being little more than a lookout to taking a more active part in enforcing the institution's discipline. To emphasize the enforcement function, the terms *officer* and *guard* were used. In the twentieth century, especially during the Rehabilitation era, the struggle for professionalism encouraged the use of the term *correctional officer*, so that such employees were rightfully included among the correctional workers or correctional staff charged with the care, custody, and improvement of the inmate.

Generally speaking, today's **correctional officers** (COs) are responsible for public safety (ensuring that criminals confined to an institution stay there), institutional security (guaranteeing that prisoners and staff are safe while in the institution), and at least in some facilities, for the treatment of the inmate. Borrowing from Lombardo (1981) we can identify six categories in which COs carry out their duties:

- *Housing unit officers*. These officers maintain order and ensure the security of the housing units. In some facilities they may also be involved in the treatment aspects of the prisoners in their unit. Their job is the one commonly pictured when correctional officer work is imagined.
- *Work detail supervisors*. Officers assigned to work detail monitor inmate behavior while they are working at general facility maintenance (e.g., kitchen, laundry, trash pick-up) in the prison or on outside details such as farming operations.
- *Industrial shop and school officers*. These officers monitor inmate activities at prison industry locations (e.g., furniture shop, street sign shop, upholstery shop) and while inmates are in academic or vocational classes.
- *Yard officers*. During recreation periods, yard officers maintain order and ensure security while inmates engage in or watch recreation activities such as basketball, baseball, weight lifting, and so on.
- *Administrative officers*. Officers with administrative duties are in supervisory positions over other correctional officers. The military structure of prison security often means these administrative officers will have ranks such as lieutenant, captain, and major.
- *Perimeter security officers*. In cell block–style prisons the perimeter officers are stationed in towers positioned along the high wall surrounding the prison grounds. In the contemporary podular-style prisons, perimeter officers often walk and drive patrol outside the razor wire perimeter.

Of these assignments, the housing unit officer probably has the busiest and most demanding job because she or he supervises and cares for inmates in their cell block or other housing area. There are cells to inspect, violent behavior to watch out for, housekeeping chores to be completed, inmate personal problems to solve, and an environment to make secure. The responsibility they carry and the management and organizational skills they demonstrate generally earn block officers the respect of other COs.

The kind of person who works as a CO has been the focus of several studies over the years. Lombardo (1981) reviews some of the pre-1980 studies that include looking at COs as one of five categories of change agents, or as one of four officer types (persistent, good, kind, or weak guard). Adler, Mueller, and Laufer (1994) comment on research that divides COs into either three groups ("Pollyannas," "white hats," or "hard asses") or five ("John Waynes," "wishy-washies," "lazy-laid-backs," "all rights," and "dirty cops"). Schmalleger (1995) lists six kinds of officers, classified according to certain characteristics they possess:

- "The Dictator," a bully CO who gains ego satisfaction by having near total control over others.
- "The Friend," a friendly officer who fraternizes with inmates and tries to control by being "one of the guys."

Help Wanted

Job Title: Correctional Officer

Position Description: Persons serving as correctional officers must be of sound moral character and able to deal with inmates in a firm manner while showing themselves to be worthy of trust by maintaining unimpeachable conduct on and off duty. Correctional officers are responsible for the custody and security, as well as the safety and well-being, of inmates. Duties include supervising the movement and activities of inmates, making periodic rounds of assigned areas, conducting searches for contraband, maintaining order within the facility, and preparing reports as necessary.

Qualifications: Applicants must pass a written civil service exam and undergo a drug-screening test as well as extensive medical, psychological, and background checks.

For examples of career opportunities in this field, check the appropriate Web page for your state's Department of Corrections (find links at ***database.corrections.com/career/index.asp#state***). For federal positions with the BOP, go to ***www.bop.gov/recruit.html***. Examples of individual state links include New York State's Department of Correctional Services jobs page at ***www.docs.state.ny.us/Jobs/jobs.html***. You will also find interesting the types of situations in which COs often find themselves at ***www.geocities.com/CapitolHill/4815/onduty.htm***.

- "The Merchant," a CO who, in exchange for money, supplies inmates with contraband items such as drugs, pornography, or even weapons.
- "The Indifferent," an officer who cares little about the working of the prison and often views inmates as worthless people incapable of changing.
- "The Climber," often a young CO planning his or her promotion up the administrative ranks and, therefore, less interested in the inmates than in ways to improve institutional procedures.
- "The Reformer," a "do-gooder" officer who believes prisons should provide opportunity for personal change and actually tries to help the inmates.

Just because one can find individual examples of COs taking these roles, that does not mean these roles are considered appropriate. The dictator, friend, and merchant especially are not tolerated by prison management or even by other COs.

Studies that categorize COs provide interesting information about the kind of person a CO might be and about the way a CO approaches his or her job. But the diversity of such categorization hides some demographic facts about COs that point to more similarity than variety among their ranks. According to Camp and Camp (1997), COs in state adult prison systems tend to be male (about 70 percent), white (about 70 percent), and non-Hispanic (about 93 percent). But despite their fewer numbers, interesting and informative research has been conducted in recent years on women COs. The remainder of our discussion about COs concentrates on these women.

Female Correctional Officers

We learned earlier that the first correctional officers were called several things—but "ma'am" was not one of them. The earliest prisoners, both male and female, were guarded by men. At times the male guards physically abused and sexually exploited women prisoners.

The process of replacing male guards with female matrons began in the 1820s but did not move very quickly. The first female jail matron was appointed in Maryland in 1822, but female guards for a prison did not occur until 1832 when Auburn prison hired women for the Auburn women's wing that had opened seven years earlier. In the late nineteenth and early twentieth centuries, as states built facilities specifically for women offenders, some legislatures required the institutions to be administered and staffed entirely by women. Later much of that legislation was repealed (because of a shortage of qualified women managers and a lack of faith by male legislators in the administrative abilities of women), thus allowing males to assume administrative positions in facilities for women (Zupan, 1992).

The situation improved in the 1970s when women began more forcefully asserting their rights to job and advancement opportunities. In 1972 Congress added the Title VII amendment to the 1964 Civil Rights Act and in doing so prohibited sex-based employment discrimination by public employers at state, county, and local levels. As a result of Title VII, the courts have generally upheld a woman's right to employment. For example, in *Grummet v. Rushen* (587 F. Supp. 913; 1984) a woman's right to employment in all-male institutions was recognized as taking precedence over inmates' rights to privacy. However, Title VII has not always been interpreted by the courts as prohibiting all versions of sex-based employment decisions. For example, in *Dothard v. Rawlinson* (433 U.S. 321; 1977) the U.S. Supreme Court ruled that height and weight requirements violated Title VII but that it was permissible to ban women from working in certain sections of prisons that are deemed especially dangerous. Today in the adult systems, about 21 percent of the correctional officers are women; in the federal system, about 12 percent are women (Camp & Camp, 1997). Figure 10.2 shows that the percentage of female officers has gradually increased during the 1990s.

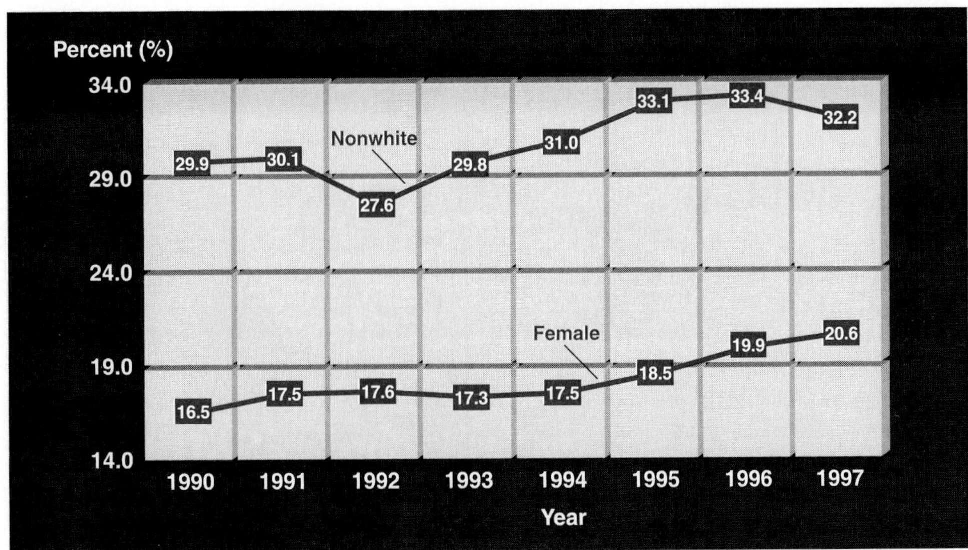

FIGURE 10.2

Percentage of Female and Nonwhite Correctional Officers on January 1 (1990–1997)

Source: Camp, C. G., & Camp, G. M. (1997). *The corrections yearbook, 1997.* South Salem, NY: Criminal Justice Institute.

Of course, a more telling percentage is for the women COs assigned to all-male prisons. By 1981 all but four state correctional systems (Alaska, Pennsylvania, Texas, and Utah) employed women as correctional officers in all-male prisons (Zupan, 1992). Today female COs are found in all jurisdictions, and one of those once reluctant states, Texas, has more female officers working in male institutions than does any other state (Camp & Camp, 1997). Data (provided by Camp and Camp) from forty-two states, the District of Columbia, and the federal system show that the majority (81 percent) of female COs are assigned to male institutions whereas about 4 percent of male COs are assigned to female institutions. Although such numbers are interesting, even more thought provoking are some perceived gender differences because those perceptions may influence the acceptance of women COs in male prisons.

Acceptance of Female COs. Female COs have always experienced resistance to their presence in male prisons—at least from the male COs. Interestingly, women COs have faced less resistance from the male inmates than they have from male officers. A study of female officers in Minnesota yielded results similar to other findings that show continuing lack of acceptance for women COs (Lawrence & Mahan, 1998). More women than men believed that women COs were accepted by male officers in Minnesota prisons, and more women than men believed that most inmates accepted women as COs. Most men believed women should be hired, but their percentage (80 percent) was significantly smaller than the nearly unanimous (96 percent) response from women who believed women should be hired.

Reasons offered for the hesitancy some male COs have about female COs include an argument that the presence of women officers in men's prisons threatens the "macho" image and behavioral norms that often characterize the prison officer subculture. Similarly, some have argued that the use and threatened use of physical force over inmates is needed to maintain control over the inmates. Female COs, the argument continues, do not possess the necessary physical attributes or attitudes to accomplish that task. The argument has been weakened as more female COs perform their duties without compromising their own or their fellow officers' safety.

Is Safety Compromised with Female COs? If female COs are more likely than male COs to be assaulted, the hiring of women for such jobs is questionable. Even if

Women correctional officers are now employed in men's and women's prisons at all security levels.

women COs are not harmed more often, an argument could be made for their exclusion from CO positions in male prisons if greater chance of injury to male officers or inmates occurs when women are on duty. That could happen if the female officer is not as able as a male officer to come to the aid of an officer or an inmate who is being assaulted. However, there is no evidence to support either of these concerns.

Rowan (1996) explains that a national survey showed that female officers in the maximum-security prisons in forty-eight states, the District of Columbia, and the federal BOP were assaulted less often than were male officers. Even in the seven states with the highest percentage of female COs, Rowan still found fewer assaults of women officers and even discovered that assaults of male officers in those seven states were below the national average. Those findings agree with other studies, which consistently indicate that women are not assaulted more frequently nor more seriously than men officers. Nor is there any evidence that male COs are assaulted more frequently when there are more women working in the prison (Lawrence & Mahan, 1998). Well, the persistent skeptic argues, maybe female COs are not assaulted as often because they are not doing the same job as the male COs.

Assigned Duties and Job Performance. Research from the 1980s found that the roles and responsibilities to which women COs were assigned were not always comparable to those given to male officers (Lawrence & Mahan, 1998). That seems to be occurring less often today, but the actual and perceived performance of those duties still have gender-related aspects.

Lawrence and Mahan (1998) review research on that topic and report findings about women officers having a calming effect on male prisoners, a perception by inmates that women officers improve the atmosphere of the institution, and a belief that the presence of female COs tends to reduce tension and hostility in the institution.

If a calming effect and reduced tension result from the presence of female COs, some wonder if that means women officers have a more positive attitude toward inmates' needs or greater understanding of inmate problems. However, existing research does not support such a view. In fact, no gender differences have been found in the attitudes that male or female COs have toward inmates. So, if differing attitudes toward the inmates do not explain the inmates' positive perception about the impact female COs have on the prison environment, could it be that the women officers are performing their duties differently? Again, existing research has not found any such differences. Simon and Simon (1993), for example, researched disciplinary write-ups (tickets) in a medium-security prison housing 650 male felons. They found that male and female COs wrote tickets for the same types of violations, prisoners were just as likely to claim they were not guilty of the violation whether it was issued by a female or male CO, the hearing officers were just as likely to uphold or reject tickets regardless of the CO's gender, and the sanctions given to guilty prisoners did not differ by the gender of the CO. Simon and Simon (1993) conclude that "clearly, gender makes no difference. . . . [and] the authority of the women corrections officers is as legitimate as that of their male colleagues" (p. 232). Similarly, Rowan (1996) found that female officers are at least as firm as male officers in managing inmates involved in serious incidents.

If women COs are doing essentially the same jobs as their male peers, are completing their job without incurring increased risk of personal harm, have similar attitudes toward the inmates, and enforce the rules in a similar manner, how does one explain the perception that female officers have a positive and calming effect on the prison? Resolution of that issue must await additional research, but it seems possible that the answer will confirm suspicions that women COs are more adept at—or at least more willing to use—verbal skills to gain voluntary compliance from inmates.

TREATMENT STAFF AND PROGRAMS

Although treatment programs in prisons may have been more prominent during the Rehabilitation era, they have existed in some form in all prison eras and regardless of which punishment philosophy was dominant. The people charged with carrying out the treatment duties range from full-time psychiatrists conducting intensive individual counseling to correctional officers charged with implementing treatment objectives in conjunction with their regular daily routine. The programs through which treatment objectives are achieved are also quite varied. Because we get a better idea of treatment in a prison environment by looking at the programs rather than at the staff in charge of those projects and services, this section concentrates on the programs themselves after brief mention of the treatment staff.

Treatment Staff

Researchers interested in prison employees have concentrated their studies on correctional officers rather than treatment staff. That may be a result of researchers' desire to find out more about those prison employees having direct and continuous interaction with prisoners. Because of the nature of their duties, employees of a prison's treatment staff may actually spend much of their workday without having direct interaction with prisoners. Instead, they may be completing paperwork, evaluating tests the prisoners completed, making arrangements for outside assistance in particular cases, and so on. Also—although there are certainly exceptions—many treatment personnel will only be at the prison from 8:00 A.M. to 5:00 P.M. on Mondays through Fridays. Finally, persons who are members of the treatment staff are often in occupations that are found in a variety of other institutional and noninstitutional settings. As a result, researchers may not be as interested in studying social workers, psychologists, chaplains, recreation therapists, and others just because they work in a prison. The occupation of correctional officer, on the other hand, is restricted to prisons and jails.

Whatever the reason, it is difficult to provide more than basic descriptive information about the treatment staff in prisons. It is much easier and probably more helpful to describe the types of programs those staff members deal with. So, attention is focused on those programs after a brief description of the staff charged with providing treatment.

Figure 10.3 shows the distribution of mental health and counseling staff in forty-eight adult correctional agencies (Kansas and South Dakota contract for mental health staff rather than have them as regular employees). The small percentage of psychiatrists making up the mental health and counseling staff may reflect the higher salary those physicians command, but it may also indicate the difficulty of providing individual attention in a setting in which people are more typically responded to in groups. When considering the percentage of total agency staff that the mental health and counseling staff comprise, Camp and Camp (1997) report an average of 3.4 percent. Nebraska (with 17.3 percent) had the largest percentage of mental health and counseling staff among its total staff, whereas Connecticut, Hawaii, Missouri, New Jersey, and Oklahoma all reported fewer than 1 percent of their total staff were in the mental health and counseling area.

To get an idea of the type of activities in which some of these treatment staff members are involved, we will look more closely at examples of typical prison treatment programs. But before doing that, we must start at the same place as the inmates—the classification stage. This is where the treatment staff help determine, in part, what needs the inmates have and which prison programs are most appropriate given those needs. Importantly, all this is done in the context of the risk the inmates present to themselves and others. So, just because some inmates would benefit from vocational training, such assignments would not be made without considering the risks posed by placing those inmates in a minimum-security facility in which vocational training is offered. These are the type of decisions made during the classification process.

Classification

The history of imprisonment has not always included a procedure for separating different types of prisoners. One reason for the absence of separation was a failure to accept the idea that there are, in fact, different types of prisoners. The earliest recog-

FIGURE 10.3

Percentage of Mental Health and Counseling Staff in Forty-Eight Adult Correctional Agencies (1997)

Source: Camp, G. M., & Camp, C. G. (1997). *The corrections yearbook, 1997.* South Salem, NY: Criminal Justice Institute.

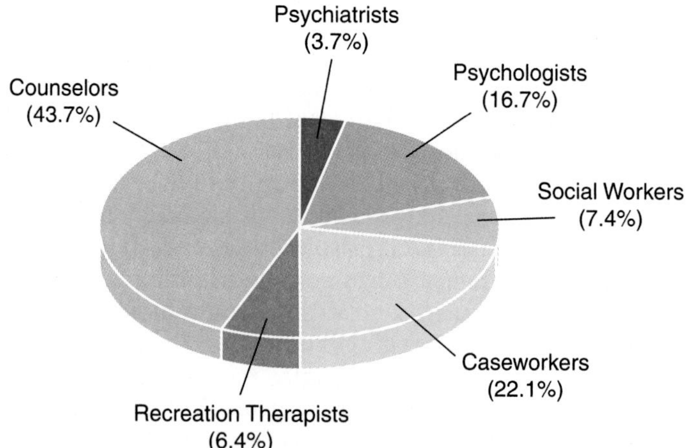

nition of this point (the 1500s) resulted in separating minor offenders from the more serious ones and women prisoners from the men. In the early eighteenth century, the Hospice of St. Michael was established specifically for wayward boys. By the midnineteenth century, separation of younger and older offenders was fairly well established worldwide. The basis for these types of separation was primarily humanitarian and moral in nature, and their appropriateness seems self-evident today.

In the twentieth century, prison officials began appreciating other reasons for separating offenders according to certain criteria. During the Industrial era, many states had procedures that distinguished prisoners who could be expected to do a good day's work from those who could not. As noted in the coverage of the Rehabilitation era in Chapter 4, the separation of offenders eventually came to have a key role in achieving a treatment goal within the prison. By this time in the early twentieth century, the process was being called **classification;** and it was used to both segregate and diagnose offenders. At the end of the twentieth century, classification continued to be an important feature of imprisonment, but its purpose had been modified to better fit the changing penal philosophies.

Contemporary classification serves two functions: management and treatment. The management purpose is like the early segregation role, but it implies more than simple separation. Similarly, the treatment purpose is like the diagnosis role, but it addresses concerns of public safety while considering the needs of the offender. In addition, classification today (for both purposes) is more objective than it was previously. To gain an understanding of contemporary classification in U.S. prisons, we will look at the issue of objectivity and then at each function of classification.

Objectivity in Classification. Until the mid-1970s, classification procedures were primarily subjective in nature. Decisions about which prisoners needed what services were made in the "professional opinion" of treatment personnel, whereas decisions about segregation of offenders were based on the "experiences" of the security staff. In the mid-1970s, efforts to make classification more objective began appearing. Those efforts were not, however, simply the result of concerns by officials to make classification more consistent and valid, although some correctional personnel certainly had such goals. Also important were some court decisions, which directed prison officials to make changes in the classification process. Throughout the latter half of the 1970s, federal courts ruled that classification, though not constitutionally required (*French v. Heyne,* 1977), must be rational and reasonable rather than arbitrary and capricious (*Kelley v. Brewer,* 1975; *Laaman v. Heigemore,* 1977; *Pugh v. Locke,* 1976). By the 1980s the courts continued to agree that there was no constitutional requirement for a classification system, but they also recognized that there may be times when classification is necessary to ensure inmates' constitutional right to a safe and secure living environment (*Grubbs v. Bradley,* 1982).

The requirement by federal courts that classification be rational and reasonable was not accompanied by specific criteria for prison officials to use in meeting those conditions. The variation in prison (and jail) circumstances, within and among the states, requires flexibility for officials to control the way that classification criteria and procedures are designed (Belbot & del Carmen, 1993). In the spirit of flexibility, state departments of corrections have tried various classification schemes that are rational and reasonable ways to meet management and treatment objectives. These **objective classification systems** base decisions on explicitly defined criteria that are organized into a classification instrument accompanied by procedures for systematically applying the instrument to inmates (Alexander & Austin, 1992).

One of the best known and most widely used of the objective classification instruments was developed in Wisconsin in the mid-1970s. Other states have adapted similar instruments, which are now used in probation, parole, and institutional settings. The common theme among the instruments is an attempt to gauge an offender's **risk level** and **needs level.** Assessment of risk helps officials in the field decide an appropriate level of probation or parole supervision, whereas institutional officials can determine better the appropriate security level and specific facility for individual offenders. Assessment of needs, on the other hand, helps officials identify areas that are likely to remain criminogenic if they are not addressed.

Classification for Management. Increasing prison populations since the 1970s required prison officials to pay particular attention to strategies that would encourage and allow the efficient use of institutional resources. Classification became a key element in this process as corrections officials, including those in both noninstitutional and institutional settings, sought to manage offender populations in rational and reasonable ways.

Of particular concern for prison officials is that their limited resources are used in the most efficient way. This means, for example, that offender **overclassification** must be kept to a minimum. Overclassification occurs when a prisoner is assigned to a level of greater supervision than that person actually needs. Offenders should be placed in the least restrictive custody level possible without compromising their own safety or the safety of other inmates, staff, or the community (Solomon & Camp, 1993). When a person actually needing only medium security is placed in the more costly maximum-security facility, the limited resources are not being effectively used, and the inmate is being treated unfairly. Objective classification should be used to reduce instances of overclassification.

Increasing prison populations have also meant that prison officials must be very prudent in choosing the programs that will be made available to prisoners. It does little good to provide vocational training in areas such as auto mechanics and air-conditioning repair if the prisoners are unable to read and write. Classification can help identify characteristics of the prison population that can in turn be used to make decisions about what treatment programs might be most appropriate at the facility. With these data, officials can allocate programs among state correctional institutions, make specific and justified budget requests for programs, or identify the need for problem-specific programs such as ones for sex offenders or violent offenders. Solomon and Camp (1993) explain that when classification is used for management purposes, "only those inmates presenting a substantial risk to others are placed in costly, high security institutions, while those demonstrating less risk and a reduced need for supervision can be placed in lower security facilities" (p. 7). In addition, classification can also provide administrators with information about current and projected populations that can be useful in facility and program planning.

Classification for Treatment. Under the medical model that was popular during the Rehabilitation era, classification was touted as the necessary ingredient for achieving the goal of rehabilitation. Without a diagnosis or classification, officials would not know what to treat or how to treat it. Identifying the offender's problems and determining his or her needs was a complicated job that required the services of specialists from the fields of medicine, psychology, education, social work, religion, and sociology. Representatives from these areas would conduct interviews and prepare evaluations of the offenders shortly after their arrival at the institution. Their reports were condensed in a classification summary to be used by a classification committee to determine such things as the inmate's living arrangements, work assignment, and treatment program. Yepsen (1975), writing in the grandest spirit of the medical model, said the classification committee should try to determine (1) what kind of an individual the offender really is, (2) how she got that way, (3) what his assets are, (4) what her deficiencies and liabilities are, and (5) how his assets can be used to his advantage while the deficiencies are corrected and the needs met.

Rather than taking a diminished role as the medical model faded away, classification maintained its importance as part of prison administration. Not only did it provide a useful management tool, it also retained a treatment aspect. The difference in its pre- and post-1970s' link to treatment is best explained by a contrast between the medical model of rehabilitation and a contemporary model of reintegration. Whereas the medical model's version of treatment sought to rehabilitate (change or modify) the offender within the prison walls, today's view of treatment emphasizes reintegration (restoration or adjustment) in the community (MacKenzie, 1989). The emphasis on reintegration over rehabilitation requires classification advocates to pay increased attention to an assessment of the offender's risk to public safety.

Although classification for reintegration has influenced the classification procedures and criteria (e.g., risk scales are of equal or greater importance to needs scales), classification for treatment is still found in most contemporary prison systems. Rehabilitation may no longer be riding high on a wave of popularity and optimism, but neither has it been sucked out to sea by an undertow. Prison systems still employ professionals in areas of medicine, education, social work, religion, psychology, and sociology, and they still prepare classification summaries that are used by classification committees to make prisoner assignments and determine program activities. MacKenzie (1989) suggests that today's version of classification for treatment falls into two types: developmental models and problem-area models.

Developmental models are classification systems that rely on deductions made from theoretical perspectives. An especially popular version of this type model is the integration level, or I-level, theory of personality development. The theory suggests that individuals pass through progressive levels of interpersonal interaction as they mature. The newborn infant, as the least mature person, is at level 1; those very few people who eventually get as mature as possible are assigned level 7. Progression to each level is not automatic with age, and arguments are made that delinquents especially get stalled at I-levels 2 through 4, where they focus on their own needs (level 2), are primarily interested in power issues (level 3), or are just beginning to internalize values (level 4).

Upon identifying an offender's I-level, the staff can design specific treatment strategies appropriate for a person at that level of development. The level might even indicate which staff member could work best with that offender. Juvenile offenders, for example, might benefit from treatment designed to help them move to a higher I-level, thus reducing the likelihood of continued criminal behavior. Adult offenders, on the other hand, may have reached their highest level and would benefit most from treatment strategies that help them adjust to their current level of development yet refrain from involvement in crime (MacKenzie, 1989).

Whereas developmental models are designed in a theoretical fashion, the **problem-area models** begin with the data and develop a theory based on an interpretation of those data. One example of this technique is the Adult Internal Management Systems (AIMS), which has been used to classify adults in prison. Factor-analysis techniques were used to identify five different types of individuals: the aggressive psychopath, the manipulator, situational, inadequate–withdrawn, and neurotic–anxious. Two checklists are prepared for each prisoner. One is completed by a trained correctional officer after observing a newly admitted prisoner. Another is prepared by a caseworker after interviewing the offender and reading supplemental reports such as the presentence investigation. The information is then used to assign the offender to one of the five types.

After treatment staff know what type of individual the new prisoner is, they can make living and work assignments based on that knowledge. For example, aggressive psychopaths and manipulators might be safely put together, but it could be undesirable to have a manipulator sharing a cell with a neurotic–anxious. Using the AIMS classification for such placement purposes gives it a classification for management aspect, but there is no reason why one strategy should not help meet several goals. The reason for discussing it here is to highlight its treatment feature, and, in the best tradition of classification for rehabilitation, AIMS categories certainly work as an important diagnostic tool. Also, because some treatment staff may have a knack for working with aggressive individuals such as the aggressive psychopath, whereas others do best with more "normal" people such as the situational, the classification can help with staff assignments as well as program development.

Whether prisons use developmental models, problem-area models, or other groupings of models (see MacKenzie, 1989) to carry out classification for treatment, it is important to realize that the classification process is still being used for rehabilitation purposes. In combination, classification for management and classification for treatment are upholding the traditions of a classification process that has been a feature of prison systems for centuries and that seems likely to continue, in some form, for the foreseeable future.

Help Wanted

Job Title: Chaplain

Position Description: Chaplains are responsible for establishing religious programs for various denominational groups and facilitating the distribution of religious materials. Chaplains also serve as liaisons between inmates and staff.

Qualifications: Graduation from a four-year college and from a recognized school of theology. Applicant must be ordained as a member of the clergy, in good standing with his or her denomination, and have satisfactorily completed one year of clinical pastoral education in a recognized training program, or have two years of experience as a parish clergyman or clergywoman, or an equivalent combination of education and experience.

This particular job description comes from North Carolina's DOC site at ***www.doc.state.nc.us/careers/programs.htm,*** and you will find similar descriptions at the various state DOC sites as listed at ***database.corrections.com/career/index.asp#state.***

Treatment Programs

As noted earlier, classification has both management and treatment objectives. In this section on treatment staff and programs, we are especially interested in the result of classification for treatment. Consistent with the rehabilitation model, after the prisoner's problems, and needs have been identified through the classification process, a treatment program must be implemented to respond to those needs. Of the many types of programs available in prisons, we will look at those in the general areas of religion, academic and vocational education, recreation, and self-betterment.

Religion. Since at least the seventeenth century, when the monastic principles of penitence and reflection were applied to offenders as a way to help wrongdoers see the evil of their ways, religious programs have been linked to prisons. In the nineteenth-century United States, the Quakers assured a connection between inmates and church personnel by including ministers among the few visitors allowed at the Eastern State Penitentiary and by limiting reading material to the Bible.

Today prisons typically provide opportunities for inmates to practice their religion, to have contact with clergy, and to access religious publications. Prisoners often participate in religious services, sing in choirs, assist clergy, have religious literature study sessions, and engage in other religion-based activities that might help them "get through" the prison experience even if it does not significantly affect their behavior after release (see "Finding Religion in Prison").

Dammer (1996) explains that most state and federal correctional institutions provide support for the four traditional religious denominations—Catholic, Protestant, Muslim, and Jewish. Regional variation and inmate interest also result in representation in some prisons by faiths such as Buddhist, Rastafarian, Jehovah Witness, Native American Church, Moorish Temple, and Black Hebrew Israelite Nation. The chaplains, volunteers, and spiritual advisors representing the various faiths may be assigned to the prison facility itself (especially for the major denominations) or might be regular visitors from the outside (for those denominations with fewer adherents in the prison). The traditional duties for the faith representatives were to provide religious services, counsel troubled inmates, and advise inmates of "bad news" from home or from prison authorities. More recently,

Spotlight ON CONTEMPORARY ISSUES

Finding Religion in Prison

Although religious programming may be the oldest type of rehabilitation for prisoners, there are cynics today who wonder why religious instruction and practices are allowed in prisons. After all, those skeptics argue, if the offenders were all that religious to begin with they wouldn't be in prison. The easy response to that statement is that just as developing vocational skills in prison may facilitate law-abiding behavior after release, acquiring a moral base for one's life may encourage virtuous conduct both in and outside prison.

Dammer (1996) asked inmates about practicing religion while in prison and received both personal and pragmatic answers. In some cases the inmates found religion provided direction and meaning for their lives and was a source of hope that their future held more promise than their past. Inmates also reported that religion improved their self-concept because the core of many religious beliefs is acceptance and love from a higher being and from members of the faith group.

Many of those reasons for involvement in religion are probably not much different than ones given by persons not in prison. However, Dammer also found some explanations that are not as likely to be found outside the prison environment. For example, some inmates reported using religion as protection from other prisoners. Without attachment to a group, as discussed in Chapter 9, inmates may be vulnerable to physical confrontations, and economic or sexual exploitation. Rather than choosing affiliation with a prison gang, some prisoners may attach to faith groups as a way to gain protection. This may be an especially attractive option for inmates who, because of their crime, are considered loathsome among the prison population (often a sex offense such as child molestation or sexual assault of an older woman). These stigmatized inmates may see involvement in religion as providing some respite from the fear of attack by other inmates. Religious services, for example, become a "safe haven."

Another prison-specific reason for involvement in religious activities is as a way to get certain prison resources that are otherwise difficult or costly to obtain. Dammer gives as examples such free goods as food and coffee, holiday items, and even musical instruments. In addition, the faith representatives may provide inmates with access to special favors such as phone access or might give written support to the inmate's request for work or living assignment changes.

There are, it appears, some prisoners who use religion to manipulate the systems. But it is equally obvious that other prisoners use religion as a mechanism for support and self-improvement. One wonders if those extremes are necessarily different from the purposes that religion serves for people not in prison.

Read "Buddha behind Bars" at ***www.westword.com/archives/1998/100898/feature1-1.html.*** Do you think meditation has a place in prison rehabilitation programs? Also review the frequently asked questions about the Federal Bureau of Prisons Chaplaincy at ***www.bop.gov/cpdpg/cpdchfaq.html.*** What are the qualifications for a chaplain? Are chaplains expected to work with persons of faiths other than the chaplains'?

Dammer explains, their role has expanded to include organizing volunteers, facilitating religious furlough visits, contracting for outside religious services, and training prison staff about the basic tenets and rituals of the different faith groups—especially the nontraditional ones about which some staff members may have limited or no knowledge.

As discussed in Chapter 14, religion presents some controversial issues for prison administrators, who are now being asked to support religious programs ranging from the traditional to the whimsical. But despite new challenges presented by resourceful inmates seeking everything from special liqueurs after dinner (Church of the New Song) to pointed objects and animal blood (Satanists), religion remains an important and supported aspect of prison programs.

Academic and Vocational Programs. Teaching and training efforts also have a long history in prisons. Even before the Reformatory era (1860s to 1900s), inmates were receiving vocational training and some academic education, but it was primarily

Help Wanted

Job Title: Academic Teacher

Position Description: Academic teachers working in a department of corrections facility must be able to function in a security-oriented environment. Duties include preparing course and unit outlines, lesson plans, educational progress reports, individual education plans, and acting as advisor to student groups and organizations.

Qualifications: Applicants must have the necessary college degrees and certification for the position being sought.

For examples of career opportunities in this field, check the appropriate Web page for your state's department of corrections (find links at ***database.corrections.com/career/index.asp#state).*** Also see the job listings at ***www.prisons.com/employ.*** General information for New York State teaching positions is found at ***www.cs.state.ny.us/announ/cr_announcements/20–740.htm.***

for the benefit of the institution, which could earn a profit from the educated prison laborer. Educational programs expanded during the Rehabilitation era, and prisons around the country offered inmates opportunities such as completing a high school education, obtaining a general equivalency diploma (GED), or receiving training in vocational areas such as welding, auto mechanics, or masonry.

Both educational and vocational programs continue today, although financial constraints are forcing some states to cut back on the number and variety of classes offered. College-level classes have especially been reduced as a result of a provision in the 1994 Violent Crime Control and Law Enforcement Act to deny all prisoners access to federal Pell Grants (see "College Classes for Prisoners"). Some benefits of vocational training are discussed later along with prison labor programs.

Academic education at elementary and secondary levels seems obviously needed when we consider how poorly educated many inmates are. Results from the National Adult Literacy Survey (NALS), the largest and most inclusive survey of English language skills ever conducted in the United States, provide information about prisoner literacy (National Center for Education Statistics, 1996). Rather than using the standard approach to studying adult literacy as being something a person either has or does not have, the NALS measures literacy based on performance across a variety of tasks encountered in daily life (e.g., reading and writing letters, filling out forms, reading information from agencies and companies, and doing basic arithmetic). A randomly selected national sample of prisoners (the prison sample) was compared with a randomly selected national sample of adults not in prison (the household sample). Some findings from the survey include (Haigler, Harlow, O'Connor, & Campbell, 1996):

- Prisoners are more likely than others to have difficulty in performing tasks that require them to integrate or synthesize information from complex or lengthy texts.
- Prisoners are more likely than others to have difficulty in performing quantitative tasks that involve two or more sequential operations and that require the person to set up the problem.
- White inmates demonstrate higher average literacy than black inmates, who, in turn, demonstrate higher proficiencies than Hispanic inmates. However, whereas the average ability for white prisoners is lower than for white householders, the black and Hispanic prisoners showed about the same proficiencies as their household counterparts.
- Inmates do not have as high an opinion of their reading, writing, and arithmetic skills as do householders.

When reviewing the survey results, Haigler et al. note that an important aspect of being literate in our society is having the knowledge and skills to process information found in documents. Being able to manage a household, apply for a job, carry out the duties of most jobs, and generally interact in an information-based society requires basic literacy skills. Because individuals with lower levels of literacy (the categorization for about two-thirds of the prisoners) are more likely to be out of the labor force, literacy programs for inmates should not be lacking. Haigler et al. point out that we should not, however, place the entire burden on the prisons. Instead, individuals, groups, organizations, schools, and businesses need to go behind the walls and assist in the efforts to improve the literacy skills of inmates.

Recreation. Prisons today include more recreational activities than just the well-known "iron pile," where inmates lift weights. Although the iron pile remains popular, some legislators around the country are trying to take away weight-lifting opportunities from inmates they fear are getting too strong and in doing so present a physical threat to staff and other inmates (see the different issues related to

Spotlight ON CONTEMPORARY ISSUES

College Classes for Prisoners

We often think about academic education in prisons as being at the high school or lower level, but college classes have been taught in state and federal prisons for many decades. Prior to 1965 there were a few such classes around the country, but in that year Congress passed Title IV of the Higher Education Act. That act permitted inmates to apply for financial aid in the form of Pell Grants to attend college (Center on Crime, Communities & Culture, 1997). The number of higher education programs in correctional facilities began expanding and peaked in 1982 when they were available in 90 percent of the states.

Since the early and mid-1980s the public's view of prison programs has become more conservative. One result was an increasingly negative perspective on prisoners taking college classes—especially with the assistance of financial aid grants. Some college students express a widely felt notion when they sarcastically suggest that they should have committed a crime so they could go to prison and get a free college education. Aside from the obvious response about the difficulty of even a college graduate ex-con finding decent employment, students are unimpressed with the argument that grants to prisoners do not really affect the monies available to nonprisoners. As the Center on Crime, Communities & Culture (1997) points out, Pell Grants are based on need rather than competition. And, because there is not a limited amount of money for the Pell Grants, it is not as though prisoners are using the funds up before law-abiding citizens can get to them. The real irritation about inmates in college classes is more likely the perception that the courses simply confirmed the perception that prisoners have it too easy.

In response to such retributive and deterrence arguments, the rehabilitationists point to studies showing a connection between higher education—including participation in prison college programs—and lowered levels of recidivism (Center on Crime, Communities & Culture, 1997; Tewksbury & Taylor, 1996). In addition, the college education programs have a civilizing influence on the more vocal and leadership-oriented offenders and in that way are a positive influence on the prison environment as well as on the individual offender (Tewksbury & Taylor, 1996). And, because educated prisoners often serve as teachers and tutors for other inmates, the college programs provide positive role models in a group for which such role models are infrequent.

In 1994 the retributive argument won out and a provision in the Violent Crime Control and Law Enforcement Act effectively denied prisoners access to Pell Grants. Results of that provision include a decline in the number of higher education programs for inmates from 350 in 1990 to 8 in 1997 (Center on Crime, Communities & Culture, 1997). The payoff, in addition to the perspective that life in prison is now tougher for some inmates, is an estimated savings of one-tenth of 1 percent of the Pell Grants' annual budget. The costs related to any increased recidivism that might result from the program's absence have not been calculated.

Read the research brief at *www.soros.org/crime/research_brief_2.html.* What is the view of corrections officials regarding correctional education programs? What arguments are presented in response to the question "Why should prisoners receive higher education?"

weight lifting in prisons at www.strengthtech.com/). Other sports attract large followings as well. Most prisons have programs for traditional softball and basketball games, sometimes against local teams from the outside; and a few prisons even have full-dress football programs. Some prisons provide activities similar to those found in school physical education programs. They offer inmates opportunities to ice skate, ski, play tennis, or even participate in rodeo events.

Both the more exotic and the traditional kinds of recreational activities are cited by some prison critics as examples of coddling criminals instead of punishing them. Prisons that offer attractive surroundings and have full-fledged recreation programs or allow televisions in the cells are referred to as "Holiday Inns" or derogatorily called "Club Fed." But the classic response from prison officials to such criticism is that the prisoners have been sent there as punishment, not for

For over thirty years the Louisiana State Penitentiary at Angola has been the site of an annual rodeo. Prisoners, many of whom are experiencing their first close encounter with horses and cattle, replace cowboys as participants. The result is one of the more unique recreational activities found in a prison.

Help Wanted

Job Title: Recreation Therapist

Position Description: The recreation therapist develops and implements a recreation therapy program in a state correctional facility. Duties include maintaining order and supervising inmate conduct while protecting and maintaining the safety of persons and property in the facility. Programs are developed for all inmates, including those with physical, mental, and developmental disabilities.

Qualifications: Applicants should have a bachelor's degree in recreation or recreation therapy and must have the necessary strength, agility, and endurance to perform during stressful situations encountered in a correctional facility.

For examples of careers in this field, see the description at the California Department of Corrections's site at ***www.cdc.state.ca.us/inside/continuous/recthrp.htm.***

punishment. What members of the public might view as pampering is often seen by prison employees as a way to encourage good behavior and to provide a safer work environment. Recreation may have a peacekeeping role by offering safe and healthy ways for inmates to exert themselves and to help keep morale high. When those kinds of goals are achieved, prison employees have a safer work environment, the inmates enjoy safer living conditions, and prison violence is less likely.

In addition to benefits that recreational programs have for the safety and security of the prison itself, recreation can also rehabilitate. Prisoners who take up a sport may have new things to do with their leisure time after their release from prison. Instead of hanging out at the tavern, they might work out at the gym. Participating in recreational programs might also help the inmates develop a more positive self-image, discover unrecognized abilities, and realize the benefits of setting goals.

Self-Betterment. Programs in the areas of religion, education, and recreation could all be called *self-betterment*, but the term usually has a more specific meaning. During the Rehabilitation era especially, prison officials sought ways to respond to the needs of prisoners as identified under the medical model diagnosis. Those needs were varied because some prisoners had substance abuse problems, others had no understanding of personal finances, some were unable to express themselves in socially acceptable ways, and still others had inadequate interpersonal skills. Self-betterment programs were, and still are, set up to respond to these types of problems.

Some of the self-betterment programs in prison have counterparts on the outside. Alcoholics Anonymous, for example, has been a standard program in most prisons for many years. The less well-known Narcotics Anonymous uses a similar strategy to assist persons with drug problems, as does the prison-born Checks

Recreational programs in most prisons include the traditional softball and basketball games. Such activities provide safe and healthy ways for inmates to exert themselves, and they help keep morale high.

Anonymous program (apparently started at the Nebraska State Penitentiary in the 1960s) that views writing bad checks as an addiction. Other programs include prison chapters of Jaycees, which involve inmates in prison and local community service projects; and prison chapters of Toastmasters International (called Gavel Clubs in prisons), which enable inmates to improve their oral communication skills through public speaking exercises.

Other examples of prison programs are found throughout the country. Some of these will be reviewed in Chapter 15 in which we discuss program effectiveness.

MANAGING PRISON INDUSTRIES

Prison labor has been of constant concern to legislators, prison officials, business and labor people, and the general public through several generations of prison development. And, as explained in the feature "Prison Labor in Other Countries," it is an important topic in prisons throughout the world. Although inmate labor issues were covered in Chapter 4 as the focus in the Industrial era of prison development, they continue to play important and controversial roles in subsequent eras—especially as those issues relate to prison management.

State legislators determine general prison labor policy as they set the rules and regulations for the type of products produced by prison labor and for the sale and distribution of those products. Prison administrators must implement the policies developed by the legislators and, in the spirit of "the more things change, the more they stay the same," we find interesting historical and contemporary similarities about the role of prison labor. In the early 1840s, Georg Michael von Obermaier, an administrator for a German prison, argued that prison labor must be organized

Cross-Cultural Corrections

Prison Labor in Other Countries

As in the United States, prison labor in other countries is recognized as having potential benefit to both the inmate and the state. And, also as in U.S. jurisdictions, other countries find it difficult to balance those benefits.

The Human Rights Watch points out that some countries (e.g., Romania and South Africa in the early 1990s) have required their prisons to be self-financing so as not to be a burden on the national budget. Other countries, such as China, go beyond economic self-sufficiency and expect their prisons to generate a profit. The Russian labor colony, called the *gulag* under the Soviet system, "continues to be considered an important part of the country's production of goods" (Human Rights Watch, 1993, p. 58). Expectations of self-financing or even profit making are not necessarily bad, but such economic goals may promote abuse of prisoners whenever goals are not met. Reports from China suggest there are occasions when prisoners who have completed their sentences are forcibly retained by prison authorities for continued employment. In addition, failure to meet production quotas is one of the most frequently and harshly punished infractions in Chinese prisons.

In some countries, France and Spain, for example, there is a statutory recognition of a right to work—implying a recognition of the social, physical, and mental health aspects of work. But its practical application is apparently hard to achieve because less than half the prisoners in France and parts of Spain actually have the opportunity to work (Dünkel & van Zyl Smit, 1991). More often a country stipulates a duty to work—emphasizing the punitive aspects of labor. That labor may occur in the prisoners' cells, in factory-like workplaces, or for those assigned to maintenance work at various locations throughout the prison. As in France and Spain, however, it seems easier to state a policy requiring work as part of a prison sentence than to actually find opportunities for work.

Japan is an example of a country that seems better able to meet its duty to give prisoners work. The Corrections Bureau reports a 95 percent employment rate for inmates sentenced to prison with forced labor. Inmates might work in their cell at simple tasks such as gluing paper bags or packing chopsticks in envelopes; or they may be assigned to a prison factory to work at industries like printing, tailoring, paper making, or metal work (Corrections Bureau, 1995; Human Rights Watch/Asia, 1995). Japanese inmates work forty hours per week. Those employed in prison industry receive a gratuity; it is not considered a wage because all necessities are already provided to them. The gratuity is saved until the inmates' release—although in some cases the inmates can use the money for purchases in prison or send it home for family support.

Japan's ability to employ 95 percent of its prisoners is a statistic not so easily achieved in other countries. Morgan (1991) reports that England and Wales require sentenced prisoners to work but have difficulty finding much more than make-work jobs, such as cleaning, for the inmates. Even those prisoners who are employed at industrial work have an average work week of only nineteen hours. Prisoners in Denmark also have a duty to work, although that obligation may be substituted with participation in an educational program, for which inmates are paid as if they were at ordinary work (Jepsen, 1991). To emphasize the "duty" aspect, work assignments are enforced by a penalty of a fine, withholding of pay, and/or by solitary confinement.

Read about prison industries in Canada at *www.acjnet.org/cgi-bin/legal/legal.pl?lkey=no&ckey=indusjhs&tkey=docs.* What are some of the advantages and concerns Canadians have about private-sector involvement in inmate work programs?

along both educational and business lines. Obermaier adhered to the following principles when he took over the prison at Munich in 1842:

- Prison labor must be useful to both prisoners and the state.
- Prison labor systems operated by the state should not interfere with the free labor market.
- Prisoners should learn at least one trade for which there will be job opportunities available after the prisoners' release.
- The work to which prisoners are put should be hard but not ruinous to their health.
- Wages paid for the prisoners' labor should approximate those received by free laborers engaged in similar work. (Hoefer, 1937, p. 36)

Few people today would disagree with any of Obermaier's points—with the possible exception of similar wages—but contemporary prison officials still have problems implementing the principles that gave Obermaier difficulty over 150 years ago. We will look next at a few of these points, by discussing the benefits of prison labor and the link between prison labor and private business.

Benefits of Prison Labor to the Prisoner. Putting prisoners to work as part of their sentence appeals to supporters of most any penal philosophy. Hard labor, the retributivists might say, is just deserts for the wrong committed by the offender. When offenders must work in ways that compensate the community or the victim, proponents of the restoration philosophy are delighted. Making offenders work hard will deter them and others from criminal activity, argue the deterrence theorists. Even the incapacitation philosophy can claim that prisoners busy at work can be locked up longer and will present fewer problems to administrators. But arguments that prison labor actually benefits the prisoner are made more likely by supporters of a rehabilitation approach. Labor, they argue, offers an opportunity to develop good work habits and learn employable skills that will help offenders become law-abiding citizens.

The types of work in which today's state prison inmates are engaged can be divided into **prison industry work** or **institutional work assignments.** Both may help develop employable skills and good work habits, but prison industry jobs are more likely to provide training that allows the offender to seek skilled labor positions after release from prison. The institutional work assignments, on the other hand, can involve training (e.g., in areas such as janitorial service or food preparation) but tend not to be in particularly skilled areas. Even though assignments to areas such as cleaning and food preparation are more frequent than to more skilled areas such as goods production and hospital or medical work, all work assignments can be rehabilitative. They can, in other words, stimulate good work habits, occasionally provide training in areas in which the offender can later seek employment, and give prisoners a sense of self-worth and confidence after completing a job.

In some of its configurations, prison labor clearly had no rehabilitative purpose. As discussed in Chapter 4, the lease system of prison labor was especially notorious for its exploitative and physically harmful nature. Some prisoners have filed suits charging that mandatory labor, especially when it is without pay, is unconstitutional. The courts have not been sympathetic to such arguments (*Wendt v. Lynaugh*, 1988), especially since the Thirteenth Amendment to the U.S. Constitution prohibits slavery and involuntary servitude "except as a punishment for crime." Although some inmates protest being made to work, even if they are paid, other inmates complain when they are not allowed to work. Again, the courts tend to side with prison officials in finding that prison inmates have no constitutional right to prison employment (*Jackson v. O'Leary*, 1988).

The issues of "shouldn't have to work" and "must be allowed to work" are interesting and important, but an even more important issue related to benefits of prison labor to the prisoner is whether it might have an effect on the inmate's behavior after release from prison.

One of the more important studies on the rehabilitative aspect of prison labor was conducted by Saylor and Gaes (1995). Their research is especially interesting because it followed released offenders for as long as twelve years after their release from prison. The sample of over 7,000 male and female offenders from the Federal Bureau of Prisons were initially selected if they had participated in industrial work within the institution setting or had received in-prison vocational instruction or apprenticeship training. A comparison group of inmates released during the same calendar quarter as the subject group, but who had not participated in the work, vocational, or apprenticeship programs, was also followed.

Help Wanted

Job Title: Prison Industries Supervisor (e.g., Reupholstery)

Position Description: Prison industries supervisor (e.g., reupholstery) is responsible for supervision of unskilled medium-custody inmates in the reupholstery of furniture, including cushions, sofas, and chairs. Duties also involve the training of inmates in the safe and proper operation of related equipment and tools used in the reupholstery trade. The supervisor will organize and direct work assignments of inmates and will conduct visual surveillance of plant operations to ensure custody and security of inmates and facility.

Qualifications: Graduation from high school or equivalent. Two years of supervisory experience over unskilled workers preferably in a production-type operation.

For examples of career opportunities in this field, see the listings for prison industries on the North Carolina Department of Corrections's job site at *www.doc.state.nc.us/careers/jobs.htm.*

Saylor and Gaes have reported on the subjects' status at four stages: during their last year at the institution, at a halfway house after release, about one year after release, and about ten years after release. Results from the first stage found that inmates who participated in the work, vocational training, or apprenticeship programs (or some combination of these) were less likely than the comparison group to have a misconduct report during their last year in prison. Even when the program participants did receive a misconduct report, it was less likely to be for a serious violation. At the second stage of the study, the researchers found that the study group participants were more likely than the comparison group to obtain a full-time job or a day labor job at some point during their halfway house stay. However, there was no difference between the groups in terms of completing their halfway house stay without committing misconduct that would warrant their return to prison.

In the one-year study, Saylor and Gaes found that 6.6 percent of the study group and 10.1 percent of the comparison group had been rearrested or had their supervision revoked. That difference was statistically significant. In addition, the study group members were more likely to have found and maintained employment and were earning more money, on average, per month.

In their most recent study of the two groups, Saylor and Gaes determined how the participants had been doing about ten years later (as few as eight years for some and as many as twelve years for others). Using federal records (so any commitments to state prisons were not included), the researchers determined whether the study or comparison group members had been recommitted to a federal facility for a new offense (one measure of recidivism) or for a supervision revocation violation (another measure of recidivism). Suspecting, based on other studies, that women would be less likely than men to recidivate, the researchers analyzed males and females separately.

Women from both the study group and the comparison group were less likely to have been recommitted than were the men (19 percent versus 32 percent). However, the men had a longer survival time—suggesting to Saylor and Gaes that although women were less likely to fail, those who did failed much earlier than their male counterparts. In fact, so few women returned to prison (52 out of 913, or only 6 percent) the researchers hesitate to draw conclusions about any differences between women from the work group and those from the comparison group. They did analyze data for the men, however, and found that males from the work group had survival times at least 20 percent longer than the comparison group members. This interesting study concludes that in-prison employment in an industrial work setting and vocational and apprenticeship training can have both short-term and long-term benefits. Specifically, the likelihood of recidivism, especially for men, is reduced by participating in such programs (Saylor & Gaes, 1995).

The Saylor and Gaes study looked only at federal prisoners, but similar results are reported in state programs. Florida found that only 16.9 percent of inmates who were involved in its correctional industries program, PRIDE Enterprises, were recommitted within two years after the study's beginning in 1996. According to PRIDE's Annual Report, the national average recommitment rate is 40 percent (Ingley & Cochran, 1999). Utah found that inmates who had spent more than eighteen months in the state's correctional industries program had a recommitment rate of 30 percent—compared to Utah's overall recidivism rate of 70 percent (Ingley & Cochran, 1999, pp. 84–85). It is becoming increasingly clear that prison labor programs can have definite and important benefits for the prisoner.

Benefits of Prison Labor to the State. The state benefits from prison labor in several ways. First, to follow the theory that "idle hands are the devil's workshop," prison work reduces idleness and, therefore, the potential for security problems.

Prison labor may accomplish several goals, but one is to provide inmates with an opportunity to develop good work habits and to learn skills that will help them become law-abiding citizens.

In addition, prison work helps ensure that the prison's day-to-day maintenance requirements are met. But important as these are, the profit motive is probably the primary benefit of prison labor to the state. And, not surprisingly, it is the profit motive that causes the most discussion by both advocates and critics of the various prison labor systems.

In Chapter 4, the discussion of the Industrial era identified four open market labor systems (lease, contract, piece-price, and public account) and two sheltered market systems (state use, and public works and ways). The Industrial era came to a close as legislators began acting on the complaints about open market prison labor systems. Although the primary complaints against leasing (and, to a lesser extent, contracting) had been the involvement of private business in disciplining inmates and controlling their employment, the objections to piece-price, public account, and contracting were directed more toward the sale and marketing of the goods. It just did not seem fair to many people that private companies should have to compete on the open market with prison-made goods. The cheap labor costs for prison products meant they could be priced lower than those made by private business, or meant that the state could sell them at a competitive price but make a significantly greater profit than private companies could make. In the late 1920s, legislators began taking action that would make open market systems less advantageous for U.S. prisons (see "Prison Labor Laws").

Under contract, leasing, piece-price, and public account systems, prisons were often profitable institutions. But by the end of the 1920s, almost all state prison systems were running large deficits (Sullivan, 1990). Reform groups were not against putting prisoners to work; they just wanted that work to benefit the prisoner (preparing her or him for life outside the walls). Labor organizations were mostly concerned that prison labor and products did not directly compete for the jobs that should be available to law-abiding workers in the community. Private businesses did not like to have their products directly competing with those made by the state with reduced labor costs. The solution most acceptable to reformers, free-labor groups, and private business was the state use system. Because prison-made products under this

HISTORICAL PERSPECTIVES

Prison Labor Laws

In 1929 the federal government passed the Hawes-Cooper Act, which made interstate transportation of prison-made goods more difficult by subjecting the products to control by the laws of the receiving state. That meant, for example, that North Carolina could protect its furniture makers by prohibiting Illinois and Michigan from selling in North Carolina any chairs made at the Joliet prison or the Detroit House of Correction. In this way, the market for a state's prison-made products was reduced. Further restrictions were made in 1935, when the Ashurst-Sumners Act made it a federal offense to transport prison-made goods into states that had barred them under Hawes-Cooper. A 1940 amendment to the Ashurst-Sumners Act prevented anything but a state's agricultural prison products from being sold in another state. In 1936, the Walsh-Healy Act (amended in 1979) added other controls by prohibiting the use of inmate labor to fulfill general government contracts that exceed $10,000. Obviously, labor organizations and manufacturers had won the battle—but at a high cost as far as state treasuries were concerned.

When the Prison Industries Enhancement (PIE) Act was signed in 1979, regulations on prison-made goods began providing more opportunities for public-private cooperation. A key feature of the PIE Act is the provision for exempting certified companies nationwide from the $10,000 restriction made by the Walsh-Healy Act. The PIE program, which allows those companies to hire prison inmates as employees, is enjoying considerable success. Armstrong (1999) reports that inmates in South Carolina are booking reservations for a travel company while prisoners at a California women's prison help manufacture electronic components for a Silicon Valley firm and some Nevada inmates restore antique cars that sit in the showroom of a Las Vegas casino—obviously quite a variety of work projects!

Future legislation on prison labor may address such issues as inmate access to personal information on private citizens and may eventually affect the work done by foreign laborers. For example, Armstrong (1999) tells of an Illinois inmate, working for a marketing firm, who used personal information from a marketing survey to write a woman a sexually explicit letter. Ingley and Cochran (1999) explain that the federal government's General Accounting Office is trying to determine where, and to what extent, inmates working in prison industries have access to personal identifying information on private citizens.

On the foreign labor issue, Ingley and Cochran (1999) suggest there is already pressure for inmates to be assigned the type of work currently being done by foreign laborers. Legislators may be interested in passing laws to help accomplish that change because doing so could lessen the impact of foreign laborers on domestic workers and on the companies themselves.

Finally, there may eventually be a move toward taking away all marketing and sale restrictions currently imposed on prison industries by state and federal legislation. Yae (1999) suggests that the primary argument for market restrictions on prison-made products is the assumption that low labor costs give correctional industries a competitive advantage. That may be a faulty assumption, he argues, because those savings are more than offset by the additional expenses associated with operating in a prison environment. Some of those additional expenses are financial in nature (e.g., slowing of production because of work stoppages for security purposes), but others are related to human resources (e.g., having to use an untrained workforce with a high turnover rate). Of course, even if legislators and private businesses can be convinced that markets should be opened to prison-made products—despite paying low wages—it is possible that private citizens and labor unions will not like the perception that criminals are taking jobs that would otherwise go to law-abiding citizens. Given these economic and public relations controversies, it seems likely that prison industries will continue to operate under strict state and federal guidelines.

Many states provide information about their prison labor programs through the World Wide Web. For a few examples, visit the sites for Florida at ***www.dc.state.fl.us/pub/annual/9899/ci_at_work.html*** and Oregon at ***www.doc.state.or.us/wrkprgms/welcome.htm.*** Describe some of the work programs available in these states. Which ones do you think are especially suited to prison inmates? Why?

system would be sold only to state agencies, the products should not compete with those on the free market. The idea that prison labor would supply state agencies and bureaus with furniture, stationery, traffic signs, clothing, and various other products seemed appealing to many legislators. By 1940 laws in twenty-two states made it mandatory that state agencies purchase products made at the state prisons rather than on the open market. But sheltered market systems were not able to keep as many prisoners at work as did the open market ones, and idleness became a common condition. World War II brought a brief flurry of Army and Navy contracts with prisons, but those contracts ended with the war and the prison labor programs returned to a condition of inactivity.

Laboring at public projects and making various items for sale to other state agencies proved to be the main labor systems used at state prisons until the late 1970s, when an interest in linking prisons and private business began reemerging. Because the interdependence of prison and private industry was the main reason for the earlier success that states had in making prison labor profitable (Conley, 1980), their reconnection was crucial to stimulate new directions and profits for prison industries. Actually, in most states prison industries still can sell only to government markets (Grieser, 1989), but the movement to private-sector involvement is having an impact that deserves brief mention.

Prison Labor and the Private Sector. New links between prison industries and private business got a big push forward in 1979, when President Carter signed the Prison Industries Enhancement Act. The act exempted prison industries from some federal restraints and also encouraged private-sector involvement in prison labor systems (Dwyer & McNally, 1993). Other projects and opportunities for cooperative efforts arose in the 1980s and 1990s; and as the twenty-first century begins, it is possible to identify new types of labor systems that supplement, if not replace, those from the eighteenth century.

Dwyer and McNally (1993) suggest four contemporary models of prison labor systems: (1) governmental use, (2) joint venture, (3) corporate, and (4) free enterprise (see Table 10.1). The governmental use model is essentially the state use system, which restricts the sale of prison-made products to state and local governmental markets. If there is any private-sector involvement, it is to serve as a consultant for management advice or technical assistance. Because the governmental use system remains the most prevalent, many examples can be found among the state departments of corrections. Typical prison-made products under governmental use systems include furniture, traffic signs, dairy products, and clothing.

The **joint-venture model** has prison industries contracting with private business. It is similar to the governmental use system in its market area, but the product being made is that of a private company. The public and private sectors

TABLE 10.1: Contemporary Labor Systems

SYSTEM	MARKET FOR THE GOODS	PRIMARY CONTROL	PROGRAM EXAMPLES
Governmental use	Restricted to state and local government	Public	Traffic signs, furniture, dairy, etc.
Joint-venture	Prison produces private-firm products for sale to state and local governments	Shared public and private	Corcraft (New York)
Corporate	Unrestricted	More private than public	PRIDE (Florida) and UNICOR (Federal BOP)
Free enterprise	Unrestricted	Private	Prison Industries Enhancement (PIE) projects

Source: From Dwyer, D. C., & McNally, R. B. (1993). Public policy, prison industries, and business: An equitable balance for the 1990s. *Federal Probation, 57*(2), pp. 30–36.

share control in this model, with the prison usually in charge of items such as organizational structure, wage scales, and inmate hiring. The private sector controls the areas of product design, marketing, and distribution within the constraints of the governmental use market area. Good examples of this program include Corcraft (New York's Correctional Industries agency) and California's Joint Venture Program (JVP). Working with the Voyager Emblem Company, Corcraft produces embroidered emblems for state agencies and local governments. Voyager employees perform the first steps in the manufacturing process, then inmates at New York's Albion Correctional Facility complete the process (Conroy, 1994).

In California, private businesses are encouraged to work with the state's Department of Corrections to match inmate employees with employer needs. Suggested ventures include having inmates doing assembly work, providing clerical services, scanning information, packaging items for shipment, and so on. Businesses are told they will benefit from this arrangement by receiving tax incentives, avoiding payment of employee benefits such as retirement, vacation, sick leave, and having a consistent and reliable workforce. Even society as a whole benefits, the California Department of Corrections (1999) explains, because the working inmates—who are paid the prevailing wage by the private business—will have money from their salary used to pay restitution to crime victims, pay state and federal taxes, defray costs of their incarceration, and help keep their families from resorting to welfare.

Under the corporate model, prison industry is a relatively freestanding, semi-independent organization looking very much like a private-sector business (Dwyer & McNally, 1993). Control lies more with the private sector under this arrangement because the prison's involvement is restricted to such areas as providing security and skilled workers. Profits become the primary goal of this labor system.

Dwyer and McNally (1993) consider the free enterprise model to present the most independent form of private-sector prison industry. Most of these examples resulted from the Prison Industries Enhancement (PIE) projects started in the late 1970s. Control is primarily with the private sector, which makes all the business and employment decisions. Under the provisions of the PIE legislation, a restricted number of prison industry programs are allowed to operate in concert with private business. By 1993 thirty-two state correctional agencies were participating in the PIE project, which meant they had agreed to:

- Make sure that a portion of inmate wages (which must be similar to those paid to private-sector employees) goes to programs aiding crime victims
- Not displace private-sector workers
- Consult with labor and industry representatives when inmate work programs are established (Sexton, 1995)

Well-publicized examples of these programs include Oregon's Prison Blues® program in which inmates at Eastern Oregon Correctional Institution make T-shirts, sweatshirts, and denim jeans under the slogan "Made on the Inside to Be Worn on the Outside."

As prison populations continue to rise, in turn increasing the financial burden on the state to house the prisoners, many people are suggesting that prison labor programs will continue to turn to the private sector to provide profitability. If a corollary benefit of that profit for the state is to lessen recidivism and provide useful and marketable skills to inmates, then it seems likely that even people with differing philosophies of punishment may agree on the desirability of prison labor. Certainly from a management perspective, the more agreement there is among divergent economic and political groups the more pleasant the administrator's day will be.

MANAGING PRISON GANGS

Prison gangs were discussed in Chapter 9 as part of the social structure of contemporary prisons. Because gang activities impact the way prisons are managed, the discussion of prison gangs continues in this chapter.

In prisons, as elsewhere, people seek out others with whom they have something in common and from whom they can expect support. There are opportunities in prisons for formal associations of this type—ranging from prison postage stamp clubs to Alcoholics Anonymous groups—but the informal groups are more likely to catch the attention of prison administrators. Sometimes the informal groups are best described as cliques because they are made up of a rather small number of people who consider themselves friends, and specifically exclude others, without identifying leaders among themselves. Other informal groups share the cliques' exclusivity but may replace feelings of loyalty for feelings of friendship and will typically attribute leadership positions to certain members. These groups, the prison gangs, are still informal rather than formal groups because they organize and operate without the approval of the authorities.

Specific identification of which groups are best identified as prison gangs is not easily accomplished. In Chapter 14, for example, members of the Nation of Gods and Earth, also called the Five Percenters, are considered a gang in some prisons but claim to be more of a religious group. The distinction, as discussed in Chapter 14, is important because recognition of the group as a religion requires prison officials to treat the members very differently than when they are considered members of a gang.

Table 10.2 identifies many of the most notorious prison gangs since the 1950s. Four traditional prison gangs—Aryan Brotherhood, Mexican Mafia, Texas Syndicate, and Black Guerrilla Family—are identified by the Federal Bureau of Prisons as certified disruptive groups and are considered especially troublesome for prison officials. Identified in a separate category, called **security threat groups** (STG), are gangs such as the Arizona Aryan Brotherhood, Black Gangster Disciples, Jamaican Posse, and Hells Angels (Orlando-Morningstar, 1997). That STG identification, which is a terminology used in many state prison systems as well, allows prison officials to place restrictions on inmates identified as members of those gangs. In South Carolina, for example, prisoners who are members of a designated STG can be removed from the general prison population, reclassified to a higher custody level, and effectively be placed in more restrictive confinement (*In Re: Long-Term Administrative Segregation of Inmates Designated as Five Percenters*, U.S.C.A., 4th Cir. 1999, No. 98-7337).

Orlando-Morningstar (1997) explains that most prison gangs recruit along ethnic or racial lines and generally have members over age twenty-five with extensive experience in criminal activities. Because the growing prison population also means a growth in the volume and intensity of gang-related problems, prison administrators are understandably concerned.

One management response to the concern about prison gangs is to ensure identification of prison gang members. That is not necessarily an easy task because prison gang members often keep low profiles and are more secretive about their gang membership than are members of street gangs. Some of the clues to be used by correctional officers and other prison officials as they try to identify prison gang members include (Orlando-Morningstar, 1997; Thorne, 1992):

- *Tattoos and other personal identifiers*. Many but not all prison gangs use tattoos as a sign of affiliation. Popular places, depending on the gang, for the tattoos are the neck, chest, outside of the calf, or the forearm. Correctional

TABLE 10.2: Origin of Prison Gangs

YEAR FORMED	NAME OF GANG	JURISDICTION	PRIMARY MEMBERSHIP
1950	Gypsy Jokers	Washington	White
1957	Mexican Mafia	California and federal	Hispanic
1958	Texas Syndicate	California and federal	Hispanic
1965	La Nuestra Familia	California and federal	Hispanic
1966	Black Guerrilla Family	California and federal	Black
1967	Aryan Brotherhood	California and federal	White
mid-1970s	Arizona Aryan Brotherhood	Arizona	White
1977	Arizona Old Mexican Mafia	Arizona	Hispanic
1980	New Mexico Syndicate	New Mexico	Hispanic
early 1980s	Aryan Brotherhood of Texas	Texas	White
mid-1980s	Bulldogs	California	Hispanic
1984	Arizona's New Mexican Mafia	Arizona	Hispanic
1984	Mexikanemi	Texas and federal	Hispanic
1984	Mandingo Warriors	Texas	Black
1985	Dirty White Boys	Federal system	White
1985	415's	California	Black
1990	Los Solidos	Connecticut	Hispanic

Source: Adapted from Orlando-Morningstar, D. (1997). *Prison gangs* [JU 13.17:2]. Special Needs Offenders Bulletin, no. 2. Washington, DC: Federal Judicial Center.

officers are warned that gang tattoos are seldom of the professional or colorful type because those might attract too much attention. More likely they are rough, amateurish tattoos made with pins, old needles, or even broken pieces of metal.

- *Photographs*. Because prison gangs often take group pictures of members while in prison, correctional officers are encouraged to look for tattoos or symbolic gestures present in photos that prisoners possess.
- *Codes and ciphers*. Many prison gangs communicate with each other through codes and ciphers. Coded messages use words or terms that have specific meaning to gang members. Ciphers involve transposing the twenty-six letters of the English alphabet or substituting figures for letters (see Figure 10.4). Finding a letter or book with codes or ciphers may indicate that a prisoner is a gang member.

Prison gangs often have considerable influence over other inmates through their use of violence and their involvement in activities such as loan-sharking, drug trafficking, protection, prostitution, and murder. Thorne (whose comments about gang members in jail are applicable to prison gang members) notes that drug trafficking by inmates is an especially lucrative activity. Being able to smuggle in drugs means that a prisoner will have money, respect from other inmates, and considerable control over other inmates. For prison officials the smuggled drugs mean heightened levels of violence and unstable, addicted inmates (Thorne, 1992, p. 3). Unfortunately, drugs are brought in by the occasionally corrupt prison employee

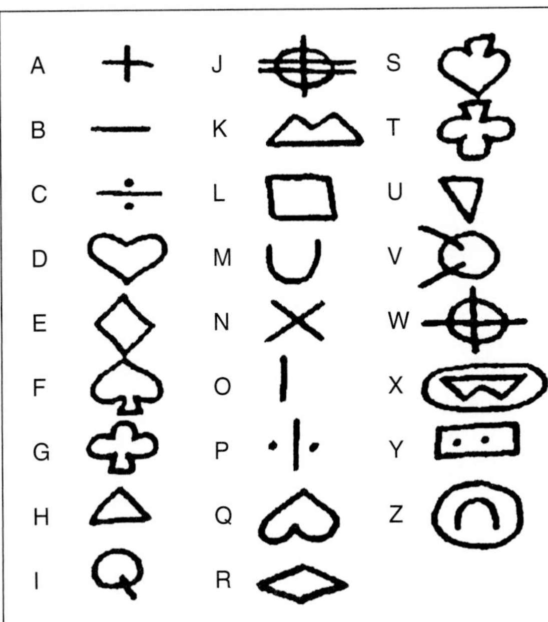

FIGURE 10.4

Sample La Nuestra Familia Cipher

This particular cipher was found during a cell search.

Source: From Orlando-Morningstar, D. (1997). *Prison gangs* [JU 13.17:2]. Special Needs Offenders Bulletin, no. 2. Washington, DC: Federal Judicial Center.

as well as by friends and relatives of the prison gang members. That situation makes it even more difficult for prison administrators to control the introduction of drugs into the prison and to negatively impact the influence of prison gangs.

Management problems presented by prison gangs are only part of a wide variety of topics confronting prison administrators. Other issues may not receive the

In many of today's prisons inmate allegiance to a gang is a way to secure protection while showing individual toughness. Shown are members of the Aryan Brotherhood prison gang at a Texas prison.

media attention that prison gangs get, but the problems they present are just as troublesome for administrators trying to provide a safe, secure, and responsive environment for staff and inmates. Some of those additional management issues are addressed in the following section.

MANAGING SPECIAL-NEEDS INMATES

Many important issues are facing corrections officials today, but one particular grouping presents problems that are comparatively new to the prison environment. These issues are linked to growing numbers of prisoners who make up special inmate populations. Roughly categorized they include prisoners with mental or physical disabilities, prisoners with infectious diseases, and an increasing number of elderly offenders. Each of the special populations requires prisons to modify procedures and facilities, add new topics for staff training and inmate education, and generally deal with issues that were not raised when inmates in these populations were fewer in number.

Inmates with Mental or Physical Disabilities

In recent years there have been both judicial and legislative actions that recognize or grant certain rights to mentally and physically disabled prisoners. Some of the early court decisions dealt with the broad issues of medical needs. For example, in *Estelle v. Gamble* (1976), the U.S. Supreme Court ruled that the Eighth Amendment is violated when there is deliberate indifference to serious medical needs of prisoners. Deliberate indifference might include never getting to see a doctor, or a long delay in seeing one, when the prisoner has a serious medical problem. Or it might include such cases as when an inmate is not seen by a person qualified to judge her problem—for example, Suzi is losing her vision but is not allowed to see an opthomologist—or did not receive medicine or therapy that had been prescribed (Manville, 1986).

The link between health care and the U.S. Constitution, as interpreted in cases such as *Estelle,* concerns the elementary principles of the Eighth Amendment's proscription on cruel and unusual punishment. The government is obliged, the courts have argued, to provide medical care for offenders being punished by incarceration. Inmates must rely on prison authorities to treat their medical needs. If the authorities fail to do so, the needs will not be met. This failure may actually produce physical torture or a lingering death—the most immediate concern under the Eighth Amendment—or it may result in pain and suffering that serves no penological purpose (60 Am Jur 2d, Penal and Correctional Institutions §91).

Because the infliction of unnecessary suffering is inconsistent with contemporary standards of decency, the public is required to care for prisoners, whose deprivation of liberty takes away the opportunity to care for themselves. As a result, the state must make available to inmates a level of medical care that is reasonably designed to meet their routine and emergency health care needs to include physical ills, dental care, and psychological or psychiatric care.

In addition to attention by the courts to physical and mental needs of prisoners, the legislative branch has also addressed this issue. The 1990 **Americans with Disabilities Act** (ADA) has been an especially important influence on prison procedures and facilities. Title II of the ADA "requires that State and local governmental entities, regardless of size, provide equal access for persons with disabilities to programs, services, and activities of the entity" (Rubin & McCampbell, 1994).

For purposes of the law, a person has a disability if he or she suffers from a physical or mental impairment that substantially limits a major life activity such as seeing, hearing, walking, breathing, or learning. The only time a government entity, such as a prison, can exclude a disabled person from a program, service, or activity is in a situation in which the person would not "otherwise be qualified." For example, if the only requirement for participation in a prison's drug counseling program is that the offender has a history of drug abuse, then a disabled inmate with a history of drug abuse cannot be excluded just because he is disabled. On the other hand, if the prison provides vocational training for inmates who have completed certain basic education classes, a prisoner whose learning disability has kept her from completing those basic classes is not being discriminated against when she is excluded from the vocational training. The key is that any disabled person who would otherwise be qualified for a program, service, or activity cannot be excluded from that program, service, or activity only on the basis of the disability. Consider, for example, the problems presented to prison officials by persons with a mental disability.

The ADA includes both mental illness and developmental disabilities (retardation) in the general category of mental disabilities. Specific data on inmates with mental disabilities are available for those who are mentally ill but not for those with developmental disabilities. Ditton (1999) estimates that about 16 percent of state prisoners are mentally ill (based on inmate self-report data). That population presents particular management problems for prison administrators because the inmates identified as mentally ill were more likely than others to be in prison for a violent offense and were more likely to have disciplinary problems while in prison.

Rubin and McCampbell (1995) offer an example of a decision that a prison official might have to make when working with inmates having a mental disability. Inmates who, despite their disability, are safely housed in the general prison population are quite likely to be eligible for any of the programs, services, or activities for which they are otherwise qualified. But what about inmates whose disability requires maintenance on psychotropic medications? Persons with a mental disability severe enough to require that level of medications could pose a threat to the health and safety of others. But simply excluding all inmates on psychotropic medications from, for example, working in the laundry or playing basketball, would be likely to violate the ADA. However, if eligibility decisions are made on an individual basis, it might be acceptable to exclude an inmate whose behavior is not stable while on such medication (Rubin & McCampbell, 1995). Obviously, the predicaments are many and difficult. The numbers of prisoners with a mental disability, especially mental illness, are likely to increase as prison terms get longer. Some of the increase may result from long-term imprisonment itself, but the numbers might also grow because more older inmates will be in prisons. We will look more closely at the older offender population after considering the problems presented by offenders with infectious diseases.

Inmates with Infectious Diseases

During 1997, nearly 2,900 persons in state prisons died (Maruschak, 1999). Deaths resulting from illness or natural causes accounted for the majority of those cases (65 percent), whereas deaths from suicide (5 percent), homicide (3 percent), executions (3 percent), accidents (1 percent), and the other/unspecified category (4 percent) made up another 16 percent. The remaining 19 percent of inmate deaths were attributed to acquired immunodeficiency syndrome (AIDS).

Some of the deaths by illness were the result of tuberculosis (TB), which was increasing during the late 1980s and early 1990s in society and in prisons but has been decreasing in both populations since 1994 (Hammett, Harmon, & Maruschak, 1999). The resurgence of TB is especially affecting inner-city minorities, injection drug users, and the poor. These populations are overrepresented in corrections in general and in prisons more specifically, so TB has become a serious problem in places of confinement where crowded conditions and poor ventilation provide ideal conditions for the spread of an infectious disease such as TB. But as important a concern as TB is, prison officials are even more disturbed by the spread of the human immunodeficiency virus (HIV) that causes AIDS.

Maruschak (1999) reports that at year-end 1997, 2.2 percent of the state prisoners and 1.0 percent of federal prisoners were known to be HIV infected. Twenty-six percent of the HIV-positive prison inmates were confirmed AIDS cases. The percentage of the prison population infected with HIV was highest in the Northeast (6.4 percent of all state prisoners in that region), followed by the South (2.0 percent), Midwest (0.9 percent), and the West (0.8 percent). New York State had the highest percentage of prisoners infected with HIV (10.8 percent), but nine states reported that fewer than 0.5 percent of their inmates were HIV positive. The number of states with so few HIV cases suggests that the overall percentage is accounted for by a relatively small number of states. In fact, four states—New York, Florida, Texas, and California—had over half the known HIV cases. Confirmed AIDS cases were also concentrated in only a few states, with New York, Texas, and Florida prisons having half the confirmed AIDS cases in state prisons (New York alone had one-fifth).

In addition to variation by region, HIV cases in prison also show a difference by sex. Male HIV cases far outnumbered those of females (20,153 compared to 2,185), but the numbers are misleading because there are so many more male prisoners. When computed as a percentage of the total population in custody, 2.2 percent of the male inmates and 3.5 percent of the female inmates were HIV positive. The percentage of HIV-positive females has been higher than the male percentage in every year since 1991 (Maruschak, 1999). Obviously, the dangers and problems presented by HIV/AIDS are not confined to prisons for men. Two of the many important questions that must be addressed in connection with the HIV/AIDS dilemma concern identifying the HIV-positive inmates and determining how to handle those who test positive.

Testing for HIV. Identification of persons with HIV infection is accomplished through laboratory tests. All fifty states, the District of Columbia, and the Federal Bureau of Prisons have at least one policy for prison HIV testing. The most frequent policy (used in forty-four of the jurisdictions in 1997) is to test inmates if they exhibit HIV-related symptoms or if they ask to be tested (Maruschak, 1999). Other frequent policies require testing of inmates who were involved in an incident that might have increased their exposure risk (twenty-nine jurisdictions). Fifteen states test inmates who belong to designated high-risk groups. Eighteen states test all inmates upon admission, and four states plus the BOP test inmates at release.

The legality of a mandatory testing policy has been challenged in the courts, and one U.S. Court of Appeals approved a policy of testing all inmates to determine if they were HIV positive (*Harris v. Thigpen*, 1991). Another federal court has ruled that mandatory testing is an acceptable policy only when prison officials are able to specify which legitimate penological interest (such as security or health) is being furthered by the testing policy (*Walker v. Sumner*, 1990).

Handling of Inmates with HIV or AIDS. Issues that have been more controversial than HIV testing policies are those related to how prison officials should deal with HIV-positive inmates and inmates with AIDS. Especially troublesome is the question of segregation. In 1985 thirty-eight prison systems segregated all inmates with confirmed AIDS, but by 1997 only three systems (Alabama, Mississippi, and California) were doing so (Hammett et al., 1999). The prevailing policy today is to segregate inmates with AIDS from the general prison population only when their medical needs require separate housing.

All HIV-infected inmates were segregated from the general population in eight prison systems in 1985, but by 2000 only three systems kept inmates known to have HIV infection from the general inmate population. Those three systems—Alabama, Mississippi, and South Carolina—have mandatory HIV-antibody testing of all incoming inmates, so they probably identify and segregate a large percentage of HIV-infected inmates (Greenhouse, 2000; Hammett et al., 1999). Alabama's procedure was upheld in 1999 by the U.S. Court of Appeals, 11th Circuit (*Onishea v. Hopper*), and left intact by the U.S. Supreme Court in 2000 (*Davis v. Hopper*).

Because the great majority of prison systems do not segregate inmates with HIV or AIDS who do not show symptoms of the illness, most inmates with HIV or AIDS are housed in the general population and participate in the same educational and vocational programs and in other activities, including work assignments. However, Hammett et al. (1999) report that some correctional programs exclude HIV-infected inmates from food service jobs. Because health professionals say there is no scientific basis for such an exclusionary policy, there is some concern that those policies encourage erroneous and dangerous perceptions that HIV may be transmitted through casual contact.

The argument that HIV-infected inmates should be segregated in housing, program, or work assignments is typically made in connection with a concern for transmission of the virus to other inmates. Shared needles, used for injecting drugs or applying tattoos, and homosexual activity are actions that dramatically increase the risk of HIV transmission. Despite the best efforts of prison administrators, these behaviors occur in prisons. But the limited studies that have looked at this issue suggest that such concerns may be overblown. Blumberg (1990) notes that states that have tried to determine if HIV is being transmitted within the institution have found very few instances of conveyance. An important limitation of such studies is that the upper limit of the incubation period for AIDS has not been established, so it is not always possible to tell whether inmates acquired the virus during or before incarceration.

Even without documentation of any more than a modest rate of HIV transmission in prisons, prison officials are obviously obliged to do all they can to achieve a zero transmission rate. This is being accomplished in prison with both agreement and disagreement regarding the best methods. Because education about the disease and its transmission can reduce fear and make normalcy of interaction more possible, HIV/AIDS education is generally routine in the nation's prisons for both staff and inmates. The problems are not so much in whether inmates and staff should receive information about AIDS; instead, they center on what that information should include. Should prison officials inform inmates about the proper cleaning of drug paraphernalia? Should condoms be distributed to inmates? Of course, these same questions are debated outside the prison as well, but they take a peculiar twist in the confines of an institution. Consider the distribution of condoms as an example.

Advocates of condom distribution argue that homosexual behavior is a fact of life in many prisons, and officials should recognize and respond to that situation by providing a means of protection from disease. Critics note that sexual activity is prohibited within institutions, and that some states have statutes making homosexual behavior illegal. Providing condoms in a situation in which they can be used only for homosexual activity places prison officials in a predicament of approving conduct that violates prison rules, may violate state laws, and might be considered by some citizens as immoral even where it is not illegal. Six correctional systems (prisons and jails) provide condoms to inmates (Vermont, Mississippi, New York City, San Francisco, Philadelphia, and Washington, DC) and these systems have been doing so for more than a decade. In contrast to the American hesitancy, many European, Canadian, and Australian correctional facilities make condoms available to inmates (Hammett et al., 1999).

In addition to concern about ways to reduce transmission of the HIV virus during homosexual activity, prison officials must also be concerned about its transmission via needle sharing by intravenous drug users. Not surprisingly, complaints that distributing condoms seems to support homosexual activity are repeated by arguments that distributing needles and syringes simply supports drug use by prisoners—in addition to violating the law or prison regulations. Making bleach available to prisoners may be one way to avoid the controversy because bleach has several purposes—including disinfecting needles. The Centers for Disease Control say bleach may be effective for HIV disinfection if it is used at full strength and specific procedures are followed. This method is much less desirable than using a new needle and syringe for each injection, but it is certainly less controversial because prisoners could also use bleach to clean their cells. In 1997 bleach was made available "for any purpose" in ten prison systems and in eight jail systems (Hammett et al., 1999). As with condom distribution, officially sanctioned bleach distribution for cleaning injection equipment is more often found in prison systems outside the United States (e.g., much of Europe and Canada).

Issues of segregation, access to programs, and health care as they relate to inmates with HIV or AIDS have been working their way through the nation's courts for over a decade. The most recent decisions are determining if prisoners with HIV or AIDS are covered under the Americans with Disabilities Act (ADA). If they are—and the U.S. Supreme Court case *Pennsylvania Department of Corrections v. Yeskey* (1998) suggests that they are—rulings under that act will affect the way prisoners with HIV or AIDS are managed (see Chapter 9 in Hammet et al., 1999).

Elderly Inmates

In 1986 there were about 17,000 inmates over age fifty-five in state and federal prisons. By 1999 that number had tripled to more than 50,000 (Krane, 1999b). That increase is consistent with the general rise in prison population, so although the actual numbers show a dramatic increase, the percentage of elderly prisoners has remained constant at about 3 percent for state prisons and 12 percent for federal prisons. Typically the percentage that a particular category makes up in the prison population is more important than the actual numbers. But in the case of the elderly and a few other groups—such as inmates with HIV/AIDS—the actual number is also very important. That is especially because of the economic impact the increased numbers (despite the constant percentage) has on prison expenses. For example, analysts estimate a geriatric inmate's maintenance costs run as much as 300 percent higher than the average prisoner's (Krane, 1999b).

The U.S. population in general is getting older, so it is probably not surprising that more older people are now found in groups as varied as tennis clubs and prisons. But the increasing number of elderly prisoners is not simply the result of there being more older Americans. A trend toward the greying of U.S. prisons began in the mid-1970s when longer prison sentences and reductions in the use of parole began expanding the number of older inmates. Today sentencing strategies such as the "three strikes and you're out" legislation and mandatory minimum sentences will continue to increase the number of elderly in prison, although many of them were not old when they began their sentence. This combination of an older general population, longer prison sentences, and decreasing use of parole leads some to believe that the number of older prisoners will continue to increase in the coming decades. Because the aging process requires adjustment both by the person getting older and by those interacting with him or her, corrections officials are beginning yet another adjustment process.

In the mid-1990s, the National Institute of Justice began a three-phase study of the management of elderly inmates in jails and prisons (Crawford, 1994). That study is examining the needs and problems of elderly inmates and the types of services and management approaches now used by corrections officials. The information from that study will be helpful in preparing prison administrators to handle a special population of inmates that has always been present but only now has sufficient enough numbers to gain specific attention. We will take a few moments to consider some of the issues that are being addressed today and that will continue to be cause for concern in the future.

Who's Old? Unlike the other special populations discussed in this section, those belonging to the group described as elderly or older cannot be identified by laboratory tests, psychological evaluations, or medical examinations. There is no agreed-upon age at which a person is said to be elderly. And of course the term *older* is even less helpful because a seventeen-year-old is "older" than a five-year-old. Upon reaching age fifty, individuals can join the American Association of Retired Persons, whether they are retired or not. The Social Security Administration lets you start drawing retirement benefits at age sixty-two. Several federal law enforcement agencies will not let a person over age thirty-four apply to be an agent. Some places of business discourage employees from working past age sixty-five, whereas others actively recruit employees over that age.

The absence of an agreed-upon age at which a person becomes elderly makes it hard to identify the extent of the problem and to determine what level of accommodation is needed. Take identification as an example. We began this section by noting that the percentage of inmates over age fifty-five is increasing. Why age fifty-five? Because that is the statistic provided by the American Correctional Association, although we could just as easily use data from the Criminal Justice Institute ("old" starts at age fifty) or data from the Bureau of Justice Statistics ("old" starts at age sixty-four).

Without an agreed-upon age for identifying the elderly, it is also difficult to plan for any special needs that population may have. On the other hand, not everyone at the same age has the same kind of needs. We all know octogenarians who are more active and in better health than some persons half their age. Just as one does not automatically become mature and responsible the morning of his or her eighteenth birthday, one does not become infirm and senile the day one turns fifty (or fifty-five, or sixty . . .). Why even bother to identify exactly how many elderly prisoners there are, if everyone in that group is not going to need the same services and accommodations? One answer is the same that can be given for many other specific populations that are identified as having special needs—a reliance on statistical generalizations. For example, not everyone suffering from schizophrenia displays exactly the same behavior or has just the same needs. Not all persons diagnosed as developmentally disabled are able to learn at the same speed or level—nor, for that matter, are persons without that diagnosis. Some people with AIDS must be hospitalized whereas others are able to live a reasonably normal life.

Despite their in-category differences, persons in these special populations share characteristics that statistically set them apart from persons in other categories. For example, schizophrenics not on controlling medication are less able to maintain normal interpersonal relationships. Persons with developmental disabilities, as a group, are more likely to need special attention and assistance in learning concepts and tasks than are those people who are not developmentally disabled. People with AIDS, even though not hospitalized, must take daily precautions that need not be taken by persons without AIDS. And, finally, as people age they experience certain physical, psychological, and social changes that are different from their experiences when they were younger. It is to these changes brought on by the aging process that prison officials must direct their attention as the greying of U.S. prisons continues. We will look at a few of these changes.

Physical Needs of Elderly Prisoners. One could argue that any increased discomfort that prisoners might experience as a result of the normal aging process is simply an aspect of their punishment and should not be of major concern to prison officials. After all, as some would argue, the victims of the murderers in prison do not get a chance to experience the aging process. Others, who are obviously taking an incapacitation rather than retribution perspective, suggest that the elderly prisoner who no longer presents a danger to society should be released from confinement—if for no other reason than to open a place for the younger, more dangerous offender. But whether the reasoning is based on practical considerations such as the incapacitation rationale, moral imperatives such as a belief that humans (even prisoners) should not be forced to needlessly suffer, or legal decisions that protect certain constitutional and statutory rights, there is growing recognition that some elderly prisoners present different health concerns, require different living arrangements, and generally need special management. Consider, for example, some of the age-related changes that may require adjustments to the way prisons have traditionally operated.

As the body ages, changes occur in the muscles, skeleton, and skin that result in a physically weaker person (muscle loses mass and tone) whose bones are more easily broken (the bones, especially of women, become more porous), and whose skin is more susceptible to being torn. These changes affect all older people's sense of safety as they complete their daily routine, but older people in the dangerous setting of a prison may be placed in even greater fear for their physical safety. Studies report that older prisoners do in fact feel unsafe and vulnerable to attack by younger inmates (Aday, 1994). But even when the danger presented by younger inmates is not present, the physical condition and structure of many prisons are themselves cause for concern about physical safety. Prisons are, after all, designed for young, active inmates. Older, frail prisoners find the environment difficult to negotiate (e.g., the stairs in tiered cell blocks) or requiring too great a distance to travel (e.g., getting from a living area to a recreational area).

Age-related changes to a person's senses can also affect the conditions under which elderly prisoners serve their sentence. Sensitivity of taste buds decreases with age, especially with men, and an accompanying decrease in sensitivity to smell can influence, among other things, a person's appetite and result in nutritional deficiencies. A decline in visual abilities and a loss of hearing can present physical and psychological problems to the elderly prisoner. Physically, a lessened ability to see and to hear may make the older offender more vulnerable to harm by the very structure of the prison. Psychologically, loss of sight and hearing loss can cause depression and result in social isolation. Hearing loss especially is problematic because it can lead to paranoia and suspicion, particularly in individuals who do not realize they have a hearing loss and instead begin to think that others are talking about them or are deliberately excluding them from the conversation (National Center for State Long-Term Care Ombudsman Resources, 1992). Responses by prison administrators might require them to make glasses and hearing aids available to elderly prisoners (as they would to any prisoner with similar impairments) but might also mean that physical examinations and other preventive measures should be more frequent for the aging inmate. In addition, staff training might include information about these sensory changes so that correctional officers and others are less likely to misinterpret the elderly offender's actions and are aware of the special communication skills needed for optimum interaction with older prisoners.

There are other physical changes resulting from the aging process, but the ones linked to our skeleton and senses provide at least a minimum understanding of how these changes might affect the elderly prisoner and the prison system. There are also changes brought on by aging that affect our psychological and social environment.

Social/Psychological Needs of Elderly Prisoners. Chapter 9 highlighted the prisonization process and discussed how all prison inmates experience some weakening or breakdown of their usual support system when they are incarcerated. Inmates adjust to the removal from familiar surroundings by finding a niche in the prison subculture. Sabath and Cowles (1988) suggest that some groups of inmates—such as the elderly—use different adjustment strategies and that it is important for prison administrators to be aware of those differences. In their review of literature on the elderly in prison, Sabath and Cowles (1998) found studies reporting that older inmates and their younger counterparts both showed patterns indicative of a behavior disorder, but "the aged inmates showed greater anxiety, despondency, apprehension, concern with physical functioning, were somewhat naive and demanding of attention and support, and appeared to want to avoid responsibility" (p. 179). In addition, older inmates are reported to be more easily influenced and intimidated by younger, more aggressive inmates; they are more depressed and dependent in their relationship with guards; and they, at least the "new" first-time elderly inmates, show better prison adjustment than do the "chronic" repeat offenders.

In their own study of the adjustment of elderly prisoners, Sabath and Cowles found that adjustment results from an interaction of both prisoner background (extraprison variables) and situational (intraprison) variables. These, of course, are similar to the concepts of deprivation and importation discussed earlier in this book. Three background variables were found to have particular impact on adjustment to prison: family contacts, education, and health. Each of these also suggests actions that prison administrators can take in developing policies regarding the elderly inmate. Family contact was shown to have a positive impact on prisoner morale, which in turn has a positive impact on adjustment by, for example, reducing the number of conduct violations. Presumably, prison administrators interested in reducing conduct violations by elderly prisoners are well advised to have programs that increase family contact and foster outside support mechanisms for those prisoners.

There are also policy implications suggested by variables that Sabath and Cowles found not to have either direct or indirect impact on prison adjustment. For example, the involvement of older prisoners in personal activities (such as reading, watching television, and exercising), and in program activities (such as clubs, counseling sessions, and vocational training) had no impact on how they viewed their own adjustment to prison, how caseworkers viewed their adjustment, or in the number of conduct violations they had. The absence of impact from participation in traditional prison programs makes sense when we remember that these programs have been geared for a different age group. Contemporary correctional programs are designed to provide an academic education, to train for an occupation, and to direct personal development for eventual return to mainstream society. Such programs are not as relevant to persons who have completed their formal education, who are retired from, rather than searching for, an occupation, and who will return to something other than "mainstream" society when (or if) they are released. For the inmates who will spend their final years in prison, some version of a prison "retirement community" might be appropriate. For older inmates who may someday return to the community, Sabath and Cowles suggest that prison programs that are geared toward community adjustment, education about available social agency support, and maintaining family contacts will be more beneficial than the programs currently available.

Geriatric Prisons. For many prison administrators, the most serious challenge presented by an increase in the number of elderly prisoners is an economic one. One estimate says the special needs of older prisoners puts the annual cost of incarceration for geriatric inmates at $69,000 per inmate compared to the national average for all inmates of about $20,000 (Krane, 1999c). Aday (1994) reports that many states routinely house older inmates apart from the general population, and several offer them unique programming or services. In most cases these special units, which are variously described as "aged/infirm," "medical/geriatric," "disabled," or simply "geriatric," mix older inmates with younger disabled ones. But operating in the belief that it may be economically advantageous to pool resources and center services, some states are using facilities specifically designed for elderly inmates.

In 1970 South Carolina prison officials began providing special facilities for the elderly. Aday (1994) points out that its harsh sentencing practices meant that before other states began experiencing similar problems, South Carolina had a large number of long-term inmates growing old in prison. In 1983 the state's prison for the elderly moved into a former tuberculosis hospital and today is able to provide twenty-four-hour medical coverage with thirteen nurses on duty around the clock and a full-time physician assigned to the facility. But some people suggest a small 200-bed prison in Alabama is even more likely to portray the way elderly prisoners will be handled in the future.

At the Hamilton (Alabama) Prison for the Aged and Infirm, prisoners are waiting to die or cannot be reasonably placed in a traditional prison setting. The

As America's prison population gets older, prison administrators must accommodate the physical, psychological, and social needs of elderly inmates.

warden at Hamilton explains that most of the men in his care could not survive in the general population—some because of physical disabilities, some because they are mentally incompetent, and some because they are just too old (Bragg, 1995). To help make his point, the warden tells of older inmates writing to beg for a transfer to the Hamilton prison—not necessarily because doing time there would be easier, but it would most likely be safer. Inmates at Hamilton help look out for each other instead of placing each other in jeopardy. The most able inmates do chores such as stripping beds and helping to clean up after those who are old and those most helpless.

In 1999 Virginia began transforming the Deerfield Correctional Center to an "assisted-living" prison for disabled and elderly prisoners (Chen, 1999b). About 3 percent of Virginia's inmates are age fifty-five and older, and about one-sixth of those require help completing daily activities such as bathing and meal preparation. A similar facility in Pennsylvania—the Laurel Highlands Correctional Institution—has geriatric wings equipped with oxygen generators and wheelchairs instead of handcuffs and stun guns. Drummond (1999) describes the inmates at Laurel Highlands as including wheelchair-bound prisoners who queue up at the medication counter to receive their daily dose of pills for diabetes, heart disease, and stroke. While those inmates await their medication, another rants about a state highway that protects him from the Martians. When inmates needing daily living assistance are housed together, the custodial staff and health staff can be fully integrated for more efficient management. As a result, we can expect more prisons of the assisted-living type to be built across the country—unless we decide such prisoners should be released to the community (see "A Clear Case of Incapacitation versus Retribution").

In addition to the specialized facilities such as those in South Carolina, Alabama, and Virginia, changes are also occurring in staff training. Correctional officers are being trained in ways to help older prisoners prevent injuries and are receiving instruction on recognizing the occasionally confusing behaviors of aging prisoners (Chen, 1999b). It is obvious that corrections officials are more sensitive to the special needs of aging inmates, but it is also obvious that special geriatric facilities and programming are only in beginning stages (Aday, 1994). There is still considerable disagreement about issues as basic as whether prison officials really are responsible for providing special consideration for elderly inmates. Some believe that older prisoners give a sense of stability to the general prison population and suggest that housing them separately would be a disadvantage for the smooth operation of traditional prisons. Also, even with the best of intentions, are prison officials the right people to be managing special units and programs for older inmates—Aday (1994) quotes one official as commenting: "I know how to run prisons, not old-age homes" (p. 53). One of the few points that everyone agrees on is that the questions raised and problems presented by the increasing number of prisoners aging in prison, and those aged at admission, will not be solved or answered without considerable planning and expense.

PRIVATIZATION OF CORRECTIONS

The last topic for this chapter is actually a variation on the management theme. Prison management in the twentieth century was primarily carried out by public employees in public facilities. In the twenty-first century it appears that management may increasingly be by corporate employees in private facilities. That situation is not so common yet as to warrant elaborate discussion of management issues in private facilities. However, it is necessary to review some aspects of the important trend.

ISSUES OF FAIRNESS

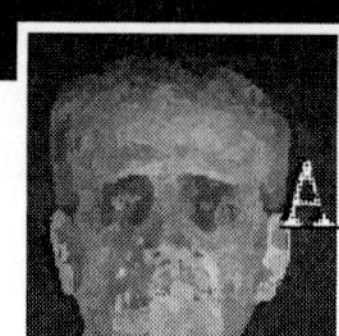

A CLEAR CASE OF INCAPACITATION VERSUS RETRIBUTION

Thus far the topic in these "Issues of Fairness" features has been race, ethnicity, or gender. An exception is made here to include another issue that increasingly draws the attention of persons concerned about inequity in society. The topic of age highlights the discrimination and abuse that some U.S. citizens face just because they are among society's oldest members. On the other hand, some people argue, just because a person is fortunate enough to be growing older, that person's criminal behavior while younger cannot simply be forgotten. Herein are the makings of an interesting dilemma that clearly portrays the incapacitation versus retribution philosophies of punishment.

The incapacitation approach toward the aging felon goes like this: The purpose of punishment is to increase public safety by restricting the offender's freedom of movement. As the offender poses less and less of a threat to the community, his punishment should be modified from more secure to less secure so that the punishment needed to achieve the goal is always being used. This means, for example, that a person sentenced to forty or more years in prison might be moved from a maximum-security facility to a minimum-security facility and eventually to community corrections as the aging process makes that offender less of a threat to the community. So, an offender with a long prison sentence could have that prison sentence replaced by a community sanction—such as parole, halfway house placement, or even home confinement—if it is determined that the offender is no longer a threat.

There are some interesting statistics to support an incapacitation approach favoring the elderly inmate's early release from prison. Krane (1999c) reports that the U.S. Parole Commission cites age as the single most reliable indicator in predicting recidivism. Twenty-two percent of the inmates between ages eighteen and twenty-four commit a new crime within one year of their release. For inmates over age forty-three, the rate drops to 2 percent. Do we really want to use prison space for a sixty-year-old bank robber who is now unlikely to continue his criminal ways—especially, when the costs associated with caring for that aging prisoner are considerably higher than for younger prisoners? The incapacitationist argues that a simple cost–benefit analysis indicates that it is poor policy to support a system in which the cost of imprisonment rises as the danger to society retreats.

The retribution approach has a different take, which is succinctly summed up as "you do the crime, you do the time." Retributionists are not impressed with the frailty or poor health of aging prisoners. Nor does the retributionist care much about the reduced recidivism of criminals over age forty-three. Instead, the just deserts perspective sees long-term imprisonment as appropriate punishment for a serious crime. Part of that punishment is growing old in prison and having that difficult life be a constant reminder of the offender's crime—regardless of how many years earlier the crime occurred. The increased cost of caring for aging prisoners and even the need to build nursing home prisons are simply expenses that society must be willing to bear in order that justice be done.

APBNews.com prepared a several-part story about aging prisoners. Go to the second of those reports at *www.apbnews.com/cjsystem/behind_bars/oldprisoners/riskcost0412.html,* and read the argument for and against keeping elderly convicts in prison. Also on that Web page is an interactive data center that allows you to identify the nation's oldest prisoners and longest-serving prisoners. Who are the oldest prisoners in your state? What were their crimes, and how long have they served? Finally, under "other resources" on that same page, view the slide show about many of the United States' oldest prisoners.

Whether you realize it or not, the history of privatization in criminal justice is a history you already know. In other books, you have read about the volunteer and private law enforcement techniques that preceded modern policing and the early reliance on victims or privately run prosecution societies to prosecute offenders. You may also have read about the historical and continued role of private bondsmen and the early use of the jail as a way for keepers to earn fees for providing services such as bedding and food. In this book we reviewed examples of the important role that private groups, such as the Quakers in Pennsylvania, played in developing the new sanction of long-term imprisonment, and the significance of private businesses' role in influencing a preference in the United States for the Auburn-style prison philosophy. Specific aspects of penal philosophies have been linked to prison labor, which in turn has ebbed and flowed as support from private business fluctuates. In the area of intermediate sanctions, the direct tie to private individuals (John Augustus in Boston and Matthew Hill in England) makes clear the widespread impact of private individuals, associations, and businesses in the area of corrections.

Importantly, no one claims that the involvement of private people in criminal justice has always been desirable. The example of the convict lease system alone prevents one from saying only positive things about private participation. But as will be argued later, many of the advances and improvements in criminal justice are the result of private rather than public maneuvers. The point to make now is simply a reminder that **privatization** in corrections is much more an old concept than a new one. And, having made that point, we can move on to a discussion of the more recent directions that privatization has taken.

Privatization in the United States Today

Figure 10.5 shows the growth in rated capacity of private secure adult correctional facilities since 1990. That nearly 850 percent rise reflects a decade-long interest by state legislators looking for alternatives to public correctional facilities—and in private corporations seeking to provide that alternative. Not all states have been attracted to the idea of privatization, however. Thomas (1999) reports that in

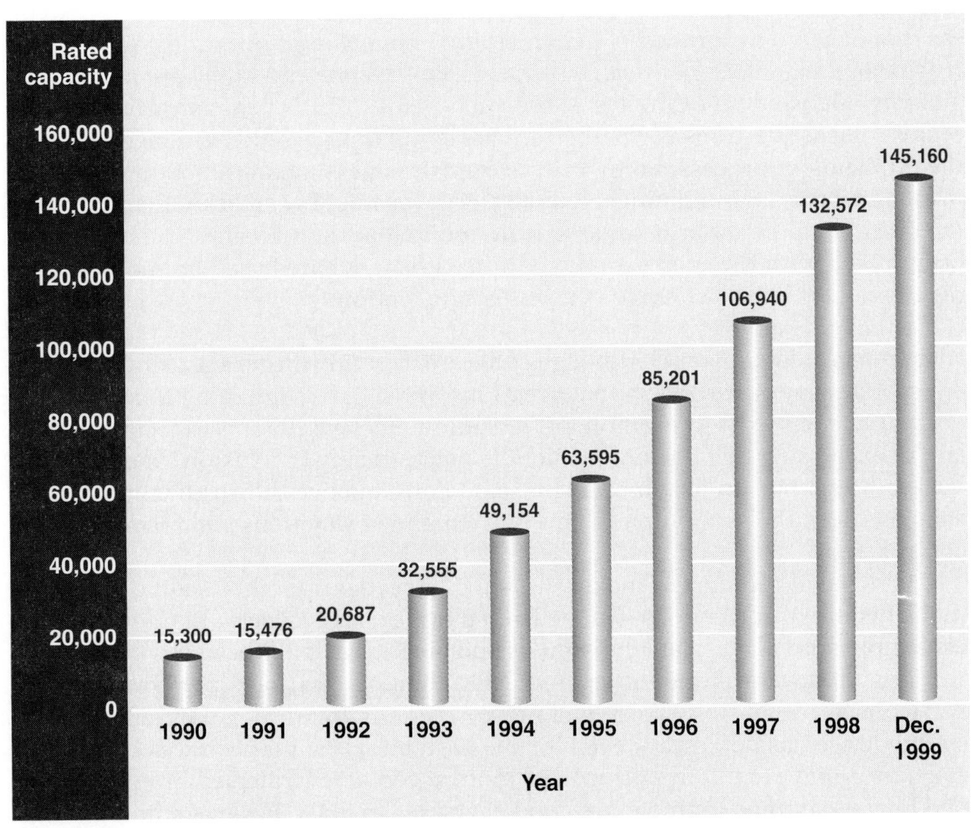

FIGURE 10.5

Ten-Year Growth in Rated Capacity of Private Secure Adult Correctional Facilities

Source: Thomas, C. W. (1999). *Ten-year growth in rated capacity of private secure adult correctional facilities.* Available: web.crim.ufl.edu/pcp/census/1999/Figure1.html. Accessed on February 22, 2000. Used with permission.

1998 there were twenty-seven states (plus the District of Columbia) that specifically authorized contracts with private companies for the full-scale management of correctional facilities. An additional eleven states seem to have statutes that at least permit such contracts. Of the remaining states, ten are without any statutory authorization, and in two states (Illinois and New York) privatization is statutorily prohibited.

Even among the states that authorize privatization, there is considerable variation in how often it is used. By the end of 1999, about 160 private facilities were distributed among thirty-one states and the District of Columbia. Most of the jurisdictions had fewer than 5 such facilities and only two states (California with 24 and Texas with 42) had more than 10. A reason for the variation in state authorization, and in the number of facilities even where there is authorization, is understood by looking at some of the issues raised by contracting for correctional services.

Issues Raised by Privatization

Even though privatization traces its ancestry to some of the earliest versions of government sanctioning, not everyone is pleased to see its return to popularity. Debates about the advantages and disadvantages of privatization cover a variety of topics (see Table 10.3). At least one point, that private facilities are more cost-effective, seems to have been decided more often in favor of proponents. Ethridge and Marquart (1993) found that private prisons in Texas were operating at close to 10 percent below the cost of a hypothetical equivalent run by the state. Sellers (1989) compared three private correctional facilities with three public facilities and found that the three privately operated correctional centers proved to be more cost-efficiently operated than their publicly operated counterparts. Other points are more controversial.

The Propriety of Privatization. Logan (1990) explains that questions of propriety may be philosophical, political, or legal. Table 10.3 presents some pro and con arguments focusing on examples of propriety issues. One of the most basic of the philosophical questions is whether private companies should even be involved in the punishment process. Some believe punishment is a core function of government and it should be administered only by government agencies. Others consider the question to be moot because private individuals and businesses have always been linked with U.S. corrections. Because it is a debate based on moral principles, it cannot be answered to everyone's satisfaction.

Privatization as Innovation. Although some are debating the legality, efficiency, and effectiveness of privatization in corrections, others are suggesting that more important reasons exist to promote privatization. Feeley (1991) is especially articulate in expressing this position, which he places firmly in a historical context. As Feeley (1991) put it: "The most significant consequence of privatization historically has been the generation of new and expanded sanctions and forms of social control" (p. 2).

As noted at the start of the discussion of privatization, this is not a new topic in the history of corrections—in the United States or elsewhere. But whereas others simply note that private individuals and businesses have been involved in corrections for several hundred years, Feeley suggests that privatization has been particularly responsible for propelling corrections forward. Admittedly, the resulting lunge has not always been for the best, but presumably it was better than stagnation and eventually encouraged more acceptable strategies. Transportation and long-term imprisonment are good examples to make Feeley's point.

TABLE 10.3: Debating Privatization

ARGUMENTS FOR PRIVATIZATION	ARGUMENTS AGAINST PRIVATIZATION
Propriety	**Propriety**
Contracting enhances justice by making prison supply more responsive to changes in demand, both upward and downward.	Contracting for imprisonment involves an improper delegation to private hands of coercive power and authority.
Contractual wardens have an incentive to govern inmates fairly in order to enhance their legitimation, induce cooperation, lower costs, and ensure renewal of contracts.	Contracting may put profit motives ahead of the public interest, inmate interests, or the purposes of imprisonment.
Cost	**Cost**
Contracting allows prisons to be financed, sited, and constructed more quickly and cheaply than government prisons; also, private firms are more apt to design for efficient operation.	Contracting is more expensive because it adds a profit margin to all other costs.
Contracting counteracts the motivation of budget-based government agencies to continually grow in size and to maximize their budgets.	Contracting may cost more in the long run as a result of "lowballing"—initial low bids followed by unjustifiable price raises in subsequent contracts.
Quality	**Quality**
Contracting, by creating an alternative, raises standards for the government as well as for private vendors.	Contracting may reduce quality through the pressure to cut corners economically.
Contracting promotes creativity and enthusiasm by bringing in "new blood" and new ideas more often than is possible under civil service.	Contracting may "skim the cream" by removing the "best" prisoners and leaving the government prisons with the "worst," which will spuriously make the private prisons look better by comparison.
Quantity	**Quantity**
Contractors can help alleviate today's capacity crisis by building new prisons faster than the government can.	Contracting, simply by expanding capacity and making imprisonment more feasible and efficient, may unduly expand the use of imprisonment and weaken the search for alternatives.
Flexibility	**Flexibility**
Contracting allows greater flexibility, which promotes innovation, experimentation, and other changes in programs, including expansion, contraction, and termination.	Contracting may limit flexibility by refusal to go beyond the terms of contract without renegotiation.
Contracting promotes specialization to deal with special-needs prisoners (protective custody, AIDS patients, etc.).	Contracting reduces the ability to coordinate with other public agencies (police, sheriff, probation, parole, transportation, maintenance, etc.).
Security	**Security**
Contracting may enhance public and inmate safety through increased staff training and professionalism.	Contracting may jeopardize public and inmate safety through inadequate staff levels or training.
Contracted corrections officers are less likely to go on strike because they are more vulnerable to termination.	Contracting may limit the ability of the government to respond to emergencies, such as strikes, riots, fires, or escapes.
Accountability	**Accountability**
Contracting increases accountability because it is easier for the government to monitor and control a contractor than to monitor and control itself.	Contracting reduces accountability because private actors are insulated from the public and not subject to the same political controls as are government actors.
Contractors are forced to be more responsive to the attitudes and needs of local communities when siting a prison.	Contracting diffuses responsibility; government and private actors can each blame the other.
Corruption	**Corruption**
Contracting gives managers more of a vested interest in the reputation of their institution.	Contracting brings new opportunities for corruption (i.e., political spoils, conflict of interest, bribes, kickbacks).

Source: Adapted from Logan, C. H. (1990). *Private prisons: Cons and pros.* New York: Oxford University Press, Copyright © 1990, by Oxford University Press, Inc. Reprinted by permission.

Transportation, especially in England, was a financially motivated innovation that provided an option to the very few punishments available at the time. Before passage of the Transportation Act of 1718, England could either execute its serious criminals or administer corporal punishment. But when banishment became an authorized punishment, the sanctioning power of the government was enormously expanded. Feeley (1991) hypothesizes that because an offender could be transported, instead of hanged or mutilated, the government's ability to sanction wrongdoers may have increased because victims were more likely to prosecute and juries more likely to convict.

And to whom is this innovation of transportation credited? Clearly, it was the work of private entrepreneurs. The act authorizing transportation even has the supplying of labor to the American colonies as a stated purpose. Much of the cost associated with transportation was borne by merchants who saw possibilities to profit in selling human cargo to the colonists. The transportees became indentured servants, and the British government gave up all responsibility for them. Distasteful as transportation was, it nevertheless provided an option falling between capital and corporal punishment. And it was an option that owed its popularity to private business.

While England was using transportation as a midrange sanction, private groups and businesses were encouraging the use of imprisonment in the United States for much the same reasons. There is no doubt that the early reformers had humanitarian motives for establishing imprisonment as an alternative to corporal and capital punishment, but it is also clear that economic factors shaped the prison sanction's form and direction. As Feeley (1991) says, "While they did not rehabilitate, some of these [prisons] came close to paying for themselves. And certainly, one of their appeals was the claim of entrepreneurs that they could pay, at least partially, for themselves" (p. 4). Imprisonment, then and now, is a sanction with many problems. In context, however, its arrival as a punishment option meant that serious offenders could be responded to with something other than execution, disfigurement, or ostracism. And to the extent that having more sentencing options is a good thing, the expansion was in no small part due to private involvement in corrections.

The argument for privatization as innovation continues today as entrepreneurs still generate new penalties that serve to expand options available to the government. Although some people may be perfectly happy with choices of fines and suspended sentences at one extreme, and execution or long-term imprisonment at another, others believe intermediate sanctions are increasingly necessary. And, as was true in the eighteenth and nineteenth centuries, many of the strategies offered at the intermediate level have a link with private organizations and businesses. Feeley suggests that supervised treatment programs, drug and alcohol abuse treatment, and job training programs were virtually nonexistent thirty years ago but are commonplace today because of private involvement.

Cullen (1986) also suggests that privatization is more likely than public owned and operated corrections to result in innovative ideas. He takes this position on the assumption that private contractors are more easily held accountable for a program's success, and they are, therefore, more likely to search for effective strategies. And, equally important given our capitalist society, reforms are more likely to be successful if they are compatible with capitalist thinking and interest. What better way is there to ensure that they will be compatible than to have private business involved in their creation, development, and implementation?

To the extent that authors such as Feeley and Cullen are correct in viewing privatization as innovation, the continued involvement of private groups, organizations, and businesses should be encouraged in the corrections enterprise. And one area that certainly needs some innovation involves the growing problems presented by special inmate populations.

SUMMARY

ORGANIZATIONAL STRUCTURE

Prisons are complex organizations that require administrators to manage their facilities with attention to the same types of issues that confront chief executives of major corporations. Personnel, economic, political, health, and security problems require the wardens' constant attention.

CORRECTIONAL OFFICERS

Correctional officers are responsible for public safety (ensuring that criminals confined to an institution stay there), institutional security (guaranteeing that prisoners and staff are safe while in the institution), and at least in some facilities, for portions of the inmates' treatment.

TREATMENT STAFF AND PROGRAMS

Treatment staff have specific duties linked to such broad areas as religion, academic education, vocational training, recreation, and inmate self-betterment.

MANAGING PRISON INDUSTRIES

As it has throughout history, inmate labor continues to play an important, if controversial, role in the operation of prisons.

- Prison labor serves to benefit the prisoner by encouraging good work habits and providing marketable skills for the inmate's eventual return to society.
- Prison labor also benefits the prison by keeping the inmates busy during the day and by providing a source of income that helps reduce the taxpayer burden for operating the prison.

MANAGING PRISON GANGS

As prison populations continue to rise, the prison administrator is being confronted with a wider variety of inmates—some of whom require special attention. Included among those could be members of prison gangs because they present a security threat that must be acknowledged.

MANAGING SPECIAL-NEEDS INMATES

The more typical categories of special-needs inmates include:

- Inmates with mental or physical disabilities
- Inmates with infectious diseases, especially inmates with HIV or AIDS
- Elderly inmates requiring assisted living and differential care

PRIVATIZATION OF CORRECTIONS

The complexity of prison management and the ever increasing cost to taxpayers for operating correctional facilities have encouraged some states to turn to private companies as an alternate way to provide some correctional services.

Key Terms and Concepts

Americans with Disabilities Act (p. 378)
classification (p. 359)
correctional officers (p. 353)
developmental models (p. 361)
institutional work assignments (p. 369)
joint-venture model (p. 373)
needs level (p. 360)
objective classification systems (p. 359)
overclassification (p. 360)
prison industry work assignments (p. 369)
privatization (p. 389)
problem-area models (p. 361)
risk level (p. 360)
security threat groups (p. 375)

Discussion Questions

1. What similarities do you suppose exist between the acceptance of female correctional officers by male correctional officers and the acceptance of female police officers by male police officers?
2. What are some problems and some possible solutions to simultaneously doing classification for management and classification for treatment?
3. The summary of recidivism research by Saylor and Gaes indicated that although women were less likely to return to prison for either a new offense or a violation of supervision, those who did failed much earlier than their male counterparts. What implications might this finding have for the design of men and women's release programs?
4. What are some advantages and disadvantages of having prison industries that make a profit for the state?
5. If you were the warden of a prison, what techniques would you use to lessen any negative impact that prison gangs might have on the security of your prison?
6. What particular problems associated with prisoners having mental or physical disabilities, infectious diseases, or those who are aging, do you see as most in need of attention? What recommendations would you make to a warden interested in developing policies and procedures for these inmates?
7. Discuss the various advantages and disadvantages of privatization of corrections. Which arguments do you feel are the strongest?

chapter 11

Responding to the Female Offender

In her 1994 book, *A Rage to Punish,* Lois G. Forer describes a visit she made to a women's prison soon after her appointment as a judge in Philadelphia.[1]

> I cannot forget one trip to a women's prison I made shortly after I was appointed to the bench. Although I had been there several times before, I was determined to see for myself the conditions my clients had described. As a judge, I thought I had the right to inspect the entire institution.
>
> The prison was in an isolated area of farmland . . . far from the cities from which most of the inmates come. The grounds were well cared for by young women inmates who

[1]From Forer, L. G. (1994). *A rage to punish: The unintended consequences of mandatory sentencing.* New York: W. W. Norton & Company. Copyright © 1994 by Lois G. Forer. Reprinted by permission of W. W. Norton & Company.

were plowing the fields, not a useful learning experience for city dwellers. . . .

We were shown the dining hall, the kitchen, the library which was empty and kept locked, and other public rooms where inmates sat idly. I asked to see the "hole" and was told there was no hole in this institution.

"You call it the 'green cottage,' " I responded. "I want to see it."

[At the green cottage I demanded to see Dorita. After some argument, I was taken to her cell.] This young woman was wearing only a T-shirt. She was lying on a bare mattress on a cot fixed to the wall. There was no book other than a Bible, no writing material, no games, no radio, nothing for her to do. She had been there for more than two weeks as a disciplinary measure for returning late from a weekend pass. Her explanation was that her child was sick and she had missed the bus that ran once a day from the city to the prison. She was denied phone calls while in the "green cottage." In despair she had tried to kill herself with a twisted sheet. Therefore, her bedding and clothes had been removed.

"Is there anything I can do for you?" I asked her.

"Please," she implored, "find out how my child is. Is she dead or alive? I have to know."

Dorita's crime was shoplifting. She had been convicted three times and . . . was sentenced under a habitual offender statute mandating a prison term. She was poor, black, unemployed, a single mother on welfare. She fit the profile of the female prisoner. On release she will still be poor, unemployable, and on welfare. Her daughter, who is a ward of the state, will be shuttled from one foster home to another. When Dorita is released, her daughter will not know her. Dorita will be alone and embittered.

Dorita's story is told to the world by a judge. Other "Doritas"—today and in the past—have also had stories about being in prison, but their stories are seldom told or heard. One explanation for the lack of attention to women offenders in general, and women in prison specifically, is that they represent such a small percentage of prisoners that they do not attract the attention of researchers, policymakers, the media, or the public. As we have seen in the preceding chapters of this book, that lack of attention is changing. In this chapter we will review reasons for the increasing attention being paid to women offenders, look at the history of society's response to those women, and then focus on contemporary aspects of women in prison.

Table 11.1 shows that women account for 22 percent of the arrests for all types of crimes, 17 percent of the violent crime arrests, and 29 percent of all arrests for property offenses. In state courts, women account for 16 percent of all persons convicted of felonies, with property offenses (23 percent female) being the area with the highest proportion. Women are 11 percent of the jail inmates, 21 percent of the adults on probation, 6.5 percent of all inmates in state and federal prisons, and 12 percent of the adults on parole. These numbers tell us that female offenders have an important impact on the U.S. justice system, but it is also clear that, compared to men, the overall role of women is statistically less significant. After all, men account for most of the arrests for all categories of crime, and they make up the majority of all felony convictions. The people in jail, on probation, in prison, and on parole are overwhelmingly male. Crime, court, and corrections issues in the United States seem clearly dominated by male offenders, defendants, and prisoners. Why devote a special chapter to female offenders?

The difficulty involved in maintaining a positive and meaningful relationship between women prisoners and their children is one of many issues presented by female inmates that differs from the issues presented by male inmates.

TABLE 11.1: Comparing Women and Men Offenders (1998)

	FEMALE (%)	MALE (%)
Total Arrests	21.8	78.2
Violent crime	16.8	83.2
Property crime	28.9	71.1
Felony Convictions (1996)	16.0	84.0
Violent crime	8.0	92.0
Property crime	23.0	77.0
Drug crime	17.0	83.0
Jail Inmates	11.0	89.0
Adults on Probation	21.0	79.0
State and Federal Prison Inmates	6.5	93.5
Adults on Parole	12.0	88.0

Source: Adapted from Bonczar, T. P., & Glaze, L. E. (1999). *Probation and parole in the United States, 1998* [NCJ 178234]. Washington, DC: Bureau of Justice Statistics; Brown, J. M., Langan, P. A., & Levin, D. J. (1999). *Felony sentences in state courts, 1996* [NCJ 173939]. Washington, DC: Bureau of Justice Statistics; Gilliard, D. K. (1999). *Prison and jail inmates at midyear 1998* [NCJ 173414]. Washington, DC: Office of Justice Programs; *Uniform crime reports, 1998.* (1999). Washington, DC: Department of Justice.

Part of the answer was provided in Table 1.1 of Chapter 1, but there are some other items to consider as well (Beck & Mumola, 1999; *Uniform Crime Reports,* 1998):

- From 1994 to 1998, female arrests were up 13 percent whereas male arrests rose 2 percent.
- From 1994 to 1998, female arrests for violent crime increased 12 percent whereas male arrests for violent crime fell by 12 percent.
- During 1998 the number of women in state or federal prisons increased 6.5 percent whereas the number of men increased 4.7 percent. That was the third consecutive year that the increase for women outpaced that for men.
- Since 1990 the number of female prisoners has grown 92 percent (an average growth rate of 8.5 percent annually). The number of male prisoners has grown 67 percent (an average growth rate of 6.6 percent annually).
- Black non-Hispanic females are more than twice as likely as Hispanic females and eight times more likely than white non-Hispanic females to be in prison. Those differences are consistent across all age groups.
- Since 1990 the number of female inmates serving time for drug offenses increased about 100 percent, whereas the number of male prisoners in for drug offenses rose about 50 percent.

The percentage of women is increasing at both the crime and the punishment points of the criminal justice system. And although their numbers may still be small in comparison to men, the increasing involvement of women in crime demands the attention of all components of the U.S. justice system.

Even if the numbers did not suggest the need to pay closer attention to female offenders, other reasons require a separate analysis for women. Females present different issues to justice officials, have different problems to be addressed by prison administrators, and have different program needs. Over the years those differences have been both ignored and highlighted. But under either of those approaches the basis for responding to female offenders has been male oriented. Women prisoners were either responded to in a manner equal to male prisoners or in a way different from male prisoners, but the one constant has been to use male prisoners as the standard. Today some authors suggest that society's response to female offenders should begin with a female rather than male orientation. In this way women prisoners can be responded to with attention to any specific needs, problems, or advantages they may present without concern for how those needs, problems, and advantages compare with ones presented by male prisoners. Before expanding on this point, we will back up and start with the first responses to female offenders.

SOCIAL RESPONSES TO FEMALE OFFENDERS

We had entertained the hope that there was not a female in Alabama so destitute of virtue and honor as to commit an act sufficiently heinous to justify the courts of the county committing one to the penitentiary. But such seems not to be the good fortune of Alabama.

—Penitentiary Inspector's Report, 1850–1851

Alabama's lack of "good fortune" was repeated throughout the country in the nineteenth century as state governments increasingly found themselves needing a place of confinement for female offenders. And for the most part, the response everywhere was just as paternalistic and patronizing as the quote from Alabama suggests. The following review of social responses to female offenders concentrates on the use of imprisonment by showing how three response models have occurred over three chronological stages identified as the **neglect response,** the **differential response,** and the **equalization response.** The section concludes with a review of a new model that proponents hope will direct the next stage of social response to female offenders by rejecting the male standard and encouraging a **female-oriented response** to women offenders.

The Neglect Response

There is a danger in attaching a name to the way society responded to women offenders prior to the eighteenth century because it implies more thought or attention was given to these women than was probably true. A later response will be called the equalization approach, but in many ways the very first response was the prototype of equality because essentially no distinction was made between women and men in prison. But this was equality based on neglect rather than equality that sought fairness.

Chapter 3 explained that Americans were hesitant to adopt the idea of imprisonment as the sole, or even primary, punishment for crimes. The criminal codes were more likely to specify imprisonment as an alternative to the standard corporal punishment of the time. An understandable result of doubting judges were prisons that held few inmates. Prior to the 1820s, when many penal codes were finally changed to make imprisonment the primary punishment, it was not uncommon for the inmate population at the state prison to be around fifty. At Newgate Prison in Connecticut, for example, the pre-1821 population ranged from forty-five to sixty (Phelps, 1845). During the first three-quarters of the twentieth century, the percentage of women prisoners never exceeded 4 percent of the inmate population.

National statistics on prisoner characteristics prior to about 1910 do not exist (Cahalan, 1986), but there is no reason to believe the percentage of women prisoners was higher than 4 percent during the eighteenth and nineteenth centuries either. This means that late seventeenth- and early eighteenth-century prisons may have had one or two female inmates per house. That number was not large enough to occasion much interest in those women at the prison, and certainly not large enough to produce discussion or action on separate facilities for female prisoners. As a result, women receiving a sentence to imprisonment were at first placed in the same large rooms that housed male offenders. Segregation of the sexes into separate cells began occurring with more regularity in the 1820s, but it was not until the 1830s that separate facilities (sometimes physically removed from the cell blocks for males) were more standard than unusual.

The housing of women in facilities built and administered for punishing male offenders presented a variety of problems for those women. Issues of privacy come to mind first, but Rafter (1993) reminds us that the women would also have been more lonely than their male counterparts, more vulnerable to sexual exploitation by guards and male inmates, and less likely to receive support from visitors, physicians, or even chaplains.[2] The physical separation of cell blocks for men and women lessened problems of isolation, because female inmates had more opportunity to see and interact with other women. They were also less vulnerable to sexual exploitation from male inmates—but not necessarily from the guards, who were still mostly male.

The process of having women supervise the female prisoners was not quickly or easily accomplished (see "Women Prison Reformers"). New York began committing females to Auburn Prison in 1825, but rather than being housed in a cell block, they were kept in a third-floor attic above the prison kitchen. Rafter (1990) explains that until a matron was hired in 1832, the women at Auburn had no supervision. A steward delivered food and removed the waste once a day, but otherwise they were left to fend for themselves in an overcrowded and unventilated space that must have made the nearby cell blocks where men were kept seem very attractive in comparison.

Although separation of men's and women's units improved some aspects of prison life for women, it presented new problems as well. As women were moved farther away from the prison's center, they had less and less access to any opportunities that were available to male inmates. Rafter (1993) explains that this meant medical advice, religious services, and exercise opportunities were not offered as regularly to the women prisoners. Even a basic need such as food was compromised because the isolated women's units had no kitchen and relied on the transport of food—usually cold by the time it arrived—from the kitchen at the men's unit. So, although it seemed that women were receiving equal treatment, that outward equality produced inferior conditions for women prisoners between about 1790 and the start of the Reformatory era.

The Differential Response

As the Reformatory era began taking hold in the 1860s, there was an interest in reforming female as well as male prisoners. Feminists[3] of the time worked hard to get all-male legislatures to fund separate reformatory prisons for women. The

[2]Adapted from Rafter, N. H. (1993). "Equality of difference" from *Female offenders: Meeting the needs of a neglected population* (pp. 7–11). Courtesy of the American Correctional Association, Lanham, MD.

[3]Unlike contemporary feminists, these women accepted a traditional restricted role for women. As a result, there is some disagreement about how appropriate the term *feminist* is to describe them. It is used here as a designation of respect for the social reforms they championed in their particular era.

HISTORICAL PERSPECTIVES

Women Prison Reformers

There have been many women activists who are important to the history of reform in the way society responded to female offenders. A brief note about some of them is provided here:

- **Elizabeth Fry** (1780–1845), along with John Howard, is one of the greatest prison reformers of modern time. As early as 1813 she was visiting London's infamous Newgate Prison in attempts to assist the prisoners. In 1817 she created an association for the improvement of the female prisoners with such goals as the separation of the sexes, classification of criminals, female supervision for women, and the providing of religious and academic instruction. Her accomplishments in these areas led her to visit other prisons in England, Scotland, Ireland, and throughout the European continent where she suggested improvements and provided counsel on how to achieve them (see www.kings.edu/womens_history/efry.html).
- **Dorothea Dix** (1802–1887) was a social reformer and humanitarian who worked tirelessly to improve the life of the mentally ill. Because the mentally ill were housed with criminals during this time period, her efforts to improve conditions of these facilities benefitted both the mentally ill and the criminal offenders (conduct a search at www.britannica.com/).
- **Jane Addams** (1860–1935) was a pioneer in the field of social work. With remarkable empathy for the poor, she and a friend settled in a shabby old mansion among Chicago's tenements and sweatshops. The place was called "old Hull house" after its builder. The name Hull House was eventually adopted for the settlements that began popping up across the United States to respond to the needs of society's forgotten, including former convicts. Addams and her associates were also instrumental in establishing in Chicago the world's first juvenile court (conduct a search at www.britannica.com/).
- **Julia Tutwiler** (1841–1916) was especially known in Alabama as the "Mother of Coeducation in Alabama" after she forced the entry of ten women into the University of Alabama. But Ms. Tutwiler was also known as "Angel of the Prisons" because she was a key figure in the separation of serious offenders from less serious criminals and in reform of the convict lease system. Alabama's Julia Tutwiler Woman's Prison is named for her (see www.awhf.org/tutwiler.html).
- **Frances Joseph-Gaudet** (1861–1934), born in Mississippi of African American and Native American heritage, spent most of her life with the Prison Reform Association in Louisiana assisting black prisoners initially, and later white prisoners, by holding prayer meetings, writing letters, carrying messages, and securing clothing. She was also the first woman, black or white, to support juvenile offenders in Louisiana, and her efforts helped found that state's juvenile court system (see www.lib.lsu.edu/soc/women/lawomen/gaudet.html).

Review the key women in corrections at *www.cj.msu.edu/~outreach/azm/hof.html,* and identify what E. D. Stewart did that started the women's movement in corrections. At that same location, find out why Clara Barton, founder of the American Red Cross, served as superintendent of the Massachusetts Reformatory Prison for Women in 1882. Another important woman in prison reform was New York's Abby Hopper Gibbons. Go to *www.ci.nyc.ny.us/html/doc/html/kbd_7.html,* and explain what Gibbons meant in her last words, which reportedly were "Be sure, Alice, thee make it a Reformatory and not a Prison."

basic arguments for separate treatment were identified by Freedman (1974) as (1) assigning the blame for female criminality to men instead of to the women themselves, (2) proposing rehabilitation as being best achieved by removing the women from the evil influences of the men, and (3) stressing the ability of women to control and reform their sisters. The call, then, was for different responses to women and men prisoners. Women were worthy of reform, and that reform was best achieved in separate facilities operated by women.

The arguments against separate treatment may not have been stated so specifically by men of the day, but Freedman (1974) outlines them as (1) the belief that women were incapable of controlling, let alone reforming, female criminals; (2) a concern that female-controlled prisons would not have a familial, or homelike, structure; and (3) a fear that women's institutions could reduce male dominance in society and would destroy femininity. But despite such concerns, prisons or reformatories specifically for women began when Indiana opened the Women's Prison in 1873 and Massachusetts opened the Reformatory Prison for Women in 1877. The women reformers who had argued for these facilities often became administrators in the new reformatories. In doing so they were able to put into practice the principles they had argued in the legislatures—women inmates should be treated entirely differently from male prisoners.

One area in which the new women's prisons were clearly different from those for men was their architectural style. The women's reformatories were built in a **cottage plan;** inmates lived in relatively small individual units (cottages) that created an atmosphere more like a home than a cell block. The cottages themselves could be set up in dormitory style or with individual rooms having windows, bedspreads, rugs, and wooden doors instead of iron bars. The goal was to project a domestic atmosphere that would focus the women's attention and interests on their expected role in society.

Programming differences were also apparent in the women's facilities, but although different from those for men, they were consistent with the cottage atmosphere by emphasizing domesticity. In their new reformatories, the women prisoners mainly received training in sewing, cooking, washing and ironing clothes, gardening, and farming. The reformers, who were primarily middle-class women, seemed intent on putting female offenders into a homemaker mold despite the fact that most of the prisoners would have to support themselves after release from prison.

In addition to different styles of facilities and different treatment programs for women prisoners, there were also differences in sentencing practices. Rafter (1993) explains that the reformers establishing the new reformatories were not much interested in dealing with felons. Those serious offenders, many of whom were black, did not draw much empathy from the middle-class and essentially white women reformers. The "preferred" clientele for reform efforts were white women convicted of misdemeanors (see "Black Women in Prison"). But for the reform efforts to be successful, it was necessary to have access to these offenders over a long time. As a result, the legislation establishing women's reformatories allowed them to hold minor offenders on sentences that were equivalent to those given to

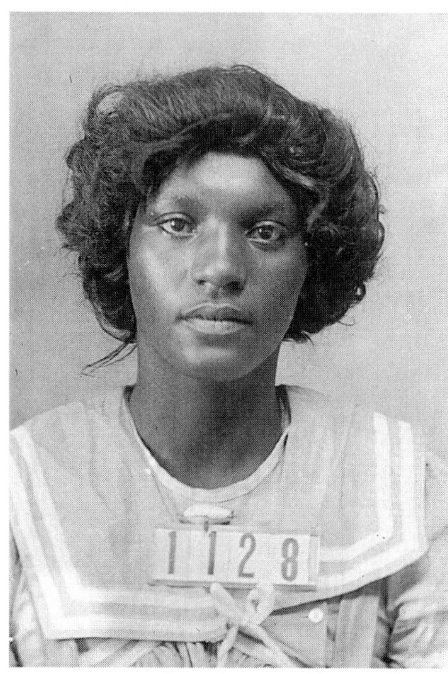

Not much is known about black women in prison during the late 1800s, but there is reason to believe that black women prisoners were more likely to serve their sentences in a prison while white women were sentenced to the new reformatories built specifically for women. Cora Thomas, shown here, served eighteen months in the Kansas Penitentiary for a grand larceny charge.

ISSUES OF FAIRNESS

BLACK WOMEN IN PRISON

The lack of clear records makes it difficult to establish the actual number of black men and women in prisons across the United States in the early and mid-1800s. Several authors believe there is enough evidence to support claims that black people were disproportionately incarcerated in the Northeast, Midwest, and West throughout the nineteenth century (Kurshan, n.d.). Blacks were less likely to be in southern prisons prior to the end of the Civil War because slaves received their "justice" at the hands of slave masters rather than the courts. Butler (1997) found an exception to that standard when, in 1851, records show the governor of Missouri pardoned a white woman who had been sentenced to prison. The one cell Missouri's prison had for women was already being occupied by a black woman. A white woman, the governor argued, should not be expected to share quarters with a slave, so the white woman was pardoned instead (p. 108, note 64).

Although we do not know very much about black women in prison during the late nineteenth and early twentieth centuries, there are some aspects that are clear. For example, there is good reason to believe that black women did not benefit as much from the Reformatory era changes as did white women (C. F. Collins, 1997; Rafter, 1990). The women who were deemed worthy of reform, it seems, were white in color. Butler (1997) points out that blacks and other minorities in the late nineteenth and early twentieth centuries were economically deprived and responded to the encouragement of white males to operate small vice establishments such as brothels. As a result, the "immorality" of black women was simply a response to the type of opportunities they were provided. In any event, while the reformable white women were serving their sentences in cottage-style facilities, the discardable black female offenders served theirs in the custodial prisons of the North or in the prison camps of the South.

By the 1930s, society was increasingly responding to white women offenders by using probation or short jail sentences, and the reformatories came to play less of a role in society's response to women (at least white women) offenders. The reformatories were transformed into more secure places and began taking some of the characteristics of custodial prisons. The decreased use of reformatories for white women occurred around the same time as increased numbers of southern blacks were migrating to the North after World War I. Before long the old northern reformatories began holding more black women, but by now the reformatories were different places than their archetype (Kurshan, n.d.; Rafter, 1990).

Today black women prisoners continue to have an unfortunately unique status. Black non-Hispanic females have incarceration rates higher than either Hispanic females or white non-Hispanic females, and black females make up nearly half the population of women in prison. As you might imagine, there are many more questions than answers. Are high incarceration rates for black women simply the result of an intensification of the conditions offered to explain the general increase in women's imprisonment? Or do different circumstances explain the rates for black and white women? Any answers to such questions must await researchers who direct their studies specifically toward the black female offender.

Read the Sentencing Project's summary policy report on young African Americans and the criminal justice system at ***www.sentencingproject.org/policy/9070.htm.*** What three recommendations does the Sentencing Project make regarding this issue? Explain why you agree or disagree with those recommendations.

felons serving time at the state prison. Rafter (1993) summarizes the disadvantages of differential treatment in the following way:

1. Women held in women's reformatories were forced into a "true woman" mold of domesticity that infantilized and ill-prepared them for self-support in an industrialized society.
2. Moreover, women who committed minor offenses were now held on long sentences—much longer than the sentences served by men who committed minor offenses.

> 3. And, of course, men were never sent to state prisons for violations of chastity. The women's prison system became a means of enforcing the double standard of sexual morality. (p. 9)

Separate and different-style prisons, different programs, and different labor assignments are just some of the areas in which the differential response was apparent. In many ways the result was a clear improvement over the neglect and mistreatment women prisoners suffered when they were housed in male-dominated prisons. But in highlighting the special needs of women prisoners and in encouraging a different response, reformers "created a new set of problems by assuming that all women inmates, as women, could be treated alike, by methods aimed at reinforcing true womanhood in an era in which a new woman was emerging" (Freedman, 1974, p. 90).

The Equalization Response

In the late 1960s, the women's movement began having some success in showing the restricted opportunities presented by concentrating on domestic skills, the unfairness of the double standard of morality, and the inappropriateness of imprisonment on minor charges. Calls were made for equal treatment of male and female inmates. Some of the calls were in the forum of public opinion, and certainly some advances were made in that area. But other calls went to the courts, and women found the justices often agreed with the legal challenges to conditions of their confinement.

But women did not often use court action to redress their concerns about prison conditions. Feinman (1986) offers several reasons for why this situation has occurred, and to some extent continues to occur:

- Women have been taught to be passive and accepting.
- Because of a commonly held idea that women prisoners are better off than men prisoners, the women end up being ignored by civil rights and prisoners' rights organizations that file class-action lawsuits on behalf of male inmates.
- Because women's prisons are often located far from urban centers where legal advice, law libraries, and legal advocates can be found, women prisoners have infrequent access to persons with the skills or resources to help build a case.
- The law libraries at the prison may not be of much help because law librarians are seldom provided and because jailhouse lawyers are not a tradition in women's prisons.

An increased use of legal action by and for women prisoners began occurring in the late 1960s and helps mark the start of an equalization response. The earliest issues taken to court dealt with sentencing disparities between men and women offenders. Muraskin (1993) identifies some of the more important issues as including several decisions holding that the Fourteenth Amendment's equal protection clause was violated when state statutes had women sentenced to indeterminate terms serving a longer maximum sentence than men serving indeterminate terms for the same offense (*Liberti v. New York,* 1968; *United States ex rel Robinson v. York,* 1968). There was also an equal protection violation in Pennsylvania's practice of sentencing women to state prison on charges for which men were held in county jail (*Commonwealth v. Stauffer,* 1969).

In the 1970s, equalization issues turned more toward the conditions of confinement. Muraskin reports that court decisions in that decade included holdings that there be substantial equivalence between women and men in such areas as (1) the opportunities afforded to participate in work-furlough programs, (2) the ability to be assigned to minimum-security facilities, and (3) the distance in the place of incarceration from the place of sentencing. These last two points resulted from the use in most states of just one prison for all female inmates. Given the size of many states, it is likely that a woman sentenced to prison will be considerably farther from home than a man sentenced to prison in a state with several male facilities. Similarly, where there is only one prison for women, that facility must house all security levels. Although men can be assigned to a minimum-security prison, the best a woman might be able to do would be to have greater freedom of movement within a medium-security prison.

In what Muraskin (1993) considers the landmark case on women's prison issues, a U.S. District Court was asked to rule on programs and facilities provided by the state of Michigan for its women prisoners compared to those for its men prisoners. Women prisoners in Michigan claimed they were not receiving access to vocational courses equal to those for male prisoners, and the numbers seemed to support the women's position (Manville, 1986). Men had access to twenty-two vocational courses whereas women had access to only five. In addition, the courses available to the men led to marketable skills, but the five for women did not. One of the prison teachers testified that the "women were taught at a junior-high level because the attitude of those in charge was 'keep it simple, these are only women'" (quoted in Muraskin, 1993, p. 218). The court (*Glover v. Johnson,* 1979) held that women inmates must be provided treatment facilities that are substantially equal, but not necessarily identical, to those provided the men. As a result of the *Glover* ruling, Michigan had to provide postsecondary education, counseling, vocational programs, and a legal-education program to its women prisoners.

Law facilities and legal assistance were also at issue in *Canterino v. Wilson* (1982), where a federal district court ordered Kentucky to improve law library facilities and increase legal assistance at the Correctional Institution for Women because such programs were found unequal to those in the state's prisons for men. But there is still much to do in this area, as indicated by the 1989 reversal of *Canterino* when the court held that the women had not provided enough information to support their claims of discrimination and had failed to prove any injury (*Canterino v. Wilson,* 1989). In another federal district, prison officials tried to argue that providing equivalent programs to women was cost prohibitive, but the court (*Bukhari v. Hutto,* 1980) held that there was no justification for disparate treatment based on the fact that women's prisons serviced a smaller population and the cost would be greater to provide programs equivalent to those in men's institutions. Cost, in other words, was not an excuse for paucity of services.

Calls for a New Model—The Female-Oriented Response

Women and men are different; so too are women and men in prison.

—Joycelyn M. Pollock

This quote from Joycelyn Pollock seems to be a simple reiteration of the "different treatment" response. Actually, it is more complex than that. Along with criminologists such as Meda Chesney-Lind, Kathleen Daly, Nicole Hahn Rafter, and Frances Heidensohn, Pollock sees a need for a new model to orient society's response to female offenders. In the absence of any agreed-upon terminology, the new model has been referred to as a "social justice approach" or a "women-wise penology." Regardless of its eventual name, there is growing agreement about its content. Essentially, proponents of a new model recognize benefits in both the differential and the equalization responses and call for a synthesis of desirable aspects from each. In this way, there is an acceptance and appreciation of differences between women and men (in prison and out) accompanied by a call for equity in response. As we will see, an equitable response is a "fair" one—although it may not be the same one for all persons.

Recognizing the need for a new kind of social response to female offenders has come with increased acknowledgment that the equal treatment response brought some undesirable consequences along with its positive results. Many women's prisons today offer both nontraditional and traditional vocational programs, some basic education and college-level programs, improved access to legal materials, and better medical care. But with this equalization has come some losses. Because the male model of imprisonment has become the measuring rod for equal treatment, women have not achieved long-term benefits. If the standard punishment for male offenders is imprisonment, equalization makes imprisonment the standard for female offenders. Legal suits requiring equal prison conditions may result in the building of new, usually large-capacity women's prisons—resulting in more women in prison. Innovations in imprisonment for men, under an equality model, become innovations for women; a disastrous example, say Chesney-Lind and Pollock (1995), being the "right" to serve their sentence "in what is perhaps the most hypermasculine setting possible—a militaristic boot camp, complete with uniforms and short hair" (p. 167).

The concern being expressed by some critics of equalization is that an undesirable consequence of equal treatment for male and female offenders is a reduction in nonprison alternatives for women. As long as the way society responds to male offenders is the standard for determining equal treatment of female offenders, women will be treated as though they are men. And that, people such as Chesney-Lind and Pollock argue, is unfortunate and undesirable because women and men are different.

A new approach to female offenders must recognize and accept differences between women and men. But to distinguish this model from the earlier differential response, it cannot be tied to male-oriented definitions. When determination of what is an appropriate response toward women offenders is decided from a female orientation, new standards and possibilities are opened. For example, the types of crimes women commit are certainly unacceptable, but they do not indicate behavior that poses much threat to the physical safety of the community. Greenfeld and Snell (1999) report that 75 percent of the violent victimizations committed by female offenders are simple assaults, but only about 50 percent of the violence by male offenders are simple assaults. Those numbers translate into about one violent offender for every fifty-six females age ten or older compared with one violent offender for every nine males age ten or older. In addition, the consequence of male violence is typically more serious for the victim in terms of weapon use, injury, and out-of-pocket losses for the victim (Greenfeld & Snell, 1999).

Because of the low risk they present, female offenders are especially good candidates for settings such as halfway houses. And, in addition to presenting little risk to the community, female offenders have the type of problems that can be best addressed in the community setting. It seems prudent, therefore, to think in terms of community-based alternatives instead of incarceration when seeking a response to women criminals.

Proponents of a nonimprisonment response to female offenders anticipate claims that it would be unfair. After all, many men are also needlessly imprisoned. One response justifying this different treatment is the argument that women are especially appropriate for community-based programs because so many of them are in prison for nonviolent offenses. Greenfeld and Snell (1999) report that about 20 percent of all women inmates in state prisons nationwide are offenders serving their first prison sentence after conviction of a nonviolent crime. Only 8 percent of all male inmates fall into that same category. But even without that rationale, it can be argued that a specific focus on this neglected population is long overdue (Immarigeon & Chesney-Lind, 1992). After all, as we noted earlier, an equitable response does not necessarily mean the same response.

In this chapter we present material in a manner consistent with the new model's (i.e., female-oriented) approach to discussing female offenders. That means an emphasis on special needs of female offenders and on differences between women and men in custodial and noncustodial correctional programs. Those differences are present and should be taken into consideration when implementing and operating prison and community-based programs for women offenders. Programs in each of those locations are covered in this chapter. But before considering program specifics, it is necessary to have a better idea about the population being served. To that end, we look at issues related to the women most likely to get caught up in the criminal justice process, the effect on those women of changes in the sentencing policy, and some of the special needs that population presents to the corrections system.

Explaining Changes in Society's Reaction to Female Offenders

Arrest data and imprisonment statistics suggest that women's involvement in crime has increased over the last decade. Media and entertainment sources might lead one to think that women are committing more violent crimes today, and that those more serious offenses require more arrests and the harsher penalty of imprisonment. But the data do not support that position. Chesney-Lind (1998) explains that the rise in arrests and imprisonment numbers for women is not explained as a result of new hyperviolent female offenders. In fact, since 1990, only 25 percent of the total growth in female inmates was accounted for by violent crimes (Beck & Mumola, 1999). Instead, the rise in female inmates is more accurately attributed to greater numbers of drug offenders (38 percent of the growth). Simply put, the increase in women being sentenced to prison cannot be explained as a result of women committing more violent offenses.

The crimes women commit tend to be property, less serious assault, and public-order offenses (see Table 11.2). The ones for which women are most frequently arrested are, in order, larceny–theft, simple assaults (no weapon used and no serious injury occurs), drug abuse violations, driving under the influence, and fraud. Similarly, the offenses for which women make up at least one-third of the arrests are also property crimes—embezzlement, fraud, forgery, and larceny–theft (*Uniform Crime Reports*, 1998). These characteristics of female crime have not changed much since the mid-1980s except that arrests for simple assault have moved into the top five to replace prostitution arrests, which was the fifth most frequent category in 1984.

Because female criminality has been primarily property and public-order offenses over the years, the recent increases in both female arrests and prison sentences have brought forth several questions. For example, are more women actually committing crime, or is the social control network simply responding to them differently? Also, because women are still mostly involved in property and public-order offenses, which in the past have not usually brought prison sentences, why is the number of female prisoners increasing at a faster rate than the number of male prisoners? The first question is important and interesting but is not central to our present discussion. We should note, however, that Merlo's (1995) review of research suggests that a significant part of the increase in female arrests is the result of more formal policing and of general improvements in the social control bureaucracy. But

TABLE 11.2: Female and Male Arrests by Most Frequent Offense Category within Gender

TOP FIVE ARREST CATEGORIES FOR FEMALES	TOP FIVE ARREST CATEGORIES FOR MALES
Larceny–theft	Drug abuse violations
Other assaults	Driving under the influence
Drug abuse violations	Other assaults
Driving under the influence	Larceny–theft
Fraud	Drunkenness

Source: Adapted from *Uniform crime reports, 1998.* (1999). Washington, DC: Department of Justice.

the question on the increasing number of women prisoners is particularly relevant to this chapter and receives closer attention. We approach it by considering how the increase might be a result of changes in sentencing policies and practices related to the country's forceful action against drugs.

THE IMPACT OF SENTENCING POLICIES

As noted earlier, one of the first areas to receive legal challenge by women concerned sentencing disparity. Statutes that provided harsher maximum sentences for women than for men were consistently overturned by the courts, and today those kinds of disparate sentencing laws no longer exist. But it appears that today's sentencing policies might be affecting women differently than they do men—even though no gender-based differences are identified in the statutes. Consider, for example, what happens if punishment is linked to act-related characteristics rather than to gender-related characteristics. Sentencing all auto thieves to prison certainly seems more fair than having longer sentences for women auto thieves than for men auto thieves. But what if the crime itself has some gender link? In fact, most crimes are committed primarily by men. For example, males make up about 90 percent of the arrests for robbery. If society cracks down on robbery by increasing arrests and penalties, men would be affected more than women. One result, especially if the increased penalty were prison time, might be that the number of male inmates increases more rapidly than female inmates. That situation is not so much a description of unfairness (arrests and penalties for women robbers would also increase) as it would be an explanation for what appeared to be a social control bias against men. Let us apply that same principle to drug-related crimes.

As you'll recall from Chapter 4, the just deserts philosophy that dominates the Retributive era has encouraged get-tough practices toward several types of crimes. This has been especially true of drug-related offenses dealing with both possession and trafficking. There is no reason to believe that increased arrests and elevated penalties for drug offenses were undertaken by state and federal legislators for any reason other than to punish, deter, or incapacitate those offenders. But it seems that the get-tough policies have affected female offenders more than male offenders. That is because women are more likely to have drugs linked to their criminal behavior. In fact, some authors suggest that the "war on drugs" has translated into a war on women (Chesney-Lind & Pollock, 1995). This is because of a more consistent and significant link between drug use and female offenders than drug use and male offenders.

Merlo's (1995) and Pollock's (1999) review of research on drugs and female criminals found that larger percentages of female arrestees than male arrestees are using drugs. In addition, women's criminality seems to increase after drug use—especially as they become involved in property crimes, and prostitution to a lesser extent, to support their drug habit. A similar profile is found when research centers on the women in prison. Reports on drug use history find that female prisoners had used more drugs and used those drugs more frequently than did men in prison (Greenfeld & Snell, 1999). Not only was drug use more prevalent among the women, but more women than men reported committing their crime to get money for buying drugs.

If female offenders are more likely to have drugs linked to their criminal behavior, a sentencing policy that cracks down on drugs will mean a crackdown on women. And that is exactly what seems to have occurred as a report from the Sentencing Project describes (Mauer, Potler, & Wolf, 1999):

- From 1986 to 1996 the number of women imprisoned for drug offenses rose by 888 percent.
- Drug offenses accounted for half the rise in the number of women in state prisons from 1986 to 1996 but only one-third of the increase for men.
- Black and Hispanic women represent a disproportionate share of the women sentenced to prison for a drug offense.

Recent policy in the United States has increased penalties for drug possession, use, and distribution. This suggests that one reason women prisoners are increasing at a faster rate than men prisoners is that changes in sentencing policies have made prison a likely punishment for behavior (drug abuse) in which women criminals are more likely to engage. It seems that the drug war policy has had a particularly negative impact on female offenders, even though there was no intent to have sentencing disparity.

The importance of drugs in explaining and understanding much of female criminality reiterates the point made by those emphasizing the need to recognize differences between women and men. To move away from a knee-jerk reliance on traditional (i.e., male-oriented) social control strategies, it is important to identify as many areas as possible in which women offenders and men offenders differ. In this way, a female orientation can develop that identifies more appropriate social control strategies than are currently used for female criminals. But such an orientation has not yet ensued. The best that can be offered is to consider how women are responded to under the traditional penalties of imprisonment and community-based sanctions. While discussing those sanctions, however, we can try to identify some of the special needs presented by women offenders and begin to work toward a female orientation that might result in totally new sanctions. Or, if this is unreasonable, at least significant modifications of the traditional sanctions as applied to females in prison or under community supervision may emerge. We look first at women in prison and then turn to community-based sanctions for female offenders. Each of those sections identifies some of the special needs and conditions that should be taken into consideration when society responds to female offenders.

Female Offenders in Prison

Although many states were placing some of their female criminals (especially white minor offenders) in new reformatories during the first quarter of the twentieth century, the women who committed more serious crimes were still placed in special units at the central state prison. This practice began changing around 1930, as the women's reformatories came to house most of the state's female prisoners. One reason for the change was the realization by states that they could no longer afford to operate institutions that held petty offenders for long periods of moral retraining. In addition, space was needed at the state prisons for the increasing numbers of male prisoners. Removing the women being held at those prisons and placing them instead at the women's reformatory became an economic necessity. But, with the arrival of these more serious offenders, the women's reformatory ceased to exist in all but name (Rafter, 1990, p. 81).

Facilities for Women Prisoners

From 1930 to 1960 there was not much increase in the number of institutions holding women in the United States. The pace picked up in the 1960s, when seven women's units were opened—primarily in the West and South—and increased more noticeably in the 1970s, when seventeen new institutions for women were established. During the 1980s, expansion went into high gear when thirty-four women's units opened (Rafter, 1990). Unfortunately, the expansion of women's facilities was often accomplished without much thought or planning. Authorities placed women with more regard to where there were spaces than to what made sense for the women. As a result, female offenders often ended up in abandoned hotels, motels, mental hospitals, and other equally unsuitable locations. States that did not build or find new facilities for the increasing number of women prisoners had to squeeze more women into existing spaces. Double- and triple-bunking occurred more frequently, and in some locations women were placed on cots in day rooms or gymnasiums. The problem did not get any better during the 1990s as jurisdictions continued to expand existing units, build new facilities, and generally scramble to house the increasing number of women being sent to prison.

As more women offenders are sent to prison, states must expand existing units or build new ones to house female prisoners. Shown is the health center at the Central California Women's Facility, which provides a full range of health services within a maximum-security setting.

Characteristics of Women Prisoners

In a 1994 report, the Bureau of Justice Statistics provided what is still the most comprehensive survey ever undertaken of women confined in state prisons (Snell, 1994). A 1999 report (Greenfeld & Snell, 1999) provides information about women offenders from type of crime through recidivism but does not include specific characteristics of females in prison. Because the findings of the 1994 report are repeated in less ambitious but more recent studies, and because of the similar findings about women prisoners in other countries (see "Profiles of Women Prisoners in Other Countries"), it is believed that the 1994 report continues to describe contemporary women prisoners.

The results of the Survey of Inmates of State Correctional Facilities (SISCF) show that female inmates are very similar to male inmates in race, ethnic background, and age. Both men and women prisoners tend to be young minority group members. There is also similarity between the sexes in the areas of marital status and education, but there is significant difference between females and males in the area of prearrest employment—female inmates are significantly less likely to have been employed at the time of their arrest.

The SISCF profile also explains that most of the women in prison were convicted on a nonviolent offense and had only nonviolent offenses as prior convictions. The women who were serving a sentence for a violent crime were most likely to have victimized a relative, an intimate (husband, ex-husband, boyfriend), or some other acquaintance. In fact, the women in prison were more likely to have committed their violent offense against someone close to them than were their male counterparts (36 percent to 16 percent).

The tendency for violent crimes by women, including homicides, to have been against intimates and relatives (nearly 50 percent of the cases) may be a result of women responding to a history of being subjected to physical and psychological abuse by that relative or intimate. Several studies have suggested that many women in prison for violent crimes are serving sentences for killing abusive husbands, ex-husbands, or boyfriends (see Moyer, 1993; Owen & Bloom, 1995; and Pollock-Byrne, 1990, for reviews of the studies). The SISCF survey did not address this point specifically, but it did find that more women inmates (43 percent) than men (12 percent) reported having been physically or sexually abused before their current incarceration (see "Prior Abuse and Female Prisoners" on page 413).

As we saw in Chapter 8, some treatment programs such as boot camps will be ineffective or inappropriate for offenders who have a history of abuse victimization. Statistics suggest that those offenders are most likely to be female, and this insight reiterates the importance of a female orientation in setting up programs for female offenders. We cannot simply take programs developed for men and assume they are appropriate for women. To elaborate that point, consider the use of drugs by women offenders and see how acknowledging that trait requires a response that differs from the traditional male orientation to prisons and prison programs.

Just as drugs affect the sentencing of female offenders, they also affect the programs that are relevant to female prisoners. Before their incarceration, women prisoners used more drugs and used those drugs more frequently than did men in prison. Women prisoners are also more likely to report that they were under the influence of drugs at the time of their current offense and to claim that they committed the offense to get money to buy drugs (Greenfeld & Snell, 1999). The prominence of drug abuse in the profile of women prisoners means that a female orientation to prison administration and programming must give considerable attention to the link between drugs and female offenders.

The characteristics of women prisoners highlighted here suggest a profile showing these women to be primarily property and drug offenders, who typically

Cross-Cultural Corrections

Profiles of Women Prisoners in Other Countries

There is remarkable similarity in the characteristics of female offenders in the United States with their counterparts in other countries. Just as women prisoners in the United States are primarily property offenders with substance abuse problems and a history of victimization by physical and sexual abuse, so too are women prisoners around the world. In their summary of imprisonment in more than twenty countries, Dünkel and van Zyl Smit (1991) note that a particular problem is that a larger percentage of women than men are drug users. Morris and Wilkinson (1995) found women prisoners in England were mainly young, in prison for property offenses, and mothers of dependent children. In addition, nearly half reported using drugs before their imprisonment (with over half of those saying the drug use was associated with their offending), about 50 percent were physically abused before imprisonment, and nearly one-third were sexually abused. Women prisoners in Scotland are committed primarily on crimes of theft, public-order disturbances, and drug offenses. In fact, their incidence of alcoholism and drug abuse is higher than among men (Adler, 1991). In Canada, women prisoners have extensive histories of physical or sexual abuse and a relatively high incidence of substance abuse (Miller-Ashton, 1993). Similarly, there are aggravated problems of drug abuse among female prisoners in Germany (Dünkel & Rössner, 1991).

Esther Giménez-Salinas i Colomer (1991) suggests that it would be simple to implement a sound penal policy for women's prisons. Given the similar characteristics and problems of women prisoners worldwide, it does seem that a policy could be developed that will respond to the specific issues of substance abuse, victimization by physical and sexual abuse, and a tendency to commit property crimes. But no single country has come up with a model approach, nor has there been any international cooperation to find a preferred way for societies to respond to female offenders. Excuses, if not reasons, typically offered are linked to the small number of female offenders in every country, but there are also some problems associated with cultural views about the role of women and with traditional practices toward women in many societies. Several of those are discussed at the end of this chapter.

Go to the Web site for the Danish Prison and Probation Service at *www.kriminalforsorgen.dk/uk_web/index.html,* and identify to which prison women are sent. What similarities and differences are there between the women in that Danish prison and those in U.S. prisons? Read about women with long-term federal sentences in Canada at *www.csc-scc.gc.ca/text/prgrm/fsw/statistical/toc_e.shtml.* What is considered a long-term sentence in Canada? What percentage of the women with long-term sentences are aboriginal?

have minor children and maintain close contact with those children, and who have an extensive history of drug abuse. These are some characteristics that should be considered when developing policies and procedures for handling women prisoners. The first step in that process, as it is when working with male prisoners, is inmate classification. After looking at that necessary procedure, we will review some programs now operating in women's prisons.

Classification Issues and Women Prisoners

Chapter 10 explained the importance of classification systems in achieving management and treatment objectives in prison. Over the last several decades many people have wondered if the typical classification systems, which were undeniably developed for male offenders, are effective tools for managing and treating female offenders. Burke and Adams (1991) tackled this issue with a nationwide study of how state prison systems handle classification of female prisoners. They began their study with an assumption that some jurisdictions had developed classification systems specifically designed for women. But they soon determined it was

Spotlight ON CONTEMPORARY ISSUES

Prior Abuse and Female Prisoners

Among state prison inmates, one in four women have been sexually abused before age eighteen. The same ratio of women was physically abused before age eighteen (Harlow, 1999). The Bureau of Justice Statistics' study that provides these data allowed the respondents to define for themselves what physical and sexual abuse meant. The 25 percent rate of child abuse for women in prison is higher than the estimated 12 percent to 17 percent of females in the general adult U.S. population who experienced abuse as children (Harlow, 1999). These data are considered important because prior abuse is often cited as one reason for the need to have a separate response to women offenders than we have to male offenders.

Males also experience abuse but, although any abuse is unacceptable and unwarranted, the abuse experienced by women seems both quantitatively and qualitatively different. First, fewer males in state prison reported either sexual (one in twenty males) or physical (one in eight males) abuse prior to age eighteen. Unlike the percentages for women prisoners, that 5 percent to 12 percent rate for male prisoners is not much different from the estimated 5 percent to 8 percent of males in the general adult U.S. population who were abused as children. In addition, Harlow reports that male prisoners reporting abuse generally had been age seventeen or younger when they suffered that abuse. The abuse suffered by women prisoners, however, occurred both as juveniles and adults. In addition, abuse of male prisoners was primarily by family members, but abuse of women was by family members and by intimates (spouse, ex-spouse, boyfriend, friend). Almost two-thirds of the abused women in state prisons reported being abused by current or prior husbands or boyfriends.

Information about abuse suffered by women prisoners is important because it offers insight regarding appropriate policies and procedures for operating a women's prison. For example, victims of abuse likely have an even more negative response to strip and pat down searches than do people who have not been abused. And abuse victims may view their privacy differently than nonvictims. If prison management and staff do not take into consideration the unique perspective of abuse victims toward what are standard procedures in a male prison—where inmates are less likely to have reason to be fearful or repulsed by physical contact or privacy violation—those officials may actually encourage misbehavior by the women inmates.

In addition to affecting prison operation, information about prior abuse may also offer some explanation for why drug offenses play an important role in bringing women into the criminal justice system. Harlow's data show that illegal drug use was more common among abused female state prison inmates (80 percent) than among those women prisoners who said they were not abused (65 percent). And abused state female prisoners (46 percent) were more likely than those reporting no abuse (32 percent) to have been under the influence of illegal drugs when they committed their crime. Is it possible that abuse victims are more likely to turn to drugs than are people who have not suffered abuse? Is the war on drugs actually a war on abuse victims? Would a female-oriented perspective on the possible link among abuse, drug use, and female criminality provide more options for responding to female offenders than does the traditional male-oriented perspective?

Read one of the versions of Harlow's report at ***www.ojp.usdoj.gov/bjs/abstract/parip.htm.*** What is the relationship between reported abuse and committing violent crime? Can the data be used to support any claim that many women in prison for a violent crime are there as a result of prior abuse?

more accurate to say that a few states have adapted or modified some aspects of their standard classification process to deal more directly with female offenders.

Little had changed when Morash, Bynum, and Koons (1998) surveyed administrators later in the decade and found that a commonly mentioned management problem was that existing classification procedures were not relevant to the needs of women offenders nor were they useful in matching women with appropriate programs. It seems likely that part of the problem was that thirty-nine states used the same classification instrument for both men and women. In seven states the instrument for men was adapted for the women. In only three states was a special instrument used for classification of women offenders. One state had no instrument at all.

The modification of existing classification systems takes several forms (Burke & Adams, 1991). In some states the **systemwide classification** process—that is, initial classification, usually at a central location, where all newly sentenced offenders are sent for the particular purpose of determining to which facility a prisoner will be assigned—remains the same for both men and women. But the **institutional classification** process—classification occurring after arrival at a particular facility in order to determine things such as cell, work, and program assignments—is different among the state's male and female prisons. Another modification, and the most frequent according to Burke and Adams, is an extensive use of "overrides" when making classification designations for women. In these situations, women offenders are classified in the standard manner, and then prison staff override the resulting classification standard (e.g., maximum security) to make it more appropriate to the staff's impression of the woman (e.g., medium security). In a third modification, some states legitimize the overrides by holding women to identical classification policies and procedures but then using different risk assessment standards. These last two modifications highlight a key issue of different classification standards for women—security risk.

In the early 1980s the American Correctional Association (1984) noted that the majority of female offenders do not need high security, even though classification systems often result in that kind of designation for women entering the prison system. Chapter 10 noted the problems associated with assigning a prisoner to a greater supervision level than the person actually needs. When this **overclassification** occurs, the prisoner is being treated unjustly, and the prison is incurring greater costs than necessary. The problem of overclassification is considered especially serious when female offenders are classified. Because most classification systems are heavily influenced by the crime for which the offender was convicted, a serious crime is likely to result in a high-security designation. But when women are involved in serious crimes, their involvement is often the result of a relationship with a man—either as an accomplice or instigator—or with the man as the victim of violence following an abusive relationship (Burke & Adams, 1991). The woman who has committed a serious crime may not actually be as violent, dangerous, or as prone to escape as is a man who committed a similar crime. But the typical classification system will result in each being identified as a high-security risk because of the similarity of their crimes. The resulting problem is to find some way to shape the system so that this difference is acknowledged without creating an environment that could be accused of being discriminatory.

Burke and Adams suggest that the problem of overclassifying female offenders is best addressed by ignoring the risk assessment issue and dealing instead with ways to make classification reflect an institution's primary focus. Their argument notes the need for all correctional institutions to be concerned with two key areas. The first, security, includes the safety of inmates, staff, the facility itself, and the community. The second, rehabilitation, addresses the education, employability, parenting, decision-making, and other life skill needs of offenders. Each institution assigns different weights to these two concerns. Facilities with large, violent, predatory, disorderly, and dangerous offenders must focus most of their resources on security. When the population is less violent, dangerous, and predatory, the focus can be more on rehabilitation (Burke & Adams, 1991, p. 14). The reason a distinction between institutions that focus on security versus those focusing on rehabilitation can affect problems of classifying female offenders is portrayed in Figure 11.1. Simply put, a classification system designed for one purpose cannot serve the other one very well.

An especially attractive aspect of having different classification systems based on institutional focus rather than on the sex of the offender is its gender neutral-

A classification system designed to support the type of institution depicted on the left will not serve well the type of institution depicted on the right.

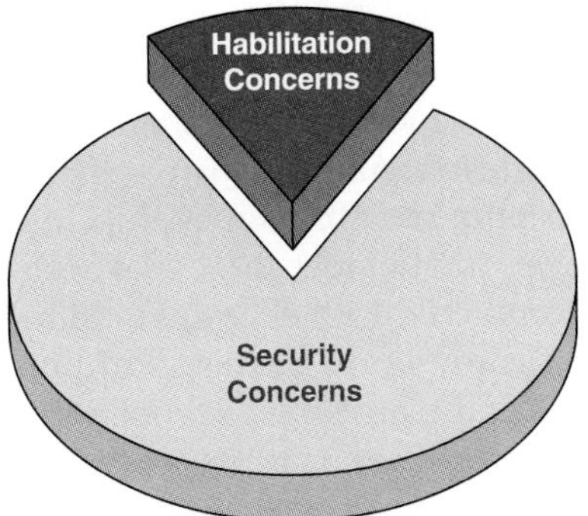

Relative emphasis on security and habilitation in institutions with high-risk populations. (Many men's institutions fall in this group.)

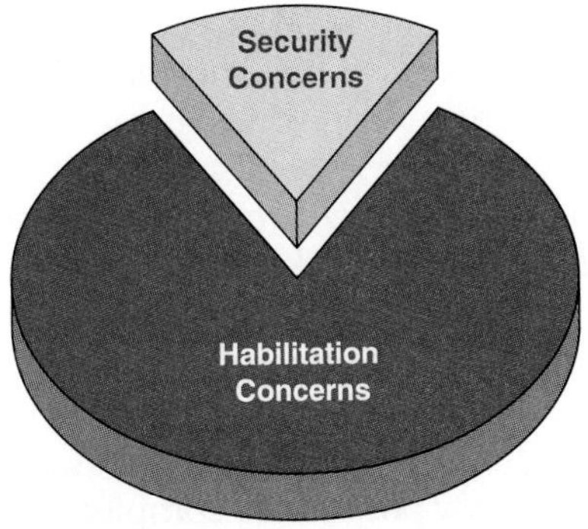

Relative emphasis on security and habilitation in institutions with low-risk populations. (Many women's institutions fall in this group.)

FIGURE 11.1

Why Current Classification Practice Does Not Work for Women Offenders

Source: Adapted from Burke, P., & Adams, L. (1991). *Classification of women offenders in state correctional facilities: A handbook for practitioners.* Washington, DC: National Institute of Corrections.

ity. Burke and Adams discovered that many prison officials do not want to see separate classification systems developed for men and women because that approach might raise parity issues and generate lawsuits by prisoners. But when classification is based less on an actual risk assessment of the offender and more on what a particular facility emphasizes, such issues are less likely to be raised. Because most women's institutions—and some for men—have lower incidences of violence and predatory behavior among their inmates, classification that emphasizes rehabilitation needs can be used. Other institutions that present greater safety risks, meaning most prisons for men and some for women, can use a classification system that places great weight on a prisoner's risk assessment.

The major obstruction to implementing this kind of strategy is that virtually all statewide classification systems are designed to support institutions that emphasize security over rehabilitation. As a result, improved effectiveness in classification of female offenders probably depends on the willingness of states to allow classification that is linked to institution-specific objectives. That, however, seems unlikely as states continue to centralize the process for receiving offenders into their department of corrections.

An alternative to decentralizing classification to the institutional level is to improve the risk assessment tools used for systemwide classification. For example, the risk/needs scale shown in Chapter 10 might be modified after researchers develop an instrument based on sufficient numbers and appropriate proportions of women and men offenders. The result might be that sex is added as a variable that adjusts the crime severity score or the overall risk score. But whatever method seems best for a particular jurisdiction, it is becoming increasingly apparent that classification systems need to consider better the different problems and issues presented by female offenders. Only in this way can classification be truly effective in helping to achieve management and treatment objectives in prisons for both men and women.

Programs for Women Prisoners

Prisons and prisoners cannot wait for all the complex issues related to classification to be resolved before implementing programs designed to educate, train, or rehabilitate. Instead, while busily working at improving the classification process, prison administrators are also designing, implementing, and revising programs for women prisoners. In the broadest sense of the word, programs encompass five categories (Pollock-Byrne, 1990): (1) institutional maintenance, (2) academic education, (3) vocational training, (4) rehabilitation, and (5) health care.

Programs linked to institutional maintenance provide the daily activity for most women prisoners. Working at either full- or part-time assignments, the inmates do clerical work, are involved in food preparation, and perform general cleaning and maintenance around the facility. The assignments are often menial and seem designed as much to keep the women busy as they are to meet some real need.

Even though women prisoners tend to have completed higher levels of education than have male prisoners, education programs for women are still important because nearly two-thirds of the women have not completed high school. Most women's prisons and most men's prisons provide adult basic education programs, and it is commonly possible to complete work that allows the inmate to earn a general equivalency diploma (GED) in place of a high school diploma.

Vocational training programs in women's prisons have been a point of controversy for many years. Under the differential response, sex stereotyping was prevalent as women prisoners received training in domestic work, cosmetology, clerical work, and food service. There is certainly nothing wrong with such occupations, but during the equalization response advocates sought vocational opportunities for women that would be beyond those of tradition. As a result of expanded offerings since the 1980s, many women's facilities have vocational training in areas such as auto repair, welding, carpentry, computers, and electrical work. It appears, however, that the most frequent offerings, and the most popular programs among the women prisoners, are still in the more traditional areas such as business education, clerical work, cosmetology, nurse's aid, and food service (Fortune & Balbach, 1992; Pollock-Byrne, 1990). Rehabilitation programs encompass a great variety of topics, ranging from art and pet therapy to psychological and psychiatric counseling. Distinctions between health care and rehabilitation programs are usually arbitrary. In fact, an argument is easily made that education and vocational programs are also rehabilitative. That means it is possible to place many kinds of programs under the heading of rehabilitation, even though they might also be related to areas such as health care or education. Some examples of effective rehabilitation programs in the prison setting are covered in Chapter 15. In this section we will look more closely at the fifth program category, health care, to see what specific needs exist in prisons for women.

Help Wanted

Job Title: Nurse Practitioner

Position Description: Provide clinical assessment and case management services to inmates. Specific duties include constructing and interpreting a medical history, performing a physical assessment, evaluating patient behavior, performing and interpreting selected lab tests, and developing and implementing treatment plans.

Qualifications: Applicants must be currently certified as nurse practitioners and should have experience working in a secure facility.

For examples of career opportunities in this field, check the various state department of corrections Web sites as found at *www.corrections.com/links/state.html.*

Health Care Programs. Women present some different health care issues to prison administrators than do male prisoners. Women in society are more likely than men to seek health care, and the same pattern is found among women in prison. Pollock-Byrne (1990) explains that the greater number of requests for medical care by women prisoners may result from their having more problems with their reproductive systems, because of problems related to the poor health care they received before coming to prison, because they may be pregnant when they arrive at prison, and because so many will have medical problems associated with drug abuse.

Ross and Lawrence (1998) identify the medical problems of women offenders as most often including asthma, diabetes, HIV/AIDS, tuberculosis, hypertension, herpes simplex II infection, chronic pelvic inflammatory disease, anxiety neurosis, and depression. The mental disorders, especially anxiety and depression, are high for both mothers and nonmothers, and one study found incarcerated women had perceived depression scores more than twice that for general population samples of women.

The problems are compounded because many women's prisons do not have a sufficiently large population to warrant a very extensive medical unit on prison

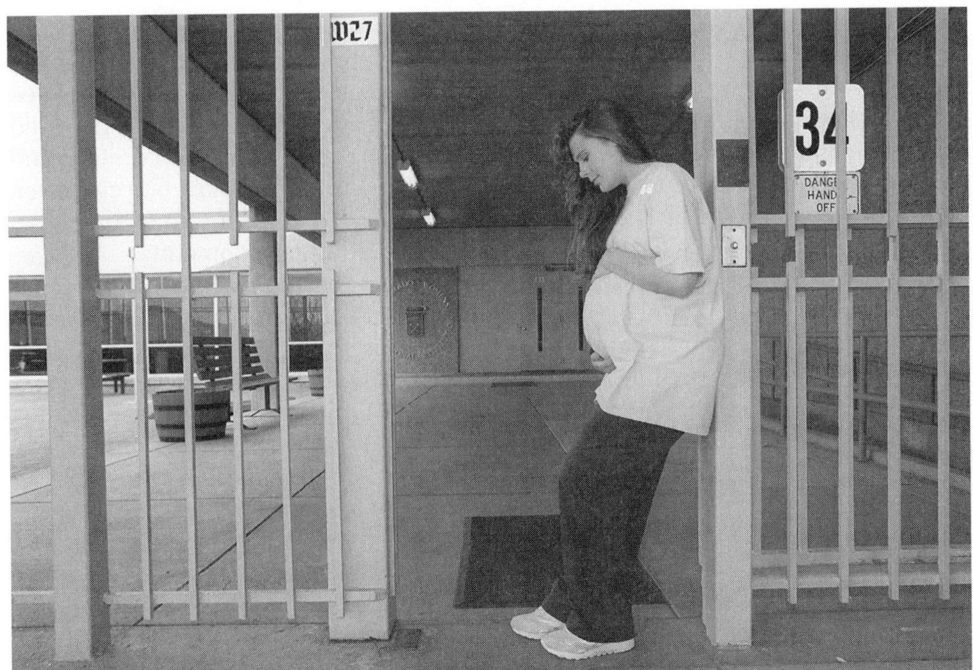

Women prisoners who are pregnant present especially difficult health concerns to prison officials. Prenatal care is often lacking in women's institutions, and pregnant women have difficulty meeting the nutritional requirements of pregnancy.

grounds. A physician is most likely on call, and examination times can be scheduled, but emergency cases and cases involving serious medical problems usually must be taken to hospitals outside the prison. Obviously, when time must be taken for arranging services and for transportation, the inmate–patient is placed in increased danger (Pollock-Byrne, 1990).

Inmates who are pregnant in prison—estimated at about 10 percent on any given day (Pollock, 1999)—present especially difficult health concerns. Prenatal care is often lacking in women's institutions, and pregnant women have difficulty meeting the nutritional requirements of pregnancy. Women who are pregnant and addicted to drugs present such additional concerns as the possibility of injuring the fetus while forcing withdrawal upon the mother. Even if the physical health concerns are met for both mother and baby, a quick separation from her newborn is in most cases extremely traumatic and can raise mental health concerns.

Because of the importance of the parent–child relationship to women prisoners, some programs specifically address this area as a health care issue. The issue has broad social implication as well because imprisoning female offenders is more likely to result in disruption of families than is the incarceration of male offenders (Bloom, 1993; Pollock-Byrne, 1990). Particularly important concerns are linked to the effect of imprisonment on mother–infant bonding, the maintenance of mother–child relationships, and the difficulty of finding a place for the children to live.

Amnesty International—USA reports that in at least forty states, babies are taken from their imprisoned mothers within a few days after birth (1999b). Exceptions include New York, where a woman may keep her baby for up to twelve months, Nebraska (up to eighteen months), and South Dakota (up to thirty days). California and Illinois have special residential programs in which eligible pregnant women are housed and may remain with the infant for up to twenty-four months (Illinois) or until the end of incarceration (California).

Because essential bonding cannot occur in the short time available in most states, future mother–child relationships are jeopardized, and the possibility for emotional, psychological, and physical problems for the children may increase. Pollock (1999) explains the process by describing the concept of **attachment or bonding** as referring to the relationship a child has with his or her primary caregiver. Attachment forms or should form between infancy and the second year as the child comes to identify the caregiver as the source of nourishment, attention, comfort, and contact. In the absence of a healthy, loving relationship with at least one caregiver, the baby does not form an attachment with anyone. That lack of attachment can have serious implications for future social and cognitive development.

As the infant gets older, the problems continue. Maintenance of the mother–child relationship is difficult at best when the mother is in prison, but because women's prisons are so often in remote areas of the state, the problem is worsened. Relatives may be more inclined than nonrelative caregivers to make an effort to ensure mother–child visits, but for both groups the distance from and lack of transportation to the prison poses many difficulties—not the least of which is cost.

Although most children of inmate mothers live with relatives, particularly maternal grandparents, some are placed in nonrelative foster homes and institutions. Results from a study by the National Council on Crime and Delinquency (Bloom, 1993) found that the relative caregivers reported having to make both financial and emotional adjustments upon assuming care for these children. The financial support for the children came primarily from Aid to Families with Dependent Children and from the caregiver's personal income. This burden was particularly demanding on grandparents who were required to use funds planned for their retirement.

In addition to having unfavorable consequences on specific individuals, mother-absent child rearing can have negative outcomes for society as a whole. Even with the best of intentions, relative and nonrelative caregivers may not be able to exert the energy and resources needed to provide necessary care and supervision. Several studies have shown that children of incarcerated parents suffer emotional stress related to that separation and often exhibit behavior patterns that include anxiety, depression, aggression, and learning disorders (Bloom, 1993). Caregivers report behavior problems and problems related to learning or school performance by the children. More specifically, the Center for Children of Incarcerated Parents reports that children of offenders are "by history and current behavior, the most likely among their peers to enter the criminal justice system" (quoted in Bloom, 1993, p. 63). Obviously, the issue of parent–child relations and separation is not something that affects only the specific persons involved—it has implications and reverberations throughout society.

To help counter some of the negative physical and mental health problems brought by mother–child separation, some women's prisons have implemented programs to address this particular need. In addition to the five states with residential programs mentioned earlier, some prisons provide parenting programs for inmate mothers. A survey of forty-three jurisdictions, including Puerto Rico and the District of Columbia, found thirty-six that offered parent–child programs (Clement, 1993). The programs emphasize communication skills, development of higher self-esteem, parenting skills, and knowledge of children's growth stages, and they assist the inmate in becoming aware of her own feelings. Some of the programs are modeled after STEP (Systematic Training for Effective Parenting) or PET (Parent Effectiveness Training), but many follow no specific model. Most of the programs allow parent–child visitation separate and apart from the regular institution visitation. Clement explains that these visits provide a "laboratory" where the parenting skills taught in class can be practiced.

Programs linked to prenatal care and to motherhood are important aspects of health care delivery for incarcerated women, but the physical and mental health problems of women offenders seldom came about in jail or prison. Instead, the women brought their health care needs with them. One reason for that is a lifestyle that places many women offenders in the illicit drug culture as alcoholics, addicts, or the domestic partners of alcoholics or addicts (Ross & Lawrence, 1998). Comprehensive health care for poor minority women (a typical characteristic of women offenders) is notoriously poor in most communities throughout the country—but it is essentially nonexistent in jails or prisons. If fact, when a comprehensive program is identified for incarcerated women, it is highlighted as both an excellent example and an unfortunate irony. Ross and Lawrence present Santa Rita County (California) as just such an example.

The Santa Rita County facility has a multidisciplinary medical team composed of a perinatal case manager, a nurse practitioner, a physician, and a nursing staff. All women admitted to the facility receive a comprehensive health appraisal and are screened for pregnancy. It is at this point that the irony of the excellent example comes into play. The tests, counseling, nutrition and exercise programs, social service information, and assistance that the women receive are possibly the highest-quality comprehensive health service provided for poor women in the community—and probably in many other communities. Some commentators wonder if the correctional institution might become the social net of last resort in which access to health and human service programs not available in the community are finally provided. Obviously the scarcity of comprehensive programs such as that in Santa Rita County makes such predictions unlikely in the foreseeable future. But it does remind us that the problems presented to jail and prison managers by women and men offenders are not isolated from problems found in the communities from which the offenders come. And that point brings us to the next section that looks at community-based sanctions for women.

FEMALE OFFENDERS AND COMMUNITY-BASED CORRECTIONS

Most women—like most men—under correctional sanction in the United States are not in prison. Instead, they are under some form of community supervision such as probation, parole, or residential community corrections. About 21 percent of the adults on probation are women, as are some 12 percent of the adults on parole. Data on successful completion of probation are not available by sex, but we do know (Perkins, 1994) that women are more likely to complete their parole successfully (58 percent) than are men (49 percent). In addition to better parole completion rates, the limited studies on predicting rates of reoffending that have female samples have found that women recidivate at a much lower rate than men (Immarigeon & Chesney-Lind, 1992). And, as we well know by now, female offenders are more likely to have committed property and public-order offenses than violent crimes. Combining this information we have a population of offenders who (1) commit crimes that, although unacceptable, pose little threat to public safety; (2) are less likely to reoffend; and (3) respond favorably to programs such as parole. It sounds like an ideal population for community-based corrections.

In her nationwide review of the participation of female offenders in the four most common intermediate sanctions (intensive probation supervision, split sentence—including boot camps, home confinement, and electronic monitoring), Robinson (1992) found that those sanctions are generally available to both men and women offenders. But IPS was the only sanction in which a majority of the programs (68 percent) accepted both men and women. For the other three programs, only 33 percent (home confinement), 41 percent (electronic monitoring), and 26 percent (split sentence/boot camp) specified they were available to both males and females. But possibly more important than how many of the most popular intermediate sanctions are available to female offenders is the question of how appropriate these programs are for those women. These are, after all, punishments that were developed for men—and as we learned earlier, there are reasons to distinguish penal responses for women from those applied to men. The following sections elaborate on that point.

Just as programs in prisons have seldom been developed with much thought about specific needs of the female offender, contemporary intermediate sanctions are basically programs designed for men and then made available to women. Robinson (1992) highlights several important points in this regard. For example, the use of intensive probation supervision (IPS) with women can present different issues than it does with men. Because much of the property crime by women is economic in nature (fraud, forgery, theft), the factors leading to those acts (survival, supporting children, sustaining a drug habit) must be considered when placing women on IPS. Expecting women to continue supporting their children (often as the children's only financial support) without doing something about the poverty prompting the crime in the first place is to invite program failure. For example, how many IPS programs were, or are, designed with child care provisions?

Even home confinement and boot camp programs may be problematic when applied to females. We know that female prisoners are at least three times more likely than male prisoners to have sustained physical or sexual abuse in their past (Beck et al., 1993), and we know that alcohol and other drug habits are often a response to physical or sexual abuse (Robinson, 1992). In instances when that abuse took place in the home, as it often does, should a female offender be confined to that home? Could the fear generated by home confinement actually aggravate alcohol or other drug habits and result in program failure?

In Chapter 8 the discussion of boot camp programs noted that female offenders who may have been in abusive relationships before being incarcerated may well be harmed more than helped under a shock incarceration philosophy. Because participation in boot camp programs is often voluntary, is it fair to offer the early release opportunity to a woman who so wants to return to her children that she actually agrees to put herself in a program that resembles the abusive home and partner she rightfully fears?

Obviously there are many questions to be raised regarding the appropriateness of applying today's popular intermediate sanctions to female offenders. Ideally, women-oriented programs should take into consideration the main problem areas for female offenders: property crimes and drug offenses. Some programs have accepted the challenge and are trying to respond to the specific needs of female offenders by paying particular attention to economic and drug-therapy issues. One of these, Project Met, provides some interesting information about the form that job-training programs might take.

Project Met

Efforts during the equalization response brought some nonstereotypical educational and vocational opportunities to female offenders. That was an important step for many reasons, but particularly important was the need to give women training in financially rewarding fields rather than the poorly compensated work of jobs such as cosmetology, nurses' aid, food services, and clerical employment. But soon after a broader range of vocational opportunities were made available, it became apparent that the product might not be what the customer wanted. Several studies found that female offenders had a positive attitude toward working, but they supported the traditional sex roles in which women were mothers and men were the primary breadwinners. It appeared that women offenders tended "to prefer traditional female occupations and white collar jobs above the skilled trade jobs" being offered in the vocational training classes (Fortune & Balbach, 1992, p. 115).

Because so much effort from the 1960s through the 1980s was directed at bringing women's prisons to a level of equality with men's prisons, not much attention was paid to community-based corrections for women. This was true in all areas, but particularly so for programs that might improve the female offender's employability in higher-paying jobs. But, given the preference among women prisoners for traditional occupations, there was some concern about how popular nontraditional vocational training might be with noninstitutional female offenders. That was the question that Project Met set out to answer.

In the early 1980s, the women's faculty at a large state university in a rural Midwest county designed a program they called Model Employment Training Program for Women Offenders in Predominantly Male-Oriented Occupations (Project Met). The goal was to provide better employment training and opportunities for women offenders in the community setting. The program began with fifteen female offenders on probation or parole, but only five remained in the program to its conclusion. Obviously the small sample size makes even tentative conclusions suspect, but in the absence of similarly structured programs with larger samples, Project Met provides important information.

The sixteen-week project focused on basic skills (writing, mathematics, reading, etc.) and vocational training. The specific vocational areas were photography, landscape care, automobile repair, and small engine repair. Interest and cooperation varied considerably during the different vocational training classes. Enthusiasm for automobile repair was not as high, for example, as it was for photography. In the landscape care class, the subject was so obviously uninteresting to the women that the instructor revised the course and incorporated floral design arrangement and greenhouse management into the curriculum. During one of these class sessions the women had an opportunity, which they greatly enjoyed, to teach mentally retarded adults how to pot plants. Small engine repair ranked at the bottom of the women's interest list at the program's completion.

Fortune and Balbach (1992) concluded that the women involved in Project Met did not respond particularly well to training in skills normally associated with male-dominated occupations. In fact, the most positive evaluations went to activities such as floral design, plant care, and teaching, which are linked to traditional female roles. That finding is consistent with studies of the attitudes expressed by women in prison vocational programs, but the authors offer some interesting opinions about what might be learned from these results. Possibly vocational training for female offenders also suffers from a male-oriented approach. The vocational training programs, both in prison and in the community, have been presented to women with a "here it is, come and get it" approach. That tactic may work with men, but the different socialization process for women might make that strategy less effective on them.

What is needed, say Fortune and Balbach, is an intermediate stage during which efforts are made to increase (1) the woman offender's acceptance of female participation in such occupations and (2) her awareness of the benefits to be gained from those occupations. Women offenders may view their economic role as secondary to that of the male in the family, but the facts are that the woman is often the primary supporter of the family and needs to have opportunities appropriate to that position. "Unless she is provided the chance to change her attitudes toward the female role, she may continue the frustration of raising a family on less adequate resources by maintaining employment in the lower paying traditional female occupations" (Fortune & Balbach, 1992, p. 127).

Programs for Drug-Abusing Female Offenders

Statistics and analysts agree that drug abuse is a significant characteristic of female offenders. Sometimes the link is because of the crime itself (drug possession or a crime committed to support drug habits); at other times the drug use is a lifestyle characteristic. In addition, there is growing evidence that some traditional—meaning male-oriented—drug treatment programs may not be effective for female offenders. But despite the growing realization that drug use and female offenders go hand in hand, and that females may need programs designed for their particular needs, only a few programs exist to provide such treatment. Also, there have been few descriptive or evaluative studies of the programs that do exist. This means we have minimal information about how programs are set up and operated, or about how effective they might be.

It is neither necessary nor appropriate to offer here an in-depth explanation of popular treatment modalities. And, although the result is certainly a simplification of a complex area, the following summary of therapeutic methods provides a basis for understanding drug treatment approaches.

Murphy, Johnson, and Edwards (1992) identify four main treatments for drug abusers:[4]

1. Detoxification, which is an entry point measure for heavy drug users that provides time and support to end the immediate use of drugs so that long-term treatment can begin.
2. Therapeutic communities (TCs) and residential treatment are long-term (six to twenty-four months) programs with a confrontational style that seeks to force addicts to face their addiction and to change their behavior so they can live without drugs.
3. The Minnesota model, which was modelled after a program started in the 1950s at a Minnesota state hospital, usually consists of three- to four-week-long residential programs based on the twelve steps of Alcoholics Anonymous. The program has a goal of breaking the avoidance and denial of addiction and providing supportive counseling and coping skills and follow-up assistance.
4. Outpatient treatment has participants involved in day programming activities while they live and work independently in the community.

The TC approach is interesting because it presents problems similar to those of shock incarceration strategies for female offenders. For example, Murphy and his colleagues determined that confrontational-style treatment programs for women with long histories of subservience and abuse are doomed to fail (Murphy et al., 1992). Wellisch, Prendergast, and Anglin (1994) reported that about 31 percent of the jail programs and some 26 percent of the prison programs they surveyed were identified as therapeutic communities. There is no indication of the particular format those TCs used, but presumably some follow the traditional confrontational style.

Murphy et al. identify other areas in which gender-specific issues suggest that it is unwise to assume that programs developed and implemented for men will also be appropriate for women. A female orientation to drug program design and implementation might lead to the recognition of several hurdles that male-oriented treatment programs fail to clear. Some of the blocks to treating women with programs designed for men include (Murphy et al., 1992, p. 14):

- Female offenders are still expected to be caregivers and that expectation can sometimes be used by the addicted woman to avoid or deny the importance of making treatment a priority for her life and the need to continue in aftercare upon release.
- Because many female offenders have been victims of sexual abuse, with high percentages of rape and incest victimization, they have trouble "opening up" in treatment sessions.

[4]Adapted from Murphy, J., Johnson, N., & Edwards, W. (1992). *Addicted mothers, imprisonment and alternatives.* Albany: New York State Coalition for Criminal Justice/Center for Justice Education.

- Many female offenders tend to suppress their anger and have a hard time acknowledging their angry feelings about loved ones. This can lead to severe depression centered around issues of abandonment and loss.
- Female offenders may become codependents in their dealings with loved ones who are addicted.

To the extent that these "blocks to treatment" are different from those for males, treatment programs that include females, but are oriented toward the male clients, will not be as effective for female offenders. It is more appropriate and probably more cost-effective to develop treatment programs specifically for women so that their special needs are recognized, and so that particular attention can be paid to conditions inhibiting successful program participation.

Two studies have attempted to identify community-based treatment programs that are presumably geared toward female offenders. In the first survey, Austin, Bloom, and Donahue (1992) gathered information on 100 community programs that provided treatment for drug-abusing women offenders. Their study was restricted to programs operating in the community as either a residential or nonresidential facility. The second survey (Wellisch et al., 1994) gathered data on custodial as well as community treatment programs serving drug-abusing women. Because these represent the most extensive and thorough studies of such programs to date, we will look more closely at some of their findings.

The majority of community programs surveyed in 1990 (Austin et al., 1992) were small operations with an average daily population of twenty-four women. They are typically operated by private nonprofit entities, although state and local governments also have some programs designed specifically for female offenders. Most of the clients in the programs were African Americans between twenty-five and thirty years old who were not married and had children under age six. The clients' service needs were identified as including alcohol/drug treatment, domestic violence/sexual abuse counseling, employment, education, housing, and legal aid. The treatment services most often provided by the programs were counseling (82 of 100 programs), living skills (76), alcohol/drug treatment (68), parenting (66), and job seeking (63). Domestic violence and sexual abuse were among the issues considered in the group and individual counseling sessions. The living skills area included training in areas such as money management, health and hygiene, meal planning and preparation, and job and housing search skills.

The Austin et al. survey attempted to identify the most promising intervention strategies for supervising female offenders in the community. They are careful to note that there are no studies proving that gender-specific programs are either more or less effective than are coed interventions, so they use the term *promising* to avoid giving the impression that evaluations have found these programs to have confirmed effectiveness. Instead, they rely on impressionistic data with face validity when they identify the most promising programs as those that address the specialized needs of female offenders by combining supervision and services in a highly structured and safe environment. The women who benefit the most seem to be those who are held responsible for their actions and who learn skills that provide them with economic and emotional independence (Austin et al., 1992, p. 21).

The programs Austin and his colleagues saw as most promising did not try to "cure" the client of an emotional disorder. They did not, in other words, rely on the medical or clinical model of correctional treatment. Instead, the programs encouraged the offenders to broaden their range of responses to various types of behavior and needs. In this way, the women's coping and decision-making skills were enhanced through an empowerment model of skill building. This approach is designed to deal specifically with women's issues such as substance abuse, parenting, gender bias, domestic violence, and sexual abuse. It seems especially effective when linked with practical skill development to prepare women for employment.

In late 1992 and early 1993, another survey of drug abuse treatment programs for female offenders was conducted (Wellisch et al., 1994). Because that survey included data on community-based programs that served both male and female clients, it provides an opportunity to contrast gender-specific and coed programs. A key finding from the survey was that services related to women's special needs were not uniformly available across programs. Instead, when programs were geared toward gender-specific problems of women, they were offered in women-only programs. Women offenders being treated in both-sex programs were more likely to be subjected to treatment strategies that ignored their special problems because the treatment was geared toward male offenders. Wellisch et al. (1994) highlight the differences in availability of services as follows:

- Nursery/child care facilities and live-in care for women and their children were found in less than 50 percent of the residential programs, but live-in care was much more available in residential than in outpatient programs. Nursery/child care facilities were more available in women-only outpatient (OP) and day treatment (DT) programs than in both-sex OP/DT programs.
- Family planning was offered in 78 percent of the women-only residential programs and in 70 percent of the outpatient programs. In the OP/DT programs, family planning was more available in women-only programs (68 percent) than in both-sex programs (47 percent).
- More women-only OP/DT programs than both-sex OP/DT programs made other family life supportive services available; these services included training in hygiene and nutrition and group meetings for parents and children.
- Training in personal empowerment was available in 76 percent of the residential and 70 percent of all outpatient programs; 90 percent of the women-only OP/DT programs offered such training. (pp. 3–4)

As research increasingly confirms that female offenders have different treatment needs and problems than do male offenders, there is a greater call for gender-appropriate programs. And, because women are more likely to receive that treatment when they are in programs for women only, it is necessary for correctional planners, policymakers, and legislators to recognize and respond to the need for gender-specific programs and facilities. The situation is improving because treatment programs for female offenders have increased since the 1970s, but most programs are still those that were designed for men by men (Wellisch et al., 1994).

Responding to Female Offenders in Other Countries

The world of prisons has been created by men for men and although it would be quite simple to introduce a sound penal policy for women's prisons, it has not been done in practice.

—Esther Giménez-Salinas i Colomer

There are few constants around the world when it comes to issues of criminal justice—but here is clearly one: Women offenders everywhere have been, are being, and seemingly will be treated poorly in relation to their male counterparts. In countries where prison conditions and treatment programs for men are stellar, they are merely average for women prisoners. In countries where prison conditions and treatment programs for men are barely tolerable, for women they are clearly inferior. Many examples indicate the extremes, but consider these for purposes of illustration:

- In Romanian lockups women are rarely supplied with sanitary napkins and most are obliged to tear up their clothing for use during their menstrual periods. Kenya provides an even more extreme example for some female prisoners are not allowed to wear underwear, nor permitted to use any sanitary protections during menstruation. (Human Rights Watch, 1993, p. 34)

- The education and work areas at the Paparua [New Zealand] Women's Prison are very modern and are equipped with clean, spacious classrooms fitted with computer stations. Recreation provisions include a modern gym as well as outdoor areas where prisoners are allowed to have gardens. (Eskridge & Newbold, 1993, p. 63)

The extremes presented by the conditions for women prisoners in Romania and Kenya, compared to those in New Zealand, highlight differences in prison systems as much as differences in the way women prisoners specifically are treated. In fact, the similarities in the way women prisoners are responded to around the world may be more striking than the differences. Much of the similarity is explained as resulting from the consistently small percentage of female inmates in all countries and the similarity of needs and problems among women prisoners. You will see quite a few parallels between the following comments and material covered in earlier pages of this chapter. That is, the countries may change, but the stories seem to stay the same.

Problems Attributed to the Small Numbers of Women Prisoners

Explanations for a country's lack of attention or concern for its women offenders are invariably based on their small percentage of the country's inmate population. Throughout the world, women constitute between 3 and 7 percent of the total prison population. United Nations data from the mid-1980s (Pease & Hukkila, 1990) found the highest European percentage of women prisoners to be in Bulgaria (10 percent) and Norway (9 percent), whereas the lowest was in the Netherlands and Cyprus (each with 2 percent). Data from countries in the 1990s suggest that the female population in prisons continues to be around 5 percent in most countries, with places such as Spain (8 percent) and Scotland (3 percent) indicating a high and low.

The most frequently stated problems attributed to the low numbers of women prisoners are linked to the condition and location of the facilities for those women. For example, Dünkel and van Zyl Smit (1991) note that most of the world accepts the principle that women and men in prison should be separated. There are some positive (such as Sweden's neighborhood prisons) and negative (some Mexican prisons) exceptions, but for the most part women in prison are housed at their own separate facility, or at a special unit in a men's prison. The Swedish exception has about 80 percent of the female prisoners housed in community prisons, where they take part in prison activities with male prisoners (Bishop, 1991). Both the men and women prisoners have an opportunity for contact with the local community, and in that manner a degree of equity might be achieved that cannot be realized in large central or regional prisons.

A review of facilities for women prisoners in most countries shows a more traditional approach than that offered by Sweden. Spain has four exclusively female prisons, but a large proportion of its female prisoners are kept in a women's section of male prisons. These sections are often quite small, with some holding as few as two prisoners. That places those women in a situation of semi-isolation that intensifies their punishment beyond what was intended by law. In India, about one-fourth of the women prisoners are kept in separate prisons, whereas the rest must stay in women's sections at prisons for men. Germany still houses some women in special annexes to male prisons, but in Mexico there have been times when women did not even have a separate annex at the men's institution.

In most Mexican prisons, male and female prisoners are housed separately, but there have been glaring exceptions. In October 1989 and January 1990, members

Prison officials respond to women prisoners in similar ways around the world. Much of the similarity seems to result from the consistently small percentage of female inmates in all countries and the similar needs and problems among women prisoners. Shown is an assembly of women prisoners in China.

of the Americas Watch (a committee of the Human Rights Watch) toured federal and state prisons in various locations throughout Mexico (Americas Watch, 1991). In La Mesa prison, male and female prisoners mingled openly during the day, and the prisoners reported that many women spent the night in the men's section of the prison. Prisoners in the women's sections of Reclusorio Oriente told members of Americas Watch that only a few months before their October 1989 visit, the directors of the men's and women's sections had operated a prostitution scheme.

> Female prisoners were sent by day to the men's section of the prison, ostensibly to visit the dentist. Male prisoners who were prospective customers made appointments to visit the dentist at the same time. They paid the directors to return the women they chose at night. (Americas Watch, 1991, p. 3)

The scandal was confirmed by a Mexican government official, who said that both directors had been criminally charged but had evaded prosecution by fleeing the area.

Many nations, and jurisdictions within those nations, have limited funds to support their infrastructure. Prisons in those countries often have low priority when budgeting decisions are made. Mexico is an example of a country experiencing these kinds of problems. In their report on Mexican prisons, the Americas Watch committee was critical of all prisons in the country but especially of the facilities for women. Women prisoners were in living quarters described as among the worst in the prison. Lack of funds meant that more women were idle because there were no programs or work opportunities to occupy their time. Even the handicrafts area was affected because fewer materials and supplies were made available to the women, with the result that more men than women did handicrafts.

In addition to facilities of poorer quality than those for men in the same country, the smaller number of women prisoners is often used to explain the fewer number of women's institutions. In the United Kingdom there are more than a hundred prisons for men but less than fifteen for women. Canada, until 1995, had only one prison for federal women prisoners in a country that has the largest land size in the Western Hemisphere. In Poland, where public transportation is not particularly good, women prisoners complain that they seldom or never receive visits. It is burdensome and costly for their relatives to travel to one of the four female institutions in this country that is almost the size of the combined area covered by Pennsylvania, Ohio, and Kentucky. Romania, which is about equal in land size to the combined area of Illinois and Indiana, has only one female prison. In Egypt (compare with Texas and New Mexico combined) over three-fourths of all female inmates are incarcerated in the urban area of Cairo—a city considerably off-center in the country—although more than half the country's population lives in rural areas.

A result of geographical isolation in these countries and in U.S. jurisdictions not only makes difficult such important things as visiting with family members but also hinders the woman prisoner's ability to develop release plans for return to the community.

Needs and Problems of Women Prisoners

Universally, there is concern about the relationship between an inmate mother and her child. There are always arguments about the desirability of caring for infants in a prison setting, but most countries have found that the benefits to mother and child outweigh the harm—at least until the child reaches age two or three. For older children the practice is difficult to support. A particularly bothersome example was found at La Mesa prison in Mexico, where elementary-school-age children, and even some teenagers, lived inside the prison walls with their mother. One mother told Americas Watch that her four- and six-year-olds had to stay with her because their father was dead and her relatives would not care for the children unless she provided money to support them. Despite that example, Americas Watch praised the Mexican policy of keeping mothers and infants together. The prison at Tepepan, Mexico, was offered as a particularly good example of attending to the mother–child relationship. At the time of the Americas Watch visit, the Tepepan prison was in a state of decay, but it featured a nursery in which more than sixty children played with their mothers and staff members in cheerful rooms resembling a small day care center (Americas Watch, 1991).

The example at Tepepan is more typical of Mexico and the rest of the world than is the example from La Mesa. In most of the world's countries, new mothers are allowed to keep their infants with them in prison. The period varies, but it is usually at least for one year so that the mother can nurse the newborn. Some prison systems allow small children, whether or not they were born in prison, to live with their inmate mother (Human Rights Watch, 1993). The laggard in this area is the United States, where most prison systems—including the federal system—do not allow newborns to stay with their mothers for any length of time. A notable exception is in New York, where state law provides that mothers be allowed to keep their infants until the baby is one year old.

A review of the policy in a few countries finds considerable agreement on the need to provide for the unique mother–child relationship. Spanish law allows inmates to keep their children with them until age seven, at which time the children are required to attend school. Mothers are housed with their children in individual or double cells. Small children stay in a nursery during the day whereas older youngsters attend a preschool outside the prison. In Belgium and Egypt, small babies normally stay in prison with their mothers until age two, at which time they are taken by the family or placed with a social service agency. Denmark allows children up to age two and one-half to remain with their mothers in prison, whereas older children may join their mothers in one of the halfway houses. German law provides that a child under school-going age may accompany his or her mother in prison if this is in the best interest of the child.

Although it seems laudable to have prison policies that allow and support the ability of inmate mothers to maintain a relationship with their infants, many women prisoners and their advocates argue that it would be better still to avoid even having the mothers in prison. The arguments covered earlier in this chapter for more community-based responses to female offenders are echoed in many other countries. Because female offenders around the world are primarily property offenders with substance abuse problems, it may be a better policy to find non-institutional sanctions that can meet their special needs. In doing so, a positive side effect would be ways to maintain the important mother–child relationship without concern for it having to be located in a prison environment.

A final area for consideration is the way cultural norms affect a society's response to women in general and female offenders more specifically. The Human Rights Watch (1993) explains that female prisoners worldwide tend to be poorer than male prisoners. One result is that there is often a discrepancy in personal possessions such as radios or TV sets in the women's cells. Some explanations for the difference are linked to cultural views of women prisoners. In Mexico, for example, families seem willing to make a larger sacrifice for a male family member than for a female. "In contrast to male prisoners, many of whose wives and families visit regularly and bring them food, blankets, clothing and other necessities, incarcerated women get much less of that type of support" (Human Rights Watch, 1993, p. 37).

In some countries there is a stigma attached to female imprisonment (although one is not similarly attached to male imprisonment) that can result in a female prisoner becoming an outcast in her own family. At times the stigma might be so twisted as to result in the female victim ending up in prison. In India some women can be kept in prison under protective custody. Most of the women held in protective custody are rape victims. Because of the stigma that Indian society attaches to rape victims, authorities apparently fear that she will not show up in court to testify against her rapist. She is imprisoned (sometimes for as long as two, three, or four years) to make sure she is available to testify at trial. But civil liberties and women's rights advocates suggest that holding victims in "protective custody" is itself a reflection of the contempt that is prevalent in India (and elsewhere as well) for rape victims (Asia Watch, 1991).

The situation in China may have improved for women prisoners in recent years, but there still seem to be some questionable expectations. For example, there are relatively new units designed for women prisoners with dormitories that are comparatively spacious. There is storage space for personal belongings, the prisoners sleep on bunk beds with matching quilts, and provisions are made for hot water and plentiful food. But in return for such niceties, certain women are required to perform in song and dance shows for visitors (Human Rights Watch, 1993). Other countries have a much longer road to travel. In Peru, the Human Rights Watch reports that sexual harassment, abuse, and rape by the security police are common in women's prisons. There are examples of women having to trade sexual favors for privileges such as extra food or access to a telephone (Human Rights Watch, 1993).

So that we do not leave this discussion with a holier-than-thou attitude, it is important to remember aspects of U.S. history and the treatment of women prisoners. As noted earlier in this chapter, the initial supervision of women prisoners in the United States was so lax and neglectful as to allow opportunities for their assault by male prisoners and male guards. We should also remember that versions of discipline were imposed on women prisoners that were at least as severe—and sometimes more so—as those for male prisoners. Rafter (1993), for example, notes the application of the "shower bath" in the mid-1800s at New York's Mount Pleasant Female Prison as one of the prison's cruelest punishments. The prisoner was bombarded by a powerful stream of water until she was close to drowning.

Just as female correctional officers can work in men's prisons, male correctional officers are employed in women's prisons. But despite the recognition of equal employment opportunities, some people believe that the presence of male corrections officers in women's prisons creates a situation in which sexual misconduct is more pervasive than if women were guarded by female officers.

In 1880 the Ohio penitentiary is reported to have been using the "humming bird" punishment, for which the naked offender was made "to sit, blindfolded, in a tub of water while steam pipes were made to shriek and electric current was applied to the body" (Rafter, 1993, p. 8).

There have clearly been improvements in the way women prisoners are treated in U.S. jurisdictions and in many other countries of the world. Just as clearly, there is room for more improvement (see "Abuse of Female Prisoners"). Even if the physical abuse and intolerable living conditions for women and for men prisoners have improved in most places, enough inequities remain to keep advocates for women prisoners very busy. The following recommendations for revising the way a society responds to its female offenders seem applicable to just about any country:

- The geographic dislocation of many women from their families and from community resources must be reduced.
- Programs must be specifically designed to (1) address such needs as maintaining mother–child relationships, (2) treat substance abuse problems, and (3) take into consideration the results of victimization by sexual and physical abuse.
- Educational and vocational opportunities must be provided that will increase the female offender's acceptance of nontraditional work areas and increase her chances to find employment that allows independent living.
- Serious consideration should be given to achieve the preceding recommendations by significantly decreasing the use of imprisonment for female offenders and by significantly increasing the use of community-based corrections.

As corrections officials and policymakers become more familiar with a female-oriented perspective toward facility management and correctional programming—in the United States and around the world—we will all come to have a greater

Spotlight ON CONTEMPORARY ISSUES

Abuse of Female Prisoners

An earlier Spotlight on Contemporary Issues, "Prior Abuse and Female Prisoners," highlighted the impact that abuse suffered both as a child and as an adult might have on women offenders and prisoners. If you were thinking that women would at least be safe from abuse upon arrival at a prison, you are mistaken. Few people would consider prison to be a safe place—but most would assume that the danger comes from other prisoners. Unfortunately, instances of abuse of inmates by staff continues to be documented in prisons throughout the country.

In 1999 the United Nations released a report prepared by the Special Rapporteur on violence against women for its Commission on Human Rights (United Nations, 1999). The report's focus was on women in U.S. prisons. The report's critical nature occasioned considerable media attention. The Special Rapporteur, Ms. Radhika Coomaraswamy, explained that she gathered information from state and federal prisons in six states and Washington, DC. In introducing her findings, she noted that wherever she went officials asked her why she decided to visit the United States. She explained that information from many sources convinced her that there were serious issues of custodial sexual misconduct in U.S. prisons. She felt compelled to investigate those reports. She found it interesting that the officials typically responded that she should concentrate instead on countries where human rights protection is less ensured. Ms. Coomaraswamy suggested that human rights protections should not be considered a certainty in any country and added that the political freedom found in the United States does not mean its criminal justice system is free from human rights violations (United Nations, 1999).

The report said that rape of female inmates by male staff was a fairly rare phenomenon in the prisons visited but that consensual sex and sex in return for favors (e.g., work opportunities, telephone privileges, or even drugs) was a more frequent occurrence. She was especially troubled that many states have no laws prohibiting sexual contact between staff and inmates. Even in states where such conduct is prohibited, it is often only a misdemeanor violation.

Much of the blame for a sexually abusive environment, the report claims, is the result of having men supervising women inmates. Ms. Coomaraswamy notes that U.N. Standard Minimum Rules for the Treatment of Prisoners requires that women prisoners be supervised only by women officers. However, the U.S. Supreme Court has deemed such a standard as unconstitutional under the equal employment statute of the Civil Rights Act of 1964. The presence of male corrections officers in women's prisons creates a situation in which sexual misconduct is more pervasive than if women were guarded by female officers. Corrections officers told Ms. Coomaraswamy that men were necessary in women's prisons to provide positive male role models. They argued that the key to success was in the professionalism of the officers and not their gender. The Special Rapporteur responded that the prevalence in U.S. society of violence against women generally, and sexual violence specifically, raises particular worries about the use of male guards in female facilities (United Nations, 1999).

Go to Amnesty International—USA's Web page on sexual abuse of women prisoners at *www.amnesty-usa.org/rightsforall/women/report/women-11.html.* Read some of the reports of abuse in several of the states. Do you think hiring practices that allow male staff to supervise female inmates are a major contributor to sexual abuse of women in prison? In October 1999 complaints of widespread sexual abuse by correctional officers at Virginia's largest women's prison were investigated. Read the story at *www.apbnews.com/newscenter/breakingnews/1999/10/12/prison1012_01.html.* Are the complaints lodged by the women prisoners in Virginia similar to or different from those reported to the U.N. Special Rapporteur?

understanding of appropriate and effective ways to respond toward women offenders. And, because women and men are different, the responses will not be identical—but they must be equitable.

SUMMARY

The involvement of women in both the commission of crime and in the number of persons subjected to criminal punishment is considerably less than that of men. But the proportion of women at all stages of the criminal justice process is increasing. That increased involvement is important to recognize because it presents justice officials with issues different from ones presented by male offenders.

SOCIAL RESPONSES TO FEMALE OFFENDERS

Societal responses to women offenders have passed through several stages.

- The neglect response, the differential response, and the equalization response brought women offenders from the earliest versions of imprisonment into the late twentieth century.
- More recently calls are being made for a new model that reflects a female-oriented penology that tries to synthesize advantages from the differential and equalization responses and provide an acceptance and appreciation of differences between women and men along with a call for equity in response. This chapter presents information about sanctioning women offenders in a manner consistent with the new model.

EXPLAINING CHANGES IN SOCIETY'S REACTION TO FEMALE OFFENDERS

Media and entertainment sources might lead one to think that women are committing more violent crimes today, and that those more serious offenses require more arrests and the harsher penalty of imprisonment. But the data do not support that position.

- The rise in arrests and imprisonment numbers for women is attributed to greater numbers of drug offenders (38 percent of the growth). The increase in women being sentenced to prison cannot be explained as a result of women committing more violent offenses.
- Female criminality has been primarily property and public-order offenses over the years.
- A significant part of the increase in female arrests is the result of more formal policing and of general improvements in the social control bureaucracy.

THE IMPACT OF SENTENCING POLICIES

- One explanation for the increasing imprisonment rate of women is the current sentencing policies that increase the likelihood of imprisonment for drug-related offenses. Because women are more likely to have drugs linked to their criminal behavior, the war on drugs may have become a war on women.
- A male-oriented approach to crime currently sets imprisonment as the best response to offenders. A female-oriented approach would suggest that it might be better and more appropriate to sanction women offenders with prison alternatives.

FEMALE OFFENDERS IN PRISON

Programs in prisons for women encompass the areas of institutional maintenance, academic education, vocational training, health care, and rehabilitation. Health care and rehabilitation programs are especially related to the different needs, problems, and advantages presented by female prisoners. Programs in two New York institutions show how a female-oriented approach might influence the design of rehabilitation efforts in prison.

FEMALE OFFENDERS AND COMMUNITY-BASED CORRECTIONS

Community-based programs designed specifically for female offenders are as rare as are prison-based programs with that focus.

RESPONDING TO FEMALE OFFENDERS IN OTHER COUNTRIES

- Upon considering responses to female offenders in other countries, the point was made that women prisoners are consistently a small percentage of a country's inmates.
- In addition to similarity in number, women offenders in most countries share the characteristics of being primarily property offenders, having substance abuse problems, and showing a history of victimization by physical and sexual abuse.
- These issues of small numbers, similar characteristics, and special needs and problems are used to discuss some ways other countries have chosen to respond to their female offenders.

Key Terms and Concepts

attachment or bonding (p. 418)
cottage plan (p. 402)
differential response (p. 399)
equalization response (p. 399)
female-oriented response (p. 399)
institutional classification (p. 414)
neglect response (p. 399)
overclassification (p. 414)
systemwide classification (p. 414)

Discussion Questions

1. Of the different characteristics attributed to women offenders (such as nonviolent offenses, history of abuse, drug-linked crimes, and role as mother), which do you believe are most important to consider when deciding how to sanction a female offender? How do you propose the characteristics you highlight should be managed?
2. The chapter raises several questions that prison administrators must handle regarding pregnant inmates. For example, what type of prenatal care should be provided? Should new mothers be allowed to keep their babies? Discuss these and other types of special concerns presented by pregnant inmates, and explain how you believe these issues should be resolved.
3. Explain your views regarding the need for classification systems designed specifically for women.
4. Although the small sample makes it unwise to generalize, results from Project Met suggest a different approach might be necessary to get women offenders actively involved in vocational training. Discuss why that might be true, and suggest some ways you could increase female offenders' acceptance of and involvement in vocational training in predominantly male-oriented occupations.

chapter 12

Responding to the Juvenile Offender

Your assignment is to divide the population of your city into two groups, those most likely to commit an illegal act and those least likely to do so. However, you may use only one variable to make your distinction. What one variable will allow you to be most accurate in your categorizing? Should you use sex—all the men and none of the women will commit an illegal act? Would economic status be better—everybody at the lowest income level versus those at the highest? How about race and ethnicity—people of color will engage in illegal behavior but whites will not? Obviously, whichever criterion you use, you will be wrong in many and maybe most cases. But if you choose age as your sole variable, you will be correct more often than if you choose any other single factor. Teenagers and young adults will commit illegal acts and older people will not.

The link between age and criminal behavior is so fundamental that the relationship is often designated as the **age–crime curve.** That curve refers to the tendency for crime to be committed during a person's younger years and to decline as the person gets older. For example, the peak age of offending (as determined by arrest data) is about age eighteen for violent crime and age sixteen for property crime. The rate falls to one-half the peak for violent offenses by age thirty and by age twenty-one for property offenses (Snyder, 1998). The age factor is so closely tied to offending behavior that some cynics have suggested (hopefully to make a point rather than to propose a real solution) the most effective crime policy would be to incarcerate everyone in the country on their thirteenth birthday and not release them until they reach age thirty. Statistically, such action should dramatically reduce the nation's crime rates. Presumably, there are less dramatic proposals to consider.

Juveniles between ages ten and eighteen constitute about 12 percent of the U.S. population (U.S. Census Bureau). That group is overrepresented among the persons arrested for property offenses (burglary, larceny–theft, motor vehicle theft, and arson), accounting for about one-third of all arrests, and in arrests for violent crimes (murder, forcible rape, robbery, and aggravated assault), where they make up about 16 percent (*Uniform Crime Reports,* 1998).

Many U.S. citizens want juvenile offenders who commit violent crimes to be treated the same as adults who commit similar offenses (Maguire & Pastore, 1995). State legislators have responded by increasing the severity of penalties for youthful offenders and by making it easier to process the most violent juveniles through the criminal courts rather than in the juvenile justice system. It appears that the twenty-first century is starting very differently than did the twentieth century in terms of views about the way society should respond to juvenile offenders.

When America's version of a separate system of justice for juvenile offenders began in 1899, the guiding philosophy of the new juvenile courts was clearly a protective and rehabilitative one. Importantly, that philosophy had the support of the public as well as the justice professionals. One hundred years later, much of the public has become disenchanted with the juvenile justice system, and several of the justice professionals seem to have a similar frustration. In this chapter we will consider how the juvenile justice system started, how it has changed, and how society uses sanctions when youths misbehave.

Our primary focus in this chapter is on the corrections component of juvenile justice. As you will see, the juvenile justice system is separate from the adult system. So, although some of the procedures by which juveniles are brought to the attention of justice officials are similar to the procedures for adults, the philosophy on which the juvenile system is based is quite different. Those differences, as we see later, make it difficult to consider juveniles in the same discussion as adults. Specific courses and textbooks on juvenile delinquency cover all aspects of that system—including juvenile corrections. Most courses and textbooks on the topic of corrections are, more exactly, on adult corrections. However, it is important and relevant that juveniles be given some attention even in these courses and books because juveniles unfortunately are responsible for much of the nation's crime. And when juvenile corrections is successful, adult corrections may not be needed. But to appreciate some of the practices and controversies associated with juvenile corrections, we must understand how the broader juvenile justice system has evolved and some of the characteristics of the youths currently in that system.

THE JUVENILE JUSTICE SYSTEM

For the most part, a separate system of juvenile justice did not appear in the United States until 1899, when the first juvenile court was established in Cook County (Chicago), Illinois. Other communities had made informal movements to respond differently to juvenile offenders before Cook County's formal action, but the Cook County juvenile court clearly became the model around the country. To understand better the reasons it took so long to handle juveniles differently from the way we responded to adult criminals, we must consider some nineteenth-century activities before describing twentieth-century practices.

Nineteenth-Century Responses to Juveniles

The seventeenth century was a turning point in the conception of childhood (see "Discovering Childhood"), but the nineteenth century was a milestone in society's response to misbehaving young persons. After the discovery of childhood, society was forced to suggest not only how the ideal child might be produced but also how the undesirable one might be prevented or controlled. Although educators, psychologists, and the clergy helped with the "producing" question, the "prevention/controlling" concern was left to a social control system unaccustomed to making distinctions based on age. The stage was set for yet another social condition to become identified as a social problem.

The first people to take a direct interest in social control of young people as a specific age group were the nineteenth-century philanthropists. Mennel (1973) describes those philanthropists as descendants of established families and prosperous members of the merchant or professional classes. They were also conservative reformers who defined themselves as God's Elect and felt duty bound to develop charitable organizations in God's name.

Several groups and people played a role at this initial stage, but the Society for the Prevention of Pauperism (SPP), formed in 1817 in New York City, had overriding influence. Two leaders of the SPP, John Griscom and Thomas Eddy, are especially noted for their interest in the moral health of the community. The poor and deviant became objects of their concern and their moral stewardship. Their intent was to regulate community morality by example and through benevolent activities (Krisberg & Austin, 1978). Such concerns required attention to a variety of social evils, but Griscom, Eddy, and the SPP were most successful in altering societal response to juvenile delinquents. Members of the SPP found the prevailing practice of placing children in adult jails and workhouses to be very undesirable. The abominable conditions of those places intensified the disgrace. In 1822 the SPP issued its Report on the Penitentiary System in the United States, which called for the building of new prisons for juvenile offenders. The youths confined in the new prisons were "to be placed under a course of discipline, severe and unchanging, but alike calculated to subdue and conciliate. A system should be adopted that would provide a mental and moral regimen" (Mennel, 1973, p. 11).

The SPP members apparently took an interest in the plight of young persons out of humanitarian concerns, but it is also likely that some of their actions were undertaken for their own protection and economic advantage (Reichel, 1979). This becomes understandable as we remember the changing conception of poverty and the poor in the late eighteenth and early nineteenth centuries in the United States. Although the colonists had accepted poverty as a normal aspect of life, Jacksonian Americans came to view dependency as abnormal and tried to control it (Rothman, 1971). The new view of poverty brought with it a fear of social unrest and chaos (Mennel, 1973), and the growing pauper class, accompanied by increases

HISTORICAL PERSPECTIVES

Discovering Childhood

The terms *juvenile* and *delinquency* are fairly new, but the people and the behavior are not. Ariès (1962) reminds us that during the Middle Ages and well into the seventeenth and eighteenth centuries, many Western civilizations did not have words to distinguish babies from bigger children. The concept of "adolescence" was not formed until 1890. Even the term *childhood* is recent; apparently, it was first used during the thirteenth century. Before that time, the child was seen as no more than a miniature adult.

Ariès (1962) sees the seventeenth century as a turning point in the conception of childhood. It was then that we begin to find a vocabulary relating to infancy; and more important, the idea of childhood innocence began to develop. Before this time, all types of language and behavior were permitted in front of children because there was no idea of an "innocence" to be violated. By the end of the sixteenth and the start of the seventeenth centuries, Protestants and Catholics in France and England began regulating access of children to certain books. Although Christianity had implied childhood innocence centuries earlier (e.g., Christ advising people to "become as little children"), the idea did not have much impact until the 1500s and 1600s.

After the discovery of childhood, and the attaching of special meaning to it, society was forced to show not only how the ideal child might be produced, but how the undesirable one might be prevented from developing—or controlled if one did develop. But describing just what was undesirable was still in the developmental stage. Just as society has always had children, whether identified as such or not, those children have always been rather consistent in their behavior. Consider, for example, three current areas of concern linked to juveniles: use of weapons, sexual misbehavior, and alcohol/drug abuse. In fact, juveniles have been engaging in these types of activities for centuries. As late as the seventeenth and eighteenth centuries, European children continued the medieval practice of wearing and using arms. The schools of seventeenth-century France had so many duels, mutinies, brawls, and beating of teachers that the result was regulations requiring that students store their weapons outside the school (Ariès, 1962). Sexual practices, portrayals, and references, which many may consider inappropriate if not obscene today, were often the norm in medieval times. That indulgence regarding sex carried over into later centuries. By 1760 Englishman Samuel Foote commented that public schoolboys practiced more vices by age sixteen than anyone else would have by age sixty (Ariès, 1962, p. 324). Finally, the young people of the Middle Ages were heavy drinkers of alcohol. After regulations forbade it in school, they simply went to nearby taverns where it was not prohibited. The absence of abundant man-made chemicals meant alcohol was the more favored drug of the time. But it is worth noting that opium use, for example, began 4,000 years ago and became an addiction, legal though it was, for youth and adult alike.

Read about the evolution of the juvenile justice system at ***www.rh.cc.ca.us/departments/academic/pubserv/leo/aj/aj207u1.htm.*** What principle from the Code of Hammurabi is relevant to juvenile justice? In what way is it relevant?

in crime, disturbed community elites (Hawes, 1971). Adult paupers and criminals were assumed to have been delinquent in their youth. Therefore, controlling the youngsters was seen as a response that had humanitarian aspects with the bonus of protecting class position by reforming potential pauper/criminals. The initial stages of that control are exemplified by development of the houses of refuge.

On January 1, 1825, the New York House of Refuge opened under the management of the Society for the Reformation of Juvenile Delinquents, as the SPP was then called. Some European institutions such as the Amsterdam House of Correction, the Hospice of St. Michael in Rome, and London's Bridewell House had housed young persons, but they were the exception. As such, this New York facility became the first institution specifically for juvenile delinquents. Boston followed New York's lead in 1826, Philadelphia in 1828, and for the next twenty-five years these three facilities defined institutional treatment of juveniles. That treatment was punitive in nature, including use of the ball and chain, handcuffs, leg irons, and whipping. The juveniles worked every day of the year (except Sundays) or were punished for refusing to work.

The exploitative nature of these early institutions becomes apparent when we consider the type of work provided for the juveniles. Joseph Curtis, first superintendent of the New York House of Refuge, set up a factory for making straw hats and baskets so the children would develop good work habits (Pickett, 1969). Important as those factories were, the primary type of labor was the lease system by which the child was "rented" to citizens who paid the institution for the child's labor. The system sometimes took the form of indenture to sea captains or farmers. Pickett notes an early request to Curtis from a judge who wanted a "black girl" to serve in his family.

By 1850 new "child-saving" organizations began condemning the houses of refuge. Like their counterparts twenty-five years earlier, these organizations had humanitarian concerns. The houses of refuge certainly stemmed the excessive use of capital and corporal punishment for juveniles, but there was growing dissatisfaction with the procedures and policies of the houses of refuge. These new reformers believed the family, not the institution, was the best reform school. The arguments were best exemplified by the work of Charles Loring Brace, whom Hawes (1971) believes was the most important U.S. citizen working with juvenile delinquents in the nineteenth century.

Brace was general secretary of the Children's Aid Society (CAS), which was a philanthropic organization attempting to help the juvenile vagrants of New York City. Formed in 1853, the CAS quickly helped to open industrial schools and lodging houses for the boys and girls of New York. Its most important project, however, was the "placing-out" system, in which city children were apprenticed out to western farm families. Brace's system differed from the indenture practice of the houses of refuge because under that system the farmers took children as cheap labor (according to Brace), whereas under the new system they would be taken as members of the family. Children from the northeastern cities were placed on trains headed for the Midwest. As the trains made their stop at farming communities, the children were paraded and presented to townspeople. Later in the day, the families went to a store or other public place to pick out children they wanted (Mennel, 1973). The first party from the CAS left in 1854, and public support enabled the system to remain strong until its decline in the 1880s.

Brace believed his system was nonexploitative, but the realities of "transportation" and "slave markets" seem only thinly veiled. However, the placing-out procedure continued to advance the identification of juveniles as deserving special attention by social control authorities and agencies. By the end of the century, a rehabilitative ideal gained acceptance and, playing on concerns about children becoming adult criminals, social reformers argued that juvenile crime was reversible. Although several cities began specialized approaches to young offenders, Chicago (Cook County) serves as the example of procedural changes. With the help of Anthony Platt (1969), we will see how the creation of a juvenile court in Cook County, Illinois, came about.

Establishing a Juvenile Court

By the late 1890s the Illinois child-savers movement was gaining membership and legitimation. The support of political and professional people was actively sought in attempts to bring about child-welfare reforms. In 1898 the efforts began paying off, and child-saving issues became a prominent issue with compassionate overtones. As Frederick Wines said before the Illinois Conference of Charities:

> We make criminals out of children who are not criminals by treating them as if they were criminals. . . . What we should have, in our system of criminal jurisprudence, is an entirely separate system of courts for children, in large cities, who commit offenses which would be criminal by adults. We ought to have a "children's court" in Chicago,

> and we ought to have a "children's judge," who should attend to no other business. (quoted in Platt, 1969, p. 132)

In February 1899, a juvenile court bill was introduced in the Illinois House and Senate. On April 14, 1899, the legislature passed "an act to regulate the treatment and control of dependent, neglected, and delinquent children" (quoted in Platt, 1969, p. 134).

The presence of the terms *dependent* and *neglected* in the Illinois act points to a topic that remains controversial today. That is, although delinquent children were reasonably handled by the new juvenile court, why should the court be interested in dependent and neglected children? Isn't that a job for the child's parents? The answer, of course, is that dependency and neglect are parental responsibilities, but under the concept of ***parens patriae*** (father or mother of the country), the court has ultimate obligation for junior citizens.

This philosophy came from the English system wherein children were taken to one of two courts depending on the problem being addressed. When the concern was one of "care," the Chancery Court heard the case. That court was concerned with protecting property rights of juveniles and the child's general welfare. The state's right to such involvement followed the philosophy that the state, or the court as its agent, is the ultimate parent of all minors and other "incompetents." The monarch as parens patriae provided guardianship and protection for the subjects. It was with this philosophy in mind that the Illinois legislators gave the juvenile court concern for, and authority over, a child's welfare. In this manner, children deemed in need of supervision, dependent, neglected, or abused are taken to the juvenile court, which has incorporated the old English Chancery Court care functions.

The additional need to control, rather than care for, some children was also obvious to the English. But other than eliminating persons under age seven from criminal prosecution, the English system provided no specific procedures for handling children. As far as the criminal courts were concerned, a ten-year-old was simply a small, misbehaving adult.

Because of the parens patriae doctrine, the initial philosophy of the juvenile court was to assume that all the court personnel were interested in the welfare of the child and constantly had the child's best interests in mind. The result was a juvenile court system with jurisdiction over three perceived problem areas: (1) situations wherein the child/juvenile has been neglected, abused, exploited, or in some other way mistreated; (2) offenses committed by juveniles that would be a crime if committed by an adult; and (3) certain offenses committed by juveniles that are deemed inappropriate or undesirable for persons under a certain age.

It is those last two items that occupy most of the juvenile court's time because they deal with actual misbehavior by the juvenile. The first type of misbehavior (behavior that would be criminal if committed by an adult) involves both petty and serious offenses, ranging from shoplifting to murder. Juvenile activity in this area must be taken seriously because arrest statistics show that persons under age eighteen are more likely than any other segment of the population to be arrested for committing a crime. Those offenses are more likely to be property crimes than violent crimes, but involvement of young people in both types is obviously a serious concern and challenge for the justice system.

The other type of misbehavior refers to activity considered wrong only because society doesn't consider the juvenile old enough for that kind of behavior. That is, the person's status of being a juvenile makes him or her unable to legally participate in certain activities. Those activities, called **status offenses,** include violating administrative rules (such as staying out past a city's curfew, skipping school, and purchasing and using alcohol and tobacco), or being "out of control" (e.g., running away from home, not obeying parents, sexual promiscuity). Before 1974 many states responded to status offenders in the same way they responded to delinquents. It was assumed that a runaway or truant would quite likely become involved in delinquent activities if some formal action was not taken. As a result, juveniles were placed on probation or put in a correctional institution for nothing more than running away from home or being unmanageable. Today it is more typical for status offenders to be handled separately under some nondelinquent category such as PINS (Persons In Need of Supervision), JINS (Juveniles In Need of Supervision), CHINS (Children In Need of Supervision), and MRAI (Minors Requiring Authoritative Intervention). These supervision categories allow the state to become involved in the child's life but do not confer the stigma of delinquency proceedings nor the effects of such formal action as incarceration.

Due Process and Juveniles

Because of the absence of adversarial proceedings, there did not appear to be a need to provide constitutional protection of due process for the juvenile. After all, because the prosecution, defense, and judge were all looking out for the rights and interests of the juvenile, why clog things up with procedural trappings? As a result, the juvenile court developed into a rather informal proceeding with a goal of treating rather than punishing the misbehaving juvenile.

The traditional absence of procedural restrictions on the juvenile court is the result of three factors. First, the juvenile court is not a criminal court. Instead, it is a statutory court (i.e., it was created in state statutes by the legislatures) with powers provided for and limited by state law. Second, because it is not a criminal court, no determination of guilt is involved. Instead, a misbehaving juvenile is **adjudicated** (pronounced) **delinquent.** Finally, the goal of the juvenile court is one of treatment rather than punishment and, therefore, procedural safeguards relevant and necessary for criminal court are neither relevant nor necessary for juvenile court.

Concern about the lack of procedural protection for juveniles did not attract much public or judicial attention until the 1960s. The U.S. Supreme Court had taken the position that the rehabilitative rather than penal philosophy of the juvenile court made it an exception to the procedural guidelines of the Constitution. As Justice Blackmun said: "If the formalities of the criminal adjudicative process be superimposed upon the juvenile court system, [then] there is little need for its separate existence" (*McKeiver v. Pennsylvania*, 1971). But by the mid-1960s it was becoming evident that in the name of treatment, juveniles were subjected to essentially the same punishments as were adult defendants. Finally, in 1966 the U.S. Supreme Court heard the case of Gerald Gault.

On June 8, 1964, fifteen-year-old Gerald Gault was taken into custody by Arizona authorities on the charge of making a lewd phone call—he was accused of asking, for example, "Do you have big bombers?"—to a woman neighbor. Gault's parents, who learned of their son's arrest from a neighbor rather than from authorities, asked about Gerald at the detention home. Gerald's mother was told what he had been charged with and of a hearing to be held the next day. A probation officer filed a petition noting that Gault was a minor under age eighteen and in need of protection by the court because he was a delinquent. Gault's parents were never served the petition nor did the petition refer to any factual basis for the court's intervention. At the initial hearing, the complaining witness—the neighbor who had received the phone call—was not present, and no record of the proceedings was made, nor was any sworn testimony offered. There was, however, testimonial conflict about whether Gault had indeed made the phone call. Gault stayed in confinement for two or three days while the judge took the case under advisement. Gault was then released and told to return to court on June 15 "for further Hearings on Gerald's delinquency" (Kittrie, 1971, p. 138).

In 1967 the U.S. Supreme Court began defining the minimum due process requirements for juvenile courts. The decision, *In re Gault,* resulted from a 1964 Arizona case involving fifteen-year-old Gerald Gault. Shown here is Gault, the day after the Court ruling, receiving instruction at a Job Corps Center in California.

At the second hearing, the complaining witness was still not present. In response to Mrs. Gault's request that the witness be at the hearing, the judge said that would not be necessary. At this hearing, the court received a "referral report" (its existence was previously unknown either to Gerald or his parents), and Gault was committed to the State Industrial School until he reached age twenty-one. Had Gerald been an adult making similar phone calls, Arizona law provided for a maximum penalty of a $50 fine or two months imprisonment. Gault's parents challenged the legality of his confinement and sought his release by a petition for a writ of habeas corpus. The U.S. Supreme Court in 1967 (*In re Gault*) reversed the Arizona court action and in that manner began a process of delineating minimum requirements of due process for juvenile courts to follow.

The tone of the decision is observed in the Court's comments that neither the Fourteenth Amendment nor the Bill of Rights is for adults only. "Under our Constitution, the condition of being a boy does not justify a kangaroo court" (*In re Gault* 387 U.S. at 28). With that thought in mind, the Court required that juveniles accused of violating a criminal statute for which institutional commitment was possible have (1) the right to fair notice of the charges to allow sufficient time to prepare a defense, (2) the right to representation by counsel, (3) the right to face their accusers and cross-examine the witnesses, and (4) the privilege against self-incrimination.

In some ways, the *Gault* decision was just as important for the things it did not say. For example, rights still unavailable to juveniles after *Gault* included the right to trial by jury, to release on bail, and to protection against double jeopardy. In addition, because *Gault* pertained only to juveniles whose delinquent actions may result in institutionalization, jurisdictions have differed in the extent to which they have carried out the decision. In some states, *Gault* guarantees such as the right to counsel pertain only to delinquent charges, whereas in other jurisdictions they have been expanded to apply to status offenders and in neglect and dependency proceedings.

In 1970 a second Supreme Court decision dealing with juveniles brought changes in juvenile court proceedings. *In re Winship* dealt with the burden of proof in delinquency hearings. The civil nature of the juvenile court proceedings meant that only a preponderance of evidence—that is, evidence having greater weight or being more convincing than the evidence offered in opposition to it—was required to establish a child's delinquency. In the *Winship* decision the Court held that the standard of proof used in criminal court was applicable to juveniles in delinquency hearings. As a result, adjudication of delinquency required proof beyond a reasonable doubt, that is, fully satisfying and entirely convincing evidence establishing the accuser's guilt.

Other decisions relating to the processing of juveniles have considered issues such as the following:

- *Double jeopardy. Breed v. Jones,* 1975, held that juvenile adjudication equated to criminal conviction, so a person adjudicated delinquent cannot be later put at risk in criminal court for the same act.
- *Preventive pretrial detention of juveniles. Schall v. Martin,* 1984, held that society has a legitimate interest in protecting a juvenile from the consequences of his or her criminal activity, and such detention thereby serves a legitimate state objective.
- *Punishment for capital offenses. Thompson v. Oklahoma,* 1988, held that execution of a person who committed a capital crime while younger than age sixteen would be unconstitutional; however, it is constitutional to execute a person who was age sixteen or seventeen at the time of committing the capital offense (*Stanford v. Kentucky,* 1989).

The Court has also been asked if due process for juveniles requires the right to a trial by jury. In *McKeiver v. Pennsylvania,* the Court found no constitutional requirement for such a right in juvenile court. But the justices went on to say that individual states should be free to experiment and may install a jury system or use an advisory jury to assist the judge. Although only about twelve states have authorized a jury trial for juveniles (Rubin, 1979), some jurisdictions have experimented with advisory juries composed of other juveniles. For example, the Teen Court in Bradenton, Florida, and the Y-Teen Court in Houston, Texas, use a teen jury and an adult judge to hear minor misdemeanor and some status offense cases. In the spirit of peer pressure, offenders who have admitted to the charges against them are "sentenced" by their age peers on the jury. Dispositions available to the jurors include counseling, community service, or even service on the teen court (Krisberg, Currie, & Onek, 1995).

The Role of Today's Juvenile Court

The history of public reaction to juvenile offenders has ranged from no distinction from any other law violators, through a period of child saving, to the philosophy of the juvenile court as "friend," to a view that places public safety ahead of the interests of individual juveniles. The impact of that transition is still felt today as American society grapples with the continuing problem of preventing and controlling misbehavior by young people. The feature "Responding to Juvenile Offenders in Other Countries" shows how other countries respond to the misbehavior of their young people. The philosophy of rehabilitation, initially accepted by the juvenile court, has continued throughout the century to guide official reaction to delinquents. Juveniles still are not found "guilty" of anything, and placement in institutions, on probation, or in community programs is typically for therapy rather than punishment (see Table 12.1 on page 443).

Cross-Cultural Corrections

Responding to Juvenile Offenders in Other Countries

A variety of approaches is used around the world for responding to young offenders. Some countries rely on what can be called an informal approach wherein the country relies on community agencies and citizens rather than a formal adult or juvenile court structure. The preference for handling juvenile offenders in these countries is with nonjudicial options that might range from a traditional reliance on family and neighbors in dealing with misbehaving youth to more contemporary strategies that use community agencies operating outside the justice system. Examples of the more traditional informality are found in the People's Republic of China where persons from ages fourteen to eighteen who commit a crime receive a lesser or mitigated punishment than would adults committing a similar act. Juvenile offenders are processed through China's lower-level courts (sometimes in a specialized children's section of the court), in which juvenile offenses are said to present "peculiar cases" that should be handled through education or punishment. The choice between education and punishment is made primarily on the basis of age and offense, with younger children committing minor offenses receiving an "education" and older children engaged in serious offenses being punished.

Countries following a legalistic approach to handling juvenile offenders place more importance on due process and formal action than on treating the juvenile. That is not to say that treatment is unimportant; rather, it simply implies that the government must deal with juvenile defendants and offenders under the same legal requirements they follow in responding to adults. In other words, legal procedure takes precedence over a parens patriae approach. For example, juveniles in Austria are handled under the criminal law and, therefore, receive all the due process rights that are granted adult defendants. However, because there is no separate legal status for juvenile offenders, they are subject to the same laws and punishments as the adult offenders.

Austria's version of a legalistic approach does, however, provide for differential treatment of juvenile offenders. For example, juveniles should be kept in special sections of the ordinary prisons or in separate institutions. But even the separate juvenile prisons may have comparatively older inmates because persons up to age twenty-two may also be detained, and prisoners already at a juvenile penal facility can stay there until age twenty-seven (Krainz, 1991). Other adjustments made for juvenile offenders in Austrian prisons include the requirement that they be made to perform only educationally useful work, receive more generous food allotments, have longer visiting periods, and be kept primarily in less secure institutions. In this way Austrian juveniles are subject to the criminal law and are considered criminally responsible—albeit at a lower level than adults.

Whereas the legalistic approach emphasizes criminal responsibility and due process over treatment, the welfare approach highlights the well-being of the juvenile—even if that means the juvenile has fewer rights under the law. A number of countries operate with a welfare approach to juvenile offenders, but New Zealand presents an especially interesting example. Morris and Maxwell (1993) describe New Zealand's juvenile justice system as stressing the well-being of children and the empowerment of families and young people. Criminal procedures are possible for young offenders, but they are to be used only when no alternative is available. A particularly interesting aspect of the New Zealand approach is its attention to the culture of its indigenous people, the Maori.

Although they make up less than 10 percent of the country's population, nearly 45 percent of all juvenile offenders are Maori. The juvenile justice system tries to respond to that disproportionate representation by taking into account the Maori culture when sanctioning juvenile offenders. For example, New Zealand's juvenile justice act incorporates Maori culture through the use of a Family Group Conference (FGC). When police detect juvenile offenders, they can warn the juveniles, arrest them, or refer them for an FGC. The FGC is composed of family members, police officials, social workers, the offender, and the victim. This group determines or recommends how the juvenile should be dealt with. Options include a simple apology, performing community work, or even a suggestion for formal prosecution. The key, however, is that the child's welfare or well-being is to be the determining factor in whatever decision is made.

Read the procedures for New Zealand's Family Group Conference at ***www.law.auckland.ac.nz/court/dc/fgc.htm***. Which persons can attend the FGC? What functions does the FGC have? What happens when no agreement is possible?

TABLE 12.1: Comparison of Terms Used in Adult and Juvenile Justice Systems

	JUVENILE TERMS	ADULT TERMS
The person and the act	Delinquent child	Criminal
	Delinquent act	Crime
Preadjudicatory stage	Take into custody	Arrest
	Petition	Indictment
	Agree to a finding	Plead guilty
	Deny the petition	Plead not guilty
	Adjustment	Plea bargain
	Detention facility, child-care shelter	Jail
Adjudicatory stage	Substitution	Reduction of charges
	Adjudicatory or fact-finding hearing	Trial
	Adjudication	Conviction
Postadjudicatory stage	Dispositional hearing	Sentencing hearing
	Disposition	Sentence
	Commitment	Incarceration
	Youth development center, treatment center, training school	Prison
	Residential child-care facility	Halfway house
	Aftercare	Parole

Source: From Senna, J. J., & Siegel, L. J. (1999). *Introduction to criminal justice* (8th ed.). Belmont, CA: Wadsworth. Copyright © 1999. Reprinted with permission of Wadsworth, a division of Thomson Learning.

The continued predominance of a rehabilitative philosophy does not mean it is without challenge. The Retributive era affected the juvenile justice system, although possibly to a lesser extent, just as it has the criminal justice system. Empey (1982) suggests the guiding philosophy of this hard-line approach is both a rejection of punishment and a concentration on doing justice. Because proponents of the just deserts model see imposing treatment or services by the court as not being beneficial to the juvenile, they reject the court's rehabilitative philosophy. Instead, as a court of law, the juvenile court would do justice better by ensuring fair proceedings than by expressing love, benevolence, and charity. Of course, that sounds like a goal of the traditional criminal courts more so than the juvenile court. But rather than modifying the purpose and procedures of the juvenile court, proponents of the "just deserts through fair proceedings" seem most successful in achieving their goal by getting cases transferred to criminal court. The increased use of such transfers warrants closer attention.

Transferring Juveniles to Criminal Court

A good example of a new mood brought by the Retributive era is the increasing number of juvenile delinquency cases that are transferred to criminal courts. All states allow juveniles to be tried as adults in criminal court under certain circumstances.

That transfer occurs in one of three ways: (1) judicial waiver (juvenile judge waives jurisdiction), (2) prosecutorial discretion (prosecutor decides to try the juvenile as an adult), or (3) statutory exclusion (for certain crimes by juveniles, criminal courts have original jurisdiction). It is possible that any particular state will have all three, or just one or two, of the strategies in place. It is important to note that several states also have provisions for transferring cases from criminal court to juvenile court under certain circumstances (called reverse waiver), but we are interested here in those cases that end up in criminal court.

Transfer by **judicial waiver** was possible in all states except Massachusetts, Nebraska, New Mexico, and New York at the end of 1997 (Griffin, Torbet, & Szymanksi, 1998). Under this mechanism a juvenile court judge can waive jurisdiction over a case and transfer it to criminal court. Prosecutors usually are the ones requesting such action, although in some states the transfer can be requested by juveniles or their parents. Statutes typically limit judicial waiver by age, offense, or offense history and might also require the judge to consider the juvenile's amenability to treatment. In addition, waiver provisions are entirely discretionary in some states, whereas in others it is either presumed or mandatory that the judge waive the case. Stahl (1999a) reports that about 1 percent of all formally handled delinquency cases are waived nationally. Since 1995 most of the cases waived are offenses against a person, followed by drug offenses then property offenses, and finally public-order offenses. Stahl also found that cases involving black youth were more likely to be waived to criminal court than were cases involving white youth or youth of other races.

In some states concurrent jurisdiction statutes give prosecutors the authority to file certain juvenile cases in either juvenile or criminal court. This **prosecutorial discretion**—also called direct file—is usually limited by age and offense criteria. For example, in Arkansas prosecutors can direct file a large range of offenses (including soliciting a minor to join a street gang). In Florida, prosecutors have discretion to file in criminal court those cases in which juveniles age sixteen or

In 1999 a Michigan jury convicted thirteen-year-old Nathaniel Abraham, shown here with his attorney, of a murder committed when he was age eleven. The case attracted international attention because Abraham was one of the youngest juveniles ever charged as an adult. His eventual sentence was for seven years in a maximum-security juvenile detention center.

older are charged with felony offenses or misdemeanors if they have a sufficiently serious record (Griffin et al., 1998).

State legislatures effectively transfer young offenders to criminal court by **statutorily excluding** them from juvenile court jurisdiction. Although this may not technically be a transfer, the large and increasing number of juveniles affected by these statutes makes it an important strategy for getting cases to criminal court. In twenty-eight states, minors accused of certain offenses cannot have their case heard by the juvenile court. In some states those offenses are only the most serious kind—for example, in New Mexico only first-degree murder by a child at least fifteen years old is excluded. But in other states the range of excluded offenses is quite broad—for example, in Mississippi all felonies committed by seventeen-year-olds are excluded (Griffin et al., 1998).

Presumably a result of having a juvenile's case transferred to criminal court is an increased protection of procedural due process. But does it also mean that convicted juveniles receive the same penalty as applied to adult criminals? The answer is yes in many states, but in an increasing number of jurisdictions, creative alternatives have been enacted that mix juvenile and adult sentences (DeFrances & Strom, 1997; Torbet, 1997). These **blended sentences** allow the criminal court to impose either juvenile or adult sanctions (six states in 1995) or a combination of juvenile and adult sanctions (Arkansas and Missouri in 1995). If the resulting sentence involves incarceration, there are three common ways it can be implemented:

- Straight adult incarceration—Juveniles are sentenced and imprisoned as adults with little differentiation in programming between juveniles and adults.
- Graduated incarceration—Juveniles are sentenced as adults but imprisoned in juvenile or separate adult correctional facilities until they reach a certain age. At that age, they may be released or transferred to adult facilities to serve the remainder of their sentence.
- Segregated incarceration—Juveniles are sentenced as adults but housed in separate facilities for younger adult offenders, usually eighteen to twenty-five years old, and occasionally with specialized programming. (Torbet, 1997, p. 123)

Processing Juvenile Offenders

The emphasis of this chapter is on how society responds to juvenile offenders rather than how it processes them. The differences between the processing of juvenile offenders through the juvenile justice system are different enough from the way adults are processed in the criminal court system that it is not possible to elaborate in detail here. Instead, a broad overview is provided simply to enable understanding of the resulting dispositions handed to juveniles either informally—usually through a probation department—or formally through court adjudication. You can also refer to the case flowchart in Figure 12.1 to get an idea of the stages involved.

The first item to identify regarding the processing of juveniles is to decide who is considered a juvenile. Unfortunately that is not easily accomplished. Figure 12.2 shows the upper age at which a state's juvenile court can have jurisdiction over the juvenile. The exceptions noted in Figure 12.2 highlight the problems in trying to place state laws into simple categories for purposes of description.

Having somewhat identified who might be processed through the juvenile justice system, we are ready to consider what they did to get them there. Again, the answer is not a simple one. Earlier in the chapter we saw that some offenses will be transferred, or immediately sent, to the criminal court even though the accused is at an age appropriate for the juvenile court. In those cases the crime takes precedence over who committed the crime. The juvenile court philosophy was established on the principle that it should have jurisdiction over three kinds of

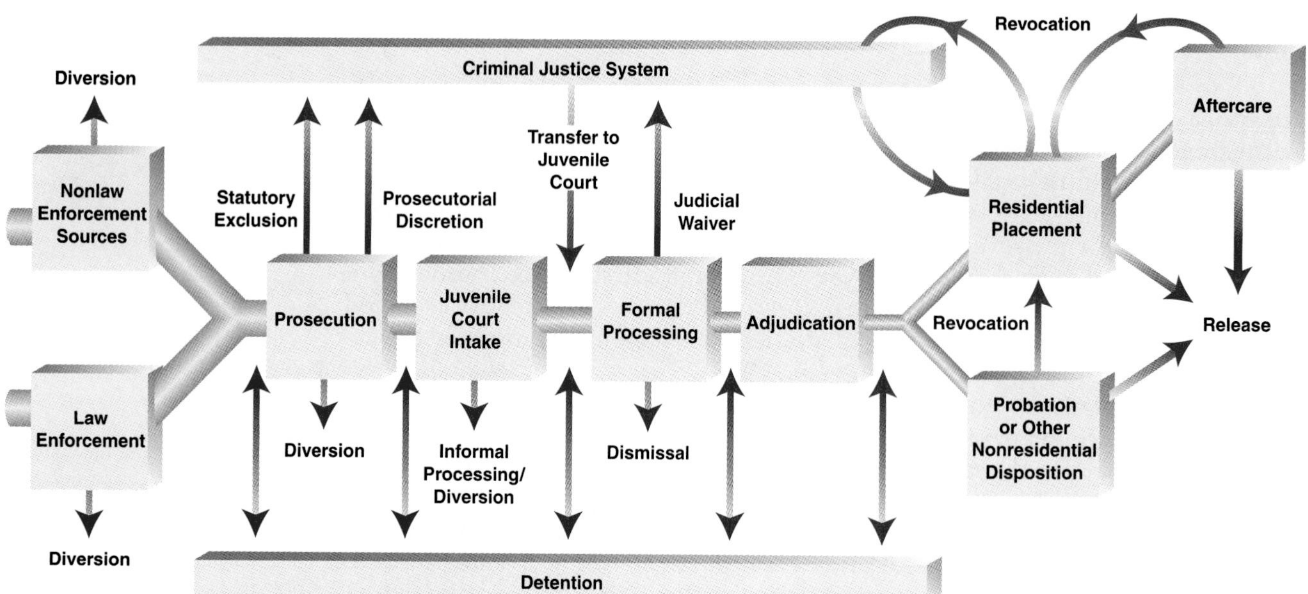

FIGURE 12.1

Caseflow through the Juvenile Justice System

Source: From Office of Juvenile Justice and Delinquency Prevention. (2000). *Caseflow through the juvenile justice system.* Available: www.ojjdp.ncjrs.org/facts/caseflow.html.

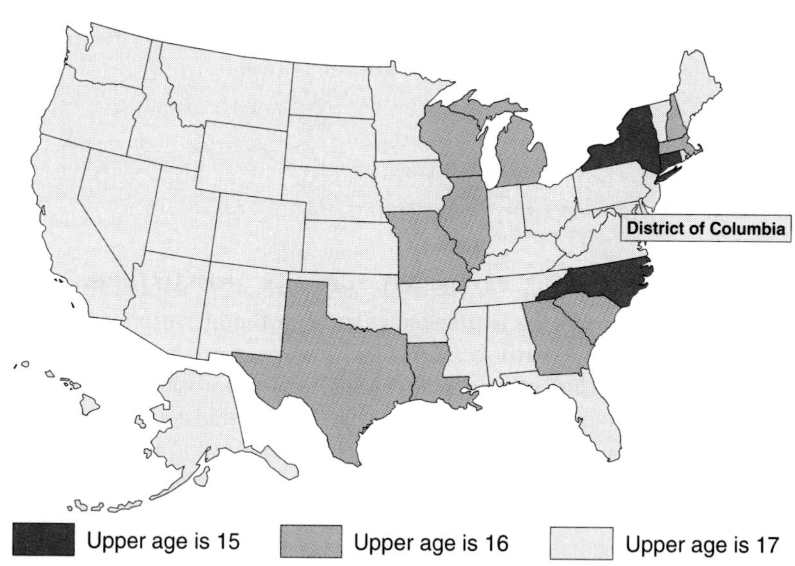

FIGURE 12.2

Oldest Age at Which a Juvenile Court Has Original Jurisdiction

State statutes define which youth are under the original jurisdiction of the juvenile court. These definitions are based primarily on age criteria. In most states, the juvenile court has original jurisdiction over all youth charged with a criminal law violation who were below the age of eighteen at the time of the offense, arrest, or referral to court. Many states have higher upper ages of juvenile court jurisdiction in status offense, abuse, neglect, or dependency matters—often through age twenty.

Source: Sickmund, M. "Upper age of original juvenile court jurisdiction, 1997." Adapted from Torbet, P., & Szymanski, L. *State legislative responses to violent juvenile crime: 1996–1997 update.* Washington, DC: Office of Juvenile Justice and Delinquency Prevention, *OJJDP statistical briefing book.* Online. Available: www.ojjdp.ncjrs.org/ojstatbb/qa085.html.

problems: (1) situations of neglect, abuse, exploitation, or mistreatment; (2) cases in which a juvenile commits an act that would be a crime if committed by an adult; and (3) certain acts that are deemed inappropriate or undesirable for persons of a certain status (in this case the status refers to being under a certain age). This chapter is more concerned with how the second (acts of juvenile delinquency) and the third (status offenses) are processed.

Delinquency Cases

Most (59 percent) of the delinquency cases processed by the nation's juvenile courts in 1996 involved youths age sixteen or younger (Stahl, 1999b). More males (77 percent) than females (23 percent) were processed, but the number of female delinquency cases showed a greater increase between 1987 and 1996 (females rose 76 percent compared to a 42 percent increase for males). And, although the number of juveniles arrested for violent crimes decreased between 1994 and 1997, the percentage of girls arrested for such crimes has almost doubled since the early 1980s. The feature "Delinquent Girls" elaborates on the increased involvement of females in delinquency. The percentage of white youths (66 percent) exceeded that of black youths (30 percent), but the number of cases involving black youth increased 68 percent between 1987 and 1996 compared with an increase of 39 percent for white youth. Half of the delinquency cases disposed of in 1996 involved property offenses as the most serious charge, followed by person offenses (22 percent), public-order offenses (19 percent), and drug offenses (10 percent). The ranking of offenses did not vary by sex or by race, but blacks were less likely to have cases related to property offenses and more likely to have person offenses than the national average for those offense categories. Drug law violations accounted for about equal proportion of delinquency cases involving black youth and white youth.

The youths and their offenses come to the attention of the juvenile court officials mainly (86 percent) by referral from the police but also by social service agencies, schools, parents, probation officers, and victims. Upon getting a referral, an intake officer, prosecutor, or judge decides whether to handle the case formally or informally. The informal response (44 percent of the 1996 cases) involves a nonjudicial disposition that is referred to as a **nonpetitioned case** (see Figure 12.3 on page 449) or is more often called **informal probation.** Nearly every state has authorized informal probation, and the practice is commonly used across the country (Torbet, 1993). Typically juveniles are placed on informal probation only when they have admitted to the charges against them, and they and their parents have voluntarily agreed to submit to the conditions of the informal probation. In the absence of such admission and agreement, the case will be dismissed or formally processed. Critics of the practice argue that it allows the imposing of substantial constraints on the youth's liberty without providing adequate due process safeguards.

Most delinquency cases are handled formally (see Figure 12.3). This involves the filing of a petition that requests an adjudicatory hearing. During this hearing, the juvenile court judge or referee determines whether the youth will be adjudicated delinquent. That decision is made after evidence and witnesses are presented by a prosecuting attorney (in some cases and jurisdictions this is done by a probation officer), and after the juvenile or his attorney presents evidence and cross-examines witnesses. The juvenile may admit to the charges at the hearing, but when an admission is not forthcoming, the judge or referee must dismiss the case or must find beyond a reasonable doubt that the juvenile is delinquent.

When a finding (adjudication) of delinquency is made, a disposition (or sentencing) proceeding follows. Sometimes the disposition stage occurs immediately after the adjudication stage—especially if a predisposition investigation has already been prepared to expedite matters—but it might also be delayed until a social

ISSUES OF FAIRNESS

DELINQUENT GIRLS

The good news: Juvenile crime, like most crime over the last several years, is dropping.

The bad news: Girls are a bigger part of the nation's crime problems than ever before.

In the early 1980s, girls accounted for about one in ten juvenile arrests. Today they are about one in four. Researchers are not sure whether it's the girls or the world that has changed—although the suspicion is that "both" is the best answer. Although the involvement of girls in all types of offenses is increasing, the rise in violent activities is especially notable. For example, a 1999 National Report found girls charged with weapons violations—although still just 10 percent of the male arrest rate—jumped from 11 girls arrested per 100,000 females in 1981 to 32 in 1997. Arrests of girls for aggravated assault more than doubled during the same period, and the rate for simple assaults more than tripled (see the report at www.ojjdp.ncjrs.org/ojstatbb/index.html).

Concern about the increased involvement of girls in juvenile offenses is matched by concern about an apparent change in the girls' motivation to commit the crimes. Kalfrin (1999) reports that some officials are noticing that more girls are committing crimes for rational rather than emotional purposes. In the past, they explain, girls committed a crime because they thought they were in love with a particular person. Today they are acting for economic gain, and they are choosing to be involved in gang activity. Both of those motivations have been more typically held by boys.

The increased gang activity is as intriguing as it is troublesome. Although males clearly dominate gang membership (90 percent by most estimates), there are some studies that report the proportion of females in gangs as large as one-fourth to one-third (Bilchik, 1999). Chen (1999c) reports on girls in Chicago gangs (estimated at about 20 percent of Chicago's gang members) and explains that they are involved in the same activities as the boys: drive-by shootings, robberies, aggravated assault, and so on.

Girls in gangs are certainly not a new phenomenon because females have been affiliated with gangs for years. However, the traditional role for girls and women has been limited to activities like hosting gang parties, having the gang members' children, and using their clean criminal record to get apartments. Today, their role is more primary and active as they are asked to carry drugs, guns, and money—based on the assumption that police officers will be less likely to search female gang members and more likely to miss contraband hidden in bras or underwear even when they do search them (Chen, 1999c). The next step, already being taken in many parts of the country, is for the female gang members to carry their own drugs, guns, and money rather than just holding the items for their gang brothers.

Read the national gang survey's section on sex demographics at ***www.ojjdp.ncjrs.org/pubs/96natyouthgangsrvy/surv_6b.html.*** Does the proportion of female gang members differ by the population size of the area? Where are there likely to be more female gang members, large cities or rural counties? Why?

history is completed. Figure 12.3 shows that most of the adjudicated cases resulted in either probation or placement in a residential facility. We will return to the placement and probation dispositions after a brief look at the processing of status offenses.

Status Offense Cases

Status offenses include acts such as possession of alcohol, truancy, running away from home, and disobeying one's parents. Status offenders handled in the nation's juvenile courts are primarily white (78 percent), male (59 percent), and their offenses involve liquor law violations (28 percent) or truancy (24 percent). Juveniles age fifteen or younger were most likely to be charged with truancy (34 percent of that age group) whereas those age sixteen or older were most likely to have liquor

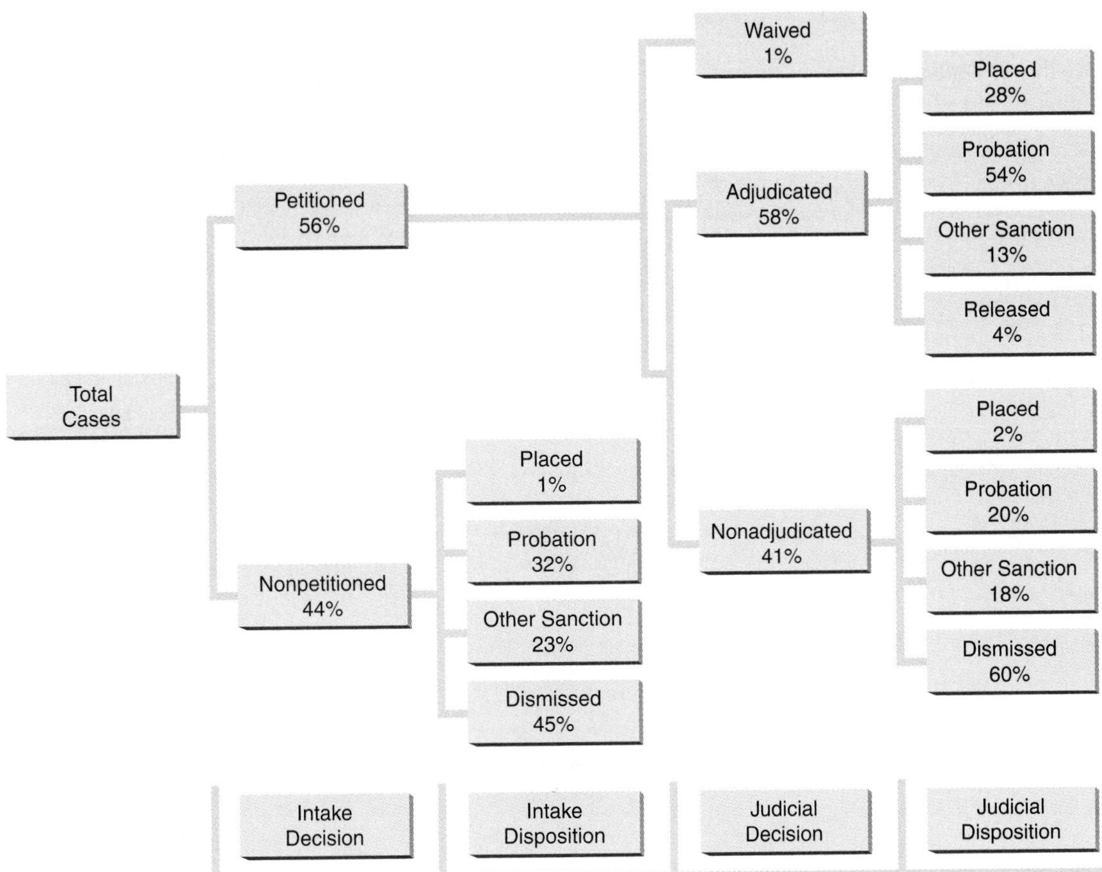

FIGURE 12.3

Juvenile Court Processing of Delinquency Cases, 1996

Note: Details may not add to totals because of rounding.

Source: Adapted from Stahl, A. L. (1999). *Offenders in juvenile court, 1996* [NCJ 175719]. Washington, DC: Office of Juvenile Justice and Delinquency Prevention.

law charges (46 percent of the cohort). Females processed as status offenders were most often charged with running away (60 percent of the runaways), and males were usually charged with liquor law violations (70 percent of the liquor charges). Liquor law charges were also primarily against white juveniles (90 percent of such charges). Truancy (34 percent) was the most common status offense among black youths (Stahl, 1999b).

Figure 12.4 shows that 52 percent of the petitioned status offense cases result in adjudication. But, as with delinquency charges, even the nonadjudicated cases can result in restrictions being placed on the status offender. Of the cases that are not dismissed, the most frequent nonadjudicated disposition is "other sanctions," such as restitution or community service. For adjudicated cases, formal probation is the most frequent disposition. A very small percentage of the nonadjudicated status offenders might end up in an out-of-home placement, as might a comparatively small percentage of the adjudicated status offenders.

Status offenses present a dilemma for society. On the one hand, it is argued that young people who are truant, have run away from home, are using alcohol, or are generally beyond their parents' control are in great danger of committing acts of a

FIGURE 12.4

Juvenile Court Processing of Petitioned Status Offense Cases, 1996

Note: Details may not add to totals because of rounding.

Source: Adapted from Stahl, A. L. (1999). *Offenders in juvenile court, 1996* [NCJ 175719]. Washington, DC: Office of Juvenile Justice and Delinquency Prevention.

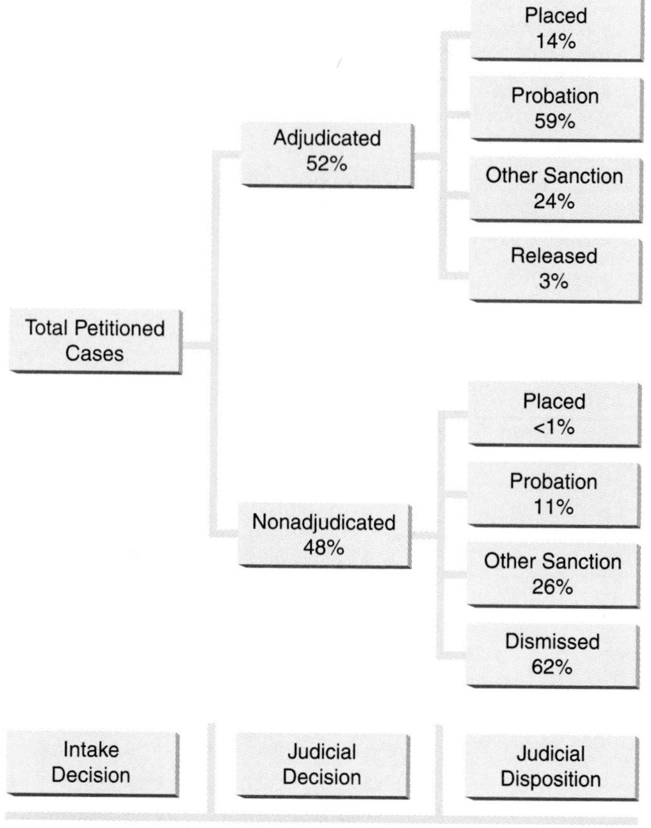

criminal nature. Property crimes might support the runaway, vandalism may give the truant something to do, or acts of violence could be a way for the incorrigible to express their continued frustration. A desire to prevent those more serious violations by "doing something" when the acts are merely at the status offense level has been the motivation for most of the status offense laws. But critics of those laws argue that "doing something" may actually push the offender further along a path toward delinquency. Because the same juvenile court officials handle both status offense cases and delinquency cases, the status offender becomes identified as a problem child or troublemaker. The juvenile is brought under the control of court officials and at times will receive a disposition that results in being treated as if he had committed a delinquent act rather than a status offense. Whether that is a desirable situation or not will depend on one's view of the juvenile court's role. But, although the situation deserves attention and serious debate, in today's version of juvenile justice both delinquent offenders and status offenders are responded to by society. So we will leave to others a discussion about the merits of processing status offenders and will instead seek a better understanding of the types of dispositions that are handed out in both kinds of juvenile cases.

Detention

Before considering the types of formal dispositions for delinquency cases, we must consider one other aspect of the juvenile justice process. For either delinquency or status offense cases, a juvenile may be placed in a detention facility at some point between referral to court and case disposition. The federal Juvenile Justice and Delinquency Prevention Act of 1974, as amended (JJDP Act), mandated that status offenders be deinstitutionalized and required that they be removed from secure confinement in either detention facilities or institutions. An exception can be made when the juvenile has violated a judge's valid court order regulating the juvenile's future conduct (e.g., attend school, obey parents, follow rules of probation). For example, if a truant who was ordered to attend school (a valid court order) fails to attend, a judge could order that juvenile to be detained. Another example would be a runaway who was ordered to stay with foster parents and then runs away again.

Standards established for determining if a juvenile should be detained typically require the court official to decide that the detention is necessary to:

- Protect the jurisdiction or the court process (e.g., ensure the youth's attendance at scheduled hearings or for evaluation)
- Prevent the juvenile from inflicting serious bodily harm or committing serious property damage
- Protect the juvenile, especially at his or her request, from imminent bodily harm (Butts & Poe, 1993; Torbet, 1993).

Of course, those guidelines are to be considered in the context of such things as the nature and severity of the offense for which the juvenile is now charged and the juvenile's prior court history.

Each state establishes time limits for processing delinquency cases, including how long a juvenile can be detained. The National Advisory Committee for Juvenile Justice and Delinquency recommends that once a juvenile has been referred to juvenile court, an intake decision should be made within twenty-four hours (excluding nonjudicial days) if that juvenile has been detained; that a detention hearing be held within twenty-four hours after a juvenile has been taken to the detention facility; and that a petition be filed within two judicial days after intake determination when the juvenile is in detention. Within fifteen calendar days of filing a petition the adjudication hearing should occur, and the disposition hearing should occur no later than fifteen calendar days after adjudication (Torbet, 1993).

Having looked at the processing of both delinquency and status offense cases, we now understand that juveniles pass through an intake process, have an adjudication hearing, and then receive a disposition from the court. We are now ready to consider examples of those dispositions, and in doing so, we look specifically at juvenile corrections.

Help Wanted

Job Title: Juvenile Detention Officer

Position Description: Detention officers in a secure juvenile institution assist in maintaining the security of that facility, provide direct visual supervision of youth, check and inspect units for contraband, and ensure the safety of staff and residents.

Qualifications: Applicants should have an associate's or bachelor's degree in criminal justice, criminology, corrections, or a related field and should have experience working with delinquent youth in a supervised setting. Good communications skills that can be used to defuse situations without resorting to violence are desirable.

For examples of career opportunities in this field, visit the various state departments for juvenile corrections. An example is the employment page for Wisconsin at ***www.wi-doc.com/employme.htm.***

INSTITUTION-BASED RESPONSES

Correctional facilities for juveniles have always had a more diverse population than other types of correctional institutions. Over the years they have held persons who have not committed—nor even been accused of committing—any illegal acts, as well as persons being sanctioned for delinquent and even criminal behavior. Cahalan's (1986) historical review of institutions for juvenile delinquents found the earliest statistical information to come from education reports from the 1850s to the 1910s. Data about juvenile offenders were sometimes kept along with information on the education of the deaf, blind, orphans, girls, and "colored" or "freedmen" categories. Factors thought to contribute to misbehavior of young people were also recorded. Some of those items are still considered important today, whereas others would no longer warrant notice. For example, reports focused on

Contemporary detention facilities for juveniles, like those for adults, are likely to be built in a podular design. This design distributes a small number of juveniles among several pods, or housing units, where they spend much of their non-school time.

such items as "idleness, use of profane language, use of tobacco and alcohol, visiting theaters, parent's employment, parent's marital status, parent's quarreling, church attendance, and truancy" (Cahalan, 1986, p. 102).

Information about how many juveniles were held in jails, prisons, and in institutions for juvenile delinquents since the late nineteenth century is provided by Cahalan (1986) from census data and data from the Department of Health, Education, and Welfare. Estimates in 1880 had about 10,000 persons under age eighteen in institutions for juvenile delinquents. Since the 1970s, the number of adjudicated juveniles held in public and private juvenile facilities has increased from about 47,000 in 1975 to around 106,000 in 1997 (Bilchik, 1999b) with most of the growth coming from a rise in the number of drug offense and person offense cases resulting in placement (MacKenzie, 1999).

Actually, it is remarkably difficult to estimate the number of juveniles in facilities around the country. Problems include deciding whether to use the state's definition of juvenile (meaning some over age eighteen are counted), what facilities to include, and whether to count juveniles held in adult facilities. Various groups have approached the problem in several different ways. The American Correctional Association provides data on juveniles under supervision that distinguish facilities as either "secure" or "nonsecure." The Bureau of Justice Statistics typically reports only on juveniles held in public facilities, but the Office of Juvenile Justice and Delinquency Prevention (OJJDP) uses both public and private facilities. The absence of agreed-upon inclusion criteria makes it very difficult to summarize the data on juvenile delinquents under correctional supervision in facilities around the country. One thing that is apparent, however, is that a disproportionate number of minority youths are in juvenile facilities. The feature "Minority Confinement in Juvenile Facilities" elaborates that point.

Once a decision is made to place a juvenile in an institution, concern is directed toward the type of programs that juvenile will experience. Some programs reflect society's desire to treat juvenile offenders like adult offenders (e.g., boot camp programs), whereas other programs are more consistent with the juvenile

ISSUES OF FAIRNESS

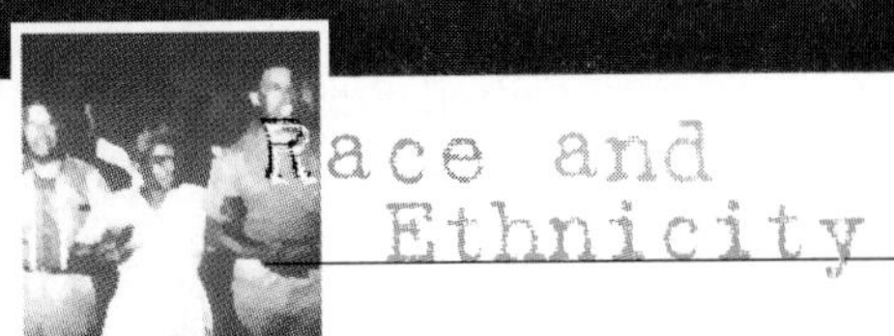

MINORITY CONFINEMENT IN JUVENILE FACILITIES

The topic of race differences at juvenile facilities deserves elaboration. Data from 1910 indicate that the early juvenile facilities were used more frequently for white than for black juvenile offenders. Of white youths sentenced to correctional facilities, 69 percent went to reformatories for delinquents whereas 31 percent were sent to traditional prisons, jails, and workhouses. The reverse was true for black youths—29 percent were committed to juvenile facilities and 71 percent to prisons, jails, and workhouses (Cahalan, 1986). The discrepancy was eased as more states built facilities for juveniles and as racial segregation in public institutions was halted.

Throughout most of the twentieth century, white youths (not including Hispanics) made up the greatest percentage of the population in public and private custody facilities for juveniles—although minority youth were still confined at disproportionate levels. Things worsened in 1989, when the percentage of minorities (blacks, Hispanics, and others) exceeded that of nonminorities, making up 52 percent of the juveniles in custody (Krisberg & DeComo, 1993). Specific analysis in four states (Devine, Coolbaugh, & Jenkins, 1998) found that black juveniles are overrepresented at every stage of the juvenile justice process (Florida and Oregon)—or at every stage except referral to juvenile court (North Carolina)—and that minority juveniles are overrepresented in secure facilities, and they tend to experience longer stays than do white juveniles (Iowa).

The Office of Juvenile Justice and Delinquency Prevention has designed specific research projects to provide answers to the presence of disproportionate minority confinement. A report on a pilot study identified four general factors that contribute to minority overrepresentation: (1) activities occurring in the juvenile justice system itself; (2) socioeconomic conditions; (3) educational system inadequacies; and (4) family dynamics (Devine et al., 1998). As you can imagine, the impact and interaction of each area are complex. Devine et al. summarize the findings by noting that family factors such as single-parent homes, economic stress, and limited time for supervision are controversial but apparent factors. Also, the absence of school programs to adequately serve minority juveniles—or the failure of minority youth to fully participate in the educational system—can encourage involvement in delinquent behavior. And poor socioeconomic conditions likely play a role by limiting job opportunities, providing low incomes, and restricting social support services.

Finally, the juvenile justice system itself contributes to disproportionate minority confinement through activities that occur well in advance of the actual confinement. Devine et al. (1998) explain that race and ethnicity are factors that seem to affect processing decisions in many juvenile justice systems. A procedure known as selection bias seems to operate wherein the actions or histories of minority youth are scrutinized more carefully than are the actions or histories of nonminority juveniles. For example, some studies show that police officers are more likely to stop and question a group of minority youth but only glance at a similar group of nonminority youth. Prosecutors, according to other research, have been found to look at prior system involvement by a minority youth as a stronger indication of a tendency toward continued crime than the same record predicts for a nonminority youth (Devine et al., 1998). When selection bias is combined with influences from the educational system, the family, and prevailing socioeconomic conditions, minority overrepresentation is one of several negative consequences.

Read the OJJDP report on disproportionate minority confinement at ***www.ncjrs.org/94612.pdf.*** At the section entitled "Synthesize Contributing Factors" the influence of each area mentioned earlier is explained. Do you agree or disagree with the report's analysis of these factors as influencing overrepresentation of minority juveniles in the system? What other factors might be important? What are some realistic efforts that can be made at the community level to reduce the negative impact the factors have?

justice system's original focus on rehabilitation (e.g., educational programs). Many jurisdictions are developing programs that respond to specific offense and offender types (e.g., programs for serious and violent offenders). We will look at examples of each type.

Boot Camp Programs

In 1995 there were at least ten boot camps for juvenile offenders operating in the United States. The oldest program, which dates to 1985, is in Orleans Parish, Louisiana. Alabama and Mississippi were apparently the only states with programs in 1995 that included beds for females in the boot camp (Camp & Camp, 1995b; Cronin, 1994). Some of the programs had capacities for over 200 juveniles, whereas others operated with as few as 24 to 30 offenders. Cronin's (1994) survey of these programs found quite a few similarities with boot camps for adults. Boot camps of both types tend to (1) accept "midrange" offenders who had failed at lesser sanctions such as probation but could not be considered hardened criminals; (2) have a 90- to 120-day duration; and (3) share military structure and discipline.

Although the similarities between juvenile and adult boot camps are predominant, there are also some important differences. The juvenile boot camps, consistent with the historical focus on rehabilitation, usually include an explicit concern for the needs and deficiencies of delinquent youths and are likely to require **aftercare** programs designed to address those needs. Also, because states mandate education for juvenile offenders, the juvenile boot camps require at least three hours per day for academic education.

The aftercare procedures for the juvenile boot camp graduates typically involve intensive community supervision. In most programs that supervision continues the rehabilitative activities started during the boot camp—with drug and alcohol counseling or treatment being especially popular. Aftercare in one Denver program requires attendance for six months at a special school that operates in the tradition of a private academy, complete with required uniform of a tie and blue blazer. Boot camp graduates in Cleveland must report to a day center for six months,

There are many types of juvenile detention facilities and programs. Training schools and group homes with vocational and academic programs predominate, but juvenile boot camps have also been popular.

where they receive case management and supervision, counseling, recreation, and other services. In Mobile, Alabama, the graduates choose from among seven Metropolitan Boys and Girls Clubs, located in low-income neighborhoods, which operate in the spirit of a day reporting center. Upon arriving at the Boys and Girls Club after school, the boot camp graduates participate in tutoring, recreation, drug and alcohol education, and other special programs (Cronin, 1994).

Educational Programs

Juvenile correctional facilities around the country offer several types of programs that might be identified or highlighted in this section. However, the importance of educating juveniles seems to have especially significant program status. Despite the widespread acceptance of education's relevance, however, correctional education for juveniles is seldom cited for its innovative and successful techniques. In fact, it is more likely to be described as needing a complete overhaul—and maybe even reinvention. This section concentrates on education for juveniles in correctional settings because of its importance and because there is good reason to believe that it can have a positive resolution. Much of the following discussion is based on reports sponsored by the OJJDP. These reports provide a good base for discussion because they recognize the poor quality of existing correctional education programs but also offer specific suggestions about how the process and procedures can be improved.

Juveniles incarcerated in correctional and detention facilities have typically had a poor experience with elementary and secondary education. Theories of delinquency have long realized the important role that school plays in relation to delinquency (Bartollas, 1993). Some studies have found school relationships and experiences to be exceeded only by family and peer group relationships as a predictive factor in delinquency. Other researchers suggest that failure in school leads to rebelliousness—which leads to more failure. Still others suggest that the school has become a prime social context for learning delinquent behavior. It is obviously an area in which intervention is important as society responds to juvenile offenders.

Concern about the relationship between juvenile misconduct and the school setting or the education process is often directed at prevention and diversion. Such attention is necessary and must be of primary importance. Also important, however, is the way correctional facilities respond to the educational needs of those juveniles placed in their care. Juveniles who have been determined to require the setting and services of a secure facility should not be written off as no longer able to benefit from the educational process. They will, after all, some day be back in free society. Without the skills and knowledge needed for today's work world, the pattern of misbehavior may not be broken. Unfortunately, many people believe that most contemporary efforts at education in correctional facilities are ill-suited for accomplishing that goal.

The Search for Effective Programs. Coffey and Gemignani cite a statement by President Clinton as a motivating factor in their search for effective correctional education techniques. In a 1993 address to the Democratic leadership, President Clinton said: "Every educational problem in America has been solved by someone, somewhere" (quoted in Coffey & Gemignani, 1994, p. 3). Coffey and Gemignani began a search for those programs that have responded to the specific educational problem presented by juveniles in correctional facilities.

The first problem encountered by Coffey and Gemignani was deciding how to interpret the word *effective*. For most educators an effective educational program

Academic education is a basic program at juvenile institutions around the world. Shown here are boys in a classroom at a primary training school in Japan.

would be one that meets certain educational goals—regardless of whether the students later commit delinquent acts. But when correctional education is evaluated, the definition of *effective* often centers on recidivism instead of on a goal such as improved writing. Realistically, the peculiarities of correctional education must strive toward both objectives. First, educators argue, it must meet educational goals—both academic and vocational. In addition, it should meet certain rehabilitative goals, as measured by things such as reduced involvement in delinquency. At present, we have only a limited idea about the kind of educational programs available in juvenile custodial institutions, and we know even less about how effective those programs are in meeting either goal.

Recognizing there is a significant theoretical and research link between school performance and delinquency, it is surprising and disappointing how little attention has been paid to identifying and addressing the specific educational needs of juveniles in custodial facilities. We know, for example, that the direct relationship between literacy level and employment earnings means juveniles and young adults who do poorly in school will have problems in the labor market (Coffey & Gemignani, 1994). Because it is clear that currently—and more so in the future—jobs must require higher levels of literacy, math, and reasoning skills, educational programming in juvenile custodial facilities requires more attention from researchers, administrators, and policymakers.

Many of the studies linking school failure and delinquency have focused on children with learning disabilities; they have also considered mild mental retardation and environmental factors such as family structure, parental supervision, and abuse. Studies summarized by Coffey and Gemignani show that **learning disabled (LD)** youths engage in more delinquent acts than non-LD youths. Also, LD youths are more likely to be arrested than are non-LD youths who also commit delinquent acts. Particularly striking is the finding that the odds of being adjudicated are 220 percent greater for LD youths than for non-LD youths. Finally, there are estimates that as many as 40 percent of youth in correctional facilities may have some form of learning disability (Gemignani, 1994).

A learning disability, which often involves difficulty in understanding or using the spoken or written language, does not appear to be the result of low IQ or poor motivation. Reasons offered to explain the link between learning disabilities and delinquency include a belief that LD children have cognitive and other deficiencies that predispose them to delinquent behavior (e.g., poor impulse control, aggression, irritability), or that the disability leads to poor school performance, which in turn leads to events such as repeating grades, behavior problems, negative peer grouping, and delinquency. Another hypothesis suggests that LD children are not really engaging in more delinquent behavior; they are simply treated more harshly by the various juvenile justice officials because they do not defend or explain themselves very well, and they may appear awkward or socially inept to those officials. Other research suggests that it is not necessary to wait for clarification regarding the causal link between learning disabilities and delinquency before doing something about it—especially when "doing something" refers to achieving educational goals if not rehabilitation ones. The best example is in the specific area of reading and writing deficiencies.

A Reading and Writing Program. Many youths in juvenile detention and correctional facilities experience reading problems. A significant number read below the fourth-grade level and are, therefore, considered functionally illiterate, and many of those reading above that level still lag as much as two to four years below grade level (Coffey & Gemignani, 1994; Hodges, Giuliotti, & Porpotage, 1994). Deficiencies at such levels are especially hard to overcome in a short time, but that is just what teachers at juvenile correctional facilities (even more so at detention facilities) must try to do.

Hodges et al. (1994) report on a project that was designed to improve the literacy level of youths in juvenile detention and correctional facilities. Language arts teachers, staff, and volunteers in the project facilities were trained in instructional methods designed to rapidly improve students' comprehension, especially those students with reading disabilities. Youths at facilities in Mississippi showed dramatic—and statistically significant—gains in the areas of spelling, word recognition, oral reading, reading comprehension, and total reading scores. These gains were particularly impressive because they occurred after just thirty-eight to seventy-one hours of instruction. The key ingredients in the gains are considered by several researchers (Brunner, 1993; Hodges et al., 1994) to be instruction in phonics along with immediate and positive feedback that encourages the students to strive for success—an approach not customarily found in schools. Figure 12.5 shows a sample of a student's writing before and after the instruction. In addition to improvement in writing, the sample suggests there might also be an improvement in attitude. It is this type of educational program that may enable correctional education to meet the challenge of accomplishing both educational and rehabilitative goals.

Help Wanted

Job Title: Probation/Truancy Tracker

Position Description: Trackers investigate incidents of reported truancies and ensure school attendance of juvenile probationers by coordinating efforts with school officials, law enforcement, and parents as all those parties seek to identify and address school truancy. Trackers also keep appropriate records, participate in grant writing, and testify in court.

Qualifications: Applicants should have an associate's or bachelor's degree in criminal justice, sociology, psychology, social work, or a related human services field. Specific skills in written and oral communication are desirable. Must have a valid driver's license and be able to pass criminal history and child abuse background checks.

For examples of career opportunities in this field, visit the various state departments of corrections or youth services. An example is the employment opportunities in Ohio at *www.state.oh.us/dys/Employment.html.*

Programs for Serious and Violent Offenders

In December 1993, the National Council on Crime and Delinquency began a search for effective programs in juvenile corrections (Krisberg, Currie, & Onek, 1995). Using both descriptive information and evaluation data, promising programs were identified in the categories of immediate sanctions (such as day treatment centers and home-based programs), intermediate sanctions (e.g., intensive supervision probation), and secure corrections. Some examples of immediate sanctions are reviewed in Chapter 15, which covers rehabilitation programs, and a few examples of intermediate sanctions are offered in the next section of this chapter,

FIGURE 12.5

Student Writing Samples—Before and After Instruction

Source: From Hodges, J., Giuliotti, N., & Porpotage, F. M. (1994). *Improving literacy skills of juvenile detainees* [NCI 150707]. Juvenile Justice Bulletin. Washington, DC: Office of Juvenile Justice and Delinquency Prevention.

Figure 3

9/17/93

Student Writing Sample—Before Instruction

David H.

What makes me angry

when people do not beliuc And they talked ... with me sometimes they want to fight so I say what ever floats your boat. make your move But does not slove thing so when I get angry I talk my friends they help out in some ways my mom always said the Bigger they are the fall. so do not people you get angry because it is thing to do so please stop before a lot of people get. Kill.

Figure 4

12/10/93

Student Writing Sample—After Instruction

David H.

It was three days before Christmas. and Santa was very sick. The little kids had their sacks on their fireplace ready for Santa, but they thought Santa was not going to deliver their presents because they heard he was sick.

"What do you want me to do?" Said Mrs. Claus. "Go get me my bag." and in his bag he had some medicine. He went to sleep for awhile. Then when He got up he felt good. Then he started to get the presents ready. Santa Claus was worried because he knew that David H.'s bad men were coming to stop him.

Santa tried to leave before they came. When Santa was going to his shop, David H. and the bad guys were there. They said, "if you move, I will steal your reindeer. Please don't steal my reindeer, because the kids need their toys. Then the bad guys said I will not steal your reindeer if you give me and my family gifts. Santa said, "I only give gifts to good boys and girls. So David asked, "How can I change?" Then Santa Said, "you can start by Saying you are sorry for what you tried to do." Then Santa said, "Come with me." They got the Sleigh. They started going to deliver gifts to the people. After they delivered all the gifts, Santa went to David H.'s house. He told David's wife he tried to stop Christmas. They had a long talk. Santa did give them gifts. Then he went back to the North pole.

David and his friends learned what Christmas was about.

"Community-Based Responses." Here we will look at one of the effective programs in the category of secure corrections—the Florida Environmental Institute.

The Florida Environmental Institute (FEI) is also known as "The Last Chance Ranch." Krisberg et al. (1995) describe FEI as a facility for serious juvenile offenders that is located in a remote area of the Florida Everglades. It is not a locked facility, but because it is completely surrounded by forests and swamp, it is considered a secure facility. FEI has a capacity of only forty youths—twenty in the residential program and twenty in a nonresidential aftercare component. When the small population and the correspondingly low staff-to-student ratio are combined with the facility's remote location, public safety is appropriately protected.

Because Florida law allows juveniles found guilty in criminal court to be treated by the juvenile justice system, the youths referred to FEI come from both the adult and the juvenile courts. On average, the youths have eighteen prior offenses and eleven and a half prior felonies. Almost two-thirds are committed for crimes against persons and the rest for chronic property or drug offenses. The typical length of participation in FEI is eighteen months, with at least nine months being in the residential part of the program.

FEI's program philosophy is set in motion using the graduated release process used in the days of Maconochie and Crofton (see Chapter 3). After a three-day orientation program in which treatment plans are established, work projects assigned, and bonding begins between staff and student, the youths enter Phase 1 of the program. During Phase 1, work and education are emphasized as the students earn points to move to the next phase. At Phase 2, students participate in paid work projects that provide them with funds to help make restitution payments. Near the end of the stage, the program's community coordinator takes the students back to their community, where the coordinator helps the students secure aftercare job placement and assists in rebuilding family relationships. During Phase 3, the students live in the community under a strict curfew. Should they break their curfew or engage in criminal activity, they are returned to the residential part of the program. Aftercare staff, working with caseloads of six, are able to contact the students at least four times per week. These aftercare workers assist the student with job searches, family problems, and other issues (Krisberg et al., 1995).

Two studies conducted with FEI students show results that are considered quite promising. Neither study used control groups designed specifically as an experimental comparison, so optimism must be tempered. In one study of twenty-one FEI graduates, only one-third of the sample was convicted of a new crime during a three-year follow-up. Studies of training school releases indicate recidivism rates of 50 to 70 percent. In the other study, which included youths in seven different residential programs, just over one-third of the FEI youths were referred again to juvenile court during a one-year follow-up period. Of the seven programs considered, the FEI youths not only had fewer new referrals to juvenile court (percentages in the other programs ranged from 47 to 73) but also had no readjudications or recommittal—compared with readjudications of 20 to 50 percent for the other facilities (Krisberg et al., 1995).

It appears that institutional programs for juvenile offenders can reduce recidivism if the program and facility are conducive to encouraging positive change in the young person. Facilities that combine (1) a residential component with small numbers of youths, as opposed to the large-capacity traditional training schools, with (2) aftercare programs that emphasize intense supervision, rather than simply returning the youth to the community, consistently show positive results. Yet despite the occasional optimism aroused by programs at some institutions, researchers increasingly point to community-based programs as the best way to rehabilitate juvenile offenders without presenting extreme risk to public safety.

COMMUNITY-BASED RESPONSES

In the early 1970s, Massachusetts made a move that was dramatic for that time and for this—the state closed its traditional training schools for delinquent youths and resorted to community-based treatment. Today Massachusetts relies on a network of small, secure programs for the most serious juvenile offenders (about 15 percent of all commitments) coupled with a broad range of highly structured community-based programs for the majority of committed youths (Krisberg et al., 1995). In 1989 the National Council on Crime and Delinquency studied the Massachusetts system and found the recidivism rates to be equal to or better than most jurisdictions throughout the country. In addition, the Massachusetts approach is very cost-effective with an estimated savings of $11 million annually by relying on community-based care. Utah's juvenile justice system also relies on community-based programs for most committed youths, and it too has resulted in large declines in the frequency and severity of offending after correctional intervention. Krisberg et al. (1995) reviewed studies of various individual and state-level programs and were led to conclude that "well-structured community-based programs are at least as effective as, and sometimes more effective than, traditional training schools, and at a lower cost" (p. 137).

Quite a few community-based programs for juvenile offenders at all levels of seriousness can be considered effective (see the review by Krisberg et al., 1995). The most frequently used disposition for all types of cases coming before the juvenile court is probation. In 1996 over half of the adjudicated cases resulted in probation (Stahl, 1999b). The work of juvenile probation officers is very similar to that of adult probation officers. As a result it is not necessary to repeat the information covered in Chapter 7. Instead, we will concentrate on how probation is modified to handle two particular offender populations—adolescent sex offenders and juvenile gang offenders—and the link between juvenile violence and drugs.

Adolescent Sex Offenses

Prior to about 1980, sexual offenses by juveniles were often dismissed as no more than adolescent adjustment reactions or as exploratory experimentation. More recently the behavior has been viewed as more serious in itself and as indicating continued problems in the future. Adolescent sex offenders are now considered an important group for offense-specific programming; research is showing that many adult sex offenders began sexually inappropriate behavior at an early age, with their adjustment problems becoming progressively more severe (McShane & Krause, 1993). Weinrott (1996) reports that juvenile sex offenders are likely to have their first offense when they are about thirteen or fourteen years old. According to Table 38 in the *1998 Uniform Crime Reports*, 17 percent of all arrests for the crime of forcible rape were of persons under age eighteen (6 percent were under age fifteen). Seventeen percent of all arrests for sexual offense (forcible rape and prostitution are excluded) were of persons under age eighteen (9 percent were under age fifteen). Research findings show that adolescents are responsible for over half the molestations of boys and for 15 to 20 percent of sexual abuse of girls (Torbet, 1993). Sex offending by juveniles is obviously an area needing close attention, and early intervention is increasingly being advocated.

Not surprisingly, the naming of juvenile sex offenses as a problem has preceded the identification of appropriate responses by justice and therapy professionals. A number of theories are suggested regarding the cause of adolescent sex offending, and a variety of factors is to be considered in treatment attempts (see Torbet, 1993; Weinrott, 1996). Thus far, the resulting treatment programs show considerable similarity in the fundamental approaches taken. That similarity is more a result of the field being heavily influenced by a core group of pioneers than by theoretical or research agreement about what techniques are most successful. Torbet (1993) explains that contemporary treatment programs for juvenile sex offenders share a philosophy that places their primary concern with the victims and community protection. Intervention strategies come from several different models (e.g., behavioral-cognitive, psychosocial, and education), and specific techniques include group, family, and individual treatment. The treatment process often strives to have the offenders accept responsibility for their acts, develop empathy for their victims, work on anger and stress management, and to recognize their thinking errors.

Some programs for juvenile sex offenders are provided in secure juvenile facilities, but several community-based programs are also found. The Adolescent Sex Offender Treatment Program, operated by the Kent County (Michigan) Juvenile Court, offers an alternative to institutional treatment for low-risk youths adjudicated for a sex offense. The program provides those youths with assessment and treatment services, using various treatment interventions to encourage them to accept responsibility for their actions and to develop healthier ways of coping with their emotional needs. Similarly, the Sexual Behavior Problems Program in Akron, Ohio, uses services such as monitoring, risk assessment, outpatient treatment, and therapy to assist youths in understanding and controlling their sexual behavior (Krisberg et al., 1995). It seems likely that the importance of targeting this offense category will continue to give rise to specific programs addressing the problem of juvenile sexual offenses.

Juvenile Gang Offenders

Today we are arresting more gang members than ever before; we are getting more convictions than ever before; and we are getting longer sentences than ever before. But ironically, we have more gangs than ever before.

—Frank Radke, Chicago Police Department

At the beginning of this chapter, we learned that juveniles between ages ten to eighteen constitute about 12 percent of the U.S. population, but they make up 16 percent of the arrests for violent crime. Of particular concern is the increased involvement of juveniles in gangs. Bilchik (1999a) reports that the juvenile gang problem is affecting communities of all sizes and in all regions of the United States. It is also apparent that gang members account for a disproportionate number of delinquent acts and a greater number of more serious crimes. The involvement of these youths in any type of crime is worrisome, but the public has expressed particular concern about these violent criminal acts.

That concern seems well placed because the increased involvement of juveniles in violent crime is changing the very nature of some of those crimes. Consider the crime of murder, for example. The *Uniform Crime Reports* record a juvenile gang killing whenever the perpetrator, but not necessarily the victim, is associated with a juvenile gang—regardless of the perpetrator's age. This means some gang leaders who are over age eighteen will be counted as being arrested for a juvenile gang killing. But despite that recording quirk, the category remains an important aspect of juvenile delinquent behavior. Prior to 1980, the number of murders categorized as a juvenile gang killing was well below 200 per year. The number peaked

Some of the increased involvement of juveniles in violent crime is attributed to their association with juvenile gangs. The gangs, as this photo shows, can be gangs of females as well as gangs of males.

at 1,158 in 1995 before declining to 627 in 1998. Also important is the weapon used in such murders. Whereas 65 percent of all murders nationally are committed with a firearm, 94 percent of the victims of juvenile gang killings were slain with firearms in 1998. Clearly, juveniles are becoming more involved in violent crime generally, in murder particularly, and in gang-related killings specifically.

In a survey of prosecutors' offices around the country, Johnson, Webster, and Connors (1995) found those court officials were often frustrated with factors that hamper the prosecution of gang members. They noted, for example, that state juvenile codes were not designed for the serious violence characterizing contemporary street gang crime. Transfers of serious juvenile offenders into the adult court system are not always easily accomplished, especially in jurisdictions with a strong tradition favoring the adjudication and treatment of juveniles only within the juvenile court and corrections systems. As a result, juvenile gang members sometimes pass through the system without serving any sentence. In jurisdictions with a shortage of detention and corrections facilities, juveniles—even those with prior convictions—may receive only intensive probation for a felony charge (Johnson et al., 1995). Los Angeles provides an example of why some prosecutors are frustrated.

Specialized Gang Supervision Program. Los Angeles County's Specialized Gang Supervision Program (SGSP) is a community-based response to gang-linked offenders. Gang membership is extensive in this county's juvenile probation population, but the SGSP is specifically geared toward the most serious and violent gang members. About forty probation officers operate in five regions throughout the county as they keep track of about fifty persons on their caseload. Because gang activity does not stop when a youth reaches age eighteen, the caseload often includes both juveniles and youthful adult offenders.

The probation officer's job in the SGSP is primarily law enforcement because a key component of the program is to bring gang participants into court for any violation of probation conditions. This is based on the assumption that violent activities in the community, especially gang-related violence, is reduced by close monitoring, swift court action for probation violations, and stepped-up surveillance of gang activity (Krisberg, Rodriguez, Bakke, Newenfeldt, & Steel, 1994). In addition to the law enforcement role, the SGSP probation officers stay informed about gang activity and potential confrontations between warring groups.

The SGSP's emphasis on enforcement, rather than rehabilitation or reintegration, highlights an important question when considering the placement of violent offenders in the community: At what point might public safety be compromised? Treating violent juvenile offenders in the community rather than at a secure correctional facility is often criticized because of the widespread perception that security and control do not mix well with community-based intervention strategies. Torbet (1993) suggests such a concern is misplaced (see "Placing Serious Offenders in Community Programs") because it is possible to have a community-based program that provides security for citizens while meeting needs and providing opportunities that are not met or provided for in an institutional setting.

The response to juveniles who commit violent crimes has always included placement in secure correctional facilities, but community-based programs are increasingly necessary if not popular. Arguments for placing violent juvenile offenders in community-based programs are often based on the understanding that most of these offenders have experienced high levels of social deprivation. As a

Spotlight ON CONTEMPORARY ISSUES

Placing Serious Offenders in Community Programs

The idea that violent juvenile offenders can, or even should, be placed in community programs is disquieting to some people. Part of this reaction is likely the result of a belief that violent juveniles are not getting their just deserts unless they are locked up. But the disturbing feeling is also probably linked to a concern for public safety. Is it really safe to have violent juvenile offenders at liberty in the community? Several programs believe it is not only safe but it is also the most effective way to respond to those juveniles.

Torbet (1993) says the notion that control and treatment are incompatible is a false belief. In fact, she argues, developing social and personal controls are part of what occurs in well-developed, community-based programs. The controls are part of a catalog of social skills that are internalized during the normal maturational process for most youngsters. Because the population of more seriously delinquent youths typically has not internalized such controls, there is actually more opportunity to transmit the skills and internalize the controls in community-based settings than in institutional facilities.

A second factor hindering the use of community-based programs for serious juvenile offenders is the belief that these programs are too lax and cannot act as a deterrent to misconduct. However, the notion of laxity is not supported in the research on the effectiveness of such programs. How lax or strict the program is for a particular youngster is determined by the level of surveillance a particular offender needs and by the youth's progress within the program. When increased physical mobility, autonomy, and responsibility are provided as privileges to be earned, limit setting and constructive reactions to stress are reinforced. Similarly, rule-violating behavior and lack of progress in the program can result in the loss of privileges. Rather than being unsuitable settings for more serious juvenile offenders, community-based programs may be the most appropriate location for encouraging the internalization of needed controls and social skills.

The Center for the Study and Prevention of Violence (CSPV) has identified ten model programs that effectively deter violence when the programs are appropriately implemented. Visit the CSPV site at *www.colorado.edu/cspv/blueprints/model/index.html*, and read about these model programs. Choose two programs to describe in detail, and explain why you think these programs are effective.

result of that deprivation, these particular youths need basic rehabilitation into society (Torbet, 1993). This is most easily accomplished in the community itself where, in a tightly knit and highly controlled community-based environment, the juvenile has access to important reintegration resources such as schools, churches, work, recreation, vocational training, and family.

Most of the violent juvenile offenders who are placed in a community-based program have first served some time in a secure correctional facility. Upon release from the facility, they may be placed in a community-based program (either residential or nonresidential) as part of an aftercare process. For an example, we return to California to consider a community-based program that has a greater emphasis on rehabilitation and reintegration than does the SGSP.

Parole Branch Services of the California Youth Authority. The California Youth Authority (CYA) is responsible for an amazingly diverse population of juveniles and young adult offenders. In an attempt to meet the various needs of that population, the CYA's Parole Branch Services operates different parole programs with specialized caseloads. The system assigns reduced caseloads to parole agents, who are thereby able to give more concentrated, in-depth services to youths with special needs and problems (Krisberg et al., 1994). Included among the caseloads are youths with problems in such specialized areas as strong gang affiliation, sex offenses, substance abuse, and psychiatric problems.

To meet the special needs of these offenders while providing for public safety, the parole agents may have caseloads as small as fifteen youths. A small caseload is considered especially important during the critical transition period from institutional living to community living. Under the Intensive Reentry Program, CYA parolees are contacted biweekly for the first thirty days after release from secure confinement, followed by weekly contacts for the next sixty days. Youths with drug and alcohol problems undergo substance abuse testing twice a month and, along with the other parolees, may receive employment, education, or job training assistance, as well as individual and group counseling.

Selected parolees, such as those newly released or those exhibiting behavior indicating a possible return to a delinquent lifestyle, may be placed under electronic monitoring. The technology is used primarily to enforce home curfews, and those curfew times are tightened or relaxed depending on the youth's compliance with rules and progress in the program (Krisberg et al., 1994). The approach here clearly emphasizes prevention and enforcement—strategies that are not typically associated with probation. However, it does highlight a tendency around the country to respond to violent juvenile offenders through increased efforts by law enforcement efforts rather than trying to "correct" the misbehavior through rehabilitation and reintegration strategies.

Response by Enforcement or Correction? At a national conference on gangs, sponsored by the OJJDP, policymakers from around the country heard presenters explain the strategies they believe are needed to respond to juvenile gangs (Bryant, 1989). Here too the main tactics are those that are directed toward prevention and enforcement. Representatives from cities were told that communities must overcome the political denial about the existence of gangs. Also, graffiti must not be tolerated because allowing graffiti to stand is simply conceding public and private property to gangs. Schools must establish clear expectations about acceptable behavior and must maintain a visible staff presence on campus to create a sense of safety that also shows gang members that they do not control the school. Changes in the juvenile justice system must also occur, so that more attention is given to the youngest kids who have committed the least serious offenses instead of concentrating efforts and sanctions on older children who have committed more serious offenses. Ira Reiner, the Los Angeles district attorney, advocated intensive attention to young offenders, including status offenders, the very first time they come to the attention of law enforcement. Under current procedures, he argued, the juvenile justice system operates "like a hospital that concentrates on terminal patients—for whom there is virtually no hope—at the expense of those who could be saved through early treatment" (quoted in Bryant, 1989, p. 5).

Rehabilitative and reintegrative responses to violent juvenile behavior have been tried over the years and continue today, but they appear less frequently than do social responses that emphasize enforcement and prevention. Siegel and Senna (1991) explain that social workers were active in rehabilitating and reintegrating youth gangs in Chicago during the late nineteenth century. In the 1950s, when Chicago reportedly had high levels of gang activity, social workers were sent into the community to work directly with gang members on their own turf. More recent examples aimed at reintegration include the House of Umoja project. This program was started by the Fattah family in Philadelphia in response to their concern about one of their children, who was a gang member. The Fattah family took into their home other gang kids and instilled in them a pride in their African heritage and culture. At any one time, groups of fifteen to twenty-five youths were provided food, shelter, surrogate parenting, and employment opportunities (Siegel & Senna, 1991).

Other urban communities are trying to reestablish strong neighborhood-based centers and programs in efforts to build a sense of community. It is believed that strong positive community ties and a sense of collective responsibility will lessen the attractiveness of youth gangs (Huff, 1995). One example of such a community effort is Cleveland's Scholarship in Escrow program. The program was designed to encourage kids to stay in school by establishing accounts for students enrolled in seventh through twelfth grades. The student's account is credited with ten dollars for every C earned in school, twenty dollars for every B, and forty dollars for every A. The money goes into an interest-earning scholarship fund from which the student can draw to help pay expenses at a college or technical school (Huff, 1995).

So far neither the enforcement and prevention nor the rehabilitation and reintegration approaches have been reported as having significantly reduced juvenile gang activity. Efforts continue at local, state, and federal levels to find effective ways to handle the problem of juvenile gangs.

Juvenile Violence and the Drug–Crime Connection

Since 1985 there have been striking changes in juvenile crime. The homicide rate has doubled, as have the number of homicides committed with guns and the arrest rate of nonwhites for drug offenses. Blumstein (1995) proposes the hypothesis that these changes are linked to the rapid growth of the crack cocaine markets in the mid-1980s. "To service that growth, juveniles were recruited, they were armed with guns that are standard tools of the drug trade, and these guns then were diffused into the larger community of juveniles" (Blumstein, 1995, p. 6). The process can be described as progressing through four stages: recruitment, guns as self-protection, diffusion of guns, and violent outcomes.

The progress toward violent offenses by juveniles begins with the illicit drug industry, which recruits juveniles because (1) they work more cheaply than adults, (2) the sanctions they face are less severe, (3) they tend to be daring and willing to take risks that more mature adults would refuse, and (4) they—especially many urban black juveniles—may see the work as one of the few ways available to achieve economic livelihood.

Because the juvenile recruits to the drug industry are likely to carry large sums of money, as well as to be in possession of a valuable product, they carry guns for self-protection. In addition, because pushers cannot call on the police if they are robbed, the gun becomes a way of resolving disputes. As these armed drug workers move about their community, including the schools, other juveniles are likely to arm themselves. Some may do so as protection from the juveniles in the drug industry, but others may take weapons as a status symbol. The escalation is similar to an "arms race" with the appearance of more guns in the community becoming an incentive for any single individuals to arm themselves.

When an increased presence of deadly weapons is combined with some of the characteristics of teenagers, violence often results. For example, in the past the combination of teenage recklessness, bragging, and a preference for settling disputes with physical force resulted in a bloody nose. Today easy access to lethal weapons means the bloody nose is replaced with more serious injury (Blumstein, 1995, p. 6). When one includes in this already harmful mix the problems associated with extreme poverty, single-parent households, educational failures, and a pervasive sense of hopelessness about one's economic situation, the likelihood of a violent outcome is worsened.

A proposed response by society to break the progression toward violence by juveniles begins with aggressive steps to confiscate guns from juveniles carrying them on the streets. Blumstein (1995) recognizes that laws permitting confiscation of guns from juveniles are almost universal, but he suggests they require more active and skillful enforcement—including the use of technology to detect concealed weapons from a distance. He also notes that the presence of guns in the drug markets results from the fact that these markets are criminalized. Blumstein does not call for the immediate legalization of drugs, but he does suggest that as people weigh the costs of criminalization against the probable consequences of greater use of dangerous drugs, they should count juvenile homicides as one of the negative consequences of the current drug policy.

This brief note on the possible link between violence by juveniles and the illicit drug industry has not suggested any real efforts at "corrections." As with the earlier discussion of how Los Angeles emphasizes enforcement when responding to gang members on probation, and the emphasis on enforcement and prevention stressed at the OJJDP national conference on gangs, Blumstein's proposal also highlights the need for prevention and enforcement to turn the tide of increased juvenile violence. We have also seen some examples of communities that are trying to accomplish change through various intervention strategies. Neither the proponents of enforcement and prevention nor the advocates of rehabilitation and reintegration would argue that their focus is the only one a community should take. Realistically, however, restricted funds will mean that communities must decide which policy can best accomplish their specific short- and long-term goals. Some communities will choose to emphasize programs that are more likely to involve the efforts of law enforcement, whereas others will offer more support to programs through corrections agencies. Until an appropriate balance of the two is found, the social response to juvenile offenders, especially violent offenders, is likely to emphasize either enforcement or corrections.

WHERE DO WE GO FROM HERE?

Public opinion polls about how to respond to juveniles who commit violent crime show that most people (68 percent) think they should be treated the same as adults. Only about one-fourth of the public believes the programs designed to protect and rehabilitate juvenile offenders, rather than to punish them, are even moderately successful (Maguire & Pastore, 1995). U.S. jurisdictions are increasingly responding to such opinions by toughening their stand against juvenile offenders. We have seen very specific movement in some states away from a parens patriae model and toward a just deserts model of juvenile justice. Of course, such a trend should not be surprising because the adult justice system is currently in a Retributive era. Presumably, legislators will continue to propose and pass laws that aim to reduce the level of delinquent behavior—especially the increasingly serious and violent versions. Hurst and McHardy (1991) note that "in our desperation, we have even begun to pass laws that would make it a crime for parents to produce a delinquent child" (p. 67).

The contemporary view of getting tough on criminals is widening to include delinquents. The pessimism is summed up nicely, if not encouragingly, by Hurst and McHardy who suggest that unless our families are stabilized, our school systems improved, and our neighborhoods regain a sense of community, the juvenile justice system in the twenty-first century may not even have jurisdiction of most youth age fourteen and older who are charged with a felony crime. The change, they say, will not be the result of any positive reason but "rather because we have grown afraid of our own children and don't seem to know quite what else to do—other than lock them up as criminals" (Hurst & McHardy, 1991, p. 67). It seems that the optimism with which the juvenile court was established has been dampened by perceived and actual increases in delinquent behavior. Taken to an extreme, it may be unnecessary for corrections textbooks in the future to have a separate chapter on juveniles because they will be treated in the same manner as adults. However, many would see those gains in convenience to be at the expense of compassion and assistance.

SUMMARY

The primary focus of this book is on adult offenders and adult corrections. In this chapter attention is turned instead to juvenile offenders and to some of the ways society responds to those young people.

THE JUVENILE JUSTICE SYSTEM

- A separate system of juvenile justice did not appear in the United States until 1899, when the first juvenile court was established in Cook County (Chicago), Illinois.
- In 1825 the New York House of Refuge opened under the management of the Society for the Reformation of Juvenile Delinquents and became the first institution specifically for juvenile delinquents.
- By 1850 new child-saving organizations began condemning the houses of refuge. These new reformers believed the family, not the institution, was the best reform school.
- They began a placing-out system, in which city children were apprenticed out to western farm families.
- The placing-out procedure continued to advance the identification of juveniles as deserving special attention by social control authorities and agencies.
- By the end of the century, a rehabilitative ideal gained acceptance and, playing on concerns about children becoming adult criminals, social reformers argued that juvenile crime was reversible.

PROCESSING JUVENILE OFFENDERS

Juvenile courts have jurisdiction over cases in which young people have been neglected or otherwise mistreated, but the court's jurisdiction in two other types of cases is more relevant to corrections:

- Delinquency cases in which the juvenile commits an act that would be a crime if it had been an adult who committed it.
- Status offense cases for situations in which a youth behaves inappropriately for a person of his or her age.

INSTITUTION-BASED RESPONSES

Sometimes the result of a juvenile's court appearance is confinement to an institution. Because there are no agreed-upon criteria for defining what constitutes a juvenile (maximum ages vary by state), what counts as a juvenile facility (public, private, residential, nonresidential, secure, nonsecure), and whether to count juveniles held in adult facilities, it is difficult to get an accurate count of the number of juveniles in institutions.

- Institution-based programs for juvenile offenders include some that are found in adult institutions, such as boot camps, but also some that are more clearly designed for young people, such as educational programs.
- Programs to address problems of learning disabilities and to increase reading and writing skills were highlighted as showing potential for meeting both educational and rehabilitative goals in the institutional setting.

COMMUNITY-BASED RESPONSES

Community-based responses to juvenile offenders rather than commitment to an institution are more frequently found in all jurisdictions. Particular types of offenses and offenders that are receiving attention in the community setting are sex offenses and gang offenders.

WHERE DO WE GO FROM HERE?

Contemporary responses to juvenile offenders seem to be moving away from the protection and rehabilitation approach of the early twentieth century and to a more punitive and incapacitative approach.

- That is consistent with current attitudes toward adult offenders and, therefore, may not be very surprising.
- But because of a continuing perception by some people that juvenile offenders need a different response by society than do adult offenders, there are consistent calls for a balance between law enforcement and corrections.

KEY TERMS AND CONCEPTS

adjudicated delinquent (p. 439)
aftercare (p. 454)
age–crime curve (p. 434)
blended sentences (p. 445)
informal probation (p. 447)
judicial waiver (p. 444)
learning disabled (LD) (p. 456)
nonpetitioned case (p. 447)
parens patriae (p. 438)
prosecutorial discretion (p. 444)
status offenses (p. 438)
statutorily excluding (p. 445)

Discussion Questions

1. Although they may not seem especially serious themselves, status offenses might increase a juvenile's involvement in criminal activities (e.g., runaways stealing food). Discuss ways that you believe school, police, court, and corrections officials should respond to status offenders who have apparently committed no other offense.
2. Suggest some reasons why educational programs offered in institutions for juvenile offenders should be structured differently than those offered in regular public schools. If a differently structured educational program is desirable in a juvenile facility, would it also be a better structure for the traditional public school setting?
3. Discuss possible explanations for why the percentage of minorities is higher in public than in private juvenile facilities. What steps could be taken to reduce that discrepancy?
4. What would be some good community-based gang intervention programs in a city with a population over 100,000? Would the same or different programs be desirable in cities with a population under 100,000? What factors other than population size might affect the success of a gang intervention strategy?

UNCONDITIONAL RELEASE FROM PRISON

Expiration of Sentence

Commutation and Pardon

CONDITIONAL RELEASE FROM PRISON

Forerunners to Parole

A History of Parole in the United States

THE CONTEMPORARY PAROLE PROCESS

Deciding Parole

Parole Conditions and Parole Officers

Parole Completion and Revocation

Criticism of Parole

REINTEGRATION PROGRAMS

Furlough

Work and Education Release

Residential Community Corrections

LOSS AND RESTORATION OF CIVIL RIGHTS

Civil Disabilities after Release

Sex Offender Registration and Notification Laws

CONDITIONAL RELEASE IN OTHER COUNTRIES

Conditional Release in Canada

Conditional Release in Asia and the Pacific

SUMMARY

KEY TERMS AND CONCEPTS

DISCUSSION QUESTIONS

chapter 13

RELEASE AND POSTINSTITUTIONAL PENALTIES

In the 1994 movie *The Shawshank Redemption,* Brooks Hatlin (played by James Whitmore) is released from prison to a world of freedom. Unfortunately, Brooks had been in prison so long that it felt as though he was being kicked out of his home and placed in bizarre and frightening surroundings. Brooks makes legitimate attempts at adjusting to his newfound autonomy. He gets a job at a market and feeds the birds in the park. But in the end, this version of freedom is too lonely, and Brooks packs his things, writes his name on the header above the door, and hangs himself.

What, if any, obligation does the government have to men and women being released from prison? At one time, upon completing their sentence, prisoners were simply given a new pair of shoes, a new suit, a bus ticket back to the county where they were convicted, and sent on their way. Even prisoners who served a relatively short sentence could find themselves a bit disoriented upon returning to their community. Just think of the changes that occur in your hometown after an absence as short as nine months away at college. Old buildings have come down, and new buildings have gone up; old friends have moved away, and at the video store—where you once knew everyone and they all knew you—unfamiliar faces are asking if they can help you.

Probably the most reasonable argument for simply opening the gate and sending the prisoner off on her own is that she has finished her sentence and the government has no right to continue surveillance or provide assistance. On the other hand, the government might share some responsibility for helping the newly released inmate readjust to life outside prison. Certainly those former inmates, like Brooks Hatlin, who have no one on the outside to turn to might benefit from some supervision. But even if Brooks had served a shorter sentence and was returning to his family, he would likely have discovered that rather than easily regaining his role in the household, his wife and children have learned to cope without him.

Professionals working with ex-offenders often explain that the desire to remain free is seldom enough to keep someone straight (Snider, 1999). While sitting in prison there is plenty of time to fantasize about a better life. The difficulties of regaining connections with family and friends, finding a job, and dealing with guilt and frustration often keep the vision of a better life from becoming more than the fantasy it was in prison.

This chapter deals with issues of release and readjustment. It begins by distinguishing two primary types of release: (1) **unconditional release,** returning prisoners to the free community because their sentence was completed (the "open the gate and send them on their way" option) or (2) **conditional release,** allowing prisoners to complete their sentence in the community (the "continue surveillance and provide assistance" option). There are, of course, other possibilities such as death, escape, and the inevitable "other" category, but all three make up only about 6 percent of the releases from state prisons. Release as a result of death (e.g., execution, suicide, illness) occurs in less than 1 percent of the releases, and release by escape in less than 2 percent. Other releases (e.g., transfers to other jurisdictions, release on appeal, temporary releases) account for another 3 percent (Bureau of Justice Statistics, 1999). We are left, then, with the vast majority of state prison releases being either unconditional or conditional releases.

As we see in Table 13.1, even conditional and unconditional releases are divided into additional types. In this chapter we are primarily interested in the con-

TABLE 13.1: Percentage of Sentenced Prisoners Released Conditionally or Unconditionally from State or Federal Jurisdiction by Type of Release, 1996

		CONDITIONAL RELEASE				UNCONDITIONAL RELEASE		
Jurisdiction	Total	Parole	Probation	Supervised Mandatory Release	Other	Expiration of Sentence	Commutation	Other
U.S. total	473,243	30%	6%	38%	4%	21%	0%	1%
Federal	22,875	8%	0%	6%	–	84%	2%	–
State	450,368	31%	6%	39%	4%	17%	0%	1%

Source: From Bureau of Justice Statistics. (1999). *Correctional populations in the United States, 1996* [NCJ 170013]. Washington, DC: Author.

ditional release types, but we will briefly review the unconditional types to provide a complete picture.

Unconditional Release from Prison

Table 13.1 shows that the total of conditional and unconditional releases from state jurisdictions in 1996 was 450,368 prisoners. Of that number, 18 percent were released because they had served their maximum court sentence (expiration of sentence), their maximum sentence was lowered (commutation of sentence), or they benefitted from some other release strategy such as vacated sentences, court-ordered releases, and pardons. Of these release types, we will look briefly at expiration of sentence, commutation of sentence, and pardon.

Expiration of Sentence

It may be surprising that only 18 percent of the state prisoners released in 1996 were released after serving their maximum sentence in prison. And, in fact, today's percentage of release by **expiration of sentence** is considerably lower than it was earlier in the twentieth century. Between 1920 and 1950 about 40 percent of the prisoners released received an unconditional release—primarily as a result of expiration of sentence (Cahalan, 1986). However, as Table 13.2 shows, since the late 1970s the number released under the expiration of sentence requirement has averaged about 16 percent. Many factors have affected whether prisoners are likely to spend their entire sentence in prison. As we see later in this chapter, releasing prisoners before their full sentence is served has been justified as desirable for rehabilitation purposes or as necessary to encourage good behavior in prison. More recently, we hear that prison crowding requires offenders to be released before completing their full sentence so that newly sentenced prisoners can be admitted.

At times the public, or at least the politicians, express frustration that offenders do not actually serve their entire sentence in prison. But before we begin thinking that there has been a dramatic shift toward leniency, we should remember that throughout the twentieth century fewer than one-half the prisoners have been released only because their sentence was completed. Certainly the 16 percent average since 1976 shows a decrease since the early and midtwentieth century. In other

TABLE 13.2: State Prisoners Released Conditionally or Unconditionally by Type of Release, 1976–1996

a) Conditional Release

				PERCENTAGE OF CONDITIONAL RELEASE			
Year	Total Released	Total Conditional	Conditional as Percentage of Total Released	Parole	Supervised Mandatory Release	Probation[a]	Other
1996	479,344	366,632	76.5	38.7	48.4	7.8	5.1
1993	437,099	350,031	80.1	46.3	37.7	6.6	9.3
1982	174,220	133,093	76.4	61.3	28.8	5.7	4.2
1976	124,511	84,225	67.6	87.5	7.4	3.7	1.4

[a]Typically in the form of split sentences of imprisonment followed by probation.

b) Unconditional Release

				PERCENTAGE OF UNCONDITIONAL RELEASE		
Year	Total Released	Total Unconditional	Unconditional as Percentage of Total Released	Expiration of Sentence	Commutation or Pardon	Other
1996	479,344	83,736	17.5	93.4	0.2	6.4
1993	437,099	56,835	13.0	87.3	0.5	12.2
1982	174,220	24,051	13.8	88.8	2.0	3.6
1976	124,511	22,703	18.2	90.5	6.2	3.4

Source: Adapted from (for 1996) Bureau of Justice Statistics. (1999). *Correctional populations in the United States, 1996* [NCJ 170013]. Washington, DC: Author; (for 1993) Bureau of Justice Statistics. (1995). *Correctional populations in the United States, 1993* [NCJ 156241]. Washington, DC: Author; (for 1982) Bureau of Justice Statistics. (1984). *Prisoners in state and federal institutions on December 31, 1982* [NCJ 93311]. Washington, DC: Author; (for 1976) Law Enforcement Assistance Administration. (1978). *Prisoners in state and federal institutions on December 31, 1976* [SD-NPS-PSF-4]. Washington, DC: Author.

words, our system of penal sanctions has a decades-long history of releasing prisoners before their sentences are completed. The real question should not be whether we should do it—it seems we always have? Instead, we should ask whether prisoners released early should have to abide by certain conditions. But before tackling that issue, we will briefly look at another type of unconditional release.

Commutation and Pardon

Commutation of sentence involves the changing of a punishment to one that is less severe. An example would be having a sentence of execution being commuted to one of life imprisonment. Similarly, a person sentenced to life imprisonment might receive a commutation to twenty-four years, or some other specific amount (often matching the time already served). The authority to commute a sentence and the circumstances under which it can be commuted vary from state to state. Abadinsky (1997) found that commutation authority usually lies with either the governor or with a state's board of pardons and parole. Sometimes the governor establishes the criteria for a commutation, but other jurisdictions have statutes setting such criteria as the minimum time an inmate must serve before being considered for commutation. Reasons that a sentence might be commuted include the finding that it is excessive, illegal, or unconstitutional, or the governor or board may simply believe commutation would be in the best interest of society and the inmate (Abadinsky, 1997).

Today's use of commutation emphasizes aspects of the sentence. Historically, commutation of sentence was linked less to the sentence itself and more to an inmate's behavior while in prison. Beginning in the 1830s and spreading quickly, commutation of sentences for good behavior was being used in more than twenty northern states by 1869 (McKelvey, 1977). In this manner, commutation provided a base for the procedure known as good time. But because good time is more typically linked to conditional release procedures, we will hold further discussion until later.

A **pardon,** like commutation of sentence, is another procedure that can result in a prisoner being released early from confinement. Because the concept of crime originated in the idea that a harm to his subjects was a harm to the king, it is not surprising that historically the power to pardon belonged to the monarch. Because the sovereign was harmed, the sovereign had the power to forgive the offense (Cromwell & Killinger, 1994). In the United States this authority to pardon was given first to the legislature, then eventually to the executive branch. Today the president of the United States has the power to pardon for federal offenses, and the state governors, acting alone or with an official board, can pardon offenders of state laws.

Although the pardon was originally seen as a method to right legal wrongs and free the inappropriately convicted innocent citizen, eventually it also became a way to lessen overly severe sentences or to recognize factors not considered at trial (Cromwell & Killinger, 1994). Today pardons for humanitarian reasons are given to old or infirm prisoners, or to those with fatal illnesses. Other pardons seem more for political reasons, such as when general amnesties (general pardons) were given to Solidarity members in Poland or to Vietnam-era draft evaders from the United States.

When pardons are given, the effect (in addition to being released from prison) it has on the offender varies by jurisdiction. In some states, as discussed later in this chapter, pardons relieve the person from the legal consequences of a particular conviction. For example, in many jurisdictions convicted felons are prohibited from purchasing firearms or being licensed to practice certain professions (e.g., attorney, counselor, or physician). A pardon may restore these civil rights in some states.

The basis for granting a pardon also varies by jurisdiction (Abadinsky, 1997, p. 276). In some states, including Florida, Georgia, and New York, a pardon can be granted to persons who prove they are innocent of the crime for which they were convicted. In Georgia, mercy is shown even to people who do not claim innocence but have completed their full sentence obligation. Florida also has some unique forms of pardon that do not imply the offender was innocent but that can restore civil rights if the person was convicted on her or his first offense (first-offender pardon) or has had no further convictions for ten years after completing a sentence (ten-year pardon).

Interestingly, pardons can also be given to persons who are not in prison at the time the pardon is given. In fact, given President Ford's pardon of President Nixon before Nixon had even been charged with a crime, a pardon may not even require a conviction. Usually, though, the person being pardoned has been convicted of a crime. But other than that common feature, the person being pardoned can be in prison, on probation, on parole, or even have completed the sentence months or years earlier.

Despite differences in their effects, to whom they are applied, and their procedures, the unconditional releases all have one thing in common. When a person is released from prison under expiration of sentence, commutation of sentence, or by a pardon, that person is free from any continued supervision by the state. An exception may be the requirement in some states that persons released under expiration of sentence from a sex crime conviction must inform local officials about their presence in the community—even though that person has completed all required sentence obligations. Typically, however, persons released through unconditional release are returned to the community without, just as the term implies, any conditions. Other prisoners are released with the requirement that they abide by certain conditions or risk being returned to prison. The most common of these is parole, which we now look at in some depth.

Conditional Release from Prison

Conditional release refers to those releases through which the prisoner, upon violating the conditions of the release, can be imprisoned again for any part of the sentence from which he or she was released. As shown in Table 13.2, 77 percent of all releases from state jurisdiction in 1996 were under some form of conditional release. Some were released to probation status (7.8 percent of all conditional releases) under programs such as shock probation. About 5 percent were released under "other" circumstances such as home arrest programs, work releases, or intensive supervision programs. The other two conditional release categories in Table 13.2 make up the remaining 87 percent: 38.7 percent parole and 48.4 percent supervised mandatory release.

Supervised mandatory release, also called mandatory conditional release, includes all inmates who—by law—are automatically released to the community when they have completed their maximum prison sentence less any good-time credit they have received. But because the full sentence is not really completed, the inmate's release is conditional and may require supervision in the community. In this manner supervised mandatory release is similar to parole, which is not mandatory but does require supervision. Table 13.2 shows a growing use of supervised mandatory releases since the 1970s. Over the same period, there has been a corresponding decrease in the percentage of releases on parole. Actually, supervised mandatory release is used most often in states where parole release has been abolished. However, discussing the abolition of parole before reviewing its origin and operation seems both inefficient and inappropriate. In the interest of chronology, we will delay further discussion of mandatory release until we better understand release on parole.

Parole is often confused with the term *probation,* but the two terms refer to quite different aspects of the justice system. Most simply, probation is a sentence imposed by the judge and usually implies the offender has not been to prison. Parole, on the other hand, happens after a person has been imprisoned and refers to an early release from imprisonment at the discretion of a paroling authority. Of course, few things remain at their simplest level. More complexly, probation is a judge's sentence that allows the offender to remain relatively free in the community under the supervision of a court official—the probation officer. Parole, which is granted by an agency of the executive branch (such as a parole board) or as a result of a statutory requirement (mandatory parole) created by the legislature, is a prisoner's conditional release to the community under the supervision of a state official—the parole officer. Probation and parole also differ in their respective goals. Probation is generally considered to have rehabilitation and treatment as its primary focus. Parole has come to emphasize its incapacitative aspect and, as a continuation of the prison sentence, often places the needs of the community ahead of the offender's needs. As a result, parole stresses control and enforcement over treatment and rehabilitation.

In addition to being confused with probation, parole sometimes suffers an identity crisis because of uncertainty about its function. Over the years parole has been used as a substitute for a pardon (a clemency function), to encourage good behavior by prisoners (a disciplinary function), to help control the size of the prison population (an administrative function), and to assist a released inmate in readjusting to the free community (a rehabilitative function). Given such a variety of jobs, it is little wonder that parole has had a stormy history. A look at that history will better inform us about how and why parole tried to be so many different things. It will also help us understand some of the attacks parole is now suffering.

Forerunners to Parole

Rather than coming into existence as part of a specific plan to achieve a particular objective, parole is more accurately seen as the end result of practical adjustments to problems that arose from the use of imprisonment as punishment. This process becomes clear when we try to identify a chronology of predecessors that clearly leads from parole's grandparent to its parent. It just is not that straightforward. Instead, parole hid in the background while attention was on procedures such as the **mark system** (a prisoner earns "marks" for good behavior) and ticket-of-leave (accumulated "marks" are redeemed for a "ticket" allowing early release from imprisonment) that were used by Alexander Maconochie (see "Parole from a Penal Colony"). But, important as Maconochie was, today's version of parole owes much of its heritage to the work of Sir Walter Crofton and the application of indeterminate sentencing.

In 1853 the English Penal Servitude Act was passed. This act provided for imprisonment in England and Ireland of persons sentenced to fourteen years or less and for transportation to Australia of persons with sentences of more than fourteen years. The act also provided for conditional release via a ticket-of-leave in England for those getting prison sentences. Sir Walter Crofton, appointed as director of the Irish Prison System in 1854, was especially intrigued with this concept of conditional release. Borrowing some ideas from Maconochie in Australia, Crofton developed what came to be called the Irish system of penal administration. Central to that system was a process of graduated release that gave prisoners the responsibility for how short—or how long—their actual time in prison would be. The initial stage in the graduated process involved eight or nine months of solitary confinement. During the first three months of that stage, the prisoner was on reduced rations and not allowed to work. After three months without labor, Crofton believed, even the laziest prisoner would long for something to do. The remaining months of the initial stage continued the solitary confinement but provided the inmate with full rations and work. In the second stage, the prisoner was transferred to another prison and put to work with other inmates. At this point, Maconochie's mark system came into play as the prisoner moved through four classes by earning marks for completing various tasks.

Crofton's most original contribution to prison administration is seen in the third stage: Inmates were transferred to a completely open institution, the first of which was founded in 1856 at Lusk, a few kilometers from Dublin. The prisoners lived in simple barracks with accommodations for a maximum of 100 men (there were not enough women prisoners in Ireland to make as thorough a system practical for them). Crofton instructed the staff of six to abide by two rules of conduct: (1) Staff

HISTORICAL PERSPECTIVES

Parole from a Penal Colony

The idea that prisoners could be released before serving their entire prison sentence has been around since the late eighteenth and early nineteenth centuries. As early as 1790, penal colony governors in Australia were granting British transportees conditional pardons, setting them free, and even giving them grants of land. The early release of prisoners under this ticket-of-leave was earned through good behavior. In 1811 the process became a more formal policy, and in 1834 it was regulated by statute. Under the formal policy, prisoners had to work off a certain portion of their sentence before being released. The 1821 version of the policy provided an eligibility formula, which made men and women serving seven years eligible for a ticket-of-leave after four years. Those with fourteen-year sentences were eligible after six years, and those with life sentences after eight years (Cromwell & Killinger, 1994).

With statutory authorization in 1834, governors could authorize a ticket-of-leave that allowed the men and women transportees to live independently. The catch was that they had to stay in specific locations of Australia rather than being allowed to return to England or Ireland. Transportees showed little interest in this option because few wanted to stay in Australia. Attitudes and procedures began changing in 1840, with the appointment of Alexander Maconochie as governor of the penal colony at Norfolk Island.

Norfolk Island in 1840 had a reputation as a horrible place, where prisoners had been known to prefer hanging to continued living at the penal colony. Maconochie had already shown a level of humanitarianism unfamiliar at many penal colonies while he was assigned to the penal colony at Van Dieman's Land (now Tasmania) from 1836 to 1840. Upon his arrival at Norfolk Island, he quickly initiated changes that he thought would establish a new atmosphere and encourage positive changes in the prisoners. His first official act was to dismantle the gallows. To show his faith in the essential trustworthiness of prisoners, Maconochie and his wife walked among them without protection by bodyguards. He encouraged self-respect among convicts by learning each of their names and by addressing them accordingly. He recorded their occupations and other interests in a little notebook and drew on that information when talking to them. Flogging and chains were abolished (except as necessary for security), prisoners were given knives and forks to eat with, schools and churches were built, and books distributed (Dressler, 1969). These changes decreased the wickedness of the penal colony and served to encourage the transportees. To take advantage of their newfound hope that things could improve, Maconochie initiated a procedure by which prisoners could earn release from the penal colony. This procedure—called the mark system—provided a structure, and even a philosophy, to the concepts of good time and ticket-of-leave.

Under Maconochie's plan, prisoners could earn marks of commendation for good behavior and labor. As they worked themselves through various grades, they were given increased liberties. After accumulating enough marks, they could receive a ticket-of-leave that would allow them to live anywhere—even back in England or Ireland. While under the ticket-of-leave, they were expected to keep the police informed of their residence, but they were not under anyone's supervision. While this sounds like parole, and it certainly is a predecessor, it falls short of being parole because of that lack of supervision and because there was no formal procedures to return to prison those persons who behaved badly on their ticket-of-leave.

Go to ***www.meertech.demon.co.uk/tol/contents.html*** where you will find a research paper on a release procedure for convicts in New South Wales from 1788 to 1850. What was a ticket-of-leave? When and how were tickets issued?

members should convince the prisoner of their faith in him and give him credit for progress that he had achieved and that had been documented by marks earned; and (2) staff should convince the public there is good reason to believe that a prisoner who is soon to return to freedom is capable of handling a job (Eriksson, 1976).

During Crofton's fourth stage, prisoners were given conditional release under a ticket-of-leave to the community. The ticket-of-leave could be revoked anytime within the span of the original fixed sentence. While in the community, the prisoner was under the supervision of the police. Such supervision was criticized by many; but by Crofton's death in 1897, a modified version of his system had been accepted in England. Today that conditional release has been reestablished in the form of parole, and the supervision is handled by parole officers rather than by police officers.

Maconochie and Crofton both made use of the existing good-time and ticket-of-leave procedures, but they each really depended on another concept that was just beginning to receive attention: indeterminate sentencing. For his mark system to operate, Maconochie had to have some level of control over how long the prisoners could be kept at the penal colony. With determinate sentences, a person must be released at a specific time. Prior to the mark system, any early release from that sentence was determined only on the basis of time served. For example, the person sentenced to fourteen years was eligible for a ticket-of-leave after serving six years. But Maconochie wanted to base the eligibility for a ticket-of-leave on the prisoners' behavior rather than on a certain amount of time. To do so he made arrangements that allowed him to control a prisoner's release date without being tied to completion of a certain number of years. For example, accumulating 6,000 marks (which would take about a year) made a prisoner eligible for release from a seven-year sentence; 7,000 marks were necessary for release from a ten-year sentence, and 8,000 marks could earn a lifer's release (Eriksson, 1976). Because early release was based on a prisoner's work and good behavior rather than on simply serving a certain number of years, the release dates could vary quite a bit among the prisoners.

Crofton had similar needs for indeterminate sentencing because his graduated release would have no meaning if prisoners were released at a certain date regardless of their stage at the time. Similarly, because Crofton's ticket-of-leave provided for supervision of the offender in the community, the indeterminate sentence had some teeth to use in carrying out the threatened bite of return to prison for misbehavior.

As good time, ticket-of-leave, and indeterminate sentencing came together, they provided the essential ingredients of parole. To complete the picture, we turn next to how these practices were used in the United States and set the stage for parole's first formal application at the Elmira Reformatory in 1876.

A History of Parole in the United States

The ingredients of parole (good time, ticket-of-leave, and indeterminate sentencing) are found in U.S. history at similar times to their appearance in places such as Australia, Ireland, and England. One of the earliest expressions of support for indeterminate sentencing is found in publications of the New York Prison Association in 1844. For example, Samuel Howe, after visiting European education, penal, and asylum institutions, wrote that the doctrine of retributive justice was passing away and taking with it all the punishments that ignore rehabilitation. An effect of that, Howe believed, would be the adoption of some system by which the length and severity of imprisonment could be modified by the prisoner's conduct (quoted in McKelvey, 1977, p. 42). With this foresight, Howe was anticipating the indeterminate sentence in which the time spent in prison depends on the prisoner's conduct.

Howe's interest in a rehabilitative aspect of indeterminate sentencing was contrasted with other reformers who were intrigued by its retributive component—that is, how could people be kept in prison longer if it seemed they were not ready for release? In an 1847 report to the New York Prison Association, the argument was made that the offender should remain confined in prison "until the evil disposition is removed from his heart; and until his disqualification to go at large no longer exists; that is, until he is a reformed man" (quoted in Barnes & Teeters, 1943, p. 817).

The debate about whether indeterminate sentencing was to be sought for its rehabilitative or retributive aspects was symptomatic of a problem that U.S. citizens had been dealing with for several years—how could determinate sentencing be given some flexibility? Since the first penitentiaries were built in the 1820s, prison officials had realized it was necessary to have ways to encourage good behavior by prisoners. With the first complaints of crowding, officials saw a need for procedures that would help control the size of the prison population by releasing some prisoners early to make room for new arrivals. Good-time procedures, first authorized by New York in 1817, became the common way to encourage good behavior; and the pardon was used to help control the prison population. But by 1870, prison officials were expressing a new concern—they were now being asked to help reform the prisoners.

The goal of reform was not one easily handled with existing procedures. Pardons had never been much help beyond the administrative function of freeing up some space for new prisoners. Good time originally had a reform aspect when Maconochie rewarded prisoners with time off their sentence after they had shown good behavior. Unfortunately, what started out as a reward to be earned by good behavior was modified so that it became a punishment for bad behavior. Under Maconochie's plan, time to be served in prison was lessened on certain dates if the prisoner had maintained good behavior during the reviewed period. In the United States, with the passage of time and the increased link to bureaucracy, the good-time concept lost its rehabilitative effect by being automatically granted in many jurisdictions (Bottomley, 1990). Upon entry to prison, the prisoners were routinely credited with the maximum amount of good time they could earn under their sentence. The prisoner's good time could only be affected after initial entry by having it taken away because of misbehavior by the inmate. Therefore, good time was no longer "earned" by the prisoner—it became something all prisoners were given until they did something to "lose" the bonus.

Because the pardon was never meant to be rehabilitative, and because good time ceased to have a rehabilitative aspect, prison officials searched for another procedure that could help them achieve a reform goal. The answer, many decided, could be found in the features of a new model of penal administration that was being used in Ireland. Prison reformers in the United States had an opportunity to hear about the Irish system in 1870 at the first convention of the American Prison Association, now the American Correctional Association, where papers were presented praising the Irish system and its reliance on indeterminate sentencing and the ticket-of-leave.

As described in Chapter 4, the enthusiasm of these new ideas spread quickly. In 1876 a new institution opened at Elmira, New York, with the specific goal of implementing the Irish system in the United States. Sentences at the Elmira Reformatory were indeterminate, so that Maconochie's mark system and Crofton's graduated release leading to a supervised ticket-of-leave could be used. The supervised ticket-of-leave was not accepted with open arms. Some U.S. supporters of the Irish system thought it might be un-American to place a person under the supervision of police (Abadinsky, 1997). But Crofton stressed that police in Ireland were allowed to delegate supervision duties to competent people in the community, so that a link to police was not a necessary ingredient. As a result, inmates released from Elmira were supervised by volunteer citizens who had to provide an account of the parolee's actions, as they were called.

After its successful use at Elmira, the indeterminate sentence and its accompanying strategy of parole became popular in several states. State legislatures provided statutory authority for indeterminate sentencing and parole, and by the mid-1890s court decisions were upholding the laws. Ohio was the first state (mid-1880s) to apply the procedures to major penitentiaries rather than reformatories, and in 1894 Massachusetts authorized the parole of any reformed first offender who had served two-thirds of a fixed sentence. The movement was afoot, and by 1898 twenty-five states had some form of parole law in operation.

THE CONTEMPORARY PAROLE PROCESS

The origin of parole in the United States had a clear rehabilitation link. In that way it came to fill the void that good time left when its reform role was set aside in favor of its disciplinary function. But it did not take long for officials to see that parole could also serve several purposes. In California, for example, within about ten years of its implementation parole was being used for some of the old administrative purposes that pardon had accomplished. Between 1900 and 1906, California experienced crowding in its prisons. As a result, parole eligibility was extended to all prisoners after they had served twelve months in prison. Rather than being a special privilege available to exceptional prisoners, parole in California became a standard mode of release for which any prisoner could be considered. Eligibility changed from the importance of showing rehabilitation to the simplicity of completing a certain portion of the sentence (Messinger, Berecochea, Rauma, & Berk, 1985).

So, is parole used as a way to help reintegrate offenders into society as law-abiding citizens, or as a way to keep prison populations at a reasonable level? The answer in most jurisdictions today would be a simple yes to each of those questions. But, increasingly, corrections officials and legislators are pointing to a third purpose for parole—protecting the public from continued crime by the offender. For example, the U.S. Parole Commission (1993) sees a threefold purpose for parole: (1) reintegrate parolees into society, (2) prevent the needless imprisonment of those who are eligible for parole and unlikely to commit further crime, and (3) protect the public. The first purpose is rehabilitative, the second is administrative (i.e., control the size of the prison population), and the third is incapacitative (i.e., restrict the released prisoner's freedom of movement by placing conditions on that release).

Keep in mind the variability of parole purposes as we look at its structure and operation. Because parole has rehabilitative, administrative, and incapacitative aspects, it is not surprising that there is also variation in how, when, and if parole is used by different jurisdictions. But despite the variation in purpose and usage, some steps in the parole process are found wherever parole is used as conditional release from prison. For parole to be used, regardless of its purpose, decisions must be made regarding who is eligible for parole, what happens on parole, and what happens when conditions of parole are violated. We will look at each of these as we cover the parole process.

Deciding Parole

There is no consistent way across the country for deciding who will be paroled. In some states prisoners receive parole as the result of discretionary decisions by a parole board—simply called parole, in Table 13.1. In other states offenders are released to parole, or at least to supervision, once they have served a specific amount of time less any good time they received—called supervised mandatory release in Table 13.1. Our concern here is with discretionary parole, which we simply refer to as parole.

The parole decision requires two important steps: (1) A prisoner must be identified as eligible for parole, and (2) someone must grant the parole.

Eligibility for Parole. In jurisdictions in which parole is at the discretion of a parole board or authority (discussed later), prisoners are given a date on which they are first eligible for early release on parole. This parole eligibility date is determined

Parole boards consist of a group of citizens, typically appointed by the state governor, who meet periodically to review the files of those prisoners eligible for parole. After hearing the prisoner's parole plan, the board members may agree to release the prisoner on parole or may decide to deny parole at the present time.

early in a prisoner's sentence—often within the first several months. Each jurisdiction develops its own formula to determine that date. For example, one state might require offenders to serve one-third of the imposed sentence before they can be considered for parole. A prisoner with a six-year sentence in such a jurisdiction would first be eligible for parole after completing two years. If the sentence is indeterminate, say three to nine years, the state specifies whether the formula applies to the minimum or the maximum time. For example, in one state parole eligibility might be after serving one year—one-third of the three-year minimum—whereas another state requires three years in prison—one-third of the nine-year maximum—before parole eligibility.

Another way to determine parole eligibility is to include good-time reductions in the formula. For example, consider an offender with a ten-year sentence, or an eight- to ten-year sentence where the maximum is used, in a state where good time is given at a rate of one day of good time for each day served. That inmate would be eligible for parole after serving five years in prison. But the emphasis is still on words such as *eligible* and *can be considered*. Parole, after all, is a privilege and not a right. In *Greenholtz v. Inmates of the Nebraska Penal and Correctional Complex* (1979), the U.S. Supreme Court held that a state has no obligation to establish a parole system, and an inmate has no constitutional right to be released prior to completion of the sentence. So the next step in the parole process is to determine who decides which of the eligible prisoners will receive a parole release.

Granting Parole. The classic design for granting parole has been to have a group of citizens, typically appointed by the state governor, who meet periodically to review the files of those prisoners eligible for parole. This **parole board** might meet at the prison, where they can interview the prisoner eligible for parole as well as review his or her file. The board members will most likely be interested in hearing the prisoner's parole plan, which may include specifics about job possibilities and places to live. If the board members agree that a person should be released on parole, they set a specific parole date—maybe a month later. The prisoner knows that, barring any infractions or problems with the parole plan, she can expect to be released on that date. If the board members do not believe the time for release is quite right, parole is deferred. The prisoner is told the next date—possibly a year later—that he will come before the board.

States using discretionary parole must decide who will make up the parole board's membership, what organizational structure the board will have, and what criteria the board will use to decide who gets released on parole. Parole board members are seldom required to have specific qualifications (Samaha, 1994). When qualifications are indicated, they tend to be quite general (e.g., "good character" or "judicious temperament") or are more concerned with the character of the board than the character of its individual members. Some states, for example, require representation of certain professions such as law enforcement or corrections, or they may stipulate that a mix of political parties be represented among the members. This last point reminds us that parole is considered an executive branch procedure because the parole board's members are typically appointed by the governor, although in a few states they are appointed from a civil service list.

Once the parole board membership characteristics and number—typically from three to twelve members—are determined, each jurisdiction must decide how that board will function. Cromwell and Killinger (1994) identify three major parole structures:

- *Institutional model.* Parole release decisions are made primarily within the institution by the staff members. This model is most prevalent in the juvenile justice field and best reflects the rehabilitative expectations of indeterminate sentencing. Because the institutional staff is most familiar with the offender's progress, the staff is best able to determine the optimum time for release.
- *Autonomous model.* The decision to parole lies with an independent authority that is not affiliated with other criminal justice agencies. This model is most frequently found in the adult system. Its advocates believe it can operate more objectively and be less influenced by problems in other parts of the justice system because of its autonomous nature.
- *Consolidated model.* Parole decisions are made by a central authority with independent powers. That authority is, however, located in the department of corrections. This model is becoming increasingly popular as jurisdictions move toward consolidating all correctional services into a single department. Consolidation is claimed to have the benefit of understanding and taking into consideration the links among the various corrections agencies. (pp. 225–226)

Determining the characteristics of the board membership and deciding under which organizational structure it will operate were the easy parts of setting up a parole system. Then the parole board must decide who among those eligible will be released.

In deciding to grant early conditional release to a prisoner, the parole board must take several factors into consideration:

- The likelihood that the person will commit another crime
- The offender's conduct while in prison
- How sufficient and achievable the parole plan is
- The extent of the offender's participation in rehabilitative programs while in prison
- The reaction of law enforcement and citizens to the offender's return to the community
- The need to provide space in the prison to receive newly sentenced prisoners
- Whether the offender has yet gotten his just deserts

Parole boards may be required to consider some of these factors as a result of statutes but others may simply be personal preferences of board members. The common goal, regardless of specific criteria used, is to predict future conduct by the offender. The prediction may emphasize public safety (i.e., the offender will not cause harm to citizens or their property), or it may emphasize offender reintegration (i.e., the offender will benefit from a supervised return to society), but it is prediction all the same.

Since the 1920s, attempts have been made to provide a level of objectivity to the prediction process. Simon (1993) describes the early efforts by academicians to develop prediction systems based on actuarial tables. Just as insurance companies determine the risk level associated with insuring different people by identifying variables correlated with long life or a good driving record, variables could also be identified that correlate with success on parole. Male drivers under age twenty-five may get into more traffic accidents, so they represent a higher risk and must pay higher premiums. A twenty-year-old male driver with several speeding tickets and involvement in two accidents may present such a risk that he cannot even get insurance—or he must pay dearly for it. Similarly, male prisoners under age twenty-five may have a hard time breaking free from involvement in crime, so they represent a higher risk for parole. A twenty-year-old male prisoner with several prior convictions who receives disciplinary write-ups in prison may present such a risk that he cannot even get parole—or he will be released only under very strict supervision. The goal of both insurance and parole prediction is to lessen the risk presented to the decision makers. The insurance companies do not want to lose money, and the parole board does not want to have someone out in the community committing crimes. To lessen either type of negative consequence, actuarial tables are developed to give decision makers information that suggests how risky it would be to insure or parole a particular person.

Despite their earlier availability, parole boards did not start using statistical prediction methods until the 1960s. Simon (1993) suggests that although the instruments were reasonably reliable in predicting recidivism, parole boards were unwilling to base their decision only on that criterion. By 1961, only two parole boards, Illinois and California, used statistical prediction methods as an official part of the process. In the 1970s the prediction methods were combined into matrices that also took crime seriousness into account; by the end of the 1970s, at least fifteen jurisdictions were using some type of actuarial prediction combined with offense severity (Simon, 1993, pp. 173–174).

Today the use of statistical prediction as an aid to parole decision making is standard procedure in jurisdictions with discretionary parole. Even jurisdictions in which parole is mandatory might use prediction methods to determine which level of supervision is required for the released prisoner. Two models have proved especially popular among the jurisdictions. One, the **salient factor score,** was adopted by the federal parole board in 1972 and continues to be used as part of the decision-making process for federal prisoners still eligible (as discussed later, federal parole has been abolished) for parole and for District of Columbia offenders. The other prediction model, developed in the mid-1970s in Wisconsin, focuses on the potential risk the offender presents to the community and on the rehabilitation needs of the offenders. This risk/needs scoring approach has become very popular around the country for determining prison placement and programs for particular offenders, and for decision making in both probation and parole matters. Because the risk/needs procedure was covered in the Chapter 10 discussion of classification, we will consider here the use of salient factor scoring as part of the parole decision-making process.

The Sentencing Reform Act of 1984 abolished parole eligibility for federal offenders who commit crimes on or after November 1, 1987, and it also provided for the abolition of the U.S. Parole Commission. However, other acts in 1990 and 1996 extended the commission in five-year increments and in 1997 the commission was mandated to make parole decisions for District of Columbia offenders. An important tool used by the commission to make parole decisions is the salient factor score. By combining the salient factor score with the other factor, offense severity, parole commissioners have a matrix to aid in their decision making (see Figure 13.1).

Because the decision to parole is expected to take into consideration both offense and offender characteristics, the commission developed guidelines for parole decision making that incorporates the two features. Figure 13.2 shows the result-

FIGURE 13.1

Salient Factor Score (SFS 95)

Item A. **Prior Convictions/Adjudications** (Adult or Juvenile) . . . . ☐
None = 3; One = 2; Two or three = 1; Four or more = 0

Item B. **Prior Commitment(s) of More Than 30 Days** (Adult or Juvenile) . . . . . . ☐
None = 2; One or two = 1; Three or more = 0

Item C. **Age at Current Offense/Prior Commitments** . . . . ☐
Age at commencement of current offense;
26 years of age or more = 2*; 20–25 = 1*; 19 years of age or less = 0
Exception: If five or more prior commitments of more than 30 days (adult or juvenile), place an *x* here ______ and score this item 0

Item D. **Recent Commitment Free Period** (Three Years) . . . . ☐
No prior commitment of more than 30 days (adult or juvenile) or released to the community from last such commitment at least 3 years prior to the commencement of the current offense = 1;
Otherwise = 0

Item E. **Probation/Parole/Confinement/Escape Status Violator This Time** . . . . ☐
Neither on probation, parole, confinement, or escape status at the time of the current offense; nor committed as a probation, parole, confinement, or escape status violator this time = 1; Otherwise = 0

Item F. **Heroin/Opiate Dependence** . . . . ☐
No history of heroin/opiate dependence = 1; Otherwise = 0

Item G. **Older Offenders** . . . . ☐
If the offender was 41 years of age or more at the commencement of the current offense (and the total score from Items A–F above is 9 or less) = 1;
Otherwise = 0

Total Score . . . . ☐

Note: For purposes of the Salient Factor Score, an instance of criminal behavior resulting in a judicial determination of guilt or an admission of guilt before a judicial body shall be treated as a conviction, even if a conviction is not formally entered.

Source: From U.S. Parole Commission. (1997). *Rules and procedures manual.* (p. 58). Washington, DC: Department of Justice. Available: www.usdoj.gov/uspc/readingroom/ProcedureManual/.

ing two-dimensional grid with the seriousness of the current offense (offense characteristics) on the vertical axis and the prisoner's risk of recidivism (offender characteristics) on the horizontal axis. The offense severity is presented as one of eight categories. The commission's Rules and Procedures Manual (U.S. Parole Commission, 1997) suggests categories for particular offenses, such as grading assault resulting in serious bodily injury as category 7, burglary of an inhabited dwelling as category 5, and insider trading with an impact of $2,000 to $40,000 as category 3.

The offender's likelihood of continued criminal behavior is identified by referring to one of four parole prognosis categories. The categories themselves are the result of grouping salient factor scores as determined by the 1995 version (SFS 95) of the prediction scale. The SFS 95 scale (see Figure 13.1) uses six items to produce a score falling along a range of 0 to 10 points. As the SFS values get higher,

FIGURE 13.2

Guidelines for Decision Making

Guidelines for Decision Making, Customary Total Time to Be Served before Release (including jail time)

Offense Characteristics	Offender Characteristics: Parole Prognosis (Salient Factor Score 1995)			
Severity of Offense Behavior	Very Good (10–8)	Good (7–6)	Fair (5–4)	Poor (3–0)
	Guideline Range			
Category One	< = 4 months	< = 8 months	8–12 months	12–16 months
	Guideline Range			
Category Two	< = 6 months	< = 10 months	12–16 months	16–22 months
	Guideline Range			
Category Three	< = 10 months	12–16 months	18–24 months	24–32 months
	Guideline Range			
Category Four	12–18 months	20–26 months	26–34 months	34–44 months
	Guideline Range			
Category Five	24–36 months	36–48 months	48–60 months	60–72 months
	Guideline Range			
Category Six	40–52 months	52–64 months	64–78 months	78–100 months
	Guideline Range			
Category Seven	52–80 months	64–92 months	78–110 months	100–148 months
	Guideline Range			
Category Eight*	100+ months	120+ months	150+ months	180+ months

*Note: For Category Eight, no upper limits are specified due to the extreme variability of the cases within this category. For decisions exceeding the lower limit of the applicable guideline category *by more than 48 months,* the Commission will specify the pertinent case factors upon which it relied in reaching its decision, which may include the absence of any factors mitigating the offense. This procedure is intended to ensure that the prisoner understands that individualized consideration has been given to the facts of the case, and not to suggest that a grant of parole is to be presumed for any class of Category Eight offenders. However, a murder committed to silence a victim or witness, a contract murder, a murder by torture, the murder of a law enforcement officer to carry out an offense, or a murder carried out to further the aims of an ongoing criminal operation shall not justify a parole at any point in the prisoner's sentence unless there are compelling circumstances in mitigation (e.g., a youthful offender who participated in a murder planned and executed by his parent). Such aggravated crimes are considered, by definition, at the extreme high end of Category Eight offenses. For these cases, the expiration of the sentence is deemed to be a decision at the maximum limit of the guideline range. (The fact that an offense does not fall under the definition contained in this rule does not mean that the Commission is obliged to grant a parole.)

Source: From U.S. Parole Commission. (1997). *Rules and procedures manual.* (p. 27–28). Washington, DC: Department of Justice. Available: www.usdoj.gov/uspc/readingroom/ProcedureManual/.

the likelihood of recidivism decreases. As a result, persons with scores of 8, 9, or 10 are considered to have a good parole prognosis and are placed in the "Very Good" category on the guidelines matrix. Scores of 0, 1, 2, or 3 suggest a high likelihood of recidivism and are assigned to the "Poor" parole prognosis category.

For each combination of offense category and parole prognosis group, the guidelines matrix (Figure 13.2) suggests a range of months to spend in prison before parole. For example, an offender with a salient factor score of 6 who is serving time for a category 3 offense should serve twelve to sixteen months in prison before release on parole. Importantly, the guideline range merely represents the Parole Commission's policy regarding the appropriate time to spend in prison given the offense and the prognosis of success on parole. The actual release on parole can occur outside that range at the discretion of the parole decision makers as long as mitigating and aggravating circumstances are followed or identified (U.S. Parole Commission, 1997).

When looking at Figure 13.2, you may have noticed a similarity between this matrix for parole decision making and the sentencing matrix found in Table 5.3 of Chapter 5. The resemblance is not by chance; there is a link between the salient factor score and the criminal history score in the federal sentencing guidelines (Hoffman, 1994). With the abolition of federal parole, the sentence imposed by the judge came to have new meaning. Because the sentences were to have incapacitative and just deserts aspects, the U.S. Sentencing Commission wanted both predictive and retributive aspects to the sentencing guidelines. The offense severity score, in both the sentencing and the parole guidelines, provides a just deserts aspect; the criminal history score (sentencing decisions) and the salient factor score (parole decisions) help predict future criminal involvement. Because the Sentencing Commission relied on the Parole Commission's salient factor score to develop its criminal history score, the concept and essential character of the salient factor score continue to have influence even after federal parole has been abolished.

Once the two steps of the parole decision process have been accomplished—deciding who is eligible and actually granting parole—the focus changes to the features of parole itself. Now, we should consider topics such as the conditions of parole and the role of parole officers.

Parole Conditions and Parole Officers

At year-end 1998, there were about 705,000 persons on parole from state or federal sentences (Bonczar & Glaze, 1999). Table 13.3 shows that most of them were white, non-Hispanic, and male. The percentage of African Americans on parole has decreased since 1993—possibly a reflection of mandatory sentences for certain drug offenses—but there has been a slight increase in the percentage of Hispanic parolees and of parolees who are female.

Despite the variation in demographics, in every case the offender was released on parole only after she or he signed a parole agreement or parole order. The term *agreement* is often used when the parole is discretionary; *order* more often suggests parole is mandatory at the completion of a specific prison sentence. Signing a parole agreement means the offender agrees to abide by certain regulations while on parole. Signing a parole order indicates the parolee is aware of the regulations that will govern the offender in the community. Colorado's Parole Agreement/Order (Figure 13.3) uses both terms on the same form because parole could be discretionary or mandatory depending on when the sentence was imposed.

The conditions that parolees must abide by are very similar to those for probationers. In addition, there is not much variation in the conditions by jurisdiction. The first nine conditions of parole for Colorado (see Figure 13.3) are typical of the federal and other state jurisdictions. Such standard conditions are applic-

TABLE 13.3: Characteristics of Adults on Parole in State and Federal Jurisdictions, 1993, 1996, and 1998

CHARACTERISTIC	1993 (%)	1996 (%)	1998 (%)
Total	100	100	100
Sex			
Male	90	89	88
Female	10	11	12
Race			
White	49	53	55
Black	50	46	44
Other	1	2	1
Ethnicity			
Hispanic	18	20	21
Non-Hispanic	82	80	79
Sentence Length			
Less than one year	3	4	n/a
One year or more	97	96	n/a
Parolees under Intensive Supervision	3	4	n/a
Parolees on Electronic Monitoring	0	1	n/a
Entering Parole			
Discretionary parole	75	46	41
Mandatory parole	21	48	53
Reinstatement	1	4	5
Other	3	2	1
Leaving Parole			
Successful completion	55	46	45
Returned to prison	34	40	42
Abscond, transfer, death, other	11	14	13

Source: Adapted from Bonczar, T. P., & Glaze, L. E. (1999). (for 1998) *Probation and parole in the United States, 1998* [NCJ 178234]. Washington, DC: Bureau of Justice Statistics; (for 1996) Bureau of Justice Statistics. (1999). *Correctional populations in the United States, 1996* [NCJ 170013]. Washington, DC: Author; (for 1993) Snell, T. L. (1995). *Correctional populations in the United States, 1993* [NCJ 156241]. Washington, DC: Bureau of Justice Statistics.

able to all parolees and usually for any other kind of conditional release as well. They include stipulations designed to incapacitate and to reform. Incapacitative, or control, conditions include those requiring the parolee to report to the parole officer; to get permission to move, change jobs, or leave the area; and to be prohibited from having weapons. Reform or treatment conditions include restrictions on people with whom the parolee can associate, prohibitions on alcohol and drug use, and requirements to obey all laws and ordinances and to be involved in work or educational activities.

FIGURE 13.3

Example of Colorado's Parole Agreement/Order

TO: John Doe 103-099999

The COLORADO STATE BOARD OF PAROLE in session in Delta, Colorado on June 12, 1995 considered your application for parole and, believing that you can abide by the conditions of your parole agreement, hereby orders your parole to become effective June 29, 1995. Your parole will discharge on June 29, 1997 unless sooner terminated by order of the Board on the motion of your Parole officer or the Parole board.

PAROLE AGREEMENT/ORDER

Parolee will be directed and supervised by Officers and Supervisors of the Office of Community Services, Department of Corrections, and will be accountable for his actions and conduct during his period of parole. Parolee must abide by all conditions of parole set forth in this agreement and any additional conditions and directives set forth by Parole Officer, consistent with the laws of the State of Colorado. Any violation of this agreement and/or any conditions thereof, can lead to the revocation of parole.

CONDITIONS OF PAROLE

1. **RELEASE:** Upon release from the Institution, Parolee shall go directly to Greeley, CO, as designated by the Board of Parole and report upon arrival to Paul Leavitt, 800 8th Avenue, Room 121, Greeley, CO 80631 Phone (970) 356-0839 in person or as directed.
2. **RESIDENCE:** Parolee shall establish a residence of record and shall reside at such residence in fact and on record; shall not change this place of residence without the consent of his Parole Officer; and shall not leave the area paroled to nor the State paroled to without permission of the Parole Officer.
3. **CONDUCT:** Parolee shall obey all State/Federal laws and Municipal ordinances. Parolee shall follow the directions of the Parole Board at all times.
4. **REPORT:** Parolee shall make written, and in person, reports as directed by the Parole Officer; and shall permit visits to his place of residence as required by the Parole Officer.
   a. Parolee further shall submit urinalysis or other tests for narcotics or chemical agents upon the request of the Parole Officer and is required to pay for all tests.
   b. Parolee further agrees to allow the Parole Officer to search his person, or his residence, or any premises under his control, or any vehicle under his control.
5. **WEAPONS:** Parolee shall not own, possess, nor have under his control or in his custody, firearms, or other deadly weapons.
6. **ASSOCIATION:** Parolee shall not associate with any person with a criminal record without the permission of the Parole Officer.
7. **EMPLOYMENT:** Parolee shall seek and obtain employment or shall participate in a full time educational or vocational program, unless waived by the Parole Officer.
8. **ALCOHOL/DRUGS:** Parolee shall not abuse alcoholic beverages, or possess and/or use illegal drugs.
9. **CHILD SUPPORT:** Parolee shall comply with any court or administrative order to pay child support.
10. **ADDITIONAL CONDITIONS:** (a) Parolee shall participate in a mental health evaluation. (b) Parolee shall participate in a drug/alcohol treatment program. (c) Parolee shall participate in a monitored Antabuse program, if feasible, and agree to pay all costs. (d) Parolee shall have no alcohol intake. (e) Parolee shall participate in Intensive supervision while on parole for 180 days. (f) Parolee shall frequent no bars. (g) Parolee shall participate in a vocational rehabilitation program. (h) Parolee shall pay restitution in the amount of $350.00, in monthly payments to be scheduled by the Parole Officer, until paid in full.

I agree to abide by all of the conditions of my parole heretofore set forth, and I do hereby waive extradition to the State of Colorado from any state or territory of the United States or from the District of Columbia, and agree I will not contest any effort to return me to the State of Colorado at any time before the expiration of my maximum sentence. I have read the foregoing document or have had it read to me and I have full and intelligent understanding of the contents and the meaning thereof; and I have received a copy of this document. I hereby affix my signature of my own free will and without reservation and coercion.

______________________________	______________________________
For the Colorado Board of Parole	Signature of Parolee
Date: ______________________________	______________________________
	Witness

Source: From Colorado Department of Corrections.

Help Wanted

Job Title: Parole Officer/Agent

Position Description: Parole officers serve dual roles as law officers and counselors. They enforce parole conditions to protect the community while providing supervision and guidance to parolees to facilitate their successful reintegration into society. Parole officers investigate inmates for parole consideration and supervise those released on parole. Parole officers are frequently called on to assist local law enforcement in a variety of endeavors.

Qualifications: Applicants must have a bachelor's degree in the social/behavioral sciences from an accredited college or university. Because parole agents are state peace officers, applicants must also be at least twenty-one years old at the time of employment and meet the legal requirements for peace officers prescribed by the Peace Officer Standards and Training (P.O.S.T.) Council. Writing skills are important because a parole agent must be able to compose concise, accurate, neat, and a well-written copy. Good organizational skills are also necessary to balance and accomplish the numerous details and urgent demands inherent in the position. Computer skills are extremely important due to the automated case management system.

For examples of career opportunities in this field, check the Web sites for the various state departments of corrections at ***database.corrections.com/career/index.asp#state***. See a specific example at Georgia's page at ***www.pap.state.ga.us/COFrames.htm***.

In addition to the standard conditions, it is not unusual for the parole agreement/order to include special conditions developed to meet the offender's particular characteristics or needs. For the fictitious example given in Figure 13.3, the parolee had eight special conditions added to the standard ones. These can also either incapacitate (e.g., be under home confinement from 7:00 P.M. to 7:00 A.M.; avoid areas where children are present; do not drive an automobile) or reform (e.g., participate in a drug treatment program; get an AA sponsor; participate in an antabuse program; pay restitution) the offender.

Just as there is similarity between conditions of probation and parole, there is similarity among the officials assigned to manage each type of case. Parole officers (parole agents in some jurisdictions) are responsible for supervising, assisting, and controlling their clients. In this way they perform tasks similar to those done by probation officers (see Chapter 7). The two positions are enough alike that in the federal system and many states supervision officers have combined caseloads of probation and parole clients.

When differences do exist between probation and parole officers, they center more on the tasks emphasized than on the tasks themselves. For example, parolees are often more dangerous and serious offenders than are probationers. Persons on parole have been exposed to prison violence and the inmate subculture, have the stigma of ex-con, and are returning to a family life that was significantly disrupted (Inciardi, 1993; Senna & Siegel, 1999). Parole supervision often has more of a control function than does probation because the parolee presents a more difficult case and may be a greater danger to the community. Parole supervisors and officials may put the needs of the community ahead of the needs of the offender to a degree that some parole officers see themselves as "gun-carrying social workers" (Inciardi, 1993, p. 658).

The organization of parole departments varies depending on things such as geography, number of parolees, and state funding. Some states have institutionally based parole officers who have primary responsibility for helping parole-eligible inmates prepare a reasonable parole plan. Helping persons still in prison line up jobs and places to live can be especially challenging. Field agents, on the other hand, are parole officers with responsibility for easing the prisoner's reentry in a way that does not compromise public safety. Some parole offices may have special units to deal with intensive supervision caseloads, parolees at halfway houses, or other parole-linked programs.

Parole officers are responsible for supervising, assisting, and controlling parolees. Parole supervision often involves more of a control function than does probation because the parolee presents a more difficult case and may be a greater danger to the community.

Parole Completion and Revocation

The length of time a person is on parole is not easy to pin down because there is considerable variation among the states. To complicate things even more, variety exists within a state because time on parole can be affected whenever legislators modify sentence lengths or good-time credit, or move from discretionary to mandatory parole. Looking only at differences among states, we can find some examples in which time on parole cannot exceed six months or the offender's maximum sentence date, whichever comes first; in other states, the parolees are discharged no later than one year after their release. States with mandatory parole typically specify time on parole as varying—for example, one to five years—depending on the crime. For example, the state legislature might determine that conviction of a class 3 felony will require two years on parole after completing whatever prison sentence is imposed by the judge.

Once the parole length is determined, the problem becomes one of successfully completing that term. Like probationers, parolees try to complete their conditional liberty through discharge rather than revocation. Table 13.3 shows that during 1998, 45 percent of those adults leaving parole status did so under successful completion of their parole. On the other hand, 42 percent had their parole revoked and were returned to prison.

Perkins (1994) reports data from twenty-nine states that provided information on parolees discharged during 1992. Reviewing that data highlights some interesting points about the characteristics of successful and revoked parolees. For example, over two-thirds of property, drug, or violent offenders completed parole successfully, but the highest percentage of successful discharges were with persons convicted of driving while intoxicated (92 percent successful). Parolees whose most serious offense was robbery represented the greatest percentage of those returned to prison (39 percent revoked).

Parole revocation, like probation revocation, can result from either the commission of a new offense or from a technical violation of the parole agreement/order. Upon becoming aware of the violation (which the feature "Eyes in the Sky" suggests may become increasingly easy), the parole officer can, depending on the jurisdiction, respond in such ways as

- Arresting the parolee without warrant
- Making an arrest with a warrant that has been issued by the parole board
- Issuing a temporary detaining order that will hold the parolee for a day or two until an arrest warrant is issued
- Issuing a citation requiring the parolee to appear for a hearing or case review

These four do not exhaust all the possibilities, but they suggest the primary formats within which states set procedures for responding to possible parole violations.

If formal revocation is sought, the U.S. Supreme Court has identified certain procedures that are to be followed. In *Morrissey v. Brewer* (1972), the Court said that the state correctly subjects parolees to restrictions not applicable to other citizens, and that the parolee is not entitled to the full array of rights due a defendant in a criminal proceeding. But, because parole revocation represents a "grievous loss" of liberty, the parolee is permitted certain due process rights. Specifically, the parolee is entitled to

1. written notice of alleged parole violations;
2. disclosure of evidence against parolee;
3. opportunity to be heard in person and to present witnesses and documentary evidence;
4. the right to confront and cross-examine adverse witnesses (unless the hearing officer finds good cause not to allow such confrontation);

Spotlight ON CONTEMPORARY ISSUES

Eyes in the Sky

In 1999 global positioning system (GPS) technology was increasingly used by average citizens to help them hike, boat, and drive with less fear of getting lost. The technology uses a satellite system to give the user, or people looking for the user, specific information about the person's physical location. (See Figure 13.4.)

Since electronic monitoring of offenders began in the 1980s (see the discussion in Chapter 8), visionaries have predicted that monitoring will someday allow authorities to be constantly aware of an offender's location. That day officially arrived in September 1999 when the state of Colorado became the test site for the global tracking system. This advanced monitoring system uses GPS technology to track a parolee's location twenty-four hours a day. That is quite an improvement over standard electronic monitoring equipment that can tell only if the parolee is within range of his base (e.g., his home or work location) or is away from the base.

Lane (1999) explains that paroled sex offenders were the first to be fitted with an ankle bracelet and battery pack that send signals, every sixty seconds, to satellites arrayed in space. Those satellites then relay the parolee's location to a parole officer. By opening her laptop computer, the parole officer can instantly determine the location of each of her parolees. The new tracking system seems especially helpful in monitoring sex offenders because those criminals typically have parole conditions that lend themselves to GPS technology. If a sex offender is supposed to stay a certain distance away from school or strip clubs, for example, coordinates of those kinds of buildings are plotted on a map. If the parolee invades the specified perimeter, a warning is triggered and the parole officer is notified by pager of the violation (Lane, 1999). The system can even be programmed with a designated route that a parolee is supposed to take between work and home. If he strays from that route, the parole officer is notified.

Another key element of the system is its ability to keep track of movements over time. Law enforcement officials are intrigued with the possibility of being able to determine the specific whereabouts of parolees after police have received report of a crime. For example, if the system shows that John was at or near the location of a burglary two days earlier, the police may decide that John should be interviewed about the crime.

Read about another company's use of GPS for tracking offenders at ***www.sierrawireless.com/solutions/protech.html.*** How is this system similar to or different from the one described in the foregoing feature? Also read the article at ***www.shire.net/big.brother/satellite.htm.*** How does the cost of GPS tracking compare with other techniques? For a critical look at GPS tracking, go to ***www.libertymatters.org/BNtradingliberty.htm.*** What are some of the issues raised in that article? Do you think they have merit?

FIGURE 13.4

Eyes in the Sky

Source: From Laue, G. "State to test satellite-based tracking of parolees." August 28, 1999, *The Denver Post,* p. 11A. Copyright © 1999 *The Denver Post.* Used with permission.

A Denver-based company, Continental Divide Robotics, Inc., has devised a tracking system using satellites to monitor paroled convicts. How the system works:

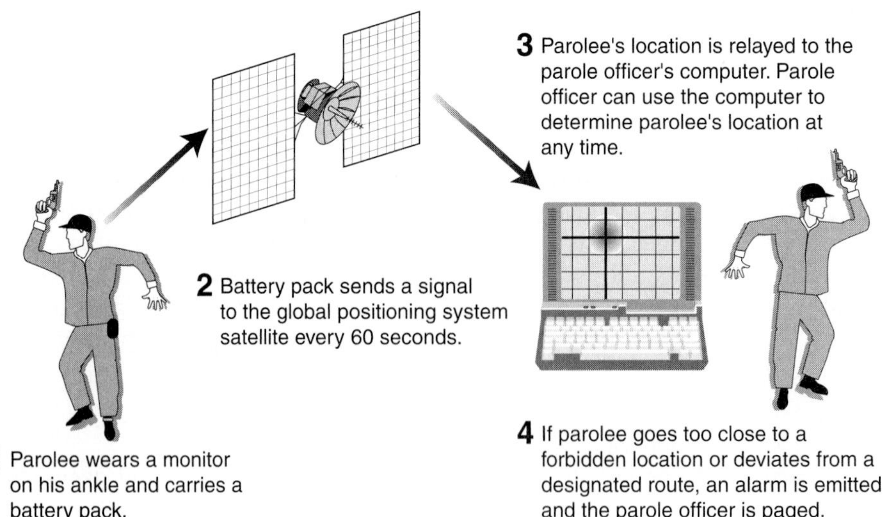

5. a neutral and detached hearing body such as a traditional parole board; and
6. a written statement by the factfinders as to the evidence relied upon and reasons for revoking parole. (*Morrissey v. Brewer,* 408 U.S. at 471–72)

The *Morrissey* decision also said there were two important stages in the parole revocation process: (1) the arrest and a preliminary hearing, and (2) the revocation hearing. The parolee is entitled to the same due process rights at both stages, and many jurisdictions have decided to have just one hearing at which the six due process rights are given. The Supreme Court has not ruled on that process, but most lower courts have considered the merged proceeding to be constitutional (del Carmen, Ritter, & Witt, 1993).

If parole is revoked, what happens to the time the parolee spent on parole? Consider Pete Padilla, who is released on parole after serving two years of his six-year sentence. Padilla's parole is revoked on a technical violation after he has spent one year on the streets. In one jurisdiction the one year of street time is counted toward the prison sentence, and Padilla has just three more years in prison. In another jurisdiction the one year is considered dead time, and Padilla is given no credit for the year on parole—he has four more years to spend in prison. Other states might give credit for a portion of the street time; still others might have a maximum amount that could be credited whereas anything over that maximum becomes dead time. As in other areas, our decentralized system provides the opportunity for states to arrange things that seem to fit best with that state's particular needs or punishment rationale.

Criticism of Parole

During the 1970s parole was a frequent target in the attack on the rehabilitative philosophy. Several issues were bothersome to the critics of rehabilitation's medical model approach (Bottomley, 1990; Rhine, Smith, & Jackson, 1991). We will consider two of them: (1) the uncontrolled discretion of parole boards to determine time served, and (2) the ineffectiveness of parole's treatment component.

A primary goal of indeterminate sentencing was to provide an opportunity to release a prisoner from confinement at the time when he or she would be most responsive to treatment in the community. Because the sentencing judge could not know in advance whether that peak time would come in one year, two years, or even five years, it seemed reasonable to leave the release decision up to the corrections system officials. This meant, of course, that parole authorities were given significant discretion as to an inmate's release date. That discretion was acceptable under the Rehabilitation era; but as the Retributive era came on the scene, it was considered inappropriate. Specifically, discretion of parole boards meant persons convicted of similar crimes could end up serving very different amounts of time in prison. When the emphasis was on the offender, such disparity was expected and accepted, but as emphasis turned to the offense, the discrepancies were deemed improper. As a result, parole boards and parole itself were criticized as exhibiting uncontrolled discretion and creating sentencing disparities.

A second criticism of parole centered on a perceived lack of effectiveness in treating offenders given an early release. Evaluation studies of parole supervision offered little evidence that it was effective in reducing further offenses by the parolee and at best served only to delay reoffending behavior (Bottomley, 1990; Rhine et al., 1991). Such faint praise was unimpressive from the critics' perspective and helped to portray parole as something that could be abolished without serious repercussion.

At the forefront in a call for abolishing parole were the Quakers (American Friends Service Committee, 1971), a commission looking into causes of a prison riot (New York State Special Commission on Attica, 1972), and academics associated with the new just deserts rationale (Fogel, 1975; von Hirsch & Hanrahan, 1979). The critics struck a chord with the public and the legislators and by the mid-1980s all fifty states, the District of Columbia, and the federal government had revised or considered replacing indeterminate with determinate sentencing (Rhine et al., 1991). As it turned out, a majority of jurisdictions retained indeterminate sentencing, but at least several others passed determinate sentencing legislation and moved away from the rehabilitation philosophy. With Maine leading the way, six states (California, Colorado, Illinois, Indiana, Maine, and New Mexico) eliminated or severely limited discretionary parole release between 1976 and 1979. Another five states (Connecticut, Florida, Minnesota, North Carolina, and Washington) followed suit from 1980 to 1984.

The pace has since slowed, with Delaware abolishing parole effective in 1990 and Virginia doing the same in 1995 (Allen, 1995; Rhine et al., 1991). There have even been signs of a reverse trend: Colorado reinstituted discretionary parole in 1985, only to change back to mandatory parole in 1993, and Florida provided a parole function under a new name—Controlled Release Authority. Rhine et al. (1991) believe the slowdown in calls for abolishing or limiting parole is, ironically, based on the very factors that started the criticism in the first place. The unprecedented prison and jail crowding that resulted from complaints against sentencing disparity and parole board discretion are now providing parole's reason for existence. Parole, with its ability to vary sentence length and the discretion it gives to corrections officials, is being called on to manage growing prison populations. Some parole boards have been given legislative authority to control the prison population by adjusting their formal guidelines for release. Other boards have received informal instructions to grant parole through a quota system by which releases on parole approximate admissions to prison (Rhine et al., 1991).

In addition to its useful role as a prison population management tool, parole is also regaining recognition as an appropriate mechanism for helping prisoners reintegrate into society. The prospect of having offenders released to the community without supervision is considered unacceptable by citizens, politicians, and corrections officials. Even those states that abolished discretionary parole have kept provisions for postrelease supervision (Cromwell & Killinger, 1994) or have turned to split sentencing with a prison sentence followed by probation (see the increasing percentage of conditional releases to probation in Table 13.2 on page 474). The goal of the supervised mandatory releases is the same as it is for parole—it should provide for public safety by supervising the prisoner's postprison release. But in addition to that purpose, both parole and the different versions of supervised mandatory release also provide an opportunity to assist the offender in his or her return to the community. Several decades ago, this process was called rehabilitation; today it is more often referred to as **reintegration.**

REINTEGRATION PROGRAMS

In 1998 nearly 6 million adults in the United States were under some form of correctional supervision. That number represents about 2.9 percent of the U.S. adult resident population and compares, unfavorably most would say, with the 1.1 percent under correctional supervision in 1980 (Bonczar & Glaze, 1999; Snell, 1995a). About two-thirds of the 6 million people were on probation or parole (4 million) with the remainder being in jail or prison. This reliance on supervision in the community, rather than in jails or prisons, is not as great as it was in the early 1990s (when it was over 70 percent) but is similar to the percentages during the 1960s and 1970s (Cahalan, 1986). Even with the movement to abolish or limit parole, the number of persons on parole grew by an average of 3.6 percent during the 1990s (Bonczar & Glaze, 1999). Obviously, correctional supervision in the community continues to be a key to U.S. corrections.

The importance of community corrections programs for persons being released from prison is highlighted by noting that most of the more than 400,000 criminal offenders released to the community will not remain crime free. National statistics show that within three years of release, 40 percent will be returned to prison or jail (Turner & Petersilia, 1996). There are many reasons for such a high recidivism rate, and a variety of community programs attempts to respond to some of those reasons. Chapter 7 discussed many community programs and explained that they were often linked to a probation sentence. Because of the already noted similarity between probation and parole, it will come as no surprise that parolees are often involved in programs similar to those linked to probation. In this manner parolees might be placed under home confinement, could be required to wear electronic monitoring devices, are sometimes under intensive supervision parole, and can be required to complete community service projects. Because there is no real distinction between parole and probation versions of these programs, we need not repeat their description. Chapter 15 reviews some of the most successful programs, but in the context of postrelease programs we can briefly note those involving furloughs, work and education release, and halfway houses.

Furlough

A **furlough** is an authorized leave of absence from prison. It is typically short—twenty-four hours to a few weeks—unescorted, and allowed for rehabilitative, reintegrative, or humanitarian purposes. Acceptable reasons for a furlough include seeking postrelease employment or housing, attending funerals, or simply establishing community contacts and maintaining family ties. Table 13.4 shows that among inmates who had received furloughs, almost three-quarters of the federal inmates and over half the state inmates visited family or friends. About 17 percent of both federal and state inmates were furloughed to attend a funeral.

Eligibility for furlough varies among jurisdictions. In some states only persons within a certain time of release (e.g., one year) are eligible, whereas in other areas eligibility is determined by factors such as institutional behavior and the type of offense. Inciardi (1993) describes the criteria as "ranging from highly specific to hopelessly vague" (p. 661).

Furloughs that allow the prisoners to visit family members at home have benefits to the family as well as the offender. Reintegration is more likely to occur when the released prisoner has positive family support. We sometimes forget that when offenders are absent from their family for months or years, the family is affected as well as the offender. Both will have some adjusting to do upon the offender's release from prison. The furlough program is one way to ease that transition by providing opportunities for offender and family members to get gradually reacquainted rather than having to undergo total immersion.

Work and Education Release

Release from prison for purposes of work has been a part of U.S. corrections since the nineteenth century. In its most general sense, **work release** refers to programs that allow selected prisoners to be released from jail or prison, during certain hours, for the purpose of private employment (Goldfarb & Singer, 1973). In this sense work release and education release are forms of furlough because the release is authorized for a specific amount of time and for a particular purpose.

TABLE 13.4: Number of Times Furloughed and the Reasons, by Sentenced Federal and State Prison Inmates Who Had Been Furloughed, 1991

	PERCENTAGE OF INMATES WITH FURLOUGHS	
	Federal (4.9% of all inmates)	State (5.4% of all inmates)
Number of Times Furloughed		
1	55.3	41.0
2	20.5	12.1
3–5	20.4	14.6
6–10	2.2	13.2
11 or more	1.6	19.0
Reasons for Furloughs		
To visit family or friends	71.6	59.1
To work/find work	7.8	22.2
To attend classes/school	0.9	1.3
To attend a funeral	17.6	17.3
Other	19.5	14.9

Source: Adapted from Harlow, C. W. (1994). *Comparing federal and state prison inmates, 1991* [NCJ 145864]. Washington, DC: Bureau of Justice Statistics.

Early examples of work furlough programs included the practice in several states of placing women prisoners in the custody of private families, where they would serve as indentured servants. Massachusetts passed legislation in 1880 that authorized this practice, and some version of it continues in a few states even today. In the early 1900s, a New Hampshire sheriff released some of his prisoners to work in the community by day and to serve nights and weekends in jail. The Wisconsin legislature passed the Huber Law in 1913, which authorized judges and magistrates to impose conditional sentences on certain minor offenders that allowed them to keep their jobs while serving sentences in local jails. But despite such preliminary efforts, it was not until 1957 that a formal work release program for felons was developed.

A 1957 North Carolina statute, especially as amended in 1959, became the first law devising and implementing a statewide work release program for state prison inmates. The amended version allowed the sentencing judge to recommend that prisoners sentenced to five years or less be given the option of serving the sentence under the work release plan. Eventually the law was modified to allow the parole board to authorize work release for prisoners (Goldfarb & Singer, 1973). By 1965, twenty-four states and the federal government had passed some form of work release laws; and by 1975, all fifty states had legislation authorizing some form of community work (Abadinsky, 1997).

Work release programs remain popular today because they have both economic and treatment benefits. Prisoners on work release are typically required to pay room and board to the state, may have to send a portion of their wages home to help support their family, and must pay income tax on their earnings. At the same time, the offenders are developing good work habits, may be learning new skills, and are possibly acquiring a more positive self-image.

Because inmates on work release are still in prison rather than having been conditionally released, prison officials are selective about placing offenders in the program. Eligibility may be restricted to prisoners within a few months of release or to those who have attained trustee status. The programs serve a reintegrative function because they give prisoners an opportunity to spend a segment of each work day in a conventional setting rather than in the prison. This experience presumably helps prisoners orient themselves to life on the outside and in that way make the postrelease transition a little easier.

Education release is similar to work release except the inmate leaves prison to attend academic (usually college) or vocational classes. Both work and education releases have reintegrative benefits, but the education release does not provide economic relief to the state because the prisoner is not receiving a wage and, therefore, is not expected to pay for items such as room and board.

Residential Community Corrections

In Chapter 8, we discussed halfway houses under the general topic of short-term confinement. The term *halfway-in house* was used in that discussion because the focus was on residential programs for persons who had not yet served prison time on their current sentence. That is, the residential setting provided a point halfway-in to prison. Similarly, there are residential programs that serve as layovers for persons moving from prison to the community. They can be called, indelicately, halfway-out houses.

The need for a transitional step between custody and freedom provided the incentive for a group of Quakers to establish the Isaac T. Hopper Home in New York in 1845. A group of Bostonians opened the Temporary Asylum for Disadvantaged Female Prisoners in 1864, and in 1889 a House of Industry opened in Philadelphia. But many agree that the 1896 opening of Hope Hall in New York identifies the beginning of halfway houses in the United States. This first Hope Hall (others were later opened in cities such as Chicago and San Francisco) provided temporary shelter for prisoners released from Sing Sing Prison. Unlike its predecessors, Hope Hall provided a place that could be considered a real home rather than just another institution (Goldfarb & Singer, 1973).

The increasing use of parole in the twentieth century led to declining interest in Hope Halls and other halfway houses. It was believed that such residences encouraged association with ex-convicts—a position hard to dismiss because the residents were in fact all ex-convicts. But after World War II, corrections officials came to see new possibilities in the halfway house concept. Parole had been adopted in every state by this time, but it was becoming apparent that many parolees were committing additional crimes, especially in the first few months after release. In the 1950s the time was ripe for a resurgence in halfway houses as a transition between prison and the community.

In 1959 Father Charles Dismas Clark, a Jesuit priest, secured funds to open Dismas House in St. Louis. Dismas House would provide shelter and assistance to recently released Missouri prisoners until they could find jobs and homes of their own (Goldfarb & Singer, 1973). By 1994 Dismas House had become a national program, with ten houses spread throughout the United States. The houses still provide shelter and support for recently released prisoners but have added a twist by mixing college students with the ex-cons in a unique living arrangement. The goal is to ease the offender's transition by having them live in a mixed community with nonoffenders. At the same time, college students studying in areas such as criminal justice, sociology, psychology, or social work are able to get practical experience in their chosen field (Dingmann, 1994).

Help Wanted

Job Title: Work Release Center Counselor

Position Description: Supervises a caseload of offenders from a wide range of socioeconomic backgrounds. The counselor will develop a program plan for each client, confirm work schedules weekly with employers, meet weekly with clients to review progress and problems, and make timely case notes to clients' files. The position may also require occasional attendance at court hearings. Monthly reports to courts, probation, and so on must be provided in a clear and concise manner.

Qualifications: Applicants must have a bachelor's degree in criminal justice, psychology, social work, or related fields. Professional experience (including internships) is desirable. Preference will be given to applicants who show effective writing skills and have word-processing knowledge.

For examples of career opportunities in this field, check your state's department of corrections (find links at ***database.corrections.com/career/index.asp#state***).

Father Charles Dismas Clark, a Jesuit priest, opened Dismas House in St. Louis to provide shelter and assistance to recently released Missouri prisoners. Dismas House became a national program, but unlike other halfway houses, Dismas House mixes college students with ex-cons in a unique living arrangement. Shown is a resident at the Dismas House in South Bend, Indiana.

The involvement of private individuals in the halfway house movement has continued today. A few states have established residential facilities in the community, but for the most part halfway houses are privately operated—by both nonprofit and for-profit organizations. Although the actual numbers of halfway houses are difficult to determine, Champion (1990) reports that about 13,000 parolees were assigned to either state-operated or private-contract community homes in 1988.

The halfway houses themselves are identified by a variety of names that might reveal links to people (Dismas House) or places (Lincoln Park House), or reflect goals such as providing a stopover between prison and freedom (Transitional Center), an emphasis on work and restitution (The Restitution Center), developing survival skills (Cope House), or providing general rehabilitative opportunities (Community Treatment Center). This variety of terminology is one reason the generic term *residential community corrections (RCC)* is sometimes used (see Chapter 8) in referring to residential facilities of both the halfway-in and halfway-out types, regardless of their funding source or the specific goals their programs emphasize.

Champion (1990) lists four major functions of residential community corrections programs that are directed toward persons being released from prison: (1) reintegration into the community, (2) provisions for food and shelter, (3) job placement and employment assistance, and (4) client-specific treatments (p. 322). The general reintegration function is accomplished by making offenders aware of and giving them access to various community services that can help them with problems such as drug and alcohol dependency or might give them life skills training in areas such as job interviewing, budgeting, or personal hygiene. The food and shelter function is important because parolees often have limited funds at the time of their release. The RCC program gives them a place to stay and regular meals until they are able to be more self-sufficient.

Job placement and employment assistance strategies are linked to almost every RCC program. RCC staff may advise *residents*—a term commonly used instead of inmate, offender, or parolee—about job leads, might help them fill out job applications, and will often provide transportation between the job site and the residential facility. Because RCC residents typically must pay room and board charges at either state-operated or privately operated facilities, they also learn about budgeting based on their income. Some persons, including law-abiders, have never developed reasonable financial management skills, so RCC staff might see such links between employment and lifestyle as an appropriate aspect of the resident's treatment program.

Responding to other client-specific treatments is a final function of RCCs. Residents with special needs or problems (e.g., drug or alcohol dependency, mental problems, deviant sexual behaviors, or assaultive behavior) can be responded to at the facility or through referral to appropriate community agencies. Residents are often expected to pay, typically on a sliding scale, for everything from testing to actual counseling services that are provided in the community. This not only makes the treatment more affordable from the state's perspective but also makes the resident financially involved in the program and possibly more motivated in achieving a positive outcome.

The various types of RCC facilities clearly offer parolees substantial support as they make the transition from prison to the community. Even poor parole risks, as identified by items such as salient factor scores, are reasonably successful when assigned to halfway houses (Champion, 1990). But despite positive reviews from corrections personnel, RCC is not always a welcome addition to the community. In classic NIMBY (not in my back yard) fashion, citizens often support the RCC concept but fight against establishment of halfway houses in their own neighborhoods. Concerns are expressed that crime rates will increase in neighborhoods with such facilities, and that the RCC residents pose a specific threat to the safety of their neighbors. No direct evidence exists to support either claim (Champion, 1990), but these are emotional issues that are seldom comforted by impersonal statistics. For the foreseeable future it seems clear that RCC facilities and programs will continue to exist and probably expand with general public support—except in the particular neighborhoods where the facility will locate.

Loss and Restoration of Civil Rights

The reintegration of offenders into the community is made difficult by many factors. Programs such as those covered in the previous section help overcome problems linked to poor work or social skills, dysfunctional family relations, or incomplete education. But convicted felons are also confronted with problems in an area in which these programs are of no help. In many jurisdictions, persons convicted of a felony will lose some of their civil rights, meaning that they are not legally full citizens, and that status hinders full reintegration.

Under early English common law a convicted offender might, in addition to his sentence, be required to lose all his civil rights and to forfeit his property. This sanction of **civil death** remains in some U.S. jurisdictions today, where the state declares persons convicted of some serious crimes as being civilly dead. Those offenders are considered to have forfeited all rights and privileges of citizenship, including things such as the right to enter in a contract (even marriage), or the right to sue.

Although the term *civil death* is still applicable in some jurisdictions, it is more common today to make reference to a convicted felon suffering **civil disabilities.** States impose these disabilities in ways that can affect an offender both during her incarceration and after her release. The disabilities during incarceration are the topic of Chapter 14. The disabilities that continue to affect the offender after release from prison are our present concern. Importantly, although civil rights include constitutional rights, the courts have not interpreted civil death and civil disabilities statutes as having completely removed a prisoner's civil rights. Instead, the statutes are considered to have placed restrictions or conditions on those rights. We can appreciate the courts' reasoning by simply realizing that a true loss of all civil (including constitutional) rights would mean that convicted offenders would have no protection against cruel and unusual punishment.

Civil Disabilities after Release

Examples of civil disabilities that affect offenders who are not even in prison include denying convicted felons such privileges as voting, holding public office, obtaining certain jobs or occupational licenses, and even obtaining insurance and pension benefits (*Black's Law Dictionary*). For example, convicted felons in Georgia lose, among other rights, the right to hold office, to vote, to serve on a jury, and to carry a pistol. Similarly, in Arizona a felony conviction suspends such civil rights as the right to vote, to hold public office of trust or profit, to serve as a juror, and to possess a gun or firearm. On the other hand, some state statutes note that convicted felons retain their rights of citizenship. In Oregon, unless the law specifically provides otherwise,

> a person convicted of a felony does not suffer civil death or disability, or sustain loss of civil rights or forfeiture of estate or property, but retains all of the rights of the person . . . , including, but not limited to, the right to vote, to hold, receive and transfer property, to enter into contracts, including contracts of marriage, and to maintain and defend civil actions, suits or proceedings. (O.R.S. § 137.275)

Palmer and Palmer (1999) explain that the courts have both supported and rejected restrictions that states have placed on convicted offenders. In *Richardson v. Ramirez* (1974), the U.S. Supreme Court held that a California provision that disenfranchised convicted felons did not violate the Fourteenth Amendment's equal protection clause. On the other hand, the Alaska Supreme Court held that an Alaskan statute barring prisoners and parolees from bringing a civil lawsuit unrelated to conviction or confinement was unconstitutional. In the Alaska case a parolee was denied an opportunity to use civil action to increase a monetary claim—a denial the court considered to be an act of taking property from the parolee without due process (Palmer & Palmer, 1999).

Loss of the right to vote has been a particularly controversial topic—especially because of its implications for black men, as discussed in the feature "Barring Black Men from the Polls." Fellner and Mauer (1998a) explain that variation among the states has resulted in a crazy quilt of disenfranchisement laws. A state-by-state breakdown of the different provisions (see Table 13.5) shows that only three states (Maine, Massachusetts, and Vermont) do not disenfranchise convicted felons. In forty-eight states and the District of Columbia, a person in prison may not vote. In twenty-nine states, convicted offenders may not vote while on probation, and in thirty-two states they may not vote while on parole. But especially troublesome to critics of felon disenfranchisement are the fourteen states where ex-felons have lost the right to vote even though they have fully served their sentence. In ten of those states the disenfranchisement is for life.

The impact of these laws is that nearly 4 million U.S. citizens, one-third of whom are black men, cannot vote because of felony convictions (Fellner & Mauer, 1998b). Those numbers mean that nationally about 2 percent of the eligible voting population is currently or permanently disenfranchised because of a felony

ISSUES OF FAIRNESS

BARRING BLACK MEN FROM THE POLLS

Is that possible? Are people in the twenty-first century United States really kept from voting because of their race and gender? The simple answer is no. There is no state where laws prohibit an otherwise qualified person from voting just because of race or gender. The more complex answer is yes—because the "otherwise qualified" restriction may have different results based on race and gender.

Individual states make their own laws regarding voting in state elections. Qualifications typically include being at least eighteen years old, a citizen of the United States, and having resided in the specific state for a minimum numbers of days or months. Another qualification, found in forty-seven states and the District of Columbia, excludes from the qualified ranks those people who are convicted felons in prison. Well, you argue, if that's where this "barring black men from voting" is coming from, wouldn't it be more correct to say that prisoners, regardless of race, are not allowed to vote? Of course, it would! And that statement is clearly more accurate. However, there are two reasons to concentrate on the impact felony disenfranchisement has on African Americans—especially men. The first reason is the history of the laws themselves, which undoubtedly were directed toward blacks. The second is the disproportionate impact the laws have on black males specifically.

Many states have prohibited convicted felons from voting since the country's founding. However, after ratification of the Fifteenth Amendment (giving blacks the right to vote), many states specifically considered whether to retain the disenfranchisement of felons. It is generally agreed that several southern state legislatures chose to keep the felon restriction as one of several tools to lessen the ability of blacks to exercise their new right (Fellner & Mauer, 1998a; Strossen, 1999). In a 1985 decision, the U.S. Supreme Court found that discrimination against blacks as well as against poor whites was a motivating factor for Alabama's felony disenfranchisement provision in its 1901 state constitution. Noting that although there were no "eyewitnesses" to the 1901 proceedings, Chief Justice Rehnquist explained that historians generally agree that the Alabama Constitutional Convention of 1901 was part of a movement that swept the post-Reconstruction South to disenfranchise blacks (*Hunter v. Underwood* , 471 U.S. 222).

In addition to being based in racist motivation, the impact of felony disenfranchisement laws on black males must also be considered. In the *Hunter v. Underwood* decision the Court noted that on its face the felon disenfranchisement law is racially neutral—applying equally to anyone convicted of one of the enumerated crimes. However, the Court agreed with the U.S. Court of Appeals' finding that evidence of discriminatory impact was indisputable. By 1903 it was estimated that the provision had disenfranchised approximately ten times as many blacks as whites. This disparate effect persists today. A national study of disenfranchisement laws estimates that more than one-third of the total disenfranchised population are black men. The report adds that given current rates of incarceration, 40 percent of the next generation of black men are likely to permanently lose their right to vote (Fellner & Mauer, 1999a).

Read the "current impact" section of the Sentencing Project's report on losing the vote at *www.hrw.org/reports98/vote/usvot98o-01.htm.* Which two states have the highest percentage of disenfranchised black men? What is the percentage in your state?

conviction. In six states (Alabama, Florida, Mississippi, New Mexico, Virginia, and Wyoming) the provisions exclude from voting over 4 percent of their adult population.

Supporters of disenfranchisement often defend their position by saying the laws prevent felons and ex-felons from voting to weaken criminal laws, or that the provisions are simply another aspect of the punishment one receives for having committed a crime. Critics of disenfranchisement argue that although there is no reason to believe that all or even most ex-offenders would vote to weaken the laws, the principle of universal suffrage cannot be conditioned on the potential content of a

TABLE 13.5: Categories of Felons Disenfranchised under State Law, 1996

STATE	PRISON	PROBATION	PAROLE	EX-FELONS
Alabama	x	x	x	x
Arizona	x	x	x	x (second felony)
Delaware	x	x	x	x
Florida	x	x	x	x
Iowa	x	x	x	x
Kentucky	x	x	x	x
Maryland	x	x	x	x (second felony)
Mississippi	x	x	x	x
Nevada	x	x	x	x
New Mexico	x	x	x	x
Tennessee	x	x	x	x (pre-1986)
Virginia	x	x	x	x
Washington	x	x	x	x (pre-1984)
Wyoming	x	x	x	x
Alaska	x	x	x	–
Arkansas	x	x	x	–
Connecticut	x	x	x	–
Georgia	x	x	x	–
Minnesota	x	x	x	–
Missouri	x	x	x	–
Nebraska	x	x	x	–
New Jersey	x	x	x	–
North Carolina	x	x	x	–
Oklahoma	x	x	x	–
Rhode Island	x	x	x	–
South Carolina	x	x	x	–
Texas*	x	x	x	x (two years)
West Virginia	x	x	x	–
Wisconsin	x	x	x	–

person's vote. Regarding the idea of disenfranchisement as simply a part of criminal punishment, the critics say that even if the state can deprive offenders of any right the state chooses (a position the critics do not accept), such punishment should only be imposed by a judge as part of a criminal sentence (Fellner & Mauer, 1998a).

The twenty-first century starts with most states adhering to felon disenfranchisement laws. However, there seems to be more people questioning the appropriateness and need for those provisions. Fletcher (1999) reports that several state

TABLE 13.5: Continued

STATE	PRISON	PROBATION	PAROLE	EX-FELONS
California	x	–	x	–
Colorado	x	–	x	–
New York	x	–	x	–
District of Columbia	x	–	–	–
Hawaii	x	–	–	–
Idaho	x	–	–	–
Illinois	x	–	–	–
Indiana	x	–	–	–
Kansas	x	–	–	–
Louisiana	x	–	–	–
Michigan	x	–	–	–
Montana	x	–	–	–
New Hampshire	x	–	–	–
North Dakota	x	–	–	–
Ohio	x	–	–	–
Oregon	x	–	–	–
Pennsylvania	x	–	–	–
South Dakota	x	–	–	–
Utah	x	–	–	–
Maine	–	–	–	–
Massachusetts	–	–	–	–
Vermont	–	–	–	–
U.S. total	47	29	32	15

*In 1997, Texas removed the prohibition on voting for ex-felons.

Source: Adapted from Fellner, J., & Mauer, M. (1998). "Losing the vote: The impact of felony disenfranchisement laws in the United States." *Human rights watch and the sentencing project,* p. 4.

legislatures (e.g., Alabama and Florida), are considering proposals to allow felons to return to the voting booth. But these efforts have an uphill battle because politicians often fear that changes to the laws will be seen as being soft on crime when the public is perceived as wanting tougher penalties for offenders.

As discussed earlier in this chapter, most states have procedures by which civil rights or disabilities can be restored (see also Burton, Cullen, & Travis, 1987). A pardon from the governor or a state board—such as a board of pardons and parole—is the typical way that civil rights and disabilities are restored, but some jurisdictions have provided other procedures. In New Mexico, for example, the governor can grant a pardon or can issue a "certificate" that restores the full rights of citizenship (NMSA

1978, § 31-13-1). Disenfranchised felons typically can apply for reinstatement of their right to vote but, critics complain, the offenders are not told about that right or the process to regain the vote is too complicated and cumbersome.

Sex Offender Registration and Notification Laws

Since the 1990s, courts have seen a substantial number of cases by felons who are testing the extent to which states can impose civil disabilities. A particularly controversial area has been the **sex offender registration law** that requires persons convicted of certain sex offenses to register their presence in a community, and the **public notification law,** an additional provision in some jurisdictions that the public then be notified of that person's presence. These laws have been challenged on such constitutional grounds as violating the offenders' right to privacy and equal protection, as being cruel and unusual, or as being a punishment that was added after the person committed the crime. That is, the notification or registration is claimed to be an ex post facto law. So far, the courts have not been impressed with the arguments provided by the challengers. A California court struck down a registration statute because it applied to even the most minor of sex offenders. But more often the statutes have been routinely upheld, as they were in Alaska, Arizona, Illinois, New Hampshire, and Washington (Campbell, 1995; Finn, 1997). Because federal legislation provides for the withholding of federal law enforcement funds from states that do not implement sex offender registration programs, every state has at least the registration laws (Office of the Attorney General, 1998). Over thirty states have taken the additional step of enacting notification laws (Finn, 1997).

The sex offender registration requirements that passed at the federal level, as part of the Violent Crime Control and Law Enforcement Act of 1994, require persons convicted of criminal offenses against minors or other sexually violent offenses to register with law enforcement agencies upon their release from prison, or as a condition of parole, supervised release, or probation. Registration laws at the state level typically give local law enforcement the responsibility for collecting the information, which usually includes an offender's name, address, fingerprints, photo, date of birth, social security number, criminal history, place of employment, and vehicle registration. Several states also collect blood samples for DNA identification. The registration requirement is for the offender's lifetime in several states, but most often it is for a period of at least ten years (Finn, 1997).

More controversial than the registration laws are those statutes that require notification to the public that sex offenders have moved or are planning to move into a community. Washington State took the lead in public notification laws in 1990 when it passed a law authorizing public agencies to release relevant and necessary information regarding sex offenders to the public (Silva, 1995). But despite Washington's lead, New Jersey's version of a public notification law received even more widespread attention. In 1994 New Jersey passed the so-called **Megan's Law,** requiring that neighbors be notified when a sex offender moves into their neighborhood. The law was passed after seven-year-old Megan Kanka was raped and murdered by a twice-convicted sex offender who had moved into a house across the street from the Kankas.

New Jersey's notification law was immediately popular and controversial. In 1995 the New Jersey Supreme Court ruled that it is constitutional to notify a neighborhood when a sex offender moves in. New Jersey's Chief Justice explained the court's ruling by saying that "to rule otherwise is to find that society is unable to protect itself from sexual predators by adopting the simple remedy of informing the public of their presence" (*Doe v. Poritz,* 142 N.J. 1, 109; 1995). But despite the Chief Justice's confidence in such a law, its value has been questioned by many other

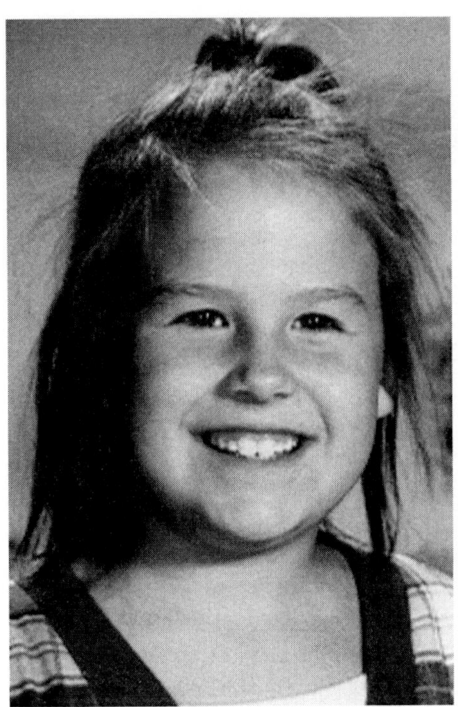

In 1994 seven-year-old Megan Kanka, shown here in an undated family photo, was raped and murdered by a convicted sex offender who lived across the street from the Kanka family. A New Jersey law requiring neighbors to be notified when a sex offender moves into their neighborhood came to be called *Megan's Law.*

professionals. Thus far, however, the state and federal courts have been more likely than not to uphold different versions of the notification laws (Finn, 1997). Megan's Law withstood a challenge at the federal level in 1997 when the U.S. Court of Appeals, Third Circuit, upheld the New Jersey statute in *E. B. v. Verniero.*

Current notification laws can be identified as falling into one of four categories (Finn, 1997, p. 5; "Sloppy 'Megan's Laws'," 1998):

- *Agency determined.* A state agency (e.g., police, probation, or parole) determines what risk the offender poses and then carries out a notification plan that reflects that level of risk. In several states, that plan provides for three tiers of risk. The first tier may involve only notification to selected local organizations (such as schools), the second could add community residents, and the third would include the media.
- *Statute determined.* State statutes specify which type of offenders are subject to notification and what notification methods to use. A designated agency carries out the notification as required in the statute.
- *Offender implemented.* Offenders themselves must do the actual notification. For example, Louisiana offenders, when victims are under age eighteen, must place an advertisement in the local legal journal, notify the public school superintendents and park superintendents, send postcards to all residences within a specified radius of their homes, and provide photographs to all those groups and individuals.
- *Community implemented.* Community groups and individuals must take the initiative to request information about any sex offenders living in their community and must ask for information about the person.

That categorization may imply more order to these laws than is accurate. In fact, an editorial in *USA Today* ("Sloppy 'Megan's Laws,'" 1998) said there is a mishmash

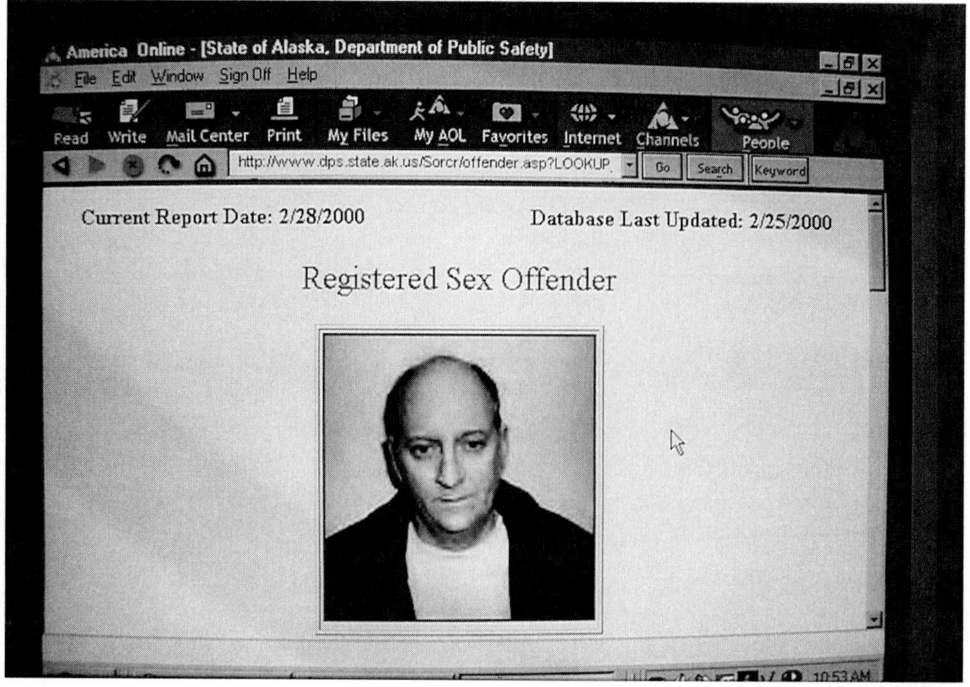

Sex offender registration laws in some states include public notification provisions that require photographs of registered sex offenders to be posted on the Internet.

of programs across the country ranging from some that do not appear to have received any forethought by legislators to others that may actually be protecting the public. But the effectiveness of the notification laws remains in doubt. Finn (1997) says there is no empirical evidence that notification achieves its stated objectives of increasing public safety. However, that study (conducted in Washington, which is the only state evaluating the effectiveness of its program) did determine that the offenders subject to notification who committed any kind of new offense were caught three years earlier on average than those who were not under notification requirements. This suggests that another goal of the notification laws—helping police with sex offender investigations—may be realized.

CONDITIONAL RELEASE IN OTHER COUNTRIES

Early release from prison sentences, both with and without conditions, is a widespread practice throughout the world. Some examples from Canada and Asia are considered next, and the feature "Conditional Freedom in Latin America" reviews some of the procedures in that region.

Conditional Release in Canada

Canada uses furlough-like programs (called temporary absences) and prerelease programs (day parole) to help prepare prisoners for eventual release to the community, but we will focus on Canada's system of parole (called full parole to distinguish it from day parole) because it offers an interesting comparison to parole in the United States. First, parole in Canada tends to operate at a national level rather than a state (provincial) level. Second, Canadians have resisted the temptation to abolish parole. We begin with parole's national-level organization and operation.

Cross-Cultural Corrections

Conditional Freedom in Latin America

In Latin American countries, conditional freedom is granted to prisoners who, having served part of their term of imprisonment, have shown good behavior in the correctional institution (Carranza, Liverpool, & Rodriguez-Manzanera, 1994). The main condition linked to this freedom is that no new offenses are committed. Should that condition, or any other that was included, be violated, the freedom can be revoked. In Costa Rica, Chile, El Salvador, Peru, and Cuba, conditional freedom can be granted when half the penalty has been served, but in Argentina, Bolivia, Colombia, Panama, and Venezuela, the prisoner must serve two-thirds of the sentence.

Carranza, Liverpool, and Rodriguez-Manzanera (1994) explain that parole also exists in Latin American countries but more so in concept than practice. Although conditional freedom places restrictions on the released prisoner, there is no supervision of the offender in the community. Parole, on the other hand, implies conditional freedom and supervision—generally by social workers and criminologists. The traditional use of conditional freedom with the lack of personnel to provide supervision has resulted in essentially no parole releases in continental Latin America. In other Latin American countries, parole is granted upon support from parole officers and at the indication of councils in the correctional institutions.

Although the absence of supervision means conditional freedom cannot be considered parole, there are still many similarities in the operation of conditional freedom in Latin America and parole in the United States. For example, conditional freedom might require the offenders to live in a designated place, maintain legitimate work—a criticized condition given the region's high unemployment rate—abstain from consuming alcohol, or avoid association with certain people.

Read more about prisons in Latin America at ***www.hrw.org/advocacy/prisons/americas.htm*** where the Human Rights Watch provides many interesting articles. Choose two countries from those listed on this page, and describe some of the important prison problems and issues of concern in those countries.

Parole's history in Canada dates to the 1899 passage of the Ticket of Leave Act, which established a system of supervised freedom similar to that introduced in the United States during the 1870s. In 1958 the Parole Act replaced the Ticket of Leave Act and created the National Parole Board (NPB).

Canada's ten provinces and two federal territories have a working relationship with its federal government that may seem too comfortable for some citizens in the United States. Whereas their North American neighbors in the fifty states resist federal government involvement in criminal justice issues, the Canadians are much more accommodating.

Following a "two-year rule" set down in the Criminal Code, offenders sentenced to two or more years fall under the jurisdiction of the federal corrections system (except in Newfoundland, where the province maintains jurisdiction over federal offenders). Offenders receiving sentences of less than two years are the responsibility of the provinces. This distinction affects parole by giving the NPB authority over parole for federal offenders whereas provincial parole boards handle their own prisoners. Actually, only three provinces have chosen to create their own parole boards—Quebec, Ontario, and British Columbia—so seven provinces use the NPB to make parole decisions for offenders with sentences under two years. As a result, the NPB has jurisdiction over all federal offenders, provincial inmates in seven of the ten provinces, and inmates in two territories. Canadian parole is essentially a national operation.

Full parole in Canada is a conditional release program that allows inmates to serve a portion of their sentence under supervision in the community (Griffiths & Verdun-Jones, 1994). Generally, inmates are eligible for parole after serving one-third of their sentence or seven years, whichever is shorter. Legislation passed in

1992 allows sentencing judges to set the parole eligibility for violent and serious drug offenders at one-half the sentence, but even then the time until parole eligibility cannot exceed ten years. The NPB reviews the cases of all inmates as they become eligible for parole and must conduct annual reviews on all cases not receiving parole until that inmate is either paroled or is discharged as having completed the sentence. Griffiths and Verdun-Jones report that full parole is not easily obtained by Canadian prisoners. Data from 1991 and 1992 show the NPB granted parole to only 33 percent of the federal offenders who appeared before the board. Provincial inmates appearing before the national board fared better, with 47 percent being granted parole. The three provincial parole boards granted parole in 37 percent (Quebec), 51 percent (Ontario), and 58 percent (British Columbia) of the cases brought before them (Griffiths & Verdun-Jones, 1994, p. 546).

In the late 1980s Canadian criminal justice in general and parole in particular came under scrutiny and criticism similar to that experienced in the United States a decade or so earlier (Rhine et al., 1991). Canadians were especially concerned about the disparate sentences imposed for similar crimes. In 1987 the Canadian Sentencing Commission recommended a just deserts sentencing framework that would have sentences imposed with attention to the gravity of the offense and the culpability of the offender. The commission suggested that parole be abolished because its rehabilitation foundation and discretionary release procedures violated the principle of proportionality in punishment.

The Canadian Bar Association challenged the call to abolish parole and urged instead a shift away from reliance on imprisonment to an increased use of community-based alternatives. A House of Commons committee sided with the bar association's suggestions and added their own conditions to tighten control on conditional releases. With its 1992 passage, the Corrections and Conditional Release Act maintained the parole option but included two specific criteria for granting parole: (1) Parole should be granted to offenders who will benefit from the reintegration aspect of parole, but (2) should not be granted to offenders who present an undue risk to the community (Griffiths & Verdun-Jones, 1994). These criteria and the addition of other criteria and conditions, as well as the standardization of risk assessment procedures, serve to calm the critics of parole and keep it as an important part of Canadian corrections.

Conditional Release in Asia and the Pacific

Sugihara et al. (1994) found two major techniques for early release from imprisonment in countries of Asia and the Pacific region: (1) remission and (2) parole. **Remission** reduces a prison sentence mainly on the basis of good behavior; parole refers to a prisoner's conditional release, under supervision, after serving part of the sentence. Some countries, such as India and Singapore, rely more heavily on remission, whereas parole has a major role in other countries (e.g., China, Japan, Korea, Papua New Guinea, Thailand, and Hong Kong). Other countries, such as Fiji, Indonesia, the Philippines, and Sri Lanka, use both remission and parole (Sugihara et al., 1994).

For examples of remission, we will look at Singapore and Indonesia. Under Singapore's criminal procedure code, the president has the authority to remit all or some part of a person's punishment. This may be done upon application by the offender and after the president receives an opinion about the application from the presiding judge of the court in which the sentence was imposed. Conditions can be attached to the remission order, and if those conditions are not met, the president may cancel the remission and require the offender to complete the unexpired portion of the sentence. Remission in Indonesia is also under the control of the president, but the process seems less case specific than in Singapore. On August 17 of each year, in celebration of Indonesian independence, the president grants remission of sentence to nonrecidivist prisoners who have shown good conduct. The wide use of this pardonlike remission is seen in statistics from 1986, when 75 percent of the persons in prison received partial reduction of their imprisonment and another 18 percent received a total reduction (Sugihara et al., 1994).

Japan presents an interesting example of parole because it displays both similarities to and differences with parole in the United States. Parker (1986) explains that prisoners in Japan may be considered for parole after serving one-third of a fixed prison term, or after completing ten years of a life sentence. Sugihara et al. (1994) report that despite the one-third minimum, most parolees have served more than 70 percent of their sentence before being released.

In addition to meeting the time requirements, prisoners seeking parole must show genuine reformation and must be nominated by their warden. Those who are granted parole will remain under the supervision of a probation officer for the remainder of their original sentence (including "life" unless a pardon is given). Parole can be revoked for either a technical violation of parole conditions or upon committing a new offense. Typical conditions of parole include residence restrictions, work requirements, and regulations affecting with whom the parolee may associate. The parole board may also provide conditions specific to the individual's needs or circumstances.

An intriguing aspect of Japanese parole is the large-scale use of government-appointed volunteer probation officers who, like their professional counterparts, also supervise offenders on parole. Upon release from prison, the parolee is assigned to both a professional and a volunteer probation officer. The volunteer probation officers (VPOs) have no authority to enforce the conditions of parole, so they can concentrate on fulfilling a helping role rather than being caught in the professional probation officer's dilemma of "cop" and "social worker." The volunteers must be healthy, active, and financially stable citizens with the enthusiasm and time necessary to supervise and assist parolees and probationers.

SUMMARY

The vast majority of persons sentenced to prison will some day be released from prison. This chapter reviews the primary ways that release might occur and some of the programs and problems associated with the reintegration of the former prisoners into the community.

UNCONDITIONAL RELEASE FROM PRISON

- When a person is released from prison without conditions attached to that release, an unconditional release has occurred.
- Unconditional release, which includes releases at the expiration of the sentence, as the result of a commuted sentence, or because of a sentence being vacated, is the less frequently occurring form of release.

CONDITIONAL RELEASE FROM PRISON

- When a prisoner is released before serving his or her entire sentence and that release is accompanied by certain conditions, a conditional release has occurred.
- Most conditional releases are under supervised mandatory release or by parole.

THE CONTEMPORARY PAROLE PROCESS

- Parole has links to procedures such as good time, the ticket-of-leave, and indeterminate sentencing.
- There is variation among the jurisdictions, but parole typically involves an early release at the discretion of a parole board. Offenders granted parole must abide by certain terms and conditions, must report to a parole officer, and risk a return to prison should they break the law.
- Some jurisdictions have abolished or abandoned parole and instead release prisoners, after they complete a required portion of their sentence, under supervised mandatory release. Persons under supervised mandatory release typically must still report to a corrections official, such as a parole officer, but their release was automatic rather than at the discretion of a parole board.

REINTEGRATION PROGRAMS

- To assist former prisoners in their reintegration to the community, programs such as furloughs, work and education release, and residential community corrections are found throughout the country.
- These programs help offenders find employment, improve relations among family members, improve their self-concept, or overcome problems with drug or alcohol abuse.

LOSS AND RESTORATION OF CIVIL RIGHTS

- In some communities convicted felons face other types of problems with which current programs cannot help. An important example are the civil disabilities statutes, found in most states, that restrict some of the offender's rights of citizenship.
- Especially noteworthy are sex offender registration and notification laws that some critics argue violate the convicted felon's right to privacy or protection against cruel and unusual punishment.

CONDITIONAL RELEASE IN OTHER COUNTRIES

The chapter concludes with a review of some conditional release programs and procedures in other countries. Some countries, such as Canada, seem very similar to U.S. jurisdictions in their use of conditional release. Others have programs—such as Japan's heavy reliance on volunteer parole officers—that are very different.

KEY TERMS AND CONCEPTS

civil death (p. 499)
civil disabilities (p. 499)
commutation of sentence (p. 474)
conditional release (p. 472)
education release (p. 497)
expiration of sentence (p. 473)
furlough (p. 495)
mark system (p. 477)
Megan's Law (p. 504)
pardon (p. 475)
parole (p. 476)
parole board (p. 482)
public notification law (p. 504)
reintegration (p. 494)
remission (p. 508)
salient factor score (p. 484)
sex offender registration law (p. 504)
supervised mandatory release (p. 476)
unconditional release (p. 472)
work release (p. 495)

Discussion Questions

1. Discuss the pros and cons of giving a state or nation's chief executive officer the power to pardon.
2. Determine whether your state uses parole or supervised mandatory release, and discuss the advantages and disadvantages of whichever procedure is in place.
3. If you were a member of a parole board, what characteristics and situations would you use to determine if a prisoner should be released on parole?
4. Identify some residential community corrections programs in your community, and discuss the appropriateness of those programs in terms of rehabilitation objectives.
5. Discuss the merits and the harms of sex offender registration and public notification laws. Are there other types of offenders who should also be required to register and about whose presence the community should be notified?

RIGHTS OF PRISONERS

Judicial Involvement in Prison Administration

Sources of Prisoners' Rights

A SAMPLING OF PRISONERS' RIGHTS ISSUES

Access to the Courts

Issues of Religion

Issues of Privacy

The Nominal Doctrine: A Return to Hands Off?

PRISONERS' RIGHTS IN OTHER COUNTRIES

Rights Retained and Rights Lost

Control of Prisons and Prison Conditions

VICTIMS' RIGHTS

Victim Participation in Sentencing

Victim Services in Corrections

SUMMARY

KEY TERMS AND CONCEPTS

DISCUSSION QUESTIONS

chapter 14

PRISONERS' AND VICTIMS' RIGHTS

You are the judge. Here are the cases:

- A prisoner in Idaho has filed suit against prison guards who refused to "tidy up" his cell after a search.
- A Florida prisoner who murdered five people is suing because lightning knocked out the prison's TV satellite dish and he must watch network programs that he says contain violence, profanity, and other objectionable material.
- A Mississippi prisoner is suing because he did not receive his scheduled parole hearing—prison officials have provided a note that the prisoner was out on escape when the hearing was held.
- A prisoner in Florida is suing because he was required to eat off of a paper plate.

- An inmate serving time on a child molestation sentence sues Nevada prison officials for not letting him subscribe to a publication of the North American Man/Boy Love Association (Irwin, 1993; 'Lectric law library, 1999).

Although it is unfair to form an opinion without hearing all the facts in these cases, chances are you are not sympathetic to most of these inmates' complaints. These are the types of lawsuits brought to court at taxpayer expense that so infuriated the public and the politicians in the mid-1990s that Congress enacted the **Prison Litigation Reform Act** of 1995 (18 U.S.C. §3626). The primary goal of the act was to limit prisoners' ability to complain about their conditions of confinement. This was deemed necessary because of a perception that inmates were increasingly engaged in what is called recreational litigation.

Prior to the Prison Litigation Reform Act, inmates could file suit in court—at no financial cost to themselves—to complain about how prison officials had violated their constitutional or civil rights. The inmates could file as many lawsuits as they wished and make claims that seemed ridiculous (e.g., an Illinois inmate filed suit for not being allowed to use his cell for drug trafficking), but the court would have to take the time to respond. As a bonus for the inmates, they were sometimes taken out of prison for a trip to court, and there was always the possibility that they might win the case and watch the court make the prison officials behave as the prisoners wished. Inmates seldom won their cases, and many were thrown out by the courts as frivolous. Even so, few people were surprised when President Clinton, in 1996, signed the Prison Litigation Reform Act (PLRA) into law.

As we see later, critics of the PLRA are concerned that it has the effect of denying prisoners access to the courts. Of course it does, you might argue! After all, "People who commit a crime give up their rights—that's what punishment is all about." But consider a few more stories:

- Prisoners at California's Pelican Bay state prison were placed naked in wire mesh cages outside in low temperatures, were hog-tied in their cells for hours on end, and received no medical or mental health care.

- Massachusetts prisoners were locked in cells that had massive vermin infestation, were fire hazards, and had no toilets.
- Female prisoners in the District of Columbia were routinely sexually assaulted by prison guards. One officer specifically was said to have fondled a prisoner who was receiving medical care in the infirmary, forced her to perform oral sex, then raped her.
- A quadriplegic prisoner in Indiana was kept in the prison hospital and denied access to all rehabilitation and educational programs offered by the prison, even though he was qualified and able to participate in them.
- Despite warnings by the Commissioner of Health, Pennsylvania prison officials failed to implement basic tuberculosis detection and control procedures. Over 400 prisoners were infected in a single prison (Erickson, 1996; Wright, 1999).

Well, those are a bit different, aren't they? It's hard to believe, but very important to remember, that these five cases are prisoner lawsuits just like the five cases beginning this chapter. Would the public have been so anxious to limit inmate lawsuits if these were the ones highlighted by the media in the mid-1990s?

Certainly there are people who read all the preceding cases and consider every one to be frivolous. They simply believe criminals gave up their rights when they committed a crime. And, they might argue, even though some of the stories present serious claims, offenders should not expect, or have, the same rights as do law-abiding citizens. Other people, however, will look at the same cases and believe that even criminals are entitled to sanitary conditions, a safe environment, and equal access to programs. Distinguishing between frivolous and serious circumstances often becomes the job of judges as they try to apply the law as passed by legislators or as it comes from other court decisions. To understand better just how legislatures and courts have responded to questions about what, if any, rights criminals retain after conviction, we will look at the sources of offenders' rights and at specific kinds of offenders' rights.

We must not forget that there are other people, also having certain rights, involved in most crimes. These persons, the victims of crimes, are too often forgotten by the justice officials and by the public. After reviewing issues of prisoners' rights, we will look at rights the victims might have. Finally, this chapter concludes with a review of how other countries approach the topic of prisoners' rights.

RIGHTS OF PRISONERS

Two positions can be taken regarding rights of persons who have been convicted and imprisoned:

- The **rights-are-retained position** argues that prisoners keep all the rights of an ordinary citizen, except those that are expressly or by necessity taken away from them by law.
- The **rights-are-lost** position says prisoners are wholly without rights except those expressly conferred by law or necessity.

Importantly, but confusingly, neither position accurately identifies the approach held by the courts. The rights-are-retained view comes directly from a federal appeals court decision (see Table 14.1 on reading court citations) in 1944 (*Coffin v. Reichard,* 143 F.2d 443),[1] but federal courts have issued many other decisions that suggest prisoners may only have rights that are compatible with the goals of prison administration. In the absence of a clear and consistent approach, it is not surprising that the public, prison officials, and even judges have difficulty understanding or describing the rights of prisoners. One way to explain the confusion is to consider how the courts have changed over the years in their level of involvement in prison administration.

Judicial Involvement in Prison Administration

Although federal and state courts have not consistently followed either a rights-are-retained or rights-are-lost position, it is possible to identify historical periods according to the courts' willingness to be involved in prison administration issues. These periods move from an initial one of noninvolvement (called the hands-off doctrine), to a time of rather active intrusion (the intervention doctrine), and most recently back to a doctrine of minimal and moderate judicial involvement (the nominal doctrine).

The Hands-Off Doctrine. Despite the rights-are-retained decision in *Coffin v. Reichard,* federal and state courts, before the early 1960s, essentially held the view that prisoners had only those rights specifically granted by statute or by policy.

[1]It has been the practice in this book to omit the full case citation in the chapter narrative. But because this chapter uses decisions from a great variety of courts, it seems appropriate to use complete citations the first time a case is noted. In this way one can easily tell which level court made the decision (see Table 14.1).

TABLE 14.1: Court Citations Using Federal Reports (Official Publications) and Federal Reporters (Unofficial Publications)

FULL NAME	OFFICIAL ABBREVIATION	TYPE OF CASE REPORTED
United States Reports	U.S.	U.S. Supreme Court
Supreme Court Reporter	S.Ct.	U.S. Supreme Court
U.S. Supreme Court Reports—Lawyers' Edition (Lawyers' Edition, Second Series)	L.Ed. (L.Ed.2d)	U.S. Supreme Court
Federal Reporter, Second Series	F.2d	Federal Appeals Court
Federal Supplement	F.Supp.	Federal District Court

A complete court citation will tell you what volume of the report or reporter you need and the page at which coverage of the case begins. So, the citation 380 U.S. 163 tells you to look in volume 380 of *United States Reports* beginning on page 163. Similarly, 142 F.2d 443 would refer you to volume 142 of the *Federal Reporter, Second Series* on page 443. Sometimes you are directed to a specific page in a court decision. In those cases the citation will include the word *at.* So, 334 F.2d at 908, directs you specifically to page 908 of volume 334 in the *Federal Reporter, Second Series.*

Prison conditions were free from outside scrutiny, and prison administrators governed without any outside interference. State and federal courts were reluctant to intervene in prison administration unless there appeared to be a clear violation of the Eighth Amendment's protection against cruel and unusual punishment.

One of the clearest and possibly most extreme examples of this **hands-off doctrine** was stated in an 1871 Virginia ruling that said prisoners were "slaves of the state."

> For the time being, during his term of service in the penitentiary, he is in a state of penal servitude to the State. He has, as a consequence of his crime, not only forfeited his liberty, but all his personal rights except those which the law in its humanity accords to him. He is for the time being the slave of the State. . . . While in this state of penal servitude, [prisoners] must be subject to the regulations of the institution of which they are inmates, and the laws of the State to whom their service is due in expiation of their crimes. (*Ruffin v. Commonwealth,* 62 Va. [21 Gratt.] at 796)

In 1948 the U.S. Supreme Court did not make reference to "slaves of the state" but still supported a hands-off policy in *Price v. Johnston,* 334 U.S. 266. In that ruling the Court held that convicted offenders should expect to be penalized for their misdeeds—and part of their punishment was the loss of freedoms that free citizens take for granted.

The hands-off doctrine espoused by the courts was justified on several grounds:

- Correctional administration was a technical matter that was best left to experts in corrections rather than to the courts, which are not equipped to make appropriate evaluations regarding the running of prisons.
- Even if judges were qualified to manage prisons, the separation of powers doctrine should keep them from involvement in prison affairs because prisons are part of the executive, not the judicial, branch of government.
- Society as a whole was apathetic to what went on in prisons, and most individuals preferred not to associate with or know about the offender.
- Prisoners' complaints involved privileges rather than rights. Prisoners were considered to have fewer constitutional rights than other members of society.

The reasons provided for nonintervention kept federal and state courts from tinkering with the way prison administrators chose to run their facilities. The hands-off policy was enduring. For example, by 1954 the federal appeals court was still taking the position that courts are without power to supervise prison administration or to interfere with ordinary prison rules or regulations (*Banning v. Looney,* 213 F.2d 771). But the end of nonintervention was in sight, and by the mid-1960s, courts were looking very differently at prison management issues.

The Intervention Doctrine. After nearly 170 years of keeping the courts out of the prison management business, the hands-off doctrine began eroding. By the mid-1960s federal district courts were seriously considering prisoners' claims. An important reason for the courts' new interest in prisoners was simply a reflection of the times—which also saw increased interest in areas such as civil rights, student rights, public welfare, and general institutional reform. Several of the earliest cases heard by the courts were ones involving racial and religious discrimination brought by Black Muslims in prison. Some of these cases are discussed in detail later, but one particular case deserves mention here as well.

In 1962 Black Muslim leader Thomas X. Cooper filed suit in Illinois against Stateville Prison Warden Frank Pate. Cooper claimed that his confinement in segregation was retribution for his religious beliefs (Jacobs, 1977). The basis for his claim was section 1983 of the Civil Rights Act of 1871. Cooper was being denied access to the Qur'an, to Muslim literature such as the newspaper *Muhammad Speaks,* and to Muslim clergy. At a 1965 trial, ordered by the U.S. Supreme Court (*Cooper v. Pate,* 378 U.S. 546; 1964), prison officials had to justify their refusal to recognize the Muslims as a religious group (see "Five Percenters: Religion, Gang, or Way of Life?"). Because Christian inmates were allowed to read the Bible, and Jewish inmates could have Hebrew literature, the prison officials found it difficult to explain why Muslim prisoners could not have the Qur'an or receive Arabic

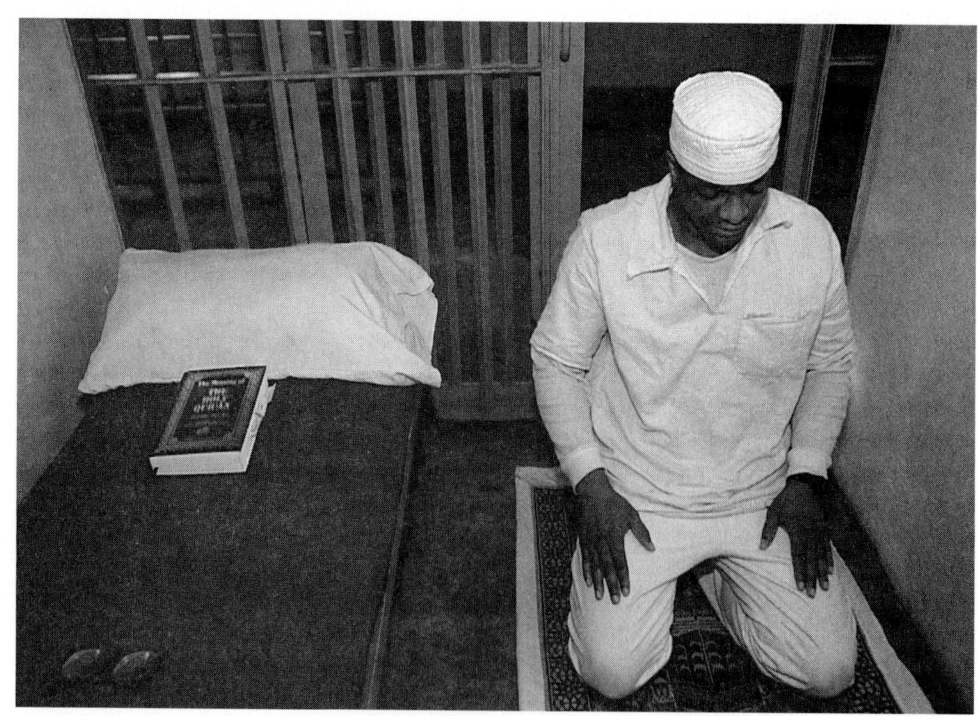

Several of the earliest prisoners' rights cases involved Black Muslims claiming racial and religious discrimination. Court decisions in the early 1960s allowed prison authorities to prohibit Black Muslims from worshiping and from studying church literature. Contemporary court decisions respond to Black Muslim cases with the same criteria used to decide cases brought by any other religious groups.

Spotlight ON CONTEMPORARY ISSUES

Five Percenters: Religion, Gang, or Way of Life?

In 1964 Illinois officials tried to convince the courts that restricting Black Muslims from practicing their religion was necessary for purposes of prison security (*Cooper v. Pate,* 378 U.S. 546). More than thirty years later prison officials are making a similar argument regarding a Harlem-born offshoot of the Black Muslims—the Five Percenters.

Five Percenters, members of the Five Percent Nation of Islam, take their name from Elijah Muhammad's explanation that enlightened followers of Islam make up a minority (5 percent) of the population and are charged with educating the foolish majority (85 percent) who are oppressed by the remaining 10 percent—who are corrupt "white devils" (Five Percent Nation, 1999). Although the Five Percent Nation of Islam (also called the Nation of Gods and Earth) shares many beliefs with the Nation of Islam (Black Muslims) and with Orthodox Muslims, the Five Percenters are not identical to either of those religions. In fact, the Five Percent Nation of Islam is considered by some members to be more a way of life than a religion. Two interesting cases reached the federal courts in 1999, and each suggests that Five Percenters will continue to raise issues regarding prisoners' rights.

In 1999 the U.S. District Court was asked to determine if Lord Natural Self-Allah, a Five Percenter and an inmate in New York, was denied his First and Fourteenth Amendment rights when prison authorities withheld delivery of his subscription to *The Five Percenter,* a religious publication of the Five Percent Nation of Islam. Prison officials argued that Five Percenters, at least in the prison context, function as a violent prison gang. They participate in extortion, robbery, assaults, and drug trafficking, and they communicate through oral and written code. Allowing access to Five Percenter literature, the officials argued, not only allows but also encourages disruptive behavior. In *Lord Natural Self-Allah v. Annucci* (W.D.N.Y., No. 97-CV-607(H); 1999), the U.S. District Court judge found in favor of the prison officials. The judge explained that although Five Percenterism in its pure, uncorrupted form may represent a belief system that does not advocate violence, it seems that the prison version does. And, because prison officials were able to show a clear relationship between Five Percenter literature and prison gang activities, the prison's ban on Five Percenter literature is reasonable.

A Five Percenter case was also heard in 1999 at the federal appeals court level. In *In re Long-Term Administrative Segregation of Inmates Designated as Five Percenters* (4th Cir., No. 98-7337) the South Carolina Department of Corrections's (SCDC) designation and treatment of the Five Percent Nation of Islam as a security threat group (STG) was deemed rational and allowed. In 1995 the SCDC classified Five Percenters as an STG after three incidents (two assaults and a riot) were attributed to Five Percenter activities. Because of their STG classification, all Five Percenters were transferred to administrative segregation or to maximum-custody confinement. In this case the inmates raised First Amendment claims (the STG designation violates the free exercise clause), Fourteenth Amendment violations (the STG designation means their group is being treated differently), and Eighth Amendment issues (the STG designation places them in long-term segregated confinement). The court of appeals, which noted there is considerable disagreement regarding the designation of Five Percenters as a religious group, simply assumed they are so the court could avoid having to examine the nature and sincerity of the inmates' professed beliefs. However, even granting religion status, the court determined that legitimate penological interests allow prison authorities to designate Five Percenters as an STG and to treat them accordingly. Furthermore, the court said there was no Fourteenth Amendment violation because Five Percenters were treated no differently than other similar groups under the STG policy. Finally, there was no Eighth Amendment violation because long-term segregated confinement does not alone constitute cruel and unusual punishment.

Read the court of appeals decision at ***www.law.emory.edu/4circuit/apr99/987337.p.html.*** Describe the reasons given by the SCDC for designating Five Percenters as an STG. Do you agree with the court that those reasons are convincing? Read about the Five Percent Nation at ***www.altculture.com/aentries/f/fivexperce.html.*** What links does Five Percent Nation have to rap acts? Read "We Are Not a Gang" at ***metalab.unc.edu/nge/notagang/.*** What would be an appropriate designation for Five Percenters according to this article?

documents (Jacobs, 1977). In the end (*Cooper v. Pate,* 382 F.2d 518; 1967), Cooper won on some points (Muslims had to have access to the Qur'an, to communicate and visit with Muslim ministers, and to attend Muslim religious services). On other points, the court sided with prison officials (contemporary Muslim literature and Arabic textbooks did not have to be allowed). But although these religious points were important in opening First Amendment rights to prisoner claims, *Cooper v. Pate* (1964) may be even more important because the suit was based on a civil rights act.

The *Cooper v. Pate* (1964) decision has had a dramatic impact on the filing of suits by prisoners. The decision serves as a good landmark to signal the end of the hands-off doctrine because it was the first to recognize that prisoners can sue if they are deprived of any rights, privileges, or immunities provided by the U.S. Constitution and by law. Because the Civil Rights Act requires that the victims receive compensatory (e.g., monetary reimbursement as a measure of the actual loss suffered) or injunctive (e.g., prison officials must stop doing something the courts found to be unjust or inequitable to the prisoner) relief, such suits became very popular. In 1966 only 218 prison law cases were filed under the Civil Rights Act, but by 1992 nearly 27,000 state prisoners' rights cases were recorded (Hanson & Daley, 1995).

Several of the cases discussed later in this chapter were brought to the courts as violations of the Civil Rights Act. The 1960s also found the courts being more sympathetic to prisoners' claims that they held on to certain constitutional rights. With the new **intervention doctrine,** courts (especially the lower federal courts) began supporting prisoners' claims to rights in areas such as privacy, communication, safety, and due process. We will look at the source of those claims after a brief note about the contemporary court views toward involvement in prison management.

The Nominal Doctrine. It is premature at this point to discuss in depth some of the recent court decisions that point to a return to the hands-off doctrine. That discussion will make more sense after we have had an opportunity to see some specific examples of court decisions as they relate to particular rights being claimed by prisoners. For that reason we will save elaboration of this topic until later.

Sources of Prisoners' Rights

Proponents of the position that inmates retain some rights during incarceration point at state and federal constitutions and state and federal laws to support their claim. State constitutions and laws are too numerous to cover here, so we concentrate instead on federal-level sources. First we will look at articles of the U.S. Constitution and two of the constitution's amendments to understand how they serve as the basis for many inmate claims. Then we consider the Civil Rights Act (U.S. Code, Title 42 §1983) as an example of a federal statute that is used increasingly often to support inmate claims of discrimination.

The U.S. Constitution. When introducing the concept of individual rights under the U.S. Constitution, John Ferdico (1996) reminds us how much easier enforcement of criminal laws would be if persons suspected of crime were presumed guilty, could be detained for long periods of time without a hearing, had no privilege against self-incrimination, and could have their bodies, vehicles, and homes searched at will (p. 2). But because the United States was founded as a direct response to what early colonists saw as British abuses in these kinds of areas, there has been from the start a strong commitment to protecting individual rights from government abuse. With the ratification in 1788 of the U.S. Constitution, and with the 1791 addition of the Bill of Rights, America's commitment to individual rights was guaranteed. As a result, persons suspected of crime are, among other things, presumed innocent, cannot be detained long without a hearing, are not forced to incriminate themselves, and have protection against unreasonable searches and seizures.

In addition to concern about the rights of persons suspected and accused of crimes, the U.S. Constitution and the Bill of Rights also express a concern about the rights of persons convicted of a crime. For example, section 9 of Article 1 provides the privilege of the writ of *habeas corpus* as a safeguard against unlawful imprisonment, whereas section 10 of Article 1, through its prohibition against *ex post facto* law, prevents imposing a greater punishment for a crime than was in effect when the crime was committed. In the Bill of Rights, the obvious example of concern for those convicted is in the Eighth Amendment's prohibition against cruel and unusual punishments. Of the subsequent amendments, the Fourteenth is of particular importance, as discussed in a moment. Habeas corpus action and complaints of ex post facto law violations are still brought by offenders today. But this overview will concentrate more on issues related to the Eighth and Fourteenth Amendments.

The Eighth Amendment. The Eighth Amendment to the U.S. Constitution says that cruel and unusual punishments shall not be inflicted. Even persons claiming that offenders forfeit all their rights after conviction are likely to make an exception to the constitutional protection against cruel and unusual punishment. The problem is not so much a question about whether cruel and unusual punishment should be used as it is disagreement about what constitutes cruel and unusual. Is it cruel and unusual to serve an inmate only one meal per day? To prohibit any out-of-cell exercise for an inmate? To keep an inmate in administrative confinement for eleven years? Does a prison violate an inmate's Eighth Amendment rights when it fails to provide adequate winter clothing, or does not supply the inmate with toilet paper, soap, toothpaste, or toothbrush? These questions represent some of the complaints brought by prisoners who believe they are being subjected to cruel and unusual punishment.

Recent court decisions reflect the difficulty inherent in dealing with these questions. Drawing from Miller, Walter, and Kelley's *Detention and Corrections Caselaw Catalog* (1995), we see how the courts have decided some of these questions.[2]

- A Kentucky jail did not violate a prisoner's Eighth Amendment rights by serving him only one meal a day for fifteen consecutive days because the one meal was sufficient to maintain normal health for the fifteen days involved (*Cunningham v. Jones,* 667 F.2d 565; 1982).
- When an Arkansas prison refused to allow out-of-cell exercise for the first fifteen days of a prisoner's time in punitive isolation, a federal court said the policy may be severe, and even harsh, but it was neither cruel nor barbaric (*Leonard v. Norris,* 797 F.2d 683; 1986).
- A Florida prisoner was placed in administrative confinement in 1975 as an escape risk. For over eleven years the inmate stayed under that status, despite the classification committee's recommendation for placement in the general population. The federal court ruled (*Sheley v. Dugger,* 824 F.2d 1551; 1987) that the inmate had not received adequate review of his status and as a result was being subjected to cruel and unusual punishment.
- In *Knop v. Johnson,* 667 F. Supp. 467 (1987), a federal district court ruled that Michigan had failed to provide inmates with winter coats, hats, and gloves and

[2]From Miller, R. C., & Walter, D. J. (1995). *Detention and corrections caselaw catalog* (8th ed.). Washington Grove, MD: CRS, Inc.

thereby subjected them to cruel and unusual punishment. Boots, however, were not required as long as the state provided adequate winter socks and kept the walkways and outdoor exercise areas free from snow.

- An Illinois inmate complained that the prison failed to provide him with toilet paper for five days, or with soap, toothpaste, or a toothbrush for ten days. The federal court found (*Harris v. Fleming*, 839 F.2d 1232; 1988) that because the inmate suffered no physical harm, merely some unpleasantness, the temporary neglect was not intentional and did not reach unconstitutional proportions.

It is not clear from these cases just what criteria the courts are using to determine if something constitutes cruel and unusual punishment. Even if more cases were cited, it would still be hard to identify a clear standard. As a federal district court explained, the term *cruel and unusual punishment* cannot be defined with specificity because it is flexible and broadens as society pays more regard to human decency and dignity. Yet, the court was able to explain that in general terms, cruel and unusual punishment is that which "amounts to torture, when it is grossly excessive in proportion to the offense for which it is imposed, or that is inherently unfair, or that is unnecessarily degrading, or that is shocking or disgusting to people of reasonable sensitivity" (*Holt v. Sarver*, 309 F. Supp. at 362; 1970).

Fourteenth Amendment: Due Process. The Fourteenth Amendment has significant importance to the concept of individual rights. Prior to the passage of the Fourteenth Amendment, the Bill of Rights served primarily to define the relationship between citizens and the federal government. Each state had its own state constitution, and many of those identified rights held by citizens against injustices by their state government. But the first ten amendments to the U.S. Constitution referred only to the protections citizens had against the federal government. This meant that a person might have certain rights when interacting with the federal government but not have those rights when associating with the state government. Such a situation was not considered inappropriate under a federal republic in which states shared sovereignty with the federal government, nor was it necessarily confusing because many of the state constitutions were modeled after the federal constitution. There were, however, some rights guaranteed in the Bill of Rights that were being denied by some states.

After the Civil War, the Thirteenth Amendment was passed (1865) to correct the obvious violation of individual rights where states continued to allow slavery and involuntary servitude. Because other infringements on individual rights continued in some states, the Fourteenth Amendment was ratified in 1868. Its importance to individual rights is best understood through the theory of **incorporation,** which argues that all provisions of the Bill of Rights are made applicable to the states (i.e., they are incorporated) by the amendment's **due process clause.** So, where the amendment says that "No State shall . . . deprive any person of life, liberty, or property, without due process of law . . . ," it is requiring each state to abide by the Bill of Rights because that is where the criteria for "due process of law" are set down. The Fourteenth Amendment also prohibits any state from denying "any person within its jurisdiction the equal protection of the law." Therefore, because of the Fourteenth Amendment, individual states must abide by the Bill of Rights and must obey federal court rulings about whether the state (1) followed due process of law when depriving a person of life, liberty, or property, and (2) provided equal protection of the law to all people within its jurisdiction. For purposes of claiming violation of their rights, offenders have often used the due process and equal protection clauses of the Fourteenth Amendment.

Prisoners' claims that their rights to due process were violated are often linked to whether a hearing is required before prison officials can discipline or transfer inmates. Although it is clear that government authorities cannot deprive suspects and defendants of their liberty without the opportunity to appear before a judge in a court of law, the ability to further affect the liberty of someone who is already a prisoner is not so clear. In other words, everyone probably agrees that it would be a denial of due process to keep suspects in jail for months, or even weeks, without having them appear before a judge to hear the charges against them and be told of their right to counsel and to a preliminary hearing. But what about inmates suspected of misbehavior while in prison? Are these prisoners being denied due process when, without a hearing, they are taken from the general population and placed in a more liberty-depriving setting such as administrative segregation? If a hearing is required, what procedures must be followed?

The leading case regarding due process rights of inmates who are being disciplined by prison officials is the U.S. Supreme Court 1974 decision in *Wolff v. McDonnell,* 418 U.S. 539. Nebraska inmate McDonnell, in a suit against Warden Wolff, claimed the disciplinary proceedings used at the Nebraska state prison did not comply with the due process clause of the Fourteenth Amendment. The Court held that because "prison disciplinary proceedings are not part of a criminal prosecution, . . . the full panoply of rights due a defendant in such proceedings does not apply" (418 U.S. at 556). However, although prison officials are not bound to the same procedures as found in criminal court, the prison disciplinary hearings must abide by some level of due process because "there is no iron curtain drawn between the Constitution and the prisons of this country" (418 U.S. at 555–556). For example, disciplinary action against a prisoner requires that (418 U.S. at 564, 566, 568, 570):

- At least twenty-four hours in advance of the hearing, the prisoner must be given written notification of the charges so that he or she might prepare a defense.
- There must be a written statement by the factfinders as to the evidence relied on and the reasons for the disciplinary action.
- Inmates facing disciplinary proceedings should be allowed to call witnesses and present documentary evidence in their defense as long as permitting them to do so does not unduly jeopardize institutional safety or correctional goals.
- There is no constitutional requirement that prison disciplinary hearings allow for cross-examination procedures, nor does the inmate have a right to either retained or appointed counsel in the proceedings. In some cases (for example, the inmate is illiterate or the case is particularly complex), a staff member or another inmate may act as substitute counsel.
- The inmate's hearing should be conducted by an impartial official or panel.

These procedural requirements present the basic ones that prison authorities must follow. States are welcome to provide more procedural protections than the Court says are required by the Constitution. In fact, many jurisdictions go beyond this minimum and, for example, allow cross-examination and appointment of counsel.

The *Wolff* case specifically concerned situations in which inmates faced punitive segregation or a loss of good time. As a result, it is considered the definitive Supreme Court position on prison disciplinary procedures in instances of serious misconduct (especially with the confirmation of *Wolff* provided in *Baxter v. Palmigiano,* 425 U.S. 308 (1976). In less serious cases in which inmates might simply lose privileges such as going to a movie or making use of the commissary, due process hearings are not required. In fact, even when a short-term segregation is possible, the *Wolff* requirements may not be needed. In a 1995 decision, the Supreme Court indicated that the *Wolff* requirements were not required for disciplinary hearings that result in a thirty-day segregation sanction. The *Sandin* decision says that unless the disciplinary segregation "imposes atypical and significant hardship on the inmate in relation to the ordinary incidents of prison life," no due process protections are required (*Sandin v. Connor;* 515 U.S. 472; 1995). Although the courts are still establishing the impact of *Sandin,* it seems apparent that the decision has severely restricted the type of hearing to which procedural due process rights apply (Palmer & Palmer, 1999).

The punitive segregation situation addressed in *Wolff v. McDonnell* and *Sandin v. Connor* is only one of two reasons that prison officials might want to isolate a prisoner from the general inmate population. In addition to isolation for punishment reasons, an inmate might also need to be segregated from others in order to protect that inmate. Such cases are ones of administrative segregation—and the Court was asked in *Hewitt v. Helms,* 459 U.S. 460 (1983), to require Pennsylvania prison authorities to grant inmate Helms a formal hearing, following the *Wolff* criteria, before placing him in administrative segregation. The Court rejected Helms's claim of due process violation and ruled that formal hearings are not required before placing an inmate in administrative segregation. Instead, an informal, nonadversary, evidentiary review is sufficient as long as the inmate receives notice of the charges against him or her and is given an opportunity to present his or her views to the prison official making the transfer decision.

Fourteenth Amendment: Equal Protection. The other type of Fourteenth Amendment claim that prisoners often use is based on the "equal protection under the law" clause. Although this phrase does not require the government to treat everyone alike in all circumstances, it does forbid discrimination or classification that is unjustified or malicious (Manville, 1986). In his self-help book for prisoners, Manville (1986) warns them that "it is very hard to win an equal protection claim in a prison case" (p. 155) because prison officials can usually come up with some rational basis for their actions. And as long as a rational basis is provided, the courts are obliged to allow the prison's practice. To make his point clear to his prisoner audience, Manville (1986) explains that the courts have not found equal protection violations when prisoners have been denied things such as temporary release programs (e.g., work release) even though other prisoners with equally—or even more—deplorable records were involved in the programs. Furthermore, having different visiting privileges for those on death row and those in general population does not violate the **equal protection clause** (*Jamieson v. Robinson,* 641 F.2d 138; 1981), nor does a pay differential between two different prisons (*Beatham v. Manson,* 369 F. Supp. 783; 1973).

The areas in which courts have been sympathetic to equal protection clause claims are in racial and gender-based discrimination and in cases of religious freedom. For example, state statutes requiring segregation of races in prisons and jails violate the Fourteenth Amendment (*Lee v. Washington,* 390 U.S. 333; 1968, and *Holt v. Sarver;* 1970) as does the subjection of black or Hispanic prisoners to disparate and unequal treatment (*Ramos v. Lamm,* 485 F. Supp. 122; 1979). Importantly, the *Lee v. Washington* decision did say that prison officials acting in good faith, and in particular circumstances, can take racial tensions into account to maintain security, discipline, and good order. But when racial tensions are used to justify actions such as segregation, those considerations should be made after a danger to security, discipline, and good order has become apparent and not before (*Wilson v. Kelley,* 294 F. Supp. 1005; 1968).

An example of something the courts have found to constitute racial discrimination was the disbanding of a prison's boxing program in Nebraska. The suit claimed that prison officials discontinued the program because most of the participants had been black. The federal appeals court agreed that the program was canceled because of racial animosity and accepted the inmates' claim (*Moore v. Clark,* 821 F.2d 518; 1987).

An interesting example of a discrimination claim that was not upheld is found in *David K. v. Lane,* 839 F.2d 1265 (1988). White inmates in Illinois claimed that prison officials, who were punishing gang activity, should also discipline nonviolent displays of gang membership (e.g., showing gang insignia). Because displays of gang membership were not disciplined, the inmates argued, a greatly disproportionate number of white inmates were in protective custody. Because protective custody meant more hours of confinement each day and fewer job opportunities, the white inmates claimed their right to equal protection was being violated. The federal appeals court agreed that the inordinately high number of white inmates needing protective custody was a result of the prison policy. But because the inmates could not show that the gang activity policy was shaped by a racially based discriminatory purpose, the court did not find the prison officials to be guilty of unlawful discrimination. The court did, however, criticize the policy and told the prison officials to take firmer control and to use reasonable methods to ultimately eliminate gang affiliation.

Gender-based discrimination and religious freedom are the other areas in which courts have heard equal protection clause claims. Chapter 11 reviewed the important gender-based discrimination cases in its coverage of the equalization response to women offenders. We need only be reminded here that, despite some court rulings supporting women prisoners' claims, neither equality nor parity has been achieved between facilities and programs for women and men prisoners.

Palmer and Palmer (1999) note that cases dealing with religious freedom often make use of the equal protection clause of the Fourteenth Amendment. This clause is especially relevant in cases dealing with minority religions, as the Supreme Court noted in *Cruz v. Beto* (1972). In that case, Texas prison officials were found to have discriminated against inmate Cruz by denying him a reasonable opportunity, compared to that offered inmates of more conventional faiths, to pursue his Buddhist faith. We will continue this discussion of religious freedom later as we discuss some of the specific rights either granted to or claimed by prisoners.

The continued existence throughout society of disparate treatment on the basis of things such as race, ethnicity, gender, and religion will, unfortunately, ensure continued claims of equal protection violations in prisons. The court decisions covered here serve as the basis from which additional decisions will try to clarify the issues and give direction to prison authorities. Similarly, legislators have tried to address issues of discrimination by passing laws to verify the fundamental value of equal protection and to provide mechanisms to force compliance with that value. Some examples of such legislative action are various civil rights acts passed in the nineteenth and twentieth centuries.

The Civil Rights Act. **Civil rights** are those personal, natural rights that protect people against arbitrary or discriminatory treatment. Clearly, the Constitution, including its Bill of Rights and other amendments, provides the first source of civil rights in the United States. However, those rights are not considered the only ones constituting the civil rights of U.S. citizens. Other civil rights not specifically mentioned in the Constitution, yet recognized by the courts, include rights such as the right to live and work where we wish, to marry and to have children, and to participate in the political, social, and cultural processes of society (Ferdico, 1996). Because the Constitution does not enumerate all civil rights, Americans can turn to other sources in which their rights are identified. Some of the most important, for purposes of discussing prisoners' rights, are the various civil rights acts passed by Congress over the years.

Important civil rights acts have been passed at the federal level in 1871, 1957, 1960, 1964, and 1968. As a result of these acts, citizens (including prisoners) and others under the appropriate jurisdiction have rights and privileges such as freedom from discrimination. But having such rights stated in a document does not always ensure they will be given. Just as the writ of habeas corpus provides a procedure by which constitutional rights can be implemented, there needs to be a mechanism that ensures access to provisions of the civil rights acts. The primary vehicle for such access is found in the **Civil Rights Act** of 1871 (originally entitled Ku Klux Klan Act because it was passed to protect former slaves from reprisal during Reconstruction), which is codified in the U.S. Code as Title 42, section 1983. For brevity, this is usually referred to as §1983. It reads:

> Every person who, under color of any statute, ordinance, regulation, custom, or usage, of any State or Territory or the District of Columbia, subjects, or causes to be subjected, any citizen of the United States or other person within the jurisdiction thereof to the deprivation of any rights, privileges, or immunities secured by the Constitution and laws, shall be liable to the party injured in an action at law, suit in equity, or other proper proceeding for redress.

The original purpose of §1983 was to guarantee the rights of newly freed slaves and to allow people direct access to the federal courts at a time when it was thought that state courts would not be sympathetic to actions brought against state officials. The act was used only sparingly until the 1950s and 1960s, when new attention to civil rights revived interest in §1983. Several obstacles make it difficult for inmates to receive monetary damages in a §1983 claim, but the provision has been used successfully in class-action suits challenging institutional conditions (Hawkins & Alpert, 1989).

As noted earlier when discussing the intervention doctrine, early recognition that prisoners could sue for civil rights violations involved cases of religious freedom brought by Black Muslims. From the rather narrow issue of religious freedom, §1983 came to be used by prisoners to bring claims of civil rights violations in cases such involving inadequate medical care, brutality by prison staff, and inmate-on-inmate assaults. Cases related to these kinds of issues are covered later in looking at specific instances of inmates' rights.

Section 1983 suits were popular, not only because prisoners could seek damages that were not available in habeas corpus action but also because class-action suits are more likely to be acknowledged by the courts as presenting an important question (Hawkins & Alpert, 1989). By 1973 the courts had realized that suits under §1983 were encompassing a wider variety of issues than might have been originally intended. In *Preiser v. Rodriguez,* 411 U.S. 475 (1973), the Court ruled that any actions in which prisoners are questioning their confinement or the length of their confinement cannot be brought under §1983.

Instead of a §1983 claim, the prisoners must use a **writ of habeas corpus,** which is the term given to a variety of writs that are used to bring a party before a court or judge. In common usage it refers specifically to the *habeas corpus ad subjiciendum,* which directs the person (e.g., the warden of a prison) detaining someone (the prisoner) to show the legality of the detention. A writ of habeas corpus is used only to determine if a person's liberty is being restrained as a result of due process. It is not used to determine guilt or innocence (*Black's Law Dictionary*). So, whereas §1983 is appropriate for complaints about the conditions of confinement (e.g., medical care, mail censorship, safety issues, and physical living conditions), it is not used to challenge the imposition of solitary confinement, administrative segregation, prison discipline, or other things that affect issues of actual confinement or duration of confinement.

A Sampling of Prisoners' Rights Issues

By the mid-1990s, more than one in ten civil lawsuits in the entire federal district court system was a Civil Rights Act §1983 lawsuit filed by state prisoners (Hanson & Daley, 1995, p. 38). Even though this is not the only source of prisoners' rights, the §1983 suits seem to dominate. Hanson and Daley reviewed the §1983 cases that were disposed of by U.S. district courts in nine states during 1992. They found that nearly half the lawsuits failed to meet the basic requirement of §1983 and were dismissed by the courts within six months of being filed. But the remaining half often involved complex issues and required two years or more to resolve. As Figure 14.1 shows, the Hanson and Daley sample found §1983 lawsuits reflect a variety of issues, but physical security and medical treatment are especially frequent.

Most of the cases (74 percent) are eventually dismissed by the courts (usually because the plaintiff has not complied with court rules or because there is no evidence of a constitutional rights violation), as a result of a motion by the defendant (20 percent) or as a stipulated dismissal (4 percent). The remaining 2 percent of the cases go to trial where less than half result in a favorable verdict for the prisoner.

We will look at several of the issues noted in Figure 14.1, although not always from the perspective of §1983 litigation. Specifically, we consider prisoners' rights in the areas of access to courts, religion, and privacy.

Access to the Courts

Possibly the most basic right for prisoners is the right to access the courts. Without it the question of any other rights would be moot because prisoners would not be able to bring their claims to the court's attention. This issue actually has two components. First, there must be some procedure by which inmates approach the courts. This involves writs of habeas corpus but must now be considered in light of the Prison Litigation Reform Act mentioned at this chapter's beginning. In addition to having a procedure to get their claims before the court, inmates must also have the necessary legal knowledge to make their access effective. These two issues are discussed under the topics of the Prison Litigation Reform Act and providing inmates with legal assistance.

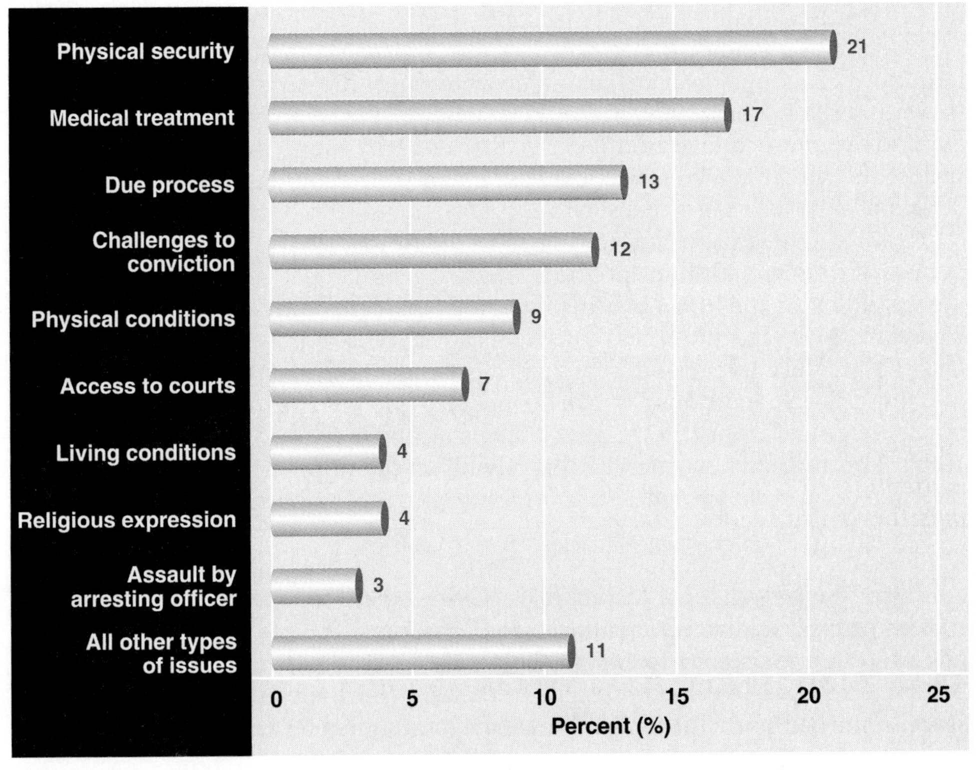

FIGURE 14.1

Issues in Section 1983 Lawsuits

Source: Adapted from Hanson, R. A., & Daley, H. W. (1995). *Challenging the conditions of prisons and jails: A report on Section 1983 litigation* [NCJ 151652]. Discussion paper. Washington, DC: Bureau of Justice Statistics.

Prison Litigation Reform Act. During the 1960s prisoners filed only a few hundred suits in the federal courts challenging the conditions of their confinement or alleging violations of their constitutional rights. By 1994 nearly 30,000 such suits were being filed, and the cases were making up more than 15 percent of the federal caseload (Palmer & Palmer, 1999). Many of the lawsuits were filed at taxpayer expense because the prisoners claimed they lacked funds to pay filing fees (i.e., they took *in forma pauperis* status). The nature of many of the lawsuits (recall the first five examples given at this chapter's start), their growing number, the increasing burden they placed on federal courts, and the expense to taxpayers having to support the judicial system's handling of the cases resulted in strong public opinion for reform.

Congress's response to the public outcry was the Prison Litigation Reform Act (PLRA). The act used several approaches as it attempted to limit the ability of prisoners to complain about conditions of their confinement or alleging violation of their constitutional rights. In addition, the act was intended to give the states more authority to manage their prison systems while reducing opportunities for federal judges to micromanage state and local prisons (Palmer & Palmer, 1999). Because only the first goal, prisoner complaints and allegations, is directly linked to court access, our attention focuses on that issue. Two of the approaches are summarized as follows (Collins, 1997; Collins & Grant, 1998; Palmer & Palmer, 1999):

- To discourage the filing of meritless lawsuits by prisoners, the PLRA requires prisoners to either pay the full fee when filing a complaint ($150 in 1998), or make an initial down payment followed by periodic installment payments. A truly indigent prisoner can still file his or her claim or appeal without paying the fee but he or she may accumulate a substantial bill over time.
- Under a three-strikes provision, indigent prisoners are prohibited from filing new lawsuits when the prisoner has previously filed frivolous or meritless claims. That provision is waived if there is an immediate threat of physical harm.

As noted earlier, critics of the PLRA contend that it inappropriately—and possibly unconstitutionally—restricts prisoner access to the courts. The three-strikes provision is especially troublesome to some, and the courts are still trying to determine what counts as a strike and at what point the number three is achieved (see Palmer & Palmer, 1999, p. 343). The paying of fees is also controversial as indicated by comments from a federal district court judge in Wisconsin who describes the new filing fee procedures as "mean-spirited and unnecessary" (Collins & Grant, 1998).

Although "mean-spirited" may be true, the "unnecessary" comment may be inexact. The number of inmate petitions filed in federal appellate courts during 1997, the first full year the PLRA was in effect, fell 5 percent—but in 1998, they were up 8 percent. When specific types of petitions are considered, the PLRA seems to have had the greatest impact on civil rights prisoner petitions (including those addressing prison conditions), which dropped 20 percent from 1996 to 1997 and another 11 percent from 1997 to 1998 ("Legislation Has Mixed Effect on Petitions," 1999). This mixed effect the PLRA is having on the number of prisoner petitions filed in federal court provides support for arguments on both sides of the "how effective is it" debate.

Providing Inmates with Legal Assistance. Having access to federal courts is only one step in the process of accessing the courts. Prisoners who are not familiar with the law may need assistance to ensure their right to access is meaningful. Similarly, prisoners who are familiar with the law can only have meaningful access if items such as law books and other legal material are made available for their use. This question of what constitutes meaningful access was addressed by the Court in *Bounds v. Smith,* 430 U.S. 817 (1977). The Court had already decided that prisoners could help each other in preparing writs in those situations in which the prison officials were not providing a reasonable alternative to the jailhouse lawyers and inmate "writ writers" (*Johnson v. Avery,* 393 U.S. 483; 1969). And, in *Younger v. Gilmore,* 404 U.S. 15 (1971), the Court ruled that California prisons were not providing sufficient legal materials to enable prisoners to have reasonable access to the courts. But the *Johnson* decision did not explain what would constitute reasonable alternatives to writ writers, and the *Younger* decision did not specify what legal materials are necessary to be sufficient. The *Bounds* decision provided some clarification.

In *Bounds,* North Carolina prisoners claimed they were denied reasonable access to the courts because the state's prisons did not provide adequate legal library facilities. The question the Court was asked to address was whether prison authorities had to assist inmates by providing them with adequate law libraries or adequate assistance from persons trained in the law (del Carmen, Ritter, & Witt, 1993). The answer regarding law libraries seemed to be yes, and North Carolina presented a plan for legal libraries that included a list of such references as state statutes, court reports and reporters, a law dictionary, and specific law textbooks. Although the Court questioned the omission of works such as *Shepard's Citations,* and local rules of court, the North Carolina plan was acceptable and thereby provided an indication of what the Court considers an adequate law library.

On the question of adequate assistance, the Court appeared to be even more specific. Reasonable alternatives to prisoner writ writers would include training some inmates as paralegal assistants to work under lawyers' supervision or using paraprofessionals and law students in formal clinical programs. Other options could include the use of volunteer attorneys organized through bar associations or other groups, or even hiring lawyers on a part-time consulting basis. For states wanting a more formal arrangement, the Court suggested full-time staff attorneys, working either in new prison legal assistance organizations or as part of public defender or legal services offices (*Bounds v. Smith,* 430 U.S. at 831).

In a 1996 ruling (*Lewis v. Casey*) the U.S. Supreme Court said that a prisoner's right to access the courts does not necessarily mean that he or she also has a freestanding right to a law library. However, most jails and prisons provide inmates with access to a law library stocked with up-to-date legal materials.

Officials in state prisons and local jails busily began providing law libraries for inmate use. But in 1996 the Supreme Court provided a clarification, if not revision, of the *Bounds* decision that gave those officials more leeway in what they provided. In *Lewis v. Casey* (516 U.S. 804; 1996) the Court said that *Bounds* did not create a freestanding right to a law library or even to legal assistance. Instead, *Bounds* simply established the right of prisoners to access the courts. So, for a violation of *Bounds* to occur, prisoners must show that the prison library or legal assistance program is hindering their efforts to pursue a nonfrivolous legal claim.

Lewis v. Casey has been interpreted by some officials as providing an opportunity to abandon well-stocked, up-to-date law libraries for inmates. Such libraries are very expensive for the state and, some believe, encourage inmates to file frivolous lawsuits by providing too broad an access to legal material. In 1999 the Iowa state corrections director decided to phase out all inmate law libraries over a two-year period (Petroski, 1999). Iowa had been spending about $500,000 a year to provide prison law libraries. Instead, the corrections department decided to contract with the state public defender's office to hire private lawyers (budgeted at $150,000 per year) who will give legal advice to inmates and do research for them.

The key in Iowa's attempt to abolish prison law libraries is providing legal assistance through private attorneys. It remains to be seen how well that programs works, how it stands up under court scrutiny, and whether it actually saves the state any money or reduces frivolous lawsuits.

Having recognized that prisoners have the right to access the courts, and being provided the necessary legal assistance to do so, we can turn our attention to some of the topics and concerns that prisoners have brought to the courts' attention. As you can imagine, they are numerous and can be categorized into seemingly endless areas. Del Carmen et al. (1993) present cases as falling under six principles of law (e.g., prison law, parole, death penalty, and sentencing), whereas Palmer and Palmer (1999) discuss cases in eleven chapters addressing issues such as visitation/association, mail, isolated confinement, and rehabilitation. In the exceptionally complete reference work, *Detention and Corrections Caselaw Catalog* (eighth edition published in 1995), cases are reviewed in some fifty different categories covering specific topics such as attorney fees, classification and segregation, cruel and unusual punishment, medical care, privacy, sanitation, and transfers. Some of these legal issues are covered in other chapters, but we should choose a few to address here. Rights to privacy and religion are particularly valued by U.S. citizens, so next we will see what happens when those citizens are put in prison.

Issues of Religion

Congress shall make no law respecting an establishment of religion, or prohibiting the free exercise thereof. . . .

—First Amendment to the U.S. Constitution

The two clauses of this amendment (the establishment clause and the free exercise clause) present a contradiction that becomes particularly obvious when the amendment is considered in terms of a prison environment (Palmer & Palmer, 1999). As a federal appeals court pointed out, prisons should provide facilities for worship and the opportunity for clergy to visit the institution because society has removed prisoners from a community where they could freely exercise their religion. In this manner the free exercise clause is satisfied. But, if a claim is made that the free exercise clause requires the state to supply the clergy, the state may be dangerously approaching the guarded frontiers of the establishment clause (*Gittlemacker v. Prasse,* 428 F.2d 1; 1970). Interesting though questions linked to the establishment clause might be, the free exercise clause has been looked at more closely by the courts and is the focus of our attention as well.

As if the potential conflict between the establishment clause and the free exercise clause were not troublesome enough, the free exercise clause itself has been taken to have two aspects: the freedom to believe and the freedom to act. In *Cantwell v. Connecticut,* 310 U.S. 296 (1940), the Court decided that "the first is absolute but, in the nature of things, the second cannot be. Conduct remains subject to [governmental] regulation for the protection of society" (310 U.S. at 303; 1940). With this decision the Court understands the First Amendment to give all people the absolute right to whatever religious beliefs they wish but not necessarily to every action they may want to carry out. Understandably, the courts are hesitant to restrict the free exercise of religious actions but have done so when (1) necessary to maintain prison discipline or security, (2) the restrictions are simply the result of prison officials exercising their authority and official discretion, and (3) based on economic considerations (see Palmer & Palmer, 1999). We will briefly look at each of these.

Restrictions Based on Maintenance of Discipline or Security. The most frequently given reason for limiting an inmate's religious freedom has been the duty of prison officials to maintain security within an institution. A clear example of this position is found by reviewing aspects of the Black Muslims' fight for recognition and rights in prisons and jails.

Smith (1993) highlights court decisions beginning in the 1960s that allowed restrictions on the freedom of Black Muslims to practice their religion. Prison officials readily acknowledge that Black Muslims were not afforded the same opportunity to practice their religion as were followers of more traditional faiths. But, the officials argued, the Black Muslims presented security problems that other religions did not present, and, as a result, the officials felt restrictions were proper. For example, the California Supreme Court (*In re Ferguson,* 55 Cal.2d 663; 1961) said prison authorities were allowed to prohibit Black Muslims from worshiping and from studying church literature because the Muslims' philosophy and assertive behavior threatened the correctional institution (Smith, 1993).

This characterization of Muslim prisoners as being a threat to institutional security was reflected in other court decisions. A federal judge in New York characterized the Muslims as an "organization dedicated to laying secret plans that were likely to lead to unrest among the prisoners" (quoted in Smith, 1993, p. 138) while another federal judge accepted a report, without examination, by the Chicago Police Department, asserting that the Muslims were dangerous (Smith, 1993). The typical position of the courts during this time was summed up in *Sostre v. McGinnis,* 334 F.2d 906 (1964), in which a judge wrote that: "No romantic or sentimental view of constitutional rights or of religion should induce a court to interfere with the necessary disciplinary regime established by the prison officials" (334 F.2d. at 908; 1964).

Black Muslims began having some success in gaining privileges similar to those granted the more traditional religions with the *Cooper v. Pate* (1964, 1967) decisions discussed earlier under the intervention doctrine. You will recall the court ruled that prison officials could not prohibit inmates from communicating, through the mail or personal visitation, with ministers of their faith. And, in *Northern v. Nelson,* 315 F.Supp. 687 (1970), the court held that the prison library was obliged to make copies of the holy Qur'an available and that prisoners must be allowed to receive the publication *Muhammad Speaks* unless it could be clearly demonstrated that a particular issue would substantially disrupt prison discipline (Palmer & Palmer, 1999).

The requirement that prison officials show a threat to prison security as a reason to restrict religious freedom continues in more recent court decisions. In

Control over prisoners' religious freedom presents difficult questions for prison officials and for the courts. A U.S. District Court decision (*Hamilton v. Schriro,* 1996) held that prison officials could prohibit Native American sweat lodge ceremonies because the sweat lodge, shown here in its early stages of construction, made it hard to monitor the inmates. Also, maintenance of the sweat lodge required inmates to have tools that could also be used as weapons.

O'Lone v. Estate of Shabazz, 482 U.S. 342 (1987), the court heard arguments on a New Jersey prison policy that prevented Muslim inmates from attending weekly congregational service (Jumu'ah). The Muslim prisoners argued that the service was central to the observation of the Muslim faith, and their participation was a necessary component to their freedom of religion. Muslim inmates with work assignments outside the prison's main buildings were unable to return for the Friday afternoon service. Seeking alternatives that would allow them to attend the services without missing any work hours, the inmates asked to be placed on inside work detail or be given substitute weekend tasks. The prison rejected these proposals as unacceptable given scarce prison personnel and potential security problems. The court, although agreeing that Jumu'ah was of central importance to the Islamic faith, said the prison policy did not violate the inmates' constitutional rights because the policy was reasonably related to legitimate penological interests.

Because prison officials are obliged to maintain security and discipline within the institution, the courts have realized that such an obligation may require that religious freedom is occasionally restricted. As a result, when prison authorities can show that such restrictions are necessary for security and disciplinary reasons, the courts will typically approve the prison policy. But, even beyond those security and disciplinary responsibilities, the courts have also recognized that prison officials should be allowed to exercise their authority and official discretion without undue interference from the courts.

Restrictions Based on the Exercise of Authority and Official Discretion. As Palmer and Palmer (1999) note, the idea that control over prisoners' religious freedom is part of the prison officials' exercise of authority and official discretion comes from the historical nonintervention doctrine. An interesting topic falling under this principle is the question of just what constitutes a religion. Are prisoners whose "religious beliefs" call for the destruction of U.S. prisons—and whose dietary requirements call for porterhouse steaks and Harvey's Bristol Cream—protected in the free exercise of that religion? Actually the courts had to decide exactly those questions when federal prisoner Harry W. Theriault organized the Church of the New Song (conveniently, CONS) under the Eclatarian faith. Theriault sued prison officials to force recognition of his new religion and to have the necessary food and drink items added to the prison menu. Federal district courts first told Atlanta Federal Penitentiary officials (*Theriault v. Carlson,* 339 F. Supp. 375; 1972) and Iowa State Penitentiary officials (*Remmers v. Brewer,* 361 F. Supp. 537; 1973) that prisons must recognize Church of the New Song as a religion and allow its members the free exercise of that religion. The federal district court in Georgia held that prison officials had to permit Theriault to hold religious services (*Theriault v. Carlson*), but the federal appeals court vacated that decision and sent the case back to the district level for further action (*Theriault v. Carlson,* 495 F.2d 390; 1974). In 1975 a different district court decided Eclatarian faith was not a religion entitled to First Amendment protection because it was merely "a masquerade designed to obtain protection for acts which otherwise would have been unlawful and/or reasonably disallowed by various prison authorities" (*Theriault v. Silber,* 391 F. Supp. at 579; 1975).

Despite the federal appeals court decision in *Theriault v. Carlson* (1974), a different federal appeals court in the *Remmers* case (*Remmers v. Brewer,* 494 F.2d 1277; 1974) agreed with its district court (*Remmers v. Brewer,* 1973) that the Eclatarian faith was a religion entitled to protection under the free exercise clause. But the appeals court added that if it were later proved that the Eclatarian faith, as practiced at the prison, was a sham, the prison administrators and the court could reconsider that opinion. Continuing the controversy, in 1979 a different federal appeals court (*Loney v. Scurr,* 474 F. Supp. 1186) found the Church of the New Song to be a bona fide religion whose adherents must be given an opportunity to worship with no more restrictions than any other religion. As Palmer and Palmer (1999) say, these decisions are good examples of the problems faced by prison administrators who must try to make sense of seemingly inconsistent decisions rendered by different federal courts.

Problems similar to those presented by the Church of the New Song have been presented by prisoners wanting to practice Satanism. In *Kennedy v. Meacham,* 382 F. Supp. 996 (1974), the court accorded religious status to Satanists but did not require Wyoming State Penitentiary officials to allow inmate followers to keep bells, candles, pointing sticks, gongs, incense, or black robes in their cells. Using a noninterference rationale, the court said that matters of inmate regulation and discipline are correctly left to the discretion of prison authorities as long as constitutional rights are not deprived in a clearly capricious and arbitrary manner. In *Childs v. Duckworth,* 705 F.2d 915 (1983), a federal appeals court denied a prisoner the right to conduct Satanic rituals and possess candles and incense in his cell. In *McCorkle v. Johnson,* 881 F.2d 993 (1989), another federal appeals court said prison officials were correct in denying McCorkle the opportunity to practice satanic rituals that included drinking blood and eating flesh.

Despite seemingly clear decisions in *Kennedy, Childs,* and *McCorkle,* the question of Satanism is not yet resolved. In *Howard v. United States,* 864 F. Supp. 1019 (1994), a federal inmate in Colorado claimed his constitutional rights were violated when prison officials refused to let him perform symbolic rituals, nor would they provide him with necessary props, related to his version of "nonviolent Satanism." Howard said he needs candles, candle holders, incense, a gong or bell, a black robe, a chalice, and an object suitable for pointing. Howard also wanted a chamber with enough room to turn around and raise his arms. Judge Nottingham noted that the Bureau of Prisons has provided, or is providing, such things as Native American sweat lodges, kosher food lines for Jewish inmates, and has accommodated a single Hare Krishna prisoner who wished to perform his religious rites. In addition, accommodations are made for inmates who are Buddhist, Rastafarian, Roman

Catholic (holding services in both Spanish and English), Protestant, Mormon, Muslim, and Jehovah's Witness. The judge directed the prison officials to stop using prison resources to provide devices to the other religious groups unless they also provided the plaintiff with the implements he requested for his religious rituals. Since Howard's version of Satanism did not advocate bloodletting or human sacrifice, the judge did not see *McCorkle v. Johnson* as a controlling case, nor was *Childs v. Duckworth* because Howard did not want to conduct the rituals in his cell.

Restrictions Based on Economic Considerations. Although less frequently than the other two reasons for restricting religious freedom, economic considerations have occasionally been accepted by the courts. In *Gittlemacker v. Prasse,* the court ruled that the state has no obligation to provide, furnish, or supply every prisoner with a member of the clergy or with religious services of the prisoner's choice. Part of the court's hesitancy to require the state to supply clergy for inmates was the danger mentioned earlier about possibly violating the establishment clause while trying to meet the free exercise clause. But in addition to that concern, the court also noted that the sheer number of religious sects made it impractical to ask each state prison to furnish clergy appropriate to each prisoner's faith.

In 1969 Muslim inmates at the Atlanta Federal Penitentiary asked that they be provided a special meal, and meal time, during the Islamic religious period of Ramadan. Because Ramadan requires Muslims to fast between sunrise and sunset, the inmates wanted the meal served after the normal dinner time and to both include and avoid particular food items. Prison officials argued that they could not afford to buy the special food items and that after-sunset meals would be cost prohibitive as well as presenting security problems. The court sided with the prison officials (*Walker v. Blackwell,* 411 F.2d 23; 1969) and ruled that considerations of expense and security outweigh any constitutional deprivation forced on the inmates.

Religious Freedom Restoration Act. Congress passed the **Religious Freedom Restoration Act** (RFRA) in 1993 as a reaction to concerns about judicial decisions (outside the corrections area) that some interpreted as restraining free exercise of religion. Although corrections officials asked Congress to exclude jail and prison inmates from aspects of the act, Congress declined. Prior to the RFRA, an inmate's exercise of freedom of religion could be restricted by prison officials if the restrictions were reasonably related to maintenance of discipline and security. Once the prison produced evidence that a particular restriction was done for security reasons, the burden shifted to the inmate who was required to show that the prison's position was without basis. The RFRA shifted the burden of proof from the inmate to the prison officials who had to show that the restriction was necessary because of compelling governmental interests (Marino, 1997).

The more stringent requirement that the RFRA placed on the prison officials gave inmates increased opportunity to bring claims that prison rules and regulations were denying prisoners their First Amendment rights. Many of those claims were considered frivolous by prison officials. For example, a Pennsylvania inmate claimed his religion forbade him from eating "pungent" foods, such as anything cooked with onions or garlic (deGroot, 1997). Pennsylvania officials offered this suit as one example of how the RFRA encouraged some inmates to have the courts legitimize behavior that ordinarily would not be allowed in a prison.

In a 1997 case, having nothing to do with corrections, the Supreme Court ruled that RFRA was unconstitutional (*Boerne v. Flores* 521 U.S. 507; 1997) except for the Federal Bureau of Prisons, which must still abide by RFRA provisions. Congress, the Court said, had exceeded its powers in passing the legislation. It is difficult to determine what impact RFRA had when it was active and what the impact of its invalidation will be. Hamilton (1998) reports the results of a survey in which corrections agencies were asked to provide information about the impact RFRA had on inmate lawsuits. Eleven agencies that claimed religion-based lawsuits increased after RFRA became law reported an average of 7.7 religion-based lawsuits being filed per year before RFRA compared with an average of 37.2 lawsuits after RFRA. Interestingly, when asked what impact RFRA had on agency operations, fifteen agencies said the lawsuits had little or no impact—largely because the RFRA-inspired lawsuits were mostly unsuccessful. Ten agencies which said they were required to accommodate changes as a result of successful lawsuits, rated the impact on agency security measures as being moderately harsh.

Just as RFRA seemed to have little direct impact on prison operations when it was the law, its invalidation does not appear to have resulted in any major changes in the prisons. One reason for that may be that some states have passed their own versions of the RFRA, and the prisons must abide by those regulations anyway. Also, prisons that made accommodations while under RFRA may not see any reason to make changes. Finally, Congress—smarting at the slap received from the Supreme Court's invalidation of RFRA, some would say—began moving new legislation through the House and Senate to restore provisions of RFRA. The 1999 version of the legislation was called the Religious Liberty Protection Act. Should that act, or similar legislation, become law, the lessons from RFRA suggest that prison officials may have to make some adjustments but there is no reason to expect sweeping changes in the way prisons try to accommodate the prisoners' exercise of religion.

Issues of Privacy

> *The right of the people to be secure in their persons, houses, papers, and effects, against unreasonable searches and seizures, shall not be violated . . . but upon reasonable cause.*
>
> —Fourth Amendment to the U.S. Constitution

> *No person . . . shall be compelled in any criminal case to be a witness against himself . . .*
>
> —Fifth Amendment to the U.S. Constitution

> *The enumeration of the Constitution, of certain rights, shall not be construed to deny or disparage others retained by the people.*
>
> —Ninth Amendment to the U.S. Constitution

The constitutional right to privacy has emerged primarily through opinions delivered by the U.S. Supreme Court. Although one cannot point to any particular constitutional amendment as specifically providing a right to privacy, it seems clear that, especially in the twentieth century, privacy has been institutionalized through court opinions and legislation (Abraham, 1988; Brigham, 1984). Building from specific references such as protections against "intrusions" (Fourth Amendment), the immunity from "disclosure" (Fifth Amendment), and the seemingly clear statement that there are other fundamental rights than those specifically mentioned in the first eight amendments (Ninth Amendment), privacy has gradually become an accepted constitutional right. But should that right to privacy extend to persons being confined for crimes they committed?

Privacy issues include a variety of topics related not only to individuals' dwellings and possessions, but also to their bodies and to their interactions with others. We consider these kinds by looking at search and seizure of the prisoner's "dwelling," search and seizure of the prisoner's body, and interference with prisoner communication.

Search and Seizures of the Prisoners' Dwellings. Generally, a prisoner has no expectation of privacy as to his place or his possessions because a loss of privacy must be considered a natural aspect of confinement. The consistent ruling of the courts has been that any balancing of inmate Fourth Amendment interests against the interests of prison officials must be struck in favor of institutional security (60 Am Jur 2d, Penal §98). After all, it would be impossible for prison officials to accomplish their objectives of prison safety, security, and sanitation while being forced to abide by Fourth Amendment protections afforded nonprisoners.

A key decision in this area comes from *Hudson v. Palmer,* 468 U.S. 517 (1984). In that case, correctional officer Hudson and a fellow officer conducted a shakedown search of inmate Palmer's prison locker and cell. Palmer brought suit against Hudson claiming the shakedown search was for the sole purpose of harassing him. The court dismissed Palmer's claim while holding that "society is not prepared to recognize as legitimate any subjective expectation of privacy that a prisoner might have in his prison cell and that, accordingly, the Fourth Amendment proscription against unreasonable searches does not apply within the confines of the prison cell" (468 U.S. at 526).

The leeway granted prison officials in searches and seizures of the prisoner's place does not necessarily extend to the prisoner's body. But even there, the prisoner's rights are considerably less than the rights of nonprisoners.

Search and Seizures of the Prisoners' Bodies. An inmate's body has only a little more right to privacy than does her or his place and possessions. Routine strip and body-cavity searches are not considered violations of the Fourth Amendment because they are not unreasonable under the circumstances of imprisonment (*Bell v. Wolfish,* 441 U.S. 520; 1979). But courts have barred body-cavity searches that are conducted in abusive, nonhygienic, or unreasonably degrading ways.

Related to the question of the privacy of one's body are situations requiring prisoners to be watched and/or searched by persons of the opposite sex. In 1984 inmates at San Quentin State Prison in California brought suit against prison officials for assigning female correctional officers to areas in which those officers could view male inmates in conditions of partial or total nudity. Prison officials argued that security considerations and the equal opportunity rights of female correctional officers supported such practices (Miller et al., 1995). The federal court agreed with the prison officials and found the practice to be reasonable (*Grummett v. Rushen,* 587 F. Supp. 913; 1984). Similarly, in *Johnson v. Phelan* (69 F.3d 144; 7th Cir.; 1995), the court said there are two justifications for cross-sex monitoring. First, it makes good use of staff because it is financially unreasonable to expect jails and prisons to employ officers who only have, for example, shower monitoring duty. And, as long as opposite-sex monitoring is conducted on the same basis as same-sex monitoring, there is no constitutional violation. "By the same token, the prison may assign homosexual male guards to monitor male prisoners, heterosexual male guards to monitor effeminate male homosexual prisoners, and so on" (*Johnson v. Phelan,* 69 F.3d 144). There are too many variations, the court explained, to place guards and prisoners into multiple classes by sex, sexual orientation, and perhaps other criteria, allowing each group to be observed only by the corresponding groups that occasion the least unhappiness.

A second justification for cross-sex monitoring is that it reduces the need for prisons to make sex a criterion of employment. If prisons had to do that, they would be in conflict with Title VII and the equal protection clause. Cells and showers, the court noted, are designed so that guards can see in as they seek to prevent violence and other offenses. Prisoners dress, undress, and bathe under watchful eyes, so officers roaming the corridors are bound to see naked prisoners. If prisons were required to use only same-sex monitoring, they would have to relegate women (at least in male prisons) to the administrative wing or eliminate them from the staff. Both are inappropriate actions under Title VII.

It is important to note that the courts have not said that the Fourth Amendment does not apply to inmates but rather that the searches and seizures of both dwelling and body are reasonable given the prison's needs of security, order, and rehabilitation (Palmer & Palmer, 1999). Security interests are especially noted by the courts, which recognize the potential for contraband to be collected while at work assignments or, regardless of its origin, to be secretly stored in a cell. Because contraband is also introduced to the prison through inmate contact with noninmates, the issue of prisoner communication must be considered when looking at privacy issues.

Interference with Prisoner Communication. Prisoners communicate with the outside world primarily through mail and visits. The control of mail to and from prisons is considered a necessary aspect of prison administration, so any uniformly applied rules that regulate mailing privileges are generally acceptable to the courts. Court decisions such as *Turner v. Safley* and *Thornburgh v. Abbott* give prison officials considerable discretion regarding what mail and publications inmates can send and receive. As long as the prison officials are acting reasonably (e.g., there is a valid, rational connection between the regulation and a legitimate state interest), their actions will be upheld.

Similar provisions are applied to regulations on visits in which institutional considerations such as security require that some limitations be placed on the entry of people into the prisons for face-to-face communication with inmates. Although security considerations generally would not allow prison officials to prohibit all face-to-face communication by prison inmates, they are important enough to require some restrictions on the entry of outsiders into the prison. So, for example, a restriction that limits visits to individuals who have either a personal or professional relationship to the inmate—such as family, friends, legal counsel, or clergy—would be constitutional (60 Am Jur 2d, Penal §78).

In addition to problems presented by the "who can visit" issue, even more questions arise regarding "what can happen during the visit" issues. Should inmates and visitors be allowed to hug, kiss, and hold hands during the visit? Should married inmates be allowed to have conjugal visits with their spouses? Given the courts' position on other items, it will not surprise you that answers to these questions center on security interests. In *Block v. Rutherford,* 468 U.S. 576 (1984), the Court was asked to rule on whether pretrial detainees have a constitutional right to contact visits. Although this case concerned persons not yet convicted of a crime, as opposed to convicted prisoners, the Court had already decided (*Bell v. Wolfish*) that for purposes of inmates' rights, jails and prisons are treated the same. In *Block,* pretrial detainees at the Los Angeles County Central Jail argued that the jail's policy of denying pretrial detainees contact visits with their spouses, relatives, children, and friends violated the detainees' civil rights under §1983. The Court disagreed and ruled that nothing in the Constitution requires detainees to be allowed contact visits when responsible, experienced administrators have determined that such visits will jeopardize the security of the facility and other prisoners (468 U.S. at 576).

The jail administrators' concern that contact visits would compromise facility security was accepted by the Court as being "obvious" because visitors can conceal guns, knives, drugs, or other contraband in many different ways and then pass the items to the detainees. Therefore, jail authorities (and prison officials as well) can reasonably prohibit contact between visitors and inmates in an attempt to prevent contraband from being introduced into the jail or prison. That restriction can be imposed even though officials have no suspicion or belief that a particular visitor is responsible for bringing in contraband. The mere knowledge that visitors in general are a chief source of contraband is sufficient to ban contact visits.

Conjugal visits (i.e., visits by an inmate's spouse with an opportunity for intimate sexual relations) can be authorized by the state as a privilege for prisoners, but they are not considered a constitutional right (*Tarlton v. Clark,* 441 F.2d 384, 5th Cir.; 1971). Many foreign countries and several states provide facilities for conjugal visits, but the general practice is not to permit such contact. Even where it is permitted (e.g., California and New York), prisoners cannot use its revocation as a basis for complaining their rights were being denied without due process (*Champion v. Artuz,* 76 F.3d 483; 2nd Cir.; 1996).

The *Bell* and *Block* decisions are important not only because they help define the restrictions that state authorities can place on prisoners but also because they point to the U.S. Supreme Court's return to a policy of less interference, if not noninterference, in the operation of jails and prisons. As such, they provide a good place to return to the historical periods identifying court willingness to get involved in prison administration issues.

The Nominal Doctrine: A Return to Hands Off?

Since 1980, an increasingly conservative U.S. Supreme Court has returned in some respects to a hands-off doctrine when handling prisoners' rights cases. The first clear indication of the Court's interest in backing away from an intervention doctrine is found in Justice Rehnquist's opinion in *Bell v. Wolfish.* Rehnquist, writing for the majority, refers to "a time not too long ago when the federal judiciary took a completely 'hands-off' approach to the problem of prison administration" (441 U.S. at 562). He goes on to note that in recent years those courts had discarded the hands-off attitude and have seemingly gone to the other extreme by becoming "increasingly enmeshed in the minutiae of prison operations" (at 562). Rehnquist found such extreme involvement by the courts as inappropriate, suggesting instead that the level of scrutiny by the federal courts into the area of prison management "must be limited to the issue of whether a particular system violates any prohibition of the Constitution or, in the case of a federal prison, a statute" (at 562). This new middle ground between hands-off and intervention can be called a **nominal doctrine.**

One of the best examples of the nominal doctrine in action is found in court decisions regarding First Amendment issues. To appreciate the contrast we first consider how federal courts in the 1970s looked at censorship of inmate mail and then compare that with court decisions in the late 1980s and the 1990s.

The constitutional right to expression (freedom of speech) can be said to provide inmates with a liberty interest in communicating by letter. Any attempts to restrict such a fundamental First Amendment guarantee might very well deserve a hearing before a court of law. In 1974 California inmates brought a class-action suit challenging the inmate mail censorship regulations followed by the Department of Corrections. In *Procunier v. Martinez,* 416 U.S. 396 (1974), the U.S. Supreme Court held that prisoners' mail could be censored only if (1) the practice furthers one or more of the important or substantial governmental interests in security, order, and rehabilitation; and (2) the limitation is no greater than that needed to protect the government interest involved. That ruling is generally seen as setting standards that make it difficult to restrict inmate correspondence or other First Amendment rights, and it provides a good example of the intervention doctrine.

Compare the 1974 *Procunier v. Martinez* decision to one in 1987. Before a more conservative Supreme Court than the one California inmates had in 1974, Missouri inmates brought suit against the prison's ban on inmates corresponding with other nonfamily inmates. The lower federal courts had used *Procunier v. Martinez* to side with the inmates because Missouri officials could not justify the ban as furthering an important or substantial governmental interest and said it was not any greater than necessary to protect that interest. In *Turner v. Safley,* 482 U.S. 78 (1987), the Supreme Court rejected the *Procunier* link and said that prison regulations that infringe on inmates' constitutional rights are valid as long as the regulation is reasonably related to legitimate penological interests. Cohen (1988) explains that the "reasonableness standard" in *Turner v. Safley* is less demanding of the government than is the "least intrusive standard" set by *Procunier v. Martinez.* Under *Turner*'s reasonableness test, the government interest need only be legitimate rather than important or substantial. In addition, *Turner* says the regulation must only be reasonably related to a legitimate interest as opposed to being the least intrusive means available. Because monitoring the inmate-to-inmate mail (the least intrusive means available) was found by the Court to be an unduly burdensome alternative that would tax limited prison resources, a total prohibition of all correspondence with a limited class of persons (other Missouri prisoners) was upheld as reasonable (Cohen, 1988).

Initially it seemed most accurate to say that the *Turner v. Safley* decision simply applied to mail censorship between inmates. But some authors (e.g., Cohen, 1988) saw in the *Turner* standards the start of a new view by the courts toward First Amendment rights of prisoners. More recent court decisions suggest that such prophecy was accurate. *Turner* has been used to allow wardens in the Federal Bureau of Prisons to reject incoming publications if such publications (reviewed issue by issue) are detrimental to the security, good order, or discipline of the institution, or if the publications might facilitate criminal activity (*Thornburgh v. Abbott,* 490 U.S. 401; 1989).

The potential broad sweep of *Turner* was emphasized in a 1990 Supreme Court decision when Justice Kennedy, writing for the majority, explained that the *Turner* principles of "reasonably related" and "legitimate penological interests" apply in all cases in which a prisoner asserts that a prison regulation violates the Constitution, not just those in which the prisoner invokes the First Amendment (*Washington v. Harper;* 494 U.S. 210). Although the courts have not rushed to apply *Turner* to every case brought forward, there have been some interesting applications.

In a 1992 case (*Jordan v. Gardner,* 953 F.2d 1137), female inmates complained that Washington State prison authorities were violating their religious freedom by requiring the women to submit to "pat searches" by male as well as female correctional officers. Because the females' religious beliefs forbid them from being touched by men other than their husbands, they argued the procedure infringed on their religious freedom. The federal court ruled that the prison policy was reasonably related to legitimate interests in institutional security and that it, therefore, passed muster under *Turner v. Safley.* The complexity of the issue was made clear a year later when the same court vacated its decision in *Jordan v. Gardner* (1992), and ruled that the *Turner* standards do not apply to Eighth Amendment cases (*Jordan v. Gardner,* 986 F.2d 1521; 1993). In other words, the federal appeals court seemed to say that claims of violation of First Amendment religious freedom rights are appropriately decided under the *Turner* reasonableness standard—and by that standard, the First Amendment was not violated by the "pat search" policy. But when the constitutional violation was claimed to have been one of the Eighth Amendment's ban against cruel and unusual punishment, the *Turner* standard is not appropriate. Although that reasoning seems to contradict Justice Kennedy's statement (in *Washington v. Harper*) that *Turner* applies to all constitutional issues brought by prisoners, the federal appeals court for the second circuit is apparently not convinced that *Turner* is quite that broad.

Whether or not the *Turner* decision has additional impact on constitutional issues, the point to emphasize here is that it indicates a move by the federal courts to return to a policy of less involvement in prison management issues. Samaha (1994) has offered an interesting analysis of the Court's movement away from the intervention doctrine by comparing the way federal courts have ruled on postconviction cases to their rulings on prearrest cases. Just as the rule of law was extended to the period prior to arrest in the mid-1960s, there was a similar extension of formal law into the prison during the intervention doctrine. Just as the courts tried to make procedural law clear regarding topics such as right to counsel, search and seizure, and other prearrest and pretrial situations, they also tried to clarify procedures to be followed after a person is convicted. The result, some have argued, was a tip of the justice scales in favor of the suspect, defendant, and offender. Since the 1970s, others have argued, the courts have ruled more in favor of justice officials at the expense of citizens' rights.

Certainly one can argue that contemporary court rulings are unsupportive of the rights of citizens caught in the system; one can also argue that contemporary courts are interfering too much in the jobs of police, prosecutors, and wardens. Probably more accurate than either extreme is a middle position that sees contemporary court rulings as an attempt to balance the formal law and informal discretion. Samaha (1994) suggests that for prison administration, rather than seeing a return either to complete administrative discretion in prison management or to the applying of more formal law to prison life, we will see attempts to adjust the balance between formal and informal action and control. In that way, "law and administrative discretion may complement each other in providing punishment in the form of safe, secure, humane confinement" (Samaha, 1994, p. 530).

Prisoners' Rights in Other Countries

When considering prisoners' rights in other countries, one is struck by the universality of two questions that governments face on deciding to imprison some of their citizens. Do imprisoned citizens have rights similar to those not in prison? Which, if any, agencies are responsible for overseeing the country's prisons and the prison administrators? We have already seen the difficult time U.S. jurisdictions have had answering such questions. We should not be surprised that other countries debate the same issues, but we may be surprised at the resulting policies and procedures. After a quick look at examples of specific areas of prisoners' rights in other countries, we will spend a bit more time on the question of how the prisons are controlled.

Rights Retained and Rights Lost

Issues of importance to prisoners in many countries around the world are similar to those of concern to prisoners in the United States. Complaints about restrictions on correspondence are expressed by prisoners worldwide. As Czech dissident, and later president, Václav Havel explained it (in his *Letters to Olga*), mail becomes very important to those in prison: "Letters are the only thing you have here, you read them ten times, you meditate them from all sides, you become glad with each detail, or—just the reverse—each detail is a source for sorrows and you become aware of your powerlessness . . . " (quoted in van Oers, 1992, pp. 62–63). Many prison systems seem to agree that correspondence is important to prisoners and have procedures that view such correspondence as a right. In Belgium, for example, prisoners have the right to receive newspapers and periodicals, to take correspondence courses, and to write and mail as many letters as they wish (van Oers, 1992). Prisoners in England and Wales can generally send as many letters as their prison earnings allow them to buy stamps for. The letters must be written on prison notepaper, are restricted in length, and are subject to some content censorship (Morgan, 1991). In the Dutch prison system, inmates may write letters to anyone and receive them from anyone without restriction. The envelope contents are checked for contraband, but the letter itself is not subject to censoring (Kelk, 1991). Censorship seems to be more specific in the prison system of the People's Republic of China, where letters to and from inmates are checked by prison officials and "those which have contents hindering the reform of prisoners or exposing the reform organs (are) detained" (Zhao, 1991, p. 437). In contrast to China, prisoners in Spain have no limit on the number of letters they may receive or send. Furthermore, that mail is neither inspected nor censored by prison officials (Giménez-Salinas i Colomer, 1991).

Control of Prisons and Prison Conditions

A country's prison system is traditionally part of its political system and, therefore, operates under the oversight of bureaus such as the Ministry of Justice, Department of Justice, Bureau of Prisons, Department of Corrections, and so on. Such placement often means that prisons are under a level of political control by the country's (or individual states/provinces) legislators. But in addition to political control, prison systems may also have to operate under the watchful eye of the country's judiciary.

Political Control of Prisons. Legislative oversight of the prison system is most directly provided through budgeting hearings. In many jurisdictions the prison officials must make annual reports to and appearances before the country's legislators. On these occasions the prison officials are questioned about the operation of the prisons, and any concerns the legislators might have regarding prison operations are expressed to those officials.

More direct political observation is provided through an office of **ombudsman.** The ombudsman is an independent official appointed to investigate citizen complaints against abuses by government officials and agencies. In some jurisdictions the ombudsman has the power to make binding decisions; in others, he or she simply makes recommendations. In Sweden, where the office of ombudsman originated in 1809, prisoners have access to the Justice Ombudsman. This particular version of the ombudsman (there are others investigating citizen complaints in different areas) is appointed by and responsible to the Swedish Parliament. Prisoners send their complaints—via uncensored letters—to the Justice Ombudsman, who investigates those complaints. The Justice Ombudsman may also, at his or her own initiative, investigate prison conditions in general and make periodic visits to the institutions (Bishop, 1991). England also relies on a prison ombudsman whose principle responsibility is to investigate complaints about the treatment of inmates throughout the system (Terrill, 1999). The ombudsman serves as the final source of appeal from the internal disciplinary system of the prison, but his or her information comes primarily from the prison staff. As a result, there is concern among some in England about how effective the ombudsman can be in evaluating the fairness of prison disciplinary proceedings.

Some jurisdictions rely primarily on these types of political control over their prisons; other jurisdictions supplement, or even substitute, judicial control for political control. Because the coverage of prisoners' rights in the United States concentrated on the role of judicial control, we will look more closely at that topic in this review of prisoners' rights in other countries.

Judicial Control of Prisons. Like prisoners in the United States, those in several other countries are able to take their complaints about alleged violations of rights to the judiciary (see "Prisoners' Rights in Zimbabwe"). Not surprisingly, prisoner access to the courts has been as controversial in other countries as it has in the United States.

Cross-Cultural Corrections

Prisoners' Rights in Zimbabwe

Access to physical exercise is a topic of seemingly universal interest to prisoners. In Zimbabwe, prisoners who were under sentence of death for a murder resulting from a 1988 car bombing complained about their conditions of incarceration. After originally having daily access to an exercise yard during daylight hours until 4 P.M., the prisoners' period of access was reduced to one-half hour on weekdays only. An additional half hour was available for cleaning and washing. As a result of the revised policy, the prisoners spent twenty-three hours a day in their cells on weekdays and twenty-three and one-half hours per day on weekends and holidays. This procedure was necessary, prison officials argued, for security reasons. Prisoner Conjwayo complained that such restriction on his ability to exercise and enjoy fresh air was inhuman treatment, and he asked the Zimbabwe court to make prison officials give him daily access to the exercise yard for one hour in the morning and one hour in the afternoon.

The Supreme Court of Zimbabwe (as reported in Naldi, 1992) agreed that the forty-seven-hour weekend confinement to the cell was offensive to one's notion of humanity and decency and involves the infliction of unnecessary suffering. In addition the Court realized that although prison officials must have some discretion in security matters, undue harshness under the pretext of prison security or discipline cannot be immune from judicial review. The Court ruled that prisoners under sentence of death must be given at least one hour of daily exercise in the open air because depriving a prisoner of access to fresh air, sunlight, and the ability to exercise properly is virtually treating him as a nonhuman. The emphasis must always be, the Court said, on man's basic dignity, on civilized principles, and on flexibility and improvement in standards of decency as society progresses and matures.

Read about the Zimbabwe judiciary at *www.mother.com/~zimweb/zim/int_judi.htm.* Upon what legal models is Zimbabwean law based? How does the Chief Justice of the Supreme Court get to that position?

In reviewing the stance of different countries regarding access to courts, Naldi (1992) notes some similarities to the rights-are-retained argument in the U.S. federal appeals court decision in *Coffin v. Reichard.* In a 1983 decision, the British House of Lords—the highest appeals level in England and Wales—ruled that "under English law, a convicted prisoner, in spite of his imprisonment, retains all civil rights which are not taken away expressly or by necessary implication" (quoted in Naldi, 1992, p. 717). Similarly, a Hong Kong court said in 1990 that "Everyone, including prisoners, has certain basic rights and these are not taken away unless the law so permits" (quoted in Naldi, 1992, fn. 13). And on yet another continent, the Supreme Court of Zimbabwe noted that a prisoner's loss of liberty does not also mean a loss of personal rights. The Court agreed that prison officials must have the latitude to administer prison affairs, and that prisoners are necessarily subject to appropriate rules and regulations, but the courts are responsible for enforcing the constitutional rights of all persons, prisoners included (reported in Naldi, 1992, pp. 717–718).

Once it is determined that prisoners have some civil rights despite their inmate status, it becomes necessary to identify a way to monitor how prison officials are recognizing those rights. Certainly the political control noted earlier can provide that opportunity, but let us take a look at the role played by the courts in this process.

Dünkel and van Zyl Smit (1991) have implied that judicial control of prison administration can be distinguished as one of three types. For our purposes we will identify those types as countries using essentially no judicial control, those having limited judicial control, and others with significant judicial control.

In the People's Republic of China, prisoners retain their constitutional and legal rights as citizens, although the content of those rights and the way they are applied differ from citizens not in prison (Zhao, 1991). Assurances that prison officials are providing those rights—for example, the right not to be tortured—are provided legislatively through the National People's Congress and all levels of the local people's congresses. These various legislators are supposed to "conduct conscientious inspections and counselling periodically or occasionally on the ways in which [prison officials] execute the law" (Zhao, 1991, pp. 445–446). Prison oversight is also provided by prison officials holding regular meetings with family members of the prisoners, and with local residents near the prison, where the officials can receive input about the way they are operating the institutions. The closest thing to judicial control of Chinese prisons is through the people's procuratorates, or public prosecutors offices. The prosecutors are expected to conduct frequent and direct inspections of the way prison rules are carried out and to quickly correct any problems they may discover as a result of their inspection. The political nature of procuratorates, and the absence of any judge or magistrate in the investigation process, suggests that the People's Republic of China provides essentially no judicial control over its prison system.

Limited judicial control over prisons is assigned to the courts in countries such as South Africa where the head of each prison must provide daily opportunity for the prisoners to complain and make requests (van Zyl Smit, 1991). The prison chief is to make a record of the complaints and requests, investigate them, and deal with them appropriately. Prisoners who are unhappy with the prison director's response may ask the prison's commanding officer to arrange an interview with the commissioner of prisons or one of his deputies. The commissioner, or a representative, "may" grant an interview during his next visit to the prison. Prisoners must be careful when making a request to see the commissioner because prisoners who "lodge false, frivolous or malicious complaints" are subject to disciplinary actions (van Zyl Smit, 1991, p. 544).

This complaints procedure is internal to the South African Prison Service, so it might seem most appropriate to place South Africa among countries providing no judicial control over its prisons. But because it is possible for prisoners to ask the local or provincial division of the Supreme Court for relief from inappropriate action by prison officials, we can point to at least some access to the courts. Importantly, van Zyl Smit (1991) notes that such access is more theoretical than actual because South African courts take a very restricted view of prisoners' rights. The courts have taken action against prison officials only when the fundamental rights of prisoners have been flagrantly abused. Another obstacle to accessing the courts is the limited availability of legal services and the high cost of those services. Realistically, only the most confident and well-funded prisoners can make use of South Africa's version of judicial control over prisons.

Countries providing significant judicial control over their prisons would include France and Spain. In France, the prison system is under the dual control of the judiciary and of the regional directors of the prison system itself. Faugeron (1991) notes that judicial control is more prominent in theory than in actuality. But to at least provide an example of how "significant judicial control" might be organized in a country, we will briefly explain the claimed role of the judiciary in French prisons.

Since 1958, each French prison has had assigned to it a judge in charge of the application of punishment (typically called the sentencing judge). According to Terrill (1992), the intended function of the sentencing judge was to provide continuity between the decision made at trial and the implementation of that decision in the prison. The sentencing judge has both administrative and judicial functions in the prison setting. As part of the prison's oversight committee, the judge is informed of all changes in disciplinary and security matters and is told of all disciplinary actions taken against the prisoners. The judge is also expected to stay informed about inmate safety and security as well as the state of various rehabilitation programs. Also, during the judge's monthly visits to the prison, he or she is to meet with any inmates requesting such a meeting (Terrill, 1992). In carrying out their judicial functions, the sentencing judges have the authority to change the prisoner's sentence, to influence the inmate's specific prison routine, and to decide or at least comment upon issues such as home leaves, transfers to halfway houses, and parole.

The sentencing judge's presence at the prison certainly provides the French judiciary with an opportunity to have direct control over the prison. But, as noted earlier, that control is more ideal than actual. Because the sentencing judge is simply informed of—but cannot challenge—the prison's discipline of inmates, the prisoners cannot use the judge to file grievances about that discipline. The result is a situation in which "judicial control hardly penetrates the walls of the fortress which is the prison service" (Faugeron, 1991, p. 258).

If the sentencing judge in France is an example of the theory of "significant judicial control" over prisons, the supervisory judge in Spain might provide a genuine example. Like the sentencing judge, the supervisory judge must be kept informed of certain administrative actions, including restrictions placed on prisoners' communication, the use of force against prisoners, or prisoner transfers to psychiatric institutions. Beyond those administrative functions, the supervisory judge has powers that create a stronger judiciary presence in the prisons than that of the sentencing judge. As Giménez-Salinas i Colomer (1991) explains it, the supervisory judges can intervene in such areas as (1) approving punishment by solitary confinement, (2) hearing cases that appeal disciplinary sanctions, (3) hearing appeals about classification decisions, and (4) reviewing prisoner complaints about the prison regime and treatment. In this manner the supervisory judge is responsible for guaranteeing prisoners' rights at such a direct level that Spain can be considered as providing significant judicial control over its prisons.

Civilian Control of Prisons. This section began with the suggestion that control over prisons is either political or judicial. Although that is essentially true for most of the world, this is at least one example of oversight that is more accurately called "civilian control." We conclude this review of prisoners' rights in other countries with a look at the Netherlands, where Dünkel and van Zyl Smit (1991) say "a well-developed right of complaint has been recognized most fully . . . (since) prisoners are allowed to appeal against a wide range of actions by the authorities" (p. 728).

Prisoners' complaints about the conditions of their incarceration are taken quite seriously in the Netherlands. To hear and respond to such complaints, legislation reforming the Dutch prison system in 1953 created supervisory committees in all penitentiaries (prisons, houses of detention, and forensic mental hospitals). These committees were to help counterbalance the relatively powerful position of institutional governor that the legislation also created. Citizens representing many parts of Dutch society make up the committee with judges, lawyers, university teachers, businessmen, social workers, housewives, and physicians typically included among the members (Kelk, 1991, p. 405). The committee exerts control of the prisons through their overall supervision of the way detainees (prisoners and patients) are treated. Access to the committee is provided by having one committee member, the "monthly commissioner," deal with all complaints filed during the month he or she is on duty.

The committee's work took on greater significance when 1977 legislation provided the formal right to complain. Under that legislation, the monthly commissioner is required to hold official office hours at least once a month. Complaints received by the monthly commissioner are taken to a three-person complaints subcommittee of the supervisory committee. The complaints committee "is authorized to change, supplement or even revise completely the decision of the prison governor in a number of precisely specified cases" (Kelk, 1991, p. 406), including complaints about disciplinary punishment imposed or about the infringement of a right to which the prisoner is entitled. Prisoners' complaints can be declared valid, unfounded, or partially valid. Valid complaints—and aspects of partially valid ones—require the prison governor to promptly implement the committee's decision. If the governor's original decision caused the prisoner damage that cannot be undone by reversing that decision, the prison governor may be required to compensate the prisoner for that damage. Compensation can take the form of a moderate amount of money or might involve granting the inmate extra visitors, telephone calls, or recreation.

Decisions by the complaints committee can be appealed by either party to the Central Council for the Enforcement of Criminal Law (an advisory board of the minister of justice). The committee generally respects the prison governor's freedom to decide his or her own policy, and as a result, both the complaints and appeal committees show a fair degree of restraint. But even with that restraint, the detainees' complaints are found to be valid in a number of cases (Kelk, 1991, p. 407).

This example of civilian control over the Dutch prisons brings our discussion of prisoners' rights to a reasonable end. And, although we may still not have clear answers to questions about whether prisoners retain their rights or lose their rights, or about the appropriate way to ensure that prisoners actually get any rights that they do retain, we have at least explored a variety of options.

VICTIMS' RIGHTS

In 1972 Marvin Wolfgang complained that "The whole criminal justice system—from police to parole—ignores the victim except as he contributes to the evidence against the offender" (p. 18). Nearly twenty years later, Deborah Kelly lamented that although "many statutes have been passed in the name of crime victims . . . in practice, most victims never benefit from these reforms" (1991, p. 22). Although it is certainly not unusual for problems related to the criminal justice system to endure, this particular example may be unique because of the attention it received in the last quarter of the twentieth century. The field of victimology in general, with the topic of victims' rights more specifically, has generated discussion, is the focus of legislation, and has been the issue in several court decisions since the early 1970s. As a balance to our coverage of prisoners' rights, let us consider, if only briefly, the important area of victims' rights.

Victimology has technically been around since the 1940s, when Hans von Hentig (1948) called attention to the relationship between criminal and victim, and Benjamin Mendelsohn (see Karmen, 1990) coined the term *victimology* in an article. Despite that history, victimology is often considered to have gained legitimacy as a subfield of criminology in the 1960s when the U.S. Congress held a hearing on the plight of crime victims (1964), the first nationwide victimization survey was carried out in the United States (1966), and in 1967 a presidential commission recommended that criminologists study victims (Karmen, 1990). Today victimologists still study the relationship between victims and offenders (see "American Indians as Victims"), but the field has grown to encompass the interaction between victims and the criminal justice system, the media, business, and other societal groups and institutions. As Karmen (1990) explains it, "crime victims may find themselves at odds not only with the offenders who directly harmed them but also

ISSUES OF FAIRNESS

AMERICAN INDIANS AS VICTIMS

In 1999 the Bureau of Justice Statistics published a focused report on the effects and consequences of violent crime among American Indians (Greenfeld & Smith, 1999). The results show a disturbing picture of American Indian involvement in crime as both victims and offenders. We are interested here in the victimization data, which show a rate of violent crime victimization for American Indians that is well above the rate of other U.S. racial or ethnic subgroups and is more than twice as high as the national average.

One finding was especially notable: "American Indians are more likely than people of other races to experience violence at the hands of someone of a different race" (Greenfeld & Smith, 1999, p. iii). Violent crime against white or black victims is typically committed by someone of the same race; that is, the crime is intraracial. Specifically, 69 percent of white violent crime victims had white assailants, and 81 percent of black victims were victimized by a black offender. American Indian victims of violent crime described the offender as white in 60 percent of the cases and as black in 10 percent. About 30 percent of the offenses were believed to have been intraracial, that is, committed by other American Indians. This interracial victimization of American Indians is especially high in cases of rape and sexual assault, which were reported as having a white offender in 82 percent of the victimizations.

Although American Indians account for a small percentage of all violent victimizations (1.4 percent in 1996), they comprise less than 1 percent of the U.S. population. As a result, their victimization rate is disproportionately high. The rate of violent victimization per 1,000 persons age twelve or older is 50 for all races. The rate for American Indians is 124—the next closest are African Americans with a violent victimization rate of 61 per 1,000 whereas the rate for whites was 49 and for Asians, 29. A rate that is 2.5 times the national average suggests that victimologists, criminologists, policymakers, and the general public should increase efforts to understand how best to address the problem of crime for this segment of our population.

Visit the Office for Victims of Crime at ***www.ojp.usdoj.gov/ovc/help/natamer.htm.*** What type of information is provided in the way of victim assistance for American Indians? Are there services provided in your state or in one near you? If so, what are some examples?

with journalists, police officers, lawyers, judges, businesspeople, and other law-abiding people" (p. 4). The field of victimology has each of those relationships as its topic of study, as victimologists try to learn more about crime victims. When attention is specifically on the victims' role in the criminal justice process, questions of victims' rights and victim services invariably come up—and those are the topics to which we turn our attention.

By the end of the twentieth-century, all fifty states had provided a "victims' bill of rights" that identifies a set of basic rights and protections for victims of crime. Twenty-nine of the states took an additional step and adopted a constitutional amendment for victims' rights (National Victim Center, 1998). Although provisions for victims' rights are present in all states, their scope and forcefulness vary. However, the procedures typically include the rights to:

- Attend and/or participate in criminal justice proceedings
- Notification of the stages and proceedings in the criminal justice process
- Notification of other legal remedies
- Protection from intimidation and harassment
- Confidentiality of records
- Speedy trial provisions
- Prompt return of the victim's personal property seized as evidence from the offender

- Availability of the offenders' profits from the sale of the stories of their crimes
- **Victim compensation** and restitution (National Victim Center, 1998)

The first right—attend and/or participate in criminal justice proceedings—has direct bearing on corrections and is the focus of this review. Specifically, we are interested in the victim's role in sentencing.

Victim Participation in Sentencing

Victim input at sentencing is considered to be an important way to involve victims in the criminal justice system and to provide them with an opportunity to influence the offender's punishment. Some prosecutors may request victim input prior to offering or accepting a negotiated plea, but more often the victim's input occurs at the sentencing hearing. In fact, every state now allows victims to provide either oral or written information at sentencing on how the crime impacted the victim, and most states allow impact information to be included as part of the presentence investigation report (National Victim Center, 1998).

The impact statements typically describe how the offense has harmed the victim—including financial, physical, psychological, and social harms—and the victim's family. The form in which the statements are made fall into one of five types: (1) a written statement either as a letter or on a designated form, (2) an oral statement (also known as **allocution**) in which the victim personally addresses the court, (3) an audiotape, (4) a videotape, or (5) closed-circuit television.

Because these statements by victims might influence the sentence given by the judge, as is their purpose, you can imagine that offenders have expressed displeasure at their use. In 1987 that displeasure reached the U.S. Supreme Court. In *Booth v. Maryland,* 482 U.S. 496 (1987), the Court heard a case involving Irving Bronstein and his wife Rose. The two elderly victims, age seventy-eight and seventy-five, were robbed and brutally murdered in their Baltimore home in 1983. One of the killers, John Booth, decided to let the jury rather than the judge set his sentence after he had been convicted of murder. A victim impact statement, as required by state law, had been prepared by the probation officer as part of the presentence investigation report. The jurors, who read the impact statement as they reviewed the presentence report, returned a sentence of death. Booth appealed the death sentence to the U.S. Supreme Court, claiming that the victim impact statement violated his constitutional rights. The Court agreed and overturned the death sentence under the reasoning that the information in the victim impact statement was not relevant for determining a capital sentence. More specifically, the Court said its inclusion presented an unacceptable risk that the jury might impose the death penalty in an arbitrary and capricious manner. But victims would still have another, if not the last, word.

In 1987 three-year-old Nicholas Christopher watched as Pervis Tyrone Payne stabbed Nicholas's mother and two-year-old sister to death in Millington, Tennessee. During the trial, the prosecution claimed that Payne, a twenty-year-old retarded man, had killed the mother and child after the woman resisted his sexual advances. Payne was convicted of both murders. At the sentencing hearing, Payne had his parents, his girlfriend, and a clinical psychologist testify to various mitigating aspects of his background and character as the defense attempted to sway the jury away from a sentence of death. The prosecution called Nicholas's grandmother, who gave a victim impact statement that told of Nicholas crying out daily for his mother and baby sister. During closing arguments of the sentencing hearing, the prosecution mentioned the continuing effect the crime was having on the victims' family. The jury returned a death sentence on each murder count.

Payne, using the *Booth v. Maryland* decision, appealed the death sentences on the basis that evidence and arguments relating to the impact that the victim's death

Help Wanted

Job Title: Crime Victim Advocate

Position Description: Victim advocates act as liaisons between victims and agents of the justice system by providing crime victims with information, emotional support, and crisis counseling.

Qualifications: Bachelor's degree in counseling or a related field and volunteer or internship experience in a victim services program.

For an example of career opportunities in this field, check the home page for the Victim Services Division at the Texas Department of Criminal Justice site at ***www.tdcj.state.tx.us/victim/victim-home.htm.***

had on the victim's family was inadmissible in death penalty cases. The Tennessee Supreme Court, essentially ignoring the *Booth* precedent, rejected Payne's claim and upheld the conviction and death sentence. The U.S. Supreme Court, in an unusual about-face, agreed with the Tennessee Supreme Court and overruled its decision in *Booth.* The *Payne v. Tennessee,* 501 U.S. 808 (1991), decision said the Booth decision was based on the faulty premises that (1) the harm caused by the defendant is not relevant to the defendant's blameworthiness, and (2) only evidence relating to blameworthiness is relevant to a capital sentencing decision.

The Court explained that information about the harm caused by a defendant has historically been relevant in determining both the particular offense and the appropriate punishment. The victim impact statement, the Court argued, was "simply another method of informing the sentencing authority about [the specific harm caused by the crime]" (501 U.S. at 808). In addition, the Court found no reason to believe that victim impact statements would necessarily lead to arbitrary impositions of the death penalty. In sum, the *Payne* decision says the use of victim impact evidence during the penalty phase of a capital trial presents no constitutional violation.

There seems little doubt that the inclusion of victim impact statements and victim allocution opportunities are victories for those championing victims' rights. A survey conducted by the National Center for Victims of Crime determined that most victims who were notified of the sentencing hearing and their right to participate attended the hearing and made an impact statement at sentencing (Kilpatrick, Beatty, & Howley, 1998). How often and to what extent that statement influences the eventual sentence is difficult to determine because the victim's opinion is only one of many for the judge to consider. Prosecutors, defense attorneys, probation officers, and even the defendants themselves make sentencing recommendations or in some way try to influence the judges' decision. Even the media and public opinion might play a role in the eventual sentence. None of this suggests that the victims' opinions are any less or more important than those of the others, but it does mean the victims have significant competition for the judge's attention.

Victim Services in Corrections

Whether they influence the sentence or not, many would agree that increased participation of victims in the sentencing process is appropriate and desirable. But do the rights of the victim end after the offender is sentenced? To the extent that rights include the right to service, the answer is increasingly no. If one reads the list of rights given earlier as simply statements regarding where the victims are allowed to be (e.g., in court), what they are allowed to do (e.g., submit a victim impact statement), and what they can expect from the process (e.g., confidentiality of records), then only one aspect of the list is being appreciated. Equally important are the rights dealing with how the victims know when and where to appear (e.g., the right to notification), receive counseling for crime-related consequences (e.g., protection from intimidation and harassment), and are paid for their financial losses (e.g., compensation and restitution). These last items are best identified as rights to service, and it is the criminal justice system's obligation to provide that service.

Not surprisingly, the first criminal justice agencies to provide services to victims were law enforcement and the prosecutor's office. Because the offender starts at those stages of the process, it is understandable that the victim will as well. So, victim services in police agencies provide victims with information about their rights in the process, about how the investigation is progressing, and about other community services available to the victim. When an arrest is made, victim services in the prosecutor's office will keep victims informed about trial dates, what to expect at the trial, plea negotiations that may be made, and how to provide a victim impact statement.

For many years victim services were provided only at the law enforcement and prosecution stages. More recently we are seeing victim services in corrections. Some of the services provided when the offender is in the corrections system are a continuation of the notification process. For example, appearance at sentencing is not the last opportunity that victims might have to make their feelings known to decision makers. Victims are increasingly given the right to attend and sometimes address probation hearings, parole hearings, commutation or pardon hearings, and even change of security status hearings (e.g., transferring the offender from maximum- to minimum-security facilities).

In addition to the continuation of the right to attend and participate into the corrections arena, corrections-based victim services are identifying other areas in which they can assist crime victims. For example, some state departments of corrections have designated a victim services representative at specific institutions and in community-based programs. Those representatives may provide direct assistance to victims, participate in local victim service coalitions, and provide training about the agency's victim services program.

A final corrections-based victim service to mention is the increasingly common use of victim/offender programs. Some of these programs reflect a restorative justice philosophy and might actually involve face-to-face encounters between offenders and their victims. They would be different from mediation meetings because the offender's sanction has already been determined; but they may serve to relieve victim anxiety about (and maybe even objection to) such changes in status as the offender's parole or transfer to a community-corrections facility.

Also growing in popularity are victim impact classes/panels for offenders. These programs are part of a treatment regimen while the offender is on probation in a community residential facility, in a prison, or on parole. In the programs, offenders are confronted by crime victims (typically not their own victims) and community members who explain to the offender how crime impacts the victim, the victim's family, the neighborhood, and the community.

The topic of victims' rights is more widely recognized as a critical issue today than it was twenty and more years ago. There is still considerable work to be done before victim advocates believe the criminal justice system has fully recognized the victim as an important player in all aspects of the process. But most would agree that improvements are constantly being made. Chapter 4 suggested that restorative justice may play a prominent role in the twenty-first century. If that occurs, it will be in part because victims, the community, and the offender are all recognized as needing to be involved in determining how balance can be restored to the community after a crime occurs.

SUMMARY

RIGHTS OF PRISONERS

Deciding which rights prisoners retain and which ones they lose is a duty that falls to the courts.

- Prior to the early 1960s, the courts generally took the position that prison officials must be given the leeway to operate their prisons as they saw fit. This hands-off approach meant that prisoner complaints about the conditions under which they were kept seldom received a sympathetic ruling by judges.

- In the mid-1960s, the federal courts increasingly showed a desire to intervene on behalf of prisoners. For about twenty years the courts actively intervened in the area of prison management, as the judges sought to ensure prisoners of certain rights to which the courts believed even inmates were entitled.
- Since the 1980s a more conservative U.S. Supreme Court has encouraged rulings that reflect only nominal involvement in prison management, as the judges seek a middle ground that allows prison officials the opportunity to run their prisons but also recognizes that prisoners retain some rights after conviction and during imprisonment.

Many rights that prisoners may have while confined are said to come from the U.S. Constitution.

- The Eighth Amendment's ban against cruel and unusual punishment is the clearest example of a prisoner's right, but the Fourteenth Amendment's due process and equal protection clauses are also applicable to prisoners.
- In addition to rights stemming from the Constitution, an increasing number of inmates' lawsuits are brought under section 1983 of the Civil Rights Act.

A SAMPLING OF PRISONERS' RIGHTS

- To exemplify some of the issues raised by prisoners, this chapter reviews court decisions in the areas of access to courts, religion, and privacy.
- The complexity of the issues involved is obvious as the chapter covers topics such as what law materials, if any, must be provided in a prison law library, whether prison officials must accommodate the worship needs of Satanists, and what restrictions can be placed on the prisoners' ability to communicate with the outside world.

PRISONERS' RIGHTS IN OTHER COUNTRIES

Like prisoners in the United States, those in other countries are also confronted with a need to bring claims against the conditions of their confinement.

- In some countries those claims are heard by citizens taking the role of a prison ombudsman. These ombudsmen are responsible for determining the legitimacy of prisoner complaints and, when appropriate, encouraging changes in prison operation.
- In other countries, prisoner claims are handled by the courts—in a manner similar to the procedure in the United States.

VICTIMS' RIGHTS

- Less controversial than prisoners' rights is the topic of victims' rights. Possibly because it is not so contentious, concern about victims' rights has a shorter history than does prisoners' rights. Advocates increasingly use the courts to gain some respect, advantage, and compensation for victims—the too often forgotten player in the justice process.
- Victims today have a more active role in sentencing through the victim impact statement.
- Corrections agencies are realizing that they also have obligations to crime victims, and an increasing number of programs and services that focus on victims are being implemented in community programs and in institutions.

Key Terms and Concepts

allocution (p. 547)
civil rights (p. 525)
Civil Rights Act (p. 526)
due process clause (p. 522)
equal protection clause (p. 524)
hands-off doctrine (p. 517)
incorporation (p. 522)
intervention doctrine (p. 520)
nominal doctrine (p. 538)
ombudsman (p. 541)
Prison Litigation Reform Act (p. 514)
Religious Freedom Restoration Act (p. 534)
rights-are-lost position (p. 516)
rights-are-retained position (p. 516)
victim compensation (p. 547)
victimology (p. 545)
writ of habeas corpus (p. 526)

Discussion Questions

1. What are the strongest arguments for both the rights-are-retained and the rights-are-lost positions?
2. As warden of a prison, you have decided to prevent an article about racial tensions in *East Cell Block* from being printed in the next issue of the inmate newspaper—an act of censorship that has not occurred in the last five years of the paper's publication. What reasons will you need to offer the court in order for the court to support your position? What arguments do you expect the inmate editor will use in his lawsuit against you?
3. What level of influence should victims and victims' families have over the decisions made in the areas of plea negotiation, sentencing, and release on parole? Should arguments from victims and victims' families who want a less severe penalty (including early release from imprisonment) be given as much weight as victim and family arguments for a more severe penalty?

chapter 15

Nothing Works—Something Works

A New York cabdriver cut across several lanes of traffic to pick up a fare and in doing so, sideswiped a red Volkswagen. Both drivers got out. The Volkswagen owner grabbed the cabdriver by the shirt and pulled him close. Poking the cabby in the middle of the forehead, the other driver said repeatedly, "This is your lucky day." He then freed the cabby, saying: "I'm on the way to my court-appointed anger-therapy group, and I don't want to go with blood on my shirt."

Well, there is an example of at least one program that works! Actually, that story highlights several interesting points regarding the question of whether a corrections program works. Most obvious, is the problem of determining what we mean by *works*. Do we mean *works* to protect society from wrongdoers, to deter offenders or others, to change offenders into law-abiding people, to teach the wrongdoer a lesson, or to restore things, as well as possible, to their prior state? The VW-driver's anger-therapy program prevented him from doing harm to the cabdriver on a particular day and at a particular hour. It is not clear if the cabby would have been as fortunate if the driver had been headed to a different appointment or if it was later in the day.

Another point about corrections programs that the cabdriver story highlights is the concern that programs are effective only while they are being implemented. Will the VW-driver control his anger as well after his anger therapy is completed? Will society be safe from burglaries by Dan even after Dan is released from prison? Will Suzi still refrain from shoplifting even after the Christmastime publicity about shoplifters being prosecuted dies down? This chapter looks at those types of controversies by returning our attention to the philosophies of punishment first introduced in Chapter 2. We do that because determining whether something works depends on the objective a person is trying to achieve. Executing a murderer may well have "taught him a lesson," and thereby pleases the retributivist, but did it serve the purpose of general deterrence? Forcing a computer hacker to do community service might change her attitude toward unauthorized access to personal records, but does her punishment deter other hackers from committing similar acts?

In this chapter we are going to review some of the research that has been conducted in attempts to answer questions about whether correctional sanctions work. We cannot review all such research, so selections are offered as they link to major topics covered in earlier chapters. The variability of the term *works* is still problematic, however. A simple explanation or definition will not be offered, although we will consider how the answer might vary depending on what punishment philosophy the questioner emphasizes. But that exercise will result in a philosophical discussion that leaves many of us wondering about practical applications. To help make the move (notice it is not a leap) from philosophy to practice, the material is presented with links to specific programs or procedures mentioned in the preceding chapters. The goal is to provide information that makes clear the link between the topics of philosophy and practice.

THE NOTHING-WORKS CONTROVERSY

In the late 1960s, Douglas Lipton, Robert Martinson, and Judith Wilks were hired by the New York Governor's Special Committee on Criminal Offenders and charged with reviewing over 1,000 studies on rehabilitation. They identified 231 studies that met the methodological standards they set and proceeded to determine what those studies showed about the effect of rehabilitation programs (Lipton, Martinson, & Wilks, 1975). In 1974 Martinson wrote a summary of their findings, providing what Hawkins and Alpert (1989) call "the academic equivalent of firing on Fort Sumter" (p. 211). The Civil War analogy is not misplaced given the ensuing and continuing controversy regarding the bombshell Martinson (1974) dropped when he wrote: *"With few and isolated exceptions, the rehabilitative efforts that have been reported so far have had no appreciable effect on recidivism"* (p. 25; emphasis in the original). Although Martinson did not specifically say that nothing works, the label stuck and has been tattooed on article, chapter, and book titles ever since.

The rounds volleyed back and forth between critics and proponents of the nothing-works charge have resulted in each side winning some battles, but the war itself rages on. A brief review of some of the major reports over the years gives us an idea of the problems associated with trying to decide what works.

The Nothing-Works Position

Actually, Martinson's 1974 article was not the first to suggest that correctional programs left much to be desired. Inciardi (1993) explains that a report in 1966 had already determined that evidence supporting the value of correctional treatment was slight, inconsistent, and of questionable reliability. Another study in 1971 seemed to suggest that persons in correctional treatment did not seem likely to act differently regardless of whether they were locked up, treated, watched more closely, or just cut loose. But despite such previous studies, Inciardi (1993) says it was the Martinson essay that created a sensation because it appeared in a prominent publication and attracted popular media attention just when politicians and policymakers were desperately searching for some response to the widespread public fear of street crime (p. 576).

Important support for the Martinson report came in 1979. In that year, a group of scientists commissioned by the National Research Council (NRC) reported on their own review of a subsample of the original 231 studies plus some studies completed after the Martinson, Wilks, and Lipton review (Sechrest, White, & Brown, 1979). The NRC scholars determined that in those places where Martinson and the others did make errors of interpretation, they were ones that benefited rehabilitation proponents. Greenberg (1977), examining evaluation studies published after those considered in the Martinson report, concluded that the Martinson report findings were essentially accurate. Wright (1994) reviews other studies conducted since 1977 that have corroborated the ineffectiveness of rehabilitation. His review led him to conclude that "there is simply no compelling evidence to suggest that rehabilitation programs implemented either inside or outside correctional institutions show much promise for reducing the recidivism rates among criminal offenders"

(Wright, 1994, p. 36; italics omitted). However, feeling more charitable a year later, Wright (1995) offered that "the research evidence at this point may be inconclusive and the [evaluation] debate may have ended in a draw; some studies show the failure of treatment programs, while others report modest signs of success" (p. 26).

The Something-Works Position

Response to Martinson has included claims that he eventually saw the light and changed his mind, criticism of the methodology used by him and his colleagues, and finally reports of other studies that found support for the effectiveness of correctional programs. We will take a brief look at each type of reaction.

Some in the something-works camp believe that Martinson retracted his nothing-works conclusion in a 1979 article, in which he said that contrary to his previous position, evidence from a new study indicates that some treatment programs do have an appreciable effect on recidivism and are indeed beneficial (see Cullen & Gendreau, 1989, p. 26). Hawkins and Alpert, however, believe that Martinson's statement that something works was taken out of context by some treatment advocates. They claim that Martinson, who has since died, is correctly remembered as holding to the stand that rehabilitation programs do not work (1989, p. 216).

Other responses to Martinson and his colleagues included challenges to their methodological techniques. They were criticized for bias, major distortions of fact, and gross misrepresentation. Inciardi suggests the criticism was well-founded because Martinson did not include all types of treatment programs, ignored the effects of some treatment programs on some individuals, concentrated on whether the particular treatment method was effective in all the studies in which it was tested, and he neglected to study the new federally funded treatment programs that had started after 1967 (see Inciardi, 1993, p. 577).

More persuasive criticism came in the form of evaluation studies that found correctional programs that did work. As will be seen later in this chapter, comprehensive analyses of groupings of studies as well as evaluations of individual programs led authors in the 1990s to write about correctional treatment as being reaffirmed and revived. An important addition to much of the work by today's rehabilitation advocates is to include in their research some comments about what has been shown not to work as well as to identify what does work. For example, Petersilia (1993) offers the following:

- Prison terms are usually imposed late in an offender's criminal career when, for most, criminal activity has ended or soon will.
- Much crime (particularly violent crime) is an impulsive response to an immediate stressful situation, often under the influence of drugs, alcohol, or both. Under such conditions the offender is not likely to consider the consequences, like a long prison term, of his actions.
- For imprisonment to deter offenders and potential offenders, it must be stigmatizing and punitive. Since about one-quarter of all males living in U.S. inner cities will be jailed at some point in their lives, there is less stigma attached to having a prison record in these neighborhoods, and that control feature of imprisonment is lost.
- There is considerable evidence that, all other things being equal, having been in prison may actually increase postrelease criminal activity. (pp. 3, 16)

Giving equal attention to what does not work is certainly helpful to policymakers, but it is also a good public relations step by persons who are still recovering from the stomach-punch delivered to their ideology in the 1960s and 1970s.

Another reaction to claims that nothing works has suggested that we direct more attention to the evaluation and selection techniques. The suggestion that problems of evaluation methods should be addressed is consistent with the position taken at this chapter's start—we cannot determine if something works until we define better just what we mean by *works*. The same point is relevant to concerns about selection techniques. Inciardi (1993), for example, notes that all correctional strategies seem to be working for somebody (p. 577). The real problem, he implies, is fitting the person with the most appropriate strategy. But this is only one side of the selection coin because it assumes the goal is to find what will benefit the offender. Borrowing from the restoration philosophy for a moment, should we also be interested in how the selection process benefits the victim and the community? If the answer is yes, we are back to an evaluation of what works that depends on first deciding if *works* means deterrence, incapacitation, restoration, retribution, or rehabilitation.

Because the nothing-works controversy has centered on defining *works* in terms of rehabilitation, we will save further discussion of research on this topic until later in the chapter. For now, we turn our attention to the other rationales for punishment. The main problem in presenting research data as being linked to specific punishment philosophies is that few corrections sanctions exist to meet just one rationale. More likely, there are several types of goals that a sanction hopes to achieve. For example, a judge may sentence Janet to probation in the hope it will be unpleasant enough to keep her from further crime (specific deterrence) and also help her in getting off drugs (rehabilitation). In the following sections, we emphasize a particular sanction for purposes of discussion. The chosen sanction is not meant to serve only the punishment philosophy under which it is discussed. Instead, consider it as simply an example with that philosophy as a goal. In other words, the attempt is to exemplify, not to categorize. As a result, despite the section's heading, you may well find comments about other punishment rationales or goals the sanction being discussed is designed to achieve. With that caution in mind, let us begin with the issue of deterrence.

THE DETERRENCE RATIONALE

In Chapter 2 the discussion of deterrence highlighted the importance of certainty, severity, and swiftness in the success of a sanction to deter. Not surprisingly, these concepts have been key variables in studies that have tried to discover the deterrent effectiveness of punishments ranging from fines and parking tickets to imprisonment and the death penalty.

Researchers have also tried to distinguish between a punishment's role as a general deterrent and its role as a specific deterrent. The results, however, suggest that any deterrent effect in operation is important for both general and specific purposes. We can see the similarities in Table 15.1, which summarizes some general conclusions that can be drawn from both types of deterrence literature. After considering some results from deterrence research, we will look at a deterrence and shock incarceration.

Lessons from the Deterrence Research

Richard Wright (1994) provides a comprehensive review and analysis of the deterrence research over the last several decades and believes it is possible to identify several lessons from those studies. Drawing primarily from his material, we

TABLE 15.1: General Conclusions from Research on Deterrence

GENERAL DETERRENCE	SPECIFIC DETERRENCE
A moderate inverse relationship exists between both the actual and perceived certainties of punishment and crime rates.	Novice offenders usually perceive a greater certainty of punishment for their offenses than chronic offenders.
The perceived certainty of punishments is a more significant factor in deterring crime than the actual certainty of punishment.	The perceived certainties of punishment among offenders are contingent on their actual certainties of punishment (or their objective likelihoods of arrest and imprisonment throughout their offending careers).
Legal/formal sanctions exert much of their influence on individual behavior through the intervening variables of informal sanctions/extralegal factors.	Punishments are more effective in deterring future individual offenders the more that one worries about reprisals from one's friends and family and/or the loss of one's job or good community reputation.
Deterrence effects are contingent for different types of offenders with lower-class persons and older persons more deterred by the certainty of punishment than the affluent and the young.	Professional offenders who are committed to crime as a way of life appear to be less deterred by punishments than amateur offenders.

Source: Adapted from Wright, R. A. (1994). *In defense of prisons.* Westport, CT: Greenwood Press.

will look at these lessons before reviewing an example of the deterrent effect of a particular program type. We begin with Wright's (1994) lessons:[1]

- Apprehension and punishment appear to be moderately effective in achieving both general and specific deterrence.
- The certainty of punishment is a far more important factor in deterring crime than the severity of punishment. To discourage most people from committing crimes, long prison sentences are unnecessary. An essential goal of policymakers and criminal justice officials should be to increase the certainty of arrest, conviction, and mild punishment/short detention for most offenders.
- Individual perceptions play a crucial role in deterring crime. The perceived certainty of punishment is more important than the actual certainty of punishment in convincing most people to behave themselves. This suggests that policymakers and criminal justice officials should place great importance on conveying the message to the public that crime does not pay. High-profile, well-publicized anticrime campaigns are an essential component for deterring crime in America.
- While average citizens and novice offenders can be deterred by well-publicized anticrime campaigns, chronic offenders usually won't be. For offenders with much crime experience, the perceived certainty of punishment mirrors the actual certainty of punishment: because experience has taught them that actual punishments are rare, chronic offenders often perceive that crime in fact does pay. Chronic offenders will also be less deterred by legal/formal sanctions because they have fewer ties to conventional society . . . and no "good" community reputations to protect. This suggests that policymakers and criminal justice officials should de-emphasize deterrence for chronic offenders, in preference to incapacitation strategies. (pp. 105–106)

[1]Adapted from Wright, R. A. (1994). *In defense of prisons.* Westport, CT: Greenwood Press.

Obviously there is a lot of information included in these lessons and an even greater amount in the research leading to them. We cannot take the time to adequately cover any of the points in a manner similar to Wright's analysis. But one point is too tempting to let pass without some elaboration. In both the lessons and in Table 15.1, Wright makes the point that deterrence research shows the certainty of punishment is more important than its severity.

To measure a sanction's certainty and severity, it is necessary to decide which variables can most appropriately reflect those concepts. In the case of the imprisonment sanction, researchers have most often measured its certainty by using the annual number of admissions to state prison. Imprisonment's severity typically is reflected in the average length of time that is served in state prisons for different felonies. These conditions, prison admissions and sentence length, are the independent variables that the researchers put against the dependent variable of crime rate. Using this general methodology in locales as varied as neighborhoods, large cities, entire states, and even the nation, a fair amount of consistency is found in showing an inverse relationship between certainty of imprisonment and crime rates. But there tends to be no relationship between length (severity) of imprisonment and crime rate (Wright, 1994, pp. 73–74).

Researchers have also distinguished between actual and perceived deterrence effects. Actual deterrence is the real probability that I will experience a certain punishment. Perceived deterrence is my estimated probability that I will experience a certain punishment. In a similar manner, it is possible to distinguish among actual and perceived certainty of punishment and actual and perceived severity of punishment. Wright's review of the literature finds that the research consistently shows that perceived certainty is related to self-reported deviance in a moderately inverse way. Perceived severity, on the other hand, has little effect. These findings are consistent with others that suggest the effectiveness of deterrence occurs because of the certainty, but not the severity, of punishment.

A final point about certainty of punishment is the agreement among most criminologists writing on deterrence that perceived certainty of punishment is more important in deterring crime than the actual certainty. Wright reminds us that because comparatively few crimes are cleared through an arrest, it is fortunate for society that most people are deterred by perceived rather than actual certainty.

All this is not to suggest that perceived or actual severity plays no role. Wright notes that some interesting studies have found that juveniles claim to have curtailed their criminal activities at about age sixteen because they feared the harsher penalties that could be imposed in adult court. Other studies suggest that perceptions of severity are not only important but that they may change over time. Citing some field studies with drug dealers, Wright explains that sanctions can come to be seen as more severe the more they threaten to disrupt the subject's life. Novice drug dealers fear that legal sanctions might disrupt their relationships with their "straight" friends and relatives. Interestingly, the long-term drug dealers were more concerned about the impact an arrest would have on their relationships with other drug dealers. The researchers suggested that because the dealers fear arrest as they start drug dealing, a general sense of paranoia causes distrust of strangers. Eventually, the dealers' social network narrows to having interaction only with a small group of trusted fellow drug dealers. Ironically, drug dealers who interact only with other drug dealers will understandably suffer losses in sales and profits. In other words, among hardened drug dealers, the fear of arrest causes the fear of strangers and the limiting of social networks, which then contributes to partial deterrence (Wright, 1994, p. 89).

Does all this make you happy that someone other than you is doing deterrence research? If so, you can appreciate the complexities involved in determining if a seemingly simple idea, such as "people won't misbehave if they will be punished," is accurate. In addition, even if people can agree that the idea is true, how can you control for things such as actual and perceived certainty, severity, and swiftness in order to put the idea into practice? Of course, the same point can be made for researching and policymaking with all the other punishment rationales as well. And, to the point that such complexities make us skeptical about theories, programs, and research, we can be assured that new theories, new programs, and new research will always be forthcoming. It will be good to keep this in mind as we look at some of the programs and their evaluations in the remainder of this chapter.

Shock Incarceration as a Deterrent

In Chapter 8 we concentrated on four types of short-term confinement: home confinement, jails, boot camps, and residential community corrections facilities. Boot camp programs especially have been the focus of media, legislature, and public attention. Researchers have responded to that attention by conducting a number of studies to help answer questions about the success of boot camps. As always, the question of success can be answered only after we know how success is being defined. Boot camp programs typically have two levels of goals that proponents hope to achieve: system-level goals and individual-level goals. The primary system-level goals are to provide an alternative to imprisonment that will (1) reduce prison crowding and (2) decrease costs. Individual-level goals are linked to (1) deterrence and (2) rehabilitation issues. We begin at the system level.

System-Level Goals of Boot Camps. Since their arrival on the corrections scene in 1983, boot camp prisons have often been promoted as a way to reduce prison crowding. Presumably, offenders who would otherwise be in prison for several years can serve an intense short-term sentence instead, but this goal has been difficult to achieve. Offenders assigned to, or selected for, most contemporary boot camp programs often have two characteristics that make it difficult for shock incarceration to decrease prison crowding. First, there are some boot camp programs whose participants would most likely not have gone to prison in the first place. This net-widening phenomenon is especially noticed in jurisdictions in

Boot camp prison programs require inmates to engage in strenuous physical conditioning as a deterrent to continued involvement in crime but also as a way to increase the prisoner's sense of accomplishment and self-worth.

which judges make assignments to boot camp programs. Research suggests that in too many cases the person sentenced to boot camp would probably have just received probation if the boot camp program were not available. Obviously a state's prison population cannot be affected when "alternative" programs are taking offenders who would not have been going to prison anyway.

Allen (1997) explains that Arizona, for example, found that judges were sending the wrong group of individuals to boot camp. Instead of using the sentence for offenders who would otherwise go to prison, they were sending to boot camp offenders who would otherwise have been granted probation. The result was an increase rather than a decrease in people in prison. Upon realizing what was occurring, Arizona officials stipulated that only 50 percent of the boot camp participants could be there because of a judicial sentence—the other half would be assigned by Department of Corrections officials.

Arizona's experience was also found in other states where judges had the ability to sentence persons to boot camp. When Colorado corrections officials realized that prison numbers were increasing rather than decreasing with boot camp sentences, they removed boot camps as a sentencing option. Instead, offenders are sentenced to the Department of Corrections, whose officials then weed through the files and select those offenders they believe will benefit from a boot camp experience.

The second offender characteristic that makes it hard for boot camps to reduce prison crowding is the type of crime for which boot camp participants were convicted. Parent (1993) used a statistical model to determine that a reduction in prison bed space can occur only when more than 80 percent of those admitted to boot camps would otherwise have been sent to prison. Because the typical boot camp program restricts eligibility to nonviolent first-felony offenders (or first-time prison arrivals), Parent figures that a state would have to observe a practice of sending 80 percent of its nonviolent first-time felons to prison—a policy most states are unlikely to follow.

Although contemporary boot camps do not appear to be effective in reducing prison crowding, there seems to be good reason to believe they can be designed to be successful at that goal. MacKenzie (1994) and Parent (1993) agree that with careful designing, boot camp programs can reduce prison crowding. To do so, boot camp programs must incorporate the following considerations:

- Selected and assigned offenders must be persons who would go to prison if the boot camp option were not available. This might require some jurisdictions to make one or both of the following changes in their boot camp design: (1) allow violent offenders and repeat property offenders to be eligible for boot camps; and (2) require those jurisdictions in which judges can sentence to boot camp to remove that option from the judge, and let corrections personnel make the selection from among persons already sentenced to prison.
- The boot camp program must involve sufficient numbers of offenders. After all, a state with 12,000 inmates will not be affected by a fifty-bed boot camp program.
- Release from imprisonment must occur earlier than it would have if the offender had been sent to a regular prison. Even though the implied trade-off for an inmate's participation in boot camp is a shorter prison term, many programs simply present that as an opportunity rather than a sure thing. If boot camp graduates are kept in confinement for the remainder of their term, the program may still result in some benefits—but reducing the prison population will not be one of them.
- Even if boot camp programs successfully implement all the preceding options, prison crowding will not be reduced if the released graduates commit other crimes upon their return to the community and are then eventually returned to prison. In other words, boot camps may provide a delay rather than a reduction in prison crowding.

A second system-level goal for boot camps was to reduce prison costs. Barr's (1995) review of research concluded that the per diem cost of boot camp is not significantly different from that of traditional prisons, but because boot campers are incarcerated for a shorter time, the overall cost is less. New York State, which operates the nation's largest shock incarceration program, estimates that for every 100 shock inmates released, the Department of Correctional Services saves over $2.5 million it would otherwise have spent on the care and custody of those inmates (Aziz & Kellam, 1998).

There are, however, increased costs of aftercare for offenders who have been through a boot camp program. Although those costs may cut into any savings that boot camps may provide, the argument is that lower recidivism rates for boot camp graduates mean the overall costs are still lower. Of course, for that to be true there must really be a lower recidivism for offenders who have been in boot camps. That brings us to the individual-level goals of boot camps.

Individual-Level Goals of Boot Camps. One of the most complete reviews of boot camp programs was a study of eight state-level programs that represented several aspects of the shock incarceration philosophy (see MacKenzie, Brame, McDowell, & Souryal, 1995; MacKenzie, 1994; MacKenzie & Souryal, 1994). The multisite evaluation sought to measure, among other things, what impact the boot camp program had on participants' attitudes and recidivism rates. Comparison groups were established so that boot camp participants could be contrasted with groups of offenders having similar characteristics but different placements (e.g., on probation or in a traditional prison). As with so many research endeavors on sentencing, the comparison groups were not the result of random assignment so there is always the possibility of critical differences among the samples.

If the prison experience demoralizes or makes people bitter about society and the justice system, those people may not be inclined to be law-abiding after their release from confinement. On the other hand, if offenders have an experience during confinement that develops in them a respect for themselves and for society, upon their release they may refrain from further criminal behavior. The multisite evaluation examined attitudes at the start of the boot camp experience and again near the end. Attitudes of inmates at the traditional prisons were surveyed at similar times.

Interestingly, consistent results were found across the programs even though different states were represented, as were programs with different designs (MacKenzie, 1994; MacKenzie & Souryal, 1994). The researchers found that offenders in boot camp prison leave the prison less antisocial than they were before entering, and they become more positive about their experiences, their future, and how they have benefited from the program. Offenders serving time in traditional prisons also became less antisocial in their attitudes, but their attitudes toward their experiences and the future did not improve.

If boot camp participants return to the community with a positive outlook, they may be more likely to have a good adjustment to any conditions of aftercare they may be subjected to, and to remain crime-free after their release to the community. Measuring those kinds of issues concerns the question of recidivism.

Research on the recidivism of boot camp graduates (the program goal most closely attached to deterrence) presents the classic dilemma of a glass being half full or half empty. Letting pessimism go first, research that compares recidivism of boot camp graduates to offenders with similar characteristics who served their sentence in a traditional prison consistently finds no significant differences between boot camp releasees and offenders in comparison groups on almost any measure of recidivism (Burns & Vito, 1995; MacKenzie & Souryal, 1994; Parent, 1993). The multisite evaluation did find some indication that graduates of boot camp programs in Louisiana, Illinois, and New York had lower recidivism on some measures. But the researchers suspected that was a result of post–boot camp supervision rather than the boot camp experience itself (MacKenzie et al., 1995; MacKenzie & Souryal, 1994). We will return to that point in a little bit.

For an optimistic view, MacKenzie and Souryal (1994, p. 30) determined that on balance boot camp graduates performed as well as similarly situated offenders who had served time in prison or had been placed on probation. Results from a two-year study in Texas found the recidivism rate for boot camp inmates was nearly the same as the recidivism rate for inmates in state jails and penitentiaries (Pesquera, 1999). Those may not seem to be glowing success stories, but consider the old "half full or half empty" analogy.

The glass is half full if we consider that similar effects can be achieved without the need for long prison sentences. In other words, if boot campers—with their relatively short prison stay of about three months—are no more likely to recidivate than are persons released from their comparatively longer prison stay in the traditional setting, then we can get by without long prison sentences.

Of course, the argument that longer prison sentences do not provide a deterrent beyond that of shorter prison sentences (at least short boot camp sentences) is impressive only for those who believe punishment should serve the purpose of deterrence. If people are seeking incapacitation or retribution, they are not likely to care if short-term sentences are as effective a deterrent as long-term sentences. But what about people hoping that punishment will rehabilitate? Is there any evidence that boot camp graduates are any more "rehabilitated" than persons who spent their sentence in prison?

The question of rehabilitation is certainly linked to the issue of recidivism. Presumably a rehabilitated offender will not commit additional crimes. But rehabilitation really deals with a much broader issue than whether an offender commits a new crime after being subjected to correctional sanctions or violates a technical condition of his or her community supervision. Law-abiding behavior may be a positive by-product of rehabilitation but so might a more positive self-image, constructive attitudes, good work habits, a higher level of literacy, and having a drug-free lifestyle.

In the earlier discussion of recidivism and boot camp graduates, we noted that programs in three states (Illinois, Louisiana, and New York) showed lower recidivism on some measures used by the researchers. But the researchers hesitated to attribute the lower rates to the boot camp programs because in each of the three states, the boot camp graduates received more community supervision than did the comparison groups. In other words, it was not clear whether the lower recidivism resulted from having been to boot camp or from being closely supervised once back in the community.

To complicate things even further, the Illinois, Louisiana, and New York programs devoted more time to therapeutic programming during their boot camps than did any of the other five programs studied. So, the lower recidivism of graduates from those three programs could be the result of the closer post–boot camp supervision, or the treatment component of the boot camp itself, or some combination of each. The one thing that does seem clear is that lower recidivism cannot be attributed to the military aspects of the boot camp experience.

Data from the multisite evaluation suggest that the military atmosphere found in boot camps does not reduce recidivism. In fact, MacKenzie and Souryal (1994) suggest that a nonmilitary program with a strong rehabilitation aspect followed by intensive supervision might be just as effective as one with the boot camp atmosphere. It also seems likely that any "rehabilitation" of boot camp participants that might occur is unrelated to the hard labor boot campers are subjected to. As Gendreau and Ross (1987) discovered, for work programs to successfully promote rehabilitation they must produce practical skills, develop interpersonal skills, minimize prisonization, and make sure that work is not for punishment alone. Few of the work assignments at boot camp programs would meet such criteria.

Continued evaluation of the New York shock incarceration program also emphasizes the importance of success as requiring more than the boot camp experience itself. In the eleventh annual report to the legislature, the Department of Correctional Services identifies the program as involving both institutional treatment and intensive parole supervision. The clear implication is that New York's success—boot camp graduates are more likely than comparison group parolees to be successful on parole despite having spent less time in prison—is a result of the shock experience combined with the intensive parole experience (Aziz & Kellam, 1998).

Summary of Research on Boot Camps. Current research on boot camps presents data that will please or disappoint people, depending on the goals they hope shock incarceration will accomplish. Persons wanting boot camps to reduce prison crowding are likely to be disappointed unless their legislators are willing to make major modifications in current boot camp designs. Proponents of deterrence who are searching for programs to reduce recidivism will not find boot camps to be any more a solution than is regular imprisonment. But there is also data that will please some people. Persons concerned about prison crowding who do not see the goal of imprisonment as primarily for retribution or incapacitation will be glad to know that shorter prison sentences can accomplish similar deterrence levels. Others who may be looking for programs that can initiate change in offenders might find some value in the philosophy of shock incarceration, although it is important that they not attribute any program benefits specifically to a military regimen and hard work for work's sake.

The positive benefits of shock incarceration are most likely by-products of the boot camp experience rather than direct results of the military regimen and hard work typical of the traditional programs. Shock incarceration may be a catalyst for change in the offender to the extent that boot camp programs encourage physical fitness and a drug-free lifestyle, provide participants with positive experience and a sense of accomplishment, and help develop prosocial attitudes and a positive self-concept. Positive results seem especially likely if the boot camp experience is followed by close supervision in the community, where graduates receive specific assistance as they make the transition to a less structured existence.

It may well be the next generation of boot camps (see the discussion in Chapter 8) that provides the clearest examples of positive benefits directly related to the boot camp experience. But, importantly, the new generation of boot camps is likely to rely less on a regimented structure with strict discipline and more on programs that help ease the prisoner's transition back to the community.

THE INCAPACITATION RATIONALE

In their review of incapacitation, Zimring and Hawkins (1995) say that "incapacitation now serves as the principal justification for imprisonment in American criminal justice" (p. 3). What they find particularly interesting about that situation is how this rationale crept up on us with little warning and less examination. What happened, they explain, is that in the 1970s both liberal and conservative crime control policies accepted the incapacitation rationale. They differed only on whether incapacitation should be selective or collective: "Confine only specific offenders or offender types," said the liberals; "lock 'em all up," said the conservatives. The resulting debates of merit contrasted two versions of incapacitation rather than comparing the merits of incapacitation with those of some other penal philosophy. With the only competition being itself, incapacitation moved to the forefront of penal philosophies during the 1980s and 1990s, and by the century's end it seemed to have been successful given the dropping crime rate.

At several locations throughout this book, comment has been made about the effect incapacitation may be having on the crime rate. The Spotlight on Contemporary Issues box in Chapter 2 ("Has Imprisonment Lowered the Crime Rate?") noted that incarceration does prevent a certain amount of crime (ones committed by high-frequency offenders) but that its effects are likely boosted by things such as aggressive policing. However, as the nation's prison population soars to more than 2 million at the start of a new century, even some advocates of incapacitation are wondering if the costs of imprisonment might be outweighing the benefits. John DiIulio, Jr., for example, is a self-described "lock-'em-up hardliner" who has written articles with titles such as "Prisons Are a Bargain, by Any Measure," that praise prisons as a way to express society's displeasure with the offender and prevent further violent incidents (DiIulio, 1996). However, DiIulio also believes we can go too far with attempts to imprison everyone.

DiIulio believes the value of imprisonment is reduced when we have so many people in prison that incarceration costs are taking money from other important justice components such as police, probation, and parole (DiIulio, 1997; DiIulio, 1999b). And mandatory minimum drug laws are the biggest culprit, DiIulio argues, because states are imprisoning large numbers of offenders whose only past felony crimes were low-level, nonviolent drug crimes (1999a). In the late 1990s, DiIulio and other hardliners believed American society was finally using prison too often—and for too many offenders who may not have needed to be locked up for the public's safety—so DiIulio called for a middle ground. As he put it, "It's time to admit that the brain-dead law-and-order right is no better than the soft-in-the-head anti-incarceration left" (1997, p. 40).

So, is there a middle ground that the "brain-dead" and the "soft-in-the-head" can agree on? Some argue that intermediate sanctions such as home confinement and intensive supervision probation (both with the use of electronic monitoring) may provide a suitable level of incapacitation. That argument draws on the restraint aspect of incapacitation.

After taking the lead among punishment rationales, incapacitation has stayed there because of two of its features: (1) It is a restraining technique that operates on the convicted offender who is presumed to be at risk of committing future crimes; and (2) it uses restraint to directly control the behavior of the potential offender rather than leaving him or her any choice in the matter (Zimring & Hawkins, 1995, p. 156). Restraint is an important concept in both features because it is an aspect of incapacitation that sets it apart from other strategies. Some punishments, at least those interested in crime prevention, use nonrestraining sanctions such as fines and community service. The behavior of persons under these sanctions is influenced by nonrestraining mechanisms such as bank video cameras, periodic drug testing, and probation or parole supervision. Incapacitation, on the other hand, uses restraining sanctions such as imprisonment. The behavior of persons under this sanction is controlled by restraining mechanisms such as correctional officers, metal doors, and razor wire perimeters. It is possible that members of the public feel safer when the behavior of convicted offenders is being controlled rather than simply influenced. Zimring and Hawkins (1995) seem to make a similar assumption when they say that "the capacity to control rather

Probation and parole clients who are assigned to intensive supervision are in more frequent contact with their supervisors and are more closely monitored for compliance with the terms and conditions of their probation or parole.

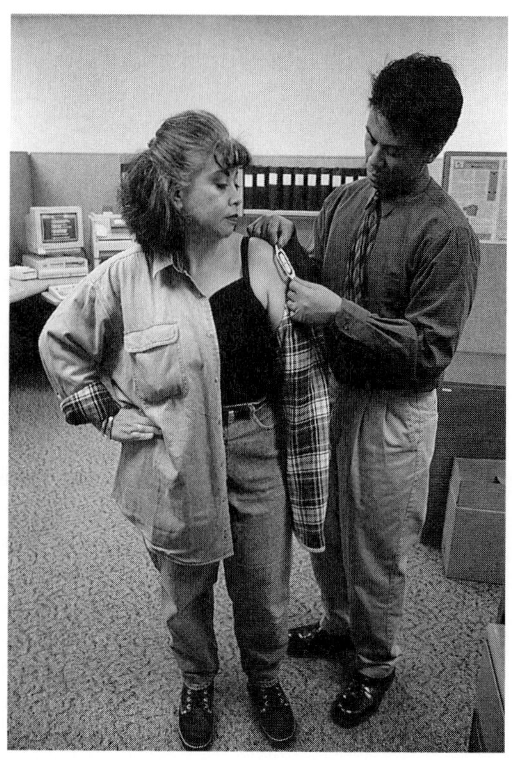

than influence is the most important reason for the great and persistent popularity of incapacitation as a penal method" (p. 157).

Jails and prisons are the classic ways by which incapacitation achieves restraint and control. More recently, efforts have been made to achieve incapacitation through technology. As mentioned in Chapter 2, such efforts might include restraining and controlling an offender through biomedical interventions such as surgery and drug treatments. Also mentioned in Chapter 2 and again in Chapter 8 is the control mechanism called electronic monitoring.

Electronic monitoring is a particularly intriguing development because it may approximate prison and jail control without the consequences and cost of full imprisonment. On the other hand, it is a technique that seems to fall between the nonrestraining and the restraining mechanisms. In doing so, it does more than influence behavior but may not be able to control it. However, that may be a limitation only for the short term. As noted in Chapter 13, although not yet widespread, today's technology includes the use of global positioning system (GPS) technology that gives corrections officials information about an offender's location in the community. Not only does GPS technology tell exactly where the offender is, but it is also possible to set up "required zones" (places the offender must be, such as work and home), "transition zones" (an approved path back and forth), and "restricted zones" (schools, bars, ex-spouse's area, etc.). It is even possible to monitor several offenders on the same screen and make sure they are not interacting. The potential is both intriguing and frightening.

Given the perception even among its advocates that we have now gone too far in attempts to achieve incapacitation through imprisonment, the twenty-first century may see increased efforts to draw on the restraining aspects of prison alternatives to achieve incapacitation in the community. So, it is appropriate in this section to determine if any existing programs work or have the potential to work at controlling behavior even though the offender remains in the community. We consider the programs as examples of community restraints.

Incapacitation through Community Restraints

Following MacKenzie (1997), this section uses the term **community restraints** to refer to those prison alternatives that provide increased surveillance and control over offenders while they are in the community. In a sense, these sanctions provide semi-incapacitation because they are designed to reduce the offenders' freedom of movement and ability to commit crime. Examples of community restraint sanctions with semi-incapacitation goals are home confinement with electronic monitoring and intensive supervision probation/parole.

Home Confinement and Electronic Monitoring. Sentences to home confinement coupled with electronic monitoring were unheard of prior to the early 1980s but are increasingly common today. But despite the growth experienced by these sanctions, there are no large-scale evaluations of home confinement on the order of those for boot camps or intensive supervision. The studies that have been conducted are small in nature, specific to particular programs, and the early evaluations suffered from poor research design and lack of program integrity (MacKenzie, 1997; Tonry, 1997). Some studies have looked at electronic monitoring specifically—regardless of the sanction it was coupled with—and report some effectiveness. Anderson (1999), for example, summarized electronic monitoring studies in three states and reports generally positive results. An evaluation of an Indiana program coupling home confinement and electronic monitoring for juveniles found that over 80 percent of the program participants successfully completed their sentence (Anderson, 1999).

Keeping all the studies' flaws in mind, they typically report positive results with persons under home confinement and electronic monitoring successfully completing their sentence and having recidivism rates similar to others under community sanctions. The early use of home confinement with electronic monitoring was typically for low-risk offenders, such as persons convicted of driving while intoxicated, but today more serious offenders and parolees are being placed in these programs. MacKenzie's (1997) summary of the best available research on home confinement with electronic monitoring concludes that it is no more effective for low-risk offenders than is standard community supervision without electronic monitoring.

Intensive Probation/Parole Supervision. As noted in Chapter 7, intensive probation (or parole) supervision (IPS) is intended to provide greater supervision and control over offenders than are provided with traditional probation or parole. Studies of IPS find that it does indeed provide increased restraint on offenders. That restraint, or semi-incapacitation, is accomplished through techniques such as increased direct contact with the probation/parole supervisor, more frequent urine testing, lengthier periods of home confinement, and generally expanded verification of probation/parole compliance.

Although there have been studies of IPS that show positive results, MacKenzie (1997) explains that the more recent and more rigorous research has found no significant differences between IPS participants and control groups, although persons on IPS were more likely to have their criminal or technical violations detected. Of course, proponents of semi-incapacitative sanctions would argue that identification of errant behavior is exactly what the programs should be accomplishing.

That is, because these offenders are being more closely monitored, we should expect that their misbehavior will more often be detected. In that sense, the programs are accomplishing one of their objectives.

Does Semi-Incapacitation Present Acceptable Risk?

For our purposes in this section on incapacitation, the key question is whether people favoring punishment for incapacitation purposes will be satisfied with semi-incapacitation programs that result in recidivism rates that are similar to rates provided by other community-based sanctions without incapacitation goals. Semi-incapacitation techniques, by definition, cannot restrict the offender's freedom of movement as much as a prison sentence would. But if we accept the idea that incapacitation can be achieved in general, even when specific instances of harm to person or property occur, the new offenses and technical violations by those under home confinement are understood as inevitable. That is, nonprison methods of achieving the punishment goal of incapacitation will necessarily result in more harm to public safety than would confinement in prison. But just as proponents of the other punishment rationales must accept something less than complete success, so too must advocates of incapacitation. By the less-than-total standard, home confinement may provide an acceptable level of public safety. Possibly, a punishment goal of incapacitation can be achieved without resorting to imprisonment.

THE RESTORATION/RETRIBUTION RATIONALES

Despite appearances, this section heading is not a cop-out because technically there is no need for an independent section on research and retribution. Our review of how different correctional strategies might be achieving the goals of various punishment rationales is based on the assumption that each rationale views punishment as serving a purpose. As we saw in Chapter 2, retribution differs from the other rationales in that it is not interested in preventing crime. The concern of retributivists is simply that society carries out its moral obligation to punish offenders. To evaluate punishment's success at meeting its obligation would require researchers to measure things such as whether citizens believed an offender had gotten her just deserts. But how would we measure such citizen beliefs? Could we use a "smugness" scale? Are citizens more self-righteous after they hear that society has punished an offender?

As Chapter 2 also pointed out, the retributive philosophy is linked to the norm of reciprocity, which in turn is an important aspect of the restoration rationale. The concept of restoration is a bit easier to measure or evaluate than retribution because it has a utilitarian aspect. Restoration's goal is to make the victim and community "whole again." It includes a retributive (nonutilitarian) aspect because it recognizes that the offenders "deserve" something; but it is also utilitarian because the victim and the community also deserve something. So, because there is really nothing that retribution accomplishes that is easily—or even possibly—measured, it is included here with restoration because of their mutual link to the norm of reciprocity.

Restorative and Community Justice

Aspects of the restoration philosophy were discussed in Chapters 2 and 4. And one of this philosophy's central features, mediation, was discussed in Chapter 5. But compared with the other philosophies, restoration has not received much attention in this text. The main reason is that U.S. corrections has mostly been oriented around the themes of deterrence, incapacitation, rehabilitation, and retribution. That may be changing, however, as restoration principles are increasingly found in legislation and programs across the country (see Kurki, 1999).

By 1995 at least two states had formally recognized restorative and community justice, as the application of the restoration philosophy is called. The Minnesota Department of Corrections has a restorative justice planner who works with communities, victims groups, and correctional managers to inform them about the nature of restorative justice and offer advice on implementing a restorative justice program. In conjunction with a department restructuring, the Vermont Department of Corrections sought to increase community participation in developing and operating sentencing options. A major principle in Vermont's restructuring is to have the state government serve and support local communities while the local communities serve and support individuals and families. Because restorative justice has a similar interest in seeking balance among individuals and the community, Vermont is relying on the restoration philosophy to be the linchpin holding things together; and reports indicate that by 1998 the state was well on its way to that goal (Immarigeon, 1995; Kurki, 1999).

In addition to statewide efforts, restorative and community justice is also found at the local level. In Austin, Texas, the Travis County district attorney drafted a state law that authorizes in each county a Community Justice Council (consisting of elected officials) and a Community Justice Task Force (with representatives of criminal justice agencies, social and health services, and community organizations). With task force assistance, the council prepares a Community Justice Plan and in Travis County that plan has established (1) victim–offender mediation for young people in trouble, (2) neighborhood conference committees that use trained adult citizens to meet with juvenile offenders and their parents to develop contracts tailored to the case, and (3) a Children's Advocacy Center that provides support and help to abused children (Kurki, 1999).

One of the points that might most surprise people when they hear about restorative justice is that victims are willing for their offender to receive something short of imprisonment. Because victims of crime have so often been portrayed as angry citizens who demand harsh penalties for criminals, it seems unlikely that these same victims would willingly participate in a mediation session. But an increasing number of studies are suggesting that the stereotypical view of an angry victim might be wrong more often than it is right.

It is clear that nearly all citizens, and crime victims specifically, want criminals to be held accountable through some form of punishment. But what is also being made clear in the research is that the citizens, including victims, also want the offenders to change their behavior. Umbreit (1989) explains that for many victims the need for justice and fairness is grounded in a deep concern that offenders, especially juveniles, receive humane treatment and assistance that can lead to their rehabilitation—especially when the alternative is lengthy incarceration at considerable public expense. Restorative justice is designed to meet these types of concerns. It does so primarily through the mediation process described in Chapter 5, but as a result of the process certain sanctions are imposed. It is to one of those sanctions that we turn our attention.

Restitution is a sanction that is quite compatible with the restoration philosophy. To make things whole again, restorative justice is obligated to the community, the victim, and the offender. Compensation by the offender to the community and/or the victim is one way that movement is made toward restoring equilibrium among the three. Compensation might be in the form of a financial payment (restitution) or by community service, but in either case it is important to note that more than just "payback" is involved. Participants in a successful mediation session come to view the work performed or the money paid as reflecting the "consequences" of a wrongful act as much as it reflects what the offender might "owe." If we think of consequences as similar in concept to just deserts, we are reminded again of the link between retribution and restoration via the norm of reciprocity. As we consider some research on restitution, keep in mind this idea of restitution as meaning "this is the consequence of my misbehavior" as well as "here is payment for what I did."

Restitution and Juvenile Recidivism

One important strategy toward restorative justice is a requirement for restitution from the offender. This sanction is among the clearest examples of an attempt to restore the losses of the victims and the peace of the community while also punishing the offender. But evaluating a sanction's success at achieving restoration is difficult at best. Butts and Snyder (1992) suggest that one way to evaluate restitution as a sanction is to see if it reduces recidivism. If it does, a strong argument might be made for its restorative aspects because citizens will have reason to believe that public safety has been increased.

Utah's juvenile court structure operates a restitution program that encourages victims to claim restitution and then incorporates a restitution order in almost every case in which a claim is made. In addition, Utah keeps one of the most comprehensive juvenile court information systems in the country. These conditions made Utah an ideal setting for a study on restitution's impact on recidivism, and Butts and Snyder took up the challenge.

The Utah study used cases in which the most serious charge was robbery, assault, burglary, theft, auto theft, or vandalism. In addition, it included only cases involving youths below age seventeen at the time of disposition to ensure that each would have at least one year remaining under juvenile court jurisdiction. The sample was divided into two groups: The first included 7,233 cases that were handled informally by the probation department (i.e., they were disposed of without filing a petition), and the second included 6,336 adjudicated cases placed on formal probation. The researchers defined recidivism as any case in which a youth was returned to court within one year of disposition for a new charge of delinquency if that charge was disposed by the court either formally or informally.

In the sample of informal cases, restitution was associated with significant reductions in the rate of new referrals. Specifically, 11 percent of the cases in which offenders agreed to pay restitution recidivated, compared with 18 percent of the cases receiving other (nonrestitution) types of informal disposition. Similar results were found with the sample of formally adjudicated cases. There, 32 percent of those ordered to probation with restitution recidivated within the year, compared with 38 percent of those receiving probation only. Butts and Snyder (1992) conclude that "for cases involving robbery, assault, burglary, theft, auto theft, and vandalism, recidivism is lower when juveniles agree or are ordered to pay restitution to their victims directly or through earnings derived from community service" (p. 1). Importantly, the difference was found whether the case was handled informally or through formal adjudicated probation. To the extent that increased public safety and even rehabilitation are important ingredients in restoration, it appears that restitution should be a desirable part of the justice process—at least for juvenile offenders.

Other studies have found only limited evidence that restitution programs reduce offending. Schneider (1986), for example, found that restitution sanctions for juvenile offenders can have a positive effect on recidivism, but not necessarily under all circumstances. But we must remember that advocates of a restoration rationale for punishment are less interested in how much a sanction reduces recidivism than they are in how well that sanction can restore balance to the community. Umbreit's (1994) evaluation of four restoration programs around the country found that restitution agreements increase both the offenders' and the victims' satisfaction with the justice process. Also important, victims report being less fearful of being victimized again. In addition, the restitution (whether financial or in the form of community service) benefits the community. To the extent that these outcomes reflect a restoration of balance and a sense of fairness having been achieved, restoration programs may well achieve their particular punishment goal—even if someone else's goal (such as the proponents of deterrence or rehabilitation) is not achieved.

Help Wanted

Job Title: Juvenile Restitution Supervisor

Position Description: Supervisors work with juvenile justice organizations to provide an opportunity for juvenile offenders to work off restitution they owe. The supervisor facilitates intakes with client families, contacts and develops appropriate work sites, organizes statistics for appropriate reports, and supervises youth work crews.

Qualifications: Applicants should have an associate's or bachelor's degree in a field related to human services and be able to demonstrate experience and skill with at-risk youth and adolescents. Bilingual skills are helpful.

For an overview of career opportunities in this field, visit Washington's Web page at *www.wa.gov/dshs/jra/jra3ov.html.*

Do Restorative and Community Justice Programs Work?

From 1998 through 2000, the National Institute of Justice and the Corrections Program Office (both in the U.S. Office of Justice Programs) sponsored a series of Executive Sessions on Sentencing and Corrections. At these sessions, practitioners and scholars addressed such questions as whether sentencing policies are achieving their intended purposes. One of the first papers commissioned for those sessions was on restorative and community justice as it relates to sentencing and corrections. The paper's author, Leena Kurki, provides an excellent overview of restorative and community corrections as the United States begins the twenty-first century.

Of particular interest for us are Kurki's comments about the impact restorative or community justice is having in the United States. Despite a proliferation of restorative and community justice principles throughout the country during the 1990s, there is no systematic evaluation of the programs based on those principles. The problem, Kurki (1999) explains, is that no one knows how many or what kinds of programs there are; how many offenders, victims, and volunteers participate; how much restitution is paid or community service performed; or the effects on victims, communities, and offenders (p. 3). Even when a specific program is evaluated, there is no agreement on how success should be measured. That, of course, has been a major point throughout this book. Some people believe a program only works when recidivism is reduced, but others claim success when offenders and victims express satisfaction in an agreed-upon outcome. Still others argue that we should be flexible in deciding whether a program has achieved its goals (see "An Idea from Japan").

But despite the similarity in deciding how the terms *works* and *success* apply to corrections programs, the restorative and community justice model presents a twist on the traditional argument. Specifically, some advocates actually don't want rigorous program evaluation. But without evaluation, you argue, how can one determine if a program works—regardless of how *works* is defined? The point, the advocates respond, is that restorative and community justice needs to be geared to specific communities and cannot be standardized. Attempts to conduct standard evaluation studies will simply result in pressure to make separate and unique programs similar—and probably less successful because of their resemblance. Because communities are unique, their chosen style of community justice must also be unique.

The twenty-first century begins with little evaluation research on restorative and community justice programs. The restitution programs reviewed earlier are unusual in that respect. There is considerable literature on the principles and goals of restorative justice and on how it differs from traditional criminal justice

Cross-Cultural Corrections

An Idea from Japan

Restorative and community justice proponents argue that traditional appraisal of program success is too limited. Measuring failure as the committing of a new crime or technical violation and success as refraining from any new crime or technical violation is not only restrictive but unrealistic. The Japanese use a broadened definition of success that may be instructive for those seeking an alternative to traditional measures.

In addition to providing recidivism statistics based on rearrest, reconviction, and recommitment, the Japanese use adjustment statistics. The adjustment statistic uses three categories to provide officials with more detailed information about an offender's performance while undergoing community-based treatment. The success category includes persons who earned early discharge from probation and parole and those who showed an improved adjustment to social life. Failure, on the other hand, refers to offenders with unsatisfactory adjustments and to those recommitted for technical violations or new crime convictions. Falling between these two categories are those who had moderate adjustment. That term is used for probationers and parolees whose standard of behavior is acceptable although it may fall short of the general community's standards of behavior (Rehabilitation Bureau, 1995).

At first glance a move away from the success-or-failure dichotomy might seem to favor the programs and potentially mislead the public. But remember that the Japanese count as failures those offenders with unsatisfactory adjustments as well as those recommitted. Used in this manner, the failure category would be expanded to include some persons who technically completed their probation or parole successfully but had not yet made an acceptable social adjustment. As a result, the case would be a statistical failure even though no technical or new crime violation occurred. On the other hand, a parolee who is returned to prison because she continued to consume alcohol, though without committing a new crime, might be considered to have made a moderate adjustment rather than be a failure because her behavior fell short of the general community's standards.

Possible benefits of using adjustment statistics might include providing corrections officials with a mechanism to indicate their unease about how well adjusted is the client who just completed his or her supervision in the community. Admittedly the moderate category could become a "cover your butt" technique for the supervisor, but it could also be a way to (1) convey to clients that they still have problems to deal with, (2) provide information to correctional workers who may work with the client when subsequent crimes are committed, and (3) encourage law-abiding family and friends of the clients to continue the reintegration/rehabilitation process that was started under community supervision.

Similarly, the success category might allow agencies and supervisors to be commended when a violent offender completes his time on parole without committing any new violent crime. At present such a person might be counted as a success if he was not rearrested or recommitted during his period of supervision. But might it also be a success if Keith, who spent five years in prison and two years on parole, were rearrested before his parole was completed because he was found in possession of marijuana? Under contemporary standards for evaluating the results of parole, Keith's case would be considered a failure (parole supervision was not successfully completed). But if working with offenders is not expected to result in a clear-cut good ending (absolutely no new misbehavior) or bad ending (any new misbehavior), citizens may be able to develop a more realistic idea about what community supervision can actually accomplish. If such a perspective is desirable, the Japanese adjustment statistic might provide ideas for new ways to evaluate whether something works.

Visit Japan's Rehabilitation Bureau at ***www.moj.go.jp/ENGLISH/RB/rb-01.htm.*** Describe the clients this bureau is responsible for and the types of programs operated through the bureau.

approaches. There are also several descriptive studies of particular programs, but there is remarkably little information on how community justice impacts prosecution, courts, or corrections (Kurki, 1999). That situation will have to change before we can evaluate whether programs linked to the restoration philosophy are working to restore the balance upset by the offender's action.

THE REHABILITATION RATIONALE

At the beginning of this chapter, we considered the nothing-works controversy as it centered on Martinson's 1974 essay. At that time it was noted that because so much of the nothing-works debate defines *works* in rehabilitation terms, further discussion of the topic would be delayed. It is now time to return to the issue. Discussion begins with a **meta-analysis,** which is a comprehensive and integrative review of research, on the effectiveness of correctional programs in reducing recidivism or changing the offender's behavior in some other positive way. Then, in order to get a better idea of the commendable programs, we consider some specific programs.

Meta-Analyses Supporting the Rehabilitation Rationale

Critics of the rehabilitative ideal argue that treatment of offenders is ineffective and should not be a primary goal of penal institutions. They simply are not convinced that institutionally based programs can significantly change the offender into a law-abiding citizen. Of course, some of the rehabilitation critics prefer imprisonment for incapacitative, retributive, or deterrent purposes—and rehabilitation, should it occur, is simply a topping. But more often the critics of a rehabilitation rationale believe that doing nothing is as effective as doing something—but doing nothing has the advantage of being less expensive.

The biggest problem with these arguments is that an increasing amount of research suggests that treatment programs do positively change some offenders. And, the rehabilitation proponents continue, treatment programs are less expensive in the long run if they reduce the likelihood that ex-offenders will engage in new criminal activities. Cullen and Gendreau (1989) note that reviews of

Many rehabilitation programs emphasize the need to develop or improve prisoners' reading skills. Here, a woman with the Retired Senior Volunteer Program (RSVP) tutors an inmate in a reading program.

evaluation studies published after Martinson's essay show that research exists to demonstrate the effectiveness of correctional treatment (p. 26). They go on to summarize the rehabilitation literature between 1973 and 1987 as including many studies that found intervention strategies frequently reduced offenders' law-violating behavior on the order of 10 percent to 30 percent—with some instances of reduced rates in the 50 percent to 80 percent range.

The critics have not been won over. Just as the treatment proponents refused to buckle in the 1970s, authors such as Wright (1994, 1995) and Logan and Gaes (1993) make it clear that they have problems with several of the methodologies and interpretations included in the studies to which Cullen and Gendreau (1989) refer. The contrast between the two positions is summed up in two statements:

- For the proponents of correctional treatment: It's ridiculous to say that "nothing works" (Gendreau & Ross, 1987, p. 395).
- For the critics of correctional treatment: Because offender treatment programs are often ineffective, persons planning careers in corrections must be warned that they are considering a job with work-related depression and stress (Wright, 1995, p. 33).

At the risk of raising false hopes among persons who might choose a career working with offenders, but also in the belief that a "save the world" mentality is not a bad way to start one's career, the feature "What Works, What Doesn't" summarizes the characteristics common to programs that have been found to reduce recidivism.

Many points in the "What Works, What Doesn't" feature are drawn from a database of approximately 500 control group studies on offender treatment programs (Gendreau & Paparozzi, 1995). An inevitable problem in linking research and practice is to somehow put into operation on the streets that which is known in the books. For example, Gendreau and Paparozzi note that maybe 10 percent of the programs on which data are being kept are receiving a passing grade in implementing characteristics known to have a desirable impact. Importantly, however, there are examples of successful programs.

Other items in the "What Works, What Doesn't" feature are from a report released in 1997 that continues to generate considerable interest and discussion. The study "Preventing Crime: What Works, What Doesn't, What's Promising" (called the Maryland Report after the researchers' university affiliation) was commissioned by the National Institute of Justice to determine how effectively Department of Justice funds have been used and to locate and evaluate various crime prevention efforts. The resulting 500-plus pages provide detailed analysis of crime prevention programs that work, don't work, might work, and need more analysis (Sherman et al., 1997), and a research brief provides a concise overview (Sherman et al., 1998) of those programs. The 1997 report has separate chapters covering programs in different settings (e.g., community, family, school, etc.). Chapter 9, which was prepared by Doris Layton MacKenzie (MacKenzie, 1997), is especially relevant for our purposes because it addresses programs aimed at offenders.

MacKenzie used literature reviews, reviews of meta-analyses, and a scientific methods score (based on a scale developed for the report) to draw conclusions about what works, what doesn't, and what is promising. She summarizes the report by noting that none of the strategies should be eliminated as an option because, in particular situations, each has some support for reducing crime. The problem is more one of identifying which offenders will benefit most from which programs and in which setting. But even with a correct match of offender and program, success requires that offenders are held accountable for their behavior, the treatment program is accountable for the expected outcome, and the criminal justice system sanctions offenders who do not comply. With that warning in mind, we turn to specific program examples.

Spotlight ON CONTEMPORARY ISSUES

What Works, What Doesn't

Although there are still those who remain unconvinced, the preponderance of evidence demonstrates that rehabilitation programs can effectively change offenders. Rather than wondering "what works?" the issue today is more accurately phrased "what works for whom?" (MacKenzie, 1997). For example, the following characteristics are found in effective treatment programs (Gendreau & Paparozzi, 1995):

- Services are intensive and last three to nine months. They are based on cognitive and social learning behavioral/psychological theories and are used for higher-risk offenders.
- Services target criminological needs, such as antisocial attitudes and values.
- There is a matching of the style and mode of treatment with the offender's learning style and personality.
- A program of reinforcements is linked to the behavior being exhibited. Positive reinforcements such as tangible rewards, activities, and social reinforcers are used more frequently than are punishments such as fines and restitution.
- The programs use therapists who relate to offenders in sensitive and constructive ways and are appropriately trained and supervised.
- The program structure and activities are designed to disrupt the criminal network by placing offenders in situations in which prosocial activities predominate.

A predominant feature of all successful treatment programs is the recognition that treatment must address factors that can actually be changed (the dynamic factors) and that are directly related to an individual's criminal behavior (the criminogenic factors). Static factors such as age, gender, and past criminal history may help predict recidivism, but they cannot be changed and should not be the focus of treatment programs. Instead, treatment must address those dynamic factors (e.g., education, peers, substance abuse, and employment behavior) that are also crimonogenic. Examples of programs that fail as treatment efforts because they are incorrectly focused, improperly implemented, or are no more effective than less elaborate measures include (MacKenzie, 1997):

- Correctional boot camps that rely on traditional military basic training to modify behavior (research findings: no difference in recidivism than what is accomplished with probation or parole).
- "Scared Straight" programs that hope to prevent future offending by having juvenile offenders visit maximum-security prisons to see the severity of prison conditions (research findings: no reduction in reoffending and may even increase crime).
- Home confinement with electronic monitoring for low-risk offenders (research findings: no difference in recidivism than what is accomplished under standard community supervision without electronic monitoring).
- Rehabilitation programs using counseling that does not specifically focus on each offender's risk factors (research findings: no reduction in repeat offending).

As a reminder, these programs are evaluated from a rehabilitation perspective. Someone with a retribution orientation, for example, might consider boot camps as successful if they make life tough on offenders, regardless of any repeat offending by the boot camp graduate. Similarly, a general deterrence proponent might wonder how many juveniles were encouraged to not commit a crime in the first place because of their "scared straight" experience. We are again reminded that an individual's answer to "what works" depends on what he or she wants to accomplish.

Read the summary of the Maryland Report at ***www.ncjrs.org/pdffiles/171676.pdf.*** This feature reviews the "what works" and the "what doesn't work" findings, but the report also identifies "what's promising." Find the section on promising programs by criminal justice agencies after arrest. Describe two of these programs, and indicate your personal opinion about them. Researchers at the Center for the Study and Prevention of Violence have identified ten model programs that successfully prevent violence. Visit the model program page at ***www.colorado.edu/cspv/blueprints/model/index.html.*** What criteria were used in selecting these programs? Choose one of the programs, and describe how it operates and why it is effective.

Specific Programs Supporting the Rehabilitation Rationale

Earlier in this chapter it was noted that we cannot really separate programs by punishment rationales because any one program is likely to have several goals. Because of that, we have already considered some successful programs that have a rehabilitative aspect even though they were discussed under other headings. Home confinement and restitution, but less so the boot camps, arguably have components that are treatment interventions. But just to provide a few other examples, we complete this section on the rehabilitation rationale by looking at programs focused on two particular areas: employment and drug abuse.

Finding a Job. Researchers are satisfied that there is a relationship between crime and employment. There is disagreement, however, about whether that relationship is causal or simply indicative of the influence of some other factor—such as stability, commitment, responsibility, or other individual social control elements (Bushway & Reuter, 1997). But the logic of linking crime prevention to the labor market seems so natural that we continue to support programs that are geared toward providing offenders with marketable skills and job opportunities.

When the Maryland Report reviewed research on vocational training and employment programs, there were only a few efforts that could be described among the "what works" category. One such program is the Job Training Partnership Act (JTPA), which attempts to help ex-prisoners by giving them assistance in finding a job, remedial education as needed, occupational skills, and other types of experiences and assistance. An evaluation of JTPA in Georgia compared ex-prisoners who enrolled in the program with nonoffender participants. No differences in employment outcome, either at the program's completion or fourteen weeks after completion, were found between the ex-prisoners and nonoffenders. Because other studies typically show that ex-offenders have greater difficulty finding and keeping a job, this program was identified as having a positive outcome. However, although agreeing that the JTPA program is effective for older male ex-offenders who are no longer in the criminal justice system, the Maryland researchers remind us that there may be some **selection bias** occurring. That is, positive results may be more likely to occur when participants are highly motivated to succeed. In this example, older male ex-prisoners may have been motivated to seek and keep employment because they are aging-out of the active crime years.

Vocational training and employment programs are popular ways to provide offenders with marketable skills and job opportunities.

Recently, Finn (1999a) reviewed four different job placement programs. He suggests that these programs may have greater success at reducing recidivism than did those from the 1960s and 1970s because the contemporary programs emphasize more than just job readiness. In addition, they address such underlying problems as substance abuse, mental illness, and even lack of affordable housing.

New York City's Center for Employment Opportunities (CEO) has a goal of providing ex-offenders with permanent, unsubsidized, higher-paying employment. It appears that the program is successful in achieving that goal because 60 percent of CEO's placed participants are still on the job after three months, and the average hourly wage of placed participants is nearly 50 percent higher than the minimum wage.

Texas started Project RIO (Re-Integration of Offenders) in 1985, and it has grown to be the nation's most ambitious state government program devoted to job placement for ex-offenders. Project RIO provides job placement services to nearly 85 percent of all prisoners released each year on parole. While offenders are still in prison, Project RIO offers inmates life skills classes, individual job readiness counseling, and assistance in assembling paperwork and documents that will be needed for job applications. On release day RIO staff give every group of departing inmates a thirty-minute orientation to the program that explains RIO services to the released ex-offenders. This program also shows promise because almost three in every four parolees in the program find employment at an average wage that is 21 percent above the minimum. There is also evidence that Project RIO clients are more likely to get jobs than are ex-offenders who do not participate in the program and are less likely to recidivate (Finn, 1999a). However, without wanting to dampen enthusiasm, we must remember that measures of success with motivated clients may reflect some selection bias in the results.

Chicago's Safer Foundation is the largest community-based provider of employment services for ex-offenders in the country. Safer not only helps ex-offenders find good jobs but also to develop a mind-set that helps ensure they will stay employed and succeed in life (Finn, 1998). Safer's clients, who are mostly referred from probation and parole officers, receive basic educational and life skills classes and job placement assistance. The way Safer provides those services is rather unusual because, in addition to its referred clients, Safer operates its own work release center (Crossroads Community Correctional Center) in which programs and services are provided, and Safer has its own school (PACE Institute) at the Cook County Jail where pretrial detainees and sentenced inmates receive daytime basic education and life skills courses.

Safer's in-house evaluation data show that nearly 60 percent of its clients are still employed after thirty days. In addition, most of the participants who complete Safer's basic education course go on to school, vocational training, or find employment. After a 180-day evaluation period in 1996, only one participant who had completed the course had been convicted of a new crime (Finn, 1998).

The final work-related program to mention here is Washington State's Corrections Clearinghouse (CCH). After starting as a way to coordinate job search activities for adult offenders being released from prison, CCH has expanded to provide services in correctional facilities and to juvenile offenders (Finn, 1999a). Services offered in prisons include prerelease employment-related courses, vocational assessments, industrial safety courses, and two programs tailored to women. Several aspects of the CCH program are interesting, and, like the other programs reviewed here, CCH has promising evaluations in terms of finding and keeping employment and possibly having lower recidivism rates (Finn, 1999a; Finn, 1999b). But rather than dwelling on those results, it seems appropriate to focus more closely on the two programs CCH has for women offenders.

Because so many women will be the sole providers for themselves and children they may have, it is important for them to have marketable skills in occupations that pay more than those traditionally open to females. But lack of training programs in women's prisons and a reluctance on the part of the women themselves have meant there are few opportunities for female ex-prisoners to be employed in the better-paying jobs. Recognizing this need, CCH offers two transition-to-trades initiatives at the Washington Corrections Center for Women.

The first strategy is an apprenticeship program wherein three trade unions (carpenters, laborers, and ironworkers) fund and staff a program at the women's prison. Women who successfully complete that Trades-Related Apprenticeship Coaching program are guaranteed union membership in one of the unions—thereby increasing the likelihood of being hired. CCH also arranges for the women to meet with mentors who provide guidance on being a successful employee (e.g., working with supervisors, being prompt, and even on dealing with troublesome male coworkers). The prison assists in the process by operating a recreation program to help women increase their upper body strength because that will benefit them on the job (Finn, 1999b).

The second trade-related program available to women prisoners is the community service work crew. Minimum-security inmates can qualify for offsite employment on work crews that have completed projects such as refurbishing low-income elderly housing, setting up and removing Christmas lights, and cleaning highways and illegal dump sites. Those may not sound like activities requiring much skill, but the more important point is that they are nontraditional work areas for women. And—although it is a sad commentary on the circumstances of women's wages in the contemporary United States—they may pay more than a female ex-offender can get in many traditional female jobs and may encourage the women to try occupations outside the norm.

The Drug War Becomes Drug Treatment. One of the casualties in the war on drugs was treatment programs for drug abusers. The "get-tough-on-crime" approach starting in the 1970s and flourishing in the 1980s saw a preference for imprisoning drug offenders rather than "wasting" money trying to rehabilitate them. The nation was especially concerned about crack cocaine, which reports claimed was the most addictive substance of all and its addicts were essentially untreatable. Fueled by desires to lock 'em up, drug users in general, and crack users particularly, began filling U.S. jails and prisons. Treatment programs never really went away during this time, but they certainly were not the focus of crime prevention or crime-fighting efforts.

By the mid- to late 1990s, calls for a return to treatment were being heard and answered. Experts who had previously declared crack the worst drug of all began changing their minds. Psychiatrist Charles O'Brien, who described crack in the late 1980s as the most addictive drug we have had to deal with, said in 1999 that his views had changed (Egan, 1999). Prompting the change were data showing 84 percent of people who had tried cocaine, in either crack or powder form, did not become addicted. Also, studies showed that at least half of the formerly habitual users of crack who received treatment were testing free of drugs a year later. Other studies were finding that crack was less addictive than some other street drugs, or even nicotine. Finally, a five-year federal survey of treatment showed habitual crack users had greater success at staying clean than did alcoholics (Egan, 1999).

As we know from the meta-analyses reviewed earlier, successful treatment programs must be individually targeted, geared toward particular needs, and address specific factors. So, any one treatment program is unlikely to work for all, or even most, substance abusers. The feature "La Bodega de la Familia" describes an interesting program that takes a family, rather than individual, approach, but most substance abuse programs are designed for individuals—even if they are individuals in groups. In addition, we tend to think of successful treatment programs as

ISSUES OF FAIRNESS

LA BODEGA DE LA FAMILIA

Findings from a broad range of social service research demonstrate the value of family support in helping to achieve behavioral goals for individual family members. But corrections officials have only recently begun to realize the family unit's potential in helping to achieve correctional treatment goals (Shapiro, 1998a). Specifically, substance abuse treatment is more successful when the abuser has the support of caring friends and family. When middle- and upper-income Americans seek substance abuse treatment, they often do so through private health care systems that often incorporate family support as part of the recovery process. Poor and minority families struggling with addiction typically do not have access to similar family-focused programs.

Shapiro (1998a) points out that although there is little difference in drug use patterns among the various socioeconomic groups, the negative consequences (e.g., violence, emotional distress, and an inability to meet basic needs) of drug use are disproportionately experienced in disadvantaged groups. In New York State, nearly one-fourth of the prison inmates have committed no other crime than possessing or selling drugs (Shapiro, 1998b). Imprisonment of nonviolent drug offenders has especially impacted New York's black and Latino citizens. La Bodega de la Familia is designed to respond to the substance abuse problem as it affects low-income minority families specifically.

La Bodega de la Familia ("the family grocery") opened in 1996 in what had been a grocery store in Manhattan's Lower East Side. Using family case management (FCM) as its orienting approach, La Bodega provides assistance to a caseload of about forty-five families (averaging four members per family) who have been referred by police, probation or parole officers, local residents, and community-based organizations.

FCM focuses on the entire family rather than just the substance abuser and incorporates both prevention and treatment by including services that address the needs of both the substance abuser and the family. The program provides twenty-four-hour support for families dealing with drug-related emergencies that might include encounters with police, drug abuse relapses, domestic violence situations, evictions, and so on (Shapiro, 1998b).

Supporters of La Bodega believe this type of program may be especially effective in Latino communities, which historically have had strong support systems based partly on the extended family. By providing counseling and other services that strengthen those existing networks—and recognize the cultural preference for them—La Bodega can help ensure successful completion of a substance abuser's treatment program (Shapiro, 1998b).

We await empirical evaluation of La Bodega, but there already is evidence that FCM, when used with drug-involved arrestees, reduces recidivism, increases retention in treatment, and reduces employment problems (Siegal et al., 1996). Hopefully, La Bodega de la Familia will report similar success.

Read about La Bodega de la Familia at *www.ncjrs.org/pdffiles/170595.pdf.* On page 6 of that report is a case story about one of La Bodega's cases. Read the case history, and describe why you think the goals set for the family are appropriate or inappropriate. In general, do you think programs such as La Bodega are appropriate and a good use of taxpayer money?

existing in the community rather than a jail or prison setting. But the effectiveness of jail and prison substance abuse programs, especially, is now well-established (Field, 1998). Among inmate treatment programs, prerelease therapeutic communities have been the most studied, and it is to an example of one such program that we now turn our attention.

California's R. J. Donovan Correctional Facility, near San Diego, is a medium-security facility housing some 4,000 men in five self-contained living areas. One housing unit in one of the living areas is designated for the Amity Prison Therapeutic Community (TC) program. The 200 men living in this housing unit are recruited for the program through the prison's reception center. The selected inmates must have a history of drug abuse, demonstrate evidence of a willingness to participate in institutional programs, have no history of child molestation or mental illness, and be within nine to fifteen months of release on parole (Lipton, 1995).

The Amity Prison TC program is modeled on New York's Stay'n Out therapeutic community that is designed for a correctional setting. The Stay'n Out program is recognized as producing parolees who have lower arrest rates, a greater chance of success on parole, and a reduced likelihood of being reincarcerated as long as they had stayed in the program for nine to twelve months (Lipton, 1995). The Amity program is showing similar success.

During the twelve-month treatment program, Amity participants move through three distinct treatment phases. Phase One, lasting two to three months, is an orientation and diagnosis phase that identifies the offender's needs and problem areas. The second phase, lasting five to six months, uses encounter groups, counseling sessions, and mentoring by other residents to encourage in the participants self-discipline, feelings of self-worth and self-awareness, a respect for authority, and acceptance of guidance for problem areas. Phase Three is the community reentry stage. During this one- to three-month period, inmates strengthen their planning and decision-making skills and—with the guidance of correctional, treatment, and parole staff—design their individual exit plans. Graduates of the Amity Prison Project are offered aftercare upon their release from prison, and they can continue in residential TC treatment for up to one year in an Amity-operated community facility. That community program builds on what was provided in prison and provides individualized treatment (Lipton, 1995).

An ongoing evaluation of the Amity Prison TC shows positive initial results with participants who completed both the prison and aftercare programs having a lower reincarceration rate than groups of (1) people who completed the prison program but not the aftercare program, (2) program dropouts, and (3) a control group of randomly selected inmates (see Table 15.2).

But are positive results from prison drug treatment programs enough to encourage the public to support more treatment efforts—both in prisons and the community? Actually, there is growing evidence that U.S. citizens not only support treatment efforts but are actually demanding them in some cases. Egan (1999) describes efforts in Arizona to change the drug laws so that treatment rather than prison was mandated for drug offenders and for certain nonviolent lawbreakers whose main problem was drug addiction. Other aspects of the proposition received greater publicity—for example, one aspect could have made drugs such as heroin, LSD, or marijuana legal for medical purposes when prescribed by two doctors. But, despite vocal opposition from politicians, the press, and national antidrug leaders, the proposition passed in 1996 by a two to one ratio. The Arizona legislature amended the measure, saying the voters had committed a serious

TABLE 15.2: Amity Prison Therapeutic Community Reincarcerated Percentages

	CONTROL GROUP (*n* = 73)	PROGRAM DROPOUTS (*n* = 48)	COMPLETED PROGRAM (*n* = 108)	COMPLETED PROGRAM PLUS AFTERCARE (*n* = 61)
Percentage reincarcerated after one year	63.0	50.0	42.6	26.2

Source: Adapted from Lipton, D. S. (1995). *The effectiveness of treatment for drug abusers under criminal justice supervision* [NCJ 157642]. Research Report. Washington, DC: National Institute of Justice.

error, but it was put up for another statewide vote and again it passed with a 57 percent majority in 1998 (Egan, 1999).

Federal restriction effectively halted the law's section allowing physicians to prescribe major drugs for medical purposes, but the treatment provision was put to work by 1997. So, are "Arizonans for treatment" in the minority among U.S. citizens? As the next section explains, they may be in the majority.

SOCIAL SUPPORT AND CORRECTIONAL SANCTIONS

In this book, we began by noting that some 6 million people were under some form of correctional supervision in the United States by the end of the twentieth century. Were all those people made to live in a single geographical area, they would become the nation's second largest city, just after New York's 7.4 million. If we just took the 2 million people in prison, they would be the fourth largest city, falling between Chicago's 2.8 million and the 1.7 million people in Houston (*Statistical Abstract of the United States: 1999*). Will the number of people under correctional supervision continue to grow and eventually surpass New York City's population?

Forecasting imprisonment rates and the general numbers of people under correctional supervision is no more accurate than weather forecasting. Deciding what weight to give such important variables as population age distribution, sentencing policies, public sentiment, legislators' interpretation of public sentiment, and success of correctional programs is as tricky as guessing where a hurricane or tornado will strike. But there is reason to believe the forecast for continued high numbers in America's correctional systems. Consider, for example, comments from a 1981 story in the London-based magazine *The Economist*, regarding the prognosis for prison crowding in the United States:

> Experts in criminology tend to suggest that overcrowding should be dealt with by probation, shorter sentences, earlier parole and more time off for good behavior. But public opinion, quickly reflected in the state legislatures, is moving in exactly the opposite direction. . . . [W]ith a law-and-order administration in Washington and a public determined that criminals shall not escape retribution, there is unlikely to be a shortage of prisoners. ("Prisons: No Vacancies," 1981)

That quote highlighted the law-and-order, or just deserts, sentiment as a leading cause for the predicted increase in the U.S. prisoner population during the 1980s. And although the annual increase in the prison population was less at the end of the 1990s than at the start (Beck & Mumola, 1999), there is still reason to believe that a get-tough-on-crime position remains a driving force. But is the get-tough approach a simple reflection of the Retributive era? A result of people frustrated in the belief that nothing works? Or an indication of raw anger? On the other hand, might the get-tough approach be a misunderstanding of public opinion and an overreaction by legislators?

Corrections in Angry Times

Table 3.1 from Chapter 3 presented six prison eras and indicated that aspects of all five punishment philosophies can be found under each era. The table also notes that one or two of the philosophies are often emphasized during particular eras. Since the 1970s, state and federal jurisdictions in the United States have been in a Retributive era. At the start of the twenty-first century, it appears that an emphasis on retribution continues. Such a forecast is suggested not only by the continued growth of the prison population nationwide but also by the treatment of the people in prison. During the Rehabilitation era, it was common to hear corrections officials explain to the public that offenders were put in prison as punishment, not for punishment. Today it seems more often that the public is explaining to corrections officials that simply being in prison is not sufficient punishment—they want the prisoners to be punished while in there as well. To be fair, the comment is more likely phrased as wanting to deny prisoners some privileges rather than administering extra punishment. The belief that inmates have it too good is escalated by stories such as the one from an Iowa jail in which the sheriff gave an early release to four Amish young people serving a ninety-day jail sentence for criminal mischief. They were getting spoiled, the sheriff announced, by conveniences such as plumbing and electricity ("'Spoiled' Amish Inmates," 1999).

Although the extra punishment idea has proponents, consider the implications of some of the following media reports:

- Under the title "Reminding Inmates That They're Inmates," a reporter explains how Mississippi plans a ban on television and air conditioning in cells. Arizona is reported to be eliminating weight lifting and will be charging inmates $3 for doctor visits ("Reminding Inmates," 1994).
- Sheriff Joe Arpaio in Maricopa County, Arizona, received national attention in the mid-1990s as he organized his prisoners into chain gangs, housed them in tents in the scorching desert, made them eat baloney as a food staple, banned skin magazines, and restricted television shows to old Disney films and Cable News Network (Lacayo, 1995).
- In a Time/CNN opinion poll, 67 percent of those questioned thought inmates were treated too leniently. Chain gangs were approved by 65 percent, and 51 percent thought inmates should be deprived of their television sets and barbells (Lacayo, 1995).
- The "no-frills" position seems summed up by comments from a Tennessee legislator: "All we are obligated to provide these criminals is a clean place to sleep and decent food—that means corn bread and beans" (quoted in Curriden, 1995, p. 74).

If the preceding are examples of no-frills prisons, the ones following might be examples of "humiliating the punished":

- Mississippi inmates, especially those on work crews, are dressed in black-and-white striped uniforms with the word *convict* on the back (Curriden, 1995; "Reminding Inmates," 1994). In Massachusetts, a sheriff who reintroduced chain gangs also puts teenage inmates in black-and-white striped prison garb ("Inmate Outfits," 1999).
- In 1999 Alabama asked a federal judge to allow Alabama prisoners to be handcuffed to chest-high metal hitching posts when they refuse to work. A year earlier the judge ruled the way Alabama was using the posts was unconstitutionally cruel (in the sun for hours without water or restroom breaks), but the state was told they could try to devise a constitutional method ("Alabama Wants to Hitch," 1999).
- By 1999 at least five states had state- or local-level chain gangs operating. In some cases proponents argued that humiliation can be an effective deterrent, but everyone was careful to avoid linking that humiliation to images of slavery that "the spectacle of shackled men, most black" brought to mind ("Chain Gangs Come," 1999; "Florida Brings," 1995).

While the public—or at least their legislators—are expanding the get-tough policies from the courtrooms to the prisons, the corrections officials are often left

Sheriff Joe Arpaio, shown here at his jail in Maricopa County, Arizona, is a staunch supporter and avid practitioner of the "make 'em miserable" school of jailing.

with the problem of implementing policies that they do not support. When Florida corrections officials began putting inmates in leg irons to work along roadsides, each inmate was shackled individually with a chain between their legs. This upset Florida lawmakers, who said they had reinstated chain gangs with the intent that prisoners would be shackled together in lines of five, as they were in Alabama. Corrections officials said you could get more work out of inmates who were shackled individually. But it won't be as harsh a punishment, countered some legislators ("Florida Brings," 1995).

A reason that many corrections officials are hesitant to hop on the no-frills and humiliation bandwagon is a very reasonable, though self-serving, one—tension and violence may increase as the "reforms" take place. For example, former warden Michael Quinn called bans on weight lifting an issue because the prisoners who exercise are the best inmates. Quinn had never encountered an inmate who bulked up just to commit crimes when he got out. Instead, he saw weight-lifting inmates as taking pride in themselves—often for the first time in their lives (see Curriden, 1995).

Other officials, taking an "idle hands are the devil's workshop" perspective, worry that without the distractions of television, weight lifting, crafts, or sports, the potential for violence is increased. Sometimes the general public and some legislators forget that what is done to and for the prisoners also affect the correctional staff.

The Myth of an Angry Public[2]

It is rather easy to cite statistics that attribute prison crowding to the retributivist philosophy and to view retribution as the rationale supporting no-frills and humiliation approaches to prison management. But often lost in this explanation is

[2]Adapted from Reichel, P. L., & Gauthier, A. K. "Boot camp corrections: A public reaction." In R. Muraskin (Ed.), *Issues in justice* (Bristol, IN: Wyndham Hall Press, Inc., 1999), pp. 73–96.

an attempt to verify several of its basic assumptions. Recalling the earlier quote from *The Economist,* we are told that public opinion was quickly reflected in legislative action. In other words, it is assumed that (1) the public held a get-tough or retributive philosophy; (2) the philosophy required a means of punishment that placed more offenders in prison; and (3) the various legislatures correctly interpreted both the public's philosophy and the preferred means of punishment as they set sentence lengths, established mandatory sentencing, and built more prisons. But what if any of these assumptions were incorrect? That is, what if the public did not really hold solely, or even primarily, to a retributive philosophy? Even if they did emphasize retribution, did the public require or prefer that incarceration be the primary means of punishment? Are the legislators able to accurately interpret and act on public sentiment when setting punishment policy? If the answer to any of these questions is "no," it is possible that America's increased prison population has been, in part, unnecessary. Let us consider this point more carefully.

Since the 1970s, the mass media, politicians, and academicians have made reference to the get-tough-on-crime philosophy embraced by U.S. society. That philosophy was oriented toward such things as stiffer sentences, less judicial discretion, weakened parole boards, increased use of imprisonment (forcing the construction of more prisons), and a return to the use of capital punishment.

Although the objective reality of those conditions cannot be ignored, the basis upon which they have been implemented may present more of a puzzle. One assumption is that because those changes are primarily the result of legislative action, we expect that in this representative democracy the legislators' votes reflect their constituents' opinions. On the other hand, some recent research suggests a lack of complete concordance between public opinion and the changes in criminal justice policy toward a solely (or even primarily) punitive stance. In other words, is American society following a get-tough philosophy because that is what the public wants, or because that is what politicians, correctional administrators, and policymakers think the public wants? In addition, if the get-tough policy is interpreted as requiring imprisonment and longer sentences, is effective use being made of unconventional methods that the public may actually favor?

Immarigeon (1986) suggests that legislators and criminal justice policymakers have shaped correctional policy according to what they see as the public's desire for a get-tough response to the criminal. Similarly, Cullen, Clark, and Wozniak (1985) believe current criminal justice policies are a reaction to the public's fear of crime and desire to punish and lock up the offenders. If it is true that criminal justice policy simply reflects public desire, we are not only secure in the knowledge that our representative democracy works, but should arguably show restraint in putting forward programs that contradict those attitudes. On the other hand, if the policy does not reflect public desire, we may stifle innovation under the mistaken impression that it violates the public will. Recent studies suggest that the latter condition may be more true.

Riley and Rose (1980) tested the assumption that a representative form of government presents a situation in which the public, at least indirectly, influences the decisions of public officials. Riley and Rose's work provides one of the first indications that public officials misinterpret public attitudes about punishment. They found that despite contrary views by correctional decision makers, the public had a positive attitude toward progressive reform rather than being predominantly punitive. The public, for example, was much more receptive to community-based programs and to parole and probation than elites expected (Riley & Rose, 1980).

Four years later, Gottfredson and Taylor (1984) surveyed policymakers and the general public and found remarkable concordance of opinion between the two groups regarding the desirability of using community-based options in response to prison overcrowding. The problem, however, was that policymakers perceived the public as being generally punitive and made decisions based on those misperceptions. Specifically, Gottfredson and Taylor (1984) found the general public to stress utilitarian goals (e.g., rehabilitation and deterrence) over punitive ones, as did the policymakers. But although both the public and the policy groups held attitudes characterized as rather liberal, nonpunitive, utilitarian, and reform oriented, the policy group attributed almost the reverse to the public. The authors refer to this predicament as an example of **pluralistic ignorance,** by which persons underestimate the extent that others share the beliefs and sentiments they themselves hold (Gottfredson & Taylor, 1984, p. 196).

Several studies have found public opinion about punishment to be a very complicated issue. Cullen et al. (1985) report on a survey of Texans' attitudes about punishment that found respondents expressing a desire for more prisons. But they were equally in favor of simultaneous development of community corrections programs. In fact, Cullen et al. (1985) suggest that get-tough policies probably do reflect—or at least do not violate—public sentiments. But decision makers seem to have missed the complexity of the public's views and failed to see an acceptance of rehabilitative and reform-oriented policies as well. Additional studies result in similar conclusions. Applegate, Cullen, and Fisher (1997) found considerable public support for the idea that rehabilitation should be an integral part of correctional policy. Skovron, Scott, and Cullen (1988) found that respondents in Cincinnati and Columbus, Ohio, surveys showed great support for community corrections and incentive good-time programs. The authors comment that public opinion is more complex than is commonly perceived. Rather than holding a uniformly get-tough attitude that demands longer prison sentences, certain types of offenders are seen as appropriate for community programs.

Because complex issues do not easily lend themselves to political solutions, it may be that legislation does not try to address the puzzle of public opinion about punishment. The studies suggest that the general public is not as dogmatic about imprisonment for all criminals as we may have thought. Furthermore, there is public support for what is traditionally considered to be rehabilitation or treatment programs. But because legislators and policymakers may be unaware of the potential for public support, pluralistic ignorance works to obstruct innovation in corrections and the development of options to imprisonment.

WRAPPING THINGS UP

In many ways this chapter summarizes this book. In the book's earliest chapters, the five basic philosophies of punishment were presented. Then a review was provided that described our passage through various eras during which the philosophies have influenced how society responds to its criminal offenders. One of the clearest lessons learned from that review was that one or two penal philosophies might overshadow the others in any particular penal system era—but there seem to be advocates of each philosophy in every period. There is, in other words, continual conflict over the purpose of punishment. Opinion polls may tell us that most people currently believe the corrections system should exist to incapacitate offenders and to exact retribution. But those same polls will also show that other citizens want punishment to rehabilitate—or to restore—or to deter.

Lack of agreement on social issues is anything but unexpected in a large, modern, industrialized society with a heterogeneous population. In fact it would be more unusual if the public voiced nearly complete agreement about the role of punishment, or about any other social issue. But the lack of consensus, expected though it is, presents some real problems for the criminal justice system as a whole and the corrections system more specifically. That is, how do we evaluate whether the justice system is doing its job and whether the justice process is working? Because society is not clear about what the justice system or the process should be doing, it is difficult to determine if the system is successful or the process is working. For some citizens, if the probation officer is not constantly monitoring her client (punishment is for incapacitation), then that probation officer is not doing her job and the intermediate sanction of probation is not working—even though the client may be attending substance abuse counseling and is successfully completing a vocational training course. For other citizens, if the probation officer is not assisting his client in overcoming substance abuse problems or providing increased job opportunities (punishment is for rehabilitation), the probation officer is not doing his job and the intermediate sanction of probation is not working—even though the client is being closely monitored on a daily basis. This issue is more important than is suggested by the response "you can't please everybody." It is more important because it addresses the basic issue of public confidence in the justice system.

One way to respond to the problems presented by conflicting opinions about the purpose of punishment is to make valiant efforts at arriving at some level of agreement. But even if significant agreement were possible, it may not be desirable. Maybe history and the occasional look at other countries have taught us that different philosophies of punishment exist in every penal era because they are supposed to. Maybe there is not a single answer to the question, "Why punish?" And if there is not just one reason for punishing, that means the answer to the question, "Did the punishment work?" will also have several answers. Chapters in the middle of this book reviewed a myriad of punishments, including corporal and capital punishment, intermediate sanctions, and confinement. Chapters near the end of the book highlighted some important issues related to those punishment types and to the people against whom they are applied. And, undoubtedly, as you were reading the chapters there were some places where you nodded your head in agreement and other places where you wondered how society could be so screwed up that such practices are allowed. The fact that a classmate nodded and wondered at different places in the chapter than you simply emphasizes the point that several reasons for punishment exist.

So what should we do? This last chapter suggests that an appropriate response might be to simply accept what seems to be the inevitable. Realize that individual citizens, legislators, judges, and corrections personnel can see different reasons for punishment. Furthermore, those reasons may change depending on characteristics of the offender or the offense. When the role of punishment is accepted as being flexible, we are able to find value in a variety of sanction types. The problem becomes one of clearly conveying to the public, the offender, and the corrections employee exactly what probation, or restitution, or community service, or imprisonment is supposed to accomplish in a particular case. As long as it has been shown that the sanction can achieve the proposed goal or goals, the public can evaluate if it was successful, the offender will know what the punishment is trying to achieve, and the corrections employee will know what she is trying to accomplish. That process begins with each of us understanding our own preferences regarding the five basic punishment philosophies and knowing the practical implications of holding those preferences. Hopefully this book has provided some information that allows you to make a more informed decision about those issues.

SUMMARY

THE NOTHING-WORKS CONTROVERSY

Drawing on examples of different sanctions mentioned in earlier chapters, this chapter looks at questions of whether particular sanctions work. Because evaluation of a punishment's success depends on what the sanction was supposed to accomplish, we considered different sanctions in terms of particular punishment philosophies.

THE DETERRENCE RATIONALE

The philosophy of deterrence was used to evaluate shock incarceration sentences.

- Results thus far suggest that boot camp programs may deter future criminal behavior but not to a greater degree than does regular imprisonment.
- But if the same level of deterrence is possible in a shorter time, the good news for deterrence proponents is that their goal can be achieved without lengthening sentences and increasing the number of prisons and the number of prisoners.

THE INCAPACITATION RATIONALE

Home confinement programs were used to consider the incapacitation rationale.

- Because incapacitation cannot be as complete outside prison as it is inside prison, persons wanting punishments to restrict the offender's freedom of movement may have to lower their standards in order for home confinement to be considered a success.
- Just as advocates of the other punishment philosophies have learned to live with something less than complete success, it seems that so too must proponents of punishment for incapacitation.

THE RESTORATION/RETRIBUTION RATIONALES

The retribution and restoration rationales were combined in this discussion because retribution, technically, views punishment as simply a moral obligation rather than as serving some utilitarian objective. But retribution also has a restorative aspect to it, making it a cousin to the restoration philosophy. As one measure of a sanction's success at providing restoration, we looked at restitution programs—typically a key ingredient in attempts to return things to a sense of balance. There is some indication that restitution helps to reduce recidivism, but even more important for restoration advocates, a restitution sanction helps to increase both the offender's and the victim's satisfaction with the justice process.

THE REHABILITATION RATIONALE

Debate continues over the effectiveness of treatment, or the rehabilitation rationale.

- Critics argue that evidence suggests rehabilitation should not be a primary goal of corrections, because there is no reason to believe it can be achieved.
- Proponents counter that there is, in fact, evidence of treatment's success, and that rehabilitation should be emphasized even more. Employment-related and drug abuse programs were offered as examples of effective treatment programs.

SOCIAL SUPPORT AND CORRECTIONAL SANCTIONS

The chapter's closing discussion of social support for correctional sanctions suggests that legislators may not understand the complexity of public opinion about punishment's role. Until that complexity is appreciated, there may not be any motivation toward expanding sanction types or in appreciating the diverse purposes that punishment can serve.

Key Terms and Concepts

community restraints (p. 567)
meta-analysis (p. 573)
pluralistic ignorance (p. 585)
selection bias (p. 576)

Discussion Questions

1. Discuss the apparent merits of both the nothing-works and the something-works positions.
2. Accept, for a moment, that certainty of punishment is more important than severity of punishment for purposes of deterrence. What implications does that have for sentencing policies in your state? How could the justice system increase the certainty of punishment?
3. If the public were more aware of the research showing that boot camps are no more a deterrent to future crime than is long-term imprisonment, would there still be such strong support for boot camps?
4. Discuss this chapter's position that proponents of punishment for incapacitation should accept less than complete restriction of the offender's freedom of movement. In other words, is it possible to use the community setting rather than a prison to achieve a punishment goal of incapacitation?
5. Discuss ways that sentencing practices could be established to reflect better the complexity of public opinion regarding the purposes of punishment.

GLOSSARY

Note: Words in **bold face** have their own glossary entry.

1779 Penitentiary Act Passed by the British Parliament in 1779, the Penitentiary Act emphasized reform principles such as secure and sanitary conditions, systematic inspection, the elimination of fees for basic needs and services, the desirability of a reformatory regimen, and the use of solitary confinement and continuous labor.

adjudicated delinquent A juvenile whom the juvenile court has found to have engaged in behavior that meets the state's criteria for delinquency. Compare with the status of *guilty* in adult court.

adolescent sex offender Adolescent offenders who have committed sexually inappropriate acts.

aftercare The process and procedures used to help reintegrate into the community a juvenile who has been in a juvenile institution or under some other form of juvenile court sanctioning. Compare with **parole** in the adult system.

age–crime curve A concept used to describe the tendency for incidences of crime to be committed more during an offender's younger years and then to decline as the offender gets older.

aggravating circumstances Events or conditions that make an offense *more* serious than it might otherwise be. When aggravating circumstances, like mutilating the murder victim, are present in a crime, juries or judges can often increase the penalty that would otherwise be applied to the convicted offender. Contrast with **mitigating circumstances.**

allocution The formal address in court before a judge sentences the offender, or at a parole hearing before the parole board decides about a prisoner's parole, when a victim is allowed to express an opinion about the offender's sentence or the offender's parole consideration.

American Correctional Association Founded in 1870 as the American Prison Association, it became the American Correctional Association in 1954. The ACA played an important role in moving American prisons into the Rehabilitation era. Today the ACA is the premier national organization for persons employed in the corrections field.

American Prison Association See **American Correctional Association.**

Americans with Disabilities Act Legislation requiring state and local governments to provide persons with disabilities equal access to programs, services, and activities. ADA requires that corrections officials make sure inmates with physical or mental impairments still have access to programs, services, and activities for which they would otherwise be qualified.

attachment or bonding The attachment or bonding process that occurs between a child and his or her primary caregiver. The process typically begins at the time of birth and is the basis for further emotional affiliation. It also is believed to influence the child's physical and psychological development.

Auburn system Along with the **Pennsylvania system,** the Auburn system defined the two main styles of prison discipline and management from the 1820s to the 1860s. The Auburn system believed correction was best achieved by keeping prisoners separate from each other at night but allowing them to work together during the day. Silence, however, was required at all times.

bail The security deposited to guarantee a defendant's appearance for court dates in exchange for the defendant being released in the community until those court dates. When that security involves a financial obligation, it is a *bail bond,* which can be one of money (*cash bail bond*) or property (*property bail bond*).

bail bond See **bail.**

banishment A response to offending acts which involves exiling the offender from the community.

benefit of clergy A forerunner to **probation** that helped, in its initial form, establish a place for more humane punishment by allowing some offenders (defined as *clergy*) to avoid harsher penalties by having their cases transferred from the state courts to the church courts.

beyond a reasonable doubt The burden of proof used in a criminal as opposed to a civil trial. When the judge or jury is asked to decide if a defendant is guilty beyond a reasonable doubt, they must be fully satisfied (entirely convinced) that the evidence establishes the person's guilt. Contrast with **preponderance of evidence.**

black rage theory An explanation for the interracial nature of prison rape (black aggressors and white victims) that assumes a link between black hostility toward whites and the inversion of power that these rapes can express. Compare with **vulnerability theory.**

blended sentences A sentence type available in some jurisdictions that allows the criminal court to impose either juvenile or adult sanctions or a combination of juvenile and adult sanctions on juveniles whose cases have been tranferred from juvenile court to the adult criminal court.

boot camp corrections Although sometimes used synonymously with **shock incarceration,** in this book boot camp corrections refers to a *program* that uses military-style discipline and activities, along with more traditional programs, to achieve specific goals.

branding See **corporal punishment.**

Bridewell House The original English house of correction, or **workhouse,** opened in the town of Bridewell in 1557. Other **houses of correction** built in England during the sixteenth century also were called Bridewell House after the prototype.

brokerage approach The method of probation supervision in which the probation officer serves as a link between the client and community resources. The probation officer helps identify the client's needs and then directs the client to community agencies that can respond to those needs. Contrast this with the **casework approach.**

Bureau of Prisons (BOP) Established in 1930 as part of the U.S. Department of Justice, the BOP is responsible for the federal prison system. Because of its willingness to be innovative, the BOP played an important role in moving America's prison system into the Rehabilitation era.

capital punishment The ultimate physical sanction in the sense that the state takes the convicted offender's life as punishment for the harm done by the offender. In the contemporary United States, capital punishment is authorized in over thirty-five jurisdictions, primarily for the crime of murder with aggravating circumstances, and is accomplished most often with lethal injection.

caseload A method of distributing clients (probationers or parolees) among an agency's probation or parole officers in such a manner that each officer has a similar number of clients. Contrast with **workload.**

case management probation A technique especially popular during the **Rehabilitation era** wherein probation officers were assigned a small enough number of probationers that each client could receive individualized attention.

casework approach The method of probation supervision in which the probation officers provide direct treatment to the clients. The probation officers will counsel the clients on issues such as substance abuse, anger management, finance budgeting, or self-esteem. Contrast this with the **brokerage approach.**

Castle Island (Massachusetts) Often considered America's first prison, this facility in Boston harbor was made the repository for convicted offenders from throughout Massachusetts in 1785. Earlier facilities cannot be considered prisons or penitentiaries because they often held both convicted and unconvicted persons, civil as well as criminal offenders, and were under local rather than state jurisdiction.

civil death The loss of all rights and privileges of citizenship as the result of conviction for a serious crime. Compare with **civil disabilities.**

civil disabilities The limits placed on a convicted offender's civil rights both during incarceration and after release. For example, while in prison the offender may suffer the civil disabilities of having his right to privacy restricted or not being allowed to vote. After prison the convicted felon may not be allowed to purchase a firearm or enter certain occupations. Compare with **civil death.**

civil law The section of law that regulates matters considered to be private wrongs rather than public wrongs, which is the realm of **criminal law.**

civil rights Those personal, natural rights protecting people against arbitrary or discriminatory treatment. In addition to the civil rights provided in the U.S. Constitution and its amendments, there are other civil rights, such as the right to live and work where one wishes, recognized by the courts.

Civil Rights Act Important civil rights acts have been passed at the federal level in attempts to ensure that citizens (including prisoners) and others under the appropriate jurisdiction have rights and privileges such as freedom from discrimination. The Civil Rights Act is codified in the U.S. Code as title 42, section 1983. Prisoners often bring suit under section 1983 when they raise complaints about conditions of confinement such as medical care, mail censorship, safety issues, and physical living conditions.

classification Considered by some to be the key to any rehabilitation efforts, classification refers to the process and procedures designed to identify things such as an offender's *needs* (e.g., education, vocational training, substance-abuse counseling) and the *risk* he or she presents to the community (e.g., minimum- or maximum-security risk). When classification is conducted for purposes of addressing the offender's needs, it is considered to be *classification for treatment.* Classification that stresses public safety and offender risk is *classification for management.*

classification committees The grouping of administrative, security, and treatment staff who meet to make decisions about the facility to which an inmate will be assigned, to determine an inmate's cell and work assignments at an institution, and to develop a treatment program for the inmate.

community corrections Programs that allow offenders to remain at liberty in the community, while abiding by certain conditions, so they can take advantage of work, educational, vocational, psychological, and other types of correctional resources in the community.

community restraints These sanctions provide increased surveillance and control over offenders in an effort to reduce the offenders' freedom of movement and ability to commit crime while they remain in the community.

community service order A sentence (order) requiring offenders to do unpaid work for the general good of the community. Types of community service include repairing playground equipment, picking up litter along the highway, or working in a nursing home.

commutation of sentence A moderation in punishment that substitutes a lesser penalty for the one originally imposed.

compensation See **restitution.**

concurrent sentencing A sentencing strategy that gives an offender a specific punishment, such as a number of years in prison, on several different offense charges (e.g., burglary, theft, and vandalism) or counts (e.g., four counts of writing bad checks), but all the sentences are allowed to be served at the same time (i.e., concurrently). For example, a person sentenced to two years for burglary, one year for theft, and one year for vandalism, will serve only two years (the longest of the three sentences) if the sentences are made to run concurrently.

conditional release At the pretrial stage this refers to a type of nonfinancial pretrial release from jail on a defendant's promise to fulfill a requirement such as staying employed or abiding by a curfew. When used in reference to an inmate's release from prison, it means that the early release is allowed only as long as the prisoner abides by certain conditions (contrast with **unconditional release**). **Parole** is the most frequent example of conditional release from prison.

congregate and silent The key words distinguishing the **Auburn system,** which required prisoners to work together in silence during the day and to be housed separately, and kept silent, at night.

conjugal visits Unsupervised visits between prisoner and spouse in a private location that allows the two to engage in more normal interpersonal contact, including sexual relations.

contract system An **open market** labor system in which a private contractor controls employment and the sale of products. The state, however, is in charge of the maintenance and discipline of the inmate workers. Contracting is especially criticized by labor unions as taking away jobs from law-abiding workers.

corporal punishment Most generally, this term refers to any kind of punishment inflicted on the body. More specifically, it refers to punishments such as branding, mutilation, and whipping that involve a direct application of pain to the body of an offender.

correctional officers Prison and jail employees who are responsible for public safety, institutional security, and at least in some facilities, for the treatment of inmates.

corrections A broad term that refers to the network of local, state, and federal government agencies that have responsibility for the pre- and postconviction custody, supervision, and treatment of persons accused or convicted of crimes.

cottage plan A popular architectural style for women's reformatories built in the late nineteenth century. Inmates lived in small individual units, or cottages, that created an atmosphere more like a home than a cell block. The cottages themselves could be set up in dormitory style or with individual rooms having windows, bedspreads, rugs, and wooden doors instead of iron bars.

crime control model A model of criminal justice that seeks to guarantee social freedom by emphasizing efficient arrests and convictions of wrongdoers.

criminal justice system Refers to a loose association of police, courts, and corrections agencies whose general goal is the control of crime.

criminal law The section of law that regulates matters considered to be public wrongs rather than private wrongs, which is the realm of **civil law.** Because a public wrong has occurred, criminal law provides the basis from which the field of **corrections** operates.

curfew See **home confinement.**

customary courts Also called "native courts," the customary courts operating in some African countries have limited jurisdiction in criminal matters, but are important because they make use of the African tradition of compensation or **restitution.**

day fine A financial penalty type of sentence that links the penalty's amount to both the seriousness of the offense and to the offender's financial situation.

day reporting center Called *probation centers* in England and Wales and *attendance centers* in Australia, day reporting centers in the United States are community-based facilities that provide an intermediate sanction where persons on probation, parole, or furlough must report for daily monitoring and for participation in required programs.

death by animal and insect, instrument, and natural elements An arbitrary categorization of death penalty methods into those that cause death by making the condemned available to lethal attack by animals or insects; by using devices ranging from the unsophisticated rock to the more technologically advanced guillotine or lethal injection; or by rendering the condemned's body to lethal exposure to earth, air, water, or fire.

deprivation model An explanation of the inmate subculture that says the subculture results from people being confined and having to adapt to conditions known as the **pains of imprisonment.** Contrast with the **importation model.**

determinate sentencing A sentencing system in which the convicted offender is given a fixed penalty, such as three years in prison. In contrast to **indeterminate sentencing,** determinate sentencing provides for little discretion as to when a prisoner can be released.

deterrence The punishment philosophy that says punishment's aim is to prevent future offenses by setting an example for both the offender and others. See also **general deterrence** and **specific deterrence.**

developmental model A treatment model using classification systems that rely on deductions made from theoretical perspectives. The idea that people progress through, and stall in, different developmental stages are examples of the developmental model. Treatment staff gain insight on a prisoner's behavior by knowing the prisoner's current developmental stage. Contrast with **problem-area model.**

differential response The term applied to society's response to women offenders when emphasis was placed on having different sentencing practices, different facilities, and different treatment programs for female prisoners. A problem linked to the differential response was its tendency to reinforce the traditional, hence limited, role of women in society.

direct supervision A type of inmate supervision in jails or prisons with a podular design. When correctional officers are positioned in the housing pod with the inmates, they have direct and continuous supervision of and interaction with the inmates. Contrast with **intermittent surveillance.**

diyya In Islamic law, *diyya* is money paid to a victim or his relatives in compensation for a felony committed against the victim.

due process clause The section of the Fourteenth Amendment to the U.S. Constitution that requires each state to abide by the federal Bill of Rights (in which due process criteria are identified) when attempting to deprive any person of life, liberty, or property.

due process model A model of criminal justice that seeks to guarantee social freedom by emphasizing individual rights and protecting citizens from inappropriate government invasion in their life.

earned good time See **good time.**

education release A correctional program that allows selected prisoners to leave the confines of jail or prison in order to attend school.

electronic monitoring A technology tool used to restrict, deter, and discover behavior of persons under supervision of court or corrections personnel. Basic electronic monitoring equipment includes *active devices*—transmitters, attached to offenders, that emit continuous signals that are in turn picked up by receivers. When the signals are expected but absent, officials are notified there has been a violation. Rather than using continuous signals, *passive devices* rely on random or programmed calls to the offenders who must then confirm their presence by signal, voice, or visual verification.

Elmira Reformatory Opened in 1876 in Elmira, New York. This facility was the first in the United States to incorporate the philosophy and procedures of the **Irish system.**

equalization response The term applied to society's response to women offenders starting in the late 1960s when calls were made for the equal treatment of female and male offenders. Relying especially on legal action, women began getting more equality in sentencing practices and in conditions at women's prisons.

equal protection clause The section of the Fourteenth Amendment to the U.S. Constitution that prohibits any state from denying any person equal protection of the law.

equity As an important aspect of the **retribution** philosophy, equity says there should be a similarity in punishment for similar crimes and similar criminals.

ethnicity For purposes of statistical differentiation, ethnicity distinguishes people from each other on the basis of cultural characteristics such as language, religion, or other common cultural variables. In this book ethnic distinction is most often one of Hispanic versus non-Hispanic. Contrast with **race.**

expiration of sentence An unconditional release from prison resulting from the inmate completing his or her entire sentence.

Federal Bureau of Prisons As an agency within the U.S. Department of Justice, the Federal Bureau of Prisons is responsible for operating nearly 100 federal correctional facilities that range from **supermax prisons** to prison camps.

Federal Correctional Complex (FCC) A new design concept being used by the **Bureau of Prisons** that places several correctional facilities of different security levels at a single site.

felonies The most serious type of criminal offense. Felonies are punished by fines, community sanctions, a prison sentence, or, where it is authorized, death. Contrast with **petty offenses** and **misdemeanors.**

female-oriented response The term applied to the way many academics and practitioners believe society should be responding to women offenders. This approach recognizes and accepts differences between women and men (including those in prison) and believes that the determination of what is an appropriate response to women offenders must be decided from a female, rather than a male, orientation.

fine A sentence requiring the convicted offender to pay the court an amount of money as the penalty for misbehavior.

folkways Along with **mores** and **laws,** folkways provide the norms or guidelines for behavior in society. Of the three, folkways are social expectations whose violation result in the least serious reaction or sanctioning by other members of society. Rules of etiquette are good examples of folkways.

formal sanction See **sanction.**

furlough An authorized and temporary leave of absence from prison.

Gaol at Wymondham The first facility in England specifically designed to implement John Howard's penal reforms and the requirements of the **1779 Penitentiary Act.** This gaol (the British version of *jail*) was built in 1785.

general deterrence The version of **deterrence** that seeks to prevent crime by using punishment to show others who are considering a criminal act that they will suffer painful consequences if they commit that act. Contrast with **specific deterrence.**

general incapacitation According to this version of incapacitation, most kinds of felons are imprisoned in an attempt to achieve large gains in crime prevention.

good time The time deducted from a sentence. When the deduction is automatically given all prisoners serving their sentence without problems, it is *statutory good time.* When the deduction is due to positive behavior by the inmate, it is *earned good time.* In some states, exceptional acts by inmates are rewarded with *meritorious good time.*

hands-off doctrine A position taken by the courts that prison administrators should be free to govern their institutions without any outside interference. Compare with the **intervention doctrine** and the **nominal doctrine.**

home confinement A requirement, usually imposed by the court, that an offender must remain in his or her residence for some or all hours of the day. Types of home confinement include *curfew* (offenders must be at their residence during specified hours, usually at night), *home detention* (offenders must remain at home at all times except for approved absences for school, work, etc.), and *home incarceration* (offenders must remain at home except for limited absences such as medical treatment).

home detention See **home confinement.**

home incarceration See **home confinement.**

Hospice of St. Michael A facility built in 1704 at Rome for misbehaving boys. The seclusion theme that was important at hospice facilities was implemented at St. Michael, where boys were required to sleep in single cells and to work in silence.

houses of correction Facilities, like the **Bridewell House** and the **Maison de Force,** that emphasized the importance of making offenders work. Along with the theme of seclusion introduced in the hospice facilities, the work theme emphasized in the houses of correction provided key ingredients of the eventual penitentiary system.

importation model An explanation of the inmate subculture that says the subculture results from people bringing certain norms, beliefs, and values into the prison from the streets. Contrast with the **deprivation model.**

incapacitation The punishment philosophy that says punishment's aim is to prevent an offender's continued criminal acts by restricting that offender's freedom to move about. Traditionally the freedom to move about has been restricted by placing the offender in prison, but recent technology suggests that incapacitation might also be achieved with tools such as **electronic monitoring.**

incorporation The theory that argues all provisions of the federal Bill of Rights are made applicable to the states (i.e., they are incorporated) by the Fourteenth Amendment's **due process clause,** which requires the states to abide by the Bill of Rights when attempting to deprive anyone of his or her life, liberty, or property.

indeterminate sentencing A sentencing system in which the convicted offender receives a penalty that covers a time range rather than a flat period. Unlike **determinate sentencing,** which requires a sentence for a specific time, indeterminate sentencing gives corrections officials some discretion as to when a person's sentence should be completed—earlier when good behavior and personal improvement is shown, and later when rehabilitation is not apparent.

Industrial era The penal system era, lasting from the 1900s to the 1930s, in which prison labor moved from an activity designed primarily to benefit the state to an activity that might benefit the prisoner.

informal probation A procedure, authorized in most states, that allows juveniles, who admit to the charges against them, to be placed under the supervision of court personnel without first having their cases heard in juvenile court.

informal sanctions See **sanction.**

inmate code Circulated by word of mouth, this informal and unwritten code stipulates the expected behavior and attitudes of inmates.

inmate roles The **inmate subculture** identifies certain social roles that inmates come to play in the prison setting. Those roles may be earned through the inmates' own efforts or might be assigned to the inmates based on some characteristic they have.

inmate subculture Refers to the existence in prison of a set of norms, values, and beliefs that can be distinguished from those in general society.

institutional classification **Classification** occurring after arrival at a particular facility in order to determine cell, work, and program assignments. Compare with **systemwide classification.**

institutional work assignments One of two broad types of work assignments in prisons. Prisoners assigned to institutional work may receive training in specific skill areas (such as janitorial service or food preparation), but they are more likely to do jobs that are considered unskilled. Contrast with **prison industry work assignments.**

intensive probation supervision (IPS) An intermediate sanction designed to provide greater supervision than does regular probation. Some IPS programs are *prison-diversion* types of IPS because they provide intensive supervision for offenders who might otherwise be in prison. Other IPS programs are *probation-enhancement* types because they provide increased supervision for high-risk offenders who would otherwise be on regular probation.

intermediate punishments or sanctions Sanctions falling between the extremes of fines and imprisonment. Intermediate punishments for offenders needing something less than incarceration might include a *prison alternative* type like **probation.** Persons who would likely go to prison were it not for overcrowded conditions might receive a *prison substitute* type of intermediate sanction like **home confinement.**

intermediate system The terminology used by Sir Walter Crofton, as director of the Irish prison system in 1854, to describe a process of progressive stages that allowed prisoners to earn increasing liberty—culminating in early release from prison—for their continued good behavior.

intermittent surveillance The typical way to observe inmates in jails or prisons with a linear design. Because correctional officers can see inmates only as they walk along the corridor and look into each cell, the supervision of and interaction with the inmates is only intermittent. Contrast with **direct supervision.**

intervention Along with **classification** and **treatment,** intervention is a key aspect of **rehabilitation.** The concept of intervention supports the idea that it is appropriate and necessary for corrections officials to act in a manner that will bring about change in an offender's behavior.

intervention doctrine The position that the courts are obliged to intervene in prison management when prison conditions, policy, or procedures inappropriately encroach on prisoners' rights. Compare with the **hands-off doctrine** and the **nominal doctrine.**

investigation See **probation officer duties.**

Irish system The penal system, incorporating a **reformatory** philosophy, that offered an alternative to the **Auburn system** and **Pennsylvania system.** Reaching the United States in the 1860s, via Australia and Ireland, the Irish system's emphasis on education, trade training, **indeterminate sentencing,** and early release from prison was first put into practice at the **Elmira Reformatory.**

jails Confinement facilities, usually operated by city or county governments, that hold persons awaiting trial and persons convicted of misdemeanors who have received a sentence up to one year (or two years in some jurisdictions). Contrast with state jails, state jail systems, and **prisons.**

jail time The period a defendant spends in jail while awaiting trial and/or sentencing. In some jurisdictions this *jail time* is deducted from the convicted offender's eventual sentence.

joint-venture model A type of prison industry in which the prison contracts with a private company to make that company's product. The public and private sector share control in this model, with the prison usually in charge of items such as organizational structure, wage scales, and inmate hiring. The private sector controls the areas of product design, marketing, and distribution—within the constraints of the governmental-use market area.

judicial reprieve A forerunner to **probation** that allowed a temporary suspension of a sentence while the offender was at liberty in the community.

judicial waiver A procedure that allows a juvenile court judge to waive jurisdiction over a case and transfer it to criminal court.

just deserts As an important aspect of the retributive philosophy, just deserts requires the severity of the punishment to match the seriousness of the offense and the blameworthiness of the offender.

labor for rehabilitation, profit, or punishment Prisoners are put to work as part of their sentence for three reasons. When the goal of the labor is to benefit the prisoner by providing him or her with marketable skills, the work is for purposes of rehabilitation. When the work is used to help make the prison economically self-sustaining, it is labor for profit. When a prisoner's labor is purely punitive in nature and without productive purpose, it is labor for punishment.

laws Along with **folkways** and **mores,** laws provide the norms or guidelines for behavior in society. Of the three, laws are social expectations whose violation result in the most serious and formal reaction or sanctioning by other members of society. A state's criminal code is an example of laws.

laying on file An early form of **recognizance** in which a defendant was allowed to remain at liberty on a promise to appear before the court at any time the judge might request. No sentence was pronounced against the defendant unless the promise to behave was not achieved.

learning disabled (LD) People who are learning disabled have a condition that prevents or significantly hinders them from learning basic skills or information at the same rate as most people of the same age. A learning disability, which does not appear to be the result of low IQ or poor motivation, is sometimes offered as an explanation for some young people's involvement in delinquency.

lease system An **open market** labor system in which a private contractor controls employment, the sale of products, and is in charge of the maintenance and discipline of the inmate workers. The lease system is often considered the most objectionable prison labor system because of the potential and actual abuse of inmates when private individuals control the conditions under which prisoners work.

lex talionis Law of retaliation. This principle requires that a wrongdoer receive the same injury he caused another to suffer. Succinctly stated in the saying "an eye for an eye."

linear facilities In a linear designed jail or prison, inmates are housed in single or multioccupancy cells that are aligned along corridors, which in turn are often stacked in tiers. Contrast with **podular direct.**

Maison de Force See **houses of correction.**

mandatory minimum sentence A broad category of sentencing types that requires judges to impose specific sentences. When the judge is required to impose a prison term (rather than probation or community corrections) for persons convicted of certain felonies, a *mandatory sentence* is being given. When legislation excludes certain offenders from being considered for parole or requires a certain percentage of a prison term to be served, *truth in sentencing* is occurring. **"Three strikes and you're out"** laws are also examples of mandatory minimum sentences.

mandatory sentences See **mandatory minimum sentence.**

mark system A procedure created by Alexander Maconochie at the Norfolk Island penal colony whereby prisoners could earn early release from the penal colony by accumulating "marks" of commendation for good behavior and hard work.

maximum-security prisons Fortress-like structures designed for the fullest possible supervision, control, and surveillance of inmates.

mediation See **victim–offender mediation.**

medical model The orienting philosophy of the **Rehabilitation era.** With a view of the criminal as "sick," the medical model requires that society's response to the offender be examination, diagnosis, and treatment.

medium-security prisons Prison facilities that are typically smaller than **maximum-security prisons,** require a less regimented routine by the inmate, and often have fences with razor wire and electronic sensors rather than walls.

Megan's Law See **public notification law.**

meritorious good time See **good time.**

meta-analysis A comprehensive review of research on a particular topic, such as rehabilitation, that provides an integrative analysis of the findings suggested by those studies.

minimum-security prisons Prison facilities designed without high walls, fences, guard towers, or other obvious security measures. These facilities are used for inmates who show little threat to themselves or others and are therefore being provided opportunities for greater personal freedom.

misdemeanors A type of criminal offense that is less serious than **felonies** but more serious than **petty offenses.** Misdemeanors are typically punishable by a fine and/or up to one year in jail (or up to two years in a few jurisdictions).

mitigating circumstances Events or conditions that make an offense *less* serious than it might otherwise be. When mitigating circumstances, such as the culpability of a younger offender who acted at the urging of older offenders, are present in a crime, juries or judges can often decrease the penalty that would otherwise be applied to the convicted offender. Contrast with **aggravating circumstances.**

mores Along with **folkways** and **laws,** mores provide the norms or guidelines for behavior in society. Of the three, mores are social expectations whose violation result in mid-level reaction or sanctioning by other members of society.

mutilation See **corporal punishment.**

needs level See **classification.**

negative sanction See **sanction.**

neglect response The term used to describe society's initial response to women offenders. During the late seventeenth and early eighteenth centuries, female offenders were often housed with males, but even when women had separate facilities or units, their needs were essentially neglected.

net-widening A situation in which a program has the effect of bringing more people under control of the criminal or juvenile justice system than would otherwise be included. When programs (e.g., electronic monitoring or intensive probation supervision) designed as alternatives to the traditional process (e.g., probation or prison) actually bring more people into the criminal justice system, the *net* has been *widened.*

new crime violation See **probation revocation.**

new generation boot camps Newer versions of **boot camp corrections** programs that retain a military-style structure and strict discipline, but that also have treatment and aftercare components.

new generation jails Jails that use a specific architectural design (podular rather than linear) and inmate supervision (direct rather than intermittent) to provide a safe and secure environment for both inmates and staff. Because of their design and supervision types, new generation jails are also called **podular direct** jails.

nominal doctrine A position that the courts should have a minimal and moderate effect on prison administration rather than the extremes of no involvement under the **hands-off doctrine** or active and intrusive involvement under the **intervention doctrine.**

nonpetitioned case An informal response to a juvenile offender wherein the juvenile admits to the charges against him or her, but no formal charges or petition is filed. See **informal probation.**

norm of reciprocity Refers to the idea that much of economic and social life relies on relationships involving mutual exchanges of goods, services, or obligations between individuals and groups or organizations. It is important to corrections in the sense that punishment is a natural response, or reciprocation, to a wrongful act.

norms The guidelines for behavior in society. Norms not only tell us how we can expect others to behave in different social situations, but they also tell us how we are expected to behave.

objective classification systems Classification procedures and instruments that try to lessen the subjectivity of classification by using a specifically designed instrument and providing precise procedures that corrections personnel can use to decide an inmate's security and treatment needs.

ombudsman An independent official who investigates citizen complaints about abuses by government officials and agencies, including prison officials and prisons.

open market Those types of prison labor systems in which inmate-made products are sold by private companies or by the state to *any* prospective buyer. Contrast with **sheltered market.**

overclassification Occurs when a prisoner is assigned to a level of greater supervision than that person actually needs. Overclassification is undesirable because it means limited resources are not being used effectively, and the inmate is being treated unfairly.

pains of imprisonment Those deprivations and frustrations, such as isolation from family and friends and the absence of personal possessions, that prisoners suffer as a result of confinement.

pardon An act of grace, usually granted by the president (for federal offenses) or a state's governor (for state offenses), that has the effect of releasing offenders from the punishment required for the offense. Additionally, a pardon may release an offender from any **civil disabilities** he or she may have suffered as a result of being convicted of the pardoned offense.

parens patriae A Latin term that is used to describe the government's legal obligation toward the children in its jurisdiction. In its role as the ultimate parent, the state must provide guardianship and protection to its junior citizens.

parole A type of conditional release from prison that requires the prisoner to be under supervision and to abide by certain terms and conditions of parole or be returned to prison.

parole board The administrative body, often appointed by a state's governor, that is empowered to decide if a prisoner shall be released early from prison under the status of **parole.**

parole revocation See **probation revocation.**

Penitentiary era The penal system era lasting from the 1800s to the 1860s that saw a movement away from public punishment in the community via corporal and capital punishment to an increased reliance on punishment through long-term imprisonment in secure institutions.

Pennsylvania system The Pennsylvania system defined one of the two main styles of prison discipline and management from the 1820s to the 1860s. The Pennsylvania system believed correction was best achieved by keeping prisoners separate from each other and requiring them to remain silent.

personal recognizance See **recognizance.**

petty offenses The least serious type of offense. The maximum penalty for a petty offense is typically a fine or short term in jail. Contrast with **felonies** and **misdemeanors.**

piece-price system An **open market** labor system in which the state controls employment and is in charge of the maintenance and discipline of the prisoner workers. The individual products or "pieces" (e.g., brooms, chairs, shoes, etc.) are then given to a private company for a specific "price" per item. The private company controls the sale of the products.

pillory A wooden frame set on a post with holes for the offender's head and hands. In this structure the more serious offenders, such as those committing fraud and cheating, were locked and exposed to public ridicule at best—and rotten vegetables and stones at worst.

play families The peer groups in women's prisons that borrow the structure, terminology, and function of families in the general society.

pluralistic ignorance A situation in which persons underestimate the extent that others share the beliefs and sentiments they themselves hold.

podular direct In a podular designed facility (which can be either a prison or jail), inmates are housed in small units containing about sixteen to thirty rooms or cells. These rooms are often on two levels, so on entering the housing unit (called a *pod* or *module*) one can look across an open area and see two rows of eight to fifteen cells each. Contrast with a **linear facility.**

positive sanction See **sanction.**

preponderance of evidence The burden of proof used in a civil as opposed to a criminal trial. When the judge or jury is asked to decide a civil case on the basis of which side has the preponderance of evidence, they are being asked to determine which side has the most persuasive or impressive evidence. Contrast with **beyond a reasonable doubt.**

presentence investigation (PSI) Prior to sentencing an offender, the judge may have the probation department conduct a presentence investigation into the offender's background and current situation. Generated from that investigation is a *PSI report* that highlights such important aspects of the offender's background and characteristics as family life, education and work history, prior convictions, and physical and mental health. After reading the report, the judge has a better idea of the type of person the offender is and can better determine an appropriate sentence.

presumptive sentencing A contemporary sentencing system that uses the fixed penalty aspect of **determinate sentencing,** but expands on determinate sentencing by adding the *presumption* that there is a relation between a crime and its sentence. Because of that relationship, judges should be handing down similar sentences for similar crimes.

pretrial detention The confinement, usually in jail, of a defendant who has been formally charged but whose case has not yet been adjudicated.

pretrial release A suspect is released from custody into the community for all or part of the time before or during prosecution.

preventive detention The practice of holding an accused person in jail prior to a trial because he or she is considered dangerous to the community.

preventive imprisonment See **preventive detention.**

prison alternatives See **intermediate punishments.**

prison-diversion IPS See **intensive probation supervision.**

prison industry work assignments One of two broad types of work assignments in prisons. Prisoners assigned to prison industry work will likely receive training that allows the offenders to seek skilled labor positions after release from prison. Contrast with **institutional work assignments.**

prisonization The process by which prisoners learn the norms and values of prison life. The term is developed from the concept of *socialization,* which refers to the process by which people in a society learn what is expected of them and what they can expect of others.

Prison Litigation Reform Act Signed into law by President Clinton in 1996, the PLRA has the primary goal of limiting prisoners' ability to complain about their conditions of confinement. The act was deemed necessary because of a perception that inmates were increasingly engaged in litigation for trivial rather than serious purposes.

prison riot A situation that represents the prison officials' loss of control over a large number of prisoners in a sizable area of the prison for a substantial amount of time.

prisons Facilities operated by the state or federal government to house convicted felons from throughout the state or federal government's jurisdiction. **Castle Island** in Massachusetts is often considered America's first prison. Contrast with **jails.**

prison substitutes See **intermediate punishments.**

privatization The involvement, often with a profit-making goal, of private individuals and companies in the management of correctional facilities and programs.

probation A sentence of conditional freedom to the community that places the offender under the supervision of a probation officer and subjects the offender to the possibility of a harsher sentence should the terms and conditions of probation be violated.

probation center See **day reporting center.**

probation-enhancement IPS See **intensive probation supervision.**

probation officer duties Probation officers typically have duties in three general areas. When they are determining an offender's suitability for probation, they are engaged in the *investigation* aspect of the job. When they are identifying an offender's needs and providing access to programs that address those needs, the *service* component of probation is being addressed. Because the probation officers must also notify the court when an offender is not complying with the terms and conditions of probation, the officers also have a *surveillance* role wherein an offender's behavior is monitored.

probation revocation Applies to both **probation** and **parole** and refers to the process by which offenders can be removed from probation or parole because they did not abide by the terms and conditions of that probation or parole. When the revocation is a result of the offender committing a new offense, it is a *new crime violation.* When the revocation is a result of the offender ignoring specific requirements of their terms and conditions (such as failure to maintain employment or school attendance), a *technical violation* has occurred. When probation is revoked, the judge may impose a harsher sentence, like **residential community corrections** or prison. When parole is revoked, the parole board may have the offender returned to prison.

problem-area model A treatment model using classification systems that develop a theory from data. The Adult Internal Management Systems technique used to classify adults in prison is an example of a problem-area model because it draws on existing information to categorize inmates into one of five different types. Treatment staff gain insight into a prisoner's behavior by knowing the *type* into which the prisoner falls. Contrast with **developmental model.**

procedural law A law that identifies the process to be followed when the government interacts with citizens at various stages in the criminal justice process.

progressive reformers Late nineteenth and early twentieth century social reformers who believed government intervention could be used to solve social problems.

proportionality An aspect of **retribution** that believes retaliation should be properly related in degree to the crime that was committed. The philosophy of ***lex talionis*** is said to express proportionality.

proportional retributivism A position taken by retributivists who are against the death penalty (despite its apparent retributive quality) because they believe ***lex talionis*** simply requires the worst crime to be punished with society's worst penalty. If life imprisonment, for example, is the worst penalty society will tolerate, then life imprisonment provides proportional retribution for the most serious crimes.

prosecutorial discretion Refers in general to a prosecutor's ability to decide if charges will be filed in a case and what those charges will be. The term is used in this book more specifically in reference to laws in some jurisdictions that give prosecutors the authority to file certain juvenile cases in either juvenile or criminal court.

PSI report See **presentence investigation (PSI).**

public account system An **open market** labor system in which the state controls employment, the sale of products, and is in charge of the maintenance and discipline of the prisoner workers. Inmates who manufacture items such as furniture, binder twine, and farm machinery and who work in mines are engaged in the public account system.

public notification law A law, like New Jersey's "Megan's Law," requiring that neighbors be notified when a sex offender moves into their neighborhood.

public works and ways system A **sheltered market** labor system in which the state controls employment, the sale of products, and is in charge of the maintenance and discipline of the prisoner workers. Inmates constructing or repairing public buildings, public roads, and public parks are engaged in the public works and ways system.

race For purposes of statistical differentiation, race distinguishes people from each other on the basis of biological or physical characteristics. In this book racial distinctions are most often made with reference to people being white, black, American Indian/Alaska Native, or Asian/Pacific Islander. Contrast with **ethnicity.**

reception and diagnostic centers Separate facilities, or defined sections of other facilities, where newly arrived prisoners are received. At the RDC, information is gathered about the inmate's educational, vocational, social, religious, psychological, medical and dental history, and needs. That information is used by **classification committees** to determine the specific prison to which the inmate will be transferred and to suggest a treatment program and security level appropriate for that prisoner.

reclamation The earliest form of **rehabilitation** whose goal was to rescue wrongdoers from the evil that had overcome them. Offenders were to be reclaimed or brought back to the correct ways of living.

recognizance Also known as *personal recognizance* and *release on recognizance* (ROR). Refers to a type of nonfinancial pretrial release in which the defendant is allowed to stay free in the community as the result of a promise to appear for trial.

reformation Like **rehabilitation,** reformation suggests that punishment can be used to change or correct an offender's behavior. However, reformation does not imply the use of individualized treatment plans or therapy procedures as does rehabilitation.

reformatory A system of prison discipline that was more humanitarian than the **Auburn system** and **Pennsylvania system** and was especially interested in preparing prisoners for their eventual return to the community. Also refers to the institutions in which such a philosophy is followed—the first of which was the **Elmira Reformatory.**

Reformatory era The penal system era lasting from the 1860s to the 1900s in which imprisonment took a more humanitarian approach and incorporated an emphasis on education, training, and preparing the inmate for release to the community.

rehabilitation The punishment philosophy that says punishment's aim is to use a treatment plan and therapy to provide offenders with skills, attitudes, and norms that can enable them to be law-abiding members of the community.

Rehabilitation era The penal system era lasting from the 1930s to the 1970s that saw criminal behavior as a pathological condition requiring the offender to be treated through a **medical model.**

reintegration Correctional programs designed to reintroduce the inmate to the community as a productive and law-abiding citizen.

Religious Freedom Restoration Act Passed by Congress in 1993, the RFRA was a reaction to judicial decision outside the corrections area that some people felt restrained free exercise of religion. The RFRA impacted prisons by giving inmates increased opportunities to file claims that prison rules and regulations were denying the prisoners their First Amendment rights. In a 1997 case unrelated to corrections, the U.S. Supreme Court ruled that RFRA was unconstitutional as it applied to the states, although the federal government (e.g., the Federal Bureau of Prisons) must still abide by the RFRA provisions.

remission A technique for early release from prison that is especially popular in Asia and countries in the Pacific region. Remission reduces a prison sentence mainly on the basis of good behavior.

residential community corrections A more contemporary term for facilities that were called *halfway houses.* These residential facilities allow offenders to live in a structured environment while still having access to work, educational, and treatment opportunities in the community.

restitution A specific sentence, or more often a condition of probation, that requires the offender to compensate the community or the victim for harm that was done. When the compensation is in the form of a money payment, it is financial restitution. When the compensation is in the form of work, it is often called community service.

restoration The punishment philosophy that says punishment's aim is to make the victim and the community whole again by restoring things, as much as possible, to how they were before the crime occurred.

Restorative era A forecasted penalty system that may follow the current **Retributive era.** If the Restorative era does begin, its key ingredient will be a philosophy of **restoration** in which punishment's goal is to make the community and victim whole again.

retribution The punishment philosophy that says punishment is a required response by the state to a wrongful act committed by the offender.

Retributive era The penal system era beginning in the 1970s and continuing to the present time. Key aspects of this era are a **just deserts** philosophy and a **deterrence** objective.

rights-are-lost position An argument that prisoners are wholly without rights except those expressly conferred by law or necessity. Contrast with the **rights-are-retained position.**

rights-are-retained position An argument that prisoners keep all the rights of an ordinary citizen, except those that are expressly or by necessity taken away from them by law. Contrast with the **rights-are-lost position.**

risk level See **classification.**

salient factor score A number falling along a range of zero to ten points that is used to predict an offender's risk of continued criminal behavior. Persons with higher salient factor scores are considered to have a good prognosis for successful parole.

sanction A technique used by society to enforce its norms. Sanctions that encourage continuation of norm-abiding behavior are *positive sanctions* while those that discourage norm-violating behavior are *negative sanctions.* Sanctions are often categorized as being ones that respond to a person's body (*physical sanctions*), financial well-being (*economic sanctions*), or to his or her social setting or psychological well-being (*social/psychological sanctions*). In addition, sanctions are *formal* when they are applied by someone acting in an official capacity and are *informal* when applied by someone acting without official standing.

security threat group Specific designations that prison administrators can assign to prison gangs that are considered especially troublesome. Members of gangs that have been identified as a security threat group can be removed from the general population, reclassified to a higher level, and can effectively be placed in more restrictive confinement.

selection bias A research problem that suggests positive results found during an evaluation of a rehabilitation program may be more accurately explained as the result of highly motivated subjects than of specific aspects of the program itself.

selective incapacitation Under this version of incapacitation, imprisonment is used only for a select group of especially dangerous repeat offenders whose freedom of movement must be restricted to protect society.

sentencing The process of assigning a penalty (a sentence) on a person convicted of a crime. Sentencing is usually accomplished by a judge but in some jurisdictions or cases may be the work of a jury.

sentencing grid See **sentencing guidelines.**

sentencing guidelines A technique used in some jurisdictions to make **determinate sentencing** and **presumptive sentencing** more consistent among judges by providing a *sentencing grid* that directs judges toward a desired punishment. The guidelines found on the grid simply suggest possible sentences to the judge or, in other jurisdictions, require the judge to abide by the guidelines' range.

separate and silent The key words distinguishing the **Pennsylvania system,** which required prisoners to be kept in isolation and to remain silent both day and night.

service See **probation officer duties.**

sex offender registration law Legislation requiring persons convicted of sex offenses to register with local law enforcement agencies on their release from prison or as a condition of probation or conditional release from prison.

sheltered market Those types of prison labor systems in which inmate-made products are produced only for the state's benefit or sold only to state agencies. Contrast with **open market.**

shock incarceration Although sometimes used synonymously with **boot camp corrections,** in this book shock incarceration refers to a *philosophy* that a military regimen with hard work and physical conditioning helps build desirable character traits in offenders.

shock probation Requires a convicted offender to spend a relatively brief time in prison (such as a few months) and then be placed on probation. Presumably the "shock" of imprisonment will encourage the offender to have a more positive probation experience. *Split probation* is essentially the same type of sentence although some use shock probation to refer to the situation in some jurisdictions where the offender is not expecting release from prison (almost "surprise probation"), while split probation is a sentence requiring prison followed by probation.

socialization See **prisonization.**

specific deterrence The version of **deterrence** that seeks to prevent crime by using punishment to show the criminal that the criminal act was undesirable because it brought more pain than pleasure. Contrast with **general deterrence.**

split probation See **shock probation.**

state use system A **sheltered market** labor system in which the state controls employment, the sale of products, and is in charge of the maintenance and discipline of the prisoner workers. Inmates who manufacture furniture, clothing, traffic signs, and license plates are engaged in the state use system.

status offenses Those offenses, such as truancy, running away, and incorrigibility, that would not be crimes if committed by adults, but are offenses for which juveniles can be brought to the attention of juvenile court officials.

statutorily excluding A procedure used in some states by which certain types of juvenile cases can be heard before a criminal court rather than a juvenile court. Minors accused of offenses specified by law (statute) cannot have their cases heard by a juvenile court.

statutory good time See **good time.**

statutory penalty Refers to the penalty (usually a range from minimum to maximum) that legislators set for each crime. When a judge imposes a sentence, that sentence must fall within any minimum or maximum penalty that the legislature has specified for that particular offense.

stocks Somewhat similar to the **pillory,** in this wooden apparatus the culprit sits on a bench with his or her legs (and sometimes hands) outstretched with the ankles (and wrists) locked into holes in the frame.

substantive law A law that defines what is criminal and stipulates a punishment.

supermax prisons Prison facilities that are either a high-custody housing unit within a secure facility or an entire secure facility in which inmates are isolated from the general population and from each other and are typically confined to a single cell for twenty-two to twenty-three hours per day.

supervised mandatory release A type of conditional release that requires inmates to be automatically released to the community when they have completed their maximum prison sentence less any **good time** credit they have earned. Because the full sentence has not been completed, the prisoner's release is conditional and may require supervision in the community. This form of conditional release is especially popular in jurisdictions that have abolished parole release.

surveillance See **probation officer duties.**

suspended sentence Used either to allow the judge to see how well a convicted offender behaves before the judge decides what the sentence will be (a *suspension of imposition* of sentence), or when a formal sentence is imposed but is not served as long as the convicted offender behaves himself (a *suspension of execution* of sentence).

suspension of execution See **suspended sentence.**

suspension of imposition See **suspended sentence.**

systemwide classification The initial version of **classification,** usually occurring at a central location to which all new prisoners are first sent, conducted for the particular purpose of determining to which state facility a prisoner will be assigned.

tariff (or fixed-fine) system A financial penalty type that imposes the same or similar fine amounts on all defendants convicted of a particular offense. Compare with **day fine.**

technical violation See **probation revocation.**

"three strikes and you're out" Based on the belief that more severe punishment should follow subsequent felony convictions, some states have passed mandatory sentencing laws that call an offender "out" (i.e., sentenced to life imprisonment) after a certain number of "strikes" (i.e., prior convictions). The title *three strikes* is commonly used although jurisdictions vary in terms of how many chances or strikes an offender is given.

ticket-of-leave The granting to British transportees an early release from a penal colony. This type of early release became more formal under Sir Walter Crofton's **intermediate system** in which release to the community under ticket-of-leave allowed that "ticket" to be revoked and the offender returned to prison. In its contemporary form the ticket-of-leave is **parole.**

torture The infliction of pain to a person's body or mind. When the pain is inflicted to coerce information from a person, it is *torture for interrogation.* When the pain is inflicted as a penalty for misbehavior, it is *torture for punishment.*

total institution Refers to a place that completely surrounds and contains the lives of the people who work and live there. The prison is a total institution in the sense that every detail of the prisoners' lives is handled within the institution and according to institution rules.

transportation A form of banishment in which the offender is sent to faraway lands often with the requirement that she or he perform labor for private individuals or the government on arrival at the new location. England, for example, transported some of its criminals to both the American colonies and to Australia.

treatment Along with **classification** and **intervention,** treatment of offenders is a key aspect of **rehabilitation.** Treatment typically involves the offender in specific programs, such as substance abuse counseling or vocational training, that will provide the offender with skills, attitudes, and motivation to refrain from future involvement in criminal behavior.

truth-in-sentencing law See **mandatory minimum sentence.**

unconditional release Prisoners receiving an unconditional release from prison have no constraints placed on their movement in the community and are not required to be supervised by a corrections official. Common examples of unconditional release are **expiration of sentence, commutation of sentence,** and **pardon.** Contrast with **conditional release.**

victim compensation Reimbursement to the victim, especially from state-supported compensation programs, for the financial hardship caused by the crime.

victim–offender mediation The aspect of restorative justice in which a neutral party (the mediator) intervenes in order to help the disputants (the victim and the offender) reach an agreement about how best to reconcile the harm done to the victim.

victimology The field of study focusing on the relationship between victims and offenders and the interaction between victims and the criminal justice system, the media, business, and other groups and institutions in society.

vulnerability theory An explanation for the interracial nature of prison rape (black aggressors and white victims) that assumes persons are chosen as rape victims because they appear vulnerable. For example, whites may be seen as vulnerable when they are loners in prison or when they are affiliated with prison gangs that are considered weak and powerless. Compare with **black rage theory.**

Walnut Street Jail Opened in Philadelphia in 1776 to house petty offenders, debtors, and serious offenders. In 1792 a penitentiary house addition was completed for the most hardened criminals. The philosophy of isolation and silence used in the penitentiary house provided the basic ingredients of the **Pennsylvania system.**

Wellspring era The penal system era lasting from the Middle Ages to about 1800 by which contemporary penal philosophies and methods began to take shape.

whipping See **corporal punishment.**

Wickersham Commission The National Commission on Law Observance and Enforcement (named the Wickersham Commission after its head, George Wickersham) was active from 1929–1931 at the request of President Hoover. The commission's 1931 report helped move America's prisons into the Rehabilitation era by calling for the rehabilitation of criminals.

workhouses See **houses of correction.**

workload A method of distributing clients (probationers or parolees) among an agency's probation or parole officers in such a manner that while each officer may have different numbers of clients to supervise, each also has a similar amount of work because some clients need more attention than do others. Contrast with **caseload.**

work release Correctional programs that allow selected prisoners to leave the confines of jail or prison in order to engage in regular employment.

writ of habeas corpus The term commonly used in reference to a written court order (a writ) demanding the person to whom the writ is directed (e.g., the warden of a prison) to show the legality of a prisoner's detention.

REFERENCES

A land of bondage. (1999, 13 February). *The Economist,* pp. 3–4.

A "more palatable" way of killing. (1982, 20 December). *Time,* pp. 28–29.

A new executioner: The needle. (1981, 14 September). *Time,* p. 80.

A quarter-million mentally ill Americans behind bars, study finds. (1999, 11 July). Available: cnn.com/US/9907/11/inmate.mental.health.ap/index.html (Accessed 12 July 1999).

Abadinsky, H. (1994). *Probation and parole: Theory and practice* (6th ed.). Englewood Cliffs, NJ: Prentice Hall.

Abbott, G. (1994). *The book of execution: An encyclopedia of methods of judicial execution.* London: Headline Book Publishing.

Abraham, H. J. (1988). *Freedom and the court* (5th ed.). New York: Oxford University Press.

Aday, R. H. (1994). Golden years behind bars: Special programs and facilities for elderly inmates. *Federal Probation, 58*(2), 47–54.

Adeyemi, A. A. (1994). Personal reparations in Africa: Nigeria and Gambia. In U. Zvekic (Ed.), *Alternatives to imprisonment in comparative perspective* (pp. 53–66). Chicago: Nelson-Hall.

Adler, F., Mueller, G. O. W., and Laufer, W. S. (1994). *Criminal justice.* New York: McGraw-Hill.

Adler, M. (1991). Scotland. In D. van Zyl Smit & F. Dünkel (Eds.), *Imprisonment today and tomorrow: International perspectives on prisoners' rights and prison conditions* (pp. 493–535). Deventer: Kluwer.

Al-Sagheer, M. F. (1994). Diyya legislation in Islamic Shari'a and its application in the Kingdom of Saudi Arabia. In U. Zvekic (Ed.), *Alternatives to imprisonment in comparative perspective* (pp. 80–91). Chicago: Nelson-Hall.

Alabama wants to hitch prisoners to posts. (1999, 15 June). Available: www.apbonline.com/911/1999/06/15/hitch0615_01.html (Accessed 17 June 1999).

Alarid, L. F. (1996). *Woman offenders' perception of confinement: Behavior code acceptance, hustling and group relations in jail and prison.* Unpublished doctoral dissertation, Sam Houston State University, Hunstville, TX.

Alarid, L. F. (1999, 17–20 November). *Understanding women prison subcultures using the case study approach.* Paper presented at the annual meeting of the American Society of Criminology, Toronto, Canada.

Alarid, L. F. (2000). Along racial and gender lines: Jail subcultures in the midst of racial disproportionality. *Corrections Management Quarterly, 41*(1), 8–19.

Alexander, J., & Austin, J. (1992). *Handbook for evaluating objective prison classification systems.* Washington, DC: National Institute of Corrections.

Allen, G. (1995, Spring). The courage of our convictions. *Policy Review, 72,* 4–7.

Allen, M. (1997, November). Boot camps fail to pass muster. *Governing,* pp. 40–41.

American Civil Liberties Union. (1997, 8 August). "Supermax" prisons minimize humanity. Available: www.aclu.org/news/w080897a.html (Accessed 9 November 1999).

American Correctional Association. (1983). *The American prison: From the beginning . . . a pictorial history.* College Park, MD: Author.

American Correctional Association. (1984). *Female classification: An examination of the issues* [NIC Grant #FG-6]. College Park, MD: Author.

American Correctional Association. (1999). *Directory of juvenile and adult correctional departments, institutions, agencies and paroling authorities.* Lanham, MD: Author.

American Friends Service Committee. (1971). *Struggle for justice.* New York: Hill and Wang.

Americas Watch. (1991). *Prison conditions in Mexico* [An Americas Watch Report]. New York: Human Rights Watch.

Amnesty International. (1995). *China death penalty figures* [AI Index: ASA 17/17/95]. London, United Kingdom: Author.

Amnesty International. (1996, 13 August). Iran: Amnesty International appeals against further execution and amputations. Available: www.amnesty.org/news/1996/51303196.htm (Accessed 12 August 1999).

Amnesty International. (1999a, April). Facts and figures on the death penalty. Available: www.amnesty.org/alib/airpub/1999/ACT/A5000299.htm (Accessed 29 July 1999).

Amnesty International. (1999b). Library Index. Available: www.amnesty.org.uk/library/index.html (choose Country Reports or Annual Reports) (Accessed 12 August 1999).

Amnesty International. (1999c, May). The death penalty worldwide: Developments in 1998. Available: www.amnesty.org/ailib/aipub/1999/ACT/A5000499.htm (Accessed 29 July 1999).

Amnesty International—USA. (1999). Killing with prejudice: Race and death penalty in the USA. Available: www.amnesty-usa.org/rightsforall/dp/race/summary.html (Accessed 13 August 1999).

Amnesty International—USA. (1999b). Mothers behind bars. Available: www.amnesty- usa.org/rightsforall/

women/report/women-101.html (Accessed 17 November 1999).

Amnesty International is dead wrong. (1999, 22 May). *New York Post* [Online]. Available: www.nypostonline.com/052299/editorial/8114.htm (Accessed 26 May 1999).

Anderson, J. F. (1999). Is electronic monitoring a successful community supervision method? Yes. In C. B. Fields (Ed.), *Controversial issues in corrections* (pp. 39–46). Needham Heights, MA: Allyn & Bacon.

Applegate, B. K., Cullen, F. T., & Fisher, B. S. (1997). Public support for correctional treatment: The continuing appeal of the rehabilitative ideal. *The Prison Journal, 77*(3), 237–258.

Ariès, P. (1962). *Centuries of childhood: A social history of family life* (R. Baldick, Trans.). New York: Vintage Books.

Armstrong, D. (1999, 22 October). Prison labor—it's not just for license plates anymore. In Fox Market Wire [Online]. Available: foxmarketwire.com/102299/prisoners.sml (Accessed 26 October 1999).

Asia Watch. (1991). *Prison conditions in India* [An Asia Watch Report]. New York: Human Rights Watch.

Auerbach, J. S. (1983). *Justice without law?* New York: Oxford University Press.

Augustus, J. (1972). *John Augustus: First probation officer.* Montclair, NJ: Patterson Smith.

Austin, J., Bloom, B., & Donahue, T. (1992). *Female offenders in the community: An analysis of innovative strategies and programs* [Report prepared by the National Council on Crime and Delinquency]. Washington, DC: National Institute of Corrections.

Aziz, D. W., & Kellam, L. (1998). *New York State DOCS shock incarceration 1999 legislative report* [executive summary]. Albany, NY: Department of Correctional Services.

Baldus, D., Pulaski, C., & Woodworth, G. (1983). Comparative review of death sentences: An empirical study of the Georgia experience. *Journal of Criminal Law and Criminology, 74,* 661–678.

Ball, R. A., Huff, C. R., & Lilly, J. R. (1988). *House arrest and correctional policy: Doing time at home.* Newbury Park, CA: Sage.

Barnes, H. E. (1972). *The story of punishment: A record of man's inhumanity to man* (2nd ed., Revised). Montclair, NJ: Patterson Smith.

Barnes, H. E., & Teeters, N. K. (1943). *New horizons in criminology.* New York: Prentice Hall.

Barnes, H. E., & Teeters, N. K. (1959). *New horizons in criminology* (3rd ed.). Englewood Cliffs, NJ: Prentice Hall.

Barr, T. (1995, 22 November). Boot camp/shock incarceration: Costs and effects on recidivism. Available: www.ncsc.dni.us/is/MEMOS/S95-1798.htm. (Accessed 11 October 1999).

Barry, J. V. (1958). *Alexander Maconochie of Norfolk Island.* Melbourne, Australia: Oxford University Press.

Bartollas, C. (1993). *Juvenile delinquency* (3rd ed.). New York: Macmillan.

Bayley, D. H. (1991). *Forces of order: Policing modern Japan* (2nd ed.). Berkeley: University of California Press.

Bazemore, G. (1998). Crime victims and restorative justice in juvenile courts: Judges as obstacle or leader? *Western Criminology Review* [Online] 1(1). Available: http://wcr.sonoma.edu/v1n1/bazemore.html.

Bazemore, G., & Umbreit, M. (Principal Investigators). (1997, August draft). Participant's module. In *Balanced and restorative justice project.* Washington, DC: Office of Juvenile Justice and Delinquency Prevention.

Beaumont, G. de, & Tocqueville, A. de (1964). *On the penitentiary system in the United States and its application in France.* Carbondale, IL: Southern Illinois University Press.

Beck, A., Gilliard, D., Greenfeld, L., Harlow, C., Hester, T., Jankowski, L., Snell, T., Stephan, J., & Morton, D. (1993). *Survey of state prison inmates, 1991* [NCJ 136949]. Washington, DC: Bureau of Justice Statistics.

Beck, A. J., & Mumola, C. J. (1999). *Prisoners in 1998* [NCJ 175687]. Washington, DC: Bureau of Justice Statistics.

Belbot, B., & del Carmen, R. V. (1993). Legal issues in classification. In American Correctional Association (Ed.), *Classification: A tool for managing today's offenders* (pp. 17–31). Laurel, MD: American Correctional Association.

Belcher, J. (1988). Are jails replacing the mental health system for the homeless mentally ill? *Community Mental Health Journal, 24,* 185–195.

Bilchik, S. (1999a). *1996 National youth gang survey* [NCJ 173964]. Washington, DC: Office of Juvenile Justice and Delinquency Prevention.

Bilchik, S. (1999b). *OJJDP Research: Making a difference for juveniles* [NCJ 177602]. Washington, DC: Office of Juvenile Justice and Delinquency Prevention.

Bishop, N. (1991). Sweden. In D. van Zyl Smit & F. Dünkel (Eds.), *Imprisonment today and tomorrow* (pp. 599–631). Deventer: Kluwer.

Bloom, B. (1993). Incarcerated mothers and their children: Maintaining family ties. In American Correctional Association (Ed.), *Female offenders: Meeting needs of a neglected population* (pp. 60–68). Laurel, MD: American Correctional Association.

Blumberg, M. (1990) *AIDS: The impact on the criminal justice system.* Columbus, OH: Merrill.

Blumstein, A. (1995, August). Violence by young people: Why the deadly nexus? *National Institute of Justice Journal, 229,* 2–9.

Bohm, R. M., Clark, L. J., & Aveni, A. F. (1991). Knowledge and death penalty opinion: A test of the Marshall hypothesis. *Journal of Research in Crime and Delinquency, 28,* 360–387.

Bohm, R. M., Vogel, R. E., & Maisto, A. A. (1993). Knowledge and death penalty opinion: A panel study. *Journal of Criminal Justice, 21,* 29–45.

Bohning, D. (1999, 4 June). Nine hangings in Trinidad end five-year moratorium. *Miami Herald* [Online]. Available: www.herald.com/content/sat/docs/016066 (Accessed 7 June 1999).

Boin, R. A., & van Duin, M. J. (1995). Prison riots as organizational failures: A managerial perspective. *The Prison Journal, 75,* 357–379.

Bonczar, T. (1997). *Characteristics of adults on probation, 1995* [NCJ 1642267]. Washington, DC: Bureau of Justice Statistics.

Bonczar, T. (1999). *Probation and parole data surveys, 1998* [NCJ 178234]. Washington, DC: Bureau of Justice Statistics.

Bonczar, T., & Glaze, L. E. (1999). *Probation and parole in the United States, 1998* [NCJ 178234]. Washington, DC: Bureau of Justice Statistics.

Boritch, H. (1997). *Fallen women: Female crime and criminal justice in Canada.* Toronto: International Thompson Publishing.

Bottomley, A. K. (1990). Parole in transition: A comparative study of origins, developments, and prospects for the 1990s. In M. Tonry & N. Morris (Eds.), *Crime and justice: A review of research; Vol. 12* (pp. 319–374). Chicago: University of Chicago.

Bowker, L. H. (1977). *Prisoner subcultures.* Lexington, MA: Heath.

Bowker, L. H. (1980). *Prison victimization.* New York: Elsevier.

Bragg, R. (1995, 5 November). Aging inmates, empty futures. *The Denver Post,* p. 14A.

Bringham, J. (1984). *Civil liberties and American democracy.* Washington, DC: Congressional Quarterly, Inc.

Bright, C. (1997). Equal protection/discrimination. Available: www.restorativejustice.org/RJ2s_Equal_Protection.htm (Accessed 19 October 1999).

Bright, S. B. (1994). Counsel for the poor: The death sentence not for the worst crime but for the worst lawyer. *Yale Law Journal, 103,* 1835–1883.

Brown, J. M., Langan, P. A., & Levin, D. J. (1999). *Felony sentences in state courts, 1996* [NCJ 173939]. Washington, DC: Bureau of Justice Statistics.

Brunner, M. S. (1993). *National survey of reading programs for incarcerated juvenile offenders* [NCJ 144017]. Washington, DC: Office of Juvenile Justice and Delinquency Prevention.

Bryant, D. (1989). *Communitywide responses crucial for dealing with youth gangs* [NCJ 119465]. Juvenile Justice Bulletin. Washington, DC: Office of Juvenile Justice and Delinquency Prevention.

Bureau of Justice Assistance. (1996). *How to use structured fines (day fines) as an intermediate sanction* [NCJ 156242]. Washington, DC: Bureau of Justice Assistance and the Vera Institute of Justice.

Bureau of Justice Assistance. (1998). *1996 National survey of state sentencing structures* [NCJ 169270]. Washington, DC: Department of Justice.

Bureau of Justice Statistics. (1995). *Correctional populations in the United States* [NCJ 153849]. Washington, DC: Author.

Bureau of Justice Statistics. (1999). *Correctional populations in the United States, 1996* [NCJ 170013]. Washington, DC: Author.

Bureau of Labor Statistics. (1925). *Convict labor in 1923* [Bulletin No. 372]. Washington, DC: Government Printing Office.

Bureau of Prisons. (n.d.). A brief history of Alcatraz. Available: www.bop.gov/alcatraz.html (Accessed 8 November 1999).

Bureau of Prisons. (1990). *State of the bureau 1990.* Washington, DC: Federal Bureau of Prisons.

Bureau of Prisons. (1991). *Facilities 1991.* Washington, DC: Federal Bureau of Prisons.

Bureau of Prisons. (1998). *A profile of female offenders.* Washington, DC: Federal Bureau of Prisons.

Burke, P., & Adams, L. (1991). *Classification of women offenders in state correctional facilities: A handbook for practitioners.* Washington DC: National Institute of Corrections.

Burns, J. C., & Vito, G. F. (1995). An impact analysis of the Alabama boot camp program. *Federal Probation, 59*(1), 63–67.

Burton, V. S., Jr., Cullen, F. T., & Travis, L. F., III. (1987). The collateral consequences of a felony conviction: A national study of state statutes. *Federal Probation, 51*(3), 52–60.

Bushway, S., & Reuter, P. (1997). Labor markets and crime risk factors. In L. W. Sherman, D. Gottfredson, D. MacKenzie, J. Eck, P. Reuter & S. Bushway (Eds.), *Preventing crime: What works, what doesn't, what's promising* (pp. 6-1–6-59 (Chapter 6)). Washington, DC: Office of Justice Programs.

Butler, A. M. (1997). *Gendered justice in the American west: Women prisoners in men's penitentiaries.* Urbana, IL: University of Illinois Press.

Butts, J. A., & Snyder, H. N. (1992). *Restitution and juvenile recidivism* [NCJ 137774]. OJJDP Update on Research. Washington, DC: Office of Juvenile Justice and Delinquency Prevention.

Butts, J. A., & Poe, E. (1993). *Offenders in juvenile court, 1990* [NCJ 113011]. OJJDP Update on Statistics. Washington, DC: Office of Juvenile Justice and Delinquency Prevention.

Cahalan, M. W. (1986). *Historical corrections statistics in the United States, 1850–1984.* Washington, DC: Department of Justice.

Caldwell, R. G. (1947). *Red Hannah: Delaware's whipping post.* Philadelphia, PA: University of Pennsylvania Press.

California Department of Corrections. (1999). Joint venture program. Available: www.cdc.state.ca.us/program/jvppg.htm (Accessed 26 July 1999).

Camp, C. G., & Camp, G. M. (1997). *The corrections yearbook, 1997.* South Salem, NY: Criminal Justice Institute.

Camp, G. M., & Camp, C. G. (1995). *The corrections yearbook, 1995.* (Vol. Juvenile corrections) South Salem, NY: Criminal Justice Institute.

Campbell, J. (1996). McNeil Island work ethic camp: Innovations in boot camp reform. In American Correctional Association (Ed.), *Juvenile and adult boot camps* (pp. 185–199). Lanham, MD: American Correctional Association.

Campbell, L. B. (1991). *An introduction to federal guideline sentencing* [Ju 10.6/2: Se 5]. Washington, DC: Department of Justice.

Campbell, S. A. (1995). Battling sex offenders: Is Megan's Law an effective means of achieving public safety? *Seton Hall Legislative Journal, 19,* 519–632.

Carranza, E., Houved, M., & Mora, L. P. (1994). Release on personal recognizance in Costa Rica: An experimental research study. In U. Zvekic (Ed.), *Alternatives to imprisonment in comparative perspective* (pp. 439–461). Chicago: Nelson-Hall.

Carranza, E., Liverpool, N. J. O., & Rodríguez-Manzanera, L. (1994). Alternatives to imprisonment in Latin America and the Caribbean. In U. Zvekic (Ed.), *Alternatives to imprisonment in comparative perspective* (pp. 384–438). Chicago: Nelson-Hall.

Carroll, L. (1946). *Through the looking-glass and what Alice found there.* New York: Random House.

Carroll, L. (1974). *Hacks, blacks, and cons: Race relations in a maximum security prison.* Lexington, MA: Heath.

Carter, R. M., Robison, J., & Wilkins, L. (1967). *The San Francisco Project: A study of federal probation and parole—final report.* Berkeley, CA: University of California Press.

Cartledge, G. C. (1986). Community service in England/Wales—organization and implementation of community service: An evaluation and assessment of its outcomes. In H. Albrecht & W. Schadler (Eds.), *Community service: A new option in punishing offenders in Europe* (pp. 15–37). Freiburg, Germany: Max Planck Institute.

Caruana, R., & Allanson, D. (1991). Attendance centres. In S. McKillop (Ed.), *Keeping people out of prison* (pp. 189–202). Canberra, Australia: Australian Institute of Criminology.

Castellano, T. C., & Plant, S. M. (1996). Boot camp aftercare programming: Current limits and suggested remedies. In American Correctional Association (Ed.), *Juvenile and adult boot camps* (pp. 233–255). Lanham, MD: American Correctional Association.

Center on Crime, Communities & Culture. (1997, September). Education as crime prevention. In Research Brief, No. 2 [Online]. Available: www.soros.org/crime/research_brief_2.html (Accessed 2 December 1999).

Chain gangs come to Massachusetts. (1999, 16 June). Available: cnn.com/US/9906/16/AM-ChainGants.ap/index.html (Accessed 17 June 1999).

Champion, D. J. (1990). *Probation and parole in the United States.* Columbus, OH: Merrill.

Chaneles, S. (Ed.). (1985). *Prisons and prisoners: Historical documents.* New York: Haworth Press.

Charles, M. T., Kethineni, S., & Thompson, J. L. (1992). The state of jails in America. *Federal Probation, 56*(2), 56–62.

Chase, S. P. (1968). *The complete works of Edward Livingston on criminal jurisprudence.* Montclair, NJ: Patterson Smith. (Original work published in 1873).

Chen, H. H. (1999a, 11 January). The "big house" of the future. Available: www.apbonline.com/safestreets/1999/01/11/fence0111_01.html (Accessed 18 March 1999).

Chen, H. H. (1999b, 5 July). For aging inmates, a place all their own. Available: www.apbonline.com/safestreet/1999/07/05/prison0705_01.html (Accessed 7 July 1999).

Chen, H. H. (1999c, 21 September). Gang girls stake bloody claim to equality. *APB News* [Online]. Available: www.apbnews.com/newscenter/breakingnews/1999/09/21/gangs0921_01.html (Accessed 23 September 1999).

Chesney-Lind, M. (1998, December). The forgotten offender. *Corrections Today,* 66–68, 70, 72–73.

Chesney-Lind, M., & Pollock, J. M. (1995). Women's prisons: Equality with a vengeance. In A. V. Merlo & J. M. Pollock (Eds.), *Women, law, and social control* (pp. 155–175). Boston: Allyn & Bacon.

Christianson, S. (1998). *With liberty for some: 500 years of imprisonment in America.* Boston: Northeastern University Press.

Chute, C. L., & Bell, M. (1956). *Crime, courts, and probation.* New York: Macmillan.

Clark, C. L. (1996). "Sisters are doing it for themselves": Women in correctional boot camps. In American Correctional Association (Ed.), *Juvenile and adult boot camps* (pp. 309–320). Lanham, MD: American Correctional Association.

Clark, C. L., Aziz, D. W., & MacKenzie, D. L. (1994). *Shock incarceration in New York: Focus on treatment* [NCJ 148410]. Program Focus. Washington, DC: National Institute of Justice.

Clark, J., Austin, J., & Henry, D. A. (1997). *"Three strikes and you're out": A review of state legislation* [NCJ 165369]. National Institute of Justice Research in Brief. Washington, DC: Office of Justice Programs.

Clark, J. P. (1989). Conflict management outside the courtrooms of China. In R. Troyer, J. Clark, & D. Rojek (Eds.), *Social control in the People's Republic of China* (pp. 57–69). New York: Praeger.

Clark, P. M. (1995). The evolution of Michigan's community corrections act. *Corrections Today, 57*(1), 38–39, 68.

Clear, T. R., & Cole, G. F. (1994). *American corrections* (3rd. ed.). Belmont, CA: Wadsworth.

Clement, M. J. (1993). Parenting in prison: A national survey of programs for incarcerated woman. *Journal of Offender Rehabilitation, 19,* 89–100.

Clemmer, D. (1958). *The prison community.* New York: Rinehart and Company.

Coffey, O. D., & Gemignani, M. G. (1994). *Effective practices in juvenile correctional education: A study of the literature and research 1980–1992* [NCJ 150066]. Washington, DC: National Office for Social Responsibility.

Cohen, F. (1968). Sentencing, probation, and the rehabilitative ideal: The view from *Mempa v. Rhay. Texas Law Review, 47,* 1–59.

Cohen, F. (1988). The law of prisoner's rights: An overview. *Criminal Law Bulletin, 24,* 321–349.

Cohen, J. (1983). *Incapacitating criminals: Recent research findings* [National Institute of Justice, Research in Brief]. Washington, DC: Department of Justice.

Cohn, A. W., & Ferriter, M. M. (1990). The presentence investigation report: An old saw with new teeth. *Federal Probation, 54*(3), 15–25.

Cole, G. F. (1986). *The American system of criminal justice* (4th ed.). Monterey, CA: Brooks/Cole.

Collins, C. F. (1997). *The imprisonment of African American women.* Jefferson, NC: McFarland & Company.

Collins, W. C. (1993). *Correctional law for the correctional officer* (2nd ed.). Lanham, MD: American Correctional Association.

Collins, W. C., & Grant, D. C. (1998, August). The Prison Litigation Reform Act. *Corrections Today,* 60–62, 160.

Colvin, M. (1992). *The penitentiary in crisis.* Albany: State University of New York Press.

Colvin, M. (1997). *Penitentiaries, reformatories, and chain gangs.* New York: St. Martin's Press.

Conley, J. A. (1980). Prisons, production, and profit: Reconsidering the importance of prison industries. *Journal of Social History, 14,* 257–275.

Conroy, J. (1994, October). New York program succeeding in today's competitive climate. *Corrections Today, 56*(6), 94–96.

Convicts in Australia. (1987). *Australians: A historical atlas* (J. R. Camm & J. McQuilton, Eds.) (pp. 200–201). New South Wales, Australia: Fairfax, Syme & Weldon Associates.

Coordination Group on Women. (1998). *Women in criminal justice.* Washington, DC: Office of Justice Programs.

Corbett, R., & Marx, G. T. (1991). No soul in the new machine: Technofallacies in the electronic monitoring movement. *Justice Quarterly, 8,* 399–414.

Correction Bureau. (1995). *Correctional institutions in Japan 1995.* Tokyo, Japan: Ministry of Justice.

Crawford, C. A. (1994, November). Health care needs in corrections: NIJ responds. *National Institute of Justice Journal,* pp. 31–38.

The criminal law and the criminal procedure law of the People's Republic of China (J. A. Cohen, T. A. Gelatt, & F. M. L. Li, Trans.). (1984). Beijing, China: Foreign Language Press.

Cromwell, P. F., & Killinger, G. G. (1994). *Community-based corrections* (3rd ed.). Minneapolis/St. Paul, MN: West.

Cronin, R. C. (1994). *Boot camps for adult and juvenile offenders: Overview and update* [NCJ 149175]. Washington, DC: National Institute of Justice.

Cullen, F. T. (1986). The privatization of treatment: Prison reform in the 1980s. *Federal Probation, 50*(1), 8–16.

Cullen, F. T., Clark, G. A., & Wozniak, J. F. (1985, June). Explaining the get tough movement: Can the public be blamed? *Federal Probation,* pp. 16–24.

Cullen, F. T., & Gendreau, P. (1989). The effectiveness of correctional rehabilitation: Reconsidering the "nothing works" debate. In L. Goodstein & D. L. MacKenzie (Eds.), *The American prison: Issues in research and policy* (pp. 23–44). New York: Plenum.

Curriden, M. (1995, July). Hard time. *ABA Journal,* pp. 72–75.

D'Amario, A. (1999, 27 July). Salem Witch Museum: Education. Available: www.salemwitchmuseum.com/learn2.html (Accessed 11 August 1999).

Dammer, H. R. (1996). Religion in prison. In M. D. McShane & F. Williams, III (Eds.), *Encyclopedia of American prisons* (pp. 399–402). New York: Garland.

Davis, R. C., Smith, B., & Hillenbrand, S. (1991). Increasing offender compliance with restitution orders. *Judicature, 74*(5), 245–248.

Davis, S. P. (1990). Good time. *Corrections Compendium, 15*(4), 1, 4–11.

Dean, C. W. (1979). The story of Newgate. *Federal Probation, June,* 8–14.

Death Penalty Information Center. (2000, 12 May). Available: www.essential.org/dpic/ (Accessed 18 May 2000).

DeFrances, C. J., & Strom, K. J. (1997). *Juveniles prosecuted in state criminal courts* [NCJ 164265]. Washington, DC: Bureau of Justice Statistics.

deGroot, G. (1997, September). Supreme Court invalidation of RFRA could reduce frivolous litigation by inmates. *On the Line* (a publication of the American Correctional Association), pp. 1–2.

del Carmen, R. V., Ritter, S. E., & Witt, B. A. (1993). *Briefs of leading cases in corrections.* Cincinnati, OH: Anderson.

Department of Justice. (1978). *Capital punishment 1977* [Bulletin SD-NPS-CP-6]. Washington, DC: Author.

Devine, F. E. (1991). *Commercial bail bonding: A comparison of common law alternatives.* New York: Praeger.

Devine, P., Coolbaugh, K., & Jenkins, S. (1998). *Disproportionate minority confinement: Lessons learned from five states* [NCJ 173420]. Washington, DC: Office of Juvenile Justice and Delinquency Prevention.

Dickey, W., & Hollenhorst, P. S. (1998, December). Three-strikes laws: Massive impact in California and Georgia, little elsewhere. *Overcrowded Times, 9*(6), 2–8.

DiIulio, J. J., Jr. (1987). *Governing prisons: A comparative study of correctional management.* New York: The Free Press.

DiIulio, J. J., Jr. (1996, 16 January). Prisons are a bargain by any measure. Available: www.policy.com/issues (Accessed 12 September).

DiIulio, J. J., Jr. (1997). Reinventing parole and probation. *The Brookings Review, 15*(2), 40–42.

DiIulio, J. J., Jr. (1999a, 17 May). Against mandatory minimums. *National Review,* p. 46.

DiIulio, J. J., Jr. (1999b, 12 March). Two million prisoners are enough. *Wall Street Journal,* p. A14 (E).

DiMascio, W. M. (1997). *Seeking justice: Crime and punishment in America.* New York: The Edna McConnell Clark Foundation.

Dingmann, T. (1994, 2 October). Dismas house mixes excons, students. *Albuquerque Journal.*

Dinitz, S. (1987). *Coping with deviant behavior through technology.* Criminal Justice Research Bulletin, vol. 3. Huntsville, TX: Sam Houston State University.

Ditton, P. M. (1999). *Mental health and treatment of inmates and probationers* [NCJ 174463]. Washington, DC: Bureau of Justice Statistics.

Ditton, P. M., & Wilson, D. J. (1999). *Truth in sentencing in state prisons* [NCJ 170032]. Washington, DC: Office of Justice Programs.

Dobash, R. P., Dobash, R. E., & Gutteridge, S. (1986). *The imprisonment of women.* New York: Basil Blackwell.

Dressler, D. (1969). *Practice and theory of probation and parole* (2nd ed.). New York: Columbia University Press.

Drummond, T. (1999, 21 June). Cellblock seniors. *Time.com* [Online] 153(24). Available: www.pathfinder.com/time/magazine/articles/0,3266,26824,00.html (Accessed 1 July 1999).

Duffee, D. E. (1989). *Corrections: Practice and policy.* New York: Random House.

Dünkel, F., & van Zyl Smit, D. (1991). Conclusion. In D. van Zyl Smit & F. Dünkel (Eds.), *Imprisonment today and tomorrow* (pp. 713–743). Deventer: Kluwer.

Dünkel, F., & Rössner, D. (1991). Federal Republic of Germany. In D. van Zyl Smit & F. Dünkel (Eds.), *Imprisonment today and tomorrow* (pp. 203–248). Deventer: Kluwer.

Dunn, S. (1999, 9 May). Offenders bypass service with donations. *Greeley Tribune,* pp. A1, A10.

Durkheim, E. (1964). *The division of labor in society* (G. Simpson, Trans.). New York: Free Press.

Dwyer, D. C., & McNally, R. B. (1993). Public policy, prison industries, and business: An equitable balance for the 1990s. *Federal Probation, 57*(2), 30–36.

Education costs by institution. (1998). Available: www.nefn.com/Content/Needs/educate/edinst.cfm (Accessed 31 October 1999).

Egan, T. (1999, 10 June). Crack's legacy, a special report: In state's anti-drug fight, a renewal for treatment. *New York Times* [Online]. Available: www.nytimes.com (Accessed 10 June 1999).

Ehrlich, I. (1975, June). The deterrent effect of capital punishment: A question of life and death. *American Economic Review,* pp. 397–417.

Eisele, G. T. (1991). The sentencing guidelines system? No. Sentencing guidelines? Yes. *Federal Probation, 55*(4), 20–25.

Ellis, R. E., & Ellis, C. S. (1989). *Theories of criminal justice: A critical reappraisal.* Wolfeboro, NH: Longwood Academic.

Empey, L. T. (1982). *American delinquency: Its meaning and construction* (rev. ed.). Homewood, IL: Dorsey Press.

Endres, M. E. (1991). The death penalty discriminates against the poor. In C. Wekesser (Eds.), *The death penalty: Opposing viewpoints* (pp. 152–155). San Diego, CA: Greenhaven Press.

Erickson, A. (1996, 11 February). Top ten list. Available: www.wco.com/~aerick/ten.htm (Accessed 30 December 1999).

Eriksson, T. (1971). Society and the treatment of offenders. In S. E. Grupp (Ed.), *Theories of punishment* (pp. 264–270). Bloomington, IN: Indiana University Press.

Eriksson, T. (1976). *The reformers: An historical survey of pioneer experiments in the treatment of criminals* (C. Djurklou, Trans.). New York: Elsevier.

Erwin, B. S. (1990). Old and new tools for the modern probation officer. *Crime and Delinquency, 36,* 61–74.

Erwin, B. S., & Bennett, L. (1987). *New dimensions in probation: Georgia's experience with intensive probation supervision (IPS).* Research in Brief. Washington, DC: National Institute of Justice.

Eskridge, C. W., & Newbold, G. (1993). Corrections in New Zealand. *Federal Probation, 57*(3), 59–66.

Espy, M. W., Jr. (1980). Capital punishment and deterrence: What the statistics cannot show. *Crime and Delinquency, 26,* 537–544.

Ethridge, P. A., & Marquart, J. W. (1993). Private prisons in Texas: The new penology for profit. *Justice Quarterly, 10,* 29–48.

Facing up to murder. (1999, 6 June). *Sydney (Australia) Morning Herald* [Online]. Available: www.smh.com.au/news/9906/02/text/features5.html (Accessed 8 June 1999).

Fairchild, E. S. (1993). *Comparative criminal justice systems.* Belmont, CA: Wadsworth.

Farrington, K. (1992). The modern prison as total institution? Public perception versus objective reality. *Crime & Delinquency, 38,* 6–26.

Faugeron, C. (1991). France. In D. van Zyl Smit & F. Dünkel (Eds.), *Imprisonment today and tomorrow* (pp. 249–278). Deventer: Kluwer.

Feeley, M. M. (1991). *The privatization of prisons in historical perspective* [Criminal Justice Research Bulletin]. Huntsville, TX: Sam Houston State University.

Feinman, C. (1986). *Women in the criminal justice system* (2nd ed.). New York: Praeger.

Felkenes, G. T. (1989). Courts, sentencing, and the death penalty in the PRC. In R. J. Troyer, J. P. Clark, & D. G. Rojek (Eds.), *Social control in the People's Republic of China* (pp. 141–158). New York: Praeger.

Fellner, J., & Mauer, M. (1998a). *Losing the vote: The impact of felony disenfranchisement laws in the United States.* Washington, DC: The Sentencing Project.

Fellner, J., & Mauer, M. (1998b, October). Nearly 4 million Americans denied vote because of felony convictions. *Overcrowded Times,* pp. 1, 6–13.

Ferdico, J. N. (1996). *Criminal procedure for the criminal justice professional* (6th ed.). St. Paul, MN: West.

Ferri, E. (1898). *Criminal sociology.* New York: D. Appleton and Company.

Field, G. (1998, February). Continuity of offender treatment: Institution ot the community. Available: www.whitehousedrugpolicy.gov/treat/consensus/field.pdf (Accessed 30 December 1999).

Finley, B. (1999, 18 June). Prison's perimeter blasted as inhumane. *The Denver Post,* p. 4B.

Finn, P. (1997). *Sex offender community notification* [NCJ 162364]. Research in Action. Washington, DC: National Institute of Justice.

Finn, P. (1998). *Chicago's Safer Foundation: A road back for ex-offenders* [NCJ 167575]. Program Focus. Washington, DC: Office of Correctional Evaluation.

Finn, P. (1999a, July). Job placement for offenders: A promising approach to reducing recidivism and correctional costs. *National Institute of Justice Journal,* pp. 2–11.

Finn, P. (1999b). *Washington State's correctional clearinghouse: A comprehensive approach to offender employment* [NCJ 174441]. Program Focus. Washington, DC: National Institute of Justice.

Five Percent Nation. (1999). Available: www.altculture.com/aentries/f/fivexperce.html (Accessed 3 December 1999).

Fletcher, M. A. (1999, 24 February). States working hard to get felons back into polling booths. *SFGate* [Online]. Available: www.sfgate.com/cgi-bin/article.cgi?file=/chronicle/archive/1999/02/24/MN8144DTL (Accessed 11 December 1999).

Florida brings back chain gangs to jangle of criticism. (1995, 21 November). *The Denver Post,* p. 7A.

Fogel, D. (1975). *We are the living proof: The justice model for corrections.* Cincinnati: Anderson.

Fong, R. S. (1990). The organizational structure of prison gangs: A Texas case study. *Federal Probation, 54*(1), 36–43.

Fortune, E. P., & Balbach, M. (1992). Project Met: A community based educational program for women offenders. In I. Moyer (Ed.), *The changing roles of women in the criminal justice system* (2nd ed., pp. 113–129). Prospect Heights, IL: Waveland.

Fox, V. B. (1971). Why prisoners riot. *Federal Probation, 35*(1), 9–14.

Fox, V. B., & Stinchcomb, J. B. (1994). *Introduction to corrections* (4th ed.). Englewood Cliffs, NJ: Prentice Hall.

Fox, V. B., & Stinchcomb, J. B. (1999). *Introduction to corrections* (5th ed.). Englewood Cliffs, NJ: Prentice Hall.

Freedberg, S. P. (1999, 4 July). Freed from death row. *St. Petersburg Times* [Online]. Available: www.sptimes.com/News/70499/news_pf/State/Freed_from_death_row.shtml (Accessed 12 July 1999).

Freedman, E. B. (1974). Their sisters' keepers: An historical perspective on female correctional institutions in the United States: 1870–1900. *Feminist Studies, 2,* 77–95.

Freedman, E. B. (1981). *Their sisters' keepers.* Ann Arbor, MI: University of Michigan Press.

French, H. W. (1997, 25 January). Ghana girls enslaved to atone for family crimes. *The Denver Post,* p. 26A.

Friedman, L. M. (1993). *Crime and punishment in American history.* New York: Basic Books.

Friel, C. M., Vaughn, J., & del Carmen, R. (1987). *Electronic monitoring and correctional policy: The technology and its application.* Research Report. Washington, DC: National Institute of Justice.

Funke, G. S., Wayson, B. L., & Miller, N. (1982). *Assets and liabilities of correctional industries.* Lexington, MA: Lexington Books.

Gallo, E. (1995). The penal system in France: From correctionalism to managerialism. In V. Ruggiero, M. Ryan, & J. Sim (Eds.), *Western European penal systems: A critical anatomy* (pp. 71–92). Thousand Oaks, CA: Sage.

Gazis-Sax, J. (1997). American Siberia: The purpose of Alcatraz. Available: www.alsirat.com/alcatraz/purpose.html (Accessed 10 November 1999).

Geddes, C. (1998). *Mini-digest of education statistics 1997* [NCES 98-020]. Washington, DC: Office of Educational Research and Improvement.

Gemignani, R. J. (1994). *Juvenile correctional education: A time for change* [NCJ 150309]. OJJDP Update on Research. Washington, DC: Office of Juvenile Justice and Delinquency Prevention.

Gendreau, P., & Paporozzi, M. A. (1995, February). Examining what works in community corrections. *Corrections Today,* pp. 28–30.

Gendreau, P., & Ross, R. R. (1987). Revivication of rehabilitation: Evidence from the 1980s. *Justice Quarterly, 4,* 349–408.

Gerety, P. (1980). French program to reduce pretrial detention—*contrôle judiciaire. Crime and Delinquency, 26,* 22–34.

Gill, H. B. (1931). The prison labor problem. *The Annals, 157,* 83–101.

Gillespie, L. K. (1997). *Dancehall ladies.* Lanham, MD: University Press of America.

Gilliard, D. K. (1999). *Prison and jail inmates at midyear 1998* [NCJ 173414]. Washington, DC: Office of Justice Programs.

Gilliard, D. K., & Beck, A. J. (1994). *Prisoners in 1993* [NCJ 147036]. Washington, DC: Bureau of Justice Statistics.

Giménez-Salinas i Colomer, E. (1991). Spain. In D. van Zyl Smit & F. Dünkel (Eds.), *Imprisonment today and tomorrow* (pp. 567–598). Deventer: Kluwer.

Glueck, S. (1928). Principles of a rational penal code. *Harvard Law Review, 41,* 453–482.

Goffman, E. (1961). *Asylums: Essays on the social situation of mental patients and other inmates.* Garden City, NY: Anchor.

Goldberg, S. (1991). The death penalty deters murder. In C. Wekesser (Ed.), *The death penalty: Opposing viewpoints* (pp. 113–118). San Diego, CA: Greenhaven Press.

Goldfarb, R. L., & Singer, L. R. (1973). *After conviction.* New York: Simon & Schuster.

Gottfredson, S., & Taylor, R. (1984). Public policy and prison populations: Measuring opinions about reform. *Judicature, 68,* 190–201.

Gowdy, V. B. (n.d.). *Intermediate sanctions* [NCJ 140540]. Research in Brief. Washington, DC: National Institute of Justice.

Gowdy, V. B. (1996). Historical Prespective. In D. L. MacKenzie & E. E. Herbert (Eds.), *Correctional boot camps: A tough intermediate sanction* (Chapter 1). Washington, DC: National Institute of Justice.

Green, A. S. (1999, 15 April). Appeals court oks city's restrictions on suspects. *The Oregonian* [Online]. Available: www.oregonlive.com/news/99/04/st041509.html (Accessed 23 July 1999).

Greenberg, D. F. (1977). The correctional effects of corrections: A survey of evaluations. In D. F. Greenberg (Ed.), *Corrections and punishment* (pp. 111–148). Beverly Hills, CA: Sage.

Greene, J. (1992). The Staten Island day-fine experiment. In D. C. McDonald, J. Greene, & C. Worzella (Eds.), *Day fines in American courts: The Staten Island and Milwaukee experiments* (pp. 11–57). Washington, DC: National Institute of Justice.

Greenfeld, L. A., & Smith, S. K. (1999). *American Indians and crime* [NCJ 173386]. Washington, DC: Bureau of Justice Statistics.

Greenfeld, L. A., & Snell, T. L. (1999) *Woman offenders* [NCJ 175688]. Special Report. Washington, DC: Bureau of Justice Statistics.

Greenhouse, L. (2000, 19 January). Justices allow segregation of inmates with H.I.V. *New York Times* [Online]. Available: www.nytimes.com (Accessed 19 January 2000).

Grieser, R. C. (1989). Do correctional industries adversely impact the private sector? *Federal Probation, 53*(1), 18–24.

Griffin, P., Torbet, P., & Szymanksi, L. (1998). *Trying juveniles as adults in criminal court: An analysis of state transfer provisions* [NCJ 172836]. Washington, DC: Office of Justice Programs, Office of Juvenile Justice and Delinquency Prevention.

Griffiths, C. T., & Verdun-Jones, S. N. (1994). *Canadian criminal justice* (2nd ed.). Toronto, Canada: Harcourt Brace & Company.

Griswold, H. J., Misenheimer, M., Powers, A., & Tromanhauser, E. (Eds.). (1970). *An eye for an eye.* New York: Holt, Rinehart and Winston.

Haigler, K. O., Harlo, C., O'Connor, P., & Campbell, A. (1996, 11 December). Executive summary of literacy behind prison walls: Profiles of the prison population from the National Adult Literacy Survey. Available: nces.ed.gov/naal/naal92/PrisonSum.html (Accessed 2 December 1999).

Hamilton, M. A. (1998, October). ASCA survey results: Religious Freedom Restoration Act. Available: www.marcihamilton.com/rlpa/asca.html (Accessed 22 December 1999).

Hammett, T. M., Harmon, P., & Maruschak, L. M. (1999). *1996–1997 update: HIV/AIDS, STDs, and TB in correctional facilities* [NCJ 176344]. Washington, DC: National Institute of Justice.

Hanson, R. A., & Daley, H. W. (1995). *Challenging the conditions of prisons and jails: A report on Section 1983 litigations* [NCJ 151652]. Discussion Paper. Washington, DC: Bureau of Justice Statistics.

Harlow, C. W. (1998). *Profile of jail inmates 1996* [NCJ 164620]. Washington, DC: Bureau of Justice Statistics.

Harlow, C. W. (1999). *Prior abuse reported by inmates and probationers* [NCJ 172879]. Washington, DC: Bureau of Justice Statistics.

Harrington, J. (1999, 11 February). Work of Protess, students free death row inmate. *Northwestern Observer* [Online]. Available: www.nwu.edu/univ- relations/ media/observer/category/1998–99 (Accessed 16 December 1999).

Hassine, V. (1999). *Life without parole: Living in prison today* (2nd ed.). Los Angeles, CA: Roxbury Publishing Company.

Hawes, J. M. (1971). *Children in urban society: Juvenile delinquency in nineteenth century America*. New York: Oxford University Press.

Hawkins, R., & Alpert, G. P. (1989). *American prison systems: Punishment and justice.* Englewood Cliffs, NJ: Prentice Hall.

Healy, W. (1915). *The individual delinquent.* Boston: Little, Brown & Company.

Henry, D. A. (1991). Pretrial services: Today and yesterday. *Federal Probation, 55*(2), 54–62.

Hillman, H. (1993). The possible pain experienced during execution by different methods. *Perception, 22,* 745–753.

Hillsman, S. T. (1990). Fines and day fines. In M. Tonry & N. Morris (Eds.), *Crime and justice: A review of research* (Vol. 12, pp. 49–98). Chicago: University of Chicago Press.

Hillsman, S. T., Mahoney, B., Cole, G. F., & Auchter, B. (1987). *Fines as criminal sanctions* [Research in Brief]. Washington, DC: National Institute of Justice.

Hinckeldey, C. (Ed.). (1993). *Criminal justice through the ages* (J. Fosberry, Trans.). Rothenburg o.d.T., Germany: Mittelalterliches Kriminalmuseum.

Hindus, M. S. (1980). *Prison and plantation: Crime, justice, and authority in Massachusetts and South Carolina, 1767–1878.* Chapel Hill, NC: University of North Carolina Press.

Hirsch, A. J. (1992). *The rise of the penitentiary: Prisons and punishments in early America.* New Haven, CT: Yale University Press.

Hodges, J., Giuliotti, N., & Porpotage, F. M. (1994). *Improving literacy skills of juvenile detainees* [NCJ 150707]. Juvenile Justice Bulletin. Washington, DC: Office of Juvenile Justice and Delinquency Prevention.

Hoefer, F. (1937). Georg Michael von Obermaier—A pioneer in reformatory procedures. *Journal of criminal law and criminology, 28,* 13–51.

Hofer, P. J., & Meierhoefer, B. S. (1987). *Home confinement: An evolving sanction in the federal criminal justice system.* Washington, DC: Federal Judicial Center.

Hoffman, P. B. (1994). Twenty years of operational use of a risk prediction instrument: The United States Parole Commission's Salient Factor Score. *Journal of Criminal Justice, 22*(6), 477–494.

House of Representatives. (1887). *Report of the Secretary of the Interior* [Serial Set 2470; Ex. Doc. 1, Pt. 5, Vol. 5] (49th Cong. 2d sess.). Washington, DC: Government Printing Office.

House of Representatives. (1906). *Twentieth annual report of the Commissioner of Labor. 1905* [Serial Set 5046; Doc. No. 906] (59th Cong. 1st sess.). Washington, DC: Government Printing Office.

Hudson, J., & Galaway, B. (1990). Community service: Toward program definition. *Federal Probation, 54*(2), 3–9.

Huff, C. R. (1995). Youth gangs and public policy. In P. M. Sharp & B. W. Hancock (Eds.), *Juvenile delinquency: Historical, theoretical, and societal reactions to youth* (pp. 457–466). Englewood Cliffs, NJ: Prentice Hall.

Hughes, R. (1987). *The fatal shore.* New York: Alfred A. Knopf.

Human Rights Watch. (1993). *The Human Rights Watch global report on prisons.* New York: Author.

Human Rights Watch/Asia. (1995). *Prison conditions in Japan.* New York: Human Rights Watch.

Hurst, H., & McHardy, L. W. (1991). Juvenile justice and the blind lady. *Federal Probation, 55*(2), 63–68.

Immarigeon, R. (1986, Fall). Surveys reveal broad support for alternative sentencing. *Journal (The National Prison Project)*, pp. 1–4.

Immarigeon, R. (1995). *What works?* [Pull-out found in *Corrections Today,* December 1995]. Laurel, MD: American Correctional Association.

Immarigeon, R., & Chesney-Lind, M. (1992). *Women's prisons: Overcrowded and overused.* San Francisco, CA: National Council on Crime and Delinquency.

Inciardi, J. A. (1993). *Criminal justice* (4th ed.). Fort Worth, TX: Harcourt Brace College Publishers.

Ingley, G. S., & Cochran, M. E. (1999, October). Ruinous or fair competition? *Corrections Today,* pp. 82–85, 98,100.

Inmate outfits get old-fashioned look. (1999, 25 September). *The Denver Post,* p. 20A.

Irwin, D. (Producer). (1993, September 24). *The great prison pastime* [20/20 broadcast]. New York: American Broadcasting Company.

Irwin, J. (1980). *Prisons in turmoil.* Boston: Little, Brown & Company.

Irwin, J., & Cressey, D. (1962). Thieves, convicts and the inmate culture. *Social Problems, 10,* 142–155.

Isokoff, M. (1995, 6 November). Crack, coke, and race. *Newsweek,* p. 77.

Ives, G. (1914/1970). *A history of penal methods: Criminals, witches, lunatics.* Reprint Series in Criminology, Law Enforcement, and Social Problems. Montclair, NJ: Patterson Smith.

Jackson, P. G., & Stearns, C. A. (1995). Gender issues in the new generation jail. *The Prison Journal, 75,* 203–221.

Jacobs, J. B. (1976). Stratification and conflict among prison inmates. *Journal of Criminal Law and Criminology, 66,* 476–482.

Jacobs, J. B. (1977). *Stateville: The penitentiary in mass society.* Chicago: University of Chicago Press.

Jepson, J. (1991). Denmark. In D. van Zyl Smit & F. Dünkel (Eds.), *Imprisonment today and tomorrow* (pp. 99–160). Deventer: Kluwer.

Johnson, C., Webster, B., & Connors, E. (1995). *Prosecuting gangs: A national assessment* [NCJ 151785]. Research in Brief. Washington, DC: Federal Judicial Center.

Johnson, M. T., & Gilbert, S. A. (1997). *The U.S. sentencing guidelines: Results of the federal judicial center's 1996 survey.* Washington DC: Federal Judicial Center.

Johnson, R. (1997). Race, gender, and the American prison: Historical observations. In J. M. Pollock (Ed.), *Prisons: Today and tomorrow* (pp. 26–51). Gaithersburg, MD: Aspen.

Johnston, N. (1973). *The human cage: A brief history of prison architecture.* Philadelphia: American Foundation, Inc.

Joseph, P., & Carton, S. (1992). The law of the federation: Images of law, lawyers, and the legal system in "Star Trek: The Next Generation." *University of Toledo Law Review, 24,* 43–85.

Judge gets grandmother to whip offender. (1995, 25 September). *The New York Times,* pp. A, 11:1.

Kalfrin, V. (1999, 21 September). Girls chase boys in lives of crime. *APB News* [Online]. Available: www.apbnews.com/newscenter/breakingnews/1999/09/21/juveniles0921_01.html (Accessed 23 September 1999).

Kamiski, M. M., & Gibbons, D. C. (1994). Prison subculture in Poland. *Crime & Delinquency, 40,* 105–119.

Karmen, A. (1990). *Crime victims: An introduction to victimology* (2nd ed.). Pacific Grove, CA: Brooks/Cole.

Katz, J. (1988). *The seductions of crime: Moral and sensual attractions in doing evil.* New York: Basic Books.

Kelk, C. (1991). The Netherlands. In D. van Zyl Smit & F. Dünkel (Eds.), *Imprisonment today and tomorrow* (pp. 393–427). Deventer: Kluwer.

Kelly, D. (1991). Have victim reforms gone too far—or not far enough? *Criminal Justice, 6,* 22–38.

Kilpatrick, D. G., Beatty, D., & Howley, S. S. (1998). *The rights of crime victims—does legal protection make a difference?* [NCJ 173839]. Research in Brief. Washington, DC: National Institute of Justice.

Kittrie, N. (1971). *The right to be different: Deviance and enforced therapy.* New York: Penguin Books.

Klein, A. (1998, May). Andy Klein's letter. *National Bulletin on Domestic Violence Prevention* [Online]. Available: www.quinlan.com/dvp/andy/andy0598.html (Accessed 17 August 1999).

Krainz, K. W. (1991). Austria. In D. van Zyl Smit & F. Dünkel (Eds.), *Imprisonment today and tomorrow* (pp. 1–28). Deventer: Kluwer.

Krane, J. (1999a, 12 April). Demographic revolution rocks U.S. prisons. Available: www.apbnews.com/cjsystem/behind_bars/oldprisoners/mainpris0412.html (Accessed 29 November 1999).

Krane, J. (1999b, 12 April). Should elderly convicts be kept in prison? Available: www.apbnews.com/cjsystem/behind_bars/oldprisoners/riskcost0412.html (Accessed 29 November 1999).

Krane, J. (1999c, 20 August). Crowded prisons, plummeting crime rates. Available: www.apbnews.com/cjsystem/behind_bars/1999/08/20/prison0820_01.html (Accessed 18 October 1999).

Krisberg, B., Austin, J. (1978). *The children of Ishmeal: Critical perspective on juvenile justice.* Palo Alto: Mayfield.

Krisberg, B., Currie, E., & Onek, D. (1995). Graduated sanctions for serious, violent, and chronic juvenile offenders. In J. C. Howell (Ed.), *Guide for implementing the comprehensive strategy for serious, violent, and chronic juvenile offender* [NCJ 153681] (pp. 133–187). Washington, DC: Office of Juvenile Justice and Delinquency Prevention.

Krisberg, B., & DeComo, R. (1993). *Juveniles taken into custody: Fiscal year 1991 report* [NCJ 145746]. Washington, DC: Office of Juvenile Justice and Delinquency Prevention.

Krisberg, B., Rodriguez, O., Bakke, A., Newenfeldt, D., & Steel, P. (1994). *Juvenile intensive supervision: An assessment* [NCJ 150064]. Washington, DC: Office of Juvenile Justice and Delinquency Prevention.

Kronenwetter, M. (1993). *Capital punishment: A reference handbook.* Santa Barbara, CA: ABC-CLIO.

Kruttschnitt, C., & Krmpotich, S. (1990). Aggressive behavior among female inmates: An exploratory study. *Justice Quarterly, 7,* 371–389.

Kurki, L. (1999). *Incorporating restorative and community justice into American sentencing and corrections* [NCJ 175723]. Issues for the 21st Century. Washington, DC: National Institute of Justice.

Kurshan, N. (n.d.). Women and imprisonment in the U.S. Available: www.prisonactivist.org/women-and-imprisonment.html (Accessed 25 October 1999).

Lacayo, R. (1995, 4 September). The real hard cell. *Time,* pp. 31–32.

Lane, G. (1999, 28 August). State to test satellite-based tracking of parolees. *The Denver Post,* pp. 1A, 11A.

Langbein, J. H. (1978). Torture and plea bargaining. *The University of Chicago Law Review, 46,* 3–22.

Latessa, E. J., & Travis, L. F. (1992). Residential community correctional programs. In J. M. Byrne, A. J. Lurigio, & J. Petersilia (Eds.), *Smart sentencing: The emergence of intermediate sanctions* (pp. 166–181). Newbury Park, CA: Sage.

Laurence, J. (1960). *A history of capital punishment.* New York: The Citadel Press.

Lawrence, R., & Mahan, S. (1998). Women corrections officers in men's prisons: Acceptance and perceived job performance. *Woman & Criminal Justice, 9*(3), 63–86.

Leander, K. (1995). The normalization of Swedish prisons. In V. Ruggiero, M. Ryan, & J. Sim (Eds.), *Western European penal systems: A critical anatomy* (pp. 169–193). Thousand Oaks, CA: Sage.

'Lectric law library. (1999). Inmate's frivolous legal actions. Available: www.lectlaw.com/files/fun30.htm (Accessed 13 December 1999).

Lee, K. R., Cole, B., & Buchele, J. P. (1998, January/February). A look at the Shawnee County pretrial release program. *American Jails,* pp. 25–30.

Legislation has mixed effect on petitions. (1999, April). *The Third Branch* [Online] 31(4). Available: www.uscourts.gov/ttb/apr99ttb/petition.htm (Accessed 22 December 1999).

Lehmann, D. J. (1999, 12 March). Porter cleared of '82 murders. *Chicago Sun-Times,* p. 8.

Lehtinen, M. W. (1978). Technological incapacitation: A neglected alternative. *Quarterly Journal of Corrections, 2*(1), 31–38.

Lepp, A. W. (1990). Note, the death penalty in late imperial, modern, and post-Tiananmen China. *Michigan Journal of International Law, 11,* 987–1038.

Leslie, L. M. (1999, 24 July). "John School" targets prostitution problem. *Minneapolis-St. Paul Star Tribune* [Online]. Available: www.startribune.com (accessed 30 July 1999).

Levinson, A. (1995, 24 September). "Three strikes" laws not used. *The Denver Post,* pp. 31A–32A.

Lewis, C. S. (1971). The humanitarian theory of punishment. In S. E. Grupp (Ed.), *Theories of punishment* (pp. 301–308). Bloomington, IN: Indiana University Press.

Lilly, J. R. (1993). Electronic monitoring in the U.S.: An update. *Overcrowded Times, 4*(5), 4, 15.

Lipton, D., Martinson, R., & Wilks, J. (1975). *The effectiveness of correctional treatment.* New York: Praeger.

Lipton, D. S. (1995). *The effectiveness of treatment for drug abusers under criminal justice supervision* [NCJ 157642]. Research Report. Washington, DC: National Institute of Justice.

Lockwood, D. (1980). *Prison sexual violence.* New York: Elsevier.

Logan, C. H. (1990). *Private prisons: Cons and pros.* New York: Oxford University Press.

Logan, C. H., & Gaes, G. G. (1993). Meta-analysis and the rehabilitation of punishment. *Justice Quarterly, 10,* 245–263.

Lombardo, L. X. (1981). *Guards imprisoned: Correctional officers at work.* New York: Elsevier.

Long, H. T. S. (1998). The "inequability" of incarceration. *Columbia Journal of Law and Social Problems, 31*(¾), 321–353.

Lurigio, A. J., Olson, D. E., & Swartz, J. A. (1998). Chicago day-reporting center reduces pretrial detention, drug use, and absconding. *Overcrowded Times, 9*(3), 1, 6–9.

Lurigio, A. J., & Petersilia, J. (1992). The emergence of intensive probation supervision programs in the United States. In J. M. Byrne, A. J. Lurigio, & J. Petersilia (Eds.), *Smart sentencing: the emergence of intermediate sanctions* (pp. 3–17). Newbury Park, CA: Sage.

MacCormick, A. H. (1926). "Send them up"—to what? *The Survey, 55*(11), 598–601, 634.

MacKenzie, D. L. (1989). Prison classification: The management and psychological perspectives. In L. Goodstein & D. L. MacKenzier (Eds.), *The American prison: Issues in research and policy* (pp. 163–189). New York: Plenum Press.

MacKenzie, D. L. (1993, November). Boot camp prisons in 1993. *National Institute of Justice Journal, #227,* 21–28.

MacKenzie, D. L. (1994). Up to speed—results of a multisite study of boot camp prisons. *Federal Probation, 58*(2), 60–66.

MacKenzie, D. L. (1997). Criminal justice and crime prevention. In L. W. Sherman, D. Gottfredson, D. MacKenzie, J. Eck, P. Reuter, & S. Bushway (Eds.), *Preventing crime: What works, what doesn't, what's promising* (pp. 9-1–9-76 (Chapter 9)). Washington, DC: Office of Justice Programs.

MacKenzie, D. L., Brame, R., McDowall, D., & Souryal, C. (1995). Boot camp prisons and recidivism in eight states. *Criminology, 33,* 327–357.

MacKenzie, D. L., Elis, L. A., Simpson, S. S., & Skroban, S. B. (1996). Boot camps as an alternative for women. In D. L. MacKenzie & E. E. Herbert (Eds.), *Correctional boot camps: A tough intermediate sanction* (pp. 233–244). Washington, DC: National Institute of Justice.

MacKenzie, D. L., & Souryal, C. (1994). *Multisite evaluation of shock incarcerations* [NCJ 142462]. Research Report. Washington, DC: National Institute of Justice.

MacKenzie, L. R. (1999). *Residential placement of adjudicated youth, 1987–1996* [FS 99117]. OJJDP Fact Sheet. Washington, DC: Office of Juvenile Justice and Delinquency Prevention.

MacNamara, D. E. J. (1977). The medical model in corrections: *requiescat in pace*. *Criminology, 14,* 439–448.

Maestro, M. (1973). *Cesare Beccaria and the origins of penal reform.* Philadelphia: Temple University Press.

Maguire, K., & Pastore, A. L. (Eds.). (1994). *Sourcebook of criminal justice statistics—1993* [NCJ 148211]. Washington, DC: Bureau of Justice Statistics.

Maguire, K., & Pastore, A. L. (Eds.). (1995). *Sourcebook of criminal justice statistice—1994* [NCJ 2154591]. Washington, DC: Bureau of Justice Statistics.

Maguire, K., & Pastore, A. L. (Eds.). (1998). *Sourcebook of criminal justice statistics 1997* [NCJ 171147]. Washington, DC: Department of Justice, Bureau of Justice Statistics.

Mahan, S. (1984). Imposition of espair—an ethnography of women in prison. *Justice Quarterly, 1,* 357–383.

Mair, G. (1993). Day centres in England and Wales. *Overcrowded Times, 4*(2), 5–7.

Manville, D. E. (1986). *Prisoners' self-help litigation manual* (Rvsd 2nd ed.). New York: Oceana.

Marcus-Mendoza, S. T., Klein-Saffran, J., & Lutze, F. (1998). A feminist examination of boot camp prison programs for women. *Women & Therapy, 21*(1), 173–185.

Marino, P. J. (1997, November/December). Supreme Court overturns Religious Freedom Restoration Act. *Corrections Today,* pp. 47–50.

Marquart, J. W., & Sorensen, J. R. (1988). Institutional and postrelease behavior of Furman-commuted inmates in Texas. *Criminology, 26,* 677–693.

Marsh, J. R. (1994). Performing pretrial services: A challenge in the federal criminal justice system. *Federal Probation, 58*(4), 3–10.

Martinson, R. (1974). What works? Questions and answers about prison reform. *The Public Interest, 42,* 22–54.

Maruschak, L. M. (1999). *HIV in prisons 1997* [NCJ 178284]. Washington, DC: Bureau of Justice Statistics.

Mauer, M. (1994). Russia, United States world leaders in incarceration. *Overcrowded Times, 5*(5), 1, 9–10.

Mauer, M., Potler, C., & Wolf, R. (1999, 18 November). Executive summary: Gender and Justice. Available: www.sentencingproject.org/news/executive%20summary.html (Accessed 18 November).

Maxwell, G., & Morris, A. (1996). Research on family group conferences with young offenders in New Zealand. In J. Hudson (Ed.), *Family group conferences: Perspectives on policy & practice.* Monsey, NY: Criminal Justice Press.

McDevitt, J., & Miliano, R. (1992). Day reporting centers: An innovative concept in intermediate sanctions. In J. M. Byrne, A. J. Lurigio, & J. Petersilia (Eds.), *Smart sentencing: The emergence of intermediate sanctions* (pp. 152–165). Newbury Park, CA: Sage.

McDonald, D. C. (1992). Introduction: The day fine as a means of expanding judges' sentencing options. In D. C. McDonald (Ed.), *Day fines in American courts: The Staten Island and Milwaukee experiments* (pp. 1–9). Washington, DC: National Institute of Justice.

McElroy, J. E. (1998, January/February). The increasing complexity of pretrial services. *American Jails,* pp. 8–14.

McKelvey, B. (1977). *American prisons: A history of good intentions.* Montclair, NJ: Patterson Smith.

McShane, M. D., & Krause, W. (1993). *Community corrections.* New York: Macmillan.

Meisenkothen, C. (1999). Chemical castration—Breaking the cycle of paraphiliac recidivism. *Social Justice, 26*(1), 139–154.

Mennel, R. (1973). *Thorns and thistles: Juvenile delinquency in the United States, 1815–1857.* Syracuse, NY: Syracuse University Press.

Menninger, K. (1971). Love against hate. In S. E. Grupp (Ed.), *Theories of punishment* (pp. 243–254). Bloomington, IN: Indiana University Press.

Merlo, A. V. (1995). Female criminality in the 1990s. In A. V. Merlo & J. M. Pollock (Eds.), *Women, law, and social control* (pp. 119–134). Boston: Allyn & Bacon.

Merry, S. E. (1989). Myth and practice in the mediation process. In M. Wright & B. Galaway (Eds.), *Mediation and criminal justice* (pp. 239–250). London: Sage, Ltd.

Merzbacher, F. (1993). Witches and sorcery (J. Fosberry, Trans.). In C. Hinckeldey (Ed.), *Criminal justice through the ages* (pp. 181–191). Rothenburg o.d.T., Germany: Mediaeval Crime Museum.

Messinger, S. L., Berecochea, J. E., Rauma, D., & Berk, R. A. (1985). The foundations of parole in California. *Law and Society Review, 19,* 69–106.

Metzger, D. H. (2000). Life in a microwave. In R. Johnson & H. Toch (Eds.), *Crime and punishment: Inside views* (pp. 138–140). Los Angeles: Roxbury.

Meyer, W. J., III, & Cole, C. M. (1997). Physical and chemical castration of sex offenders: A review. *Journal of Offender Rehabilitation, 25*(¾), 1–18.

Michalowski, R. J. (1985). *Order, law, and crime.* New York: Random House.

Miethe, T. D., & Moore, C. A. (1988). Officials' reactions to sentencing guidelines. *Journal of Research in Crime and Delinquency, 25,* 170–187.

Miller, D. (1994). Revocation: "The good old days." In P. F. Cromwell & G. C. Killinger (Eds.), *Community-based corrections* (3rd ed., pp. 160–161). Minneapolis/St. Paul: West.

Miller, R. C., Walter, D. J., & Kelley, T. L. (1995). *Detention and corrections caselaw catalog* (8th ed.). Washington Grove, MD: CRS, Inc.

Miller-Ashton, J. (1993). Canada's new federal system for female offenders. In American Correctional Association (Ed.), *Female offenders: Meeting needs of a neglected population* (pp. 105–111). Laurel, MD: American Correctional Association.

Mills, S., & Armstrong, K. (1999, 18 May). Yet another death row inmate cleared. *Chicago Tribune* [Online]. Available: www.chicagotribune.com/news/metro/chicago/article/0,1051,ART- 28731,00.html (Accessed 19 May 1999).

Milner, A. (1969). Sentencing patterns in Nigeria. In A. Milner (Ed.), *African penal systems* (pp. 262–292). New York: Praeger.

Montgomery, R. H., Jr. (1994). American prison riots: 1774–1991. In M. C. Braswell, R. H. Montgomery, Jr., & L. X. Lombardo (Eds.), *Prison violence in America* (2nd ed., pp. 227–251). Cincinnati, OH: Anderson.

Montgomery, R. H., Jr., & Crews, G. A. (1998). *A history of correctional violence: An examination of reported causes or riots and disturbances.* Lanham, MD: American Correctional Association.

Moore, L. E. (1973). *The jury: Tool of kings, palladium of liberty.* Cincinnati, OH: Anderson.

Morash, M., Bynum, T. S., & Koons, B. A. (1998). *Women offenders: Programming needs and promising approaches* [NCJ 171668]. Research in Brief. Washington, DC: National Institute of Justice.

Morgan, R. (1991). England and Wales. In D. van Zyl Smit & F. Dünkel (Eds.), *Imprisonment today and tomorrow* (pp. 161–202). Deventer: Kluwer.

Morris, A., & Maxwell, G. M. (1993). Juvenile justice in New Zealand: A new paradigm. *Australia and New Zealand Journal of Criminology, 26,* 72–90.

Morris, A., & Wilkinson, C. (1995). Responding to female prisoners' needs. *The Prison Journal, 75,* 295–305.

Morris, N. (1974). *The future of imprisonment.* Chicago: University of Chicago Press.

Morris, N., & Tonry, M. (1990). *Between prison and probation.* New York: Oxford University Press.

Moyer, I. L. (1993). Women's prisons: Issues and controversies. In R. Muraskin & T. Alleman (Eds.), *It's a crime: Women and justice* (pp. 193–210). Englewood Cliffs, NJ: Prentice Hall.

Muraskin, R. (1993). Disparate treatment in correctional facilities. In R. Muraskin & T. Alleman (Eds.), *It's a crime: Women and justice* (pp. 211–225). Englewood Cliffs, NJ: Prentice Hall.

Murphy, J., Johnson, N., & Edwards, W. (1992). *Addicted mothers, imprisonment and alternatives.* Albany, NY: New York State Coalition for Criminal Justice / Center for Justice Education.

Naldi, G. J. (1992). Prisoners' rights as recently interpreted by the Supreme Court of Zimbabwe: A comparative study with international human rights. *African Journal of International and Comparative Law, 4*(2), 715–727.

National Center for Education Statistics. (1996, 12 November). 1992 National adult literacy survey. Available: necs.ed.gov/naal/naal92/ (Accessed 2 December 1999).

National Center for State Long-Term Care Ombudsman Resources. (1992) *Comprehensive curriculum* [A training resource for state long-term care ombudsman programs]. Washington, DC: (Copies available from NCSLTCOR at 2033 K Street NW, Suite 304. Washington, DC 20006).

National Victim Center. (1998). Rights of crime victims. Available: www.nvc.org/ns-search/indolink (Accessed 23 December 1999).

Neudek, K. (1991). The United Nations. In D. van Zyl Smit & F. Dünkel (Eds.), *Imprisonment today and tomorrow* (pp. 703–712). Deventer: Kluwer.

New York State Special Commission on Attica. (1972). *Attica: The official report of the New York State special commission on Attica.* New York: Bantam Books.

Newman, G. (1985). *The punishment response.* Albany, NY: Harrow and Heston.

Newman, G. (1995). *Just and painful: A case for corporal punishment of criminals* (2nd ed.). New York: Harrow and Heston.

NIC Information Center. (1993). *Women in the community corrections workforce* [Accession no. NIC-period 104]. Topics in Community Corrections. Longmont, CO: National Institute of Corrections.

Nieves, E. (1999, 18 March). For patrons of prostitutes, remedial instruction. *The New York Times* [Online]. Available: www.nytimes.com/yr/mo/day/news/national/calif-johns-school.html (Accessed 18 March 1999).

O'Shea, K. A. (1999). *Women and the death penalty in the United States, 1900–1998.* Westport, CT: Praeger.

Office of the Attorney General. (1998). *Megan's Law: Final guidelines for the Jacob Wetterling Crimes Against Children and Sexually Violent Offender Registration Act, as amended* [A. G. Order No. 2196-98]. Washington, DC: Department of Justice.

Oldest woman allowed off death row. (1999, 10 August). Available: www.apbonline.com/911/1999/08/10/overturn0810_01.html (Accessed 11 August 1999).

Orlando-Morningstar, D. (1997). *Prison gangs* [JU 13.17:2]. Special Needs Offenders Bulletin, no. 2. Washington, DC: Federal Judicial Center.

Otterbein, K. F. (1986). *The ultimate coercive sanctions: A cross-cultural study of capital punishment.* New Haven, CT: Human Relations Area Files, Inc.

Owen, B. (1998). *"In the mix": Struggle and survival in a women's prison.* Albany, NY: State University of New York Press.

Owen, B., & Bloom, B. (1995). Profiling women prisoners: Findings from national surveys and a California sample. *The Prison Journal, 75*(2), 165–185.

Packer, H. L. (1968). *The limits of the criminal sanction.* Stanford, CA: Stanford University Press.

Paddock, R. C. (1999, 26 June). Amid public outrage, the Kremlin shuts doors of Russia's death rows. *Los Angeles Times* [Online]. Available: www.latimes.com (Accessed 28 June 1999).

Palmer, J. W. (1991). *Constitutional rights of prisoners* (4th ed.). Cincinnati, OH: Anderson.

Palmer, J. W., & Palmer, S. E. (1999). *Constitutional rights of prisoners* (6th ed.). Cincinnati, OH: Anderson.

Parent, D. (1993). Boot camps failing to achieve goals. *Overcrowded Times, 4*(4), 1, 12–15.

Parent, D., Byrne, J., Tsarfaty, V., Valade, L., & Esselman, J. (1995). *Day reporting centers* [NCJ 155060]. Issues and Practices in Criminal Justice, vol. 1. Washington, DC: National Institute of Justice.

Parent, D., Dunworth, T., McDonald, D., & Rhodes, W. (1996). *The impact of sentencing guidelines* [NCJ 161837]. Key legislative issues in criminal justice. Washington, DC: Office of Justice Programs.

Parent, D., & Snyder, B. (1999). *Police-corrections partnerships* [NCJ 175047]. Issues and Practices in

Criminal Justice. Washington, DC: National Institute of Justice.

Parker, L. C., Jr. (1986). *Parole and the community-based treatment of offenders in Japan and the United States.* New Haven, CT: University of New Haven Press.

Paternoster, R. (1991). *Capital punishment in America.* New York: Lexington Books.

Pease, K., & Hukkila, K. (Eds.). (1990). *Criminal justice systems in Europe and North America* [Publication Series No. 17]. Helsinki, Finland: Helsinki Institute for Crime Prevention and Control, affiliated with the United Nations.

Pellicane, A. W. (1991). New Jersey saves money without compromising security. *Corrections Today, 53*(4), 146–148.

Perkins, C. A. (1994). *National corrections reporting program, 1992* [NCJ 145862]. Washington, DC: Bureau of Justice Statistics.

Perkins, C. A., Stephan, J. J., & Beck, A. J. (1995). *Jails and jail inmates 1993–94* [NCJ 151651]. Washington, DC: Bureau of Justice Statistics.

Pesquera, A. (1999, 11 May). Study shows boot camps not doing job. *San Antonio Express-News* [Online]. Available www.expressnews.com (Accessed 13 May 1999).

Peters, E. M. (1995). Prison before the prison: The ancient and medieval worlds. In N. Morris & D. J. Rothman (Eds.), *The Oxford history of the prison* (pp. 3–47). New York: Oxford University Press.

Petersilia, J. (1988). *House arrest* [NCJ 104559]. Crime File Study Guide. Washington, DC: National Institute of Justice.

Petersilia, J. (1993). More prisons are not the answer. *Overcrowded Times, 4*(3), 3, 16.

Petersilia, J., & Turner, S. (1993). *Evaluating intensive supervision probaton/parole: Results of a nationwide experiment* [NCJ 141637]. Research in Brief. Washington, DC: National Institute of Justice.

Peterson, R. D., & Bailey, W. C. (1998). Is capital punishment an effective deterrent for murder? An examination of the social science research. In J. R. Acker, R. M. Bohm, & C. S. Lanier (Eds.), *America's experiment with capital punishment: Reflections on the past, present, and future of the ultimate sanction* (pp. 157–182). Durham, NC: Carolina Academic Press.

Petroski, W. (1999, 15 February). Law libraries to close in Iowa prisons. *Des Moines Register* [Online]. Available: members.tripod.com/~Brother_Swartz/page-6.htm (Accessed 17 December 1999).

Phelps, N. A. (1845). *A history of the copper mines and Newgate prison, at Granby, Conn.* Hartford, CT: Press of Case, Tiffany & Burnham.

Pickett, R. S. (1969). *House of refuge: Origins of juvenile reform in New York State.* Syracuse, NY: Syracuse University Press.

Platek, M. (1990). Prison subculture in Poland. *International Journal of the Sociology of Law, 18,* 459–472.

Platt, A. M. (1969). *The child savers.* Chicago: University of Chicago Press.

Pollock, J. (1999, March). *Parenting programs in women's prisons.* Paper presentation. Academy of Criminal Justice Sciences, Orlando, FL.

Pollock-Byrne, J. M. (1989). *Ethics in crime and justice.* Pacific Grove, CA: Brooks/Cole.

Pollock-Byrne, J. M. (1990). *Women, prison, and crime.* Pacific Grove, CA: Brooks/Cole.

Powers, E. (1985). *Supplement to the American prison: From the beginning . . . a pictorial history.* College Park, MD: American Correctional Association.

Pratarelli, M. E., & Bishop, J. L. (1998–99). Perceptions of estimated pain experienced during execution: Effects of gender and belief in capital punishment. *Omega, 38*(2), 103–111.

President's Commission on Law Enforcement and Administration of Justice. (1967). *The challenge of crime in a free society.* Washington, DC: Government Printing Office.

Preston, R. K. (1992, December). Evaluating abuse claims of Americans transferred under exchange treaties. *Corrections Today,* pp. 134, 136.

Prisons: No vacancies. (1981, 8 August). *The Economist,* pp. 20, 23.

Probation Division. (1989). Implementing community service: The referral process. *Federal Probation, 53*(1), 3–9.

Propper, A. M. (1982). Make-believe families and homosexuality among imprisoned girls. *Crime & Delinquency, 20,* 127–138.

Radelet, M. L. (1999). Post-Furman botched executions. Available: www.essential.org/dpic/botched.html (Accessed 12 August 1999).

Radelet, M. L., Bedau, H. A., & Putnam, C. E. (1992). *In spite of innocence: Erroneous convictions in capital cases.* Boston: Northeastern University Press.

Rafter, N. H. (1990). *Partial justice: Women, prisons, and social control* (2nd ed.). New Brunswick, NJ: Transaction Publishers.

Rafter, N. H. (1993). Equality or difference? In American Correctional Association (Ed.), *Female offenders: Meeting needs of a neglected population* (pp. 7–11). Laurel, MD: American Correctional Association.

Reaves, B. A. (1998). *Felony defendants in large urban counties, 1994* [NCJ 164616]. Washington, DC: Bureau of Justice Statistics.

Reaves, B. A., & Perez, J. (1994). *Pretrial release of felony defendants, 1992* [NCJ 148818]. Washington, DC: Bureau of Justice Statistics.

Rehabilitation Bureau. (1995). *The community-based treatment of offenders system in Japan.* Tokyo, Japan: Ministry of Justice.

Reichel, P. L. (1979). Nineteenth century societal reactions to juvenile delinquents: Preliminary notes for a natural history. *Mid-American Review of Sociology, 4*(2), 39–54.

Reichel, P. L. (1999). *Comparative criminal justice systems: A topical approach* (2nd ed.). Upper Saddle River, NJ: Prentice Hall.

Reinhard, D. (1988, 13 March). Shape up, son!! *The Oregonian.*

Rejali, D. M. (1994). *Torture & modernity: Self, society, and state in modern Iran.* Boulder, CO: Westview Press.

Reminding inmates that they're inmates. (1994, 3 October). *U.S. News and World Report.*

Renzema, M. (1992). Home confinement programs: Development, implementation, and impact. In J. M. Byrne, A. J. Lurigio, & J. Petersilia (Eds.), *Smart sentencing: The emergence of intermediate sanctions* (pp. 41–53). Newbury Park, CA: Sage.

Renzema, M., & Skelton, D. T. (1990). *The use of electronic monitoring by criminal justice agencies 1989: A description of extent, offender characteristics, program types, programmatic issues, and legal aspects* [NCJ 126159]. Rockville, MD: National Institute of Justice.

Restorative justice: An interview with visiting fellow Thomas Quinn. (1988, March). *National Institute of Justice Journal, 235,* 10–16.

Rettig, R. P., Torres, M. J., & Garrett, G. R. (1977). *Manny: A criminal-addict's story.* Boston: Houghton Mufflin.

Rhine, E. E., Smith, W. R., & Jackson, R. W. (1991). *Paroling authorities: Recent history and current practice.* Laurel, MD: American Correctional Association.

Rideau, W. (1992a). Angola's history. In W. Rideau & R. Wikberg (Eds.), *Life sentences: Rage and survival behind bars* (pp. 35–42). New York: Time Books.

Rideau, W. (1992b). The sexual jungle. In W. Rideau & R. Wikberg (Eds.), *Life sentences: Rage and survival behind bars* (pp. 73–107). New York: Times Books.

Riley, P. J., & Rose, V. M. (1980). Public vs. elite opinion on correctional reform: Implications for social policy. *Journal of Criminal Justice, 8,* 345–356.

Riveland, C. (1999). *Supermax prisons: Overview and general considerations.* Washington, DC: National Institute of Corrections.

Robinson, R. A. (1992). Intermediate sanctions and the female offender. In J. M. Byrne, A. J. Lurigio, & J. Petersilia (Eds.), *Smart sentencing: The emergence of intermediate sanctions* (pp. 245–260). Newbury Park, CA: Sage.

Robison, J., Wilkins, L., Carter, R., & Wahl, A. (1969). *The San Francisco Project: A study of federal probation and parole.* Berkeley, CA: University of California Press.

Ross, P. H., & Lawrence, J. E. (1998, December). Health care for women offenders. *Corrections Today,* pp. 122–124, 126, 128–129.

Rothman, D. J. (1971). *The discovery of the asylum.* Boston: Little, Brown and Company.

Rothman, S., & Powers, S. (1994, Summer). Execution by quota? *The Public Interest, 116,* 3–17.

Rowan, J. R. (1996). Who is safer in male maximum security prisons? *The Keeper's Voice* [Online] *17*(3). Available: oicj.acsp.uic.edu/spearmint/Public/Pubs/kv/kv170331.cfm (Accessed 5 December 1999).

Rubin, H. T. (1979). *Juvenile justice: Policy, practice, and law.* Santa Monica: Goodyear.

Rubin, P. N., & McCampbell, S. W. (1994). *The Americans with Disabilities Act and criminal justice: Providing inmate servies* [NCJ 148139]. Washington, DC: National Institute of Justice.

Rubin, P. N., & McCampbell, S. W. (1995). *The Americans with disabilities Act and criminal justice: Mental disabilities and corrections* [NCJ 155061]. Washington, DC: National Institute of Justice.

Ruggiero, V. (1995). Flexibility and intermittent emergency in the Italian penal system. In V. Ruggiero, M. Ryan, & J. Sim (Eds.), *Western European penal systems: A critical anatomy* (pp. 46–70). Thousand Oaks, CA: Sage.

Sabath, M. J., & Crowles, E. L. (1988). Factors affecting the adjustment of elderly inmates in prison. In B. McCarthy & R. Langworthy (Eds.), *Older offenders* (pp. 178–195). New York: Praeger.

Samaha, J. (1994). *Criminal justice* (3rd ed.). Minneapolis/St. Paul: West.

Sanad, N. (1991). *The theory of crime and criminal responsibility in Islamic law: Shari'a.* Chicago, IL: Office of International Criminal Justice.

Saum, C. A., Surratt, H. L., Inciardi, J. A., & Bennett, R. E. (1995). Sex in prison: Exploring the myths and realities. *The Prison Journal, 75,* 413–430.

Saylor, W. G., & Gaes, G. G. (1995, 6 November). The effect of prison work experience, vocational and apprenticeship training. In Long-term recidivism of U.S. federal prisoners [Online]. Available: www.bop.gov/orepg/prep95.html (Accessed 30 November 1999).

Scacco, A. M. (1975). *Rape in prison.* Springfield, IL: Thomas.

Schafer, S. (1970). *Compensation and restitution to victims of crime.* Montclair, NJ: Patterson Smith.

Schmalleger, F. (1995). *Criminal justice today* (3rd ed.). Englewood Cliffs, NJ: Prentice Hall.

Schmidt, A. K. (1991). Electronic monitors—Realistically, what can be expected? *Federal Probation, 55*(2), 47–53.

Schneider, A. (1986). Restitution and recidivism rates of juvenile offenders: Results from four experimental studies. *Criminology, 24,* 533–552.

Schulz, K. (1991). Electronically monitored home confinement: The Canadian experience and the issues. Criminology Research Centre, Simon Fraser University (Available as item "VF 1020.10 Electro 010221" from NIC Information Center, 1860 Industrial Circle, Suite A, Longmont, CO 80501).

Schwitzgebel, R. K., Schwitzgebel, R. L., Pahnke, W. N., & Hurd, W. S. (1964). A program of research in behavioral electronics. *Behavioral Science, 9,* 233–238.

Sechrest, L., White, S. O., & Brown, E. D. (1979). *The rehabilitation of criminal offenders.* Washington, DC: National Academy of Sciences.

Seidman, R. B. (1969). The Ghana prison system: An historical perspective. In A. Milner (Ed.), *African penal systems* (pp. 431–472). New York: Praeger.

Seligman, K. (1996, 15 September). Chemical castration costly, won't work, experts insist. *San Francisco Examiner* [Online]. Available: www.sfgate.com (Accessed 19 October 1999).

Sellers, M. P. (1989). Private and public prisons: A comparison of costs, programs, and facilities. *International Journal of Offenders Therapy and Comparative Criminology, 33,* 241–256.

Sellin, T. (1967). A look at prison history. *Federal Probation, 31*(3), 18–23.

Sellin, T., & Wolfgang, M. (1964). *The measurement of delinquency.* New York: Wiley.

Senna, J. J., & Siegel, L. J. (1999). *Introduction to criminal justice* (8th ed.). Belmont, CA: West/Wadsworth.

Sexton, G. E. (1995). *Work in American prisons: Joint ventures with the private sector* [NCJ 156215]. Washington, DC: National Institute of Justice.

Shapiro, C. (1998a, February). Family-focused drug treatments: A natural resource for the criminal justice system. Available: www.whitehousedrugpolicy.gov/treat/consensus/shapiro.pdf (Accessed 30 December 1999).

Shapiro, C. (1998b). *La Bodega de la Familia: Reaching out to the forgotten victims of substance abuse* [NCJ 170595]. Washington, DC: Bureau of Justice Assistance.

Sharp, D. (1995). *Boot camps—punishment and treatment* [Pull-out found in *Corrections Today,* June 1995]. Laurel, MD: American Correctional Association.

Shaw, A. G. L. (1966). *Convicts and the colonies.* London, England: Faber and Faber.

Sherman, L. W., Gottfredson, D., MacKenzie, D., Eck, J., Reuter, P., & Bushway, S. (1997). *Preventing crime: What works, what doesn't, what's promising* [NCJ 165366]. Washington, DC: Office of Justice Programs.

Sherman, L. W., Gottfredson, D., MacKenzie, D., Eck, J., Reuter, P., & Bushway, S. (1998). Preventing crime: What works, what doesn't, what's promising [NCJ 171676]. Research in Brief. Washington, DC: National Institute of Justice.

Shilton, M. K. (1995). Community corrections acts may be the Rx systems need. *Corrections Today, 57*(1), 32, 34–36, 66.

Siegal, H. A., Fisher, J. H., Rapp, R. C., Kelliher, C. A., Wagner, J. H., O'Brien, W. R., & Cole, P. A. (1996). Enhancing substance abuse treatment with case management: It's impact on employment. *Journal of Substance Abuse Treatment, 13*(2), 93–98.

Siegal, L. J., & Senna, J. J. (1991). *Juvenile delinquency: Theory, practice and law* (4th ed.). St. Paul: West.

Silva, T. L. (1995). Dial "1-900-Pervert" and other statutory measures that provide public notification of sex offenders. *SMU Law Review, 48,* 1961–2058.

Simmons, A. M. (1999, 22 July). Ghanaian practice under fire. *The Denver Post,* pp. 21A–22A.

Simon, J. (1993). *Poor discipline: Parole and the social control of the underclass, 1890–1990.* Chicago: University of Chicago Press.

Simon, R. J., & Simon, J. D. (1993). Female guards in men's prisons. In R. Muraskin & T. Alleman (Eds.), *It's a crime: Women and justice* (pp. 226–241). Englewood Cliffs, NJ: Prentice Hall.

Skovron, S. E., Scott, J. E., & Cullen, F. T. (1998). Prison crowding: Public attitudes toward strategies of population control. *Journal of Research in Crime and Delinquency, 25,* 150–169.

Sloppy "Megan's laws" hinder goal of boosting public safety. (1998, 13 May). *USA Today,* p. 6A.

Smith, C. E. (1993). Black Muslims and the development of prisoners' rights. *Journal of Black Studies, 24,* 131–146.

Smith, N. E., & Batiuk, M. E. (1989). Sexual victimization and inmate social interaction. *The Prison Journal, 69,* 29–38.

Smylka, J. O. (1981). *Community-based corrections: Principles and practices.* New York: Macmillan.

Snell, T. L. (1994). *Women in prison* [NCJ 145321]. Survey of state prison inmates, 1991. Washington, DC: Bureau of Justice Statistics.

Snell, T. L. (1995a). *Correctional populations in the United States, 1992* [NCJ 146413]. Washington, DC: Bureau of Justice Statistics.

Snell, T. L. (1995b). *Correctional populations in the United States, 1993* [NCJ 156241]. Washington, DC: Bureau of Justice Statistics.

Snell, T. L. (1998). *Capital punishment 1997* [NCJ 172881]. Washington, DC: Bureau of Justice Statistics.

Snell, T. L. (1999). *Capital punishment 1998* [NCJ 179012]. Washington, DC: Bureau of Justice Statistics.

Snider, E. (1999, 17–23 June). The road to freedom. Available: www.exoffender.org/road_to_freedom.html (Accessed 13 December).

Snyder, H. N. (1998). *Juvenile arrests 1997* [NCJ 173938]. Washington, DC: Office of Juvenile Justice and Delinquency Prevention.

Solomon, L., & Camp, A. T. (1993). The revolution in correctional classification. In American Correctional Association (Ed.), *Classification: A tool for managing today's offenders* (pp. 1–16). Laurel, MD: American Correctional Association.

Sorensen, J., Wrinkle, R., Brewer, V., & Marquart, J. (1999). Capital punishment and deterrence: Examining the effect of executions on murder in Texas. *Crime & Delinquency, 45,* 481–493.

Spierenburg, P. (1995). The body and the state: Early modern Europe. In N. Morris & D. J. Rothman (Eds.), *The Oxford history of the prison* (pp. 49–77). New York: Oxford University Press.

"Spoiled" Amish inmates go free. (1999, 28 August). *The Denver Post,* p. 20A.

Spread of boot camps menaces black males. (1996, October). *African American Male Research* [Online] 1(1). Available: http://www.pressroom.com/~afrimale/bootcamp.htm (Accessed 12 OCT 1999).

Stahl, A. L. (1999a). *Delinquency cases waived to criminal court, 1987–1996* [FS-9999]. OJJDP Fact Sheet. Washington, DC: Office of Juvenile Justice and Delinquency Prevention.

Stahl, A. L. (1999b). *Offenders in juvenile court, 1996* [NCJ 175719]. Washington, DC: Office of Juvenile Justice and Delinquency Prevention.

State Department. (1999, February). Prisoner transfer treaties. Available: http://travel.state.gov/transfer.html (Accessed 28 May 1999).

Stohr, M. K., Self, R. L., & Lovrich, N. P. (1992). Staff turnover in new generation jails: An investigation of its causes and prevention. *Journal of Criminal Justice, 20,* 455–478.

Stone, W. E. (1990). Means of the cause of death in Texas jail suicides, 1986–1988. *American Jails, 4*(1), 50–53.

Streib, V. L. (1999a, June). Death penalty for female offenders, January 1973 to June 1979. Available: www.law.onu.edu/faculty/streib/femdeath.pdf (Accessed 12 August 1999).

Streib, V. L. (1999b, June). The juvenile death penalty today: Death sentences and executions for juvenile crimes, January 1973–June 1999. Available: www.law.onu.edu/faculty/streib/juvdeath.pdf (Accessed 12 August 1999).

Strossen, N. (1999, 20 May). Black Americans and the right to vote. Available: ic.voxcap.com/issues/issue233/item4518.asp (Accessed 11 December 1999).

Struckman-Johnson, C., Struckman-Johnson, D., Rucker, L., Bumby, K., & Donaldson, S. (1996). Sexual coercion reported by men and woman in prison. *The Journal of Sex Research, 33*(1), 67–76.

Sugihara, H., Horiuchi, K., Nishimura, N., Yamaguchi, A., Sato, S., Nishimura, I., Nagashima, Y., Nishikawa, M., & Saito, F. (1994). An overview of alternatives to imprisonment in Asia and the Pacific region. In U. Zvekic (Eds), *Alternatives to imprisonment in comparative perspective* (pp. 95–202). Chicago: Nelson-Hall.

Sullivan, L. E. (1990). *The prison reform movement: Forlorn hope.* Boston: Twayne Publishers.

Sumner, W. G. (1907). *Folkways: A study of the sociological importance of usages, manners, customs, mores, and morals.* Boston: Ginn.

Sutherland, E. H., Cressey, D. R., & Luckenbill, D. F. (1992). *Principles of criminology* (11th ed.). Dix Hills, NY: General Hall.

Swain, J. (1931, 1995). *The pleasures of the torture chamber.* New York: Dorset Press.

Sykes, G. (1958). *The society of captives: A study of a maximum-security prison.* Princeton, NJ: Princeton University Press.

Sykes, G., & Messinger, S. L. (1960). The inmate social system. In R. Cloward, D. Cressey, G. Grosser, R. McCleery, L. Ohlin, G. Sykes, & S. Messinger (Eds.), *Theoretical studies in social organization of the prison* (pp. 5–19). New York: Social Science Research Council.

Tak, P. J. P. (1986). Community service orders in Western Europe—a comparative survey. In H. Albrecht & W. Schadler (Eds.), *Community service: A new option in punishing offenders in Europe* (pp. 1–14). Freiburg, Germany: Max Planck Institute.

Tamaki, J., & Gladstone, M. (2000, 25 February). State puts all prisoners on security alert. *Los Angeles Times,* pp. A-3 (Home Edition).

10,000 witness negro hanging; crowd orderly. (1936, 15 August). *Augusta Chronicle.*

Terrill, R. J. (1999). *World criminal justice systems: A survey* (4th ed.). Cincinnati, OH: Anderson.

Tewksbury, R., & Taylor, J. M. (1996, September). The consequences of eliminating Pell Grant eligibility for students in post-secondary correctional education programs. *Federal Probation, 60*(3), 60–63.

Thomas, C. W. (1999, 10 October). Numbers of private facilities by geographical location. Available: web.crim.ufl.edu/pcp/census/1999/Chart3.html (Accessed 30 October 1999).

Thorne, C. (1992). *Gangs and gang indentification.* Jail Operations Bulletin, vol. 4 no. 1. Hagerstown, MD: American Jail Association.

Timasheff, N. S. (1941). *One hundred years of probation 1841–1941, Part one.* New York: Fordham University Press.

Timasheff, N. S. (1943). *One hundred years of probation 1841–1941, Part two.* New York: Fordham University Press.

Tjoflat, G. B. (1991). The untapped potential for judicial discretion under the Federal Sentencing Guidelines: Advice for counsel. *Federal Probation, 55*(4), 4–9.

Tocqueville, A. de. (1981). *Journey to America* (G. Lawrence, Trans.). Westport, CT: Greenwood Press.

Tonry, M. (1997). *Intermediate sanctions in sentencing guidelines* [NCJ 165043]. Issues and Practices in Criminal Justice. Washington, DC: National Institute of Justice.

Torbet, P. M. (Ed.). (1993). *Desktop guide to good juvenile probation practice* [NCJ 128218]. Washington, DC: Office of Juvenile Justice and Delinquency Prevention.

Torbet, P. M. (Ed.). (1997, June). State responses to serious and violent juvenile crime. *Corrections Today,* pp. 121–123.

Trafzer, C., & George, S. (1980). *Prison centennial, 1876–1976: A pictorial history of the Arizona Territorial Prison at Yuma.* Yuma, AZ: Yuma County Historial Society.

Trager, J. (Ed.). (1979). *The people's chronology.* New York: Holt, Rinehart and Winston.

Turner, M. G., Sundt, J. L., Applegate, B. K., & Cullen, F. T. (1995). "Three strikes and you're out" legislation: A national assessment. *Federal Probation, 59*(3), 16–35.

Turner, S., & Petersilia, J. (1996). *Work release: Recidivism and corrections costs in Washington State* [NCJ 163706]. Research in Brief. Washington, DC: National Institute of Justice.

Uganda defies last-minute appeals, hangs 28 prisoners. (1999, 1 May). Available: www.anc.org.za/ancdocs/briefing/nw19990503/66.html (Accessed 9 May 1999).

Umbreit, M. S. (1989). Crime victims seeking fairness, not revenge: Toward restorative justice. *Federal Probation, 53*(3), 52–57.

Umbreit, M. S. (1994). *Victim meets offender: The impact of restorative justice and mediation.* Monsey, NY: Criminal Justice Press.

Umbreit, M. S. (1998). Restorative justice through victim-offender mediation: A multi-site assessment. *Western Criminology Review* [Online] *1*(1). Available: wcr.sonoma.edu/v1n1/umbreit.html (Accessed 17 August 1999).

United Nations. (1999). *Violence against women* [E/CN.4/1999/NGO/71 and E/CN.4/1999/68/Add.2]. Integration of the human rights of women and the gender perspective. Geneva: Economic and Social Council; Commission on Human Rights.

United States Parole Commission. (1993). *An overview of the United States Parole Commission* [J27.2:OV2]. Washington, DC: Department of Justice.

United States Parole Commission. (1997, 11 March). An overview of the United States Parole Commission. Available: http://www.used.gov/usa/overview.htm (Accessed 28 May 1999).

U.S. Sentencing Commission. (1998). *Guidelines manual, 3E1.1.* Washington, DC: United States Sentencing Commission.

U.S. urban public transport summary of national trends 1983–1995. (1995). Available: www.publications.com/ut-95sum.htm (Accessed 31 October 1999).

Useem, B., & Kimball, P. (1989). *Stages of siege: U.S. prison riots, 1971–1986.* New York: Oxford University Press.

van den Haag, E. (1975). *Punishing criminals: Concerning a very old and painful question.* New York: Basic Books.

van den Haag, E. (1991). Guilt overrides the importance of death penalty discrimination. In C. Wekesser (Ed.), *The death penalty: Opposing viewpoints* (pp. 156–159). San Diego, CA: Greenhaven Press.

van Kalmthout, A. M., & Tak, P. (1988). *Sanctions-systems in the member-states of the Council of Europe, Part I.* Norwell, MA: Kluwer Law and Taxation Publishers.

van Oers, H. (1992). Concerning the Belgium prison system. *Tilburg Foreign Law Review, 2,* 49–66.

van Swaaningen, R., & de Jonge, G. (1995). The Dutch prison system and penal policy in the 1990s: From humanitarian paternalism to penal business management. In V. Ruggiero, M. Ryan, & J. Sim (Eds.), *Western European penal systems: A critical anatomy* (pp. 24–45). Thousand Oaks, CA: Sage.

Van Wormer, K. (1995, March). Those who seek execution: Capital punishment as a form of suicide. *USA Today Magazine,* pp. 92–93.

van Zyl Smit, D. (1991). South Africa. In D. van Zyl Smit & F. Dünkel (Eds.), *Imprisonment today and tomorrow* (pp. 537–566). Deventer: Kluwer.

Vass, A. A. (1990). *Alternatives to prison: Punishment, custody and the community.* London: Sage LTD.

Vesey, B. M., De Cou, K., & Prescott, L. (1998, May/June). Effective management of female jail detainees with histories of physical and sexual abuse. *American Jails,* pp. 50–54.

Vicenti, C. N. (1995). The reemergence of tribal society and traditional justice systems. *Judicature, 79*(3).

Vito, G. F., Koester, P., & Wilson, D. G. (1991). Return of the dead: An update on the status of *Furman*-commuted death row inmates. In R. M. Bohm (Ed.), *The death penalty in America: Current research* (pp. 89–99). Cincinnati, OH: Anderson.

von Hentig, H. (1948). *The criminal and his victim: Studies in the sociobiology of crime.* New Haven, CT: Yale University Press.

von Hirsch, A. (1976). *Doing justice: The choice of punishments.* New York: Hill and Wang.

von Hirsch, A., & Hanrahan, K. J. (1979). *The question of parole: Retention, reform or abolition?* Cambridge: Ballinger.

Walker, N. (1991). *Why punish?* Oxford, England: Oxford University Press.

Wallace, B., Podger, P. J., & Van Derbeken, J. (2000, 24 February). Guards kill prisoner in brawl at Pelican Bay. *San Fransisco Chronicle* [Online]. Available: www.sfgate.com (Accessed 25 February 2000).

Wallace, C. P. (1994, 1 April). Youth's appeal against caning fails. *The Denver Post,* p. 2A.

Weigend, T. (1983). Sentencing in West Germany. *Maryland Law Review, 42,* 37–89.

Weihofen, H. (1971). Punishment and treatment: Rehabilitation. In S. E. Grupp (Ed.), *Theories of punishment* (pp. 255–263). Bloomington, IN: Indiana University Press.

Weinrott, M. R. (1996, June). Juvenile sexual aggression. In CSPV Fact Sheet [Online]. Available: www.colorado.edu/scpv/factsheets/factsheet2.html (Accessed 22 November 1999).

Weitekamp, E. (1992). Restitution: An overview. *Overcrowded Times, 3*(3), 6.

Weitekamp, E. (1993). Reparative justice: Towards a victim-oriented system. *European Journal on Criminal Policy and Research, 1,* 70–93.

Wellisch, J., Prendergast, M. L., & Anglin, M. D. (1994). *Drug-abusing women offenders: Results of a national survey* [NCJ 149261]. Research in Brief. Washington, DC: National Institute of Justice.

Werner, R., Frazier, F. W., & Farbstein, J. (1993). Direct supervision of correctional institutions. In *Podular, direct supervision jails information packet* (pp. 1–8). Longmont, CO: National Institute of Corrections.

Wheelchair to be boy's punishment. (1994, 9 January). *The Denver Post,* p. 6A.

Wikberg, R. (1992). The horror show. In W. Ridear & R. Wikberg (Eds.), *Life sentences: Rage and survival behind bars* (pp. 284–303). New York: Times Books.

Wilber, D. Q. (1999, 24 April). Prisons swap problems for other states' inmates. *The Baltimore Sun* [Online]. Available: www.sunspot.net (Accessed 1 May 1999).

Willing, R. (1999, 5 February). More on death row opting to die. *The Denver Post,* p. 39A.

Wilson, J. Q. (1975). *Thinking about crime.* New York: Basic Books.

Winfree, L. T., Jr., & Wooldredge, J. D. (1991). Exploring suicides and deaths by natural causes in America's large jails: A panel study of institutional change, 1978 and 1983. In J. A. Thompson & G. L. Mays (Eds.), *American jails: Public policy issues* (pp. 63–78). Chicago: Nelson-Hall.

Wolfgang, M. E. (1972). Making the criminal justice system accountable. *Crimes and Delinquency, 18,* 15–22.

Wooden, W. S., & Parker, J. (1982). *Men behind bars: Sexual exploitation in prison.* New York: Plenum.

Wright, M. (1991). *Justice for victims and offenders.* Milton Keynes, England: Open University Press.

Wright, P. (1999). The department of corrections' dirty dozen. Available: www.prisonlegalnews.org/doc12.htm (Accessed 21 December 1999).

Wright, R. A. (1994). *In defense of prisons.* Westport, CT: Greenwood Press.

Wright, R. A. (1995). Rehabilitation affirmed, rejected, and reaffirmed: Assessments of the effectiveness of offender treatment programs in criminology textbooks, 1956 to 1965 and 1983 to 1992. *Journal of Criminal Justice Education, 6,* 21–39.

Yae, M. (1999, October). An analysis of correctional industries programs. *Corrections Today,* pp. 94–97.

Yepson, L. (1975). Classification: The basis for modern treatment of offenders. In L. J. Hippchen (Ed.), *Correctional classification and treatment: A reader* (pp. 13–16). Washington, DC: American Correctional Association.

Zawitz, M. W. (Ed.). (1988). *Report to the nation on crime and justice.* Washington, DC: Department of Justice.

Zedner, L. (1995). Wayward sisters: The prison for women. In N. Morris & D. J. Rothman (Eds.), *The Oxford history of the prison* (pp. 229–361). New York: Oxford University Press.

Zehr, H. (1985). *Retributive justice, restorative justice.* Elkhart, IN: Mennonite Central Committee, Office of Criminal Justice.

Zeno, T. E. (1991). A prosecutor's view of the sentencing guidelines. *Federal Probation, 55*(4), 31–37.

Zhao, G. (1991). The People's Republic of China. In D. van Zyl Smit & F. Dünkel (Eds.), *Imprisonment today and tomorrow* (pp. 429–454). Deventer: Kluwer.

Zimbardo, P. G. (1972, April). Pathology of imprisonment. *Society,* pp. 4–8.

Zimring, F. E., & Hawkins, G. (1995). *Incapacitation: Penal confinement and the restraint of crime.* New York: Oxford University Press.

Zipp, Y. (1999, 25 June). Chain gangs arrive—in Yankee country. *Christian Science Monitor* [Online]. Available: http://www.csmonitor.com/durable/1999/06/25/p1s3.htm (Accessed 28 June 1999).

Zupan, L. L. (1991). *Jails: Reform and the new generation philosophy.* Cincinnati, OH: Anderson.

Zupan, L. L. (1992). The progress of women correctional officers in all-male prison. In I. Moyer (Ed.), *The changing role of women in the criminal justice system* (2nd ed., pp. 323–343). Prospect Heights, IL: Waveland.

TABLE OF CASES

Artway v. Attorney General of New Jersey, 876 F. Supp. 666 (D. N.J. 1995)

Banning v. Looney, 213 F.2d 771 (10th Cir. 1954)

Baxter v. Palmigiano, 425 U.S. 308 (1976)

Bearden v. Georgia, 461 U.S. 660 (1983)

Beatham v. Manson, 369 F.Supp. 783 (D. Conn. 1973)

Bell v. Wolfish, 441 U.S. 520 (1979)

Block v. Rutherford, 468 U.S. 576 (1984)

Boerne v. Flores, 521 U.S. 507 (1997)

Booth v. Maryland, 482 U.S. 496 (1987)

Bounds v. Smith, 430 U.S. 817 (1977)

Branch v. Texas, 408 U.S. 238 (1972, No. 69-5031)

Breed v. Jones, 421 U.S. 519 (1975)

Bukhari v. Hutto, 487 F.Supp. 1162 (E.D. Va. 1980)

Canterino v. Wilson, 546 F.Supp. 174 (W.D. Ky. 1982)

Canterino v. Wilson, 869 F.2d 948 (6th Cir. 1989)

Cantwell v. Connecticut, 310 U.S. 296 (1940)

Champion v. Artuz, 76 F.3d 483 (2nd Cir. 1996)

Childs v. Duckworth, 705 F.2d 915 (7th Cir. 1983)

Coffin v. Reichard, 143 F.2d 443 (6th Cir. 1944)

Coker v. Georgia, 433 U.S. 584 (1977)

Commonwealth v. Stauffer, 214 Pa.Super. 113 (1969)

Cooper v. Pate, 378 U.S. 546 (1964)

Cooper v. Pate, 382 F.2d 518 (7th Cir. 1967)

Cruz v. Beto, 405 U.S. 319 (1972)

Cunningham v. Jones, 667 F.2d 565 (6th Cir. 1982)

David K. v. Lane, 839 F.2d 1265 (7th Cir. 1988)

Dothard v. Rawlinson, 433 U.S. 321 (1977)

E. B. v. Verniero, 119 F.3d 1077 (3rd Cir. 1997)

Doe v. Poritz, 142 N.J. 1 (1995)

Estelle v. Gamble, 429 U.S. 97 (1976)

Ex parte Hull, 312 U.S. 546 (1941)

Farmer v. Brennan, 114 S.Ct. 1970 (1994)

Ford v. Wainwright, 477 U.S. 399 (1986)

French v. Heyne, 547 F.2d 994 (7th Cir. 1977)

Furman v. Georgia, 408 U.S. 238 (1972)

Gabel v. Lynaugh, 835 F.2d 124 (5th Cir. 1988)

Gagnon v. Scarpelli, 411 U.S. 778 (1973)

George v. King, 837 F.2d 705 (5th Cir. 1988)

Gittlemacker v. Prasse, 428 F.2d 1 (3rd Cir. 1970)

Glover v. Johnson, 478 F.Supp. 1075 (E.D. Mich. 1979)

Godfrey v. Georgia, 446 U.S. 420 (1980)

Greenholtz v. Inmates of the Nebraska Penal and Correctional Complex, 442 U.S. 1 (1979)

Gregg v. Georgia, 428 U.S. 153 (1976)

Grubbs v. Bradley, 552 F.Supp. 1052 (M.D. Tenn. 1982)

Grummett v. Rushen, 587 F.Supp. 913 (N.D. Cal. 1984)

Hale v. Arizona, 993 F.2d 1387 (9th Cir. 1993)

Hamilton v. Schriro, 74 F.3d 1545 (8th Cir. 1996)

Harris v. Fleming, 839 F.2d 1232 (7th Cir. 1988)

Harris v. Thigpen, 941 F.2d 1495 (11th Cir. 1991)

Hewitt v. Helms, 459 U.S. 460 (1983)

Holt v. Sarver, 309 F.Supp. 362 (E.D. Ark. 1970)

Howard v. United States, 864 F.Supp. 1019 (D. Colo. 1994)

Hudson v. Palmer, 468 U.S. 517 (1984)

Hunter v. Underwood, 471 U.S. 222 (1985)

In re Ferguson, 55 Cal.2d 663 (1961)

In re Gault, 387 U.S. 1 (1967)

In re Kemmler, 136 U.S. 436 (1890)

In re Long-Term Administrative Segregation of Inmates Designated as Five Percenters, 174 F.3d 464 (4th Cir. 1999, No. 98-7337)

In re Winship, 397 U.S. 358 (1970)

Ingraham v. Wright, 430 U.S. 651 (1977)

Jackson v. Bishop, 404 F.2d 571 (8th Cir. 1968)

Jackson v. Georgia, 408 U.S. 238 (1972, No. 69-5030)

Jackson v. O'Leary, 689 F. Supp. 846 (N.D. Ill. 1988)

Jamieson v. Robinson, 641 F.2d 138 (3rd Cir. 1981)

Johnson v. Avery, 393 U.S. 483 (1969)

Johnson v. Phelan, 69 F.3d 144 (7th Cir. 1995)

Jordan v. Gardner, 953 F.2d 1137 (9th Cir. 1992)

Jordan v. Gardner, 986 F.2d 1521 (9th Cir. 1993)

Jurek v. Texas, 428 U.S. 262 (1976)

Kelley v. Brewer, 525 F.2d 394 (8th Cir. 1975)

Kennedy v. Meacham, 382 F.Supp. 996 (1974)

Knop v. Johnson, 667 F.Supp. 467 (W.D. Mich. 1987)

Laaman v. Heigemore, 437 F.Supp. 269 (D. N.H. 1977)

Lee v. Washington, 390 U.S. 333 (1968)

Leonard v. Norris, 797 F.2d 683 (8th Cir. 1986)
Lewis v. Casey, 516 U.S. 804 (1996)
Liberti v. New York, 28 Conn.Supp. 9 (1968)
Lockett v. Ohio, 438 U.S. 586 (1978)
Lockhart v. McCree, 476 U.S. 162 (1986)
Loney v. Scurr, 474 F.Supp. 1186 (S.D. Iowa 1979)
Lord Natural Self-Allah v. Annucci, 000 F.Supp. No. 97-CV-607(H) (W.D.N.Y. decided March 25, 1999)
McClesky v. Kemp, 481 U.S. 279 (1987)
McCorkle v. Johnson, 881 F.2d 993 (11th Cir. 1989)
McKeiver v. Pennsylvania, 403 U.S. 528 (1971)
Mempa v. Rhay, 389 U.S. 128 (1967)
Miles v. Bell, 621 F.Supp. 51 (D. Conn. 1985)
Mistretta v. United States, 488 U.S. 361 (1989)
Moore v. Clark, 821 F.2d 518 (8th Cir. 1987)
Morrissey v. Brewer, 408 U.S. 471 (1972)
Nicholson v. Choctaw County, Alabama, 498 F.Supp. 295 (S.D. Ala. 1980)
Northern v. Nelson, 315 F.Supp. 687 (N.D. Cal. 1970)
O'Lone v. Estate of Shabazz, 482 U.S. 342 (1987)
Onishea v. Hopper, 171 F.3d 1289 (11th Cir. 1999)
Payne v. Tennessee, 501 U.S. 808 (1991)
Pennsylvania Department of Corrections v. Yeskey, 524 U.S. 206 (1998)
Penry v. Lynaugh, 492 U.S. 302 (1989)
People v. Romero, 13 Cal. 4th 497 (1996)
Preiser v. Rodriguez, 411 U.S. 475 (1973)
Price v. Johnston, 334 U.S. 266 (1948)
Procunier v. Martinez, 416 U.S. 396 (1974)
Proffitt v. Florida, 428 U.S. 242 (1976)
Pugh v. Locke, 406 F.Supp. 318 (M.D. Ala. 1976)
Ramos v. Lamm, 485 F.Supp. 122 (D. Colo. 1979)
Remmers v. Brewer, 361 F.Supp. 537 (S.D. Iowa 1973)
Remmers v. Brewer, 494 F.2d 1277 (8th Cir. 1974)
Rhodes v. Chapman, 452 U.S. 337 (1981)
Richardson v. Ramirez, 418 U.S. 24 (1974)
Roberts v. Louisiana, 428 U.S. 325 (1976)
Ruffin v. Commonwealth, 62 Va. (21 Gratt.) 790 (1871)
Sandin v. Connor, 515 U.S. 472 (1995)
Schall v. Martin, 467 U.S. 253 (1984)
Sheley v. Dugger, 824 F.2d 1551 (11th Cir. 1987)
Sostre v. McGinnis, 334 F.2d. 906 (2nd Cir. 1964)
Stanford v. Kentucky, 492 U.S. 361 (1989)
Tarlton v. Clark, 441 F.2d 384 (5th Cir. 1971)
Theriault v. Carlson, 339 F.Supp. 375 (N.D. Ga. 1972)
Theriault v. Carlson, 495 F.2d 390 (5th Cir. 1974)
Theriault v. Silber, 391 F.Supp. 579 (W.D. Tex. 1975)
Thompson v. Oklahoma, 487 U.S. 815 (1988)
Thornburgh v. Abbott, 490 U.S. 401 (1989)
Tison v. Arizona, 481 U.S. 137 (1987)
Turner v. Safley, 482 U.S. 78 (1987)
United States ex rel Robinson v. York, 281 F.Supp. 8 (D. Conn. 1968)
United States v. Salerno, 481 U.S. 739 (1987)
Walker v. Blackwell, 411 F.2d 23 (5th Cir. 1969)
Walker v. Sumner, 917 F.2d 382 (9th Cir. 1990)
Washington v. Harper, 494 U.S. 210 (1990)
Weems v. United States, 217 U.S. 349 (1910)
Wendt v. Lynaugh, 841 F.2d 619 (5th Cir. 1988)
Williams v. New York, 337 U.S. 241 (1949)
Wilson v. Kelley, 294 F.Supp. 1005 (N.D. Ga. 1968)
Wilson v. Seiter, 501 U.S. 294 (1991)
Wolff v. McDonnell, 418 U.S. 539 (1974)
Woodson v. North Carolina, 428 U.S. 280 (1976)
Younger v. Gilmore, 404 U.S. 15 (1971)

Name Index

SUBJECT INDEX

Photo Credits

p. 3: Mediaeval Crime Museum, Rothenburg Ob der Tauber, Germany; p. 4: Donna Binder/Impact Visuals; p. 7: Jana Birchum/Impact Visuals; p. 8: Gary Wagner/Stock Boston; p. 16: A. Ramey/PhotoEdit; p. 21: Liaison Agency; p. 22: Corbis/Bettmann; p. 40: John Coletti/Stock Boston; p. 44: James Prince/Photo Researchers; p. 49: Kean Collection/Archive Photos; p. 63: Corbis/Bettmann-UPI; p. 67: The Granger Collection; p. 70: Capital Features/The Image Works; p. 75: The Library Company of Philadelphia; p. 77: The Library Company of Philadelphia; p. 87: David Woo/Stock Boston; p. 88: Kansas State Historical Society; p. 97: The Granger Collection, New York; p. 99: Courtesy of American Correctional Association; p. 102: A. Ramey/Stock Boston; p. 106: Hulton Getty/Liaison Agency; p. 117: Michael Newman/PhotoEdit; p. 142: Scott Manchester, Petaluma Times/Sygma; p. 146: Michael Newman/PhotoEdit; p. 148: AP/ Wide World Photos; p. 154: Gamma Tokyo/Kaku Kurita/Liaison Agency; p. 179: Culver Pictures; p. 182: AP/Wide World Photos; p. 187: AP/ Wide World Photos; p. 189: Jack Kurtz/Impact Visuals; p. 196: Bob Daemmrich/The Image Works; p. 222: U.S. Department of Justice, Federal Bureau of Prisons; p. 230: Michael Newman/PhotoEdit; p. 242: John Barr/ Liaison Agency; p. 246: C. Takagi/Impact Visuals; p. 259: Philip Reichel; p. 268: Mary Kate Denny/PhotoEdit; p. 274: J. M. Moynahan/Historic Jail Study Project; p. 282: AP/Wide World Photos; p. 287: Joel Gordon; p. 288: Philip Reichel; p. 290: Gary Wagner/Stock Boston; p. 292: AP/Wide World Photos; p. 314, top: Philip Reichel; p. 314, bottom: Philip Reichel; p. 315: Philip Reichel; p. 318: Liaison Agency; p. 335: Liaison Agency; p. 356: Joel Gordon; p. 366:Louisiana State Penitentiary; p. 367: Joseph Sohm/ChromoSohm, Inc./Corbis; p. 371: Liaison Agency; p. 377: Andrew Lichtenstein/ Corbis Sygma; p. 386: Grace Wojda; p. 397: Grace Wojda; p. 402: Kansas State Historical Society; p. 410: California Department of Corrections; p. 417: Helen Davis/The Denver Post; p. 426: Liaison Agency; p. 429: Grace Wojda; p. 440: AP/Wide World Photos; p. 444: AP/Wide World Photos; p. 454: AP/Wide World Photos; p. 456: Correction Bureau Ministry of Justice, Japan; p. 462: Deborah Copaken/ Liaison Agency; p. 482: AP/Wide World Photos; p. 492: California Department of Corrections; p. 498: Paul Rakestraw; p. 505: Courtesy of the Kanka Family; p. 506: Joel Gordon; p. 518: Corbis/Sygma; p. 529: Joel Gordon; p. 532: Ziggy Kaluzny/Liaison Agency; p. 560: Mike Okoniewski/Liaison Agency; p. 566: Spencer Grant/PhotoEdit; p. 573: Joel Gordon; p. 576: A. Ramey/ PhotoEdit; p. 583: AP/Wide World Photos.